The Bee Gees

Tales of The Brothers Gibb

Exclusive Distributors:
Book Sales Limited,
8/9 Frith Street,
London W1V 5TZ, UK.

Music Sales Corporation,
257 Park Avenue South,
New York, NY 10010, USA.

The Five Mile Press,
22 Summit Road,
Noble Park,
Victoria 3174, Australia.

To the Music Trade only:
Music Sales Limited,
8/9 Frith Street,
London W1V 5TZ, UK.

Front cover photo: Angela Lubrano
Back Cover: Rex & L.F.I.

Typeset by Galleon Typesetting, Ipswich.
Printed by Creative Print & Design (Wales), Ebbw Vale.

A catalogue record for this book is available from the British Library.

www.omnibuspress.com

The Bee Gees

Tales of The Brothers Gibb

Melinda Bilyeu, Hector Cook & Andrew Môn Hughes
with assistance from Joseph Brennan and Mark Crohan

OMNIBUS PRESS
LONDON · NEW YORK · SYDNEY

In memory of
Mildred Boyken,
1926-1999

Contents

Acknowledgements

A LL THREE OF them were showing signs of anxiety and trepidation as they entered the plush London offices of the company who were keen to sign them. After all, this was an important contract they were being asked to sign, carrying with it a great deal of responsibility. The deal concluded, the trio immediately agreed that they could benefit from some additional help, and their number quickly swelled to five following the recruitment of two men who were recognised as specialists in their fields.

As familiar as the above story may sound, for once, we are not talking "Bee Gees" here. For Barry, Robin, Maurice, Colin and Vince, instead read Melinda, Hector, Andrew, Joe and Mark. It required a great deal of conviction on the part of our publisher to entrust us with the task of writing this book, especially when you take into account the fact that none of us had ever attempted such a venture before.

Therefore, to Chris Charlesworth, we extend our gratitude for providing us with the opportunity to tell a story that needed to be told, for being there when we needed you, but also for allowing us the freedom to write without the pressure of feeling that someone was looking over our shoulders as we did so. He was assisted by Nikki Lloyd who assiduously tracked down many of the previously unpublished photos which are seen here for the first time. Many of these were provided by Harry Goodwin, for many years the official photographer for *Top Of The Pops*, where he first came into contact with the Gibbs.

Joe and Mark, we doubt whether we could have done this without you. Joe, not only for your welcome expertise of The Bee Gees' recording history, but also for your in-depth knowledge of the music industry as a whole. Mark, you managed to track down so many people who knew the Gibbs from their early Australian years, and come up with so much new information, we could almost have written a separate book on that period alone. We salute you both.

There are a number of individuals who have provided us with help and encouragement over the years, and who are also deserving of our gratitude. Thanks to Dick Ashby of The Bee Gees' personal management and his assistant Pat Gulino, to Carol Peters of Left Bank Management, and also to The Bee Gees' lawyer, Michael Eaton.

And then there are the cast of thousands who all played their part in making this book become a reality.

A great number of people graciously gave of their time by allowing us to interview them, and all the following should take great credit for their personal contributions: Ahmet Ertegun, Alan Bates, Alan Simpson, Albhy Galuten, Andrew Jenkins, Andrew Sandoval, Angus Deayton, Arif Mardin, Athol Guy, Barbara Wood, Barrington Davis, Bev Harrell, Beverly Burke, Bill Gates, Bill Inglot, Bill Levenson, Billy J. Kramer, Billy Lawrie, the late Bip Addison, Bob Saker, Brian Walton, Bruce Davis, Bryan Davies, Carl Savona, Carlos Olms, Cheryl Gray (Samantha Sang), Clem Cattini, Clive Powell (Georgie Fame), Colin Blunstone, Colin Petersen, Damon Lyon-Shaw, Dave Berry, Dave Wyatt, David Browning, David English, David Harman (Dave Dee), David Leaf, David Mackay, David Martin, David Stead, Del Juliana, Dennis Williams, Dennis Wilson, Diana Murphy, Dorothy Gliksman, Dorothy Wilson, Dougie Davidson, Eileen Callaghan, Elaine Blatt, Fred and Joan Marks, Frederic and Christine Tanner, Gary McDonald, Geoff Bridgeford, Geoff Bruce, Graham Bonnet (and the webmaster at www.bonnet-rocks.com), Graham Knight, Helen Kenney, Ian "Tich" Amey, Jan Trew, Jenene Watson, Jerry Greenberg, Jim Caine, Jimmie Haskell, Jimmy Little, Joan and Ted Hill, John Alderson, John Bywaters, John and Lori Vallins (Lori Balmer), John Macbeth, John Manners, John McNally, John Pantry, Johnny Ashcroft, Johnny Devlin, Johnny Young, Jon Blanchfield, Jonathan Ledingham (Jonathan Kelly), Julie Park, Karen Witkowski, Kelli Hartman (Kelli Wolfe), Ken Griggs, Kenny Horrocks, Larry Salters, Lonnie Lee, Lynne Fletcher, Mike Brady, Mike Mayer, Mike Vickers, Ned Sherrin, Noeleen Stewart (Noeleen Batley), Pamela Brown, Pamela Buhner, Pat Fairley, Paul Frost, Paul Nicholas, Peter King, Peter Mason, Peter Robinson, Ray Galton, Reg Gray, Roland Rennie, Ron Watford, Ronnie Burns, Rosalia Black, Sara Salt, Sir Louis Clark, Steve Groves, Steve Kipner, Terry Nelhams (Adam Faith), Tom Dowd, Tony Brady, Tony Cope, Trevor "Dozy" Davies, Trevor Norton and Vince Melouney.

In particular, we should like to register our appreciation to Blue Weaver, John Stringer, and Tom and Stephanie Kennedy for their additional support and encouragement, let alone their friendship, all of which we greatly value.

Then there are those who spent many hours transcribing the vast amount of taped audio and video interviews of the Gibbs which had been accumulated over a number of years, and praise is indeed due to Angela Hughes, Anne Simpson, Cliff and Chris Banks, David Ellis, John Pethers, Lee Meadows, Linda Egan, Lynda Gillies, Pat Todd, Paul Martin, Sara Williams and Sarah Horner for all their efforts.

We were also reliant upon the co-operation of those who took on the task of additional research on our behalf, and congratulations are particularly due to the wonderful Ann Grootjans and Graham R. Gooch, and most certainly not forgetting Andrew and Kate Laing, Billy Taggart, Dan Box, Darrin Mitchell, Herman Verbeke, Kay Barclay, Kevin Johnson, Kevin Murphy, Kim Lowden, Mark Byfield, Patrick Cowley, Sterling Bower, Suzanne Bodle and Yuko Nishihara for all going about such important work in such a conscientious manner. Specialist research relating to the Isle of Man was provided by Bernie Quayle and Keith Handley, whilst Kristi Shadrick, Alycia Apostolides, Dawn Legere and Judy A. Stephenson shared their extensive knowledge of the career of Andy Gibb. Good luck with your own book on Andy, ladies!

We were indeed fortunate to be able to call upon the expertise of Bob Sommerville in the specialist area of cover versions, and we are grateful to him for his diligence and attention to detail.

Thanks also to the following who have provided general assistance throughout the years: George McManus and Chareen Steel of Polydor UK Ltd, Hazel Shacklock, Masaya Uchimura, Peter Kington, Redcliffe City Council, Richard Saunders, Saul Davis, Sharon Jadick, Shirlee Faur, Nancy Powell and Tessa Le Bar. We also received help from Sue Kurz, Kate Satteson, Shirin Thobani and Stephen Morgan who were all kind enough to provide us with access to their carefully compiled scrapbooks. These were supplemented by the additional clippings that Dorothy A. Taylor, Linda O'Connor, Marty Lam, Richard Atkinson and Jean-Anne Corbin took the trouble to send us.

Although they do not form part of the text itself, the Appendices contain a great deal of information, and Arne Moen, Carlos Alberto Lacayo, David Dasch, Georges Zuger, Göran Nilsson, Jostein Hansen, Manfred Baumann, Norbert Lippe, Rod Lane, Tore Eriksen and Willie Bléfari all provided important information which was used when compiling these.

In addition to all the above-mentioned, further acknowledgement should be made of the supplementary contributions made by Graham R. Gooch, John Stringer, Jonathan Ledingham and Paul Martin who loaned their scrapbooks, and again to Dan Box and David Ellis for additional assistance with the appendices.

Let us not forget too all the hundreds of fans who took the trouble to provide little snippets of information here and there. Too many to mention, but nonetheless appreciated, you know who you are.

A vote of thanks too, to our professional advisers Ken Harkness and Martin Smith for guiding us successfully through the various pitfalls which presented themselves in our first venture of this sort.

Our families and friends are also due our gratitude not only for your love and support, but also for your patience during a time when our everyday lives were put on hold. At a personal level, in addition to those we have already mentioned, we should like to extend our appreciation to the following:

From Melinda and Hector – thanks to our extended family: Nora Cook, Martha, David and Seth Rurup; Samantha and Andy Eder; Janine, Loren and Sarah Brandt; Andy, Ben and Emily Gray; Amelia and Rob Coates; and never forgetting our very own "babies", Ceilidh and Milngavie, as well as their Auntie Kate and Uncle Charlie Loughlin, and Mary Katherine Whitman. Although Fraser Cook, and Arthur and Mildred Boyken didn't live to see the day when we unexpectedly became authors, they are undoubtedly pleased to know that their indulgence of our musical tastes was not in vain. The Leask family may also be similarly delighted that something finally came of their neighbourly tolerance.

From Andrew – thanks to Jonathan Môn Hughes (who arrived mid-project on June 13th 1999) and in time-honoured fashion – the long suffering wife, Wendy (it could have been worse – you could have been a golf widow!); to my mother and father, Enid and Mervyn (for the 15 years of research which they tolerated – I told you I'd do it . . . eventually!); to my mother-in-law, Eileen, and my sister-in-law, Linda (who never quite understood my obsession); to my colleagues at BGQ, who are so much more to me than that, the inimitable Renée Schreiber (gosh, how things change – now Renée Di Nicola – "Hi!" to new hubby Nick too!), and the quite extraordinarily talented Wim Swerts; to Sandi Hunt, Roy & Thea Wringer; Carol & Terry Morgan; John Simcox and Vikki Hughes for your friendship; to my oldest friends, David Davies & Karen Lacey, Kenneth Bevan (caricaturist extraordinaire), Robert, Kathryn, James & Rebecca Hall, Paul Dooling and Melfyn & Julie Williams; to my friends in the media – Bernie Quayle (Manx Radio), Chris Savory & Mike Adams (The Record Collectors), Lee Henshaw (Granada – Live Challenge 99), Brian Hansen (VH-1) and Faye Dicker (C4, Collectors Lot); to all at the Isle of Man Post Office Philatelic Bureau especially Dot Tilbury, Janet Bridge and Ian Curphey; and last, but by no means least, Martin Swift (is he the missing link in our story?) – I think I owe you a pint or two matey!

Our colleagues Joe and Mark have also neglected their friends and families on our behalf and so, on their behalf:

Joe says: Thanks to my wife Helen Schreiner and daughter Megan Brennan for tolerating (more or less!) my incessant use of the good computer and my other time spent away from them. I also thank my alma mater and employer Columbia University for providing the space for personal web pages, and Chris Mathis for his work running the 'Words' internet mailing list – without both, I would not have come in contact with so many Bee Gees fans worldwide including my four collaborators on this book.

Mark says: Many thanks to my wife Jacinta, three children Bree, Edan & Daina, and son-in-law Dale Grant for their patience not only over the period of this book's creation, but for the times that I have without doubt force fed them Bee Gees trivia, and of course their music. Many thanks to all other Bee Gees fans for their support on this project. It's been great to be a part of it.

Finally, and most fittingly, a big thank-you from the five of us to Barry, Robin, Maurice and Andy Gibb for writing and performing the music which touched all of us as individuals, and yet which inspired us collectively to produce this account of their lives and careers.

Foreword

A S MANAGING DIRECTOR of Festival Records, I could only marvel at the raw talent of the three young boys who were signed to Festival almost 40 years ago.

As I now look back on the intervening years, I am honoured to have this opportunity to pay tribute to Barry, Robin and Maurice Gibb. Although they are now in their fifties, I still look upon them as fine young men, and I shall always regard them as such. They are in the top bracket of lyric and melody writers, and whether live or in the studio, they perform that material to perfection. Their songs continue to stand the test of time as showcased by the recent resurgence of their music in the *Saturday Night Fever* stage shows.

I am proud to have been able to play a small part in their fabulous career, which I am sure will produce many new classic Bee Gees songs in years to come. Along with the rest of their millions of fans, I look forward to being there to see and hear those hits of tomorrow.

Frederick C. Marks

Introduction

ONCE UPON A time, three young brothers set their course for success in the music world. "We made a pact between the three of us that, hell or high water, we were going to be a famous pop group and that nothing was going to stop us," Barry Gibb declared. In a fairy tale, the boys would have found overnight success; in the real world it took a little longer, but for more than 40 years, nothing *has* stopped The Bee Gees in their quest for recognition in their chosen field.

Unlike many conventional rock biographies, much of the content of this book revolves around the musical careers of Barry, Robin, Maurice and Andy Gibb. This is not because the brothers' lives are without their share of controversy and tragedy. On the contrary, there are elements of the typical rock star's life within these pages. Sex, drugs, booze, divorces, lawsuits, and most regrettably, premature death, are all areas examined within these pages in their proper context.

However, the main theme of the book is the music, because the brothers' lives revolve around it. Almost everything they do is based on their constant desire to develop their skills, and in particular their songwriting abilities. It is this dedication to becoming absolute masters of their craft that sets them apart from so many of their peers.

Tales Of The Brothers Gibb is not just the story of The Bee Gees. There are in fact three completely separate stories to be told, with easily recognisable divisions in each.

The main story, of course, deals with the pop group known as The Bee Gees, and their journey from the most humble of beginnings imaginable to their current status as world superstars. It details the family musical background which encouraged their love of singing; their initial five year struggle to gain some sort of recognition; how they achieved international success, only to throw it all away again; the five years it took them to rebuild their career; the unprecedented success and fame that followed; the inevitable backlash; and finally, their general acceptance by both the public and the music industry.

Then there are The Brothers Gibb, the prolific songwriting trio who have had more than 2,500 artists cover their compositions, with many of those songs remaining unreleased by The Bee Gees. Sir Tim Rice enthused, "I rate the Brothers Gibb as one of the greatest songwriting combinations of the 20th century. I think that they're up there with Lennon & McCartney, Cole Porter and George Gershwin of their eras. Their songs have penetrated all classes and creeds, enormously successful."

There can be no denying their success as composers. From 1963 to the current day, exactly the same period as their more publicised career as recording artists and performers in their own domain, the Gibbs have been writing material specifically for the use of others, and again there are distinct periods in this parallel career. Australia was crying out for new songwriting talent and, for Barry in particular, it offered a greater opportunity to write different types of music than Britain or America could possibly have done at that stage of his development. Later, he, Robin and Maurice discovered they had the ability to write songs with the intended recipient's individual style very much in mind. By the late Seventies, they had perfected this into an art, and there was a brief period when their Midas touch produced a succession of hits for a lucky few. When it became appropriate during the early to mid-Eighties for The Bee Gees to take a sabbatical, they wrote and produced a string of entire albums for already internationally established acts, providing them with hitherto unknown levels of success. Although this activity diminished during the Nineties, occasional hits were still forthcoming and, at the time of writing, more are anticipated.

Andy Gibb also deserves to have his own story told. Once condescendingly thought of solely as "The Bee Gees' baby brother", he went on to prove that he too had inherited the same musical and composing gifts of the more celebrated members of his family. By 1977, he had embarked on his own meteoric rise in the music industry. His career paralleled his older brothers' for a few short years, when Gibb compositions dominated the charts. As Maurice put it, "We were so saturated at the time. We weren't on the charts; we *were* the charts!"

After a period when Top 40 radio belonged to the Brothers Gibb, the phenomenal success brought with it problems of its own.

Andy's first three American singles all went to number one there, and platinum albums and sell-out tours followed. But the golden boy image was merely a façade that disguised a personality dominated by self-doubt and a huge lack of confidence. His insecurity manifested itself in bouts of depression and substance abuse, before the final irony. With his recording career a casualty of his growing addiction, he moved to musical theatre and then to television, but in each case, personal problems destroyed a bright start. Having bottomed out, bankrupt and his professional reputation in tatters following a whole series of missed engagements, he had slowly regained his health and had begun to rebuild his career. He had achieved a long-held ambition by gaining his pilot's licence, and had also signed a new recording contract. Just when it looked as if his star was in its ascendancy again, his past caught up with him and it flickered briefly before being extinguished forever, although his memory will always linger.

The public that couldn't get enough of The Bee Gees rejected them suddenly and absolutely at the beginning of the next decade, but by the late Eighties, most of the world was ready for their return. Andy's unexpected and tragic death spurred on his older brothers to prove themselves once again.

The Nineties saw them finally gain the recognition and acclaim they had always sought, with accolades from their peers and the public arriving in rapid-fire succession. The Bee Gees had finally achieved that longed-for time when "we can feel comfortable as human beings, that our music is accepted, not jeered at because it's been played a lot," Barry said wistfully. "We'll be striving for credibility after 10 more albums if I know anything about us. Every record we put out is still like the first record. It never ceases to be exciting for us if it makes the charts, and it never ceases to be a great disappointment to us if it doesn't."

Their ability to change with the times has rewarded them with an ever widening circle of admirers that defies any attempt to stereotype a "typical Bee Gees fan". It encompasses every age, sex, race, nationality and walk of life. As Barry noted, "Language doesn't seem to be a barrier. Even people who speak no English sing along with us and seem to understand perfectly what is going on."

For Robin, the most important thing is that the brothers continue to play their part in the music world. "Anyone that writes music is contributing," he explained. "I don't think it's necessary to want to change anything, but just to be a part of it. As long as we are part of it and people can appreciate it, that's all I care about; you know, as long as people will say, 'That's a significant item,' or, 'That's a significant group.' If you can always maintain that . . . The Bee Gees want to create a form of music that is always there to be reckoned with. I think that's equally important as trying to change everything."

Barry, Robin and Maurice may be brothers, but they are all very different individuals. As their friend, David English, pointed out, "Maurice is a wonderful comedian, very good soul, very good heart, very funny and very witty. Robin is extremely sensitive . . . zany . . . eccentric . . . He's got this most wonderful off-the-wall sense of humour. Barry kind of harnesses these qualities, he's the steady captain of the ship. That's why I always call him 'the skipper'. He's an immensely creative person. If you are his friend, then he would do anything for you . . . Then you put all those qualities together, in the three of them, and it's unbelievable, but the humour is the thing that I've always thought has been exceptional. They make me laugh and laugh and laugh."

Few would argue that there is strength in the trinity. Their father, Hugh Gibb, once said, "I always sum up by saying individually they're good; together they're brilliant – they're a team." In recent conversation, the group's former drummer, Colin Petersen, agreed, "The Bee Gees are like a tripod; they need all three."

★   ★   ★

When we were first given the opportunity to tell The Bee Gees' story, it was, by necessity, only in the briefest of forms for the official tour programme for the *One Night Only* series of concerts and for the Isle of

Man Post Office's commemorative Bee Gees stamps presentation packs issued in 1999. In both cases, the challenge was to condense a musical legacy which has spanned four decades into fewer than four pages of text. While it was possible to detail the career highlights in such a fashion, we were frustrated that there was little scope for the bigger picture: the stories behind the music, the characters who make the tales come to life. It was, however, an even greater challenge which awaited us when we were approached by Chris Charlesworth with a view to writing this book. Chris echoed our own thoughts that the time was right for a serious, in-depth biography of the Brothers Gibb. For him to entrust such a project to a most unusual team of would-be authors required a gigantic leap of faith on his part, and for that we are all grateful to him.

The writing of a book by a team has been a unique experience, made possible by e-mail. Apart from the initial meeting of Melinda, Hector and Andrew with Chris in London exactly one year ago to discuss the possibility of the biography, only Hector and Melinda have actually seen each other during the 12 months of research and writing, although they have remained in constant contact with Andrew by means of many hours of telephone conversations, in addition to the e-mails which connected all five of us. Neither Joe nor Mark have ever met any of the other participants, but their individual areas of expertise made them a vital part of the operation. The truly global nature of the team, with Brits Hector and Andrew, Melinda an expatriate American living in Scotland, Joe in the USA and Mark in Australia, sparked many fascinating discussions as we worked together towards mutual agreement on international vernacular. Bearing in mind that the Gibbs have lived on three separate continents, it was also important that we were able to call on local knowledge whenever the need arose.

All five members of the research and writing team are unashamed fans of the group and, between us, have accumulated 133 years of following their fortunes. The one thing that linked all five Bee Geeologists was the desire to write the definitive history of the Brothers Gibb, detailing not only their career but also the men themselves. We hope that we have succeeded.

The Authors - April, 2000

1

ALL THIS AND WORLD WAR TOO

THE TALE OF the brothers Gibb opens in Manchester, England, during the dark days of the Second World War. As Hitler's Luftwaffe sought out cities on which to drop their bombs, Manchester, 200 miles north of London and just 35 miles east of strategically important Liverpool, was considered by many to be a safe city; indeed, the BBC even evacuated many of its London staff there as a precaution. But the BBC was wrong. When the blitz came conditions in the industrial capital of Lancashire were as terrible as in London, Coventry or anywhere else.

Manchester's first major air raid was on December 22, 1940, when German bombs struck Albert Square and Bridgewater Street. There were fires in the buildings around Deansgate: the Royal Exchange was burning and the Victoria Buildings were so badly damaged that they collapsed into the road. A lack of firefighters exacerbated the problem – 200 had been sent to Liverpool the previous night to help deal with bombing there. Fires spread to Portland Street and Sackville Street. The following night the bombing began afresh, and although the emergency services (including extra helpers from the London Fire Brigade) struggled to contain the resultant fires, strong winds quickly spread the conflagration. Royal Engineers had to blast fire breaks to prevent the huge wall of fire around Piccadilly from spreading further.

Manchester Cathedral, the Free Trade Hall, Exchange Street and Victoria Station were all bombed out. Hundreds of businesses and 30,000 houses were destroyed. In Stretford, where Barbara May Pass lived with her family, 106 civilians died and 12,000 houses were damaged or destroyed. In January 1941 Old Trafford, the famous Manchester United Football Club ground, was hit during a three hour raid. Another heavy air raid at the start of June 1941 damaged the Gaiety Theatre, police headquarters and Salford Royal Hospital, where 14 nurses were killed. On Christmas Eve, 1944, the Germans launched a volley of V1 flying bombs at Manchester.

For the generations born after the war, the incendiary bombs, the air raid and all-clear sirens, blackouts, fuel and food shortages, rationing and complicated points systems are difficult to comprehend, but in 1941, when Hugh Gibb met Barbara Pass, they were a way of life. In a Britain thrust into war, patriotism took the form of a willingness to endure sacrifice for the good of

1

the cause. The nation pulled together to fight the evils of Nazism, with all strata of society, rich and poor alike, pitching in side-by-side for the first time.

Many Mancunians undertook civil defence work. By 1940 one and a half million, a quarter of them women, were involved in Air Raid Precaution. Wardens would assess the damage and help bomb victims to safety, first aid workers ministered to the injured and emergency rescuers searched for survivors and the dead amongst the rubble of bombed-out homes. There were more than 50 Auxiliary Fire Service stations in Manchester, all of them indispensable in helping the regular Fire Brigade battle the effects of incendiary bombs. The Home Guard, so often the stuff of *Dads' Army* jokes, were actually a vital part of the war effort, guarding factories, railways and other strategically important sites, leaving the army free to concentrate on the more important business of actual fighting. Some eventually made their way into the army; by the end of the war, men up to 40 years of age were being conscripted.

Even those not fighting were drawn into the war effort, zealously working long hours to keep production levels high. Manchester's strength in engineering ensured that it made great contributions to the war effort. The Ford factory was restructured to produce engines for British Merlin planes. By the war's end, it had 17,000 workers, of which only 100 had ever worked with aero-engines before.

Until 1941, war work for women had been voluntary but as labour shortages became critical, women aged 20 to 21 were required in March of that year to register for war work at Labour Exchanges. This was soon extended to include women aged up to 40 years old. The Essential Work Order meant that women could not leave their employment nor employers release them without the authorisation of the National Service Office.

By December 1941, the Minister for Labour, Ernest Bevin, conceded that it was necessary to conscript women into the armed services. Women were urgently needed to fill the formerly male domain of factory work and support services of the military. There was very little equality of the sexes though; female civil defence workers received only two-thirds the pay of their male counterparts, and female factory workers faced long hours and poor conditions.

Entertainers were in high demand during the war, many being called up to ENSA, the Entertainment National Service Association. Music was seen as a morale booster, and a radio programme called *Workers' Playtime* was even broadcast in factories in the hope that it might encourage employees to work more efficiently. Young soldiers and their sweethearts, desperate to leave behind the hardships and horrors of the war if only for an evening, would crowd the local ballrooms and dance to the big band hits of the day.

Hugh Leslie Gibb was 23 when war broke out but because he was a musician, the leader of a dance band no less, he avoided conscription. As Maurice Gibb would laughingly say more than 50 years later, "He accompanied the

2

war. He did the soundtrack to World War II." Although Hugh didn't serve in the forces, he did contribute to the war effort by working in Metro's Gun Shop, where he operated a radial arm drilling machine in a department where searchlights were made. He was born on January 15, 1916, in the Chorlton district of Manchester. "I was the oddball in my family, 'cause I liked music and the attitude was that it would never do you any good," he said. "The main theme then was go to work, have a steady job, and bring your wages home every weekend. A side-track from that wasn't right in their eyes. To be a musician was like the old days, you know, when they were considered vagabonds; and that's all I ever wanted to do."

Instead of following the more conventional career paths open to a young man in the Thirties, the self-confessed "oddball" sought fame as a drummer and bandleader. By 1940 The Hughie Gibb Orchestra was firmly ensconced on the circuit of Mecca ballrooms, playing mainly in the north of England and Scotland. So it was that 20-year-old Barbara May Pass came to meet her future husband in a Manchester ballroom in 1941.

Barbara was born in the Bolton district of Manchester on November 17, 1920. She has often been erroneously described in Bee Gees-related literature as a "big band singer" but takes pains now to set the matter right. "Here, this has got all out of proportion!" she says. "My sister wrote and said she read that I was a big band singer. That escapes me altogether. I sang locally, but I didn't make a career of it. After I got to know Hugh, I didn't . . . The funny part is, he wouldn't let me sing with his band. He used to say one [musician] in the family was enough." It was ironic then that he would end up with a house full of them.

Of that first meeting, Barbara said, "We met at a dance in Manchester at the Stretford Trades and Labour Club. He was a bandleader there and I used to go dancing with friends, and that's how I met him. He came down and danced with me and that was it – we just went on from there."

Hugh Gibb told reporter Cynthia Heimel, "At the time I was teaching a young lad to play drums, running him ragged. He always stood in the wings, waiting for his chance, so I spotted Barbara, said 'Come on, Alf, here's your chance.' So he went and played and I went and had a dance."

Hugh escorted Barbara home that night and thereafter romance blossomed. Ironically, despite the nightmare of war, Hugh Gibb has fond memories of the time he met his future wife. "People enjoyed themselves more," he maintains. "Kids today . . . think they've done everything by the time they're 18 and have nothing to look forward to."

It was a long courtship. "We went steady for about three and a half years," Barbara says. "We both lived at home with our parents, you know, right up to getting married." The wedding took place in Manchester on May 27, 1944. Photos show the happy couple posing beneath an arch of instruments formed by members of Hugh's band.

On January 12, 1945, their first child was born; a daughter, whom they christened Lesley Barbara. Soon after, the family relocated to Scotland where, according to Barbara, Hugh was offered a job by Mecca at the Palais in Edinburgh. "We lived just at the outskirts of Edinburgh," she says. "Funnily enough, Barry's wife's mother and father used to dance to our band. We didn't know them, but they used to dance to the band."

When World War II came to an end in the summer of 1945, the Gibbs returned to Manchester. "We went back and stayed with my mother in Stretford," recalled Barbara, "and then Hughie was offered the job at the Douglas Bay Hotel and that's when we went to the Isle of Man. However, he played at the Alexandra [Hotel] for old Mr Raineri first and then he played for Mr Leslie [Raineri] at the Douglas Bay Hotel."

Hugh Gibb's new employer, Carlo Raineri, was born in Northern Italy but came to Britain at the end of World War I. After learning the catering trade in Glasgow, he took a summer job on the Isle of Man around 1920, fell in love with the island and returned there to live in 1922. In 1925 he bought a single hotel in Douglas, the Alexandra, in a block called Metropole Mansions. As his business prospered, he added one hotel after another until he had a total of six hotels on the same block which, when joined together, became the biggest on the island. In 1938 he expanded further and bought the Douglas Bay Hotel. By then the Raineri hotels could accommodate over 700 guests.

During the war, all foreign nationals in Britain except the French were interned, many of them on the Isle of Man, with suspected Nazi sympathisers indiscriminately interned with Jewish refugees by virtue of their foreign birth. The massive size of the Alexandra made it ideal for an internment camp and, isolated behind barbed wire, it became the site of one of the largest in Britain.

A tiny island in the Irish Sea, the Isle of Man is not part of the United Kingdom, although the UK is responsible for its defence and foreign relations, and for the purposes of custom duties and postal services, it is also considered part of the mainland. It has its own government, the Court of Tynwald, consisting of the Lieutenant-Governor, the Legislative Council, the upper house, and the Keys, a 24-man body elected by universal adult suffrage. Laws of the Tynwald nevertheless require the approval of the Crown. The Isle of Man has its own postal system, issuing its own stamps which must be used on the island, and mints its own currency although British sterling is also accepted. Nowadays the island is best known as a low tax area, where wealthy individuals take advantage of tax rates that rise no higher than 20p in the pound. The general rate is 14–15p in the £.

The island takes its name from the Celtic god Mannanan mac Lir, a pre-Christian deity known and revered in both Ireland and Britain. According to legend, Mannanan throws a magical mist over the island in winter to protect it from invaders. In the summer months the lush green island becomes a bustling tourist resort and the sounds of the TT (Tourist Trophy) motor bike races fill the air in the hills above Douglas and Ramsey.

Ellan Vannin, as the island is known in Manx Gaelic, is where the saga of The Bee Gees really begins.

2

CHILDHOOD DAYS

"OH, WE MOVED about a lot!" Barbara Gibb would tell Manx disc jockey Bernie Quayle. The family's first home in the Isle of Man capital of Douglas was a little house "over the hill behind Duke's Garage . . . Then we moved down to Strand Street over Maley's Chemist. From there it was [St] Catherine's Drive, then it was Spring Valley, and from Spring Valley we went to Chapel House on the Strang Road and then from there . . . we got the house in Willaston and we were there for quite a while."

It was in the little flat over Maley's Chemist at 17 Strand Street, in Douglas' main shopping street, that Hugh and Barbara were living with baby Lesley when their first son was born at 8.45 a.m. on September 1, 1946 at the Jane Crookall Maternity Home in Douglas. He was given the name Barry Alan Crompton Gibb. The "Alan" was in honour of Hugh's second youngest brother, who died in infancy. According to Hugh, in a mingling of fact and fiction, the third name was given to the eldest son of the family in honour of the Gibbs' illustrious ancestor, Sir Isaac Crompton, the inventor of the mule spinner, whom he claimed had been immortalised in a statue in Manchester though no such monument to a Crompton actually exists.

In fact, there is no Sir Isaac. It was *Samuel* Crompton (who would be Barbara's great-great-great-great-grandfather, give or take a generation) who invented the spinning mule in 1779 in Bolton, Lancashire.

Hugh was kept busy with his music at the various hotels in Douglas when Barry was a baby. "I stayed there for [about] 10 years, and Joe Loss' band used to be there . . . That *was* the big band era," he said.

Rosalia Black, the daughter of hotel owner Carlo Raineri, recalls that "the band must have been popular because the ballroom was always packed, even though the Joe Loss Orchestra was at the Villa Marina and Ronnie Aldrich with The Squadronaires was at the Palace Ballroom."

Hugh Gibb was always on the lookout for work as even an extremely popular musician did not earn very much, and he often put together bands for one-off gigs. One such dance might have been the Invitation Dinner Dance held at the Metropole Hotel on Thursday, February 24, 1949. The tickets, priced 8s/6d each advertised that the reception was at 7.00 p.m. with dinner commencing at 7.30 p.m. prompt. "Hughie Gibb And His Music" would keep the revellers entertained until 1.00 a.m.

5

Barbara stayed home looking after the children. "I had little ones then – Lesley was 17 months and Barry was a new baby," Barbara said. "Most of the time Hughie was working, I didn't see much of him. You know, he was up there [at the Raineri hotel complex] all the time. I couldn't go out as much as my husband could because I had the children."

The first year of Barry's life passed without incident, but at 18 months he was injured in a near fatal accident which would seriously affect his development. "He was only a baby then – he was only a little baby," Barbara Gibb told Bernie Quayle. "We lived at Strand Street at that time . . . I'd just made the tea, I put it on the table and he pulled the chair up and climbed on it, pulled the tea cosy off and pulled the whole thing all over him. He was in a terrible state."

Barry was rushed to Noble's Hospital with serious scalding and fell into a coma for a short while. It was a terrifying time for the family. "Then gangrene set in," says Barry, "because in those days, the advancement of medicine simply didn't apply to people with bad scalds, so you didn't have skin grafts, you didn't have things like that. But this was a particularly bad scald, and I think I had 20 minutes to live at some point. The incredible thing for me is *that* whole two years is wiped from my memory, the whole period of being in hospital . . . The idea of being burnt is in there somewhere, but I have no knowledge of it. I've got the scars but I have no knowledge."

"He was seriously ill for about three months, and he didn't talk until he was nearly three because of this," recalled Barbara. "It upset him rather badly. I think this is one of the reasons he used to be quiet because he didn't learn to speak until quite late."

She remembers him as a quiet little boy who followed her around. If she turned suddenly, she would nearly fall over him and tears would stream down his face, though he never made a sound when he cried.

The family moved to Chapel House on the Strang Road. Hugh Gibb brought over a number of his musician friends from Manchester to play in his band, often inviting them to stay with the family. One of them was Arthur "Archie" Taylor who came out of the army in 1948, and whose first work was playing in a big band at the public swimming baths in Manchester. In those days it was common practice to put ballroom floors over empty swimming pools in the winter months. "You could go down during the day," he recalled, "and look at the tiled bottom of the baths with all the struts of the sprung ballrooms which might dance several hundred people. Then, when the swimming pools re-opened, many Manchester musicians would go on summer season to the Isle of Man.

"So I went too and spent the summer of 1949 at the Glen Helen Hotel, playing in a trio band comprising myself on sax, Arthur Thompson on drums and a pianist, Don Franklin.

"Part of the time, I stayed in a rented house called Chapel House, and it was there that I met Hughie who was staying there too."

An occasional visitor to the house was his then fiancée, Alma Varnom, who used to go across from her native Rochdale to visit him. Alma observed, "They certainly weren't poor when we knew them although they weren't rich either. The money was good for those people who worked at Glen Helen in the summer, but in the winter it would be very different. Life would have been tough on the island so I'm not at all surprised to learn that Hugh would take on lots of different jobs. I only met him a couple of times but the impression I got is that he would be a bit of an entrepreneur if he got the chance. My memory of Hughie was that he was fairly tall and that he looked like a man who was going places. That's probably why he was so ambitious for the boys."

Hugh Gibb also had the concession to provide music on board a small ferry, *The Thistle*, which ran the full length of the harbour to a jetty at Douglas Head. There, the tourists disembarked and took the inclined railway to the top of the headland where they could visit the open-air amphitheatre. Hugh had musicians on board who entertained the passengers, and Archie still has a photo which shows himself on saxophone and Don Franklin on accordion. Hugh himself didn't actually play on board the ferry, and the band were not paid by Douglas Corporation, who ran the ferry, so it was up to Hugh to collect "tips" from the passengers. In the trade, this job was referred to as the "bottler" or "bag man" and close inspection of Archie's photo does indeed show Hugh in the process of collecting the half crowns, or 2s/6d, which were deemed the norm at that time. Another of Archie's photos shows a young Barry playing in the garden at Chapel House with Arthur Thompson's son, Chris. A third child in the photo is most likely Rex Chambers, Barbara's nephew, as her sister Peggy was a frequent visitor.

Not only did Archie share the same temporary residence as Hugh, and play at the same venues, albeit on different days, they also had something, or someone, else in common too. Archie explains; "I also used to play jazz at the Alexandra Hotel with a local barber called Charlie Whewell who played a very good jazz trumpet. We used to go back to Douglas with the last coach party returning from the Glen Helen, then go up to the Alexandra and play till all hours of the morning."

Archie Taylor saw out the season on the Isle of Man before returning to Manchester to marry Alma and begin a six year run in a big band at the Levenshulme Palais in Manchester where it was not uncommon to have up to 1,300 people paying to get in. Like the Gibbs were to do a few years later, the Taylors settled in Chorlton, where their daughter Julia was born.

Apart from trumpeter Charlie Whewell, others who played in Hugh's band around this time included Arthur Crawford (accordion), Jim Caine (piano), Tommy Cowley (bass), Albert Metcalfe (tenor saxophone) and John Knight (trombone), but not all at the same time as the line-up would vary from a three-piece up to a five-piece. They would play at a number of other venues, including the aforementioned Glen Helen Hotel, a very popular tourist spot on the TT course that was especially famous for its afternoon tea dances. The Hughie Gibb Trio played there quite frequently. The Glen Helen Hotel, which is roughly in the middle of the island, still has a concert room in use today.

Jim Caine joined The Hughie Gibb Band as the pianist in 1949 and played with him in Hugh's various groups until 1954. By coincidence, Don Franklin would be his normal "stand-in" on piano, on the odd occasion that Jim was unavailable for a particular gig. Jim still cherishes a recording made at the Villa Marina in 1949 when he was the pianist and Hugh was the drummer for a band put together just for the occasion. During the winter months, he recalls, all the musicians had to scrounge around looking for other work just to stay alive, so when gigs came up such as a dinner dance, bands were put together from whoever was available on the night. It could be just a quartet or a full dance orchestra, made up of members of Hugh Gibb's band or Jim Caine's or Harold Moorhouse's. Jim's acetate contains four tunes, three of which – 'Sweet Georgia Brown', 'Moonglow' and 'I'm In The Mood For Love' – were considered as standards by Hugh and would be played regularly by his bands.

Jim's wife Edna has very fond memories of the Gibb family. She married Jim a year after he had joined The Hughie Gibb Orchestra, which was a very busy summer season for the band. As a result she spent a lot of time with Barbara while their respective husbands were off playing at the various hotels in Douglas and often baby-sat for the young Gibb children.

It was a friendship which would last through the years. In the late Sixties Jim Caine was playing in the bar of the Castle Mona Hotel, when he felt a tap on his shoulder and a friendly voice saying, "You play just as well as ever." It was Hugh Gibb. Jim was staggered and said, "I thought you were in Australia!" Hugh said the whole family were on the island for a few days holiday.

Hugh and Barbara asked Jim and Edna to join them for dinner the next evening which they did. When Edna saw Hugh she couldn't believe her eyes – he looked 20 years younger. It took a while to realise that he had acquired a toupee that looked so natural she thought it was real!

Another friend with good recollections of those times is Dougie Davidson, whose parents originated from Glasgow, but who settled on the island before his birth in 1934. He first joined his father's band, The Jock Davidson Trio, as a saxophonist at the age of 13 along with his sister Anne. "My father actually played sax as well but he wasn't very good, to be honest, so we sort of got him on to string bass eventually."

Although Jock never played in Hugh's band himself, on a couple of Saturday nights in 1953, Dougie got to play at dances in The Majestic Hotel in Onchan Head, overlooking Douglas Bay. The Majestic was a very popular venue during the Fifties and Sixties for dancing and cabaret shows. The ballroom even featured a telephone on every table with the phone number on the lampshade. This way a young man could phone a girl and say, "Hey number 17, this is number 29, fancy a dance?"

Dougie remains impressed by Hugh's ability. "I remember he was a good drummer, and he could have been a pro or a good semi-pro. He was a little bit outspoken . . . he used to gig around quite a bit with the local bands. I think he was one of the better drummers on the scene at the time."

In the Seventies, when Hugh and Barbara ran the Union Mills Post Office, Dougie would sometimes pop in to buy a newspaper, but Hugh failed to acknowledge the identity of his customer. "He didn't recognise me actually . . . I didn't think I'd made a lasting impression!"

In the early Fifties Dougie witnessed a very rare occurrence. "I remember [Barbara] singing on the stage once. I wasn't playing on that occasion – I went there to listen, and I didn't even know she was his wife till afterwards. I don't even remember her singing more than one [song]. Folk groups were very, very few and far between. I can't even remember any local band having a vocalist."

The advent of synthesizers would eventually bring about the decline of the hotel bands that offered employment to musicians like Hugh Gibb and his colleagues. By the Seventies an electronic keyboard player who knew which knobs to press could reproduce the sound of all manner of instruments, and by the Eighties dance band music, the elegant waltzes, foxtrots and quicksteps, had entered into terminal decline on the Isle of Man, as it had elsewhere. "Summer seasons" of the type that offered a living to Hugh Gibb and so many professional musicians like him were no more.

★ ★ ★

Back in 1949, the Gibb family had relocated to 50 St Catherine's Drive. Barbara was expecting again and, about four weeks before the birth, the doctor confirmed her suspicion that she was expecting twins when he detected two heartbeats.

On December 22, 1949 Robin Hugh Gibb came into the world at 3.15 a.m. at the Jane Crookall Maternity Home. At 3.50 a.m. his fraternal twin Maurice Ernest Gibb arrived. The first of what would eventually amount to millions of press cuttings was a simple birth notice in the local paper: "GIBB – December 22nd, to Barbara and Hugh Gibb, 50 St Catherine's Drive, Douglas – twin sons. (Thanks to Dr McPherson and Sister Carine.)"

As Barbara put it, "We had this little girl, Lesley, who could talk to [the family] like a little lady, the baby twins, and poor old Barry was in the middle of this. I think he got a little introverted at the beginning . . . That was only for a period, and then he came out of that. He was the boss of the twins, and Lesley was the boss of the lot." Parents and grandparents were delighted with what seemed like the perfect family: a girl, a boy and then a set of twins.

But elder sister Lesley remembered that three-year-old Barry was singularly unimpressed with the new arrivals, especially as the family cat Tatty had produced *six* kittens rather than what he saw as a rather paltry two! She added that differences in the twins' dispositions were immediately obvious: as she recalls it, Maurice was a quiet, contented baby and Robin began exercising those famous vocal chords right from the start.

9

Lesley recalled an occasion when Barry, annoyed by Robin's crying, tried giving him a shake in an effort to quiet him, a lesson in child-care which he learned from watching his beloved Tatty with her kittens. When this proved to be ineffective on his brother – baby Robin screamed all the louder – Barry begged his mother to give the twins back. It would take a few years for Robin and Maurice to get past the crying stage, and only then did Barry look upon his young brothers as friends.

When the twins were still quite young the Gibb family moved to Smedley Cottage in Spring Valley, on the outskirts of Douglas. The Bell family lived next door to them, and their daughter Barbara, who was just a few years older than Barry, remembered playing with all the Gibb children.

All three of the boys have very clear first memories dating back to their birthplace on the Isle of Man. "My memories start in a pram obviously, but I have very early memories," said Barry. "My childhood is fairly vivid to me. I remember standing in Spring Valley . . . Being about four or five, I remember standing on the loading dock at the back of the ice cream factory pretending to perform." Barry's recollection is slightly inaccurate – he recalled the ice cream factory as Wall's (an easy mistake to make as, at the time, Wall's Ice Cream was *the* leading manufacturer of ice cream in the U.K.), when in fact it was actually Ward's, a local company.

Their neighbour Barbara Bell (now Barbara Wood) distinctly remembers seeing him up there on the loading dock of the Ward's Ice Cream factory singing. On one particular occasion Barry had gone missing as evening fell, and his mother asked the Bells if they had seen him. When Barbara Wood told her that she had seen Barry at the Ward's factory singing 'Home On The Range', she recalled that Mrs. Gibb retorted, "I'll give him 'Home On The Range'," and she smacked him all the way home that night.

The non-identical twins have identical earliest memories, even though they occurred on two separate occasions. Robin said, "I remember being stung by a bee – it's my first . . . sort of memory because the pain and memories sort of go together, you know – you always remember horrible incidents in your life and that was being stung by a bee in Spring Valley. I must have been . . . younger than two or three, which is before we moved to Snaefell Road. I can remember that very vividly – perhaps if I hadn't been stung by the bee, I wouldn't remember it, but it sort of brings a picture . . ."

"The only major one was getting stung by the bee for the first time – I think every kid remembers that when they get stung, especially when you're three or four years old," Maurice said. "And falling in the water – I remember walking home backwards because I didn't want anyone to see my bum because it was wet, going all the way home to Snaefell Road."

On that occasion, Maurice's fall into the water had a comical twist to it, but on another occasion, it could have had tragic consequences.

When not under the watchful eye of adults, the Dhoo river was a favourite place for the neighbourhood children to play. "We lived in wellies all the time," Barbara Wood recalled. A path of stepping stones was built across the river and the children tried to make their way across the precarious crossing. "The dog fell in first. It was a Pomeranian, a little posh dog. Then Maurice fell in next. [The twins] were only very little. They used to go round with these siren suits on . . . like little Eskimos. He toppled off the stone – it was a slimy stone and he went in the river. There was a bit of a swell on that day and he just got tangled up and carried down. Face down he was – when you think back it was very frightening."

The little dog was rescued, but the terrified children left Maurice. "We all just ran home and got his dad, and he had to come fish him out," Barbara Wood recalled. "We were all there, and we panicked a bit, and we just went screaming hysterically. Don't forget I wasn't very old myself, and I was the oldest of the lot of us. I got the blame for the lot of it because I was the oldest there."

Barbara Gibb herself remembers the incident in even greater detail. "Maurice had been weighed down by his hooded 'siren suit' so he was unable to lift his head out of the water. The river was only 20 feet from the back door of the cottage, but he'd floated almost 100 yards before Hugh came to the rescue." It was the second time that Barbara had been close to losing one of her sons before he had reached his second birthday.

Barbara Gibb's parents, Mr and Mrs. Pass, also stayed in Douglas for a short time. They were equally accommodating, watching over the neighbourhood children who all used to visit them on Saturdays at their flat in Victoria Street over the tobacconist's shop while their respective parents did the week's main shopping.

Barbara Gibb described her sons as little rascals: "Yes, of course they were. They were normal kids, you know. Children really didn't get into a lot of problems like they do today . . . They were pretty good kids, but they were little devils – they were into everything."

As the twins grew, Barbara recalled that, "Robin used to call Maurice 'Woggie', and Maurice used to call Robin 'Bodding'. It was always, 'It's not me, it's Woggie.' If you mentioned anyone to them, they used to say, 'Oh yes, it's a friend of him.' If it was to do with the twins, anybody they knew was a friend of him!"

With such a rapidly growing family to support, Hugh Gibb found additional employment to supplement his meagre income as a musician, with Barbara also playing her part by taking on cleaning work at the Quarterbridge Hotel. Winter months were especially slow for a musician on an island where the entertainment business is dependent on the tourist trade, and Hugh took jobs as a nurse at the mental hospital at Ballamona, an insurance agent and also at Quirk's Bakery, where he helped ice the cakes at Christmas and drove a delivery van. Young Barry sometimes accompanied his father on his delivery rounds, and was often tempted by the heavenly aroma of freshly baked bread.

"He used to take me to work in the van," he recalled, "and the most fantastic thing was the smell. You'd sit in the bread van all day . . . What my father didn't know, and what the people he was delivering bread to didn't know was that I was eating out the insides of the loaves, and so a lot of people in those days were getting hollow loaves of bread."

Barry started school on September 4, 1951, just three days after his fifth birthday, attending Braddan School. Big sister Lesley was his staunch defender in those days. "When he was at school, he was always such a baby, always crying," she remembered. "You only had to look at him and tears would stream down his face. They used to call him Bubbles at school – it sort of suited him. There was always one girl in the street who would pick on him and give him a belting, and I'd have to go and give her a good hiding."

Lesley wasn't on hand the day that an even older girl took Barry's shirt off though. "I was 11 years old, he must have been five years old," Pamela Brown (neé Gribben) revealed gleefully. "I had to strip the little ones down to the waist for the school doctor. I think his name was Souter. I remember Barry because his chest was badly scalded. Mr Little, the headmaster, said it was because he'd tipped the kettle over. We used to have the kettle sitting on the hob at the side of the fire then. He had exactly the same smile then as he has now. He's only aged, not changed at all. My party piece when I was younger was how I'd stripped Barry Bee Gee! I never mentioned that he was only five. I always wondered about his hairy chest, until they said they were chest rugs."

The following year, it was Tynwald Street Infants School for Barry, and on his seventh birthday in 1953, he went to Desmesne Road Boys School, where he stayed until the family left the island in early 1955.

In 1952, the family relocated to number 43 Snaefell Road in Willaston, which was to become their home for the next two years. The Willaston estate was a close-knit Douglas community, with neighbours frequently popping in for visits. Joan and Ted Hill, the Gibbs' next door neighbours at number 45, became close friends of the family. Ted, as a merchant seaman, was often away for lengthy periods of time, but when his career at sea ended, he was elected to the Douglas Town Council and later became Mayor of the Borough.

Joan said she didn't see much of Hugh Gibb because he was working two jobs at that time, playing in the band at night and delivering bread by day. However she remembers that he always brought home cakes and buns, which had not been sold but would have been too stale for the following day, as treats for the children. The neighbours benefited from this as well. "We were all very poor in those days and Mr Gibb was a godsend," she said. "He used to bring home dozens of loaves that had to be sold before the end of the day – bread must have been much more wholesome in those days, didn't have all the preservatives it does today. Hugh would then be able to sell these off to neighbours at a fraction of the normal cost."

She also recalled that Barry, Robin and Maurice loved their jam butties. "I must have made hundreds for them – but that's the way it was, kids were in and out of everyone's houses, we all chipped in to help each other."

There was also the excitement of the very first television which arrived at number 43 just before Christmas 1952. "I think it must have been the first one in the whole Willaston estate, certainly the first on Snaefell Road," Joan said. "It didn't matter what was on, the living room would be packed with neighbourhood kids, they'd even sit and stare at the goldfish during the interludes. *Bill and Ben, The Flowerpot Men* was the twins' favourite programme." "Flob-a-lob" thus entered the language of all the Gibb children's playmates.

In 1953 the Coronation of Queen Elizabeth II was televised and number 43 was packed to capacity, with the overflow standing in the garden peering through the window at the Gibbs' tiny 12 inch black and white television. Later that day a street party was held in the next street, Keppel Road, coincidentally the same name as a street in Manchester where the family would later live. This might explain Barry's confusion of later years when he would tell Bernie Quayle that he had watched the Coronation in Manchester, when in fact it was probably the Isle of Man Keppel Road street party that he recalled.

Joan Hill reflected, "When I look back at those days, I realise how very kind and generous the Gibb family were, and from what I'm told, they're still the same."

Another neighbour from the Willaston estate was Marie Beck, who was friendly with Barbara and her sister Peggy. They all popped in and out of each other's houses regularly. Sadly, Marie passed away in 1995 and is no longer around to tell her story, but her good friend Helen Kenney, although then living up at Douglas Head, was a frequent visitor to the Beck household.

Helen recalls, "Barry and the twins used to come into Mrs. Beck's house and we would mind them. Barry often used to sing and always had a tennis racquet across himself, strumming and humming or singing. Robin once said to me, 'We're going to be rich one day, we're going to form a band!' Little did I realise he meant it.

"We'd cook chips for them and Marie Beck used to love the company as her hubby was away doing his guitar night, and Mrs Gibb had gone to meet her hubby for an hour out with him. The boys were lovely and I can still visualise them smiling and putting little shows on even then. I think Barry was about seven or eight and Robin and Maurice five. Lovely children, full of fun."

"Robin had a lovely smile, and he was very lively and took some watching, but brother Barry, still strumming on his tennis racquet, said, 'I'll get him!' He used to watch over Maurice and Robin even then. They were good days," Helen said.

Elsewhere on the Willaston estate, close to Snaefell Road, stood an old barn which was connected to the old manor house (now a pub). This became the favourite place for the neighbourhood children to play. "There was a gang of us," recalled Robin, "and I remember one day Barry had a Scout's knife, a pen knife, and accidentally cut a boy's finger off by throwing it into the ground. They were doing one of those games, you know, but we were just young kids having fun . . . It wasn't actually cut off, it was just badly cut . . ."

The boy in question, Brian Walton, also chose music as a career in the Sixties becoming the lead singer for a local band called The Cheetahs. They were one of the very first bands to be featured on the fledgling Manx Radio which began operations in 1964.

Brian, who was just a couple of months older than Barry, remembers the knife incident even more vividly – he still has the scar to remind him. He recalls that it was a game they used to play called 'Split The Kipper', in which a piece of wood was placed on the grass and the boys took turns throwing knives at the wood to see who would be the first to "split the kipper". When excitement was running high, sometimes a knife couldn't be retrieved quickly enough. Brian stooped down to pick up his knife when Barry, all too quickly, threw his. The knife almost severed Brian's finger. Brian was rushed to hospital where he received a number of stitches to repair the wound. He says that he looks at the scar today and thanks Barry for a permanent reminder of all the good times they had as children.

Brian also remembers playing commandos, where they would go on raids. In the weeks leading up to Bonfire Night, November 5, these raids were often to the "dens" of other kids who were storing up rubbish for the bonfire. There was always stiff competition for the biggest and best bonfire.

"I remember Barry getting a rocket up his trouser leg on Bonfire Night," Barbara Gibb said. Rockets were the fireworks of choice among the Gibb brothers and their friends, small rockets which cost about sixpence at the time. "We'd prop them up in a milk bottle," Brian Walton said, "but one of them toppled over just as it was about to take off. Everyone scattered, but it managed to hit Barry in the leg."

Robin added, "There was many a great Bonfire Night on Snaefell Road – well, not *many* because we were very young."

It seems fitting that Robin would remember the bonfires. "In a quiet way, Robin was the mischievous one. He used to light fires under his bed," Barbara said. Collections of leaves and twigs would be secretly carried into the house, hidden away under the bed and lit, while the fascinated youngster would watch the bottom of the mattress scorch. Caught in the act, he would attempt to pass the blame onto his hapless twin. "He used to sit there quietly and say, 'It was not me. It was Woggie,'" Barbara added.

Maurice has recollections of a peculiarly Manx tradition. "I remember loud noises of TT bikes and things like that. Our dad used to take us down and watch them in the pits and things . . . and driving around on Mad Sunday. My dad drove around the TT course and I was on the front of the tank of the bike – I think it was a Norton he had, and I remember it was bright green and I would hang onto this tank and my dad used to fly around that track. That's probably why they called it 'Mad Sunday'. It was like yesterday – I can remember it like it was yesterday."

Mad Sunday was the one day of the year when the TT Races were open to anyone, not just the seasoned racers. This meant that ordinary people who either owned or had access to a bike could participate in – rather than just watch – the races.

Although the brothers never saw their father perform with his band on the Isle of Man, music was still a big part of their lives. Barry remembered that, "When we were just babies and Mum was doing the ironing . . . she used to sing these songs all the time . . . there was 'Answer Me', 'Yours' and there was 'You'll Never Know' . . ." These old songs obviously made an impression – Barry Gibb still loves to sing them at parties.

In the spring of 1954, pianist Jim Caine was offered a job with a major dance band as was another musician in Hugh's band. It would prove to be Hugh's last summer season at the Hotel Alexandra. Having lost two of his best players, he put together what was described as a scratch band that summer, but it wasn't as good. His contract with Carlo Raineri was not renewed for the summer of 1955. "I think a lot of our father's frustration for not quite making it goes into us," Barry has said. "We carry on from him."

By then Hugh Gibb was finding life on the island difficult. With the winter months, his work seemed to dwindle, and at the start of 1955 he decided that his hometown of Manchester might give him more opportunities.

According to an interview Barry gave to the *Daily Mail*, on their arrival in Manchester, Maurice, Robin and Lesley moved in with their mother's sister, and he and his father moved in with his dad's family. "It made me extremely lonesome," Barry said. Life wasn't any easier for him when he began at Manley Park Junior school on January 24 either. "I didn't have any friends," he reflected wistfully. "It's a year I'll never forget. I never understood why we weren't all split evenly. It left me with a complex that I'd been singled out. I'd be left in the house all alone, playing in the streets with a broken bike that had no tyres."

Manchester itself was also a bit of a culture shock for eight-year-old Barry. "It was an adventure and, more than that, what was interesting to me as a child was the amount of buildings in ruins," he recalled. "If you hadn't seen the war or . . . if you were born after the war, it was quite a shock. In the Isle of Man, of course, there were no ruins, but when you get to Manchester you'd see all these buildings in ruins and just foundations of buildings, and on the way to school, I would see these ruins and not understand why . . ."

During the first week of September 1955, the family was reunited on the second floor of a boarding house at 161 Withington Road in Whalley Range.★ On September 5, 1955, Lesley and Barry both started at Oswald

---

★ It had previously been thought that the correct address was 261, but this conflicts with their school records, which were re-discovered in December, 1999.

Road Junior School with Robin and Maurice attending Oswald Road Infants School. Barbara remembers sending the children off to school in the morning, only to have Robin reappear at the door a few minutes later, complaining of the cold or a blocked nose. She would send him off again and he would be fine, she says, but she maintains that he was always the one who was a little bit clingy and dependent on her.

Happy as he was to be back in the company of his siblings, there was one particular aspect of the move which Barry did not enjoy. "I had a very bad experience at school," he related. "The headmaster was particularly unkind to children and he terrorised me for a good few months. Because of my fear of this man, I started playing truant, and me and about two other kids never went to school from that point. For about a year, we were always being chased by the truant officer who would come knocking on the door . . .

"I never had the nerve to tell my mother it was because of this headmaster who had been terrorising me, you know. It's funny what you don't tell your parents. If I had, maybe something would have been done about it. I would go to school but never get there."

Lesley became a willing co-conspirator with Barry in truancy. "We were always skipping school," she said. "We'd get to the bus stop, the bus would come and neither of us would make a move to get on. Then we'd go home and tell Mum the bus just never came.

"Of course, she just sent us off to school again, but by that time we were frightened to go because we were so late and we'd just go to the park. Other days Mum would give us our dinner money and we'd start off for school, wait until she'd gone to work and then spend the day playing at home. Then we'd go out and come home as though we were returning from school. At one stage we were doing that about two or three times a week.

"One day Barry and I were at home and there was a knock on the door," Lesley continued. "Barry opened it and it was the truant officer, and like a fool, he told him where Mum worked. Of course, the officer went round to see her and told her we'd had so many days off school. She didn't know and was very cross. We just got one hell of a good hiding and that was it.

"Rows never dragged on in our family; we just got a telling off and then everyone would forget it."

Barbara Gibb remembers the first time she became aware of the brothers' budding musical talent. She had come home and heard what she thought was the radio in another room. "We used to bring Hugh's father over to our place to watch the cricket on television," she recalled, and she offered to turn off the radio in the next room if it was bothering him.

Their grandfather, who had heard them regularly, replied that it was the boys rather than the radio, so she went into the bedroom and found nine-year-old Barry and the six-year-old twins sitting on the bed singing.

Barry recalled the fateful day when the three boys started singing "with three hairbrushes with cans on the top, pretending they were microphones. That was the same day we found out we could sing in harmony. The three

16

harmonies, as such, was a beautiful sound. We wanted to do that, we started finding out what harmonies were. It was all instinctive. It wasn't a matter of looking at music or learning in school, though you did sing in assembly."

In the way of older siblings everywhere, Lesley delights in recounting her younger brother's mishaps. "I've never known a kid like him, always doing stupid things," she said. "We used to play in this park which had a building in the middle. We were always being told to stay away from there, but of course, Barry wouldn't. It had a corrugated roof and he just went straight through. We thought he'd broken his back, but he'd only bruised himself."

"It was quite a bad fall," Barry protested, "and probably the core reason my back is still bad to this day. I landed flat on my back from about 20 feet."

Lesley Gibb remembered another incident in Manchester, which also contributed to his back problems. It was just before Christmas in 1955 and Barry "was going to have his first guitar for a present. I chased him into the road and he got hit by a car . . . I went to the house and was trying to think of a way to tell Mum what had happened.

"I stood on the doorstep for ages thinking of what to say and all the time Barry was lying in the road. I just said, 'Mum, don't be shocked but Barry's been hit by a car.' I can remember as they bundled him off to hospital, I just kept saying to him, 'Don't worry, I'll bring your guitar to the hospital — that's how Tommy Steele got started. He became a big star and you will too.' "

Tommy Steele, Britain's first rock'n'rolling, guitar-playing singer, was Barry's earliest hero, though compared to the hip-swivelling American Elvis Presley he was a lightweight impersonator whose real talent lay in straight showbiz. But Lesley also remembered that Barry had a talent for swivelling his hips, which suggests that Elvis, who was making inroads on the UK charts by the summer of 1956, might have had some influence as well.

The following Christmas was also filled with drama. "It was Christmas night and Mum and Dad had just taken some visitors home," Lesley said. "I was playing with an Alsatian puppy I'd been given as a present, and he kept jumping up at the Christmas tree. I bent down and my nylon dress got sucked up the chimney and caught fire. I was running around the room in flames.

"All I can remember is seeing Maurice crying and then Barry yanked the back of my hair, pulled me down on the bed and rolled me over and over to squash the flames. Then he wrapped me up in a rug because the sparks kept starting up again and phoned for an ambulance. I can't remember much. I know he ran to the next-door neighbours and asked them to go to the hospital with me. Someone phoned Mum and Dad . . . and they went straight to the hospital."

Lesley had third degree burns and required skin grafting. She then contracted scarlet fever. Children weren't allowed to visit in the ward, she said, so "Barry used to talk to me through a window. He just kept saying, 'I'm the one that saved your life, and nobody will buy me a bike!' "

17

By now they had moved to 51 Keppel Road in Chorlton-cum-Hardy, Manchester. Keppel Road was a very close-knit community and the Gibbs got to know most of their neighbours very well. While the Gibbs occupied the ground floor at number 51, Joan and William Burton were upstairs in Flat 2, Walter and Rona Chew were in Flat 3, and Harold Hunt was in the attic flat. William "Billy" Burton fancied himself as a bit of a trumpet player, a view – particularly late at night – that the other occupants of the building didn't always share.

Just across the road at number 50 were Alfred and Elizabeth Horrocks, who had a young son called Kenny about the same age as the Gibb twins, so it was only natural that a strong friendship would quickly form.

Down the road at number 23 were Denis and Florence Dilworth, and Kenneth and Hilda Haggett. It wasn't until 1957 that they would move out to be replaced by Reginald and Betty Holdcroft, and William and Sarah Frost, together with their son Paul.

These neighbours in Manchester remembered the Gibb family as struggling to make ends meet. Hugh was working two jobs, mainly as manager of a TV shop but additionally employed by a Mrs. Gillespie for whom he sold fridges. Barbara also worked to provide for the family.

Phyllis Cresswell, who lived two doors away said, "They were puny little rats – the twins in particular. They looked half-starved."

Katherine Kulikowski, another Manchester neighbour, agreed. "The kids were very pale and fragile looking," she said. "I used to give them sandwiches, biscuits and orange juice. They never refused food."

The impoverishment of their family background is something that all three brothers have never tried to hide. "I think a lot of people tend to think that [because] we have had phenomenal success, that you always had phenomenal success, and that it was always like that for you." Robin said. "That you've never had to work hard before that. They always have the idea that as children you had a silver spoon in your mouth and that you were living on beautiful manicured lawns of suburbs. I mean it was never like that for us, we had come from a very working-class background and we worked damned hard. So, everything we've done in our lives has been for the love of the art, of the music. We've never, as we started so early, we've never once thought it was gonna be for money. It has to be a by-product of what you do."

Barry has laughingly said that, "Even though we were aged eight to 11, the Gibb name in Manchester was like the Krays in London." It may be a slight exaggeration, but the boys did seem to have a knack for finding themselves in trouble in those days. "We were street kids. Our parents had no control over us. I had a great fear of the law, which . . . you did have in those times, but I was also very rebellious," Barry admitted. "Life on the street became more fun, and we wouldn't come home until 11 at night, 12 at night, because you know in the summers it didn't get dark until 11 o'clock at night, so kids around my age didn't *go* home. We'd be on the streets every night."

Kenny Horrocks told reporter Malcolm J. Nicholl, "Barry was tough. He was small and wiry, but he would never back down from a fight and he nearly always won. Barry and Robin became friendly with a bad kid who'd been in trouble with the police before. They were breaking into houses."

Their other main friend, Paul Frost, added, "I remember going to their house quite often at night, and the only light they had was candles. The power was cut off frequently because they couldn't afford the bills." Maurice has always claimed to be the "goody-two-shoes" of the group, saying his only crime in those days was once stealing a bottle of orange juice. Paul Frost had a slightly different memory of the orange juice incident, claiming that he and Maurice "once stole a dozen bottles of orange juice from the doorstep of an old lady's house. Someone saw us and reported us to the police. The police came and interviewed us and gave us a half-hour's bawling out. They never pressed charges, and my parents had to pay for the juice. We also stole from Woolworth's on about half a dozen occasions. We used to head straight for the toy counters. We did it for the sake of doing it, not because we particularly wanted those things."

Their sister Lesley also remembered other occasions when Maurice blatantly demonstrated his fondness for taking other people's property. Apparently he thought it great fun to take away bikes and prams, especially when they were standing close to the nearby police station, and put them a couple of blocks further down the street. One time, he is even said to have moved a pram when a policeman was standing in front of a window with his back to it. Lesley didn't mention whether the pram was occupied or not but noted that Maurice was proud of his success in this daring raid. Barry and Robin, on the other hand, merely spent that evening debating how many years Maurice would get in prison once discovered.

Barbara Gibb recalls another early theft by the twins. The dustbin man had brought his wife flowers, and Barbara complained to Hugh that, "'You've never even bought me a bunch of flowers since we've been married. I never get flowers from anybody!'

"My mother used to come up to the house every afternoon for a cup of tea with me. We used to sit in the window watching the traffic go by. On the other side of the road was a cemetery. So we're sitting in the window and my mother says, 'Whatever is this coming down the road?' All you could see were four little legs. And it was the twins. They were coming down the road with a big wreath they had pinched off a grave. It said 'Rest In Peace'. They came in and said, 'Here you are, Mummy. Now then, you've got your flowers.' They were so pleased with themselves."

Barbara recalled another time that . . . "Hugh left some money to pay the electrical bill, about £12 in pound notes, on the mantel shelf over the fire-place. After the children had gone off to school, I got ready to go out to pay the bill." She went to the mantelpiece to find the money had "disagone", to use one of Robin's childhood words. Her only thought was that the little twins might have helped themselves so she dashed to their school. It was playtime when she arrived, and the children were all outdoors. "I called Maurice over and said, 'Did you see some money on the mantelpiece this morning?' " Barbara recalled. A wide-eyed Maurice denied seeing any money, but told her, "Robin's got some paper he found on the mantelpiece. He put it in his windjammer, but it's gone now. He's given it to everybody. Everybody got some."

Barbara recalled that Maurice's earliest career ambitions were to be a decorator and he always had his own supply of ready cash. "He used to keep paper money – bits of paper he'd made himself – and he'd keep them in his 'office'," she said. "He was always giving people a job. And he really believed this. He put you on the payroll for £20 a week."

The twins had a way of melting their mother's heart: "They always used to look at me so innocently," she said, "[with their] great big eyes."

Kenny Horrocks confirmed that Robin's career as a junior arsonist continued into their time in Manchester. "Robin was crazy about fire. He was always playing with matches. He'd set fire to anything. A TV and radio shop went up in flames once. There were two or three fire engines on the scene. Nobody knew at the time, but that was Robin."

Paul Frost agreed. "One time Robin and I went to play in a parking lot. There was an old car there and we set fire to it. The car was completely gutted within twenty minutes. Police were looking for the culprit but they never found us."

Barbara and Hugh remained blissfully unaware of their sons' activities for quite some time. "We took them for a drive one day and commented on the billboards at a train station," Barbara remembered. "They had been burned down. I didn't know until later that it was my kids who had done it."

Barry remembered that occasion well. "We built a fire behind a set of billboards," he confessed, "and it took the whole lot down into the main road. I remember us going to the baths to go swimming after we started the fire and watching the police and the fire brigade and the crowd all filing out on the road and watching. We just stood in the crowds as well and we were standing next to a policeman and we said, 'What's happening?' and the policeman said, 'Don't worry, we'll get 'em.' "

They escaped the law that time, but soon the police were on to the chief fire starter. "Robin burned down a shed at the back of a butcher's shop. The police came and said, 'Your boys set the fire. There's quite a bit of damage,' " Barbara said.

Robin Gibb believes that music was ultimately their saviour. "I think it was the environment, especially in Manchester because there were a lot of young restless kids on the street, as there still are in inner cities," he said. "I think we were sort of a very early product of that environment . . . but the fortunate thing with us is that we had something that we wanted to pursue even that early and that was our music. We didn't have anybody on the outside saying, 'Boys, you mustn't do this' or, 'You mustn't get into trouble.' We actually did it instinctively from within ourselves. We'd act up occasionally and then we'd say, 'Look, we don't really want to do this, we want to make music.' "

Chat shows and tabloid newspapers often focus on the exploitation of children in show business, often castigating inappropriately assertive attitudes of parents with show business ambitions for their children, but all three brothers say that this was never the case with them.

"We weren't that kind of family," Robin insists. "Our father couldn't quite understand where we were coming from at first because we weren't taught anything. We suddenly ended up in the bedroom just harmonising together . . . Dad was never sort of a show business kind of father saying, 'Now you've got to do this and you've got to do that, and you're gonna sing, by God. We're gonna have you on that stage . . .' We were singing on street corners and cinemas before the film started – it was kind of a grass roots kind of thing, very natural. My parents were a bit worried at first because they didn't know where it was going to end or whether they should encourage it . . ."

★ ★ ★

Robin and Maurice joined Oswald Road Junior School, starting on September 2, 1957. Barry had already left on July 27, 1957, when he moved to Chorlton Park School to begin his secondary education. His younger brothers would remain at Oswald Road Junior until the start of the Easter holidays on April 25, 1958.

Unfortunately, their ability to harmonise didn't impress many at school, as Maurice recalled. "I remember the entrance [to the playground at Oswald Primary School] where we first stood by the wall and sang to the other kids," he said. "They didn't like us much, but we used to stand against the wall, tell jokes and sing. In fact, most choirs we were in at school, we were thrown out of so it is interesting that we ended up doing what we did. Most of the schools didn't like us harmonising to 'God Save The Queen'. We didn't mean to. It's just that we sang it that way, and naturally [they] said, 'What are you doing? Get out of my class!' "

Their parents were somewhat more appreciative, if a little taken aback. "It was a shock to us when we heard them singing in harmony," Barbara Gibb said, "but after that, Robin always laughingly says his father got dollar signs in his eyes when he heard them sing, but he didn't. I mean, he just thought it was great, he just thought they could sing at parties and things like that. He used to play The Mills Brothers' records to them."

Although Hugh recalled that his sons "had an uncommon ability to sing in this unique harmony", he didn't take their ambition too seriously. "Bearing in mind that they were still school kids, and you know how some kids get ideas about being ballet dancers or . . . want to be train drivers at one time or another, but singing was the only thing the boys ever wanted to do. We just couldn't stop them. Even in those early years their whole lives revolved around waiting to be discovered. Not that we ever put pressure on them. They'd stand on street corners singing songs like 'Wake Up Little Susie'. They had to have an audience . . ."

"He didn't push us," Barry agreed. "We had natural harmony and we'd all sing together. We were constantly trying to call his attention to our singing, saying, 'Please listen.' We had a three part harmony going. At that age, it's pretty ridiculous. We didn't know then why we were doing it, but we knew we wouldn't want to be doing anything else when we grew up. So our father wasn't the main cause of our going into show business. He didn't do anything about it until he heard us singing in the lounge. He was in another room, and he thought it was the radio. About two years after we started singing, he became involved in our careers.

"From the age of Maurice and Robin being about six and me being about nine years old, that was our objective in life . . . we knew that that's where we were going. It's drive and determination, because that creates talent if you're determined enough and you love something enough. The ability to do it seems to come with that, it doesn't come on its own. It's the determination to succeed that creates talent."

Hugh recalled that Barry tried his hand at crafting a musical instrument. "[He] got the bottom of an old cheese barrel, put a piece of wood on it, a piece of household fuse wire and made a guitar. Then, when I saw things were heading that way, I bought him one. Four quid for a second-hand guitar and that's where it all started."

"It was after hearing Elvis that I decided I wanted a guitar. My father got it for my ninth Christmas – it was on the bottom of my bed. I begged him for it basically," Barry remembered. It was obviously better than the home-made effort he had been using up to that point which "turned out more like an obscure banjo!" he once conceded. "It was then that I wrote my first pop song. I didn't know how to write music, but I managed to play the tune I wanted."

"A serviceman who had been stationed in Hawaii lived across the road in Keppel Road in Manchester," Barry continued. "I was a friend of his younger brother and he took me inside and started showing me chords that he'd learnt in Hawaii, playing Hawaiian guitar. So basically, I play the guitar completely wrong. I play totally unconventionally, much more in a country music sense. If you watch Dolly Parton play the guitar, it's the same as me. We bar all our chords – there's very little fingering going on, it's just all barring, which is basically steel guitar, open D or open E . . . A lot of country artists play the same way. So, I think when you're a kid and you live up in the mountains in America, there's no one to tell you how to tune a guitar so you do it by ear and you end up with that kind of tuning."

Barry set the scene for their first public performance. "What was happening at the Gaumont Theatre in Manchester – it was probably happening in other theatres, too – where, between *Laurel & Hardy* and *The Three Stooges* and whatever, kids could get out of the audience and go on stage and mime to an Elvis Presley record, 'Blue Suede Shoes', or a Tommy Steele record and we liked this," he said. "We'd see this and look at each other and say, 'Oh, we should try and do that – that's fun.'

"I was on my bike going down Buckingham Road in Chorlton-cum-Hardy. A boy called Paul Frost, another called Kenny Horrocks and another called Nicholas were running after me with the twins. We were joking about kids miming to records at the local theatre before the matinee started on Saturday morning. The kids used to mime to Elvis Presley records with plastic guitars."

"I suggested that we did this with an Everly Brothers disc. It was just nearing Christmas. We asked the cinema manager and he said okay. We decided to do it the week after Christmas."

Memories of that fateful first performance vary. The brothers seem to agree that it was after Christmas, in either 1955 or 1956, but here their story becomes cloudy.

Barry has said that the first song they performed was Paul Anka's 'I Love You Baby', which he remembered as the B-side of 'Diana' (it wasn't), but in 1968 he remembered it as the Everly Brothers' hit, 'Wake Up Little Susie', which had been Lesley's Christmas present from her parents.

"When the great day came," Barry said, "all of us – including Kenny and Paul – went down to the theatre at 10 o'clock. I was clutching the record. We were going up the steps outside the cinema when I dropped the record and it smashed. We said, 'What now? No record – no miming.' Someone replied, 'We'll have to sing for real.' One of us said, 'If we haven't got the record then we'll really sing.' The thought was unimaginable. Anyway, we did and it was awful.

"The manager gave us a shilling each and told us to come back the next week. The next time we got ourselves more organised. Us three brothers did the singing while the other two moved about clapping their hands."

Robin's recollections agree with Barry's up to this point, but he added, "The Saturday came just before Christmas, and we were going up the stairs of the Gaumont when Barry dropped the record . . . Barry had a guitar, which he had taken along to help the miming, and he suggested that we go out and really sing. So we went out and sang 'Lollipop' by The Mudlarks, and it went down well. We ended up doing five more, including 'That'll Be The Day', 'Book Of Love' and 'Oh Boy', and that was how The Bee Gees began."★

As there was not enough room in the Gibb's ground floor flat, Paul's mother, now Mrs. Sarah Salt, allowed the youngsters to practice in her cellar, where the expensive £150 drum kit she had bought as a 1956

★ The passage of time has obviously distorted the brothers' memories of the precise details, since none of the songs mentioned here were released before November, 1957. In January, 2000, in separate meetings with long time fan of the group, Graham R. Gooch, Paul Frost and Kenny Horrocks were happy to complete the missing gaps in the story, which actually began some weeks earlier.

Christmas present for her son was kept. "I must have been one of the first to recognise their talent when I think back," she says. Her younger sister, now Mrs. Dorothy Wilson, occasionally minded her young nephew Paul, and heard some of their early rehearsals. Although she maintains that she's a big fan of the group today, she was unconvinced when she first heard them. "What a racket!" she exclaimed.

They were certainly capable of "pumping up the volume" with Paul on drums, Barry on guitar, Kenny on a tea-chest bass, and the twins Robin and Maurice singing – and sometimes "playing" on toy guitars. Their skiffle era tea-chest bass was also stored there and Kenny says that Barry hand-painted the band's name, "The Rattlesnakes", on the side of the tea-chest bass. After months of faithful service, the tea-chest box was eventually left out at the side of Paul's house, where it lay for several months before it was finally thrown away in the latter half of 1958. Paul still remembers it fondly, describing it as "a tea chest with a long broom handle fitted with strings. We used it as a bass," he added, "every group had a bass in those days."

After several weeks of practice, Barry proposed that they join the ranks of other kids who performed at the Gaumont, the venue where all the local children spent their Saturday mornings. Nicholas Adams was with them when Barry made the suggestion about performing themselves, but he was never a member of The Rattlesnakes quintet, just one of their increasing gang of friends.

The Rattlesnakes' first "professional" performance was given on the first Saturday after Christmas, December 28, 1957, at around 11.10 a.m. Like Barry, Paul is confused about the details of the broken record but Kenny is certain that it was indeed Lesley's Christmas present, 'Wake Up Little Susie' by The Everly Brothers – released in the autumn of 1957, and that it was dropped in the street before they even reached the Gaumont Cinema.

The usual procedure on Saturday mornings was that the Gibbs always popped over the road for Kenny first, before setting off to collect Paul at number 23. On this occasion, they also collected the tea-chest bass from Paul's basement before undertaking the short trip to the Gaumont Cinema. This was negotiated via a back alley to Selborne Road which joins Barlow Moor Road / Manchester Road just opposite from where the Gaumont was situated.

The logistics of the operation narrow down the identity of the butter-fingered culprit. Barry was carrying his guitar, Paul and Kenny were carrying the tea-chest bass between them . . . which leaves either Maurice or Robin carrying the record until it was dropped. As Robin has never previously been linked with the incident, Maurice may well be deserving of the credit for kick-starting their career, as he has often claimed. While the songs they sang at their weekly performances during January and February of 1958 would vary, it seems safe to assume that 'Wake Up Little Susie', the record they were due to mime to, was also the first song they sang live.

The routine was that the Saturday morning kids' film started at 10.00 a.m.

At approximately 11.00 there was an interval, during which the manager of the cinema encouraged anyone to get up on the stage and perform while the audience tucked into ice cream and refreshments. Most performers usually mimed to hits of the day in front of an announcer's microphone. Kenny remembers a Brian Lewis who regularly had the first 10 minute spot, and who sang Cliff Richard songs. The Rattlesnakes, singing Everly Brothers' songs, would be up for the next 10 minutes. After some adverts, the films resumed until 12:00 noon when everyone went home.

It would be nice to imagine that their performances were met with the enthusiastic adulation they enjoy today. Sadly, that was not always the case. Kenny confirmed that there was a small group of lads, including two brothers who called Barry "Smelly", who thought it very funny to boo and hiss whenever The Rattlesnakes came on. Somewhat peeved at this lack of respect, Barry asked Kenny to come along to help "sort out" the two brothers, who he knew had to go home via a narrow passageway between some houses. When these two brothers appeared, Barry bashed them both together at head level. That was the end of the heckling!

A couple of photos of these early performances survive. The earliest first appeared in the 1979 *Authorised Biography* but more recently, Hazel Shacklock née Gibb, the daughter of Hugh's brother Roy, rediscovered a slightly later one. Although no longer in pristine condition, it is a remarkable relic from the time and clearly shows all five, not just the three Gibbs, singing their little hearts out for all they are worth.

Another from those days with a good memory is Eileen Callaghan. "I remember them at the Gaumont Picture House when I used to go on a Saturday morning, but I don't remember them at school.

"[Barry] wasn't in my class," Eileen continued, "but I think his teacher would have been a Mrs Brown or a Miss Reeves. Mrs Brown had very straight hair but [wore it] in a bun, and was a rather busty lady. Miss Reeves must have been about six foot tall, she was huge, very slim and very tall. The headmaster at the time was a Mr Jones and my teacher was called Mr Jurski. Oswald Road was a very friendly school, the kids were nice there."

Eileen can recall events at the cinema too, and cites "*Hopalong Cassidy, Flash Gordon, Buster Crabbe* and things like that," as films she watched during that period. They might even have watched the 1956 film *Smiley,* which featured an Australian child star who would later play a major role in The Bee Gees' career.

"The Gaumont Picure House was on the corner of Manchester Road and Nicholas Road in Chorlton, it's now the [Co-Operative Funeral Service]. There was a little lady called Mrs McLellan who was the paybox lady, and then the lady with the torch was called Maureen, she was the usherette.

"When it was your birthday, you got a birthday card about a week to 10 days beforehand which enabled you to get in free, and you could also go up for a free ice lolly! And there were things like pet shows, you could take your pet one Saturday morning, and I can remember the cats and the dogs were all screaming at each other one morning; it was really good fun! There was an interval when everyone went wild and then they used to have these talent competitions."

In early March 1958, an opportunity arose for Barry to appear on television, but circumstances conspired against him. A solo audition was arranged for 7 p.m. at the old BBC TV premises in Piccadilly, Manchester. Because dad Hugh was out playing with his band every evening, Barry asked Kenny to go along with him. Their plan was to catch the 5.30 p.m. bus, but when Barry called for Kenny at around 5.00, it was already dark and Kenny's mother said, "There's no chance of you going into Manchester. Not at your age, and certainly not at this time of night!"

So Barry, being only 11, decided to forego the audition.

This temporary setback notwithstanding, the Gibbs continued to seek out other places to sing. "We would find empty churches," Barry recalled.

"We used to look for public conveniences," Robin added. "We used to love singing in the toilets."

"We used to go down to Lewis' Department Store and sing in the gents' toilet because of the echo," Barry said. "You couldn't get echo anywhere else in your voice, and that was the place that was our favourite spot. And now, even today, we get a microphone and fill our writing room with echo like a big toilet, if you would, and it can look like that too.

"So it's just like doing a live performance; you get the echo of the theatre. That's an inspiration if you're writing a song because if you have musicians in the room as well, and you're playing, it sounds like a record. You get an impression of a finished record without it having any of the sophistication or quality of a finished record."

If an empty church or a lavatory could become a concert hall, so their basement could become a television station. With a television camera made of an old box and parts salvaged from broken binoculars, the twins would take it in turns to film elder brother Barry as the newsreader.

"We were like the Brontë sisters in that we created our own world and fed off our fantasies and ideas," Robin said. "Once we created this inner world, we immersed ourselves in that. The Brontës wrote stories, we wrote songs. Outsiders thought we were mad, but once we discovered music, we never doubted we would succeed. It was never about money, it was about being recognised and liked."

The age difference between the brothers barely seemed to exist. "We always call ourselves triplets, only something went wrong with Barry," Maurice said. "The three of us have the same way of thinking, the same mentality, the same sense of humour, the same love of music that we've always loved. We looked up to big brother Barry, but you see, we started so young we were sort of never apart – we were like all more or less the same age."

Lesley recalled that the other "children of hardly six years old" were nine-year-old Barry's great admirers, although as a typical elder sister she says that she thought that in those days he was just a strapping lad with dirty fingers, nothing out of the ordinary. Still, how many ordinary nine-year-olds are budding composers? Barry recalls that his first effort was a song called 'Turtle Dove', but he insists today that all he can remember of it is the title so he can't be persuaded to sing a few bars.

However, another original Barry Gibb composition may well have pre-dated it. Kenny Horrocks remembers how Barry wrote what he believes was the very first Gibb song. It was called 'Hopscotch Polka'. "Barry was just making up words aloud, while strumming his guitar in the Gibb's front garden, for several days until the song was finished." Kenny says it was a good song, but unfortunately cannot recall any of the words. However he did confirm that, even back in those early years, "Barry was always music-minded."

One Saturday evening, Barry's guitar, like Lesley's record, met with an unfortunate accident. Paul Frost had gone over to the Gibb's house with some candles – the house was in darkness as Hugh was unable to pay the electricity bills at that particular time. Without lights to see, Paul sat down on a chair and promptly broke Barry's guitar which was lying there. Paul recalls it was "broken in the middle" and almost completely irreparable. Fortunately for all concerned, the word "almost" proved to be accurate, and the guitar was soon back in use.

"Our next date was at the Whalley Range Odeon, when Maurice and I added [toy] banjos," Robin recalled.

"They used to give us a shilling a week and our lunch," Barry said. "Our pocket money was sixpence a week, and we reckoned we were rich."

In early May, 1958, the family were on the move, resettling in Northen Grove, just off Burton Road in the West Didsbury district of Manchester. The move brought with it new opportunities and venues for the brothers, as well as a change of name, as Robin explained. "We did the Palatine [Cinema] as Wee Johnny Hayes and The Blue Cats – Barry was Johnny Hayes."

At this point, Paul and Kenny left the band just as the brothers were beginning to broaden their horizons, although the two would maintain close contact with their former neighbours. Kenny can recall that Barry did a solo spot as Wee Johnny Hayes at a "Minor 15", a talent contest for under-fifteen's held on Thursday nights, between 7.00 and 9.00 p.m. at the Princess Club in Chorlton, so this may well be where the change in name originated.

David Stead was nine years old and in his next to last year at Cavendish Road Primary School, when he was given some additional responsibility. "Two boys," he said, "I can remember quite distinctly, they were twins, Maurice and Robin, came in as new boys to the school. When any new people used to come to the school, they were always assigned somebody to look after them and, for that period of time, I was that person, although I became particularly more friendly with Maurice than Robin.

"They got quite well known in a short period of time, the three of them. I never really got to know Barry – Maurice was the one that I used to pal around with the most. The three of them used to have this acoustic guitar; they used to go into the park [on Cavendish Road], and the thing everybody knew about them was the way they harmonised to a song called 'Lollipop'.

"The other place where people knew them very well," David continued, "was a picture house called the Palatine Cinema at what they used to call West Didsbury Terminus, which is a bus terminus at the crossroads of Palatine Road and Lapwing Lane. It used to be sixpence on a Saturday afternoon to go and watch all these old films, but the three of them used to sing, and more often than not, all they used to sing was 'Lollipop' with this acoustic guitar. They used to get up before the start of the Saturday afternoon matinée."

As David says, the brothers were now becoming quite well known locally. This was not lost on Hugh who began to recognise his sons' potential and decided to intervene. Hugh's band was playing at the Russell Street Club in Manchester, and one night he smuggled his three young sons into the club, where they sang a few songs to thunderous applause from the patrons. "We did our first sort of evening live thing for the audience," Barry recalled, "and goodness, they liked us!"

They were given the princely sum of two and sixpence★ by the manager and were once again smuggled out the back door of the club. Barry Gibb says he now realises the audience's response had very little to do with their talent and a great deal to do with their age. "We were doing something nobody had ever seen before, we were three kids singing in three part harmonies. Kids and animals," he laughed, "you can't go wrong! From then on our father became devoutly supportive of what we were doing. He played on the drums for us that night and did do after that, even when we went to Australia."

Hugh Gibb was hardly the doting father when it came to praising his children. "One thing about Dad is that we would come offstage, and he will always find the criticisms," Barry recalled. "He would never say, 'Great show!' He would say, 'You messed it up again, didn't you?' Our objective became to please Dad. And if we pleased him, we knew we were on the right track . . . These things would become implanted in our minds. It's not that he never gave us a pat on the back 'cause I'm sure he did in his own way . . . But he always complimented the audience. When we came offstage and it had been a good show, he would always say, 'The audience was great tonight.' That was his way of complimenting us."

Maurice was of a similar opinion. "Our father never once told us that we were good. Every time we came offstage, he told us we were terrible and I think this is what stopped us from being bigheaded."

★ About 13 pence or 20 cents in today's currency.

Although Hugh Gibb's musical background is widely credited as The Bee Gees' inspiration to follow a musical career, his influence on his sons was actually more indirect. "What Dad did, unknowingly, was to play a lot of music that was inspirational to writing," Maurice said. "I would say The Mills Brothers, regarding my dad's input from them to us, was probably when you are on stage, smile. If you feel like crap and look like crap, people will feel like crap too. Dad would always be down the back holding a smiley face because that's what The Mills Brothers did. I really did think that Dad wanted us to be little white Mills Brothers."

"My father was always bringing great records home," Barry added. "He was actually an opera fan as well as a big band fan, and it would either be Bing Crosby, who was his idol, or The Mills Brothers. It was from The Mills Brothers that we heard all about harmonies, and he would play these records non-stop."

The boys added songs like 'Alexander's Rag Time Band' to their repertoire, with big brother Barry strumming his guitar and Robin and Maurice providing the sound effects to the song's "bugle call like you never heard before". Although they would reprise this part of their act in the early Seventies on television shows such as *The Midnight Special*, Robin cringes at the thought today. "The sight of a grown-up man trying to do a trumpet is not quite . . ." he said, his voice trailing off in embarrassment. "When you're about 10 or 11 years old and you're doing these in clubs, you can get away with that stuff," Maurice added, "but when you turn like teenagers, they all go 'what the hell are they doing?' "

While it's tempting to visualise the young Bee Gees as little white Mills Brothers or an early version of The Osmond Brothers, they are the first to quash that squeaky clean image. "We were never like The Osmonds! The Osmonds are Mormons, we're morons! Totally different religion," Barry laughed.

★   ★   ★

The brothers' new found love of performing didn't keep the boys out of trouble. Along with a friend, Barry stole a toy pedal car. The friend already had a police record, and his mother was afraid he would be sent to reform school, so Barry agreed to take full responsibility for the theft.

"I took the rap for a kid named Graham . . . He ended up getting sent down later, and I would have gone the same way, I'm sure . . . I ended up with two years probation, and that put the fear of God into me. The policeman came to the door to tell me that I was under arrest and at the same time to basically say to my mother that there must be another country that you can take these children to," he said jokingly.

The remark by the policeman was light-hearted enough but it presaged the next great adventure in the life of the Gibbs, the decision to emigrate to Australia. "It was mum and dad basically [who decided to emigrate]," said Barry. "Don't forget that we were kids, and it was mum and dad that made all the decisions, and they were looking for a better way of life. You know, rather than sitting in the back streets of Manchester which was not all that pleasant at the best of times. That's not really a put-down on Manchester because we love Manchester, but . . . at that period of time dad wasn't earning an awful lot of money."

Hugh Gibb has credited Barbara's sister, Peggy, with the idea of emigrating to Australia, as she eventually did with her family, though it was Hugh's family that arrived down under first. The decision was based largely on economics as supporting the growing family was proving increasingly difficult. "Life hadn't been very good to them since the War," said Barry. "Dad hadn't been able to get very good work, and the New Life scheme came around where you could emigrate to Australia for about . . . £10 in those days."

It was against this background that the Gibb family began making plans for emigration. For Hugh and Barbara Gibb, a fresh start in a new land seemed like the answer to all their problems. The idea of leaving behind the cold, damp English winters appealed to the whole family.

"What I remember vividly about Manchester is how cold the winters used to be and how the water was always freezing in the taps when you got up in the morning to go to school, and wearing shorts and not really wanting to because it was always freezing," Barry said.

Hugh and Barbara applied for passage to Australia but did little to prepare for the move, "Because they say, 'Don't dispose of your property until you know what you're doing,'" Hugh said. "Sometimes you have to wait two years, we got it in six weeks."

Matters were complicated by the fact that Barbara was pregnant again. "I was having the baby and we had to wait until we got our papers to get on the ship you see," Barbara added. In the event the new addition to the family, a boy they named Andrew Roy Gibb, arrived on March 5, 1958, at Stretford Memorial Hospital, Manchester. Andy's middle name was given in honour of his uncle, Roy Gibb, Hugh's youngest brother.

And so at the beginning of August 1958, the Gibb family, now numbering seven, set sail for Australia, leaving behind more than just a few memories. Before leaving, Barry told Kenny, "I'm never going to work for anyone else . . . I want to be my own boss . . . I'll make it by myself, somewhere."

Kenny requested, "When you do, don't forget me," to which Barry replied, "I'll come back, I won't forget."

3

CHILDREN OF THE WORLD

FOR THE GIBB family, as with so many others on board, excitement mingled with apprehension as their ship, the *Fairsea*, run by the Italian shipping line Sitmar, began its voyage from Southampton to the other side of the world. Although making ends meet had been a constant struggle for Hugh and Barbara in both the Isle of Man and Manchester, there was no guarantee that the future would be brighter for them and their children in the new life that lay just four weeks ahead.

While five-month-old Andy slept blissfully unaware of his surroundings, Lesley, now 13, Barry, now 11, and eight-year-old twins Robin and Maurice could all let their imaginations run wild. Andy would be christened en-route while the journey presented a wonderful opportunity for his brothers to demonstrate their musical talents to an unsuspecting, but captive, audience.

That audience included two other budding musicians. Peter Watson would later form a group called MPD Ltd and would even record with the brothers on one occasion. Redmond 'Red' Symons, about the same age as the twins, would have to wait until the Seventies for his moments of fame when he would come to prominence as the guitarist in Skyhooks, Australia's biggest and most outrageous band of the period. Thereafter, he would forge a successful career on Australian television. His memories of the journey include water pistol fights with Robin and Maurice, and an image of all three of them sitting in the prow of *The Fairsea;* Barry playing guitar and the twins singing with him. These private performances for Red would quickly develop into something more entertaining.

As Hugh Gibb explained, "We used to put them to bed because kids were supposed to be off the decks by 9.00 p.m. Then we would find a crowd had gathered and in the middle were our little boys in pyjamas singing away. It happened every night. We couldn't do a thing about it."

Perhaps these nocturnal performances, reputedly as 'Barry & The Twins', were a blessing in disguise. After all, there were no reports of mysterious fires or ship's property going missing, and the sight of three bleary-eyed children across the breakfast table was of little concern to their parents, as was their relief at the absence of contact with the ship's pursers. In any event, there were other distractions quite literally just over the horizon.

Had the Gibbs made the journey less than two years earlier, the Suez

Canal crisis would have forced them to endure the alternative and more arduous route down the west coast of Africa and round the Cape of Good Hope, a passage not usually associated with calm waters. Instead their voyage through North Africa's coastal waters led them to Egypt and a brief lay-over in Cairo where the opportunity arose to view one of the seven wonders of the world. The experience clearly made a lasting impression on Barry. "I think it was the journey as well. I mean we saw the Pyramids and all these exotic countries at such an early age. So we've always had a feeling that that's had something to do with our songwriting you know. We drew on all of that experience when we got older."

The second week of their journey was spent navigating the relatively narrow Red Sea where Arabia lay to port and East Africa to starboard. The Gulf of Aden lay ahead and thereafter the Arabian Sea which offered them safe passage to India, just one of the exotic countries Barry referred to.

The final leg of the journey was by way of the Indian Ocean. To their north lay Indonesia, a country the brothers would have particular cause to remember later in their careers.

A twelfth birthday is not necessarily a landmark occasion but for Barry Gibb it was his first day on Australian soil. The ship finally reached Perth on September 1, by which time Maurice's health was in a very poor state. Nowadays the journey can be made by plane in less than a day, but travellers experience jet lag (Perth is eight hours ahead of British time) and a temporary difficulty in acclimatising to the increase in temperature. There were no such difficulties for those who disembarked – four weeks on the ship had enabled them to gradually adjust to both factors. The weather on that first day was more typical of what they had left behind, with rain sweeping the boat and visibility poor. The boys were still excited, although Maurice definitely recalls feeling let down as the family took their first steps on Australian soil. "All we knew of Australia was kangaroos and koala bears, and we expected to see them going down the main streets of Perth," he mused, "and aborigines running everywhere, [but] it was a big city." Although Maurice remembers their point of disembarkation as Perth, the *Fairsea* continued on to Melbourne, then Sydney, where it would have made more sense for the family to get off.

By whatever means they arrived there, the Gibb family settled in Redcliffe which overlooks Moreton Bay, to the north of Brisbane on Australia's east coast. This was in Queensland, the Australian equivalent of Florida, which was known as "The Sunshine State". Here Hugh found work as a "bush photographer" – a job description which has been an endless source of schoolboy-type humour for the brothers ever since.

"[Dad] used to go out into the small towns and photograph people's families," Robin explained.

"That's right, people who had never even seen a camera," Barry agreed, if somewhat inaccurately, as Australia was far from an undeveloped country by then.

Maurice could even remember "the caravan where they developed their own film. They would shoot pictures of people and their families," he continued, "where they wouldn't go to a local chemist because they couldn't send it off to get fully developed."

It quickly became apparent to Hugh and Barbara that Redcliffe was an ideal place to bring up their children. They would move houses many times in a short period but, initially, they would remain in either Scarborough or Margate, the two districts that form the Redcliffe area. The Gibbs made their first home at 394 Oxley Avenue with all three boys attending Scarborough State School. While Barry was noted as 'Barrie', the enrolment records for February 12, 1959, do correctly note their dates of birth although a curious inaccuracy would appear on future occasions. The assisted passage scheme meant that many families were going through the same process at that time. Timothy, Pamela and Susan Wheatley had all enrolled the previous day and some or all may have made friends with the brothers.

Hugh's photography assignments were not as frequent as he would have liked, so he took on extra work for the Scarborough local council. By this time, they also had their own transportation in the form of a station-wagon which their father had purchased from a Mr Pepper. Hugh took the twins with him when he went to buy it, but their appearance failed to impress the vendor. His daughter Karen can still recall him telling her, "They were the ugliest kids I've ever seen!"

Although Brisbane was Australia's third largest city behind Sydney and Melbourne, it was somewhat in need of modernisation and was said to be five years behind the rest of the country. However, it did have certain facilities that only a large city could provide.

One benefit was the proximity of radio stations and it was only a matter of months before three young voices attributed to 'The Gibb Brothers' were heard harmonising on *Talent Quest*, an aptly named show, broadcast by 4KQ. Ever keen to develop that talent, the brothers shunned the usual activities of boys of that age, preferring instead to exercise their lungs in a more co-ordinated fashion. "All we wanted to do was sing," explains Barry. "We used to organise little concert parties for our friends. Times were pretty hard for us then because our dad was travelling round the country." Given the choice, the brothers would seek to perform for their playmates, but that choice was not always theirs to make as their school sports teacher promoted the belief that being proficient in physical pursuits would stand you in good stead in Australia's predominantly masculine environment. For Barry, it wasn't a particularly pleasant experience. "I used to get killed," he said. "We ran around in bare feet and built up big calluses on our feet."

Robin and Maurice didn't play. "But we were always hit by the ball when Barry was kicking it around."

Another advantage of city dwelling was the speedway, the increasingly popular sport of motorbike racing, which was held at the nearby Redcliffe Speedway Circus. Barry and his pal Ken Griggs used to go to the Speedway every Saturday night to sell Coke and Fanta. Even now, Ken can remember the fine details as if it were yesterday. "We would each grab a case, with a strap around our shoulders, and walk around selling them. Then we came up with a better idea."

Ever the opportunist, Barry noticed that there were often lengthy gaps between the races and came up with an idea to fill them. Ken continued, "We would grab a few cases at the interval and set up a little stall under the grandstand. Barry and the twins would sing, and I would do the selling. People would stop to watch the singing and we'd get quite a crowd and sell the drinks. It went quite well, much better than walking around selling! Eventually Bill Goode noticed the singing, and they got to sing at the microphone and that's how it all began."

"I happened to be rushing around the pits, organising motorcycles for the first event after the interval," is how Bill Goode himself remembers things. "I heard the kids singing, and the absolutely beautiful harmony of the voices just made me stop dead in my tracks, and I said, 'Holy smokes, this is good!' "

Brisbane disc jockey Bill Gates takes up the story. "One night I was driving a race car in a charity meeting at the Redcliffe speedway, which was run by a guy called Bill Goode, who now owns the most successful speedway complex in Queensland. Bill introduced me to a youngster named Barry Gibb and his buck toothed twin brothers, who said they were singers. Bill Goode arranged for them to sing a few songs on the public address system during the intervals between races and that's when I first heard them. Even under such primitive conditions their sound was remarkable."

Their father Hugh also had fond, if slightly different, memories of the occasion. "They have what the Australians call duals – stadiums with a speedway track around the side – miniature Wembleys.* We found out that the boys were going over to one, and they put a microphone up for them, and they were singing for the crowd in between races . . . This was the beginning of how they were christened. The organiser was named Bill Goode – the first B.G. He popped his head out and at first he wondered what all the fuss was about, so he came out of his office and saw these three young kids singing. He was so knocked out that he introduced us to a Brisbane disc jockey whose name was Bill Gates – another B.G. In those days the name was just the two initials, B.G., then it was elongated to Bee Gees."

Bill Gates continued. "The actual naming of the group took place at the Redcliffe Speedway. Barry pointed out that his initials, Bill Goode's and mine were all B.G. so the name 'B.G.s' almost wrote itself."

Explaining the original shortened form, Barry said, "Initials were 'in', like dj." The naming process left out the twins initials but, at their young age,

---

* England's national soccer stadium.

they were doing little more than singing along. Later, as their involvement increased, the name was recast to mean Brothers Gibb.

Their unofficial mini-concerts also helped to supplement the brothers' pocket money, Maurice remembered. "We still weren't working professionally, being managed by our father, and they [the two Bills] got us jobs between the races at a speedway track; not during the races of course otherwise you wouldn't have heard us. So people threw money on the track and we'd run over and grab it, once again between the races, not during them!"

"We just sang for the love of it," Barry recalled, "but the crowd threw us coins and we usually went home with our pockets bulging with about £3 worth."

By now the family were living at 12 Fifth Avenue in Scarborough. The house remains much as it was then and, when up for sale in 1999, even had a "Bee Gees Place" wooden sign hanging from the very same sprawling tree they used to play in.

It wasn't long before they were on the move again though, travelling the short distance to the adjacent district of Margate. Here they resided at the Orient House Flats, on The Esplanade, just a 10 minute walk from Humpybong State School, where Lesley and her brothers again made new friends. Another student at Humpybong State School was a very young Colin Peterson who was in the same class as Barry. The paths of Colin and the Gibb brothers would cross again on further occasions.

'Humpybong' is the original aboriginal name for Redcliffe, home for Queensland's first European settlers in 1824. The name certainly conjures more pleasant images than its literal translation, 'deserted huts', taken from the Aboriginal words 'oompy bong'. Nowadays, Redcliffe is a thriving community with a population in excess of 60,000. The area obviously made a tremendous impression on Barry in particular as the following letter written by him on July 9, 1999 for The Redcliffe Museum reveals:

> *If you ask me about Redcliffe I could tell you a hundred stories about my life here in this wonderful place.*
>
> *As a 12 year old emigrant, I was a stranger in a strange land, from England where we came to live without any real idea of where we were going, Mum and Dad and us five kids in search of a 'new life', and we found ourselves here in paradise.*
>
> *It was 1958 and Johnny O'Keefe was singing 'Shout' on the radio and Col [Joye] was singing 'Bye Bye Baby' and Johnny Cash was singing 'Teenage Queen'.*
>
> *And I was there when Princess Alexandra visited Scarborough State School and we all sang 'Life Is Great In The Sunshine State' in our khaki shorts and bare feet, and it was a wonderful tropical existence that I re-live over and over in my heart and mind. 'Humpybong State School' and swimming at 7.00 a.m. every morning off the dock on*

Deception Bay, fishing for that tiger shark off Redcliffe Pier at night, only to be disappointed with that two foot grey nurse at 7.00 in the morning. Playing between the fishing boats when the tide was out at night. Listening to the insects while sleeping beneath white mosquito nets, eating fruit from the trees, singing and playing on the beach on those soft warm summer nights.

Thank God I will always be 12. This incredible place was ours, our world, ours to explore. Very little has been written about these times, but I was there with my brothers and our family, and this was to be our home. It is held in time deep inside my soul. It will always be 1958 for me.

The Saturday afternoon matinee at the theatre at the top of the hill was something we never missed. The 4KQ talent quest we never won, the Saturday night dance which always ended with a pie floating in peas from the pie cart across the road.

Redcliffe Pier was the main attraction for all the kids, with its pinball arcade nestled halfway down the walkway. There were many cracks between those planks inside the small arcade, and many is the time we would dive for the lost pennies which fell through the cracks, the water was clear and blue and provided excellent vision for the best divers, that was us!

During the summer days beneath that pier became our domain, whilst at night the various large sharks would glide and rest and watch us watching them watching us. Nobody would dive for pennies at night, but we would fish from the beach and of course there was 'Redcliffe Speedway' where the stock cars roared, and the little nats used to race that dusty oval. The smell of the oil, the noise and the atmosphere was incredible, and we were always there.

This was the first public appearance Robin, Maurice and I ever made in Australia. We sang through the PA system and people threw money onto the track, and we met Brisbane's leading DJ and racing car driver Bill Gates, who suggested we call ourselves the BGs and even played our songs on his radio show, 'Swingin' Gates Platter Chatter'; hence, Redcliffe became the birthplace of The Bee Gees.

I returned here in 1989 and was delighted that it had not really changed. I have changed, but the child inside me has not. I'm still here on Redcliffe Beach. I'm still fishing for the tiger shark on a pier long swept away by time and tide.

I can still see the pie cart, the Saturday night dance, and the speedway, and first love. I remember visibly my childhood days here and I will dwell on my Redcliffe for as long as I live.

Although the original jetty at Redcliffe was replaced by a new one in November 1999, Barry would be pleased to know that the nearby Woody Point jetty remains intact, still used by local youngsters unaware of the famous family who fished from there some 40 years ago.

Redcliffe Speedway has become famous as the venue for the brothers' first public appearance, but there is some doubt about where their first proper indoor show was held. A strong possibility is the bar in Filmers Palace Hotel, run and owned by Mrs. Mavis Filmer who proudly shows new guests the same stage on which three toothy youngsters performed in 1959. The hotel is situated in Woody Point, another part of Redcliffe, and is perhaps the same place Maurice refers to. "We started singing in a local pub just up the road from our house and our father had to drive us. My father just had to drive us around everywhere we went."

Meanwhile, Bill Gates had been very impressed with what he had heard at the speedway track. "I tape-recorded six songs of theirs and played the hell out of them on 4BH. The response was so good that I sent [a tape of] the songs to [top Sydney DJ] Bob Rogers on 2UE and he played them to death too. The raw talent of The BGs was apparent. The harmonies were fantastic . . . Barry was able to write a new song in five minutes. It usually was the best one of the four songs [he'd] previously written."

Sadly the 4BH tape no longer exists and Bill cannot remember all the songs that were on it. Over 40 years later a framed copy of the acetate that Bob Rogers had made from the tape was presented to Barry on the 1991 Bee Gees *This Is Your Life* British television programme. The acetate now hangs proudly in Barry's English home. Likely title candidates for the original tape were 'The Echo Of Your Love' and 'Twenty Miles To Blueland', as well as 'Let Me Love You' which he had heard them performing at Redcliffe Speedway. However, Bill had wanted two more songs over and above the four that Barry had already written. "I sent the two kids out to buy a hamburger and gave Barry an hour to write them. He did it in half the time." One was '(Underneath The) Starlight Of Love' which would have greater significance later. Not yet old enough to assist Barry with his writing, Maurice and Robin often had to find ways to amuse themselves until their turn to participate came. The memory is a painful one for Bill. "The twins were real hell in the studio. They used to kick the wastepaper basket around!"

Maurice has a more selective recollection of the studio. "I just remember seeing that glass booth and I remember that booth particularly because it was like being in a spaceship – very futuristic."

The six songs gained an enthusiastic audience on Bill 'Swingin' Gates' *Midday Platter Chatter* programme as well as on Bob Rogers' show down at 2UE in Sydney but Barry remembers that in the case of 'Let Me Love You' in particular this became a bit of a problem. "Bill began bashing our recording of the number across the air in Brisbane. It became very popular. People kept requesting it and asking where they could buy it, which was funny because there was only the one copy which Bill had made himself. He played it every day on his programme. Soon the local television studios started phoning and saying, 'Loved that song. Will you come and do it on the show?' "

Even the newspapers picked up on the growing interest in the boys. Under the heading of "Yes, They're Real Cool Cats", one feature included a photo with the caption, "Three boys from Redcliffe who have jolted the radio and record world with a 'rockabilly' song . . . Barry Gibb and his nine-year-old twin brothers, Maurice and Robin. The song they're singing is their own."*

The family had been in their new homeland for less than a year but, even at this early stage, Bill could see that the boys had a big future ahead of them. With Hugh often away from home for weeks at a time, it was important that his sons had someone to nurture their careers so Bill took the task upon himself and offered to become their 'promoter'. The title was chosen carefully as, with Barry not yet turned 13 and still at school, they had to be careful to avoid using terms like "manager" that had professional connotations which might attract the unwanted attention of vigilant Children's Welfare staff.

Their new 'promoter' did not endear himself to their elder sister however. "When the boys were first starting in Australia, Bill Gates wanted me to sing with them. I was 14 at the time and every time Bill came round to the house, I used to lock myself in my bedroom to avoid being brought into the group," Lesley admitted. "I was scared stiff of the idea."

Bill was able to book Lesley's brothers onto the bills of small outdoor concerts in Brisbane called 'tent shows' such as the EKKA Exhibition where he officially launched The BGs and also the Fosters one where they appeared with singer Toni McCann. Long time fan Tony Brown, now living in Norway but a native of Brisbane, is a year older than the twins and well remembers his first sighting of the trio in 1960. It would probably be fair to say that his initial impressions were not favourable.

"Every Easter time Brisbane had an exhibition for what Queensland primary industry [farming] could produce. My father moved his office to this huge cricket ground known as The Show Grounds. There he and two assistants issued insurance for the two week duration of the show. This was dreadfully boring for me and I found it dull. Everything was so bloody primitive and the noise and smell repugnant."

As Tony explains, "The Brisbane Show had a number of small shows on the side that were called side shows. These stands, attractions, entertainers etc. attracted hooligans, pick-pockets and criminal types who'd come 'down for the show'. This atmosphere was so cheap and in bad taste that I did prefer the primary produce area . . . The side show really was a filthy area."

Obviously these days Tony is well aware of the group's history but, at the time, he just did not know what to make of them. "The BGs were typical of

---

* An interesting aside to this story is that photographic evidence exists of a meeting around this time between the brothers and renowned English singer/actor Tommy Steele. Rumours have long persisted that Tommy's version of 'Let Me Love You' lies unreleased in the depths of Decca's record vaults but, to date, these remain unsubstantiated.

the side show mob – a family affair – brothers or cousins no doubt . . . In Scottish tartan waistcoats, dumb expressions and Brylcreemed hair they were well at home. Trouble was they looked so dumb and would be doing these shows all their lives because they couldn't do anything else. Later on they turned up on Saturday afternoon television's *Opportunity Knocks.* They were corny, still bristling vanity and believing they were on their way. Someone, I thought, should take them to one side and point out that this TV programme is really just an exploitation show. Surely they know when they are being made fools of? This really exposed the dreadful state of television in Brisbane. Cheap and tacky and far too much light. It really showed them up unlike the dark in the side show."

To put things in a proper perspective, Tony admits to having changed his views by 1965. "I had become a fan of theirs for sure, but I didn't have the attitude to be a fan." It wasn't easy for him to demonstrate his affection for the group in the midst of macho Australian men-folk, as Tony recalls that they considered "men who were fans of men groups were a little kinky".

Summing up, he says "They were charismatic and believed in themselves I thought, so many fans would have Kodak Brownie snaps of them lying in attics around the outback towns. Many things are possible."

At this time Australia, in keeping with much of the civilised world, was still some way behind Britain and America in the field of technological advancement. This was highlighted by the fact that it was only now that the first TV stations began to spring up beyond Melbourne and Sydney, where Australians had first seen television on home soil in 1956, due in part to that year's Olympics. TV presented Bill Gates with another arena to showcase their precocious talent although that is not quite how Nancy Knudsen, hostess of the TV programme *Swinging School* describes them. "They were an incredibly dirty group," she says. "They always turned up at the studio in dirty chequered shirts and jeans, and boy, could they swear! They were only about 10 or 12 years old, but four-letter words would be flying around everywhere! And this was at the time when four-letter words were just not acceptable, even in private conversation. I warned them about it several times, because my audience had a lot of mums and teachers and school kids in it, and they were getting very upset. But the boys kept swearing – so I fired 'em! Now when The Bee Gees describe the early days . . . they always mention radio but never TV – maybe that's the reason."

Their first Brisbane TV appearance came in March 1960 on Russ Tyson's *Anything Goes* on ABC when Robin and Maurice were made to perch on boxes so they would appear the same height as Barry. There was no repeat of the controversy that attended *Swinging School,* thus enabling them to appear on several other programmes. Indeed, they soon obtained their own show, broadcast live on Friday nights. Filmed in Sydney, the boys needed to get permission from their school for time off to go and do it. "We were on all the local television shows," recalled Barry, "and were eventually given our own show called *The BG's Half Hour* which later ran to an hour a week! We used to do all this Monkee-comedy type stuff, with special guests each week. Dad thought up the idea of the show. We were in such demand, but after a year or so, the child welfare people stepped in and had our show reduced to once a month. Naturally it lost ground and was eventually killed." Barry remembers that the reason given by the Children's Welfare Department was that "they did not consider we were old enough to do this kind of work".

As compensation they were offered regular spots on two other shows, BTQ7's *Cottie's Happy Hour* and *Strictly For Moderns*, both hosted by well-known local presenter Desmond Tester. Barry chose their first appearance to showcase another of his compositions, 'Time Is Passing By', and existing footage reveals that they were in every sense an act, dressed in matching zipped jackets with synchronised (well, almost) finger-clicking movements by the twins to accompany Barry's guitar-strumming.

By now The BGs were gaining quite a high profile on Brisbane TV and Bill Gates began to worry about their continued growth and development. "I'm not a businessman, I'm a disc jockey," he told their father, "and I've done all I can for them on my side."

It now began to dawn on Hugh Gibb that things were becoming serious. "That's when I began to realise that it wasn't just a flash in the pan craze, just as I did when I came home from work one day when the twins were seven and heard these voices harmonising to a song. I thought it was the radio playing because the sound was so good."

The group needed someone working full time on their behalf but who could Hugh and Barbara rely on to fill such an important role? Hugh was an obvious choice but the concerned parents faced an unavoidable complication.

"Suppose you were a booking agent. If I go on about the boys you'd say to me, 'It's all very well you saying that – they're your kids.' I don't believe in that because I think it's wrong for a parent to manage his own children."

Barbara put forward the other side of the argument, "You couldn't let them go with complete strangers! You never know . . ." Barbara's inability to contemplate even finishing that sentence left Hugh with little choice. There could only be one outcome.

"My father had to give up his job to take us everywhere because we were under-age," Maurice confirmed. "He had to take us into the place, and it was all down to pointy-toed shoes and polish and bow ties and nicely dressed. We did that for about three years."

Hugh now had to turn his full attention towards making his sons household names in places further afield than Brisbane. This meant that his young prodigies would soon become exposed to things he had hoped to shelter them from. The majority of Australia's venues in the early Sixties consisted of either sports or veterans' clubs. At one you would find men who drank hard and played hard, open warfare being deemed acceptable on playing fields when the situation demanded it, while at the other you would find those who had been used to warfare of an entirely different nature. These were the RSLs which became almost a second home to Hugh and his sons over the next few years. Barry paints a typical picture. "We used to play Returned Soldiers [League] Clubs and there'd be a juggler, a guy with dancing dogs, a comedian and us. We'd do a lot of comedy; in fact, we were billed as 'The Bee Gees Comedy Trio'. We'd sing 'Does Your Chewing Gum Lose Its Flavour (On The Bedpost Overnight)?' and do little comedy routines. If you were going down badly, the secretary would come on stage and pay you in the middle of your act. Then we worked in places like dockside clubs where sailors would actually have beer drinking competitions during the show.

"We played one night in a place with a huge hole in the roof. It was absolutely pissing down and a great torrent of water was falling straight on to our heads and all the audience were playing one-armed bandits which were positioned all around the stage. Then these two blokes started having a fight in the audience, but they were so drunk they had to fight sitting down! Australians are great. They'll get into a fight for any reason whatsoever. That's the way it was back then in the Fifties and Sixties. Brutal. It really was an amazing place to be a kid."

Warming to the theme, Barry continued, "The big time to us, back then, was working in clubs, hotels, the RSLs. Let's face it – that was our life from the pre-teen years onwards. Australia also toughened us up as The Bee Gees. An Australian audience is the hardest to please in the world, and I always found that if you could please an Australian audience, you could please any audience in the world so it was a good training for us as a group.

"We were into Col Joye, Johnny O'Keefe, Billy Thorpe and Normie Rowe, though I wouldn't say they influenced us a great deal musically. Maybe they did in the sense of competition. We really wanted to get out and prove ourselves against those acts. We were three kids, and everybody loves kids, you know – a great dog act. I honestly feel synonymous with Australia. It's really everything I learned about songwriting."

Nowadays parents and social workers alike would most likely question the wisdom of such an upbringing but Hugh knew the dangers and shielded his boys from them. "They had to be supervised by me. They couldn't mix with the audience and I didn't drink and still don't."

Barry remains extremely appreciative of his father's guidance. "We had very strong parents. When we were young, there were a lot of places we weren't allowed to be in. When we went some place where drinking was taking place, our father was always with us. We weren't allowed to come from backstage and blunder into the audience. We were all well protected from the kind of adults who might have tried to talk us into drinking or anything like that."

Maurice takes a different stance from his eldest brother when reminiscing about his formative years. "We had a great childhood. I always refer to the time when I was 11, in the changing room of a stripper and I think to myself, 'Will I be a normal child?' No! We never had friends our own age.

Most of them were 10 years our senior and things like that and most of the kids I went to school with I couldn't relate to."

Barry tends to agree with Maurice about having a great childhood, although the highlights for him are less seedy than his those of the younger twin. "I often wish my childhood upon those people who say, 'Didn't growing up in show business take away from your childhood?' For me it was the best childhood anyone could possibly want." Obviously with Redcliffe in mind, he continued, "I lived on the beach and was always on the beach. It was a fantastic time. Amazing."

Hugh's involvement with the group went even further as they began to travel throughout the state of Queensland. By taking them into various nightclubs as well, their act needed a more professional approach and their father often appeared on stage with them, resurrecting his career as a drummer. Later, Maurice (bass) and occasionally Robin (piano) would complete the instrumental quartet. It may sound as if it was all work and no play for the boys but it wasn't. One month short of his fourteenth birthday, Barry Gibb would find his first love.

★   ★   ★

For nearly 40 years, Ann Blackmore had kept quiet about her secret love. However, to coincide with The Bee Gees' Sydney concert of 1999, she finally decided to share some memories with readers of *Take 5* magazine.

It was a Saturday night in August 1960 and Ann was getting ready to go out on her first date at Brisbane's Woolloongabba Church Hall.

She had never heard of The BGs, but later as she and her partner Jimmy bopped along to their songs, she decided that the group was really good. The Blackmores didn't yet own a television set so, unlike some of her school-friends, she had yet to see Brisbane's hottest new act.

During the break, while Jimmy was talking to some other girls, the handsome lead singer introduced himself. "Hi, I'm Barry Gibb. Would you mind if I joined you?" he asked with a smile.

Barry spent the next 30 minutes chatting away with Ann, explaining his English background and how he and his brothers were going to make it big in the music business. They even shared a dance together before Barry went back on stage to continue performing with his younger brothers.

But that wasn't the end of things and the pair became particularly close over the next couple of years and saw each other as often as the BGs' schedule would allow. They were introduced to all the members of each other's family; Barry to her parents, brother Brian and sisters Pamela and Susan – Ann to the other six members of the Gibb clan. On occasion, sleeping in Lesley's bedroom, she was even permitted to stay overnight at the Gibb's family home, first in Kallangur, an inland town to the north of Brisbane, and then in Nundah, situated near the city's airport. They would keep in touch on the phone a couple of times each week and meet up on Saturdays, Barry greeting her at the train station before they would head off to the nearby

Nundah picture theatre, often accompanied by the twins. Ann especially remembers one afternoon when Robin, without Maurice for once, seemed upset.

"What's wrong?" she asked him.

"All the girls like Maurice more than me," he confided before tears began to trickle down his cheek.

Putting her arm around the distraught youngster, she reassured him, "These girls don't know what they're missing out on," as Barry grinned quietly in the background.

A typical Saturday evening would see all four boys and Ann descend into the makeshift studio in their den under the house of the Gibb's home while Barbara prepared dinner. Barry would pull out the notebook he took everywhere, hum and sing a few lines from his latest song. Maurice and Robin would join in as Ann bounced baby Andy on her knee, keeping time with the rhythm of the tune. Later, once his younger brothers had gone off to bed, Ann and Barry would steal a kiss before Ann retired to Lesley's room for the night.

On the Sunday Barbara and Hugh would drive Ann home and once, to Ann's total embarrassment, Barbara casually mentioned to her husband, "You should have seen Barry and Ann on the couch kissing – just like two lovebirds!" Ann visibly shrunk in the back of the car. She'd thought that no one had seen them the previous night.

Illustrating the depth of his feelings, the normally private Barry shared many of his secret thoughts with Ann, even showing her the scars on his chest from the early incident on the Isle of Man when he had pulled the pot of scalding tea over himself. However, he had another love in his life, which was to cause the break-up of their relationship.

★　★　★

Boxing Day, December 26, is traditionally a day of rest when families can recover from the excesses of food and drink consumed the day before. In 1960 however, the young Gibbs were using their school holidays to expand their repertoire to include a new activity . . . pantomime. *Jack And The Beanstalk* opened at the Rialto Theatre in Sydney that afternoon and the boys were the undoubted stars of the show. For the next two weeks, the show played twice daily, at 10.15 a.m. and 2.15 p.m., to seats filled with enthusiastic children and parents. When schools reopened, they returned to their usual routine of grabbing one-off gigs wherever Hugh could book them and countless miles were clocked up during 1961 as they continued to travel the length and breadth of Queensland in their search for new and appreciative audiences.

Now living in Cribb Island, a suburb east of Brisbane and part of the current site of Brisbane International Airport, the brothers were even said to have run their own "ham" radio station. But other things were occupying their parents' minds. Barbara and Hugh knew that a landmark in the life of their eldest son had been reached when Barry turned 15 and left Cribb Island State School. He now had to find employment but his first attempt did not fare well. "I never had much of an education and my first job was carting things about for a tailor. I got sacked from that job because I forgot to hand some money in one morning. I really forgot it, but the tailor thought I had nicked it so that was that."

Shortly thereafter, Barry signed a "composer's agreement", another name for a publishing contract, with Belinda Music for a five-year period. At the time, Belinda was very active signing up home-grown talent such as Lonnie Lee and Johnny Devlin. Tony Brady, who brought Barry down to Sydney to put pen to paper, said, "[Belinda] had heard about him even then as Barry was an amazingly quick songwriter." Barry found himself under the management of one Norman Whiteley who had left the UK on contract for Jean Aberbach of Hill & Range Songs. The choice of publisher was probably more than just a coincidence, as Norman and Hugh had known each other since the Thirties when they were both playing the Manchester band circuit, Hugh on drums and Norman on piano.

Another piece of good fortune wasn't far away, about an hour's drive to be precise. "We got a break when we moved to a place called Surfers' Paradise, which is [60 miles south of] Brisbane," Robin recalled. The Gold Coast, a 20 mile coastline filled with hotels and clubs, is the ideal place for any manager looking to find regular bookings for his clients. Enjoying bright sunshine for nine months of the year, its centre is Surfers' Paradise; a four mile stretch between the surf beach and the Nerang River. "The three of us played Surfers' Paradise at the Beachcomber Hotel for six weeks, six shows a night," Robin continued.

"Surfers' Paradise is an Australian-style Honolulu, an incredible place where it's hot all the time," Barry confirmed, fondly recalling happy times at their Cambridge Avenue home. The old block of flats also holds pleasant memories for the Lane family, and two of them in particular.

Diana Murphy, née Lane, was just 12 years of age when she met 11-year-old Maurice Gibb at one of those early Bee Gees performances. "They were wearing their little tartan vests and singing at the Church Of England Hall in Hamilton Avenue in the Broadbeach suburb of Surfers' Paradise," she recalled. "In fact, I eventually got married in that same church hall!" she exclaimed. After the Gibbs' performance, Maurice asked her for a dance and they later went for a coffee at the Blue Danube Restaurant in Surfers'.

Diana's sister, Pamela Buhner, née Lane, also well remembers that evening because, while Diana and Maurice were off having coffee, she was sharing a kiss with Robin under the carport! "I got the kiss off Robin which made this relationship with his family happen. They were a great family, full of tricks and jokes. They loved to play around all the time, and laugh and laugh." Pam also remembers four-year-old Andy, whom she described as "gorgeous, just like Barry."

Although Pam and Robin didn't go steady, Maurice was quite taken with Diana and followed up the coffee by taking her to see *Love Is A Many Splendored Thing* – starring William Holden and Jennifer Jones – at the local Surfers' picture theatre. Diana also remembers that Maurice gave her lots of little gifts including a Box Brownie camera and a guitar pick, and can also recall swimming with him in the pool of Lennon's Broadbeach Hotel.

She also recalls that even though the Gibbs had left Brisbane, they still went back the following Easter to again take part in the EKKA Exhibition where this time Lesley participated as a go-go dancer.

Both Pam and Diana hung around with the Gibbs quite a bit during this time. On one occasion, at Maurice's request, the Gibb family took Diana to Brisbane for a Bee Gees concert at The Festival Hall but forgot about her in the confusion after the show. Diana's parents had to get the only taxi driver in Surfers' at the time to go and pick her up. It cost Mrs. Lane £10 to get her daughter back, and that was not cheap in those days. Later, when the Gibbs moved away from Surfers' Paradise, Diana spent a week visiting with the family in Sydney, but thereafter her little romance with Maurice fizzled out, and life moved on for both.

The Bee Gees were such a success that their residency period at the Beachcomber Hotel was indefinitely extended and they continued to perform in the hotel's nightclub for 18 months. They would perform additional one-off shows at other local venues like The Garden Paradise Hotel, right in the centre of the town, which is now a Hard Rock Café.

Their success was due in no small part to Hugh's knowledge of what their public desired of them. "My father knew exactly what those audiences wanted," Maurice admitted. "If we were cute little kids, any bit of comedy would have them laughing their heads off . . . I was always the one who got suckered, always the straight man. Robin was the funny one, the cheeky little cute look. Barry was the older brother, looking after us. It was always visual comedy. Sort of like Abbott & Costello."

Barry continued, "We sang all sorts of material, from 'My Old Man's A Dustman' to Ray Charles' 'What'd I Say'. Big artists would come to top the bill but we were so young and sweet that we were doing great and killing their acts." Although he undoubtedly relished the applause, there was also sadness in Barry's heart.

Deep down, Ann Blackmore had always known that the day would come when Barry must leave Brisbane to pursue his dreams but he promised to write often. For over a year, his letters dropped through her mail-box every second day. "My dearest Ann . . . I don't know why you should doubt my feelings. I told you how I felt about you the day I went away. I still feel that way and I always will," he wrote. "Remember how much I love you every time some boy makes eyes at you." He ended with, "All my love for you now. Yours forever, Barry."

There can be no doubting the sincerity of Barry's words. In 1990, in an interview with *Australian Playboy* magazine, he revealed, "I like music that moves you emotionally, music where if you're in pain, it works for you. The first record I bought was 'Crying' by Roy Orbison, and that destroyed me. I bought it because I was in love at the time and that record applied to every part of me. I figured, 'There's a guy who's writing for people, who's writing for emotions.' " Given that 'Crying' was released towards the end of 1961, it is possible to appreciate the circumstances that led Barry to attempt to gain solace from the knowledge that someone else could also understand his pain.

It would be easy to assume that Ann was the girl in Barry's thoughts were it not for Lesley's own recollection of the period just seven years later. In a magazine article she stated that Barry's first girlfriend was Theresa, a small slight girl who adored Barry and would often go to Lesley in tears to express a desire to run away from home and move in with the Gibbs. She would write Barry little love letters but, according to Lesley, these were received with indifference by Barry, who was apparently relieved when Theresa's parents moved house, taking their besotted daughter with them.

It is difficult to know what to make of all this. The events were relatively fresh in Lesley's memory at the time of the article, although she may have got the names confused in which case the conflict between the two stories can be explained by differing perspectives. A naturally shy Barry may also have concealed the extent of his feelings in front of his family. Alternatively, by his own admission, Barry confessed to having several girlfriends on the go at the same time during his adolescence.

"When I was about 15 or 16, I got myself engaged to about six girls at one time. My sex life was amazing for about six months until they all found out." Asked nowadays how he achieved this feat, the former lothario flippantly replied, "I had a bike!"

Gradually, the frequency of Barry's letters to Ann ceased as the couple lost contact but their paths would cross again a couple of years later. Then 17, Ann was working in Brisbane when she suddenly saw a familiar figure standing in the doorway of the city's Festival Hall.

"Ann!" Barry cried with undisguised glee. They quickly hugged and Barry took her in to allow the rest of the family to share in his delight. "You've got to come back and see the show," Barry insisted and gave Ann tickets. Although they met for coffee after the performance and corresponded again for a while, the group's hectic lifestyle meant they would never be able to build on their early relationship.

Ann seems to have no regrets. "I feel privileged to have known them before they were big. They were good people then and they still are. They really do deserve their success and I have such sweet memories."

This would not be the first time that a Gibb would discover that the price of fame can sometimes prove to be very high indeed.

4

TAKE HOLD OF THAT STAR

As with all long careers, the Bee Gees' career encompasses many highs and lows with certain years more readily identifiable than others as particularly significant. 1962 is not readily associated with their success but, in its own way, it offered the three brothers as big a launching pad as at any time in their lives.

For Barry Gibb, one particular September's day of that year remains as clear in his mind as if it were yesterday. "We were in Surfers' Paradise doing these shows and on the road, coming into Surfers' Paradise to do one show, right opposite where we lived, was Australia's biggest pop star, Col Joye and his brother Kevin Jacobsen." This was too good a chance to miss and Barry was quick to seize the initiative.

Born Colin Frederick Jacobson on April 13, 1937, Col Joye grew up in Sydney, forming a band with his brother Kevin and some friends who played in a few small clubs. By the mid–Fifties he had his own band called The Joy Boys and, together with Sydney singer Johnny O'Keefe, they were the stars of Australia's fledgling rock'n'roll business. Between 1959 and 1963 Col had 10 Top 10 records including four number ones and toured regularly to packed audiences.

While Col was the star of the show, his brother Kevin had the business acumen to steer the band through the pitfalls of the notoriously shaky pop business. It was while on a mini-tour of Australia, performing on Queensland's Gold Coast in 1962, that the Jacobsen brothers first met Barry Gibb. "[Col Joye] happened to be rehearsing no more than 100 yards from our house, in a hall for his show," Barry recalled.

"We thought, 'This is the next step. If we can meet this guy, we can sell him a song and we're on our way.' We all talked about it, but nobody would go over and say 'hello'. So I said, 'I'm going. It's the only chance we've got.' I said to this man that I would like to meet with Col Joye. What I didn't know was that I was speaking to Kevin Jacobsen, Col's brother. Kevin replied, 'Hang around for a minute; Col is on his way out.' Col came through, and I said, 'I'd like to sing you some of the songs we've written with a view to you recording them if possible.' He said, 'Oh sure.' I couldn't believe it. [When] we played for him, he wasn't totally knocked out by the material as much as he was mesmerised by the

47

way we were singing and harmonising at that age."

Col's own recollection of events is that he was assailed at a party by a very determined Hugh Gibb demanding that Joye listen to his sons. Unable to hear them properly, Col invited the boys to attend the local church hall the following day where they played the songs to him using gear set up for Col's own show. As he remembers it, "In come these three kids with their little shirts with these little felt badges that said BG. I've still got the original tape where he says, 'My name is Barry Gibb, I live at 23 Cambridge Avenue, Surfer's Paradise. My first song is 'Let Me Love You'' . . . and they had these magic harmonies."

Whichever version of events is the more accurate is irrelevant. What mattered more is that they did well, much to Barry's surprise considering that, "We were shivering like leaves because he was such a big star!"

Col was so amazed by the distinctive vocal blend and original songs that he gave a tape of the entire proceedings to younger brother Kevin. Col still has the original tape in his possession.

Both the Jacobsens liked what they heard but they impressed on the Gibbs that Sydney was where the music scene was centred and that the boys would stand a far better chance of being successful if they moved south. Col even went further, suggesting that the Gibbs' relocation to Sydney would allow him and Kevin to become their agents with a view to gaining them a recording contract. Hugh agreed with the suggestion. "Surfers' is marvellous," he stated, "but there you can go so far in the entertainment world and no further."

Barry remembers that the clincher came while performing one evening. "While we were playing, a guy from Sydney came up and said we were great and that we'd make a fortune working in the Sydney clubs. So off we went."

In 1962 making records was the 'Golden Ring' as far as The Bee Gees were concerned and that was all they wanted to hear. Certainly the family were now so used to moving that another upheaval was less of a problem than it might have been for others in a similar situation. So the shift 500 miles south was completed in January 1963. Their first home, named 'Swingin' House', was at 23 Colin Street in Sydney's suburb of Lakemba. Here, with the help of Lesley's fiancé – comedian-compere Alan Curtis – they created a rehearsal room, complete with stereo tape recorder, out of an old tin shed. They also had a mock-up TV studio under the house and used their own movie camera and projector to indulge in their hobby of 'Goon' film-making, writing crazy scripts and acting them. The set-up was similar to the one in their Nundah home in Brisbane where they had made a Goon version of *African Queen*. Now, in their spare time, they were working on a short horror film.

Curtis had once shared the same bill with Lesley's brothers and Bruce Sacre at The Hotel Grande where posters had pronounced that the BGs were "Back again – you asked for them!" Now a member of the household, he commented on the usual hive of activity by saying, "Generally most of us are practising. It's nothing to have three radios going at once, the TV on, two guitars playing."

Hugh indicated that he would prefer to have a little bit more peace and quiet than he was getting. "You've got to have a tin ear around here," he complained.

For now, Lesley preferred more sedate activities – she was running the first Bee Gees fan club and, in *TV Week* magazine, she apologised for the delay in sending members their photos and membership cards which was due to printing problems.

Moving from the holiday town of the Gold Coast to the big city environs of Sydney was not without some trauma, however, and Robin described their new surroundings as being "[a bit] like moving to London."

It was also a time when he would become the third of Barbara's sons to narrowly escape the Grim Reaper's clutches. "I had been out for a ride on my bike and was on my way home. I had to come down a steep hill and suddenly remembered I had no brakes. There was a delivery van just in front of me, and the driver signalled to pull into the kerb. Quick-witted as ever," Robin quipped, "I decided to get between the van and pavement, and slow down by holding on to the door of the van. Well, I managed to get between the van and the kerb, but my back wheel just touched the van's wheel and that was the last I knew for a while. Even my bell couldn't save me that time! I was unconscious for two hours, and I had amnesia for another six. People passing by thought I was dead, there was so much blood all over the road." Taking into account his temporary loss of memory, Robin does well to recall these events in such fine detail.

Thankfully, he made both a quick and full recovery. One benefit, according to local journalist Dale Plummer, was that Robin's resultant gold filling in a front tooth made it easier to tell which twin was which.

The move to Sydney, coupled with their association with the Jacobsens, paid dividends almost immediately, for around that time impresario Lee Gordon was finalising arrangements for a Chubby Checker tour with Col Joye and Johnny O'Keefe as support acts. As a favour, Kevin Jacobsen asked Max Moore, the General Manager of ATA Records, to use whatever influence he could bring to bear on Lee in an attempt to squeeze The BGs onto the bill. Whatever Max's powers of persuasion were, they did the trick and Lee agreed to see what he could do. Robin remembers the next time they heard from Col. " 'Would you be interested in doing a show with me and Chubby Checker at Sydney Stadium because we don't have a fill-in act?' Chubby Checker was very, very big at this time. He was very hot, we were very young."

Against that background, it would have been a major surprise had the boys not felt a little bit out of their depth. "When Kevin Jacobsen first dragged us out of Surfer's Paradise and took us to Sydney, he put us on at the Sydney Stadium . . . the opening [concert] for the Chubby Checker tour. It was totally mind-blowing for us," admitted Barry. "It was the first time we had worked with – in terms of what was going on in Australia at the time – an overseas star. You had a crowd of screaming teenagers and these three kids – us – playing this stadium sandwiched between Johnny O'Keefe and Chubby Checker. We protested that we were unknown and would be murdered, but we were stuck with it. It was a complete nightmare." To make matters worse for the already nervous trio, an attendant had pulled them up in the dressing room before they went on, demanding to know who they were. Their response was immediate and collective. "Just wait 'til after the show, and you'll know!" Evidently they were a hit, for afterwards they accepted an invitation to join Johnny and Chubby on the remainder of the tour in Melbourne and Brisbane.

Although the twins were still at school, the group's career now began in earnest as a regular support act for Col Joye. They endeared themselves to his audiences, particularly with their zany sense of humour. A "juvenile Marx Brothers" is how one member of the tour party remembered them.

Around this time they made the first of many appearances on Brian Henderson's national TV show *Bandstand*. 'Hendo' was described by one colleague as the "patron of family pop when skin lotion was a by-word of his television career". It was also said that those connected with the show enticed its pimply faced stars to sign up for an initial mandatory six appearances by boasting, "Half a dozen *Bandstand* appearances and the whole of Australia will know you, you'll be *big*."

The brothers also appeared regularly on TV shows like *Sing, Sing, Sing* and *Saturday Date* as well as making live appearances at clubs, the dates being secured through the Jacobsens' agency. Although the money sounds poor, £15 – £20 for anything up to five hours work, it wasn't bad for those days and was enough to meet the family's bills. The boys' own weekly allowance was meagre, Barry being allowed to keep £10 and the twins half that amount each. Money aside, the most important thing was that the bookings enabled them to hone their act and develop into true professionals.

Col certainly took every opportunity to boost their confidence, regularly announcing them as "the only Aussie group good enough to make it overseas". Even allowing for his undeniable ability to recognise young talent, it was a remarkable piece of foresight on Col's part.

At the same time the boys were also exposed to other important aspects of life. Bob Taylor, one of Johnny Devlin's Devils, fondly recalls a very aware young trio, still in short pants, delivering a hilarious spoof of 'Puff The Magic Dragon' called 'Drag The Magic Poofter' at the Three Swallows Hotel in Bankstown, an unfortunate choice of name for the venue given the circumstances. Tales abound of the boy's sexual precociousness, some quite startling. There can be no question that early exposure to the backstage traditions of show business provided Hugh's elder sons with a personal maturity well beyond their years.

Kevin Jacobsen's name was the one on the management contract, although in reality it was Hugh who effectively 'managed' them at this stage. He demonstrated considerable intelligence, foresight and drive in his dealings with those who might otherwise have taken advantage of the boys' lack of show-biz experience, something Mr Gibb was not short of himself. It was said that what Hugh wanted, Hugh got, regardless of whose toes he stepped on.

As with other showbiz families, like The Osmonds and the Wilsons from The Beach Boys, music was in their blood and ruled their lives. "Music was a part of life," Andy reflected. "I took it for granted and didn't really take much notice until [I was] about [eight]. My brothers were always writing or singing or playing about with music. Robin was forever singing in the bath, the family all called him 'a quavering Arab.' "

The Jacobsens were as good as their word with regard to a recording contract and the brothers' baptism of fire at the Sydney Stadium turned out to have a happy ending. "Our first recording contract came the following year as a result of the [Sydney] concert," Robin continued. "Sydney is where all the labels are – you don't get signed up anywhere else."

The offer came from Festival boss Fred Marks, probably tipped off by Lee Gordon, who had been monitoring the boys' progress since the Sydney Stadium show. There had also been some prodding by the Jacobsens who were also on the Festival label. Kevin had allowed Marks to hear the tape of the boys' audition for Col, but the Festival managing director was not at all impressed. "Vocal groups don't sell", he proclaimed. Not to be thwarted, a crafty plot was hatched whereby Kevin offered to demonstrate his faith in the trio by dropping one of his own recording acts, Judy Cannon, and replace her with the Gibbs although, truth be told, Judy was going overseas anyway. Impressed by Kevin's "sacrifice", Fred Marks agreed to sign the brothers to a contract, delegating their records to Gordon's own label, Leedon, a Festival subsidiary.

★   ★   ★

Fred Marks was born in Melbourne on September 26, 1924. During the Fifties, he was based in Adelaide in the cinema industry but in the final year of the decade, he moved to Sydney, working as Rupert Murdoch's assistant at News Limited, a company which organised the distribution of free newspapers and continues to do so today. Within a year, News Limited had bought Festival Records and Murdoch installed Fred as its managing director.

The significance of this was twofold. Murdoch invested heavily in the label and was responsible for bringing Festival's studio facilities up to a more than professional level. Secondly, Marks was shrewd enough to realise that Festival's future lay not in solely looking inward and signing home grown talent, but in attracting major overseas record companies who wanted to do business in Australia. Rupert Murdoch's money enabled Fred to travel and meet his overseas counterparts, thus striking many deals which were beneficial to both parties. These foundations, laid by Marks, would be crucial to

The Bee Gees' development a few years down the line.

In May, 1970, Marks was head-hunted by the Philips label and moved to London to become managing director of their UK operations. During the next seven years, he became the international MD of Pye Records, the British MD of Fantasy Records of California, as well as a stint with the music division of the Disney Corporation. In 1977, he was appointed MD of *Billboard* magazine in the UK before retiring after a long and distinguished career in 1979.

If Marks is to be remembered for anything in this world, he says it should be for discovering Herb Alpert before anyone had ever heard of him, and he reckons that the $500 he spent to acquire the Australian rights to 'The Lonely Bull' was the best value for money Festival Records ever had. At the age of 75, he was living in Surrey, England, with his wife Joan, who was assisting in his recovery from a fourth operation to remove a brain tumour.

★   ★   ★

The Bee Gees' first recording session in January, 1963, took place in Festival's studio at 52 Harris Street, Pyrmont, and the engineer in charge was very likely the ubiquitous Robert Iredale who supervised many of Festival's recordings. Documentation for the session appears not to exist which can probably be explained by the fact that much of the brothers' studio time was unbooked; they were allowed to record during small time-frames when the facilities were not being used by the major acts on Festival's roster. At the time Festival did not use the title of "producer", and in addition to Iredale, there was probably an A & R (artists and repertoire) man who reviewed the material before recording (Lee Gordon may have played this role). One man definitely present was Col Joye himself who, to all intents and purposes, could rightfully have claimed production credits, while backing vocals and instrumentation were provided (again uncredited) by his very own Joy Boys.

Iredale, "a bespectacled rather studious person with a cutting sense of humour", was known for his ingenuity with the limited capabilities of the equipment on hand. The late Rajahs' guitarist Jon Hayton recalled from sessions in 1959-60 that Robert was "a very clever engineer, probably the best in Sydney at that time, but unfortunately he had the attitude of most engineers that musicians and singers are total ignoramuses who have to be pushed and prodded throughout the session to get anything artistic out of them at all. At that time in Australia, we were all just learning recording techniques; not only musicians and singers but also producers, engineers and the record sales department. Hampered by inadequate, outdated equipment, we plodded on, always behind the Americans, desperately trying to catch up."

Leon Isackson, drummer of The Rajahs who were another Festival act, goes even further, describing Iredale as "bossy, used to getting his own way". Apparently, the only guy who stood up to him was Johnny O'Keefe and tapes still exist of the following conversation from an O'Keefe recording session:

O'Keefe : "What do you think Robert?"
Iredale : "Sounds a bit noisy, John."
O'Keefe : "It's rock'n'roll, Robert. It's supposed to be fucking noisy!"

The product of the Gibbs' initial session, their first single, was released on March 22, 1963, under the banner of "The Bee-Gees". This name, reminiscent of nomenclatures being given to new American groups like The Lettermen and The Four Seasons, perhaps reflected Lee Gordon's desire to market them to the teenage audience which was becoming increasingly responsible for a record's ability to make the charts. A fact sheet proclaiming "two great sides with definite Top 10 potential" accompanied sample copies of the disc, issued in advance to disc jockeys. It also provided brief biographical details of the brothers and advised that the group "have really hit the top since their arrival in Australia, with many TV appearances to their credit and several triumphant personal appearance tours". Barry's age was noted as 17, a year older than he actually was, this probably being a deliberate ploy on Festival's part to lose any schoolboy comparisons and thereby make him more appealing to teenage girls.

While the song failed to turn out to be the hit that their record company had hoped for, it wasn't the abject failure that Robin later made it out to be. "We recorded our first flop which was a record called 'The Battle Of The Blue And The Grey' based on the old story [of the American Civil War]. Now this record was very hot with one guy at 2SM in Sydney. He was playing this all the time and, of course, it didn't do anything." In fact, although not making any noticeable impact, it did creep into the top 20 of the local Sydney chart, a national chart being some years away.

Barry's first person narrative, from the perspective of a Confederate veteran recalling his youth, is a remarkable account considering that he was still only 16 when he wrote it.

The song featured Barry on lead vocal and guitar with the twins providing the harmony and backing vocals, and its subject matter made it an unusual choice for a first single. In retrospect, it sounds very much like a tribute to Johnny Horton who had a hit record with the similarly themed 'Battle Of New Orleans' four years earlier in 1959. Though short in its length (2.05) like most of their Australian releases, it's a cleverly crafted song full of interest, albeit somewhat violent for the time with references to shooting people "full of lead" as part of its war theme. In an attempt to promote the single, stories appeared in Sydney newspapers about the new "singing group" and its young songwriter. Indeed, footage of its television début on *Bandstand* still exists.

While their début release achieved a reasonable amount of publicity, the music press also made mention of one other member of the household. Tucked away in the small print, was news that sister Lesley had also embarked on a show business career in Surfer's Paradise . . . as a snake-dancer! In an unfortunate accident, Helene The Snake Dancer had been bitten and the club's owner asked Lesley to fill in. "I said, 'Okay, but you'll have to clamp the snake's jaws with sticky tape. I don't want to end up in hospital, too.' Everything went fine, and I started to keep snakes as pets after that." However, by 1980, Lesley had decided that she would just stick to breeding dogs, claiming, "[Snakes] have such short life spans, and I get quite upset when they die."

The flip side to 'The Battle Of The Blue And The Grey' was a pretty enough little ditty entitled 'The Three Kisses Of Love'. Bearing favourable comparison with Herman's Hermits' 'Silhouettes', it is also similar to the unreleased 'Let Me Love You' and provided Robin and Maurice with a better opportunity to demonstrate their vocal ranges than its companion. This was even shorter at 1.46 but a catchy song nonetheless and The Bee Gees have been known to do brief renditions of it during radio and television interviews, even as late as 1990. At the time, according to Barry, "It got more plays [than the A-side]!"

Both sides sound as if they have some orchestral backing, but the absence of session records means this cannot be confirmed. Aural evidence suggests that the arrangements comprise only violin, string bass and drums with the violin (or possibly damped guitar) played pizzicato, plucking strings instead of bowing. If this is the case, then Robert Iredale and/or Col Joye deserve full credit for the clever use of an echo chamber, a favourite trick of Iredale's which probably featured on some of the boys' next few singles too. By placing a speaker and a microphone in a small side room adjacent to the recording booth, Iredale could make a solitary violin sound more like a string section and fool all but those in the profession who knew what to listen for.

Having a recording contract most certainly did not mean that they had hit the big time, and live performances at strange venues were still the order of the day. A fine example was the show they performed that year at the Oval Showgrounds in Wollongong, about 50 miles south of Sydney. Situated in a predominantly industrial area Wollongong is itself attached to the steel-making town of Port Kembla whose two largest employers were BHP and John Lysaght.

The latter company had sponsored a day out at the Wollongong Oval for its thousands of workers and their families and, according to John Macbeth, appropriately now returned to his native Scotland, "Lysaght's, the company my father worked for, paid for the whole day. There was free admission, free candyfloss, ice cream . . . everything. It was like the kids' Christmas day out type of thing," he remembered with all the enthusiasm of the 10-year-old schoolboy he was at the time.

"There were all sorts of side-shows, and on one stage was a young singing group. I was with a bunch of people and there was a girl saying, 'I'd love to have their autographs.' She was 12, ready to go to High School, and she promised me a kiss if I got them for her. I can remember running up the side of the stage during one of their breaks, there wasn't any security or anything like that, and one of the smaller singers said, 'Yep, okay.' So off he went taking the leaflet that the lassie had given me and got the other ones to sign it, and then I brought it back down and got my kiss off the girl. I can't remember much about their performance, but I noticed the influence that having a guitar had over all the girls. I can remember afterwards going and looking in all the music shops and thinking I should learn how to play a guitar. Never mind the music, it was the being adored by all those girls that I wanted!"

The remainder of the Macbeth family was there that day too. At just seven and three years of age respectively, John's younger sisters Ray and Annette were too young to remember this landmark Bee Gees concert, but Mum Ella recalls the trio only too well. "Was that those skinny boys with the long hair?" she queried, displaying her preference for "a short back and sides", before adding emphatically, "They were awful!"

Ella apart, the group's growing number of fans had to wait only two months 'til May 1963 for their next song to be released. It wasn't by the Gibbs themselves on this occasion but by their mentor at the time Col Joye. Joye recorded one of the songs he had first heard Barry play the year previously back on the Gold Coast. Col recorded Barry's '(Underneath The) Starlight Of Love' as the B-side to his 'Put 'Em Down' single on Festival records. More than 35 years later, '(Underneath The) Starlight Of Love' remains a bright, cleverly produced song well sung by Joye that is a nice testament to an emerging but still young and learning songwriter. It was a considerable feather in 16-year-old Barry Gibb's cap to have one of the country's top performers record his material and its release gave Col the distinction of being the first artist anywhere to cover the Gibbs' material. Before the decade was over other singers, including Elvis Presley, Nina Simone, Wayne Newton and many many more, would join him.

Meanwhile Andy, aged four, was already considering his own career options. He wanted to be either a doctor or a Bee Gee. Hugh and Barbara expressed their preference that he should pursue the latter option. "He sings in perfect pitch with the boys when they're practising," enthused Barbara, "and we'd like him, one day, to join the group."

'If at first you don't succeed, try, try, and try again' goes the old saying and, over the next three years, nobody would accuse the boys of any lack of effort. On July 29, they did indeed try again.

With the benefit of hindsight, Robin wonders whether their next release was the right choice in the circumstances. "We went back into the studio and cut our second one, 'Timber', which did exactly what the title suggested!" While it certainly comes across as being somewhat trite today, the A-side's lyrics of 'Timber baby 'cos I'm a falling for you' were actually reflective of the period. One group, Steve & The Board, even went so far as to entitle their 1965 LP *I Call My Woman 'Hinges' Cause She's Got Something To Adore*. In contrast to their first effort, 'Timber' was an extremely up-tempo number and sounds almost like a 33 rpm record being played at 45 rpm speed. Produced by Robert Iredale, this time without the studio assistance of Col Joye, and with a time of only 1.46 minutes, it was almost over by the time it began.

This time, Festival's generosity in providing "orchestral" backing, sounding suspiciously like a solitary violin, was limited to the A-side only, and it would be over a year before the budget-conscious label would see fit to do so again. On the reverse side was 'Take Hold Of That Star', a rather impressive ballad where the trio's harmonies are well to the fore. This is a fine song with an almost Fifties feel to it. The arrangement is entirely different to that on 'Timber' with Barry's first instrumental contribution of strummed guitar, a lounge-style piano, and string bass and drums suggesting that it came from a different recording session. The evident maturity of Barry's full vocal during the solo bridge section, belies the fact that he is still only sixteen years of age. Unfortunately, it was consigned to the anonymity of the reverse side and remained generally unheard.

For this release, the group had discovered their third and final variation of their name by dropping the hyphen. "The Bee Gees" would serve them well, lasting to the end of the century and beyond.

Perhaps, at that age, their songs relied too heavily on visual presentation because they continued to go down well whenever they had their audience in front of them. In September, 1963, they appeared at their first Sydney 2UW Spectacular, a four-hour concert at Lane Cove National Park sponsored by a local radio station. Over 40,000 were in attendance to watch not only The Bee Gees but Warren Williams, Lonnie Lee, Col Joye & The Joy Boys, Johnny Rebb, Laurel Lea & The DeKroo Brothers, Judy Stone and Noeleen Batley.

They must have acquitted themselves well because they were invited back to another Spectacular just four months later, early in the new year. The bill saw the return of The Bee Gees, Warren Williams (this time with The Courtmen), Johnny Rebb, Judy Stone and Noeleen Batley being joined by The Atlantics, The Dave Bridge Trio, The Denvermen, Johnny Devlin and Digger Revell. During the remainder of their time in Australia, some of these names would become even more familiar to the brothers.

In between these two concerts, Robin and Maurice left school on December 22, at the close of term immediately before their fourteenth birthday. However, the education authorities were firmly of the belief that their departure coincided with the approach of their fifteenth birthday, the strictly enforced minimum legal school leaving age. Indeed, all three brothers had been economical with the truth about their ages for some time and many press cuttings from this period and beyond all quote their ages as a year older than they actually were. Defending accusations that they received virtually no education at all, Maurice gives the game away. "We actually did fill some forms out and passed some tests and left at 13. The school said, 'They can't concentrate – they're too involved in show business.' In fact, a lot of people say to us, 'Don't you think you feel a bit left out not having a normal childhood?' I had a fantastic childhood because all the people we mixed with were adults, so we heard dirty jokes long before we should have and all the bad language!"

Encouraged by the success of their 2UW Spectacular appearances, the boys bounced back into the studio, the resulting recordings appearing as their third single on February 10, 1964. Robin is dismissive in his recollection of the event. "So we went back to the studio . . . to record a follow-up, 'Peace Of Mind', which didn't give us any when it flopped!" The lack of success was despite an attempt on Festival's part to boost sales by cashing in on Barry's growing popularity with young teenage girls and also to reflect his status in the group. Nonetheless, the new release by "Barry Gibb & The Bee Gees" was to suffer the same fate as its predecessors! This was something of a shame, as the Mersey influenced 'Peace Of Mind' deserved to be appreciated by a wider audience. Sounding less like children, it had a raunchier, more adult feel to it, highlighted by a couple of screams not dissimilar to those heard on some Beatles songs of that period. A lead guitar augments the now usual Barry on rhythm guitar, and string bass and drums.

By 1964, The Beatles sound had well and truly hit Australia. While The Bee Gees unique harmonies had actually predated The Beatles, the success of the Liverpool band certainly gave The Bee Gees the impetus and confidence to use their own harmonies in a more R&B style.

However, in stark contrast, for the first time but certainly not for the last, they ventured into country and western territory on the B-side with yet another Barry Gibb composition. 'Don't Say Goodbye' is a much slower paced number with piano, Barry on guitar, string bass and a coconut-like percussion.

By now, itchy feet had got the better of the family again, and they settled within the city boundaries at Lane Cove, on the north side of the Parramatta River that divides Sydney. The Bee Gees were also starting to appear in the local Sydney newspapers, not only because of the "singing brothers" aspect, but also focusing on teenager Barry's songwriting success.

According to Belinda Music's promotion manager of the time, Tony Brady, between September 1963 and March 1964 Barry had 12 songs recorded by other artists. "This makes him one of the few songwriters in Sydney who has material constantly recorded. He has the greatest potential of any songwriter in Australia. In fact, I'd go so far as to say he could become the first Australian songwriter to make a living from composer's royalties alone. Barry is one of the few songwriters in Sydney who can satisfy this great demand from the record companies."

Tony continued by revealing that one of Barry's latest compositions, 'One Road' was being reviewed by 19 record companies in America, "And we expect it to be recorded by at least three or four companies. If the song becomes a hit in the States, Barry could earn up to £2,000 from this song alone."

To an impressionable young man, such a glowing tribute could have been the catalyst to breaking out on his own, but Barry had no thoughts of leaving his brothers behind. "The two careers are equally necessary to me. Without either one I would be dissatisfied. [I began songwriting] to express a desire to create rather than copy the songs I sang." Barry did concede that the royalties money lay in the pop field, but this had not prevented him from trying his hand at ballads and semi-classical music. In fact, he had just completed work on a piano concerto, the whimsically titled 'Concerto With No Name'.

Another song, said to be written from around this time, has recently surfaced. Entitled 'Double Dating', it comes from a scrapbook kept by one of their most fervent fans from that period. There is no doubting, whatsoever, Dorothy Gliksman's credentials – there are many examples of letters written to the radio stations and music press by her in those early years, requesting more airplay of The Bee Gees' music – and she states quite clearly that she can recall the song being gifted to her by Barry in 1964. So far, Barry has declined the opportunity to validate the claim that 'Double Dating' is indeed one of his compositions but, then again, he hasn't denied it either.

Although typed, and without music, the word "Love" is written at the bottom, accompanied by a signature which could indeed be Barry's. If this is the case, the song's lyrics provide a fascinating insight not only into Barry's thought process towards his brothers at the time, but also the extent to which his spelling had suffered from such a fragmented education. Indeed, future manager Robert Stigwood, asked what it was about the group that he found so appealing, would state: "This may sound corny," he replied, "but it's their poetry. These boys are completely uneducated. They don't even know how to spell. They write the lyrics out spelled phonetically. And the simple poetry of the words appeals to the public."

Spelling mistakes and grammar aside, "Double Dating", whoever wrote it, is actually a fine example of uncomplicated poetry.

DOUBLE DATEING

Now we are twin bothers and when things are done
We do them together we do them as one
But I have a girlfreind and he has one to
So we go double dating what else can we do

Chorus

Double dating theres nothing like this
When you can't help but wink at your twin brothers miss
And when hes not lookinn your stealin a kiss
Double dating thers nothing like this

Chorus

Well we drive through the city with the big burnin lights
Lookin fir somewhere to have a good night
We don't want a movie we don't want a show
We just wanna go where the lights are down low

Chorus

Now there can be trouble if you have a twin
And theres no telling what kind of trouble your in
Yes we have a problem our heads in a whirl
For we are in love with each others girl.
And

Chorus

In the circumstances, unless an out and out denial is forthcoming, 'Double Dating' could be regarded as an original Barry Gibb composition.

By now the boys were said to be earning £150 a week for their regular slots on *Bandstand* which had seen their recent repertoire extended to include performances of 'Please Please Me', 'Blowin' In The Wind', 'Da Doo Ron Ron', 'Little Band Of Gold', 'I Want You To Want Me' and the classic 'Hilly Billy Ding Dong Choo Choo'! While £150 might sound like a lot of money for those days, with so many hungry mouths to feed in the Gibb household, the boys didn't have that much left for themselves by the time all the bills got paid. Regular performances on other popular television shows ensured that they were becoming increasingly well known across Australia.

In an unusual display of optimism, Festival elected to release their first EP comprising the four tracks from their first two "flops". Entitled *The Bee Gees,* the disc was contained in a picture sleeve cover which showed the three brothers identically dressed in white shirts with dark ties, dark trousers, black "winkle-picker" shoes and tartan waistcoats. The waistcoats were augmented by "BG" lettering on the left breasts which would become a trademark of their TV appearances over the next two years.

In Brisbane, they were feted in April 1964 by the local Channel 9 who offered them a half-hour special in a move designed to persuade them to transfer their loyalties from Channel 7. They were not always so highly regarded by their new suitors as Barry J. Whalen, writing in *On Air*, a book to commemorate the twenty-fifth anniversary of TV in Queensland, reveals:

"I was watching their first try-out for *Brisbane Tonight* with Wilbur Kentwell, Nine's musical director . . . We watched The Bee Gees thump through a couple of numbers and I asked him: 'What do you think of 'em, Wilbur?' Wilbur tugged his lower lip, then said with great deliberation, 'They'll never make it – they can't even carry a tune.' Oh well, that's show biz!" Wilbur would see the error of his ways at their second audition and they became regulars on the show thereafter.

Their TV special brought them into contact with a record producer called Nat Kipner, an American brought out to Australia by Festival Records to be their A & R (Artists & Repertoire) man. Nat was also talent co-ordinator and producer of the television show *Saturday Date*, another programme that The Bee Gees had regularly appeared on. His natural energy and drive, matched with his enthusiasm for The Bee Gees and their songwriting skills, were to have a big impact on the Gibb brothers' achievements over the next few years.

Another name that kept cropping up throughout the duration of the Gibbs' stay in Australia was that of Johnny O'Keefe. Host of *Sing, Sing, Sing* he was more responsible than anyone for the brothers' appearances on that show. One show in particular, broadcast during the second week of June, 1964, is of special interest.

Even in those days, it was not uncommon for artists to mime to recordings of current hits, which they would tape at a studio a few days prior to actual filming. In October, 1983, 42-year-old Bill McSorley came across some oddly labelled records at a garage sale in the Sydney suburb of Rushcutters Bay. He was recommended to world renowned Australia rock historian Glenn A. Baker who was able to confirm that Bill had discovered original Festival acetates of rare and priceless pre-recordings for O'Keefe's show.

The acetates contain Bee Gees performances of 'From Me To You' (Lennon & McCartney), 'Can't You See That She's Mine' (Smith & Clark), 'Yesterday's Gone' (Stuart & Kidd), 'Just One Look' (Payne & Carroll) and 'Abilene' (Brown, Gibson, Loudermilk & Stanton). Although it took several years of negotiation, and much work to clean up the sound to an acceptable level, the first four listed of the five recordings were made available on a compilation CD in 1998.

By now the Gibb family had moved yet again. Their International Fan Club was receiving 500 letters per week at their new residence at 8 Kent Street, Bronte, just south of the famous Bondi Beach, on the south side of the Parramatta River. Their rise in popularity was due in part to exposure in teenage magazines which often featured the obligatory "fact file" type information. Here you could read that Barry was into The Mills Brothers and The Shadows, loved go-kart racing and deep-sea diving, wanted to reach worldwide standards in his own right and preferred small blondes. Robin was a fan of Roy Orbison and The Tornados, also liked go-kart racing and was fond of small redheads. His ambition was to tour the world in his own right. Maurice, or "Morrie" as he was becoming known, listened to The Beach Boys and The Preachers and his preference was for small brunettes, with big soft jumpers. His ambition was linked to his hobby . . . to win a go-kart race! Such "star dossiers" also revealed that "they design all their own clothing and shoes", a statement they would have done well to disassociate themselves from on occasion.

Of even more interest was the identity of their fan club secretary, Miss M. Bates, c/o the same Bronte address. Maureen Elaine Bates, a small blonde, was born on April 30, 1947. Her mother, a Watson by birth, had settled with her husband in Birmingham but, in an amazing coincidence, the Bates family also emigrated to Australia in 1958, although it would probably be stretching things a bit far to suggest that they may have shared the same ship as the Gibbs. Lesley and Maureen used to dance on the same Australian TV show, and this was how she came to be introduced to Barry. Her title of "fan club secretary" disguised the fact that Barry was in love again, and this time there would be no leaving her behind. When he moved, she moved.

Romance was also in the air for Robin who had a girlfriend called Margaret whom Lesley described at the time as being from a rather rich family. She also revealed that her brother was reluctant to express his feelings to a girl lest she made fun of him. Margaret didn't seem to bother too much about the lack of affection, showering Robin with gifts. She bought him a ring which he merely commented on as being a bit striking. A complete leather travelling set was apparently useless – in those days he never used a brush – while he also received an expensive watch. Apparently, even then, Robin had a loathing of appointments. No problem to our Margaret . . . she sent a taxi from her Lidcombe home to collect him.

Perhaps Margaret's attraction to Robin stemmed from the physical side of their relationship; either Lesley was completely unaware of the extent of it or it was Robin's bravado talking when he alleged, "We screwed every night!"

The incident that Lesley felt best summed up Robin's apathy towards his relationship with her was when he spent an entire evening in front of the TV, hardly uttering a word to Margaret. When he grew tired of watching, he asked her to fetch him another glass of milk, which he drank before heading straight to bed. Not surprisingly, as soon as she met a boy who was nice to her in return, Margaret promptly disappeared from Robin's life.

Always well-mannered and polite, Margaret made a courtesy call to Lesley to let someone know the reason why she wouldn't be coming round to their house any more. When Robin learned of this he was furious and declared that he would forgive her one more time! This was the straw that broke the camel's back as far as Lesley was concerned, and she launched into a furious tirade against her younger brother, pointing out to him in no uncertain terms his need to change his attitude. Pig-headed, moody and insolent were just a few of the accusations levelled at the startled youngster, who was caught completely off guard by his sister's aggressive reproach.

If Lesley's memory is accurate, it was another three months before a smile returned to Robin's face and, of course, he never uttered Margaret's name again. Instead, to Lesley's regret, he became completely withdrawn in all his dealings with the fairer sex. Although he would accompany his sister to dances, he would never once take to the floor. Interested only in the music, he would declare that dancing was stupid. That attitude would change when he met his first real love, but that was some years and several thousand miles away. Before then, Maurice would also discover that making friends with girls was not without its difficulties.

★   ★   ★

On July 31, a small column in a Sydney newspaper revealed that there were plans for the boys to visit the USA in January, 1965, to coincide with an appearance on *The Ed Sullivan Show*. Sadly, it would be another few years before that particular ambition was realised.

As they had already done so spectacularly elsewhere in the world, The Beatles had now made a considerable impact on Australian pop culture. "Col was always number one," Barry explained, "then, all of a sudden, bang! The Beatles started happening. It changed our whole attitude towards show business. Col fell flat as a tack. Nothing happened to him after The Beatles arrived! We were in Tasmania when their record 'Love Me Do' was released. It never got a scrap of air play, but we loved it. The flip-side, 'I Saw Her Standing There', did get lots of plays. We thought 'The Beatles! What a stupid name!' Stupid name or not, The Bee Gees were influenced by their Liverpudlian "cousins" as much as any other up-and-coming artists of the time.

Robin took a pragmatic view. "Then we started our experimental stage because The Beatles were happening and we thought, 'Let's get some inspiration from this group that are doing so well overseas. It's a British group, we're British – living in Australia, surely we can do something so let's experiment.' "

Their father Hugh saw things from a different perspective. "When [my sons] started recording, they were singing in their own style. Then The Beatles began to hit, and we had trouble because the recording companies were saying, 'Oh, they sound too much like The Beatles,' and I said, 'They've always sung like that.' Bearing in mind that they come from thirty miles away from The Beatles, it's a similar type of sound. It is rubbish to say that we copied The Beatles' sound, it wasn't their sound, it was an English sound that began with Tommy Steele and skiffle."

Barry agreed. "People were playing our records and The Beatles' and found that we sounded very similar, so we were banned right off the air! If Australia gets someone good from overseas, they'd rather push their own artists out."

Whatever the case, the indisputable fact remains – that The Bee Gees were unashamed Beatles fans and still are.

"The Beatles came to Australia, and that was a very important moment for us being a group," Barry stated. "When they arrived in Melbourne, there were a million people in the city centre and we thought, 'We gotta do this, if we got to England we could become like The Beatles.' I think to this day, people not of our generation do not realise how huge The Beatles really were. Even people like Michael Jackson, I don't think, have the same aura. Whatever they did to the world, they did it to all ages, they didn't do it to one age."

62

"When The Beatles came on the scene it was like, that's us, that's what we've been trying to do," Maurice enthused. "Our first record, the flip side was called 'The Three Kisses Of Love'. We were going, 'Kiss me once, oh yeah, baby.' This was all pre-Beatles stuff and we were going, 'Wow, it's them . . . She loves you yeah, yeah, yeah.' They're doing what we're doing . . . and they were English to boot. Also, there was a mystery about them. The *With The Beatles* cover blew me away totally. This is what I would like to be like, the black polo necks, the half-shadowed faces, the moodiness, the mysteriousness, touchable but untouchable and Paul was my mentor. His bass playing was amazing and every single Beatles record, even now, I can play every bass line that Paul played and that's how I learned bass from The Beatles' records. We modelled ourselves on them, a lot of kids did, a lot of groups did, in those days."

The Beatles' Australian tour followed the release of 'Can't Buy Me Love' which had flown spectacularly to the top of all the local charts at the beginning of May. Ironically, by the time of their arrival in Melbourne on June 14, 1964, it had slipped in the ratings and the number one in most areas was 'Poison Ivy' by Billy Thorpe & The Aztecs. For their lead guitarist in particular, one Vince Melouney, there would be further opportunities to compete against 'The Fab Four' but on a bigger stage altogether.

For The Bee Gees, however, the novelty of the flattering comparisons quickly began to wear off. Desperate for the group to create its own identity, a clearly irked Barry told Australian *Cash Box* music magazine, "Stop referring to us as 'The Australian Beatles', you can quote me on that," which, of course, they did!

"Everywhere we went," Barry reflected some years later, "we saw notices saying we were 'Australia's Beatles'! There was only one DJ, called John Laws, who would stick up for us and play our records. He said that although we sounded 'Beatley', we had been there before The Beatles. But the public just didn't want to know. We had a very bad time. Every show we did they shouted, 'Get off Beatle imitators!' We couldn't wait to get back to England again. We thought, 'If they're going to slam us in our face, we'd rather get out.'"

His brother "Morrie" was quick to support his remarks. "We have our own sound, and actually recorded our first single in January, 1963, long before The Beatles became famous."

The result of their experimentation was their fourth single, again under the supervision of producer Robert Iredale, released on August 17 under "The Bee Gees" banner. Worthy of comparison with 'Please, Please Me', 'Claustrophobia' has a fuller sound than previous releases due to the presence of The Delawares, a Sydney based band, comprising Bruce Davis (guitar), Leith Ryan (guitar), Bill Swindells (bass) and Laurie Wardman (drums).

In those days the recording details could be decidedly casual. In this instance, the (uncredited) Delaware's support came about after the Gibbs had seen the band play at a dance in Wollongong. The band would also support the Bee Gees on television shows like *Saturday Date, In Melbourne Tonight, In Brisbane Tonight, Seventeeners* and *Sunnyside Show* promoting the single. The Gibbs would return the favour the following year by providing two songs for the group, fronted by lead vocalist Dennis Williams. Maybe, all these years later, the lyrics sound a little bit corny "I get claustrophobia, 'cos there's too many boys on your mind". Bruce Davis recalls that Robin played the brief instrumental solo on "recorder", actually a reeded instrument that looks like a recorder with a small keyboard. Maurice also makes his first instrumental appearance, playing rhythm guitar. The B-side, also with The Delawares and again with Maurice on rhythm guitar, was called 'Could It Be' and was probably the nearest thing to rock'n'roll they had thus far attempted.

Yet again the record failed to sell in any appreciable numbers but hindsight is a wonderful thing and it is easy now to appreciate the reasons for its failure. Tony Brady confirmed that "selling" their songs to the radio programmers was difficult because their material was too close to The Beatles and so airplay was difficult to get; an attitude he describes as "stupid".

Another theory is that when on the road, the group was performing to a predominantly adult audience and delivered a polished cabaret act. Meanwhile their record company wanted to promote them as a teenage band while TV shows viewed them as a young Mills Brothers. *Bandstand*, the last bastion of conservatism in Australian music, did more than anyone to prolong this unwanted image, even requiring their studio audiences to wear coats and ties. The brothers were perhaps slightly guilty of trying to be all things to all people and ended up suffering from the inevitable consequence of failing to completely please any. Barry now accepts the reasons for their lack of chart success despite his immense frustration at the time. "I have to say that there was a lack of interest in the group," he conceded. "In those days kids did not buy kid's records, this was definitely pre-Osmonds. We were too young for the teen market . . . so we had to have an older act and sing older songs."

Sometimes, however, they were their own worst enemy. "It was dreadfully difficult getting them on television for a while because they were considered cheeky young upstarts," revealed Kevin Jacobsen in a slightly more tactful manner than Nancy Knudsen. "It was almost impossible to get *Bandstand* to take them. Robin was such an extrovert, he frightened people." Both *Bandstand* and *The Tonight Show,* another show that Kevin had to struggle with, were mainstream programmes and as such they portrayed The Bee Gees in a light that was unlikely to impress the audience that Festival targeted for their records. They needed something, or someone, to get them out of a rut. Festival thought they had the answer and sent them back into the studio to record their fifth single.

The problem, Festival wrongly concluded, was with the songs themselves so, even while Barry's own work was being successfully marketed to other artists, it was decided that the group should record material written for the American market. The 'plug' side was 'Turn Around Look At Me', a 1961 Jerry Capehart ballad recorded by Glen Campbell (who was possibly involved in the writing process too) although it was The Vogues who first charted with it in 1967. Capehart has written numerous country-rock hits, perhaps the best known being 'Summertime Blues' which he co-wrote with (and for) Eddie Cochran. Festival spared no expense for the Gibb's return to the studio, hiring not just an orchestra but also a choir. The flip side was the theme tune to an American television show called *The Travels Of Jaimie McPheeters* (Winn Harline) which had run for only six months between September, 1963 until March, 1964. Kurt Russell starred in the title role and the cast list not only included Charles Bronson, but also Alan, Jay, Merrill and Wayne Osmond, who had sung the original version. The series was based on the novel by Robert Lewis Taylor, which won him the Pulitzer Prize in 1959.

Again, the group's lead singer was pushed into the spotlight and the new single by "Barry Gibb & The Bee Gees" found its way into record shops on October 12.

On this occasion, 'Theme From *The Travels Of Jamie McPheeters*' (note the minor change to the Christian name) appears to have been recorded at a different session from its companion. All three brothers share the same theory about the reason why.

"We weren't what you might call priority," Barry said. "In those days it was Normie Rowe or it was Ray Brown & The Whispers. Normie Rowe was the king of Australian pop and Johnny O'Keefe was the king before him.

"It was like another world over there. There are big stars in Australia but they remain inside Australian record boundaries. We didn't get much time in the studio. In fact, being an English group in Australia wasn't the thing to be which is the weirdest thing. Even when The Beatles came up, still being an English group in Australia didn't do us any good at all. They tend to think of us as pommies and all that business and you become second down the line as far as favours, or as far as help, or as far as getting a break anywhere [goes]."

Picking up on the studio theme, Maurice continued, remembering one time in particular. "We'd done the back track and the [engineer] says, 'Hurry up, the pub opens in six minutes – you've got the time to do the vocal in six minutes and that's it!' In those days, [the record company] paid for the studios, they paid for the musicians and if you wanted strings on it, they paid for it. And they would say, 'Who the hell do you think you are? Khrushchev?' and they wouldn't give you the strings although it's obviously the opposite in England. We never knew that but, in Australia, when the pub is opening and one's got to catch a train back to somewhere outside Sydney and he had to leave and six minutes we had. We did the vocal in six minutes and double tracked it!"

Robin echoed his brothers' sentiments. "I don't think there was anybody more frustrated. We were kids and part of it *was* the fault of the record company. We all blame the record company but part of it was in so much as the studio that we recorded at was at the label.

"We'd ring up and say, 'We'd like to make our new record next week – how much time can we have?' and, if you didn't have a hit record or anything, then you'd get about an hour. An hour! Believe it or not, we'd cut a record in an hour. It's atrocious but we did and this was the way things were in Australia and, if we didn't do so well there, then this was one of the reasons."

Barry conceded though that it wasn't an easy situation for the label either, "Festival was under the same situation we were. We did not appeal to kids because we were kids and it was hard for the people at Festival to sell us." One solution was to sell themselves, so they embarked on a tour of Adelaide and Brisbane in an attempt to broaden their appeal. This didn't entirely work either. "The Australians have no great love for the English and that made things even more difficult," Barry continued. "To a few we were just precocious kids who ought to be playing with toys, but we kept hard at it." As he told *FAB 208* magazine in 1968, "It isn't money that keeps us going even now, it's the same drive to be successful."

They could always rely on their mother for reassurance, as Barbara never doubted her sons' ability or determination for a minute. "I always knew, given the opportunity, that they would be world stars. I always knew that without hesitation."

Now relocated to Middle Cove, just to the north of Lane Cove, Hugh and Barbara became grandparents for the first time when, on September 29, 1964, Lesley (19) gave birth to Bernice Barbara Gibb. Only six years younger than her uncle Andy, the two became inseparable, and it was therefore hardly surprising that people often assumed that Beri was Andy's sister, especially when he referred to her as such. Indeed, Hugh and Barbara adopted her and raised her as if she were their own daughter, a sensible and practical decision under the circumstances. It relieved Lesley of the pressures of motherhood at a time when she was least equipped to handle them, while simultaneously offering her daughter a loving family environment. In time, Lesley would go on to raise more children than her parents or any of her brothers, an achievement in itself.

As the year drew to a close, Barry issued a statement on behalf of Robin, Maurice and himself. "I'd like to wish you all a very happy Christmas and New Year. We've had a gas year, and we certainly hope you have too. We hope the year ahead is going to be marvellous and want to thank the fans for having made this one such an exciting time for us. Christmas cheer to everyone."

The message expressed a mood of optimism and rightly so. They had achieved a great deal in the six years that had elapsed since they first set foot on Australian soil, and the future looked rosy.

5

BIG CHANCE

THE NOMADIC GIBB family began 1965 at yet another new address, this time in Castlecrag, a suburb just north of Sydney. The three brothers also the released their sixth single. For this they had teamed up with Trevor Gordon Grunnill, a friend from their early days in Brisbane.

"I first met The Bee Gees [a couple of years] after I emigrated to Australia with my parents in 1961," says Trevor. "They'd just made their first record . . . and the main thing that struck me was how small they were! They were about 14 and I was 13, but Maurice and Robin were even tinier than me! We were both sort of novelty acts as we were so young and used to meet on the *Johnny O'Keefe Show*, Australia's *Top of the Pops*. I got very friendly with them and used to visit their house. Maurice was a fanatic for home-made magic and spent hours showing me all his new tricks.

"Also, we were all mad keen on making home-movies in which we all starred with a tiny girl singer called Little Pattie."

The home-movies in which Pattie appeared were actually more than a hobby . . . the brothers even went so far as to form an 8 mm film company with Trevor, though nothing would come of this particular venture.

Even at such a tender age, Trevor had demonstrated his precociousness by landing a job as a childrens' TV show host in Brisbane and The Bee Gees had appeared on his show when they were resident there. When making their own special guest appearances on the programme and others like it, the brothers formed friendships with other budding young performers such as Colin Stead, April Byron, Jon Blanchfield and Bryan Davies, all of whom would have further involvement with the Gibbs in years to come.

Released under the guise of "Trevor Gordon and The Bee Gees", 'House Without Windows' was of a slightly different style than previous Bee Gees releases. While the famous Gibb harmonies are present, they certainly weren't being used to their full advantage. Gordon had a nice, if not terribly distinctive, voice and carried the song well.

The B-side 'And I'll Be Happy', was one of those curious but interesting Barry Gibb songs which has no big commercial hook with it but throws in the title almost as an ongoing summary of his (the singer's) feelings. It sounds very much like a Cliff Richard type ballad of the late Fifties. It's a very pretty song that is only dated somewhat by lyrics such as "happy boy" and "lovely girl".

Both sides featured four vocals instead of the usual three and this was the only occasion during the Australian portion of their career that the group would share performing credits with someone else on record, despite there being many other instances of collaboration during this period.

Meanwhile, Barry, Robin and Maurice decided to register, along with 2,000 other aspiring "casuals", at the Automagic Carwash on New South Head Road in Edgecliff, an eastern suburb of Sydney, right next to Abe Saffron's Lodge 44 motel.

Former carwash Manager Kevin Murphy has many fond memories of the brothers' time there.

"The three wet fellows seen from the overhead walkway so regularly toiling away on their cars were The Bee Gees! The three elder Gibbs – I never knew Andy – worked for me for over twelve months and were among my most regular casuals at the 'wash. They were unknown to me other than I knew they were doing gigs around Sydney.

"They were out-front most weekday mornings, looking for some hours. They were most amenable to the worst jobs in the place, I can recall. I had them working 'the mitts'. Now the mitts was the dirtiest, steamiest, wettest, most uncomfortable part of the automated line that made up the carwash and my memory of them is that they put up with that section of work better than most."

The three boys worked there on and off for the best part of that year but it was their last day working for him that Kevin best recalls. "As demand fell away in the afternoon or when rain threatened, casuals would be stood down. My mistake that day lay in picking one of the three working in the mitts to go home and was I surprised when all three marched out? Not at all. It was the risk you took in letting friends work together."

Within a few days of the incident, Kevin was walking in Pitt Street, Sydney when he came upon a familiar Volkswagen Kombi van. It was emblazoned with hand-written legends such as 'BGs' first tour of England.' "I knew then that all was okay. They were ready to tour anyway, and I wasn't really the catalyst for their leaving town."

It had quickly become apparent that their collaboration with Trevor Gordon was unlikely to trouble the chart compilers so, in February, Festival sold the group on the idea of recording another non-Gibb composition. 'Every Day I Have To Cry' was written in 1962 by American rhythm and blues singer-songwriter Arthur Alexander, incidentally one of John Lennon's favourite composers. Since The Beatles recorded 'Anna', and The Rolling Stones covered 'You'd Better Move On', Alexander became the only composer to have material recorded by all three groups. 'Every Day I Have To Cry' had become a minor hit Stateside for Steve Alaimo, and obviously the hope was that the Gibbs could reprise this and use it as a launching pad for their stuttering career down-under.

Certainly the Bee Gees cover of 'Every Day I Have To Cry' was a fine attempt. Both Barry's lead vocals and the harmonies are well used. It was possibly the best example of their distinctive vocal sound to date. For the first time on record, Robin's unique voice really asserts itself at the end of the song.

At least this time Festival allowed Barry to write the B-side. 'You Wouldn't Know' is quite a contrast. Barry's John Lennon style vocal continued and the fast beat to it shows a real R&B influence. Robin and Maurice's vocals really stand out in this song. The engineer/producer on both of these songs is uncertain as, by about this time, Bill Shepherd – just freshly arrived from England – had replaced Robert Iredale.

Shepherd was a proven studio engineer with great experience from working in England. With more musical training than Iredale, and a sparkling personality, his rapport with the boys and appreciation of their potential had an immediate positive result on their records. By coincidence, Shepherd had previously worked with famed British producer Joe Meek but, more significantly, with an entrepreneur called Robert Stigwood. Fate and good timing would soon bring all three, Shepherd, Stigwood and The Bee Gees, together in another land, with extraordinary results.

The single was released in March, both sides credited to "Barry Gibb and The Bee Gees", a format which would continue for all their records for the remainder of the year. Once again, sales were dismal and it would be a long time before The Bee Gees would issue another record without their own songwriting credits. As Barry himself put it, "Well, if we're going to have flops, we may as well have flops with our own songs."

Back at Belinda Music Publishers, Tony Brady had continued to work hard at promoting Barry's songs in the USA and his labours were starting to bear fruit. During his first Silver Spade shows in Australia in 1964, popular 22-year-old American singer Carson "Wayne" Newton had agreed to meet with Tony. A native of Virginia, and proud of his Cherokee and Powhatan Indian heritage, Newton had also been something of a child star, having performed since the age of five and having his own radio show just one year later.

Following Wayne's performances in the Silver Spade Room of Sydney's Chevron Hilton, the American was persuaded by Brady to visit the Belinda office, where he listened to Barry performing some of his own compositions on acoustic guitar. Newton was so impressed that he took some of Barry's songs back to the States and gave these to a friend, the singer and actor, Bobby Darin. Darin, uniquely amongst his generation of performers, took an active role in his own management, had his own publishing company and was actively seeking new talent. Wayne and Bobby agreed they would keep a close eye on the young Gibb's progress over the next few months, agreeing that he would clearly be a considerable asset to Darin's expansion plans.

One of the batch of songs was 'They'll Never Know' which Wayne himself recorded on November 5 for his American album *Red Roses For A Blue Lady*. Released by Capitol on April 12, 1965, it became Newton's best selling LP to date, reaching a respectable 17 in the US charts. Terry Melcher, the album's arranger who also contributed back-up vocals and happened to be the son of actress Doris Day, particularly liked one of the other songs that Wayne had passed on to Darin and offered it to an actor/vocalist that he was working with at the same time.

Although 'They'll Never Know' earns the distinction of being the first Gibb song to be released outside of Australia and New Zealand, Jimmy Boyd's 'That's What I'll Give To You' became the first such composition to appear as a single, being released by the Chicago-based Vee-Jay label in late May, 1965. Boyd had come to prominence in 1952 when, in the last week of the year, he hit number one on the USA pop charts with 'I Saw Mommy Kissing Santa Claus'. By so doing he became the youngest solo artist to have a number one song, a record that still stands. However by the mid-Sixties, his commercial successes had declined considerably, and he failed with this attempt to rejuvenate his career.

With one eye on the chart progress of Wayne Newton's LP, Barry unfortunately had a patch over the other at this time. Curious to see the effect, he fired an air gun point blank at a brick wall. The pellet ricocheted off the wall and hit him in his left eye. "The eye was an awful mess at the time," Barry told *TV Week,* "but I'm hopeful the sight can be saved. At the moment it is causing splitting headaches, particularly when it is exposed to light."

The accident couldn't have come at a worse time as the group was performing every day at Sydney's Royal Easter Show for its week's duration, doing as many as 21 shows a day. However, Barry was glad to be kept so busy claiming, "This has helped take my mind off worrying about whether I'll lose sight in the eye."

A doctor's report to determine whether the sight in his injured eye could be saved was anxiously awaited during the last week of April, and Barry was concerned about an additional complication if it couldn't. "What I'm most afraid of is that, according to the doctors, the loss of sight from my left eye could affect the sight in the right eye in time. Meanwhile, if I do lose the sight from the eye, I will just have to face up to wearing a patch permanently." He added that he didn't think this would greatly affect his singing career. "It'll certainly teach me to be more careful with guns in the future."

It no doubt came as a great relief to all the family to learn that, given time, the eye would heal of its own accord.

Mid year in Australia is winter, but the boys and their father continued to travel far and wide in search of the audiences that their studio output had clearly not been reaching. The major engagement of that winter, however, was right on their very own doorstep, "The Gala Night of Stars", with all proceeds going to *Torchbearers For Legacy.* A crowd of over 5,000 raised more than £1,250 for the locally based charity. The list of performers read like a "Who's Who" of Sydney pop artists of the time: Johnny O'Keefe, Billy Thorpe & The Aztecs, Col Joye & The Joy Boys, The de Kroo Brothers, The Blue Jays, Judy Stone, Little Pattie, The Showmen,

Johnny Devlin & The Devils, The Rajahs, Johnny Reb & The Atlantics, Max Merritt & The Meteors, The Easybeats and various comedy acts. Barry was sufficiently moved by the occasion to say, later that evening, "We've never enjoyed a show more."

The following month, one booking took them to Goulburn, about 130 miles south west of Sydney. The concert passed without incident and the family set out for home as normal. "It was a nice straight road," recalls Robin, "we were in a good mood, and dad pushed the car up to 80 [miles per hour]. Suddenly it overturned and we were flying through the air. None of us had time to do anything except close our eyes and put our hands together.

"Eventually the car stopped. When we climbed out we had a good look at each other and were so surprised that we still had all our limbs, that we burst out laughing. Later we discovered the car had skidded into a fence and ripped it right away from the posts.

"Somehow, and to this day I don't know how, the word got back to Sydney that The Bee Gees had been killed. The radio stations started playing all our records and reading out messages of sympathy. When we got home safe and sound, it was almost as if they were annoyed to see us after crying their eyes out for nothing."

It had been a narrow escape but not without injury after all. Troubled by a pain in his side for some weeks, Barry eventually went to see the doctor who advised the startled teenager that he had sustained a broken rib in the crash but that it had just about healed itself by now. Commented Barry, "I reckon I'm better than Tarzan." Maintaining his fitness was a worry for him, spending as much time as he did on less active pursuits. "Sometimes I feel I should take up some sort of sport to keep fit, but working the strange hours that I do, it's hard to organise," he admitted.

Festival Records were now fully utilising the skills of new house producer/arranger Bill Shepherd, who greeted the brothers on their next return to the studio. While Barry continued to write for other artists, Robin and Maurice had spent the six months since their visit developing their instrumental skills. Using Shepherd's expert musical direction, the new Bee Gees sound was first heard on the A-side, 'Wine And Women'.

For the first time Robin Gibb shared lead vocals with Barry and their alternating, yet contrasting, styles added a new dimension to their vocals. Musically too there were changes. Barry's rhythm guitar sound was more prominent as were Maurice's McCartney-inspired bass playing. Robin Gibb also appears for the first time playing organ.

By contrast, 'Follow The Wind', also written by Barry, had quite a folk sound to it. A song quite obviously influenced by Australian band The Seekers, who had just achieved the first of many successes in the UK, it remains one of the most underrated songs of the period. Ironically, The New Seekers would go on to record this song in 1970.

From time to time, particularly on slow news days, completely unfounded stories appear in the press as if by magic with nobody quite sure from where they emanate. It came as something of a surprise, therefore, for Hugh to read in the paper one morning that his boys would be opening a record shop in the Sydney suburb of Kogarah that summer.

There were also murmurs that Festival was close to dropping the boys and that this might have been their last single with the label had sales not picked up. That the figures did show a marked improvement owes little to Festival, who barely raised a finger to promote it, and more to the Gibbs own ingenuity as they resorted to desperate measures to ensure that their best record to date would at least be heard.

"'Wine and Women' went to number 19," Barry explained, "mainly because we went out and bought it! You could do that in those days."

Their new record entered the radio 2UE sponsored local chart thanks to some very precise market research which the brothers had discreetly conducted themselves. As Robin tells it, "First of all, we found out the shops of the radio station's survey . . . Walton's, Woolworths, about six in all. That's all [the information] we needed. You didn't have to sell very many records to get on the actual Sydney charts. We arranged for our fan club to meet us on the steps of Sydney Town Hall. It wasn't hard to rendezvous with them 'cause there were only six of them."

Barry elaborates further. "We knew if we could sell 400 records on that [September's] Saturday afternoon, by the next Wednesday chart, we'd be at number 35. We only had £200 so it could be no higher than 35. Sure enough, the next week, the record was 35 with a bullet. We were going to get there eventually, but we had to find a way to make it happen and we did."

Once in the Top 40, the disc began to receive airplay and, while there was no guarantee of subsequent sales, at least the record buying public had the chance to decide for themselves. The gamble paid off and the brothers were able to recoup their investment although the money wasn't the main issue according to Barry. "It did an enormous amount for us. It made momentum for us in the country. Even if it was just one hit, it was something." There was also a lesson to be learned for Festival's marketing department, as they were about to miss a wonderful opportunity by failing to adequately promote the next Barry Gibb song, which would shortly attract the attention of the Australian music industry.

It had taken The Bee Gees eight singles to achieve their first goal. Now that they had tasted chart success, they wanted more of the same and rushed back into the studio in search of it.

At 3.35, 'I Was A Lover, A Leader Of Men' was easily their longest recording to date at more than double the length of their shortest song. Having found a successful formula with 'Wine And Women', Barry had obviously decided that more of the same was required. Again built around a strong rhythm guitar sound much like that on its predecessor, 'I Was A Lover . . .' was their strongest vocal performance yet. With a neat piece of guitar work in the middle, it was also their "rockiest" sounding release to date.

For the B-side, Barry would break what would become the golden rule of his songwriting technique. In 1997 he confirmed, "At some point we establish exactly what the melody is, note for note, and then when we do our lyrics, we don't detract from that melody. We don't change the melody to go with certain words we may like, we really make the words fit the melody we have pre-established." His latest song, 'And The Children Laughing' was lyrically deserving of being the exception.

Obviously a song influenced by current world events of the time, 'And The Children Laughing' also has elements of the protest song style of Bob Dylan and particularly Barry McGuire's 'Eve Of Destruction'. While today's poets could say that it's lyrically naïve, it's in essence a very thoughtful, if somewhat wishful, song from a very observant eighteen year old.

Sadly, though deserving of better, this October release failed to build on the limited achievement of its predecessor. It did, however, win Barry his first award, Adelaide radio 5KA's "Top Talent Award" (Composer Of The Year) for 'I Was A Lover, A Leader Of Men', proving that the music industry thought more of him than did his own label. This did not diminish his pride in accepting it. "That was a very big moment for us. That told us we were going somewhere. We knew not where, but we were going somewhere."

Now formally recognised as one of Australia's leading songwriters, Barry conceded that one aspect of his composing set him apart from the rest. "The words come fairly easily. Whenever I think of a tune, I record it on tape and pay someone to write it down for me. It would probably make things a lot easier if I did learn how to write music. Anyway, I've still managed to write hundreds of songs one way or another."

By now, Festival had quite a few Bee Gees recordings in their vaults, sufficient for them to issue the first real Bee Gees LP. It contained 14 tracks, all written by Barry and all performed by The Bee Gees. If it needed a snappy title to catch the public's imagination, they certainly didn't get it from Festival's marketing department who, in a rush of creativity, decided on the ultra bland *Barry Gibb & The Bee Gees Sing And Play 14 Barry Gibb Songs*. This first ever Bee Gees album found its way into all good record shops that November. Anyone in possession of all nine Bee Gees singles to date, and there were precious few, if any, would have been pleasantly surprised to learn that the compilation included three new songs specially written for it.

'I Don't Think It's Funny' is notable for being the first Barry Gibb composed Bee Gees song on which he did not sing lead, this being Robin's first chance on record to showcase his unique vocal style. 'How Love Was True', one of the most mature songs from their Australian recordings, is often cited as an example of how similar The Bee Gees sound could be to The Beatles. The last of the trio, 'To Be Or Not Be', is a raucous piano pounding rocker sounding very much as if Jerry Lee Lewis was in the studio with them at the time.

The other 11 songs comprised the Gibb compositions to be found on the singles with the exception of both sides of their first single and their collaborations with Trevor Gordon. The album's lack of sales mean that *Sing And Play* is today arguably the most sought after and expensive Bee Gees album to buy in its original form. Curiously, the rear sleeve of the LP cover shows a photo of a Farfisa portable electronic organ and states "which is featured on this album".

It would have been simple for the brothers to record an album of entirely new material had Festival allowed them sufficient studio time. Certainly there were sufficient suitable Barry Gibb originals as, by now, other artists had recorded and released 25 of his songs, none of which had been recorded by The Bee Gees themselves. By looking at the list of unrecorded songs that Barry had registered during that period, there were obviously still many more lying unused on the shelves.

Unrecorded, published titles from 1965 like 'Boy With A Broken Heart', 'My Love Won't Take The Time', 'Run Right Back' and 'When A Girl Cries' all seem to capture the mood of the period and would have been more representative of the group at that time. The decision to plunder their back catalogue and reissue material from up to two years before suggests that Festival had simply taken the easy option and missed another opportunity to promote the Gibbs properly.

Domestically, the last 11 months had seen the family move house again not once but twice. They were now residing in Fenton Street, Maroubra, south of Bronte, to the east of Sydney Airport, having briefly stayed in Strathfield, just north of Lakemba, in between times. Barry did not have fond memories of their interim dwelling. "Was I glad to get out of there. The house itself was okay, but it was what was inside that worried me. It was haunted! All the family at some stage or other heard weird sounds."

Wherever they happened to be living in or around Sydney, their real ambitions lay outside of Australia. They knew all too well that America and Great Britain offered the best prospects. There was even an offer on the table from Wayne Newton to sponsor the entire family's removal to America, so impressed were both he and Bobby Darin by Barry's writing. It was talked about at length within the family but eventually Hugh gracefully declined the invitation on the grounds that such a move might involve too many complications. In reality, he was concerned about conscription – "the draft" as it was known in the United States – and that his sons might end up as US soldiers sent to fight in Vietnam.

There remained the possibility of a short-term visit to the US, but Barry was at pains to tell reporters that they had no intentions of leaving Australia for good. "Don't think that we will be going there to hit the big time or anything like that," he said. "It's more for the experience than anything else. I've seen a few kids set off for overseas with great hopes and ambitions, not realising that it's much more difficult over there."

Also up for discussion was a trip to Japan. Australian artists were very much in demand in the Far East at that time and papers announced that negotiations were being finalised to take the group to the Land of the Rising Sun in February, as part of a group of entertainers selected by Kevin Jacobsen. Barry enthused over the possibility. "After hearing of the fabulous times other performers have had there, I'm really looking forward to it."

The talks must have been extremely protracted as the press made a similar announcement in March, mentioning also that the Far East tour was going to wind up in England.

January of 1966 saw the group entertain their new "home" crowd at Maroubra Surf Life-Saving Club with a new segment to their act. They had always impressed their friends with their ability to do imitations, everyone from Rudy Vallee to Elvis, but were reticent to do so in public. It was all change now though and they pledged to "send-up" some of the biggest names in the business including Billy Thorpe and Col Joye. The highlight, however, was when one of the twins donned a blonde wig and became . . . Little Pattie! Presumably their targets, on the surface at least, just smiled and took it all in good humour; something the boys would have done well to remember when the shoe was on the other foot some 15 years later.

While the brothers were out polishing their new act, Festival were refurbishing their studios and upgrading their equipment from two-track to four-track. If Barry's memory serves him correctly, they apparently also had an eight-track recording machine, "but they didn't have anyone who knew how to use it". The label needed some guinea-pigs to test their new gear and in February The Bee Gees were afforded "the honour" of inaugurating Festival's new recording facilities. The label also made a half-hearted effort to squeeze a little more income from their only hit to date by issuing their second picture sleeve EP, *Wine And Women* which comprised both sides of that single and their February 1964 release, 'Peace Of Mind'/'Don't Say Goodbye'.

After the booming up-tempo feel of their last two singles, which had at least made some impact, it seems as if Barry made a conscious decision to go as far as possible in the other direction with his latest offerings. The mournful 'Cherry Red' was probably aimed at the same market that had bought Roy Orbison's 'Crying', a song that much impressed Barry. A pretty ballad, it again featured the now familiar and unique Gibb harmonies. In contrast the B-side 'I Want Home' was a real rocker, with a distinct R&B feel. Released as their new single that March, both recordings were mixed only to mono, even though Festival had the ability to produce stereo records.

A number of other recordings were made around this time but nobody is really sure what their purpose was as they were never intended for release. Almost by way of contradiction, these seven songs – all "standards" from the mid–late Fifties – benefited from full orchestral backing and chorus. Whatever the original intent of the label or the Gibbs, these demos would resurface further down the line.

Although 'Cherry Red' was destined to become another notch on Robin's "flop belt" that he would wear with such pride once he was rich and famous, times were not all bad for the trio. For a start, they now joined the long list of celebrities who had appeared at the celebrated Silver Spade Room in the Sydney Hilton, then widely regarded as Australia's most prestigious venue. It must have been particularly thrilling for the brothers, as it was at this same venue that they had first met their idols, The Mills Brothers, three years previously. Now here they were on that very same stage.

An entirely different stage altogether, but nonetheless enjoyed, was that provided by *Six O'Clock Rock,* a new TV show fronted by Aussie wildman Johnny O'Keefe. Variously described as raw, unpolished and unconventional, their new environment became a haven for their offbeat humour and cheek. Whereas the conservative attitude of *Bandstand* meant that they always had to work within the confines of strictly enforced parameters, this new environment allowed them behave as they chose. There would be no going back to the show which has often since claimed to have launched them. *Six O'Clock Rock* welcomed them with open arms and booked them often. Perhaps Australia couldn't have its own Beatles but, to the show's growing band of regular teenage viewers, The Bee Gees were a more than acceptable compromise and the Gibbs took full advantage.

It must have been like a dream come true for Maurice, in particular, who was used to having his father maintain a watchful eye over his electric guitar playing. Their first appearance on the show also marked the point when their trips to the local barbers would become less and less frequent.

They had also attended a séance, a peculiar thing for boys of that age to be doing but, nonetheless, "Ian" (or "Noel" depending on which brother's version you take) contacted them and forecast great success in a new venture overseas. "England" would become an increasingly used word in the entire Gibb family's domestic vocabulary during the winter months that lay ahead.

Whatever the temperature outside, at Festival Records offices the atmosphere was decidedly chilly. By now, Hugh's sons had 10 flops to their name and the growing antagonism between their father and Fred Marks now rose to the surface. With Barry at his side, Hugh descended on Marks' office one day, and the sound of their ensuing argument grew to such a level that it could be heard throughout the entire building. Interestingly, Fred Marks has no memory whatsoever of there being any such argument.

The basis of Hugh's discontent was the apparent lack of interest being shown by Festival in furthering his sons' careers. Both RCA and EMI had tabled lucrative offers, promising to properly promote the group into the bargain, so Hugh questioned the legality of what he termed a "stranglehold" contract. However, this was one of those few occasions that the senior Gibb wouldn't get his own way, encountering a determined Marks who was prepared to be equally resolute.

Fred countered that there were unpaid bills for record stock that had been supplied for tour sales and claimed that Hugh was generally belligerent to

work with. He also pointed out that he was probably one of the most travelled men in the world at that point, regularly circumnavigating the globe to
promote Festival Records and its artists. Indeed, he was probably the
best-known record company executive anywhere in the world, such was the
extent of his travels. Each time he left the country, he would take a parcel of
Festival releases and, as he reminded the Gibbs, every single one of their
singles since 'The Battle Of The Blue And The Grey' had been personally
promoted by him way beyond Australia's shores. Eventually a compromise
was reached.

Ambitious Frank Baron, sometimes described as a "press baron" in the
great Australian tradition of the likes of Rupert Murdoch, published a
semi-pop magazine called *Everybody's*. Always on the look-out for new ways
to expand his empire and increase his media presence, he decided to launch
a record label of the same name. However, he lacked an understanding of
the fickle nature of the marketplace in which he was investing so heavily,
and the label released but a handful of singles before his conservatively
minded backers, Consolidated Press, pulled the plug on the whole project.

A casualty of his over-optimism could have been the Everybody's house
producer, Nat Kipner. However, the alert Kipner, loosely in charge of the
day-to-day running of the label, had seen the writing on the wall and bailed
out before the end to set up his own record company and booking agency,
which he named Spin. When Everybody's went belly-up, Nat quickly
moved in to sign most of his previous company's roster and arranged a distribution deal with Festival, the label who looked after three lads he had
worked with just two years before.

While all this was going on, Bill Shepherd was packing his bags and
booking passage back to his native England. There were murmurs from
within the company's walls that his departure from Festival was not entirely
of his own choosing, one even going so far as to connect his exit to a romantic entanglement with one of the label's secretaries, although this remains
unsubstantiated. With Kevin Jacobsen now on his back about his protégés in
addition to Hugh, and with the Gibbs having lost their producer, it looked
as if Fred Marks had more than enough problems on his plate with The Bee
Gees alone. It was at that point that the wily campaigner pulled off his
master stroke. Not only did he get rid of all his Bee Gees related problems in
one go, but he also, quite literally, negotiated the deal of a lifetime.

Realising their potential to a far greater extent than Festival, Nat Kipner
was more than happy to take The Bee Gees off Fred's hands but there was a
catch. Kipner had to agree to extend the current distribution deal between
the labels, thereby granting Festival the exclusive distribution rights for all
Spin releases in perpetuity.

Marks was equally skilled when it came to The Bee Gees' contract.
Although the group's original obligation now had less than two years to run,
the Festival boss demanded his pound of flesh in return for his agreement to
sub-contract them to Spin. In a deal brokered by Kevin Jacobsen, Marks

secured an extension into the mid–Seventies, thereby ensuring that, no matter where they might be at the time, revenue from the Australian release of future Bee Gees material would still filter through to Festival's coffers. Fred's shrewdness, or obstinacy – take your pick – would secure his company millions. The Gibbs, on the other hand, were simply glad to be free.

There remained the problem of how to find another Bill Shepherd. Bill had been a great influence on the brothers and they wanted to work with him again at some stage. At this point fate played its trump card when a saviour walked into their lives. Robin explains. "We met a man in 1966 called Ossie Bryne, and he owned his own studio just outside Sydney.

"He'd always been a fan of ours but thought that we should have been handled a bit better, so he said, 'Come to my studio, you can have all the time you want.' We used to record all night till seven in the morning. We could experiment for the first time. We felt great, we wrote all our own music, and it was like a whole new door had been opened."

Byrne, an occasional associate of Nat Kipner, had created his own recording studio next to a butcher's shop in the St Clair strip mall just off Queen's Road in Hurstville, another of Sydney's sprawling suburbs. Commercially available for £5 per hour, Ossie magnanimously offered to allow the trio unrestricted recording time there for free. It was an offer that may have inspired some lyrics written in the following year, "all our Christmases came at once". The boys gratefully accepted their new friend's hospitality which, in time, they would repay with interest.

Another group who recorded at Ossie's studio were Steve & The Board, a band formed by Nat Kipner's son, Steve. "Ossie just ran the tape equipment," said Steve Kipner. "The Bee Gees really directed themselves and they always knew just what they wanted to do. It was just a couple of mono tape decks, not even two-track. You might make an instrumental track and then bounce it to the other tape while singing to it. You could do it again to add something else but there was a limit because you'd start to lose sound."

As Barry would explain years later, "You just kept balancing things until you had enough things on the track that you wanted, but every time that you did balance something, what you already had on the record was fading away because in those days you couldn't bring everything up to the same volume on all the instruments. So it was difficult."

Ossie would soon upgrade his facilities though. Singer Jon Blanchfield recalled that at the back of the butcher shop, "the old Coolroom was the control room with the two track player."

The remainder of March, the whole of April and the early part of May was spent in their new "home" – they spent more time there than they did at their own house. They were often joined in their lengthy sessions by a fellow classmate from Barry's old school, who had met up with the brothers again by way of an unusual coincidence.

Colin Petersen was now a drummer in Steve & The Board. One evening when chatting to Maurice in a local discotheque, the youngest Bee Gee invited Colin to sit in on one of their sessions. "[Shortly after] I moved to Melbourne with my group, but I used to fly to Sydney for sessions with them," he says. "That's quite a distance – over 600 miles. I used to be out of pocket, but I did it out of friendship." Colin's choice of words cleverly disguised part of his motivation for going to such lengths to participate. He and Lesley Gibb were more than "just good friends". He was treated more like a member of the family than a musician, and often stayed at the Gibbs' house. He remains very appreciative of all the times that Barbara made him a cup of tea, or cooked meals for him. In all, he reckons he played on about 12 tracks during this period, 'Coalman', 'Lonely Winter', 'Exit Stage Right', 'I Want Home' and 'Cherry Red' being the ones which spring most immediately to mind.

Another musician, guitarist Vince Melouney, also popped in and out of these sessions. Robin dabbled with the harmonica on occasion as well as continuing his piano development while Maurice had added mandolin to his existing repertoire. Eleven songs are known to have originated during this period with three, in particular, deserving of special mention. 'Where Are You' by Maurice and 'I Don't Know Why I Bother With Myself' by Robin were the first recorded instances that Barry's younger brothers had songwriting ambitions of their own. The third, 'Tint Of Blue' also marked the first occasion that two Gibbs, in this case Barry and Robin, would share credits.

The songs were jointly produced by Nat Kipner and Ossie Byrne, and the two selected for their first Spin release at the end of May were 'Monday's Rain' backed with 'Playdown'. In truth this was a false start because the single was quickly reissued in early June with a new catalogue number and a new B-side, the newly submitted 'All Of My Life' now deemed to be the more appropriate supporting number.

As Festival had done with their initial Bee Gees release, an information sheet accompanied promotional copies of the re-pressed version. This told deejays that, "There's no doubt at all these boys have top talent, and past record releases such as 'Wine And Women', 'Turn Around Look At Me' and 'And The Children Laughing' all served to place the boys several steps higher up the ladder of success."

In case that wasn't sufficient to have radio jocks drooling, there was an additional message at the bottom, "It's a beauty! Spins please. It will make your programmes sparkle like candle light on crystal!" They don't write 'em like that any more!

'Monday's Rain' was possibly the most soulful and musically adventurous song they had recorded to date. It was an interesting choice for a single. Barry's breathy vocal, which was to become a Bee Gees trademark, gets its first hearing on this song. In contrast, 'All Of My Life' is a very commercial song containing some very Beatles-like vocal inflections.

The 12 new songs were lined up for their second album, *Monday's Rain*. However, sales of the single had been disappointing and its release was put on hold while they went back into the studio to see what else they could come up with.

'Where Are You' had drawn Nat Kipner's attention to Maurice's potential as a more than competent songwriter although, by his own admission, he felt more comfortable writing the music than the words. Kipner spent much of the Australian winter collaborating with him and four of their songs were given to other artists for release on his other label, Downunder. Something or someone had obviously motivated Maurice to come out of his shell and make a name for himself in his own right . . . her name was Kathy.

Lesley Gibb recalls her as a singer with long fair hair and an innocent look that belied her real demeanour. "Maurice was terribly fond of her and got the craziest ideas. One was to kidnap her and take her to a deserted island so that he could be alone with her but, like most of the time, Kathy only laughed at his suggestion. Eventually, Maurice realised that he was just being made fun of by her and remained terribly disappointed for the remainder of his stay in Australia." Thankfully, for his sake, he wouldn't have to endure his torment much longer.

Returning to England remained high on the agenda as a topic for conversation in the Gibb household. Egged on by Ossie Byrne, Barry, Robin and Maurice beseeched Hugh and Barbara to uproot the family and sail back to the land of their parents' birth. For now their pleas fell on deaf ears as Hugh and Barbara still had unpleasant memories of Manchester, and were convinced that to return was a retrograde step. Hugh even went so far as to threaten to confiscate the boys' passports if they didn't drop the idea altogether. Though they backed down, they remained convinced that England was where their future lay.

Taking their frustration and energy back into Ossie's studio, they continued to write and record. Robin showed no inclination to write for anyone other than the group while Maurice, with Nat, and Barry continued to do so. All three brothers also sang (uncredited) on other artist's recordings, and it remains anyone's guess just how many such releases actually do exist from this time. MPD Ltd, Ray Brown & The Whispers, Vyt & The World and Tony Barber are just some of those identified thus far, none of the songs being Gibb compositions. It must have been "old home week" when they were recording with MPD Ltd as the bass player of that three person group, Pete Watson, was on the same ship that brought the Gibb family to Australia in 1958.

There can be no doubt that Barry was coming under increasing pressure on various fronts at this point in time. Including the first release of 'Monday's Rain', by August 1966, the harsh statistics were that The Bee Gees had released 12 singles, and only dented the charts twice. More than twenty different acts had released Gibb compositions as singles, Jimmy Little's 'One Road' being the only one to have Top 10 success, and that in New South Wales alone. There were serious question marks over the commercial appeal of Barry's songwiting and Spin still had no prospect of making a return on their considerable investment. As Robin tells it, "They thought we were finished – a financial loss."

It seemed like make or break time for the group but a lifeline arrived when Barry heard a sequence of notes that would inspire him to create something which would propel The Bee Gees to new heights. While recording another Barry Gibb composition, 'Upstairs Downstairs' with singer Jon Blanchfield in the Hurstville studios, Maurice was fiddling around on the piano, heading in no particular direction, when Barry heard something he liked and immediately picked up his guitar and developed it into a melody. The title, 'Spicks And Specks', came from a name the boys dreamed up for an imaginary pop group and, in little more than an hour, the song was finished. Whether a coincidence or not, a newspaper article from the time revealed that 'Specks', or specs to be more precise, were Maurice's latest hobby and he now had a collection of more than 300 pairs of weirdly shaped glasses!

Finally, Barry had found the sound that not only Australian radio liked but also that the Australian record buying public wanted. Supported by television appearances on new and popular music television shows like the *Go!! Show*, the record took off immediately. It had the unique Barry Gibb vocals over simple yet effective piano chords, with the lyrics nostalgically recalling lost love of past days.

A solo trumpet also adds some real quality to the song, but there is some confusion over the trumpeter's identity. According to the Gibbs, it was played by Ossie Byrne, but singer Bip Addison, who had worked with them shortly beforehand, is certain that it belonged to Billy Burton. Since there is no way that Bip could have known that Burton was the Gibb's Manchester neighbour almost a decade previously, the only explanation is that Burton followed the Gibbs to Australia. Alternatively, the Gibbs might have still been bemoaning his nocturnal blaring all those years later and confusing Bip in the process.

The single was released that September, reluctantly from Spin's perspective, with the B-side featuring a stunning solo Robin vocal on his own composition, 'I Am The World'. Again featuring the mystery trumpeter, the song has a haunting feel reminiscent of Roy Orbison's best work.

Both these songs came from their second set of sessions with Ossie and Nat. Colin Petersen was not involved this time as, by then, he had followed Bill Shepherd and emigrated to Britain, travelling on a ship called the *Fairsky*. Before leaving, and while on his way back to Brisbane to bid farewell to his parents, Colin popped in to see the Gibbs and agreed that if his acting career didn't turn out as well as he hoped, then he would certainly consider joining the group when they themselves made the same move.

Colin's replacement as drummer in Steve & The Board was another Australian, Geoff Bridgeford, who would also play a role in The Bee Gees in years to come. The drummer on 'Spicks And Specks' was a sixteen-year-old local by the name of Russell Barnesly, who so impressed the Gibbs that he was offered the chance of seeking international fame with them. However, Russell's parents insisted that he finish his butcher's apprenticeship before undertaking such a risky venture. Regrettably, Russell's known participation on a finished Bee Gees record is limited solely to 'Spicks And Specks'.

Vince Melouney could well have contributed a few guitar licks as he remained in Australia until October before he too, quite independently of Colin, decided that his musical future lay in London. Also aware of the Gibbs intention to return to England one day, he made what he terms "loose arrangements" to meet up with them again when they did so. In what was probably a common occurrence at that time for budding musicians preparing for a new life overseas, Vince married his girlfriend before he departed. On October 21, in Crowulla, Dianne Mitchell became Mrs. Melouney.

To date, twenty recordings have surfaced from these sessions and a motley collection they are too. There's three Beatles songs, Lovin' Spoonful's 'Daydream' (John B. Sebastian), individual solo compositions and, for the first time, collaborations involving all three brothers. One of Barry's solo contributions, 'Morning Of My Life (In The Morning)', had actually been written the previous year when he managed to find a few spare moments prior to the group's appearance at the inspirationally named Wagga Wagga (pronounced Wogga) Police Boys' Club in central New South Wales. It is also one of the few compositions from their Australian period which was frequently recorded by other artists in later years and, unusually for a group who prefer to look forward than back, it was re-recorded and re-titled in 1971 for a film soundtrack.

There was also 'Lonely Winter' by "Keats" whose real name was actually Carl Groszman, a member of Steve & The Board. This is the only known song that The Bee Gees recorded which was written especially for them, and was a payback for The Board being allowed to record one of Barry's compositions, 'Little Miss Rhythm And Blues'. The lives and professional careers of both Carl Groszman and Steve Kipner himself would cross again with the Gibb brothers within a few short years.

Another of Barry's "little pressure cookers" came close to exploding now too. Even before the release of their new single, the family had finally resolved to return to England early in the following year. Hugh had been persuaded that his sons could follow the example set earlier by The Easybeats, but the threat of Australian conscription and eventual service in Vietnam for Barry may also have been a factor. It was not until 1972, when Labour came into office, that conscription ceased in Australia.

Maureen Bates was unhappy. Despite Barry's best efforts to reassure her, she harboured doubts that Barry would come back for her if allowed to leave without her. Of course, as she was quick to point out, there was only one way that she would be able to go with him.

According to Lesley, Maureen's manipulative nature did not endear her to Hugh who couldn't stand her. "Maureen had an equal loathing of TV, to which Barry was nearly addicted," she says. "For hours at a time, Barry could sit, eyes glued to the screen, without saying a word. Other women might have quarrelled with their men in such circumstances but not Maureen. On one occasion, she dressed up in the smallest bikini she could find, put on one of mum's hats from the Thirties, two different shoes and danced provocatively right before Barry's eyes, apologising in a hoarse voice for being such a monstrous temptress but far more interesting than television."

Barry's alleged response says much about the nature of their relationship. "Hi sweet, do you wanna make a nice cup of tea for me?"

Their obvious incompatibility notwithstanding, Barry and Maureen were wed at The Holy Trinity Church in Kingsford, immediately north of Maroubra, on August 22, 1966. Their eldest boy was not the first of Hugh and Barbara's children to get married. Earlier that year, Lesley herself had tied the knot with Keith Evans, an advertising executive. Although Lesley and Keith would remain behind for now, they would follow the family to England in 1968 and remain there for a couple of years before returning to Australia to settle permanently. During that period, Keith would become Barry's personal assistant while, albeit for "one night only", Lesley would also become a Bee Gee.

Barry's five-year contract with Belinda had expired in September, an event that coincided with the end of Norman Whiteley's management contract with Hill and Range Songs Inc. The two old chums, Hugh and Norman, quickly got their heads together and formed their own publishing company, Abigail Music (Australia) Pty. Ltd which they registered in the UK as Abigail Music (London) Ltd. It seemed a simple enough transaction, but it would soon become a complicated affair.

With their passage home now all but booked, 'Spicks And Specks' was actually receiving airplay. They even made the front page of Australia's then premier music paper, *Go-Set*, whose October 26 edition announced, "One of the fastest rising records on the charts the past two weeks has been 'Spicks And Specks' by The Bee Gees, who leave for England in February." The article also mentioned that, on arrival, the group intended to change its name.

To capitalise on the immediate success of 'Spicks And Specks', Spin appear to have had a last minute change of mind about the title of the album that was to accompany their new single. *Monday's Rain* contained their new single and the original eleven songs from their March–May sessions. Manufacture had commenced in early October but no sooner had the master been placed on the presses than it was taken off again and all copies of the album destroyed. As usually happens in such instances, a few copies still managed to find their way out of the factory and are highly prized by those fortunate enough to possess them.

The reason behind the decision was that Spin had noted a change in public attitude and wished to repackage the album with same title as the single. In the event, production of the *Spicks And Specks* LP had initially not gone smoothly and, in the haste to make the change, the first batch bore the same catalogue number as the unissued *Monday's Rain*, and side one still bore the original title. Needless to say, a couple of these escaped destruction and are even rarer than the original pressing. The reverse of the album sleeve has liner notes penned by Nat Kipner, describing the brothers as having "a myriad of musical abilities" and adds "as instrumentalists, they have mastered practically every instrument in the book". Warming to his task, he enthuses, "As for personality and stage presentation, their act is a sight to behold," before he amusingly signs off, "Yours swingingly".

The songs show a richness in their writing, and even some experimentation in the vocals. Robin's unique vibrato was now a feature of the group's sound, and the songs where he and Barry alternated lead vocals were a highlight. Brother Maurice also makes his début lead vocal on his own composition 'Where Are You'. What was so refreshing about the album was its diversity. There is a nice range of styles from pop to R&B to ballads and proof of the value of the songs was shown by the immediate rush of Australian artists to cover the various album tracks. Over thirty years later, 'Spicks And Specks' remains a concert highlight for any Bee Gees appearance, both in Australia and New Zealand.

Sounding more like The Beatles at this stage than they had ever done, a few of these would find their way onto the second side of an Argentinian album first issued in 1973. Entitled *The Beatles versus The Bee Gees*, it attempted to make a comparison between these recordings and the ones recorded by Tony Sheridan & The Beatles in Hamburg in 1961. It seems strange in retrospect that the six Bee Gees tracks chosen by Karussell were ones that instead highlighted the Gibbs own individual sound. This of course could have been a deliberate ploy on the label's part, as The Beatles had now gone their separate ways, and the public was waiting to see who would assume their mantle.

Determined to squeeze every penny they could out of 'Spicks And Specks' before the group departed Australian shores, Spin even financed a video, or as it was called then, 'a promo film,' to boost sales. It was filmed at Essendon Airport in Melbourne and featured Denise Drysdale, one of Melbourne's best Go-Go dancers of the time. Another mimed recording was filmed for *Go!! Show* at ATVO's studios in Nunnawading, the venue where the famous Australian soap opera *Neighbours* would later be filmed.

Ironically, The Bee Gees "lucky thirteenth" single was now finally earning them the recognition that years of toil and struggle deserved. "We knew we could make it internationally, we could just feel it," Barry confirmed, "but we knew that to do it, we'd have to go to America or back home. There was just no way of getting Australian records released outside Australia, New Zealand and a few other places in the neighbourhood. We could have spent forever down there and got nowhere."

For all of his public verbal swagger, deep down, Barry had the normal lack of confidence found in most 20-year-olds. "See you in 12 months," he had predicted when bidding farewell to his friend Colin Stead.

Immediately prior to leaving Australia, The Bee Gees had never been busier. With the success of 'Spicks And Specks', all of a sudden every television show and magazine wanted them. They were also frantically busy in the Hurstville studios producing artists such as Bip Addison, Jon Blanchfield, April Byron, Mike Furber, The Twilights, Jenene Watson and Ronnie Burns, all of whom had requested Gibb compositions, as the brothers rushed to get as many of their songs recorded before they left. Ironically, as a result of these late recordings, for the next few months the Australian charts would be dotted with successful cover versions of Gibb songs. Too late for the Gibb family, Australia had finally discovered The Bee Gees.

It was time for a change and arrangements were finalised even quicker than originally anticipated. Just three days into the New Year, they set sail for England, the country they were once again calling "home".

6

THE SINGERS SANG THEIR SONGS

As creative as the brothers have been since Barry's first stabs at songwriting during the late Fifties, the story of The Bee Gees – the group fronted by Barry, Robin & Maurice – tells only part of the tale. Indeed, on many occasions they have confirmed that the group's recording and performing activities are secondary in importance to those of their alter ego, The Brothers Gibb.

In the early Sixties, Australia was very much in need of local writing talent so the Gibbs lived in an environment that actively encouraged and nurtured their desire to be songwriters. Had they been living in either the UK or USA at the time, they might have been swamped by the size of the competition, and perhaps would not have enjoyed the same opportunity that Australia offered. Many Antipodean artists and groups benefited from having one or more of the Gibbs write material especially for them. Indeed, during the period from 1963-66, the brothers would write more songs for others than they would for use by themselves. Initially, they would all emanate from Barry, but by the end of their stay in Australia, Maurice and Robin would join their elder brother on a career path that would very much run alongside that of The Bee Gees.

The very first artist to release one of Barry's songs was Col Joye. Because he had such a considerable influence at the start of the group's career, it seems only fitting that he should likewise launch their songwriting one too. '(Underneath The) Starlight Of Love' was issued as a single by Festival in May, 1963 and reached number 31 in the Victoria State charts.

August saw the release of the second Barry Gibb composition, this time by another Leedon recording artist, Lonnie Lee. Norman Whitely, the head of Belinda Publishing Group who had the rights to Barry's songs, suggested that Lonnie listen to this new artist who had just moved down from Brisbane, and he was given a tape of several Gibb songs. Lee said that the demo he was given sounded great, with Barry's unusual guitar sound (i.e. tuned to the open E chord) and that he had a great voice. He said, "Even then, you could see he was destined for great things." Lonnie particularly liked 'I'd Like To Leave If I May' and produced the song himself. In 1998, he was still able to recall that Barry was in the studio with him at the time he recorded the song and that, although only 16, the young Gibb had a "fair idea of what he intended the song to sound like."

Lee's desire to record "Australian material" reflects how being a local songwriter assisted Barry Gibb in getting his music heard at that time. It was quite common for Australian artists to record local versions of overseas material for hit records. Lee was one of the pioneers of the Australian music industry, and was also one of those artists who at the time fought strongly to give the Australian music scene its own identity and to use and encourage Australian songwriters. To illustrate the point, the words "Australian Composition" were clearly marked on all such releases. Nowadays, Lonnie Lee is probably one of the only Australian rock'n'roll singers of the Fifties still working actively. He has his own record company, Starlight Records, still records and tours, and even has his own web site.

While records by The Bee Gees themselves weren't having much success, other artists were more than happy to have the Gibbs as backing vocalists. In November, they appeared uncredited on Johnny Devlin's 'Stomp The Tumbarumba', a Top Five hit for the Kiwi who recorded in Australia. Tumbarumba is a town in northern New South Wales, about as unconnected with Scandinavia as you could possibly imagine, but the Olga label released it there nonetheless, technically making it the brothers' first release outside Australia.

There was more chart success soon as the Gibbs provided backing vocals on an early February 1964 number two record by popular Australian television host Jimmy Hannan. His first single, 'Beach Ball', backed by 'You Gotta Have Love', featured the voices of all three Gibbs on both sides. Jimmy was also the first artist to be signed by Reg Grundy for his RG label, and this release was a huge success for Hannan, who at the time was the host of the teenage music television show, *Saturday Date*. With The Bee Gees' own producer Robert Iredale also working as musical co-ordinator for the television show, The Bee Gees' involvement in Hannan's single seems only natural. This record was also the first occasion on which Americans were exposed to The Bee Gees' distinctive vocal sound. As with the Australian release, they were again uncredited on the record when 'Beach Ball' was issued in the USA on Atlantic 2247, this time without any chart success.

The Gibbs also provided back-up vocals for Hannan's follow-up single, 'You Make Me Happy'/'Hokey Pokey Stomp', released at the very end of March. While it was not as successful as its predecessor, it still made number 21 on the Sydney charts.

Even though they couldn't find chart success as The Bee Gees at that point, Jimmy Little's cover of Barry's 'One Road', released by Festival on February 3, 1964, made the Top 10 in some states. 'One Road' was the follow-up to Little's number one, 'Royal Telephone', a few months before. Barry changed it from a love song to a religious theme to suit the gospel style that Jimmy was after. Little, another who was signed to the Festival label, also included Barry's 'Walkin' Talkin' Teardrops' on his *New Songs From Jimmy* LP at about the same time.

Although Jimmy knew of the Gibbs through the industry, these two songs were actually suggested to him by Ken Taylor in Festival's A&R department. Jimmy says that he always liked Barry's work but that he never really got the chance to say thanks as none of the Gibbs were in the studio with him for the recordings which were produced by Robert Iredale with assistance from Hal Saunders. One of the nicest guys in the entire entertainment industry, he is still very busy as a performing artist and is even sometimes asked to include both Gibb songs in his act.

Later that February, another Festival act, Sydney born Noeleen Batley, released the first of four songs that Barry would write for her, as the B-side to 'Forgive Me'; a number 34 in New South Wales. Now Noeleen Batley Stewart, and still a good friend of the Gibb family, her records had uncommonly good arrangements for the time and these, combined with her young voice, brought the most out of Barry's songs. The years have been kind to her, and she retains an excellent memory of those far-flung days. "I met the Bee Gees when I did a big concert at Lane Cove National Park. Their mum and dad and the three boys were there, and we were introduced by Col Joye. The songs that Barry wrote were especially for me. I went to Belinda music and met with Tony Brady, who was in charge of the company, and Barry played many songs to me which I wasn't really impressed with at the time. So we made another appointment, and he came up with 'Surfer Boy', my first recording by him. I loved it. [All four] records were produced by Robert Iredale, of Festival Records. I remember the fun we had, the three boys and myself together."

Tony Brady had worked hard to promote Barry's songwriting abilities, so it seemed only fair that he should get a slice of the action too. 'Let's Stomp, Australia Way', another title reflecting the new Australian dance craze, was released by RCA in March and was the first cover version single to contain two Gibb compositions, as the reverse side was 'Lucky Me'. Brady embarked on what one newspaper described as "a barnstorming television tour round Australia in an attempt to push it high into the charts", but he failed to catch the mood of the record-buyers who had put him into the Top 30 on two separate occasions just two years earlier.

All was quiet on the Gibb front for the next three months but June witnessed a proliferation of releases. By then, Tony had switched to the Parlophone label and launched his career there with another offering from Barry entitled 'I Will Love You'. Nat Kipner, a key figure in Maurice's writing development, wrote the B-side. Thankfully, Kipner would soon turn to serious writing – 'I'm Gonna Buy My Mother-In-Law A Block Of Land On Mars' might have appealed to Brady but would surely have looked out of place on a Bee Gees record. Tony now works for Col Joye's ATA Records in Sydney.

All three brothers were called upon once again by Johnny Devlin to contribute backing vocals on his next release. This time they appeared on both sides, but their voices are far more audible on the B-side, 'Whole Lotta

Shakin' Goin' On', than on the plug side, 'Blue Suede Shoes'. The single was rush released to capitalise on the announcement that Devlin and his band, The Devils, would be supporting The Beatles on their 1964 Australian tour. As Johnny is honest enough to admit, the Gibbs were not his first choice for these recordings. "I remember at the time we wanted the Delltones, who were big back then," he confessed, "but they were unavailable, so we settled for what we thought was second-best, The Bee Gees."

Devlin's good fortune came as the result of a strange decision by another artist. Del Juliana is famous in Australian pop music folklore for turning down an opportunity to tour with The Beatles at the height of their fame on that same 1964 tour. No reason has ever been given for her knockback of the Fab Four. A New Zealand born female singer, Del made 'Never Like This' almost sound like a Beach Boys tune. Produced by fellow Kiwi, Johnny Devlin himself, in Sydney, Del recently recalled that when the song was released, it was criticised by local deejays for sounding too much like a Phil Spector recording, a sound that Devlin had intentionally attempted to re-create. 'Never Like This' was only one of a number of Barry Gibb songs that RCA suggested to Del, and she remembers that she recorded another one, 'Boy On The Board' at the same session. Sadly, no copies of Juliana's version of this latter song exist. She now lives in the tranquillity of The Blue Mountains in New South Wales.

Later that summer, Tony Brady also collaborated with Barry on a radio advertising jingle for *Surfing World* magazine called 'It's A Surfing World'.

Like the Gibbs a decade later, another young artist, Bryan Davies, emigrated from Manchester at the age of four in 1948, and first came to the attention of teenage rock fans in 1959 when he became a regular on *Bandstand*. He was soon heard from again, and Barry wrote both sides of his October release on HMV, 'I Don't Like To Be Alone' backed with 'Love And Money'. Both numbers belong to the emerging rock'n'roll genre and returned the Gibb name to prominence by reaching the Top 40 in several state charts, number 22 in New South Wales being pick of the bunch.

Also in October, Columbia released 'Scared Of Losing You' as the B-side to Reg Lindsay's 'Lonely Road'.

Before the end of the year, two more New Zealand acts got in on the Barry Gibb act too. The Pleasers were sufficiently impressed by Bryan Davies' version of 'I Don't Like To Be Alone' to record their own one for release on their native Red Rooster label. The other was country singer John Hore who included 'Tribute To An Unknown Love' on his *Hit The Trail* album for the obscure HMV-distributed John Brown label.

The start of 1965 saw a couple of solo artists come back for second helpings. Bryan Davies chose 'Watch What You Say' as the A-side of his next single, while Noeleen Batley did likewise with 'Baby I'm Losing You'. In hindsight, it is particularly frustrating to see how good a job Batley did with Barry's songs because, with a little bit more time and expense, substantial improvement could have been made to The Bee Gees' own releases.

One of those Bee Gees releases was their collaboration at the end of 1964 with Trevor Gordon. This time Leedon chose to promote Trevor on his own, albeit that one Gibb – Robin – and possibly more, again provided vocals. 'Little Miss Rhythm And Blues'/'Here I Am' was released on April 18, 1965 and the A-side, a fast Chuck Berry-like tune, was also covered by two groups.

Mike, Tommy and Albert Williamson had all been merchant seamen from the UK who whiled away their spare time on board by fooling around with music. In 1961, the three guitarists jumped ship together in Australia and formed a rock'n'roll band called The Steele Brothers as a tribute to their hero, Tommy Steele. Working out of Sydney, they moved to Auckland, New Zealand in 1963, taking drummer Dave Camp and lead singer "Judge" Wayne Harrison with them. Thus, Judge Wayne & The Convicts were born and they recorded 'Little Miss Rhythm And Blues' for Viking Records, also recording 'Here I Am' as its B-side. Even before the record was released, Wayne took up the offer of a solo career in Australia and the band split. The other four would at least have the satisfaction of seeing Wayne's career nose dive rapidly, before they too moved back to Australia where they are still involved in the music industry.

The same song was released on Spin by Steve And The Board, the band formed by Nat Kipner's son Steve and which included drummer Colin Petersen. The group was one of the few examples of genuine overnight success that surfaced during this period as their début record, 'Giggle Eyed Goo' had reached the Top 10 in some states. However, after Petersen's departure, even though he was replaced by ex-Nomads drummer Geoff Bridgeford, the band dissolved without ever realising their full potential.

Bryan Davies recorded his fourth Barry Gibb song, 'I Should Have Stayed In Bed' for an April release, and he can recall Barry being in the studio for all four, not only to provide backing vocals, but to harmonise with him as well.

Two new Leedon female artists came knocking on Barry's door that June. Michelle Rae was presented with 'I Wanna Tell The World'/'Everybody's Talkin' ' which was put out as a single by Leedon, apparently with some Gibb vocals on the B-side, while child singer Jenny Bradley received 'Who's Been Writing On The Wall Again'/'Chubby'. Neither record made any impact nor, for that matter, did the careers of either singer. In Rae's case, it appears to have been her one and only release.

Barry now embarked on a brief hiatus as far as writing for others was concerned, and the period coincided with The Bee Gees' first chart success in the form of the Bill Shepherd produced 'Wine And Women'. His batteries were sufficiently recharged by October to resume.

Noeleen Batley still had faith in Barry's abilities and returned for another song. Festival relegated 'Watching The Hours Go By' to the B-side of 'Padre', a non-Gibb composition, which failed to chart. 'Watching The Hours Go By' lacked the impressive arrangements of Batley's earlier releases; on the other hand, it does have substantial accompaniment from The Bee

Gees to redress the balance, and is another source of pleasant memories for the lead singer. "The boys joined in and played their instruments," Noeleen recalled. "I remember Maurice on the organ working out all of the chords. Even then at their young age, they were brilliant and Barry was such a perfectionist, especially rehearsing the song over and over again." This was a trait that the eldest brother would demonstrate on many an occasion during his career.

Barry, Robin and Maurice were also heard alongside Vyt on 'Why Do I Cry', a song that was a hit for The Remains a few years earlier. Vyt is a shortened version of this Lithuanian's real name, reputed to be so long that they didn't have room to fit it on the record itself.

Denis Williams' band, Denis And The Delawares recorded a pair of lively rock numbers and were rewarded with an HMV release of 'Bad Girl'/'They Say'. Delawares lead guitarist Bruce Davis confirmed that the recording of these songs came about through their manager, Chris Dipler, chasing Barry Gibb, who was by then getting a name around Sydney as a hot songwriter. Barry was not present during the recording although he was at Bruce's house when they were rehearsing the song, and he did make a few suggestions. Robert Iredale, whom Bruce described as "a nice approachable man who would quite often join in on piano and maracas when necessary", again produced the record. Barry additionally helped to promote the single's release by also attending its launch.

Two months later, as 1965 drew to its close, another HMV artist, Lynne Fletcher chose 'You Do Your Loving With Me' as the A-side of her new single. The song was sent to her by HMV, but Lynne already knew the Gibbs through her appearances on *Bandstand*. Highlighting the friendships that readily grew in those halcyon days, Noeleen Batley was Lynne's bridesmaid when she got married.

There would now be almost a six month gap before Barry could spare any time to resume his writing for others. Ossie Byrne had provided him and his brothers with a new playground, and it proved virtually impossible to tear them away from the recording studio during that entire period.

★   ★   ★

The first to receive a new Barry Gibb composition after his sabbatical was female singer, Lori Balmer, who reprised Jenny Bradley's 'Who's Been Writing On The Wall Again' and backed it with 'In Your World'. Born in Victoria to showbiz parents, Lori was working professionally by the age of six. "When I was living in Sydney, I was picked up by RCA at seven and was their youngest recording star. My parents, being British (Irish & Scottish), were good friends of the Gibb family – Brits stick together – so I've known them since I was seven. Andy and I used to play together," she reminisced fondly.

"Barry wrote some songs for me, and the Gibbs played on [them], which were recorded at EMI studios in Castlereah Street, Sydney. I was eight years of age. The house producer of RCA was Ron Wills, but Barry really produced [them] under Ron's eye. We did the vocals with the Gibbs providing the background vocals on one tape. The day before we did the demos for the songs at the Hurstville studio."

Emphasising the strength of the bond that developed between the two families, Lori revealed that when the Gibbs left Australia for England in less than a year's time, they had their going away party at the Balmer's house.

In May, The Richard Wright Group – the lead singer was no relation to the Pink Floyd keyboard player – recorded 'Neither Rich Nor Poor' as the A-side of their single. Guitarist Gary McDonald confirmed that the song was actually recorded prior to the group's formation. 'Neither Rich Nor Poor' reached Sydney's Top 40 and he also clearly remembers having to learn the song so that they could go out and play it at concerts.

By now, The Bee Gees had determined that their future lay outside Australia's confines, and the only thing to be decided was when. Rather than sit idly twiddling their thumbs while awaiting confirmation of their passage, the brothers took an entirely opposite view and attempted to cram as many recordings as possible into the short space of time before their imminent departure.

The writing for others showed no signs of drying up either, and August 1966 witnessed a landmark occasion with the near simultaneous release of three singles. All three were on Festival's Down Under label and had consecutive catalogue numbers.

The first, UK 1454, was allocated to Bip (his younger brother couldn't pronounce 'Phillip'!) Addison's 'Hey'/'Young Man's Fancy' and had the honour of being Maurice's first efforts at writing for others, both of Bip's songs having been co-written with Nat Kipner. Nat had first met Bip on *Saturday Date*, the TV show for which Nat was talent co-ordinator and producer. Bip also knew The Bee Gees, describing them as "just like the rest of the young artists in the pop music world that you ran into at other television shows."

Ossie Byrne's St Clair Studios in Hurstville was where artists did the recording for songs that they sang/mimed on *Saturday Date*. It was here that Nat and Maurice played their two new songs for Bip, and he recorded both of them that same day. The precise details are still fresh in his mind. "For most of ['Hey'], Maurice and I were the singers, double tracked so there were four voices. On the middle eight, it was just me." Barry was on guitar, drums were provided by Colin Peterson while bass, piano, harmonica and maracas all came courtesy of Maurice. The line-up on 'Young Man's Fancy' was similar but all three Gibbs sang back-up vocals while Maurice played a solid electric 12-string guitar unplugged to achieve a "Byrds" effect.

Apparently, over and above the impressions that Maurice performed along with his brothers as part of their new stage act, he also bore a striking resemblance to the lead singer of The Easybeats, and Bip still chuckles at the memory. "He used to get annoyed as people kept mistaking him for Stevie

Wright because they both had long hair and English accents."

Although Barry was workmanlike and interested in observing Nat's and Ossie's production techniques, Robin's attention was sometimes elsewhere. "I remember I was amazed as he ate a whole [family size] Vienetta ice cream that day," recalls Bip, "and I felt that sort of diet wouldn't help his skin too much. Remember, they were pimply youths then," he added.

Bip describes Nat as a "nice enough guy, very busy, almost hyperactive in some ways" but he concedes that he didn't know Ossie all that well. "He seemed a generation apart from us then. He was at least 20 years older with Brylcreemed hair, and we all had longer scruffy hair. I do remember he had only one eye or a glass eye! I can't remember him ever playing an instrument."

Towards the end of the decade, Bip decided to give the recording business another try. "I was about to go and record another song with Robert Iredale as producer, but unfortunately he'd committed suicide. I had also done some recording with my previous band, The Fugitives." Bip himself passed away suddenly in March, 2000.

Next in line was Sandy Summers and Maurice and Nat wrote 'Messin' Round' for her. This time, all three Gibbs provided backing vocals, with Maurice additionally contributing piano and bass while Barry was on his usual rhythm guitar. The B-side, 'A Girl Needs To Love', was written by Barry and can almost be considered a Bee Gees recording as Barry sings along with virtually all of Sandy's lead vocal, while the twins are clearly heard providing back-up.

The last of the Down Under trilogy was Anne Shelton's 'Talk To Me', which was written by Maurice and Nat. The Bee Gees influence again predominates with vocals and instrumentation to the fore, especially on the B-side, a Kipner/Byrne composition entitled 'I Miss You', where the Gibbs even sing a verse on their own. Little is known of Shelton. Barrington Davis referred to her as "a fine singer" but said that "she left the pop world to work in the lucrative club scene" and Ossie Byrne was not sure if that was the best career move for her. She is no longer in the musicians' union and no one appears to know her.

According to their Spin label stablemate Tony Barber, the brothers were also involved on his Nat Kipner produced *Someday . . . Now* album, but any vocal accompaniment is undetectable so it is likely that the participation is solely restricted to instrumental contributions, possibly from Barry and Maurice only. Like the Gibbs, Tony had emigrated to Australia on the *Fairsea*; in his case following the break-up of a serious relationship when his girlfriend left him for another man.

"We recorded a lot of my album at Ossie Byrne's studio," he said. "I used The Bee Gees on quite a few of those tracks. It was a great little studio. We got some remarkable sounds out of it, a lot of it due to Ossie's ingenuity. Ossie was great. We recorded 'Spicks And Specks' at his studio [and] I helped out with the arrangements and recording."

It wasn't long, a month to be precise, before another M. Gibb & N. Kipner writing credit appeared on a Down Under release. This time it was The Mystics turn and 'Don't You Go, I Need Your Love' was the end product, with a non-Gibb song, 'Turn The Lamp Down' appearing on the B-side. The ear suggests that the brothers sang on both sides but, if this is indeed the case, it has never been confirmed.

The Mystics lived up to their name by maintaining a low profile. Originally from Cooma in New South Wales, the band won the Canberra division of *Hoadley's Battle Of The Bands* competition; their prize being a one-release contract with Festival. Sadly, 'Don't You Go, I Need Your Love' failed to launch their career, but mention of the song still brings back happy memories for lead singer Ron Watford, who maintains that, for one week, it actually outsold The Beatles' 'Yellow Submarine' in Cooma. Okay, so it only was 70 copies, but what a great claim to be able to pass on to future generations! Only 19 then, Ron also remembers Maurice's amazing ability to notice little details, telling Ron that his guitar's "G-string was flat".

October brought the final Down Under release to have Gibb involvement. Like all four of its predecessors, Ossie Byrne and Nat Kipner produced it at the Hurstville studios. The singer who sang their songs on this occasion was Adelaide born April Elizabeth Potts. She was discovered by Johnny O'Keefe who heard her sing, and who persuaded her to leave school early, and take up her hobby as a full-time career in Melbourne. Her new manager, Horrie Dargie, patiently groomed her for stardom, and was rewarded when, as April Byron, she had a big hit in May 1964 with 'Make The World Go Away'. She became much in demand for television appearances, as well as live performances at discos dances and hotels. Her follow-up Leedon single, 'Listen Closely', was backed with 'What Does A Girl Do' which was co-written by April herself with Bill Shepherd. It is likely that it was Shepherd who introduced her to the Gibbs.

Once again, it was a Maurice and Nat collaboration on the A-side, 'He's A Thief' while its companion was Barry's 'A Long Time Ago'. All three brothers provided backing vocals and instrumentation on both sides.

There was a whole collection of Bee Gees demos lying unreleased in Festival's vaults, recordings that would eventually be released against the Gibbs' wishes. One that never did see the light of day on a Bee Gees record was 'All The King's Horses', written by all three brothers, which 20-year-old singer Ronald Leslie Burns paired with 'Coalman', preferring Barry's song as the A-side of his January, 1967 single. The Bee Gees' backing vocals are apparent on both sides, as indeed is Barry's guitar, Maurice's piano and bass, and Colin Petersen's drums. Spin's press release predicted that its latest release "was all set to burn up the charts", describing it as "a red hot item with Ronnie's searing vocal of 'Coalman' given a tremendous musical backdrop featuring haunting guitar and male vocal chorus. A winner for sure!"

As with their own 'Spicks And Specks', 'Coalman' would become a hit in the Gibbs' absence, reaching a very commendable number seven in both the

Sydney and home town of Melbourne local charts. Ronnie plundered the demo tapes, firstly releasing a four-track EP where he combined the single with 'Top Hat' and 'Butterfly'. He then had another hit single with 'In The Morning' / 'Exit Stage Right'. All of these songs would be joined by 'Terrible Way To Treat Your Baby' and 'I'll Know What To Do' on his début LP, *Ronnie*; resulting in eight of its 14 tracks having flowed from the pen of a Gibb hand.

Peter Robinson, former bass guitarist with Ronnie's Melbourne-based backing band, confirmed that The Strangers were involved as unaccredited session musicians in the recording of the two singles, as well as on 'Terrible Way To Treat Your Baby.' These songs may have also have been co-produced by fellow band member, guitarist John Farrar, famous later for teaming up with Hank Marvin and Bruce Welch of The Shadows, and producing and writing for Olivia Newton John.

The versions of these songs are very similar to The Bee Gees' original demos, but they are new recordings. "I was given the demo's for 'Coalman' and 'Exit Stage Right'," says Ronnie, "and I was really impressed. I went back to my manager at the time, Jeff Joseph, and said that the songs were really good and can we get some more? So all the other demos arrived, which I really liked also. I went up to Sydney at the Hurstville Studios to record the songs, and while Nat Kipner is given the credit as producer on the records, it was really The Bee Gees who produced the songs. I was relatively new as a solo singer having left my previous band, The Flies. I had just had two reasonable hits ('Very Last Day' and 'True True Lovin' '), so I was looking for some other material."

One demo, which particularly caught Ronnie's ear, was 'Terrible Way To Treat Your Baby'. "I was really into the Scott Walker sound, and that's why I liked the song. I spent some time with them while we were recording the album, and even spent a night at their house, I think. I remember their old green Kombi van, [but] what I really recall is they had this guitar at home with only two strings on it, and they were too poor to afford the other four strings." Perhaps displaying a hitherto well disguised sense of humour, but then again perhaps not, Ronnie went on to claim, "That's how they came up with the 'Spicks And Specks' song, because that's all they could make of two chords!" Ronnie continues to perform today with his band, Burns, Cotton and Morris, with his colleagues Daryl Cotton and Russell Morris.

Maurice and Nat managed to squeeze two more songs out of their available time together, with 'Raining Teardrops' and 'As Fast As I Can' comprising both sides of a single for Barrington Davis. Displaying their versatility as writers, the A-side is a rock number while the reverse is a slow ballad. This time Spin's press-release was somewhat wide of the mark. Although it did earn the solid airplay predicted of it, it was much to Maurice's chagrin that he discovered that both the R&B flavoured numbers were "penned by two Australians, Nat Kipner and Barry Gibb, aimed at the teen set".

While Barrington did make some other records that do sound like they had Gibb vocals on them, this was definitely not the case. Maurice played bass and piano on this record though. While recording with Nat and Maurice, Barrington remembers Barry was busy in another corner of the studio working on a new song which had a strange title. It was called 'Spicks And Specks'. One member of Powerpact, Dennis Wilson, also regularly recorded at Hurstville, and often played on The Bee Gees demo recordings, although not on the finished product itself.

Like the Gibbs, Barrington himself originated from Lancashire, in his case from Blackpool, and he returned to England in 1969 where he met up with the eldest brother again while Barry was recording with P.P. Arnold. He remembers driving around London with Barry in his Rolls-Royce convertible.

As The Bee Gees 'Spicks And Specks' began to make an impact, the brothers quickly found themselves in greater demand than ever before. In most cases, the actual release of these late 1966 recordings came after the boys had left Australia, and some would even be delayed until the latter part of 1967.

Jon Blanchfield, simply referred to as "Jon" on disc, went to Hurstville and recorded 'Upstairs Downstairs' and 'Town Of Tuxley Toymaker, Part One'. Barry alone wrote the more often played side, which reached number 32 in Queensland, but all three are credited on 'Tuxley'. It is ironic that, on the back of the success of 'Spicks And Specks', Jon should receive more promotion than The Bee Gees ever got during their time in Australia. Leedon purchased a full page advert in the February 1 edition of *Go-Set* which contained nine photos of Jon and contained near embarrassing accolades from three prominent deejays. The "Bee Gee's" (sic) 'Tuxley' was described by 4GR's Ross Weldon as "a very haunting and absolute up-tempoed ballad", whatever that means. Almost 35 years later, fans are still waiting for Part Two.

Jon met The Bee Gees while they were doing *Countdown*, a TV show which he hosted in his native Queensland; an entirely different show from the one that Molly Meldrum hosted in the Seventies. "They liked my voice and invited me down to record a song in Sydney on the Leedon label (which he thinks was owned by Johnny O'Keefe at the time) and which they had an 'arrangement' with. They also asked me to stay at their house in Maroubra for a period of three weeks. They may have written 'Upstairs, Downstairs' for me, but they were working on 'Town Of Tuxley Toy-maker' while they were recording the TV show back in Brisbane." Legend has it that this backstage composition took them just ten minutes to finish.

"I also toured with them a couple of times in Queensland," Jon added, "and not always to a good response. I remember once in particular where Robin had an egg thrown at him in Toowoomba in Queensland, and he let the egg stain remain for the whole tour. I was also at the studio when they were recording 'Spicks And Specks', and while they were waiting for the brass section from the nearby Oceanic Hotel to arrive, Barry wrote

'Coalman'." At least something good came out of that incident – the brass section's recording remained unused.

Living in the Gibb household obviously allowed Jon to gain a better perspective of the family than most. "They were a very different sort of people. You got the impression you couldn't get close to them. They had a very 'us against the world' attitude, that they were very determined to make it. They were totally driven."

Another example of their extrovert behaviour was forthcoming from Jon. "The Gibbs took full advantage of their Myers – a huge department store – credit arrangement before they returned to the UK, buying things they would need [for] when they [got there]. They then paid it back when they returned four years later!

"I saw them off on the boat," he continued, "and Barry was very supportive of me to the end, telling me I had the necessary talent to make it, and to stick at it." Despite this good advice, Jon ceased singing after he got married in 1971 and is now into management, with several bands on his books.

Trevor Hales, a New Zealand male solo singer of British origin, released his own rendition of 'Town Of Tuxley Toymaker, Part One' as a single on the obscure Zodiac label shortly after Blanchfield's version. Formerly a member of The Aussie Pleazers, who folded after completing a three month contract working the Auckland club circuit and who should not be confused with The Pleasers, Trevor used 'Tuxley' to launch his solo career as Shane; the highlight of which was a huge hit in August, 1969, called 'Saint Paul'. Shane continues to be involved in the music industry to this day.

Another visitor to Ossie's studio was Jenene Watson, and she too, in what was quickly becoming a trend, was only referred to by her Christian name on her Spin release. Again the label made a reasonable effort to promote this up-and-coming artist, described as "star of ABC's television programme *Crackerjack*, accomplished singer, dancer, versatile entertainer, a trouper in Australia and overseas." The formula of a Maurice and Nat song on the A-side, and a Barry one on the reverse, was once again repeated on 'So Long Boy'/'Don't Say No', the songs being described by Spin's release sheet as "a novelty, semi R&B" and "a big ballad" respectively.

Barry remained as prolific as ever, quickly churning out four more songs. Adelaide formed but Melbourne based band, The Twilights, included 'Long Life' on their self-titled album for Columbia, a song which bass guitarist John Bywater recalls that Barry wrote for them while they were recording their own 'Come Back Baby' at Hurstville, when Barry was in the back room of the studio.

John De Jong was born in Indonesia, but he grew up on his parents' farm in Kalamunda in Western Australia, later making live appearances with The Nomads. By 1965 he had become the host of local television pop show *Club 17*, and within a year he had signed to Clarion and formed Kompany. Within months they had a massive number one hit in Perth, Sydney and Melbourne with The Easybeats' penned 'Step Back' and suddenly, Johnny

Young was the hottest name in the land. After another big hit in January 1967, Johnny left to pursue a solo career and used The Nomads – now renamed The Strangers – on his recording of Barry's 'Lady', a single that was also issued on the Decca label in Britain. In fact, within weeks, he had travelled to London where he recorded three songs already released by The Bee Gees themselves. He returned to Australia in January 1968 and, neglecting his own singing career, Young spent the remainder of the Sixties and early Seventies concentrating on writing for other artists, penning hit singles for the likes of Russell Morris, Ronnie Burns and Ross D. Wylie, as well as 'Here Comes The Star' for Herman's Hermits. He then moved into TV production and later operated a successful school of music.

In September, Noeleen Batley released the fourth song written for her by Barry, and 'The Wishing Song' became the second of the quartet to be issued as an A-side. "We laughed a lot and had so much enjoyment," she recalled. "My friendship is still close, and they are like my brothers to me." This is hardly surprising when you consider that they've been friends for almost 40 years now.

Country singer Johnny Ashcroft's career took off as the result of even more uplifting emotions. He is best known in Australia for his 1960 release, 'Little Boy Lost', which tells the true story of a young boy who survived a number of days lost in the Australian bush, and which was co-written by him with Sydney DJ, Tony Withers. It was also released in the USA by Capitol, as well as being covered in the UK by Tommy Steele.

Whenever Johnny was recording, he was on the lookout for new local material. The fourth in this batch of Barry's songs was given to him by his record company Columbia/EMI, but Johnny is unsure of whether this was prompted in any way by Barry. "I had previously worked with The Bee Gees on *Bandstand*," Johnny explained, "and had performed with them on a show in a Sydney club. I chose 'Don't Forget Me Ida' from a heap of material submitted by various music publishers, on the basis that it is a lovely song, not simply because it is a Barry Gibb song." The late Eric Dunn was the producer, but the Gibbs were not present.

Even when they didn't have time to write, the brothers were always prepared to lend support, and the trio can be clearly heard accompanying Festival's Ray Brown & The Whispers (originally called The Nocturnes) on 'Too Late To Come Home', located on the flip side of 'Respect'. Lead singer Ray Brown died of a heart attack in 1996, but former Whispers' members, guitarist Laurie Barclay and bass player John Manners were prepared to go "on record" in July 1998 about the problems besetting the band at the time of recording. Firstly, they wanted to concentrate on the recording itself. They said that the Gibbs' appearance came about simply because they were Festival label mates. They can recall that the song sounded pretty average before the brothers came in and did their overdubs. The recordings took place in August, 1966 with Joe Halford as the producer, and Barry Neagle as the engineer.

John Manners spoke very highly of Bill Shepherd, who was the producer of most of The Whispers' previous recordings and called him a "lovely guy". He said Shepherd was a brilliant musician and a very patient producer. In contrast, he remembers Robert Iredale as being somewhat arrogant and intimidating at first, appearing to be disinterested in them until they had some success. Manners also said that The Bee Gees had great respect from their peers, and at the time, fellow musicians couldn't understand their lack of commercial success. However, when presented with cute kids' ditties such as 'My Old Man's A Dustman', it may have been hard for record buyers to accept them as a legitimate rock or pop act. Relations between the band and Ray Brown were not good, and in fact the song was recorded at three sessions, one where the music was recorded and then separately when Ray, and then the Gibbs, recorded their vocals.

Indeed, Hurstville-born Ray left before the single was actually released. Although they produced five good albums and a number of singles, the group lasted for less than two years. The band broke up acrimoniously with Ray, and their parting of the ways eventually required litigation to settle a few issues.

It had taken eight long years for the MPD Ltd's bass player, the late Pete Watson who died in 1972 following a long illness, to finally team up with his fellow "10 pound tourists" from that fateful August 1958 voyage. 'Absence Makes The Heart Grow Fonder' and 'I Am What I Am', released on the Go! label, are two more songs that contain some very recognisable vocals or instrumentation. Guitarist Mike Brady, another English immigrant, said he could never forget one moment in particular from yet another Hurstville session. He related how, on 'Absence Makes The Heart Grow Fonder,' Maurice sort of played piano with a plectrum in an attempt to create a unique sound, while stamping the pedals with his foot. Mike went on to become Australia's most successful advertising jingle writer. The group took its moniker from the Christian names of its members; drummer Danny Finley completing the line-up.

The single was also released on the Ariola label in Germany, but it would take some time before that nation's Bee Gees fans of the future would recognise this connection to their heroes. 'I Am What I Am' had previously been released by Ray Brown & The Whispers as the B-side to 'Tennessee Waltz' amidst much suspicion that the Gibbs featured on their version. However, while sharing the same title, Brown's was a completely different song altogether and John Manners has since confirmed that the Gibbs most certainly did not participate on that version.

Neither did Barry, Robin and Maurice have time to write anything specifically for Mike Furber, but they were delighted with his choice of 'Where Are You' and 'Second Hand People', two tracks from their new album, for his latest Kommotion label single. Again the brothers' vocals are clearly evident. Furber had first come to prominence in 1965 when he united with Brisbane band, The Bowery Boys, and they became well known in The Bee

Gees' old stomping ground of Surfers' Paradise. However, it was Ivan Dayman, ironically a harsh critic of The Bee Gees, who set them on the road to fame when he signed them to a contract. Sadly, it was short lived and they only had two minor hits to show for their efforts, but 'Where Are You' wasn't one of them. Indeed, by the time of its release, Mike had suffered a nervous breakdown, and in 1973 he was found dead, having committed suicide.

★ ★ ★

The fact that the majority of these many releases went largely unnoticed by the Australian record-buying public matters little. It was more important that the Gibbs develop their songwriting, and there was no better way to do this than to write for and record with as many different artists and groups as they possibly could, thereby exposing themselves to styles of music that they would not otherwise have encountered. Perhaps one of the best barometers of the progress they made during the May, 1963 to December, 1966 period lies in an obscure LP released in Australia by Columbia, shortly after their departure. Orchestras are generally spoiled for choice when assembling titles for an album, usually selecting the better known hits of the day. It is therefore no surprise to find instrumental versions of 'Spicks And Specks' and 'Coalman' on The Johnny Hawker Orchestra's *Out Front* collection of 12 tunes. More relevant, though, is that 'Wine And Women' and 'Exit Stage Right' were virtual unknowns to the general public, and their inclusion suggests that Johnny Hawker had a pretty good idea of the Gibbs' potential in an era when melody remained the key to a writer's success.

Many of the cover versions of Gibb material that were recorded during this early stage of their careers eventually appeared on a compilation CD in 1998 on the Spin label, and so successful was it that a second volume is being planned. The recordings were lovingly and painstakingly restored to their original condition on the instruction of the then Festival Records' group deputy managing director, Warren Fahey. However, it appeared that the brothers were not in favour of his efforts. "I don't think any artist anywhere wants to be reminded of their gawky period," as Warren put it slightly untactfully.

Gawky or not, the release of this compact disc opened up an area of The Bee Gees' career which had previously lain in the domain of the dedicated few collectors who knew what to look for, where to find it, and who were fortunate enough to be able to afford it. More importantly, it preserved some of the best examples of the fledgling Gibbs' songwriting for the benefit of future generations. Indeed, there may be instances of the brothers' involvement on other recordings that have not yet come to light, such was the extent of their energy and enthusiasm during this particular stage of their development.

7

BACK HOME

"THE VERY LAST month we were in Australia, our first single got to number one in Australia . . . and other strange places," Barry said. "You can get locked into Australia because it has a great record market of its own. Anyone who has success in Australia doesn't really have very much outside Australia because the links overseas are too distant. Our objective was to become known in other countries and the best place to do this was the US or England. At that time the British boom was at its fullest and we headed to England . . ."

Fading memories can play strange tricks, especially on pop musicians. Research reveals that 'Spicks And Specks' wasn't a national number one in Australia simply because no official overall Australian chart existed until the early Seventies. Australia consists of six states and two territories. The most populated is New South Wales, followed by Victoria, Queensland, Western Australia, South Australia and finally Tasmania. There is no trace of 'Spicks And Specks' achieving top slot in any of the six states although, admittedly, it did top the hit parade locally in places like Melbourne, where such statistics perhaps mattered most. Its best placing in any state appears to have been number three, so to New Zealand goes the honour of being the first country to have a Bee Gees chart topper, Spin having also released it there.

"The thing about Australia is that it's such a big country," said Hugh. "There's a lot of inter-state rivalry between cities like Sydney, Brisbane and Melbourne. Brisbane is about 550 miles north of Sydney and Melbourne is right down south, so what hits in one place doesn't necessarily go in another. You can have a number one in Sydney, that doesn't mean a thing in Melbourne, or Perth, which is nearly 3,000 miles away. Really, each state is like being in a different country. There are 1,500 clubs in New South Wales [alone]."

Whatever the semantics, the record was undoubtedly a massive hit and its success brought with it an unexpected intrusion. Festival Records, claiming that the boys' impending departure was in violation of the terms of their agreement, tried to prevent The Bee Gees from leaving Australia by bringing an injunction against them. Hugh has always maintained that he was served with the court documents at the ship's gangway, but he treated Fred Marks' parting gesture with the contempt he felt it deserved. In reality there was no such confrontation and Fred Marks professes never to have served a writ on anyone in his life. Indeed, the many friends he has made over the years describe him as an extremely mild-mannered gentleman for whom such action would be unthinkable. In fact, it was very much in Fred's interests for the group to go on to be successful internationally as Festival's revenue from their future Australian releases would be significantly higher than if they just remained successful solely in Australia. For their part, in spite of what was said then, the brothers bear Fred no ill will at all and greeted him with open arms on their last encounter.

At the time, Robin claimed to find the whole situation ironic. "Festival Records once said, 'Change your name and move to Melbourne.' Festival Records once said, 'Forget it, fellas. If you can't do it here, what makes you think you can do it anywhere else?' And Festival Records, once said, 'Quit, it's finished.' It hadn't even started, and they said it's finished!"

As Barry recalled it, Festival wanted the group to return to promote 'Spicks And Specks', "But we were already across the Indian Ocean," he recalls. "There was no bitterness. We wanted to show everyone here [in Australia] that it could be done, but not in a nasty way; we needed to search out the opportunities and we did."

One Australian record man – Normie Rowe's manager who ran Sunshine Records, another Festival subsidiary – did offer disparaging remarks that irritated Barry intensely. "There was this bloke, Ivan Dayman, and he said, 'If King Normie [Rowe] can't make it in England, nobody else can,' and that spurred us on because I thought that was the most senile remark I'd ever heard."

"We were tired of being ignored," Robin added. "A new Bee Gees record would come out, and the record people would take it round to the radio people, and they'd say, 'Oh yeah, another Bee Gees song.' We were still seen as a bunch of kids who played on *Bandstand*, while we were already full of ideas."

For The Bee Gees, it was a time of "frustration mixed with ambition, I think, because we were a very ambitious pack of brothers really," Barry said. "And all we could see was ahead, we would not look back at anything. We wanted to go ahead and try our luck in England. We even prepared ourselves to fail, completely. We didn't have any money when we arrived in England."

"Had we failed [to achieve success in Britain], we would have come back to Australia," Robin said. "We went over there to find out whether we could or not. It wasn't whether we were going to make it because we didn't broadcast that at all. To anybody."

"We didn't do a 'Look out Beatles, here come The Bee Gees,'" Maurice added. "After 13 records in Australia and endless TV appearances, we decided to try our fortune in England. We had good managers and plenty of luck."

Barbara Gibb was something of an amateur fortune-teller, and before the Gibb family left Australia, she consulted the cards. "She told us that before five months or five years or five something, we would have everything we wanted," Barry recalled. "She also described Robert [Stigwood] long before we ever met him."

Having heard that The Seekers had worked their way to England on a ship called *Fairsky*, the same ship on which Colin Petersen had left for England, Hugh had approached the Italian shipping line Sitmar, with whom they had first travelled to Australia in 1958, and made them an offer: The Bee Gees would entertain the ship's passengers in return for free passage for himself and the boys. The deal was done, and on January 3, 1967, the Gibb family (minus Lesley, who stayed behind in Australia with her husband Keith), accompanied by their Australian producer Ossie Byrne, boarded the *SS Fairsky,* setting sail for what they hoped would be the start of a fresh career.

Things got off to a strange start when, on the first day aboard, Hugh went to the ship's purser to establish the boys' performance schedule and discovered that the bewildered man had no idea that The Bee Gees were on board or were supposed to be performing. Other entertainment had already been booked, but a compromise was finally reached whereby the group would perform a 20-minute set on a few evenings of the voyage.

They had set sail by the time that news filtered through that 'Spicks And Specks' had reached pole position in Sydney. "We found out on the boat that it was number one and we just couldn't believe it," Barry said. "We hadn't been able to get a solid hit record in that country since the moment we arrived [in] '58.

"Nothing had happened to us," he continued, his frustration obvious. "We'd done a lot of club work, a lot of experience." He did concede that the experience was invaluable though. "That's the one thing Australia has done for us. We worked a lot of stages, did a lot of shows, never really made hits, [but] it made us into, I think, a good band."

The first port of call was a brief stop at Thursday Island. The boys took the opportunity to send postcards to Sydney deejays, many of whom didn't know the group had left. The message was short. "We're on our way to England."

On January 7, The Bee Gees gave their first performance of the voyage home, commencing at 11.30 p.m. As the ship was full of young Australians who were familiar with the group, they got a fantastic reception. It was a far cry from the voyage from England, when three little boys had to sneak out in their pyjamas to sing their songs perched on the anchor. Now they really were a group. They were still performing their nightclub act of original material with occasional covers of hits like 'Puff The Magic Dragon' and 'Twist And Shout' and the odd bit of comedy thrown in.

One interested onlooker was fellow-passenger David Browning, who described their daily performances as, "Partly rehearsal, but partly entertainment for the boat. The thing that used to be sung more than anything else by them was 'Yellow Submarine', which was a great laugh! They used to sing that a lot."

Other family members joined in too. "I know that their father was on drums," recalled David, "and there was the wife of one of the chaps, a slim blonde girl, and she once did an act with them, but I didn't see much of her. It was a bit of a magical disappearing act, sort of thing from a wardrobe or something like that." It is often said that life imitates art: this particular part of the act would soon be reprised, for real.

Mysterious poems began to appear on the notice-board of the day's activities. Intrigued passengers would gather each day to read the latest work of the phantom poet of the *Fairsky*. Watching from the distance as they speculated on the poet's identity was the phantom himself, Robin Gibb, who composed the nonsense poems on a portable typewriter in his cabin.

Barry and Robin also wrote a complete book of short stories during the five-week voyage. The book, which they planned to publish under the title *On The Other Hand*, was one of many proposed Bee Gees' projects which would be shelved along the way.

The *Fairsky* docked at Southampton on the evening of Monday, February 6, 1967. As Maurice explained, "We were there for the night, and everyone was going to be disembarking the next day, so we decided to go off for the night and go round to find our first good fish and chip shop."

Barry continued the story. "We met this group who were all dressed like The Beatles were in *A Hard Day's Night* with the black cloaks, you know, and all that business. And they said, you know, 'Go back, go back. Groups are out.' That was the statement which is pretty amazing, considering that groups still do all right, you know! 'Groups are out, go back.' So we didn't, but that was the message . . ."

The events of the following morning remained in Andy Gibb's memories for different reasons. As he recalled, "I went running down the gangplank, nine years old . . . and I left at five months old so I'd never even seen [England]. I was running down there and kissed the ground . . . and my brothers all kissed the ground. After a few months, we wondered why, but we did it."

The Gibb family had only about £200 between them and after making their way to London they spent their first few nights in what Maurice unkindly describes as "a crummy hotel in Hampstead". As Barry recalls, "I had two pounds and ten shillings to my name."

They wasted no time in contacting their Australian friend, Colin Petersen, who was already in London and who helped the family find a semi-detached house. "I had a letter from Hugh Gibb," he explained, "and sorted out somewhere for them to stay and stored their equipment in my flat." Colin's help proved invaluable. "We [disembarked] on a Tuesday and by Friday we'd moved into a furnished house in Hendon," Hugh Gibb confirmed.

The underground journey to Colin's flat was memorable for some bemused passengers. Maurice was carrying a sitar purchased in India on a stop-over on the journey back from Australia. Quickly realising that he was no budding George Harrison, it was one of the first things he sold on returning to Britain.

On their first Monday in London, Barry and his dad travelled by tube to see Eddie Jarrett, of the Lew Grade Organisation, who was managing The Seekers at the time. "He painted a very black picture about the possibility of touring but offered to put us into clubs to keep the boys working," said Hugh.

Dejected, Barry and Hugh returned to the semi-detached house in Hendon, where Barbara was waiting with the news that a "Mr Stickweed" had been ringing all day. While in Australia Hugh had sent acetates of their records to Beatles manager Brian Epstein's NEMS office in London. He in turn had passed them on to Robert Stigwood who worked with him at that time. "We didn't know at the time that Brian didn't handle that side of the business," Barry explained, "and that [the discs] were passed to Robert Stigwood instead. He played them and liked them. He had our date of arrival in England and tried for days to contact us but couldn't find us. We tried every agency in the book but none of them wanted to know. At last Robert contacted us."

"I don't know how he got that telephone number because I didn't tell him," Hugh said. "We only moved into the house on Friday and on Monday he was ringing all day." For years, Hugh's question remained unanswered, but in 1999, the missing piece of the jigsaw was discovered.

★　★　★

In 1965 The Deutsche Grammophon Company created a new subsidiary in London called Polydor UK Ltd, appointing 35-year-old Roland Rennie as its first Managing Director. It was during a previous employment with EMI that he had first encountered Robert Stigwood, a relationship which would serve both well in Roland's new job.

One of EMI's subsidiaries was a company called Top Rank which itself had previously founded the "Rank Co-operative". This had originally been set up on behalf of all the small record companies around the world so that they could combat the monopoly of Decca and EMI, giving them a fighting chance to acquire American repertoire for their various companies. When EMI bought Top Rank, the co-operative folded and Roland, then of EMI, travelled the world meeting all the various company heads. One of these was Fred Marks.

In late 1966 Roland was approached by an Australian music publisher, one of the titles on offer being 'Spicks And Specks'. Noting that The Bee Gees were a Festival act, Roland immediately contacted Fred and acquired the rights to it with a view to issuing it as a Polydor single. It was already in the process of being pressed when, according to Roland, "Totally out of the blue, [Barry Gibb] came into my office one day. He virtually came off the street, as I remember. He was a very together young man, it was incredible at his age to come in and talk about a record deal – he was very impressive."

Alan Bates, Polydor's marketing manager, remembered that this was the first time he had ever heard of The Bee Gees. He was shown an acetate, probably one of the ones sent to NEMS by Hugh. "I know that the acetate came via Roland – where he got it from, I couldn't say," Alan explained. "There was a white label and on it; it just said 'Spicks And Specks' and 'Bee Gees'. I didn't know what to make of it – the way that 'Bee Gees' was spelled on the thing, it wasn't obvious to me which one of those two was the title and which was the group. I actually thought that the band was called 'Spicks And Specks'. That just shows that they were completely unknown."

As impressed as Roland Rennie had been by Barry Gibb's presence, it was clear to him that the young Gibb was very inexperienced when it came to business acumen. He had his own thoughts on how best to promote the interests of not only his company, but also The Bee Gees.

Alan Bates provided the details. "Well, what happened is that Roland decided to give The Bee Gees to Robert Stigwood. Roland knew Stigwood from his EMI days, and Stigwood had actually gone bankrupt either once or twice, and there was a certain amount of eyebrow-raising when it was suggested that Stigwood, who at that time was down and out, should be brought into the picture. But Roland was insistent because he thought that Stigwood was the right guy to break them, and so that is what happened. Roland actually *gave* The Bee Gees to Stigwood."

"[The group] needed some management," Roland Rennie resumed, "so then I got hold of Robert, who I'd worked with in my EMI days. He had already heard about them and said, 'I know something about this,' so I left him to take things on."

★ ★ ★

"So at about half ten in the morning, the phone rang again," Hugh told *Record World*, "and the boys were sitting on the stairs saying, 'Who is it, Dad?' So I get on the phone and he says, 'Good morning' – you know the way Stiggy speaks – he said, 'I'm Robert Stigwood, Brian Epstein's partner.' The boys were saying, 'Who is it, who is it?' and I told them, and they started grinning all over their faces.

"He said, 'I'm very interested, could you come up and see me?' I said, 'Sure, okay, would you like to see the boys?' and he said, 'Bring them along by all means' and that's how it started . . .'"

It was an auspicious start to their life in London. While Brian Epstein had his Beatles, Robert Stigwood was still searching for a group he could mould in the same way when the parcel arrived from Australia.

"We sent all our records which we made in Australia, all the LPs, acetates of new songs, tapes of new songs, all to the Epstein agency," Maurice recalled. "We sent them all to Brian Epstein. Robert was the managing director of NEMS, Brian Epstein's company. Brian and he had a few drinks one night and started to play all the tapes and things they had received from all over the place and ours came up and Robert saw something in the songs and thought 'these guys are good.'"

Maurice exaggerates the amount of material shipped to NEMS as Hugh had actually sent only two discs, the *Spicks And Specks* album and an acetate with additional songs including some The Bee Gees never released, such as 'Mrs Gillespie's Refrigerator', 'Deeply, Deeply Me' and an early version of 'Gilbert Green'.

Along with the parcel, which arrived at NEMS on December 3, was a letter saying that the group wrote all their own songs. The letter, dated November 25 and signed Hugh L. Gibb, began:

> *This is just a preliminary letter to advise you of the arrival in London of a young vocal group, who, having reached the top of their field in this country, are returning home to the U.K. to further their career. They are the "Bee Gees", who consist of three brothers, Barry Gibb, aged 19 and twins Robin and Maurice, aged 16. I am writing to you on the sugges-tion of Mr. Harry M. Miller of Sydney, who feels you are the best person to look after the interests of this talented young group.*
>
> *The boys migrated from Manchester as schoolboys and made their TV début in March 1960 and have been in the business ever since. Although still youngsters, the boys have had an enormous amount of experience in all facets of show business; TV, recording, pantomime, hotel and club work, etc. Naturally, their records have been aimed at the teenage market and at the time of writing, they have a hit record, 'Spicks And Specks', which has just reached the number three position in every state in Austra-lia. We quite realise that this does not mean very much overseas, but considering the enormous size of Australia, this is considered quite a feat here.*
>
> *Another side to this talented group is the fact that all their records, plus three albums and several EPs, have all been written by themselves. The eldest boy, Barry, is acknowledged to be the top songwriter in this country. Practically every 'name', top recording artist here, has recorded his material. In addition, Barry cracked the American market by submit-ting six numbers and then having two recorded, one by Wayne Newton and one by Jimmy Boyd.*

Hugh went on to mention Barry's 5KA composer award and explained that they had unreleased material on the acetate and 'about another 20 num-bers' besides. In reality, only two albums and the same number of EPs had actually been released. To be fair, there was an album's worth of material in the can, and *Turn Around, Look At Us* was issued by Festival in late 1967, after *Spicks And Specks* had gone out of print. Immediately following the boys' departure, Spin had also rush-released a *Spicks And Specks* EP which included three other tracks from the album: 'Jingle Jangle', 'Tint Of Blue' and 'Where Are You'.

Stigwood was intrigued enough to listen to the material that Hugh had sent. The first song he remembers hearing was 'Jingle Jangle'. "I heard it and was astounded," he recalled. "It was some of the best harmony singing and composing I had ever heard. I was absolutely knocked out with their writing. I thought it was sensational . . . It was pointed out to me that the boys had been barely sixteen years old when the songs had been written. So I figured that if boys of that age had been able to turn out material of that calibre, they must have immense potential. They were probably the best new writers to emerge since Lennon & McCartney . . .

"After they arrived [in England] I had a meeting with them and offered them a deal for recording, management and publishing. They were incredibly amusing. Often when people are just starting up in the business they're fairly nervous when they meet managers. I was amazed at their relaxation; they were polite, but just totally relaxed, cracking lots of gags. I thought with their harmony singing, that natural quality that you only get with brothers really, and with their writing ability, it would be very difficult for them to go wrong."

The first person they met at NEMS was a 20-year-old receptionist named Molly Hullis. A small brunette, Molly was born February 16, 1947, one of seven children brought up in a council house near Hastings. She had left her village home looking for the excitement of the city life in London and found a position as personal assistant to a London shipping company executive. It wasn't exactly the stimulating career which she had envisaged. One day she answered an advertisement for a receptionist position at Brian Epstein's NEMS empire and became involved in the pop music scene almost by accident.

Having worked in the office which was home to The Beatles, she was not particularly impressed with the three Gibb brothers at that first meeting. Molly recalled, "They arrived late one afternoon, very bedraggled looking, very old-fashioned clothes as far as England was concerned . . . They were all sort of terribly shy and didn't know how to conduct themselves. So I said, 'Who do you want to see?' They said, 'We've come to see Robert Stigwood. We're The Bee Gees.'"

After speaking to the boys and their father, Stigwood told the group that he would like to hear them perform live before signing them.

"We did an audition at the Saville Theatre," Barry said. "Well it's gone now, but it was in the basement of the Saville Theatre and Robert was sort of brought in. We think he'd had a bad night the night before because he was helped in by two men and sort of sat down in front of us with his arms hanging limp at his side. He had a hangover like you would not believe. He put his head in his hands and said, 'Carry on.' So we did what we had worked up in Australia."

"We did our nightclub act and he watched and listened and never smiled once," Maurice recalled.

Barry elaborates even further, describing a "Peter, Paul & Mary segment" of 'Puff The Magic Dragon' which "concluded with Maurice kissing Robin on the cheek. It used to be funny. As you get older, it's no longer funny. It's highly suspicious and shouldn't be repeated!"

The brothers, watching Stigwood closely to try to gauge his impressions, saw only his miserable expression. "He never saw a minute of [the audition]," Barry remembered. "He heard something, told us to come and see him in his office later and staggered out again."

"He said, 'Be at my office at six o'clock,' and we were, and we signed contracts," Maurice added.

"Robert's an Australian," continued Barry, "but we'd never heard of him when we were there. It was purely coincidental. When we asked him where he was from and he said 'Adelaide,' we said 'Adelaide's beautiful.' After we'd signed the contract and had a glass of champagne, we said 'Adelaide stinks.'"

"It's a funny thing, but not long before we left Australia, there was an article in one of the papers saying that Brian Epstein was looking for the new Beatles," Hugh Gibb pondered. "I thought, 'You've got them here if you only knew it.' Then it happened – they were signed up by the Brian Epstein office within a week of arriving in England."

On the voyage from Australia, the brothers had again discussed a change of name for the group which they hoped would bring about a change in their fortunes as well. Having already had some posters printed, they told Robert Stigwood that they would like to change their name to Rupert's World (inspired by the cartoon bear), a change which Barry now likens to "changing your name from Charlie Shit to Fred Shit" but in the psychedelic Sixties, it seemed to the brothers to be a good choice. Stigwood was not convinced and suggested that they bring out their first record under the name The Bee Gees, then if it "stiffed", they could change their name later and no one would be the wiser. No such change would occur although Barry's friend in Australia, Colin Stead, would use the concept to title his group, Lloyd's World.

Strangely enough, a British psychedelic band by the name of Rupert's People surfaced in July of that same year. This was probably nothing more than a coincidence although, just months previously, Howard Conder, one of Robert Stigwood's understudies, had tendered his resignation solely to take on the management of the trio who would shortly form the nucleus of that new group.

"There are many intricacies as to whatever became an agreement between us and Robert," Barry recalled. "There were so many side deals to which we had no knowledge . . . even memories of details are no longer there . . . We signed a record agreement and a publishing agreement with Robert and a management agreement at Robert's offices . . . For us it was the opening of the doors to the world. Robert's faith in us was the equal to having a hit record. It wasn't having a hit record then, it was the fact that someone had signed us up. That was more important than anything else . . . It was a very exciting period."

Robert Stigwood offered them a five-year contract, almost unprecedented for a new group. He says that in those days, he often offered new artists a one-year contract with the option to extend, but so convinced was he of the Gibbs' songwriting and performing talents that he never considered anything less than a firm five-year deal. The contract was signed on February 24, 1967, only three weeks after their arrival in England.

Seen against the background of the comment made by Alan Bates that Polydor, through the good offices of Roland Rennie, "gave" The Bee Gees to Stigwood, it appears more than just a coincidence that The Bee Gees' contract with Polydor should also expire in 1972. Again, thanks to Alan Bates, the complex question of just who "owned" The Bee Gees can be answered.

"Polydor went into joint ventures with people such as Chas Chandler,"★ Alan explained. "There was Chris Stamp and Kit Lambert, who we also went into a joint venture [for The Who] with as well. It might be that that was some sort of a joint venture that we went into with Stigwood.

"The essence of it was that Polydor put up all the money as an advance, and the management paid themselves out of the advance, which was then in itself an advance against the future royalties.

"We would advance [the manager] a substantial chunk of money, out of which he had to do everything – produce the records, pay himself, keep the band going, and then the theory being that in the end results, the profits would be shared."

Stigwood announced the signing with a press conference, and described the brothers' audition to gathered journalists with genuine enthusiasm. "The Bee Gees put on one of the most exciting stage shows I've ever seen. They have a tremendous versatility, an unbelievable professionalism. It's impossible to overstate their international potential both as performers and composers." The announcement was timed to coincide with the Polydor release of their Australian single, 'Spicks And Specks', to introduce the group to the world.

Meanwhile, in the land that could rightly claim to have created The Bee Gees, Spin released the brothers' fourteenth Australian single with barely a whisper. 'Born A Man' and 'Big Chance' were the chosen tracks. Spin would now require to negotiate a licensing agreement with Polydor if they wished future output bearing the group's distinctive sound to be released on their label in Australia again.

There was also a certain irony in the news that Barry had collected another writers' award and that The Bee Gees had won the 1966 National Radio 2UE award for best group. They might not have won Barry's treasured 4KQ talent contest but they now had something far more important – tangible proof that they did indeed have the ability to go to greater things. Full of confidence, and with their creative juices flowing, they went into the studio to commence their first British recordings.

★ Chandler was the former bass player in The Animals, who became co-manager, along with Mike Jeffery, of The Jimi Hendrix Experience. He later managed Slade.

8

A MAN CALLED STICKWEED

FOR THE GREATER part of their career, one man in particular has been responsible more than any other in bringing The Bee Gees success on a scale they never dreamt of, and the Gibbs widely acknowledge the importance of his influence on them.

There was little in the family background of Robert Colin Stigwood to indicate the theatrical flair and shrewd foresight that he would bring to his glittering career as a popular music impresario. He was born in Adelaide, Australia on April 16, 1934 where his father was an electrical engineer and his mother ran a nursing home. His parents, descendant from Scottish, Irish and German Protestant roots, divorced when he was 12 and attending a private school. He converted to Catholicism at age 15 and later considered becoming a priest, spending three years at Adelaide's Sacred Heart College. However, he decided he didn't have the calling and left to become a copy writer for a local advertising agency, progressing to the grade of junior account executive.

Robert also walked the boards in his home town. "I did appear on stage myself as an amateur," he admitted. "I played Toad in *Toad Of Toad Hall*. That was my first assessment of talent, the elimination of myself as an actor. I got wonderful notices, but I knew it was typecasting." There is talk that he trained as a hypnotist during this period too.

In 1955, aged 21, he left Adelaide for London.

His reasons may have been as simple as a young man's desire for a change of scene and the Australian desire to experience the British homeland. A romantic story has been told about pursuing a girl he wanted to marry, only to be stood up for their rendezvous in Paris.

The journey was a difficult one because he travelled overland on "the most ill-equipped expedition of all time" as he later called it. At length, he arrived in London with £5 and dysentery, two stone lighter than when he left home. He settled at first in what was known as 'Kangaroo Valley', the small Australian colony at Earls Court, and embarked on a variety of jobs from selling vacuum cleaners to working at a hostel for delinquent boys.

He appears to have been at loose ends about what he wanted to do with himself, but something brought him into the theatrical business, which has attracted many men of genius on or behind the stage. His first such job took him south of London to Southampton, but by 1959 Robert had found a position running a theatre in the East Anglian city of Norwich called the Hippodrome, and here he not only began his managerial career but also found his first business partner, Stephen Anton Komlosy.

Robert Stigwood never married or had children. Many have said that his best clients became his family, and he looked after them like a doting father, or perhaps a favourite uncle. One thing he tried a few times was to find a handsome young man to turn into a star, and perhaps it is not too much of a leap to speculate that this came from the same feelings as parents who work for their children's success. He eventually found his concept of a talented teen idol in Barry Gibb, but that was a few years off yet.

"The idea was I was going to be a pop star," Stephen began, "but there were a few problems. I'm too nervous and I can't sing." Komlosy had taken a job painting scenery at the Hippodrome before planning to head off to University, which he never did do. Despite his being the wrong person for Stigwood's starmaking plan, "we got on very well, and I left school and we ran that theatre together. It went on for about a year . . . both of us doing everything from management to scene painting to a bit of acting."

Hoping for better things, they quit in 1960 and moved to a cottage in Hampstead near New End Hospital. They opened the Robert Stigwood Associates in a tiny office at 41 Charing Cross Road with £5,000 from Komlosy's mother and Komlosy himself as the only model. In retrospect, Robert can't quite believe his own naïveté. "It was a lunatic thing to do," he admitted, "because I didn't know anybody."

The only reason it succeeded was that Stigwood found an angle that was being overlooked by others. "The big theatrical agencies treated the advertising agencies very badly," he recalled. "Even though TV commercials were only 30 seconds long, the [advertising] agencies wanted those commercials to be like feature films. Vast amounts of money were spent on time buying, after all." So it became a specialty agency, casting actors for television commercials. The advertising agencies were delighted to find someone who gave them the respect they thought they deserved, and business flowed into Robert Stigwood Associates. It wasn't only brief commercials, but longer "advertising magazines" similar to today's infomercials, and as Komlosy recalled, "In time, there were about eight presenters and we had them all."

In addition to the commercials however, "we started handling a few actors in series on television like Emergency Ward Ten," Stigwood said. "From that, I first got involved in music – through John Leyton."

Robert Stigwood's first musical client was born in 1939 in Frinton-on-Sea. Leyton had Komlosy's heart-throb good looks, but more importantly to Robert, he had the voice as well. Even Stephen Komlosy agreed that John could become what he himself could not. "He looked exactly right," conceded Stephen. "He was an actor, and he could sing well enough. It was the formula we'd talked about."

The John Leyton recordings were made by the legendary engineer and producer, Joe Meek. Leyton's first record, 'Tell Laura I Love Her' was released in August 1960 but it was his next release a year later which really brought him to prominence. By then Robert Stigwood Associates had quite a few mainly serious actors who worked in the legitimate theatre. John Leyton was still there too, and RSA had landed him the lead in a prime-time show called *Harpers West One*, a latter-day soap set in a London department store with a striking resemblance to Harrods. Stigwood's influence would even extend onto the set itself.

"The first episode was about a pop singer opening the record department. I had lunch with the director, played him the song we had just recorded, which was 'Johnny Remember Me'. He loved it, and it became the theme music. We rather changed the show around – built John a more lavish staircase to walk down and sing." Leyton appeared on the show playing the role of Johnny St Cyr (pronounced "sincere") and by the very next morning, record shops up and down the country were being deluged with requests for the record.

The song was written by Geoff Goddard, a young man from one of the instrumental groups Joe Meek had worked with, the Flee-rekkers, and whose publishing just happened to be handled by RSA, so RSA got a share of that too. The lyrics were toned down though, so that "the girl who died" became "the girl I lost".

Stigwood finally had both feet firmly planted in the music business, but his agency remained the heart of the operation.

"We conceived the idea," Komlosy boasted, "that in show business, you can monopolise all areas of income by controlling and managing the artist. If you start with the star, you can control when and where he appears, so if you promote him yourself, you get the promoter's share. If you record him yourself, you become the record company. If you publish his music, you get the publisher's cut. And we always had the B-side of records. In terms of mechanical royalties, they make just as much money as the A-sides. The idea was not to let anyone in from the outside."

Leyton's follow-up release, 'Wild Wind' was almost as successful, reaching the number two spot in November, but December's offering, 'Son This Is She', another Goddard composition, peaked at number 15.

Another Stigwood discovery, Mike Berry, also tasted chart success, his 'Tribute To Buddy Holly' climbing to number 24 in November 1961. In January 1963, 'Don't You Think It's Time' would reach number six but 'My Little Baby', a number 34 three months later, would be his last chart visit until the Eighties.

Robert and Joe Meek had a falling out in the middle of 1962. The credit on John Leyton's records changed from 'Lonely Johnny' in October 1962 to read "A Robert Stigwood Production for RGM Sound". RGM Sound was Meek's independent production company, named from his initials Robert George Meek, but the credit seems to have been purely contractual, as was

113

perhaps their relationship, from this point forward. Robert was now an independent producer like Joe Meek, but he was neither an engineer like Meek nor a musician. He simply had an ear for what the public would like.

The next RSA artist to hit the charts was Michael Scheur, a German who was instrumental in providing phonetic transcriptions to enable British pop singers like Adam Faith and Johnny Leyton to sing in German. Renaming him Mike Sarne, Robert teamed him up with his secretary, 15-year-old Wendy Richards who, like Mike Berry, would go on to have an extremely successful career in *Are You Being Served*.

The money enabled Stigwood to move his operations to plush new offices in Edgware Road, from where he embarked on an aggressive expansion campaign. A talented girl singer with a distinctive voice, 16-year-old Carol Hedges, was his initial target, but first he had to steal her away from Meek.

Hedges had won a talent contest early in 1962 and had been referred to Joe Meek by Cliff Bennett whose Rebel Rousers had been the backing band for all the contestants. Meek worked with Carol on and off over the next 6 months, but Joe appeared more interested in testing her voice with different effects than actually recording her, a prime example being his apparent infatuation with "fiddling around with microphones in the bathroom", as she described it.

Eventually Meek did get round to recording a couple of songs where Carol was backed by The Tornados but, by this time, she had already come to the attention of Robert Stigwood, a frequent visitor to Meek's studio at 304 Holloway Road. Never one to pass up an opportunity, Robert offered to sign her up. The volatile Meek was less than impressed. "There were huge arguments going on in the back room," Carol confirmed. "Although I hadn't signed a contract with Joe, Stiggy poached me, if you want to put it that way."

Perhaps it was this argument that was the cause of the cold war between Joe and Robert. Whatever, Stigwood's determination prevailed and Carol became the newest addition to his growing roster. As the pair got to know each other better, Robert learned that two of her musical inspirations were Billie Holiday and Sammy Davis. Thus, his latest creation, Billie Davis was born. At this stage though, Billie was still lacking the polish that Stigwood felt was necessary to allow her to become the star that her potential deserved. He arranged for her to attend two elocution classes with a drama teacher each week and encouraged her to enrol in a fashion school in Leicester Square where, to her considerable embarrassment, she had to put on bright pink indelible lipstick. Robert did nothing to lessen her self-consciousness, teasing her with remarks like, "Have you been eating jam again?"

One day in the winter of 1962, Robert returned from America clutching a copy of the latest hit by The Exciters. In January 1963, Decca released her début single, 'Tell Him', which gained her a top 10 hit. Not bad, but actually quite remarkable when taking into account that it was promoted in direct competition to The Exciters' original, which became a UK number one at the same time.

Either side of this, Mike Sarne had two more visits to the Top 30 and then Billie's follow-up achieved the Top 40 in May. By August, when John Leyton's latest release reached number 36, Robert Stigwood's four discoveries had provided him with 17 Top 40 entries in just two years; an incredible tally for a novice to the recording industry.

In September 1963, the Glasgow *Daily Record* attempted to discover the secret of his amazing success. "The business calls them kids because mostly teenagers buy and dictate the record market," he explained to reporter Donald Bruce. "But don't kid yourself about the kids. They are the most discerning of all buyers. The kids are no fools. They buy a sound and, unless the sound is individual and live, you are wasting your time flogging it to anyone . . . Hits, anyway, are a lottery. No one really knows what the public wants. You can guess a trend, but at the end of the day the kids can make a mug of you. They know. You don't. That's what makes this business so exciting."

One of the least known of the RSA recordings is of interest even though it was not released. In late 1963, US rocker Gene Vincent went to Joe Meek's studio to record two versions of a song called 'Temptation Baby'. One was for inclusion on an album, the other to be used in a movie, which went by the name of *Live It Up* in the UK and *Sing And Swing* in the States. But Stigwood paid Vincent to record a third version which was taped at Olympic Studios on November 14 with backing provided by The Bill Shepherd Orchestra. Bill Shepherd had first come to prominence in 1959 on the soundtrack of a film titled *Idle On Parade* and also with his own orchestral album *Shepherd And His Flock*. In 1964 or early 1965, Shepherd left for Australia where he went to work for Festival Records and, of course, produced The Bee Gees.

In 1962, record production and RSA Publishing were just two aspects of Robert Stigwood's rapidly expanding empire. He had been very active on other fronts too, as Stephen Komlosy confirms. "By then we really had the embryo Robert Stigwood Organisation – everything under one roof."

★ ★ ★

Robert Stigwood Associates lasted till the end of 1964. The company was short of cash because they kept using the profits to finance the next step in its rapid growth. The commercials operation took a fatal loss when the film technicians' union ACTT took job actions to stop the use of videotaped commercials. Meanwhile the recordings side was not doing well either because the company misjudged the popular interest in the beat groups that had followed The Beatles in a procession from Liverpool to London, a phenomenon noticed even thousands of miles away by three Gibb brothers.

Stephen Komlosy recalled that, "Suddenly, we weren't successful any more. It took us a while to understand what had happened in the music business – that it had really changed. The single hip-swivelling artist was no longer what was wanted. It was all groups – and they really flooded in. Our cash flow from that area had gone because we were a year behind."

Robert had fancied himself as a concert promoter and had invested heavily in that area. A Rolling Stones tour did well, a Chuck Berry one didn't, but the unreliability of trouser-splitting P.J. Proby on an expensive one caused a loss on tour promotions as well.

The company had been used to dealing in hundreds of thousands of pounds. With the benefit of hindsight, the manner of its demise appears to have been completely avoidable. "When you think what our turnover and our profits had been," Komlosy protested, "to go under for a measly £50,000 was unbelievable."

The winding-up of a company's affairs is a strange business. While the appointed liquidator would spend 10 years unravelling the mess, within days, Stigwood and Komlosy were back in business, working from the offices of Starlite Artists, owned by Tremeloes manager Peter Walsh, who wanted them to develop and promote his younger talent. This was a somewhat ironic set of circumstances when Stigwood's later association with NEMS is considered. In January 1962, Brian Poole and The Tremeloes were one of two groups who had auditioned for Decca. They were chosen over The Beatles, much to the disappointment of their new manager, Brian Epstein.

The pair promptly discovered The Graham Bond Organisation – according to Robert, the first group to use a mellotron on record – and with them, bass player Jack Bruce and drummer Peter "Ginger" Baker.

It looked as if they were back on track until, one Friday morning, Robert failed to appear. The previous night he had collected £400 in commission from Graham Bond, which was needed by the Friday afternoon to pay staff wages. Stigwood eventually turned up at two in the afternoon and said he was terribly sorry, but that he had lost the money at The Twenty-One Room, a gambling establishment.

It was the final straw for Komlosy. "I left," he said simply.

It would be easy for him to harbour a grudge against his former colleague and friend, but the opposite is nearer the truth. "He has an uncanny political judgement, this ability to judge very quickly how people will react in any given situation. It is a vital ability. He's a genius, and he is immensely charming and funny and nice. And I like him, immensely."

But Stephen's obvious affection does not allow his judgement to be clouded into failing to recognise Robert's modus operandi. "He is a Svengali. He dominates you. He dominates your mind. He imposes his will. He is like a father, and the children are all jealous of the father's attention. That's how RSO works – they all respect and admire him."

★ ★ ★

Another who respected and admired Robert Stigwood, for all his recent failings, was David Shaw, one of London's brightest moneymen.

When RSA folded, Shaw saw an opportunity and Stigwood became a frequent topic of discussion between Shaw and his friend Andrew Gordon. Between them, they decided that Robert might be worth backing, and wrote him cheques for £25,000. Stigwood took offices in Walden Court just off Oxford Street and The Robert Stigwood Organisation was up and running (again?). The remainder of 1965 was discouraging but Shaw still had faith in Stigwood's ability to turn things around and, early in 1966, David put in another £15,000.

Slowly, things began to happen. Learning from his previous mistake, Robert launched his own record label, Reaction Records, with distribution by the German company Polydor, which may have been backing him as early as this date. Reaction's emphasis was firmly on groups with The Who as one of its first acts. Co-managed by his friend Kit Lambert, The Who were signed to a production deal with the US producer Shel Talmy, but the deal was heavily weighted in Talmy's favour. Lambert – and The Who – wanted out but Talmy refused to budge, so in early 1966 Lambert simply breached the contract and took The Who's next single, 'Substitute', to Stigwood who released it on Reaction. For The Who, the move was financially catastrophic, triggering a lawsuit from Talmy, who in return for bowing out obtained a 5 per cent royalty on the group's recordings for the next five years. Although North American rights reverted to Decca after the one single on Atco, in Britain The Who were now on Reaction Records. For Stigwood, his label was up and running.

An attempt to do something similar with The Small Faces met with an entirely different kind of "reaction". The group's fearsome manager Don Arden was not the kind of man who took kindly to poaching, nor was he interested in courtroom battles. By his own account Arden assembled a team of "persuaders" to accompany him to Stigwood's office. "We arranged that first thing we would do . . . was ask the girl to move away from the switchboard because nobody must be able to make phone calls. We formed this triangle. I was at the point of the triangle, and I said, 'Each step I take, you follow. I'll do the talking and I'm gonna say if it ever happens again, we're gonna throw him through the window.' And you must say, 'Fuck him, let's give it to him now!' "

But even Arden had underestimated his henchmen's enthusiasm for their work. "They decided amongst themselves for laughs to go one further, and let me think that they were gonna throw him over, and I must admit at one time I thought, 'Fucking hell, these guys have gone nutty or something!' " Poor Stigwood must genuinely have heard his maker's voice calling him whilst being dangled out of his office window.

Eventually, the police were called, but by this time Robert had been convinced to see Arden's point of view. As Arden himself has since confirmed, Stigwood informed the police, "Mr Arden did come here, but he was a perfect gentleman."

Robert's next move was his most propitious thus far. In response to the trend for more musically sophisticated groups, he created Cream, the world's first supergroup. The combined talents of Jack Bruce, by then with Manfred Mann, Ginger Baker, and former Yardbirds lead guitarist Eric Clapton, who had just quit John Mayall's Bluesbreakers, would prove immensely successful, even if their personalities were at loggerheads.

Stigwood also had Crispian St Peters, Oscar, and Screaming Lord Sutch on his books too. Sutch had also been a Meek act before succumbing to Robert's charms.

In the later part of 1966, Robert became involved in a remarkable business deal with Brian Epstein, who as The Beatles' manager was unquestionably the most successful impresario of the beat boom. Epstein's company NEMS Enterprises – named after the Epstein family's North End Music Stores in Liverpool – also looked after the affairs of many other acts, and he had branched out into promotion and even theatre management with the Saville in London's Shaftesbury Avenue. Thanks to the success of The Beatles, Epstein had the world at his fingertips . . . but he didn't want it. The Beatles were giving up touring after August 1966, greatly diminishing his role with them, and while he took a personal interest in two other artists, Cilla Black and Gerry Marsden, he was far less interested in running a company. The sheer scale of his business had outgrown him and he dreamt of an early retirement, browsing around picture galleries and passing his time with bullfighters in Spain.

Brian, Robert, and David Shaw arranged to go off to Paris for what Shaw openly described as "a dirty weekend". The pair put it to Brian that RSO could provide NEMS with representation in Europe, but Brian surprised them with a much bigger offer – he wanted out! Clearly concerned for his friend's well-being, Stigwood said, "He was responding to pressures the wrong way. He was taking uppers to keep himself going, to sustain himself through all the travel and pressures, and he was taking sleeping pills to counterbalance that at night. It had become a vicious circle."

On their return from Paris, Shaw and his high-powered finance friends in the City put NEMS under the microscope. It didn't make for pleasant examination, what with the plethora of unresolved lawsuits stemming from Epstein's naïve mishandling of Beatles merchandising, including the American Seltaeb suit, by then in its third year.

No bank would fund the purchase of NEMS so a compromise deal was negotiated. Conversely, NEMS would buy RSO but Stigwood and Shaw would be given a legal option to buy 51 per cent of NEMS a year later if they could help to clean the company up. Epstein willingly agreed and on September 30, 1966, papers were signed, though kept a secret for a time.

It is doubtful whether two music industry entrepreneurs had ever been handed a greater incentive. Work your butts off for 12 months and then own the company that managed The Beatles. All seemed well again, but there was one little problem on the horizon. "The trouble was," Robert confided, "that [Brian] hadn't told The Beatles. He said that he wanted to do that at the right time."

Shaw now had a year to line up the necessary financial package but bankers remained nervous about the prospect. Polydor and their parent company, Philips/Siemens, however, were very interested in the idea of gaining management control of The Beatles for a bargain price, and promised the duo £500,000 when their option fell due. Now that RSO had the financial clout to back up their little agreement, Epstein publicly announced a merger of the two companies on January 13, 1967. Sadly, fate would intervene before the original 12 month period had elapsed.

★ ★ ★

On August 26, 1967, Brian Epstein's personal assistant, Joanne Newfield, received an urgent phone call from his concerned household staff at his Belgravia home. Joanne drove at once to Chapel Street, phoned a doctor and, when repeated pounding on Brian's locked bedroom door failed to get a response, the doctor and Epstein's Spanish manservant Antonio broke down the door. Joanne went into the room to find Brian's lifeless body lying on the bed. "Even though I knew he was dead, I pretended to the others that he wasn't, 'It's all right,' I said, 'he's just asleep, he's fine.' "

While it was widely supposed that Brian had committed suicide, the Coroner, Mr Gavin Thurston, ruled that it was an accidental death caused by "incautious self-overdoses" of Carbitol, a bromide-based drug which he used to help him sleep.

With Brian Epstein's death, the future of NEMS seemed uncertain. As he had left no will, his entire estate passed to his mother, Mrs. Queenie Epstein. Having lost both her elder son and her husband in a matter of months, Mrs. Epstein was in no state to deal with the business, so the responsibility fell to Brian's younger brother, Clive.

After two weeks of discussions between the interested parties, it was finally agreed that Clive would take over as Chairman of NEMS Enterprises. A new company, Nemperor Holdings, was formed to administer NEMS, with former bandleader Vic Lewis as its Managing Director, whilst Peter Brown took over from Epstein as The Beatles personal manager. In reality, of course, they managed themselves from this point on.

In a statement released to the press, a NEMS company spokesman said, "Policies agreed between Brian Epstein and Robert Stigwood are now not practically possible. In the circumstances it has been agreed on the most amicable basis that NEMS and the Robert Stigwood Organisation will go their separate ways. Towards the end of November Messrs Stigwood and David Shaw will resign from the board of NEMS."

They were rumoured to have left NEMS with a settlement of £500,000. "Having left NEMS, he was determined that he was going to have a Beatles of his own, and The Bee Gees were it," Dick Ashby said. "In those days, Robert gave his total attention to their career. He was a manager in the finest sense of the word. He did everything: he was in the studio with them, travelling with them . . . The Bee Gees and Cream, those were his two loves, as it were."

Philips/Siemens still saw Stigwood as a worthwhile investment and, in February 1968, they handed over their original £500,000 stating, "We are interested in all forms of show business and are backing Mr Stigwood because we feel he has the necessary ability to deliver us business we never got before." Robert would put their money, and that received from NEMS, to very good use.

★   ★   ★

Over and above the success he has enjoyed with the acts he managed, which included comedians Spike Milligan and Frankie Howerd, Robert Stigwood boasted other achievements that, even if viewed in isolation, would make him the envy of his peers.

Firstly, in 1968, there was his first West End production *Hair*, a play which opened at the Shaftesbury Theatre, then ran for six years. He bought out Beryl Vertue and Associated London Scripts, and then the Gunnell Brothers agency, both of these take-overs bringing him writers and performers of the calibre of Ray Galton and Alan Simpson, Johnny Speight, Georgie Fame, Alan Price and John Mayall. There were also film versions of *Steptoe And Son* and *Up Pompeii*.

Then 1970 brought the shocking *Oh! Calcutta!* This was soon followed by the equally notorious *Jesus Christ, Superstar* which started life as an album, hit Broadway in 1971, and finally opened in 1972 at London's Palace Theatre where it ran for eight years. The big screen version followed in 1973. A year later Stigwood produced the movie version of The Who's *Tommy*, a film that nobody else would touch. Directed by the controversial Ken Russell, it would premiere on March 26, 1975 and star Oliver Reed, Ann-Margret and, in the title role, Who singer Roger Daltrey.

Other equally well-publicised successes would follow, and Robert enjoyed a lavish lifestyle, unthinkable just a decade before.

He shows no signs of slowing down yet either. In February, 2000, his *Saturday Night Fever* musical completed a successful run at The London Palladium. It only took 10 months for the production to recoup its estimated four million pounds costs, a figure in excess of 25 million pounds being anticipated when final accounts are drawn. A touring version of *La Cage Aux Folles* is being planned, together with another musical based on the work of the celebrated horror writer Anne Rice, best known for *Interview With A Vampire* which became a Tom Cruise film. His assets include real estate business in Australia, and a Louisiana oil and gas exploration company.

Stigwood's achievements are well known, but less so the man himself. Once he had their confidence, he seldom imposed his management on The Bee Gees, preferring to think of them in more sociable terms. "[They] are friends. I'm godfather to their children. We [didn't] have formal business

120

meetings. We [would] sit around socially and debate what they should and shouldn't do. We worked on a committee basis, really."

Freddie Gershon, former worldwide President of RSO, once described him as "father, confessor, hand-holder, baby-sitter, and he has the bedside manner of the greatest medical practitioner in Middle America. He looks after his flock, his boys."

Julie Barrett saw Robert frequently when she worked for him in 1967 and says, "I found him quite a fair man. One of the girls who actually helped me at the time became pregnant, and being a single mum at that stage was just not on. He was very good and arranged for her to go into a 'mother and baby' home and he paid for all her expenses. I think he was quite caring, and though he'd come such a long way in his business dealings, he was quite down to earth in his attitude towards people."

"Down to earth" would certainly fit one tale his great friend Ahmet Ertegun likes to tell of him, and it reveals a side of Robert that all but his closest acquaintances never see. "Robert can be very cutting you know, just awful. There was a manager and concert promoter, Sid Bernstein, best known for The Beatles' Shea Stadium shows in New York, who was manager of an Atlantic act, The Rascals, and he told me that he wanted to meet Robert. So I arrange that we go out to dinner, and Sid starts saying to Robert, 'My boys love your boys – those Bee Gees sing like angels and so many songs, and Cream, the way Eric Clapton plays', and on and on and on repeating, 'my boys love your boys'. Then nature calls and he goes off to the toilets and Robert says to me, 'I'm going to tell him that my boys hate his boys,' and I said, 'No, you'll kill him.' Robert says, 'I'm going to tell him that my boys think his boys are a bunch of fucking Italian shoeshine boys!' I begged him not to say that, and he didn't, but he wouldn't compliment Sid's boys either."

Perhaps it is fitting that the last words should come from two of Robert's boys themselves.

"Believe it or not," Barry began, "even though he probably doesn't even realise it, [Robert] is still a great influence on our careers. Whatever the moves we make or whatever we do with our careers we always think to ourselves, how would Robert have handled this, how would he have had us do this? Would he have let us do this? It really has an effect on our decision-making."

"He was one of the old school of managers," Robin continued, "that worked on gut reaction. You know, he had an instinct or something. And he went on feelings, and a lot of people today don't go on feelings, they go on technical data and numbers, where in those days you see, a lot of people went on gut reaction. That was the old school of thinking and it was always, to us, [that] the best way to go with anything is the feeling that you get in your gut. There's a lot less of that [now] and I think that business is richer for them, those kind of people."

It was left for Barry to sum things up nicely. "Robert is irreplaceable," he confirmed. "There is no question about that."

9

BEE GEES 4TH?

"THERE WERE A whole bunch of highlights that all happened in that six-month period in 1967," Barry Gibb told Marc Baker in 1997. "Meeting The Beatles, being signed to NEMS, Brian Epstein's label, thus being in The Beatles stable – that's what everyone called it. It was incredibly inspiring to be among these people and to be suddenly in the game, in the competition.

"But without a shadow of a doubt, the highlight was meeting Robert Stigwood. I think that apart from our father and mother, he is the man who made things happen for us – who opened doors for us. He is the man who gave us the opportunities – who made us believe in ourselves, much more so than even we had done, who changed our lives.

"What glowed was the belief; whoever this man was he believed in us and that elevated us. It made us go to work, it made us think on a much higher level than we had before."

Robin echoed Barry's sentiments when he said, "The whole industry is about flag flyers, champions who champion your cause and one voice that can actually move mountains for people. Robert Stigwood was a blessing, he was the man."

One of Stigwood's early priorities was to smarten up his new protégés. "He gave us £300 and said, 'Go and find some clothes because the clothes you are wearing are completely unacceptable,'" Barry recalled. "So he sent us to Carnaby Street, and we came back with clothes that were completely unacceptable because we didn't know – we couldn't have been greener."

In the early days of his stewardship Robert Stigwood introduced them to Richard Clayton Ashby, better known as Dick, whom the brothers would often refer to as "the fourth Bee Gee". Dick Ashby would become their right-hand man, their tour manager and general liaison between them and Stigwood. He began his career in the music business as road manager to The Birds★, a rock group whose most celebrated member was Ronnie Wood, who later found fame with The Faces and The Rolling Stones.

Robert Stigwood became involved with The Birds as their agent and also

---

★ Not to be confused with the better known California-based group, The Byrds, who had hits with 'Eight Miles High', 'Turn! Turn! Turn!', 'Mr. Tambourine Man', etc.

cut a couple of tracks for them on his Reaction label. When the group eventually disbanded, Dick found himself in something of a quandary.

"I had got involved a little bit financially with the group, in as much as I'd lent them some money for equipment," Dick recalled, "and obviously when the group folded there wasn't any money to share around so I came to see Robert, cap in hand, with a van load of equipment trying to get some of my money back. He'd signed The Bee Gees virtually the week before, and that evening they were in Polydor putting down some demos. He took me round there and that was it. I became their road manager from 1967 . . . So as soon as they came back to England I virtually started work for them straightaway. They lived in Hendon for a while.

"I got to know them on a very personal level, whereas if you're just in an office and the group is signed up by the head of the company and they say, 'Here's The Bee Gees, here's Dick Ashby, he's going to be looking after you,' it would take the amount of time I spent on the road with them to really get to know them, how they work and be able to keep the wheels turning in the best possible way."

With Dick looking after the day-to-day affairs of the fledgling group, Robert Stigwood and Brian Epstein travelled to America to choose an American label and negotiate terms for The Bee Gees.

Ahmet Ertegun, the president of Atlantic Records, recalled, "It was just prior to this trip that I first heard some of the tracks that Stigwood had produced with the group, and needless to say, I was extremely impressed. When they arrived in America, there was a bit of a tug of war between Epstein and Stigwood. Since Epstein had had several acts with Capital and Columbia, he was inclined to go with one of those labels as he knew the people who were working there; and Stigwood was leaning in favour of Atlantic as we were working hard at that time to break another new group that Robert had put together, called Cream.

"Luckily for us, Robert's will prevailed and we had the pleasure and honour of releasing the first of what was to be many hits by a group whose singing style and whose songs were of an originality and brilliance rarely heard on record. Our enthusiasm for the group, which must have made Stigwood and Epstein go along with us, was matched by that of our record buyers throughout the world."

Atlantic Records' legendary engineer/producer Tom Dowd was already on the trail of The Bee Gees. In March 1967, he accompanied a Stax recording artists tour across the Continent and on to London. "At that time Atlantic's contact at Polydor in London was a guy called Frank Finter, and he was anxious to meet all the guys . . . Otis, Sam & Dave, Booker T. and so on . . . He played me a tape [of The Bee Gees] and said, 'You gotta hear these guys – they are gonna be big!'

"He played me a few songs and I said, 'Listen, I want them, but I don't have the authority to sign anybody.' He said there were other people interested, but he would try to hold off.

"I immediately tried calling Jerry Wexler and couldn't get a hold of him," Tom continued, "and I tried calling Ahmet and nobody knew where he was, and I'm telling Frank Finter, 'Hold them, hold them,' 'cause I had zero authority. Meanwhile I finally get hold of Jerry and say, 'I've heard this great band – we have to sign them,' and he says, 'Don't talk to me about groups – I've got a great group that I'm gonna sign,' and then I get hold of Ahmet and he says, 'Don't talk to me, don't talk to me, I'm going to sign a group that's going to be the biggest thing.'

"What had happened was that earlier I did *Disraeli Gears* with Cream, and Robert became a big fan of Atlantic so he had gone to Ahmet with the deal. So we're all on the trail of the same group and didn't know it! I didn't meet the guys until about six months later, but I heard that tape and I knew they were going to be big."

In spite of all the confusion, The Bee Gees were eventually signed to Atlantic Records for a staggering £80,000, the biggest deal ever made with a new group at that time.

★ ★ ★

Carlos Olms, born in Germany in 1930, joined Deutsche Grammophon DGG in 1952 from an electro-acoustic engineering company called Telefunken. He started in the electro-acoustic laboratory before being trained in the art of recording itself. He went on to learn how to record classical music and was then sent to Hamburg to learn about the pop recording side of the business. Here he worked with Germany's top producers and artists like Bert Kaempfert.

In the early Sixties, he was sent to Venezuela to work in a recording studio for Polydor. When he returned to Germany, he was offered a job by Roland Rennie in London and he arrived there in January 1967. His remit was to create, and then run, a recording studio in an office floor at 19 Stratford Place – in the midst of the producers offices. It was very much built "on the cheap", the recording electronics consisting of obsolete valve equipment shipped over to England by Polydor's parent, DGG.

In late February, after the studio's completion, Carlos was called up to Roland's office and introduced to a new act that had recently signed to Polydor. By early March, he was working with them.

"They came in one evening," he recalls, "and we started recording a backing track at about seven o'clock. But the whole concept was in the early stages. They had not even the words together for the song. But in the quietness of our old staircase – there was no one else in the building – in this atmosphere with the old goods lift and the folding zig-zag doors, sitting on the cold stone steps, there they composed and found the right words to the new song, which they called 'The New York Mining Disaster 1941'.

"When they started to put the vocals on the backing track, it sounded absolutely great. No matter that it was four o'clock in the morning.

Everybody had the feeling, this would be a hit. Roland Rennie loved it at first hearing in the morning, but if ever something is great, others come along with ideas to improve it, and so the original demo was re-recorded at IBC with strings and other sounds added. Still it was a great song."

One thing that astonished Carlos was the amount of technical recording knowledge the boys possessed. Firstly with Robert Iredale, and then with Ossie Byrne, the Gibbs had obviously been paying attention.

As Carlos himself admits, he learned one thing in the session: "How to place the vocals into the backing track, to get the balance right in mono and stereo. You just listen in mono on one speaker! Everything falls into place."

Although he never worked with The Bee Gees again, Carlos did bump into the brothers on several occasions, and remembers these moments with great fondness. His connection with the group did not end there however, as he also worked with Lulu and Yvonne Elliman in years to come.

Prior to 1967, The Bee Gees had always been just the three brothers with two guitars, but beginning in late February, in preparation for live dates, the group was expanded to include some old friends from Australia.

Colin Petersen was born March 24, 1946 in Kingaroy, Queensland. A child actor in his native Australia, Colin entered show business at the age of seven and made his film début in the title role in the film *Smiley* in 1956. The circumstances that propelled him to stardom must rank amongst the most unusual of anyone in the entertainment business.

"Thousands of guys were being tested for the part, and I went along to a theatre in Brisbane and lined up with the rest in my best suit, with a collar and tie and shoes and socks, clutching my scrapbooks. All the film people walked straight past me! Never gave me a second look. I went home and played with my cousin. I took my shoes off and got dirty, the way kids do.

"But I was very curious to see who had got the part," Colin continued, "so eventually I went back to the theatre. I was just going past a side door when the director came out for a cigarette and a breath of fresh air. I asked him what was going on, and he took me inside the theatre and offered me the part."

The film made a star of the engaging little lad with fair hair and brown eyes, whose earnest delivery and wide-eyed innocence made him a scene stealer even from a veteran like Ralph Richardson. A year later he co-starred with Richard Attenborough in *The Scamp* and in 1958 with Max Bygraves in *A Cry From The Streets*. The latter film also starred another child star in the making called Dana Wilson, who became a good friend of Colin's, and who went on to star in another big film of the day, *The Shiralee*, with Peter Finch.

With three films in as many years, Colin's busy schedule meant that his education was often disrupted, and by 1959, his mother decided that it was time to concentrate on school instead of acting. He had been tipped to play the lead in the film *Tiger Bay*, but the part was rewritten for a girl, giving Hayley Mills her first role. The loss of the part still rankled in 1967, when

Colin listed it as the biggest disappointment of his career in a *New Musical Express* questionnaire.

Although Colin, like the Gibb brothers, attended Humpybong State School, they didn't remember each other in their schooldays. Colin studied piano for two years and trained as a jazz drummer for three, before joining Steve & The Board as their drummer in the early Sixties. From then on, The Bee Gees' paths often crossed with his, and he played drums on some of their sessions.

In 1966 Colin decided that Britain offered more scope for advancing his career. "When I decided to come to Britain, I stopped off in Sydney to see the Gibbs," he recalled. "Barry asked me to be their drummer when they came over. I arrived and was interested in films."

When the Gibb brothers contacted him, he was sharing a flat in London with Bill Shepherd. True to Barry's word, Colin was hired as their drummer, even being used at their famous audition for Robert Stigwood, and Bill, who had first worked with The Bee Gees in 1965, was brought in as their musical director and arranger.

The band's number was increased to five the following month with the addition of a new member, lead guitarist Vince Melouney.

Vincent Melouney was born on August 18, 1945 in Sydney, Australia. In the late Fifties, a chance visit from a door-to-door guitar salesman sparked his interest, and after a few lessons, he decided to teach himself from then on. Vince began playing at school dances when he was 14 years old, forming his own group. He moved from band to band in Australia, playing with The Vibrators, Vince & Tony's Two, The Vince Melouney Sect, Billy Thorpe & The Aztecs and latterly The Blue Jays. Most notable of these were Billy Thorpe & The Aztecs, who were one of the top groups in Australia, with the hit singles 'Poison Ivy', 'Mashed Potato', 'Sick 'n' Tired' and 'Over The Rainbow'. Vince also worked as a session musician and had worked with the Gibbs on occasion.

"I was like a thousand other Aussies," he said. "I felt that the streets of Tin Pan Alley in London were paved with gold." He worked hard to earn the money to emigrate to Britain, hoping for his big break.

But stardom hadn't come his way. He was sharing accommodation with The Easybeats and working in a nine-to-five job at Simca Motors in London which was breaking his heart. A casual conversation with one of his flatmates would bring about a dramatic change in his fortunes. "He said that The Bee Gees had arrived, so I got their number and rang them up. I spoke to Maurice and he said to come down as they were recording that day.

"I didn't even have a guitar at the time having hocked it to pay my fare over there. So I borrowed Harry Vanda's of The Easybeats and went to the studio and started playing. The first track we recorded which I was on was 'New York Mining Disaster 1941'. Me using Harry's guitar!" Melouney exclaimed, thrilled to have played Vanda's Gibson.

Originally hired for just the one session, Vince was invited back for more.

It didn't take long for the brothers to appreciate the value of securing his unquestionable talent on a full-time basis, and he jumped at the opportunity to go back to his first love, music. The band had exactly one afternoon to rehearse before their first London show, at The Cromwellian on Cromwell Road in South Kensington. It was an unpaid gig before an audience comprising mainly of music industry executives. An interested spectator was Atlantic Records chief, Ahmet Ertegun. "We killed 'em!" recalled Colin Petersen.

With the group now numbering five, and accompanied by Dick Ashby, they set out for their first British concert at the Palace Theatre back in their old hometown of Manchester, opening for Gerry & The Pacemakers and Fats Domino.

A few days later, April 1, 1967 saw The Bee Gees playing the first of six nights at London's Saville Theatre, once again opening for Gerry & The Pacemakers and Fats Domino. The group were something less than a resounding success with the rock'n'roll audience.

"All they wanted was Fats Domino," Barry said. "They were all Teddy Boys★ and hated us. Robin got an egg thrown at him that hit him right in the chest." In the best show business tradition, Dick Ashby remembers that Robin manfully "carried on with this thing dripping down him."

It would be another nine months before they would exorcise the ghosts of that concert when they returned to the Saville Theatre in triumph.

With Ossie Byrne in Australia, The Bee Gees had begun to experiment with their music. One of the group's biggest frustrations in those days was the lack of time and money that their record company was willing to invest in their recordings, so for them, it was another dream come true when Robert Stigwood gave them free rein in the Polydor studios which they would often use when nobody else was about.

"We found out what we really wanted to hear was strings," Barry said, "and we couldn't really get that in Australia. So when we got to England we knew we wanted to hear our music with an orchestra behind it. When we got a manager situation going with Robert Stigwood he asked us what we wanted to do with our music and we asked him for an orchestra. We always loved orchestras and, being in Australia, we were pretty starved of that. Tommy Tycho★★ was about the limit of where you could go and we couldn't have afforded him anyway. So I think it was the starvation over those years that had us use orchestras with such enthusiasm when we finally had a manager and record company prepared to pay for them."

More than 30 years later, Barry reflected, "We knew for quite a while

★ Teddy Boys was the name given to British rock'n'roll fans who were easily recognised by their uniform of drainpipe trousers, a long drape jacket, winkle-picker shoes, black shirt and bootlace tie.
★★ A well-known Sydney bandleader of whom it was said, "If the Queen were to visit, and they were having a gala performance, it would be Tommy who would conduct the band."

before we could do anything about it, that there was only one way for us and that was out. The only way was to go to one of the hubs, like London or Los Angeles, and try your luck there. We believed we were as good as any international group and, if you're going to believe something like that, you have to do something about it. We thought we could make better records than we were hearing, and that wasn't necessarily true at first, but we did do *Bee Gees 1st* which I would always regard as our most inventive album – within our first year in England . . . and we did make a world-class album, so I think our point was proven."

The group's first British album was recorded in a fairly short time, between March 7 and April 21. A first album often amounts to the best of the artist's work to date, as demonstrated by their first Australian album, and The Bee Gees could have been forgiven for starting their international career off with a bang by reworking some of the many dozens of songs they'd done in Australia, especially the demos from 1966 that had not even been released there. But they did not do so. Instead, with the exception of 'I Can't See Nobody' which dated back to a ballroom in Brisbane, they used exclusively new songs from just the past few months, which made this supposedly first album all the more impressive. "We can write a song about almost anything, to order," claimed an enthusiastic Barry. "We write all the time. I suppose we finish about four or five songs a week on average but a lot of the material we write is thrown away."

Their first official sessions included the original demo of 'New York Mining Disaster 1941' and other rehearsals at Polydor's studios, although the final recording proper is credited solely to IBC Studios, which Robert Stigwood had used for clients as far back as 1962. IBC (owned by the television company, Independent Broadcasting Corporation) had four-track recording equipment by the time The Bee Gees came to it and was regarded as a first-class facility. It was very much on a par with EMI's Abbey Road, as The Beatles were still using four-track then too. It would be another year at least, before both studios could offer their clients eight-track facilities.

Robert Stigwood spared no expense to announce the release of the first new Bee Gees single. "The most significant new musical talent of 1967" proclaimed the full page advertisement for 'New York Mining Disaster 1941'.

It was both an unlikely title and subject for a pop single – two miners trapped, hoping to be saved, yet fearing that the rescuers may have given up on them – but the pop-folk ballad served to display their harmony singing against a simple arrangement of guitars. The song is immediately accessible, yet certain details remain elusive, and this combination makes for a good choice as a single. As far as any song can serve as an example of the group's style, their UK début conveyed exactly what they were about – the harmony singing, the solid melody, the quirky lyrics. It also highlighted a shift in their attitude towards their writing.

"The old concept of writing about love and romance as the basis of every pop song has changed," Barry told a music press naturally curious about the new kids on the block. "We still do write romance songs, but most of our writing is about contemporary things, situations, people. The Beatles have started to write about subjects not connected with love. We do too. 'New York Mining Disaster' is about some people trapped in a mine."

Robin Gibb recalled the events of that long night spent recording with Carlos. "It was written at Polydor Records on a staircase . . . It was in the dark and it was echoey and we had this strange inspiration to write this song about a mining disaster that occurred in New York in the year 1941. I suppose, you know, because it was the atmosphere . . . It was right in the middle of the offices of Polydor at the very time. But the lights were out anyway. There was in fact a mining disaster in New York but it wasn't in 1941 . . ." Actually, unbeknownst to Robin, there *was* a mining disaster in 1941 which took place in McIntire, Pennsylvania, in which six people were killed.

"We couldn't see each other," Barry added. "We made it up, we were just sitting in the dark and that was where the idea sprang from. So, what would it be like trapped in say a mine, for instance, and you can't see each other. Can we write something about that? Well, we were very tragic orien-tated, and in those days we wrote a lot of tragic songs . . . It was written about the time of the Aberfan mining disaster★ so it's a little bit gory but it still works today. People still love to hear it and people still ask us to play it."

This differed from their normal writing style which Maurice was happy to detail. "We arrive at the studio and begin. No sitting round a table and talking. It comes *there* or not at all. I usually use a piano to help with the 'sound' of the whole number. I don't have anything to do with the lyrics; pure music is my line."

The single's extra-lyrical title, while adding an interesting touch, caused minor sales problems since people who'd heard and liked the song might have found it hard to identify in the shops. The Atco release in the United States was rather long-windedly labelled 'New York Mining Disaster 1941 (Have You Seen My Wife, Mr Jones?)' in an attempt to overcome this, but Robin explained, "At the same token . . . as it was our first single [outside Australia], we wanted something to draw attention as well. So a title like that was not to be dismissed, you know. I mean, Matt Monro could not have recorded this song!"

Maybe Matt Monro couldn't have recorded it, but what about The Beatles? The group were dogged for some time by the idea that they were imitating the Fab Four, for which some responsibility may lie with the

★ On October 21, 1966 a waste tip slid down the mountainside into the village of Aberfan in South Wales. It first destroyed a farm cottage, killing all its occupants, and continued on to engulf the Pantglas Junior School and about 20 houses in the village before coming to a halt. Almost half of the children at the school and five of their teachers were killed. In all, the death toll was 144; 116 of them were children.

action reportedly taken by Atlantic Records in the United States. Legend has it that white label copies of the disc were circulated amongst radio stations without any clues as to the identity of the group, although none have ever been discovered, thus raising doubts as to their existence in the first place. However, Ahmet Ertegun himself kept the story alive by suggesting, "You know what . . . I wouldn't put it past our promotion department. They might have done that, with just a few radio stations, like that, to create a 'wonder who they are' [scenario]. The reason to do that would be to get airplay. The reason you've never seen one would be they are probably in some radio station, and eventually they would discard them." Curiously though, as if to raise further doubts, at this point Ahmet began singing, "I started a joke . . ."

Adding credibility to the tale, Atlantic's Jerry Wexler confirmed that the action was one of his trademarks. "I resorted to the old tricks," he wrote, "sending out white label acetates to deejays and programme directors, hyping the market with advance copies of singles."

"['New York Mining Disaster 1941'] was a total rip-off of The Beatles," conceded Maurice. "We were so influenced by them. In fact it started a mystery [in the USA] about us, because they started playing [it] and saying, 'They're this new group from England that begins with a B and finishes with an S' so they all said, 'Ah, it's The Beatles, not naming it, they're doing that trick again.' The disc jockey would play it and play it and play it and, 'Guess who it is?' and people would guess, and they wouldn't get the answer. I heard [the idea] came actually from Ahmet Ertegun . . . and Jerry Wexler. To us it was an honour, to actually think we were as good as The Beatles."

Two years later, while in Australia, Maurice would retract his initial remark. He told 'Molly' Meldrum that, while "stuck in a corner with George, Ringo and Eric Clapton" at a party, George had owned up to buying a copy of 'Mining Disaster' "because it sounded so much like [The Beatles], it was untrue." Maurice's response to George was that "it was unintentional" to which George was said to have replied, "I knew that, I admire your work."

It's important to recognise that at this time, nearly all pop and rock bands were strongly influenced by The Beatles, whose every remark was picked up by the music press and made into the new trend of the hour. "If you sounded like The Beatles and also could write a hit single, then the hype of the machine would go into action, and your company would make sure people thought you sounded like The Beatles or thought you were The Beatles," Barry explained. "And that sold you. Attracted attention to you."

"It was good for us because . . . everyone thought it was The Beatles under a different name," Robin added. "And all the deejays on radio stations in the US picked it up immediately thinking it *was* The Beatles, and it was a hit on that basis. It established us in those early years. It helped our following record which was nothing like The Beatles."

Still, it rankled when *Disc & Music Echo* reported "widespread rumours" that 'New York Mining Disaster' had been written by Lennon & McCartney. "Rubbish!" Robin retorted. "We've always written our own songs. I've been writing since I was ten – before Lennon and McCartney were even on stage. People can say what they like. If they don't believe us, they can ask The Beatles."

The single went on to achieve number 12 in Britain and number 14 in the American charts, a more than respectable showing for a new group.

The success of 'New York Mining Disaster 1941' owes a lot more to the perseverance of Robert Stigwood than he has previously been given credit for. "We had quite a hard time at getting The Bee Gees played," conceded Polydor's Alan Bates. "We weren't all totally convinced that Stigwood was picking the right song to plug . . . but at the end of the day, he was a very forceful character. All of these guys were – Chas Chandler [manager of Jimi Hendrix] was the same, Kit Lambert [manager of The Who] was the same. They all argued their case with passion, you know, they *lived* it, they were like that."

In addition to finishing work on the album, the boys found time to record their first BBC session at the Playhouse Theatre, Northumberland Avenue, London, with producer Bill Bebb. They naturally performed the single, 'New York Mining Disaster 1941' and also gave listeners a preview of what the album had to offer with 'In My Own Time', 'One Minute Woman' and 'Cucumber Castle'. When the BBC Light Programme's *Saturday Club* presented by Brian Matthew was broadcast on April 22, it was noted that there were "rave reviews from the audition panel".

Barry, Robin, Maurice, Colin and Vince made their first British TV appearance on *Top Of The Pops* performing 'New York Mining Disaster' on May 11 and were rather awe-struck at the company they were keeping.

"Jimmy Savile was on it," Maurice recalled. "That was amazing because . . . we'd seen pictures of him in The Beatles fan club book so we thought we were really there! That show had Lulu, us, The Move and the Stones doing 'Let's Spend The Night Together'. You have to remember this was really before the superstar was invented so you were all in it together."

Scottish singer Lulu performed, 'The Boat That I Row', and a smitten Maurice was quick to make her acquaintance in the BBC canteen, although the relationship wouldn't develop for quite some time.

"I thought they were all rather flash then," Lulu recalled.

"And I thought, what do I say to this big pop star?" Maurice added.

By now the brothers had been introduced to someone who thought of herself as anything but a big star. Julie Barrett, who worked in the same NEMS office as Molly Hullis, had requested that she be allowed to run an official Bee Gees fan club, which would begin that July.

"My first memories are of the twins," she recalled, "who were enjoying the success of it all, becoming very excited, and I found them to be what I called 'normal' at the time. Having a lot of acts go through the press office, there were some that really were above themselves, and you were lucky if they spoke to you."

In her privileged position as their fan club secretary, Julie got to see the group in a completely different working environment than others who worked with them, and is therefore uniquely positioned to comment on their individual personalities at that time.

"In Brook Street they had a small recording studio just next to where my office was," she revealed, "and they used to pop in there all the time. Whenever they came into the office, it was always very lively. Barry was more withdrawn at times – probably because of problems in his personal life, but Robin had a very strange sense of humour, and it always took a while for the penny to drop and realise that he was actually joking. Maurice was always a sort of, very hands-on, practical joker.

"I always thought Vince was the most genuine, he was down to earth and very sincere in everything. He and Dianne even sent me red roses at Christmas. They were always very considerate and always made me feel as though I wasn't just a silly fan club secretary, not that any of them did anyway, but Vince was the one who considered me more as a friend rather than just an employee.

"Colin I liked as well," Julie continued, "though he was very quiet and had a dry sense of humour. A bit like Robin, you didn't always know what he was thinking. He was very likeable and more down to earth than the others, maybe because he had been a star from a very early age. He was used to dealing with people, and I just felt that the scene with The Bee Gees hadn't gone to his head because, being a drummer as well, he was always in the background, although I think he got as many fan letters as the brothers anyway. He was definitely more level headed, and I think that's why he didn't go off the rails. He was always very un-star like, he didn't give the impression of being a superstar, which he was at the time; a bit bemused perhaps by the fact that he'd become a big pop star. Joanne, his future wife, was Brian Epstein's personal assistant, and I got to know her, maybe more when she actually started work with Robert Stigwood. She was definitely sort of a high-flying woman then, and I felt that she was, like Molly, very strong and knew exactly where she was going, and she sort of led Colin all the way but obviously they have a very good relationship. I wasn't really a friend of hers as such, because she was definitely in a higher league than me.

"Barry was the most extrovert and you could see that he took charge of situations. He didn't divulge a lot about himself, but he was definitely the one who you reckoned was in charge and who would have the last say on whatever was going to happen. He was very much aware that he was older and perhaps the most forward of the three but that was obviously what was needed and he did have the looks at the time as well which attracted the girls.

"Maurice to me always played the part of a clown, always joking around.

He enjoyed having jokes with you and it was him who instigated any little practical jokes. He was quite naïve and very immature in some ways, but he'd make a point of coming and making certain that he'd sent cards, and I'd always get a card from him. He was quite thoughtful in his ways. He often laughed and joked with me and read the letters – I think it highly amused him that someone should be that interested in him. A down to earth guy who liked a joke."

One Maurice prank was to cover Vince's sheets with shaving soap and toothpaste while he slept. But sometimes Maurice would be on the receiving end too, as on the occasion when he was trapped in a hotel bathroom before an important interview with a New York deejay. He made the meeting with moments to spare, but it had taken a carpenter's saw to free him.

"Robin had a very warped sort of sense of humour," Julie continued, "and he took his music very seriously. I remember that a fan gave Robin a little black Labrador puppy, but he couldn't keep it and so my Mum and I took him. I'm sure he was half wolf – he nearly drove us round the bend – and in the end we had to give him to the dog home, and that was sad particularly because someone had originally spent a lot of money for this dog. When I went to Robin's flat to pick up that dog, I think he was playing the cello at the time, and I was quite surprised and Molly was saying, 'He's really very good at it, he's learning and he's always trying to learn something new.' I think Robin is the deepest of all of them, and I think that perhaps is the reason why sometimes he was unpopular. He wasn't actually being unfriendly, but he couldn't always communicate with people. He found it quite difficult, but when he did, and it took a while, then you realised that he was quite a funny guy as well, but that he just found it difficult. He didn't seem like a 17 or 18 year old; he seemed far more mature than Maurice. No way would you have thought they were twins!

"But none of them treated you as though you weren't an important person," Julie concluded. "With some of the stars I'd met before – there were a few who weren't even particularly big stars who had only made a couple of records – it was always, 'Oh, we are great and you are down there.' "

The Bee Gees followed their début *Top Of The Pops* performance with a concert at Liverpool University on May 25 and then, on June 13, the group appeared again on television on ITV's *As You Like It*.

Robin remembers that on one of their early television appearances, they shared the bill with a little known Japanese performance artist who became a household name that year. "Actually, it was funny because we'd met Yoko Ono . . . on a TV show that we were doing. She was doing this thing where she got out of a bag. That was her act. She got out of a bag. It was weird at the time. Pretty weird now, come to think of it!" he laughed.

The group's frenetic pace caused their mother more than a little inconvenience. Their rented house, although furnished, lacked both a washing machine and a tumble dryer. "I had to wash all their shirts in the bathtub," Barbara recalled. "Oh, my aching back! I'd start after dinner and work until I finished at midnight. Then I had to get up early to contend with Andy's mischief."

★ ★ ★

Barry Gibb seemed elated with the five-man Bee Gees' line-up, saying, "Vince is a brilliant guitarist, Colin is a brilliant drummer. I don't think they'd ever leave the group, and I'd never think of replacing them with anyone else because I don't think anyone else is as capable as these two guys are."

The group released their second single, 'To Love Somebody' in June. A fine ballad that has gone on to become one of the most recorded and played songs of The Bee Gees' entire catalogue, for some reason it failed as a single. The instrumental introduction used for both verses was not repeated in subsequent versions, perhaps indicating that they were unsure of the best way to open the song, but the melody is strong with Barry's vocal and Robin's support in good form.

According to Barry, "It was written for Otis Redding . . . in [early March] 1967 at the Waldorf Astoria Hotel. I was on my own and Robert Stigwood had brought me to New York to meet Nat Weiss and the people at NEMS, because they had signed the group. I'd never been to New York before so it was a great thrill for me. I met Otis Redding early in the evening, and Robert Stigwood had sort of suggested I write a song for Otis Redding, and I said I would try. I was inspired because I had just met him. That first flash you get – you meet somebody like that who you really admire and something happens. The rest of the evening I was alone and I sort of concocted most of it in that time. Of course, he died . . . later in a plane crash,★ so he never recorded the song. But the song was then finished with Robin and Maurice."

"Everyone told us what a great record they thought it was," Robin said. "Other groups all raved about it but for some reason people in Britain just did not seem to like it."

"I think the reason it didn't do well here was because it's a soul number," Barry added. "Americans loved it, but it just wasn't right for this country."

An enduring classic from their début album, 'I Can't See Nobody', was wasted as the B-side of the single. Some may have felt Robin's soulful vocal was an acquired taste, but it conveys the song's emotional impact very well. As all three voices roll into that final chorus, and Bill Shepherd's string arrangement pours it on, it's a little masterpiece.

Bee Gees' 1st was released on July 14, 1967, and issued in both mono and stereo versions (in most markets), as was the common practice of the time. The mono version is not simply a reduction of the two stereo channels to one; each song's four-track master was remixed separately to mono and

★ Otis Redding and his backing band, The Bar-Keys, died on December 10, 1967 when his twin-engine Beechcraft plane crashed into Lake Monona near Madison, Wisconsin.

stereo. The mono version was important because it was the one heard on singles, AM radio, and jukeboxes; and because in Britain in 1967, mono still dominated the LP market.

Ossie Byrne continued to encourage the use of the overdubbing techniques, which he had first employed with the group in 1966, to build up layers of vocals and to provide Maurice with an outlet as a multi-instrumentalist while Barry and Robin took the lead vocals.

In addition to Barry on rhythm guitar, Robin probably on organ, and Maurice on bass, piano, harpsichord, mellotron, and you name it, the band for these sessions included Colin Petersen drumming on some of the songs, and Vince Melouney is quick to stress that he was involved in all of them, despite not *officially* joining as lead guitarist until after much of the recording of *Bee Gees' 1st* had been completed.

The arrangements are credited to Bill Shepherd and Phil Dennys, and it is tempting to assume the Dennys' ones are the earliest, since Bill continued to work with the Gibb brothers till 1972, but this is conjecture. Four songs have no orchestral backing, which would be a rarity in the years to come.

There were some strong Beatlesque features on the album. The most obvious is the lead guitar riff on 'In My Own Time' which is similar to The Beatles' 'Taxman' (1966), but a riff is not a melody, and the two songs are markedly different.

"We started off with a mellotron and we used that on . . . 'Every Christian Lion Hearted Man Will Show You' . . . I had to repeat that on stage, but I used an organ," Maurice revealed.

The three-part Gibb harmony was likewise compared to The Beatles, although Bee Gees fans familiar with the voices have not always agreed. Possibly it was not so much in the voices themselves as the application of harmony singing to rock music, where a single lead vocal with backing was more common.

There is one way in which The Bee Gees have forever carried on The Beatles' legacy, and that is the value they place on eclecticism. Like The Beatles, The Bee Gees freely combine elements of songwriting and arranging from any musical style they happen to have come across. The downside at times is that The Bee Gees' wide-ranging styles do not fit well into the market categories used for radio play and consequently the charts, but they are keeping alive what could be reasonably called The Beatles' tradition of all-inclusive pop music.

While the album is very much a collection of diverse songs, it is well-paced with a mix of straight ballads and some looser pieces like the slightly chaotic 'Red Chair Fade Away' and 'I Close My Eyes'; both Phil Dennys' arrangements. By contrast, the most well-known songs are the straight pop ballads like 'To Love Somebody' and 'I Can't See Nobody'.

Shortly before the album's completion, Barry implied that Ossie Byrne and his production team were deserving of great credit, just for their patience alone. "We drive the producer and technicians mad. We have nothing worked out. We sit about and think up a subject, then write a song on the spot. We did the whole of the LP like this. It's really the only way we can work – spontaneously, off the cuff." Years later, he would add, "Ossie was a good producer. I think he was crazy to go back to Australia."

Driven mad perhaps, but nonetheless still retaining his sanity to this day, is one of those IBC technicians, Damon Lyon-Shaw who well remembers those sessions for *First*.

"Just sensational," is how he describes them. "As far as I was concerned, the combination of Barry Gibb's weird tuning – not to mention how long he took to tune his guitar, and Colin Petersen's phenomenal style of drumming was certainly unique at the time." Vince's guitar playing was not entirely his personal cup of tea although, conversely, he does go on to say, "but it fitted in so well.

"The whole combination was so good, it was so simple. I mean they were very simple writers, I'm not saying that they're not brilliant, but the lyrics were simple, the music was simple, they just had that knack of bringing out that commercial sort of stuff. At that stage they, the original Bee Gees to my mind, were just unique. It was just phenomenal.

"To my mind The Bee Gees were [at their best] around the *First* album when they were all together as a unit, the five of them. Live they were sensational, they could play it live, and they sounded just like the albums. They used to just turn up. Barry could either tune his guitar, or if he didn't, they went home! But if they got it together, they used to just have a rough idea a lot of the time. I mean I wasn't privy to their writing process, but I think a lot of the time they just came in with an idea and it just matured in the studio. They had the money to do it then, I don't think you could do it nowadays."

Contradicting Barry's earlier praise of Ossie Byrne as a producer, Damon insists that he knew Ossie as well as anyone and offers a fresh perspective.

"I did more stuff with Ossie Byrne without The Bee Gees than I did with The Bee Gees. Ossie had a knack of keeping quiet and letting people get on, and then he went adrift a bit and got some bands that weren't quite so good, and it all sort of petered out from there really. I had a lot of time for Ossie, he was a nice chap.

"The thing with someone like Ossie, he didn't have much talent as a producer I have to say, but he had enough talent to see the band. He had this talent of keeping people together and making them productive, and when they threw him out they didn't have anyone, they only had themselves. If they wanted to get lazy or do stupid things, they got on with it because there wasn't anybody there to push them, whereas Ossie was their mentor or father figure in the early days. But [The Bee Gees] outgrew him very quickly sadly, because as I say he wasn't a producer. They had enormous talents and obviously they could see things that he couldn't see, so I can understand why he went."

His colleague John Pantry held a similar view. "Ossie was a nice guy. He didn't know a great deal technically and initially relied heavily on the engineers. It wasn't long before The Bee Gees knew as much as him and started doing sessions without him." John also contributed an unexpected piece of information about Ossie. "He did a great trick with his glass eye, which he could pop out!"

John thought equally highly of Bill Shepherd too whom he described as "a smashing guy. Really knew his stuff, an excellent arranger who helped shape their early sound."

The album's sleeve design was the work of Klaus Voorman, the bass guitarist with Manfred Mann. A friend of The Beatles from their days in Hamburg, Voorman designed the cover of their *Revolver* album.

The Beatles themselves were interested in the NEMS newcomers. "They wanted to come in on one of the boys' earlier sessions," Robert Stigwood recalled, "but I asked them not to because I didn't think it would be particularly good."

The summer flew by with a two-week promotional visit to the United States. Before leaving, Colin reassured anxious fans that they would return. "We came to Britain because the scope in Australia was so small, but we don't just regard it as a stepping stone to the States. Even if we make it there, we still regard ourselves as a British group."

The group found time to see some of the sights, but Hugh Gibb revealed that the trip was not without some minor drawbacks. "Robin is a very nervous person; for example, he hates lifts," Hugh revealed. "He'd sooner walk up ten flights of stairs than use a lift. I think it's claustrophobia as well as fear. When we went to America, he wouldn't go up the Empire State Building. He tried three times but each time couldn't make it. He hates planes. I think it's fear again, but we travel so much he has to put up with them. But he'll never go on these charter planes; he hates small planes, but he can just about stand the big jets. He always wears a St Christopher; all the boys do."

The Fourth of July was spent in New York talking to music journalist Nancy Lewis. Although they had joined the group in March, both Colin and Vince formally signed five-year contracts with Robert Stigwood and The Bee Gees that day. Like Brian Epstein, Stigwood shared a flair for the grandiose and the group was launched with an enormous all-day press party on a yacht rented especially for the occasion. That little detail appears to have been omitted from conversation on the day, as all present were clearly left with the impression that it was Stigwood's own vessel.

Less impressed was Epstein himself as the following extract from Ray Coleman's *Brian Epstein: The Man Who Made The Beatles* reveals:

> *"Who are you going to charge it to?" asked [Nat] Weiss.*
> *"Bill it to my personal account," Stigwood replied.*
> *Epstein phoned Weiss from London that night. He had heard of the extravaganza shindig. "Who is paying for this?" he asked tartly.*

> *"Oh Robert told me to charge it to his personal account," Weiss*
> *answered. "Those were his words."*
> *There was a silence before Epstein spoke icily. "Number one, he*
> *works for me," Brian began. "You're my partner. Number two, you're*
> *going to have to pay for this. Number three, Robert owes me £10,000*
> *on a personal loan already. Number four, when The Bee Gees have*
> *come to America and earned a million dollars, then they can take a*
> *yachting trip." Then he hung up.*

This seems to imply that Brian Epstein wasn't a Bee Gees fan. In fact, the opposite was true, and he also expressed his admiration for acts like Cream and Georgie Fame. But Epstein did resent Stigwood's attempts to manoeuvre The Bee Gees into a status befitting his own major act. As Nat Weiss admitted, "[Brian] liked their music, and liked them personally, but when Robert described them as 'the next Beatles', Brian was furious."

The following day plans were announced for the first Bee Gees' film project commissioned by NEMS Enterprises, entitled *Lord Kitchener's Little Drummer Boys*. The screenplay was being written by Mike Pratt, a television scriptwriter. The film, to be filmed on location in Africa, was the story of five young men who enlist in the Army as musicians and are pressed into service in the Boer War. With Colin's previous acting experience, it was suggested that he would take the starring role, whilst Barry, Robin and Maurice would compose the musical score.

"There will be songs in it, but we don't know how yet," Barry said. "We're writing both the background score and one or two songs for us to sing. We want everything to be authentic so you really couldn't use electric guitars and still be in keeping with the time."

Colin appeared his usual laid-back self. "I take things as they come. It won't worry me at all if the others all come off better than me. It's a completely new concept for me, anyway. As there will be songs in it, and a story line that fits our pop image, I'll be working in a completely new field.

"When I first joined the brothers, they used to send me up . . . mainly about the film bit. They don't now. I think they've said all there was to say. I couldn't make the most of my contribution to the group if I didn't get on with the other people in it. I don't see how you can create anything nice together if you're not nice in others' eyes."

The demands on up-and-coming pop performers were far more strenuous then than now, and no sooner had their feet touched the ground after the American trip than they were off to Scandinavia for a three-day promotional jaunt. A weary but elated Maurice barely had time to tell waiting journalists, "America is great. We were all treated like gods over there. It really was a knockout. Funny, when American groups come here, the kids seem to respect them. But, when British groups go to the States, the kids go real wild! We liked America very much."

The young group had begun to move in exalted social circles, with nights out at exclusive clubs in impressive company. In Swinging Sixties London there were numerous clubs where the pop stars of the day could relax after hours in congenial company. One of the best known was The Speakeasy near Oxford Circus.

"I met John and George down at The Speakeasy," Maurice related. "I walked in and John Lennon said, 'Bee Gees!' like this. And I said, 'Hi.' Paul had just walked out then. He'd gone with Jane Asher somewhere. And I just sat and talked to John and he said, 'I dig your act,' and so forth, which I thought was very nice of him to say. Then I went and joined my other table. I thought the best thing to do was not just to sit there and say, 'Gee, I think you're the greatest,' because I really didn't want to do that. It's just best to say, 'Okay, nice to have met you; I must go now; cheers,' and that's all. Because if I would have sat there all night talking to them, they would have thought, 'Oh, he's a real rave-on,' so I just walked away and that was the end of it."

"It was strange," he reflected later. "One moment I was in Australia poring over The Beatles' fan club books and two months later I was in The Speakeasy Club in London getting drunk with them. Or Lennon was showing me how to use the mellotron he played on 'Strawberry Fields'. The first time we met them at The Speakeasy, they'd just come back from doing the *Sgt. Pepper* album cover and they were wearing those brilliant clothes. That was a fantastic night – Keith Moon, Otis Redding, Pete Townshend, all drinking scotch and coke, which was *the* drink then."

"I remember that night," Barry added. "That was the first night I met Lennon. He was sitting with his back to me in the *Pepper* gear talking to someone, and Pete Townshend said, 'Do you want to meet John?' So he took me over and went, 'John, this is Barry Gibb from the group The Bee Gees' and – I'll never forget it – he never turned round, didn't look at me at all, just reached over his shoulder and shook hands with me and said, 'Howyadoin?' and then continued his conversation. I felt like digging a hole and burying myself."

Those feelings of embarrassment didn't last long, though. An exuberant Barry Gibb told Norrie Drummond of *New Musical Express,* "When we arrived in London, we had nothing. We were unknown. We had no recording contract and no work. We could have been sleeping on park benches now but fortunately everything turned out well – much better than we had ever hoped."

★ ★ ★

But by August dark clouds were gathering.

The first blow came when Roy Jenkins, the Home Secretary, declared that, as native Australians on temporary work permits, Colin Petersen and Vince Melouney would have to leave Britain by September 17 when their visas would expire.

"The Bee Gees' solicitors received the instructions from the Home Office on Tuesday evening," Robert Stigwood announced. "It is absolutely scandalous! The Government is continually asking for help in the export drive, and this group is potentially one of the biggest foreign currency earners for years."

"In the last 12 weeks, we estimate we've brought into this country or earned from foreign royalties around $250,000," Robin said. "Others who earn dollars are awarded the MBE or invited to a nosh at Buckingham Palace. Not us. They hit us with a stupid rule and treat us like criminals."

"Before I left Australia I went to the British Embassy and asked if I needed a permit to work in Britain," Colin said. "They said I didn't. All I had to do, they told me, was to get a visitor's visa. 'When you get to England,' this official said, 'just take it into the Home Office and they'll stamp it.' Unfortunately I found out there was a lot more to it than that."

Meanwhile Maurice, already the proud owner of a Rolls-Royce and an orange Morris Cooper S with blacked out 'celebrity' windows, failed his driving test for the first time. In the middle of that first test, the examiner suddenly recognised him and said, "You're one of The Bee Gees, aren't you – the ones getting deported?"

"I was just about to say this applied to only two of the members," Maurice recalled, "when this bloke says, 'Then why the hell are you taking your test?'

"That got me. My blood really boiled and I thought, 'Right, mate.' I gave it to him at 80. We were going along like there was no tomorrow.

"When he got out, he said, 'Mr Gibb, I'm happy to say you've failed.' " Unfortunately for Maurice, it would take three more attempts before he got that coveted driver's licence.

In a show of solidarity, Barry, Robin and Maurice discussed plans for the entire group to relocate to the United States, Spain or Germany rather than see two of their members deported. Vince and Colin even toyed with the idea of becoming Spanish or Italian citizens as this would mean that they would then be able to work in Britain almost immediately.

"It is a ridiculous state of affairs," Stigwood said. "But it is one we are having to consider seriously. Another possibility is that The Bee Gees may settle in Germany, as it would be easier to commute to and from Britain than if they were living in the States."

Finally, it was left to Robert Stigwood to take on the British government. He appealed to the Home Office and was turned down, although he did manage to get the boys' visas extended until the end of October. It was a temporary reprieve which bought Colin and Vince a little more time.

The death of Brian Epstein during the last week of August had a marked effect on one Bee Gee in particular. Poignantly, Maurice Gibb says that he remembers the last time he saw Brian Epstein. "It was on the Saturday – no, the Friday, because on the Sunday he was found dead. He came out and he was supposed to join us in Cannes the next day, he came out of his office and said, 'That 'Massachusetts' is going to be the world's number one. It's beautiful,' and walked away. That's the last words he ever said to me."

10

FIRST FAME

"FIRST FAME IS a very dangerous thing," explained Barry. "You believe what you read about yourself, you believe what people say about you. You believe that you have something very special to say and that God's talking through you and the public need to know. This happens to you when you become famous for the first time, especially on an international level."

The Bee Gees had just begun to get a crash course in the dangers of international success at a major level.

'Massachusetts' was released just six days after Brian Epstein's prophetic words, giving The Bee Gees their biggest hit to date. In Britain it held the number one slot in the singles chart for four weeks; in Germany three weeks, and Japan an incredible six weeks. In addition, it reached number one in Malaysia, South Africa, New Zealand, Singapore and Australia. In America, where 'Holiday' was released as the third single without the group's knowledge, 'Massachusetts' just missed entering the Top 10, rising only to number 11.

According to Athol Guy of The Seekers, The Bee Gees didn't even originally plan to record 'Massachusetts' themselves. He told Richard Saunders, "['Massachusetts'] was offered to our manager by The Bee Gees for the group to record, before they did it. There was some discussion about publishing rights which I think got in the way of us ever finding out about it. While they made a huge hit song of it, I don't know if it would have meant a great deal for us. I love The Bee Gees – they're a fantastic band – but the lyrics in some of their earlier songs . . . er . . . what does it mean?"

Maurice confirms Athol's story, implying that the attempt to offload 'Massachusetts' had been without their own manager's knowledge. "We sat on the demo . . . and actually never wanted really to record the song but then Robert, our manager, said it was *the* disc for us and we must record it. He was right."

By the time the single came out, 'flower power' and its attendant culture was in decline. "It's a business!" declared Maurice somewhat cynically. "Of course the idea is good, but there is so much commercialisation happening that the movement is dying a sad death. Bells being sold in Carnaby Street . . . urgh! When we went to the States in July, flower power hadn't

141

really begun here, but when we came back the flowers had started to grow. Naturally, there was nothing like this hitting the Australian scene when we left, but I guess flower power is there as well."

How The Bee Gees came to write their answer to the movement, immortalised by Scott McKenzie's pop classic, 'San Francisco', varies according to which brother is telling the story.

"The first time the group went to New York and stayed at the St Regis Hotel, and while our luggage was being moved into the suite, we were writing 'Massachusetts', sitting on a sofa, the three of us. It came from our first exposure to America, our first thoughts of writing a song about flower power, which the song is about. Or it's basically anti-flower power . . . because we were getting tired of it long before everybody else did. 'Don't go to San Francisco, come home, for Christ's sake,'" Barry laughed. "We wanted to write the opposite of what it's like to lose somebody who went to San Francisco . . . Well, we thought, 'Why not write a song about everybody going home?' The lights all went out in Massachusetts because everyone went to San Francisco, because they left. There was something very special about that thought."

According to Robin, "Ninety per cent of it was mental telepathy. I had had this line in my head all day, 'The lights all went out in Massachusetts.' Later that night I mentioned it to Barry and he said, 'Yes, I know. I've already got the tune for it.' So we wrote the rest of it together, and Maurice did the arrangement. 'Massachusetts', in fact, is not talking about people going back to Massachusetts. It represents all the people who want to go back to somewhere or something. It is all about people who want to escape."

However, as Maurice remembered it, "We worked out the basic melody in about five minutes when we were in New York. Robin and I began, then Barry started throwing in ideas. We wrote 'Massachusetts' in 15 minutes and recorded it in three takes. I'm not quite sure why we thought of 'Massachusetts' in the first place because we weren't even sure how to spell it. It's untrue that 'Massachusetts' was geared for the [American] market. We were just fooling about, and we thought that it would be fun to record a number like Engelbert or Tom Jones. After all, they do get the number ones."

The memory of how the song was written may have faded, but one moment remains crystal clear for Maurice. The Bee Gees were standing on a revolving stage, waiting to perform. "The Merseybeats were performing," he recounts, "and Dick Ashby, who was our road manager at that time, came rushing up just as the stage was about to turn around and said, ''Massachusetts' just went to number one' . . . We were so high from that news because that was the first number one we had in England. All that time we were in Australia, dreaming of that, it was such a kick for us that I couldn't stop crying. We did the lousiest show you ever saw, we were so excited. That moment of being told – that stands out like it was this morning."

In fact, Maurice had received similar news a week earlier, but an error resulted in the charts being immediately recalled and, within 12 hours, they were demoted to number three. Perhaps preparing himself for disappointment, he told *Music Makers* that it actually wasn't the kind of music they liked, and he wouldn't have bought it himself. "The disc was meant to be a commercial proposition and it paid off," he explained, "but we are much more thrilled about 'World', which isn't released yet. Now that is great. A lot more work went into it than into 'Massachusetts'." Number one status was finally achieved on 11th November.

These were heady days indeed for the young group, but Robert Stigwood ensured that they remained focused and grounded. "Robert was very good with us, he was almost like a parent," Barry recalled. "He wouldn't let us get big-headed about it and he would always bring us down to earth and say 'One hit does not a career make.' He was always there to tell us that, 'Two hits does not a career make,' and even on our third hit he would say, 'Stay calm.'"

The success of 'Massachusetts' further elevated The Bee Gees' status among London's social elite, and the boys became part of the social scene that had grown up within London's pop industry. They began to spend more of their nights in the central London clubs, mixing freely with the premier division of rock superstars.

One of the most unlikely friendships to spring up came on the heels of an insult in the press. "When we first came out, Jimi Hendrix said we were two-year-old Beatles," Barry said. "He was just giving an opinion at the time. People just like to have a go at other artists. But we are very good friends with Jimi now.

"He was a great mate of mine," he recalled years later. "He came to my twenty-first birthday party. He was an extremely polite bloke. I never knew about the drugs then. I thought he was acting a bit weird and saying kind of *remote* things, but I was too naïve to even consider that it might be drugs . . . I never cottoned on with Jimi and the drugs. I saw him drunk a few times because I remember thinking he was always really quiet until he had a few drinks."

"I'll tell you how naïve we were," said Maurice. "I went out drinking with Lennon once when he was on LSD, and I never even noticed! He covered it very well, and he was much funnier. He wasn't sarcastic, but he was very witty. He also got *very* creative. He'd keep running off into a room to draw or write things down. We were that green. I was at a party one night . . . and someone passed me a joint, and I got my fags out and said, 'It's all right, I've got plenty! There's no need to share one!'"

"The pressures on us at that age were incredible," Barry said. "The guys were about 17 when all this happened, when we first started making hit records from England, 'Mining Disaster' and those things. We didn't really know where we were at because we never had hits all over the world before and it all happened so fast for us. There were so many people around us talking to us, filling our ears with nonsense."

Robin agreed that the sudden burst of fame turned his head, adding that if he met the young Robin Gibb walking down the street now, "I think I'd grab him by the collar, belt him around the head and tell him to learn something . . . I was very selfish then. I was arrogant and condescending to a degree.

"When I think back to myself at [that time], I see a young boy who didn't want to know about anything and who was all wrapped up in all the little things . . . like ego problems . . . I kept wanting to know what somebody was really thinking about me, or what they really meant by what they were saying. If we had a new record out, it was important to get it mentioned in a music paper . . ."

To nine-year-old Andy Gibb it all seemed very strange but, to his credit, he didn't allow his brothers' success to affect him. "It didn't change my life that much. I knew they were in the business and I had always known they were in the business. Not being anything extra special to me, and at [that age] you don't think about show business, you don't think glitter, you don't think that you have 400 or 500 kids outside the front door because your brothers are big stars. I just walk in after school, pass the 500 kids at the front door, go in the back door, my brothers would all be sitting, watching television with the curtains drawn, girls banging on the windows and that was their whole life, you know."

The roller-coaster lifestyle of the rich and famous was beginning to consume them, and The Bee Gees would soon discover that their working-class roots and sensible upbringing would offer little protection.

★   ★   ★

Although only 17 years old at the time, Robin Gibb was addressing his future wife when he introduced himself to Molly Hullis at the NEMS office when the brothers first met with Robert Stigwood. Molly didn't have any indication of future events either because, as Robin says, "I didn't get around to being sociable until four weeks afterwards at a party in Kensington. Then the real thing started about May, 1967."

Molly remembered, "Robin would come and sit in the reception area and talk. At that time, he was very concerned about the number of late nights I was keeping up. I would only have maybe a couple hours of sleep and get into work the next morning and carry on."

But as she recalled it, Robin wasn't the first Gibb brother to ask her out. "One day, Maurice invited me to this party," she said. "When I arrived, Maurice was with somebody else. So I thought, 'Ah, nice one here, I'm off.' Robin said to me, 'Don't go. You might just as well stay now that you've got here.' And that was really the first time we went out. We went from the party to a club, and then we started going out on a regular basis . . .

"It was something that sort of grew. Robin's a dreamer, a romantic person. Therefore, he makes a situation romantic even if it isn't. He is very sensitive. People say he's shy, but he's not. He's just very sensitive about everything, whether it's good or bad . . . And terribly kind and considerate, not just to me and the family but to strangers. Always concerned, always prepared to take time out to talk to fans."

Colin Petersen also found romance at the NEMS offices, in his case with Brian Epstein's personal assistant, Joanne Newfield, while Vince Melouney was already married to Dianne when he joined the group.

For Barry and Maurice it was The Bee Gees' appearances on *Top Of The Pops* that led them to meet girls they were destined to marry. Not long after their first *Top Of The Pops* performance, Colin's girlfriend told her close friend and former flatmate, Lulu, that Maurice Gibb was very impressed with her. "He keeps talking about you," Joanne added.

"I thought Maurice was cute," Lulu recalled, "so I said, 'In that case, tell him to stop talking about me and take me out.' He did just that.

"I never expected much to come from this, but in fact our relationship grew – after a fashion . . . Going steady is quite the wrong way to describe what was happening between us. Going *un*steady might better sum up the way we fell in and out with each other."

Lulu recalled one instance when she even attended a concert with The Bee Gees' manager. "I knew Robert," she explained, "and he offered to take me to see Pink Floyd at the Saville Theatre because he said Maurice would be there too. He was . . . with another girl! So I tried to be all tactful and asked him the name of his girlfriend. 'She's not my girlfriend and her name's . . .' he replied, so I breathed again.

"I think I may have fallen in love with The Bee Gees' music before I fell for Maurice . . . I always liked Maurice, and in the early days I thought he was uncomplicated. It was only later that I realised how wrong I was. When you are a child star, you are encouraged to be loud so as not to be ignored, and I must have been rather intolerant and spoiled . . . But Maurice saw the good side of me, and I of course saw the good side of him."

Lulu was born Marie McDonald McLaughlin Lawrie on November 3, 1948, the eldest of four children, in a two-room Glasgow tenement flat with no bathroom. At 13, Marie joined a band called The Gleneagles who performed in clubs and pubs. The pint-sized singer with the big voice was spotted in 1964 by record company talent scout Marian Massey. She became her manager and renamed the band Lulu & The Luvvers. Lulu had her first Top 10 hit at age 15 with her début single 'Shout' and quickly became an enormous star in Britain.

Barry also fell for a Scottish lass. The guest hostess on *TOTP* on the evening of September 21, 1967 was a 17-year-old beauty queen named Lynda Ann Gray. Lynda was born on May 11, 1950 in Musselburgh, on the outskirts of Edinburgh, in Scotland. After winning the Miss Edinburgh pageant, she went to London to work as a "colour girl" on *Top Of The Pops,* where she was chaperoned by Jimmy Savile, the show's disc jockey. Being a colour girl involved posing while the camera and lighting men adjusted their settings. The contrast of Lynda's fair skin and dark hair made her ideally suited for the job.

At rehearsals for the show, Lynda was embarrassed by the teasing of the other girls at the show, who insisted that Barry was staring at her. He introduced himself, took her down to the restaurant for coffee and invited her to a party at Robert Stigwood's house in Adam's Row. Jimmy Savile took his responsibility to Lynda's parents seriously and refused permission for her to attend. He hadn't reckoned on Lynda's rebellious streak though – when she got back to her hotel, she jumped into the nearest taxi, with Savile's personal assistant in hot pursuit in the next cab.

She arrived in tears at Stigwood's house, where his servant Victor, undoubtedly accustomed to hysterical fans, was understandably reluctant to let the distraught teenager in.

Lynda remembers, "I said, 'I've come to see Barry.' Mascara was running down all over my face, and Victor said, 'I don't know who you are.' Just then, Barry came running down the stairs and said, 'It's okay. I'm expecting her.' We didn't go straight into the party; we went into the study. Barry was on the phone to his mother, and his wife was threatening to come to the party. I thought, 'My God, he's married. Oh no!'"

When Barry finished his telephone conversation, he told Lynda, "Don't look so worried. You tell me your problem and I'll tell you mine."

Barry's marriage to Maureen was rapidly falling apart. Obliged to keep the marriage a secret from fans and the press, Maureen was kept out of the public eye and away from any of the group's appearances. Barry's burgeoning career, his single-minded quest for success and recognition for the group, was placing an intolerable strain on the relationship. Inevitably, he had come to regret his hasty marriage and wanted his freedom. Indeed, in an effort to distance himself from the stressful situation, he had separated from Maureen and was living at Stigwood's Adam's Row home.

Lynda says, "He told me all about his relationship, how he was separated, and then I told him how I shouldn't be there." But she didn't leave. At the party she says that Barry "gave me all the usual crap. 'Oh, I love you,' this and that. And I said, 'Oh yes? How many people have you said that to today?'"

Lynda returned to the Musselburgh council house, where she lived with her parents, and found a job as a typist, which reportedly earned her £8 a week. The couple saw each other a few times after that when Barry went to Scotland; then, after Lynda turned 18, their paths crossed again. "I came down to do some modelling in London," she recalled. "We met again, and shortly after that, we started living together. I stopped working then because Barry didn't want me messing around with photographers. I thought, 'He's so sweet; he's really nice.' And he *was* very nice. He was so polite and well-mannered which you don't always find in young guys. He was very romantic, opened the door for me and things like that."

The couple moved into a lavish penthouse flat built for the millionaire property developer, Bernard Sunley, just a few years before he died. The flat boasted panoramic views of London, with a quirky Gibb decorating touch of a foam rubber model of the New York skyline hanging upside down from the ceiling, with lights flickering in the skyscraper windows.

Then there was the problem of how George and May Gray would react to the news that their daughter was moving in with a married, albeit separated, pop star, but as Lynda explained, it was only a minor glitch. "I've told my parents about us. I never lie to them. I thought they'd be upset, but they have both been marvellous about it. In fact, my mother even stays with Barry and I from time to time. She loves the flat, as you can imagine."

★　★　★

The Bee Gees had begun writing songs for their second album of 1967 almost as soon as the first was finished. The recording sessions were scattered over a few months from July, the month when *Bee Gees 1st* was released, to as late as November or December.

The group's personnel was now stable for touring and recording, with Bill Shepherd arranging, Barry on rhythm guitar, Robin on occasional organ, and Maurice on several instruments, bass on all songs and piano on many, in addition to Vince Melouney on lead guitar and Colin Petersen on drums.

But a question mark still hung over the future of the group. Despite having won an extension for Colin and Vince to stay in Britain, legal battles continued to obtain unlimited visas for the boys. With the flair for showmanship that has become Robert Stigwood's hallmark, his mighty publicity machine rolled into action, organising a series of events to bring the case into the public eye.

"I had fans chaining themselves to the railings of Buckingham Palace," he recalled. "I marched an elephant on the Home Office in Whitehall, a procession that tied up London's traffic for a day. I landed a helicopter full of fans in the Chancellor of the Exchequer's garden. They ran and [verbally] assaulted him and told him what a terrible thing it was. I had the Prime Minister's holiday residence picketed . . . We blew it up so much that in the Home Office itself that dealt with immigration, all the secretaries started putting up 'Save The Bee Gees' posters."

Whilst Stigwood undoubtedly pulled the strings, Julie Barrett was in the front line. For a 19-year-old girl, whose day-to-day job more often than not involved replying to fan letters, that September was quite an ordeal. "When all the deportation stuff started, that's when it got a bit heavy," she conceded.

"Tony Barrow was the press officer at the time and he was the one who'd say, 'Right, today Julie, you're going to Carnaby Street to walk up and down with placards saying "Do not deport The Bee Gees"' and we got a good press coverage. I was just told each day what I was to do, and it was all done in my name. He would phone the press and say, 'Julie Barrett says today (this is going to happen),' and I remember for the chaining at Buckingham Palace we had actually Deirdre Meehan from the office chained up instead. I'd had a couple of threats from the police to the effect that I must not keep doing this kind of thing, and I was warned that if it continued, I could be in trouble, so I was a bit scared.

"We went down to Buckingham Palace and I can remember being petrified because Deirdre stood out so much – she had this great big '10 gallon' Stetson hat on – and there were policemen walking by. I thought, 'I can't do this, I can't do this,' and we went up to the railings a couple of times and I pulled her back and then I said, 'Well, we've got to do it.' I did it very quickly, and when I chained her to the railings, I didn't realise that I'd chained her in the end to one that didn't go all the way up because it was broken off at the top. But it was quite good because, by the time all the photographers had taken all their photos, and there was a lot of hoo-hah, the police eventually realised, 'Oh we don't need to saw her out after all,' which Tony Barrow was a little bit upset about. We were able to just lift her arm out, but it made the papers, well all over the world actually. It was pretty hair-raising although it was quite exciting too.

"Then with the elephant, I chickened out. I didn't mind my name being there, but I wasn't going to be prosecuted, I didn't want anything going against me. So we got another girl from the office, and she was a beautiful girl as well, with long lovely hair, and we went down Whitehall with this elephant and that was quite amazing. We also went to the Scilly Isles in a helicopter to see Harold Wilson with our petition. He lived in a little council house with his bike outside, and I remember speaking to him and being flabbergasted that I was presenting something to the British Prime Minister, and I made some silly comment like, 'Oh you're a nice little man!'

"Then Tony came up with his classic, which he said would finish the whole campaign off. He said that I had to stand on a window ledge, about three storeys up and next to The London Palladium, and threaten to throw myself off unless Vince and Colin were not deported. That was getting to the silly point and I told Tony I wouldn't do it."

As an alternative to Tony Barrow's dramatic stunts, Stigwood took a more astute approach to solving the deportation issue, and played a winning hand in presenting the authorities with a detailed account of The Bee Gees' dollar earnings which amounted to over a million dollars so far that year. "Finally, there was such an uproar in the press that the Prime Minister had to intervene, and he declared The Bee Gees a national asset," recalled Stigwood. In October, the Home Office rescinded the expulsion order, and Colin and Vince were given unlimited work permits to stay in Britain. The Bee Gees were staying together.

On September 30, BBC Radio One began broadcasting, taking over from the Light Programme. Most pop aficionados know that the first song played by DJ Tony Blackburn was 'Flowers In The Rain' by The Move. Less well known is the fact that the second was 'Massachusetts', and The Bee Gees were there in the studios waiting to tape their appearance on the first ever *Saturday's Club*, hosted by Keith Skues, which was broadcast later that day.

The Bee Gees appeared on *Let's Go* as guests of Dave Symonds on the new station during the first week of October and also taped their second BBC session at 201 Piccadilly, Studio One, in London with producer and engineer Dave Tate. They performed with a small backing group, and the session featured 'In My Own Time' (once again), 'I Close My Eyes', 'New York Mining Disaster 1941', 'Massachusetts', 'Mrs Gillespie's Refrigerator' (an original song which the group would never release themselves), 'To Love Somebody', 'Cucumber Castle' and 'World'. The show was broadcast on Radio One's *Top Gear*, which was presented for that show only by Pete Drummond and Tommy Vance.

They made an appearance in Manchester on *The Joe Loss Pop Show,* where Barry was astonished to see Loss march over to their father and say, "Hello, I know you, don't I?" The show gave Hugh Gibb a chance to catch up with his fellow bandleader years after the time both had spent on the Isle of Man, just after the war.

They also appeared on Radio One's *Pete's People* with Pete Murray on October 21 and on *The Jimmy Young Show* the following week.

The Bee Gees turned down an offer to write and perform the soundtrack for the film *Wonderwall*. According to director Joe Massot, "The Bee Gees were interested in doing something and came to Twickenham Studios to see me. It seemed the movie had created a vibe as Graham Nash [of The Hollies] also wanted to join in." After the Gibbs had turned down Massot, the director turned to George Harrison. "George told me that he had been working on *Magical Mystery Tour* helping out, but that was Paul's project, and that he would like to do something solo." Harrison agreed to take on the project – a strange turn of events for one of The Beatles to take on a project rejected by the Gibbs.

They seemed to be flying high, but Barry Gibb insisted that they were not becoming complacent. "In England, at least, you might say we've had a lot of success for the group, but none of us see it that way," he insisted. "None of us ever will, because if you see success, you stop trying. And that's the whole secret. Success is not a symbol – it's seeing our music recognised. That's the important thing."

11

FOR FAWKES' SAKE!

Today's eco-warriors have nothing on Guy Fawkes. On the night of November 5, 1605, Guy and his cronies attempted to blow up the Houses Of Parliament but were caught in the act and sentenced to death in the most unpleasant of circumstances. Since then the Gunpowder Plot has been celebrated annually in Britain with fireworks and bonfires, but on the night of November 5, 1967 near Hither Green in South London, sights and sounds of a different sort filled the air.

It should have been the end of a pleasant outing. Robin Gibb and his girl-friend, Molly Hullis, had been to Hastings to visit Molly's parents; a chance for Mr and Mrs. Hullis to get better acquainted with her boyfriend. "They're ordinary folk who've never before had any connection with celebrities," Molly said. "When they first realised that Robin was famous they were very overwhelmed. My mother kept asking me, 'Are you sure he's the right person for you?' It was just that Robin was so different from any other boyfriend I'd taken home before."

The weather had been unseasonably fine, and the young couple spent the afternoon walking on the beach in the autumn sunshine. As evening approached, Robin and Molly prepared to return to London. That night, he needed to see Robert Stigwood to pick up some tapes, believed to consist of demos of 'Sinking Ships' and 'When Things Go Wrong', so they climbed aboard the 7.43 Hastings to London express, carrying a suit-case, a bread pudding made by Molly's mother and some apples for the journey.

The ride began unremarkably, but as the train approached Hither Green it began to shake. Robin was afraid that something was wrong and reached for the alarm cord. "What I didn't realise was the engine had just become uncoupled. Then the carriage rolled over and big stretches of railway line came crashing in straight past my face."

"Suddenly it felt as if we were going over great boulders," he would tell reporter Camilla Beach the following day, the horror of the accident still fresh in his mind. "Rocks were hitting the side of the compartment. Molly and I held on to each other as the train turned over and over, still going forward along the line.

"It almost seemed as if the train was going to pieces around us," he recalled. "One minute we were in the luggage rack, the next we were on the floor. The train finally came to a halt on its side 1,400 yards from where it had come off the rails." The official inquiry would reveal that the actual distance covered by the derailed carriages was half that which Robin had claimed but, to those on the train itself, the time it took for the train to stop must have felt interminable.

The signalman at Hither Green, Albert Norman, observed a flash from the direction of the Hastings train. "All the wheels appeared to be red-hot and then they became white-hot. Then, as one of the coaches went straight up on its end, there was a big flash," he said.

Donald Purvis, the driver of the train, later told the inquiry into the accident that, "The ride up to Hither Green was no different from on any other day. At Hither Green I experienced dragging, then snatching. This became far more violent. I didn't know what had happened. Everything happened so fast. I could not get an impression which part of the train the drag was coming from. The whole thing seemed to rear up and there was a terrific bang. We broke away and the brake pressure shot up. The brakes were hard on because the pipes were severed."

The leading pair of wheels of the third coach became derailed and the second, third, fourth and fifth coaches turned on their sides. Passengers were tossed like rag dolls as the coaches overturned. The leading coach broke away and came to a stop some 640 yards further on. Survivors mentioned a strange silence before the screams of the injured and dying split the night air.

Robin recalled, "When the train finally stopped, there was just a hissing sound, then finally the gut-wrenching screams. We were fortunate to have been in a first-class compartment near the front of the train.

"I may owe my life to . . . 'Massachusetts' . . . If our hits were not making so much money, I would not have been able to buy first-class tickets. Most of the people who died in the train wreck were in the second-class compartments, which had no corridor to protect them. Our compartment window was broken. I tried to push Molly out first but she panicked. So I got out first and then lifted Molly out."

The compartment doors in their carriage were jammed, so Robin and Molly walked along the top of the train, which by then was lying on its side, opening doors and asking if anyone was badly hurt. Such was the shock that they didn't realise they themselves had been injured until they saw blood.

Five minutes after the first emergency calls, the first ambulance arrived. In all 33 ambulances and 28 London Fire Brigade appliances and vehicles came to the scene. Firemen put up ladders and helped the victims down from the top of the train.

"They pulled 24 people from the second-class carriage with railway lines through their bodies," Robin remembered. "Some were unconscious; some had no legs. I was lifting very badly injured people about three times my weight out of the compartments."

There was nothing anyone could do for one young man, hopelessly trapped in the twisted wreckage, whose screams of "don't let me die" eventually trailed off into silence.

"We were all put into ambulances and taken off to the local hospital . . . People were brought in badly cut, dying and suffering badly from shock. The three hours until my father arrived to collect us was a nightmare," Robin recalled.

Molly said, "I had this vision of the whole of the train being engulfed in flames. I was petrified." Her most vivid memory was pulling a young boy from the wreckage, "a real little Billy Bunter, and he started shouting, 'The driver's dead! The driver's dead!' "

Surrounded by all the carnage, that was the very last thing that Molly needed to hear at that particular moment. She probably regrets it now but, at the time she had admitted thinking, "I wanted to push him back in again."

Molly also remembered that Robin managed to stay calm until ambulances arrived, adding, "Robin has the knack of being able to cheer people up. The night of the train disaster was typical of that. There we were, sitting on top of an upturned carriage and like the others about us . . . badly shaken and aware of a complete shambles, when Robin suddenly remarked, 'All this, just to get to Battersea Funfair.' It eased the tension for everybody.

"But when we got to hospital," she continued, "he just broke up. When Mr Gibb was driving home from hospital, Rob could not stop crying from shock."

Hugh Gibb took the shaken young couple home with him to Buckinghamshire.

Years later, Maurice Gibb cited the incident as an example of what he calls "a twin thing" empathy with his brother, explaining to Timothy White in *Record Mirror*, "I definitely have a kind of ESP with him. When Robin was in the Hither Green train disaster, I said, 'There is something wrong. Something has happened to Robin.' And Barry said, 'What do you mean?' And then we found out. We watched the news, saw the train disaster and I said, 'Robin was on it.' We went to Hither Green Hospital and there was Robin – Molly was having X-rays – sitting there going, 'I didn't think I was going to see you guys again.' "

A gifted storyteller, Maurice turned Robin's realistic account of events into a tale of epic proportions. "He pulled six people out of a carriage, and he said, 'I never knew I had that much strength.' He laid them on the lawn, and they were all dead. I knew he had been through a strenuous thing – my arms were aching."

The next morning the NEMS offices issued a press statement: "Robin, after getting Molly and himself clear from the train, spent a lot of time helping with the rescue of other people, sustaining cuts and bruises. Molly had to have her shoulder X-rayed, and today she and Robin were put under sedation, suffering from shock."

Julie Barrett was ideally placed to assess the effect the incident had on Molly. "I knew Robin's wife Molly 'cause she was a receptionist with

NEMS at the time," she confirmed. "I really got on well with her, but she was quite a forceful character, even though she was very young at the time. She was a nice girl, always bubbly except for the morning after that awful train crash. She came into the office the very next day. She was a big strong girl anyway, it took a lot to ruffle her feathers, but she was shaking, she didn't know what she was doing." Little wonder that Molly was sent home, though why she had gone to work in such a state in the first place is a mystery. Perhaps her boyfriend had some influence.

"I had been told to spend three days in bed," Robin said later, "but that is the worst thing you can do. You should get straight back into reality."

Reality, for him, meant expressing his emotions through songwriting, with 'Really And Sincerely' the result. "I wrote that song on the first day and recorded it on the second," he explained. "It doesn't mention anything about a train crash but it does reflect the mood I was in."

The already sensitive 17-year-old became even more introspective in the weeks after the crash. "When that train crashed, the first thought which came into my mind was God . . . It's a very strange thing – that my first thought was of God. And that, more than anything else as far as I'm concerned, proves the existence of God – just something up there that's watching over us all the time. I've never been tremendously religious, going to church and all, but this crash has certainly made me think," he mused. "I mean, we've travelled on that line so many times and noticed the tremendous jolt just where we crashed before but it wasn't until that train went off the rails that I discovered things about myself I'd never been aware of before. I'd always thought that if I was involved in that sort of horrible situation, I'd just run from it all, but no, my first impulse on finding that I was safe except for scratches, was to run back to help the others. I just had to."

There were 550 passengers on the Hastings to London express that night and the death toll eventually reached 53, with 78 severely injured, making it at that time the fourth worst rail accident in British history.

Neither Robin nor Molly gave evidence at the official inquiry into what became known as the Hither Green Train Disaster, conducted by Colonel Denis McMullen, but other passengers mentioned the swaying of the train just before the derailment and the noise. The inquiry ruled that the cause of the derailment was a broken rail and neither the driver nor the guard was in any way responsible, but the events of that night would haunt survivors for years to come.

After the Paddington train crash on October 5, 1999, counsellors were called in to help the crash victims, their relatives, train company staff and rescue workers come to terms with the scale of the tragedy. Great Western wrote to all those taken to hospital offering individual or group counselling if requested. Its staff was also offered the sort of help which was widely taken up after the 1997 Southall tragedy, which occurred on the same stretch of track.

But for the survivors of Hither Green, there was no organised counselling;

in the late Sixties, this sort of psychological care was unheard of. Those crash victims who were injured were treated; those with minor injuries might be sedated to help them recover from the shock, but were then left to get on with their lives.

Robin seemed to adopt a rather fatalistic resignation, telling *Flip* magazine, "Since the crash I've stopped worrying too much about petty little things. Being brought close to death like that has made me realise how pointless it is to get too hung up on trifling matters. Things which seemed so important to me before have lost their significance.

"And another thing – there have been people I've considered friends and looked up to but even when they knew I'd been in this awful crash in which I could so easily have been killed, they never even asked after me, how I was, or anything. I'm certainly reassessing them now."

More than 30 years after the crash, Robin still has horrifying memories. "People had to be amputated on the railway line and I was talking to them as they were being injected. All I wanted to do was escape . . . I was covered in blood, had glass in my eyes and mouth. But when I got to the hospital, it was like a scene from World War I. I felt so guilty being there . . . Later, I got a delayed shock, didn't sleep for a long, long time afterwards . . .

"I went through a guilt trip of feeling people were hurt, so why wasn't I? I've travelled in trains since but I don't like it, always keep listening for a change in the sounds . . . I've learned to appreciate the little things in life. I still remember that train crash and thinking that I was going to die. I don't have nightmares about the accidents, but when I do think of them, a cold shiver runs up my spine."

Barry noticed the changes in his younger brother after the crash, but seemed almost dismissive when approached to comment. "Robin is very deep," he explained. " . . . It seems to have marked his character somewhat, because he hasn't been the same since. He's twice as serious about everything – he can't take life as a joke any more. And he's very quick to criticise everybody at every moment – he's usually right, but he's too fast to jump. Being his brother, I worry about him because he gets into terrible tempers and sometimes terrible moods . . . but that's Robin. He's a very nervous person now, but he writes better music!"

It was perhaps an attempt to make light of a sensitive subject, but there's a ring of authenticity there as well. There can be no doubt that an experience of the magnitude of Hither Green leaves its mark on all its victims.

★ ★ ★

On the evening of November 17 The Bee Gees switched on the specially designed Christmas illuminations in Carnaby Street, London's fashion centre, and dancing to other groups followed. As a mark of those less health-conscious times, *New Musical Express* announced that free soft drinks and cigarettes would be provided for the young fans in attendance.

The date also marked the announcement of their plans to film a Christmas television special, and the release of their latest single, 'World', which reached number nine on the British charts and gave them their first number one in both Holland and Switzerland.

Barry explained their new song by contrasting The Bee Gees' philosophy to that of the Fab Four. "I'm afraid that I can't agree with The Beatles recording of 'I Am The Walrus'," he said. "They never had to use dirty words before but they are using them now. What's the point? I didn't altogether agree with their flower-power scene either – it wasn't realistic. They were only escaping from reality which doesn't work. That's what our record 'World' is about. It goes, 'Now I've found that the world is round, and of course it rains everyday.' What we are saying is that you can't live in your own little world, because somewhere there is trouble – rain – and you must face up to it. It may be sun, flowers and beauty in England today, but it's rain and misery somewhere else. It's always raining somewhere in the world for somebody.

"I think that The Beatles did themselves a lot of harm by admitting they took LSD. I think they were living in a fool's paradise. You don't need drugs if you're happy, and you're happy if you're working hard at something you love. I love my work, every aspect of it, and therefore I don't need drugs. I don't mind doing picture sessions and interviews, I enjoy them and pop stars who complain or don't turn up for them are fools, they are only hurting themselves. We've got a long way to go and I won't be content until we're there, which means I'll have to work day and night."

Maurice added that they try to avoid flower power and prefer "fantasy clothes". "We'll be wearing that type of thing when we play at the Saville Theatre on November 19. We're having a 30-piece orchestra and a hundred extras . . ."

"We're all very excited about the Saville show," Barry declared. "It's now beginning to take shape and it's really going to be something that people have never seen before."

The following day it was announced in *Melody Maker* that The Bee Gees would perform a special concert to benefit victims of the Hither Green train crash but, in spite of genuine intent on the brothers' part, this never took place.

Just one day later, The Bee Gees made their triumphant return to the Saville Theatre, this time as headliners, with support acts Tony Rivers & The Castaways, The Flowerpot Men and The Bonzo Dog Doo Dah Band. They played two shows that night, with compere Tony Hall announcing to the audience at the second that the crowd from the first house were so knocked out they were still dancing in the street outside.

"The Bee Gees put on one of the most exciting stage shows I've seen," Robert Stigwood said. "They have a tremendous versatility, an unbelievable professionalism. It's impossible to overstate their international potential both as performers and composers."

Barbara Gibb remembers watching the show in rather exclusive company.

"We sat in the box with Paul McCartney and Jane Asher," she said. "He was raving about The Bee Gees. When we came out after the show, all the girls were outside, and they all pushed past Paul to get to the boys. And Paul said to me, 'Oh well. It's their turn now, we've had our day.'"

The very next day the group was off to Paris for three days filming of five television shows, followed by a trip to Bremen to appear on *Beat Club*. It was also announced that negotiations were nearly completed for Spike Milligan to write the screenplay for the *Lord Kitchener's Little Drummer Boys* film, replacing Mike Pratt.

The storyline of the film was beginning to take shape, as Barry revealed. "We're playing five little lads who get caught up in the Boer War . . . We get sort of shipped out from London to the war. I play a bank clerk who gets chased around by a lot of birds and eventually has to leave the country. Colin is a pickpocket, which figures! Robin and Maurice are street photographers – real sharp characters. And Vince is a diamond miner, already working in South Africa when the rest of us turn up there to fight the good fight. We try to get out of the army – actually, we desert the army at the front. Then we run into the enemy, but we don't know it's the enemy. We're trying to make this film as farcical as possible."

Barry said that the movie was all to be filmed on location in either Africa or Spain. Filming was scheduled to begin the following May, but in the meantime, the group planned to rectify their apparent neglect of Britain. "We've been filming TV shows and travelling abroad so much, it's just been impossible to do much here," Barry said. "The dates we have played have all been great. We found that all types of people were coming to see us. From teenyboppers right up to adults – and this is exactly what we want. We want everyone to come and see us – not just one particular age group.

"I think the visual impression given by a group on stage is perhaps more important in some ways than the sound they are laying down. The glamour started to go out of pop when groups began wearing jeans and any old clothes on stage. We believe a pop group is essentially an entertainment. We have to project something that's entertaining visually and musically. We spend a lot of time before a gig deciding what to wear. We want to give a good show for an audience who have paid, so we can go back there again."

By the beginning of December plans to release 'Swan Song' as their next single had been dropped. However, the change of decision didn't influence the producers of an Austrian TV special who commissioned an out of doors film where the group just about managed to convince viewers that they were as insulated by their coats as the swans were by their feathers and down.

In the pop music business, there is an unwritten rule that the latest teen heart-throb should appear to fans to be available, so when the news broke weeks later that Barry Gibb was married, young hearts were broken. The problem wasn't just that Barry was married and had kept it a secret; he had specifically denied being married.

To be fair, Barry had given broad hints about the end of "a long and deep relationship" in earlier interviews, adding, "The reason we split up was, I suppose, 50-50 between us . . . I can't see it being patched up. The kind of person I am – obsessed with my career – it runs my whole life." Once the news was out, he seemed relieved to unburden himself.

"I admit I kept the marriage a secret because I didn't want to spoil my image," Barry confessed. "It seemed the best way. Since the group became a success, the pressure has been enormous. I'm glad it is now out in the open. I could not have taken her with me as a girlfriend because if we had split up over here, she would have been on her own, so we got married three months before we left and that was the biggest mistake I ever made in my life.

"Everything was fine for a while. We thought we were in love but these things never last unless you are really solid . . . There is such a thing as loving someone and being in love. You can love another person but that doesn't mean you are lovers.

"Show business is one of the biggest destroyers of a marriage there is . . . After we arrived in Britain, I was working most nights and she would hardly ever see me . . . but show business is my life. I am in love with my career and I mean *in love*. I would come home at three and then we would fight until six and then I had to be back in the studio again.

"It went on until I didn't know what day it was and I was falling asleep at the piano. There would be arguing as to where I had been. It was destroying me physically. Destroying me because I could not sleep," he continued.

"On tours, I couldn't take my wife, and we were spending lengthy spells in America. We were incompatible as regards horoscopes and stars and I believe in those things. It took just a year to come to a head.

"I really think we were both unaware of what marriage would mean to us. I told her what it could be like, but she didn't know that she wouldn't be able to go around with me. I couldn't take her with me because she made me nervous."

The stress of trying to live in a marriage he increasingly viewed as a mistake had evidently become intolerable for him. "I had a mental, not a nervous breakdown," he said. "I couldn't take any more. When people start throwing things around and shouting at each other . . . it got so I would lie awake at night. My hair was falling out and my head was falling off. She was the same.

"We were in the flat, and I think I had just come back from America. She would question me. She mistrusted me, with good reasons. I didn't do things like that, but I was a pop artist, and pop artists are notorious for that kind of thing because there are so many groupies around. On the final row, I was bursting for freedom and I just walked out. I left her but I did not desert her," he admitted.

"The marriage lasted just over a year. I think we were just too young. The parting was mutual. We will just wait a couple of years and then get divorced. It is all unfortunate."

Despite Barry's protestations of innocence regarding groupies, Maureen may have had good reason to distrust him. While his relationship with Lynda turned out to be a lasting one, Lynda recalled that at one point their relationship almost broke down because of previous dalliances with groupies. "After I was living with him, the girls used to come to the door, and they were all engaged! One time, Barry was doing this TV thing. I was at home cleaning the flat, so I'm in a scruffy old dress, no make-up. Just how you generally are doing housework. The doorbell rings. It was the penthouse apartment, and the door wouldn't open unless I buzzed the person in. You could look through this eye and see who it was. I saw this chick there and thought, 'Oh?' because she looked as if she was expected. I opened the door and said, 'Can I help you?' So she says [in a Swedish accent], 'Oh yes, I have come to see Barry.' I knew there was some press expected that afternoon so I said, 'Come on in, he won't be long.'"

According to Lynda, the girl made herself at home, tossing her coat over a chair, lying back and saying, "Barry and I, we are so in love."

Lynda was seething but managed to ask levelly, "Oh really?" only to be told, "Oh, we had such a wonderful time at the *Top Of The Pops*."

"I said, 'Oh, you did, did you?' . . . She said, 'Are you the girl who answers the phone and does things for Barry?' I said, 'Well, you could say that.' She says, 'How long have you worked for Barry?' I said, 'Well, I've just stopped,'" Lynda recounted.

Lesley's husband was at that time working for Barry as his personal assistant, so he took the call when Lynda phoned to speak to Barry. "Keith . . . said, 'Lynda, you sound a bit upset.' 'Who is this girl?' I screamed. 'What are you talking about?' he says. I say, 'The girl who had such a wonderful time with Barry last night.' He says, 'Oh no. Are you upset?' I said, screaming, 'Am I *upset*?'"

She told Keith that she was packing her bags to leave when Barry came to the phone. "I said, 'Barry, there's some Swedish girl telling me about you and her last night.' He says, 'Oh, she arrived at *Top Of The Pops* last night. It wasn't my fault. It had happened on a tour before you were around. I said, like I usually said, 'When you come to England, come to see me.' I said, 'I don't believe you.'"

Lynda went back to her packing, as Barry and Keith rushed to the penthouse flat. "After that incident," Lynda said, "Barry started taking me on tour. He said, 'You're coming on tour; then you can't get misled that there's anything going on.' I said okay and unpacked my bags."

From then on, Lynda became a fixture of The Bee Gees' tours.

★ ★ ★

Julie Barrett won't forget the NEMS office Christmas party of 1967 in a hurry. "I remember Maurice drinking quite a lot. He had his cousin Chris who was his chauffeur at the time, and Maurice volunteered that I could have a lift home. We were going from Brook Street, and Maurice had this

Rolls-Royce and we drove along, and obviously they decided that we couldn't go all the way to Wandsworth, which is where I lived at the time. So they stopped at a bus stop, and I had to get out of this big posh car, and then stand and wait for a bus."

Not one to bear a grudge, Julie looks back on the memory of this lack of consideration with fondness. "I liked Maurice," she confirmed, citing the group's sudden rise to fame as a factor. "When I look back on it now, they had far too much to contend with, they were very young."

After all the stresses of their personal and professional lives, it seems little wonder that later that month both Barry and Robin collapsed from nervous exhaustion on a flight from Australia to Turkey.

The two brothers had left England for Australia on December 23, "But due to the time difference we arrived on Christmas Day," Barry explained. "We missed Christmas Eve altogether!"

With Robert Stigwood's promotional flair, there was no way that the boys would slip quietly into the country, unnoticed by the media. "It was supposed to be a holiday," Barry said, "but there were people waiting for us to arrive – press and television people were wanting us all the time. Not that we mind the interviews – it's great that somebody is taking an interest."

The boys did manage to celebrate Christmas with Robert Stigwood's family, but the Australian pop journalists continued to focus attention on the returning pop heroes. "We went on to Sydney," Barry continued, "where it was just press and photographers morning, noon and night. We were beginning to get very tired and weary, but we were loving every minute of it . . . When we left Australia, we had had barely any sleep."

Nor would they find any relaxation on their return flight, as both were tense passengers. "We just cannot sleep on planes. Robin is as nervous as a kitten. You hear of so many crashes . . . I know that you can say there is more chance of a crash on the roads, but it can happen in the air, too. Or on a train, like Robin in the Hither Green tragedy. He could well have been killed.

"I hate flying. It just worries me because it's not a natural thing to do. We were due to stop in Istanbul, anyway, but we had been flying for 28 hours solid, and we were really fagged out. About an hour or so before we got there, we just couldn't keep awake any longer.

"Robert advised that we should go to hospital for a check-up. They told us there that we were suffering from mental and physical exhaustion. So we decided to rest up. There wasn't anything else we could do."

Maurice, on the other hand, was ebullient. His relationship with pop star Lulu had become public knowledge, and the pair seemed to be the perfect show business couple. "Lulu and I met on the *Top Of The Pops* TV show three months ago, and then at the Saville Theatre in London last month," he told *Disc*. "We got on very well and that evening went with a crowd of people to the Speakeasy Club. Lulu admired a ring I was wearing and I gave it to her to try on. Then she couldn't get it off, so I thought, 'Might as well get her phone number to arrange for the return of the ring . . .'

"We've been seeing one another nearly every night since then. It's difficult because we're both working so hard. It means grabbing a few hours when we can. Marriage? I think we are a bit young for that."

The Bee Gees finished the year off with their Christmas Eve special *How On Earth?* filmed by ABC TV ten days earlier at Liverpool Anglican Cathedral. The programme, broadcast at 6.35 p.m., featured special seasonal material such as their own composition 'Thank You (For Christmas)' – recorded in the studio on December 1 – as well as their own arrangements of the traditional Christmas carols 'Silent Night' and 'Hark The Herald Angels Sing'. The English folk group The Settlers were also part of the proceedings which were conducted by The Very Reverend Edward H. Patey, Dean of the Cathedral.

Before the concert, the TV crew took background footage including some where children walked into the main hall, miming to some music. One of the boys, Dave Wyatt, remembers that during a break in filming, he and a friend, John Davies, decided to explore the building and wandered down some steps where they encountered two of the Gibbs having a cup of tea. They chatted for a couple of minutes. Later that evening, after the performance, Dave recalled thinking that this new group were good singers but "would never be as good as The Beatles".

Perhaps unseen by the group, the progressive nature of Patey's service attracted considerable hostility both before and after the event. Not only did it feature one of the top pop groups of the day, it also had DJ Kenny Everett reading the Gospel in scouse,★ and pictures of teenage girls dancing and screaming in front of their idols, and embracing their boyfriends. There were also reports of beer drinking and smoking.

Although the show was considered controversial at the time, the Dean should now be thought of more as saint than sinner for his innovative ideas, as many religious programmes nowadays use rock music as part of their format. Indeed, it would be a good few years again until groups like The Resurrection Band and Petra became accepted as part of Christian music as a whole. The Gibbs themselves probably got it just about right when they sang . . . "Every Christian lion–hearted man will show you".

★ Dialect of inhabitants of the Liverpool region.

12

HORIZONTAL

JANUARY 1968 began with a promotional trip to the United States. Los
Angeles Police Department were on alert in anticipation of a Beatles-type
reception, and special security arrangements were being put in place even as
the group boarded their plane for the long flight, with bodyguards waiting
for them on their arrival. Police were there in their dozens to hold back the
anticipated crowds, and police cars were standing by to convoy them to their
hotel and to public appearances. Thankfully things went according to plan
and, on this occasion, there were no noteworthy incidents.

Shortly afterwards, The Bee Gees made their first ever appearance on
American television on *The Smothers Brothers Show* on CBS. Tommy
Smothers had first encountered The Bee Gees on a trip to London and
immediately became a friend as well as a fan. On the show that evening,
Tommy wore a shirt which Maurice had bought for him at The Beatles'
Apple boutique.

In an interview around that time, Colin Petersen spoke of the contrasting
dispositions of the brothers, saying, "They have totally different personalities. Robin is a very temperamental and very highly strung person. His
music is his whole life and he is highly sensitive to criticism. Barry is a very
easy-going and receptive type. He adapts himself to the situations he finds
himself in at the time. He is very interested in the potential acting possibilities of the group. I think he would like to be a film star more than a singer.
Maurice is closer to my attitudes and ideas. He has the same kind of humour
as I have. We have other common interests like playing chess. He's the kind
of guy who will come over and give you a hand washing the car. As brothers, they really have very little in common, except the feeling that they are
living for the day."

Barry agreed with Colin about the differences between him and his
brothers. "Although I write songs with Robin, I'm the complete opposite of
him in a way," he said. "I can take life seriously and as a joke, because I
believe that the moment we're born, we're dying, and there's no use going
through it looking miserable! If you think you can do better, then fight like
hell to do it! But don't let yourself be dragged down by your own moods –
just enjoy what you've got.

" 'Mattress-back' Gibb, which is Robin, is currently getting out of bed.

Probably got his second sock on by now . . . I wouldn't say he's slow – I'd just say he was dead. Actually, he's probably halfway dressed and having some breakfast, and then he's coming straight in here, which at this point you'll be amazed! This is typical – it happens every morning. And night."

On the other hand, Barry felt that he and Maurice had a little more in common, adding, "Maurice is a Gay Young Blade . . . Maurice likes going out and having fun. Which is like I am – I like to go out and have a lot of fun . . . Maurice likes to have a good time too . . . I'm not the raver Maurice is – Maurice would stay out all night every night if it were humanly possible. But it's not, so he doesn't."

The rest of the Gibb family added their comments to Barry's summary. "Maurice just lives for today," said Hugh Gibb. "He's the one of the three of them that likes a bit of night life now and again. He likes to have a good time, and he doesn't worry about anything. He's everybody's friend – he's got a super sense of humour, and he's so talkative. Barry and Robin are the two artistic ones, Maurice is much more practical – he takes after me more . . . If I had something important to be done, I'd ask Maurice because he is reliable – the other two are dreamers."

"As soon as you meet Maurice, you know him," Barbara added. "He's a very outward person. He doesn't have a care in the world. Maurice spends his money, whereas Robin hoards it. Maurice will spend until he's told to stop. Maurice is the only one to have a drink now and again."

Ten-year-old Andy came right to the point, saying, "Maurice is . . . most friendly and plays with me when he comes home. I don't like Robin – he doesn't talk to me."

Elder sister Lesley described Robin as "very difficult to get to know . . . very reserved. We went to Rome and he only came out of his room once. It isn't that he's unsociable – he's just like that. You have to be content to do what he wants to do, otherwise you have to do things on your own."

"He's a fanatic about his food," Barbara said. "He always inspects his knife and fork to make sure they're clean; many's the time he's sent a fork back to me because he thinks it's dirty. He's more artistic than the others in every way. He has got beautiful hands and really looks after them. His nails are long and slender, and in general he's very particular about his person. He uses his hands to express himself; if you cut them off he couldn't talk. He wears suits all the time; he'll never wear anything casual even in hot weather."

"He's basically lazy, but not with his music," Hugh asserted. "When it comes to anything physical, he can't be bothered. If there was a wallet on the ground with £100 in it, he'd walk over it rather than bend down to pick it up. He's a bit of a hypochondriac too. He worries about his health and if he gets a little pain, he thinks it's the beginning of something awful.

"Another thing about him, he always thinks he's right. It's just his generation, I think, although the other boys aren't like it. Maybe he'll secretly know he's wrong, but he's just so stubborn he won't give in . . ."

While in the US The Bee Gees made an appearance on NBC's *Rowan & Martin's Laugh-In,* and on January 27 they played two concerts at the Anaheim Convention Center in Orange County, California, each to an appreciative audience of around 8,000. The fee was $25,000, an astonishing amount at that time.

Ann Moses, editor of *Tiger Beat* and LA correspondent for *New Musical Express,* wrote, "The Bee Gees gave Los Angeles *the* greatest pop show it has ever witnessed! The LA audience, which is usually rudely blasé (to the point of booing Jimi Hendrix on The Mamas and Papas concert last summer), showed their appreciation and complete admiration by giving The Bee Gees a standing ovation at the close of their second show.

"The Bee Gees followed the same format as at their Saville show and worked beautifully with the 30-piece orchestra, with whom they had only rehearsed twice. The audience couldn't resist clapping wildly at the intro of each familiar tune."

The concert was noticeable for the inclusion of their version of 'Gilbert Green', a song which they never released themselves, but which would crop up in occasional performances during the following year.

Barry explained their decision to play in Los Angeles alone, rather than doing a full concert tour. "Our manager thinks we should limit our appearances here. I think this is not to overexpose ourselves. We have been very lucky that the Americans have accepted our records, and the fastest way to spoil this would be to come into America and work all over the country for about six weeks. Then they'd say, 'Oh yes, we've seen them. We're not interested.'"

The trip was arranged to coincide with the release of their latest single, 'Words', written especially for the soundtrack to a movie called *The Mini Mob.*

Georgie Fame had a starring role in the Robert Amran directed film, but it never actually gained release. "It might not have been good enough!" speculated Barry. "I don't know whether it was edited, I never saw a completed version of it. It was all rather embarrassing – most of it was shot by the river at Maidenhead, I think. We were meant to be kidnapped on a boat."

Turning to The Bee Gees' music for the aborted project, Georgie Fame considered, "I think they did write about half a dozen tunes. At that time it was considered a good move to try and get into movies. I always liked their harmonising, their vocals, and Barry Gibb's written a lot of good tunes. It wasn't my kind of music, but I admired them, especially the high voices. They had a very distinctive sound which is important if you want to make inroads. You could always tell The Bee Gees apart from anybody else because of their own individual sound."

In the States, the film was given a good deal of advance publicity. Re-titled *The Mini-Affair,* promotional flyers asked, "Can the country that survived the Vikings, the Romans, Napoleon, two World Wars, and The Great Train Robbery, survive . . . The Mini-Affair?" Maybe, all things considered, it was just as well that the question would remain unanswered, although it is a shame that with the exception of 'Words' and another performed by The Majority called 'All Our Christmases', the remaining Gibb compositions have never been heard.

Another film to which they were invited to contribute compositions was *Pippi Longstocking*, inspired by the storybook legend, first published in Sweden in 1945. Three songs, 'I Can Lift A Mountain', 'Four Faces West' and 'Treacle Brown', were written specifically for the project but the project was aborted – although a non-Gibb related version would finally appear in 1970. The first song would be reworked by The Bee Gees for possible inclusion on their own 1970 album, while the other two titles were given to a young friend from Australia, Lori Balmer, for her 1968 UK Polydor single.

For well over a year, until the release of *Best Of Bee Gees,* 'Words' was available only on a single. There was a six-day halt in sales due to an export injunction in the UK, but the single still reached number one in the charts in Germany, The Netherlands and Switzerland.

Vocally, it was a solo spotlight for Barry. Robin does not appear to sing on the song at all, the first Bee Gees single not to feature both of them audibly. Yet it was Robin who offered the story behind the song. " 'Words' . . . reflects a mood," he explained. "It was written after an argument. Barry had been arguing with someone, I had been arguing with someone, and happened to be in the same mood. [The arguments were] about absolutely nothing. They were just words. That is what the song is all about; words can make you happy or words can make you sad."

The recording sessions for this particular track were especially memorable for two other members of the group. "I remember the [first] session so clearly," Barry recalled. "Robin and I were in the studios at 9 o'clock in the morning, and Robin kept on falling asleep over the piano. I wanted him to write the piano part of the song and play it because I'm not much of a pianist, but he just couldn't keep his eyes open, so I ended up doing it myself."

'Words' was also the showcase for a new piano sound, as Maurice explained. "We accidentally discovered the sound on 'Words'. When we were recording [it], after everyone had gone to lunch, I was sitting at the piano mucking about and I wrote a riff. I went upstairs and switched on the mike for the piano, and then I started playing about with the knobs in front of me. When I played the tape back, I had all these incredible compressed piano noises . . .

"Mike Claydon at IBC Studios, who engineered all our records, then said, 'What the hell was that?' when he heard the piano sound. 'Come up here and listen to this sound.' It was just compression, but he didn't know what to call it then. I think he called it 'limited' . . . It made the piano sound like it was about 40 pianos playing at the same time and very, very thick. In 'Words' it was very beautiful but that sound on it made it sound like the LA Symphony on it. If you listen to all our records, that piano sound is on it."

Damon Lyon-Shaw has more to say on this matter. "I was the one that actually devised it . . . Mike Claydon was the one who took the credit for it, but I was actually piddling around at the time as his junior. On the mixer at the time, we had compressors . . . Maurice was playing the piano at the time, just piddling around [and] I started feeding the piano into a series of these compressors and then screwed them up until he got this lovely metallic sort of sucking sound, and that was the birth of that sound. Maurice . . . assumed it was Michael, so he took the credits."

Another IBC engineer, John Pantry, offered to put things in a proper perspective. "Well, Damon didn't make the compressor/limiter, and my memory is that we all used to use that sound once we discovered what it did to piano notes. As to who got there first is open to debate. The sound was unique because it was a home-made device that was made by a guy called Denis King."

Following a week after the release of the single, the album *Horizontal* seemed to get mixed reactions from fans. It has a darker tone than most Bee Gees albums, both in the lyrics and what was called a heavy musical sound. Nothing is light and cheerful on this disc, not even the "nonsense" songs, in which lemons trying to forget and the crowd being proud to see Harry Braff win the race have an almost desperate sound to them. The Bee Gees' first priority was to convey a consistent mood and from this point of view the album is a success. They also found a sound that is distinctly theirs, and not like any other group. This was the last Bee Gees album for some time that critics didn't accuse of being lightweight.

The American release of the album differed slightly in the sleeve design, featuring a larger unadorned version of the front cover photo, compared to the "framed" photo on the sleeve released elsewhere.

Compared to *Bee Gees' 1st*, the songs sound a little closer to the band's live arrangements, despite Maurice's overdubs. Another difference this time out was a greater reliance on solo vocals on most of the songs. Barry and Robin sound distinctively different here, and as strong as they ever had to date.

Bill Shepherd was closely involved in the creative process and probably served to give the Gibb brothers critical feedback on the songs they were writing, as well as to assist in realising the sound they wanted. Bill's "accompaniment" is not just added to finished tracks but an integral part of the arrangement. The demos from this period that have leaked out show full arrangements for orchestra just like the released songs. They seem to have recorded all the better songs first and decided what to release afterwards, a highly unusual method for that time or this.

The recordings were actually made between July 17 and November 29 specifically for the Robert Stigwood Organisation who officially determined which to send to Polydor for release and which to shop as demos for RSO's publishing arm Abigail Music.

A fans' favourite was 'Harry Braff'. "It was written during a very, very –

165

what shall we call it? – drunken night," Barry admitted. "The guy who used to be the president of Polydor Records in England had invited us out to his house. This guy could really knock it back, you know? So we had no choice. We spent the whole day and night at this guy's house and he was legless. And we were all legless by the end of the night. 'Harry Braff' came from that. In the middle of the night, coming back from this guy's house, we went and woke Robert up in his London flat, and got him out of bed at three in the morning, so we could sing him this song. It's amazing how young and enthusiastic you can be," he laughed. "You think it means something to somebody else, but it probably didn't mean a thing to anybody." Easily the most strident song on the album, it was sung by all three brothers in unison for a change, with horns as well as strings, and was first recorded as far back as April 26 according to archive sources. While it's the one Bee Gees song that Vince Melouney professed to hate, it does have at least one famous fan: another Manchester musician who found musical success with his brother, Noel Gallagher of Oasis.

Horizontal is considered by some to be the heaviest album ever recorded by The Bee Gees, due for the most part to an increased influence asserted by Vince and Colin, which didn't always sit well with Robin. "I was right into the blues," admitted Vince, "and while Colin – who was essentially into jazz – and Mo liked it, Robin and Robert certainly didn't. I particularly had issues with Robin about it and, in the end, they were right because they weren't a 'blues band.' "

All three singles had B-sides not on the album: 'Barker Of The UFO', a short Barry tune featuring tuba, probably a reference to the London club; 'Sir Geoffrey Saved The World', a 'Penny Lane'-like tune with Robin singing about The Clean Air Act; and 'Sinking Ships', which appears to have solo lines by all three. The first two were probably just too peculiar for the album, while the last is structurally a little too close to the song 'Horizontal', with three verses and a false fade at the end of verse two.

Barry explained the group's approach to making records. "Firstly, I think we give the public melodies," he said. "And secondly, we don't attempt to preach at people. There are so many groups which try to change the world. We, I think, are simply a pop group which writes all its own songs. We write songs about people and situations – we tell stories in our songs, but we don't give sermons."

He shrugged off any suggestion that he was an unusually perceptive young man. "I assume that some people have it and others don't. I've always been interested in people and I suppose that helps. Some people are sensitive and sentimental while others aren't – it's the same type of thing. I don't think it's necessarily because we've seen more than some people our age. It's more a case of being interested in the other bloke – a sort of understanding, if you like."

By the end of 1967, the group had begun making plans for a film or television feature to be called *Cucumber Castle*, and a set of further songs copyright early in 1968 may have been intended for this, or possibly for *The Mini Mob*. One of the songs, 'Turning Tide' (written by Barry and Robin), appeared eventually on the album of that name in 1970, but credited to Barry and Maurice. Another one, 'End Of My Song', similar in style to 'The Change Is Made', was re-recorded in 1969 but not used. Additional titles are known but the songs never appeared.

Coinciding with the release of the *Horizontal* album was a Scandinavian tour, with concerts in Copenhagen (where they concurrently had four records in the Danish Top 20), Stockholm and Gothenberg.

On their return to Britain, The Bee Gees recorded their third BBC session at the Playhouse Theatre, in London's Northumberland Avenue, utilising an orchestra of 19 under the direction of Bill Shepherd. All songs performed were from the new album: 'Birdie Told Me', 'With The Sun In My Eyes', 'The Earnest Of Being George' and 'And The Sun Will Shine'. The session, again produced by Bernie Andrews, was broadcast on Radio One's *Top Gear* presented by John Peel, on February 18.

On February 27, The Bee Gees, backed by the 17-piece Massachusetts String Orchestra, began their first tour of Germany with two performances at Hamburg Musikhalle. The group were supported on the tour by Procol Harum, who had topped the British charts the previous year with 'A Whiter Shade Of Pale'.

Molly Hullis recalled that, "Germans were wilder than the fans in England at the heights of Beatlemania. But I also think the police in Germany antagonised the fans with guard dogs and guns. There was one point where they hosed the kids down to sort of clear them off the street. They were great concerts, very wild."

The rigorous tour schedule took them to 11 venues in as many days with 18 concerts played, finishing with a brace of shows at the Braunschewig Stadhalle.

With only a day off, the group was off to Switzerland, for what Maurice described as the scariest tour date. "There were over 5,000 kids at the airport at Zurich," he recalled. "The entire ride to Bern, the kids were waving Union Jacks. When we got to the hotel, the police weren't there to meet us, and the kids crushed the car. We were inside and the windows were all getting smashed in, and we were on the floor . . ."

Talk to Barry about it and the number of fans quadruple. "I was terrified that day . . . when 20,000 kids suddenly surrounded our car," he said. "They climbed on top, and we had to put our feet up against the roof to keep it from collapsing. I said to Robin, 'What do we do now?' and he said, 'Sing, you fool!' "

The police eventually turned up but, "The incident had a terrible ending," as Maurice remembered, uncharacteristically solemn. "With all those kids around us, the driver suddenly moved the car forward and one girl's leg was broken and another girl was thrown through a plate glass window and killed."

"We tried to get to her," Robin added, "but the police just waved us off. They were very cold about it." It was a sobering finish to the tour, which drew to a close the following day.

Although Robin and Maurice apparently left the scene convinced that the girl had been killed, there were no reports of a fatality in the newspapers and even today, Dick Ashby is of the belief that she recovered from her injuries.

In any event, the brothers were obviously upset by the incident, and Julie Barrett solemnly recalls the next time that she saw the group. "I can remember them coming into the office, and they were quite devastated by that and very down about it all. It was as if they felt very responsible for what had happened."

Meanwhile, plans for *Lord Kitchener's Little Drummer Boys* continued. Johnny Speight, best known as the *'Til Death Us Do Part* dramatist, became the latest writer commissioned by Robert Stigwood to write the screenplay for the film, following Mike Pratt and Spike Milligan.

Spike Milligan, meanwhile, was soliciting contributions for an album to benefit the World Wildlife Fund. The Bee Gees and The Beatles were among those who pledged songs, with 'Marley Purt Drive' and John Lennon's 'Across The Universe' making their débuts on this highly collectable album. The Bee Gees' contribution, originally conceived as 'Marley Purt Drive (Area Code 213)' would reappear the following year on the *Odessa* double album.

They made a brief promotional trip back to the United States, making their début appearance on *The Ed Sullivan Show* on CBS where they performed 'Words' and 'To Love Somebody'. "Promotion is all important," Barry commented. "Not in the matter of gimmicks and stunts but in doing the right work at the right time. You have to have a basic talent and also the right promotion. We do what we think boosts our career – avoid that danger of sitting back and saying, 'Right, we're number one so there's nothing more we can do.'"

The Bee Gees were flying high, which made what happened next seem inexplicable. Although it reached number five in Germany (following three consecutive number ones), their next single only reached a disappointing 25 in the British charts and a devastating 57 in the American equivalent.

"We've been attacked for apparently never changing our style," Barry said. "Well, remember that we write all our own material. We try for unusual song lyrics, but obviously we have a bias towards one particular style of song. Our single . . . was going to be 'The Singer Sang His Song' as the A-side, but we heeded the criticism. We switched to 'Jumbo', which is a distinct change of direction for us. A simple sort of idea – every kid has an imaginary pet animal – but scored differently. As it happened, a lot of people thought we were wrong to change and said they preferred 'Singer' even if it was on the same lines as earlier ones . . . But when we study other groups . . . we know the dangers of staying on one direction."

"The only time Robert was wrong was when he said to release 'Jumbo' as the A-side instead of the flipside, 'The Singer Sang His Song'," Maurice added. "We thought *that* was going to be the A-side, but Atlantic convinced Robert, and Robert had been convinced by Vince and Colin 'cause they liked playing a bit more bluesy stuff. Robert said, 'Never again will I let anybody talk me into anything.'"

"As far as record sales go, 'Jumbo' was aimed at the American market," Stigwood explained. "I also now realise it was a mistake to release it as an A-side in Britain because the public still want big, emotional ballads from the boys."

Strangely enough, all copies of the British release traced thus far, *do* have 'The Singer Sang His Song' as the A-side. One possibility is that, at the very last minute, Robert realised his mistake and, in Britain at least, destroyed the original pressings. Vince Melouney lends credence to this theory. "It was always Stigwood's call. The only exception was 'Jumbo' where we pushed for that. Robert wanted the other side as the A-side. When that started to go wrong, he quickly tried to make 'Singer Sang' as the A-side."

It was left to Robin Gibb to have the final word on what he considered a dismal failure. As Nairobi was the proposed location for the filming of *Lord Kitchener's Little Drummer Boys*, he had gone on holiday there to familiarise himself with the country. "Thank you in Nairobi is 'jumbo,'" he related. "I remember getting off the plane – I was very disappointed that this record's success was nil – and this big sort of Nairobian came up to me and he took my bags. I tipped him and he said, 'Jumbo.' And I said, 'Don't rub it in.'" It seems a shame to spoil a good story but, in fact, "jambo" is Swahili in origin, and means "hello".

Meanwhile, Maurice's love life had taken a turn for the worse after he confided to a music journalist that Lulu had made a Leap Year proposal to him during a telephone call from her American tour. When his remarks were published, an irate Lulu declared that their three-month romance was officially over. "It's absolute rubbish," she told reporters. "I would never propose to anyone. Our friendship is over."

In America, Lulu was receiving rave reviews for her appearances at Hollywood's famous Coconut Grove, where she was introduced on stage by Tommy Smothers, of The Smothers Brothers. Critics for the *Los Angeles Times* raved that, "This mini-gowned young woman is another amazing production of modern show business. A stage presence unusual in one so youthful," and the *Hollywood Reporter* said, "She has an unaffected charm which is contagious, and the capacity to approach the meaning of her lyrics with a quality of communication rare for singers in the rock pop genre."

Lulu was later seen out on the town with Davy Jones of The Monkees, whom she described as one of the nicest boys she'd ever known.

There was a certain irony to this as Davy Jones was already a good friend of Maurice, who took the news hard. However, Barry told reporters, "He's got over it now and doesn't care any more, but I was in the room when Maurice was talking to her on the phone to the States about the row over his saying she had proposed to him . . . except that he didn't get a word in edgeways! He just didn't get a chance to speak. She monopolised the conversation and just wouldn't listen to him.

"It seems to me that if they can argue halfway round the world, there can't be much of a romance going in the first place," he added. "If there was, surely they would wait and talk it out together when she got home?"

Although Barry insisted he had fully recovered, Maurice professed to be devastated by the end of the relationship. "I was so much in love with her that I didn't give a damn for myself," he said. "I didn't wash my hair for weeks. I drank rather too much . . ."

Eventually, Maurice turned to man's best friend for company. After seeing Dave Dee's Pyrenean mountain dog, he bought one of his own: a fluffy, white giant of a puppy which he named Aston de Maurice de Beaudier. "I used to sit and watch TV with him asleep on my lap . . . Aston was the only friend I had," he added plaintively.

Barry was so taken with Aston that a few days later, he became the second Pyrenean mountain dog owner in the Gibb family when he bought one he christened Barnaby.

Maurice was soon seen around town with a Hungarian pop singer, Sarolta Zalatnay, in what appeared to be a rebound romance, but he later insisted, "I'm not a Casanova and it's all most unfortunate. I've never been publicised to be available. Because of the stories of my affairs with Lulu and Sarolta, the fans feel, 'Oh, we won't bother about Maurice because he's always got a steady girl.'

"So I seem to be the Gibb brother who gets left out in the cold. The teenyboppers come to see Barry because he's pretty and got the sex image, while Robin's got the voice and all I do is stand there and play my guitar. I'll have to change all that. I'll have to learn to keep my mouth shut. That supposed affair with Sarolta, for instance. It was a publicity idea for her and I agreed to play along." Good thing then that the press were unable to substantiate rumours that linked Maurice with "Tiger" Mathis.

Maurice claimed to have little time for romance anyway, adding, "So many groups fail because, having got quite well known, they decide to spend all their time in the clubs. Work pours in and they can't handle it because of late-night drinking. I went to bed at 11.30 p.m. the other night, which is incredible for me. But we worked for 11 years to get where we are today, and I want to take our work seriously so that, later on, I'll be able to appreciate the money we've made."

★ ★ ★

On March 27, 1968, The Bee Gees began their 26-date UK tour with a concert at London's Royal Albert Hall which, according to Robin, "had everything on there except The Bee Gees. It was like a Roman spectacular, a bit overdone. But it was exciting . . . Robert's usual flair for putting on a show."

"It was a particular stage of their career, and I wanted to create a big event," Stigwood explained. "These boys are brilliantly talented and their music shows this. Big things are happening for them, and therefore there is no reason why their affairs shouldn't be treated with a certain amount of flamboyance."

With Robin's introduction, "We'll now sing for you something we have never recorded," the group went into the opening strains of 'I've Decided To Join The Air Force.'

"They did that once through," Stigwood continued, "and then I had the doors of the hall open in all different directions, and this Air Force band marched through the audience playing a reprise of the song. I had a choir of 40 or 50 planted in the audience for a song called 'Birdie Told Me'. They looked like the audience because there was no equipment around them. When it got to the reprise of the song, I had sound booms produced and this section of the audience stood up and performed the chorus. Quite a night."

Adding to the festival atmosphere, The Bee Gees employed a 30-piece orchestra, conducted by their musical director, Bill Shepherd.

Robin's then girlfriend Molly said, "It was such a display of showmanship, one of the first stage-managed pop shows. It was the first group ever to have an orchestra on stage . . . very impressive to see the group standing there, sort of young and nervous, because it was the biggest concert they'd ever done at that stage. It was really an incredible show."

Bob Farmer wrote in *Disc & Music Echo:* "Sixty-seven dinner-jacketed gentlemen file in from behind the stage and sit down, row upon row of them, in a semi-circle around a deserted stage. Musicians to a man. With violins and cellos, harpsichords and big bass drums, you name it – the instruments are there . . . Bill Shepherd, The Bee Gees' arranger and conductor, has come to control the horde of penguin-like figures, preparing to provide the most costly accompaniment any pop group – sorry, quintet – has had the nerve to hire.

"Down go the lights and on stage slip five furtive figures who need no introduction . . . Suddenly up come the lights and there they are! Maurice in mauve shirt and trousers. Robin in wine-red velvet jacket. Barry decked from head to bell-bottom toe in blue shot silk. Vince in inevitable black shirt. Colin crouched over his drums with fawn sweater and white trousers.

"That night five boys, 67 musicians, 45 RAF bandsmen and 40 mixed voices fed the 5,000 the most sumptuous meal of music any British pop show has produced. But was it really worth it? It would be absurd to say 67 musicians were necessary to enable The Bee Gees to recapture exactly their sound on record. Half the number would have been adequate, and in any case the screams often swamped those violins. And The Bee Gees themselves, smartly turned out and singing finely, did little more than merely stand and sing.

"But it was worth it. For this was a spectacular, an occasion of prestige, a concert which will not be forgotten."

Not everyone was completely bowled over by the event. The supporting acts for the show were The Beatles-backed Apple band Grapefruit, The Foundations and Dave Dee, Dozy, Beaky, Mick & Titch, with the latter planning a walk-out less than five minutes before the concert was scheduled to begin. Dave Dee & Co were known for their elaborate stage routines, and were expecting time to rehearse their act, but because of the extensive rehearsal time taken up by The Bee Gees and their orchestra, were unable to do a lights rehearsal until 15 minutes before the public were admitted. As the lighting was an integral part of their performance, the results could have been disastrous.

"I was seething," Dave Dee recalled. "When the audience started filing in, we just had to pack up rehearsals. There was a storming row backstage, and we were ready to quit there and then. We cooled enough to realise we would be letting down the public, and in the end our act went off all right.

"There were actually no problems at all on the tour [itself]," Dave admits. "We always got on very well with the boys, but this Albert Hall gig, it was important for both of us, because there we were, young bands starting off – the Albert Hall was the pinnacle in those days.

"We got wind of the fact that they'd got this great big military band in, so we thought, 'Well, we've got to do something.' Our show was good anyway, because we used to use UV lights and all sorts of stuff which was way ahead of its time for those days, but of course we needed to rehearse it, or at least to set it up to see if it would work, and of course we didn't get the time . . . We got six [soldiers of our own in] and right in the middle of 'Bend It', they all marched on stage with their guns, pointed them up, shot, turned around and walked off the stage. That was like the total opposite to what The Bee Gees were doing, and we just thought that was subtle and a bit funny, and it was just our way of at least doing something."

Immediately after the show, he told reporters, "We don't need a huge orchestra and choir to get across." Despite his acerbic tone, Dave now claims, "There were never any problems, it was really a question of one-upmanship I think. Are they going to do that – well we've got to do something, and then of course you get your road crew winding you up, and you get your managers winding you up, and you get everybody else winding you up. [Robert Stigwood] wanted to go one better than everybody, and he did, and to be quite honest, he was doing the right thing for his band."

Much of the rumpus was down to DDDBMT's publicist, Brian Sommerville, a former Beatles publicity man. Recognising an opportunity when he saw one, Sommerville created the impression that here were two groups about to go on the road for two months together, but who hated each other. Dave likens it to modern day sports hype. "It's a bit like boxing isn't it? It creates interest."

Barry was quick to have his say after the show too, and defended The Bee Gees' use of the orchestra. He also used the event to take another shot at

The Beatles, saying, "We hear so much about The Beatles being unable to appear on stage anymore because they could not reproduce their record sound on stage. But what we're doing now completely defeats the argument, and they should follow suit.

"We didn't hire this huge orchestra simply to be flash. We did it to provide audiences with as near as possible [a] reproduction of our sound on record. If we can do it, then I see no reason why The Beatles shouldn't take up our challenge and hire themselves an orchestra and do a few concerts. It's not as if they can't afford it!"

With such a spectacular start, it was perhaps inevitable that the tour itself was anticlimactic. Ticket sales were disappointing, and Robert Stigwood shouldered the blame himself. "I accept full responsibility for the fact that it wasn't a sell-out tour," he announced. "I did overestimate their drawing power in Britain. While The Bee Gees were playing all over the world, I neglected their appearances on British TV. Apart from things like *Top Of The Pops,* they were never seen. I now accept they should have done far more TV shows before going out on a British tour."

The use of the orchestra was still a sensitive issue for Barry. "In Germany, then at the Albert Hall and later on tour, we carried a large orchestra with us. Okay, at the Albert Hall we gave the cynics a certain amount of ammunition," he admitted. "An RAF band, a choir, a near-symphony orchestra . . . it was obvious that some knockers would say we overdid it – and worse that we got ourselves outnumbered, simply because we couldn't depend on our own music to get us through.

"But this is surely unfair thinking. My feeling is that it is the song, not the group, that sells records nowadays. If a really established group came out with a very bad song, their disc sales would slump. With us, we've been on the big ballad scene . . . But to present those big rather sad songs on record, you have to have a full-scale arrangement. And we think it is only fair to go as far as possible to present those same sounds on stage.

"We're spending the money, remember. We could go on, just guitar and drums, and do the same dreary old thing and make much more. Thinking big must produce, in the end, big results. Taking a big orchestra round the country causes problems, especially with small stages, but problems can always be overcome.

"We built our reputation on the Continent . . . and our tours have been ambitious, whether you like what we do on stage or not . . . it's not a question of trying to show anybody else up. We're not the flash-Harry types . . . But we do feel we have this debt to people who buy our records . . . and are determined to give them the best possible sound."

Frederic Tanner was present at the fourth concert of the tour at the Manchester Palace Theatre on March 31. "I was in the stalls, and the girls in the circle were screaming their heads off. In between the songs, various items were thrown down from the circle onto the stage, mostly flowers, but also rings, bras and knickers. It was an amazing atmosphere."

Nearly 20 years later in 1985, while on honeymoon, Frederic was amazed to learn from new bride Christine, that she too had been to that same concert, accompanied by her best friend Marilyn.

Impatient as they were for The Bee Gees to come on stage, both appreciated Dave Dee, Dozy, Beaky, Mick and Titch. However, Christine conceded that they were not even an appetiser for what they had come to see. "For us, The Bee Gees were the starters, main course, dessert and creme de la creme all rolled into one. The roses which we were each clutching looked worse for wear, and as they walked on, we went mad. I loved Barry while Marilyn was crazy about Robin, so we each had our quiet swooning sessions as they sang their own songs like 'Words' or 'I Started A Joke'. Otherwise we just screamed along with everybody else whenever possible.

"I vaguely remember objects flying past us and landing on the stage," Christine continued, "but funnily enough cannot remember throwing my own rose at Barry. I do remember one landing in front of him, and like to think it was mine. We were on cloud nine throughout their performance and lived on it for months afterwards . . . what a night. Little did I realise that a total stranger, who was also in the stalls, would one day become my husband."

As the tour continued, so did the pranks. Ian "Tich" Amey still chuckles at the memory of one little jape in particular. "They used to all take a little solo spot, and Robin was due to go on stage and do his bit. They used to frequent our dressing room a lot, go in and out, and he said, 'Oh, I must go now, I'm [due] on stage,' and we said, 'No, you're not going,' and we literally closed the door on him. 'You're not going anywhere,' we repeated. 'Ahhhh!' he cried followed by a loud 'Bang, bang, bang, bang.' 'I must go on!' he said, 'I *must* go – you have to let me go!' 'No, no, sorry, stay there!' We did let him go in the end but the band were playing away like good 'uns, waiting for the 'singist' to come on stage."

As Trevor "Dozy" Davies recalls, the fraternising between the two groups was in spite of Stigwood's attempts to keep the bands apart, concerned that over-mingling would diminish The Bee Gees' top billing status. "There was this thing at that time, where the powers that be wanted them just to stay in their dressing room and be the stars of the show! But they didn't want that – half the time they were in our dressing room. Even though their management still wanted them to stay away and just be the superstars. It didn't happen."

Their socialising wasn't just confined to show time either. Maurice has long been associated with Aston Martins from those days of heady excess and Tich accepts some responsibility for Mo's infatuations with that particular make of car. "I had an [Aston Martin] DB5, and we were actually on tour with them at the time, and we happened to be in Salisbury, which is our home town. We had some time off and [Maurice] saw my car, and he says, 'Ooh! I'd like to have a little spin in that.' So I took him out to a place called the Amesbury Flats and got him up to about 120mph. He quite liked it, and decided that he would have one. I was driving, because he was still a learner, and I didn't have any L-plates! And no, I wasn't going to let him drive it.

"So, he quite enjoyed the ride," Tich narrated, "and next minute he went out and bought a DB6, which was the next one up. I can remember seeing him, with one of the roadies sat next to him, and it seemed quite strange, somebody learning to drive in an Aston Martin DB6, going down the Bayswater Road!"

The tour concluded at the Belfast Ritz on May 3, with The Bee Gees staying at the Grand Central Hotel before taking a well-earned holiday.

While the boys had been out on the road, Polydor had released the first in a series of three compilation albums. Roland Rennie had acquired from Festival the licensing rights to 35 of the Australian recordings from 1967, under a five-year deal. Concerned about the damage that the release might have on the group's trendy image, Robert Stigwood argued vociferously with Roland against the wisdom of doing so. "He was against putting them out because, of course, he didn't want any energy wasted on something that he didn't have a part of, and of course, they had moved on since then, as well," said Alan Bates.

"You shouldn't be doing this," Stigwood protested. "I mean, they're rare, they're precious, they're beautiful!"

Both Roland and Alan thanked Stigwood for airing his concerns and promised to consider his comments carefully. That April, *Rare Precious & Beautiful* was released in the UK, followed in November by *Volume 2*, and in February 1969 by *Volume 3*. Each of the albums' covers had a different coloured background, but each featured the same large butterfly. In the USA, the releases were staggered so that the first volume appeared in November 1968 and *Volume 2* in February 1969. Atco never released the third collection.

13

SUCH A SHAME

THE GROUP BEGAN work on their next album almost as soon as the tracks for *Horizontal* were completed. With tour dates the only break from recording, holidays were long overdue. The Gibb brothers therefore took time off in the early summer to travel to different parts of the globe and, according to Robin, "met up again, unfortunately, in different parts of the globe."

Barry picked up the story, adding, "Strangely enough, none of us knew where the others were going. I went to Los Angeles and got a bit fed up with the scene there. A few people I knew there, I found to be phoney, and I wasn't enjoying myself. So I came home and then went to Rome, and when I got to the airport, Robin was standing there. And it was a strange thing because I had just decided to go there on the spur of the moment. It was very weird because I could have gone anywhere.

"I thought Robin was in India, but apparently he got fed up with it and decided to go to Rome as well. It's the telepathy thing again. It crops up all the time between us."

Vince Melouney and Colin Petersen headed for the Bahamas, where Colin married Joanne Newfield in a ceremony in Nassau, with Vince acting as best man. The couple managed to keep the press unsure as to whether the wedding would actually take place.

Robert Stigwood gave his approval to the match, saying, "Colin is a very level-headed person, despite being a racing car enthusiast. I was very happy to see my personal assistant, Joanne, whom I'm very fond of, marry Colin because I knew that she was in good hands. He's a very sophisticated person. He has a good appreciation of good food and wines . . . He's 100 per cent professional in everything he does and he's an old professional like the Gibbs because he's been in entertainment as a child as they were, too."

After the wedding, Colin and Joanne jetted off for a honeymoon in Majorca, which was spoiled somewhat when Joanne fell ill with German measles.

Between June 12 and July 12, it was back to work again for all the boys, completing recording on the *Idea* album. However the first two days in the studio were more of a warm-up in preparation for the four weeks ahead. The eight-track tape of their first day's efforts was titled "jam session" and consisted of 'Let There Be Love', 'Kitty Can', 'I O I O', 'Stepping Out' and one untitled song. The first two became the opening two tracks on the album, 'I O I O' would appear two albums down the line, and 'Stepping Out' remains unreleased. The following day's session was bizarre to say the least. The studio tape box refers to the tracks as "Robin demos", so where the other members of the group were is anyone's guess. 'Indian Gin And Whisky Dry', credited as written by all three brothers on the album, is listed alongside six other titles: 'Band Will Meet Mr. Justice', 'The People's Public Poke', 'The Girl To Share Each Day', 'My Love Life', 'Heaven In My Hands' and 'Come Some Christmas Eve Or Halloween'. This latter title would resurface later as 'Halloween Or Christmas Day', but is undoubtedly the same song.

The group also filmed a television special with veteran comedy actor Frankie Howerd, another of Robert Stigwood's clients. *Frankie Howerd Meets The Bee Gees*, written by Ray Galton and Alan Simpson, gave the group the opportunity to show off their own comedy skills in sketches with Howerd, as well as showcasing their music.

The Bee Gees were due to begin a seven week tour of the United States on August 2, 1968, but on July 27, Robin got up from the settee to change the television channel, collapsed and fell unconscious. He was admitted to a London nursing home suffering from nervous exhaustion, and the entire American tour was postponed due to his illness. Or was it?

Years later, Molly Gibb was adamant. "There was no 'nervous exhaustion,'" she insisted. "It was just a thing Robin did for the group, a way out of the tour. Whatever anyone said to them, they did it. They didn't know any different then, didn't know anything about the business world. If it's good for the group, then you do it."

Robin himself now admits that he and his brothers' intense desire for recognition for the group drove him to take amphetamines, a not uncommon habit in the pop world. "I did things like stay up all night and I wish I knew at 18 that living like that wasn't necessary," he said. "I was taking pills in those days, uppers – nothing that anybody else wasn't taking then, and probably a good deal milder. But there were times when I never seemed to go to bed. It was lunacy. We used to go to America for a tour and I would stay up all night, collapse and then wake up in hospital suffering from exhaustion. I didn't know what the hell I was doing. I suppose teenagers tend to do that sort of thing, especially if they're a bit in the limelight. But I could have killed myself. I look back on that period now and realise I might easily have not come out of it alive. I'd collapse from staying up from one show to the next and there was absolutely no reason for it. I just hated going to bed. I wish I had known at 18 that, in the end, success comes from hard work and sacrifices. We knew we didn't want to be just a group that came along in the Sixties and then faded away. We wanted to achieve longevity."

Robin was moved from the nursing home to a health farm in Sussex on July 31 to continue his "recuperation", while his twin brother Maurice told the press, "I could see this coming. Robin is such a highly strung person, he was bound to snap eventually. We have just come back from holiday but he never moved out of his hotel room. He also went with Barry to Rome and Nairobi. But in both places, while Barry went sightseeing, Robin just stayed in his room writing songs. Robin seems totally unable to relax. He always has to be writing. Yet, instead of sitting back after his songs have been recorded, he immediately turns to new writing. So he gets tense and tired, with the result that he collapsed last week. We may be twins, but I'm not a bit like him."

Harley Madison of *Hullabaloo* had his suspicions about Robin's delicate health, writing, "A basic economic fact of touring is that you have to sell tickets to make money. One wonders why Robin Gibb collapsed from nervous exhaustion only hours before the group was to begin the tour. They missed four dates, then Robin had another illness, a relapse, and had to fly back to Britain for a few days rest. Just more concerts missed or more tickets that didn't get sold?"

The group's latest single, 'I've Gotta Get A Message To You' was released at the beginning of August. Another unlikely topic for a pop song, the subject matter sounds like a Robin concept, although Barry has used the theme of doomed individuals many times since. Barry explained, "It is not about death although a lot of people think that it is. It's about a person who is about to die. He's going to his death because he's committed a murder."

"It's quite sick," Maurice added.

"It's not sick at all," Robin protested in an early example of how the brothers would occasionally disagree in public and in the press. "It doesn't mention death and doesn't mention how he's going to sit there and the guy who pulls down the thing. It doesn't mention the circumstances of his death or how he's going to die. It just tells that he is talking to a preacher, and he wants to get a message to his girlfriend or wife that he is sorta sorry and wants to apologise. He's killed a man who's been carrying on with his wife, and he wants to get a message to her before he dies."

"We recorded it the same night as we finished the song," Barry explained. "Robert came in late that night, and what we hadn't done was . . . we sang the whole song without three-part harmonies in the chorus. Robert made us come back and sing the choruses again. We said, 'Well, why?' and he said, 'Because you've got to sing in three-part harmonies. You cannot sing it in unison and have no harmonies in the chorus.' So back we all drove to the studio and sang the choruses in three-part harmonies, and that's the record as it stands today." It is also worth noting that 'Message' was the group's first ever eight-track recording, IBC having only just upgraded their equipment to what would soon become the new industry standard.

Released just weeks before the *Idea* LP, 'I've Gotta Get A Message To You' was for some reason not actually on the album, except in the United States, but at least its B-side, 'Kitty Can', was. 'Message' was the Bee Gees' biggest hit yet in the United States, reaching number eight, making it their first Top 10 hit there. It topped the British chart for one week before being nudged out of the peak position by The Beatles' 'Hey Jude'. In Germany, it was their fifth consecutive Top 10 hit, reaching number three.

By August 10, Robin was fully recovered. "There was nothing mentally wrong with me," he said. "I just wanted some sleep. We'd just finished the *Idea* album and we'd gone many nights without sleep, often writing songs right through the night." Following his release from the Sussex health farm, the rescheduled American tour began at Forest Hills Stadium in New York.

Robert Stigwood was delighted. "[The Bee Gees'] original breakthrough in the States was the most exciting thing," he said. "The concert I most enjoyed them doing was when they played at Forest Hills in New York. This was when they were using their full orchestra. It was an outdoor concert and it rained and they did about an hour and a half in the rain, but I don't think one person in the audience moved. I've never seen a reaction at a concert like that. The audience just wouldn't let them off the stage and gave them a 30-minute ovation at the end. That was their first big New York appearance and it was really tremendous to see."

The group received 13 curtain calls, and Maurice remembers looking out and seeing a proud Hugh Gibb watching them with tears (or was it rain?) streaming down his face.

One fan in the audience that evening was Fredric Gershon, who years later would work with The Bee Gees when he became president of the Stigwood Group. He vividly recalled the Forest Hills concert. "It was stunning," he said. "There was a full orchestra supporting them, and I had never seen anything like it. I don't believe there *was* anything like it. That powerful orchestral sound was awesome and the three brothers used their voices in an almost classical way; making sounds instead of words. That was before I had any business relationship with the brothers. I was a fan."

While in the United States, The Bee Gees appeared on *The Ed Sullivan Show* alongside actor Cary Grant, who described them as his favourite group. The twins also made a very different sort of television appearance as contestants on *The Dating Game*, the American television series which was the inspiration for Cilla Black's long-running *Blind Date*. Despite (or perhaps because of) Maurice's response that he would "smash his face in" if the girl's father announced that he would be taking his daughter's place on a date, he was the winner that evening, and the chosen date was a trip to the diamond mines of South Africa.

Ostensibly because of its delayed beginning, the American tour was severely curtailed, but years later Barry would admit that: "The first tour of America was a washout. Forest Hills was a nice moment, LA as well. I think both shows were papered to an extent. It wasn't a good show musically; we didn't do a good show then. The band was still not a band; we really didn't have the years of playing as a band that makes it work. And all the gigs in between New York and LA had to be cancelled. Nobody bought tickets. They tried to make it look good. We spent the time hiding out in LA while

Robert was juggling the publicity to make it look like we were invading the country. They got Robin to go into hospital for a couple of weeks and play the game." "The game", as he explained it, involved Robin feigning a relapse to give the group an excuse to cancel more concerts.

"The bookings were so disastrous that the group hid out," Dick Ashby revealed. "They weren't worried about the American press so much, but they didn't want the British press to find out they hadn't cracked it."

The group arrived back in Britain after the American tour and Barry immediately dropped a bombshell, announcing he was leaving the group to pursue an acting career. "It is now or never for me," he declared. "If I do not try it on my own now, I shall never try. It is worth giving up all the success we have, just to try for one dramatic part in a film. It is something I have been considering for some time. The American tour finally made up my mind for me. I received several film offers in Los Angeles."

Robert Stigwood attempted to pour oil on troubled waters. "Barry has talked about going out on his own, although he doesn't want to leave us altogether," he said. "I think he will feel differently when he's had a rest. I can't let him go this year. It's the group's best year yet. All the boys were very exhausted after the thirteen-hour flight from Los Angeles. Barry said more than he really meant. Although he hasn't seen the script yet, he has the starring romantic role in *Lord Kitchener's Five Little Drummer Boys*. That will please him."

"I have said I shall be leaving The Bee Gees, and I stand by that," Barry countered. "I shall fulfil all existing commitments with the group which will take up about the next two years. The group scene is not an everlasting thing, and in the pop business you can only go so far.

"In films, I shall have as much contact with the fans as in the group. More even . . . I don't know whether I'll make a good actor. I've never tried it. But in Hollywood, I passed the screen test.

"I want to be a star and that's why I want to do films. I'll sacrifice anything to do it. I'm not a big star at the moment, and that's not being modest. Merely realistic. I think a star is someone who can go to anywhere in the world and people will jump. Bob Hope and Bing Crosby, for example, and it has taken them a long time. Makes my 11 years in show business just mere chicken feed . . ."

At the same time, he seemed torn between his desire for film stardom and his loyalty to the group. "It's frightening," he added. "The group are succeeding. Should I leave them? And I don't just mean, 'Would I make it as a film actor?' because, all right, I haven't had acting lessons, but James Stewart and Clark Gable and Errol Flynn never did either. No, what worries me most is my personal obligation to The Bee Gees. This will be the only thing that will stop me. I owe too much to my brothers, especially as it would only be an attempt at movies."

Maurice also indicated that all was not well with the group when he said, "We had a couple of arguments while we were away. I forget what they were about. When I saw Barry at Mr Stigwood's, he didn't seem to be on speaking terms. He didn't say hello – let's put it that way. I definitely don't want to split. I hope the five of us keep together and remain good friends."

The *Idea* album was released in September amidst the "will he or won't he leave?" fiasco in the music press. The personnel were all the same as for *Horizontal*, but the sound was quite different. *Idea* is much lighter, more pop than the bluesy rock sound of the previous LP, with less electric guitar, lighter lyrics, more flowery orchestration, and more of the breathy vocal style that Barry had displayed on 'Words'. This did not sit well with the critics, some of whom began to question the group's "rock" credentials. There was a backlash against the flower-power style of 1967, and while The Bee Gees were moving away from it, unlike many groups they were not so much a rock band temporarily experimenting with pop eclecticism as harmony singers finding their element and continuing to experiment with different pop forms. Critics following the mainstream back-to-rock movement left them here.

This is the only Bee Gees' album of the LP era with different contents in the US and abroad. Even the album covers were different, with the American album featuring Klaus Voormann's design of a collage of a face compiled from features cut from photos of each of the five Bee Gees, while the rest of the world saw a photo of the group in the base of a light bulb against a purple background. The American version dropped the song 'Such A Shame' in favour of 'Gotta Get A Message'.

This was the first and only Bee Gees' album to go on sale (outside the USA) with no lead-off singles on it. *Idea* is also the only Bee Gees album to note who sings on each song, but the CD version lost this useful guide. A couple of their other albums give the lead singer, but no others give all the singers.

A memorable moment is the inclusion of Vince Melouney's 'Such A Shame'. Asked in February, 2000, whether getting one of his own songs on the album had been problematic, Vince replied, "No, Barry really liked it and wanted to sing it. Whether Robert behind the scenes wasn't happy, I don't know," he added, implying that Stigwood might have been concerned about the fact that the inclusion of 'Such A Shame' was the first time that an entirely non-Gibb writing credit would appear on any of their internationally released albums. Vince was probably right to assume that Stigwood wasn't happy, as it was also the last time a writing credit that excluded the Gibbs ever appeared on a Bees Gees' album.

Another song worthy of comment is 'I Started A Joke', one of Robin's classic moments. It comes on quietly, so simple, so deep, one of their most requested songs. It wasn't even a single in many countries, and only followed the album, as if no one had noticed it ahead of time. On its December release in the States and parts of Europe (but once again, not in Britain), the song reached number six in the US, and it fared a little better in Holland and Austria, making the Top Three in both countries.

Although Robin has claimed that the melody was inspired by the sounds he heard in a jet engine, he has always steadfastly refused to explain the evocative lyrics. 'I Started A Joke' has to be the prime example of the pure abstract Gibb lyric that everyone can read something into and, it would seem, nearly everyone did. "There was a lot of that in those days," Barry laughed. "There was a lot of psychedelia and the idea that if you wrote something, even if it sounded ridiculous, somebody would find the meaning for it, and that was the truth.

"People used to ask us if we took LSD. And we suddenly realised that that's what it really was about. People hang on what you say because they think you've taken drugs when in fact you haven't taken anything. They get carried away with it more than you do. It's like The Beatles and songs like 'Strawberry Fields', where people assume that it was drugs that concocted those songs – and we all know for a fact that some of it was – but I think there's a very rare gift that existed inside John Lennon and also inside Paul [McCartney] when they were together. I think it came from more than drugs or drink."

A special album for Polydor's anniversary was released in Germany which featured an instrumental called 'Gena's Theme' recorded around this time and credited to The Bee Gees, but it would be more accurate to credit it to Bill Shepherd. Bill also recorded two whole albums of covers of Bee Gees songs in "easy listening" style, one with voices called *Aurora* by The Bill Shepherd Singers and the other, an instrumental album, *Bee Gees Hits* by The Robert Stigwood Orchestra. Although neither album was marketed as "by The Bee Gees", each carried an official seal of approval.

When Bill Shepherd asked Robert Stigwood if he could make an LP of Bee Gees' songs with a large lush choir, the impresario waved an expansive hand and said, "Go away and make it." Bill then inquired about the budget allowance and song selection, but Stigwood countered, "Just go and do what you like and give me the bill with the finished tape." This was not a lack of interest on Robert's part but rather an expression of complete confidence in Shepherd's ability to do the project justice.

Bill was delighted to be given carte blanche and he described the *Aurora* album as, "My own personal choice of some of The Bee Gees' songs, using one of my favourite musical means of expressions – a choir – and what better way to show off the songs of the Fabulous Singing Gibb Brothers. I first worked with the boys in Australia and have been with them ever since. It's not easy for any musical arranger to see into the original, sharp, quick thinking minds of Maurice, Barry and Robin; always changing direction, seeking new things and forever cheerful and confident. But I detect in their work a simplicity which makes it possible to do virtually anything with their music. At the rate they are turning out such good material today, I would say they will become the Rodgers & Hart, Rodgers & Hammerstein and Irving Berlins of tomorrow."

Robin Gibb was equally effusive about The Robert Stigwood Orchestra compilation. "Barry, Maurice and myself are completely thrilled by this LP, a life-long ambition has been fulfilled to hear our music played by a full orchestra. They have done it splendidly and I shall cherish it always and I hope it will be the first of many such albums." In actual fact, The Robert Stigwood Orchestra did not exist; it was simply an assembly of top musicians, specially brought together for the album.

★   ★   ★

On September 12, The Bee Gees flew to Brussels and spent the next two weeks recording a television spectacular with Jean Christophe Averti to promote the *Idea* album on French television. The resulting hour long special featured guest appearances by The Brian Auger Trinity with Julie Driscoll and Swedish pop singer Lill Lindfors, who performed her version of 'Words' in her native language. Compared to today's music videos, the programme looks simplistic and at times rather comical, with the group performing songs from *Horizontal* and *Idea* against pop art backdrops. There were even fairly primitive special effects used in 'Indian Gin And Whisky Dry' to make it appear that the boys are bouncing up and down in their respective shot glasses and floating question marks during 'I Started A Joke'.

At one point during their stay in Brussels, the Belgian Police would not allow The Bee Gees' limousine to stop outside their hotel, The Metropole, due to a fashion show being held there by the French pop star Johnny Halliday's wife, Sylvie Vartan. Maurice's leg was injured as he attempted to get out of the car, leading to a formal complaint being filed with the Chief of Police by Robert Stigwood.

Back in Britain, Vince Melouney announced, "In future I intend to have much more to say and do because people think that Colin and I have the least talent in the group, and I'm out to prove them wrong. Both outside and inside the group I want to prove that I am capable of doing successful things as well. I came over to England because of the lack of appreciation in Australia. I used to practise a hell of a lot, and the more I did the less musical respect I've got. It was either going back to playing simple stuff or come to England. We Australians, you see, looked up to England like Buddha.

"Certainly I get frustrated," he added. "Everybody does, whatever they do. But to have the initiative to keep going you must get uptight about things. If everything was rosy all the time it would be a bit of a drag. I honestly enjoy being in the group. I get as much of a kick out of being in The Bee Gees as I would being in a blues group. And because I have different musical ideas to the Gibb brothers, it's fine. If we had all the same ideas it would become a drag. Being different makes it all the more interesting."

Colin Petersen also spoke out about the pop scene. "There are many people in groups who take it upon themselves to make social comments, which is stupid," he said. "One minute you work at the butcher's, the next minute you're a pop star and asked to make social comments. What has made you any the more intelligent? Of course there are exceptions, but there's a lot of rubbish spoken.

"I do try and write songs, but it's no good competing against the brothers. Maurice and I try and write something, and in the meantime Barry's written 53 songs. So you can see what I mean! I write but my songs are very Dylanish and country inspired. Very odd lyrics in fact. Some turn out very ambiguous. 'Everything That Came From Mother Goose' is the best we've done and Manfred's Klaus Voormann is knocked out with it. Before joining The Bee Gees last year I had various offers of films. I nearly got a part in *Round The Mulberry Bush* in fact; although I couldn't tell you whether it was the starring role that Barrie Evans landed. You see, I came over to England to get back into films. I had no intention of joining The Bee Gees. But their success hasn't surprised me. They were the only group in Australia, apart from Billy Thorpe & The Aztecs when Vince was with them, who I thought capable of making it internationally."

Maurice explained his own role in the group in *Disc & Music Echo*, saying, "I do less singing, of course. I only come in on high harmonies. I'm more of the musician, playing the piano, bass, mellotron or organ on records, which saves money on hiring musicians, for one thing. It's the same when it comes to writing. I write the music, because I cannot really write lyrics. But I can write chords like Robin's never heard of. So I provide the music for them to write the lyrics to. It's the same as on stage – when we write we complement each other. To prove that, we wrote six songs, Barry and I, while Robin was ill during the American tour, and they were terrible until Robin came back, and then everything worked out. It's very hard to write a song alone, and it's only by jamming that you can get a song together. That's the way we do it. At the same time, I've never liked many of our records. I positively hated 'Massachusetts' and 'Message', and yet they have been two of our biggest hits."

★ ★ ★

Barry's girlfriend Lynda Gray had been receiving harassing calls at the couple's penthouse flat in Ave Maria Lane near St Paul's Cathedral in London. The mysterious caller made another appearance when Barry was at home with Lynda on October 20, and Barry, armed with a pistol, ran to the door.

"When I opened the front door, this man was still speaking on the intercom," Barry related. "He was a big guy – aged about 35. I asked if he was the person who had kept calling at the flat. He said he was. Then he started running down the street. I chased him and fired a blank from my .38 in the air. At that point the police arrived. We both went to the police station and were questioned. I don't know what will happen now."

No charges were filed against the unnamed Edinburgh man, aged 34, but Barry was charged with possessing both the .38 pistol and a German Luger without a firearms licence. He was ordered to appear in court on December 3, where he was fined £25 on the firearms violation. In an amusing footnote to the affair, the chairman at London's Guildhall Court commented after the hearing, "Besides possessing two pistols, about the only thing I can see Mr

Gibb has done wrong is wearing a white suit to court." Barry had also been guilty of ignoring good advice – his own, from three years earlier, when he had sworn "to be more careful with guns in future".

Meanwhile Robin was also making headlines in the music papers for a non-musical reason: his ever-lengthening hair, which one writer noted was beginning to resemble that of the eccentric American pop star, Tiny Tim. From America, where he was supervising Cream's farewell tour, Robert Stigwood issued the order to Robin, "Get your hair cut before I return from America in a week's time or there will be trouble!"

"I have no intention of getting my hair cut," Robin hotly retorted, as the group left for Amsterdam for the first leg of the European tour. "I like it the way it is. After all, even Jesus had long hair. If they don't like me for what I am, then that's their choice. But if they are going to knock me just for my hair, I don't want to know them. The length of a person's hair should not have anything to do with his capabilities as a singer. The rest of the group haven't complained to me. They don't mind at all. If my hair was dirty and full of grease, then they could knock me. But I shampoo it twice a week; in fact, I'm a fanatic on showers and baths. I really don't know why Robert is so insistent about this, and I don't know what he means about trouble!"

Barry discussed his recalcitrant younger brother with the *New Musical Express'* Nick Logan, "He won't talk about it. He's just got this mental block on the whole subject. Yet he's conservative in other ways. He wouldn't dream of stepping out of his front door without his suit and tie and the whole bit. Yet he *will not* get his hair cut, and I don't think anyone in the business should criticise him for it."

Robin's fiancée Molly refused to become embroiled in the great hair debate. "It looks nice long, besides which I wouldn't try to influence him," she said. "He is very stubborn and when his mind's made up, nobody can change it."

Robin had also come under fire for his stage presence. Standing perfectly still in the spotlight with his right hand cupped to his ear, his left arm out-stretched, he looked, according to one writer, "like a gawkish village bobby on point duty".

"My concentration is fully on a) my voice and b) my audience, which is why I don't prance around on stage," he explained defensively. "I can't be something I'm not. I'm a songwriter and a singer but not a performer. It's not within my character to move about. My confidence is not in my body but in my voice. I feel very embarrassed if I try to move about a bit. That's for Barry to do, not me."

The proposed European tour had run into problems in Germany where The Bee Gees were turned down by 31 hotels. The country's innkeepers evidently feared a repeat of the fan riots which had dogged the group when they toured the country earlier in the year. In an attempt to find a solution, Robert Stigwood announced plans to rent a "complete portable hotel" for the group and staff, with each Bee Gee having his own luxury portable caravan suite, and 10 more mobile homes to house the staff. Protection for the group would be provided by 100 security men.

On his return to Britain the following week, Stigwood conceded defeat in the battle of the haircut. "I have given up," he said. "If he feels so strongly about it, then okay, let him keep his hair as it is."

His attempts to keep the three members of Cream together were no more successful, but he intended to keep trying, as he told *Disc & Music Echo*. "I have not made any progress as yet in my attempts to prevent the Cream from splitting, so their current American tour can still be regarded as their farewell tour, but I am going back shortly to discuss it again with them."

Stigwood also abandoned his plans to hire the caravan convoy for The Bee Gees' tour of Germany in November, announcing that the group and security men would travel and sleep in the train used by the Queen and The Beatles during their visits to Germany.

The grandiose plans raised some eyebrows, but Stigwood fended off the criticism, saying, "England seems to be on such a very self-destructive kick these days. In the beat boom everyone was proud – the press, the DJs, the public – but now everyone is a bit cynical. Yet The Bee Gees have sold 10 million singles and three million LPs which is an unparalleled achievement and selling records is what it's all about. I suppose on their current sales rate, The Bee Gees could be millionaires in two more years, but they live like such already which causes a little bitterness with other groups because so few of the others happen on an international level. I make The Bee Gees live on the level they can afford and I'm very tough with them."

Next it was Vince Melouney's turn for the headlines when, after protesting how content he was as a member of The Bee Gees the previous month, he suddenly announced that he would leave the group at the close of the tour. "The talent I had didn't come up to the talent of the Gibb brothers," he explained. "I realised that my ideas, within the context of what they were doing, didn't augment their ideas.

"I learned one thing in Australia and that was that if I was in a group that didn't appear to be progressing, I always left it even if they were earning big money, because I would feel I was letting myself down as a musician. I'm leaving The Bee Gees because now is the time I feel I must try my own musical policies. I feel I can express myself a lot more outside The Bee Gees than within them. There are certainly no bad feelings between us, we've all been good friends for years and I'm sure will remain so. It's the simple question of all groups having to or needing to break up sooner or later, either for musical or personal reasons. For me, it's the music, and the right time, I feel, just happens to be now."

With Cream on the verge of splitting and the precociously talented Steve Winwood having left the successful Spencer Davis Group, it certainly wasn't uncommon for groups to fragment. Indeed, it was quite the fashion to either go solo or join up with evacuees from other bands. Vince's need for musical independence was inspired by a visit by Tony Ashton & Roy Dyke, formerly of The Remo Four, and Kim Gardner, formerly with The Creation, to a Bee Gees recording session. Vince became friendly with them and offered to lend an ear to their own output.

"I heard the tracks they were doing, said to them that I'd like to produce their discs, and this they let me do. We got a lot of stuff recorded. The more I got involved with them, the more I appreciated what they were about and what they were trying to do. I just felt that I wanted to join in with them because I felt strongly about what they were playing.

"Of course being with The Bee Gees gave me a very safe and secure feeling. I know it will be a great financial risk to leave such a great money making group. But this really doesn't matter, because I'm sure we are going to be successful. We're all convinced. Let's face it, nothing in pop is easy. It's all a great big gamble. I feel musically that we have something great to give the public, something which they will appreciate and understand and like.

"The Bee Gees were and are a very happy group even though Colin is my best friend and I see more of him than the others. I don't foresee the end of the group in the near future. Barry has said that in two years The Bee Gees will have a rethink about what they're doing. My decision was nothing to do with the fact that Barry, really the musical mainstay of the group, would possibly leave them eventually. Colin is staying, I believe, despite all the rumours. I think they will carry on as a foursome and just manage without a new lead guitarist."

For his part, Colin was quick to pay tribute to his departing compatriot claiming that his role in the band was underrated. " 'World' would have been nothing without Vince's guitar," he stated. For all that Robin didn't share Vince's love of blues music, Colin felt that Robin's "beautiful soulful voice went hand in glove" with Vince's unique sound.

Barry was philosophical about Vince's announcement. "We will go on, of course, but eventually The Bee Gees must come to an end – the Gibb Brothers will always exist but The Bee Gees were formed with the intention of a short-term future. Get in, get some money and get out. Vince has been a big blues fan since we started. He felt stifled because the rest of us are only interested in commercial numbers and it's no good having somebody in the group who's not really with you in spirit. Obviously he will be a great loss to us, but our loss will be someone else's gain because he's a brilliant guitarist. I don't think he realises just how good he is himself yet."

Following a concert at Houtrust Hall, The Hague, where they topped a bill featuring Riggich, The Sharons and The Motions, and television dates in Sweden, Denmark and three shows in Austria with The Marbles, it was on to Germany.

For the tour, the group was joined by a young man who would become a lifelong friend and a loyal employee for many years. Thomas Patrick Kennedy first met Dick Ashby when Dick was working as road manager for The Birds and kept up the acquaintance. "I used to fix the van for Dick, and that's basically how I got into [working for The Bee Gees]," Tom said. "I did a few bits and pieces in the studio with the boys, and then I started off with the German tour. I was going to be there for six weeks, and it just went on for 20-odd years!"

He enjoyed those years on the road with the group. "They're easy people to work with, and you have to like the music as well . . . I did like their music before I worked for them . . . Vince Melouney was a nice guy – I used to play chess with him back in the hotel after the gigs. Colin was quite nice – they were all very nice. I suppose in those days Barry was the most reclusive . . . Maurice was the fun-loving type. Robin, of course, was a law unto himself and still is today.

"I've always believed, and I can honestly say this, that Barry decided to get famous, and everybody got sucked along with him. The support Robin and Maurice gave him was invaluable, and he probably couldn't have done it without them, so although he may be seen as the leader, it doesn't diminish the part that the twins played. As a triumvirate, they work well together. There is something almost telepathic between them."

After the shows, Barry would often play his guitar and sing rather than going out. Tom remembers these impromptu concerts fondly, especially his own particular request. "Much to Barry's chagrin, one of my favourites was 'Jumbo'," he said, "and when he used to get his guitar out, I'd always say, "Come on, Skip, play 'Jumbo' for us" and, under duress, he used to play it. I always thought it was a lovely song. It's one of my personal favourites. He's got total recall – you could shout out songs and he could play and sing every one of them." Barry's nickname, Tom said, was short for 'Skipper' because he was always the group's unofficial captain.

The German leg of the tour opened in Bremen on October 31. The country's young fans couldn't do enough to show their appreciation for their heroes, sometimes carrying their adulation to a riotous extreme. At the Bremen airport, excited fans trampled over barriers and police, with several people, including Robin, injured in the fracas. When they arrived in Hamburg, fans had strewn the airport with flower petals. In Frankfurt they were greeted by 7,000 replicas of themselves with the fans wearing Bee Gees masks. In Cologne they were met by a sea of orange-clad fans, who were somehow under the impression that it was the group's favourite colour.

Nor was the tumult confined to the group's comings and goings. Hugh Gibb recalled, "One time the boys had to pull me on stage when the fans trampled the barriers. We had to have police escorts all the time just to get away from the hotels."

The riotous German tour came to a premature halt after the group's concert at Munich Deutches Museum when both Barry and Robin were taken ill with acute tonsillitis, forcing the cancellation of the remaining dates. Vince's days as a Bee Gee ended with a whimper instead of a bang.

14

BROTHER, CAN YOU SPARE A SONG?

IN AUSTRALIA, the Gibb brothers had become as well known for their songwriting and guesting on other artists' records, as they were for appearances and recordings in their own name. Barry, Robin and Maurice have always considered themselves songwriters first, recording artists second and performers last, and this will always be so. In England, they still clung dearly to that principle and time that could have been spent promoting The Bee Gees was often put to other use.

Even before 'New York Mining Disaster' began its ascent of the charts in April 1967, some of their Australian recordings were catching up with them. In 1966, Ronnie Burns had discovered a treasure trove of demo recordings from which to select songs for his new album, and as the names of Barry, Robin and Maurice Gibb increased in prominence, so did requests to sample their back catalogue. The release of The Bee Gees' own renditions was still some years away, so at the time these songs were very much regarded as new compositions.

As early as March 4, in what was their first proper recording on English soil, all three brothers and Colin Petersen were in the studio for Billy J. Kramer's second solo single following his split from The Dakotas. The session had come about through a mixture of circumstance and Robert Stigwood's perseverance on behalf of the Gibbs. "What happened was," Billy began, "Brian Epstein said to me that George Martin was very tied up with a lot of projects and would I mind doing a record with Robert Stigwood. I had a meeting with Robert, and he played me Bee Gees' tapes, demo's, all sorts of things that they'd written. 'Spicks and Specks', things like that. Then I think I had a copy sent to me of 'Town Of Tuxley Toymaker (Part One)'.

"I remember saying to him that they were great. I'd seen these fellas in the office and had been told about them and what they did, and how they were popular in Australia, and I heard some of the songs, and they said, 'Well, this one would be a good one for you.' And then we got with a musical director and we set the key, which was something I'd never done before.

"I was very inexperienced," Billy continued. "If I recorded with The Dakotas, they could transpose a key if it was in the wrong key, they could do it mentally, instantly! If it was in D, and I said that's too low, I want it in E, or if it was in E and it was too high, I'd say put it in D and there was no problem – but when you've got a big orchestra, well, you can't do that, it all has to be written out.

"So, I thought at the time, the day of the session when I had this huge orchestra with me that I'd pitched the song too low. But everybody thought that it was fine. That's the only thing that unnerved me. And I'd never worked with session men before, it was the first time I'd ever been in a studio without The Dakotas, with all these top session men. It was a Saturday morning, which was unusual in them days. Sessions now go on all night and all day, but this was 10 o'clock in the morning to one o'clock finish – all wrapped up. The Bee Gees did the vocal backing. They had very distinctive voices. I thought it was a great song."

Billy was generous in his praise of the Gibbs. "I think that they must rate alongside The Beatles for their songwriting. You think of the amount of songs that they've written both for themselves and other people. Some people just don't get the acclaim, it's just the way it is. There's no answer to it, I've given up on trying to work that one out, why the press are kind to some people and horrible to others."

Next in line were The Peppermint Circus about whom little is known. Their April single 'All The King's Horses' appeared on the obscure Olga label, but on this occasion the release lacked any Gibb involvement.

One of the best of the demos recorded by Ronnie Burns was 'Butterfly', and it received the first of several British airings in June from Unit Four Plus Two. The Hertfordshire based psychedelic group had scored some very minor hits either side of their big 1965 number one hit, 'Concrete And Clay' and their version of 'Butterfly' deserved a lot more attention than it received. The band split in 1969, Russ Ballard being the only member to achieve any kind of fame in later years.

In August, it was the turn of a Sheffield artist, David Holgate Grundy, to try his hand at one of these early Bee Gees' demos. Better known as Dave Berry, he faced the same dilemma as several other British teen idols of the era: R&B was obviously nearest and dearest to his heart, but he needed to record blatantly pop material to make the hit parade. "As we did at that particular time, it was a matter of my A & R man sending material through to me, because I'm not a songwriter," Dave explained. "All my recorded material was sent to me by different music publishers. I had done a few TV shows and concerts with The Bee Gees at that time, and they came up with this song that was sent to me by their music publishers at the time."

Ronnie Burns had passed on 'Forever', and even though it was over a year old by the time of its release, it still captured the mood of the era. "I remember it was just after the *Sgt Pepper* album," Dave continued, "so that's why there was that phasing on the voice. We were all listening to what other people were doing, the new albums, the new singles, and obviously everyone was going in and wondering, 'How did [The Beatles] get that effect?' So that's why there's that sort of phasing on the vocals and on the backing.

"I've performed quite a few of their songs live and I do think that their Sixties songs are very underrated, they're not played as much as they should be. I think they're classic songs, but for some reason you just don't hear them played."

Albert Hammond is remembered by many in Britain for his big 1973 hit, 'Free Electric Band', but elsewhere in the world he is better known for its immediate predecessor, 'It Never Rains (In Southern California)'. However, in 1967 he was the guitarist in an unknown five-piece band called Family Dogg. Named after their début single of the same name, they selected 'Storm' as its B-side thus ensuring that this particular cover version would remain consigned to obscurity, where it languishes to this day.

Family Dogg did manage to score a number six hit a couple of years later but two groups who didn't even achieve one solitary hit were The Montanas and The Sounds; their versions of 'Top Hat' being as anonymous as its performers.

By the end of 1967, the Gibbs were almost as well known in the USA and Europe as they were in Britain and a Spanish band were next to get in on the act. Los Bravos were far from being an unknown entity in the UK though; their version of 'Black Is Black' having provided Decca with a number two in the summer of 1966. The previously unreleased 'Like Nobody Else' joined its predecessors by failing to even make a slight dent on the hit parade. They also recorded a Spanish version, 'Como Nadie Mas', for release to their home market.

American soul singer Nina Simone recorded 'In The Morning (Morning Of My Life)', but her time to have a hit with a Gibb song was yet to come.

Although its release was delayed until the following year, one other of the Australian demos appeared before the Gibbs' own version did. The Brigade were a Melbourne based quartet who recorded two singles on the Australian Astor label before they disappeared as quickly as they had appeared, although they did support The Rolling Stones on their first tour down under. Maurice's 'All By Myself' was the A-side of their début single which was an early production credit for Ron Tudor who became well known both as a producer and for the success of his Fable label.

With the exception of the Billy J. Kramer recording, on which the brothers were actively involved, Barry, Robin and Maurice had little or no say in these releases. Where they were far better placed to exercise control over their work was when they had written it either specifically for, or at the request of, another artist, and there was no shortage of such releases during this period either.

★ ★ ★

The Monopoly were a four-piece outfit from Birmingham that had been formed by lead singer Raymond Froggat and which comprised Hartley Cain on guitar, drummer Len Ablethorpe with one Lou Clark on bass. Now Sir Louis, in recognition of his subsequent years as conductor of The Royal

191

Philharmonic Orchestra, not forgetting his work with The Electric Light Orchestra and the *Hooked On Classics* albums, the April '67 recording of 'House Of Lords' was a somewhat inauspicious start to his musical career.

"From what I recollect, it was the first record that we ever made, the first record that I ever made in my life," recalls Sir Louis. "We were youngsters, in our teens in the Sixties, and we were signed up by Polydor. They had another office in Birmingham where they had some talent scouts. The Polydor scout guy phoned up the people in London, and they came up to listen to us; gave us a recording test and offered us a deal.

"Then it was a matter of material. The Bee Gees had just been signed up and they were much more important at Polydor than we were, and I think a few Bee Gees things were presented to us to have a go at. I'm pretty sure we did 'Red Chair Fade Away' as a demo, or maybe even recorded it, but it never got released. 'House Of Lords' was one of the things we considered. It was given to us by the record producer [Terry Kennedy]."

Raymond Froggat described The Bee Gees' own version as being "in a definitive Beatles style, with two-part harmony encompassing the whole of the lyric. We found this very disconcerting as the style was completely out of character with the direction we had hoped to follow." Displaying the lack of confidence one would expect of such relative novices, Raymond confirmed that the band's own musical interpretation was a note perfect copy of the demo version, such was their desire not to offend. The recording took all day and most of the night to complete but Raymond was unhappy with the outcome, claiming embarrassment at the final result, and even going so far as to say that he was thankful that the record itself didn't get any airplay. Interestingly, he revealed, "We also felt that we could write a better song than the one The Bee Gees wrote for us."

Having left The Monopoly pretty much to their own devices at Advision Recording Studio in New Bond Street, the brothers, and the eldest one in particular, were determined to have a greater influence on the next song they chose to give away.

"To prove that we could make it as composers," Barry said, "it became an ambition for us to have a hit by another artist singing one of our songs. Gerry Marsden did one. Don't forget that he'd set a new record when his first three releases [with The Pacemakers] all went to number one on the charts. But the mixture of our song and Gerry's voice didn't work. The trouble was that we knew how the song should be done, and the whole character of it was completely changed at Gerry's session.

"We realised that it would be better if we actually went along to the session and explained exactly how the song should be done. Unfortunately, that's easier said than done. Really, the composer doesn't even expect to be allowed to dictate how one of his songs should be done."

The song Gerry recorded for CBS/Columbia, Barry and Robin's 'Gilbert Green', survives in a Bee Gees version on a concert tape, and is so good that it is hard to imagine why it was given away. The concert arrangement is presumably what they recorded, with a Robin lead vocal joined by Barry for the short choruses, and an unusual extended orchestral ending. While Bill Shepherd arranged Gerry's recording, which Robert Stigwood produced on June 27, the live Bee Gees' take blows it away, mainly for Robin's outstanding delivery on the four verses of strange storyline lyrics and his high notes at the chorus. If the Gibbs ever do consider letting out some unreleased songs, this should be one of them.

The Sands were five young men from Middlesex, former school friends of Brian May of Queen fame, who were signed by Brian Epstein for NEMS after he had spotted them performing at the Cromwell Club in London. Their first incarnation was The Tridents before they changed their name to The Others which earned them a single-release deal with Fontana Records in 1964. Now, three years on, Robert Stigwood picked them up for his Reaction label and, on July 24, they recorded 'Mrs. Gillespie's Refrigerator' as the A-side of their only single after Robert had played a Bee Gees' demo version to them.

Esther and Abi Ofarim were also relatively unknown during the summer of 1967; the release of their smash hit 'Cinderella Rockefella' still being some months away. Although Barry's 'Morning Of My Life' occupied the A-side of this Philips release, and soared to number two in the German charts, of more interest was the flip 'Garden Of My Home', again written by all three brothers. It seems an unlikely alliance, but the ease with which the Ofarims were able to interpret both compositions gave clues to the future ability of the brothers to adapt their style of writing to almost any type of music that was called for. Both titles were obviously favourites with the duo as both reappeared on their *Live 1969* album.

August found the Gibbs inside a little studio just off Denmark Street to assist Adam Faith with his recording of the heavy psychedelic guitar ballad, 'Cowman Milk Your Cow', which is far from being as crass as the title suggested. Upon its release on September 22, it deserved a far better fate than the thumbs-down it received from a disinterested public, which was witnessing the decline of a brightly shining star.

Born Terry Nelhams, Adam had 24 chart hits for Parlophone, starting with two number ones, in a seven year period up to late 1966. "I think ['Cowman'] came to me through one of The Roulettes, my backing group at the time," Adam said. "They'd heard it and thought it would make a great record. I think we did hear a demo. I loved the song – it was one of those mad moments where you hear somebody, a writer, sing their own song so brilliantly, it fools you into thinking that you can achieve the same effect. Of course, who's going to sing it better than those boys? Fantastic, amazing group! Brilliant!" The Roulettes' guitarist was the same Russ Ballard who had been part of Unit Four Plus Two when they recorded 'Butterfly'.

Barry agreed with Adam's admission that the Gibbs were a hard act to follow vocally and expressed frustration that the performers of the Gibbs' work didn't possess the same degree of extrasensory perception that the brothers claim plays an important part in their collective writing process.

Admitting to *NME*'s Norrie Drummond that he didn't particularly like any of the cover versions that had been released prior to the interview's publication that September, Barry concluded, "I think every songwriter must feel as we do. Somehow no one who has recorded one of our numbers has made as good a job as we had hoped. When you write a song you have an idea of how it should be sung, but it doesn't work out that way if someone else records it. No one so far has been able to get the proper feel of a song. Maybe in time we'll come to accept that this is the way it's got to be. Playwrights must feel the same way, I suppose, when they see actors portraying the characters they have created."

1967 was a busy year, as the boys had also helped out on a couple of singles where the performers released material that had recently been recorded by The Bee Gees for their own use. Upon his arrival from Australia, Johnny Young was given 'Craise Finton Kirk (Royal Academy Of Arts)' and 'I Am The World' for a Polydor release in August. Although it made no impact in the UK, he was rewarded with a Top 30 hit back in Australia, thanks in part to the obvious inclusion of three extra voices on the A-side. 'Every Christian Lion Hearted Man Will Show You', September's follow-up, failed to chart.

Paul Oscar Beuselinck, the son of a show business lawyer, was born in Peterborough shortly after the end of World War II and first came to Robert Stigwood's attention while playing piano with Screaming Lord Sutch and The Savages in 1964. Robert himself launched Paul's solo career in 1966 with the first of four single releases for his Reaction label. The second, 'Join My Gang' was written by Pete Townshend and the third, 'Over The Wall We Go', by David Bowie. "Robert Stigwood decided to do this campaign on me," Paul said. "He'd done it with a singer called Simon Scott, and he'd put out a lot of busts and things; so he'd decided that I'd be called Oscar – my middle name is Oscar – so that's how it came about. And he put out a lot of sort of Oscars, busts of me that looked like Oscars."

The fourth in the series was 'Holiday', where he took advantage of the decision by Polydor not to release The Bee Gees' version in Britain, despite its success elsewhere in Europe and the States. Robin was only too glad to lend some very evident vocal support as Paul explained. "I'd heard the record, because Robin sang it on their album. It was recorded in a studio in Portland Place I remember, and [he] came down and did the backing on it. I'm not sure if Barry was there, but Robin was certainly there, and I think Maurice was [too]." Robert Stigwood regained production credits again, while musical direction was courtesy of Bill Shepherd. Paul's next single was released on Polydor a few months later before his manager cottoned on to the fact that the Oscar nomenclature just wasn't working. He was re-launched as Paul Nicholas, and although his first chart success was still eight years away, film stardom was just around the corner. Indeed, between 1969 and 1999, he would appear in 19 films or TV series, with *Tommy*, *The Jazz Singer* and *Just Good Friends* perhaps being the most representative.

Whilst The Bee Gees' 'Words' climbed steadily up the charts in January 1968, the other simultaneous single release from the film *The Mini Mob* didn't fare nearly as well. 'All Our Christmases' was the eighth and final flop for Decca outfit, The Majority, who originally hailed from Hull. A harmony group like The Bee Gees, they did a very nice job with this pleasant little ditty that had flowed from the pen of all three brothers. Discouraged by this latest failure, The Majority disbanded not long afterwards.

Meanwhile, across the other side of the Atlantic Ocean, another harmony-oriented group, a New York quintet of Italian descent called Sounds Of Modification, had included Barry's 'You' on their album of the same name for Jubilee Records, which also popped up in the UK on the EMI subsidiary, Stateside.

Even though Barry protested tongue-in-cheek to the contrary, financial gain was never the main consideration for his interest in how other artists interpreted Gibb compositions. "It's interesting when another singer does your song," he suggested, "because when you write something, you kind of sing it in your mind, and it's your own voice you hear. So when someone else puts their ideas into it, it often comes out very different. It's great that an artist such as Paul [Jones] should want to record one of our songs. Same with Billy Fury doing one. Artists of that calibre know good from bad. Of course, it's not only the prestige we like, but the money!"

The songs he referred to in this instance were 'One Minute Woman' by Fury, but it was the one by former Manfred Mann vocalist and harmonica player, Paul Jones, that must have thrilled him most. Barry's hero then, and probably still today, was Paul McCartney, and although uncredited on the Columbia single release of 'And The Sun Will Shine', the appearance of Macca on drums, and Jeff Beck on guitar for that matter, must have been a source of pride to the eldest Gibb brother.

Barry and Robin had spent their first Christmas after leaving Australia . . . in Australia! They had travelled there at the invitation of Robert Stigwood who was keen to introduce them to his mother and, indeed, his mother to them. The brothers also took the opportunity to ingratiate themselves with the Australian music press in Sydney and, while there, met up again with the Balmer family. Lori, by now just 10, had maintained a close contact with Andy and they wrote to each other regularly. She still wanted to pursue a musical career, and Barry did nothing to discourage her, promising to help if her parents ever returned to Britain. Less than a month had elapsed before Barry's word was put to the test.

"We arrived in the UK in January '68, and I signed to the Robert Stigwood Organisation." Lori reminisced. "We stayed with the Gibb family on arrival and it was a very exciting time. I worked on all the TV shows, radio – for example, *BBC 1 Club* – regularly. Kids love to see other kids sing, and I was dubbed the 'bush baby' by the British press." Sometimes, she even appeared on the same shows as The Bee Gees.

On July 23, she was given more assistance from Barry than she could possibly have imagined. Taken into a recording studio, she was given the complete Bee Gees treatment. First off, she was presented with two songs, 'Treacle Brown' and 'Four Faces West', both of which were composed by all three brothers. Although originally written for the abandoned *Pippi Longstocking* film, they were given to Lori as her own and, apart from an Italian language version of 'Treacle Brown' released the same year by Anna Marchetti, neither were recorded by anyone else. Not only were the Gibbs there to provide encouragement, guidance and vocal backing, they were joined by Colin and Vince on drums and guitar respectively. Barry played rhythm guitar whilst Maurice tickled the ivories. To complete the family atmosphere, Bill Shepherd took control of musical arrangements while Barry tried his hand at producing, although the subsequent Polydor single release credits his brothers as well.

The downside to all this could have been that she might have been dominated by the large Bee Gees presence, but if anything the opposite is true as young Lori steals the show. It is only recently that those fortunate enough to have heard both songs have been able to establish that the powerful voice belongs to an 11 year old, and not a teenager as had previously been suspected. Little wonder, therefore, that a bright future was predicted. It wasn't to be.

"My contract came unstuck," she revealed, "as often happens when lawyers, parents and a child are involved. But, for my part, my affection and gratitude to the whole Gibb family is far-reaching and unwaning. Andy and I remained in contact by letters and phone for quite some time."

Back in her parents' Sydney home, Lori discovered another means of keeping up with the latest news from England. "Lesley, the boys' sister, and [her husband] Keith had kennels in Sydney breeding bull terriers for many years, and so I stayed in contact with the family's goings-on."

Her experiences in England would appear to have served her in good stead as her career is one many would envy. She toured or recorded – under pseudonyms – with the likes of Cliff Richard, Tina Turner, Brian Ferry, Joe Cocker, Lionel Ritchie, U2, George Harrison, Van Halen and Johnny Rotten. She continues to perform on Australia's Gold Coast, appearing with Johnny Vallins as the duo Short Notice. She first met Johnny back in England in 1968 when he was a member of Tin Tin and, 13 years later, they were married and now have a four year old son called Sam who appears to have inherited his parents' and, indeed, his maternal grandparents' talent.

The high hopes that the brothers, and Polydor for that matter, had shared for Lori, had been dashed by some legal rigmarole. There would be no such problems for their next protégés, and again another collaborator from their Australian recordings would be involved.

15

LET THERE BE LOVE

"I WAS MARRIED, and I've owned up that it all went very flat, and that was the end of it," Barry told *Rave*'s Chris Webb. "I'd not recommend getting married early . . . because you make a mistake, and it's something that you've got to live with for the rest of your life. If they are in love, there is only one thing to do and that is to get married. Neither I nor anyone else would stop them. They have to learn from their mistakes."

Barry was speaking in general terms about couples marrying too young, but it's also likely he had two very specific young people in mind. But neither Robin nor Maurice was willing to concede that their elder brother might have a valid point, or that they might even learn from his mistake.

Maurice's off-again-on-again romance with Lulu was definitely back on, with Davy Jones and Sarolta completely out of the picture and Maurice trying to play down the extent of Lulu's relationship with the Monkees' vocalist.

"Davy Jones was a good friend of mine," said Maurice. "I broke it off with Lulu over the phone and Davy called me up and said, 'I am going to ask Lu to dinner with some friends, is that all right?' I said, 'Yes, I am not going out with her any more, have a ball,' and threw the phone down. They then took so many photos of them and made it look like a six-month romance, but she had only been out with him that one night – she did not even want to go out. She phoned me the next day and she was crying, saying she was sorry."

Maurice later regretted not accepting her apology. "We just grew up, that's all," he admitted. "We were miserable apart and when we started going out again, it got so that I didn't want to be with anyone else. I used to phone her up from Los Angeles about twice a day. Then she'd call me back. We used to make about 90 minute calls . . ."

Maurice recalled the first meeting with his future in-laws. "I went up to Glasgow to meet Lu's parents, and I was told that Billy, who is younger than Lu, would be at the station to meet me. I got off the train and was walking along the platform when I saw him. I didn't need to speak – I knew it was Billy and I went up to him and said, 'You're Billy, aren't you?' He said, 'You must be Maurice,' and we had met."

For Billy Lawrie, his first meeting with Maurice stood out in his mind for quite a different reason: the yellow jacket imprinted with yellow and grey giraffes that his future brother-in-law was wearing.

In the other corner, Robin and Molly had been engaged for a year when Robin set the wedding date. They had lived together for a while in a tiny flat in Paddington. "That was to prove Molly wasn't only after my money," Robin joked, but Molly said they deliberately took plenty of time before getting married.

"I was determined that getting married would not harm Robin or the group," she explained. "I didn't want to risk it having a disastrous effect on the group's popularity, although I think kids today grow up at a much earlier age and have a more adult outlook at their pop favourites getting married. They accept it much more readily than in the past.

"Mind you, we still talked about whether to marry for three months before Robin finally named the day. It was December 4 and that was that. Typical of him," she added.

Molly had envisaged a quiet wedding, hoping to keep their plans out of the press. "Only my family and Robin's knew initially," she said. "Then the papers got hold of the news and, of course, there was no peace after that."

"We got married in a registry office because I do not believe in any particular religion," Robin explained. "I would have felt very hypocritical getting married in a church. I do believe in God but in my own God, not anybody else's."

So the new Mr and Mrs. Robin Gibb stepped out of London's Caxton Hall to a barrage of camera flashes before leaving for the reception at their new home in exclusive Montpelier Square in Knightsbridge.

"I don't know how many people were there," Robin said of the reception. "Judging by the cigarette ash they trod into the carpets, it must have been thousands. We put ashtrays all round the room but nobody used them. They stubbed all their cigarettes straight into the carpets; it was incredible. I suppose there must have been about 150 people there – and we knew 10 of them. The others had all been invited by Robert Stigwood. There were a lot of journalists."

With the benefit of hindsight, Robin said, "I was married at 18, but that didn't have anything to do with my unhappiness. I wasn't happy before and I wasn't happy later. Still it was probably one of the several mistakes I made of the time. I wish I knew at 18 what a responsible state marriage was. I met my wife . . . after we arrived in England, and she was working with The Beatles and Brian Epstein and all those people. We were married in the way people did things in those days – without thinking about it. We didn't have any children until I was 22, and until then we lived a strange yo-yo kind of life. We were living on our nerves. I tended to be a bit of a recluse and a bit wayward, so I probably wasn't suitable to be married to anybody. I certainly didn't give my wife an easy time."

Later in December, Robin and Molly left for a Swiss honeymoon which, according to Robin, might well have spelled the end of their marriage. "We had booked a chalet near Geneva," he explained, "but it just so happened that the travel agent had forgotten to tell me it was right in the middle of the landslide season. The chalet was nothing more than a wooden hut, stuck on the side of a mountain miles from anywhere. One night, the snow came down in a solid sheet. With it came half the mountain, right outside our little hut . . . We had no telephone . . . one tiny stove and a little fuel. There was no central heating in the chalet, and we had to make home in the kitchen. A blizzard was blowing, but I went out and got trapped in the snow. I almost suffocated until this French guy saw me with his torch and shouted to hold still while he threw a rope. He couldn't pull on the ice, and by now the snow was almost up to my neck and they had to get a truck and a chain to pull me clear. I nearly died that night."

No stranger to brushes with death – his childhood bicycle accident, the car accident in Australia, Hither Green – Robin quipped, "I don't know why I've been picked out, but I hope whoever is responsible for almost killing me off has realised that I'm not quite ready for it yet."

Suddenly serious, he added, "Because I've had these narrow escapes, I've learned to appreciate the little things in life. I still remember that train crash and thinking I was going to die. I don't have nightmares about the accidents, but when I do think of them, a cold shiver runs up my spine."

It was a cold and hungry Robin who finally made his way back to the chalet, where the only food was one egg and a piece of cheese. "I had that egg raw. There was nothing to cook with – and I tell you it was the nicest thing in my life. Molly was ill and I was very sick the following day – New Year's Day," he continued. "It wasn't a very happy start to the New Year . . .

"[Then] a taxi drew up outside the front door . . . It was a friend I had invited up and forgotten about. He produced a bottle of Scotch from his pocket, and we set about welcoming in the New Year right away. Then we all jumped back in the taxi and flew on to Paris for a real honeymoon."

Back in Britain Molly revealed that the couple had no immediate plans for any little Gibblets. "I come from a big family – there are seven of us – and although we obviously won't have the hardships that my parents suffered in struggling to bring us up, Robin and I don't want to be involved with lots of children because we couldn't then lead our own lives together. We do want two or three children, but not for a few years yet."

Nor did she intend to accompany Robin when The Bee Gees toured. "I went on the German tour . . . with him," she said, "but it's not much fun for a woman travelling around all the time. I don't like being with Robin when he's working. If I go abroad with him, or to a television studio, I'm always left on my own. He's much too busy to spend time with me so I just feel as though I'm in the way. You don't really get much time to see each other so I shall stay home."

"I know just how Molly feels," Robin agreed. "I know she would rather stay at home, so that's the way it is. But she knows that if she ever wanted to come with me, she could."

While Robin was battling snowdrifts in the Swiss Alps, Maurice and Lulu announced their engagement on the first show of her new two-part Saturday night BBC TV special, *Happening For Lulu*, which followed her hugely popular series for the Corporation, *Lulu's Back In Town*. Broadcast live on December 28 at 6.15 p.m., the 43-minute show featured Lulu's performances of tracks like 'Cry Like A Baby', 'Why Did I Choose You', 'My 'Ain Folk', The Bee Gees' 'To Love Somebody' and Stevie Wonder's 'For Once In My Life', before reappearing to sing with Maurice.

Although Maurice confessed to a bad case of pre-show jitters in his first television appearance without the rest of the group, his nervousness wasn't evident as the couple performed a romantic duet of Donovan's 'What A Beautiful Creature You Are'. A delighted Lulu declared it "the best thing in the show – but then I'm biased! I was thrilled that we did a bit in the show together. Maurice wants to concentrate more on his piano playing. He really is terribly serious about becoming a well-known pianist. Maybe we will go on writing some songs together."

The show provided Maurice with the opportunity to demonstrate his keyboard prowess when the 32-piece Johnny Harris Orchestra backed him on 'Seven Seas Symphony'. Other guests included The Cartoons who performed 'Penny For The Sun' before dueting with their host on 'Toby Jug'. Also present were The Tremeloes with 'Nothing But A House Party' and, backed by Harris' orchestra, a version of Bob Dylan's 'I Shall Be Released'. Throughout the show, Pan's People, aided by two male dancers, provided additional visual entertainment. The highlight, of course, was the announcement of Lulu's forthcoming wedding.

"About four months ago, I decided I wanted to [propose] and a week before Christmas I said, 'Let's get married,' " Maurice revealed to *NME*'s Richard Green. "But Lulu said, 'Let's get engaged first,' and I said okay. It wasn't a rush, it just happened. Nobody pushed us into anything. I can't honestly say when we're going to get married. When we get time, I suppose."

If finding time for the wedding was problematical, a honeymoon seemed out of the question. "I don't honestly know if there will be time," Lulu said. "We may just have time for a few days' holiday somewhere. I can cut down on work if I want, but Maurice has got three other guys to think about. I expect we'll have a holiday together sometime, but at the moment I've got my TV series, then they're off filming and when they finish I begin mine, so we will keep missing each other."

"I hope Lu can come to Spain during the filming [of *Lord Kitchener's Little Drummer Boys*]," implored her future husband. "Even if it's only for weekends, it'll be worth it. It's going to be very hard for us when we're married being apart so much."

Perhaps sensing troubled waters ahead, Lulu agreed. "Yeah, it's something we're gonna' have to work out. Maybe it can be arranged so that we're working near each other, but I don't think that'll happen often. I suppose the phone bills will start going up again!"

Maurice remained optimistic about the couple's future, although it was apparent that friends did not share his confidence. "Everyone says you should not marry anybody in the business, but it's great because she understands when you have to go away, say for a week on tour."

Lulu showed off her engagement ring, saying, "Maurice loves driving, and I love window shopping. We went round a lot of Kent villages, and I saw it in a little shop. It's a sapphire with diamonds round it. It's Edwardian and in cabochon style, which means the stone hasn't been cut. I like it because it looks just like a mountain."

She disclosed that her manager Marian Massey had been wonderful about the news. "She was as excited as I am about it, and she suggested that I give up the business in about a year. She's not like the image of a manager that is usually built up. She didn't worry about herself, she just wanted to be sure that I'd be happy.

"At first, I couldn't agree with her, but the more I thought about it, the more I saw her point of view and saw what she was thinking. I won't stop yet, maybe later when we start having babies. Can you imagine me with my hair in curlers, and a pinny on sweeping the house? What a gas!"

"When she has her first baby will do," Maurice added. "She wants five and so do I. We're agreed on that. It's a good thing to agree on, isn't it?" They also agreed on the timing of their first born, which Maurice confirmed would be planned for "about two year's time". Continuing, he revealed, "If we had one now, it would be by accident. We want to get to know one another first. Once the child comes, the attention goes away from the wife or husband to the child and that is why a lot of marriages split up by having children too young."

Meantime, Barry continued to muse over the changes taking place in the group. "I thought the time had come when we should make some kind of move . . . not leaving pop entirely but by going into films. That way you can stay with the kids but be seen by more people . . .

"Instead of us doing this, we have found a more sensible way. We have found that we can get to the kids in different ways and still stay together. Like Maurice was on Lulu's show playing the piano with an orchestra. None of the kids would have expected to see him there without The Bee Gees. Another time it may be Robin on his own. Maurice is with Lulu now most of the time. If he hadn't fallen in love with Lulu, we would be together more. And Robin is now married so it cannot be like it was."

Barry maintained his role as the older and wiser brother. "Both Robin and Maurice knew my thoughts on the subject of marriage," he said with resignation. "What I said to Maurice was that you are going to do this anyway and you don't have to listen to my advice. It was the same with Robin. The reason it worried me was because they both married younger than I did. I have learnt from my mistake. I hope and pray that Robin and Maurice don't have to learn the same way."

Maurice blithely disregarded this brotherly advice. "Barry's blast-offs don't bother me, purely because half of what he says doesn't really mean anything," he responded. "What I mean is that what he says is true, but he exaggerates it. He has the chance to say more because he has most of the interviews – and he doesn't let you down, does he? When Lu and I announced we were getting married and he turned round and announced in *Disc* that we were too young, I simply said, 'Look, Barry, we're in love and we're getting married whatever you think. If anyone had said you were too young when you got married, you wouldn't have listened to brotherly advice either.'"

Barry and Lynda had spent the Christmas holidays in Australia, and he had used the trip in part to seek out new talent, saying, "I've signed up a girl group who are going to be the next big thing in pop. I'm going to mould them myself and write songs for them. I know what I'm talking about – look at The Marbles . . . They're normal, attractive, nice girls. They're English actually . . . these girls are completely different. They've got a wonderful sense of humility and a wonderful sense of humour.

"I've also got another boy probably coming over in three to six months. He's an old friend called Ronnie Burns, and he's a very big teenage artist in Australia. I know that doesn't mean anything here – don't I know it! But I think he's got a great voice and the market is right at the moment for a good male singer."

The holiday got off to a bad start when £8,000 worth of jewellery was stolen from Barry and Lynda's room at the Chevron Hilton Hotel in Sydney. Barry said wryly, "[The thieves] kindly unpacked all my cases and even took my trousers!"

Barry's love of jewellery was well documented. He was once interviewed wearing jewellery worth £16,350 and claimed to have another £5,000 worth in a bank safe deposit. "I used to go into Woolworth's and buy anything that sparkled," he said. "Over the years the collection built up. I like rings with unusual settings. I don't get stared at too much when I'm wearing a lot and I don't think I'm ostentatious. I don't think I'm spending money when I buy jewellery. I believe in assets so I collect securities. You can always sell them for more than the cost price."

The Sydney police recovered the goods, which were duly returned to Barry, but the saga did not end there.

On their return to Britain on January 19, Barry was stopped when he attempted to go through the "nothing to declare" exit at Heathrow. Her Majesty's Customs Officers pounced, and a search revealed that tucked away in his pocket was a gold and diamond watch worth £3,000 which he had bought while the couple were away. Frightened and confused, Barry claimed that he had bought the watch in London and signed a paper to that effect.

According to his lawyer, David Harter, Barry was tired after the 25-hour trip and "had panicked and told lies" but that it was not premeditated – he had only put the watch in his pocket because it was snagging Lynda's stockings. He was charged with trying to evade customs duty. The case was eventually settled the following June, with the watch confiscated and Barry fined a punitive £2,000 for evasion of customs duty and £500 for filing a false statement.

With no time to recover from his ordeal or jet lag from his long flight, the following day The Bee Gees began recording a Tom Jones television special. Two weeks later, on Valentine's Day, Maurice presented the *Disc & Music Echo* Awards, with Lulu winning four of them.

Both Maurice and Lulu maintained that they wanted a small intimate wedding. "It's something you can look back on in 20 years' time. It's a personal thing, the most important day in your life," Lulu said, whereupon she issued statements to the press naming the date, time and place, thus ensuring that the wedding would be anything but a quiet, low-key affair.

Barbara and Hugh Gibb had settled in Gerrard's Cross in Buckinghamshire and, when visiting them, Maurice and Lulu had much admired the picturesque St James' Church there. It was, they believed, the ideal place to hold their wedding.

Lulu arrived 20 minutes late at the church on February 17, 1969 to find the police desperately trying to hold back a crowd of nearly 3,000, all pushing and jostling to catch a glimpse of the diminutive singer in her wedding finery of white mini dress, white boots and a long, hooded white coat trimmed in mink.

Robin acted as best man for his twin brother, and Lulu's manager Marian Massey's daughter Sharon, six-year-old Beri Gibb, and Lulu's 10-year-old sister Edwina were the bridesmaids. The couple's young brothers, 10-year-old Andy Gibb and six-year-old Gordon Lawrie were pages, looking adorable in their kilts and velvet jackets, according to the bride. Guests included Cynthia Lennon, Kenny Rogers, Mickie Most and, of course, elder brother Barry.

"When I came out in my wedding dress, my father looked at me and cried," Lulu recalled. "Of course, I was telling everyone that I wasn't nervous and how confident I felt, then when I walked into the church and saw Maurice . . . oh, I don't know, I just felt the tears coming.

"I asked my father if he had a handkerchief, and he pulled one out and wiped his own eyes and put it back again. So there I was, walking down the aisle with tears running down my face, not to mention mascara. Then when I stood at the altar with Maurice I looked at him and I was laughing and crying all at the same time. I felt such love for him."

Afterwards, Lulu said that for her, "Marriage was almost an impulse. I am not one to mess around and, having made up my mind, I went ahead as quickly as I could, and that was it."

Living together was not an option they seriously contemplated. "Perhaps it was our upbringing," she said. "I think one or two people were surprised, particularly in this day and age. There is the danger in marrying young, but there's also the advantage of being able to grow up together."

Three days after the wedding, it was business as usual, with Lulu returning to rehearsals for her television show, and preparing to represent Britain in the Eurovision Song Contest the following month. Maurice and both of their mothers accompanied Lulu to Madrid for the contest, which ended in an unprecedented four-way tie. Lulu got the last laugh though, since her entry, 'Boom Bang-A-Bang' got into the Top 10 and became a big hit, and as she pointed out, "The other three songs did nothing."

Maurice enjoyed his new role as Lulu's husband. He claimed, "I was always the one left behind. Out in the streets, people would point and say, 'That's Robin with the big teeth' and, 'That's Barry, the good-looking leader of the group.' But when they saw me they'd simply say, 'That's just one of The Bee Gees.' But at least I ended up with the best looking wife. No one knew me until I met my wife. Even Lulu's mother used to ask, 'Which one is Maurice?' For six months after we were going out she thought Lulu was dating Barry. In Birmingham . . . where Lu was appearing in cabaret we went into a shop and a woman came up and asked Lu for her autograph. Then she turned to me and said, 'Yours too, Barry.' This happened again five times before the day was out. I'm sure people in faraway places like Dundee are quite convinced she married Barry. Stands to reason she'd marry the best looking guy in the group."

Years later, Lulu laughed, "Sometimes I think Barry and I were destined to be together. So many people make the same mistake and think I was married to him. I told my mother I was dating one of The Bee Gees. She asked if it was the good-looking one. I said yes, meaning Maurice, but she thought I meant Barry. From that point on, I think she thought Barry should have been the appropriate one for me!"

With Eurovision out of the way, Maurice and Lulu were finally able to go off on their postponed Acapulco honeymoon. Barry and Lynda accompanied them.

With his divorce from Maureen not yet final, Barry was unable, and perhaps also reluctant, to commit himself completely. "At the moment I have a perfect partner," he said. "I am in love with Lynda. I don't just love her. But I won't marry her until I am sure. She is the kindest person I have ever met in my life. She will do anything for you.

"I will be contradicting myself, but I know I have the right woman this time. But we will wait, and in a couple of years I will know if Lynda can put up with me. The best thing is always to wait."

★   ★   ★

Rumours still abounded that Barry was planning to leave The Bee Gees behind in favour of a career in films, but Robin firmly denied any question of a split.

"He's not going at all," he insisted. "We'll stay together because we're not like a pop group; we are writers and we like to perform and record the things we write but we don't do one-night stands or anything like that. I hope we all stay together singing. I'd like to direct films; I'd get a lot of enjoyment out of that. I've got film and videotaping equipment in my house and I can show my films through my own television. This is something I enjoy as an individual but as far as the group is concerned, I think we'll stay together for years. We've got a very close bond."

But Barry was beginning to feel that he was an outsider in the group, complaining, "The brothers' scene is different now that two are married. It makes me a lone ranger. They are both married, so is Colin, and I am on my way out of marriage.

"In about seven months my divorce will be through and I will be single again. I have always believed that kids don't really like the idea of stars being married. It still does make a difference . . . I want to stay single for a while, but there should be at least one bachelor in the group.

"I cannot see my brothers any more as much as I would like to. When we work, we are together, but rarely otherwise . . . It hurts a lot but I have to face the fact that my brothers are married . . . It could have a damaging effect; it could have a good effect. We might now be more happy when we are together."

Tom Kennedy recalled that there was some internal bickering with the group, but as often occurs in families, outsiders' advice was decidedly unwelcome. "No matter how big the argument those three boys could be having," he said, "you could never intervene because they would, as a whole, attack you. You know, 'What's it got to do with you, pal?' – they would be united. Obviously, that's the sort of thing that affected the band members as well, because they would always be united in their cause."

The group remained friendly with Vince Melouney in the months following his departure. He visited some of their recording sessions, and Barry attended some of his sessions with Ashton, Gardner & Dyke. Vince was quick to acknowledge the fact that his Bee Gees career would assist, rather than hinder, his new one. "I know it's a great advantage and in our favour that I have been with such a world-known group. I hope it will be a great help to get us launched."

Revealing his intention to take a more behind the scenes role in future he confirmed, "I won't be the front man, the one on stage to sell the group."

As much as he was looking to the future, it was clear that he would carry the baggage of his past with him for some time to come. "It was no use, I never fitted in as a Bee Gee," Vince said ruefully. "I was just a prop for the talents of the Gibb brothers. I had to get out and do something on my own. The blues has always been my music, I was just adapting myself to a musical style that was not really me.

"I'm not complaining. I had a good run with The Bee Gees and saw the world but the time to split has come. The boys all knew of my decision and my breaking away is a very amicable thing, no nastiness at all. To be honest, the Gibbs are three extremely talented fellows. Barry is a fantastically beautiful songwriter, Maurice is a great arranger of material and Robin comes up with some fantastic song ideas.

"I wouldn't say that I was unnecessary in the group but obviously, because they have such great ability, the emphasis all round has always been on them. Publicity-wise, both Colin and I never did bother too much about being left out or ignored. We never really cared. There were times, naturally, when musically we didn't agree, but never anything serious enough to cause arguments. Of course [the Gibbs] had more power than me, but all major decisions made for The Bee Gees were finally decided by our manager Robert Stigwood. I've learned a lot from Robert about how to handle things."

One of the things he hadn't learned from Robert was the value of tact and discretion. Adding fuel to an already smouldering fire, he revealed to a vulture-like press, "Just between you and me, it would not surprise me if the group split again later."

Colin Petersen also sensed trouble ahead, saying, "I think . . . that Vince's leaving did more damage than people think it did, and I don't think The Bee Gees could possibly stand another person leaving. It would not be possible for any of us to leave now without breaking the group up. All we have to do this year is the film, and I think after this year The Bee Gees' work will be limited to recording. I might be wrong, but I think that is the case."

After his marriage, Colin was beginning to branch out into other areas; setting up a management company with his wife Joanne, making plans to produce records and reactivating his writing partnership with his Australian friend, Carl Groszman. "I am not like any of the others," he added. "I have got more interests apart from the group than the others. I am tighter with money than them, in the respect that I worry about the future. The brothers most times just live for the day."

Whatever professional tensions there might be, all three brothers seemed contented in their personal relationships. Robin professed to find married life "wonderful", adding, "Coming back to Molly and a proper home is like having a rock to rest on. I can leave The Bee Gees and pop outside the front door any time I want, and sit on the floor and play ludo with Molly.

"Before I met Molly, I had never really thought of getting married. Well, I'm only 19 now. But you know how it is, I started chatting her up, and all that. Then I asked her out, and to my immense surprise, she said 'yes.' I've always kept an open mind on the type of girl I wanted to marry. I never said she must have a perfect figure, be brunette, petite or intelligent. I was just going to accept the girl for what she was."

As for Molly, it was taking some time to get used to the change from a busy office to the house in Kensington. "Now and again I miss all the people – there were so many coming and going at NEMS. But being a housewife is a pretty near full-time job. I like looking after the house myself. I do all my own cooking and apart from that, it's my job to file all Robin's songs and correct any spelling mistakes. I'm his unpaid private secretary."

Molly also revealed that the couple were looking for a new house at that time. "This place was already furnished and you just don't feel like putting yourself out to keep a place nice that isn't really yours," she added. "We don't want to live too far out, but we want a nice old house with some ground. Robin has looked at some, but the leases were too short. He knows more about these things than I do."

Her biggest problem seemed to be The Bee Gees' devoted admirers. "The main [disadvantage] is the fans," she revealed. "They come to the door and call me all manner of names. At first I wanted to have a go at them and take a broom to them, but I got used to it. It's Robin who stands to lose if I tell the fans to go away. After all, they are only kids, envious of something I've taken away from them."

Lynda Gray was also having problems with fans. "Photographs of Barry and I together have appeared in the newspapers quite a lot recently," she said. "Some fans have found out my name and make malicious telephone calls. They're bad enough, but it's the poison pen letters that I can't bear. I never believed people could really be so sick."

Still, she was blissfully happy with her new lifestyle. "My feet have hardly touched the ground. Musselburgh seems a million miles away. I hadn't been anywhere or done anything then, nor did it seem I ever would.

"The first thing I wanted to do when I met Barry was see London. Well, I saw it all right. I found out about things that I never knew happened. We went to all the in clubs, ate at the best restaurants, were invited to premieres and party after party, and I met some of the stars whose fan I had been. Since then I have been almost around the world with Barry. We've seen Los Angeles, Hollywood, Rome, Nairobi, Sydney, Singapore, Vienna . . . there's hardly a country I haven't visited with him," she added.

Maurice and Lulu were settling into their Tudor cottage near Windsor. "Maurice and I are getting to know each other," Lulu told *FAB 208*'s June Southworth. "It takes time for two people to know each other – *really* know – even though you love each other. It isn't an instant happening. We know we like the same things . . . clothes and music and fun and babies.

"Much of our time together before we were married, we used to spend buying things for Maurice's flat. And I always kissed him goodnight on the doorstep. I don't disagree with people living together when they're not married, but marriage is better!

"I'm a wife first before anything else. Life is falling in love and getting married and having babies. We hope to have three or four in time, a girl first – Maurice wants a girl – then a boy. Maybe in a year or so, but who knows?

"We've been told the first year of marriage is the worst," Lulu concluded. "If that's so, we just can't wait for the next year. I mean, how could we possibly be happier than this?"

16

YOU'LL NEVER SEE MY FACE AGAIN

T HE FIRST CANDIDATE for the next Bee Gees single was 'Odessa (City On The Black Sea)', originally titled 'Odessa (On The White Sea)', which remains one of the most ambitious songs The Bee Gees have ever done. Its title inspired by a travel brochure Robin had seen, the song is built around a simple verse-chorus, but with added opening and closing sections, all performed in a stately tempo that gives it a feeling of genuine power. The lyrics are in their best stream of consciousness style, telling the story of the sole survivor of the fictitious British ship *Veronica*, floating on an iceberg in the Baltic Sea. After an orchestral opening, and some introductory lines sung by the group (which never repeat), the song settles into verse one, Robin singing solo to sparse accompaniment of rhythm guitar and quiet piano, and the rhythm cuts out as voices build to a big, slow chorus of all three voices led by Robin in operatic style. Verse two adds electric bass guitar and proceeds at a faster pace through the same melody, into an even more intense chorus, augmented by a featured cello part played by Paul Buckmaster and some high wailing notes by Robin. The extended closing section has a rhythmic instrumental and wordless group vocal, building in power, and then dropping off and back to the opening orchestral and vocal part to finish.

The group discussed splitting the song's seven and a half minutes over both sides of a seven inch disc, although the traditional three minutes limit for a single had been broken the previous year by two seven-minute-plus hit singles, Richard Harris' 'MacArthur Park' and The Beatles' 'Hey Jude', neither of which was split to two sides. The idea to release it as the lead-off single was dropped, apparently because The Bee Gees were unwilling to be seen to be following a trend for long singles.

"I worked and worked on that 'Odessa' track," Robin said bitterly, "and I got a ring from Robert Stigwood to say it was the greatest pop classic he had ever experienced. He said it was stupendous, and I used to get calls from him at three and four and five and six in the morning telling me the same thing. I thought it was going to be the new single . . ."

Robert Stigwood's final choice for the single was released under a cloud of acrimony. "It all started with 'First Of May' being the single and the flip-side was 'Lamplight'," Maurice recalled. "I was in the middle of this.

208

Robin was singing the lead on 'Lamplight' and Barry was singing the lead on 'First Of May'. There was also a bit of management problems going on too at the time. Each one was being told, 'You don't need the other brother' and all that stuff was going down. Egos got in the way and when you're 19, 20 years old . . . It's like when managers promise you the world and what they can do for you, you really can do it alone. I never got told that, only Robin and Barry did. I was in the middle and the next thing I hear was that we were doing the *Cucumber Castle* film for television and Robin's quit because 'First Of May' is going to be the A-side."

"If Robert says 'First Of May', then 'First Of May' it is, whether it is a flop or a hit," Barry said, "because I never try and pick our singles. I can't. I always leave that to Robert."

"I haven't released a single yet that the whole group have liked," Stigwood shrugged. "Somebody is always going to be unhappy. This time it was Robin, yet fortunately I usually make the right decision because 25 million singles later, no one can be really unhappy about my choice.

"The fact is that [Robin] has an incredible and wonderful imagination. This is shown in the lyrics of his composition 'Odessa' . . . which is, I think, one of the finest pop songs ever written."

Certainly Stigwood's choice of single on a commercial basis could not be questioned as it made number five in the UK and number three in Germany. While it only just breached the US Top 40 at number 37, it was also Top Five in other places in the world such as Australia and New Zealand, and several European countries.

The choice of single didn't bother Maurice so much as the promotional appearances. "I was always the sexy bass player in the background while Robin stood centre . . . and I've never had the opportunity to prove on TV that I could play the piano," he complained. "I'm quite proud of my piano playing, and I had a good chance to express it on 'First Of May'. What happened? Robert Stigwood, our manager, decided that since Barry did the singing, we couldn't have Robin standing there doing nothing, so he sat at the piano and pretended to play while I was back on bass again. I mean to say, Robin's never played a note on the piano at our recording sessions. So I just wish I could be appreciated musically now."

The sessions for *Idea* were scarcely separated from those for the *Odessa* album, and these began at Atlantic Studios in New York as early as August 13, 1968, with the mixing taking place between October and December. This time The Bee Gees were going to try for something more ambitious and create a concept album, to be called *Masterpeace* (sic) or *The American Opera*. The album notes name IBC Studios for the fourth consecutive album, but some of it was recorded in the United States.

In the event, growing dissension between Barry and Robin caused the album to lose its concept, and it became *Odessa*, another collection of songs. It was released in a lavish red velvet gatefold sleeve embossed in gold, an extravagant touch which brought problems of its own.

"The early records came in the flocked cover," Tom Kennedy recalled, "the later ones came in just a red gloss cover because the fibres were like itching powder, and they brought the whole plant to a stop. When they were making the album covers and were sticking the flock on, it was getting in the air . . . causing rashes, and they had to stop production on it. At the end of production, they did go over to the non-flocked cover because of the problems they were having."

Odessa was a double album spread over two LP discs and running 65 minutes, almost twice the length of *Idea*. As with many such albums, there are many who feel it would have been better trimmed to a single disc, and Barry Gibb is among them.

"Robert Stigwood wanted a double album and we didn't know why," he said. "I think it was basically a financial deal. If we do a double album, everybody makes more money except the group. So we were doing something that we weren't motivated to do, because of somebody else wanting to have a double album go out. So it became full of all this stuff that didn't necessarily blow me away at all. I like some of the first sessions in New York. Everything was done for tax reasons, you know? You'd go to New York to record so you wouldn't have to pay taxes in England. We didn't even know these things. This was our management and record company. There were so many things going on in those days that had to do with how you lived your life, and you didn't know about them. So the *Odessa* album to me was not a good experience. It was an album that was made over many, many months, and we didn't really want to do it. A single album would've been perfect. A double album, it just seemed there was too much stuff that wasn't that good."

The problem with reducing a double album is that very rarely does everyone agree on what should be left out. In fact, a version trimmed to one LP was released in certain countries in the Seventies. Rather surprisingly, most of Robin's songs were cut.

"We were trying something there," Robin said. "No way can it be said to be commercial, but it wasn't done as a commercial thing so it was risky. From a recording angle, I think that we could have recorded it a hell of a lot better, but . . . 'Odessa' the actual song is still one of my favourites."

"People thought it was an in-depth album," Maurice recalled, "like, 'What do they mean by those lyrics?' and 'What's this all about?' There's all sorts of different areas on it. It went up and down in places, but a lot of people regard it as our *Sgt. Pepper*. To us, I don't think it was the best album we made, but the main title 'Odessa' I loved. I thought that was beautifully played by Paul Buckmaster, who eventually became Elton John's musical director. He was a cello player on one of our tours and sat in the room with us, and we wrote it all with just a cello and an accordion, so it was great memories from that album."

Barry disagreed with Maurice about the great memories. "I guess I have strong personal feelings about it because it was a time when the group was splitting up," he said. "We were in tremendous crisis with each other. You know, maybe it's because there was so much trouble and strife going on at the time the songs were written. I think there's probably a little bit of that in every song . . .

"I realised it was over when I turned up at the studio one night and realised I was the only one there. The engineer said, 'Let's [record] anyway' and I said, 'I can't,' and picked up my guitar and walked out. I went to Robert's house and then I found out that Robin and Maurice were recording somewhere else. I thought, 'This is the end.' "

The style of *Odessa* was a definitive shift from the pop of *Idea*, and the group were now without Vince Melouney, although he was involved in the initial New York recording sessions. The Bee Gees did not go so far as to offer the vague philosophical advice or quotations from classic literature that might have made it art rock, but they did provide a different kind of bridge between pop songs and the sound of an orchestra. Bill Shepherd must have had his hands full doing the charts as some of these songs are set in the lushest orchestration of any Bee Gees recordings. With both the lead-off single and opening album song among them, it seems as if all of the songs had large arrangements, but they don't. Some are basic rock and veer towards country. "It was my idea that we do that sort of thing," Colin Petersen claimed of the country influence on *Odessa*, "and Maurice is the one who will take more time out to listen to what I have to say, although within the group, the okay has to come from Barry."

"Barry is The Bee Gees co-ordinator," explained Robert Stigwood. "I use the word advisedly, as there is no leader of the group as such. He has a tremendous feel for soul music à la his composing work for The Marbles, but he is also a fantastic solo singer in his own right."

The musical ideas seem to have taxed the ability of the technical team. Some of the arrangements of orchestra, rock band, and lead and backing vocals are so lavish that they lose clarity, as if too much musical information is being crammed into a small space. Perhaps less would have been more. Depending on how clear the multi-track is, the *Odessa* album may be a good candidate for a remix some day.

One of the album's high spots was 'Melody Fair', a heavily orchestrated song where Barry trades off lead vocals with Maurice in the way he usually does with Robin. "I think 'Melody Fair' was written in the studio," Barry said. "We used to write a lot of stuff on the spot in the studio. We often used to go to recording studios without any songs at all. Because the time was booked [and] we had to be there. So we'd turn up at seven at night, and we'd basically start writing and cutting the backing track of a song that wasn't finished. We would just create it in that way . . . A lot of [the early] albums were done in one month, or five weeks. The first one was three weeks. It really makes you think about whether the technology has made things more complicated. It seems like everyone takes much longer now, and in fact, some of the best stuff I ever heard put on record was done at a time when people didn't even construct a song before they started recording. There was this flashing creativity that had to go on and you just did it. You didn't think about where it would end up. You just did it. 'Melody Fair' was probably influenced by 'Eleanor Rigby' – I was wanting to make the same kind of statement.''

Particularly unusual is the inclusion of 'Give Your Best', a square-dance with guitars and fiddle which Colin Petersen described as "the best recording session I've ever been to". Whether this was due to the influence of two anonymous bluegrass musicians on the song, he didn't say. It's followed by something even more unexpected, a pair of instrumentals; the first, 'Seven Seas Symphony', with Maurice's simple piano playing a complex (for them) melody line, and the second a string arrangement of the short 'For All Nations (International Anthem)'.

There was also 'Never Say Never Again'. "I wanted a line to go, 'I declared war on Spain'," Robin said of it. "Instead Barry wanted something so normal it was ridiculous. He said my words were so unromantic. But what could be more normal than a man in love wanting to declare war on anything that was to him unlovely?" In this instance, Robin was successful; the line stayed.

That the leading single 'First Of May' comes way back in the penultimate spot, shows how late it was chosen, and that no one wanted to re-sequence the album to fit it into a more commercial place in the order.

Maurice recalled the session in which that song came about. "Barry and I were sitting at the piano," he said, "and I started playing the chords, and Barry started singing, 'When I was small and Christmas trees were tall,' and started singing along with it . . . We put a demo down with a vocal and we kept the piano track. Went back to England, and went into IBC studios in London, added onto that piano track and Barry's vocal stayed on as well – he just redid bits of it. We had a choir and an orchestra all on this one piano."

Barry's tender, wistful vocal and the song's simple but strong arrangement perfectly complement its theme of childhood and lost love. The title came from an unexpected source, according to Barry. " 'First Of May', that was my dog's birthday. How that song came about was that I had a Pyrenean mountain dog called Barnaby and his birthday was the first of May."

The final song is a third instrumental, 'The British Opera', built around a simple organ part that might possibly be Robin, and if so, it could be that each brother took charge of an instrumental section, Barry being the 'International Anthem'.

Although Maurice has described it as a "heavy" album, some light relief could be found on Japanese copies of *Odessa*. Japanese pressings of records have always been much sought after by European collectors for a variety of reasons. The vinyl is of a superior quality, singles appear with lavish picture sleeves, and albums and singles both contain lyrics. More often than not, the lyrics appear not only in native Japanese but also in their original English form. Despite the words often being available from the songbooks which were commonly available in Britain at that time, the English lyrics which appeared on Japanese releases were often transcribed direct from the songs themselves. Consequently, mistakes would occur, often amusingly so. Bee Gees songs were no exception, and fans of the group were often amused by these "alternative" versions. The song 'Odessa' perhaps suffered more than most as the following comparison reveals:

> *Fourteenth of February, eighteen ninety-nine*
> *The British ship Veronica was lost without a sign*
> *Bah bah black sheep you haven't any wee [wool]*
> *Captain Odessa [Richardson]*
> *Kept himself a lonely life enclosed [wife in Hull]*
> *Cheryl [Cherub], I lost the [a] ship in the Baltic Sea*
> *I'm on a nice hird [iceberg] running free*
> *Sitting-filing this bird [berg] to the shape of a ship*
> *Sailing my way back to your lips*
> *One passing ship gave word that you have no doubts of your oath*
> *[moved out of your old flat]*
> *That you love the victor [vicar] more than words can say*
> *Tell him to pray that I won't melt away*
> *And I'll see your face one day [again]*
> *Odessa how strong am I*
> *Odessa how time does fly*
> *Trever [Treasure] you know the neighbours that lived next door*
> *They haven't got their dog anymore*
> *Freezing sailing around in the North Atlantic*
> *Can't seem to eat [leave] the sea anymore*
> *I just don't understand*
> *Why you just moved to Finland*
> *You love that victor [vicar] more than words can say*
> *Ask him to pray that I won't melt away*
> *And I'll see your face again*
> *Odessa how strong am I*
> *Odessa how time does fly*
> *Fourteenth of February eighteen ninety-nine*
> *The British ship Veronica was lost without a sign*

Lyrics by B., R. & M. Gibb © 1969 Abigail Music Ltd.

The *Odessa* album marked the beginning of a period that all the brothers would rather forget. Although Barry had been the first to indicate that he might soon leave the group, it was Robin who quit the group first, thus triggering a sequence of events that led to the entire group disintegrating. For a while all three brothers appeared to be at loggerheads with one another, and although they placed the blame for the bickering firmly on the media, without their own almost daily statements to the press there would have been little to write about.

"It was a lot nastier in the press than it was in actuality," Barry has protested. "We were nervous wrecks at the end of the Sixties; touring, recording, promotion. I was living in Eaton Square and my neighbours must have thought I was a bit freaky. I can remember a time when I walked out my front door and there were six cars and they all belonged to me. That's madness. The break was a traumatic experience. Long after we fought, the press had us fighting and reopened wounds."

"I used to be very insecure," Robin said. "There was a lot of pressure around me, and I had trouble coping with initial stardom and touring. We were very young and we didn't know how to handle [fame], and that was all it was. It was like a kettle that just had to boil. I think that it was good for us to split up when we did. Groups can split up all the time now and come back together again, and no one bats an eyelid or says anything or even thinks of it as any importance.

"It was never a hoo-hah in America when we split up, but it was in England. For some unknown reason, it was murder. It was the biggest nightmare that I've ever, ever gone through, and it has been for the three of us. I mean, the press, the trade papers and everyone just made our lives hell, and they made it so bad for us when we got back together . . . Those days left a sort of mark on me. I could never understand why people wrote and said the things they did about us when all we did was break up. It was such a dreadful situation at that time that nobody knew what was going to happen from day to day. I never even enjoyed the success of 'Saved By The Bell' even in this country because I was too busy in my lawyer's office. Everyone was suing each other. It was ridiculous and the only people that were benefiting were the lawyers."

"It was more of a spontaneous blast," Barry added. "It was sort of what we call our first fame. When somebody gets famous for the first time and your ego gets out of control, you start to get too much money. The Bee Gees were a casualty of the pop business. We started arguing in the press. This is a big pitfall for most groups, when you start fighting with each other through the newspapers. Instead of talking to each other, we would actually argue through the newspapers."

Robin has described the break as "a clash of personalities. We realised at the time that our personalities were all the same. We all had the same goals. The only difference being that we wanted to do it on our own. When we were on our own, we realised the goal we were trying to make on our own was the same goal we were trying to make together."

"We stayed to ourselves, surrounded by hangers-on," Barry explained. "Each had his own camp of 'friends' who said he was the real star, he should go solo. When we became isolated, the problems started. We stopped seeing one another as brothers. We were three stars unto ourselves.

"The pressure and fame got to Robin the most. He's a very deep thinker with a serious, sensitive side to him. He gets in moods that last quite a while. I remember when things were coming apart . . . I went over to his house to talk to him, try to straighten things out. All these people were sitting around him. And every time I said something they'd look at him like, 'Don't listen to him.' This was happening to a family, not just to a rock band. It was terrifying.

"It's doubly hard to be brothers in show business because our private life was magnified and made public. Our family squabbles were blown out of proportion. It was harder than ever being apart, for – unlike ex-business colleagues – you never become an ex-brother. We were never brother against brother, face to face. We just went mental about the things we read in the press. We'd read about each of us slandering the other, but we saw one another during the break and it wasn't anything like that. The press eventually turned us against each other and that's the main thing I blame them for – provoking it – breaking up a family for the sake of gossip stories," he concluded.

Lulu said that at the time, she believed her own career to be much more secure than her husband's. "There seemed to be strange tensions in the group which I sensed but could not really understand," she wrote in her autobiography. "Barry was undoubtedly the dominant force, and it may be that the others resented this. I know that Maurice thought that Robert Stigwood favoured Barry, and perhaps this created some undercover problems. Later I came to realise that nearly all the jealous remarks I heard people make about Barry were unjustified. The better I know him, the more convinced I am about this."

"I was more or less in the middle," Maurice recalled. "It was always between Barry and Robin, and the trades were to say one brother said this one week, and one brother would say something about the other brother the next week. And it was, 'What's your opinion about that Maurice?' 'Well, I don't know!' "

"We . . . have a reputation here [in Britain] as the arguing brothers. I don't think we mishandled anything at the time of our problems because when our solo records came out, we were friends again. But stories of the arguments were still coming out. The press built it up fifteen times more than it was," he added.

"I think we were all a little highly strung as a result of our enormous success," Robin reflected poignantly. "I said things at the time that were just said in the heat of the moment, and I think that goes for the rest of us too."

Even Andy Gibb, only 11 years old at the time, said, "It was a very shaky thing, a bit of a sore point as far as our family went because my brothers weren't talking to each other, and they all wanted to because they're so close. They can't get by a week without talking to each other. They wanted to call, but no one wanted to swallow their pride and do it. So I knew the family was going through a real tight moment because it affected my parents and everything . . . For families to split up, it's a really strange thing. I knew they were going to get back together again, and our family knew. There was no doubt in that, but it's hard for the public to know that."

★   ★   ★

The growing signs of disquiet were revealed by Molly Gibb shortly after the release of the *Odessa* album. "It's not fair," she protested. "Robin does 90 per cent of the work on the album, and I bet he doesn't get the same amount of credit. While the others were leaving the recording studios about eleven at night, I never used to see Robin until four or five in the morning."

Barry took up the challenge, retorting, "He has said that he was not getting enough credit, but he never said anything to us. If we had sat down and discussed it . . .

"The press are closer to him than we are. I just get abused. But I would remind him that he only wrote four songs on this new LP. That may be a reminder to him. I have been writing for the past nine years. He's been writing only a few years. Over the past year there were different things, but we never argued about him not getting enough credit. I saw something coming because we were arguing a lot. It is a fact that we've grown up together and never been out of each other's sight. Three brothers are not usually like that because they will have different jobs. That is one of the reasons why this happened.

"But Robin was very lackadaisical about sessions. He would turn up at the last minute or an hour after we'd finished. So we didn't get anything from him to put down. I liked 'Lamplight' but I liked the other side as well. The next thing is that we read in the papers that Robin has said the 'First Of May' shouldn't have gone out."

Indeed, for much of the following year, the only communication the rest of the Gibb family would have with Robin was conducted through the music trade papers.

On March 19, 1969, Robin announced he was leaving The Bee Gees to pursue a solo career, in breach of the five-year contract he had signed with Robert Stigwood. That same day, Barry, Maurice and Colin were in the studio laying down tracks for 'Tomorrow, Tomorrow' and 'Sun In My Morning'.

"The last time I slammed out was three months ago when I said I couldn't work with Robin again," Barry said. "Since then, he's had the daggers out for me. I didn't know he had left until I read it. He didn't say goodbye or tell our parents he was leaving – that's what annoyed me. It's all a bit upsetting and bewildering when none of us really knows what is happening and are unable to reason with Robin, but I think he knows that it would be a mistake to leave the rest of us."

The three remaining Bee Gees – Barry, Maurice and Colin – made a scheduled appearance on Lulu's television variety show on the following Saturday evening, and at the end of the programme, Barry and Maurice waved to the camera and sent get well wishes to their absent brother. Earlier that day Robert Stigwood had received a medical certificate from Robin's doctor claiming that he was too ill to appear. "The certificate says he is suffering from nervous exhaustion," Stigwood told the press, "and we hope he will be well soon."

Soon the pretence of illness was set aside, when a press officer issued the statement, "Solicitors acting on behalf of the Robert Stigwood Organisation have issued a writ against Robin Gibb and Robin Gibb Ltd claiming a declaration, damages and injunctions. This is now being served. The company's solicitors – Messrs. Wright and Webb – have retained Mr Quintin Hogg, Q.C., and Mr David Sullivan, Q.C."

A month later it was announced that: "The writs were purely an interim measure to prevent Robin and others claiming he had actually left the Bee Gees."

"It definitely does look as if there is little hope of Robin staying," Barry said. "But Robert Stigwood doesn't give up easily. None of us knows what the outcome will be. But speaking personally, I would have thought he'd have been on the side of the brothers. He may be married but he's still the same blood.

"We've been recording without him in the past few days in the hope of finding something suitable for a new single, which shows that we're still determined to keep the group going whatever happened. When he has fully recovered, I think his feelings will change. He'll realise it would be daft for The Bee Gees to break up – or, at least, for him to leave us."

Robin denied that his leaving the group had anything to do either with Molly's ambitions for him, or with his wanting more credit within the group. "I just could not take The Bee Gees any more," he said. "Everyone has a point in his life when everything about them gets confusing. I felt like a prisoner, like I was in a whirlpool.

"We used to be very compatible on everything and then we started to clash. I stayed on the same level. I'm not saying they became big-headed but I found the simple things we used to talk about were not happening. In Australia we used to work till four in the morning for usually six pounds. Barry had one pound; we got ten shillings each." Although by his own admission, arithmetic was not Robin's best subject, the balance of four pounds can be explained by the fact that the boys were supporting the family at that time.

"On the ship over here," Robin continued, "we were going to try and become the biggest group in the world. Success changes quite a lot of people and I think it left me alone in The Bee Gees. Where it did change others, maybe unfortunately, it didn't change me. There became this false aura in the recording studios where they were more publicity conscious than work conscious. I found myself working by myself for half the time. It turned slowly to hatred after a while because they didn't care if I was interested in the work or not. Their heart wasn't in their work but it is now because I have left.

"Maurice and I were neglected publicity wise. It had been all Barry. What

217

were Maurice and Colin and I – just Barry's backing group? When I left they thought I was being selfish and wanted all the credit, but it was the group I was thinking of."

Barry was quick to offer his own opinion in the press. "Robin wants to sunbathe in the spotlight while the rest of the group stand in the shadows," he declared. "The things he has said have been extremely rude, from my own brother, and I would not forgive him for that. I would say that he is unwell. He's got a very, very big persecution complex. He thinks everybody hates him. But it is a family matter now, and it is getting to the stage where we should be thinking of going in and smashing the door in.

"I picked up the paper like everybody else and I wondered what it was all about. I phoned him and I was told to bugger off. He wouldn't speak to me.

"We don't know where he is; all we know are the things he has said about us. If he wants us to get together he can contact us. Many attempts have been made to contact him, but he has made no answer. So we have stopped.

"He has been grasping for freedom. His attitude is, 'I want to do this and I want to do that and bugger the guys next door' – who happen to be his own brothers. His head has become too big for him. The wife should have nothing to do with the husband's business affairs. I've never got on with Molly. I've tried very hard, because she is my brother's wife. He is being pushed around. They are accusing me of all kinds of things I have never heard of. Foul things, well below the belt. You couldn't print them.

"He still has one of the greatest voices I have ever heard. He has a far better voice than I have. And he is a great songwriter too. I don't think he knows what is going on. One day he's going to find out the truth. He has not only made a mistake, he has ruined his career."

Not to be outdone, Robin countered with: "The thing that really hurt, and was the deciding factor on my splitting from The Bee Gees concerned a feature which was conducted between a reporter and my wife. It took things entirely out of context which she had said and slandered both my character and her own. It made it look as though Molly was a bad influence on me instead of the inspiration she is."

Rightly or wrongly, Molly seemed destined to become the scapegoat for the split in much the same way that Yoko Ono would be blamed by Beatles' fans for her part in the break-up of that group. Molly was accused of turning Robin against his family and Robert Stigwood and, more bizarrely, of holding him a virtual prisoner, isolated in their Kensington home.

According to Tom Kennedy, Molly was "a very down-to-earth, forth-right person, and she may have put people's backs up. She was despised by everybody in the other camps because they thought she had more power over him, and she obviously had his ear, as well. Over their cocoa last thing at night, she was his confidante. She probably had the best at heart for him at the time, but in the long run, his path with his brothers was definitely the best for him."

"The game", as Barry had dubbed it, now came back to haunt Robin. With the well-publicised attacks of "nervous exhaustion" used as excuses for the cancellation of undersold tour dates and his failure to appear on Lulu's television programme, a few carefully uttered words to the press could cast aspersions on his mental health.

"Robin has been under a great strain recently," said Robert Stigwood, "but as soon as he is recovered, we hope to have business discussions which will resolve the problem."

"Robin has an incredible persecution complex," he later told reporters. "He tends to think the whole world is against him. He has no confidence at all and can be hurt by the pettiest of remarks, which is silly since every artist must expect to receive a few knocks. Robin, though, gets unbelievably upset. For example, if a journalist with whom he is friendly turns round and says something bad about his performance, Robin takes it as a personal grudge against him.

"I don't think Robin is at all well at the moment," Stigwood added, "and he is not capable of making decisions."

The ruse was kept up for The Bee Gees' scheduled appearance in concert at The Talk Of The Town in London when, just five weeks after giving birth to twin daughters Tiffany and Debra, their elder sister stood in for the supposedly indisposed Robin. "I suppose the idea was to keep it in the family while Robin is ill," Lesley said.

"I couldn't believe it when Mr Stigwood asked me to stand in for Robin at the TV spectacular from Talk Of The Town on Sunday. I'm not worried about coming in with all the controversy raging. I'm just going to get on with the job and do the best I can. Although I know I shan't be with the group for long, I'm very excited.

"I'm hoping to carry on singing after The Bee Gees have found a permanent replacement by going solo. While the family was in Australia, I was singing professionally and once played where my brothers were topping the bill. I am married to Keith Evans, an advertising executive, and have four young children so obviously I am not going to be able to devote my whole life to staging any sort of return to show business. As far as live appearances and recordings with The Bee Gees go, I really am not sure what is going to happen."

"We were rehearsing 'Gotta Get A Message To You' and we just could not tell the difference with Lesley's voice," Maurice said. "If it turns out that she does record with us, I'm sure the sound will hardly change. But Barry and I will be doing most of the singing. The songwriting won't change either, as Barry and I have been doing most of the numbers for some time now."

The concert was recorded and broadcast in colour on BBC 2 on May 17 with a set list devoid of any of the songs strongly associated with Robin: 'New York Mining Disaster 1941', 'Kitty Can', 'With The Sun In My Eyes', 'Suddenly', 'To Love Somebody', 'Seven Seas Symphony', 'First Of

May', 'Morning Of My Life', 'I've Gotta Get A Message To You', 'Spicks And Specks', 'Sun In My Morning' and 'World'. 'Morning Of My Life', although originally recorded in Australia in 1966, remained unreleased at that point, but the audience obviously liked what they were hearing for the first time and it received the most applause of any song that evening.

It was a nerve-racking time for Lesley, who confessed to praying that Robin would just walk out on stage at the last minute to spare her, but she said afterwards, "It seemed to go well, although I nearly burst into tears when it all began.

"I haven't spoken to Robin," she added, "but he's being a bit stubborn. I think it will all get settled amicably in the end."

Their road manager, Tom Kennedy, recalled that, "It was strange, there was no doubt about it, because Robin was such an integral part of it. They weren't really The Bee Gees just with Barry and Maurice, with Robin missing. It was just something that was tried . . . [Lesley] hasn't got the same sort of power of voice that they have. Although it was nice and a family thing, it wasn't something that could go on, they couldn't build a career on it."

Another who watched the concert with interest was their former fan club secretary Julie Barrett, who had resigned from the job and was preparing to fly off for a new life in Greece later that month. "I saw Lesley at The Talk Of The Town, and I think I was surprised that she could actually sing. I'm certain she kept in tune, and was genuinely surprised because I thought it was strange that they would bring her in to replace Robin anyway. She was definitely a performer, and she knew exactly what she was doing, so the show didn't stop just because Lesley was in it. Maybe she was nervous underneath, but she looked as if she was enjoying it and gave the impression that she was a born performer."

A party for the group's friends and various members of the press was held at Barry's flat following the recording of the show. Lulu took the opportunity to perform her latest song, written by Maurice and Barry, for the gathering. Although expected to be her next single, 'Please Don't Take My Man Away', described as "a slow, soulful number away from the usual up-tempo mood of her hits", was never actually released.

Robert Stigwood, who announced that he would launch Lesley's solo career with a single to be released soon, didn't hold out much hope for an expeditious solution to the break-up. "It may be another six months before we know one way or another with Robin," he commented.

The break-up was taking its toll on the whole Gibb family. "When the boys broke up, they all had a rough time of it," Barbara Gibb said. "There was Stigwood in Barry's ear, and Molly in Robin's ear, and poor old Maurice was on his own – he had nobody's ear!

"It's terrible when brothers don't get on, and we didn't either – not from one day to the next. The result was that we didn't even see Robin for two years."

"The people round Robin have cut him off from everybody – including his own mother and father," Hugh Gibb said. "We first read about the split in the papers. Then when we tried to find Robin, he had vanished. By then I was in a bloody fury."

Hugh said that he tried to telephone Robin at his home, only to be told that he was "unavailable". Next, he related, Barbara and Lulu went round to Robin's house and had the door slammed in their faces. The next time Hugh saw Robin, "We hardly had a chance to say hello, but I could tell from the way he spoke that he wasn't happy.

"Of course there were rows. They are three brothers; there are bound to be some problems. It would be unnatural if there weren't. But they never came to blows . . . I am his father . . . I had hoped that he felt he could talk to me about anything that was bothering him. I've always tried to bring the boys up to confide in me. Perhaps I am partly to blame . . . I honestly don't know. The door is wide open. We all hope and pray that Robin will come back. You have no idea how worried we are about what is happening to him. But I believe he will come back . . .

"Robin had some feeling against Robert Stigwood for some reason. I don't know what it was. I don't understand it at all. Robert doesn't understand it either. We both want to talk to Robin to find out what was going on in his mind. But he has been completely cut off from us," he added sadly.

A spokesman for the Robert Stigwood Organisation concurred. "We can't even get him ourselves. When we phone his home, we get Molly and she won't let us speak to him."

Robin had no intention of returning to the fold. On April 16, he announced his plans to launch an organisation called Bow & Arrow to handle his solo career. Nor did he intend to continue on as merely a singer/songwriter. With characteristic intensity, possibly fuelled by amphetamines, he revealed just a few of the projects on the burner. "I've written several books and I hope to get them published. One's about early England and one's about how England would have been if Hitler and Germany had won the war.

"I'm planning an overland trip from Tangiers to Timbuktu which is something I've always wanted to do. It's something I'm to write a book about, too.

"I've got an uncle called Brian Pass who was 21 when he went missing in Burma in 1952. No one's found out what happened to him since but I'm sure he's still alive. I think he's probably in East Germany or Russia. He was the sort of person who'd answer back. I'm going to the War Office and the Russian Embassy about him to see if I can find him through his regiment or something. I'm thinking of getting a private detective to go out to East Germany and Russia to see if I can find Brian that way. I'm damn sure he's still alive."

A spokesman made a statement to the press on Robin's behalf that he planned to bring out a solo single, adding, "Robin tried to leave The Bee

Gees in a peaceful way and bring about an amicable solution, but negotiations finally broke down last weekend."

Robert Stigwood hotly denied that negotiations had taken place. "We have not heard from Robin Gibb since we read of his announcement in the newspapers that he intended to leave the group, so it is impossible to see how he can say there have been negotiations. Both myself, his brothers and his parents tried to contact him well before litigation started, but his wife would not let us speak to him. There is still no real reason why he cannot speak to myself, his brothers or his parents since litigants can always speak to each other.

"Immediate proceedings will be instituted in the UK and USA against anybody who purports to issue a recording by Robin Gibb, in breach of the Stigwood Group of Companies' exclusive rights. It is believed that the proposed recording may contain material by Maurice Gibb and, if so, he will join in any proceedings to restrain the record's issue since he and Robert Stigwood have given no consent. Meanwhile, that action against Robin Gibb is proceeding."

"I was getting too hurt where I was," Robin insisted. "I liked working with The Bee Gees, but they started to sit in judgement on my songs and I couldn't stand that. Something else occurred which hurt my wife, and there is only one thing which hurts me more deeply than being hurt myself — having those I love hurt.

"I wanted to leave because I wanted to leave and I left. There wasn't any feud. There was a time when there was talk of Barry leaving to pursue a film career, and in those days I didn't know what was going on. This was never mentioned in private, and I had to buy the trade papers to find out what The Bee Gees were doing. Well, now I've left and I'm sure they'll make out fine without me."

When it eventually became clear that Robin was determined to go it alone, Robert Stigwood said, "We agreed to allow him to release solo records and for his solo activities to be handled by Chris Hutchins on behalf of the Robert Stigwood Organisation."

Former pop journalist Hutchins, with the London firm Enterpress, announced, "The ten lost weeks of Robin Gibb are over. With his Bee Gees days behind him, he is set on a solo career launched on Friday (June 27) with the Polydor release of his first solo single, 'Saved By The Bell'. And so ends the two and a half months during which he has been 'in hiding' as lawyers wrangled over his future."

The new recording and songwriting deals were said to guarantee him almost £200,000 over the next five years. The recording and publishing deals were arranged by his new manager Chris Hutchins with Robert Stigwood.

Nineteen-year-old Robin said, "I'm happy. I have the freedom I wanted and now I can work alone. The ten weeks have not been wasted. I have written more than a hundred songs during that time. I have also burnt the midnight oil answering as many as possible of the thousands of letters that have come in since the split."

It was announced that although he'd left The Bee Gees, Robin would still work with the group on mutually acceptable projects. The key word was mutual.

"Don't forget Barry has said he will never work with Robin again," reminded Hutchins.

The battle continued, as always, in the press. Week after week, headlines appeared that would have been ludicrous were they not detailing the destruction of a family. "Barry Says Robin 'Extremely Rude' ", "Happy Robin Not Gloating Over The Bee Gees' Miss", "I Don't Want Robin Back", "I'm Not Guilty" – the music press couldn't get enough of the feuding brothers.

"I have left The Bee Gees," Robin told one reporter emphatically. "There won't on any account be any get-together with them again. I don't regret leaving and I don't think they will miss me. The only thing I do regret is that we couldn't have come to a compatible settlement at the beginning when I first left."

Barry confirmed that Maurice had played on 'Saved By The Bell', adding, "I don't see how Robin can go ahead with this single in view of this fact. As for its being a very commercial hit record, I've heard it and frankly I just can't agree." If Barry appeared miffed by the fact that two "Bee Gees" had appeared on the single, it's probably just as well that he wasn't aware of Colin Petersen's involvement in several tracks on the forthcoming album.

The single was much anticipated both in Britain and Europe. It is an instructive example of how a great record can be made from such a simple song: a simple verse-chorus number with a rather predictable melody and minimal lyrics is arranged with a sweeping orchestra and vocal dubs for a very successful result. The single has a fairly obvious edit to get in an extra repeat of the chorus; which would not be included on the album version.

The B-side for Robin's first solo effort was intended to be the stately 'Alexandria Good Time', but this was withdrawn at the last minute and the B-side changed to the calypso style 'Mother And Jack', an unusual song unlike anything by The Bee Gees. The lyrics suggest a story line but include many evocative stream of consciousness elements.

"Robin had always wanted to go solo, so when it happened I wasn't really angry at all," Maurice said philosophically. "I simply understood the situation. But Barry is so full of pride and just couldn't understand why Robin had done it. I suppose being his twin made me understand Robin that much more easily, anyway. So the silence between us went on and Barry went on blasting away – he blasts away much better than me, in any case . . .

"I hope [Robin's] single is a hit. I wouldn't stop it. I read somewhere that I was supposed to be against it but I wouldn't do that; he's my brother."

Maurice still held out hopes that the brothers could reconcile their differences. "For myself, I'd love Robin to come back to The Bee Gees," he added. "Whether it will happen, we'll have to wait and see. It's rather premature to pose that question."

But a furious Barry blustered, "If he walks back into the group, I walk out! With me, it's a matter of pride. Saying the things he's said about me, he has made himself a stranger as far as I'm concerned. Letting him back into the group would be letting him walk all over us. I wouldn't stand for that whatever settlement may have been reached."

Almost lost in the fracas surrounding the group was the latest single release, 'Tomorrow, Tomorrow', by the three remaining Bee Gees. A bit of a departure from the accepted Bee Gees formula, Maurice said, "I don't think it's *us* but I quite like it." Maurice was right in saying that the song wasn't "us" because 'Tomorrow, Tomorrow' had originally been written for Joe Cocker, who was desperate for a new song. Barry rushed the track through, but it never reached Joe, who was given 'Delta Lady' by his management instead.

Robert Stigwood attempted to rescue this particular 'phoenix' from its ashes by demanding that 'Tomorrow Tomorrow' be recorded for release as The Bee Gees' new single. This insistence came in spite of Barry's protests that, having been written for Joe Cocker's style of singing, it didn't suit their style. Barry would later agree that, "This was a mistake that Robert very rarely made."

This single, released a month before 'Saved By The Bell', gave Barry and Maurice a jump on Robin's first solo single. It was not a big success but together with the B-side, 'Sun In My Morning', a guitar ballad, it showed where the group were going musically. Neither side of this single appeared on the next album, which was released almost a year later.

Seeming to anticipate the 45's failure, Maurice revealed, "We've got another one that we'll put straight out if it doesn't make it."

As Robin's 'Saved By The Bell' rose in the charts, 'Tomorrow, Tomorrow' made its descent after reaching a disappointing number 23 in Britain and number 54 on the American charts, although a bright spot was in Germany where it made number six.

"It is a bit of an irony but I don't think it has anything to do with the clammy hand of fate or anything. It is just a coincidence," Robin said.

"I always expected 'Saved By The Bell' to go in [to the Top 20] though I thought it would either do it very quickly or I would be in for a long wait. But I always had the confidence in it."

"I thought 'Tomorrow, Tomorrow' was a lovely single, and I'm sorry it didn't get as high as it should have," Robin said. "If I was still in the group, I'd have recorded the number. I don't really think my single has any bearing on theirs.

"When I left, it was a complete split and they all understood. I have my own life, my wife and family to think of as well as my own ideas. When I left we split up professionally but not as brothers. I'm not even going out of my way to alter my style. I write all my own material, but if it sounds to someone like The Bee Gees, that's just me. I'm trying to get rid of the Robin Gibb, Bee Gee title. I was a member for 13 years but I'm not trying to push the title either. Of course I get nostalgic about the group, but I don't think I've put a black cloud over them. I honestly don't know what they're doing, other than working a lot. I just want to be me now."

Of his own single, he said, "I made that record back at the end of March – immediately following my split from The Bee Gees. I'm not bored by it at all – I obviously have confidence in the song . . . It's been a long wait for my freedom, but now I feel fully independent and self-assured. I have a sense of wellbeing, without the feeling that there's someone obstructing me. As a solo singer I command much more attention than merely being a member of a group.

"I haven't had a single word of congratulations from my brothers for 'Saved By The Bell'. I don't feel alone and cut off though. I have good friends around me, and I can go over to Maurice and have a jam like in the old days."

As far as The Bee Gees were concerned, he added that he thought their next single would be an immense success. "Like 'Jumbo', 'Tomorrow, Tomorrow' was just one of those records, and the next one will be big. I would not call it a failure, just a black spot. We," he went on, undoubtedly finding the habit hard to break after years of being a member of the group, "have had failure before, but they weren't really failures. The Bee Gees don't have to depend on chart records. But the next will probably go straight into the Top 10."

Despite all the highly publicised fighting and backbiting in Britain, The Bee Gees' popularity in Germany had never waned. In *Bravo* magazine's annual music poll, they received 197,497 votes as favourite pop group. The Beatles came in second with only 85,862 votes – in fact, votes for The Bee Gees' exceeded the total number of votes for all of the other 19 groups nominated.

Best Of Bee Gees, a compilation of the group's greatest hits to date, was released in June in Britain, although its release was delayed until October in the US. It marked the first time that fans outside the US could buy 'I've Gotta Get A Message To You' on an album, and the first LP appearance worldwide of 'Words'. The album was certified gold in seven countries, proof indeed of the popularity of the united group.

Robin maintained that going solo had been a very slow process, mainly because of all the legal hassles, but added, "Now my new record seems to be establishing itself, so things are starting to move. [It] started happening in September 1968 and just mushroomed from there.

"All of us have always had things we wanted to do – and things that could only really be done individually. I'm happier now than I've ever been. It wasn't so much a split in the group as a progression. We've been professional since the age of seven, and so this is really a graduation into something else for all of us as individuals. I personally want to do a lot of things . . . I shall be

225

writing some musical scores for films in the New Year, and I've also completed a book called *On The Other Hand* which is to be published soon. It's a collection of poems and stories, all very classical. I'm a great admirer of Dickens . . .

"I really want to try and influence people towards a more patriotic feeling. The nearest I've got to it at the moment, as far as recording goes, is a song called 'The Statesman', dedicated to Winston Churchill. It's not on my new album, but it's on a special album which is to be released early next year."

Robin began a whirlwind tour, making television appearances in a dozen countries to promote 'Saved By The Bell', which eventually rose to the second spot on the British charts and topped the Irish charts for two weeks.

On July 19 the *New Musical Express* announced "Tonight [Robin Gibb] is fronting a 97-piece orchestra and a 60-piece choir in a recording of his latest composition 'To Heaven And Back', which was inspired by the Apollo 11 moonshot. It is an entirely instrumental piece, with the choir being used for 'astral effects'. The single will be billed as by The Robin Gibb Orchestra and Chorus and it will be rush-released as soon as possible by Polydor."

The single was one of many Gibb projects which would never see the light of day. Robin later described a track recorded for his first solo album called 'Heaven And Earth' as "a musical piece of mine [which] features a 100-piece orchestra and a 70-piece choir. It should have been a 73-piece choir, but three were working in Tooting!" It seems likely that this was another title for 'To Heaven And Back', but the composition was cut from the finished album.

Robin originally planned to entitle his first solo album *All My Own Work*, for obvious reasons, and announced that the tracks would be 'Alexandria Good Time', 'The Flag I Flew Fell Over', 'I'll Herd My Sheep', 'The Man Most Likely To Be', 'Love Just Goes', 'Make Believe', 'I Was Your Used To Be', 'The Complete And Utter History', 'Seven Birds Are Singing', 'Sing A Song Of Sisters' and 'Beat The Drum'.

But in August, when he returned to the studio to complete work on the album, the title and tracks had changed, and the assiduous Mr Gibb had even more projects on the go. "I've got fifteen tracks in the can for the LP, titled *Robin's Reign*. There isn't any universal theme to the tracks, just a series of my compositions.

"I'm also doing the musical score for a film called *Henry The Eighth* and I'm making my own film called *Family Tree*. It involves a man, John Family, whose grandfather Sir Catarac is caught trying to blow up Trafalgar Square with a home-made bomb wrapped in underwear. He is taken away by ten policemen and left in a cage at the zoo, where after a considerable length of time he begins to enjoy his abode. The rest of his relations dislike seeing him in a zoo, so knowing his partiality for cages, John Family has one installed in his lounge at home and keeps the old man there. The theme of the film is John Family's attempts to get into his past and trace his ancestors."

In addition, it was reported in *New Musical Express* that Robin had written half a dozen songs for Tom Jones, and that the Welsh singer would be recording one of them as his next single. A meeting between the two stars was said to be arranged for Robin's return from a three-day promotional trip to Germany.

At this point, it was also announced that Robin had signed a new management and agency contract worth £400,000 a year with Vic Lewis, the former top bandleader, who was then managing director of NEMS Enterprises. Chris Hutchins was still on the scene but, from this point onwards, adopted a more behind-the-scenes role due to a combination of Lewis' increasing prominence and Stigwood's diminishing influence. Molly Gibb, who was 22 years old, countersigned the contract on behalf of her 19-year-old husband, still legally regarded as a minor. However Molly was quick to point out, "My countersigning the contract today was a formality. I'm not the boss at all. I don't make Robin's decisions for him. He has a mind of his own."

Years later, Robin would laugh about what happened next. "Dad came to me and asked me to make it up. I told him, 'Go 'way, Dad, or I'll put a pair of cement shoes on you.' Then he tried to make me a ward of the court," he quipped.

The whole scenario sounds suspiciously like evidence of Robin's offbeat sense of humour, but the latter remark was no idle jest. Hugh Gibb, who had countersigned Robin's five-year contract with Robert Stigwood, *did* announce that he would try to make Robin a ward of the court. "My wife Barbara and I are being kept away from Robin," he said. "We believe he is almost a prisoner in his own home. He is under pressure. We've tried ringing him but can't contact him. My wife can't take anymore . . . I last saw him two weeks ago at a TV show. We said hello, but you could have cut the atmosphere with a knife. He was very heavily guarded. I don't want anything. Making him a ward of the court is the very last thing I want to do. I have never been a stern father . . ."

"At the time it was just poisoning everything," Tom Kennedy said of Hugh's lawsuit. "There were just a lot of bad vibes around . . ."

Hugh insisted, "The fact is that Robin just couldn't go on on his own. He's a ballad singer. He needs the others, besides which, he's under contract.

"Robert Stigwood has told me he is going to fight tooth and nail to keep Robin in the group, and we are right behind him. The fans should realise that Robert is acting entirely in Robin's interests. It's not a selfish thing at all. He knows, and we all know, that Robin can't expect to be as successful as a solo singer.

"Robin is only 19 and has always had his frustrations and rows with the other brothers. I've seen them having a stand-up fight, break it off to appear on stage, then carry on fighting afterwards. But these things have always blown over.

"What's upsetting and significant to me is that there has been no official word from Robin himself. My wife and Lulu both phoned up last night to

227

try to speak to Robin, but each time they spoke to Robin's wife who told them, 'You can't come round; I've got friends here.' And she would not put Robin on the phone either."

And so it went on, with Robin next calling a press conference to air his views. "There's no chance of my going back with my brothers in The Bee Gees," Robin told the assembled reporters. "That's all over. I don't see how my father can make me a ward of the court. I have my own family and career and don't have to cater for my father and mother. I'm not fighting my family. They are the ones who are fighting. For a father to interfere is ridiculous. He is just making a fool of himself. It is ridiculous to suggest I'm not well or for my father to think I'm a prisoner in my own home. If that is prison, I'd like to throw away the key. I'm having a lovely time. I feel sorry for my father.

"I make my own decisions," he reiterated. "I love her, but my wife is second to me in my own house. Maturity isn't a question of age, it's a question of mind. Molly and I have a partnership, not a dictatorship. She's a wonderful person and these stories that she's some kind of demon . . . they make me sick."

"Certain people around him were trying to rip him off, but he wouldn't listen," Hugh said years later. "They were trying to make Robin a big star. I wanted him made a ward of the court for his own protection. That was the only answer at the time."

Robin flatly disagreed with Hugh's assessment of the situation. "[All my] years in show business have gained me insight," he claimed. "Otherwise I might have been conned, but I know what I'm doing, have an ability for instant analysis of a situation, a sixth sense about people which enables me to tell whether to trust them or not."

"Dad and Mum didn't have evil in them," Barry insisted. "They didn't have anything against Molly. They were only trying to save Robin from what he was doing to himself, and that was taking too much speed. They tried to stop it to get him in his right mind. They thought somebody was doing everything for him. Robin wasn't doing anything. He was vegetating. He didn't know one way or the other what he wanted to do. That's the way I saw it.

"But unfortunately, it alienated Molly from our parents. For forever, I suppose," he added sadly.

"I think the whole thing was blown up out of all proportion," Molly said. "Robin has got a mind of his own, always has. He wanted to leave the group and as his wife, I was behind him. If your husband wants to do something, you're not going to kick him in the teeth. He wanted to do it, so I stood by him, no matter what. I don't know why his family and people surrounding him thought he wasn't capable of making his own decisions. That's when the nervous exhaustion bit came back and was thrown in our faces.

"To make your son a ward of the court when he's a married man, to me, was just absolutely crazy," she added. "And I took it because I'm that kind of person. It was terribly unpleasant, and it was very upsetting for my family. We're just an ordinary family, and to pick up the papers and read this and that . . . And of course, we had no money. Our money was stopped. The whole thing was like a crazy nightmare. All Robin wanted was to have more recognition of himself as a songwriter and singer, not as a personality."

The arguments dragged on but the crazy nightmare was far from over. The agreement which Hugh had countersigned with Robin meant that he was legally under exclusive contract to the Stigwood Organisation for agency, management, recording and publishing for another two years. Citing this, a spokesman for RSO stated: "The Robert Stigwood Organisation has issued writs against Vic Lewis and NEMS Enterprises claiming damages. The claim arises out of certain contracts alleged to have been made by Vic Lewis and NEMS with Robin Gibb."

Vic Lewis countered, "We always take advice about all our contracts, and I am satisfied that the one I signed with Robin is completely valid."

Eventually, Robert Stigwood was compelled to drop the claim. "Barry and Maurice were so upset by Robin's departure that we had to release him from the company," he related. "That was really the most difficult part of it. I always instinctively knew that they would get back together – there's a great bond there for them as brothers. But when brothers fight, it's worse than strangers fighting."

A NEMS spokesman issued a statement that clarified the situation: "An amicable settlement has been reached between the Robert Stigwood Organisation and The Bee Gees with Robin Gibb and NEMS Enterprises Ltd. The basis of it includes provision that Robin Gibb relinquishes his shares in The Bee Gees' songwriting and publishing companies in return for his release from the Robert Stigwood Organisation in all areas."

The statement went on to say that . . . "Robin will continue to record for Polydor with Vic Lewis as his personal manager and NEMS providing exclusive worldwide agency representation."

In July, Robin sold his shares in Abigail Music to Robert Stigwood for £40,000 and collected his first instalment of £30,000 from his recording contract with Polydor. "I put it straight into the bank," he said. "I'm not going to spend it just because it's there. When I see something I want, I will go out and buy it."

At the time, he claimed to have few vices. "Well, I don't drink. But I might go out and buy a few thousand records," he admitted. "I'm quite a record collector."

Looking back now, Robin says that he was very much in denial of the situation. Most of his money was spent before he got it, but he was a pop star and pop stars had money and all the friends money could buy. Looking back, he says ruefully, "I wish I knew you couldn't buy friends . . . At the time, it wasn't as if I even had any money. I was living in this big house in Virginia Water [Surrey] with no money in the bank. People never knew you could have a number one record and still be broke. You had your advance, and it had gone before the record was a hit."

At that time, his personal assistant was a man named Ray Washbourne. "One day we went off to buy a Mercedes," Robin recalled. "He kept telling me I didn't have any money, but my attitude was that it didn't matter so long as I was happy, and I rather liked the idea of a blue one. It cost about £6,000, which was a lot of money in those days. Then two weeks later it was his wedding anniversary, and I gave it to him as a present.

"I couldn't see at the time why it's not the sort of thing you go and do. I can imagine giving a car now to someone who was really special. But you have to learn not to be like that and that you can't buy friends by giving them a Mercedes Benz. If you do, of course, they just think less of you. I did so many silly things in those days . . ."

But in those days, Robin had his own theories of what the public wanted from its recording artists. "In entertainment and music being a star, not just a pop star, means you have an obligation to your audience. The public wants an artist who is unreal to them. And it is the artist's duty to endeavour to be unreal. The mystique of an artist has to be there. The kids love that. They don't want to see you out smoking and drinking like they do. They want someone who has this glamour. Somebody straight out of the television tubes. Not like Harry Blogsworth next door.

"I work on the philosophy of accept me like I am if you want to or forget it – either like it or lump it . . . It's when you take a middle course that you are finished."

Plans were announced for an ambitious promotional tour of 22 countries. "The tour has been arranged for me to promote 'Saved By The Bell' on TV in the various countries, but also to establish me as Robin Gibb, the solo artiste. I shall be appearing in the major cities in the countries, such as Vienna, Berlin, Munich, Milan. Then I'll be over in the States for two weeks doing New York, Los Angeles, Chicago, San Francisco, etc. After that I'll go over to Japan and play Tokyo.

"In all, the tour lasts for two months. I won't be away from Britain for that period. The dates I have on the Continent I'll fly across to, then return home. But for the States and Japan, I'll be away for a little time.

"A solo artist's scope is incredible . . . there are so many things one can do. One thing I won't do is one night stands. For the concerts, I'll sing backed by a 33-piece orchestra or more. I don't want to be like Cliff or anyone else – I'm just aiming to be simply Robin Gibb. In the future, singing and writing will be given equal attention. I'll be recording two or three singles a year and one album at the most. Then, later on, I'll give individual concerts at major cities.

"When I start doing live appearances, they will be at least three months apart and there won't be any of those club and ballroom gigs . . . I want the whole thing to be an event, a performance. I'll have an orchestra behind me but no chorus. I might possibly do one in Prague first, because I have a lot of fans out there and I'd really like to do one for them."

Although Robin claimed that there was no reason why he and his brothers could not get along socially, it was evident that the rift between them was far from healed. "I haven't heard from them for a long time," Robin continued. "The reason we didn't talk during the split business was because my lawyers advised me not to make contact.

"The first time I met Maurice after that was at the *NME* Poll Concert in May and we were very friendly and chatty. He asked me if I was coming back and I said 'no.' That was that as far as he was concerned."

As he rehearsed for his upcoming concert tour, he admitted, "The feeling that you are all alone is there. But that is countered by a feeling that the group is still there with me. However, I have all the confidence I need and have no worries apart from any profession's worries.

"I'm used to doing a lot of singing on my own because Barry's more aggressive, powerful voice has given out with laryngitis and so I've had to do the singing. I do know my business and I have all the confidence in the world. I regard myself as an artist and a musician, and if I cannot do what I'm paid to then I have no right being where I am."

★　★　★

While Robin continually expressed enthusiasm for his new found freedom, Vince Melouney was finding life outside the group a bitter disappointment. "Things have really gone sour on me," he admitted.

"Everything went wrong after I left The Bee Gees. My whole scene started to crumble. I tried to form a new group [Ashton, Gardner & Dyke] and negotiated a recording deal with The Beatles' company, Apple Records. But first we were stopped from recording because of my contract with The Bee Gees. Then, when that was sorted out, our first record was scrapped before it was released.

"I knew I had already spent a lot of money keeping the group in hotels, food and wages. But suddenly I found I'd got through £15,000 in under four months. I reckon another £5,000 had gone on entertaining and buying clothes.

"Then I found I had a number of unpaid bills. Nearly all had been incurred by one of my companies and the reason they hadn't been paid is that one of my business associates owes me a lot of money. Everyone will be paid as soon as I get things sorted out."

"Vince was a hell of a nice guy, I have to say, and I got on with him very well," said Tom Kennedy. "I did some bits and pieces with him after he left the band, just to help him out, when he went to Ashton, Gardner & Dyke. He managed them, but it was a half-hearted thing really. Although he was a very good guitarist, management skills are another thing altogether.

"Management expertise is knowing how best to use the money. There's a lovely story, and I'm sure it is true, that he gave Ashton, Gardner & Dyke £500 to go out and buy stage clothes. They were party animals, and they came back with a jumper each for £500. They were quite a talented trio of

231

musicians and probably given the right management they would have done very well."

Vince's wife had left him, and was sharing a basement flat in Chelsea with four other girls. "I'm still very much in love with Vince and I hope we can get together again," Dianne Melouney told reporters.

Despite living in a cheap hotel in Guildford with a Swedish model, Vince said that he still cherished hopes that his marriage could be saved, but added sadly, "I don't know whether there can be any reconciliation with Dianne now."

He had quit The Bee Gees to pursue his first love, the blues. In a bitter twist of irony, his very existence now reflected the mood of the music which inspired him most.

★　★　★

Looking back on those days, Vince is quite philosophical about the impression he gave, to some outside observers at any rate, that his decision to leave was the wrong one. "I had a feeling it was all coming to a close," he explained. "Musically, I was *so* frustrated and there were tensions in the band, Barry getting all the lead vocals etc. Mo all of a sudden had a driver, and all of these other people started having their say. You know, Vince should be doing this and shouldn't do that.

"Robert also presented us with a new second and very wordy contract," he continued. "While the boys signed it, Colin and I got some legal advice and that caused some problems too. We never signed the contract. Lots of tension started to appear. I wasn't getting on with Robin because he didn't like the blues, and their father always made Colin and I feel like outsiders."

Vince is the first to admit that he didn't get on with Hugh. "I thought he was a troublemaker. Overbearing. At times [Colin and I] would tell the boys, 'He's your dad, not ours. Tell him to stop telling us to do things.' I think they had a word with him at some point to back off. [He was] very forthright in his opinion. Colin and I were always made to feel like outsiders. He dictated things to us . . . drove us crazy. Barbara, on the other hand, was lovely."

His memories of those times remain good ones nonetheless. "Fantastic, [we had a] wonderful time travelling in first class [and staying in] great hotels, and we had a lot of fun initially and had a good rapport.

"Robert Stigwood was a good guy [who] treated people with respect. A very polite man [who] put a lot of time and effort into The Bee Gees. When I said [that] I wanted to leave, he asked me to complete a German tour they were about to do, and if I did then he would relieve me from my contractual obligations. So I did and he did. When I left he made the comment, but not in a nasty way, that he never wanted me in the band at the beginning but I never asked what he meant by that."

It is clear that Vince still regards all four of his former fellow band members with great affection and has maintained some kind of contact with them since his departure. Ever affable, he prefers to look at the positive side of people's characters as his retrospective appraisal of the brothers demonstrates.

"Barry was the driving force behind the band. He was always working. I visited him in 1976 and stayed with him at the Isle of Man for a couple of days, and he was always doing things. We co-wrote a couple of songs 'Morning Rain' and 'Let It Ride', but they were never published. [He's a] nice guy, very gentle, thoughtful, extremely diplomatic. Barry was always on my side. When I first joined the band, because I joined after Colin, for the first five months I was on a wage. It was Barry who went in to bat for me. It was on his instigation to Robert that it wasn't fair, that I was an equal part of the band, [that] I should be getting equal money."

Vince never socialised with either Barry or Robin at all. In the case of Robin, whom Vince can best describe as "extremely eccentric and intro-verted", this was probably due mostly to their differing musical taste. Ask him about Maurice though, and you get a different response altogether.

"Flamboyant, extremely extroverted, prone to exaggerate things. If you bought a Rolls [Royce], he'd buy a bigger one. I think he had issues to deal with Barry and Robin with their voices and where he stood in the band. Mo, Colin and I would socialise quite a lot and would have these great blues jams, just the three of us."

Of the four, he was closest to Colin whom he described as "introverted, very intelligent, [but] would go out of his way to get publicity."

Vince Melouney no longer receives royalties from Bee Gees' recordings, having sold his interest in them around 1981, apparently because he was short of money at the time.

17

AND THEN THERE WERE NONE

"SINCE ROBIN LEFT . . . Barry and I are a lot closer," Maurice claimed, "we're working much more together. We're having a ball, we can bring anyone we like into things.

"I did the majority of the backings anyway, even when Robin was with us, but there's more work for me now. It's bringing me out more – I do six leads on the next album; before I think I only sang three all told. I write soft, and Barry keeps telling me to write harder music. I'm progressing more to the arranging side and Barry is getting more ideas-wise – he's freer with his words.

"At the moment, we'll go on as a three-piece [group], and if we find someone suitable to take Robin's place, we'll take him in . . . We've only seen two people. We're getting tapes from Wapping and Nottingham and Stoke and all over, but . . . we want to get someone who can sing nice. We can take care of the hair and the clothes and all that. We're not looking for a copy of Robin though."

Dave Dee was instrumental in finding a possible stand-in for Robin. "[Barry] was looking for a replacement – and I found him one," he recalled. "A guy called Peter Mason . . . He was a Scouser, but he lived in Salisbury where we lived. Barry was looking for somebody who had a similar voice sound but also wrote.

"So Pete Mason went up to London and Barry really liked him. Barry actually took him out and bought him a couple of suits 'cause he wasn't quite as trendy as they were. I'll always remember, he took him to Carnaby Street and bought him some suits and got him all decked out before he met Robert Stigwood . . . Anyway, it was all on, and he was going to go into the band as Robin's replacement – and Robert Stigwood blocked it.

"Never really got to the bottom of it, but it all just fell apart, because, I think, as far as Robert Stigwood was concerned, and quite rightly so, he wanted to get Robin back."

"It all started because people said my voice was very much . . . like a Bee Gees' voice," said Peter, "probably because it was a high nasally sound – coming from the north . . . I suppose . . . There was a thing in one of the musical papers, the *Melody Maker* or *New Musical Express*, that Robin Gibb had left [The Bee Gees], and Barry was looking for a replacement. It didn't matter who it was as long as they could do it! It didn't have to be a name or anything like that. So basically anybody could apply.

"I mentioned it to Dave – I don't know whether I said it in joking or whether it was in earnest, and he spoke to Barry Gibb. Dave reckoned that I could do that kind of thing. I always remember when we went in to meet Barry, he'd got into The Band (the Bob Dylan band), and they were playing, laying tracks down in that kind of way, because I always liked that sort of stuff, it led on to Little Feat and things like that, but The Band were a very rootsy type of band, which is what I was into, even now.

"He was very, very nice, Barry Gibb; he's a real gentleman. We ran through some songs there and then, things like 'Massachusetts' and 'New York Mining Disaster' which is my all-time favourite. He said, there and then, 'Well, as far as I'm concerned, you're in. Obviously, I want you to meet Maurice.'

"I can't remember whether I met Maurice before I went into the studio with them. I remember spending one night with Maurice; he introduced me to some people as Robin's replacement. Barry had taken me shopping and wanted me to meet Robert Stigwood. He said, 'I've just got to sort everything out with Robert, so you've got to look good for him; let's go and get you some clothes.' He took me into the West End, to Soho, bought me some clothes, fitted me out from top to bottom and then we sort of hung around.

"It was one of those very 'in' shops at the time. He just pulled his Rolls-Royce Corniche onto the sidewalk and we walked in. Everybody just bowed to him, and he said, 'This is Peter, I'd like you to fit him out real nice!' and they did! I've still got that suit hung up in my wardrobe."

Peter recalled going to the studio with Barry and spending time at his home with Lynda. "[Barry] had two servants who, when I was at his home, they fussed around me; he made sure that they looked after me. He was actually charming, I was very impressed, and Maurice was very nice too.

"I always remember being in the studio with Maurice one time because he was on the phone to Lulu, and he was saying that he'd just written a song for her. I did speak to Lulu on the phone when I was at Barry's. The phone went, and Barry said, 'Could you answer that for me?' I didn't know who it was – this lady said, 'Can I speak to Barry?' 'Yes, just a minute,' I said. 'There's a lady wants to speak to you,' I said to Barry, and he said, 'Can you ask who it is?' So I said, 'Can I have your name, please?' and she said, 'Tell him it's Marie Lawrie!' so she was a little bit irate I think!"

Barry took Pete to IBC Studios and during July they worked on some of the tracks for the *Cucumber Castle* album. "I did some harmonies, I remember doing three songs . . . There was 'Don't Forget To Remember' and I put the harmony down on that and two other songs. [I don't know] whether it was a tryout, although he'd said before that he wanted me, because we sat and sang together.

"When I sit and listen to 'Don't Forget To Remember' I can't really tell whether it's me or not. He ran the tracks and said, 'Can you put a harmony to that?' They already had backing tracks, and Barry had put his vocal down. Obviously, because it was the hit, 'Don't Forget To Remember' sticks out in my memory.

"Barry played this track for me a few times, and it sounds to me like it could have been 'Bury Me Down By The River'." The third song is likely to have been 'Who Knows What A Room Is', which was demoed at the same time as 'Don't Forget To Remember' on May 7.

"I was hanging around, and hanging around and I think there was talk going on with Robert Stigwood who was trying to arrange a meeting, and I think that Robert Stigwood was still hoping that he'd get them all back together again . . . It went on a few weeks and I was kind of hanging around then.

"It came to a point where [Barry] said to me, 'I don't know what's going to happen, but one thing's for sure, I'll make an album with you if this doesn't work out.' This was further down the line, two or three weeks maybe, because we just didn't seem to be getting this meeting together and I was hanging around; I wasn't getting fed up, but I was starting to think, 'What is [happening]?' I said, 'Well look, I think I'll go on back to Salisbury, you sort it out,' and he said, 'Whatever happens, I'll make an album with you and we'll do something.'

"In a way I didn't really expect it. I don't know why, I just didn't. I was there, it was taken seriously, we weren't playing games or anything. I always felt that, okay, I was very flattered to be asked but I always felt that it was the brothers, and I always think deep down that they would get back together . . . I think I was right about that, because I think that's why [Stigwood] was holding off not meeting me and so I wasn't surprised. It was a big thrill, it was just nice being with them, they made me feel so welcome, I think *that* as much as anything impressed me. I think that in the end it wasn't such a big shock . . . I went back to Salisbury, and then I never heard anything."

It was the end of Peter Mason's brief career as a wannabe Bee Gee, and no more was ever mentioned of the album Barry promised to make, although, ever the optimist, even to this day, Pete says, "I'm still ready and waiting, Barry."

Around that time, Dave Dee decided to leave Dave Dee, Dozy, Beaky, Mick and Tich and, knowing that Peter was still waiting and available, Dave offered him a job. He wanted a guitarist and harmony singer and also asked him to be his personal assistant. "So I was involved with him all the way down the line in that way when he went solo," Peter said.

Meanwhile The Bee Gees had decided that they could carry on on their own. "We did at first think we should replace Robin," Barry admitted, "and we even considered asking Jack Bruce to join us, but after working in the studios we've decided we don't need an outsider."

Completely unaware and unconcerned that his brothers were attempting to replace him, Robin jetted off to the United States, keeping busy with a round of scheduled appearances on *The Ed Sullivan Show, Kraft Music Hall, The Glen Campbell Show* and *The Andy Williams Show*.

The Bee Gees released a single from the soundtrack of the forthcoming Cucumber Castle film called 'Don't Forget To Remember'. This release, a song Robin would never have recorded, was probably to keep The Bee Gees in the public eye after Robin hit big with 'Saved By The Bell'. It was the first real country number from The Bee Gees, with Barry singing down in Maurice's natural range, very smooth and full. This wasn't exactly what the public expected, but it did very well in Europe, and in Britain it matched Robin's achievement of reaching the number two spot on the charts.

"The thing is," said Maurice, "that it is Jim Reeves-ish, it's rather like 'Oh Lonesome Me' and that sort of song, and you'll never forget the melody. It wasn't a deliberate dedication to Jim Reeves – it just worked out that way."

It's not clear how close to an album they were in August when this was released, since there are several song titles from this year that have never come out. The B-side was originally planned as 'I Lay Down And Die', but it was changed to 'The Lord' days after tape of the former had been sent out to the record companies. For some reason Atco of Canada put out copies with the original B-side, a different mix with much more backing vocal than what was finally heard on the album in 1970.

At the time of its release Maurice was promoting group unity amongst the remaining three, saying, "We know we don't want to split up . . . maybe Colin will want to leave sometime in the future, but we all have different things we're involved in . . ."

Barry and Maurice were involved in their own individual production companies and a proposal to launch their own Bee Gees record label. Maurice revealed they had planned this out in every detail except for the fundamental problem of what to call it. "We thought of all sorts of names . . . We thought of 'BG' and even 'Lemon'. We had decided a long time before then that the label colours would be blue and white – just because we like blue and white – but we couldn't think of a good commercial name.

"Years ago we had a record about apples and lemons and at the time we thought what a good label 'Lemon' would be. But we scrapped the idea because everyone would have thought we had only chosen 'Lemon' because of The Beatles and 'Apple'.

"We don't want our company to be another Apple. While they have produced a lot of hit records, I also feel they have lost their way a little. They employed too many of the old school friends in the beginning, even though they weren't doing a proper job. Our company has no room for people unless they know what they are doing."

P.P. Arnold, Samantha Sang and The Marbles were among artists proposed for the new label. "Maurice and I plan to record The Marbles solo," Barry revealed. "Maurice will record Trevor [Gordon] – who has a voice exactly like Cliff Richard though he's never been able to use it before – and I'll produce Graham [Bonnet], whose voice is phenomenal."

Maurice advised any up-and-coming performers that one of the most important ingredients for success was a strong ego. "They should have complete faith in themselves and be a little big-headed. It does help if you really believe you have something worthwhile.

"Anyone who thinks he could make a go of the business can write to Barry and myself at our office and if we think they are good we will sign them up. Once we have signed them to our label we will do the production ourselves. We have done quite a lot of production, not only on records but also for television films."

Colin and Joanne Petersen had joined forces with another friend, Slim Miller, to launch no less than five companies, with Joanne handling management, Colin production and Miller looking after the variety subsidiary. "Obviously, The Bee Gees won't last forever," Colin said, "and whenever they do finish, I want to have this as a backbone to carry me on."

Plans for the long delayed *Lord Kitchener's Little Drummer Boys* film had finally officially been dropped, but Barry still harboured fantasies of making his début on the big screen. "It's something I've always dreamed of – to be more free within yourself," he said. "I pulled out of *Lord Kitchener's Little Drummer Boys* because I thought it would be a catastrophe. I'd like to do a Western, but it takes a long time to arrange everything. I know I shouldn't say it because I've never appeared in a film, but I wasn't keen on the story for a start. It was a much too colourful film and reminded me too much of The Beatles' *Help!*"

Keeping the public informed, he hinted, "Maurice and I have star parts in a big movie that is to be made in three months' time. It isn't *Hair* – that's all I can say at the moment."

Weeks later, he announced that he would play the starring part of Claude in the film version of the rock musical Hair, and that Maurice was set to play the part of Wolf, who falls in love with a picture of Mick Jagger, but he added, "Maurice doesn't like at all the idea of being seen nude on the screen and may back out of the film because of it."

As for Barry himself, he had no such qualms about his role because "in the nude scene, Claude is kept covered up in a white shirt," he said. "My own first reaction to the offer to appear in Hair was to turn it down as well – because I love stories, and there's no real story in this show. I also think that the bulk of the public hate hippies, which is what it's all about. Still, the show has been a huge success and I will do the film. But later on, I'd love to do a film with a real storyline."

An RSO spokesman said that any talk of the Gibb brothers starring in *Hair* was "extremely premature", adding, "It is true that Robert Stigwood's company is bidding for the film rights of the show. But we haven't yet got the rights – and let's face it – practically every other major company are after them, too."

"It was one of those things that were bandied about at the time – I don't know how serious any of that was," Tom Kennedy said of the project. As it turned out, it would be years before a film version of *Hair* was made, with no Gibb participation whatsoever.

★　★　★

On July 12, 1969 Barry, who was said to have spent £1,500 in one week in Carnaby Street and claimed to have a £16,000 a year clothing budget, received the Best Dressed Pop Star award in a competition organised between Radio Luxembourg's 208 People Club and the John Stephen Organisation. He was presented with a silver statuette worth £500 from actress Tsai Chin at a Carnaby Street party with dozens of other pop stars in attendance, including The Tremeloes, Family Dogg, Billy Fury and Status Quo.

Accepting his award, Barry said, "It is one of the nicest things that has ever happened to me. I try very hard to dress well, not too loudly or flashily. If you dress like a bum, they don't want to know. This award will be one that I shall always treasure." He would later point to the award as a symbol of his useful excess, an acknowledgement of the fact that he had spent more money on clothing in Carnaby Street than anyone else, but in those days, he said, "Money to me is something you swap for something else, and to have lots of it is nice. I always buy in bulk – I have never gone shopping for, say, just one shirt."

"Barry spends money crazily," Lynda added. "It means nothing to him. Cars, flats, clothes . . . he has to have the best of everything – and as we're always together, I get the best, too. He's fantastically generous . . . It has come to the point that I daren't say I like anything when we're out together because he buys it for me."

Not to be outdone by his big brother in the sartorial elegance stakes, Robin chipped in with tales of his own extravagance in this area, informing reporters that he had 20 suits from Bailey and Witherall, 50 to 60 shirts, 50 pairs of shoes, and countless ties. "I'm only extravagant up to a point, and then it's always in connection with work. It's extremely important to look good. It makes me feel good. I never wanted to be a handsome guy. I love being ugly . . . In that respect, I think I have a characteristic face. But I do like to look nice."

Part of looking nice meant that the hair which had been the bane of Robert Stigwood's life was shampooed and now neatly trimmed before each television appearance. "I let it go really long that time, didn't I?" he admitted. "I finally had it cut to make it healthy. I'm growing it again, but I'll keep it shaped.

"I bathe as soon as I get up and before I go to bed. It's so relaxing . . . And I like to change my aftershave." His favourite, he said, was Eau De Cologne 4711 Ice, which he had first picked up in East Africa. "Now I fly to Amsterdam for it specially. It's terribly hard to get. It's like trying to get drugs. It's about £10 a bottle but works wonders!"

When it was reported that Barry cleaned his cars with his cashmere sweaters, Robin claimed to shine his shoes with his suits before sending them to the cleaners. "And why not?" he reasoned. "The suits are dirty anyway – that's why they're being cleaned."

Maurice, meanwhile, was nursing two black eyes, the result of a car crash just 10 yards from his home in Kinnerton Street, Belgravia. On May 28, 1969, he was driving home in his grey Rolls-Royce Silver Cloud with friends Roberto Bassanini (who later married Cynthia Lennon) and Brian Duffy after a meal at Mr Chow's restaurant. He said that he saw a car attempting to overtake him at high speed and, swerving to avoid it, he lost control of the car and smashed into a high kerb. "The driver of the other car," Maurice said, "drove on without stopping."

Maurice hit his head on the windscreen, fashion photographer Duffy hit the car's mirror, breaking his nose, and Bassanini's face was badly cut.

Rushing out, Lulu and her close friend Cynthia Lennon found the three men battered and bloody. Lulu recalled in her autobiography that she was almost hysterical, praying that Maurice hadn't been drinking. They phoned Barry, who lived nearby in Eaton Square and he rushed Maurice and his passengers to St George's Hospital. Fortunately none were seriously injured; all three were treated and released, and a grim-faced Barry drove them home again.

"I'm lucky," Maurice said. "I was the least hurt of the three of us."

The Rolls-Royce, however, was not so fortunate. "The chassis was bent, so [my insurance company] wrote it off," he added. "Now I suppose they're spending twice as much as it was worth putting it right. Rolls just don't get written off."

It was a sign of his new, sensible lifestyle, he claimed. "I don't live anywhere near as extravagantly as I used to. At one time, I would buy a new car every week, and if I damaged one I wouldn't bother to get it repaired – I would just order a new one."

This would be the same Maurice Gibb who left IBC's John Pantry somewhat bemused with his account of that day's events. "I remember Maurice turning up to say that he had written off his Rolls-Royce and, after it was towed away, [he] went straight down to the showroom and bought another one. He told me his accountant had said he shouldn't have done that, and [then] he laughed."

On August 6, with the discoloration barely faded from his blackened eyes, Maurice took a tumble down the stairs of Robert Stigwood's Brook Street office, breaking a bone in his arm. Upon his release from hospital later that same day, instead of heading straight home, he made his way to Nova Sound Studios to sit in on a Tin Tin session. By that evening, a couple of drinks, on top of the painkillers taken at the hospital, ensured that he was "feeling no pain". This unwise combination resulted in some rather interesting recordings, to say the least, and may have contributed heavily to Maurice's distorted memory of the evening's events.

Barry. (*Glenn A. Baker Archives*)

The Hugh Gibb Orchestra during Summer Season, Isle Of Man, 1949. Back row: Jim Caine and Hugh Gibb; front row: Albert Metcalfe, Archie Taylor and Charlie Whewell (*Edna Caine*)

The *Thistle* ferry at Douglas, Isle of Man, in 1949, on which Hugh Gibb 'bottled' for cash while the band played. (*Archie Taylor*)

Barry Gibb, aged three, in the garden at Chapel House, Strang Road, Isle of Man. (*Archie Taylor*)

Maurice (left) and Robin, aged about 18 months, on the Isle of Man. (*Courtesy Gibb Family*)

The Rattlesnakes in Manchester, early 1958. Left to right: Paul Frost, Kenny Horrocks, Maurice, Barry and Robin. (*Courtesy Gibb Family*)

Robin, Barry and Maurice in Brisbane, c. 1961, shortly before moving to Sydney. (*News Limited*)

Maurice in Brisbane in 1961, photographed by his girlfriend Diana Lane. (*Diana Lane*)

Fred Marks, managing director of Festival Records, the first man to sign The Bee Gees. (*Courtesy Joan Marks*)

The Gibb Brothers in readiness for signing their contract with Sydney's Festival Records, 1963. (*Glenn A. Baker Archives*)

Barry, Robin and Maurice on the *Bandstand* TV set where they performed their first single 'The Battle Of The Blue And The Grey', 1963. (*Glenn A. Baker Archives*)

The Bee Gees appear on the Australian TV show *Thank Your Lucky Stars* in August, 1964, promoting their new single 'Claustrophobia', backed by The Delawares. Left to right: Bruce Davis, Leith Ryan, Maurice, Bill Swindells, Robin, Laurie Wardman and Barry. (*Courtesy Bruce Davis*)

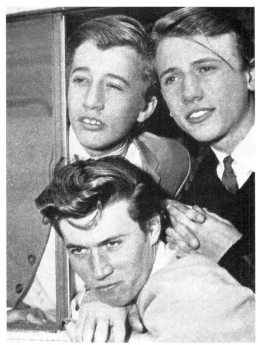

Barry inspecting his injured left eye after his shooting accident, April 1965. (*Graeme Roberts*)

The Gibbs in 1965, on the road, surveying the world from the window of their van. (*Glenn A. Baker Archives*)

Barry, Robin and Maurice with their Kombi van on the streets of Sydney, 1966. (*Courtesy Gibb Family*)

Barry in Sydney in 1966 with Maureen Bates, whom he would marry four months before the family returned to England. (*Glenn A. Baker Archives*)

Lesley Gibb, at an EKKA Exhibition – a tent show - in Australia in 1966. (*Diana Lane*)

The Brothers Gibb, shortly before departing for England, 1966. (*News Limited*)

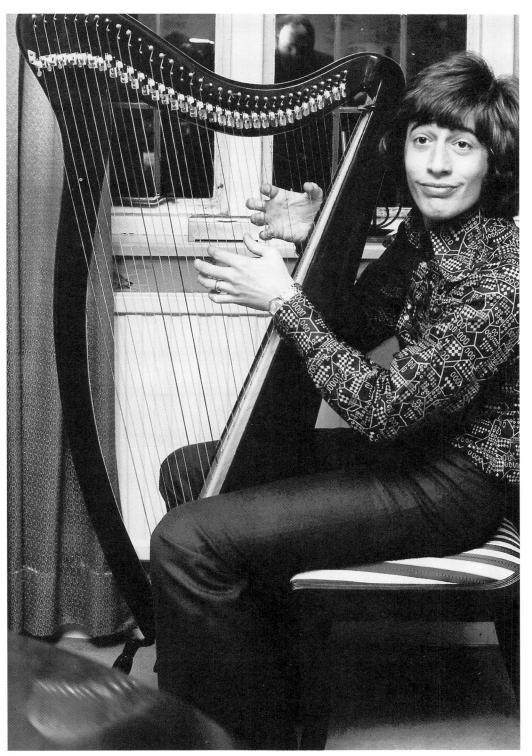

Robin. (*LFI*)

New drummer Colin Petersen with Robin, Barry and Maurice in London in March 1967, shortly after signing with Polydor. (*Rex*)

The Gibb family, less father Hugh, backstage in London. Left to right: Barry, Maurice, Lesley, Andy, mother Barbara, and Robin. (*LFI*)

Vince Melouney joins in the band. Left to right: Barry, Vince, Robin, Colin and Maurice. (*Rex*)

Frankie Howerd Meets The Bee Gees, 1968. (*Rex*)

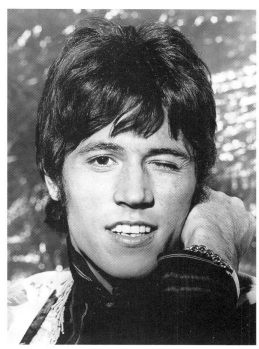

Barry winks for the camera. (*Harry Goodwin*)

Maurice with his girlfriend, Hungarian pop-star Sarolta Zalatnay. (*Pictorial Press*)

Robert Stigwood. (*Rex*)

Robin weds Molly Hullis at Caxton Hall, London, December 8, 1968. (*LFI*)

Maurice marries Lulu at Gerrards Cross, Buckinghamshire, February 18, 1969. (*PA News*)

Vince Melouney with wife Dianne. (*Pictorial Press*)

Colin Petersen with wife Joanne, secretary to Beatles manager Brian Epstein. (*LFI*)

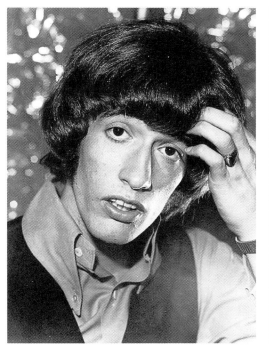

Robin goes solo. (*Harry Goodwin*)

Peter Mason, Robin's would-be replacement, in 1969, wearing the suit that Barry bought him in Carnaby Street. (*Courtesy Peter Mason*)

Lesley Gibb Evans on stage with Maurice, Colin and Barry, at The Talk Of The Town, London, May 1969. (*Barry Plummer*)

The cast of *Cucumber Castle*, with Andy Gibb in the bath. (*Rex*)

Colin Peterson, wearing his *Cucumber Castle* outfit, two days before he was fired from The Bee Gees. (*Harry Goodwin*)

Barry in a scene from *Cucumber Castle* that was cut from the final film. (*Rex*)

Clockwise from top left: Barry, Maurice, Andy (aged 12) and Robin. (*Harry Goodwin/Barry Plummer*)

Robin in 1969, with wife Molly and Hedgehog the basset hound. (*LFI*)

Barry in the bath. (*Pictorial Press*)

Maurice with Barbara Windsor arriving at the Garrick Theatre, London, for *Sing A Rude Song*, June 1970. (*LFI*)

Colin and Robin in the control room at IBC Studios recording 'Make A Stranger Your Friend' for Jonathan Kelly. (*Barry Plummer*)

Then, heaping injury upon injury, on August 11 at the start of filming for The Bee Gees' colour television spectacular *Cucumber Castle*, Maurice cut his neck on a jagged piece of armour. After refusing a doctor's advice to get hospital treatment for the injury, he discovered that he couldn't get the headpiece off when the crew decided to break for lunch. Maurice was spoon-fed through the visor, solving one little difficulty, but he soon discovered that the headpiece was not the only problem with wearing a heavy suit of armour. "It's these clothes I'm wearing!" he exclaimed. "A major operation when I suddenly want to go to the loo." A mere 45 minutes after his scene was finished, film crew technicians managed to free a relieved Maurice.

Maurice and Lulu's careers had often taken them in very different directions, but *Cucumber Castle* was a chance for them to work on the same project and Lulu remembered it fondly as a great time.

Originally conceived as the pilot episode for a 13 week series with such guest stars as Sammy Davis Junior, Richard Harris and Hermione Gingold, the television special was filmed on the 36 acre grounds of Robert Stigwood's estate at Stanmore with its own authentic Scottish castle, removed brick by brick and rebuilt in its original form. The film co-starred Vincent Price, Eleanor Bron and Spike Milligan, amongst others, and even featured cameo appearances by Stigwood himself and a very young, freckle-faced Andy Gibb.

"Before we made *Cucumber Castle,* Barry, Lu and myself went right through it and had it all filmed on my video," Maurice said. "Then we watched the result and changed anything we didn't like. So, by the time we went into the actual production, we had tested every little facet of the production.

"The concept was of a *Laugh-In* type of show but set roughly in Tudor England," Barry explained. "The way that a lot of the sketches worked out was that the punch-line was in the sudden contrast between the Tudor times and a confrontation with the 20th century.

"It was basically very simple . . . Maurice and I are the princes who quarrel over the division of the kingdom when our dad dies." Their father, in all his melodramatic glory, was played by their old friend and co-star from The Bee Gees' first television special, Frankie Howerd.

Barry continued, "It was when we began to really work on the story that we both realised that the outline of the story contained so many parables relating to reality. So it worked out that several of the sketches, for us anyway, have a meaning above and beyond the obvious joke.

"We wouldn't claim to be very profound thinkers, but we have always carefully considered the words of our songs, and we have put many of our deepest beliefs into them. We have done the same in a humorous way with the sketches in the show."

"Dressing up in all these period costumes does something to you," Maurice added. "You feel like the person you're supposed to be playing simply because of the clothes. Errol Flynn admitted in his autobiography that he couldn't act. He simply found he could be convincing when he was dressed in period costumes. So we're quite pleased with our acting, and the whole project is turning out far funnier than we ever thought. Mind you, with people like Frankie Howerd and Spike Milligan in the film, it could hardly be anything else but funny . . . A lot of what we did . . . was ad-lib and we had a fabulous time making [it]. Spike and Frankie were always up to something weird every time we went before the cameras."

"We are very pleased with the results we have seen so far," Barry agreed, "but we know that the real art of making a comedy film is in the editing, and we are getting the best professional help that we can in that department."

It was during the filming of *Cucumber Castle* that Barry discovered something that had been missing in the life of a young pop star: mornings!

"To tell the truth, I think that [Maurice and I] found that the hardest part of all was getting up so early in the morning. After years of working late at night you get into the habit of having a sleep-in in the mornings. To suddenly have to get up at six is a bit shattering. But after three weeks we began to realise what we had been missing. I didn't even know that there was a six o'clock in the morning – I thought it only happened in the evening," he quipped.

One of those early morning treks to Stanmore nearly led to his arrest when a conscientious policeman spotted a sleepy Barry Gibb loading a gun into the boot of his car, parked outside his home near the Irish Embassy. Springing into action, the officer took Barry to the local police station.

Fortunately for Barry, he had a perfectly reasonable explanation. He was Frederick, the King of Cucumber, and needed the gun to fight a duel with his brother Marmaduke, the King of Jelly. Amazingly enough, he was neither charged nor detained pending psychiatric examination.

The project was not without other obstacles. A proposed tour of the United States and Canada was cancelled as filming of the show fell behind when heavy rains meant the location set was awash in a sea of mud. According to Maurice, "After only a week, the £50,000 budget had already been spent. But we've waited two years to do this film. People never thought it would ever happen, in fact, but we've always wanted to do something like this – a period comedy, with breaks for our songs and top-line guests."

In another incident it was reported that The Bee Gees lost an estimated £10,000 worth of equipment (including, according to Maurice, his prized 22-year-old Les Paul guitar), when a thief walked into the grounds of Stigwood's lavish estate and drove off in the group's Ford Transit van.

Tom Kennedy, The Bee Gees' road manager, laughed heartily when reminded of this incident and said, "I'm not so sure about the 22-year-old Les Paul guitar, but the van *was* stolen, and it was my fault . . . I was despatched to buy some chamber pots . . . I came back, left the keys in while I delivered them to the house, came back and it was gone. Whoever was there must have seen me get out and got straight in. Because there was a film crew there, they probably could have wandered up the drive and no one knew who anyone was. The van was found somewhere in the Midlands and we got a couple of the amps back from somewhere else . . . It probably was just an opportunist thing. It was literally done in five minutes.

"Everyone just thought, 'Oh well, these things happen' – it was a bit like that in those days. At the time, I felt a bit stupid, but you know, everything was insured and there wasn't anything of great value in there anyway." Reminded of the legendary Les Paul guitar, Tom added, "It probably belonged to John Lennon at the time as well! Maurice is a colourful person."

In the midst of filming came another dramatic turn in the saga of The Bee Gees when it was announced that Colin Petersen had left the group. Scenes involving Colin which had already been filmed were scrapped. There were suggestions that Colin wanted to appear only in the musical scenes – with one wag claiming that perhaps this was because he had seen the script – and had later complained that he wasn't given enough to do.

A Robert Stigwood Organisation spokesman pulled no punches, stating: "Colin has been fired. The Gibb brothers will continue to perform and record as The Bee Gees." Barry was somewhat more diplomatic. "This is all part of the natural progression of The Bee Gees, as we become more and more involved in our separate interests," he said, implying this was all part of a master plan. "Since our brother Robin went solo, Maurice and I have been working more closely together even than before, while Colin has been spending increasing amounts of time with his own interests. We are naturally sorry that he won't be with us, but we all have to progress.

"Colin lost complete interest in the group," he continued. "During the last recording session he didn't turn up once. He said, 'Call me if you need me.' A dedicated Bee Gee doesn't do that. He also told some [journalists] that he was only interested in the money. He said The Bee Gees wouldn't survive when Robin left – I was never under the impression that Colin Petersen was a fortune teller!"

Colin retorted bitterly, "Why do people keep saying I left The Bee Gees? I was fired! I really cannot see that [remark] about me losing interest. If I had, I would have left on my own accord just as Vince and Robin did. I suppose he was referring to the fact that I was producing records. At the time Maurice was producing two artists and Barry was also producing a couple. In fact, they started before I did. You could take it, if they go out and start producing people, this is how a Bee Gee should act.

"Naturally, everyone in the pop business is interested in money. You'd be a bird brain if you weren't. But I never put the money before my work as a Bee Gee. You get to the stage where you are successful and are earning a considerable amount of money, and then money doesn't matter that much any more.

"Barry's reference to the last recording session is unbelievable," Colin added. "I turned up to every one, although on one occasion I got there and Barry said I wasn't needed because it was a Cheryl Gray session . . . I can remember quite clearly speaking to the press and saying Robin was a big loss to The Bee Gees. Now I'm quite sure the public in general was aware of that, and I was only expressing my admiration for Robin's talent. If I thought the group couldn't continue, I wouldn't have stayed with them."

As when Robin quit, the war of words continued in the press, dragging on to such an extent that fans could be excused for thinking that all The Bee Gees ever seemed to do was criticise one another in public. "The only way to continue as The Bee Gees is to continue as two people," Barry announced. "A lot of songs on our albums haven't had a drummer at all. That's no reflection on Colin; they just haven't needed a drummer.

"Maurice and I will make records together. I don't think we'll make records individually as far as I can see. The only thing that's likely to separate us is if I'm living in America where I would like to live for the filming. There's always pressure there, you suddenly realise that your nerves are bad. Robin's leaving the group hurt me a lot. It's a shame he's not feeling the same ambitions now that we held together as three brothers. He's left me bewildered, but I think his success is fantastic, and I hope Colin succeeds."

Maurice diplomatically said, "Colin has his own business interest while we are spreading into television and films. We have all been aware for some time that our ways were separating. Mr Stigwood has offered to release Colin from his contract so that his career will not be held back."

Colin still professed to be stunned by the decision. "After The Bee Gees did *Top Of The Pops*, everything was fine," he insisted. "Then I suddenly get this letter delivered by Robert Stigwood's chauffeur saying I'm out of the group. Just like that. No phone call or anything.

"From the other week backwards, we all got on well. And this really came like a bolt from the blue – a real shock. It's not as if I hadn't been pulling my weight. I believe if you're in a group, it's a business partnership.

"Apart from the odd illness, I've always turned up for gigs and things, and I've always put the group first and foremost . . . I've even cancelled things which would have brought me money from outside so I could appear with the group.

"I have received a letter from Barry and Maurice Gibb to the effect that they no longer desire to be associated with me. I am deeply hurt. I am a partner in The Bee Gees and as a result of receiving this notice I have no alternative but to turn this matter over to my lawyers and ask them to dissolve the partnership known as The Bee Gees. Barry and Maurice are welcome to go out as The Brothers Gibb. I don't think they or anyone else can replace The Bee Gees.

"The brother trouble was felt by Vince and this forced him to leave. Robin left because he couldn't get on with his brothers. He wasn't really suited to the group. But I can't quite understand why this has happened to me. We were a successful group and got on well and were making money. I feel I've done just as much performance and image-wise for the group. I don't see why I should have to give it all up and hand the group name over to the other two."

Attorneys working on Colin's behalf filed a writ declaring that he and the Gibb brothers were equal partners in The Bee Gees; that the name Bee Gees was property of that partnership; and that Barry and Maurice had broken their obligations to him under that partnership. He was also seeking an order to prevent Barry and Maurice from appearing as The Bee Gees without him. It was even reported that he planned to form a new Bee Gees.

An RSO spokesman issued the terse statement, "The Bee Gees will go on performing as The Bee Gees, and if Mr Petersen instructs any proceedings, they will be turned over to their lawyers. If Mr Petersen wishes to try and form a group known as The Bee Gees, that matter will be dealt with in due course.

"When Colin Petersen joined The Bee Gees in 1967, the brothers Gibb had been appearing under the name of The Bee Gees – which are Barry Gibb's initials – for many years. The brothers Gibb have no objection to Colin Petersen performing under his own initials or any other name."

The High Court ruled against Colin in the suit, adding, "It is a situation which often develops when people have been in a long association and no discredit is cast on anyone."

"This is very disappointing to me of course," Colin said. "I always looked upon The Bee Gees as a mutual thing between the Gibb brothers and me and I didn't think it was possible or proper for them to dismiss me in this way.

"I still feel part of the group because I've been a Bee Gee for so long," he insisted. "It's a question of being Colin Petersen or Maurice Gibb. You have an identity as a Bee Gee after working seven days a week. I can't see how they'll get across to the public on their own."

Nowadays, more than 30 years later, Colin still remains slightly bitter over the circumstances of his departure. "I got fired by Robert Stigwood for questioning his business. I went to Mo and asked him, 'What's going on with the money?' How could Robert have negotiated a decent fee on The Bee Gees' behalf when he had conflicting interests?"

Colin was ideally placed to raise such an issue. He and Joanne were now in the management game themselves and understood that Robert's role as manager was to negotiate the best possible deal for his clients. However, he also had to look after the publishing and recording interests of The Robert Stigwood Organisation and they would not necessarily coincide with those of The Bee Gees. Often a generous man, money might not have been an issue for Robert, but Colin's question struck right at the heart of his management technique of completely controlling all aspects of his artists' careers.

A few days later, a letter was delivered advising him of his dismissal. He now recalls that Dick Ashby was the unfortunate messenger, perhaps driven by Stigwood's chauffeur. "Dick was a decent bloke and was very upset," Colin continued. For the first time too, he revealed the contents not only of the initial letter, but also of the follow-up correspondence some months later.

Devoid of any heading and undated, although it would have been written towards the end of the third week of August, 1969, the first note read, "To Colin Petersen, After having given considerable thought to the situation, we have decided that we do not want to continue our association with you. Accordingly, your association with us is hereby formally terminated." It was signed by Maurice, Hugh (as Maurice was still a minor) and Barry.

Noticeable by its absence from the letter is any mention of the part that Colin claims Robert Stigwood played in the whole messy business, but a second letter leaves him in no doubt as to who was really pulling the strings. Dated January 13, 1970, and headed 68 Eaton Street, London, it reads, "Dear Colin, On consideration I must apologise on the way I behaved towards you when I wrote to you and told you that I no longer wish to be associated with you as a Bee Gee. I did this after being pressured to do it by Robert Stigwood who advised both Maurice and I to treat you in this way and the whole idea came from him. On reflection now, I sincerely believe that if it weren't for Robert Stigwood's actions The Bee Gees would all be working together for a long time to come."

Of course, the mere existence of this letter is not proof that any of its contents are true. It was signed by Barry, but curiously was then witnessed by Jim Morris. This immediately begs two questions – why would Barry feel the need to have the letter witnessed, and why would he choose Robert Stigwood's driver to do so? Perhaps the answers will be revealed in one or other of the books that Barry and Colin are now said to be writing.

Colin is adamant that his sacking had nothing whatsoever to do with the *Cucumber Castle* film. "I had told Barry that I didn't want to be in the comedy sketches as I didn't think they were very funny. Barry had no problems with this," he confirmed.

As regards his suing for The Bee Gees' name, something which followers of the group had always thought to be a strange move, Colin now reveals that there was more going on behind the scenes than previously made public knowledge. "I had no intention of stopping them using their name forever, but I had other litigation going on with Robert Stigwood and I was advised by prominent lawyer Marty Machat, a former partner of Allen Klein, to take this course of action to have my litigation finalised."

Barry pleaded for a little understanding from the group's followers. "I have no hard feelings against Colin. We wish him well in anything he may do. Though we've given the public a confusing time, we should have the chance to prove that we are The Bee Gees. The Bee Gees are not dead and don't intend to be. I just ask the critics to back off a bit and give us a chance. We just want a little leeway.

"It's given us a lot of freedom both musically and personally. Maurice and I will become a complete partnership in business and everything else we do. Out of the whole mess comes the new true Bee Gees. We intend to stick together like glue. There are only two of us now, we won't be fighting each other. Neither Maurice nor I started any fight within the group, we've always been the closest, he's always talked about the personal things with me. He discussed his marriage with me. There are no more reasons to fight."

This new-found brotherly harmony applied to their musical taste as well. "Maurice and I love ballads – you can't make us do rock and roll," Barry said. "We listen to rock and roll, we like it, as we like all forms of music especially Chopin and Beethoven, but we'll stick to what we can do with our hearts not with our heads. The songwriting will be done between us. I write the lyrics and Maurice comes up with some beautiful chords. Robin is a strong songwriter and a strong singer, but Maurice is the backbone musically of the group. He always has been. There are guys who are very talented would give their right arms to be in Maurice's position."

Barry reminded everyone, "Maurice is capable of playing about seven instruments – most of the back tracks on the records were all him, and I sang lead on four or five of the hit singles. So how can The Bee Gees sound be finished?" he asked.

As a gesture of gratitude to the fans who had supported the group through all the tumult, the brothers planned a series of live performances. "We want to go out on a concert tour of Britain before Christmas with a big orchestra," Barry revealed. "I want to give people value for money and if they hear an orchestra on record, why shouldn't they expect to hear the same sound on stage?

"We'll get another record out and gain a bit more confidence from the kids and thank those who bought the last one . . . The tour will more or less be our début as The Bee Gees – I mean, The Bee Gees as they are going to stay. If we split anymore, we won't be The Bee Gees.

"You see, the one advantage of only being two people in a group is that we can do things separately and not split up. One thing is certain. Now there's just Maurice and me, nobody need be afraid we're going to split up. I can tell you, we'll be together for the next 10 years!

"Maurice and I will continue working as The Bee Gees."

In the event, Barry's confidence was misplaced. All the feuding had inspired a joke that circulated among the pop business to the effect that by Christmas, it would be The Bee Gee. It therefore probably came as no real surprise when, at the beginning of December, Barry announced, "As from today, I'm solo."

For Barry, things came to a head when Robert Stigwood booked studio time for Barry and Maurice to begin work on The Bee Gees' next album. "I got to IBC studios. Maurice knows well and truly about it. And there's nobody there!" he exclaimed. "So I called up Robert and said, 'Where's Maurice? We're supposed to be doing an album.' Robert said, 'He's in Australia.' I said, 'Robert, you've lined all this up for us to go in the studio and make an album. Why didn't Maurice even tell me he was going to Australia?' And he said, 'Well, he went with Lulu quickly. It had to be done quickly. They've gone to promote *Cucumber Castle*.' I said, 'What!?' Things

247

were pretty crazy, but nothing as crazy as this. I honestly felt . . . I was being worked against."

Although it failed to dissuade Barry from leaving the group, it was quick thinking on Stigwood's part to mention *Cucumber Castle* in an effort to disguise the fact that promotion of the film was far from Maurice's and Lulu's minds. The trip was purely "for pleasure", the couple had told officials as they passed through passport control.

Part of their 'world tour', their visit involved a nostalgic trip to Sydney. Maurice had been looking forward to driving Lulu around Bronte and Maroubra so she could "see all the old places we used to hang around [because] I wanted to show her where it all began". This was the first sighting the Australian press had had of Lulu, and Maurice was quite content to keep a low profile. "It never bothered me a bit when photographers pushed me aside because they wanted to photograph my wife without me. Or when I was introduced as 'Lulu's husband'!"

A weary looking Lulu, exhausted by the long flight, was interested primarily in getting a good night's sleep. Before they left Britain, even that little luxury had been denied her as Maurice grew impatient for the day of their departure. "He's been so excited, he hasn't been able to sleep," she confided to reporters.

Back in Britain, Barry was determined to go despite The Bee Gees' reported earnings of £3 million a year. "But the money doesn't come into it," he said. "I haven't been doing anything for the past three or four months. I feel isolated and rejected."

Contrary to his earlier statement, he remarked, "I just didn't believe in two people being a group. Colin, Vince and Robin have put the lid on it for me. They all left for their own reasons. I had nothing to do with them leaving, despite the things they have said. Vince said that my music got on his nerves; Robin said he was a better singer than me; Colin said that I wanted to be king. What Maurice does is his own business. We'll still work together but it won't be as The Bee Gees."

A music paper of the time announced the final collapse of the group with a tongue-in-cheek poem:

> *Five little Bee Gees, but many shocks in store,*
> *One left to form a group – and then there were four.*
> *Four little Bee Gees, not good company,*
> *One became a soloist – and then there were three.*
> *Three little Bee Gees, not sure what to do,*
> *Decided drums weren't needed – and then there were two.*
> *Two little Bee Gees felt it wasn't fun,*
> *One got fed up with things – and then there was one.*

"The trouble is they were surrounded by people saying, 'You're the star, you're the star, you're the star' to ingratiate themselves," said Tom Kennedy, their road manager. "The managers were sort of sucking up to their egos. Living in Barry's shadow can never be easy for the other two . . . and the people who were around Robin at the time fed on that. Although Robin enjoyed a minor success and the others did as well as a duo, they were never very happy with the situation, and I think they were glad when they got back together. I think it was the most natural thing and something they wanted to do, but their pride wouldn't let them. Maurice and Barry were stung by Robin doing this, and I think Robin . . . if someone had made a phone call, it might have gone a long way to stopping this thing happening. When it's family, it becomes even more bitter – there's a kind of hatred that builds up that between strangers would never happen. Luckily their rift didn't go on that long and Robin came back to the fold, so to speak.

"I think the others really missed him. Barry became more reclusive and Maurice went on doing what he does. Maurice was always more the sort of outgoing, social person, and Barry retreated to Eaton Square for 18 months.

"Maurice went off and socialised and just generally did music with other people, which he enjoyed. In those days, he would just phone me up and say, 'I've booked Nova Sound for six o'clock tonight.' I was actually in Devon once and I phoned him just to check in, and he said, 'Where are you?' I said, 'I'm in Devon,' and he said, 'I've got a studio booked for tonight' so I came home!" Tom laughed. "That's just the way Maurice was."

Maurice's chief collaborator was Lulu's younger brother, Billy Lawrie. "Billy was a fun character and probably very good for Maurice at the time because Lulu was away. He was very supportive of Maurice. Although Billy's been quite successful in the music business, singing was not really his forte – the singer in that family was always Lulu. Their little sister had some minor success with a group, but once again Lulu was always the person that the spotlight was on."

With Maurice otherwise occupied, Barry was retreating into himself. According to friends, he had become practically a recluse, rarely venturing out from his plush London home. "He's not a person to this day who is compelled to go out to have a good time," Tom Kennedy said. "TV, books, things like UFOs and mysticism . . . he can immerse himself. He just literally stayed home. People like David Garrick and Peter Wyngarde used to go to his house and they would just entertain themselves at home rather than go out, which was never really up Barry's street. He used to read the *TV Guide* – he would actually peruse it."

Australian pop star Ronnie Burns recalled his stay with Barry and Lynda during this period. "I came over to London and Barry and his male assistant picked me up at the airport. I stayed with them for about 10 days. In retrospect, it was a hard time for Barry. He didn't know where he was going, or what the future held for him at all. In the time I was with him, he never left the apartment at all, living a very reclusive lifestyle. I remember he would get up at strange times of the night and cook sausages, and as I was still on Australian time, this suited me.

"I wanted to go and buy some clothes at Carnaby Street so he took me down there and we both bought matching jackets. When we got back, Lynda thanked me, saying it was the first time he had been out of the apartment for 18 months.

"I grew quite close to Barry, and the more time we spent together, the closer we became," Burns related. "Remember he didn't have his brothers there, and I think he was missing them."

Barry insisted that he was not interested in retaliating against the other Bee Gees. "Although they have all had a damn good go at me," he added bitterly. "I was nine years old when I asked my brothers to play with me. That was 14 years ago. Something happened after we came to England. We lost enthusiasm. We had to leave Australia to become international stars. You can be tops in Australia and be unheard of everywhere else. It was a family thing with us, and that maybe is what destroyed it. The Bee Gees no longer exist."

Barry added that he was fed-up with the "phoney" image that had been built up of him – "I just want to get down to reality.

"By going solo I could lose a fortune but money is not important. I couldn't give a damn. I will always have my songs and I don't think I will ever dry up. I would be content if I had nothing but a tape-recorder. I could still write songs and record them."

He maintained that he was still keen to get into acting, preferably in a Western or a period drama. "Five or ten scripts a day are coming into the office," he said, "and we are just waiting for the right one." He had a promotional television tour of Europe lined up and intended to do more television appearances in Britain on his return. He was also looking forward to working more in America.

A spokesman for the Robert Stigwood Organisation stated, "We are not opposed in principle to Barry going solo, and we will be meeting with him and Maurice later this week – following Maurice's return to Britain – to discuss the matter."

Commenting on what appeared to be the final break-up of his old group, Robin said: "It looked as if it was going to happen anyway. One of them was going to leave; they couldn't go on with just two people. But it looked so silly the way it happened. They should have just let the news leak out on its own instead of Barry announcing it the way he did. I don't think Maurice knew anything about it; it was just a case of Barry leaving on his own accord. He was very bitter because Maurice was out of the country with Lulu getting things done by himself, and he was just sitting around at home."

Robin still insisted that the family ties were still there, even though they had been strained. "There are certain feelings that you can convey only to brothers and relatives . . . The only thing I regret about leaving is that there might have come a time in the group when we'd all have been having a good time together," he said.

"But that certainly wasn't the situation when I left, and I'm much happier now I'm on my own. At last I've got to make my own decisions and can attract individual attention, rather than just being part of The Bee Gees . . . By leaving I didn't do anything to jolt the cog of the working harmony. It was for the benefit of all really."

Robin claimed that he and Maurice had managed to bury the hatchet. "Maurice and I are twins and have our birthday at Christmas. We got together then and are now on extremely good terms. Maurice is incredibly happy about my success. But communication between Barry and me is nil."

The twins' reunion had come at Maurice's instigation. "Recently I saw that Robin was appearing on *Top Of The Pops*," Maurice said. "I'd heard that he was a bit sorry to find he was losing contact with his brothers so I rang the studio and asked to speak to him. They wouldn't let me. I said, 'This is ridiculous – Man has just got on the Moon and yet I can't even speak on the phone to my twin brother!' But a couple of hours later there was a knock on the door and there was Robin, saying he'd heard I'd been trying to contact him. So we embraced, all emotional, sat down and had a drink . . ."

After the reunion, Maurice added, "I find it easier to talk to Robin than to Barry. I can get together with Robin any time, but it seems difficult with Barry.

"I don't know what it is, but he just seems to have a basic distrust of me. I just can't understand why. I'd like to be able to talk to him about it. But he seems to be the sort of guy who believes everything he reads in the papers, whereas I will read something and say, 'What a load of crap!' But Barry won't talk to me and I can't find out what's wrong with him."

★ ★ ★

New Musical Express announced that the final three days of November and first five days of December were provisionally set aside for Robin's British solo concert tour. Although no venues were confirmed, there were to be eight concerts with an opening date in London. "I took a gamble on my own abilities," he said. "Now it's come off and I'm spreading my wings."

The proposed UK tour never did take place, but Robin was somewhat surprisingly scheduled to play two concerts, on January 31 and February 1, at the outdoor Silverstream Bowl as part of the Redwood Festival at Redwood Park in Swanson, Auckland, New Zealand. The concert poster for the event proudly proclaimed "Robin Gibb – The Voice Of The Bee Gees".

"It's a place where I have had about eight number ones. 'Massachusetts' and 'Saved By The Bell' and other numbers I recorded . . . were number one out there," Robin explained. "I ought to put in an appearance, but I don't like being on the other side of the world for too long."

Ordinarily, artists would play various dates along the way, but Robin made the gruelling flight halfway around the world for what was virtually a "one-night stand", flying directly to New Zealand immediately after an appearance in the United States on *The Andy Williams Show*.

251

"He was completely out of context," Tom Kennedy recalled, "appearing between Maori dancers or some such. The Maoris were throwing beer cans at him! Robin tells this story with great glee. Robin will tell you anything – if he's done it, he's honest about it . . ."

Earlier, Robin had insisted that when he began making his solo appearances, they would be something out of the ordinary. "I want them to be concerts that will run like my own version of a carnival," he explained. "An evening with Robin Gibb will be something full of unexpected events. I want the whole thing to be an event, a performance."

Robin couldn't have chosen a more apt description for the first of his two Redwood Festival concerts. Backed by his trademark orchestra, he took the stage late in the evening to the opening strains of 'Massachusetts'. He greeted the audience, but before he could sing a note, a tomato sailed through the air and struck the side of his head.

Undaunted, Robin brushed the remains of the tomato from his hair and, accompanied by flying debris, sang the song without missing a beat. At its conclusion, as he thanked the audience for their appreciative applause, a teenage girl suddenly leapt onto the stage and with an enthusiastic embrace sent the slight young singer reeling into the astonished orchestra. Robin was rescued by the police, and the young girl escorted away. Then a young man jumped onto the stage and was thrown roughly back into the audience. By now the security guards realised that they had lost control of the crowd, and Robin and his orchestra hastily exited the stage. Police efforts to calm the furore were futile as the mutinous mob lobbed bottles, beer cans and whatever else was at hand.

Robin's second appearance was scheduled for the following afternoon, and that morning the promoter tried desperately to assure him that this time everything would run smoothly. The audience was moved back 25 feet from the stage, and two security vans waited on either side of the stage in case he had to make another expeditious escape. Police were planted in the audience about 30 feet away from the stage, with security guards on stage with Robin and guard dogs backstage at the ready.

"I can't say I really felt scared – I was terrified!" Robin quipped later. "No, I can't say I felt scared; it's quite natural that something like that should happen after a crowd of such vast amounts had been there all day. It was quite late when I appeared, and they had sort of had the weather all day – it was sort of heated and they had the yen to do something physical."

At any rate, Robin added, "I have an obligation to my audience not to look scared – even when they hurt me!"

Noting that Robin was much calmer about the whole incident than he was, the promoter tried to downplay the episode, saying, "The thing has been blown out of all proportion because – what were there? Ten cans, two bottles and half a dozen tomatoes."

"A smorgasbord," suggested Robin helpfully.

With a cheerful reminder that "This is a new suit", Robin stepped out into the bright New Zealand sunshine and performed his set unscathed. He ended the concert with a moving rendition of 'I Started A Joke' and, with an almost audible sigh of relief, said, "Thank you, everybody, and this is where I take my leave."

After this eventful live début, it was back to Britain and the business of promoting records. Robin's second single, 'One Million Years', was somewhat in the same mould as the first, and he even admitted to reporters to playing it safe, hoping for a repeat. The lyric is actually daringly morbid; a dead man telling his lover he's waiting, but melodically it is more flat, and it failed to make any impact on the British or American charts, although it reached number 14 in Germany. Robin claimed that this came as no surprise to him. "I never expected the single to do anything," he explained, "because it was released over Christmas at a time when all the radio and TV producers had already pre-set their plugs for the programmes over the festive season. It got lost in the avalanche of record releases over that period, which is exactly what I expected."

The song would not even be included on Robin's album for some reason, leaving it with 11 songs at a time when most albums had 12. It did, however, appear on the German LP and is on the CD reissue from Germany, both in mock stereo made from the mono single master.

★   ★   ★

Jonathan Ledingham was raised in a house overlooking Drogheda, near Dublin. On leaving the Royal Irish Academy of Dramatic Arts where he studied dancing, fencing and method acting, he arrived in Britain in late 1968. By mid-1969, he had become Jonathan Kelly, and was a struggling musician living in The Madison, in London's Paddington area, which had gained some notoriety for its clientele. Amongst the hotel's other guests were Joe Cocker and The Greaseband. One day he received a visitor. "The person was like an archetypal Mafioso guy," he says. "Seriously! I think he had a patch over one eye, he had a limp; he wore his coat over his shoulders, but not through his arms. This guy was absolutely, 100 per cent mafia.

"He got me this gig in The Hotel International [in Lancaster Gate], and the score was, that I would sing, and get paid – £15 per week, and I'd also get my meal in the evening. So that was quite a good gig. But it was a posh hotel, and I was not the kind of singer who entertains posh people. I was singing songs like 'The Lonesome Death Of Hattie Carol', songs about changing the world. These people didn't want the world changed, they wanted it just the way it was, only with more money for them.

"One night Colin and Joanne Petersen came in with a party of other people, and I had just done a song called 'Sailor'. Colin invited me over to the table and asked, 'Who wrote that?' I said I had and he asked me whether I had written any more. I sang him some; I think I even did a Bee Gees song, for crying out loud! Then he ordered champagne, it was marvellous. And then he said, 'Let's do a song together, now!' So we made up a song right there, which is what I would do all the time, so I was quite happy doing that. So we got on really well.

"He asked me to come around to the mews, and then of course he talked about doing music together and that sort of thing. So I just got involved with him and doing their new project, which was for Joanne to be managing and for Colin to be assisting and producing, and it was really nice, and they gave me excellent opportunities. They were very kind; very nice," recalls Jonathan.

"Nice" barely describes Colin's attempts to make his protégé feel special. Jonathan's first promotional photo shows him smartly dressed and sitting in a Jacobean chair whilst holding an exquisite looking instrument. "That was Barry Gibb's guitar, a custom built [Gibson] J-200, a beautiful guitar! I dropped it on stage and broke all the side and a guy invisibly mended it down in Brighton." In actual fact, the guitar was one which Colin had bought himself, but as Jonathan was so impressed by the guitar's background, it seemed a shame at that time to destroy his illusion.

Jonathan Kelly was in the right place to observe Colin's reaction to his departure from The Bee Gees. "He was a bit cross about it, but he was also a bit excited by the whole thing because it was in the papers and things like that, and no publicity is bad publicity. So I think he felt . . . it meant something was happening. He always wanted a full diary of things happening. When things weren't happening, that's when he was unhappy. So he wasn't unhappy to be in the limelight as it were, through this. Being the drummer with writers like Robin and Barry around, all that he was doing was playing over the tracks. They were coming up with all the creativity."

Giving him expensive instruments aside, Joanne and Colin did well for Jonathan professionally too. "Colin organised a recording contract with Parlophone," explained Jonathan, "with an Australian called Ken East who was head of EMI or something at the time, he was a nice chap. He also organised a publishing deal with Carlin with Freddie Beanstock."

By then, Colin had also started his own music publishing company, Hercules, named after the couple's little Yorkshire Terrier, and he produced Kelly's album, which was preceded by two singles, also produced by Colin. 'Denver' was the first release, but the follow-up, 'Make A Stranger Your Friend', is of more interest, both from a musical and non-musical perspective. "What a crazy song," Kelly concedes. "None of my friends liked it. [It's] just about ending human conflicts and racism. Racism is the ugliest face of mankind that people express. They made me write a letter to [The Reverend Ian] Paisley!" Tory M.P. Enoch Powell was another recipient of the plea for better understanding between people of all religions, colours and races.

The recording session for Kelly's new single was also the cause of some friction between Robin Gibb and his new management, as Vic Lewis refused to allow Robin permission to participate in the "super-session" organised by Colin Petersen. Mick Taylor of The Rolling Stones, Klaus

Voormann of Manfred Mann and The Plastic Ono Band, Madeleine Bell of Blue Mink, Carl Wayne formerly of The Move, Christine Holmes, Steve Rowland and Albert Hammond of Family Dogg, Jackie Lomax, Tony Ashton of Ashton, Gardner & Dyke, Leslie Duncan, Peter Sellers and Spike Milligan were others who had all been invited to participate in the recording, and Colin had included Robin on the list.

"I wanted Robin because his high voice is just right for the record," Colin explained. "We're both friends – despite all The Bee Gees business. It's a pity he couldn't take part."

"There should be a clause in recording contracts which allows artists to work with whoever they wish," Robin protested. "Music shouldn't be tied down in this way. Companies should have got together long ago to break down this barrier. It's all furiously frustrating. I was dying to get down there and join in. But I'd only have to open my mouth and I'd be in breach of contract!"

Even the thought of one of his signed artists working for another label infuriated Robin's manager. Vic Lewis complained, "It's a load of tripe. I don't put people under contract so they can record for other people! All these stars think they should be allowed to record like this without getting paid. But they'd soon be worried when they hadn't any money."

A photo of the session shows one young man with wavy hair wearing a conservative dark suit, the only one of the group who is facing away from the camera. The hand cupped to the ear is a powerful clue as to his identity, but for contractual reasons, officially Robin did not participate. The passing of 30 years has diminished Jonathan Kelly's memory of exactly who was present, but he too clearly has his suspicions, although he has another theory about "the hand".

"I'm sure he came down and sang with us," he said. "I think that [shot's] very interesting because, when he saw the photograph being taken, that's why he put his hand over his face. That's what happened – he's actually hiding! It would make sense that he was hiding from any photographer taking pictures."

The one man who knows for sure ain't saying. In a weekly column he was writing at the time, his entry for Friday, January 16 reveals, "Surprise, surprise! Today I received a telephone call from ex-Bee Gee Colin Petersen, now personal manager of the fantastic new singer Jonathan Kelly – soon to be celebrated. Colin asked me if I would like to visit Jonathan's recording session that night, which Colin himself was producing. As one good friend to another, I did not hesitate in saying 'Yes.' So, at 7 p.m. I arrived at the IBC recording studios in Portland Place and found the session already underway."

Robin then goes on to claim that he spent the remainder of the session "sitting in the control room with Colin and commanding a view of the whole proceedings." That may well be the case, but one indisputable fact is that the various photos which appeared in the Sunday newspapers clearly show Colin at the microphone singing along with all and sundry.

Colin even attempted to get all the artists together for an appearance on *Top Of The Pops* but it was something of a nightmare for him. Peter Sellers was overseas, whilst Spike Milligan was "indisposed". Although the performance was filmed, it was never shown.

Jonathan's next single, 'Don't You Believe It' also had an anonymous but equally famous participant. Eric Clapton agreed to play lead guitar because he disagreed with the way that Colin had been treated by both Robert Stigwood and The Bee Gees. Eric was also due to appear on *Top Of The Pops* for the single's TV début but had to call off at the last minute and Tim Staffel played instead. Clapton's absence didn't over adversely affect sales as it shifted about 4,000 copies over the following weekend.

If *Record Collector* magazine is to be believed, there is a suggestion that the alleged appearance by Robin on 'Make A Stranger Your Friend' was not the first time that he had shown a disregard for his contractual obligations by making an incognito performance. In February, 1969, the Tonbridge based band Jason Crest released their fourth single, 'Waterloo Road', recorded at Philips' headquarters in Stanhope Place in West London. According to a 1999 article in the magazine, a "contractually anonymous Bee Gee contributed euphonium." Although Maurice is usually considered the undisputed instrumentalist of the Gibb brothers, Robin has always been a keen collector of musical instruments, making up in enthusiasm for what he may lack in musical proficiency. Indeed, the recording session was interrupted by an over-zealous policeman who considered that the sounds emanating from the studio constituted a disturbance.

18

GOING UNDERCOVER

A T THE SAME time as The Rattlesnakes were strutting their stuff in Man-chester, two boys of roughly the same age were doing likewise in The Blue Sect in Lincolnshire's seaside town of Skegness. Trevor Gordon Grunnill was on piano whilst his cousin Graham Bonnet sang and played guitar. Trevor emigrated to Australia with his family at the beginning of the Sixties, and enjoyed some success down there, but in the latter half of 1967 he returned home at his cousin's request. Graham had decided to form a band and wanted Trevor Gordon – he had dropped his surname by then – to be an integral part of it.

Progress was slow during those formative months, and there could have been a temptation to look for outside help, but the thought didn't even cross Trevor's mind. "When Graham wrote to me in Australia asking me to join his group back home in Skegness, it never occurred to me to contact Barry Gibb, who was a very good friend of mine. In fact, it was quite by chance that we got a booking in London's Revolution Club. Barry was there and saw us, and from that night came . . . our new manager, Robert Stigwood.

"But when Graham and I formed the group which we called Bonar Law after an unknown British Prime Minister, I never thought of 'bludgeoning' The Bee Gees to take an interest in us. It's what you do yourself that is important and we were determined to make it on our own."

In any event, Trevor was delighted to meet up with the group again. He said, "The most amazing thing to me is that The Bee Gees have not changed at all over the years, despite their dizzy rise to fame. Barry's still the organised one. He's the business mind of the group and used to have most of his time taken with keeping the other two in order. I also knew Vince and Colin quite well before they ever joined the group."

Although Trevor was fulsome in his praise of the brothers' talent, he was less impressed with the Australian music scene than the Gibbs themselves had been just 12 months earlier. "I don't think their music has changed much either. They're like The Beatles and Bob Dylan – you can always recognise their songs. I wasn't surprised when they decided to come back to England. Australia is a terrible drag scene for pop! You have to play cabaret all the time, and the bands are awful."

Trevor and Graham quickly booked recording sessions and, at Barry's

257

suggestion, the name Bonar Law was ditched in favour of one which Barry himself had come up with . . . The Marbles. An early result of one of these first sessions, a demo recorded in March 1968, remains in Polydor's vaults and is marked on the tape box as 'Burning Candals' (sic). This would later appear as the B-side to their first single under its full and correct title of 'By The Light Of The Burning Candle', written and produced by all three brothers.

As the sessions continued, it quickly became clear to Barry that he was grooming an extraordinary vocal talent. "You know that guy Graham Bonnet has got the most powerful voice I have ever heard," he enthused to music journalists. "He has to stand six feet from the microphone in the studio. There is a metal plate in the mike itself, which can be bent if the voice is powerful enough and his voice can bend it. The engineers tell me they have never known it to happen before." While certainly a rare occurrence, the event itself had been observed elsewhere before, The Moody Blues' Ray Thomas being just one example.

If there was no doubting the quality of the performers, then they would require a very special song to bring that talent to the fore, and Barry, Robin and Maurice set about the challenge with enthusiasm. What they came up with was almost too good to give away, and fans have long mourned the lack of a Bee Gees version.

The power-ballad, as it would nowadays be termed, 'Only One Woman' was released in September 1968 as the A-side of The Marbles' début single. It rapidly climbed the charts in Britain, where it reached number five, Europe and Australia, but it made little impact in the USA, where it appeared on Atlantic's Cotillion label.

They now had an impressive platform on which to build, but the opportunity was wasted when momentum was lost amidst some petty squabbling and ego driven bickering which resulted in a temporary parting of the ways between The Marbles and their mentors. However, by February 1969, the rift had been healed and Trevor announced to reporters, "As things have turned out, we're back with The Bee Gees again, and very happy about it too!"

Barry confirmed that all was well again. "At the moment we're recording their new single, 'The Walls Fell Down', which I wrote. We've patched up all our differences." Then, referring back to his childhood days spent with Trevor in Australia, he continued, "If our association is helping The Marbles get a foothold in the business, then it is good because that is a difficult thing to do. But we went to school together in Australia, and we made a pact that if we made it first, we would help them and if they made it first, vice versa. If they had made it first they would now be helping us."

Further good news came in the form of the announcement in June of the formation of The Marbles Fan Club. It should have been a time for celebration as, properly promoted, their début album had sufficient quality on it that it could have earned them recognition as artists in their own right, and not just The Bee Gees clones they perhaps felt they were in danger of being regarded as. Old problems rose to the surface, release of the album was post-poned, and by August, 1969, The Marbles were no more. Their self-titled album was eventually released in Germany and America in 1970 though.

Tom Kennedy appeared to share the frustration felt by many when he said, "The Marbles were both very fine singers . . . Given proper manage-ment and everything else, they could have done a lot more than they did. Barry's involvement was obviously well meant, but he didn't have the time to actually invest in their career. I think they saw that, and just said, 'Let's go our separate ways' and just called it a day."

Tom's presumption was always believed to have been the case, but Graham Bonnet has recently confirmed that there was more to it than that, and that their manager must shoulder some of the responsibility too. "We broke up because Robert Stigwood wanted to make me into a solo artist," he revealed, "but I didn't want to be what they wanted me to be . . . another Tom Jones type." With the benefit of hindsight though, he now hints that the break-up could perhaps have been avoided, citing "over-confidence in one's future" as a contributing factor, but adding that he has "too many regrets to mention". Graham retains a deep respect for what the Gibbs have achieved over the years, and claimed that their success is because "they always keep up with the trends, and also at the same time try to do some-thing new, but it's always them . . . individual!"

Trevor went on to release a Polydor album, *Alphabet*, in the early Sev-enties but little was heard of him after that. He is now believed to be a music teacher in London. Graham's career went from strength to strength, and he eventually found his niche alongside hard rockers like Ritchie Blackmore, Cozy Powell, and Michael Schenker. Graham never forgot his roots though, and recorded further Gibb material in each of the next three decades.

★ ★ ★

The two songs covered by The Marbles, but which The Bee Gees had previ-ously released, were released in January, 1969 by Nina Simone. 'To Love Somebody', backed with 'I Can't See Nobody', provided the American soul singer with a number five placing in the UK charts.

The following month, Pye recording artist David Garrick released a single featuring a song that had been written specially for him. He was born Philip Darryl Core in Liverpool in 1945, but like so many others with artistic flair, he found London to be better suited to his flamboyance. His circle of friends included Peter Wyngarde and Barry Gibb, and many an evening was whiled away in the company of either or both.

"I used to sit with Barry Gibb, in his flat in Eaton Square, drinking his scotch," he mused. "One night he said, 'I'm gonna write you a song,' and he dashed off 'Maypole Mews' in around twenty minutes, while I was out buying more scotch, or mixers, or something. We did a great version and it was a big hit in Germany . . . but it didn't do anything over here." Quite what David meant by "big hit" is unclear as 'Maypole Mews' didn't chart in Germany either!

While David was correct when he later advised, "Another Bee Gees song I recorded was their first hit 'Spicks & Specks', but I don't believe it was ever released," that matter was rectified when the song finally appeared on his *The Pye Anthology* double CD in 1998.

In May 1969 though, there was further chart success for the Gibb brothers as songwriters. Jose Feliciano released 'Marley Purt Drive' as a single, only two months after The Bee Gees own version had first become available on the *Odessa* album. Number 70 in the USA charts may not sound like much of a success, but bearing in mind that the best cover version placing prior to that was number 74, achieved by Sweet Inspirations with 'To Love Somebody' in July 1968, it was gratefully acknowledged in the Gibb camp nonetheless. Jose obviously liked the Gibbs' style of writing. In October he released 'And The Sun Will Shine', and it eclipsed his previous single by climbing to number 25 in the British ratings.

Another *Odessa* track appeared as a single around that time too. Following the issue the previous year of 'Every Christian Lion Hearted Man Will Show You', Tangerine Peel released 'Never Say Never Again' as their first MGM product. A psychedelic five piece band, their most prominent member was Mike Chapman who went on to have phenomenal success with Nicky Chinn writing hits for the likes of Sweet and Mud during the Seventies.

June 20, 1969, witnessed the birth of one of the great mysteries to have plagued collectors of all things Gibb for more than 30 years. On that day, Decca issued a single by Clare Torry, 'Love For Living'/'Love Tomorrow, Love Today', clearly stating "Producers : Robin Gibb/Ronnie Scott". However, Robin has always vehemently denied his involvement and, indeed, it transpires that Ronnie Scott is not the late jazz nightclub owner, but a record producer of the same name who lived in Frith Street in London. Whether there is another Robin Gibb lurking in the shadows remains to be seen, but there exists the possibility that the Gibb in this instance could be Mike Gibbs, a composer and arranger of the time.

Another extremely collectable item appeared on the scene in July. Few in Britain had ever heard of The Tigers, but the Kenji Sawada fronted band were very popular in their native Japan, and had visited London in the hope of achieving similar levels of success in Britain. Polydor introduced them to Barry who delved into his bag of unreleased material and pulled out 'Smile For Me', originally an outtake from the *Horizontal* album. With a little bit of rewriting in which Maurice participated, it was soon ready. Strangely, after going to such bother, Polydor relegated it to the B-side of 'Rain Falls On The Lonely', but this failed to provide The Tigers with the hit they craved, and they headed back east. The Japanese issue reversed the status so that 'Smile For Me' became the A-side. It was accompanied by the usual deluxe photo-sleeve expected of that market, and shows the group in various poses from their London trip. Barry appears in four of them, perhaps the one in the go-kart being the least damaging to the debonair image he was trying to promote at the time.

Another recording that was being touted for possible single release during 1969 was Elvis Presley's rendition of 'Words', and the prospect had Maurice positively drooling. "He has done it just as you would imagine Elvis would, but I like it because it is more up-tempo and rock'n'rollish. It will be a smash because he's done it, I hope." Whether Maurice was referring to a studio or a live version remains unclear. At the time Elvis was finalising the line-up of tracks for a double album entitled *From Memphis To Vegas – From Vegas To Memphis*. The first album was recorded live at The International in Vegas, whilst its companion consisted of studio sessions recorded in Memphis. In any event, by the time of the set's release in November – the British release was delayed until March 1970 – the only version of 'Words' was a live one.

During their lengthy careers, there would be very few instances where the Gibbs would provide an artist with songs to record, and then revisit the material at a later date to produce a Bee Gees release of its own. American female vocalist Pat "P.P." Arnold had four British chart entries on the Immediate label when she was taken under Barry's wing. Studio sessions between June 12 and July 12 resulted in 'Give A Hand Take A Hand' and 'Bury Me Down By The River'. 'Let There Be Love' had also been recorded on July 9, but this was rejected in favour of the other two songs which formed both sides of her September release for Polydor in Britain and Atco in the US. Barry and Maurice composed both, and Barry additionally took on the producer's role. Bill Shepherd took responsibility for the arrangements. Release had originally been planned for August as the first record on a new label being launched by Barry and Maurice. Originally called Diamond, and then Gee Bee, something or someone must have intervened and plans were dropped.

Although the single made little impact, none of the participants were discouraged and a further visit to the recording studio on November 3 saw demos of 'Piccaninny', 'High And Windy Mountain' and 'Turning Tide' deposited in Polydor's vaults. The first two later appeared as poems in a booklet issued by the Barry Gibb Fan Club in 1970, while the last one was included on the *Cucumber Castle* album the same year. Pat recorded two more demos on April 4, 1970 but 'Born' and 'Happiness' would only ever be heard as outtakes from Barry's unreleased solo album recorded at that time. Two Blood Sweat & Tears songs were also laid down at the same session.

Exactly the same writing, production and arrangement credits on P.P. Arnold's single were seen on both sides of the British début single of a young Australian singer called Cheryl Gray. She had made her first TV appearance at the age of 11 in her hometown of Melbourne, and had a Shirley Bassey style hit there in 1967 called 'You Made Me What I Am', which made the Top 10. Having been brought to London by her parents in search of stardom, the seventeen year old became the next visitor to IBC studios in July 1969.

"I had not met The Bee Gees before. We had been in London and were about to return [home], we had our tickets booked. I had done some recording in London with David Mackay in London also. Barry rang my house about 1 a.m. out of the blue – remember I hadn't met him before – and said he had just heard my record, 'You Made Me What I Am', and wanted to work with me. He said, 'Don't do a thing before Robert Stigwood signs you.' What had happened was Barry had had an old friend of mine from Sydney around to his place for dinner, and he had taken over my record to Barry's house and played it.

"So I met with Robert Stigwood," she continued. "He is a most brilliant man, very clever but amazingly shy. There was an absolute aura about him. I firstly auditioned for Robert with Barry playing acoustic guitar singing 'To Love Somebody' at Robert's amazing big mansion, then they arranged for me to go and sing in a studio to see what my voice was like in a recording atmosphere.

"Then Robert arranged for me to do a show at Caesar's Palace in London because he wanted to see what I could do on stage. I remember they held the show up in front of hundreds of people until Robert arrived. He was a very important person in the entertainment scene.

"Anyway, Robert signed me and was going to do big things for me. He said I could be as big as Streisand. It was quite a deal, as I was the only woman on his books at the time."

It's tempting to think that Robert may have been looking for his own Cilla Black, and perhaps thought Cheryl could fill that role. Her name was a problem though, as it didn't fit the image required. To provide for her future, she borrowed from her past, changing her name at the last possible moment to Samantha Sang – a surname of her ancestors. In fact, her great, great grandfather was a Manchurian surgeon and herbalist.

It took about a week for her to record her vocals over the backing tracks that had already been laid down, but Bill Shepherd was there as usual to handle the arrangements.

The release of her Parlophone single was accompanied by full-page ads in the music press announcing "Samantha Sang, and the world listened to 'The Love Of A Woman' ". In contradiction to the composer credits on the disc's centre, which included Maurice, the advert also noted that the A-side had been "written and produced by Barry Gibb". 'Don't Let It Happen Again', another song credited to both Barry and Maurice, was on the flip side.

Given both the extent of the hype and the quality of the record itself, it was a major surprise that it failed to become a hit anywhere, even in her native Australia. She was taken back into the studios by Barry at the end of October, and recorded demos of 'Please Don't Take My Man Away', which might have originally been written with Lulu in mind, and 'The Day Your Eyes Meet Mine', a song that would later be considered by Andy Williams. However, an all too familiar problem reared its ugly head at this point.

Samantha's visitor's visa was about to expire and immigration officials were hot on her trail. Encouraged by his previous success with Colin Petersen and Vince Melouney, Robert Stigwood decided to take them on a second time. To buy himself some time, Robert arranged for her to go to Polydor in Germany. Anxious to protect his investment, he then sent her, her family, Bill Shepherd and a whole entourage to Atlantic Records in America to look after her whilst the visa problems were sorted.

Ahmet appeared to be unsure of his role in the affair and, as Samantha described, asked her, "Vhat does Vobert vant me to do vith you?" To cut a long story short, on this occasion the authorities' will prevailed over that of Robert's, and he was forced to let her return to Australia.

As Tom Kennedy recalled, even a last-ditch desperate attempt failed. "Robert was trying to get someone to marry her at the time so she could stay in the country. I think it was all family connections."

The sad outcome was that it was a great opportunity missed, and even after 30 years of reflection, both Samantha and her father remain affected by the treatment handed out by the British Government to a 17-year-old girl.

★ ★ ★

For Ohio born Steve Kipner – his family moved to Australia before he had graduated from cot to pram – Steve & The Board was not fulfilling his musical ambitions. Steve Groves, a member of the Melbourne band The Kinetics, was in a similar position. In conversation the pair discovered they also shared a love of composing, so they left their respective bands to form a new songwriting partnership, with one eye very much on the forthcoming 1967 *New Faces* show.

As luck would have it, they won the competition with their own 'Melissa Green', which they performed under the guise of Tin Tin. As many Australians had done before them, they too decided to seek their fame and fortune in London, finding a benefactor in Phil Solomon, then boss of the now defunct Radio Caroline. Phil also ran the Major Minor record label, and paid for their flights to England where they cut an album for him in 1968, now calling themselves Steve & Stevie.

The duo toured Britain throughout the remainder of the year, earning themselves a reputation on the cabaret circuit, but were devastated when violence flared in a club in London's Leicester Square and one of their audience was battered to death. Disillusioned, the pair quit, understandably letting music take a back seat for a while.

Early in 1969, gazing out of their apartment window, both of them recognised a familiar face. Barry Gibb had literally parked his car right outside their door, and the pair dashed out to extend their greetings. Barry explained that he was busy working with The Marbles, and with Robin pursuing his solo career, Maurice was on the lookout for someone he could produce. A reunion with Maurice was arranged, and all went splendidly well. Robert Stigwood bought out their contract with Major Minor, and they signed with the Stigwood Organization, being put under the charge of John and Rick Gunnell.

Re-christening themselves Tin Tin, the two Steves quickly came to appreciate that working so closely with a Bee Gee brought them several advantages. Like the Gibbs, they both loved using strings on their recordings, so it was a delight for them to be able to introduce Maurice to a young pianist and arranger, with whom they had worked on their *Steve and Stevie* album. Steve Kipner described Gerry Shury as "a lovely man, very talented", but his praise was tinged with sorrow as Gerry died in a car crash in the mid-Eighties. Kipner believes that he would have gone on to do great things if he had survived.

Another benefit, Kipner recalled, was the amount of free studio time they enjoyed. Sometimes Maurice would call them in because "Barry had a sore throat, or something, and the time was already booked and paid for." Maurice was equally cost conscious when it came to the strings too. Steve Kipner still fondly recalls the way a few of the songs were arranged, because Maurice would wait until an orchestra was hired to do Bee Gees songs, and then he'd have them play on the Tin Tin songs too.

Polydor released Tin Tin's début single in Britain in August 1969 and Maurice, as he did on three other tracks on the album, contributed instrumentally, if not vocally on both sides. The songs chosen to launch their new career were 'Only Ladies Play Croquet' and 'He Wants To Be A Star'.

But it was their second single, their first in the USA, that would focus international attention on the duo. Although issued in Britain in March 1970, it was a year later before the Stateside release of 'Toast And Marmalade For Tea' provided Tin Tin with a massive hit where they perhaps least expected it. Americans took them to their hearts and the single peaked at number 20 during its 11 week stay in the Top 100. The song, also a Top 20 entry in Australia, was never properly finished, and featured an unusually distinctive sound as Steve Kipner explained. " 'Toast And Marmalade For Tea' was an unfinished song with just verses by Steve Groves, and we had been thinking that we would write a chorus for it together," he said. The first demo had been taped on June 27, 1969, but as was often the case, Maurice called them into the studio at short notice the following month, and had them record it properly because studio time had suddenly become available.

"We modulated the verses," Kipner continued, "since it was all that we had." He and Steve Groves had originally recorded the basic track on guitar and piano. They would usually try using whatever was in the studio, improvising where necessary. "There was a drum kit there that day, but the pedal was broken, so I pushed it by hand to make us a drum track. Then Maurice put bass on it, playing with his broken arm." The sound effect which made the song so instantly recognisable is a piano played into a tape loop that was manipulated live by hand to distort it. "It was fun," Kipner concluded.

The single bombed in Britain, a failure that Steve Groves attributed to technology, more than anything else. "We got some airplay, but I don't think any Robert Stigwood Organisation people had hits that year. RSO and Polydor were changing to a new computer driven distribution system, and it wasn't working." If true, the remark certainly goes some way to explaining why The Bee Gees 'How Can You Mend A Broken Heart' fared so badly, when it became their biggest seller in the States, up to that point in their career.

Tin Tin were also involved in another recording which, for a while, attained a near legendary status. It was called 'Have You Heard The Word' by The Fut, and was released in 1970 on the obscure and now defunct Beacon label. There was no promotion or hype but, gradually, it became a massively sought after collector's item as rumours grew that there was a considerable Beatles involvement. So, were any of The Fab Four really involved? American copyright would have you believe that they were. Under reference number Pau-765-317, can be found the following entry:

TITLE : Have You Heard The Word? / words & music John Lennon
PHYS : 4 pages
CLNA : Lenono Music
DATE CREATED : 1980   DATE REGISTERED: 20 Sep. 1985
ECIF : 3/M

It is interesting to note that the alleged creation date is 10 years after its release, and that the registry date is five years after Lennon's demise. However, it had originally been filed Stateside in May, 1974 by Abigail Music for Kipner and Groves whilst the British equivalent, PRS, currently list it as Kipner, Groves and Billy Lawrie.

Many different tales of the now infamous August 6, 1969, recording session abound. Maurice is first to plead his case. "I don't know how the tape [of 'Have You Heard The Word'] even got out, I really don't," he insists. "The last time I heard of it was on an interview on Capital Radio and the disc jockey asked me, 'What about this Fut record?'

"It was me, Steve Kipner, and Steve Groves, Tin Tin guys. [John and Paul] turned up and we were having drinks. We were just jamming, everyone just started jamming, and the tapes were going. John was smashed as usual, and everyone was pissed. It was just a big pisser. We were just getting ready to do some tracks and we were just doing nothing and I was fartin' around on the bass. I was a big Paul freak. He was a great teacher for me. When I was a young kid, I listened to the early Beatles records, and I could play every bass lick he played. Some of the things like 'Michelle', the bass line, really tasteful stuff, and way ahead, way ahead of his time. All of them were. That's why their records were so different. [Lennon] denied [his involvement in Fut]! Paul didn't. He didn't deny it in England. That was many years ago."

Billy Lawrie was also heavily involved in the session and can at least solve

Maurice's quandary of how the recording achieved its initial legitimate release.

Apparently Mark London, manager of Stone The Crows, heard the tape and thought it ripe for a release. Although it took a bit of persuasion, eventually Lionel Conway of Island Records was sufficiently enticed to take a chance with it, via a subsidiary label. It also provided him with the means to "dispose" of an entirely unconnected trumpet-led reggae instrumental, an early Island niche area, onto the B-side which was cunningly retitled 'Futting Around'. The release was arguably not one of his better business decisions perhaps, but at least it provided the music industry with enough ingredients to create a new myth, which some have been only too glad to perpetuate.

Given Maurice's tendency towards embellishment, the search then begins to establish what can be substantiated and what cannot.

"That was done at Nova Sound," Tom Kennedy confirmed. "We did lots of sessions with Tin Tin, and they were all very entertaining affairs, which all involved lots of alcohol."

Steve Kipner can even remember which brand they enjoyed that particular evening. "Maurice and Billy showed up with a bottle of Jack Daniels, and the engineer must have switched the tape on. They were singing in funny voices, and talking like The Beatles. Maurice does quite a good Lennon, you know."

Steve Groves claims that the song began earlier in the day as a nice little composition by himself and Steve Kipner called 'The Word'. Enter Maurice, released earlier that day from hospital with his broken arm, but "feeling no pain".

On hearing 'The Word', Maurice had decreed immediately that it had to be "a real John Lennon number" and proceeded to start playing slide guitar using his plaster cast before putting down a vocal track à la Lennon. It would probably be fair to say that things went downhill from that point onwards, and the two Steves abandoned the session in favour of an early night. What happened in their absence is anyone's guess.

The record itself provides few clues. A thumping bass, effectively combined with rhythm and electric guitars, catches the listener's attention from the beginning before a familiar piano sound emerges. The opening vocals unquestionably belong to Maurice but, after a mid-song increase in tempo where the piano changes to a saloon sound, it becomes less clear as the lead vocal screeches out the lyrics and is followed by an overlapping repetitious backing vocal which matches the lead word for word. The word of course is the "F" word, heard in all its glory at the end of the record when the music fades out to allow a brief conversation in what purports to be Liverpudlian accents.

With John Lennon unable to issue any further denials and Paul McCartney presumably disinterested in doing so, Maurice's claims cannot be completely refuted, but therein lies the beauty of his achievement. For over 30 years, so-called experts have pulled his creation to pieces and yet, for all their unravelling, sufficient doubt remains. Of course it started out as a deliberate attempt to imitate his heroes, and an effective one at that, but could two legends have popped into Nova in those twilight hours just to see "what was happening"?

The final words on the matter appropriately belong to the two co-originators. Steve Kipner, who himself has also come across a Beatles' bootleg album that had 'Have You Heard The Word' as the opening track, said, "I always wanted to be on a Beatles album, and now I can say I was on one!" Steve Groves was likewise delighted to find out, nearly 30 years after the event, that he had supposedly co-written a song with John Lennon!

The *Tin Tin* album finally appeared in Britain in late 1970 – its American release being held over to the following year – and the sleeve notes revealed that Maurice could add organ to his already impressive list of instruments. One name notable by its absence was that of Billy Lawrie, who was very much part of the sessions, albeit in a behind the scenes capacity. His talent would not go unrecognised by Steve Groves in particular, and Billy would soon be rewarded for his endeavours.

A third British single appeared towards the end of 1970, comprising two non-album tracks. A co-writer on 'Come On Over Again' was new band member Geoff Bridgeford, former drummer with Steve & The Board, so he was obviously well known to Steve Kipner. His time with Tin Tin was short-lived, as was that of Carl Groszman who had also been a member of Kipner's Australian band.

Recordings for a second album commenced in earnest in May 1971, by which time the first one had been issued in the USA. The group numbered three again following the addition of former Kinetic's member Johnny Vallins. Steve Kipner announced the signing when he stated, "After four years as Tin Tin, we have decided that it really is time to get a proper working band on the road."

Right through June and July, writing and recording was conducted at a hectic pace, and with good reason. They were booked to support The Bee Gees on a 24 date USA tour and Atco were looking to use the tour to promote the album. With Maurice fully committed to working with his brothers, and Geoff Bridgeford for that matter, Tin Tin had put Billy Lawrie in charge of production, and he didn't let them down, also appearing as co-writer on two tracks. With no disrespect whatsoever intended to Maurice, both founder members of the group were actually glad of the change, as Steve Groves explained. "We preferred Billy, as Maurice's production was a little too 'Bee Gee-esque' at times." Picking up a favoured Robert Stigwood mantle, Maurice retained an involvement as "Executive Producer".

Without any further Gibb association, Tin Tin continued to release singles each year up to and including 1974. At that point the band split and its members went their separate ways to pursue solo writing careers.

★ ★ ★

Billy Lawrie's introduction to Tin Tin had come about as the result of his close working relationship with Maurice. Intermingled with the tapes of Tin Tin's recording sessions are several of Billy's compositions, and one of these, 'Come Back Joanna', found its way onto the B-side of his first single. The song chosen to launch his recording career was Chuck Berry's 'Roll Over Beethoven', perhaps a more suitable choice than one of Billy's first efforts, 'Super Duck', which he attempted at different sessions in August and September 1969. This had been dropped in favour of the Berry song, recorded on October 6 and released the following month. As you might expect from your brother-in-law, Maurice produced the record and helped out with the arranging too. Despite the appearance of a half-page advert in *Record Mirror* on November 15, the single did not realise the young Scot's dreams of achieving the levels of success enjoyed by his contemporaries or, for that matter, his sister.

Another Caledonian export was Pat Fairley. His first band of any note was formed in his native Scotland in 1963, calling themselves Dean Ford and The Gaylords. By 1967, they had signed to CBS and changed their name to Marmalade. They experienced their first success in May of the following year and, within a four year period, had achieved 10 UK chart entries from 11 singles releases, of which seven made it to the Top 10. So what happened to the one single that bombed?

" 'Butterfly' was the last record we recorded for CBS before our contract expired," Pat explained. "CBS released it in competition to our first Decca hit and it died." Pat couldn't remember how Marmalade had come to receive the song in the first place, but Graham Knight was on hand to live up to his name and come to the rescue.

"We got it from Robert Stigwood – who was [not only] The Bee Gees' manager [but also their] music publisher at the time – as a demo, and we just liked the song. It was the usual thing in the Sixties when you didn't write your own songs. You went to a music publisher and they gave you songs, and this one just cropped up. What used to happen was, you'd go into the publishing company, ask what songs they had, and they knew the band, so they'd root out some tracks that were suitable for us. Stigwood would go into the little cutting room – well, *he* wouldn't – but one of his eunuchs would go in and play the tape and cut it straight to an acetate. You'd play it 20 times and it was gone. We thought ['Butterfly'] was going to do more than it did.

"[The Bee Gees] had a unique sound. When we heard them first, we thought it was quite funny because they had these unusual voices. They're good at what they do, it's as simple as that; there's no secret to their success. A good song will always come through, they just happen to write particularly good songs."

Pat Fairley eventually left Marmalade to work for RSO, which brought him very much into contact with the Gibbs and their associates. Renowned as Scots are for their frugality, it was an Englishman that Pat singled out for a bit of friendly abuse. "One story sticks out about the early days," he recalled. "When Dick Ashby handed in his receipts, there was always charges for newspapers; e.g. LAX 24th 3 x LA Times 75 cents. Guess it soon mounts up!"

"Americans love titles," he continued, shifting up a gear to take on an entire nation. "In the first few weeks, I got a letter signed 'Bill Oakes, PRESIDENT.' I wrote back and signed 'Pat Fairley, PRIME MINISTER.'"

The amount of time that the Gibbs spent writing for and working with other artists during this period was mostly due to the fact that they were no longer working with each other. Robin's profile in this regard was particularly low because he was spending all his waking hours on his solo career. His manager/producer, Vic Lewis, had ambitions in that direction too, and both took time out from working on *Robin's Reign* to collaborate in the writing of 'No Other Heart' with Ken Thorne, who was best known as a writer of instrumental music for films including The Beatles' *Help!* The song was issued by NEMS on December 12 as the B-side of a single by The Vic Lewis Orchestra & His Singers while, in the USA, it appeared on the Epic label. For both issues, the A-side was McCartney's 'Come And Get It'. Also written by Robin and Vic at the same time was 'Prelude, Beverly Hills', but this was never released.

There were several other significant releases, none of them in Britain, during 1969.

Dutch group Soft Pillow followed Gerry Marsden's example and recorded 'Gilbert Green'. Orchestra leader Max Greger, or "Orchester" as he was referred to in Germany, released Barry and Maurice's 'The Square Cup' on a now virtually impossible to find Polydor single. Equally hard to locate, there is a compilation album celebrating Polydor's anniversary called *Eine Runde Polydor*. The hidden treasure here is a 1:30 version of 'Gena's Theme' by Bill Shepherd, although it is actually credited on the album to The Bee Gees themselves. The tune resurfaced in 1983 on a bonus album entitled *Rarities*, which was only issued as part of a German box set which re-issued all The Bee Gees' albums up to that point. Completing the succession of Continent only releases, a Belgium-based band, The Vipers, became the latest in line to attempt to score a hit with 'Town Of Tuxley Toymaker (Part One)' which continued to defy expectations of its worth.

1970 was a quieter year for cover versions and productions and, P.P. Arnold and Tin Tin excepted, there was very little by way of activity during the first nine months of the year.

A visitor to the Barry Gibb household during this time was his Australian friend, Ronnie Burns. "I came over to London and Barry and his male assistant picked me up at the airport. Barry always impressed me. I'm into fashion, I like nice clothes, and Barry looked sensational at the airport. Beautiful high collared white shirt."

On arrival at Barry's flat, he gave his host a gift replica gun, as Ronnie was aware of his fondness for them. Barry then took his guest downstairs to show him his gun collection. Handing Ronnie a German Luger, Barry uttered the immortal words, "Careful, it has a hairline trig . . ." For those familiar with Barry's history of misfortune with guns, what happened next was no surprise. Before Barry could finish what he was saying, the gun went off and its bullet parted his hair, missing his head by millimetres. It seems almost comical now, but at the time it was no laughing matter. "Barry just went white," Ronnie recalled.

Ronnie returned home with a demo version of a recent Barry Gibb song safely locked away in his suitcase. The song was one of several which were eagerly recorded by other artists once it became known that The Bee Gees had reformed, and that release of Barry's solo album *The Kid's No Good* would be shelved.

'One Bad Thing' was a particularly popular choice, and Ronnie was fortunate that his visit to London had put him at the head of the queue. However, like all those that followed, the Festival single didn't become the commercial success that it was anticipated it would be.

There was often talk that Richard Starkey and Maurice would eventually work, as well as play, together, and Maurice finally made his mark on a (former) Beatle's record. Included on Ringo Starr's *Sentimental Journey* LP, a George Martin produced compilation of cover versions which Apple released in March, was the old Dixon–Henderson standard, 'Bye Bye Blackbird', and Maurice hadn't needed to be asked twice whether he would like to take responsibility for the song's arrangement.

Philips recording artist, and friend of the stars, Lou Reizner released his eponymous album in late 1970, and it contained the song that Samantha Sang had recorded the year before, the previously unreleased 'The Day Your Eyes Meet Mine', written jointly by Barry and Maurice. The album also included Barry's 'In The Morning (Morning Of My Life)'.

Maurice and Billy Lawrie had recorded a lovely demo of their own composition, 'Touch And Understand Love', which somehow found its way to Nashville where it was recorded by Myrna March and released by Starday-King Records.

Only provided with a limited distribution, it stood little chance of following up the chart success that Engelbert Humperdinck had achieved on both sides of the Atlantic with 'Sweetheart' in September 1970, six months after The Bee Gees own version had been released as a B-side. Number 47 was its zenith in the States, but it fared a bit better in Britain, where it peaked at number 22.

It also signalled the last occasion that a cover version of a Gibb song would enter the charts in Britain or America for the next five years, although there would be no shortage of attempts to do so.

19

LONELY DAYS

"FOR THE PAST six months I have done no work except record making for myself and Lulu's brother, Billy Lawrie," Maurice said in March 1970. "During this time I travelled the world with Lulu."

Home again in England, Maurice worked with Billy as commercial jingle writers and performers for such products as Start-Rite shoes – with Lulu's assistance on vocals – and Ultrabrite toothpaste. They also provided the music for a commercial for a package holidays company, which featured a glimpse of Hugh and Barbara Gibb waving from a balcony in Ibiza. Nowadays, this is a profitable area of the music business, and one where Maurice could probably be very successful, as his particular skills and talents seem ideally suited to that environment.

In addition, Maurice began to work as a record producer for Tin Tin, teaming up with brother-in-law Billy. "They were always quite busy in the studio with bits and pieces," Tom Kennedy recalled, "and I think some of them were quite lucrative for them. Billy was a fun character and probably very good for Maurice at the time, because Lulu was away a lot. He was very supportive of Maurice. Although Billy's been quite successful in the music business, singing was not really his forte – the singer in that family was always Lulu."

Lulu was pleased with the alliance that had developed between her husband and brother because it helped to keep Maurice occupied. In those days, Maurice's boredom was often relieved by spending vast sums of money. "Maurice literally showered me with presents," she said. " 'Every week is an anniversary for us,' he used to tell me. But he spoilt himself too, and perhaps that was part of the problem. He was always buying cars, clothes, jewellery and more cars, as well as cameras, tapes, records, guitars and gadgets. The house was positively polluted with them. When he was not on tour or in the studio, he spent his time spending money. If he became bored, he might go out and buy a Bentley; four weeks later he would buy an Aston Martin."

Maurice and Billy's partnership had recently become official with the formation of their company, Moby. "Billy and I have worked on a number of things together and have even written some songs together," he explained. "It seemed right to get the relationship onto a business footing and Moby seemed an ideal name."

The formation of the company seemed to give Maurice a new stability in his life. "Lu and I don't like to be apart and the new company has helped me in that," he said. "At one time I used to be charging about all over the country and so did Lu. Since we got married we have both settled down.

"Lu doesn't do as much work as she did before she married me, and I don't leave London as much as I used to. If she ever has to go away, I always try and be with her, but if I can't make it I will always set my watch at the time it will be where Lu is performing. She does the same. If I'm in London and she's in New York, my watch will show New York time and hers will show London time.

"It's not because of any silly little thing; just that it is easier then to phone each other. I might think I would like to phone Lu and look at my watch. If it was early in the morning I would remember not to."

Despite his wife's celebrity status, Maurice claimed, "We have a happy working relationship – just like any ordinary working couple. Lu puts all the money she earns into an account, and I give her housekeeping and personal spending money each week."

Lulu revealed that Maurice was an old-fashioned husband in other ways as well. "He really is unbelievably possessive and sometimes he gets unduly annoyed," she said.

On one occasion, a shopping trip to Oxford Street nearly became an embarrassing scene. Maurice waited in the car while Lulu and Billy went off on their own to a shop. When Lulu took her brother's arm to cross the street, she recalled that Maurice "reacted violently and jumped out of the car like Superman to drag us apart!"

She thought at first that he was joking, but he was serious. "There are people looking," he told her sternly, "and they don't know Billy's your brother. They'll think you're a harlot!"

Lulu laughed as she related the story, adding, "Maybe he's right. There are always people looking for something nasty to say."

Maurice admitted that Lulu was the driving force in their marriage. "She is determined and strong-minded, whereas I am placid," he said. "I have never been pushing or jealous. My big asset, I suppose, is that I get on with people. I keep my mouth shut and stay in the background."

Lulu agreed that Maurice was "placid, easy-going, very nice to live with, generous, warm, affectionate," but she claimed he could still fly into a temper. "Maurice stamps up and down the stairs and flings his clothes down to the bottom if he's really roused. But usually if he gets annoyed, then it's because I bring it out in him. I'm a bit of a bitch, and I can really needle him. I might fling a dirty old ashtray," she admitted, "but I'd never aim to hit him. Two minutes later, I've forgotten everything, and we're soon kissing and cuddling. I always say I'm sorry because I know what I'm like."

The couple had moved to a new home in Hampstead the previous August; quite a house for a couple barely out of their teens. "It's like my mother said when she first saw our house," Lulu laughed, putting on her thickest Glasgwegian accent, " 'Would you ever have believed it, hen? It's like a mansion!' It's on three floors with two sitting rooms, six bedrooms, three with their own bathrooms, and the kitchen."

The couple immediately began adapting the house for their own use, converting one bedroom to a cinema, another to hold Lulu's clothes, and Maurice converted an old air raid shelter into a home studio.

"I can make as much noise as I like with Ringo as my next-door neighbour," he said. "I'd never met him before. I introduced myself when I moved in and said, 'Hi, neighbour!' Now we've become great pals. He's certainly mellowed a lot, I'd imagine. He's certainly one of the most likeable guys I've ever met. We've been having some great times together. As a matter of fact, I did the arrangement of 'Bye Bye Blackbird' on his *Sentimental Journey* LP."

Some of those "great times" Maurice refers to included the pair discussing, on an on–off basis for almost two years, the possibility of recording an avant garde album of electronic music. "It didn't happen," said Ringo, but one title called 'Modulating Maurice' does exist, although Maurice's only contribution to this was random spoken words over Ringo's instrumentation.

Instead, they pursued one of Maurice's other great loves, film-making. "[There] was a little movie, actually, that we were working on," Ringo explained to *Record Collector*'s Ken Sharp. "It was like *The Chase*," he continued. "We had one camera between us and we'd chase each other all round the area in Britain where we were both living at the time. We went into the studio and I just overdubbed all the sound effects from the movie *Yellow Submarine*."

Unlike many such ventures that the Gibbs have been involved in over the years, this one actually saw the light of day, appearing on a limited edition video in February, 1995 – the proceeds benefiting charitable causes.

Lulu said that she and Maurice and Ringo and his wife Maureen became "an almost inseparable foursome". The friendship was so close that they used to laughingly suggest building a bridge or a tunnel to connect the Gibb and the Starr homes.

Ringo and Maureen, who married in 1965, seemed to have "a fabulously happy relationship", according to Lulu. "They were so comfortable with each other and were my idea of the ideal couple . . . I realise now that I idealised their relationship because I was comparing it to mine with Maurice. They always appeared at ease whereas we operated in a state of constant tension." It came as a great shock to her years later when the couple divorced.

On February 18, 1970, Maurice opened in the stage musical, *Sing A Rude Song*, at the Greenwich Theatre. The musical was based on the life of the famous music hall performer, Marie Lloyd, played by Barbara Windsor, with Maurice starring as her third husband, the Irish jockey, Bernard Dillon. "I first saw the script in Robert Stigwood's office," Maurice recalled. "Robert asked if I would like to take it home and read it. Then the very next day, he asked me if I would like to play the part of Marie Lloyd's third husband, Bernard Dillon."

"Maurice came in [to the show] in the first place simply because The Bee Gees had split up," the musical's co-writer and director, Ned Sherrin, explained, "and this was, I think, Stigwood's therapy for keeping Maurice interested; giving him something to do while the break-up was going on. I don't remember the ramifications of it, but I do remember that Maurice needed to be kept with something in his mind. So I think that was the main reason for Robert's investing in it."

Sing A Rude Song was originally written for actress Millicent Martin, but an engagement at The Talk Of The Town prevented her from taking the role of Marie Lloyd. Georgia Brown was next considered but was similarly unavailable, according to Sherrin, "so hence Barbara [Windsor], who was very good."

Maurice professed, "I've always wanted to do a musical because it's invaluable experience. I've always wanted to act to gain all-round show business experience." From most reports, his vow that he "would never give up pop music because it's in my blood. I will still always write and record – whether as a Bee Gee or under my own name," was probably the wisest course to take.

Sherrin diplomatically observed that Maurice was not, perhaps, a natural stage performer. "In retrospect, I think you could say that it wasn't *quite* his métier," and Maurice himself would in later years agree with that appraisal.

At the time, however, Maurice was enthusiastic about the role. "I had never done any [stage] acting before," he admitted, "but it presented a new challenge so I thought I'd have a go. I never believed acting on stage could be such hard work. The directors of the show, Robin Phillips and Ned Sherrin, gave me every help and I think I handled the part as well as I could.

"The only thing I ever did fight for was a part in this musical show, although I was up against competition from more experienced artists. I shall be upset if I am no good, more so than I ever was at being described as 'Barry's brother' or being mistaken for Robin."

The world of musical theatre proved to be an eye-opener for Maurice. "I used to think it was pretty hard work during all those hectic Bee Gees days," he admitted. "But – no kidding – I didn't know what hard work was then. Believe it or not, we have been rehearsing an average of 12 hours a day for the last three weeks or so in preparation for opening night."

"I always remember the first day of rehearsals," Ned Sherrin said. "Everybody arrived and were changing from their shoes into their sneakers or whatever they were going to dance in. Maurice was still travelling with his road manager, who was there at his feet putting on his [shoes]! I think he quite enjoyed it because it was different and a whole new experience. It was quite an important [part] because he was playing the nasty third husband, but I think it was just therapy from Robert, and it was enough for that. I think the understudy had to go on once or twice and brought it much more to life."

The musical, written by Caryl Brahms and Ned Sherrin with additional material by Alan Bennett and featuring music composed and arranged by Ron Grainer, did not exactly open to rave reviews. Pearson Phillips of the *Daily Mail* wrote, "Barbara Windsor tried hard, perhaps too hard. She just didn't put across the simple magic that I am told 'our Marie' had. Ron Grainer's music was not memorable – certainly no match for the old song-writers. Dennis Quilley had moments as Marie's second husband, but pop singer Maurice Gibb was disappointing as her final, caddish one. There were some hilarious moments, particularly when she appeared before an LCC licensing committee. But mostly it all fell really short of a satisfactory tribute."

Barbara Windsor was amused by her co-star's inexperience. "Maurice had never done theatre before," she said, "and he wasn't quite putting it across – he lacked grit or confidence or something." The tale of how she attempted to overcome the problem has grown into something of a showbiz legend.

"Maurice was a bit lifeless on stage," Sherrin agreed, "so I said, 'Oh come on, you'd better give him one, Barbara, and brighten him up a bit'. "Unfortunately, she did, and it had no effect; it didn't get any better! He didn't sound very convincing, I don't think."

The musical proved to be exhausting work for Maurice, but he enjoyed the experience overall. "We had great fun working in the show. I'm definitely going to America to do a series of syndicated TV shows. It was very hard work in *Sing A Rude Song*, I used stagger through the door every night and Lu would say your bath is ready and I literally would fall into a hot bath! I used to be exhausted. Each evening I arrived home absolutely flaked out. We've already recorded the original cast album for release on Polydor."

Despite the lukewarm reviews from the critics, the show's run at the Greenwich Theatre was an overwhelming success. "People couldn't get in at the Greenwich, they were terribly keen to come," Sherrin remembered. "We were playing to full houses all the time at Greenwich – it was absolutely packed. I don't think we had a spare seat at Greenwich, but then there was this long hang about before it came to the West End."

During the show's hiatus, the original cast album, which Maurice produced, was recorded for release in May, to coincide with the West End transfer to the Garrick Theatre on May 26.

February also saw the release of Robin's third solo single, 'August October'. Possibly the most predictable song on the whole of his solo album, it again featured a very basic melody with simple lyrical content, and did little to demonstrate the range of musical ideas Robin was experimenting with elsewhere on the album.

Robin said that he had intended to release it a month earlier, adding, "I have said before that I do not like to release tracks from an LP as a single, but 'August October' was never intended to be on the album, and the principle I was against was of releasing a single from an LP which had been out so long that the particular track was already over-exposed. *Robin's Reign* has only been out three weeks so that does not apply to this single.

"It is not a deliberate single – I'm not trying to pull the wool over the public's eyes by releasing something commercial which I don't believe in myself. It's a very catchy, waltzy sort of song, and that is just the way it was intended to come out.

"There is no question of my sacrificing quality for commerciality as has been suggested. I apply the same degrees of quality to everything I write, and my final analysis is that if the milkman can whistle it – that's it!"

Although Robin has since stated that he considered his first LP, recorded during September and October, to be unfinished, at the time, he claimed, "I'm completely happy with the album. The only regret is that it couldn't have been longer.

"All my songs are the product of my imagination. I write the words and music at the same time and keep them in my head. It's always been a hobby of mine, and it's just fortunate that I can turn it to good use. Songwriting is like an addiction to me; it gives me peace of mind, and my love for it is unlimited. I just can't see that there will be a time when music will fall away.

"You could be talking now and a phrase you use like 'and now today' or 'my word' or 'you stole the show' are titles right there. I don't think about titles, but you could be talking and something will click right there. Then again, I never think of a song all the time. I may do a song and go back to it two days later. I feel my songs are deep enough to be of personal value, and although it takes a while, the public do accept it and get into it. And that's not meant to sound big-headed."

Although Robin seemed happy with the way the album was received, it received a mixed response from fans. This may have been due to Robin's distinctive voice – inescapable since he sings all of the lead, harmony, and backing vocals – and also his artistic approach, which ranges from the mundane to the genius. Unlike his more workmanlike brothers Barry and Maurice, Robin seems to rely on flashes of inspiration and is less able to turn such moments into fully realised songs.

Most of the songs on *Robin's Reign* feature a large orchestra as on *Odessa*, and many overdubbed vocals and, artistically, there are some inspired moments.

The album credits Robin as the sole producer, but his manager, band-leader Vic Lewis, must have been more involved than he gets credit for. Arrangements are by Kenny Clayton and Zack Lawrence. Robin has said he plays numerous instruments on the songs, including organ and guitar, and Maurice probably also contributes piano and bass.

Arguably the highlight of the set, 'Lord Bless All' is completely solo. Robin's double-tracked lead vocal and organ are accompanied by a choir of Robin's multi-tracked voice, a real tour de force of vocal overdubbing with a good supporting arrangement. Robin himself described it as "a kind of carol with a Christmas flavour". He then went on to say, "It's got a 40-piece choir behind it consisting of 40 Robin Gibbs. In the end, I'd put about 28 tracks down." The closing song, 'Most Of My Life', is a return to earth, its repetitious length running to a fade-out ending.

Under extreme pressure to release the album as quickly as possible, *Robin's Reign* could have benefited from being delayed to allow Robin more time to polish off some of its rough edges. Nonetheless, while it disappointed some fans who had been brought up on a diet of group releases, it served its purpose as a showcase for Robin's individuality.

Other Robin solo songs have circulated on tape among fans but it is hard to say which are from the *Robin's Reign* sessions and which are from his incomplete 1970 album. Dozens more song titles are known from the many interviews conducted during the split period, and must have remained unfinished.

★ ★ ★

Despite the demise of the group the previous December, March saw the release of three Bee Gees' singles. 'Let There Be Love' was released in Belgium and also in Holland, where it reached number 14. In the United States 'If I Only Had My Mind On Something Else' was released, while in Britain 'I.O.I.O.' was the latest single, a month before its American release.

Barry and Maurice had split up just as the last *Cucumber Castle* recording sessions were underway between July and October, and Maurice has said that 'I.O.I.O.' was not even quite finished, but it still had Barry's guide vocal on it. It has a very sparse arrangement indeed, mainly guitar and drums, and it's not obvious how Barry would have bettered the lead. The "I.O." chant is, to date, Maurice's most vocal part on a Bee Gees' A-side. The song managed to make number six on the German charts and reached the Top 20 in both Australia and New Zealand. It even got a little airplay in the United States, and Barry and Maurice were on good enough terms to make a few promotional appearances for the album, but no follow-up single was issued after the album came out.

The film songs and others were intermixed freely, which mattered little since no one could see the film yet anyway, but they did mark with an asterisk which ones were in it. The album package was again a gatefold, with photos of Barry and Maurice in costume for the film.

Several other songs from this period were copyrighted as by Barry and Maurice but never appeared. One that received a mention from them in an interview in 1969 was 'Who Knows What A Room Is', a bluesy wail with electric guitar that must have come close to being included on the album.

With the future of the group uncertain, there seemed to be an effort by the record company to cash in on past success by releasing the first half of the *Odessa* album under the title *Sound Of Love* as part of the budget Polydor 99 series. The second LP, *Marley Purt Drive*, followed in October.

Also in 1970, *Inception/Nostalgia*, a two LP set of previously unreleased recordings from The Bee Gees' early days in Australia, mysteriously appeared on the German Karussell label and the French Triumph label. Described since as a collection of song demos, warm-ups and vocal tests, the songs all seem to be re-mixed into mock stereo. What is particularly intriguing about this set of songs is that while some are quite obviously demos, many of the tracks seem well supported by an orchestra and even background chorus. While it is extremely unlikely that Ossie Byrne's small studio could accommodate such support, it would also be most out of character for Festival to fund such support for a band which at that date had not tasted chart success. The orchestra and chorus has never been adequately explained, and the general belief is that The Bee Gees sang over pre-recorded tracks of some of the established hits of the time. Whether these songs were recorded in any serious attempt to cross into a more mainstream audience or just some 'fun' recordings made with no intention of their eventual release is not known.

What is known is that when they were released, some three years after The Bee Gees achieved international success, it was not with the group or their management's sanction.

Maurice only discovered about the album when he and Ringo Starr and their wives had gone on a skiing trip to Switzerland, and Ringo chanced upon the album in a shop. Pointing it out to Maurice, he commented that he had never seen that one before; nor had Maurice until that moment!

Inception/Nostalgia was withdrawn within a few months, popping up again later as a Japanese release. It quickly became the most sought-after of all The Bee Gees' albums since the songs were unavailable anywhere else until the 1998 Australian CD set, *Brilliant From Birth*.

★ ★ ★

Following the dissolution of the group, all three Gibb brothers opened the year working on solo albums. None of the three albums was ever released, but enough songs for each were written and recorded, and two singles were issued in the spring.

By the time the *Cucumber Castle* album was released in April, Maurice had launched his first solo single, 'Railroad'. Written for a Bee Gees' album but never used, the song featured a big sing-along chorus like Robin's three singles, and resembled 'Don't Forget To Remember', with its similar country feel. The least familiar ingredient was the voice, since Maurice had never sung lead on a Bee Gees A-side, and he needed to establish an identity more than Barry or Robin. Part of the problem was that his creative work had been hidden inside songs identified with them.

"People have said that my single sounds like The Bee Gees. I sang the higher parts usually, and the other vocal parts I've added to 'Railroad' could be the others," Maurice explained. "It's hardly surprising there could be a similarity because I used to work out the back tracks for The Bee Gees, and I'd play piano, bass and rhythm acoustic guitars, and sometimes even drums. It's my piano on 'Words', you know – it gave it that distinctive sound."

Lulu offered critical input to the recording, according to Maurice. "I couldn't stand the type of wife who said everything I did was beautiful," he said. "Lulu first said the piano was too loud, then something else was wrong. Would you believe it? I mixed it six times just to please her!"

'Railroad' is structurally more complex than usual for The Bee Gees, though the lyric – about going home – is less interesting. The B-side song, 'I've Come Back', drifted in a looser presentation than Bee Gees fans would expect but is wonderfully understated.

"Billy and I have written a lot of album material," Maurice revealed. "I will probably be forming a group to work with me. There is something in the air. There will be a few lost friends, but I can't say too much about it."

Although Maurice's plans for his solo career were accelerating, he remained nostalgic for the old days. "I'd seriously love to get back to the old Bee Gees again," he said wistfully. "I really loved the group, and I miss the unit a lot. It's things like sitting in hotel rooms together after a show and taking people off that made working in a group such fun. I miss all that being solo."

Tom Kennedy was present for the recording at Nova Sound Studios of *The Loner,* which ran from December 9, 1969, following immediately on from the last Bee Gees sessions, to March 23. "Billy Lawrie was involved in it, of course, and the various members of Tin Tin," Tom revealed. "It was just a good, fun time, really – working in the studio with Maurice always was. It's quite a nice piece of work for someone who . . . no one really sees as a singer, really. He's more of a musician, really, than a singer, although he can sing harmonies."

Also present were drummer Geoff Bridgeford, who had replaced Colin Petersen for the last Bee Gees sessions, Stone The Crows guitarist Les Harvey, pianist Johnny Coleman and arranger Gerry Shury, who had done songs on the Tin Tin album Maurice produced in 1969. As usual, Maurice played various instruments, and sang all the vocals.

Interviewed by Nicky Horne on Radio 1 two years later, Maurice appeared to have less than happy memories of the project. "My solo LP is one thing that, well, to tell you the truth, I don't think it should be worth releasing because I did it a while ago . . . and I was under a great depression at the time when I did it, because I missed the boys very much. I just did it because I thought I had to do it."

Maurice announced that he would be writing and performing the sound-track to Richard Harris' latest film, *Bloomfield*, prompting an immediate denial from musical director Johnny Harris, who stated, "I am contracted to score the picture and write two songs for it. There will be four other songs in the film – one by Maurice Gibb, one by Glen Mason, one by the Tony Colton & Ray Smith team and one by Bill Wheelan and Niall Connery."

But an RSO spokesman defended the claim, saying, "Maurice has a con-tract from the producers John Heyman and Wolf Mankowitz to write five songs, including the title number. As far as we are concerned, that adds up to the entire score, although admittedly someone else may be adapting them to the needs of the film." One such song was 'Danny', again co-written with Billy Lawrie while another might have been 'Till I Try', an instrumental located on the reverse side of a 'Danny' acetate. Eventually a whole album's worth of material was recorded with Richard Harris, but the master tapes still languish in The Bee Gees' studio in Miami, and the material will probably never see the light of day. Bob Saker recalled being present for one of those sessions at London's Nova Studios in Bryanston Street. "I remember going to a session with Richard Harris, and I remember being there, and he was pissed out of his head and he knocked a pint all over the [mixing] desk. Gone! Goodnight!"

Bob can recall just one of these unreleased recordings. " 'Half of every dream is Mary, Half of every dream is she'. I remember the song."

In July, Billy Lawrie and Maurice re-recorded 'The Loner', and the song, credited to The Bloomfields, was released on the soundtrack of the Richard Harris film. The film was called *The Hero* in the USA, after the Joseph Gross novel of the same name. It was also the recipient of a Golden Globe nomination.

The first Barry Gibb single followed a month after Maurice but was not issued in the United States. 'I'll Kiss Your Memory' was a country weepie in the mould of Bobby Goldsboro's hit single, 'Honey', a widower recalling his happier days. As a simple song with verse and chorus of essentially the same melody, it is disappointing both lyrically and musically, from the man considered The Bee Gees' main songwriter.

"It's not the same orchestra as we used with The Bee Gees," Barry explained. "But Bill Shepherd is the only arranger I'll ever work with. On the single I double-tracked my voice seven times, because I knew exactly how I wanted everything done. Now I want to make one mark on my own, before I get too involved in anything else. I don't think my past associations with The Bee Gees are a bad thing to have as far as it affects my solo efforts, because people already know me. And also in this business, it's who you know!"

'This Time' on the B-side was a little more hopeful, another country style ballad, as are many of the songs considered for the album. "I love country music and I probably allowed a little more than I should have to influence me," Barry admitted. "But I do music that I enjoy and hope that everyone else will enjoy it too. If you try to work for whatever everyone else wants, I think that you get lost. I think you've got to be in love with what you've done and then see what happens. That's what helps for me anyway."

A second Barry Gibb single, 'The Day Your Eyes Meet Mine'/'One Bad Thing', came very close to release around August 1970. Barry performed the latter song on German television, and in the United States an initial batch of Atco singles were pressed but destroyed. Needless to say, at least one copy escaped unscathed, and was offered up for auction during the Eighties.

Barry's album may have been near completion by August, but no definite song selection or sequence is known. Recording began using eight-track facilities on February 15, but in less than a week, master tapes were being submitted in 16-track. The title *The Kid's No Good* was rumoured, but no song by that name is known. Tapes leaked out to fans since show predominantly the country-with-strings style of the first single. An exception is 'One Bad Thing', an upbeat pop number which, according to a US copyright filing, was written with Maurice in September, 1969. Some are story songs, such as 'Clyde O'Reilly', and others are mood pieces, such as 'Mando Bay', possibly the best of them. Another, 'Victim', sounds as if it could have been written for Gene Pitney, perhaps inspired by 'Something's Gotten Hold Of My Heart' as Barry's vocal delivery is virtually identical to the American singer in several portions of the song.

Fan reaction to the tracks is generally lukewarm. Something seemed to be missing. Many of these songs were at least published, and most of those were recorded by other artists, but none were hits.

Robin's work during this time is not even represented by a single officially, but again many tapes have since been passed around fans. One song that seems an obvious choice for a single was the very commercial sounding 'Engines Aeroplanes', the only one received by Atlantic. A few are clearly identifiable as outtakes from either *Robin's Reign*, or from his second album said to be called *Sing Slowly Sisters*, although it is not clear which. The song, 'Sing Slowly Sisters', has an unusually good melody and a strong vocal performance, and it may have been the planned single.

There are a few songs, best exemplified by the six-minute 'Cold Be My Days', in which he touches upon his Isle of Man origins with the words, "You can see Snaefell from Peel Castle Tower". The song features Robin singing to orchestra alone, and with no rhythm section he is free to vary the tempo on different lines, something he started to do in 1969 on 'Lord Bless All'.

Two effective songs with no orchestra also seem to be from 1970, 'Very Special Day' with piano and a war theme seemingly related to 'Sing Slowly Sisters', and 'Sky West And Crooked' with guitar and Robin's most inscrutable lyrics. In many cases, the arrangements are far superior to those on the *Robin's Reign* album, and great care appears to have been taken in the recording. On the other hand, the available tapes also include numerous very strained songs of questionable worth, and what he was going to make of all this is unknown. Many of the songs, including good ones, were never even published, and few of those were recorded by anyone.

★　★　★

Robin and Molly had settled into their new home in the Surrey countryside with their basset hound puppy, Hedgehog. "I don't think he liked London very much – too much concrete and not enough mud," Robin said. "He finds life much more exciting chasing rabbits, squirrels and an assortment of other creatures found at the bottom of the garden. Mind you, he hasn't caught up with anything yet. His new-found playmates are all much too fast for him – and they certainly lead him a merry dance. He comes in exhausted at the end of the day, trots off to his bed-basket and we don't hear a woof out of him all night."

Robin had begun writing a column for *FAB 208* magazine, in which he detailed his views on anything and everything: patriotism ("Britain and all its glory! Our beloved Union Jack soiled and tattered. A flag that can only be seen in one piece on people's carrier bags."), life in Australia, Hedgehog's exploits and eating habits, travel advice – nothing was safe from Robin's running commentary.

Britain's change to decimal coinage particularly worried him. "My arithmetic never was above average at the best of times," he wrote, "and as for decimal points, they always did make me a bit dizzy. I can see now that I will easily be 'done', and even when I'm given the right change, it's going to be hard to convince me it is correct. I do hope they don't do away with the six-penny bits too quickly. Whatever are we going to put into our fruit machines? I hope they don't make us use those horrid little metal discs. For a start it's a nuisance having to change them back into money and the game is just not as exciting.

"I've already acquired nostalgic thoughts about the now redundant half-crowns – I seem to need 2/6 change quite frequently, and I don't like messing around with the two bob bit and a sixpence. Of course, I shouldn't be thinking of shillings – it's all going to be new pence, isn't it?"

It was reported that Robin would release 'Great Caesar's Ghost' as his next single; this was then dropped in favour of 'The Statesman (Sir Winston Churchill)', Robin's tribute to his "greatest hero" which was to be recorded with a 100-piece orchestra. Once again, it was not to be.

Next he planned to release 'The Ghost Of Christmas Past', from his original musical based on Charles Dickens' *A Christmas Carol*. "I'm an ardent admirer of Charles Dickens. I read this piece in one of Dickens' books where he was trying to get published an article condemning the spectacle of public hangings. The laws of the day slapped a writ on him for interfering with public entertainment."

Robin's musical, entitled *Scrooge,* suffered the same fate as his earlier *Family Tree* (or *Family Circle*), but undaunted, he wrote yet another, *Henry VII*. Somewhat predictably this, too, would never materialise. "I'd like to write lots of musical scores and appear in serious and happy-go-lucky films," he revealed. "I'd like to write music where I can use my imagination to the full and also act in a typical British type of film, preferably of the last century.

"I get the feeling that I was born in the wrong century, but I'm a hypochondriac really, and they wouldn't have had the apparatus and equipment to deal with me a hundred years ago," he added.

Robin was reported to be rehearsing at the London Palladium for an upcoming 22-country tour and a concert to be broadcast on ITV.

★ ★ ★

In March 1970, the youngest member of the Gibb family was given a gentle nudge towards a musical career. For Andy's 12th birthday, Barry presented him with his first guitar. Up to this point, Andy had shown little interest in music, most of his attention having been lavished on sport and horses. Barry also gave his youngest brother his first horse, which Andy named Gala.

"[Andy] was a little devil," Barbara said fondly. "A little monster. I'd send him off to school but he'd sneak off to the stable and sleep with his two horses all day. He'd wander back home around lunchtime smelling of horse manure, yet he'd swear he had been at school. Oh, he was a little monkey!"

"Andy was always around – he was this cheeky little lad," said Tom Kennedy. "Hugh and Barbara doted on him, so he would have a limo to go around London with his pals and twenty quid to go to the cinema. It was unheard of in those days! But he was just a cheeky little lad with a heart of gold . . . He used to try to get me to buy him beer when he was underage – he would only have been about 11 or 12. He was always there, a lot of fun. He was good as gold. Very talented little lad, Andy . . . He always had a lot of freedom. I suppose if he had had a little more discipline in his life, he might still be with us today."

Armed with his new guitar, the small, freckled-faced boy began to emulate his hero, his big brother Barry. Despite more than a decade's difference in their ages, the youngest and eldest of the Gibb brothers had formed a strong bond. "I think he's my favourite brother," Andy said. "He's so kind and generous, and when he comes to visit us, he plays with me. I've only got to ask for something, and he'll buy it for me. I think he's too soft-hearted, people can talk him into things, and he hates hurting anyone. I see him about twice a week. He takes me out for rides in his Bentley, but he doesn't let me have a go at driving it, though! I go up to his flat sometimes, and we play together. He's very kind and generous, and when I grow up, I hope I'm like him."

For his part, Barry described Andy as his "consolation prize". During those years when he felt excluded by the closeness of the twins, he had Andy to turn to, an adoring but equally adored youngest brother.

★　★　★

In July 1970, Barry and Maureen's divorce decree was made absolute. It had been a particularly acrimonious divorce, as Maureen had blamed Robert Stigwood and The Bee Gees' busy professional schedule for the break-up of their marriage, and saw herself very much as the injured party. Barry chose not to contest the divorce, as there could have been bitter courtroom battles, with the press turning the whole dispute into a media circus.

Barry therefore agreed to Maureen's demands which were settled "amicably". The financial cost was perhaps greater in the long run, but Barry was desperate to get out of a marriage he considered a youthful mistake. He was also eager for everything to be done with a minimum of publicity.

"I don't think divorces should be put in the public eye," he said. "It is nothing to do with the newspapers." As Maureen and her legal representatives probably knew all along, it was the only sensible option and to the benefit of all three parties.

Although everyone connected with the group (himself included) describes Barry as reclusive in those days, he continued to be in demand. He appeared on the panel of judges and performed for the *Miss Teen Princess Of The World* pageant in Germany.

"I've not appeared on stage for at least a year and three months," Barry said, "and I really miss people, seeing an audience in front of me. You know, without that crowd, I'm lonely. As it is, I know I'm going to get back to doing stage work, but if the time came when I couldn't, then I'd take twenty sleeping tablets! Believe me, I know just how guys, who can't get out on stage when they need to, feel."

The Australian pop singer Ronnie Burns accompanied Barry when he and Lynda went to Germany for the pageant. Ronnie, it would seem, was a little star-struck by his old friend. "It was fantastic," he recalled. "We were treated like kings. I remember him warming up and singing a few songs, and being in awe of the guy . . . Beautifully dressed, magnificent voice – he had the lot . . . We became, I thought, very close . . ."

When the time came for Ronnie to return to Australia, he remembered, "On my way home, the plane stopped in Amsterdam, and I wrote him a letter thanking him for his hospitality and the time we had spent together.

"When I got home, there was a letter from Lynda with some negatives of some photos of Barry and me taken together. The letter just asked me to choose which ones I wanted and send it back to them and that was it. After that, nothing!"

Maurice had taken advantage of a gap in his schedules to have a quiet holiday visiting his sister, Lesley, who had by now returned with her family to set up home in Sydney. On landing at Melbourne, however, Maurice found himself stranded at the airport by strikes affecting internal flights. Eventually, when the press discovered a celebrity in their midst, he was persuaded to emerge from the VIP lounge and give an impromptu conference.

"[The Australian pop scene] is absolutely fantastic," he declared. "I used to say anyone in Australia, who wanted to get big, had to go overseas. Now I don't agree with that. In a few years, I hope people will be coming to Australia to get big."

In July it was Barry's turn, and he travelled to Australia to act as compere for *Go-Set* magazine's pop poll awards. While there, he gave an exclusive interview for the magazine which revealed that some 16 months after the initial split, he was still not ready to make peace with his brothers.

"Obviously we're still brothers, but we are no longer one as a group. Over the last year, there's been a lot written about the Gibb family and The Bee Gees. In fact, at one stage, I was beginning to think that the English public knew more about our family and our personal problems than they did about the *Coronation Street*★ crew. Every week, the music papers in England report splits between major groups. It's reported as news and it's treated as such. But when it comes to The Bee Gees, they want to see something insidious or vindictive because of the family relationships within the group.

"Regardless of what publicity comes out in the future about The Bee Gees, I can assure you that I am going to stick to my solo career regardless of what Robin and Maurice do," he insisted. "I've yet to have the big hit as a solo artist. I was disappointed that Robin's 'Million Years' and Maurice's 'Railroad' failed to make the charts in England, but perhaps they were too much like the old Bee Gees sound. I think I have fallen into the same trap. There are so many records released, and it's so hard to get a single off the ground [in Australia] because of the limited airplay."

A royalties war was being fought out at the time. UK record companies wanted big royalty payments from Australian radio stations to play their records. The radio stations then retaliated by refusing to play UK record companies' records. US releases were unaffected as were the majority of Australian record companies; but not, for example, EMI Australia whose head office was in the UK. The ban lasted about a year until a compromise agreement was reached.

Barry claimed that not only had he been concentrating on his songwriting and recording, but he still also hoped to branch into films. "I have already had offers to play different parts but without appearing swell headed, I haven't found the right part yet."

In the meantime, his first love, music, occupied much of his time. "There is nothing that I like more than to while away my time in a recording studio putting down songs that I have written. Writing by myself, it becomes easier to fit into a pattern, and in the long run, it has been more rewarding," Barry claimed. Conversely, he admitted that he did miss the cross flow of ideas which came from working with Maurice and Robin; the interaction "which converted a couple of lines or the beginning of a melody into a big hit record".

He added, "Ever since I can remember, I have written songs with Maurice and Robin, and it has been hard over the last year writing songs without the help of the Gibb team.

"After going through the mill of the international pop scene, one does tend to become a little silly," he confessed to *Go-Set*'s readers. "The pressure of competition is all go and non stop. It affects everybody – pop singers, record producers and even pop journalists. Perhaps your own writer Ian ['Molly'] Meldrum could recommend a good psychiatrist for Robin – or myself for that matter!"

★ Britain's longest running soap opera.

20

REUNITED

B Y THE SUMMER of 1970, the word was out: the battling Bee Gees had buried the hatchet . . . fortunately not in each other.

Just as he had been the first to leave the group, it was Robin who made the first move towards patching things up, phoning Barry – although, being Robin, he gives the story his own twist, claiming that Barry told him to, "Piss off!"

Barry, being Barry, offered a more thoughtful account. "Robin rang me in Spain where I was on holiday," he recalled, "and he gave me his views on being alone. When I got back . . . Robin came to see me . . . and we sat down and we talked and he said, 'Let's do it again,' because he had had some success himself. He had had 'Saved By The Bell' which was a really big hit record for him, but it was not the same as the three of us. As Robin coined it then, 'It's not nice when you have success on your own' . . . We realised we had forgotten our original arguments which started the whole splitting thing off. When Robin came round that day, both of us had a bit of a strum and then Maurice joined in . . .

"The most important thing to me is that we're all friends again, but with my solo single only just having been released, I feel I'd like to see how it goes before committing myself to anything. When The Bee Gees do reform, we'll still be free to work on our solo plans, but for me particularly, joining the group again would look like I can't make it alone. Robin has had a big hit, and Maurice has been successful with his stage work, but I've just been waiting for what I thought was the right time," Barry said wistfully.

"All I know is this time it will be better than before. There's a much better feeling now. Oh no, it wasn't all publicity; it was true. Have you ever seen a boxing ring? It was that bad. Every family will have arguments but because we were a group, and it got in the press, it became an incident."

Robert Stigwood was credited with instigating the actual reunion, although he was quick to point out that an end to the quarrels did not necessarily mean that The Bee Gees were back together. "There are definitely no plans at the moment for the boys to reform," he announced. "However, they are meeting, have patched up their differences and are very good friends again. We regard this as more important than anything."

Stigwood's statement sounds somewhat hollow if Barry is to be believed.

"Robert, our manager, was also included in the break-up, and that's something that nobody ever mentions, and I think he has to be honest about it these days, you know. He played favourites too, and that can be disruptive within the group. It was like a popularity contest and I'm sure it happened with a lot of groups."

Robin was still under contract as a solo artist to NEMS, and his manager Vic Lewis was less than eager to release him. "They all want to get together again," Lewis said, "but there are still some technicalities to sort out. I've had discussions with Robert Stigwood, who manages Maurice and Barry, and there is a suggestion of making an LP and single together again." Lewis proposed that a possible solution might be for Robin to continue as both a solo performer and a group member.

The brothers' initial business meeting came about when shares in Robert Stigwood Group Ltd, RSO's parent company, were offered for sale to the public. "We didn't get together in a burst of brotherliness," Barry admitted. "Instead, there was a great roomful of lawyers present. It was terrible. The coming back together was conducted in about as silly a fashion as when we broke up. When you have a split like that, the 'brother thing' goes out the window. Because you're brothers, it becomes more of an issue and you can become dire enemies, and this is what happened to our heads. The way we treated each other was terrible."

"It was pretty nasty in the boardroom," Dick Ashby recalled, "but it wasn't really the boys so much . . . NEMS lawyers and RSO lawyers were having pretty hefty meetings on Robin's behalf, splitting his wares, as it were. Barry was unavailable in his apartment in London. But as far as the three brothers were concerned, it wasn't heavy because they weren't seeing each other. There was some obviously hairy business going on, but at the time, the boys weren't too business-minded. So it was more or less left to lawyers. History has shown it was whether they had a good or bad lawyer in those days as to how they came out of it, with what slice of the pie they got.

"At the time RSO was going public, and with their shares in the company, they were very much involved financially. Robert had to get them in one at a time to sign papers, discuss their new share deal and their new parts in the company. I think, once again, Stiggy's got to be credited with it. He said to them, 'Look, we're going public . . . What a great thing it would be to launch the public company press-wise if you all came back together.' "

It was not to be that easy. "The three of us were sitting in the office in London," Maurice recalled. "We had split up, and the lawyers and accountants were all there, trying to sort out all our affairs with Robert. We all looked at each other like, 'What the bloody hell are we doing here?' All these people are trying to fight over who owns what, and who gets this and that, and our manager is sitting there trying to sort them all out. We're sitting there together on the couch going, 'What's going on?' We wanted to get back together again, and all of a sudden, the four of us, Robert as well,

287

realised these guys were trying to break us up, not keep us together. And when we got to Barry's part, I broke up and cried because I couldn't believe how stupid we'd been . . . My first wife [Lulu] just sat there going, 'Take it easy.' I said, 'I just don't believe all the rubbish we're going through . . .' "

"There were all these people giving us this, 'Don't speak to anybody until you speak to me' business," Robin added.

Although at the time, they presented a united front to the press, Barry said later that, "Spiritually, our heads weren't in it. We were still upset with each other. Things hadn't been resolved. And Robert was putting us back together in his way, meaning well, of course, but really to the end of seeing the company going on the market united. Everything we did was for the corporation. I honestly think the will was there for us to come back together. I don't think the time was right for us. It was all done legally. Everybody had his lawyer in the room, and nothing was resolved . . . At that point there was a battle going on over who could get the most amount of shares before the company went public."

According to Barry, some major players in the financial world began to put pressure on the brothers in an effort to persuade them to sell out. "None of us were left alone night and day," he recalled. "Other people, other major people, other important people were trying to buy our shares. They were harassing us and persecuting us. All kinds of death threats, threats to our families. Things like that.

"It got to be where we were in danger of being physically injured. Heavies would appear late at night, banging on the door, saying, 'Sell . . . your . . . shares.' One night I was lying in the hallway with a gun, pointing at the front door . . .

"We always seemed to have enough money so that during the time the pressure was on, we were all right. Providing we didn't give way to those people who threatened physical violence. They didn't actually commit physical violence but sent heavies to our door, just to bang on the door. Not to get in, not to do anything but frighten the lives out of us. I can't say who sent them . . . various major concerns."

It was worse for Robin, following on the heels of Hugh's suit to make him a ward of the court. "I think it hit us hardest," Molly revealed, "because there were times when there was no money at all around, and Robin wasn't working. It was like, 'What are we going to pawn this week?' "

According to Robert Stigwood, "Robin had the crucial one per cent controlling share, and he was threatened by some heavies to give it up."

Lynda recalled that the sale of the company had a sobering effect for another reason. The day of reckoning came for the extravagant lifestyle that the brothers had been leading. As she said, they "did a lot of spending when they didn't actually have it in liquid cash. It was advances and loans, and one day, the office goes public and they say, 'Well, you have this debt with us,' and all of a sudden, you're asked to pay it. I think that brought them all back down to earth."

Apart from Polygram/Polydor, the major financiers of RSO, Robert Stigwood and David Shaw, had the greatest number of shares in the company. "Then me, Maurice and Robin and Eric Clapton, Jack Bruce, Ginger Baker and Frankie Howerd, down the line," Barry added. "What was going on was a major corporate battle. The Bee Gees couldn't survive during that. No one was looking after The Bee Gees. It was a total financial struggle. Except you couldn't have put that in magazines. Nobody would have listened to you."

What you *could* put in magazines were the Gibb brothers' efforts to explain the break-up and reunion and to plead their case to the public. On August 21, 1970, weeks after they had got back together again, it was finally made official. "The Bee Gees are there and they will never, ever part again," Barry announced. "If a solo record comes out, it will be with the enthusiasm and great support of each of us. We *are* a musical establishment."

"We just discussed it and re-formed," Maurice said. "We want to apologise publicly to Robin for the things that have been said. We just want to stop boring the public without squabbles and do the music."

"All that 'Robin said this' and 'Barry said that' and 'Maurice did this' stuff was written by the press anyway," Barry contended. "We didn't say most of it at all. When we broke up, we each found that we were going pretty much the same way as each other, but it was taking us all more time to get things done."

"The [British] public didn't take kindly to the break-up because of the press," said Stigwood. "They really had a field day with it. So there were lots of unpleasant quotes from one brother about the other one. That didn't win any sympathy from anyone because from the public's point of view, they were sort of riding high, earning a lot of money. And then to see that go on, we decided the best thing was to focus on their recording and not worry about publicity."

Robin acknowledged the harm that their very public battles had done. "We hope we haven't lost the public's confidence with all this," he told *Melody Maker*'s Chris Charlesworth, who interviewed the brothers at Barry's Eaton Square flat. "I think we were afraid of losing each other as brothers. When brothers fight, it's worse than friends. The fighting is more violent. It's far worse than friends fighting, and anyway we were making mountains out of molehills."

More recently, Robin looked back on the split as a natural progression of growing up. "I think a lot of people that remember [the break-up] don't remember that we were very young at the time, a lot younger than people realise. And that we were also very green to the kind of success that we had initially. And I don't think each of us individually knew how to handle it. We had a lot of egos that young people develop very fast and very quickly, and a lot of things that are of value to a young person are very superficial. Relationships don't mean a thing for instance, or how close someone is, or whether the fact you are brothers don't mean anything."

"When you were hurt at that age, you're hurt forever as opposed to when you get older, when you mellow out, and you realise that there are situations, you can get around these situations," Barry added. "I think individually when you get depressed now and again you think, 'God, I think I'll toss it in, this is ridiculous,' you know, 'It doesn't work.' But I'm glad we didn't. We never did. We remind ourselves of, maybe it's a bit radical but sort of a Three Musketeers type situation. It is pretty radical . . . Oh, all right, The Three Stooges is probably closer!" he laughed.

The brothers were full of plans for the future. "I'd like the three of us to write a feature film," Robin revealed, "ideally within the next three years. There's a multitude of things to do," and prophetically he added, "The Bee Gees have scarcely begun."

In fact, as far back as June 13, The Bee Gees, albeit unofficially, had begun, but without the eldest brother. Robin and Maurice recorded nine songs in June and a dozen more in August, before Barry joined them, of which only 'Sincere Relation' and 'Lay It On Me' ever appeared. Barry had revealed his intention to remain solo despite the fact that his brothers had "just completed a recording session under the name of The Bee Gees, and I guess that it will be released within the next six weeks". While many would regard it as a moot point, perhaps the truth of the matter is that it was Barry who had rejoined The Bee Gees.

There were still unfulfilled plans to publish *On The Other Hand*, the book of short stories that Barry and Robin started in Australia. "They sometimes sit up until four in the morning writing stories," Maurice said. "When we're at a hotel, they share a room and sit and scribble until all hours."

The enforced togetherness of their past schedule had been one of the major causes of the split, according to Maurice. "We'd toured for two years without a break. We were with each other every day and every night. You couldn't say goodbye and go home to the wife . . . it was like two years solid. That's why we stopped touring.

"Now we're more mature. Now we're honest with each other. But before, there were things we wouldn't bring out and say to each other . . . We've been working now for about three months and in that time, we've got together an LP and a single and the music for a film and even some solo stuff."

The brothers all agreed that the major drawback of being on your own is having no one to share your successes with. "You could turn around and say, 'Guess what, love,' you know, to the wife, 'the record's number one.' She goes, 'Oh that's nice, dear, what do you want me to do?' you know, but when you can share it between the three of us, we missed all that," Maurice said.

But Robin, as usual, had the final word on individual accomplishments. They had achieved success apart when 'Saved By The Bell' and 'Don't Forget To Remember' both reached number two on the charts, but there was no one there to help commiserate over "the fact that some bastard was keeping us out of number one!"

★　★　★

290

The group promised that their new album would contain no dramatic changes or shocks for their old fans. "The Bee Gees sound will be pretty much the same as it always was," Barry explained. "We are not going progressive or anything like that. I think the change while we have been away has been good for musicians because before people were successful if they had the glitter and gimmickry. Now the underground [movement] is taking over, and the majority of people are buying their records."

"I think we appeal to these people," Robin added, "and they will buy our records . . . because of the words we use in the music. The words mean things, and I think the underground people will realise that."

Maurice said that he considered his solo career to be a good experience. "I suppose it was a good thing to get it out of my system," he added, "but at the same time, I never thought we would never sing together again. I started off intending to make a go of it, but I soon found something was missing. I'd write songs and want desperately to play them to my brothers, but because of all the squabbles I didn't feel I could. Then our record company unintentionally seemed to be trying to sabotage our solo careers. Distribution problems hit my solo single, Barry's first single and Robin's second single.

"Then I found I was rehearsing in Eaton Square, just round the corner from Barry's flat, and the temptation was too great. So the two of us would get together just to talk – and one day I arrived and found Robin there too. We looked at each other and said, 'What are we doing? Why have we been so silly? Why don't we get together again?' "

Although the most important matter was to re-establish themselves as The Bee Gees, Maurice revealed that the brothers were reluctant to give up entirely on seeking individual glory. "We intend carrying on with our solo careers," he said, "but we want to start things as a group again. There will just be the three of us, and we will use a session drummer. Now that we have resolved it, we will go into the studio and record a new single and an album in the near future."

Robin insisted that the split had never been based on any sort of musical incompatibility. "It was just a matter of politics within ourselves," he explained. "It might be that one of us was planning to have a recording session tonight somewhere, and the rest of us hadn't heard about it. It was a lack of communication. I might think . . . or Barry or Maurice might think . . . 'Somebody is keeping me out of something.' You start to ask yourself, 'Why aren't I there?' and you say, 'Well, it won't happen again,' and suddenly everyone is getting different messages and you're in trouble."

★   ★   ★

With his divorce made final the previous month, on August 27, 1970, Barry and Lynda decided to get married. Lynda chose the date, September 1 – Barry's birthday – reasoning that this would ensure that he would never forget their anniversary. It didn't allow them much time for planning the wedding, especially since Barry had a scheduled television appearance in

Zurich, Switzerland, on Monday, August 31. Lynda, as usual, accompanied him.

Their flight from Zurich was scheduled for 7.00 on the morning of the wedding, which meant that they should have been up before 5.00 to get to the airport in time. They should have been, but they overslept.

Fortunately for them, also appearing on the programme the night before was their old friend, Dave Dee. "Believe me, if it wasn't for me, he wouldn't have made his wedding!" Dave recalled. "It was the typical things, we'd done a show, I think it was a telly show, and we were all staying in the same hotel . . . It was the usual heavy night, and we'd sort of partied the night away. We had to make a flight because they were getting married. And anyway, I'm about to go out and they're not there! Barry's not there, [Lynda's] not there, and I thought, 'I'd better check their room.' So I checked their room, and the buggers are still in bed! And I said, 'Hey! It's your [wedding day] – c'mon, you'd better [hurry up]!'

"So I waited and held a taxi, because everything in London was all organised. Everything in London was all buzzing, and we were all going to the wedding, except there wouldn't have been one without the bride and the groom."

The wedding took place at Caxton Hall at 2.00 p.m., where a crowd of more than 300 had gathered. Barry arrived in his maroon Rolls-Royce with John Stephens (owner of the Carnaby Street boutique where Barry bought most of his clothing), who was the best man, and Lynda's mother, May Gray. Living up to his fashion icon image, Barry wore a blue and aqua check suit with matching waistcoat, white shirt, white raw silk tie and high heeled red and black boots.

Minutes later, Lynda and her father, George Gray, along with her sister-in-law Shirley Gray, who was to be matron of honour, arrived in Barry's white Bentley convertible. Lynda wore a white floor length gown with a heavy guipere lace overslip, which she had bought just three days before the wedding, and carried pink roses. A family friend recalled that Barry remained perfectly calm during the ceremony, but his blushing bride was more nervous and mixed up the words of her wedding vows, even getting Barry's name wrong. The wedding guests included Barbara and Hugh, Andy, Beri, Lynda's parents George and May Gray, Tommy and Shirley Gray, Robert Stigwood, Vince and Christina Melouney, scriptwriters Ray Galton and Alan Simpson, Barry Ryan, Dave Dee, Peter Wyngarde and reporter David Wigg of the *Daily Express*.

Maurice, Lulu and Robin avoided the crush of fans and reporters outside Caxton Hall and chose instead to wait at Barry's flat for the reception. As it turned out, it was a wise decision, as after the wedding, when the photos were being taken outside the hall, a fight broke out between a reporter and policeman.

"Lynda and I have been together for nearly three years now, and we're very happy and very much in love," Barry told the waiting pressmen.

The new Mr and Mrs. Barry Alan Crompton Gibb and their guests returned to their flat at Eaton Square for the reception. The guests even included the couple's Pyrenean mountain dog Barnaby and Afghan hound Snoopy.

They postponed a honeymoon, but since Lynda's family were spending the night in the flat, Barry and Lynda had planned to spend their wedding night in a London hotel. Unfortunately, after driving around for what seemed like hours in an unsuccessful attempt to find it, they abandoned the search and went home. Instead of reclining in the bridal suite at a posh hotel, their wedding night was spent in the somewhat less romantic surroundings of their small spare bedroom, in single beds.

★   ★   ★

The response to the sale of shares in the Robert Stigwood Organisation was disappointing – in fact, it was deemed "the biggest flop in recent years" by a top finance writer of the time. The newly public company needed a quick promotion, and The Bee Gees were up for the task. "This is a real challenge," Barry said. "One hit from us could change the whole situation. Shareholders and speculators apparently need some confidence. Well, they are going to get it."

The manager who had dubbed them "the most significant new musical talent of 1967" was no less effusive at their return to the fold. "Individually The Bee Gees are creative people," Robert Stigwood said. "Collectively they are, for my money, the best pop group in the world."

When The Bee Gees made the decision to put their differences aside, each of the brothers had been working on new solo recordings for about nine months. In fact, two of Barry's solo efforts were touted for single release around this time. 'The Day Your Eyes Meet Mine' was withdrawn at the last minute in the USA, while Polydor planned to release 'One Bad Thing' on October 2. Despite Barry's longing to prove himself as a solo artist, it was decided instead that the next single should be a group effort. The solo works of all three were set aside in favour of quickly recording a new Bee Gees album together and getting it to the market by the end of the year. Incredibly they used none of the songs they'd completed, but all new ones. The song total for this period encompasses over a dozen each from the solo albums, and the sessions together had yielded over a dozen more, amounting to over 70 total recordings of which only 13 were released. Atlantic's master tape list shows the songs for the album arriving in two groups, with the tape for Barry's single arriving between them. Most of the songs recorded for the solo albums and the duo album were not sent out to the record companies.

'Man For All Seasons' was the early favourite for the lead-off single, but in the end, it was relegated to the B-side in favour of 'Lonely Days' as the A-side. "It's like a spiritual thing when we write," Robin explained. "We know what the other one is thinking, as if we have a language between us. 'Lonely Days' was written in 10 minutes. It was that quick. I was at the piano 10 minutes."

"Robin came to my place," continued Barry, "and that afternoon we

293

wrote 'How Can You Mend A Broken Heart', and that obviously was a link to us coming back together. We called Maurice, finished the song, went to the studio and once again, with only 'Broken Heart' as a basic structure, we went in to the studio with that and an idea for 'Lonely Days.' And those two songs were recorded that night."

In 1998, Barry also revealed, "A manager we had about five years back heard 'Lonely Days' in a restaurant and he said to a friend, 'That's one of my favourite Beatles songs.' And he was managing us!" he added incredulously.

The single was rush released as soon as possible after the reunion, hitting the shops on November 6. Both sides are quality songs, written by all three brothers. It was their first such created in almost two years – thus the album's title, *2 Years On* which also became available to impatient fans, only three weeks after the issue of 'Lonely Days'.

The A-side of the single has no solo vocal apart from lines called out in the concluding chorus, and the B-side features the trademark alternation of Barry and Robin solo parts. This contrasts with what is on most of the album, but politically – within the group – it would have been difficult to feature anything on the single that highlighted one brother. That aside, 'Lonely Days' is clearly the catchiest song for a single, and 'Man For All Seasons' makes a good case for their genius when working together. Another reason for the selection of these two songs, both pointedly credited to B., R. & M. Gibb, was to emphasise that The Bee Gees were back together as the success of RSO shares was likely to be heavily influenced by sales of the single.

The songwriting was done separately for just over half the songs, and while Maurice is playing on all songs, the vocals seem to be restricted to the writers, and it's not clear that Barry and Robin are present on songs they did not write. Although The Bee Gees in general do their best work together, it's interesting for once to have their separate creative approaches on one disc.

Maurice brought in the two musician partners from his solo work, drummer Geoff Bridgeford and arranger Gerry Shury, but the latter was replaced by the returning Bill Shepherd for most of the songs.

'Lonely Days', with its combination of sweet melodic verse and a great big stomping chorus, raced up the charts in the United States. Much of its initial momentum was due to the innovative thinking of Atlantic's then head of promotion. Jerry Greenberg had joined the label in 1967, promoting their product in Hartford, Connecticut. Had he been based just 25 miles further north, he would have been able to promote 'Massachusetts' in Massachusetts, that being the first Bee Gees record he handled. However, it is the events of the month of November, 1970 that he prefers to remember.

"I heard that song ['Lonely Days'] and I went crazy. I thought it was going to be an amazing number one record. In those days we had our own recording studio, right down the hall from the main offices. Now the record was pressed and ready to go, but what I did was, I made up about 30 tape copies, just put the song on a tape on a regular plastic reel, and I called up a bunch of my promotions department friends.

"I said, 'The Bee Gees just came out of the studio and they cut this record, and I don't even have time to press it up yet, but I wanted you guys to hear it, and I'm going to send you, you're the only one I'm sending, this tape, right from the studio.' I mailed it out special delivery and I have to tell you, within a week, thirty radio stations were all over 'Lonely Days', and it busted the record wide open. I was very proud of that. Ahmet [Ertegun] and Jerry [Wexler] were both talking about it. In those days, you had to come up with some creative ideas, how to promote a record. That record took off!" he exclaimed with justifiable pride.

The song sequence on the album seems to balance contributions as much as anything else: side one has two by all three, two by Robin and Maurice, and two by Barry; while side two, after 'Lonely Days', has two Robin songs bracketing two Barry songs bracketing Maurice's one song.

The remaining song by all three – not on the single – is 'Back Home'; short, fun, with three-as-one vocals and a sparse arrangement of just guitar, bass, and drums. The dated reference to Lyndon B. Johnson (President of the United States from 1963 through 1969) makes it sound like an old song. "We wrote this one at the time of the hijacks," Barry explained, "and it's all about that particular time. We more or less did it in the studio."

There's confusion in the credits in different releases, but Robin wrote either 'Sincere Relation' or 'Alone Again' with Maurice. They are both reminiscent of Robin's solo works and both are marred by distortion in the piano and vocal.

Although no solo version of the song was ever recorded, Robin's handwritten lyrics for an early version of 'Alone Again' were published in Germany's *Bravo* magazine in 1969 and provide a rare glimpse of a work in progress.

> *Baby, you've hurt me for the very last time,*
> *And you show it;*
> *Everyone around me just knows it, baby,*
> *Could be, you really had me tied up in string,*
> *And I believe it;*
> *And now I'm the one who must leave it,*
> *I could be wrong.*

Chorus

> *People, the sun is going down on your heads*
> *So read your paper*
> *I said you've been complaining about your legless beds.*

Fortunately, by the time the song appeared on *2 Years On*, Robin had reworked the lyrics to such an extent that the original bears little relation to the finished work.

There also exists another fine example of how a song can change midstream, although this time it required outside intervention. One of the "Bee Gees sessions" tracks that Robin and Maurice had written and recorded before Barry's decision to team up with them again was called 'Distant Relationship'.

The lyrics suggest that the song's subject matter was the Prince Regent, later King Edward VII, who was notorious for a string of affairs both before and after his ascension to the throne. His conquests included Lilly Langtry, the famous actress, and Mrs. Alice Keppel, equally infamous in her day as a royal mistress as her descendant Camilla Parker Bowles is now. Indeed, some of these original lyrics, were it not such a serious matter, might well bring a wry smile to the present heir to Britain's throne:

> *Sheila, Sean, and I lived in Sennen Cove,*
> *Drawing pictures in our dining room,*
> *She could run like Alice In Wonderland,*
> *She would speak like Charles Dickens planned . . .*
> *Then came the Crimean War and I had to sail,*
> *Waving from the shore like Florence Nightingale,*
> *And the people's prince,*
> *Cannot have what's rightly his,*
> *And he's convinced,*
> *It's a distant relationship.*

Before Robin and Maurice could advance the composition beyond the demo stage, Molly's father, George Hullis, died unexpectedly at the age of 60 a short time before the album was recorded. "He spent the last three days of his life in my house," Robin said, "and he told me he was going to die." And so, 'Sincere Relation' became Robin's tribute in song to his late father-in-law, with this set of lyrics bearing little resemblance to the first version:

> *George was born somewhere inside London town,*
> *Working, as he grew for that extra pound.*
> *Respected by all, he married and made a home*
> *To give his children more than he had known . . .*
> *Years before, a fire sent him in the street.*
> *It took him months of work to make ends meet.*
> *But then he died without an explanation.*
> *He never lied; a very sincere relation.*

(lyrics R. Gibb © Robin Gibb Publishing Ltd. 1970)

Barry has four solo songs. Two are in the folk country style he used in much of his solo album, of which 'Tell Me Why' is the simplest and purest. "I wrote this with Ray Charles in mind," Barry said. "It was written just before a session, with the lights down."

Maurice goes for a no-risk little country rocker, 'Lay It On Me', his voice growling and with as many instruments as he could dub. "This is a Maurice Gibb solo – backing and all," Maurice said proudly. "It's sort of swamp soul, and I recorded it at ten in the morning. I love the whole feel of it."

The thirteenth recording of 1970 alluded to earlier was the timeless 'How Can You Mend A Broken Heart', but fans of the group would have to wait until the following year before they would hear it.

★ ★ ★

The group's former drummer, Colin Petersen, was also making a fresh start with a group he named Humpy Bong, a two-word variation of the name of one of the schools that he and the Gibb brothers attended in Australia. The group's first single, 'Don't You Be Too Long', featured Colin on drums, Tim Staffell on guitar and lead vocals and Jonathan Kelly on bass, but the group was unable to play any live gigs until they added two new members.

The spectre of Colin's Bee Gees' past was making the task of recruitment even harder. "I've just auditioned my 200th applicant," he groaned. "People are assuming the new group will be a carbon copy of The Bee Gees. I must have heard 'Massachusetts' 50 times."

"I am *still* looking for a good lead guitarist and a pianist to finish the line-up," Colin said. "We can record with the three of us by double-tracking, but we can't appear on stage. Live radio shows are also a problem . . ."

For Jonathan Kelly, of course, it was simply an extension of his existing relationship with Colin, who had produced three singles and an album for the Irish born singer.

Jonathan Kelly went on to release two more RCA albums while under Colin and Joanne's management, *Twice Around The Houses* in 1972 and Wait *Till They Change The Backdrop* a year later, although neither release had any musical involvement from Colin. Looking back, Jonathan still retains strong views of his time with the Petersens, and is not afraid to express them, although much of it is tempered with regret.

"[Colin's] main interest was music, and I think he would have liked to produce, but I don't know if that was gonna be his forte. He was a very active producer, he wanted certain sounds, he wanted lots of things, so he was good, but I think you've got to have a very deep musical knowledge to produce well. And you've probably got to know about electronics a bit, you've got to know about sound and how it translates. I don't think Colin had ever really got involved in sound to that degree.

"I think Colin liked the good times, he liked living it up. I don't know whether he was going to be a serious student of music or production, because that's all about hard work."

Taking into account his own persona and political beliefs, Jonathan reflected, "Colin and Joanne were different to me; different, different, different! They loved fame and glory and being in the midst of the pop industry. I hated the pop industry actually. I saw it as totally ruthless and callous.

297

Not to say that there aren't good people [in it], because music is the most wonderful thing, and I've met so many good people. They were quite happy to go along with the system, but I wouldn't.

"They used to always take me to lovely restaurants, so kind, I couldn't believe these places I was going to. We went to a Greek restaurant, and the Greek owner started coming over to Joanne and saying, 'We Greeks and you Jews, we will get together and we will kill the Palestinians!' She never made a big thing out of that, she didn't think in those ways. In fact they weren't political at all, I don't think they thought politically. I did! I couldn't help it, and this guy was talking all this racism at my table. I know he owned the restaurant but it was my table while I was in his restaurant, so I told him! I said, 'Can you please go away from this table.' I will not sit, joined to somebody who is talking racial hatred.

"That's why we were so different; they would just have gone along with those things. I can't go along with those things, so we were never ever going to mesh, never going to come together really. And that was the trouble; and that was the trouble for Colin and Joanne. They needed some guy who wanted to be famous, who would just toe the pop line. But I was awkward and a troublemaker and I understand from their point of view that was a real problem."

After breaking away from Colin and Joanne in 1974, Jonathan went on to do two more solo albums, *Waiting On You* and 1975's *Two Days In Winter* which he produced himself. He had his problems with drink and drugs, then found religion, but seems to have reconciled himself to the manner in which his errant, restless personality was incapable of embracing pop success.

Colin Petersen returned to Australia with his family in 1974. Their son Jaime, christened Gideon, would soon have a younger brother, Ben, born the year after the family's move. Colin and Joanne would go on to have one of showbiz's longest running marriages before their unexpected break-up, 25 years after their departure from England.

Colin's bad luck extended to financial matters. He lost his right to royalties in a deal made after his unsuccessful High Court case against the brothers. He remained close to Vince Melouney, who sympathises with his friend's predicament. "He's a painter now. Colin Petersen a painter, can you believe it? [He's] pretty bitter about it all and when they met in 1989, he mentioned [the royalties aspect] to Barry. Barry was going to check up on it, but Colin never heard back."

★ ★ ★

As Jonathan Kelly and the Petersens went their separate ways, another threesome were coming to terms with being back together again.

Although the brothers all agreed that they were happier as a group, getting back together was not without its complications. All three agree that they spent most of the next five years getting to know one another again – and trying to explain to the press, suddenly bereft of their squabbles to sell magazines, the reasons for their break-up and re-formation.

"It's funny that in the first week of recording, we sat around and looked at each other and smiled," Maurice remembered. "But we were all afraid to suggest something – it was a case of, 'Who's going to try and take control?' We had to get back together because the formula was between the three of us, but the image of The Bee Gee brothers had been smashed."

"We were all willing to give ground though," Barry added. "It was a case of, 'Whoever pushes the first idea, we'll accept it.' And we started to ask each other's opinions and generally think about the other person a bit more. In the past, we were just three kids. We couldn't respect each other as men and for each other's talent.

"I think we reformed because we were tired of being on our own," he added. "We didn't split in the first place because we wanted to be solo acts, we just wanted to be alone for a while because at that time we'd been together for 10 years. We were young men and it only struck us because of our ages. Now we're the average age of a pop group."

"The break-up was an adolescent action," Robin agreed. "We were going through the puberty stage. Each wanted his own recognition. Breaking up did us a lot of good. If it didn't happen, we wouldn't be as good a group as we are now."

"It made us grow up. We needed it," Barry added. "We needed to see if we could go out and make it on our own. Most groups can't go back because they're not brothers. Their heads are in a different space."

Molly Gibb agreed that the time apart had been essential for the three brothers. "If the break-up hadn't have happened then, they wouldn't be together now. I'm convinced of that," she said. "The time away gave them all breathing space, time to grow up. And to realise that as a team, they worked better. Everything had been so intense. They had almost been manipulated like puppets, and they were very much indulged in. I think this type of break made them realise what it was all about."

On Boxing Day, 1970, British fans got a double treat when the group appeared on a comedy special with Peter Cooke and Dudley Moore, and the long awaited *Cucumber Castle* was finally screened on the BBC. The delay in showing *Cucumber Castle* was explained by the fact that the group had reconciled, and there was some talk of re-shooting some scenes to include Robin. He suggested that he would like to play a court jester, but in the end, the film was shown in its original version.

As the year drew to its close, tucked away in a small corner of the music papers was the news that Ashton, Gardner & Dyke were to release a new single. Entitled 'The Resurrection Shuffle', it would spend 14 weeks in the UK charts reaching a very respectable number three. It appeared that Vince's faith in the group had been justified but, sadly, he had now departed. In the event, AG&D would join the list of acts with the unwanted nomenclature of "one hit wonders".

21

TO WHOM IT MAY CONCERN

W ITH 'LONELY DAYS' topping the charts in America's *Cashbox* magazine and placed number three on *Billboard*'s chart, The Bee Gees had their biggest hit in the States to date, and late in January 1971, they set off on an extensive promotional tour to prove to the American record-buying public that the Brothers Gibb were definitely back.

"We don't feel rusty because we've been playing all our lives," Barry said. "But it is a little bit apprehensive to be getting back to live dates, and I have a feeling that in the next week or two we'll probably be rehearsing harder than we've done before, and probably working a lot harder at it than actually being on tour."

They admitted that they really didn't know what to expect of the American audiences. "I'm very confused about them because none of us knows if they'll be the people who have bought our records in the past, or if they'll be deeper, more progressive, or what," Barry added.

"We'll just have to go there and see what happens," Robin said philosophically. "We haven't changed ourselves, at least not in a way we can notice. It's very hard for any group to see itself. It's easy to get too involved – and not see the faults anymore."

"We're now all married and have a stable place in life," Maurice added. "We have more understanding between each other, no hang-ups and no hassles. We don't enjoy doing things on our own. If Barry got a number one and I didn't, it would cause a bit of a hassle, then the next person would say, 'I'm going to stay out until I make it.' We've got to have a hit together rather than separately. When I made a solo album – it's in the can and hasn't been released – I was dying to come home and play it to the boys. I'd play it to Lulu and she'd say, 'That bass is a bit too loud' and walk out! And I couldn't take it to the boys, although I wanted to, because at the time we weren't talking!"

The group, with Geoff Bridgeford in tow as a hired drummer, flitted from one to another of the top television shows of the time, performing 'Lonely Days' on Johnny Carson's *Tonight Show*, *The Ed Sullivan Show* and *The Johnny Cash Show*. For *The Andy Williams Show*, they performed both sides of the latest single.

In February the group travelled to New York for an appearance on *The*

Dick Cavett Show and the start of a seven-concert tour. It was their first time on the road since the close of the German tour in December 1968, and the boys were understandably nervous. The opening concert was originally intended to be held at Carnegie Hall, but inexplicably the venue was changed to the Albany Palace Theatre.

Hugh Gibb was present in his official capacity of lighting director, but at the soundcheck before the show, he was very much the father chiding his sons, with comments like, "Keep the guitar down, Maurice. You can't hear the fiddles with the guitar that loud and it ruins the effect."

Following a set by another family group, The Staple Singers, Barry, Robin and Maurice took the stage. Standing in front of the curtain backdrop, they opened the show with 'New York Mining Disaster 1941' and followed it with 'To Love Somebody'. The third song was 'Really And Sincerely', and as the crescendo was building, the curtain was raised to reveal what Hugh Gibb had so cavalierly dubbed "the fiddles": a 20-piece orchestra in full evening dress. The Bee Gees played all their previous hits with this orchestral backing, finishing off with a triumphant 'Lonely Days'.

"When we did Albany, it was incredible," Maurice recalled. "It was the first time we'd actually been on stage in two and a half years. And once you make one mistake, that's it, you just wait for the next one. Nothing is spontaneous on stage. Everything is made to look spontaneous, but it's all carefully calculated. Robin forgot the lyrics in 'Really And Sincerely'. He used some from 'I Started A Joke'. So when we got to 'I Started A Joke', he just used the lyrics to 'Really And Sincerely' that he'd forgotten, and no one knew the difference. They think you've rewritten it for the stage."

The tour progressed with the press dedicating almost as much space to Lynda as her famous husband and brothers-in-law. The latest fashion craze was for hot pants, and Barry's young wife was a most dedicated follower of fashion in those days. *Rolling Stone*'s Robin Green mentioned that Lynda "stayed on the sidelines filing her nails but attracted lots of attention in red patent leather boots, pink shirt and red leather hot pants, cheeks hanging out the back", and various photos duly appeared in most of the pop magazines. Barry and Maurice were described as looking like everything a rock star should be in "painful-looking too tight pants", while Robin "gave the group class by wearing a grey wool three-piece suit" as he "stood stiff and skinny, moved spastically like a puppet on strings and sang in this touching trembling sweet voice."

The mini tour came to its conclusion on February 21 in Portland, Oregon, and the group returned to Britain, where 'Lonely Days' had failed to make much of an impact on the charts. Barry admitted his disappointment with sales but added, "That's not to say that I think 'Lonely Days' has had its day here. I'm still waiting for it to do better, and I'm not convinced it's going to drop away without trace. Maybe the American success will revive some of the interest."

Following their return to Britain in March, Geoff Bridgeford was asked officially to join the group. "Naturally I am very, very pleased," he said. "I sort of drifted into it . . . I was gigging around with Tin Tin and, at the same time, I was doing a lot of session work for [The Bee Gees]. I played on all of their solo albums while the break-up was in force. When they got back together again, I played on *2 Years On* and the single 'Lonely Days'. It just seemed natural that we should stick together for a tour but I was very surprised when they asked me to become a member. I'd expected to be on sessions with them but not as a fully fledged Bee Gee.

"We all get on so well, it seems the natural thing to be joining them. I feel a bit guilty about leaving Tin Tin, but I am really happy for them that their record 'Toast And Marmalade For Tea' is doing so well in the States. It was at 24 last week and is still going up fast. I'm happy with [The Bee Gees] style of music – I think I'm meant to play like this. And the brothers are working well together and striving for the same thing."

With his wife Caryl and their young daughter Emma to think of, the stability of a position in an established group made a welcome change to picking up session work. "At last I'm in a group that's going on the road. I like the security because I have a family to look after," he added. "Playing on stage is terribly important to me. As a musician, that's the climax. I was afraid I wouldn't get the opportunity to go out on the road and play, but Robert Stigwood promised there would be plenty of stage work. I thought I would be back in Melbourne in just six months, but after a couple of weeks in London I just knew I wasn't going to go back."

Having already worked on *Cucumber Castle* and *2 Years On* as an uncredited session musician, Geoff was similarly frustrated when the next "Bee Gees" LP was released in May. Due to the high predominance of Gibb compositions on it, many regard the *S.W.A.L.K.* album as one of theirs when it is actually the soundtrack to the *Sealed With A Loving Kiss* film – or *Melody* as it was called elsewhere in the world – initially released in Britain. The film, a sweet and sentimental drama about two 10-year-olds who declare their intention to get married, starred Tracy Hyde as Melody and Mark Lester as Daniel. It also reunited Lester with his *Oliver!* co-star Jack Wilde.

The soundtrack to the film featured music by The Bee Gees, The Richard Hewson Orchestra and Crosby, Stills, Nash & Young. It contained 'In The Morning', 'Melody Fair' and 'First Of May', with instrumental reprises of each performed by the Richard Hewson Orchestra, as well as 'Spicks And Specks', 'Give Your Best' and 'To Love Somebody'. For 'In The Morning', it was the first official release of the Barry Gibb composition from the group's Australian days, which they had first performed for the general public at their Talk Of The Town performance with Lesley. Although the song itself was unchanged from its original 1966 recording, it was specially re-recorded for the film, and the new arrangement took it a little slower and featured some bass and piano from Maurice, as well as smoother harmony vocals. One reviewer described it as "a song worth seeing the film just to hear."

'Every Second Every Minute' from the *2 Years On* album was originally written for the film but wasn't used. In retrospect, its aggressive vocals and raucous style would seem completely out of place in this gentle story of young love.

Recognising the reluctance of the British public to forgive and forget the past, Robert Stigwood issued a gentle admonishment in the form of a press release to accompany the launch of their new single, 'How Can You Mend A Broken Heart', due out on May 28.

> *'Lonely Days' was the first single from the Gibb Brothers after the settlement of their family quarrel. And for anyone else the fact that it reached No. 1 in fourteen different countries, gave them their first chart-topper in the United States and became a gold for a million sales, would have been cause for unqualified rejoicing. But there was just one dark cloud. In Britain their fans, perhaps overfed on the diet of almost daily public squabbling, did not welcome them back with exactly open arms.*
>
> *Robin Gibb said, "Of course it meant a lot to us to get to number one in the States. And in terms of money it means far more than having a hit in Britain. But for me I would have sacrificed all of that to know that the fans here had forgiven us. We hope this new record will help them forget. It means more to us than I can tell you."*
>
> *Certainly the Bee Gees fans with long memories will find something in 'How Can You Mend A Broken Heart' to take them back to the golden days. All of the Bee Gees' lush romanticism is there, with the sweeping strings and Bill Shepherd's instantly recognisable arrangements. The song was written by eldest Gibb brother Barry, together with Robin. Maurice shares the writing credits on the disc, however, with his own composition 'Country Woman' on the B-side. Both tracks have been selected from the twenty songs that the Gibbs wrote and recorded for us on their next album, which is titled* Trafalgar.
>
> *With a two-month tour of America scheduled for the autumn, it seems almost certain that this latest release will become another monster success in the U.S. charts. But this time the Bee Gees are anxiously watching the hit parade a little closer to home.*

Stigwood's prediction for the American release would prove to be correct. 'How Can You Mend A Broken Heart' would surpass its predecessor in sales there, but in Britain, the response remained lukewarm.

"The Bee Gees were always respected until the break-up. I think I lost a little respect for them when they broke up," Geoff Bridgeford admitted. "The trouble is that they are brothers. They have hassles other groups don't have.

"Our tour of America was a success because there hadn't been so much publicity about the break-up. But there's no doubt that The Bee Gees would like to be accepted in Britain again. It would mean they had been forgiven. Still, I think they'd like to feel a little more confident of a good reception before doing a British concert. If the new single is successful, they may be tempted to try," he added.

Robin's emphatic patriotism was still evident. "We want people in Britain to take us seriously now . . . What I mean is, we're willing to work all the hours we can," he said. "I'm all Churchill and the Union Jack, and I'd like to have a number one in my home country."

Unfortunately, regaining lost ground in Britain would turn out to be more difficult than they had anticipated. "It seems to be taking us a long time after the row to convince the public that The Bee Gees are alive and together," said Barry. "Of course, we still have a go at each other, but we don't argue. Arguments are a malignant growth and we crush them from the start. It's things like that which break up groups. By no means are we on the way down. We've kept up our morale and the fan letters have helped."

Barry admitted to a certain reluctance to face the public in their homeland. "It has been too long between tours and it's been so long since we met a British audience, I don't know how they'll take us. I'm nervous about it. To be honest, if we saw one of our records in the charts here, none of the number one records in all the other countries would matter a bit."

"If we had another hit, we could probably do another tour of England," Maurice said. "But at the moment it's not really worth the audience coming to see us, because they would be living on the memories of each song . . . I think the people in the business feel, 'Why should they come back and try and make it again?' We already have a reputation here as the arguing brothers. I don't think we mishandled anything at the time of our problems because when our solo records came out, we were friends again. But stories of the arguments were still coming out. The press built it up 15 times more than it was.

"I can see what is happening. Every time we make a record, people say, 'That's The Bee Gees again,' but half the people in the country don't think we're still together. I'd love to do some concerts in England, but I don't want to go on stage and do 'Words', 'To Love Somebody' . . . and all those old songs and have people saying 'Do you remember that, Edith?' It's very hard to get back again, we want another number one before we do concerts."

His twin disagreed about the negative aspects of people's memories. "There will never be a vocal change in The Bee Gees. People remember your sound and that is what they want," Robin insisted. "They associate sounds with times in their lives; perhaps they stood in Earls Court when they heard a song and it brings back memories.

"We're a very closed up group. We firmly believe in what we are doing," he added. "To us, our music is the ultimate thing – we don't like outside influences and we don't believe we need them. We never have and we've been doing this for 15 years. You can get enough influences just by reading the papers or watching television. We'll go on until we drop. We'll all do separate things, but The Bee Gees will always be The Bee Gees. We're not just a group – we're an establishment within ourselves, and we're a family as well. The Bee Gees are more to us than our second name. We were born into music, and we'll go on the road even when we're 60."

Maurice was disparaging about the glam rock movement that was sweeping Britain. "I've seen Roxy Music, David Bowie, Mott The Hoople and Alice Cooper," he stated and, ignoring the fact that the last named was American, continued, "If you play those British artists' records one after the other you never know the difference. Nobody will ever be as exciting as the Stones."

"We sold the same number of copies of 'Lonely Days' as 'Ride A White Swan' did, but our records weren't in the shops that are used to make up the BBC charts," Barry challenged. It seems somewhat ironic that Barry would get on his high horse about T. Rex's first big hit in light of the ploy used by The Bee Gees themselves to get 'Wine And Women' onto the Australian charts just a few years earlier.

★   ★   ★

One bright spot on the horizon was their return to Australia in July for their first tour since finding international success. After being greeted by their sister Lesley and her young son Barry at the airport, The Bee Gees faced the press on their first day back in the Land of Oz.

"We've been waiting for five years to tour back here," Maurice said. "At our first hit we said, 'Right, now let's go to Australia.'"

"But we've always thought it was a little bit too soon to come back," Barry added, "because we didn't want to come back and say 'Hello' and appear on shows here and there, we wanted to come back with a bang because we left with such a dent . . . nothing. As soon as 'Spicks And Specks' was number one, we made plans and we left."

To emphasise the change in their fortunes since they left Australia, the Gibb brothers agreed to the tour only on the stipulation that they be backed with a full orchestra for all the concerts. "I suppose you could call it value for money," Barry explained. "It's the only way the kids can hear the same sound we put on our records."

The group told the Australian press that their management had been forced to hire bodyguards for the upcoming American tour, their second that year. This was due to the activities of the so-called Rock Liberation Movement, which had started after Bob Dylan's 1969 comeback concert at the Isle of Wight festival when thousands rioted as they tried to gain access without paying.

The movement was clearly well organised, as highlighted by an episode on The Bee Gees' recent American tour. According to Maurice, "They knew where we were when nobody else did. One of them phoned me when we were in Los Angeles and said he had planted marijuana in my hotel room."

"Bob Dylan was attacked in the US because he doesn't practice what he preaches – freedom. It's a kind of liberation movement," Barry explained. "There are thousands of people involved and their main feeling is against paying money to see entertainers who sing message songs about freedom. It's an underground movement which wants all music to be free. There have been death threats against pop stars and, when we were in New York during February, there was a bomb scare in our hotel. Death threats against pop stars are useless, and they don't worry me. Anyway, death couldn't be any worse than living," he added cryptically.

Maurice alleged that the cost of a Bob Dylan concert ticket was $20, while The Bee Gees charged only $6. "It's the same with John Lennon and Yoko," he added. "They say 'Power To The People' but charge enormous prices for seats at their concerts."★

The brothers joked about the fact that RSO's status as a public company meant that anyone could now buy stock in The Bee Gees. "Our public company is worth about twenty million dollars," Barry said. "We are major shareholders. We have enough security for us to live in comfort for twenty years or so. Once we had to pay $80 to get our photo on the front page of a magazine. Of course, then we were a struggling group in Australia, with only one hit to our name."

They admitted that they weren't sure what to expect of the Australian audiences after such a long absence. They needn't have worried. Every concert of the nine-day tour was a complete sell-out, and pleas for more encores continued long after the group had left the stage.

Between concerts, the Gibbs found plenty of time for an exclusive interview with *Go-Set* magazine about their past and future projects. Referring to *Sing A Rude Song*, Maurice revealed, "I ended up doing a musical with Barbara Windsor, which was the worst part of my life." However, he declared, "It was a great experience for nine weeks but . . ."

"I got a lot of kicks out of going to see Maurice," Barry said, "and Robin had his single 'Saved By The Bell'. I had a lot of baths and waited. I produced other artists and did a lot of writing, which is in the can. I spent more time in reclusion than anything else, and I wrote and I wrote. There's two years of writing because I didn't do anything else."

For Maurice, the future held the promises of delving more heavily into production. "I've always wanted to produce my wife, Lulu, on record and I'm doing that now," he revealed. "I have a production company called Moby Productions and I'll have Tin Tin and Richard Harris and Lu. I'll basically stick to that. I'm more the technical side of it, I love doing tape recordings and things like that, I've got my own studios and I

★ Maurice was incorrect. Though Dylan concerts were a rarity at this time, it was possible to see him in America for less than $10 in 1974. Maurice may have been referring to the cost of a three-day ticket for the Isle of Wight Festival on which upwards of 20 'name' groups and performers were appearing. John Lennon and Yoko Ono rarely performed concerts anyway. When they did it was usually for charity.

guess I just want to make good records. ['Toast And Marmalade For Tea'] was done two years ago. It must be the only record produced two years before it's a hit."

For Barry, Hollywood still beckoned. "I like acting," he said. "Whatever happens in the future, well I'll just wait and see but I want to do dramatic acting. We all want to . . ."

"To be or not to be!" Robin interrupted.

"We all want to in a way, but I'm a fanatic about it," Barry continued, ignoring the outburst.

Robin revealed a far more intriguing plan for the future. "I want to put the World Domination League on the map," he disclosed. "So far we've only one member . . . perhaps I'll be doing some dominating this afternoon. It's not very popular, but I'm sure after a few years I'll get it together. There's a lot of dominating to do, but until then I still want to act . . . but that doesn't stop me behind the scenes promoting the World Domination."

What more could be said?

★ ★ ★

The group's concert at Melbourne's Festival Hall on July 15 was the main focus of an ABC-TV spectacular. The producer of the show, Bruce Wilson, had accompanied them on the tour to familiarise himself with the group. "The audience was terrifically responsive," he recalled. "Following The Bee Gees on their Australian tour, I got to know their show so well that I knew where to point the camera. The result is that we have captured on-stage jokes and conversation."

For native Australian Geoff Bridgeford, the tour was a chance to catch up with his family. While he was glad to be back, he said he planned to stay in Britain. "I think London is the best place in the world to live, after Melbourne," he added diplomatically. "And London is the entertainment centre of the world for me, anyway. The challenge there for entertainers is what I imagine Hollywood would be for film stars.

"The public have come round in the cycle, The Bee Gees have never wavered . . . I was a big fan long before I was in the group. I had played with them before in Australia, and I always wanted to be in the group with good songs and good lyrics. No one can touch them, and I also dug their dedication. I don't think the group has changed – the music is more important than the line-up."

After the excitement of filming the television special, the Perth concert on July 17 should have proved anti-climactic. Instead, a riot broke out in the audience when, during the third last number, some young girls attempted to scramble up on to the stage. A roadie snatched one girl back and roughly threw her from the stage, injuring her as she landed on her back. The crowd raged but seemed to calm down as Maurice told them to shut up.

For Robin with his ill-fated New Zealand début, things began to take on a serious flavour of déjà vu. When the group returned for an encore, so did the angry mob. One young man leapt to the stage and began smashing the group's equipment. More joined in the destruction, followed by the police. One officer was dragged from the stage but helped back up. As the first young man was arrested and led off in handcuffs, the crowd went berserk with angry cries of "Kill the pigs!" ringing out.

The Bee Gees shunned the after show press conference. It was an unfortunate end to what began as a triumphant homecoming.

★　★　★

According to Maurice, after the Australian tour was completed, "We have about three week's holiday, which isn't really three weeks because we'll be doing other things as well, and then we do a three-month tour of America which is about 38 cities and that should just about kill us."

"We're looking forward to visiting the places we didn't before, Oklahoma, Texas, Nashville," Barry added. "We want to go south where we haven't been before to hear the music down there."

The tour, with Tin Tin as the supporting act, began on August 28 and took them to 22 cities, playing 30 concerts and a guest appearance on the *Tonight Show* with Johnny Carson, in only 36 days. The tour concentrated this time on the eastern half of the United States, finishing up in the Midwest at Keil Auditorium in St Louis, Missouri.

Robin joked that the punishing schedule of the tour would be "very brain draining, and our mental output and physical output will equal four nervous breakdowns. But we'll have days off – we get back in time to see the Rolf Harris show at Christmas!"

It seemed less of a joke, as Barry told the story in 1979. "Robin was still doing speed, still on the way down," he recalled. "We arrived in Greensboro, North Carolina one night. The next morning, I walked past Robin's room and the door was slightly open. My father was standing in the middle of the room, and Robin was lying out on the middle of the bed. He'd collapsed. The stress of overwork combined with the pills was too much for him."

That evening's concert was cancelled. Barry continued, "Robin spent a few days in the hospital, taking it easy . . . Five or six days later, he appeared on stage with us again. He was a very weak person, and he could hardly sing a note. But the fact was that he was on stage! Molly flew over from England when she heard all about it, and she was with him on tour from then onwards. He started putting on weight slowly, and he's mellowed out over the years, and now he's fine. He became a normal human being again."

Barry had a hospital visit of his own on the tour, when a dive into the hotel swimming pool resulted in a broken nose. Tom Kennedy recalled that he appeared on stage with his nose taped but didn't miss a show.

Barry had been scheduled to play the part of a murderer in his friend Peter Wyngarde's series, *The World Of Jason King*, but his actor's equity card ran out just as he was about to start filming and couldn't be renewed in time.

It was frustrating after cherishing the idea of an acting career for so long. "I had the script at home and everything. I needed a scooter for the part and had arranged to have my own brought from England. It was a big disappointment, but there might be a next time."

The tour came to a close and The Bee Gees returned to Britain and a well-deserved break in October. "It was the longest tour we've done," Maurice said. "We did 37 shows and, initially, it was going to be a longer tour, but we cut it down to five weeks. By that time, we all had funny nervous things happening to us anyway. Never again! It was exhausting, very trying and I had a nervous collapse. It was hard to do and not worth it when you get to the stage where you break down. So the most we'll do for a tour is two weeks now."

"There's still a demand for open-air concerts [in the United States]," Barry explained, "and we did a couple of those as well as concert halls and universities. But people go out there to see big [American] football matches, and they want somewhere like the open-air concerts to go to."

Returning to one of his favourite themes, Maurice added, "If we had another hit we would probably do another tour of England but at the moment it's not really worth the audience coming to see us, because they would be living on memories of each song, and they'd be coming to see what we did. I'm sure we would draw an audience though."

Since 'How Can You Mend A Broken Heart' topped the American charts, it obviously pleased people far beyond the small group of dedicated Bee Gees fans in America. However, the single bombed in Britain where, unlike 'Lonely Days' which had at least made number 33, it completely failed to chart.

Its lack of success still niggled, but Barry tried to look on the bright side. "Everything is going just as before – we've only had two singles out since we last made the charts," he pointed out. "We were never conscious of what we were going to record until we got to the studio. All the songs were written there, while we thought about the arrangements at the same time."

Even though the British public remained cool, their success in other countries was undiminished. In Germany *Bravo* magazine awarded them yet another Golden Otto award, while "In the US, we're regarded as a heavy band," Barry asserted. "Soft rock. We've had a Grammy nomination [in the category of "Best Vocal Performance by a duo, group or chorus"] for 'How Can You Mend A Broken Heart' along with George Harrison's 'My Sweet Lord' – the only two British bands nominated. What we do it isn't just a product; some companies forget that. Underground people think commerciality means where we're only in it for the money; they hate capitalism. But this is not true of us and it's a very pretentious attitude, anyway. We've struggled for so long that we just enjoy people appreciating us. There are other sides to the profession though, like Jonathan King. He has his finger in a lot of pies and it just brings you down to talk about it.

"Of course, there are the number ones in other countries – like the two gold singles for 'Lonely Days' and 'How Can You Mend A Broken Heart' in the States. And there are number one records which have been taken off our albums and released in places like Israel without us even knowing."

In fact, 1971 had seen the single release of 'When The Swallows Fly', from their 1968 *Idea* album, reach number 18 on the charts in Holland. Additionally, 'Melody Fair' and 'In The Morning', both plundered from the *Melody* soundtrack, were successful singles in Japan.

Following the group's July tour of Australia, in spite of Maurice's then hopes for an extended holiday, The Bee Gees made a whistle-stop tour of Israel, performing a few shows. In a cute piece of marketing, Polydor had placed 'How Can You Mend A Broken Heart' on the B-side of its single release there, promoting another track from the forthcoming album to the plug-side. 'Israel' became the A-side in its namesake country but unfortunately, failed to make any impact in the local chart.

However, when released in January of the following year in Belgium and Holland, backed with 'Dearest', it made a creditable showing as a single, reaching number 22 in the Dutch Top 30.

After the quick work of *2 Years On*, the reunited Brothers Gibb had worked on the follow-up that became *Trafalgar*, which was recorded between January and April 1971, interrupted only by their American jaunt. Although available in the USA in September, to coincide with their autumn tour there, its release in the British Isles was delayed until November, perhaps with the Christmas market in mind.

They have admitted that it took time for them to learn to work together again. While Maurice is clearly playing instruments on all songs, Robin had decided to concentrate entirely on his vocal contributions. On the writing side, only one song is credited to all three brothers; the vocals on each number seem to be done almost solely by the writer or writers, thereby effectively leaving Robin out of half the album.

Trafalgar now officially marked the inclusion of Geoff Bridgeford as the fourth member of The Bee Gees, although his name was misspelled "Joeff" on the sleeve of the American release. The album also noted the first appearance of Alan Kendall on lead guitar, credited by name although he really has little to do on this particular album. Alan had been in the RSO band Toe Fat (who toured the US as the support act for Eric Clapton's new band, Derek & The Dominoes), until they disbanded at the end of 1970, and he was transferred to The Bee Gees sometime early in 1971. This would be the first of many appearances by Alan Kendall, and in recent years, Maurice has taken to introducing him at concerts as "the man who's been with us longer than we have."

"I had obviously been aware of their music," Alan said. "I enjoy melody and they are possibly the most melodic of all writers, so it's a perfect match. In fact, working with them for so long has given me a real curiosity about music theory and composition."

The sound is distinctly their own, but as Geoff Bridgeford pointed out,

"We could record any song and it would sound [like The] Bee Gees, but they've been doing rock'n'roll type of things all the times anyway. It's just a tag someone put on music in the Fifties."

The sound on this album, recorded once again at IBC, was a great leap forward in clarity over previous recordings. It was probably chosen for a special gold CD reissue because it sounded so good – that, and because it contains a best-selling US single. The well thought out arrangements should probably be credited to Maurice as much as to Bill Shepherd (who definitely scored the orchestral parts), and all three brothers are in fine voice.

But in 1971 The Bee Gees were being marginalised as artists, especially in the United States where more performance-oriented artists were winning critical attention. It may seem odd that the Gibb brothers were not classed as singer-songwriters, but their focus on recordings and supporting musicians, and having pop standards as part of their inspiration instead of mainly rock and folk, set them apart from a movement of which they should have been part. This manifested itself in the fact that while their singles sold well, the merits of their albums tended to be ignored. Some of the blame could be attached to a song like 'How Can You Mend A Broken Heart' which did little to suggest the livelier music to be found in the album.

Written the same day as 'Lonely Days', 'How Can You Mend A Broken Heart' has often been mentioned when the brothers discuss their method of songwriting. "We might imitate somebody in our own privacy like you sit around and imitate a certain group," Barry explained. "Later on, the group will pick up on the song and say that suits us. When we were writing 'How Can You Mend A Broken Heart', we thought of Andy Williams. So we did it in that feel and he cut it." Soul singer Al Green subsequently recorded a delicately expressive version of the song that became a highlight of his emotive concert performances.

The B-side was a lively Maurice song, perhaps assisted by Billy Lawrie, which did not appear on the album. 'Country Woman' seems to have been cooked up separately from his brothers with Bridgeford and Shepherd on hand to complete it.

The album's cover is Pocock's painting *The Battle Of Trafalgar*, and its gatefold sleeve opens to reveal the group's enactment of the famous 'Death Of Nelson' scene, with Barry taking the starring role, comforted by a newly bearded Robin. As Geoff Bridgeford rather incongruously reads *The Beezer* comic, Maurice and Hugh Gibb gaze down on the dying Barry. Hugh's part in the picture was unplanned, according to Tom Kennedy. "He was just there at the time," he recalled. "[The photo shoot] was actually done on a barge on the Thames. The photographer needed someone and thought Hugh will do."

Maurice recalled that there was "a great deal of giggling about Nelson's purported last words and who was kissing who", during that photo shoot, and revealed that the album's cover might lead to some confusion about the songs' actual subject matter. " 'Trafalgar' is a song about a very lonely guy who lives in London and spends a lot of his time feeding the pigeons in Trafalgar Square. In fact, a lot of people are going to think that the album has a general historical theme running through it because, apart from 'Trafalgar', there are other titles like 'Walking Back To Waterloo'. I'm afraid that it's slightly misleading because none of them have any bearing on history at all.

"What I will say though is that this is our best ever album. *2 Years On*, which we made just after we got back together again, was just an experiment to find out whether all of the tensions which had caused the original break-up had gone, so we were all a bit wary about giving our best on that album. Gradually, throughout the session, the tensions and hang-ups disappeared and, as a result, the whole scene's back together again as it should be."

"*2 Years On* was a hesitant album," Barry agreed. "We were just getting used to each other again . . . Our new LP *Trafalgar* was made up virtually as we went along and we've got a whole lot of good songs on it. Some of them are fairly old like 'How Can You Mend A Broken Heart', but the actual album wasn't finished until two or three months ago. It doesn't really matter when the material was written – The Beatles are releasing stuff they wrote at school."

★   ★   ★

January 1972 saw the release of the latest Bee Gees single. "It's called 'My World'," Barry said, "and it's not from the album." The song, written backstage at ITV's *The Golden Shot*, followed along some of the same musical ideas as 'How Can You Mend A Broken Heart', with the same arrangement of Barry's guitar, Maurice's piano and bass, Geoff Bridgeford on drums, and Bill Shepherd's string section. The Tin Pan Alley-style verse lyrics sound almost meaningful compared to the invariant chorus of "My world is your world and your world is my world" and so on. Undeniably catchy, the song had little foundation and seemed like a holding action.

"Whether something is a soft ballad or an up-tempo thing, we would record it if we thought it was going to make a good single," Maurice said.

"When you've been writing for so long, you know you've improved, and after years most artists get better, they don't get worse," Barry reasoned. "If they do, it's something that happens to the person inside, not musically. People said Cat Stevens was deteriorating, and he came back and showed them.

"[Our older songs are] not as good as the stuff we do now," Robin added. "Even last year's recordings aren't as good as this year's."

The B-side of the single was a contrasting Maurice "solo" number, 'On Time'. A tune from the time which he described as his "Swamp period", it was a choppy electric guitar number with Maurice playing lead guitar among other things.

'My World' was a minor hit in the United States, but although it reached number 16 on the other side of the Atlantic, the British public appeared indifferent to the group. Well, if the British public wanted to ignore The Bee Gees, The Bee Gees could very well ignore the British public. Their plans for the New Year called for the group to tour Japan, the United States and Australia (where 'My World' had been a top four record) and play selected dates elsewhere.

On their arrival down under, Maurice announced, "Basically we're here because of great demand. Everyone looks forward to coming here but not the journey. We said, 'Oh great, we're going back to Australia,' then, oh that flight! It's a letdown in a way, but once you've done it you know what to expect. The first time we were out of our heads, we wanted to kill each other! We'd seen each other for twenty hours, but I'm sure when Concorde gets in, it'll be about the same flying time as from London to New York."

He revealed that Lulu wasn't travelling with the group. "She's rehearsing for a musical in England called *Vanity Fair*. It's about to start in March. She plays Becky Sharp and it's a demanding role so she's pretty busy. Mind you, I wouldn't like to take her on a trip to Australia because it's such a trip. Especially for a girl, it'd just knock her out," he added with artless chauvinism.

For the Australian leg of the tour, The Bee Gees were travelling light, having reduced the size of the orchestra to 16 musicians. "Expenses are so high coming to Australia," Barry explained. "We carry four roadies, a lighting man, a musical director and so on. The air fares alone are huge. We can make more by whipping over to Germany for a gig, but we wanted to come to Australia again because the demand has been great and it's another chance to promote our records."

Once again, the Australian tour passed by lightning fast, with seven concerts in eight days. Geoff Bridgeford remembered that, "It was a buzz to come back to a sell-out tour."

Barry revealed that, after the Australian tour, "we go back for a week and then we go to Holland for the Special European Gala which The Beach Boys are doing and The Carpenters, Johnny Cash, there are a lot of people flying in. Then we have another week off, then we do a Japanese tour, which should be fun."

And for all those *Go-Set* readers breathlessly waiting for news of the World Domination League, Robin divulged, "Since I spoke about it last, [it] has blossomed into a very prosperous organisation. We have dominated about 50 new members since, we hope to dominate another 100 people in 1972. It's going to be a big year for us, 1972. [As for future plans], this is something I have to speak with the directors about."

He refused to disclose the identities of the directors as "they're all silent!" but he promised that he would "be doing a bit of dominating while I'm here."

On March 19, 1972, The Bee Gees played their first ever concert in Hong Kong, arriving at the airport to mob scenes reminiscent of their early

German tours, as police tried to hold back their ardent teenage fans.

The concert drew even more enthusiastic response. "After more than six months of negotiations, The Bee Gees, the darlings of the pop fans, came, saw and conquered a 16,000 strong audience of screaming fans," the Hong Kong *Star* reported after the show at the Government Football Stadium in Sokonpo. The *Standard* raved, "Memories of those hazy crazy days of the Sixties and Beatlemania were revived last night when The Bee Gees, by sheer professional talent, captivated and won the 16,000 fans (the largest ever to attend a pop concert in Hong Kong) at the Government Stadium."

Geoff Bridgeford's term with the band was drawing to a close. "My last concert [with The Bee Gees] was at the Pallazzo de Sports in Rome," he recalled. "It was a wild concert – almost a riot with chairs being thrown about."

Geoff admitted that being with The Bee Gees had been everything he wanted in the beginning. "They were successful, having two huge records in the States. I was staying at the best places like the Waldorf Astoria and getting well paid. But looking back, I can see it was unsettling, but an important time for both myself and the brothers. We were young, successful, famous, wealthy and fully involved in the early Seventies music business of sex, drugs and rock'n'roll. The brothers were still getting used to being back together after the break-up and at the same time achieving greater success than they had before.

"And with that came more, new and different business and personal concerns that subtly affected the situation. I had been going through some problems with my marriage, and there was an extreme amount of substance abuse which was taking its toll on everyone in its own way," he added. "As you do in life, I simply found it was time to move on, time to make a change."

Mindful of the problems that personnel changes had caused in the past, Robert Stigwood tried desperately to persuade Geoff to change his mind. "I left just before the tour of . . . Japan with the brothers," Geoff said. "That's when Robert Stigwood called me in to try and convince me to stay because they had the tour all planned . . . While I was with The Bee Gees, I was on a weekly retainer and a substantially larger wage when on tour. I was never included in The Bee Gees royalty situation, but when I was leaving the band Robert did get together with me to offer a royalty deal at the time."

Geoff now looks back fondly on his time with the group. "The Bee Gees are one of the most popular bands of our time, and back then in 1970, '71, '72 it was a great experience to be a part of it. There were some magical moments in the studio and performing live. It was a high creative transitional period for The Bee Gees and myself and some great songs came out of that time."

When The Bee Gees' tour of Japan began in Tokyo on March 23, 1972, Chris Karon had replaced Bridgeford on drums. After four successful concerts, the entourage moved on to Kuala Lumpur for two shows and then a further two gigs in Singapore. These latter two performances were under threat of cancellation due to a strict government's policy on men's hair styles.

"It was against the law to have long hair," Tom Kennedy explained, "so, to play there, we had to have permission from the authorities . . . We *did* have to carry passports with our photographs wearing long hair."

Dick Ashby confirms that the government conceded ground by granting special 48 hour passes which allowed the group just enough time to fulfil their commitments and leave.

Ask anyone in The Bee Gees entourage what show sticks out most in their minds, and you're likely to get the same answer: April 2, 1972 in Jakarta, the show which concluded their Far East tour. Although everyone's recollections vary, with attendance estimated at anywhere between 15,000 by Hugh Gibb's reckoning to 80,000 by Tom Kennedy's and nearly every figure in between, everyone agrees on one thing – it was a most memorable concert.

Dick Ashby recalled, "The weirdest [concert] of all was Jakarta in Indonesia. We did a tour of Australia and one promoter in London who bought the whole tour asked if we'd like to do a few gigs in the Far East on the way home. I thought it would break up the flight so I called them and they seemed quite excited about visiting Indonesia, Hong Kong and all these places. The only particular details I had about this was that it was under cover and had 10,000 seats, so we set the fee accordingly.

"I got in a taxi with the road manager to go and look at the venue before the band came down to get the stage and everything together, and the taxi driver takes us to a most enormous place . . . So I said, 'Oh no, this can't be right,' but sure enough, there was a stage there, and it turned out that somehow the venue had been switched on us, and there was a Seneghan *inside* stadium and a Seneghan *outside* stadium, and it appeared that we were playing in the latter."

"We were supposed to play 10,000 seats indoors and we arrived at this Wembley sized stadium outdoors," Tom Kennedy added. "I actually did ask the promoter if they should have a roof on it, and he said, 'I'm a Catholic and I've prayed for eight days – it's not going to rain!' "

Apparently, it was a task requiring more than eight days of prayer. "We got everything out of the cases and laid the cables out, and the heavens opened," Tom said, "and we just abandoned the idea."

"Obviously, there was a lot of tension going on through the day with me trying to get the fee up," Dick Ashby continued, "and equipment and staging is very difficult out there, so we had a very hard day at the gig. Then about an hour before the show was due to start there was a torrential downpour of rain so all the equipment had to be bunged under the stage . . . total disaster.

"By this time all the people were coming in, including the Prime Minister of Indonesia, who was in the royal box. I worked it out in the end that the

315

final call was 38,000 people in the stadium. Anyway, [Tom Kennedy] came to me and said, 'Look, I'm scared of the group going on – it's wet. A guitar's only got to touch something and someone will get electrocuted.' So I went back to the hotel with this in mind and said we're not going on. The promoter's wife burst into tears saying, 'You must go on, the Royal family is there . . .'

"So in the end the promoter says to me, 'Right, well if the support group goes on and they don't get killed, will you go on?' What could I say to that?"

"The thing was actually said, 'If the support band go on and they don't die, will you go on?' " Tom said incredulously, "and that's what happened."

"All our people told us we would be electrocuted," confirmed Maurice. "The system was really bad, so we were a bit worried about that. We thought we might do an acoustic set, but no, they didn't want that. Eventually . . . it calmed down, and we did go on, but it was crazy. That was the wildest place I think I've ever worked."

As Robin put it, "We were doing this show, and Sukarno★ was there and there were about 60,000 people. And . . . just before we went on, a monsoon hit . . . dreadful . . . and the makeshift stage, of course because they didn't have permanent stages at that particular time, completely got washed out. There was . . . at least 3 feet of water up to . . . or past the amplifiers. And the audience got pretty angry, and Sukarno ordered that soldiers should go in front of the stage to stop the audience attacking us . . .

"We said we wouldn't go on you see because we didn't want to get electrocuted. So the promoter came backstage – well, backstage, he came into this *shed* where we were. And he said to us, 'Listen,' he said, 'we know it's pretty bad, the water and everything on stage and you could get electrocuted, but there's 60,000 people out there and it could be worse if you don't go on. However,' he said, 'I do have a remedy,' and we said, 'What's that?' And he said, 'We have this little supporting act that have come up from Bali. If they go on first and they live, will you go on?' "

"I think the reason we went on was because the promoter sent his wife round to see Hughie. I believed it at the time, and it probably was true," Tom Kennedy insisted. "The promoter and his wife were Australian, and they persuaded them, against everyone's best judgement, to go on."

The support group went on and lived, impressing Dick Ashby with the bravado of their performance. "I can't remember the [band's] name now, but Mick Jagger had nothing on this cat. He was throwing the microphone stand up in the air, and they were rubbing guitars against the mike stands and all sorts of things, and they didn't get blown up, so we agreed to go on."

At various times the brothers have changed the story so that the soldiers were facing The Bee Gees with machine guns to keep them from leaving

★ It must have been Suharto – Sukarno died in 1970, and at any rate, was under house arrest from 1966 until his death. The names are similar so it would be an easy mistake to make.

the stage, but Tom Kennedy refutes this. There were guns, he said, but for crowd control rather than Bee Gees' control. Concerts in Indonesia were always an event, as he recalled. "We had a four star general driving us around – they always took you around in a car to show the people you were there because in the past, the promoters had advertised Tom Jones, and there's a little speck on the stage pretending to be Tom Jones, some local lad who got lynched when the crowd figured out what was going on. Meanwhile, the promoter was on his way to the airport with his ill-gotten gains," he laughed.

The Bee Gees finally took the stage. "By this time the concert was running hours late," Dick Ashby recounted, "and half the orchestra we'd rehearsed with in the afternoon had gone home, as they thought the concert wasn't going on. Even some of The Bee Gees' band, who shall remain nameless, didn't think they were going on either, so they got pissed because they were fed up with the whole thing anyway. I think when the concert went out we had three live mikes on, and though I didn't let the orchestra leader know, nobody could hear what was going on. Every time that Maurice moved from his stand-up mike where he was playing bass, to play the piano, someone had to go on stage and take his vocal mike across to him and put it on the piano. It was an amazingly good sound and it was quite a good show. We just did one show and got out the next day."

Tom Kennedy disagreed with Dick's memories of good sound quality. "They weren't allowed to touch the microphone – we had *one* live mike . . . The fact is, we went on, and there were 80,000 people all screaming and shouting. You couldn't hear anything, anyway. They were there in the spotlight, and that was all that mattered."

It was a show reminiscent of the early days of Beatlemania, he recalled. The performance was immaterial to the event; the crowd wanted The Bee Gees, and the fact that *they* were there was all important.

★   ★   ★

In early 1972, tragedy struck when Molly Gibb's young brother, David Hullis, was killed in a fire on board a ship returning to London from South America. Robin flew back from LA to be with Molly for the funeral.

The group had begun recording sessions for their new album, as usual doing most, but this time not all, of their composing on the spot. Maurice provided some details. "We recorded for, like, two weeks and I got a bit of sunshine, thank God. [We] recorded from eight o'clock in the evening onwards . . . . and recorded eight tracks that have really turned out nice. It's called *To Whom It May Concern* . . . which means if anyone wants to buy it, they can buy it. It's a multitude of tracks which have been cut during the years of breaking up and getting together, and rewriting songs that we wrote years ago. I mean . . . they're all new tracks really, as far as the public is concerned but to us they've been written quite a while ago. I mean, there's about seven tracks on the whole LP which are new. We did them hoping that people will say, 'Oh yes, they're back together again.' We are definitely together and I doubt very much we will separate again."

The group met up again in London's IBC Studios in April to finish off the recordings, which marked the end of an era in The Bee Gees' recording career: the last sessions with Bill Shepherd, the last album produced by Robert Stigwood and the last album in which Geoff was involved.

The gatefold sleeve of the album opened to reveal pop-up figures of the three brothers, with a backdrop of many of the people with whom they had worked through the years depicted as members of the orchestra. The LP package gives "special thanks to those pictured on the inside liner for their contributions over the years". Unfortunately, the identities of those featured was never revealed, leaving many a frustrated purchaser, unable to work out who was who . . . until now. Although a good few of the original buyers will now have replaced their vinyl copy with the compact disc, for those still in possession of the original album, here are the names that fit the faces on the inner of the gatefold. Going from left to right in the back row are Chris Cooke (Maurice & Lulu's Assistant), John Davidson (RSO head of publishing), Ahmet Ertegun (head of Atlantic Records), Peter Brown (director of RSO in New York), Beryl Vertue (Frankie Howerd's manager), Frankie Howerd, Robert Stigwood and Rik & John Gunnell (RSO – USA). In the front row are Lynda Gibb, Lulu, Molly Gibb, Ruby Bard (RSO booking agent), Mike Housego (RSO press officer), Tom Kennedy, Ray Washbourne (Robin's personal assistant), David Shaw (Stigwood's partner) and John Taylor (RSO office manager). Lurking behind the speakers and mixer is Dick Ashby himself, while the man behind the speaker stack in the bottom right of the sleeve is Ray Cane (RSO). The conductor, naturally, is Bill Shepherd, new boy Chris Karon is on drums, and the guitarist, who has been with the group longer than they have, is none other than Alan Kendall. Hugh Gibb completes the picture, literally, as he is manning the movie camera and lights.

The back cover of the LP (and of the CD booklet) has a 1963 Bee Gees photo and insets of Barry, Robin and Maurice from 1972. The "album idea" is credited to their longtime personal manager, Dick Ashby.

Alan Kendall stayed on but again was needed on only a few songs, as Maurice played much of the additional guitar as well as unusual items like mandolin and harpsichord and even a then avant-garde Moog synthesizer on one song. Geoff Bridgeford played on 'We Lost the Road' "as a result of that song being carried forward from the *Trafalgar* sessions," he explained, and on 'Paper Mache, Cabbages And Kings', 'You Know It's For You', and 'Alive' (although when the album was released on CD, the booklet missed out the asterisk credit for the last three), which dated from around October, 1971. Session drummer Clem Cattini played on the other songs but did not tour with the group; Chris Karon did, and is the drummer shown in the inner sleeve, though much to Clattini's chagrin. "On the album, it's got a photograph of Chris Karon which is ridiculous really," he bemoaned, "because it wasn't Chris playing on the album, it was me!"

Although he would cease working with the band the following year, even today, Clem remains one of their greatest admirers. "As far as I'm concerned," he states emphatically, "I think they have an unbelievable talent – I'd give anything just to have written one of the songs that they've written, especially the latter stuff."

Musically, *To Whom It May Concern* is a much more diverse offering than *Trafalgar*. Bill's arrangements are relatively toned down, and the backing vocals sometimes seem to take the place of what could have been string sections. In fact, the ratio of musical parts played and sung by the Gibb brothers personally is at an all-time high here, aside from the more simply arranged recordings of 1966. Many of these songs, like 'Paper Maché, Cabbages And Kings', do not appear in any way to be calculated for commercial motives; this is purely The Bee Gees being The Bee Gees and doing much of it themselves.

For these reasons, many fans find the album very personal and appealing, while others are put off by the somewhat less polished and definitely less consistent sound. The great importance of the album sessions is that the brothers were finally really working together again. The fine backing vocals echo the close personal harmony that Barry, Robin and Maurice had rediscovered.

'Run To Me' was the first single, released three months before the album. The B-side was the sort of up-tempo throwaway song usually associated with Maurice but 'Road To Alaska' is a group number, with Robin singing what sounds like Robin's lyrics, and Alan Kendall's lead guitar duetting along with Maurice's bass in the break.

Like *Trafalgar*, the album opens with the obvious: the single, although inexplicably, the early British pressings lacked 'Run To Me' and had a sticker stating "Track One Side One is omitted from this album".

The final track is one of the most unusual selections ever to appear on a Bee Gees album. Titled 'Sweet Song Of Summer', one reviewer unkindly described it as "abuse of a Moog synthesizer".

Maurice commented more than a year later, "We used the moog synthesizer once, and most groups really can't afford to get such an instrument in to do a whole album with, because it's such an expensive instrument to rent or buy or get made up or whatever," while that same year, Robin dismissed "electronic music" as a "very limited field because people today haven't really got the access to the equipment that people are using to record in the electronic field." In hindsight the song is of course an early outlying entry in what would be a long list of Bee Gees songs with synthesizer; the instrument had to undergo technical improvement for a few years more before becoming practical for regular work.

There's nothing subtle about the synthesizer part on 'Sweet Song Of Summer' but Maurice keeps it musical, and it is somewhat reminiscent of a Seventies style guitar solo in the way it varies from the melody and bursts into odd sounds here and there. Closing songs on albums often look forward, and the idea here probably was that they were about to move forward to new things, having said goodbye with this album.

★　★　★

The Bee Gees' American tour, in which they performed with a 40-piece orchestra, came to a close, and the brothers began work on their next project at the Record Plant in Los Angeles. "It's been a pretty hectic '72 for us," Barry said. "We've been working on a new album due out next spring called *Life In A Tin Can*. We've been experimenting with lots of new sounds; we've tried an entirely different approach. The best thing we've ever done, we think, and everyone who has heard it agrees."

According to Robin, the timing of this was crucial as he had planned to be back in Britain by October to be with Molly for the birth of their first child. "Everything had been arranged months in advance so that I could be near when the baby was born," he recalled. The baby had other ideas, though. "I went off to America, and the next thing I knew there was a call to say I was a dad."

Their son arrived on September 21, 1972, nearly four weeks early, weighing four pounds and two ounces, and was given the name Spencer (in honour of Robin's hero Winston Churchill) with the middle name David as a tribute to Molly's late brother.

Tom Kennedy recalled that the band and crew were staying in a rented house in Los Angeles while recording. After a late session, he returned to the house with the others. "Robin was at home and when we came in, he was asleep on the floor," Tom said. "He'd been waiting up just to tell us about Spencer. He woke up and he was really excited."

The proud new father rushed home to meet his son. "Molly and I have been longing for a baby," he said. "I feel as though I'm living on cloud nine."

Robin returned to the States where The Bee Gees performed in the "Woodstock Of The West" festival organised by a Los Angeles radio station. Other participants included The Eagles, Stevie Wonder, Mott The Hoople and Sly & The Family Stone.

Early in the year, the *New Musical Express* announced that The Bee Gees were said to be set to star in an American TV series, a Western spoof based on the film *Zachariah*. The theme song was to be a Gibb composition, but the series itself was not intended to be a musical.

Later it was revealed that the brothers were scheduled to fly to Yugoslavia to begin work on a horror movie called *Castle*. "As well as acting, we'll be writing the music for the film," Barry said. "We finish the movie by the end of the year, then we start planning our US trip."

Neither of these potential cinematic masterpieces would ever see the cameras roll.

★　★　★

Early in 1971, Barry and Lynda had moved to a new home in Gerard's Cross, Buckinghamshire, near the home where Hugh and Barbara Gibb were living with young Andy and Beri. They were pleased with the new proximity, although the touring schedule of The Bee Gees meant that they were away for much of the year, but in November of 1971, the Gibb parents decided to take the two youngest members of the family to live on the Spanish island of Ibiza.

Although bright, Andy was an indifferent student at best and said that he felt singled out in school when he was in England because of his famous brothers. "I have never had a good day at school ever in my life," he said. "I mean there were kids there that I would do anything to get on normally with . . . If I would do something outstanding in the game or sport, it was, 'You think you're great, don't you?' 'Because you're The Bee Gees brother, you think you can do that fabulously.' To have that for quite a few years thrown at you, I mean, it just got to me so bad in the end, I just couldn't handle it anymore. I had to leave it. Everyone said that most people in that position would say, 'God, my brothers are responsible for all this, damn them' . . . but not for one second did I ever think that. I always decided to take everything myself and not consider it as their fault. Naturally, I was always going to be related to them in any conversation or anything, so that has never bugged me really."

His brothers weren't the only famous faces in the family. Following the holiday commercial featuring both Barbara and Hugh, Hugh could be seen on television advertising for Clarksons.

Unable to fit in with his peers at school, Andy became involved with a rougher crowd and acquired a less than desirable circle of new friends. "I was moving about with my own gang, the skinheads, wearing steel-toed army boots and kicking in shop windows," he admitted. "With the skinheads, the main thing was football matches. You take a hammer into the stadium and throw it as high as you can into a capacity crowd of 30,000. And wherever it lands, it lands. We were really very nasty."

It's tempting to blame Andy's new mates, and they may have played a small part in his parents' decision to relocate, but the Gibb family had never stayed in one place long enough to put down roots.

"As far back as I can remember, we always moved," Andy said. "We never even stayed in a house more than eight or nine months. We never lasted a year at any one house, I don't know what it was, we would have to get up and move somewhere else . . . I didn't have permanent friends in many places for long. All my friends were older than me, I never had friends my own age. I left school at 13, so I've always been surrounded by people in the business."

Because they were a British family living in Spain, it was easier to persuade the authorities to turn a blind eye, and the move to Ibiza basically spelled the end to Andy's formal education. "I never got round to going back to school because I knew I wanted to be a singer," he said in 1977.

"My brothers left school when they were thirteen, and they were doing all right. Everybody said that I would regret leaving school but I haven't so far and I don't think I ever will now."

Hugh Gibb said that, "Andy was later starting [in the music business]. Andy is the oddball of the brothers; he is a real sports freak. He tackles everything and, once he masters it, he starts on something else. First it was show jumping in England – he was the youngest member of the team, only 11. He had two horses. Then we go to Spain and he got interested in scuba diving, still a kid, you know, about 12."

Shortly after arriving, Andy met a young man named Tony Messina, manager of a local night spot called Debbie's Bar. "He had a bar on the island at the time," Andy recalled. "He invited me down to the bar for St Patrick's Day. The bar had a big cavern cut into the rock underneath. It was cool in summer, warm in winter. The party was down there, and I sang for the patrons. It was a big crowd.

"Tony passed the word to other friends with clubs. One club handled package tours from Sweden, Germany, Denmark and such. They'd come in once a week, stay a week, and the next week a new party would arrive. They like entertainers to meet them and I started to sing to them as they arrived – a little acoustic guitar, a couple of songs. I did that for a couple of years and played piano bars."

One of the tourists whom he serenaded caught his eye. "There's something about those Swedish girls," he laughed. "I was 13, and there was this Swedish girl who was sixteen. I was head over heels in love, but she seemed like an adult. I wrote this song. I told Barry about it one night when just the two of us were together. He asked me to play it for him, but I said, 'No, no, not for you of all people. You've written good songs – you know what good songs are.' He insisted and when I finished, he said that he was amazed, that I'd proven to him that I could write. Then he told me the important thing was to keep writing."

Andy took his brother's advice to heart. "I was writing material," he said, "but not particularly from an artist's standpoint because the customers in the club were on vacation and they wanted to hear Spanish love songs or songs they knew from the radio."

He was rarely without a gig in those days. "I know I was only 13, but I handled it well," he said. "I was playing the hits of the day for the tourists, and there was never any trouble getting work because I wasn't being paid then. I started to take more of an interest in music, and my brothers began to take notice of it and we started to get together more musically."

Later on, Andy said, "My brothers, Barry, Robin and Maurice, would come down to the club and get up and sing with me. We'd have a four part harmony going that sounded absolutely amazing, although we hadn't had a chance to do it in front of a large audience."

Andy was underage so rather than being paid for his club work, he was given free beer. Ibiza's beaches and holiday atmosphere provided ample entertainment for a youngster barely into his teens, and his indulgent parents even allowed him to drive on the island. As Tom Kennedy put it, "Young Andy was leading the life of Riley."

Ibiza's sunny weather and sandy beaches attracted more of the Gibb family. Maurice and Lulu and Barry and Lynda bought holiday villas near to where their parents lived, and Barry and Lynda even planned to make it their home.

"Hughie and Barbara moved out there," Tom Kennedy explained, "and then Hughie came back – Barry was living at Gerard's Cross at the time – and invited Barry and Lynda along. I helped Hughie move and they said, 'Why don't you come along?' so off we went to Ibiza. We went back and rented a villa – Alan Kendall came out as well – so it was Barry and Lynda, Alan Kendall and myself. They quite liked it, and they decided they would move over there.

"So [Barry and Lynda] sold their house in Gerard's Cross and bought a house in Ibiza. It was off the beaten track. All their stuff was shipped over and when it arrived – under Spanish law, if you ship 100 pieces and 99 arrive, they impound it. I actually did go . . . and I got the stuff cleared, but by that point, Barry had decided he didn't like it because the power would go off, the TV was in Spanish . . .

"It looks like an idyllic lifestyle but everything is *mañana* . . . The lights have gone off – 'They'll be back on tomorrow' – or the water . . . It's one of those places where nothing is hurried."

Barry and Lynda returned to Britain without ever unpacking any of their furnishings. "Their belongings never actually left the airport," Tom said, "and I came home on the flight with their dogs." After their brief holiday abroad, the dogs, Barnaby, Kim and Snoopy, had to go into the required six months of quarantine on their return to Britain.

It was the worst part of the whole affair, having to visit the dogs in quarantine. According to Tom, "Lynda probably hated it even more [than Barry] because she's a softie for dogs. That's why their house is filled with dogs today – she's always been a softie for waifs and strays."

22

SAW A NEW MORNING

*L*IFE IN A TIN CAN was released January 19, 1973 in the United States and March 1 in the UK, officially launching Robert Stigwood's new RSO record label.

RSO, whose logo was a red cow, was what is known as a vanity label, since there was no manufacturing and distribution company behind it. Instead RSO's discs continued to be handled as they had been before, by Polydor in most of the world and Atlantic in the United States and Canada.

By the end of October 1972, The Bee Gees had recorded 20 tracks in Los Angeles, which had been sequenced into two albums by November 5. The second album was not released. Of the personnel they used, only Alan Kendall was kept on, and as usual he appeared on only a few songs. It was meant to be a change of pace to set them off in new directions. The credits for *Life In A Tin Can* list six top session players, most notably Jim Keltner on drums for all eight songs; for two songs each, Sneaky Pete Kleinow on steel guitar, Tommy Morgan on harmonica; and for one each, Jerome Richardson on flute, Rik Grech (formerly of the RSO act Blind Faith) on bass and violin, and Jane Getz on piano. The strings were arranged by Johnny Pate, and production is credited solely to "The Bee Gees".

Life In A Tin Can was issued only months after *To Whom It May Concern*, and it seemed odd that writers known for voluminous output had come up with only eight songs, four by Barry solo. Robin would be more prominent on the second of the albums, but Maurice has almost no lead vocals and begins here his gradual slump that lasted until about 1980.

Sometimes it is hard to figure why a single would not be a hit. 'Saw A New Morning' was the best Bee Gees lead-off A-side in years, musically inventive yet catchy enough to attract attention. The soft/loud dynamic card had been played before on 'Lonely Days' with great success, and 'Saw A New Morning' glides even more effortlessly between the extremes. Maybe the punch of the loud parts didn't come across in compressed radio sound, or maybe this wasn't what people expected from The Bee Gees.

Unfortunately, *Life In A Tin Can* also did not do well in the marketplace, selling especially poorly in the States where the hit singles since 1970 had been keeping modest album sales going. The new musical direction did not seem to be working commercially. It would have depended on album orientated radio, which was overtaking Top 40 by 1973, but The Bee Gees had never been popular in that format with their Seventies albums. It never moved above the lower portion of *Billboard* magazine's Top 100, but Maurice protested indifference, cheerfully adding, "Don't worry, we'll have a lot more flops!"

On February 19, The Bee Gees played their first British concert since 1968, a single performance with The London Symphony Orchestra at the Royal Festival Hall. Explaining the decision to make it a one-off performance before leaving for their North American tour, Barry said, "Basically it's down to finance. Most people in England have no conception at all of how expensive it is for a band to tour here. If the whole thing is going to be done properly there's hardly any way that the group can make money. By the time you've paid for the expenses, the promoter and the other 'in-betweeners', you're left with almost nothing . . .

"In the States the whole financial end of affairs is far more worthwhile. Your salary is higher because the cost of living is higher. They charge more for the kids to get into the concerts but then again the kids earn a lot more money – so it's fair. In England you have the situation where the kids are charged too much to get into the gig in the first place, and yet the group often seem to end up losing as well."

The Bee Gees had added a new drummer to their line-up. Dennis Bryon was born March 14, 1948 in Cardiff, Wales. His first group was Brother John & The Witnesses, but he enjoyed great success in Britain in the late Sixties as the drummer for Amen Corner, with four Top 10 hits in less than two years, including their 1969 number one, '(If Paradise Is) Half As Nice'. Dennis did a two-year non-playing stint as a truck driver following the break-up of Amen Corner, before a neighbour in his apartment building, Alan Kendall, suggested that he should audition for The Bee Gees. The Festival Hall concert with The London Symphony Orchestra was his first appearance with the group.

Colin Blunstone opened the show that night and remembered it as "a very interesting evening, and obviously, I think it was an important concert for them . . . They had a full orchestra and . . . from a personal point of view, I mean I really enjoyed their show. I'm a big fan of theirs, I think they're wonderful. They're wonderful writers; they're amongst the best in the world . . . They were lovely guys – I didn't have a chance to talk to them that much, but when we did talk they were lovely.

"I remember having a beer and talking to Robin Gibb and saying, 'I feel quite apprehensive about this. How do you feel?' and he said, 'Yeah, I feel quite apprehensive about this as well.' I don't like to use the word 'nervous' – it's not a word you want to use before a show – and I thought that was quite nice that he was open and honest enough to say.

"It was very nice to share that moment with Robin Gibb. I remember it because it was very nice, 'cause it was their show. Sometimes people don't even talk backstage, but he was very friendly and open, and I appreciated that."

As it had for Dave Dee, Dozy, Beaky, Mick & Tich in the Sixties, The Bee Gees playing with an orchestra played havoc with the support act's sound check. "We ran into a slight problem in that they had so much to rehearse, that most of the day was taken up with the orchestra and everything," Colin recalled. "We were doing a half hour set before them, and the problem is trying to work out what half an hour's set is. We didn't get a chance to play until the actual show.

"I think we did slightly over-run. I think some of the road crew and stage managers were getting a bit fraught because they were worrying about how they were going to get this orchestra on and get the main part of the evening going. From our point of view, we were just getting towards our big songs at the end of the show, and desperate signs were coming from the road crew, 'Wind it up! Wind it up!' I was going, 'No way! I'm not going without doing 'She's Not There'; it's the only one I know the words to!'

"It did get a bit frantic towards the end, our keyboard player Pete Wingfield, he was practically being pulled off stage by the stage manager – he wanted us gone, and I was saying, 'No, we're staying!'"

For Elaine Blatt, a fan then and now, the concert holds very special memories because it was the first time she had ever seen the group perform live. "The venue was perfect because the RFH is not that big, and it has a very intimate atmosphere, with wonderful acoustics and excellent views of the stage from just about every seat."

To great anticipation, eventually The Bee Gees came on stage to a huge cheer and, even after all this time, Elaine can recall many little details of the performance. "Barry was wearing a light coloured shirt and dark trousers, Robin was all in black, but I seem to remember that Maurice had on something a bit more sparkly and glittery. The new songs they performed were from *Life In A Tin Can*, which was just about to be released. I still remember how 'Saw A New Morning' knocked me out, but all the old favourites were there too."

One of the Gibb family's closest friends was sitting in the row in front of Elaine and she recalls that he admitted to being just as caught up in the wonderful atmosphere as any that were present that evening. "At the end of the show Neil Sedaka was up on his feet, applauding and cheering as enthusiastically as all of us. My sister and I asked him if he had enjoyed the concert, and he said he had and that he was a big Bee Gees fan. A small number of fans, myself among them, ran down to the stage to try and meet the band: I managed to shake hands with Barry and Maurice. Meanwhile my sister, who was and still is a fan of Neil Sedaka, had persuaded him to autograph and give her his concert ticket, which she still has to this day!"

After the concert, Robin's earlier feelings of apprehension had disappeared. "Things have never been better," he said. "The show was sold out and everyone thoroughly enjoyed themselves."

Dismissing the media speculation that the group had declined in popularity in Britain as rubbish, he countered, "Three years ago the critics said the same thing, and we proved them wrong with more records. Eventually we'll do it again because that's what we are if you come right down to it – songwriters.

"We've become very anti-press. I think anyone would if they'd been treated the way we have since the split. People still want to talk about it. Can't they realise that thing happened well over two years ago? The Bee Gees aren't interested in the past, only in the future."

Their disenchantment with the press spilled over to the trend in British music. "The kids here just don't wanna be interested in the music, just the faces," Maurice declared. "Take Marc Bolan, for example. He'll last as long as his face" – a somewhat unfortunate if apt choice of words.

"England is now far behind the rest of the world's music scene, whereas it used to lead," Robin claimed. "The kids here are spoiled and it's sad . . . We can't understand why we're treated like we are in this country. In America our music has become an institution. The music business in general respects us, yet the people don't. The break-up lost us a lot of fans but they're gradually coming back . . . The American people understand what we're about. They appreciate what we do, whereas in England people tend to disregard us. For some reason, they don't accept that we progress."

"Basically we are songwriters who perform our own music. Many people have covered our songs. But our versions, being the originals, are always the best," Maurice insisted. " 'To Love Somebody', for example, has been covered well over two hundred times. Yet strangely, it wasn't a particularly large hit for the group. Why?"

"This is it," Robin added. "Take Gilbert O'Sullivan, for example. His record gets to the top of the American charts, and it hits the front page of just about every paper. We had . . . consecutive number ones and not a word is written about it. People in England don't value their art. I mean, there's no other group like us. We are always original and never use other people's material. People should value it, but they don't because they're spoilt.

"We're pop stars and now we're content. All we want now is for people to realise that our music is a lastingly progressive thing."

Describing the various styles of music they have written, Robin said, "Really, The Bee Gees' songwriting is for The Bee Gees, and we sit down and think of other artists, but what we're really writing is for us."

"We don't do it on purpose," Barry added. "We just do it with someone else's feel and it comes out on their album."

"We recorded 'Run To Me' and Andy Williams cut it on his LP," Robin continued. "If Andy Williams came up to us and said write me a song and we wrote 'Run To Me' for him, he probably wouldn't have recorded it. But we recorded it and then he recorded it."

Maurice dropped even more famous names. "I went [to Las Vegas] with Lulu when she was working at the Riviera Hotel. We arrived to find a note from Tom Jones asking us to join him for a drink across the road," he said.

"Well, we sat down at the table and I suddenly realised that the chap sitting next to me with the gorgeous Chinese girl was none other than Frank Sinatra. Tom introduced us, and we sat up chatting 'til about five in the morning. Eventually he recorded 'First Of May' and 'Words'. I haven't heard either of them yet though." Nor has anyone, apparently.

The North American tour kicked off in Canada at the end of February with performances in Montreal and Toronto before moving south for 16 dates across the United States.

An interested observer on the tour was young Andy Gibb, who celebrated his fifteenth birthday on the road with his famous brothers. "He's basically on this tour watching us and studying us so he knows what to do when he joins us, which will probably be in about a year," Maurice said.

Just five days after their final date of the tour in Portland, Oregon, The Bee Gees were guest hosts of NBC's *Midnight Special*, a popular late night music programme, which – in spite of its name – only appeared at midnight in the central time zone of the United States. There was a guest host each week, along with the show's announcer, the gravelly-voiced deejay Robert Weston Smith, better known as Wolfman Jack, for a blend of music from the current top of the chart acts, plus some veteran rockers.

Their blend of music and lively repartee struck a chord with the audience, and the show reported its highest ratings ever. The show's producers were understandably pleased, and The Bee Gees were asked back to host three more shows. No other act did as many guest host appearances.

"We did one, and I think it was a mark of their popularity . . . They got a great reaction the first time so they were invited back and back and back," Tom recalled. "One thing that set them apart, they played live . . . as opposed to just lip-synching. It worked well, but I think in the end they stopped doing it because they were almost regulars – along with Wolfman Jack. They were good shows, and of course, they were done in Hollywood, which is a nice place to spend some time."

On August 10, they hosted a "British Rock Revival" which teamed them up with, amongst others, fellow Mancunian Peter Noone, the former "Herman" of Herman's Hermits, whose parents had been friends of Barbara and Hugh Gibb all those years ago. While The Bee Gees technically came after the original British Invasion, they performed an excellent Beatles medley of 'If I Fell', 'I Need You', 'I'll Be Back' and 'She Loves You' with only Barry on guitar.

The *Midnight Special* performances are another example of the brothers' inconsistencies in their memories of events; while they apparently loved doing the shows at the time, they now look back on it as an embarrassment and feel they were made to look foolish. "I don't think being serious musicians and being in comedy really, really mixes," says Robin.

"You can't say at eight o'clock tonight, The Bee Gees will be funny," Barry adds. "It just doesn't work for us that way."

The group were one of many who participated in a concert sponsored by a new Los Angeles radio station, KROQ to raise money for the United Free Clinics of Southern California which offered treatment for drug addiction. The headliner of the show was to be Sly Stone, who was flying in directly from a Madison Square Garden concert. As was so often the case with Sly Stone, the concert was fraught with problems from the very beginning, and a two and a half hour delay meant that Sly didn't get on stage until after two in the morning. Los Angeles city codes prohibit the playing of live music after two but a special dispensation allowed him to stay on until 2.30 a.m. The time problem was the least of the LAPD's concerns for the concert, with more than 400 drugs arrests made at the gig.

It was a memorable show for The Bee Gees, but not for reasons they care to remember. Yoko Ono had called the radio station to explain why she and John Lennon couldn't be there in person and to give support to Free Clinics. Rather than saving the message until there was a change in acts, a deejay walked on stage and took over the mike to play it while The Bee Gees were actually in the middle of a song.

"KROQ – that was a fiasco!" Tom Kennedy recalled. "It was completely unprofessional. This deejay came out and literally had a Walkman and played this message from Yoko Ono. You couldn't hear a thing."

The group walked off in disgust but were persuaded to give it another try. "They did finish their songs," Tom said, "but the whole show degenerated at that point, and as I was going through the tunnel with their equipment, the riot police were coming down. It was just *so* badly organised."

★   ★   ★

The Bee Gees' return to Britain in April might have passed without much fanfare were it not for the fact that Lulu was waiting for Maurice with the news that she wanted to separate. She said later that she couldn't bring herself to use the word "divorce", but she knew that, for her, the marriage was over.

A friend to both, Clem Cattini was one of the first to hear the sad news. "I got a phone call at two o'clock in the morning, I was working with Lulu, and it was Maurice on the phone saying that him and Lulu had split up, and he was out of his mind. He was crying and all that, 'What can I do?' and all this. I'll always remember, we were working at Southend. I was doing a week down there with Lulu, doing a cabaret thing down there, and he was really devastated. Unfortunately it was because of his drinking problem at the time."

Once the tears had dried, a stunned Maurice claimed, "She slapped it on my lap after I had returned exhausted from a five-week tour of America. I did the manly and stupid thing of walking out and saying I was off to Ibiza. There was no one else involved."

This was no sudden whim on Lulu's part. It had been a long time coming. She wrote in her autobiography that although the marriage lasted just over four years, she believed after the first year, and was certain after 18 months, that she had made a mistake. They were attracted to one another but were completely and utterly unsuited to be married to one another. Yet she tried to make a go of it, refusing to admit to anyone that the marriage was rocky. She later described the situation as "mental torture".

In the first year of the marriage, the constant clubbing and drinking seemed a fun, almost natural way of life for two bright young pop stars. Gradually, however, she began to see that Maurice's drinking was out of control. A bottle of scotch in the afternoon before hitting the clubs in the evening had somehow become the norm, and Lulu finally realised that it could destroy them both.

The cosy house and five children of their dreams would never be, but although she knew it in her heart, Lulu found it difficult to admit it to herself, never mind anyone else. "Ours was not what my parents would have considered a 'proper' marriage," she wrote. "It was a showbiz dream gone wrong . . . It took me a long time to admit to myself that I had been trying to create something that was impossible, but it was when I thought about having a child, that it all came into perspective. I already had one, and his name was Maurice Gibb. I could not cope with another . . ."

By the end of 1972, she said that to all intents and purposes, the marriage was over. Still, she went on giving interviews which confirmed the myth that they were happily married, partly in an effort to convince herself that it was true.

The strain of living with the deception was affecting her nerves and when she burst into tears during a visit to her doctor, he recommended that she see a colleague who specialised in women's emotional problems. The therapist listened as Lulu tried to describe the problems in their marriage as honestly as she could. For someone used to putting on a bright face for the public, it was an emotionally exhausting and painful experience.

"It was much more difficult to let it all out than it had been to bottle it all up, even though I was talking to a professional consultant," she recalled. As she spoke, the therapist realised that Lulu already knew what she had to do, but Lulu was still hesitant to admit failure in the marriage and suggested that perhaps a trial separation would improve things.

"Only you can make that decision but after what you've told me, I don't see the point. I think you know that yourself. You're both still young," Lulu recalled being told.

She protested that she was frightened to tell Maurice what they had discussed, so the counsellor offered to speak to him on her behalf. "That would be wonderful, but I don't think he'll ever come," Lulu told her.

Going home to face Maurice took all the courage she could muster, but she managed to tell him that the marriage was over and begged him to see the consultant. His first reaction was to refuse, but eventually he agreed to speak to the woman, albeit grudgingly. "I'll sort her out," Lulu recalled him saying.

She said that she had learned not to rely on Maurice keeping his promises, but this time he did. He returned from the appointment in a bad mood, and she suspected he had been drinking. He then told Lulu that the doctor had said that there was something wrong with her, and that the couple should stay together.

It was then that Lulu realised that he would never recognise the truth of the situation. She said later that it was "an experience beyond my worst nightmare". She carried on with her career in a daze, and her manager and close friend, Marian Massey, grew very concerned about her. Still the public and most of her close friends were stunned at the announcement which came when The Bee Gees returned from their American tour. Lulu said she finally convinced Maurice that the marriage was over, and after a "heart to heart" talk, they decided to separate. They agreed to keep the parting as amicable as possible, with a simple statement to the press that they had parted and nothing more.

It seemed like a betrayal when Maurice made tearful speeches to reporters about what a bombshell it had been and how much he wanted her back.

"I agree that I had not been honest with the press about my marriage, partly because I did not want to admit to myself that it was going wrong but also because I did not really regard it as their business. The actual announcement of the break-up therefore stunned even those closest to me," Lulu said. "We had agreed to give no interviews, and although the press were camped outside the house, down the road and round the corner, I had said as little as possible, and I was very annoyed with Maurice. He had obviously had one too many in the airport VIP lounge, I thought."

From his parents' home in Spain, Maurice blamed Lulu's career for the breakdown in their marriage, saying that he had flown there "to discuss the matter with my parents because I feel they are the wisest people to talk to.

"Of course, I would like a reconciliation," he said. "I am very much in love with her. There has been a strain on our marriage for two years. I am afraid Lulu is not well. She has had to put up with a lot of pressure in her work and worries more about her career than she does about me.

"Our marriage was called the happiest in show business. But there is no business like show business. It has ruined a lot of marriages.

"She sometimes considers that I am getting in her way and what she really needs is a good rest. The last thing she told me was that she was going on holiday to Marrakesh in Morocco. I would adore it if she would change her mind and come here. I would love Lulu to fly out here on the next plane. If she did, we would probably go straight to bed, then go to the local and get drunk."

Lulu threw herself into her work, although it was reported that she appeared to be under a great deal of strain at her concert at Preston's Guild Hall that evening. Before launching into the Bill Withers song, 'Ain't No Sunshine', she announced, "This is my favourite song. It is for all girls who are sad tonight when their man goes away for too long."

Although she didn't allow personal problems to interfere with her sched-uled performances, Lulu resented Maurice's allegations that her career was responsible for the failure of the marriage and issued her own statement to the press: "The reasons [for the break-up] are private and personal, but it has nothing to do with my work.

"For the past two years there has been a terrific strain on our marriage. It's really very private – the way two people act together. But personal problems are the worst. I wouldn't wish this on my worst enemy."

Maurice's reported remark, that if she were to join him in Ibiza, they would probably go to bed and then get drunk, seemed to emphasise how far the couple had grown apart. "This is typical of Maurice," she said. "I have repeatedly pointed out to him that this is an immature way of settling our problems."

It was the only time she spoke in public of the break-up of their marriage, apart from saying that it was "too personal to discuss in public", telling even a close journalist friend, "I'm trying very hard to find a way to be happy, but I can't talk about the marriage. Not just to you. To anyone."

She steadfastly continued to refuse to discuss the problems the couple had been going through until she bared her soul in her 1985 biography. By 1999, she had managed to find a way to simplify what must have seemed complex emotions at the time. "He was as cute as a button, but we were too young," she admitted. "Splitting up was awful. We weren't fighting, but I still became distraught."

Maurice revealed that he himself had threatened to leave Lulu during blazing arguments, but as he said later, "Men say those things all the time but never mean it the next day. When a woman says it, boy, does she mean it!

"I don't know if a baby would have helped, but Lulu does not want children at the moment," he added.

He continued to profess his undying love for her, seemingly to anyone who would listen. Lulu's annoyed response to a persistent reporter asking her about this was, "I certainly don't hate him."

Looking back, she said of that terse response, "I think I used to put up a tough exterior . . . Actually, Maurice's line was, 'I love you, Lu, more than life.' Would you rather I had said that I love him, and it would have been like, 'Ooh, they both love each other and can't be together.'"

Lulu said that her father was not completely surprised at the end of the marriage, but for her mother, it was traumatic. Despite all the evidence to the contrary, she adored Maurice and wanted to believe that the fairy-tale marriage was true, and Lulu didn't want to distress her with the explanations of what had gone wrong. Hugh and Barbara Gibb seemed to be equally incredulous and upset by the whole affair but remained supportive of both Maurice and Lulu.

Maurice eventually adjusted to life on his own by fully committing himself to The Bee Gees' latest project. "We're still tossing ideas around," he said. "But we all have this feeling that the next album is going to be very special and very good. We'd like to be at the top in Britain again. Although we still mean a lot in America, it isn't the same.

"At least I have plenty of time to write now. The trouble is I get so lonely sometimes," he added gloomily.

Later, he would complain, "It was all over the papers, Lulu being their darling. I was the mean, miserable old bastard who treated her like shit, you know? And belted her about now and again. Believe you me, she had a great right hook."

With the age and maturity that they lacked when they were married, Lulu and Maurice have managed to put the problems of the past behind them, and Lulu has remained on good terms with all the Gibb family.

★   ★   ★

Despite the disappointing reception of *Life In A Tin Can*, plans went ahead for the second album, the whimsically titled *A Kick In The Head Is Worth Eight In The Pants*. Recorded at the Record Plant on 3rd Street in West Hollywood, LA, its running order was known as early as December 4, 1972.

This was the first and only time that renowned musical arranger Jimmie Haskell would work with the group, although he would also be involved in solo projects of both Barry and Maurice in time to come. The word "arranger" hardly does credit to a man who is a legend within the music industry and who is equally well known as a conductor and a composer of film scores. In addition to winning three Grammys as Best Arranger Of The Year, Jimmie has been involved in more than 100 Gold and Platinum CDs and records, and has worked with artists as diverse as Barbra Streisand, Elvis Presley, Tina Turner, B.B. King, Simon & Garfunkel, Foreigner, Damn Yankees, and mostly recently Sheryl Crow, to name but a few.

As Jimmie himself explains, it is clear that rapport developed quickly between himself and the brothers. "They put me at ease immediately with their calm, laid-back manner, and yet they did move rather quickly and accomplished a great deal of meaningful music, as opposed to some groups who spend many hours and even days accomplishing what The Bee Gees do in a very few hours. They were writing songs so fast that one of the songs they had me arrange had no lyrics! They told me, 'Just call this the "La La Song",' because they sang the melody to me singing La La La, (etc) instead of lyrics. After we completed the orchestra recordings they completed a lyric and sang to the recording, and it turned out great."

The lead-off single 'Wouldn't I Be Someone', like its predecessor 'Saw A New Morning', is a beautifully arranged pop song with considerable dynamic range, but like 'Morning', it did not reach its potential market. It appeared to be a great lead-off single, and very fairly represents the level of quality on the album itself. The B-side 'Elisa' is a slow piano ballad typical of several songs on the album, similar in mood to 'My Life Has Been A Song' but with a better lyric that avoids needless repeats. Germany got a different

B-side, 'King And Country', another five-minute song shortened for the single to fade out quickly after the second verse. It may have been a little late for an anti-war lyric, and actually plays better in the short version than in the full-length LP version.

The album opened with both sides of the lead-off single, 'Elisa' and 'Wouldn't I Be Someone', then into 'A Lonely Violin', another piano ballad featuring Barry solo. An acetate of the next two suggests they may have been planned for the next single. 'Losers And Lovers' has a mixed Barry and Robin vocal over a lively rhythm guitar and gypsy-ish backing. 'Home Again Rivers' is a country ballad with a Robin solo, repeating the same short melody many times over as he works through a long series of verses, resolving in the different final harmonised verse.

Side two opened with two songs run together, 'Harry's Gate' and 'Rocky LA', the second sharing some of the same lyric. 'Harry's Gate' is a bittersweet meditation on ageing and old times irretrievably gone, quite remarkable for writers only 27 and 24. It links into choppy electric guitar for 'Rocky LA' repeating the "back in 1958" lines in Robin's rawest voice and adding "but it's all gone!" Next was 'Castles In The Air', covered by Graham Bonnet within the year, which opens with a Barry vocal accompanied by a solitary piano and remains a memorable song. 'Where Is Your Sister' follows, a simple but effective song with a beautiful acoustic guitar opening supported by Barry's finest soft vocal. The final track is 'It Doesn't Matter Much To Me', which the group re-did the next year with a slightly faster and much bigger rhythm arrangement. It represents the first appearance of genuine falsetto screams – so beloved by their next producer – courtesy of Robin, who more than amply demonstrated his capabilities in that regard. Most of the album's songs feature solo sections by both Barry and Robin, and the only Maurice solo is the verse in 'Elisa'.

Four additional songs were submitted in January 1973, 'King And Country', '(Life) Am I Wasting My Time', 'Dear Mr. Kissinger', and 'Jesus In Heaven'. These were appended to the ends of the album master tape reels of sides A and B, but most likely they were not intended to appear on the album but rather were for B-sides.

Kick is a generally stronger album than *Life*, because it mostly avoids the worst excesses of overblown arrangements and repeated verses, as if they were now in command of this kind of material. The care taken with the recordings, and the genuine emotion in the vocals, belie any claims that this was an ineffectual piece of work. Unfortunately few have had the pleasure of hearing it as it was meant to be heard.

★   ★   ★

On August 25, 1973, *Billboard* magazine reported that, "[The Bee Gees] have apparently reached a final decision to junk their last album master, a six month project which no longer satisfies them."

"We could remix and get some of the cuts more to our liking," Barry commented, "but if we feel the music doesn't best represent what we are capable of today, it makes much more sense to go on to another project. The record companies aren't happy at this decision of course. But they aren't pushing us."

Some believe that Atlantic rejected the album. "After all those years, to send an album to the office and have them say, 'Sorry, lads, it's not good enough,' " Dick Ashby said, his voice trailing off in disbelief. But asked in early 2000 about it, Ahmet Ertegun said, "I don't recall that we rejected an album", and Jerry Wexler and Jerry Greenberg, while both cautioning that Ahmet handled The Bee Gees, also do not recall any such incident. Mike Mayer, Atlantic's counsel at the time, seconded Jerry Greenberg's views that music came first and business second in those days. "Ahmet and Robert had formed a friendship years before and always discussed releases together. It was never a question of just submitting a tape and seeing what Atlantic would do." While not recalling the album specifically, Ahmet suggested that he and Robert might have agreed that "we didn't hear any hit songs in there", which is close to what Barry said in 1973. Given the similarities in style of *Life* and *Kick*, and what had happened to *Life In A Tin Can* and its lead-off single, the chart failure of the excellent lead-off 'Wouldn't I Be Someone' signalled the same fate.

The Bee Gees didn't see it coming since they had completed *Kick In The Head* even before *Life In A Tin Can* was released. As Barry said, they might have tried tinkering with the *Kick* songs to salvage the sessions, but RSO was evidently willing to scrap the whole project and move on. Nonetheless The Bee Gees' pride and their confidence had been badly damaged by so much hard work being wasted.

While David English, the former president of RSO Records and Barry's close friend, says that the album *could* have been released outside the United States, America's dominance of the world market would make it unwise to do so. "You make your money in America, and at that time there was a [record industry] cake [which showed] that 48 per cent of all record sales were in America. Second was Japan, then Germany and only nine per cent of all sales worldwide came from Britain. That is why . . . we wouldn't release it [elsewhere]. If we're going to make money, record sales in Britain wouldn't be that important on a world scale."

A Kick In The Head Is Worth Eight In The Pants would probably have been a fans' favourite judging by the reaction of those who have heard the tracks by way of cassette tapes which have managed to make the rounds, or more recent bootlegged CDs. Much of the credit for the album's overall appeal belongs to Jimmie Haskell whose arrangements proved him to be a worthy potential successor to Bill Shepherd. If The Bee Gees had been aiming at the cult group approach, it would have been an important release. But they had never been pitched at that kind of audience, and wanted Top 40. A change of direction followed.

'Wouldn't I Be Someone' was released on June 22 to coincide with their first British tour in more than five years, but on the eve of the tour, it was announced that, "The Bee Gees have now cancelled the whole of their British concert tour, with the exception of their performance at the London Palladium on June 24. Also cancelled is their guest spot in the Royal Charity Gala at the Royal London Festival Hall (June 25) as the whole show is now scrapped."

The official reason for the tour's cancellation was that the group's new drummer, Dennis Bryon had injured his shoulder, but there were some murmurs that perhaps the injury was not the real reason. "I admit some of the ticket sales for the early dates were not as good as they could have been," Dick Ashby said, "and the group is perhaps not as popular in Britain as they once were, but they were quite willing to play to non-capacity audiences."

For the concert at the London Palladium, their support act was Jimmy Stevens, the singer-songwriter whose *Don't Freak Me Out* album (released under the title *Paid My Dues* in the United States) had been produced by Maurice. Stevens fell victim to one of The Bee Gees' entourage's little wind-ups, as Tom Kennedy recalled. "With Jimmy Stevens, we actually wired an alarm clock under his piano above the pick-up mike. When he was halfway through a love song, the alarm went off, but being the trooper that he was, he carried on," he said.

The story of the prank became legendary, and would be passed on to subsequent generations of band members. Blue Weaver, who would not be involved with the group for another two years, well remembers being told about the incident, emphasising, "It was his most important song!"

Autumn found the group on the road again, with the start of another Far East tour at Kurashiki, Okayama-Ken on September 6. Nine days later, the last Japanese show of the tour took place in Tokyo at Shinjuku Koseinenkin Kaikan and was filmed for Japanese television's *Love Sounds Special*, to be broadcast at the end of the month.

The two outdoor shows in Hong Kong were cancelled due to torrential rain and had to be rearranged for a week later. Two further concerts in Singapore were cancelled when authorities there denied The Bee Gees the 48-hour passes which the group had used the previous year to bypass the "long hair" restrictions vigorously enforced at that time.

★   ★   ★

Looking back on *Kick In The Head*, the brothers tend to disparage it, dismissing it as a weak album. "It was some nice music but just totally mainstream pop," Barry said. "They were downers, written about ourselves and things like that. One song on it was called 'Harry's Gate', which was about a gate we used to swing on when we were kids. It was *definitely* a wrong direction."

In August, another song was submitted for consideration as a single, but this apparently received the "thumbs down" sign too. Recorded at DeLane Lea studios, a tape box dated August 1 contains 'You're My Heaven' with a handwritten note, "demo of possible single".

With *Kick In The Head* out of the picture, The Bee Gees needed another studio album and a change in musical direction. "Most people have classed us as classical pop because we use an orchestra," Maurice said. "The reason we use one is because the strings add the colour to a song we think is a beautiful melody. It fills it out so you go back and you hear it and you say, oh yeah, that's lovely. It fills it all out. That's why we go on tour with an orchestra to produce the same sound as we do on record."

"We don't use an orchestra just for the sake of using it," Robin added. "We use it because it complements the music we're writing. If we didn't think so we wouldn't use it. There have been plenty of songs where we thought an orchestra wasn't warranted. We won't use it on every song."

"We don't want to talk about it yet but we're going to attempt a concept album that's a major departure from our usual Bee Gees trademarks," Maurice revealed. "And if that doesn't work out, we'll do something else."

Robert Stigwood turned to Ahmet Ertegun for ideas on possible producers, and after discussing it with Jerry Wexler, Ahmet suggested their own house producer Arif Mardin, renowned for his work with Atlantic artists such as The Rascals, Aretha Franklin and Roberta Flack. Arif was well known as a fine arranger too, something The Bee Gees needed. Robert was happy with the idea. "I just felt that Arif Mardin was a terrific producer," Stigwood said. "I knew him because of our Atlantic connection. I asked him if he would come in and start recording them, and he did . . ."

★   ★   ★

On the home front, Hugh and Barbara Gibb were on the move again, after their plans to open a nightclub in Ibiza fell victim to red tape and the political climate of the Franco government. They left behind the sunny island of Ibiza for the somewhat less temperate climes of the Isle of Man in the summer of 1973. They settled in Rose Villa, a large white house in a peaceful residential area of Douglas. For Andy and Beri, it was just one more upheaval, as they left behind the friends they had made to start again in a new place.

Andy's budding musical career had sparked his brothers' interest, and in 1973, The Bee Gees' fan club reported that Andy had recorded a song written and produced by Maurice. The track, alternately referred to as 'My Dad's A Rebel' or 'My Father's A Rebel', was considered for release as Andy's first single but was set aside.

Plans to publish Robin and Barry's book, *On The Other Hand*, were also dropped around this time. "I've got streams of poetry at home," Barry added, "but I don't publish them. I just hold on to them because I think they'd be exploited if they were put out now. I'd rather have a book of poems published in about 10 years because I'd be older and my thoughts would be more mature. Right now it would be a part of The Bee Gees."

Barry may have had "streams of poetry" on his mind, but Robin, on the other hand, expressed an interest in "water music", but not the Handel variety. While there was little he enjoyed more than a lengthy soak in a hot bath, it caused him some frustration that he had often forgotten some of his best ideas by the time he had towelled himself dry. Never one to be concerned about appearing unconventional, he solved the problem by having a battery operated recorder and microphone installed in the bathroom of his Virginia Water home.

Barry and Lynda had settled into their new home in Ascot, still missing their dogs, who remained in quarantine after their Ibiza adventure. But on December 1, a new addition arrived. Barry was with Lynda when the five pound eight ounce boy was born and told reporters, "It was the experience of my life!"

Tom Kennedy recalled that, "The night his first son was born, Barry was up all night ringing people."

"We were all ready with some girls names, but a boy has taken us by surprise," Lynda added. One newspaper even claimed that the newborn Gibb went nameless for several weeks, but in the end, he was duly christened Stephen Thadeus Crompton Gibb.

23

A NOT SO GOLDEN GARTER

STEPHEN WAS BARELY a month old when he moved with his parents and maternal grandparents to a rented house on Glencrutchery Road in Douglas on the Isle of Man. It was a move inspired not so much by any longing to return to the land of Barry's birth, but for more practical reasons: the prohibitive tax situation in the Britain of the early Seventies.

"We were all born on the Isle of Man which . . . helps us enormously if we live there, tax wise," Barry explained. "The Labour government in England had raised the taxes to something like 83 per cent in the pound, which was terrifying to anybody who was actually making good money. The Isle of Man was our original home, so I think it was a bridge in a way to us moving to America because we'd done quite well up to this point. We'd had four really quiet years between '70 and '74. We couldn't get arrested, I tell a lie, we could get arrested! But we were lucky, we didn't get arrested! We weren't selling records and the media were sort of saying, 'Well, that's enough of The Bee Gees.' You know, you had them in the Sixties and you know what happens in this business at the end of every decade, it's anyone who was big in that particular decade gets ejected unless they've got a few tricks up their sleeve.

"So it was the end of the Sixties, it was the end of people like us, and four years went by. We had some money put away from our success in the Sixties. This was our way of trying to save some money, and [although] we didn't know it at the time, we were going to move into America. We were going to have another shot at the whole thing in a different country. But we went to the Isle of Man for about two years, and I stayed in that little semi-detached at the top of Bray Hill and then [the] little white house at the top of Princes Road, which I fell in love with."

Maurice also had a new home, a five-acre estate in Sussex, following his separation from Lulu. "Of course I still think of Lulu and I still love her," he confessed. "It took a long time to get over the shock, and when her TV series started I just couldn't watch it. But I did catch one show and thought she looked like a million dollars and was singing really well.

"I feel I'm much more grown-up and independent now," he continued. "I don't think I'd have moved down here unless we'd separated, but it really is a fantastic place. Our home always used to seem to be full of pop people.

339

And that doesn't help when you just want a bit of peace and quiet. Living away from it all has taken away the pressure."

With the new house in the country, he'd added a new hobby. "I've really got the horse-riding bug," he revealed. The Bee Gees fan club dutifully reported that Maurice had bought a racehorse, called Royal Nash.

"It wasn't *actually* a racehorse," Tom Kennedy disclosed. "Some people in a pub sold him a horse, which they purported to be a racehorse. It *was* a nice looking horse – it had a goat for company," he added.

For Maurice, the horse-riding bug would last only a few years before he reluctantly sold Royal Nash in October, 1976.

February was an eventful month for Maurice. He and his business partner Chris Cooke formed a publishing company, Shetland Music, and signed a management deal with Soliloquy, a five-piece group that Maurice had discovered the previous year when The Bee Gees appeared in Kuala Lumpur.

These events were overshadowed by another little mishap. In one of the bizarre episodes which Maurice seemed to attract in those days, he was punched in the eye at the Montcalm Hotel in Great Cumberland Place, London, seemingly over his choice of entrée. "At this particular hotel they always make me corned beef hash – I just love it," Maurice explained. "And it's never caused me any trouble before – not even stomach-ache. This American, a bit bigger than me, took exception when I ordered the food. I think he thought I was trying to send him up because they use the word 'hash' in the States. The American said, 'Fancy eating that garbage.' I told him to belt up, and he belted me. I didn't hit him back or take any other action. I think he'd had a few to drink."

Even Monsieur Claude, the hotel manager, was drawn into the controversy, not to offer any enlightenment on the altercation which resulted in Maurice's black eye but to clear up any misconception which might arise from mention that the Montcalm Hotel would serve such a plebeian dish as corned beef hash. Insisting that it did not appear on the hotel's menu, he added, "It's not something we are asked for very often. But we have provided the hash for Mr Gibb on almost every visit. He calls in advance and says what time he would like it, and I send out for tins of corned beef. It's not what you would call a classical dish. We just like to please our clients."

The next Bee Gees' American tour began with a concert at the Philharmonic Hall in New York City on March 4, less than a week after recording sessions for their next LP were concluded. The group had changed their act from previous tours; rather than playing the whole show with orchestral backing, the first half was more akin to a conventional rock concert. This may also have been the only occasion when songs from an as-yet unreleased album were performed; the set was also memorable for the inclusion of 'Butterfly', a rarity from their Australian days. "We have a rule on this tour," Maurice announced. "It must be fun. No hassles, no fights."

The visit also included appearances on American television programmes such as *The Mike Douglas Show*, where they performed their new single, the title track of the forthcoming *Mr. Natural* album.

As always, Hugh Gibb was in attendance, running the lights and acting as unofficial supervisor-consultant-advisor – being a father, in other words. "Dad taught us how to be professional," Maurice admitted. "How to shine our shoes, how to act on stage, how to be ourselves."

"I'm one of the few guys the boys listen to," Hugh said. "If I say they're out of tune, they listen. Anyone else, they'd get mad. They've never forgotten the things I've taught them: how to walk on stage, how to bow, how to be nice people."

The tour's penultimate show at the Municipal Auditorium in Nashville had a special guest watching from the wings. Roy Orbison dropped in to tell the boys that he was recording 'Words' on his next album. Another Nashville musician called the group before the show to offer his studio and instruments in case The Bee Gees felt like jamming with any friends. The boys were finding it easy to stick to the tour rules of fun and co-operation.

★   ★   ★

The group returned to Britain on a high and went straight into what Barry has called "the lowest point of our careers", the cabaret circuit of Northern England.

Molly Gibb recalled that Dick Ashby had suggested that the group should "do one or two club dates", and with a new baby on the way, Robin had little choice but acquiescence. Still, it wasn't an easy decision.

"Robin had always hated nightclubs because of Australia," she explained. "They didn't like to go into a nightclub and see beer-swigging men talking and ignoring what you're doing. Robin wasn't very keen on the idea, but there was nothing much else happening. It was quite a lucrative fee, and it was ready cash.

"After they'd signed the contract, Robin knew that it was a mistake, and he didn't want to do it. He would have done anything not to have done it.

"They were at a really low point in their careers. And it was getting to be, 'What are we gonna do?' There was no way they would have fallen into a trap of doing one-night stands again, and sort of becoming a nothing group and struggling on. Robin's a positive thinker and will not be defeated. If a record doesn't go, it's not going to bring him down. He will be more determined that the next one is going to go," Molly added.

For all three brothers, it felt like a giant step backward in their careers. On April 28, 1974, they played the first show of a week of appearances at The Batley Variety Club in Leeds. They had gone from playing concerts at prestigious halls backed by the finest orchestras to a nightclub act backed by the clinking of cutlery, clatter of crockery and the occasional sound of breaking glass, as people chatted, ate and drank their way through the shows.

"We ended up in – have you ever heard of Batley's, the variety club in England?" Barry asked. "It was a little club up north, and if you ended up working there, it can be safely said that you're not required anywhere else.

341

In those days that was the place *not* to work in, and we ended up working there.

"We were back doing the Northern clubs. We realised we'd come full circle, and we were *back doing clubs again*," he emphasised. "It was the most horrible sinking feeling."

In a review from the first show at Batley, Chris Salewiez cited Robin, in his bright blue jacket, as "definitely the one to watch under the spotlights" although pointing out that his "gauche rag doll dancing" made him "the most unlikely pop star ever". The group's comedy routine was panned as "so super-kitsch that the audience were baffled rather than amused". Not exactly the accolades of their American reviews.

Although The Bee Gees have a particular horror of the place, to be fair, it's not quite the career death knoll they make it out to be. They were certainly not the only big names to play Batley, though the biggest names were more generally comedians.

At any rate, things could get worse – and they did. Having enjoyed a week's break to recover from playing the Batley Variety Club, they resumed their cabaret tour with a week at The Golden Garter in Wythenshaw, Manchester, and followed that with another at The Fiesta Club in Sheffield. A further week at Bailey's Club in Liverpool was cancelled.

"Robin said, 'Nothing has changed about performing in front of night-club audiences.' He came back from that very down," Molly recalled. "He said, 'It can't be like this. It's not going to be like this. Something has got to happen. I'd rather give up than do that again.' It's like a nightmare to him. He really hated every minute of that."

"We thought, 'We've come to this,' and we just walked out of that club and we never looked back," Robin continued. "We said, 'That is never *ever* going to happen to this group.' We knew we've got so much to offer."

Barry remembered thinking, "This is it. We've hit bottom. We are has-beens. We have to get back up there. It has to happen. We'd lost the will to write great songs. We had the talent but the inspiration was gone. We decided right then we were going to do it, and honestly, it took us five years to get to know one another again. Those five years were hell. There is nothing worse on earth than being in the pop wilderness. It's like being an exile. And the other artists treat you like crap. They say, 'Hey, I didn't know you were still together.' It's then you realise they haven't thought of you for years. It's all ego. This whole business is ego."

"We were in a real dead zone," Robin agreed. "No one wanted to hear us; the record company wasn't interested . . . It was a real down period, a wilderness."

Notwithstanding their negative feelings about their surroundings, fans who saw them during this period say that despite poor attendance at some of the dates, The Bee Gees' professionalism never wavered.

Frederic Tanner, a veteran from the 1968 tour, was again in attendance to provide another eye-witness account. "I was horrified to find the club virtually empty, with no more than 30 or so fans dotted around it. When they came out to sing, their hearts must have sank, yet they performed as if the club was packed, giving the few of us there a performance to remember. They were superb and totally professional throughout.

"Another fan who was at the same table as me had spent up, on the obligatory chicken & chips in the basket, so I agreed to give him a lift back into town. As we left, we saw Robin at the end of an alley at the back of the club walk past looking totally dejected."

By a remarkable coincidence Frederic was to meet the same Manchester fan again at a Bee Gees convention. "As we chatted, I learned that he had also been at the 1974 Golden Garter Concert and had been given a lift back into town after seeing Robin down an alley at the back of the club. After 25 years . . . we meet again!"

Although Frederic remembers The Golden Garter theatre-restaurant as being "almost empty" on the night he attended, Graham R. Gooch definitely recalls that the place was virtually full on Thursday, May 16, the evening he was there. He also remembers that, mindful of their new surroundings, the brothers had made some changes to their regular concert tour act, although a contributory factor may have been the popularity of their *Midnight Special* appearances.

"I saw them sing 'Alexander's Ragtime Band' as part of a medley of three old vaudeville/music hall type songs, where Maurice clowned around and tried to put the other two off their singing, copying Robin with his finger in his ear, and Barry brushing his hands through his glossy mane of hair.

"Funnily enough, the tickets all had a clause which said that you 'must' buy a full-price meal during the evening as a condition of entering the club. But I'd spent almost all my money on the ticket and bus fare, and so I had to convince the waitress that I was feeling unwell, and she agreed to let me order just a Coca-Cola. This left me with no money at all. Luckily we got a lift home with some people at our table who were also huge fans.

"It was amazing that some of the people there had only come to have a meal like at any other restaurant and grumbled that they couldn't hear their conversation when songs like 'Heavy Breathing' were blasting out. And blast out they did!" Graham exclaimed. "The 15-piece orchestra, which included a brass section, together with the group's amplification was almost deafening in that medium-sized hall, which had a low ceiling. Sheer bliss."

Setting the scene, Graham continued, "There weren't any ordinary concert seats – just large dining tables complete with paper tablecloths, cutlery and menus. People were still eating after The Bee Gees started singing their old hits and selections from the newly released *Mr. Natural* album. It was noticeable that the new songs were not applauded as much as their chart successes.

"After the show ended, we were leaving the car parking area just as the brothers emerged from the club's backdoor and they walked over to two waiting cars . . . no security, no writhing mass of fans and almost total darkness . . . but I could still recognise their shadows." It seemed an appropriate way for them to leave the venue, as by their own admission, they were indeed shadows of their former selves.

As much as they hated going back to club work, Tom Kennedy believes that the nightclub dates had a positive effect on the group. "It was a good thing in one way because it showed them what not really trying could do and where you could end up," he maintained. "If you try and do something and it doesn't happen, you think maybe it's finished. And I think maybe they were beginning to accept that when Batley came around. That was so bad for them – young people eating while they were performing. They thought, 'How can anyone do this?' From that point on, they went for broke. And they made an album that was worthy of being called a Bee Gees album."

It was a wake-up call for the brothers that they had to make the effort to get their career back on course. "I remember us talking about it backstage at that place," Barry affirmed, "and I said, 'If this is the bottom, there's no further we can fall. Something's gotta happen for the positive.' I think it was positive thinking that got us back to where we are now, refusing to accept anything negative. Like, making a three-week album became a negative thing. It was time to start working on three-month albums and making the very best of them. It was a frightening time.

"Now I still believe in what I started to think about then . . . A characteristic I noticed about us at that time was that we were very negative in our thinking. I think that changed The Bee Gees, and we got ourselves in a rut. The worst part about that was that we refused to come out of it for a while. We shut the door on everybody and said, 'We like what we're doing . . . go away!' That did us a lot of damage. When we realised that negative thinking was destroying us, we came out of it."

One other positive result came from the week at Batley's. "Derek Smith, the booking agent for Batley, came backstage after the Tuesday show," Maurice recalled, "and he brought Yvonne in to say hello . . . She just smiled, and I thought, 'What a beautiful smile!' "

Yvonne Spenceley was born on September 24, 1950 in West Yorkshire. "She was the manageress of the steak house [attached to Batley's]," Maurice recalled years later, "and she told me that when she first saw me on stage, she thought I was gay. I never wore that suit again, I can tell you!"

But of that initial meeting, he said, "It was love at first sight. I couldn't believe that smile, that sort of shimmer in her eyes, laughing teary eyes. When she smiles, you don't know whether she's laughing or crying. That smile really knocked me out. I thought, 'What a lovely girl.' There was a pure innocence about her, which is what I loved. She was something that I never thought I'd come across. I was quite thrilled. Changed my life as quickly as that."

Maurice wasted no time in letting her know his feelings. With their week at Batley drawing to its close, Yvonne recalled that, "On Friday night he asked me to live with him. I wouldn't go straight away. I went out with him for a few months. He seemed really nice, a very warm person. That's what struck me first of all. The first night, all I remember was he just kept looking at me and chatting away. Of course, I was more quiet then – all I did was smile."

★   ★   ★

After the New York Philharmonic Hall concert Barry had raved about working with Arif Mardin. "He's marvellous . . . He has a wonderful ear. This album will be a distinct new sound for The Bee Gees."

Engineer Damon Lyon-Shaw, back twiddling the knobs again, claimed that Barry's praise for Arif, while genuine now, represented a shift from the eldest brother's original standpoint. "Stigwood brought in Arif Mardin, which they weren't very sure about; in fact they were furious I think, because they thought that they could do it all, and they'd just lost their direction. The bloke who has been genuinely fantastic throughout this, was old Stigwood. He gave them that chance, and I think it was a real master stroke to get Arif in."

Just who recommended Arif to Robert Stigwood in the first place is another question. Ahmet Ertegun and Jerry Wexler recall having a discussion between them, and each put forward the names of expensive independent producers before they looked closer to home, remembering that not only did they have a very good producer in their own backyard, but also already on the payroll.

"They still had the talent obviously," Damon continued, "which was shown after that, but they needed a new direction, and Stigwood was clever enough to think that Arif would actually guide them without actually putting pressure on them. In fact he did very little, he very tactfully guided them away, and into this American sound that they went onto, which I thought was amazing.

"[They were] still a very difficult band to work with. Barry was always the professional and very easy-going, but the two younger brothers were hard – difficult band! They were a problem in the studio. They were very grumpy with Arif Mardin, [but] he was fantastic trying to keep them together, he was a real gentleman.

"They were not easy, because I guess they didn't want to particularly go that way, and maybe they were disappointed that Atlantic had dared to say that their [previous] album wasn't [good enough]."

For their fans, a new sound perhaps, but still classic love songs, sentimental favourites; some things never change. "We are all romantic," Maurice admitted. "Whenever we write a song, alone or together, it's romantic."

Echoing his twin brother's thoughts of three years earlier, Maurice continued, "But the advantage is, people hear us singing, and they remember what they were doing when they first heard the song. Five years later, they still remember it. And that's the advantage of sentimentality, our songs stir up memories in people, and so they remember them, and they remember The Bee Gees."

345

The album they recorded with Arif Mardin, *Mr. Natural,* was released in the United States on May 13. The Bee Gees do not appear in the cover photos, which were shot at a bar and restaurant called the Corner Bistro, still in business 26 years later at the same location, 331 West 4th Street in Greenwich Village. Both sides depict a pudgy middle-aged man who seems to "smile secretly" as he sits with a glass of beer. On the front, he gazes dreamily into space; on the back, he seems barely disturbed about the bartender lifting him out of his seat to eject him.

The new album had been recorded in a series of sessions, starting in November, 1973, fitted in between their various live engagements, in London and New York. A harder electric sound emerged on many of the tracks, the closest The Bee Gees have ever come to rock and roll, mingled with a few ballads featuring Arif's beautiful horn and string arrangements.

In retrospect, it can be seen as the key transitional album between the old Bee Gees sound and the new rhythm and dance music that they would soon begin recording. Because it failed to spin off any chart hits, the record is relatively little known, but taken in context it is fascinating to listen to the band take such a big step. While not generally well received by critics, by its very transitional nature, *Mr. Natural* is a favourite of many of the "old guard" fans, for whom each of the following albums was a shift away from the sound they had grown up with. Commercially, however, the change in direction was a necessity, and for each old fan lost, there would be several new ones to replace them.

The band now consisted of permanent drummer, Dennis Bryon, Alan Kendall on lead guitar, who benefited from a much increased role, and for the first time a keyboard player, Geoff Westley, as Maurice stayed with bass guitar on stage. The live band were becoming more important, and on this album they began to record arrangements that could be substantially duplicated on stage.

Mr. Natural wasn't the monster hit they had hoped for with the new change of direction. "We simply were not devoting enough time to our albums," Maurice admitted. "We recorded *Mr. Natural* while on tour. Every time we had a few days off, we'd be shooting back to New York to do a few tracks. When we finally finished, we knew we could do better work."

The promotional blurb for the album quoted Arif Mardin as saying that *Mr. Natural* "brings The Bee Gees' sound and identification into today's vein . . . while there are fresher and newer techniques used, the group still retains their individuality."

Robin called it a "transitional album", the tentative first step towards the R&B direction they would later follow, and Barry has dismissed it as an album that, once finished, he never listened to. Once again, lack of commercial success seems to have coloured the group's feelings about their work and prejudiced them against it.

In June the second single from the album, 'Throw A Penny', was issued, although not in Britain, where even the album release was delayed until

July. Unlike its August successor, 'Charade', where the removal of a segment was at least subtle, 'Throw A Penny' was mercilessly edited by the removal of its slow section for single release and was not the chart success the group had desperately wanted.

Robin and Molly had cause for celebration when their daughter, Melissa Jane, was born at 5.00 a.m. on June 17. Newspaper reports at the time dubbed the new baby 'Little Miss Natural' as a nod to the group's album.

★   ★   ★

Two months later her father and uncles were back on the road, beginning the group's most extensive tour of Canada with a concert in Halifax, Nova Scotia, on August 21. "My brothers and I wanted to come back," Maurice said. "It's like one of those ideas you have as a kid. When I used to think of Canada, I would picture lumberjacks and that sort of thing. When we finally played there and saw the actual things, it was mind-boggling."

He added that the audience response from the previous Canadian concerts they had played had been "terrific, and we've never fully worked Canada. This time we'll also be working places we've always wanted to see – places like Moneton, Saint John, Winnipeg . . ."

While the group planned to draw heavily from the *Mr. Natural* album, Maurice reassured fans that the old favourites wouldn't be neglected. "We have to do the tunes like 'To Love Somebody' and 'Massachusetts' because people expect to hear them, especially in places we've never worked before." The group opened with a rock set supported only by guitar, drums and piano, with a drastically rearranged 'Marley Purt Drive' as the only "early" Bee Gees number, before adding the orchestra for their hits.

The Bee Gees played to sold out houses all over Canada, finishing off with a show at the Centennial Concert Hall in Winnipeg, Manitoba with the Winnipeg Symphony Orchestra on August 31. After the concert, the group went to Eaton's Warehouse for a party to celebrate Barry's birthday. Although it started a few hours early, the party went on until 2.00 a.m., by which time his birthday had actually arrived.

The group went on from Canada to do a short tour of the United States, then jetted off to New Zealand, but with so many concerts in such a short space of time, Tom Kennedy recalled that The Bee Gees and their crew were often unsure of where they were on any given date. "In Canada they have these halls which are virtually identical," he explained. "In conditions like that where it's car to hotel, hotel to venue, day after day after day – it starts to look just like the place you were yesterday.

"Barry used to walk on stage and say, 'Where are we tonight?' Still some nights he would say, 'It's nice to be in Cincinnati' and we were in Boston. The audience thought it was some sort of joke – they hear someone saying something like that, it's got to be a joke because it's not in their make-up to be nasty."

Even the best organised tours can run into problems and keeping up with the gruelling schedule can be difficult. "On one occasion," Tom said, "we flew to Los Angeles, missed our connection so we had to stay overnight there. Went on to Honolulu the next day, get to Honolulu and the plane breaks down, so we were there for 10 hours getting shipped to hotels while they fixed the plane.

"So we arrived in Auckland the day of the concert. Once again, down to the hall, set up, they come in for sound check. They're tired and jet-lagged as well so they go back to the hotel, come back and do the show, and then it's back to the hotel and straight to bed because they've been up for about 48 hours."

The hectic pace continued, as the group made their way to Australia. They were greeted at the Sydney airport by Andy Gibb before a press conference. It was Yvonne Spenceley's first time in the spotlight as Maurice's girlfriend, as the smiling couple were photographed arm in arm.

The first show of the Australian tour was September 21 at Brisbane's Festival Hall, with Mr George as the support act. For their Melbourne concerts nine days later, Maurice's protégés Soliloquy opened the shows.

As with their July 1971 show, Melbourne TV filmed sufficient footage to make up a one hour colour special. This time Channel 7 made a heavy financial investment, and when it aired, one reviewer noted that "with the aid of brilliant television production and direction, The Bee Gees stamped themselves in that one programme as masters in their field. They played, sang and clowned their way through all their hits, and when the visual action slowed, outdoor shots of the group were delicately cut in. Seven Network obviously gave its producers full rein on resources and allowed a sizeable budget."

The outdoor scenes were filmed in the picturesque countryside at Yarra Glen, an hour away from Melbourne, as the lads also took time out from touring for riding horses and being pulled along in an ancient horse and cart. The group was pictured lunching on spit roasted meat at The Winery, a low-beamed wooden restaurant which, true to its name, was renowned for its own wine.

The Australian leg of the tour ended in Perth, and the group flew on to Kuala Lumpur, The Philippines and Hong Kong, followed by 15 dates in Japan, where The Bee Gees' popularity had never waned.

The last Japanese show of the tour was at Sapporo Koseinenkin Kaikan, Hokkaido, and Lynda Gibb recalled that, "Dennis, Barry and I all decided we were going to do something silly because it was the last night of the tour." The three made up hundreds of "bombs" of rice and flour tied up in paper towels with elastic bands. Alan Kendall found out about the conspiracy and made his own supply.

When the support act, a Japanese group, took the stage, the "silliness" began. "While they were singing 'It Never Rains In Southern California', we went on stage," Lynda confessed. "Dennis had one drum, somebody else had a triangle and I had a tambourine. We went on singing, and they thought we were nutters."

The beleaguered Japanese group struggled on with their act, only to be interrupted when, Lynda said, "we dressed up like stagehands and started hammering on stage while they were singing."

The Bee Gees began their set with Robin dressed entirely in black, centre stage as usual. As the stage lights heated up, he picked up his towel from its usual place by the drum kit to blot the perspiration from his face, never suspecting that his mischievous sister-in-law had carefully massaged flour into its folds. "When Robin opened [the towel] up that night, the flour went all over him. Everyone was hysterical on stage. The Japanese didn't know what was going on; they thought we were loonies. And Robin said, 'What are you laughing at?' and then he saw himself."

Unfortunately, he jumped to the wrong conclusion. Assuming that this was payback from the support act for the earlier disruptions to their set, Robin sought revenge. "[He] thought it must have been them that played a trick on The Bee Gees. He ran off stage, chasing this Japanese group all around," Lynda laughed.

It was then that the first flour bomb was fired and then pandemonium. "They were going in every direction. Barry was singing 'Words' and Dennis was behind him, firing the bombs and drumsticks. And as Barry sings, 'It's only words' he ducks his head and a rubber arrow sails over his head and into the audience, then he stands up and sings 'And words are all I have . . .'

"Robin wouldn't go back on stage. Dick had to talk to him for at least two or three numbers before he finally talked him back on stage. By then, the flour bombs died down a bit. We were running out," she added.

Robin wasn't the only member of The Bee Gees' entourage to fall victim to a practical joke that evening. Yvonne's quiet nature made her an ideal subject for a prank. "We were trying to get her to climb in a box," Lynda said, "and at the medley in the show, come out and throw confetti all over Maurice . . . We told her we were just going to push her across the stage to the other side, and we'd tap on the box when it was time to come out."

Instead of pushing the box to the other side, she was left in the middle of the stage, and of course, no one tapped on the box. "And she sat in there," Lynda continued. "Finally, she came out, and she was so embarrassed because she was such a shy girl."

The Bee Gees arrived in Anchorage, Alaska, for the final show of the tour somewhat less encumbered than they would have liked. "The pilot said, 'Welcome to Alaska, ladies and gentlemen. The bad news is your bags are still in Japan.' So we all just stood there in the clothes we were stood up in," Tom Kennedy recalled. Their bags and all the equipment had to come in the following day on a later flight. It may seem a strange choice to finish a Far East tour with the northernmost State, but as Tom explained, "Anchorage is halfway between England and Japan so it makes sense in that way – it just breaks the journey up."

24

A MANX TALE

THE GIBB FAMILY's relocation to the Isle of Man was not easy for Andy. Although Barry, whom he idolised, had a home on the island as well, The Bee Gees' intense touring schedule of the early Seventies meant that he was rarely there.

Talk of Andy joining his brothers as a member of The Bee Gees had died down. "I almost joined the group a couple of times," he said. "Over the past few years we've made plans for me to join them, had shows worked out and been ready to go.

"But somewhere along the line negotiations have always fallen through. The boys are travelling so much that it's hard to pin them down long enough to finalise anything. The only way I think I'd get to join now is if one of the group left," he added wistfully. "I'm a sort of ready-made understudy. I can do any of their voices and sound just like them, particularly if I do their material."

But waiting around for another Bee Gees split was hardly Andy's idea of fun. "The boys were all away [on tour] and Andy wasn't seeing anybody," Barbara Gibb recalled. "All his friends were in Spain." Nine-year-old Beri was, of course, at St. Francis School in Douglas so Andy's days passed slowly.

"One night he was really crying," Barbara continued. "So I said, 'Look, love, in the morning we'll go out and buy some amplifiers and get some good players and we'll start our own group.' And we did exactly that. His father came home and got him a job at one of the local hotels for the season and that was that."

It does seem to have been exactly that simple for 16-year-old Andy Gibb to form his first band.

His first recruit was drummer John Stringer, formerly of Bootlegged, who joined Andy on February 13, 1974. John was born on June 1, 1954 in Cyprus, where his father was stationed in the Army, later moving with his family to the Isle of Man.

"I can remember exactly how I got involved [with Andy] because my mother went to collect my cymbals which I'd ordered," John explained, "and when she came back, she said, 'Terry [Clough, who owned a recording studio in Douglas] said that there's a guy called Andy looking for a drummer,' and I thought ah, it was Wednesday, I couldn't really be bothered – I was watching the telly or something. But she kept nagging at me to go down to Douglas to this place, Rose Villa, Alexander Drive.

"When I went there, I just walked in, and he said, 'There's the drum kit' and I sat on it and played a bit. He strummed along a few chords, and I drummed along a bit, and he said, 'Right, you'll do.' Only then did I start finding out who he was when he started showing me all these LPs and said, 'They're my brothers, The Bee Gees.'"

A few days later, Andy and John Stringer were joined by lead guitarist John Alderson who, like Andy's brothers, came into the world at the Jane Crookall Maternity Home in Douglas. Born on March 29, 1948, Alderson was a familiar face on the island's musical scene, formerly playing with local outfit, Jygsaw.★

For Alderson, "This was the sort of opportunity that only comes along once so you take it. There were no guarantees, of course, but I'd do it again given the same set of circumstances." By coincidence, John had also played in The Ray Norman Combo alongside Dougie Davidson, who had occasionally played in the same band as Hugh at the start of his career.

In 1964, Britain's first casino opened at the Castle Mona Hotel but fell foul of the law and was forced to close two years later. However, towards the end of 1966, Sean Connery performed the official ceremony when the Casino reopened next door in the Palace Hotel. The band that night, and every night for the next nine years, were The Ray Norman Combo. Towards the end of their residency at the Palace Hotel Casino, John Alderson joined the band as their lead guitarist. The Combo went on to release an album, which marked the recording débuts of both Davidson and Alderson.

The group set up their equipment in Terry Clough's recording studio in Duke Street in Douglas to rehearse and audition new members. Over the next few weeks several other guitarists tried out for the group. John Stringer's friend Michael Craine rehearsed with the boys for a while, but by the end of the month, Andy wanted him out of the group. Dicky Caine from Roadhouse briefly came on board as bassist, but was later replaced by Jerry Callaghan, then working as a croupier at the Casino but formerly of the local group Nelson Sound.

Barbara Gibb christened the group Melody Fayre, a variation on The Bee Gees' song title, 'Melody Fair'. According to Alderson and Stringer, the name was not one they would have chosen for themselves. "We didn't exactly . . . I thought, 'I've got to live here in the island – Melody Fayre, what a soppy name!'" Stringer laughed. "I remember saying that there was a group called Vanity Fair. She said, 'Well, Melody Fayre's different' and we thought, 'Well, it *isn't* - not *really*.'"

Barbara put her foot down. There was to be no further discussion.

★ Not to be confused with Jigsaw, who came to fame around the same time with their hit, 'Sky High'.

On March 1 an article about the Gibb family appeared in a Manx newspaper, describing Hugh and Barbara's purchase of the Central Stores and Post Office in Union Mills on the island. It went on to say that Hugh would be leaving to accompany The Bee Gees on an extensive tour of North America and carried on a family tradition started in Australia of adding an extra year to ages. "Not to be outdone, the Gibbs' youngest son Andy, nearly 17 and living with his parents, has just formed his own group and will be recording later in the year. He plays guitar lead and also sings." It was Andy's first mention in the press on the island, and he was just four days away from his sixteenth birthday.

These were heady times for the young band. For the impressionable young men from the Isle of Man, it was quite exciting "that we were actually with someone who we knew had very important, famous brothers". The group moved their equipment to the Palace Lido in Douglas and rehearsed there on a daily basis, adding such standards as Mud's 'Tiger Feet', Paul McCartney & Wings' 'Helen Wheels' and The Bee Gees' 'Every Second Every Minute' and 'Down The Road' to their repertoire.

The group jetted off to London and hired a red Avenger to drive around for the day. John Alderson recalled, "We all went off to be measured in Carnaby Street" at Barry's friend John Stephen's boutique for their new stage suits. While there, Andy and John Alderson had their hair cut at Smiles Hair Salon where they were awed to see Michael Parkinson and Paul Jones being styled at the same time.

Andy's decision on the colour of the band's suits caused some mild friction in the group, although it never became a full-blown argument. "Andy wasn't an arguer," John Stringer recalled. "He would sulk, sometimes, if he didn't get his own way, but he never argued." Andy had decided that as front man for the group, he should stand out from the rest.

"We all wanted white – well, we wanted white with him," Stringer said, "but he said, 'No, I've got to be different – I'm wearing white, you two have red' – well, us three, 'cause Jerry didn't come with us because he had to work every evening as a croupier so we knew roughly what size he was. It was a take it or leave it job for him. So we got measured up properly and then we went to Cranborne House, Barry Gibb's home in Windsor," where Lynda's parents, George and May Gray, made them a lunch of eggs, chips and bacon.

While in England, the three lads set about seeing the sights of London. They had a couple of pints in a strip club ("Andy paid!" Stringer noted in his diary) and went around Madame Tussaud's Wax Museum. They drove to Gerrard's Cross to see Andy's old house there, and just made it back to the airport in time for their 7.15 flight back to the Isle of Man.

The suits arrived by the end of April, and on May 2 the group posed for their promotional photos; Stringer, Alderson and Callaghan in the despised red and Andy in dazzling white.

On May 5 and 6, 1974, Melody Fayre recorded their first demos at Island

Music Centre with Terry Clough as engineer. The Bee Gees' 'Wouldn't I Be Someone', 'The Most Beautiful Girl' and a song called 'Whiskey', which John Stringer remembered as being mooted as a likely début single. The Bee Gees' song 'Dogs' from their *Mr. Natural* album was also considered a possible candidate. The group were interviewed on Manx Radio by Alan Jackson on May 28, and their demos were broadcast.

The group found a new rehearsal spot, Marown Riding School, later that month and added new songs, The Everly Brothers' classic, 'Bye Bye Love', Neil Diamond's 'Song Sung Blue' and a song called 'Never Going Back' to their burgeoning set list. " 'Never Going Back', that was done as a demo by Maurice for Lulu, that little demo record he had," Stringer said. The Beatles' 'Norwegian Wood' and 'The Long And Winding Road' were often rehearsed as well.

'Crunchy Granola Suite' and 'Sweet Caroline' were other favourites of Andy's. "That's right – he went through a phase of Neil Diamond, didn't he?" Stringer reminisced. "Plus Neil Sedaka – he had a craze on him as well."

On May 26, the group was featured in the local newspaper. "Here's a unique opportunity for you to be at the début of an island formed pop group already poised on the brink of fame. Melody Fayre is a group that is going places," wrote Penny Black. "They've been together only four months, but they are already booked for a four week tour of Britain to be followed by a six months extensive tour of South Africa . . . Their music, which is melodic harmony, features Andy's very distinctive vibrato vocals backed by highly capable instrumental work. Material is already afoot for their first LP and due for recording now is their maiden single, 'Dogs'.

"For the host of islanders who have been asking when the launch is to be, the news is that Andy Gibb and Melody Fayre are to give a one night charity concert in aid of the Carnane Children's Ward of Ballamona Hospital at Rushen Abbey Ballroom [Ballasalla, Isle of Man] on Tuesday, June 4."

Barry Gibb arrived on the island on Sunday and helped the group to compile a set list, which mixed Bee Gees' standards with covers of other pop hits. This revealed that Andy's influences included not only his brothers but also Leo Sayer, The Hollies and Elton John, amongst others. The final set list consisted of 'Down The Road', 'Road To Alaska', 'The Show Must Go On', 'How Come', 'Last Song Together', 'I've Decided To Join The Air Force', 'Most Beautiful Girl', 'Rocket Man', 'Whisky', 'Words', 'Guitar Man', 'The Air That I Breathe', 'I've Gotta Get A Message To You', introduction of the group, 'Every Second, Every Minute', 'Goodbyes' and 'Down The Road' with an encore of 'Benny And The Jets' ending with the scrawled instructions "GET OFF!"

Rehearsals the day before the big event were less than encouraging. John Stringer's diary noted: "Everyone arrives late, Andy runs out of petrol. Practice list. Not very good. Too many mistakes."

But on the day of the show, things looked more promising. The group, minus Jerry Callaghan, arrived at Rushen Abbey at 8.00 a.m. to set up their gear and rearrange the tables in the ballroom. John Stringer recalled that it took them three hours, but the finished result looked impressive. Andy, Alderson and Stringer returned in the afternoon to run through 'Guitar Man' and 'Road To Alaska' and "have chicken and chips there free!" as John Stringer duly noted.

Melody Fayre went on stage at 9.00 p.m. before an audience of about 400 people. In the audience was an entertainment manager from Manchester, who had come to check the new group out with a view to signing them for cabaret work in the North of England. Stringer observed that the gentleman in question shared the band members' feelings about the red suits, adding that Melody Fayre were "not a cabaret group but a pop group and should be promoted as such."

The small disappointment from not being signed by the manager couldn't dim the excitement of playing in front of the one person whose opinion mattered the most. It was a proud time for Andy, performing before his idolised eldest brother.

"He was besotted with Barry – absolutely worshipped him," Stringer recalled. "I don't mean that disrespectfully, I just mean that he worshipped Barry, and therefore I think he was gonna be influenced from the word go by his elder brother. [His voice was] very like Barry Gibb. I suppose 50 per cent of it would be deliberate because he did idolise [him], he even copied the way Barry played his acoustic guitar."

He also copied the way Barry tuned his guitar, but not always with the greatest success, according to his former Isle of Man bandmates. John Stringer recalled, "I can remember of an evening . . . before we'd go on, not to make too big a thing of it, but [John Alderson] would be getting [Andy's] guitar in tune, because he'd *think* it was in tune, and John would be saying, 'Well, hang on, it's still not quite . . .' and a few more strums, [John] would say, 'That's all right.' "

"He'd spend about an hour getting ready," Alderson agreed, "then pick the guitar up and hit it, and I'd say, 'Now tune it!' "

On June 13, the group rehearsed for two and a half hours at Hugh and Barbara's home with Barry in attendance. The eldest Bee Gee told the young men that he enjoyed listening to them play, as they ran through their new numbers, including The Bee Gees' 'Heavy Breathing'.

"The first few days, I couldn't believe it," Stringer said. "I was actually talking to Barry Gibb, and then as he started watching us . . . and we'd go back to his house, or we'd actually call at his place . . . of an afternoon. This one day he showed us this new thing called a video. We'd call at his place socially and watch him strumming his guitar and when Maurice came over, they'd be having sing-songs together. We got to know them, I think, quite well."

Videos seem so commonplace now, but in 1974, these were amazing things. The boys would spend afternoons at the Gibb house, watching videos of *Cucumber Castle* and Hugh Gibb's behind the scenes movies of The

Bee Gees' tours. "We used to go over there every night, and when The Bee Gees were over, they'd always end up with guitars, strumming and singing away," Stringer recalled.

"Eventually we used to open the show with 'Down The Road' because it started with that drum beat, and then Andy would walk on stage," John Stringer recalled.

In those days, Andy was far from the teen heart-throb he would become a few years down the line. "Andy was always very shy with girls, almost to the point of being silly at times," Alderson said. "I don't remember him going out with any girls at all."

On June 15, Melody Fayre played a concert at a small club in Ramsey on the Isle of Man for the Buffalo Club charity. John Stringer recalls it as the strangest gig the band played. "We were playing for a charity do with a magician, and there was a very small triangular stage inside. It was a very small building anyway, so we put our gear up, did a sound check and played through a couple of numbers, then we went to the Chinese [restaurant] for a meal. When we came back, all our gear, every single last piece of it was on the pavement outside. The magician had a lot of big boxes to do the party tricks with, and of course, he had put all his equipment on the stage, and all ours had been relegated to the pavement. So, the minute he'd finished his tricks that night, we then had to lug all our gear back in which caused quite a bit of chaos."

Eventually, all the gear was back in place, and the group once again were well received. In addition to their own set, they also backed local man, Bill Caine, on the Tom Jones' hit, 'Delilah'.

Melody Fayre's first paid concert was held at Port St. Mary Town Hall on June 17. By this time, Andy's friend from Ibiza, Tony Messina, had re-entered the picture as the group's roadie. The Clerk for the Commissioner's Office granted permission for the group to hold a "Disco Dance . . . subject to good order being maintained, the event finishing at 11.30 p.m. and any necessary clearing up being carried out afterwards." It was obvious that the lads were not in it for the money – after paying for the hall and posters, the band members and Messina each collected the princely sum of £3.56!

On June 20 Melody Fayre went to Liverpool for one week, followed by a week in St. Helen's before returning to Douglas, where on July 2, they began the summer season at the Peveril Hotel on Loch Promenade. The Peveril is no longer there, demolished to make room for a large office block, but in those days, it was a major step for the fledgling group: a residency at one of the largest hotels in Douglas. Particularly in later years, Andy would demonstrate the hereditary Gibb tendency to embellish the truth when it came to PR, claiming, "I spent a year there after living in Ibiza, one full year performing in a club for money. The profit at the gate, and what have you, we did pretty well there, made a bit of money . . ."

Posters failed to mention Melody Fayre, advertising only "Appearing

Nightly: The Youngest Brother of The Famous BEE GEES, ANDY GIBB and his music: The Show For The Young At Heart".

As it turned out, Andy didn't appear nightly for the whole season. On August 12, Andy burned his face badly while using a sun lamp to try to compensate for the poor Manx weather. "He got the instructions and it said you were supposed to give it so many seconds the first time," John Stringer recalled. "He said, 'It doesn't seem very long, that,' and straight away he started upping the time. The next day, you could see his face was red, but he said, 'I'm going to give it a bit more today – that doesn't seem long enough.' The next night he appeared at the Peveril and his face was blistering – there was liquid running down all over his face. They rushed him to hospital, and his mother was in a hell of a panic because, of course, he was a good-looking kid, wasn't he? Obviously, for future fame, he had to keep his looks. And his face was blistered all over, and in fact we did one night without him – we played without him because he was too burnt . . . Even for several performances after, he had to have all this ointment or powder to hide all the blotches and that."

By now the group were playing a 90-minute set each night, often to a stellar audience. 'Run To Me', 'Road To Alaska', 'Words', 'Down The Road', 'New York Mining Disaster 1941' and 'I've Gotta Get A Message To You' regularly featured in their set list, which could prove disconcerting for the band. "Maurice used to sit and watch if he was over, and Barry would come every night of the week when he was here. It was weird, playing Bee Gees songs with one of them sitting watching up in the balcony," Stringer added.

Alderson and Stringer both recall that Hugh Gibb would occasionally have a go at the drums, sitting in on a song or two. "He was very much a swing drummer," John Stringer said.

For the young group, it was becoming apparent that although they could find steady work on the island, the future prospects there were limited. They were beginning to see the potential was there, and Hugh and Barry Gibb began to encourage them to consider moving on to The Bee Gees old training ground.

For Andy, there was a feeling of predestination. "At the end of that year, Barry and my Dad said 'Australia'," he recalled. "Barry and my father suggested that I go out there . . . and try to become a big name there like [The Bee Gees] originally did. They reckon Australia is the hardest training ground in the world. Barry told me if I could make a start [there] I would be all right anywhere.

"So they controlled it even from that point, so that even before I had any single [released] at all, they were guiding it, and they were planning for the future. They were planning for me to eventually come back to America, for Barry to produce me at the right age and to sign with RSO. So, therefore, even when I was very, very young they told me basically how they had it all worked out and I let them do it.

"I was too young to break in on the American or English scene," he added. "I didn't have the experience. I mean, with all due respect to the Australians, it is a great training ground because you can be the biggest name in Australia and without outside help you will not get heard outside of Australia – that's just the way it is. So, you can make a lot of mistakes there, and there are also very tough audiences there. You can become the biggest name in Australia and never get heard until you leave to do something elsewhere."

"It was an opportunity not to be missed," John Stringer said. "Once we realised that, hang on a minute, this fella's the brother of The Bee Gees, and he's not got a half bad voice. Once we started getting the practising together and the playing together, we sounded good. We thought we did sound good, we could go somewhere. And The Bee Gees used to come and watch us and they'd say, 'Yeah, you sound all right.'"

Plans were made, and Jerry Callaghan left the group when he was told he would not be required for the trip to Australia. The final few nights at the Peveril were played as a trio, although one evening, a honeymooning tourist played bass for the second half of the set. On September 9, Melody Fayre played their sixty-ninth and final gig on the Isle of Man, and John Stringer, John Alderson and Tony Messina set off for Australia with Andy.

"John and I went down with so much promise," John Stringer said sadly. "We both knew it was a gamble, and we both had a limited amount of savings. We thought, 'This is a gamble, this is a one-off, to go to Australia and set up where The Bee Gees became famous.'"

They weren't alone in that feeling. "I think my whole youth was kind of a risk in a way, a big gamble," Andy confessed. "I didn't have any education to fall back on if things didn't work out. I can hold my own conversationally, I think, with just about anybody because travelling has educated me an awful lot but, getting down to degrees or having qualifications, if I didn't make it in singing or didn't make it in show business, I didn't think there was anything else I could do."

The adventure began before the boys ever left Britain. "Before we went out to Australia, we stayed a night at the Skyline Hotel in London," Stringer recalled. "When you go to the bar, there's little stools to sit on but they're submerged in water, so you're actually sitting at the bar and you're up to your waist. It was beautiful and hot – there were all tropical trees all around, little bridges over the different pools. We were drinking Harvey Wallbangers . . . [John Alderson] went to bed and Tony went to bed, and Andy came up with this incredible idea. I must have been drunk or gullible because I went along with it.

"'Listen,' he said, 'Australia is such and such a time now and we are at this time. If we go to sleep now, we're going to be tired when we get to Australia. If we stay up all night, we'll be wide awake.' This is honestly a true story. So me and him, we stayed up all night – and what a job that was, trying to keep your eyes open. The next morning, we were *absolutely* knackered, and on the plane – obviously, there's a bit of excitement so you wake up again, then you doze again, but when we got to Australia, we absolutely went out for the bloody count, me and Andy. We just couldn't wake up at all! It's a true story – not all true stories are funny!" he added.

They arrived a few days before The Bee Gees' 1974 Australian tour and were there to greet the band on their arrival at the Sydney airport. "We stayed the first week or ten days in this town house – the best hotel you could stay in, on the same floor as The Bee Gees," Stringer continued. "We felt important because we were on exactly the same footing as The Bee Gees. We went everywhere with them. I mean, when they went to the concerts in the evening, we joined in the entourage. They had a [limousine] for us as well, and we thought, 'This is tremendous.'"

After The Bee Gees' concerts, the lads would return with them to the hotel. "We sat there . . . on the floor," Alderson recalled, "and they were just singing around us, with Barry on the guitar, and I just sort of sat there in awe."

"It was lovely to be party to that . . . to just sit and watch, famous people just jamming," Stringer added. "They were always jamming. They used to have some right sing-songs."

Their own accommodation at the deluxe Sydney hotel was as lavish as The Bee Gees'. "This double suite was hired for us," John Alderson remembered, "and they brought in a camp bed. There was quite a heated argument as to who should have to sleep on this camp bed."

Tony Messina eventually drew the short straw. "There were more of us than there were of him, so he ended up on the camp bed. He used to come in every night and sort of throw himself on it – 'Aaahh . . .' We couldn't help noticing this. Now down the sides of the camp bed were a row of springs so I took them out," he continued.

"And I kept watch!" his co-conspirator added.

"So he came in and threw himself on this bed and hit the deck," Alderson went on. "We thought, 'This is good fun!' so we didn't let it rest."

From then on, the hapless Messina was the brunt of many a prank. "We always would sort of seize on an opportunity that if he came in cold or he was tired, we'd let him sleep and we'd warm him up," Alderson said. "He came in one night and said, 'Jeez, it's cold out there!' . . . so we told him, 'Oh, you should get some sleep, Tony.' So we put the central heating on full, then we thought, 'Well, maybe he's not hot enough,' so we put some blankets on him . . . We thought he'd wake up fairly quickly, but he slept like a pig!"

Ever solicitous, they noted that poor Tony was sweating and losing a lot of salt so they helpfully poured salt on his head. Then there was the matter of Messina's favourite tipple, Southern Comfort. "We diluted it . . . but not with water!" he confessed. All in a day's work for musicians on the road!

They agree that their main problem with Messina was his influence on Andy. "This was one reason we didn't particularly like Tony because he was his crutch, really . . ."

They remember going with Andy to see *The Exorcist* and sleeping with the lights on for days afterwards. Andy's sister Lesley provided John Stringer with a little light reading after that experience. "She got me all these books – proper Roman Catholic books about cases of exorcisms – and she said, 'You take those and read them.' And I remember reading all those blooming things because I was so scared by the film," he laughed.

On other occasions, Andy would suggest seeing a film in the afternoon, and John Stringer would happily accompany him. They would watch that, come out and Andy would suggest another film. Stringer, pleading poverty, would demur, but Andy would insist and then offer to pay. On one such day, they saw four films. "He was very juvenile in some of the things he did . . . He'd been shielded, he'd been looked after, decisions had been made for him."

The Bee Gees' old friends, Col Joye and his brother Kevin Jacobsen, represented the young group, and there were plans for recording a single and album for Col Joye's ATA label. They shared in Andy's dreams for stardom and recognition as a songwriter and performer in his own right, not just as "The Bee Gees' Little Brother".

"He used to write the words – I mean, he had words up in his head for everything," Stringer said, "but when it came down to sitting down and swapping ideas, it was very much a mutual collective thing."

"His chord knowledge was a bit limited so we slotted a few chords in," Alderson added.

There was one song that both consider the highlight of their work with Andy, but sadly neither has a copy of the finished studio version.

" 'To A Girl', that's right," John Stringer agreed. "[Maurice] came in on that. God, we did some work on that song. We spent days and days and days getting it right."

"I couldn't get my track right – I kept getting a buzz," Alderson added.

Stringer continued, "The bass guitarist we had down in Australia was a Dutch fella, and his dad played in the Sydney Symphony Orchestra."

"He said, 'My dad is the lead cellist in the Symphony' and we said, 'Oh yeah, we believe you,' " Alderson laughed. "So he came in, put some strings in, and the whole thing just came alive. Then he put down a harmony track. It was incredible."

"It was superb – it was a good song, it really was," Stringer insisted. "But then they said it was too long."

'To A Girl' was recorded at Col Joye's studio, where the group did all their rehearsing. Andy made his first television appearance, performing the song on Ernie Sigley's show, *In Melbourne Tonight*, and a live recording exists, but the record itself was never released. Six tracks from the demos which Andy recorded with Melody Fayre have survived. All original Andy Gibb compositions, they are 'Flowing Rivers', 'Westfield Mansions', 'Words And Music', 'You've Got To Live Your Life', 'Mr. Mover' and 'Turn Me On'. Andy went on to re-record the first three, but the latter compositions exist only in their original form.

The Melbourne *Sun* reported that "[Andy] has been compared in vocal tone to Neil Diamond and Perry Como" – which made a change to the usual Bee Gees comparisons.

When interviewed, Andy said, "I've just finished a season on the Isle of Man but I only brought two of my current boys with me – lead guitarist John Alderson and drummer John Stringer. I'm looking for two others to make up a combo."

Yet another variation on the title of the song written by Maurice was mentioned. 'My Father Is A Reb' – described as "a catchy little number" would be recorded as a single by the group the following day, and once again the song was dropped. Andy added, "I hope this one will lead to a lot more. My father Hughie and the boys think I'm doing the best thing by recording it here. They reckon Australia is the best grooming ground in the world.

"And I know Sydney so well, having lived here with the family for so long. I was just nine when we left to go back to the UK, but I'm no stranger to the music scene abroad. I started seriously in Spain about four years ago and despite my brothers' success, I've been doing pretty well on my own."

The high life of the established rock group definitely appealed to all the lads, but it couldn't last. When the time arrived for The Bee Gees to set off for the next leg of their tour, Stringer said, "Mrs Gibb called us in and said, 'Right, boys, I'm afraid you can't keep staying here,' " Stringer recalled, "and she said, 'I have a nice place for you down in Newtown in Sydney.' "

"When we got to Australia, we had this list of gigs, and one by one they fell away . . . Mainly, Mrs Gibb was sort of promoting Andy at the rate she wanted him to go at, sort of keeping him under her wing.

"But our problem was we played literally a handful of performances and there was always this promise of more to come. You're gonna back Paper Lace – it was all set, we were gonna back them on an Australian tour, and of course, they never came so that went down the Swanee.

"It wasn't just one thing that made us pack it in, it was lots of little things – it was a build up. We had low finance. We asked Mrs Gibb – we had a board meeting and asked, 'Could we have a retainer?' – just a little bit of money to help us with food and everything every week, and she said, 'No, because the performances will be coming soon, and we've got lots of bookings for you.' Well, of course, they never came. Then everything would go right again because we'd have a performance somewhere and it would go well . . . I remember that shopping precinct – that was a superb performance," Stringer said.

"I signed an autograph!" Alderson remembered. Both men insist that in those days, the band certainly didn't have any groupies – or at least, none that they noticed. "Considering our roadie didn't 'road', by the time we had finished packing all our gear up, everyone else had gone!" he added.

The lads from the Isle of Man decided to try another tack with Barbara Gibb. "We used to spend hours and hours in the recording studio," John

Stringer said, "so we had a nag at that – we said we're spending hours and hours a day but we're not getting anything for this. Then everything would go right again because we'd have a performance somewhere and it would go well. That was great. Then it would go back to the old ways, you know, we'd be in the doldrums again.

"There would be another period of where we weren't doing anything, and all Andy wanted to do was lie on the beach. Of course, we lay on the beach with him, but the trouble with him was he didn't need money because he had it all. You know, he obviously had money when he wanted it from his mum or whatever, but we had to keep dipping into our funds . . . and eventually we said, 'What are we doing here?'

"We got very serious heads on us all of a sudden, because we thought, we're not playing anywhere, there's no proper promise of backing any group on a tour of Australia or anywhere else, we're not being paid a retainer, and it just got to a head and we thought we've got to make some money from somewhere.

"I just thought about you and me queuing up to go on the dole," Stringer said to Alderson. "We went on the dole because we didn't have any work, so we thought we could legitimately go on the dole . . . Because we weren't getting any money from Andy, and we thought, 'We're not breaking any laws – we're not getting a retainer' and we queued for hours and hours . . .

"Just by chance, we were walking past Kentucky Fried Chicken and we went in to get some food, and this girl from behind the counter said, 'Oh, are you boys from England?' We said, 'Well, we're from the Isle of Man.' She said, 'Oh, I'm from Birmingham' and one thing led to another and she said, 'Well, they're looking for staff here.'"

John Stringer went on a training course to become an assistant manager, and John Alderson started several days later. The boys finally had a dependable source of income in Australia.

"It wasn't a case of making the money to go home in the first place," Stringer said. "We liked the country, but I think we were starting to get homesick. We were stuck down thousands of miles from home, we'd got no proper plans made, and Andy kept disappearing off to do TV interviews and game shows – disappeared off to Melbourne for a week and never told us. We suddenly started to feel that we weren't really part of it," he said.

"Time after time he wouldn't show up for this and that, and what we considered to be the big break as far as we were concerned was this television spot," Alderson revealed.

"Yeah, so one of us went round to his sister's house and asked, 'Where's Andy?'" Alderson continued, "and she said, 'Oh, he's gone out in the bush, hunting.' This was about Tuesday and he was supposed to be there on Saturday, so we were to have rehearsals and that sort of thing. And he never came back – well, obviously he did come back *sometime*, but not before the show on Saturday, so we said, 'That's it.'"

The lads who had left the Isle of Man with such big dreams returned to their homeland older and wiser. "I sold my drum kit down there in a shop in Sydney," said Stringer, "just for a pittance, a bit more money to come home with. I had sold my car before we went . . . and gave [Barbara] £100 towards my fare.

"When I came back to the Isle of Man and I was filling in my tax forms for that year, they did not believe how little I earned," Alderson admitted. "They said, 'You *must* have earned more – you couldn't have lived on that,' but it was true. They wouldn't have it, but it was true."

Both men regret the loss of a friendship more than what might have been. "We were good friends – it was a social life as well as musical," Stringer said. "We knew his ways – we'd grown up with him and knew his songs. We got on well personally and musically, and I would have loved to have been able to go around the world and play in halls . . . I would have liked to have gone on further.

"I would have liked Andy to have come back here on holiday and come to see us and say, 'Hello, how are you doing?' That's the type of recognition I would have liked – just to have him come back and say hello to me and go out for a pint with me . . . I'm not worried about the fame because what we did, we went as far as we had done, and I'm sure if we had got a whole set of bookings . . . or gone on a tour somewhere, we'd have stayed together a lot longer than we did. Nobody could say how long it could have gone on."

John Stringer did run into Barbara Gibb when she returned to the island, although their chat was somewhat strained. "She said, 'How are you, John? And what are you doing with yourself?' and she said, 'Andy's doing very well for himself, but he does miss you and he'd certainly like to have you back as a drummer.' . . . Half of me wanted to believe it and say that's a nice gesture or thought. I just said to her, 'The trouble is the fare of getting back to Australia again,' and the conversation sort of petered out."

★　★　★

With Stringer and Alderson back in the Isle of Man, Andy needed a new band behind him. Still managed by Col Joye and Kevin Jacobsen, he advertised for new band members.

Jim Towers of the Cordon Blue Agency responded to the appeal for players. At that time, he represented a rock group called Zenta; a four man group consisting of Glen Greenhalgh on vocals, Rick Alford on lead guitar, Paddy Lelliott on bass and Trevor Norton on drums. Glen recalled, "We were working at the Stagecoach, a club in Sydney. Apparently, Andy had a band but he wasn't too happy with them, and our agent at the time asked us to go and audition."

A meeting was arranged and took place at Rick and Glen's tiny two-bedroom apartment in Auburn, Sydney, and although Glen says that they never really auditioned, when it was finished, the group was hired as Andy's live band.

The Jacobsen brothers continued to manage Andy. "Col Joye and Kevin Jacobsen, they were around all the time. They were his managers when he was here. As far as [Zenta] were concerned, they didn't have much to do with us at all, because we came under Cordon Bleu, with Jim Towers, but as far as Andy was concerned, they were totally behind Andy. They got him a car and everything."

After rehearsals together, Andy and the group began playing small club dates, shopping centres – anywhere they could get a gig. Zenta would usually play a few sets on their own, then Andy would come on and play with them.

On the first show that Zenta ever performed with Andy, Paddy Lelliott fell victim to two flat tyres on his way to the gig. It was time for Zenta to go on for their first set, before the set with Andy, and there was no sign of the bass player. "We were all in a panic," Trevor recalled. "We were all saying, 'Where's Paddy? What are we going to do?'

"Andy said, 'It's all right, man. I'll play bass from the side of the stage, behind the curtain. No one will see me.' Glen, Rick and myself said, 'Can you play bass?' Andy said he could, but added that he hoped Paddy got there before the start of the next set. We all thought that the audience would wonder who is playing the bass – where's it coming from? Don't forget this is 1975 not 2000."

In the end, it all turned out fine – for everyone apart from Paddy. "He arrived just at the end of that first set, and he had to put up with one *huge* verbal from me – he has never forgotten it," Trevor added.

As in Andy's Isle of Man days, the set list changed almost on a nightly basis, although Glen said, "We always started out with 'Nights On Broadway' and 'How Can You Mend A Broken Heart' was always in the middle and then it was all mixed up . . ."

"He had 'Words And Music' towards the end there," Trevor added, "and 'Westfield Mansions' . . . The set would always change . . . There'd be 'Winds Of Change' and 'Words'."

Zenta didn't record with him, however. "He used session musicians," Trevor explained.

Glen added, "We were in the studio with him when he was recording at times, but that was it."

Drummer Trevor Norton recalled that one evening during rehearsals, Joye and Jacobsen dropped in and told Andy that he needed to write another song. "Andy went to the toilet and 10 minutes later came back and said, 'Here it is – it's called "Words And Music"!'" The speed in which the song was composed might have been impressive, if it weren't for the fact that he had demoed the song with John Stringer and John Alderson months before.

At any rate, Col and Kevin were sufficiently impressed with the song this time around to choose it to be Andy's début single in Australia.

Perhaps Alderson's and Stringer's defection acted as the jolt Andy needed to get his career back on track; at any rate, the young men from Zenta all remember him as a true professional. "With Andy, he was always on time, very professional," Glen Greenhalgh recalled, "and many a time he was there before us."

Australia was indeed proving the hard training ground that his brothers had experienced. "One afternoon around four o'clock I got a call in Sydney," Andy recalled, "[saying] 'Would you please come to Adelaide tonight?' So we drive 1100 miles across Australia and about 500 miles outside of Adelaide, we stop to do a little concert in a town . . . that was literally in the outback, in the bush country. These were like kids who had never seen a group before. They were very starved for talent of any kind and that was a memorable show we did there, a great response we got from them. Anyway, we leave [the town], we get to Adelaide, arrive at the gig there and find out they've never even heard of us. We drove 1100 miles, and we weren't even booked to play the place. Those are the little things you have to put up with in Australia, if you are struggling along," he laughed.

On August 18, 1975, their big break came when they opened for the British glam-rock group, The Sweet, on the opening date of their Col Joye promoted Australian tour at Horden Pavilion in Sydney. It was a high profile gig, and capitalising on The Bee Gees' connection, Zenta were backed by a small orchestra.

The group opened with The Bee Gees' 'Nights On Broadway' and followed it with a Bread song, 'Down On My Knees'. Harry Nilsson's 'Down', 'Edge Of The Universe', 'How Can You Mend A Broken Heart', 'Road To Alaska', 'Words And Music', 'Westfield Mansions' and 'Madman In The Night' completed the set list. The latter three songs were all Andy Gibb originals, later recorded for inclusion in his first album.

Andy's versatility proved challenging for the group at times, and The Sweet concert was a case in point, when the group played 'Madman In The Night' for the first time. "You'd go to the job to play," Glen explained, "then he'd pop up all of a sudden and say, 'We're doing this tonight.' You know, you'd be standing there like a stunned mullet, like, 'We're doing *what*?' But we'd handle it, and I think that's what he liked about us, that we all sort of got together. The classic was that 'Madman In The Night', I couldn't believe that. I still talk about that to this day, here we are in front of 5,000 people and our Andy's written a song about half an hour before we went on . . . and he just said, 'This is the way it goes.' "

After the show, Andy got his first taste of what stardom would be like. "There were about 200 girls waiting for me at the back door after the concert, and when I came out, they were all over me," he exclaimed. "Their hands were feeling me everywhere . . . and I do mean everywhere. My manager saved me. He pushed me through the crowd into a car to escape them. They would have had all my clothes off if he hadn't helped me!"

The romantic ballad 'Words And Music' was finally released in November, 1975, with the rocker 'Westfield Mansions' as the B-side. It was slow to take off but did receive airplay, and boosted by a Sunday evening performance on the top-rated TV show, *Countdown*, managed to reach number 26 on the Queensland charts. But there were the inevitable comparisons to his older brothers to contend with.

"We weren't all that close for a start," Andy protested. "They were much older than me; I was just a little kid who hung around. When Maurice married Lulu, I became quite friendly with her younger sister, and she told me she had the same problems. Barry has told me I'm 100 per cent better than he was at my age, so that's pretty encouraging."

The positive response to their concerts and club work led to the group being hired as support act for The Bay City Rollers five-day tour of Australia beginning with two shows in Melbourne on December 12.

The tour programme noted, "Barry [Gibb] predicts Andy will become an international recording star and believes his distinctive sound will be among Australia's future international hits. A good-looking boy with the obvious Gibb flair for entertainment, Andy is no doubt destined to be a star in his own right. He is at present writing more songs for an album and of course, being a Gibb, Andy writes all his own material."

Zenta opened the show for the next three nights in Canberra, Sydney and Newcastle. Andy later referred to the experience as "hell" – opening the concert for thousands of screaming Bay City Rollers fans who only wanted to see their idols. He got an unplanned reprieve at the last show of the tour. Zenta's truck broke down on the way from Newcastle to Brisbane, and the group were stranded. There was a mad rush to get a substitute support band for the Rollers at the last minute. If the tour promoter, Garry Van Egmond, can be believed, the management for the boys in tartan were probably secretly relieved. He recalled getting Andy on the bill as support. "After three nights," Garry explained, "the Rollers' management came up to me and said, 'You've got to get him off, mate. He's no good.' Of course, what they were saying was he was *too* good for their boys. He had a great voice." By a strange coincidence, they got their request.

Another episode that stands out in their memories was a trip back to Sydney after a gig in Brisbane. At that time, Paddy Lelliott was away from the group, replaced by a young man named David Furby. "Typical Andy at the time," Glen laughed. "We were coming back from Queensland, and Dave Furby . . . had just bought a guitar in Brisbane and we're coming back and we ran out of petrol. Andy said, 'I'll go and get the petrol.' Andy Gibb, you know, just walk down the road and get the petrol! . . . He said to Dave Furby, 'You better put the guitar underneath the car to protect it from the heat.' He said, 'Yeah, all right.' The truck had been in front of us with all our gear and all that. So Dave put it under the car, Andy comes back with the petrol, puts the petrol in the car, starts the car up and runs over the guitar. Unbelievable! You've never seen anything like it in your life. Furby never spoke to us all the way back to Sydney . . ."

"He spent every cent he had on the guitar," Trevor added. "Every bit of money that he made on the trip, he'd spent on this guitar."

The days on the road with Andy were memorable for other reasons. Trevor recalled, "There was one amazing thing about Andy . . . When we were away on tour and the show was over . . . back at the hotel, he would love to sing with his acoustic guitar. He could sing any song – anything – from the Twenties, right up to that time. It was amazing – he knew every word and every chord. He would play and sing for a couple of hours, and we would all be sitting around on the floor listening to him. We loved it and so did he."

In those days, Andy was living in West Ryde near Sydney. Trevor Norton lived just five minutes away in Dundas, so the two got together frequently even when the band wasn't working. In the autumn of 1975, Barbara Gibb had moved to Australia to be closer to Andy, while Hugh remained at their home in the Isle of Man. She settled in Gladsville, just down the road from Andy. "I always remember him with his mum," Trevor said. "He totally adored his mum. I know there was a guy around called Tony Messina, who was sort of his protector, but he thought more of his mum than anybody else, I think."

Also living nearby, in Rydalmere, was a petite, pretty blonde named Kim Reeder. Andy had first met her at a dog show. The Reeder family bred Staffordshire Bull Terriers, as did Andy's sister Lesley and her husband Keith Evans, so Lesley introduced the teenagers.

It seems Andy was immediately smitten, and as for Kim, she thought, "He was a very plain, ordinary, good person. He was *nice*," she added simply.

It was an assessment that Glen and Trevor are quick to verify. For Trevor, just a year older than Andy, he was his best mate, "Terrific bloke, great to get along with."

"The thing is when we were with him, he was like one of us . . . we saw the other side of Andy, where the people on TV and all that saw the star side of Andy, we saw the other side of him," Glen said. "He was just like a little boy playing in a marble pit – he was just an incredible little guy. And everybody in the band, from me down, and I was the oldest, everybody could talk to him . . . He was just a very, very funny little bloke at times, he loved a joke."

Trevor added, "Andy never drank back then – he only drank cans of Coke. I only ever saw Andy drink one beer the whole time we were with him."

"We started going out together," Kim continued. "I was working as a secretary in a doctor's office in Parramatta. He used to pick me up and take me to work, pick me up and take me out to lunch, pick me up after work. He was so good to me. He wouldn't let me out of his sight. If we were walking across the road, he'd take my hand . . . Of all the people in the world, he would look after me."

Kim's mother, Yvonne Reeder, remembered Andy playing with the kids in the street while Kim was working, turning up at their house so often that her husband feigned exasperation. "He was lovely then – he was just a big kid. He was so young. He used to be here all the time. Kim's father used to come in and say, 'Are you here again?'

"One day he got fed up and threw him out. Andy went round the back over the fences and when Ron went into the kitchen, there was Andy sitting at the table. He gave up then!" she added.

Kim said that the couple had a simple courtship, taking pleasure in doing little things together. They enjoyed going to dog shows, taking in a film, even going fishing at 4 o'clock in the morning.

The Reeders' normal family life seemed to hold a great attraction for Andy after years of the Gibbs' nomadic lifestyle. They were a solid, middle-class family, breeding dogs as a sideline whilst Kim's father Ron worked as a bricklayer and Mrs Reeder worked four days a week as a machinist. With Kim and her twin sister Kerrie, they formed an exceptionally close-knit family. It was a normality that appealed to a teenager who had wistfully commented that he'd never lived in one place for a whole year.

Andy celebrated his eighteenth birthday with Kim's family, and the Reeders fondly remember him opening the present they gave him and declaring it to be the best birthday of his life. That is "the old Andy" that they like to think of today. "I don't want to talk about the bad times," Kim said. "There were some good times . . .

"He sort of latched on to our family in those early days like a lifeline," she added. "None of us were impressed with his brothers or his background . . . It's hard to impress people like us, so we loved Andy for what he was – a bright, enthusiastic and considerate person."

Kim did remain remarkably unfazed by Andy's career choice or his family background. "I had no interest in pop groups. I used to call them The Gee Bees!" she said.

In May, 1976, Andy was playing "Buttons" in a production of *Cinderella* in Newcastle, about 90 miles from Sydney, so the couple saw each other less often. When Andy and Zenta were playing in the metropolitan Sydney area, Kim would go along to watch them perform; otherwise she didn't follow him. "I never stuck my nose into his business. That was his work, his area, and I never involved myself in it," she explained.

The young couple could have continued quite happily dating for several more years. "We were always going to get married, but I wanted to wait until we were older," Kim said – but in June, 1976, a call from his brother Barry changed those plans. Barry believed that Andy was ready to start his career on an international level, and Robert Stigwood agreed. They wanted him to come to America immediately.

"The first call came from Barry in Anchorage, Alaska on tour," Andy said. "He said he'd just been sitting there after the show, and he said, 'I want to produce your records and Robert wants to manage you.' I thought, 'Manage, oh that's incredible!' 'Plus he wants to sign you up for the label.' So, what could I say? 'Two weeks.' So a date was arranged and Barry insti-gated it."

The phone call really had come as a surprise to Andy. "In a way, he didn't really want to go, but he knew he had to go," Trevor said.

It was obviously the next step in his career, something that his mates in

Zenta had always half expected. "He told us all that he knew what he was going to do, and we all knew before he left us that he was gonna be number one because *he* knew that. He was totally professional – the most professional person I've ever met in my life. Very much so," Trevor added.

"We were supposed to play a surf club that night, and then we got a phone call that Saturday afternoon saying that Andy had gone," Glen added. "We knew and we didn't. It was one of those things that we knew he was gonna go eventually."

Kim recalled Andy phoning her at work and telling her, "We've got to get married. I've got to go to America, and I won't go if you don't come."

She said later she didn't recall ever saying yes – "I said I'd have to think about it, and I'd ring him back. But he rang every two minutes . . . He gave me two dates to choose from, and two weeks notice. I could have July 4 or July 11. I chose July 11." Andy's brothers and parents all tried to convince him that at 18 years old, they were too young for marriage, with Barry's and Maurice's early marriages held up as examples. But just as none of his older brothers would listen to reason, Andy remained headstrong and determined.

Kim recalled, "He gave me the money from his Christmas club account to buy a wedding dress. I'd shown him how to work those accounts the year before and taught him to save money for the first time in his life."

Ron and Yvonne Reeder were also afraid that the couple were too young, but Mrs Reeder said, "They loved each other. They really did."

The wedding was held on July 11,1976 at the Wayside Chapel in Potts Point, a suburb of Sydney, with a reception for 60 guests following at the Chevron Hilton Hotel in Sydney.

After the reception, the new Mr and Mrs Andrew Roy Gibb left for a honeymoon in Bermuda at Robert Stigwood's lavish home there. Barry and Robert Stigwood were there to meet them and to begin making plans for turning "The Bee Gees' Baby Brother" into the teen idol, Andy Gibb.

Andy and Kim found plenty of time to themselves to enjoy their honeymoon. They rode motorbikes all over the island, went shopping and took sightseeing trips. They went swimming in the crystal clear water and went out in catamarans. An entire day was spent out on a big game fishing boat.

Kim enjoyed Bermuda and loved Stigwood's house and its garden with a huge pond with a map of Bermuda in it. Stigwood's culinary skills also impressed her. "We ate five course dinners," she remembered. "Robert Stigwood imported nothing but the best and he cooked the food himself. He's a pretty good chef."

While there, Andy signed a recording and management contract with RSO. Kim was excited and happy for Andy, but she stresses that this was because it was so important to him. "I always wanted him to be successful because *he* wanted to be successful so much, and I wanted him to be happy," she said. "I never wanted to change him."

25

THERE AT LAST

WITH THE MEMORY of their discouraging British club dates fresh in their minds, The Bee Gees went into 1975 with a new determination and drive to succeed. "We went into the studio determined to make a strong album," Maurice said. "It was more important to us than touring. We tried to come up with a different sound, a more disco sounding style, yet incorporating pop and rock. It seemed to work."

"We had a conversation with Eric Clapton about making a comeback because *he* was trying to make a comeback," Barry recalled, "and we were *always* trying to make a comeback. Eric said, 'I've just made this album called *461 Ocean Boulevard* in Miami. Why don't you guys go to America and do the same and maybe the change of environment will do something for you?' I think it was really good advice . . ."

Maurice's version of events cites Robert Stigwood as suggesting Miami. "He showed us the picture on the cover [of *461 Ocean Boulevard*] and said, 'You can rent that place and live there and record *and* get a sun tan. We decided that it was our big chance to get serious about our music again so we went out there and did *Main Course*."

Before they thought about recording, the group did some serious re-evaluation. The first tentative steps they had taken towards a more R&B orientated sound with *Mr. Natural* had felt right, and they began to think of themselves as more of a band, with Alan Kendall and Dennis Bryon now part of the picture. They were also using the services of musical director Geoff Westley, a classically trained conductor and arranger, who listed his instruments played as keyboards, flute and "short white stick with cork handle". Geoff was the conductor for another Stigwood project, *Jesus Christ, Superstar* so his time for the group activities was more limited. The idea was broached to tour without the crutch of an orchestra behind them, but something was still missing.

Late in 1974, Dennis Bryon suggested an old friend, Derek "Blue" Weaver. Blue was born on March 11, 1947 in Cardiff, Wales and had played with Dennis in both Brother John & The Witnesses and Amen Corner, with whom he acquired the distinctive nickname. He left Amen Corner, and in 1971 joined The Strawbs, replacing Rick Wakeman, who had moved on to Yes. From The Strawbs, Blue went on to join Mott The Hoople and toured the US with Queen as the support band. By 1974 he had built up a fine reputation as a session player and was reluctant to give that up.

Blue Weaver recalled, "Ever since Dennis was with The Bee Gees, he would always say to me, 'Let me have a word with them and see if we can get you in as a keyboard player.' It was Dennis who was always contacting me . . . [He] was saying, 'Oh, come on, let's get a band together.' I think they all most probably said, 'Let's get a band together, let's get rid of the orchestra, let's try to do something a bit different.' So Dennis kept phoning me and saying, 'Let's do something.' Well, at that time I was playing with . . . Mott The Hoople and also doing a lot of sessions with Dennis . . . playing with lots of different people."

But Dennis was persistent, and Blue was persuaded to meet with the group. "I went over to the Isle of Man," he recalled, "and stayed with Barry for the weekend – went over on Friday night and came back on the Sunday night."

Blue's personality gelled with the rest of the group and the weekend turned into more a social gathering than an audition. Barry played and sang, they discussed songs and arrangements. "As I'm leaving, Hughie and Barbara, everybody's around, and George and May, they're all there, and we'd all had a good drink and a meal and a laugh, I'm walking out the door, and Barry says, 'Here! I haven't heard you play piano yet!' I was actually putting my bags in the car, and I said, 'Oh, do you have a piano?' They had this old thing in the back – it was all out of tune – I can't even remember what I played. I mean, they knew I could play, I suppose. I rattled out a quick tune on the piano and they said, 'Fine, can you come to Miami next month?' " he recalled. Easy as that, Blue Weaver was in.

Looking back, it was an easy decision for him to make, although he admitted, "When I joined, I think it was the lowest ebb that the three brothers had been. I'd actually heard *Mr. Natural* as well, and I thought that was great, and there were elements in that that I obviously felt we could take further."

Despite the relative lack of success of the previous album, Blue said, "I think we were all optimistic. We were going off to Miami to make an album in the winter, we were going to stay at 461 Ocean Boulevard, you know, Eric had had a massive hit from that, we were going with Arif – you know, it was all looking positive. There had never really been any problem with The Bee Gees – I mean, they were always capable of writing songs."

The fact that Eric Clapton had named his successful album after the house where they were staying brought its own little inconveniences. "The drag is that everybody who bought *461* used to start coming into the grounds, because by the beach, there was access," Robin explained.

Maurice picked up the tale, "So all the fans of Eric would come past this house and go . . ."

" 'Is Eric in?' " they said in unison.

" 'Can Eric come out to play?' " Robin added, laughing.

The combination of all the new elements was coming together, as Barry recalled, "And so here we were in this new environment and at the same time falling in love with Miami."

"We didn't sit down and decide to make any radical departures," Robin insisted. "Something happened one night; we booked Criteria Studios . . . and went in there and it started happening. The change wasn't immediate, but as the group worked together, they became a more cohesive unit."

The other musicians in the group were never made to feel like session musicians to the Gibb brothers. "I think it most probably started off like that, but I never thought of it like that," Blue said. "Even though we were only being paid a wage on *Main Course*, it didn't matter – we were *there*, we were all working. I didn't feel as if it was *them* and *us* at that time. I mean, there always has been [a division], but I always felt that we were more *with* them than anyone else was, if you like. There was no one closer to them musically than we were at that time."

Blue admitted that it wasn't easy in the beginning. "I got a little bit worried at first . . . we all have personal problems, but sometimes the personal problems overrun into – well, we were all living in one house so there was no way that you could hide anything that goes on. If one person drinks a little too much, everybody else is gonna know about it.

"There were a few things to overcome, and obviously politics as well, if you're going to change something. If Maurice, for instance, had been playing the piano, and suddenly you decide that I'm going to play the piano or something like that, then you have to be a little diplomatic and break things in gently. As soon as they could see the potential, as soon as we started doing things, there was no problem."

"We wanted to move into an area of better, tighter rhythms and become more of a band than just three brothers," Barry added.

"We wanted it to change" Blue added, "that was the whole brief . . . the whole thing was to change it, to do something that was different than ever they'd done before, but we didn't really know what."

The very first track recorded on January 6, the first day of the *Main Course* sessions, was a ballad called 'Was It All In Vain'. "I always remember the first line," said Blue, "because in the house where we were staying, in 461 Ocean Boulevard, the dining table, above it was a chandelier, and I think Barry must have got the opening lyric . . . he must have been sitting there, looked up, and the first line was, 'As I gaze into the chandelier' – or 'my chandelier' or something, which I think a day or two later, I read and changed it to, 'As I gaze into my can of beer.' It was actually put onto tape . . . but I haven't got a copy of it. They'll think it wasn't important because it wasn't worthy – it was important to me, though, because it was my introduction to The Bee Gees.

"Nobody's ever heard that – so obviously, it *was* a bit all in vain. We knew after a couple of days, because then we started getting better ideas."

'Country Lanes' came out of day two of the sessions, but it was on day

371

three that the band had their first real breakthrough with 'Wind Of Change'. It would need to be re-recorded at a later session though, before it had the feel of the new Bee Gees' sound.

Blue was directly responsible for a serious attempt at reviving an old Gibb classic that The Bee Gees had never themselves released. "We re-did 'Only One Woman' when we were recording the *Main Course* album," he later confirmed. "I just said, 'Barry, I've never heard you sing this.' We did a fair bit of work, but it was never released. I love that song with Graham Bonnet singing it."

On day four they recorded 'Your Love Will Save The World' which was, for over 20 years at any rate, destined to remain on the cutting room floor.

Lynda Gibb also recalled those early sessions, saying, "They were in the studio putting some tracks down. Dick [Ashby] and Tom [Kennedy] and I were the onlookers, and we were looking at each other and thinking, 'This isn't what's happening now. They've got to write something more up-tempo.'"

Their record company had lost patience with them as well, according to Robin. "Ahmet [Ertegun, the head of Atlantic Records] was so quick to turn off to us, to say, 'This is it?' We thought they weren't even going to give us a chance," he recalled. "They were burying us. Only Arif, of all the Atlantic people, kept faith in us."

"When they arrived in Miami . . . we started to record and some of the songs were *still* in their old ballad style," Arif Mardin admitted. "But The Bee Gees were listening to a lot of American groups, especially R&B groups, and since my background was R&B, I was well suited for the affair."

"When they started the second album with Arif, I didn't like a lot of the tracks," Robert Stigwood said. "I flew down to Miami and told them I wanted to scrap a lot of the things they'd done, and I'd like them to start again. I would swallow the costs, not to worry, but to really open their ears and find out in contemporary terms what is going on."

Arif urged the group to "look at what's happening now, rather than what's happening to you. Your minds seem to be stuck in one place . . . We decided to change a little bit. I suggested they listen to current R&B artists who had hit records, like Stevie Wonder and the other groups."

Soon his faith in the group and gentle encouragement began to pay off. "They started writing different songs . . . and we had a fantastic rapport," he recalled. "We spent fifteen or eighteen hours in the studio every day for two months, and it became like something out of a movie, with everybody being incredibly creative and dynamic.

"Usually, when Barry writes the songs, or actually the three brothers write them, Barry would have the electric guitar or the acoustic guitar, and the song would take shape with the instruments they used. And Maurice would go to the piano and play the chords. So it was what they thought the song needed, usually, sometimes acoustic guitar, sometimes electric guitar, that really dictated the sound . . . It's not like one brother goes into seclusion and comes out with a song. They write them together. In the beginning, their process is that they have nonsensical syllables to accommodate the melody, and then the lyrics come after that. Like 'Yesterday' was 'Scrambled Eggs' for The Beatles. They do the melody first. Most songwriting teams have their own system."

Robin credited Arif with "drawing out what we loved the most," explaining, "He said, 'Don't hide what you love, don't try and do the things you think people will love, do what *you* love . . . and stay true to yourself, and the rest will take care of itself.' And he was right."

As the group worked on composing the new material for the album, their new surroundings began to affect the music they were creating. "Being in America when we recorded helped us," Barry added. "When we wrote the album, we were listening to a lot of radio, and we tried to get an idea of what people wanted to hear – from anyone. The main vein at the moment is soul – R&B – disco, so we moved into that area. There's so much of this kind of music going on around us and we want to do it, but we want to do it better if we can.

"We're into music now that is better than anything we've ever done. Therefore, it's our 'main course'. It also means we're on the right track."

"The Bee Gees have always had an unmistakable sound," Arif explained. "It's their collective singing and beautiful vibrato and their unique solo vocal strengths. The three all together are incredible with their melodies, and come up with hooks that will be remembered internationally. These melodies . . . Robin has a different distinctive vocal sound to Barry, very soulful. Maurice is mainly singing the high harmonies and being the musical instrumentalist, and he sings lead sometimes, and when he sings, he's great, has a great sound. It's that sibling sound – when they sing harmonies, it's like they're breathing it. They're truly terrific melodists and creative harmonists.

"And what happened was that there was a happy marriage of their sound and the orchestral strings, punctuated by a strong beat, which is part of my style."

"Quite simply, [Arif is] the best producer in the world for us," Barry declared. "In that studio with him is magic. There isn't any certain kind of technique or attitude that he uses. He's totally like an uncle. He rolls in there with you.

"As far as a song is concerned, you take it to him. He says the song is fantastic; however, put that verse there, that chorus there. He's *that* kind of producer – doesn't take the song away from you, he just places it where he thinks it should be. He brought it out of us again.

"We've always been capable of writing that kind of music," he insisted, "but we were too scared of having the confidence that we could play it as good or better than others. I think the main lesson we learned from Arif was that the music has to be vibrant. It has to have some magic about it."

"We *were* always afraid to do this type of music before," Maurice agreed. "People wouldn't accept it of The Bee Gees. We had to stick to the same type of music we were known for. Now we're finally able to start fresh."

Although 'Jive Talkin'' is often cited as the turning point in the sessions – and of reigniting The Bee Gees' career – Blue Weaver thinks otherwise. "The first one that we all realised that we'd hit on something that was going to develop was 'Wind Of Change'. I *knew* that we were going to come away with a hit album no matter what – I mean, we *all* did, I think. It was just finding our direction . . . I mean, nobody had any doubts about things *not* happening.

"I expect The Bee Gees felt the pressure [to make a comeback], but on the other hand as soon as the new thing started happening, the pressure was off," he added. "You felt you could relax because you knew there was something new there. We all knew there was no way it could *not* be successful. It was amazing! So it was a great pleasure to be around. Everyone was up; everyone was on a high."

"Positive thinking means success . . . people have proven it over and over again," Barry reiterated. "It isn't just a statement. If you *really* hold a positive thought in your head, and you really *believe* in what you're doing, and you say to yourself when you're doing it, 'This is going to be successful,' when you tell that to other people, they'll believe you. If you tell them, 'I'm worried about this record . . . I don't think it's going to make it,' they'll believe that too. And the more you pass that on, the more destructive it is. That thought transfers to someone else's head, and that person transports it on one step further and ultimately you have a flop on your hands."

For the first time on a Bee Gees' album, they teamed up with a musician outside the family group, collaborating with Blue Weaver on the ballad, 'Songbird'. "Blue Weaver had a beautiful chord progression while we were in the studio cutting *Main Course*, and that's how there's a four-way collaboration on 'Songbird'," Barry explained. "And in the future, who ever's there that could be creative could become collaborators."

"Most of that melody I'd had for a long time, since just after Strawbs," Blue recalled. "It's a chord sequence I had for a long time and not done anything with because I couldn't write lyrics at that time. One night, I was just sitting at the piano just playing that, and Barry walked past and said, 'Oh, that's nice' and started humming along, came up with a melody, and then he sang the word 'songbird'. He's very quick, and usually the first things that come out of his mouth end up actually being part of the lyric and usually the hook."

Barry explained the collaborative process further. "I started to write when I was nine – when Robin and Maurice were six," he said. "They started to join me when they were about 14. After that point, nobody ever decided exactly who was going to write what. No one ever said, 'Go away – I'm writing this one.' Sometimes two of us spend more time on one song; whatever, it just happens accidentally. But a collection of ideas is better."

Main Course also introduced a new vocal sound for the group, the beginning of what would become known as "The Helium Years". "We would try many things, like synthesizers," Arif Mardin explained, "and probably because of my background with Aretha Franklin and all the R&B greats, I said, 'Hey Barry, why don't you sing a *high* note here?' He said, 'Okay, let me try it.' And that was the first falsetto, which he sang on 'Nights On Broadway'. It all just happened in the course of a day's work. So when people say, 'How did you bring it about?' I must say we did it all together. It shouldn't sound like *The Glenn Miller Story* or something, where someone discovers a new sound overnight."

"Arif said to me, 'Can you scream?' I said, 'Under certain circum-stances,'" Barry said with a laugh. "He said, 'Can you scream in tune?' I said, 'Well, I'll try.' So he said, 'Go out to the microphone and try some ad-libs on "Nights On Broadway" and see if you can do it in a falsetto type music, scream type voice' . . . I was the one who volunteered to go out there and in doing so, sort of discovered that this voice was hidden back there. Then I started developing it and started singing real songs with the falsetto instead of doing ad-libs with it. It just developed from there."

Arif has a slightly different version of the story. "I said to Barry, 'Why don't you take it up an octave? I think we need more energy,' and Barry said, 'But I can't!' So I said, 'Try falsetto' – Barry keeps telling it, that I said this, which, obviously if he says that, it's true. But I remember just saying, 'Take it up an octave.' And the only way he could do that was to go into his falsetto. And a certain style was born after that."

While everyone in the studio felt confident about the new direction the music was taking, it took a visit from Robert Stigwood and Ahmet Ertegun to make them recognise just what that new direction was. "We didn't realise, for example, when [they] came to Florida to visit us at the studio, and we played them 'Nights On Broadway' – we were just having a great time, and it was a time to be very creative . . . They said, 'Wow, this is dance music!' And we said, 'Is it, really?' But it was, because we cut it to a click, and the tempo was appropriate for the club scene. So that is when we realised that we really were doing a lot of stuff, energetic music, having fun, trying to create powerful songs, that at the same time, the end product on one or two songs was danceable. We really didn't set out to do that."

The Bee Gees had played an early version of 'Nights On Broadway' for Stigwood which contained a slow section, but they had decided to drop this from the version they were recording at Criteria. Stigwood requested that they put "the dreamy part" back in to the song. Nowadays, this could be done easily with computer editing, but then it was a very different story, according to Arif. "We physically edited the track and put the slow section in there," he explained. "It was a very cumbersome and very dangerous process. We were cutting the multi-track. It was added like an afterthought. But we hadn't finished the record yet."

After the ad-libs of 'Nights On Broadway', Barry recalled, "Arif called me in and said, 'You know, you really should try to develop that because it's like The Stylistics, it's like Brian Wilson and people like that. They're not afraid to do that. Go and think about it and expand. You know, write with that voice.'"

Barry took his advice and sang the entire verse of 'Baby As You Turn Away' in falsetto. "It was a feat I was not aware I was capable of until [then]," he said.

Falsetto also featured heavily in the third single from the LP, 'Fanny (Be Tender With My Love)'. Through the years, The Bee Gees have gone through phases with the falsetto. While the immediate reaction was positive, in the disco backlash of the Eighties, it became something of an albatross. Most recently, they have taken the defensive position again, insisting that they've never had a moment's doubt about it. "I do it when I love it and I don't do it when I don't feel like it," Barry said in 1998. "To tell you the truth, I've never had reservations about using it . . . When I look back it's actually something I ought to be proud of. Brian Wilson, Frankie Valli and even Prince – they don't make any bones about doing that. I think if you go back far enough, the first rock'n'roll record I ever heard was 'Little Darlin'' by The Diamonds, and that was falsetto. So I think that falsetto in a way has been an integral part of rock'n'roll, as far as doo-wop is concerned and that kind of singing. So when I look back far enough, I don't feel bad about it at all. I feel quite good about it. I think it's nice to be one of those falsetto voices that's quite well known."

Another feature of 'Fanny' is its distinctive change in key at the end, courtesy of Blue Weaver. He was influenced by Hall & Oates LP *Abandoned Luncheonette*. "The key change in 'Fanny (Be Tender)' was a complete rip-off from *Abandoned Luncheonette* from 'She's Gone'," he admitted. "I only had it on tape, and I didn't know that *Arif* had produced it, and I'm pinching all these ideas. . . . After we finished the session, I went out and got the album and Donny Hathaway as well, was a big influence, and Arif produced *Donny Hathaway Live* as well. We're doing this thing and I'm pinching all these licks, all these ideas, and he said, 'Well, you listened to them, you're influenced by that, you take that and then you go on.'"

While all the brothers, and indeed, all the members of The Bee Gees' band, have their own opinion as to what made the *Main Course* sessions different, all agree that the major factor was the influence and encouragement of Arif Mardin. Maurice is quick to pay homage to the man he refers to as both "a producer and a referee . . . Arif showed us the right track," he said. "*This* was the track leading to R&B and hits, and *that* was the track leading to lush ballads and forget it. He just shoved us off that track and right up this one."

"Arif was incredible to work with," Robin agreed. "Especially with Maurice. He changed our style of recording. We would start with one instrument and build up from there, as opposed to all playing at once. It is a clearer process."

"We'd say, 'What kind of bass can we do on this?'" Maurice explained, "and then sit down and talk about it, instead of just putting down the bass and saying, 'That's fine for that track.' He'd rather sit down and ask me what I'd like to do. I'd say, 'I'd like to do it like this,' and he'd say, 'Why don't you try it like this?' We'd sit down and put the two ideas together. If we didn't like it, we would try something else again. And sometimes the bass went on last on some of the tracks, because I want to work around some of the other instruments – the lead guitar, bass drum."

While there is no denying that Mardin's production was a major ingredient in the success of *Main Course*, it was only that: an ingredient. Arif had also produced the previous year's *Mr. Natural*, which Barry said "was an album that we made but never listened to. You know something is wrong when you don't bother to listen to your own albums. If you're not going to bother, other people may not bother either. There are a few nice tracks on it actually, but nothing stands out as a hit.

"After we made that album I went home, and I didn't have a good hi-fi set-up at the time so I never put it on. A month went by, and I actually forgot to play it. The new album I keep playing all the time, and I've listened to it more than I've listened to any one before."

Blue Weaver believes that science played a big part in the new sound. "During *Main Course*, the sound changed so drastically because synthesizers were used, and technology was introduced rather than just an orchestra and a piano," he explained. "That was a change as well. There hasn't been musically much change since then because nothing new has been invented to make such a tremendous difference to the sound as the synthesizer did, compared to an orchestra. Oh, sometimes I'd try to make the synthesizer sound like a real orchestra. I got heavily involved in technology; days would be spent on it. With the early albums, we liked being advanced, and we liked using technology, but we were ahead of technology then. I think now technology always stays one step ahead of you."

Another vital ingredient for the success of the album was Karl Richardson, a veteran of Miami discos and sound and light shows, who eventually moved on to become a top engineer at Criteria. During the recording of *Main Course*, Karl introduced the group to one of his friends, a young man named Albhy Galuten. According to Maurice, the initial meeting was inauspicious. "Karl knew this guy Albhy, who'd worked with Clapton and such," he related. "At first, I saw him barefoot and all, eating his bloody grease tree [avocado] sandwiches, and I was a bit frightened."

"When we first went to Criteria, Karl was the house engineer," Tom Kennedy explained. "Albhy was a sort of hippie keyboard player who had his own studio and did a few things. He got on quite well with Barry . . ." Although he didn't participate in the recording of *Main Course*, Albhy would soon play a major part in The Bee Gees' story.

The first single from the album emerged from the daily drive between Criteria and 461 Ocean Boulevard. "We were on our way back from the studios, Criteria Studios, in Miami . . . and, as the car takes us back to the house we had rented, it was going across this bridge," Barry said. "We'd recorded a lot of songs at that point. As we crossed the bridge, the bridge went 'tickety, tickety, tickety tick' and it just gave us a thought and I don't know where it came from, I just started singing 'Just your jive talkin' '. That's a great groove, we gotta remember that groove. In those days you didn't tape something, you never did. You just had to remember it so the next day, when we were going across the bridge again, we started singing along to it. The same night, we got back about midnight and we sat down and we wrote the lyrics to the song. We finished it in the studio, but when we played it for Arif Mardin, our producer, he asked us if we knew what 'jive talkin'' meant in America. We said we didn't and when he told us, we had to change the lyrics so they'd make sense. That's also why the first line of the chorus is 'Jive talkin', so misunderstood.' That's how it really came about."

Maurice was even more forthcoming about the problem with the lyrics. "When we did 'Jive Talkin'' . . . we were talking about rock and roll jive, the dance," he revealed. "[Arif] said, 'No, I've got to tell you it's a black expression for bullshitting somebody.' We had 'Jive talkin' you dance with your eyes' and we changed it to 'Jive talkin', you're telling me lies.' So we just changed the lyrics around and he even gave us the groove, he said, '*This is what the tempo should be.*'"

"On 'Jive Talkin'' I remember we used . . . it was very interesting, we did it to a click, but it was a metronome with a light flashing," Mardin explained. "The drummer would look at the light flashing to play it, not an audible click but a visual click. So we weren't really getting into cutting edge sounds on *Main Course.*"

The intense creativity in the air spurred the group on. "But the actual track that started it all off was 'Jive Talkin'','" said Robin. "That snowballed one night and the energy went on for a couple of weeks."

Blue Weaver explained the distinctive bass sound on the track. "I thought, 'Oh, we can't go back home tonight and listen to the demo without bass, so I'll copy a sort of bass guitar thing and do it with the synthesizer because Maurice wasn't there at the time. So I got the ARP in, there was one in the studio, and I started playing the bass part. We took it home that night and we thought, 'That's it, that's an angle – that's great!' Then instead of going for a guitar sound, to make it sound like a bass guitar, we went for something totally different. We all got into the studio the following day, and Arif as well, we were all saying, 'Well, we've hit on something here – how do we approach it?'

"Well, I thought, 'We'll do it first and then we'll see how we overcome the point of Maurice not playing bass on it. It was actually in C so we got Maurice to tune his low E string down to a C so he plays the down beat, the C to add the extra weight to the synthesizer, so he's still involved. But I think he would have gone along with it even if he hadn't been involved because everybody could see that it was right."

"On *Main Course* we were still exploring." Arif explained. "However, I had some ARPs and such, which were state of the art at that time. We used bass lines, and we had that instrument play, the keyboard player play bass lines. Some of them, I wrote down. Definitely, on 'Nights On Broadway' or 'Jive Talkin'', Maurice was playing bass too, but the synth bass was playing some active stuff. So obviously that influenced him. We had two basses going at the same time."

If Maurice is to be believed, the choice of 'Jive Talkin'' as a single was far from unanimous, but that the group decided "to live dangerously" and release it anyway. "A lot of people were against it being the first single but Robert got his way as well as ourselves. Robert knew it was going to be the first single. He knew it was going to be a smash."

Because of the apparent prejudice against The Bee Gees, RSO is said to have famously shipped out blank white label copies of 'Jive Talkin'' to allow the song to sell itself without DJs knowing who it was. However, no blank label copies of the single are known to exist; in fact, when VH-1 was putting together its *Bee Gees Legends* television documentary in 1998, they had to create one to perpetuate the myth.

"There might not have been white label copies," Tom Kennedy admitted, "but I think there were some tapes sent out to radio stations . . . I think it was to do with Al Coury, one of his bright ideas, because we were suffering."

Maurice offered another variation. "We were over the moon about 'Jive Talkin'', but when we played it to people at the record company, they didn't want it . . . Stigwood was fighting with them, telling them they were mad and it was a guaranteed number one single, and we were getting secret phone calls from the record company asking us if we could talk him out of it. Robert came up with a way round it, which was that he sent out some unmarked cassettes to DJs and critics. That way they wouldn't know who it was, so they'd only come back to us if they liked the music. Then, having said they liked it before they discovered it was The Bee Gees, it was very hard for them not to play it."

Blue Weaver did a little promotion of his own. "When I got back to England, I took one down to the Speakeasy and Roger Chapman of Family was there," he recalled. "I got the DJ to put it on without telling Roger who it was, and he loved it. Then he said, 'So who was it?' I had to actually tell him it was The Bee Gees, it was that different."

The single was definitely accompanied by a plea from Polydor's press officer David Hughes: "If you've never liked The Bee Gees before, and there seems to be some who now have a mental block when it comes to their records, please give this single a chance. It is totally unlike anything they have recorded in their entire career. That's a bold statement but it's not wrong. Produced by Arif Mardin, this is actually almost unrecognisable as the Gibb brothers and is an extremely funky piece of music. If you don't like The Bee Gees (or rather if you haven't in the past liked The Bee Gees), please pretend it's not them."

Whatever the reason, the public listened. "Because it was a departure from the ballad style that most people associated us with," Barry said, "when it became a hit people started saying that we had stepped down to be a disco group which was a sort of put-down to disco music as well. We don't think disco is bad music. We think it's happy and has wide appeal. We decided we would try something light-hearted. We didn't cunningly go into the disco market to gain greater strength in the record market as some people implied at the time."

According to *Rolling Stone* magazine, an unlabeled test pressing released in Britain found that only 20 per cent of the DJs who heard it were able to identify 'Jive Talkin'' as The Bee Gees.

More importantly to The Bee Gees themselves was that as 'Jive Talkin'' entered the American pop singles chart at number nine, it was simultaneously entering the rhythm & blues charts at number 90. While not the highest rating, to them it was significant, symbolising the recognition they had been seeking that they were, according to Robin, "an R&B group with a lot of soul music in our hearts. Our dream is not to be the best group of the Sixties, but the best group of tomorrow," he added. The success of 'Jive Talkin'' was not just limited to the United States, where it eventually hit the number one spot on June 18. It also made number five in the UK as well as the Top 20 in Germany, Australia and many other places around the globe.

On May 21, 1975, just weeks after 'Jive Talkin'' had been released, Robert Stigwood threw an outdoor party on the skating rink at the Rockefeller Center to celebrate The Bee Gees' twentieth anniversary in show business, complete with a huge piano shaped cake. Although the claim that Barry, Robin and Maurice had actually begun performing in public in 1955 had never been fully substantiated, why let that spoil a good party?

Rumour had it that while there were 250 invited guests, more than 450 attended the bash, and the searchlight pointing straight up into the Manhattan sky drew even more sightseers. Guests included Atlantic Records boss Ahmet Ertegun, The Average White Band, Broadway star Ben Vereen, and, of course, the guests of honour, The Bee Gees and band members with their wives and girlfriends. Even Molly Gibb had flown in from England for the event.

Despite the fact that Stigwood arrived in his usual understated fashion in a stretch limousine, the joke of the evening was that many of his guests went through the entire five hour party without seeing him, while many of those who did catch a glimpse of him didn't recognise him. The Bee Gees arrived in a hired car driven by a former construction worker called Marvin, who told the swarming reporters, "The boys don't mind what they drive in. They're just as happy in a little Cadillac."

The ubiquitous Marvin also divulged that "the boys" didn't care for Stigwood's choice of the evening's entertainment, the 20-piece Lester Lanin Orchestra, who had previously played for four Presidents at 11 White House parties. "They want something you can move to," he added.

As the group mingled with the guests, a proud Hugh Gibb told reporters, "I knew they'd do it if they got the breaks. It was frustrating. One thing about being with them around the world, I've had the opportunity of meeting so many people, big people, I never thought I would in a fit. Who'd ever thought of three kids from Brisbane in a place like this?"

With that, it was time to turn the evening's festivities over to the man who made it all possible, as band leader Lanin announced, "Ladies and gentlemen, your host, Robert Stigman!"

★   ★   ★

The *Main Course* album was released three days later in the US and the following month in the UK and Europe. "It's the quickest reaction we ever had to something different," Robin said. "Our fans know us as writers; they'll accept anything we do. Writers can't limit themselves; they must explore all areas of creativity. The hard-core fans will appreciate our music just as much; they're still getting their type of music. The whole thing is, we're picking up new fans, not just keeping the old. We want to keep the old, but we want to get new ones as well."

For the second album in a row, The Bee Gees do not appear on the cover, which uses the same artwork background on both sides, on the front a drawing of a young woman in a large hat and nothing else bathing in a large spoon. Al Coury, the head of RSO Records, recalls the cover as someone's deliberate strategy to help the R&B flavoured songs gain an edge on the R&B charts. "Atlantic didn't want black people to know the group wasn't black. If they saw three white guys on the cover, that might be a major problem." If so, it would all depend on young record buyers' memories being too short to recall the *Midnight Special* shows only one and two years earlier. At any rate, the inner sleeve included a small monochrome photo of the group. Barry holds a cup of tea.

Maurice insisted that the public hadn't been ready for the new Bee Gees' sound in the past. "When we were going with softer material such as 'How Can You Mend A Broken Heart' and 'Run To Me', I think that's all people wanted to hear from us," he said. "I don't believe that our audience would have accepted our new songs then."

It wasn't just their old fans who were surprised by their new sound. David English, Barry's close friend, revealed, "Jack Bruce sent a telegram to the boys saying he'd just heard the record, and he had thought it was the best new black band he'd heard. This was before he knew it was The Bee Gees."

English singer/actor Paul Nicholas added, "I remember being on holiday and there were a load of people including Robert Stigwood, myself and lots of other people down in Brazil . . . I remember Robert saying to me that he was trying to get them to . . . listen to other people's music. Because I think that he felt they had lost touch with what was currently going on. I remember him playing this kind of new sound from them, which was this kind of disco thing and the high pitched falsetto stuff and thinking, 'God, this is fantastic!' "

Maurice had yet another story. "There was a party the other night and the Stones were in Robert Stigwood's apartment. He just put the album on and didn't tell them who it was," he claimed, "and Mick Jagger says, 'That's fucking dynamite, who's that? Some new group you've signed up?' "

On May 30, The Bee Gees were due to begin a 40-date tour of the

United States in Dayton, Ohio, the first time in nearly eight years that they would perform without an orchestra. Initial rehearsals with the new band took place in the Isle of Man. "The whole situation was new . . . not having to think about an orchestra," Blue Weaver said. "We were trying to play together as a unit as well. Before the *Main Course* tour we rehearsed in the Isle of Man for a week or two, a couple of hours a day, and then a couple of days actually in America with the whole set-up."

Geoff Bruce, the manager of the Douglas Bay Hotel at that time, remembered exactly how long the group rehearsed on the island. "Barry and Maurice approached me one day and asked, 'Could we use the hotel restaurant to rehearse in winter?' because we were closed in winter," he explained. "I said we were having it redecorated so it would be quite empty. I asked if they would have a lot of gear to bring, and they said, 'No, no, there won't be a lot of gear,' so eventually, I said fine, they could use it."

Apparently the Gibb brothers' idea of what constituted "a lot" of equipment differed radically from Geoff's. "A furniture van arrived and it had a piano, keyboards and *stacks* of equipment. I remember Alan Kendall was with them then, and Blue Weaver was on keyboards. They rehearsed 'Jive Talkin'' and 'Fanny (Be Tender)'.

"It was really strange that they were rehearsing in the room that their father had played in some 30 years before. Their mum and dad would often come and listen to them rehearse, and time the sets for them. Hughie used to tell the boys how it used to be when he was there. Barbara used to come to most of the rehearsals.

"They would start about midday – it was quite strange – I became the world's authority on 'Jive Talkin'' because my flat was above the restaurant, and I listened to 'Jive Talkin'' for about two weeks until midnight every night. In fact, the opening riff still sends a cold shiver down my back!" he added.

"For years people said that because we always travelled with an orchestra, they never knew if we were any good as a band," Robin admitted. "It was time to let everybody hear us as a band and judge for themselves."

Dick Ashby agreed that the new band was very important to The Bee Gees' new sound. "Without a doubt, [Blue Weaver] has given everyone else in the band and the three brothers themselves a big lift this time. He's a fresh person in there injecting ideas.

"There's Dennis Bryon on drums . . . and we're moving into synthesizers and just having a small brass section. Geoff Westley's responsible for scoring the songs brass-wise, and we're also using ten keyboards this time so he and Blue are playing keyboards. There's about six synthesizers, electric piano, a regular piano and Hammond organ, so it needs ten pairs of hands in there. Obviously in London, Geoff is very busy so we're hoping to bring in yet another keyboard player [who isn't available until the end of the year]."

With Dennis, Blue and Geoff added to the core Bee Gees musicians of Barry on rhythm guitar, Alan Kendall on lead guitar, and Maurice now

382

mainly on bass, The Bee Gees were, at last, a band to be reckoned with.

At the time, there were plans for Dennis, Alan, Blue and another keyboard player to form their own group and open the shows for The Bee Gees. "It will be a permanent thing inasmuch as they'll be doing their own thing, as well as working for The Bee Gees," Ashby said. "It will give them goals to aim for." A recording contract for the group apart from their Bee Gees' work was in the talking stages, but it never progressed any further than that.

The tour was the first time that anyone had seen the group performing their new falsetto sound, but 1975's *Main Course* might have proved confusing for the fans seeing 'Nights On Broadway' performed live for the first time and seeing the falsetto ad-libs done – by *Maurice*.

Robin's wife Molly had returned to England after the anniversary party at the Rockefeller Center, as usual shunning the touring life in favour of spending her time at home with the couple's children, three-year-old Spencer and one-year-old Melissa. The years hadn't changed her opinion that touring was a complete bore, and she claimed she would rather not have children at all than to turn their care over to someone else. Reasoning that when he was working, he didn't have time to spend with her anyway, she preferred to stay behind and keep in touch long distance. "Robin and I are in constant contact," she said. "He phones me every night, and we always chat for a quarter of an hour or so."

While Molly and Robin kept the telephone lines busy, Lynda Gibb and Yvonne Spenceley once again chose to accompany their men on the tour. For Yvonne, the novelty was still there. "I'm only just getting used to the life of a pop star – but I don't mind it at all. We first met in a restaurant when the group were having a night out. I was disappointed in The Bee Gees at first, but they got better as their week in Batley went on. I wasn't a Bee Gees fan then," she admitted, "but I definitely am now. Maurice has a very amiable disposition and we get on very well."

The American tour got off to a poor start when, in Cleveland, Ohio, on the second night, the group played to an audience of only 500 people. *Main Course* had barely been released, and the group was still suffering from the slump of the past few years. As the group made their way across the United States, everything was about to change dramatically.

There was a special concert in Chicago taped for the Public Broadcasting System's *Soundstage* programme. In addition to the usual concert material, the group answered questions from the studio audience and reprised some of their childhood favourites, 'Bye Bye Love', 'Lollipop' and 'Happy Birthday, Sweet Sixteen'. They also performed 'To Love Somebody' with their special guest and RSO stablemate, Yvonne Elliman.

On the West Coast, they made yet another appearance on *The Midnight Special* where they received a Gold Record award for 'Jive Talkin' ', presented by Wolfman Jack. This time they performed 'To Love Somebody' with hostess, and fellow Aussie ex-pat, Helen Reddy. The Bee Gees' offbeat senses of humour mixed with their music once again proved popular with television audiences, and once again the idea of a film was discussed.

"It *is* possible that we'll be staying after this tour for a TV film that will lead to other things," Barry said. "I don't know whether we're going to like it or not – Robin, Maurice and I – since we've never acted before. From what I've heard – this is nothing definite – it's about three immigrants who come to America at the turn of the century. Something like *Little House On The Prairie* – but I hope different enough – because I certainly won't say those things in front of a camera to anybody! From what I hear, it starts after we've arrived. But I guess we would have had to come over by boat. There weren't a lot of planes around at the turn of the century!"

The film, titled *The Bull On The Barroom Floor*, was described as a Western about three young Englishmen who emigrate to America in the early days and, according to Barry, "bring a bull with them and mate it. It's very fast. It's supposed to be a 'chase film' which hasn't been done for a few years. Something along the lines of *Mad Mad World.*"

With a plot with the unlikely combination of *Little House On The Prairie* and *It's A Mad Mad Mad Mad World*, it was no surprise that this film, like *Lord Kitchener's Little Drummer Boys* and *Castle,* never saw the light of day. "They were just ideas, once again, that never came to fruition," Tom Kennedy said of the project.

Fortunately, The Bee Gees didn't have to depend on their film career to earn a living. Their old fans were still there, and the new sound was bringing in more fans. Barry Gibb believes that the secret of their success is mainly down to one thing. "It's the songs, basically, that sold us," he said. "We have a large 'listening' audience – people who just like the things we've been writing and the music we've been performing. Whether somebody comes to 'adore' us because of the way we look or the way we dress – or anything like that – I don't really know. Our fans, whether it be [in the US] or in Germany – where once they take a liking to you they really stay hooked – or in Japan – where they told us that the audiences would just clap politely, but where we always get standing ovations and really enthusiastic responses – I'd have to say the audiences are very similar. We've developed a 'listening' audience."

★   ★   ★

Maurice's divorce from Lulu became final on August 21, 1975, and they got together for the first time in two years to discuss the sale of their £88,000 Highgate home. There was some tension on both sides before the meeting, but as it turned out, it was completely unnecessary.

"When Lulu and I met to talk things over, I thought it would turn into a cat-and-dog fight, but it was lovely," Maurice revealed. "I am glad that Lu and I can still be good friends. Our attitude now is that we have to go ahead and live our separate lives."

Maurice still maintained that their marriage failed because he and Lulu had their separate careers going on under the same roof. "I found it was very difficult for two show business people to be married because we were always apart through work. And I suppose when Lulu and I were married we were so young we didn't have the experience to make it work. She couldn't join me on tours because of her work and then when I was off, she was working hard.

"With Yvonne I can feel much more relaxed and we've hardly been away from each other since we met. I'd miss her terribly if we were separated for even a few days."

Maurice said that the couple had always planned to marry once his divorce from Lulu became final, but it would need to wait until after the end of The Bee Gees' tour of Canada in early October. He revealed that the couple were planning a much different wedding from his first in church with thousands of fans outside. "This one is going to be in the registry office with just a few family and friends."

"My mother wasn't too happy when she heard I was going off to live with a pop singer," Yvonne admitted. "But she changed her mind when she met Maurice." Not only had her parents given their blessing to the match, but they had also moved in with the couple, living with them in Maurice's Sussex home.

"We have been very happy for the past 18 months and hope to have children soon," added Yvonne. In fact, she was already nearly three months pregnant when she and Maurice spoke to reporters.

"My personal life is a lot happier," Maurice said, "and work is going well too – our single 'Jive Talkin'' is number one in the States and number five [in Britain]."

For Lulu's part, she professed to be very happy that Maurice had found a girl whom he wanted to marry, adding, "I wish them both all the happiness." She dismissed any suggestion that she may have been put off by her first experience of married life, saying, "I still want a man in my life – a normal man living in a normal house who I can have normal children by."

For a time, anyway, she would find that man in hairdresser John Frieda, whom she married in 1976 and with whom she has her much-loved son, Jordan.

★　★　★

The release of 'Nights On Broadway' coincided with the first concert of The Bee Gees' Canadian tour at the Memorial Arena in Victoria, British Columbia. The record gave them their second American Top 10 single from the *Main Course* album, perhaps in this case assisted by the editing on advance American promo copies. These omitted "the dreamy part" which Stigwood was so rightly fond of but which destroyed the song's momentum as a snappy potential hit single. Regular copies of the single retained this bridge section and it was the last occasion, before the advent of 12-inch remixes, that any of their singles would be tampered with in such obvious fashion.

'Nights On Broadway' was yet another Top 20 hit in Germany although, this time, they pitched wide of the mark in the UK. However, less than two years later, Candi Staton would rectify this glitch when she charted with her own version.

The tour came to an end at the Forum in Halifax, Nova Scotia, and The Bee Gees returned home. Barry and Lynda left behind their rented semi-detached house at the top of Bray Hill in Douglas on the Isle of Man and bought a larger house at the top of Princes Road called "Sherdley", where they lived with Lynda's parents, George and May Gray.

Maurice officially announced his engagement to Yvonne, and on October 17, the wedding took place at Haywards Heath registry office. Barry, on crutches and with his leg in plaster after a fall on his front steps, acted as best man for his younger brother. Maurice was kept waiting nearly 15 minutes before his bride-to-be arrived in a silver Rolls-Royce. Following the four-minute ceremony, the new Mr and Mrs Maurice Gibb and their guests returned to the couple's home for a champagne reception.

The final two months of 1975 were spent promoting the *Main Course* album in Europe with press parties held in Copenhagen, Hamburg, Amsterdam, Brussels, Milan and Paris. The album earned them their first AMPEX Golden Reel award in the US with $1,000 going to the charity of their choice, The Children's Health Council.

Meanwhile, convinced that it made good business sense to do so, Ahmet Ertegun had recommended the purchase of RSO to his board. Jerry Greenberg believes that Warner Communications were thinking about doing a deal, but declined because Stigwood's price was too high. In any event, Polygram stepped in with a much bigger financial commitment, and Warner's were left to rue their inability to conclude the deal. As Greenberg less than subtly put it, "Of course it was the biggest fucking mistake they made!"

Robert Stigwood thus changed the American distribution of RSO's recordings from the Warner's subsidiary Atlantic to the Dutch record company Polygram, of which Polydor was a part.

In January, 1976, as the group flew to the US to begin work on their next album, the third single from *Main Course,* 'Fanny (Be Tender With My Love)' was released. It was issued a month later in the US, where it entered the Top 20, eventually peaking at the number 12 spot. Once again, the group credited Arif Mardin's production for a major part of the single's success, but as they went into the studios this time, they could no longer count on Mardin's guidance.

Arif Mardin was contracted to Atlantic, and since The Bee Gees were now effectively signed to Polydor under the new RSO arrangement, he would no longer be available to produce the group's albums. The Dream Team partnership of Mardin and The Bee Gees had come to an abrupt end. A new challenge was suddenly thrust on The Bee Gees.

26

SHOULD YOU BE DANCING?

"Everybody at atlantic was telling [Arif], 'They won't do anything without you.' And Arif was saying, 'Don't worry. These guys will do it,'" Maurice remembered.

Despite Mardin's faith in The Bee Gees' ability, they weren't immediately confident that they could produce their next album themselves. Barry recalled that they phoned Arif and asked, "Who do you think can continue where you left off?' He said, 'Listen, I've worked with you guys. You can do it. You don't need anybody else. Go away and do it, the same as you did for *Main Course*.' I didn't really believe that . . . We didn't like it because we'd just had our first successful album in years, and we didn't want to have to start looking for another guy that was compatible to us."

The Bee Gees flew to California to begin work on the new album with veteran producer, Richard Perry, but it became apparent almost immediately that Perry's personal style and The Bee Gees were not a happy mix.

"We were in the studio in LA for three days with Richard. His constant position of sitting in the studio was this," Barry said, slouching in his chair and narrowing his eyes to sleepy slits to demonstrate. "And he had a phone on his console that he always talked on, so things were either constantly out of it or constantly disturbing. What he does, I'm told, is that he's out of it most of the time, but when it comes time to cut the tracks and actually *function*, he gets it done. And then he goes back to being out of it again."

The group played 'You Should Be Dancing' to Perry on three separate occasions, but even by the end of the third rendition he could not appreciate its hit potential.

Once again, they phoned Mardin to relate the experience. The situation seemed desperate; they didn't feel that they could work that way. "Arif said, 'You've got to do it yourself. *You* know what you want.' So that's what we did," Barry said.

"A producer's job is mostly just to be there and to encourage the artist's creativity," Blue Weaver explained. "I mean, what Arif did was to *be* there, to *guide* and to *influence*. It helped just to have his presence there . . . he didn't tell you what to do. Sometimes, he would stop you and say, 'Oh, you've gone a bit too far, you've lost it there. What you were doing half an hour ago was great,' and you think, 'Oh, what was I doing half an hour ago?' and he would be able to tell you exactly."

The group flew back to Miami and the familiar environment of Criteria Recording Studios, determined to use what they had learned from Arif to produce the album themselves. They continued to draw on their environment as he had encouraged them to do, to take inspiration from all types of music.

"You listen to all the radio stations – FM, AM, black, MOR – and you find out exactly what is happening . . . Then we go into the studio with four ideas only," Barry explained. "It takes about two weeks, maybe three, to cut the four tracks – to cut them well, I mean, as far as finished items are concerned."

He denied that this was a crass, commercial approach to music, insisting, "If you are a natural songwriter and your feeling is in it, it's not a cold calculating thing at all. You listen not to steal, but to find out what little things are happening in songs and making hits."

Karl Richardson, whose engineering work had helped Mardin make *Main Course* the success that it was, was enlisted as co-producer as well as engineer this time around. "We knew we would come back here to Miami and work with Karl, who's a genius engineer and knows us from *Main Course*," Barry said.

"We would actually get physically involved," Blue added. "I mean, Karl was the engineer; he would get the vocal sounds, and we would give suggestions to him, but in those days, Karl was a brilliant engineer." The new production team set forth to begin recording their new album.

It wasn't easy at first. "We knew what we wanted, but we didn't know how to get it technically," Barry admitted. "But the problem was, we needed ears in the box. Someone to listen and give us help while we were recording . . ."

"We got two basic tracks down. I was having a lot of trouble just keeping my hands on the knobs and getting the sounds they wanted, and they were having a hard time communicating to the musicians what they really meant. So I saw the need for somebody else to be in the control room," Karl Richardson agreed.

A phone call was made to Richardson's best friend. Albhy Galuten had just finished recording a Bees Make Honey album and had no projects in the immediate offing, so he caught a plane to Miami.

An alumnus of Berkeley School of Music, Albhy was just what was needed. "He was musically trained, had a very wide musical knowledge, which was invaluable at that time," Tom Kennedy explained. "When they started producing themselves again, Albhy was brought in with Karl as a co-producer."

"As it turned out, some of Albhy's ideas were really good for some of the songs we were working on," Karl said. "So the relationship was struck up. They recognised the need for somebody else in the control room, somebody who could musically interpret what they were trying to say. It works well as a team because when they hear something, Albhy can say to the musicians,

'Let's try it like that.' The musician's paying a lot of attention to his instrument, what he's trying to do, and he's not thinking about the song, so to speak. Whereas the brothers are thinking about the song. They're not playing the instruments, so they don't know the technicalities of trying to get a particular sound out of an instrument. Myself, I'm involved in trying to capture it on tape. So Albhy is really the extra hand, he's in 'cause he can interpret what's going on."

"Albhy was a musician," Blue conceded, "but we didn't *need* Albhy there to interpret their ideas – we'd already been working with them, we'd already done *Main Course*. I was responsible for actually pulling Albhy in because Karl said to me, 'Oh, I need somebody there' – because if you talk to him about music, he couldn't relate to it. Albhy was Karl's sidekick, and Karl said, 'I'd like Albhy to be there so that when you ask me a question about music, you can ask Albhy,' so he was Karl's guide, if you like, for when none of us were in the studio. That was initially it, and maybe Albhy saw dollar signs and went to . . . a big lawyer and got a contract straight. He most probably couldn't believe his luck because here was a guy whose luggage consisted of a cardboard box tied up with a little piece of string. In fact, when we went to Canada to mix the *Children Of The World* album, we arrived in Montreal in the middle of a snowstorm. They must have set the luggage down on trolleys on the runway because by the time the luggage came in on the carousel, Albhy's cardboard box had disintegrated and his t-shirts and pants were just lying there. I can't remember exactly how he gathered his belongings together but it was most probably a duty-free carrier bag that he stuffed them into." To be fair to Albhy, he wasn't one of Atlantic's big wage-earners at that point. Jerry Wexler recalled paying him something in the region of $50 a week, as he put it, "to hang around".

"Albhy and Karl also got themselves down as producers. Good luck to them for getting the business side of things sorted out first. They think they got their priorities right, whereas Dennis, Alan and I have only ourselves to blame. We were into the music first and were genuinely excited about what we were creating. Production credits were the farthest things from any of our minds and perhaps, with the benefit of hindsight, there was a certain amount of naïveté on our part. Karl and Albhy were very clever in getting a co-production credit for *Children Of The World* and future albums, and that is still a contentious point with me because some people put more into the production side than others . . . We could have done it without Albhy, it most probably wouldn't have been a lot different."

The album was given the working title *Pacer*. Somewhere along the line, as the recording progressed, the working title for the album was changed to *Slipstream*, but this was then used by Sutherland Brothers & Quiver. Next in line was *Horizon* which, in turn, became *Response* when it was decided that that might have been too close to their 1967 album *Horizontal*, but by the time it was completed, the LP took its name from its final track, *Children Of The World*.

"We do about two weeks work before we go into the studio," Barry explained, "which is all preliminary ideas . . . which seem better written at the moment rather than three months before. Then, just before recording, you are really fresh, whatever you think of is right now." The first song which emerged from the sessions with the new production team was 'You Should Be Dancing'.

"The bass riff on 'You Should Be Dancing' – that's all Maurice – only he could have done that," Blue observed. "He just goes out and sings stuff to the brass players . . . the string lines as well, Barry would sing the string parts and I'd sit and play those."

The group had begun work on the track before Albhy came into the equation, but he suggested a looser feel, adding percussion. Stephen Stills was also in Miami recording at the time, and he was brought in, along with session player Joe Lala, to play percussion on the track. "Stephen was pretty loaded most of the time, but I had known Stephen from before, so I kind of made the introductions," Albhy recalled. It was the beginning of a long friendship.

"I was always hanging around with Stephen," Blue Weaver said. "Stephen was in one studio, we were in another. I'd go in and do things for him, he'd come in and play with us . . ."

"Barry Gibb and I were just sitting around saying whatever happened to the good old days when we sang each other's songs," Stills recalled. "If you nicked something from someone, they'd nick something back later. Everybody got so protective and competitive which really destroyed a lot of great music. That destroyed the artistic end of the business that was essential to the great upheaval of music in the Sixties."

Stills would go on to play bass on the demo for The Bee Gees' 'Rest Your Love On Me' and even got involved with collaborating with the group on an unreleased song. "We wrote a song together one day," he recalled. "We made an *incredible* track. Incredible! I've yet to finish the lyrics. They wanna use it in the movie of *Grease*."

"We did a track with Stephen as well – The Bee Gees, myself, Dennis playing drums, and Alan," Blue said. "'Walk Before You Run' . . . was a collaboration, we wrote it in the studio."

"Then Robin – all three of 'em – fell in," Stills continued, "and we sang the chorus one evening in four part harmony and everybody went, 'Oh oh, we better not, this would be *too* much to deal with!' Gorgeous sound though."

Albhy's memories of the tune are a little less enthusiastic than Stephen's; as he put it, "I don't think it was a particularly auspicious song."

"I've played on so many Bee Gees songs I don't know which ones I played on and which ones I didn't," Stephen Stills said in 1979. "Because Barry Gibb is an old friend of mine, and I just sat in and played chickum-chit, chickum-chit, a little wacka wacka guitar, then said, 'Use 'em or don't use 'em, I had a great time. You don't even have to use my name.'"

His percussion work on 'You Should Be Dancing' was spot-on, although it took some work to convince the record company. They felt that the percussion breakdown in the song wasn't commercial enough. It was up to Karl Richardson to create a processed version of the track to simulate how it would sound when played on the radio to persuade them not to cut it out of the song.

Richardson's engineering expertise would also come to the forefront for Alan Kendall's brief guitar solo in 'You Should Be Dancing'. According to Albhy, the apparently seamless performance was actually superbly edited by Karl from approximately 12 guitar tracks.

"When I listen to a Bee Gees tune for the first time, I listen for its overall picture of excitement," Richardson explained. "I'm not that technical on the first listening. I listen mainly for the overall 'get-off' point; where does it take me, how do I feel after I've heard it."

Albhy Galuten operated in much the same way, his job as a producer involving listening to a song written by the brothers, played simply to him on acoustic guitars, to "get a vibe on the emotion, like take an emotional photograph of how it moved with the dynamics, and what the important places were . . . Then my job was to make sure, when we had a finished record recorded and mixed and everything, that it created the same emotion.

" 'You Should Be Dancing' is not a song that can stand in a vacuum, but it's based on the way it's recorded and sung. So in those kinds of songs, if you change the vision from what it's supposed to be, even how it's supposed to feel, the songs often don't survive. Particularly up-tempo soul songs. A ballad is a ballad."

Barry agreed with Albhy's theory that the execution of a song could make or break it. "If we had written [the songs for *Main Course*] two years before, we might not have got such a hit LP because we were not giving them the right framework," he added. "Even though the songs themselves might have been good, they would not have been in the 'what is happening now' framework."

As the recording of the album progressed, Maurice was drinking heavily, and it was becoming evident to the others that they could not always rely on him to play his part. With this in mind, Albhy brought in George "Chocolate" Perry to play bass on the song 'Subway'.

"A producer of records is very similar to a producer of films," Galuten explained. "The producer is responsible for hiring the right musicians. You have to arrange the music, the strings, the horns, sometimes choose the songs, get performances out of vocalists and get the sound down on tape. You also have to share in the engineering duties, recording techniques and sound mixing.

"Chocolate was someone who was hanging around at the time . . . and playing, I think, with Crosby, Stills and Nash and other musicians we knew. He was a great bass player, and I thought this would be cool to have him. He seemed like the right bass player for the job. I don't think there was anything particularly nefarious about it."

391

Even though it was done out of a desire to get the best sound for the individual song, it did cause some hurt feelings. "Albhy was always a little blunt," Tom Kennedy recalled. "He wasn't a person who thought about his words, he just said them."

Galuten maintained that, while production credit was given to the entire Bee Gees band with Karl Richardson and himself, "Karl, Barry and I were the main ones. We had a vibe," he said, "very powerful and very creative." The three worked so well together that when Barry went on to do outside productions, he once again enlisted Karl and Albhy's help.

Galuten said that in those days, "Maurice was usually out in the lobby holding court, drinking Perrier, which much of the time had vodka in it . . . being social and hanging out."

Although Robin didn't play any instruments on the records, "He was pretty active in the writing," he added, "and then he and Maurice were usually not in the studio. Robin was often not around at all, except when he came in to sing, but Robin often had good incisive comments. He'd come in, maybe at the end of the day every day, like we'd work during the day, and they'd come in for dinner . . . Then Robin would make some comments and listen to whatever we'd done that day."

"Robin is the objective production ear," Karl Richardson agreed. "The rest of us – me, Barry, Maurice and Albhy Galuten – get so close to the music, we do so many different experiments, that we can't always tell what sounds good. Robin comes in and calls it in a second; it doesn't work or it's great."

"His comments were often quite useful and sort of objective in certain ways. Maurice's comments in that time period frequently were not," Albhy added bluntly. "He was really not paying attention, and having difficulty with his alcohol problem."

Albhy likened Robin's input on the album to "the way A&R people and executives work. The person who's not in the trenches can come in and say, 'Hey, did you notice . . .' Somebody being objective and outside is often valuable, and there was a voice in there with Robin, and even at a higher level was Stigwood. He'd also come in and listen every month or two to mixes we had put together, and say, 'Great, more hits!' "

For the second time in as many albums, Blue got a composing credit. " 'The Way It Was' was something I'd had for awhile as well," he explained. "That stretched most probably back as far as the 'Songbird' riff did as well. I thought, 'This is a good one – I'll throw this one at him as well and see what happens.' That was just myself and Barry there, and Chocolate playing bass – George Perry played bass."

Although Blue, like most musicians, finds it difficult to choose one album over another, he said, "Of the ones I worked on . . . I think *Children Of The World* most probably [is my favourite]. It was *special*; I don't know why. I suppose it's the amount of work that went into it. Every time I listen, it has a special attraction."

Blue recalled that an unwillingness to accept second-rate performances spurred them on in those days. "I wouldn't let anything go without agreement, or I'd have to be persuaded. But then, I think that's why things turned out so well," he added. "I think we were all a bit like that really – nobody would let anything go. Nobody was lazy; if there was something we weren't quite happy with, no matter how trivial, we'd do it again. And vocally, they're all perfectionists as well, so they wouldn't have anything they weren't happy with."

That perfectionism sometimes caused some heated discussions in the recording studios, but he believes it's all part of the creative process – and part of being a family. "Of course, all families argue, but they'd always come back together, no matter what," he said. "We always argued but that's just the way things are – if people just sat back and were complacent and never aired their views, things would just get left. If you think something's important, you push for it."

"We've all grown more mature about things like who's going to sing the lead on what song, and we don't argue anymore," said Maurice. "We have an occasional difference of opinion, but it's usually two or three of us saying we'll do this or that, and the majority rules. In the old days when the publishing credit said 'B., R. & M. Gibb', and I had nothing to do with it, they would say, 'What's Maurice's name doing on it? Why's he getting paid?'

"We went through all the little stupid arguments. 'Who sings lead?' Who cares, as long as it's a hit? I don't care if I don't have a solo track on the entire album. It's still a Bee Gees record. All that sort of thing is past – we can handle it now."

★   ★   ★

The year 1976 saw the appearance of two films that featured the music of The Beatles. *All This And World War* is a documentary which uses Movietone newsreels and 20th Century-Fox feature film footage to trace the chronology of World War II, against a backdrop of Lennon & McCartney's music as performed by various artists. Recorded at Olympic Studios in London, the soundtrack music was arranged by Will Malone, and directed by Lou Reizner who had assembled an impressive array of performers, including The Bee Gees.

The double-album was released in Britain by Riva, and in the USA by 20th Century Records, where a limited edition boxed set was also available. Both releases contained a lavish booklet containing lyrics to all the songs as well as pictures depicting scenes from the movie. Less than a year after the film's release, Lou Reizner was dead, aged 43.

The Bee Gees shared top billing with Leo Sayer; each performing three songs, while Roy Wood got two of the 28 tracks. 'Golden Slumbers'/ 'Carry That Weight', 'She Came In Through The Bathroom Window' and 'Sun King' were all delivered immaculately by the Gibbs, who had also recorded 'She's Leaving Home' at the session too. Ultimately, it was Bryan

Ferry's rendition that prevailed, although a version with Gibb vocals was in the pipeline.

★   ★   ★

During a break in the recording of *Children Of The World*, Robin and Maurice returned to England to spend some time with their families, while Barry stayed behind in Miami to mix the new single. For Maurice, the timing was critical as it enabled him to be with Yvonne for the birth of their first child. "I wouldn't have missed it for anything," he said.

"He was great," Yvonne declared. "He'd been working during the back of my pregnancy. They were away two and a half months, and I'm getting bigger and bigger. I didn't really mind because he used to phone me every night. He came home about three days before I was to go in hospital. When I went into labour, he came in with gloves on, and he cut the cord."

"I got him as he came out, and the doctor grabbed him with me as well," Maurice added. "And he said, 'You cut there,' and I cut the cord. They gave him to a nurse, and we washed him down. Then I saw it was a boy."

"The doctor said to me, 'Congratulations, you've got a son,'" Yvonne recalled. "And Maurice came over to me and said, 'It's a boy!'"

The six pound nine ounce boy, born at Penbury Hospital, Royal Tunbridge Wells, Kent on February 23, 1976, was named Adam Andrew; had he been a girl, Samantha Louisa were the preferred names. "It makes a great year for me as our latest single ['Fanny (Be Tender With My Love)'] is in the US top 10 and we're touring there later this year," Maurice added.

With little Adam just one week old, Maurice and Yvonne, along with Yvonne's parents, moved from their home, Kidborough House in Danehill, Sussex, to a townhouse at 10 Stanley Terrace in Douglas, Isle of Man. Thus they would now join Barry and his family as tax exiles. Maurice told reporters that he would not be back in England for some time.

Although he admitted to a growing frustration with the tax situation at that time, Robin and Molly remained firmly committed to living in England. "I wish people in the pop world and similar scenes were given greater financial encouragement to stay in Britain at the moment," Robin said. "But I'm prepared to sacrifice some income as the price for staying in the country I regard as home. Molly and I are British to the core, and we just refuse to become tax exiles, although it would be more profitable to do so. While I like the professional excitement of America where we do most of our work, I feel safer and physically more relaxed in England. We believe there is no better place to raise our children. Even though I have to work out of Britain for a large part of the year, it is now easier than ever to fly home to my family."

Molly added, "We both want our children to grow up in the surroundings they were born in."

In 1993, Maurice gave journalist Pamela Coleman a colourful account of those times. Despite the fact that when he moved to the Isle of Man in 1976, the group were more successful than they had been in years, he maintained, "The Bee Gees were in a rut, tax was terribly high, and we were in a valley of depression. I sold my big house in Sussex and moved to the Isle of Man. I ended up with £5,000 in the bank and a blue Rolls-Royce, living in a terrace house next to a fish and chip shop."

Although rich in assets, Maurice was cash poor at the time, though he did have his share of the group's royalties to look forward to, as well as the sale of his shares in RSO. This would soon enable the family to move to a very nice detached house, then called The Old Vicarage, on Belmont Hill in Douglas, Isle of Man. Maurice and Yvonne changed the name of the house to Kidborough after their previous home. In a strange twist, Jim Caine, who had played with Hughie Gibb's band in the Forties and Fifties, did the refurbishment of the house for the couple.

Rather than sell the townhouse, Maurice saw the opportunity not only to retain his investment but also to use it as a source of regular income, renting it out during the remainder of his stay on the island.

His financial position contrasted with a statement from Barry during this period. "The three of us have made a lot of money . . . Even during our quiet periods, our tours grossed a lot of money. No problem there," said the elder brother.

"[We all] are dollar millionaires. I don't want to say I'm a pound sterling millionaire . . . but there is no doubt that The Bee Gees are financially secure. Myself, I'm the fourth largest shareholder in the Robert Stigwood Organisation, followed by Maurice and Eric [Clapton] and people like Frankie Howerd.

"I think we'd rather build up our income over the years, rather than be hit the way Robin is at 83 per cent. We're here [in the Isle of Man] because we'd like to live in England if the tax situation eases off."

With his typical flair for embellishment Maurice contradicted his brother, telling Melvyn Bragg on *The South Bank Show*. "Our careers have been like mountains and valleys, it's been up and down like a yo-yo. We had a great period from '67 to '71; that was just unbelievable. We had lots of hits, everything went really well. We had our first two number ones in America, 'Lonely Days' and 'How Can You Mend A Broken Heart'. Then 'Run To Me' came out, and I think that did fairly well, and after that boom, nobody wanted to know us, they weren't interested.

"Our management lost interest, everyone moved out. All of a sudden, we were left alone. Our manager got interested in musicals with Andrew Lloyd Webber and Tim Rice. All of a sudden, we didn't have a career.

"We were living on the Isle of Man . . . I got really bad in the drink and stuff like that."

Maurice continued in his riches-to-rags vein, his latest account differing slightly in detail to his version of three years before. "Even though we lived on the island, Robin was still living in England because he managed to put more aside than we did. I ended up with a blue Rolls-Royce and about eight grand in the bank. That was it after all the years I'd been working, and then I had to sell the Rolls, of course, and live in a little townhouse next door to a fish and chip shop. That's all I could afford, nothing in the bank. My marriage to Lulu had broken up by then and I'd remarried, and we had a little six-month-old boy called Adam and living in this townhouse. We couldn't even afford a cot. Mind you, the fish and chip shop was good, but it was really rough living there, it was really cold."

While one can feel some sympathy for Maurice, cut off from the social life he used to revel in, his remark about not even being able to afford a cot is surely stretching things a bit too far. For all that he had to suffer a short term cash flow problem, *Main Course* had been the group's most successful album in years, spawning three hit singles in the United States, so even if there was the usual delay in royalties filtering through, the family would hardly have been living hand to mouth.

★   ★   ★

On March 22, Maurice and Yvonne flew back to Miami, leaving one-month-old Adam behind in Douglas with his maternal grandparents. In May, the group left behind Criteria and the Miami sunshine to complete the *Children Of The World* album at Le Studio in Montreal, Quebec, Canada. As non-resident aliens, there were limits to the time they were allowed to work in the US, and with Barry and Maurice as tax exiles, working in Britain was not an option. Le Studio was Canada's finest recording facility at the time and in high demand; The Bee Gees were working evenings and nights there because another artist was booked for the daytime hours. This in itself caused some minor inconvenience – Dick Ashby recalled standing on a step ladder to take photos of the console so they could duplicate all the settings the following day.

Blue recalled that the early mixes of the album were disappointing. "Everything was there, it's just that we weren't happy with maybe the balances, the levels, the way things had been done . . . the mixes sounded very flat, there was no life to them. We just felt that if we want it to be the way that we wanted them, we better go in and do it ourselves."

The album was completed in late May, and the group returned to their homes. For Barry and Maurice, this meant a roundabout route via Paris, then Ireland and on to the Isle of Man, since they weren't allowed to set foot on British soil. When Maurice and Yvonne left for their belated honeymoon in July, their route was equally circuitous. They travelled from the Isle of Man to Dublin, then on to Madrid. From Madrid, they caught a flight to Mexico City and finally on to their ultimate destination, Acapulco.

Back in the Isle of Man, boredom set in for Maurice, and the drink took over. He became a familiar face in the Douglas pubs, just as his blue Rolls-Royce was a familiar sight parked outside. On one such evening out, he met up with a friend who was involved in the planning of the island's famous TT Races. "He asked me if I would like to be a marshal and, as I have had fire rescue and first aid training while in Miami, I decided to give it a try," Maurice recalled. He was given the position of fire marshal at Creg ny Baa, a famous corner section of the TT track, where there is a pub of the same name. Unfortunately, that portion of the track was the scene of a major disruption during the races, when it was suspected that someone had tipped nails all over the track.

During the Seventies Maurice began collecting police uniforms. "He used to bag these uniforms from policemen in the States, badges and everything – I don't know how he would do it – they would walk out in their under-wear, he was so persuasive," Tom Kennedy marvelled. "He had a whole collection of these bits and pieces and used to dress up as a State Trooper and drive around in his Rolls-Royce while inebriated.

"He was arrested in his Rolls-Royce, dressed as an American policeman, by a [real] policeman on a push bike. I think he was driving on the pavement – that's why the policeman got suspicious," Tom added.

Tom's account of the incident was accurate. Maurice left the Casino in Douglas at about 1.00 a.m. on June 20. A suspicious policeman followed him until he stopped his car in the middle of the road near his house. Maurice was charged with driving while his ability was impaired by drink or drugs. He was fined £80 and banned from driving for the next two years.

When Maurice was not busy marshalling TT races or getting arrested, the brothers spent much of their time making absurd home movies to alleviate the monotony. Their interest in home movies had started back in Australia, and has never waned. They enlisted the services of nearly everyone they knew; friends, family, in-laws, all were drafted into co-starring in the epic *Day Of The Kipper*, a play on the film, *The Day Of The Jackal*.

"We made a lot of home movies," said Maurice, "and we had some smuggling of kippers in, so Barry played the chief sergeant type of thing . . . We had to check it out, and there was someone smuggling kippers out of the Isle of Man, and that was the whole story. We went around the whole island, filming everywhere and interviewing different people about the Manx Kippers. It was like a big send-up."

Day Of The Kipper was not the end of their movie-making. "We had another one called *The Million Dollar Cop* which was this guy, 'cause I had a flashy blue Rolls, and I drove around the island a lot in it. I know a lot of the police knew me from the pubs anyway. I know one sergeant in particular did!" Maurice laughed. "Anyway, I would just drive around in it and we filmed it, and we called it *The Million Dollar Cop,* and we had police uni-forms and all sorts of crazy stuff."

David English recalled those daft days of film-making. "Maurice said, 'Come over.' So I went to the Isle of Man," he recounted, "and as my plane touched on the tarmac, this blue Rolls-Royce roared up to the plane with a red light flashing, out gets Maurice, dressed entirely as an American cop, and escorts me off the plane into the Rolls-Royce. So we went back . . . and we made a film called *Million Dollar Cop*. Hughie Gibb was on camera, George and May Gray were in it, Herbie Spenceley was in it. It's a good little 8mm film, we had all the props and all the costumes, and then when Yvonne came out with Adam, she was straight in the film. We were always making little films together, all of us, always a lot of fun. Whenever we went on tour, particularly the promotional tours, we always had a camera and we all made films with Lynda there, Yvonne was in there, all going on, you know. Then the kids came along and we did a wonderful thing [based] on *The Sound Of Music*, lots and lots of little films."

Tom Kennedy recalled that any visitors would be subjected to private screenings of these their cinematic masterpieces. "It's just something that was never meant to be commercial – just one of those things that was done because there was nothing better to do," he added.

★   ★   ★

'You Should Be Dancing' was released on June 21, 1976 in the UK and the following month in the US, and rapidly began its ascent up the charts. Maurice explained how the singles were chosen. "We don't really release anything just for the commercial sake of it, like it would be good just because it's a dancing number – we don't think of things like that. We release songs that mean something to us. The three of us sit down with Robert Stigwood and we listen to the tracks we've done and usually Robert picks out the right one. He always has a good valid reason for releasing.

"It was great to do the ballads and so forth, there were all those strings. But we could have stayed in that groove all the time, we wouldn't have advanced any further. We would have just ended up staying there and doing the same old thing."

Robin told *Record World* magazine that the release of the album was delayed because, "When the president of our record company heard the album, he said it was not to be released until the single got to number one in the United States. This week, it shot up to number five, and only Elton [John] and Kiki [Dee] look like keeping it off the top spot!

"We'll be back on the road touring the States, Canada and Japan by the end of the year. It's a pity we can't work in Britain, but the tax situation is such that when we did a recent BBC radio programme, we had to waive the fee or the tax man would have clobbered us!"

'You Should Be Dancing' did reach number one in the US, and like 'Jive Talkin' ', achieved another very respectable number five in Britain. It was also a Top 20 success in many other countries. There was never any doubt this was going to be the lead-off single, with its insistent dance floor beat and the first whiff of Barry's amazing falsetto lead. 'You Should Be Dancing' is one of those songs that could never be performed any other way, a striking example of the pop music ideal of "writing a record".

Children Of The World was ultimately released on September 1, 1976, although in Australia, record company altercations would delay its release until the following April. On the album, Robin had moved somewhat out of the spotlight which was now solidly on Barry, while Maurice was less involved with the recordings than at any time before or since.

Blue Weaver played synthesizer in place of the strings The Bee Gees had used for years but the new technology was not yet up to the task, especially on the ballads, and sometimes this sounded closer to a cheap organ, unlike the touch of class Arif's arrangements had given them. The real problem was that instrumentally, this album was ahead of its time and can be seen as a worthy experiment. The synthesizer backing, the horn section, and Barry's ubiquitous falsetto give the whole album a lot of high end sound.

In America, some of their new releases featured an interesting addition to the credits. Blue Weaver explains: "Dick Ashby put a blackboard up to put all the credits on; at the end of course it always had 'By arrangement with The Robert Stigwood Organisation', and that was always the final thing. Our roadie at the time was Tom Kennedy, so we added 'and Tom Kennedy', and it got into print! Millions of records went out with 'By arrangement with The Robert Stigwood Organisation and Tom Kennedy.' Have a look at the [first American pressings of the] singles of 'Love So Right' [and 'Boogie Child' as well as the *Children Of The World* album]. There was a gold album with the label on it, as well, all saying 'and Tom Kennedy.' Robert wasn't too pleased about that!"

Tom Kennedy pointed out the obvious. "Nobody had proof-read the liner-notes! That's the sort of pranks we'd get up to . . . I've got the gold record where it's actually on the label."

As praise came in for their production work on the new LP, Maurice was modest, paying credit to their mentor. "We could never say that Arif Mardin didn't do 50 per cent of the groundwork for the hits we have today," he admitted. "Everyone knows what a great producer he is. We don't pretend to produce like Arif does now, but we've learned to write our music more like he would produce it."

Maurice revealed that as they began work on the album, they had sought Mardin's input. "We were saying, 'Can we send you the tapes to see what you think?' He said, 'Well, I have to hear them sometime, but don't tell anybody.' So we sent him the tapes and he sent a note back saying, 'They're fantastic. Don't do a thing to them.' "

As *Children Of The World* raced up the charts, The Bee Gees' "second" career was moving from strength to strength. "This album doesn't just have disco and R&B," Barry said. "To us, there are other tracks on the album and on *Main Course* that could be hits as well. For The Bee Gees, it's not right to put out these tracks as singles yet."

The Bee Gees have often described their songwriting as almost telepathic. 'Love So Right' was a case in point. "No line ever looked so right to me as, 'I thought you came forever, but you came to break my heart.' But we didn't think of it," Barry revealed. "We sat there singing along and there it was. Maybe we did think of it but not on a conscious level."

"It just comes . . . Sometimes we surprise ourselves," Robin added. "It's as if somebody had said, 'Put that line there.' It's like we're picking it up from somewhere . . . as if somebody is trying to get hold of us and tell us that that's the line to use."

'Love So Right' became the second single from *Children Of The World*, issued to coincide with the album's release, and RSO also released a special promotional 12-inch containing four *Children Of The World* tracks, including extended versions of 'Boogie Child' and 'You Stepped Into My Life', the seven inch version's B-side. The release eventually climbed to number three in the US charts, their fourth American Top 10 single in two years. Once again, Europe and the UK markets were harder to crack, with the song barely breaking into the Top 40 in either region. However, by now, The Bee Gees were beginning to become a bit sensitive about the disco label. "The new single is an R&B ballad and you certainly couldn't dance to it," Barry said. "We always have the fear of falling into that bag with these new records because we're not *just* a disco group."

"We won't put out two disco songs in a row either," Maurice added. "Disco music isn't that bad, as long as it progresses with new sounds and lyrics. But The Bee Gees aren't a band that will do disco for the rest of their lives just because we've clicked again with it. We clicked with other kinds of music as well. We'll go on trying other kinds of music if this stops working. Our music will always go on. We might get too old one day to sing it, but until then we don't intend to stop."

"We had to become an R&B band," Barry agreed. "If you look at our past history, it's gone from one form of music to another. We're a band that likes most kinds of music, and in five years you may not find us doing this any more. *Children Of The World* is a mixture, as was *Main Course*. Side two wasn't played so much because it's oldish Bee Gees. Right now it's a very vibrant band, and the songs are pouring out. In the old days, we took three or four weeks to cut an album, and now we're taking three months. It makes a hell of a difference, especially when you're in there with the right people. The band – Dennis Bryon, Alan Kendall, and Blue Weaver – are more like Bee Gees than side musicians, these guys have been with us for years. On *Children Of The World* everyone gets a cut, not just a wage."

A two-week stint in Las Vegas was cancelled due to "increasing commitments elsewhere in the USA", much to the brothers' relief. For them, nightclub work, no matter how deluxe, still brought back horrible memories of failure. The Bee Gees also cancelled a proposed concert at the Palace Lido to raise money for the Isle of Man's Olympic participants.

After rehearsals in the Isle of Man, The Bee Gees flew to New York on November 8, accompanied by a blaze of publicity. In *Melody Maker*, Chris Charlesworth wrote, "A casual visitor to New York this month could be excused for thinking that The Bee Gees are currently running for elected office.

"It has been a campaign worthy of a presidential candidate, the purpose of which is to trumpet to the nation the fact that The Bee Gees, after a very shaky period at the beginning of this decade, are currently bigger and more popular than at any time during their career."

To celebrate their success Robert Stigwood threw a stylish party for them at his sumptuous triplex apartment on Central Park West and, in an unprecedented move, RSO combined their massive publicity drive with The Bee Gees opening their "International Headquarters", a shop on busy 57th Street. The shop sold their albums, tickets, posters, clothing – anything and everything Bee Gees. "It's the sort of place you can buy souvenirs, t-shirts, records that are collectors' items, things like that," Maurice said. "It also tells you where we are touring, [in case] anybody wants to know where we are at a certain time."

Barry described it as "a gathering place for the people who are interested in the music and the oddities they may want to collect. It was our management's idea."

"We didn't see it until we came to New York," Robin added.

The shop certainly drew its share of visitors. There seemed to be no escape from the group for the people of New York City with posters of the *Children Of The World* album cover adorning the backs of the city's buses.

At the opening ceremony, policemen struggled to contain the crowd of predominantly teenage girls as the group stepped through a gigantic replica of the *Children Of The World* album, which had been reproduced with Blue Weaver's little amendment. The disc was "literally six or eight feet tall," Tom Kennedy recalled, "and at the bottom it said, 'Robert Stigwood & Tom Kennedy.' I didn't know anything about it at that time. Later on, Robert found out it was Blue, and he saw the funny side of it."

For the better part of the month, Barry, Robin and Maurice held court in a suite at the Sheraton Hotel on 7th Avenue, giving countless interviews. "Publicity is a key factor," Robin explained. "People say if the music is there, you don't need publicity. But tasteful publicity, well done, isn't harmful. People in America love this kind of thing. They like to have things put smack bang in their faces."

"The fact is that the music is succeeding, and our record company wants to promote us," Barry added.

They announced their plans to donate the net proceeds of their Madison Square Garden concert to New York's Police Athletic League, a charity to provide sporting facilities for underprivileged children via police sponsored youth clubs. Maurice explained, "A lot of gigs come here and take a lot of bread out of the city and never give it back. We want to leave the money here this time."

The Bee Gees were invited as the guests of honour for a gala luncheon party on the lawns of Gracie Mansion by the mayor of New York, Abe Beame. It was the first time a party for a pop group had ever been held at the mayoral mansion, and Mayor Beame was more than a little bemused by it all. "Rock Music? The only notes I know about are the ones they put on

Wall Street," quipped the diminutive mayor. He later proved his point by referring to his honoured guests as "The Jay Pees" and "The Gee Bees" before presenting them with the key to the city.

New York in November is not the usual venue for a garden party, but Robert Stigwood picked up the bill of nearly $15,000 for the Mayor's "midi dansant"★, including heating the giant yellow and white marquee against the near freezing cold outside. He reasoned, "It's hard to get 300 of the beautiful people out for a pop group, but an invitation from the mayor is an offer they can't refuse."

James Taylor, Carly Simon, Andy Warhol and Paulette Goddard were among the 1,000 guests – the celebrities mingling with journalists from both the political and pop world – who dined on beef wellington, hot smoked salmon, pâté and lobster mousse and danced to the music of Peter Duchin. Despite the mayor's wife spilling tomato juice on his shoulder, Maurice gallantly asked Mrs Beame to dance, but she declined, saying she had an ingrown toenail.

It was also a rather shrewd – but nonetheless generous – promotional stunt to kick off the tour, which took them across the country, collecting the keys to the cities of New Orleans and San Francisco along the way.

"The tours certainly were gruelling, I have to say," Tom Kennedy admitted. "It was bags at 9.00; bodies at 10.00, on and on and on."

Gruelling or not, Maurice claimed he wouldn't have it any other way. "I think if we weren't allowed to tour," he declared, "or at least go on stage any more, I'd be very upset. I love going on stage and having a good time and pleasing the audience that buys the records. I think if we just stayed a studio group and didn't perform, I'd be, you know, a bit down about it. I would find it boring just sitting at home, going to the studio to record and then back home again. You don't meet the other people, the people who buy your records."

"We have come pretty close to our recorded sound on stage because we have some good people who do our sound, and we go for the best we can. In fact, somebody said to us once, 'Are you miming?' We try to get the best stage effects, the best sound, the best lighting and so forth," he added.

At the pre-concert sound check for the Madison Square Garden concert, the group nostalgically performed 'Let Me Love You', Barry's early composition from their Redcliffe Speedway days.

After the concert, Barry, Robin and Maurice Gibb presented Robert Morgenthau of the Police Athletic League with a cheque for $31,000. In addition to donating the net proceeds of the concert, The Bee Gees personally paid the costs of lighting, stage and sound crews, as well as all musicians and production fees.

"I hope this sets a precedent for the other groups," Barry said. "It would

★ Dancing at lunchtime.

be nice if every band gave one concert for charity. A really big band would never miss the money."

Maurice added, "We did it because New York has given us so much inspiration for writing, things like that, and all sorts of people have been great to us. We thought we'd pay the city back. It was not because the Police Athletic League was the one we picked; it was just the one that needed help most, because they're the ones that look after people.

"They take [young people] off the streets so there's not juvenile delinquents growing up to be desperate criminals or whatever. The Police Athletic League are the people who grab these kids off the street and give them something to do."

Nevin Graham, the director of developments for the PAL told reporters, "The Bee Gees' donation was the largest we received from one source the entire year. And The Bee Gees' donation was the most pleasing we have ever received because it was done out of the goodness of their hearts."

The Muscular Dystrophy Foundation also benefited when the group received their second AMPEX Golden Reel award, this time for *Children Of The World*.

The final concert of the tour at the Forum in Los Angeles on December 20 was recorded for their contractually obligatory live album, and the group returned to their homes to spend a quiet Christmas with their families, before returning to a hectic pace in the coming year.

27

SEX, DRUGS & DISCO!

WHILE THE MOVE towards R&B had proved so successful with *Main Course* and *Children Of The World*, by 1977 The Bee Gees were all too aware of the jeopardy of becoming complacent. "It was a good change, but it's by no means the last," Barry said. "We have no intention of stopping in this one area. We're going to try to embrace all kinds of areas as long as we exist as a band. It's not something you can put into words. It's just a feeling between the three of us, and how our writing is stepping up in scale.

"The next album will be more progressive and have more variety. We want to get a little more intricate; we want to add a little more melody and place more importance on the lyrics. Last year we had a pop hit, an R&B hit and a country hit, which must prove that you shouldn't dwell in one area. We just want to keep developing."

One of the proposed new developments for the group was to branch out into films, but for the moment there was the task of mixing their first live album and writing the songs for their next studio album.

In April, 1977, The Bee Gees flew to Paris and began work at the Château D'Herouville in the north of France, the studio which Elton John immortalised when he recorded *Honky Chateau* there in 1972. According to all accounts, when they arrived at the studio, it was not exactly what they were expecting.

"I recall that the Gibbs thought the Château was going to be some elaborate production like Versailles," said Fredric Gershon, then President of the Stigwood Group. "Instead it was a cold, depressing place. They were more than a little cranky."

"When Elton did his album, the studio had just been built, and it was fabulous," Maurice recalled. "By the time we went there, we felt like we were waiting for the Americans to come and liberate us. The place had gone downhill, and the studio itself had no atmosphere."

"One of the reasons they were put in D'Herouville was because there were few distractions," related David English. "It was in the middle of nowhere. It's very strange because the studio is haunted. There was an axe through the console of one of the rooms of the studio, and that studio had never been used again. There was also this cook who was crazy on Keith Richards, and he used to get up and do impersonations, jump up and down and sing."

"It *was* a pretty funky studio," Albhy Galuten agreed. "[It] had a window that didn't really close all the time 'cause you needed the air, and it was right by the piano, so it was very hard to keep the piano in tune, by an open window, as you can imagine.

"We got it because it was cheap, and also because we'd originally gone there to record and mix the live album. Something about by recording it outside the United States and mixing it, they didn't have to pay American taxes or some such thing."

Nonetheless, they soldiered on and began work on their next album. "We started recording our new album with a track called 'If I Can't Have You'," Maurice said. "About a week after we got there and started warming up and getting used to the studio, Robert phoned us."

Barry recalled that Stigwood told them to press on with mixing the live album, putting the studio album on the back burner until it was finished. Only a few days had passed when their manager phoned them again. "Robert called me up and said, 'I'm doing this film called *Tribal Rights Of A New Saturday Night* from an article by Nik Cohn in the *New York* [magazine] . . .'"

★   ★   ★

As in most undertakings in which many people are involved, there are contrasting recollections about how the project that would become *Saturday Night Fever* actually started. Ask a hundred participants, and you'll get a hundred different answers, most equally convincing in their sincerity.

According to Robert Stigwood, about six months before the story was published, Nik Cohn, a former London based music writer now living in New York, had come to him with an idea. He told Stigwood, whom he had known from his days in England, that he wanted to write a screenplay or at least the story for a film. Stigwood said, "Okay, if you have an idea, come and see me again, and we'll talk about it."

Half a year passed by with no word from the aspiring screenwriter, when by chance a magazine cover caught Stigwood's eye. He recalled, "I picked up *New York* magazine and saw this cover story and Nik's name. So I immediately read it, and I thought, 'This is a wonderful film subject.' So I called Nik up and said, 'You're crazy! You come to me about writing a story for a picture. This is it!' And I made a deal with his agent in 24 hours to acquire the rights."

"There'd been a hit record called 'The Hustle', Van McCoy's record, that suggested there was a club culture . . . that wasn't being written up," Nik Cohn explained, "but I started to go to discotheques in Manhattan . . . I met this . . . black dancer, and he became my guide to the scene . . . With him we started going to gay clubs, watched the dancing there, and he said, 'Well, there are these Italian kids over in Brooklyn, you ought to take a look at them.'

"It was a very different kind of disco dancing than [in] the Sixties with everyone sort of waggling themselves around and waving their arms in the air. As soon as 'The Hustle' came in, I suppose it was a primitive version of line dancing . . . That's what it was, everybody would line up and do pre-ordained steps. The leader would sort of call out the claps, and that was the earliest form of disco dancing."

Nik Cohn's account of how the film came about included the story that his wife took a call for him, which she said was from a "Rabbi Stigfeldt". He didn't bother to return the call, thinking a local synagogue was seeking donations, but Robert Stigwood persisted. "He called until he got *me* on the line," Cohn said. "We talked, he said he wanted to do the film. He called my agent to make the deal and she had his papers from his lawyer the same day.

"The whole thing was completely baffling to me," he added. "I mean, people didn't make films out of articles or short stories, films were films, magazines were magazines, sometimes books were turned into films but never magazine stories. I didn't feel that my article or story was a sacred document. It wasn't the most important thing I'd written, certainly not to me . . ."

According to Anthony Haden-Guest in his book *The Last Party: Studio 54, Disco And The Culture Of The Night*, Nik Cohn was fully aware of the film potential of his article and in fact had given a pre-publication copy of the story to Kevin McCormick, with whom he had been collaborating on another film project. McCormick read it and turned it over to Robert Stigwood.

Stigwood read the story and phoned his lawyer and partner, RSO chief Freddie Gershon. Stigwood told him, "I see a hundred-million-dollar movie."

"There *are* no hundred-million-dollar movies," Gershon retorted. "You are crazy."

At that time, Gershon said, disco was happening but had not yet become the worldwide sensation that it would later. "It was the very smart set and the gay set, which was sometimes the same set," he continued. "It hadn't spilled over. But Robert saw this was happening in Brazil. The year we went on the maiden voyage of the Concorde from Paris to Rio, Rio was rough and very exotic, and the music never stopped. He saw it happening in England, France, Germany. It was going down the social strata. Five years earlier it would have been deemed effete for men to even be on a dance floor. Now men were becoming peacocks. It was Robert's instinct that a Tony Manero existed in every community in the world."

Gershon got an option on *Tribal Rites Of The New Saturday Night* for $10,000, with Kevin McCormick assigned to produce, but before the deal had been finalised, seasoned producer Ray Stark expressed his interest in the story. Stigwood clinched the deal by offering Cohn the option of writing the first draft of the screenplay for a guaranteed $150,000 and agreeing to Cohn's demand for a percentage cut of the soundtrack royalties. It was unprecedented for a writer to be given a share of the soundtrack royalties, but Stigwood was determined to make the film. Anyway, soundtrack albums were hardly big sellers.

Stigwood and Gershon travelled to Los Angeles and hired a director, John Avildson, whose work on *Rocky* Stigwood admired. Avildson insisted on working with *Serpico* scriptwriter Norman Wexler. Stigwood acquiesced, and Wexler was hired, although no one bothered to inform Nik Cohn, busily working on his script.

Not that Cohn minded. "I was just riding on its coattails, extremely pleased whatever happened, that was just fine. I could see that Norman Wexler was extremely skilled, and he'd made a commercial film," he said graciously. "He got [the dialogue] right! He got it as right as I got it wrong."

"The person that did the most research was Norman Wexler," Stigwood admitted, "and he really did hang out at all those clubs, the rhythm of the dialogue, he got it perfectly. I wouldn't touch it, you know I wouldn't water it down. Because he wrote *Serpico*, he knew it had to be gritty – you can't gloss over the way those kids talk."

Gershon and Stigwood were staying at the Beverly Hills Hotel during the negotiations. One evening as Gershon was sitting in the living room of their bungalow, he recalled, "I hear a screaming in the bedroom! 'Quick! Quick!'"

He dashed into the bedroom and found Stigwood watching *Welcome Back, Kotter*. Stigwood had found his Tony Manero.

John Travolta had previously auditioned for Robert Stigwood when he was casting *Jesus Christ, Superstar* for its Broadway run. Stigwood liked what he saw but felt that Travolta was too young to fit in with the rest of the cast. "But I remembered his name," Stigwood said, "and I was intrigued a few years later to see him pop up on *Welcome Back, Kotter* as Vinnie Barbarino. I could see the potential building for him, so I offered him a firm three-picture deal, pay or play guarantee of a million dollars. That came from left field.

"[John] made a great crack at the press reception when his film deal was announced. He said, 'I auditioned for him five years ago, and I just heard back!'"

Although at that point John Travolta was best known for his role as the educationally challenged Barbarino, he had a wealth of experience in TV, stage and film work and had even recorded an album. Still, the contract with Stigwood was quite a coup for a young actor as yet untried as a leading man.

"It was very unusual, but very typical of Robert's belief in himself," Freddie Gershon said. "It guaranteed that John Travolta would be paid for three pictures, even if the first one bombed. But Stigwood owned him, the way the old studios used to own an artist. Like a chattel."

Shooting for the film was scheduled for January 1977 at Paramount. Stigwood was dealing with the studio chief, Barry Diller. Diller's reputation as a shrewd, tough businessman preceded him, but according to Freddie

Gershon, "He also had the ability to step back and say, 'I don't agree with you but I will defer to you.' Had he not done that, there would have been a debacle, because he was under a lot of pressure to make this a PG movie."

For a film targeting the youth market, making the film an R-rated picture seemed incomprehensible. The language used in the film was the main objection. "How are the kids going to get in? There were many fights," Gershon explained. "I think Robert allowed a few 'fucks' and 'sucks' to be taken out as a concession."

"I was a *bit* worried about the language," Stigwood conceded.

The next problem to be solved was the music – there wasn't any. Stigwood and Gershon had lost their concentration on the film and were occupied with negotiations to poach The Rolling Stones from Atlantic Records to sign with RSO. Proposals flew back and forth from their suite at the Plaza Athenee to the Stones at the Georges V Hotel and their long-time business manager, Prince Rupert Lowenstein at the Beverly Hills Hotel. Lowenstein was keeping Atlantic Records founder, Ahmet Ertegun, informed of each new offer, using Stigwood's bids to try to raise their stakes with Atlantic.

"Robert finally said they were getting very, very greedy. Very, very, *very* greedy!" Gershon recalled. Stigwood conceded he had had enough and dropped the idea of signing Mick Jagger and company for RSO. Stigwood was nothing if not gracious in defeat, and in typical fashion, he concluded the negotiations with a flourish.

"Robert and Ahmet were very old friends," Gershon said. "Robert had had it. He said, 'I've gone the limit on this deal,' and he sent Ahmet a bottle of Louis Roederer on his account."

Stigwood turned his attentions back to his film project and the task at hand of providing music. He made a simple phone call to a recording studio outside Paris. Enter The Bee Gees.

As far as *Saturday Night Fever* is concerned, there is a discrepancy between what the Gibbs said *then*, what they say *now*, not to mention fluctuating opinions during the Eighties. To date, Barry, Robin and Maurice Gibb have spent more than 20 years alternately defending and disparaging the film, its music and its impact on the group.

Maurice's memory of events is sometimes clouded by the alcoholism which gripped him at the time. "We wrote the entire musical score of *Saturday Night Fever* in a matter of hours," he boasted in 1978. "We spent as much time at the premiere party as we did in composing the music!"

Barry gives a more considered version of events. He says that the songs for *Saturday Night Fever* were born out of four or five weeks of horrible weather and being miles from civilisation. "All of those songs were for our own album," he said in 1989. "They weren't for *Fever* at all. Robert just happened to hear those four or five songs and said he wanted them for the movie, and 'Please don't make an album, this will be your new album.' So we said okay. 'How Deep Is Your Love', 'Stayin' Alive', 'More Than A

Woman', 'If I Can't Have You' – these things were all done in a chateau in France in really bad weather, with nothing else to do . . . Not even having television was actually very conducive to songwriting. It really worked well. There was no other form of entertainment, so you literally *had* to go to work. We couldn't be lazy. The record for 'How Deep Is Your Love' was mixed about six times. 'Stayin' Alive' was mixed about six times."

Ten years later, Barry claimed that when Robert Stigwood called about the film, he asked for suggestions for songs because The Bee Gees had never done any songs for a movie, and it might be a good experience. "So I said, 'I'll call you back, let me just think about it.' So, about an hour later, I called him back and said, 'There were three titles come to mind. One is 'Stayin' Alive' and one is 'Night Fever', and I suggest you don't call the film *Tribal Rights Of A New Saturday Night*. You've got to give it something people will remember, and something much shorter.' I suggested 'Night Fever' as perhaps being the title of the film, and I remember Robert retorting . . . 'No, that's too pornographic, that's too hot, we can't use that.' I said, 'But those are the suggestions I have right off the bat.' "

Maybe there was no TV to keep them amused, but there were other recreational pursuits. Two years further down the line, they would reveal to *Rolling Stone* magazine that their clear-cut image wasn't completely deserved, and that for "Barry, Robin and Maurice" you could substitute "potty, pilly and pissy".

For Robin, "speed" was but a distant memory and he confessed that "grass" made him confused, forgetful and paranoid. "If you can't face reality and be happy with it," he explained, "what's the point of living?

"But we're not choirboys either," he hinted.

It appeared that success was not the only thing that had been going to their heads. Barry admitted to having tried cocaine, but clearly the chemical experience wasn't pleasant for him either. "My nose was like a block of concrete for a week," he told *People* magazine.

Marijuana appeared to be an acceptable alternative but Hugh Gibb was confused by its appeal. "There's nobody yet explained to me what pot does for them," he said.

His wife Barbara also entered the debate agreeing, "I've had a puff with Barry, and it doesn't do a thing to me. I don't say to people, 'Don't do it,' but it wouldn't do for me."

It was left to Hugh to put things in their proper perspective. "Barry doesn't smoke it *neat*," he clarified. "He pulls a cigarette to pieces and mixes it. Somebody said to me, it makes you more aware. I said I'm quite bloody well aware without it!"

This unusual procedure came as something of a surprise to Aerosmith's rhythm guitarist, Brad Whitford, who worked with them the following year. "Barry Gibb was rolling cigarettes out of a plastic bag full of tobacco, pot, and hash, which kept something light going all day."

For Maurice, drugs were less of an issue, as he stated rather pointedly, "I consider marijuana no worse than having a bloody drink," before claiming that he hyperventilated on grass and, despite so much time spent in the company of individual Beatles, didn't even know what LSD looked like.

The youngest Bee Gee was facing an entirely different demon altogether and his mother was evidently very concerned about the long term effects of his alcohol problem, after being persuaded by New York reporter Cynthia Heimel to compare the respective effects of booze and coke. "[Cocaine's] not as bad as whisky," she felt provoked into saying, "because whisky makes you really ill." Concerned about the potential of liver damage, and perhaps feeling cornered into justifying her remark, she added naïvely, "Your sinuses can always be repaired."

When the *Rolling Stone* discussion turned to their music, Barry insisted, "I didn't know that anyone was going to call it disco but they did. It certainly wasn't in our minds, and we certainly wouldn't have called it disco, we thought it was R&B. We liked The Stylistics and The Delphonics and people who sang in falsetto. That was interesting to us because of our new found falsetto thing. So we weren't thinking in terms of what you might call the music, and 'Stayin' Alive' was born of those feelings and the lyric of '*New York Times* effect on man'. New York was, in fact, having that effect on the whole world at that point. Not so much California but the Studio 54 and the nightlife and the young people trying to find a future for themselves where without this nightlife, there might not be a future. I think the 'Tony' character in *Saturday Night Fever* depicted that."

"We weren't looking at *Fever* as a career vehicle," Maurice insisted. "We just got caught up in the Robert Stigwood syndrome. Anyone he managed, he also wanted involved in his film projects as opposed to keeping them separate, and I think we got blinded by that. He asked for three songs, we gave him three songs off what would have been our next studio album. We played him demo tracks of 'If I Can't Have You', ['Night Fever'] and 'More Than A Woman'. He asked if we could write it more discoey. We'd also written a song called 'Saturday Night' but there were so many songs called 'Saturday Night', even one by The Bay City Rollers, so when we rewrote it for the movie, we called it 'Stayin' Alive'. Then we wrote 'Night Fever' and Stigwood changed the movie's title from *Saturday Night* to *Saturday Night Fever*."

In 1989, Barry claimed, "We didn't know what the film was about. We didn't know there was a conflict of images which could perhaps hurt us later on. In those days you didn't think too much about images. It sort of grew, blew out of proportion. We didn't realise that's what was . . . gonna happen."

In 1997, Robin gave a typically facetious reply as to how The Bee Gees came to write the music for *Saturday Night Fever*. "We had been down on our luck, and someone said, 'Would you write some songs about a painter who goes out dancing in the evenings?' so we did. If we'd known Travolta would make such a good job of it, we wouldn't have knocked out any old rubbish and sung in those stupid voices!"

Shifting gears into serious mode, Robin explained, "We'd had successful albums right up until *Saturday Night Fever*, and what was happening when *Fever* came about was, we were recording our new album in the north of France . . . And we'd written about and recorded about four or five songs for the new album when Stigwood rang from LA and said, 'We're putting together this little film, low budget, called *Tribal Rites Of A Saturday Night*. Would you have any songs on hand?' and we said, 'Look, we can't, we haven't any time to sit down and write for a film.' We didn't know what it was about . . ."

"When Robert explained this plot about some Italian kids in Bay Ridge, I never thought it would come together," Gershon recalled. "But as Robert played me the tapes of just the vocals and acoustic guitar, it was clear something very, very special was happening. They were all hits."

Robin said that the group offered the four songs already written for their next studio album to Stigwood, telling him if he liked the tracks, he could put them in the film. "We sent them to him, he reviewed them, he said he liked three or four, which was 'Stayin' Alive', 'Night Fever', 'How Deep Is Your Love' and one that we didn't do ourselves, but Yvonne Elliman did, 'If I Can't Have You'. And that was used, so then we didn't see any more about or hear any more about the film till they asked us about the title. They put Saturday on the front of one of our songs, *Saturday Night Fever*, at our suggestion and then that's when the film came out. Of course, it was a low budget film without any hype. It was word of mouth that completely took the film off."

Somehow the group and their co-producers Albhy and Karl found the time to finish mixing the recording of the Los Angeles Forum concert, in between writing and recording the new material. The double album, *Here At Last . . . Bee Gees . . . Live*, was released in May, 1977, with the live single from the LP, 'Edge Of The Universe', following in July. It almost seems an afterthought, overshadowed by *Fever*.

The soundtrack's ballad, 'How Deep Is Your Love', was "one song where Blue [Weaver] had a tremendous amount of input," Albhy Galuten admitted. "There was a lot of things from his personality. That's one where his contribution was quite significant, not in a songwriting sense, though when you play piano, it's almost like writing the song . . . Blue had a lot of influence in the piano structure of that song."

"One morning, it was just myself and Barry in the studio," Blue said. "He said, 'Play the most beautiful chord you know,' and I just played . . . what happened was, I'd throw chords at him and he'd say, 'No, not that chord,' and I'd keep moving around and he'd say, 'Yeah, that's a nice one' and we'd go from there. Then I'd play another thing – sometimes, I'd be following the melody line that he already had and sometimes I'd most probably lead him somewhere else by doing what I did . . . I think Robin came in at some point. Albhy also came in at one point and I was playing an inversion of a chord, and he said, 'Oh no, I don't think it should be that inversion, it should be this,' and so we changed it to that, but by the time Albhy had come in, the song was sort of *there*.

"We started work about 12 o'clock maybe one o'clock in the morning, and that demo was done at about three or four o'clock in the morning . . . Albhy played piano on the demo – I'd drunk too much or gone to bed or something . . . Then I woke up the next morning and listened to that . . . and then put some strings on it and that was it. Then we actually recorded it for real in Criteria. The chords and everything stayed the same – the only thing that changes from that demo is that when we got to Criteria, I worked out the electric piano part which became the basis of the song. It was the sound of the piano that makes the feel of that song."

Despite his unexplained absence, Albhy agreed that Blue's spirit remained integral to the song. "Even though I did the demo because he wasn't there, there were a lot of things from his personality [on the track]."

"A lot of the textures you hear in the song were added on later," Barry revealed. "We didn't change any lyrics, mind you, but the way we recorded it was a little different than the way we wrote it in terms of construction. A little different for the better, I think . . . The title 'How Deep Is Your Love' we thought was perfect because of all the connotations involved in that sentence, and that was simply it."

"Every now and then a song comes along that has universal appeal," Robin said. "Not every song has it but I think that one has, it's either in the music itself or in the lyrics, but there is something about what someone says in a lyric that gives it automatic universal appeal every time you hear it. Personalities are examined in that tune, but female or male aren't even mentioned in it. It has universal connotations and it clicks with everyone. It's like a song you hear and never get tired of, and I think that 'How Deep Is Your Love' is one of those sort of songs that you can hear over and over again and not get tired of for the same reasons."

"It was something that was special to me at the time," Blue said, "because I had been involved in the conception of the thing, and I was away from home, I think a lot of my emotions went into that song as well, even though lyrically I didn't do anything."

There was some talk of Yvonne Elliman débuting 'How Deep Is Your Love', but Robert Stigwood soon quashed those ideas. "Robert said, 'You've got to do this song yourself, you should not give it to anybody,' " recalled Barry.

"I felt very strongly about that because when I heard The Bee Gees themselves, it was one of the most moving ballads I ever heard," Stigwood added. Yvonne Elliman was given 'If I Can't Have You' instead.

At this time it was still very unusual to release a movie soundtrack song ahead of the movie but, as RSO intended, the song built up interest in the coming film. The B-side was 'Can't Keep A Good Man Down', a song from *Here At Last . . . Live*, so nothing else hinted at what was about to happen.

★   ★   ★

A tale so often told that it has passed into Bee Gees' legend is that Robert Stigwood said, "Give me eight minutes – eight minutes, three moods. I want frenzy at the beginning. Then I want some passion. Then I want some w-i-i-i-ld frenzy!"

In fact, after hearing the demo for 'Stayin' Alive', Blue Weaver said, "Stigwood came in and said, 'Oh, they're on the dance floor at this time and suddenly he sees her across the floor and it goes in slow motion and they walk towards each other . . .' So we wrote this whole section in 'Stayin' Alive' where it goes down into slow section . . . but we threw it out in the end . . . There are obviously reasons why it never went on there in the first place."

"Robert has this thing about songs that break up in the middle with a slow piece," Robin observed. "He did the same thing with 'Nights On Broadway'."

"Robert wanted a scene that was eight minutes long," Barry explained, "where John Travolta was dancing with his girl. It would have a nice dance tempo, a romantic interlude and all hell breaking loose at the end. I said, 'Robert, that's crazy. We want to put this song out as a single, and we don't think the rhythm should break. It should go from beginning to end with the same rhythm and get stronger all the way. To get into a lilting ballad just doesn't make sense.' The film got changed."

Blue still has fond memories of the extended version of the track. "I want to mix the long version of 'Stayin' Alive'," he said in 1999, "because I think it would do them a lot of good inasmuch as I think it would be very interesting to people to know that little story . . . they're going to see each other across this dance floor, it's going into slow motion – I think it's a great version. And the end, as well, is different because it's actually got synthesizer bass."

Next Stigwood asked them why they were singing 'Stayin' Alive' rather than 'Saturday Night', according to Maurice. "We said because there are so many bloody records out called 'Saturday Night'. It's corny; it's a terrible title."

Barry added, "We said, 'Either it's "Stayin' Alive" or we'll keep the song.'"

Albhy Galuten recalled that after Stigwood had phoned the group, they agreed to get together some songs for him. "So of course, none of us had seen the film or even read the article, let alone the screenplay. 'Stayin' Alive', when we first heard it, was just the three brothers singing with Barry on guitar. By the time they finished playing, I had the guitar lick that was used in the song figured out.

"So we were working on writing the song, sitting out in the studio. So that we could practise the groove, we had some little drum machine, like an organ drum machine, awful sounding, and that would just run in a little loop, and [Barry] would strum the guitar and work on lyrics and the melody. I think the other brothers were there, the three of them sitting. This was kind of exciting."

"As writers you have to use a certain amount of imagination," Robin explained. "Everybody thinks that sometimes writing is biographical and sometimes it is, but you would be exhausted if every song was about you, you know, if you actually *experienced* everything you write. The amazing thing about writing songs like 'Stayin' Alive' is that we never actually saw the script. We never really knew what was going on, it just so happened that the songs worked, especially 'Stayin' Alive' . . . It's a very straightforward song about survival in the city that's what it was and that's really the statement." Another of those amazing songs was also under construction.

" 'Night Fever' started off because Barry walked in one morning when I was trying to work out something," Blue recalled. "I always wanted to do a disco version of 'Theme From *A Summer Place*' . . . by The Percy Faith Orchestra or something – it was a big hit in the Sixties. I was playing that, and Barry said, 'What was that?' and I said, " 'Theme From *A Summer Place*'," and Barry said, 'No, it wasn't.' It was new – Barry heard the idea – I was playing it on a string synthesizer – and sang the riff over it."

Albhy continued, "For 'Night Fever' the group had the hook-line and rhythm – they usually pat their legs to set up a song's rhythm when they first sing it – and parts of the verses . . . They had the emotion, same as on the record. We put down drums and acoustic guitar first, so the feel was locked in. The piano part was put on before the bass, then the heavy guitar parts. We had the sound, but we needed something there to shake it so we used the thunder sound."

Echoing the beginnings of their first international hit 'New York Mining Disaster 1941', the writing of 'Night Fever' was completed sitting on a staircase, utilising the natural echo. The only difference was that 'Mining Disaster' was written in Polydor's London studios, and 'Night Fever' had the more atmospheric setting of a thirteenth century French château.

That staircase had other claims to fame, according to Robin. "You know, years ago there were so many pornographic films made at the Château," he revealed. "The staircase where we wrote 'How Deep Is Your Love', 'Stayin' Alive', all those songs, was the same staircase where there've been six classic lesbian porno scenes filmed. I was watching a movie one day called *Kinky Women Of Bourbon Street*, and all of a sudden, there's this château, and I said, 'It's *the* Château!' These girls, these dodgy birds, are having a scene on the staircase that leads from the front door up to the studio. There were dildos hanging off the stairs and everything. I thought, 'Gawd, we wrote "Night Fever" there!' "

'Night Fever' was the movie's big dance number, and besides the drums, it is full of rhythms played on guitars and keyboards. 'Night Fever' uses two different verses and is so feverishly fast that it runs through verse-chorus pairs four times in only three minutes.

After 'Night Fever' had been recorded, there was a serious illness in Dennis Bryon's family so the drummer jetted back to Cardiff. Barry was anxious to complete the recording of 'Stayin' Alive', but they had no drummer. Albhy said, "I think [Barry] was thinking about using that drum machine, which really sounded terrible, to put it down. So I had the idea . . . I said to Karl, why don't we make a tape loop out of one bar of the drums from 'Night Fever' and set it to the right tempo and use that, and then we can replace it with Dennis when he comes back.

"It's one of those happy accidents. We picked a bar out of 'Night Fever' that sounded pretty good, and Karl took a seven-inch plastic reel and we used a two-track tape machine. We took this bar, recorded some drums from 'Night Fever' – Barry and I listened and picked out a bar with a particularly good feeling [then] recorded that bar of drums. Karl spliced it together into a long loop and then, on the two-track machine, had it going around through the capstan, and had a mike stand turned sideways, and the tape hung over that, and he had a seven-inch tape reel in the bottom hanging from the tape loop. It goes around through the tape recorder on one side, the other side goes over the thing and hangs, so that seven-inch tape reel was just enough balance so it stays in place while the motors turn it around. He made this drum loop that became 'Stayin' Alive'. We overdubbed to that, thinking we'd replace it with Dennis's drums."

Galuten explained that when The Bee Gees are working on a song, very few lyrics are done in the early stages of composing. "Only the chorus and key words are locked in, and the rest is scat vocals, because they find nice holes rhythmically to put words in that way. So they end up putting different lyrics in different places, which is often very creative."

Galuten credits himself with the distinctive bass 'Stayin' Alive' line in the finished record. "The result was it got recorded very quickly," he said. "I showed the guitar parts to Alan [Kendall], and we punched them in. The bass line was mine as well, and I used to joke, for the songs on that album, if I had to name every note on every track, I could do it. By the time we had overdubbed the pieces, Dennis came back, but we could never change the drums. It happened to be a great feeling loop. We ended up using that same loop on 'More Than A Woman' . . . It was a great feeling bar."

As happens all too often when artists are in creative mode and ideas are flying around, disagreements over who actually did what are common. It therefore comes as no surprise to learn that Blue Weaver's memories of this important event differ slightly. "First of all," he said, "Maurice deserves a lot of the credit for the bass part because I believe Albhy picked up on a bass line that Maurice originally played. Also, I believe the guitar riff was possibly inspired by my trying to sound a bit like Stevie Wonder's clavinet. I think Albhy thought (quite rightly) that we shouldn't use the clavinet because it was too much like 'Superstition' and he came up with a similar riff inspired by one of his favourite Miami recordings."

The veteran record producer, Sir George Martin, said, "The great thing about 'Stayin' Alive' is that it had a great guitar hook to start with which set up the theme, that pulsating beat. It's no coincidence, by the way, that the disco beat of 120 beats per minute coincides with the heartbeat of your heart when you're excited. This was a key thing which underlined the whole tune, and when the vocals came in, the vocals were so designed that they pushed that beat further. They anticipated in many cases, they came in before the bar line. All the time it was surging forwards to go with it which also accentuated that it leaned on the words. When you have that, combined with [The Bee Gees'] impeccable three part harmonies, it was electrifying. Their harmonies also have a kind of paradox because everybody knows they have quite high voices, but this was a very macho song but portrayed by almost feminine voices, but beautifully done."

The original source of 'Stayin' Alive' can be traced to a few lines of the lyric scrawled on Robin Gibb's Concorde ticket. "The subject matter of 'Stayin' Alive' is actually quite a serious one," he said. "It's about survival in the streets of New York, and the lyrics actually say that."

"People crying out for help. Desperate songs. Those are the ones that become giants," Barry explained. "The minute you capture that on record, it's gold. 'Stayin' Alive' is the epitome of that. Everybody struggles against the world, fighting all the bullshit and things that can drag you down. And it really is a victory just to survive. But when you climb back on top and win bigger than ever before – well, that's something everybody reacts to. *Everybody.*"

Barry's keen observation would ring true for Gloria Gaynor, whose number one smash 'I Will Survive' spent 15 weeks in the UK charts, three weeks longer than 'Stayin' Alive' did.

"It became such a phenomenon, the whole *Saturday Night Fever* thing," Robin added, "that very few people realise it's to do with anything but dance. The lyrics don't talk about dance at all. The lyrics very obviously state the scenario of survival in the city, and it's not about disco dancing at all."

Whether or not it mentions dancing, the opening of the film with the image of John Travolta strutting down the street to 'Stayin' Alive' remains one of the most perfect and enduring marriages of film and music. Yet it almost didn't happen.

Just a few weeks before filming was due to begin, the director whom Stigwood had hired, John Avildsen, decided that he didn't want to use The Bee Gees' music in *his* film. With the success of his earlier work, *Rocky*, the director had become imperious in his demands.

Kevin McCormick brought Stigwood the news. Stigwood called Avildsen and McCormick to a meeting in his apartment. "There's good news and bad news," he told Avildsen. "The good news is that you've been nominated for an Academy Award [for *Rocky*]. The bad news is that you're fired."

John Badham was rapidly hired as Avildsen's replacement. "I checked that he worked fast," Stigwood explained. "He didn't mess around and could keep to time so I called him and arranged for him to fly to New York. I said, 'I think it's a bit long, John. On the plane read Wexler's screenplay and tell me where you think the cuts should be,' which he did . . . He met me in New York, and he was 100 per cent on time so I hired him then." The shooting began, with The Bee Gees' music very strongly in the foreground. Judging from the public's reaction, it was the right decision.

'Stayin' Alive' was issued as the second single, close to the release date of the movie. The amazingly steady rhythm from the drum loop made it perfect for John Travolta's walk down the streets of Bay Ridge in the opening sequence, and yet some feel that it is actually quite hard to dance to this rhythm. This is somewhat ironic for a song that epitomises the disco era.

The B-side was indirectly from the movie. Yvonne Elliman's version of 'If I Can't Have You' appears both in the movie and on the album, but The Bee Gees' version appeared only on this single until the *Greatest* album in 1979. This sounds more like a demo, with piano and a really high falsetto by Barry.

Yvonne's hit version of the song is really not that different from The Bee Gees' original recording and she was quite naturally thrilled by the outcome. "The Bee Gees are phenomenal songwriters and performers," she enthused in an impromptu tribute. "They are not motivated by money. One of the things I admire most about Barry, Robin and Maurice is their genuine love for music."

'More Than A Woman' was originally written and recorded as a demo for the group Tavares to record for the soundtrack and they went on to have a hit single with it. Like Yvonne Elliman, Tavares were grateful not only for the song but also for the friendship which developed as a result. A spokesman for the group said, "There are two primary areas of appreciation that we have for The Bee Gees. The first lies in their character as people. They are gentlemen of the first order and, in our opinion, they are the most creative and innovative musicians, writers and singers that we know."

The Bee Gees' own version of 'More Than A Woman' featured both on the album and in the film, and also found its way onto the B-side of 'Night Fever', which followed 'Stayin' Alive' to become the third Bee Gees' single from the album. It would be reasonable to conclude that the brothers had spent as much time recording 'More Than A Woman' as their single releases, but this was actually far from being the case.

"We overdubbed on it because they wanted it on the album, which was probably worth a lot of money, because every song was another piece of the royalty," Albhy Galuten explained. "The person who made the most money in the shortest time, for the least amount of significant work," he continued, referring to David Shire, "was the guy who scored the film. They had a side of an album, because they wanted to make a double album, [and] had a side empty so they had him write filler, stuff like 'Night On Disco Mountain'. Can you imagine how much money he made, for going in *one* day and scoring that?"

Rick Dees, at various times in his career a writer of novelty songs, a DJ and a television chat show host, has had years to contemplate just how much money the album made. He wrote and recorded a novelty song called

'Disco Duck' and put it out on a small record label, Fretone Records. "Then we sold the master tape to Robert Stigwood through his representative, Al Coury, for $3,500. *Three thousand five hundred dollars*," he emphasised.

The song topped the American charts for nearly a month, beating out established artists such as Paul McCartney and Chicago. "To ride that wave was an amazing experience . . . Can you imagine the angst of having one of your masterpieces at number four, and you look, and something called 'Disco Duck' was at number one?" Dees said.

His penny a copy royalty on the song added another $40,000 to his original fee of $3,500. Next RSO asked him if he would mind if they used 'Disco Duck' in the soundtrack to *Saturday Night Fever*. The young man was ecstatic. His agent negotiated the deal, and 'Disco Duck' can be heard in the background of John Travolta's dance class in the film. For Dees, there was one small problem, which he learned only through bitter experience. "Negotiating a deal that you're in the soundtrack is *not* the same as that you're going to be on the soundtrack *album*. It would have been easy to say, 'Just make sure you put it on the album.' The Stigwood organisation would have said, 'No problem!' Lo and behold, the *Saturday Night Fever* album comes out. I run out to get the album. It's got The Bee Gees, KC & The Sunshine Band, The Tramps [but] nowhere, Rick Dees."

Royalties for a song's inclusion on an album at that time would have been approximately 10 cents an album. The album's sales topped 25 million. "Now we're talking about a loss of $2.5 million," Dees said. "So the 'Duck' became an albatross, hanging around my neck."

Two more tracks were written during the recording sessions, but not destined for the *Fever* soundtrack. The first, 'Warm Ride', "was the only song from France we didn't want," said Barry. "We thought it [wasn't] a hit, thought it was a bit too sexual, thought it was a bit too hot under the collar, and we didn't make anything of it. We cut it as a demo and left it. Roger Daltrey's . . . producer rang us up and asked if there was a song for Roger . . . We had the song 'Warm Ride' because it's right down Roger's alley. It's the same chords he likes to use, it's the kind of thing he might turn into a hit. We didn't know, we didn't think it was a hit, and we said, 'We've got this one song – everything else has gone into the film, and we're not writing right now.' We sent him 'Warm Ride', and Roger didn't want to do it – they turned it down."

"Roger Daltrey . . . didn't like it," Albhy recalled. "You can see why. Barry is brilliant, but he doesn't understand rock'n'roll. It's not his genre. The idea of somebody like Roger Daltrey doing a song called 'Warm Ride' – I mean it's not rock'n'roll sensuality, it's an Australian pop star's opinion of what rock'n'roll sensuality would be like." Eventually, the song would be released as a single, firstly by Rare Earth, then by Graham Bonnet, and it was also included on Andy Gibb's third album, although Albhy said, "I don't know why that got on there."

The remaining song from the Château sessions was 'Our Love (Don't

Throw It All Away)'. Written by Barry with Blue Weaver, the song would later become a hit single for Andy Gibb.

"That was me playing around again," Blue said, "and Barry said, 'Let's try to write something.' It wasn't done for [*Saturday Night Fever*] – it was just something that we did . . . When Andy actually went to record it, Barry listened to it again, and thought, 'Oh, it's not finished,' so Barry wrote the whole of the middle eight."

Released in the USA in October and two months later in the UK, no one could have predicted the success of the *Saturday Night Fever* soundtrack, least of all The Bee Gees and their personal manager. Dick Ashby recalled, "We had no idea *Saturday Night Fever* was any big deal until album sales passed two million. When we saw the film the first time, the initial reaction, especially from some of the wives, was, 'What awful language!' You know, swear words."

Although Robin maintains, "Total word of mouth was all *Saturday Night Fever* was about. There was no money for actual promotion so they couldn't hype it. It was one of the few films in history that was as big as it was that actually did it on word of mouth."

Al Coury of RSO claimed that the company concentrated a promotional drive on the film right up until its actual release. "Then we converted the campaign to selling the soundtracks and piggybacked onto the success of the film," Coury explained. "The music that [The Bee Gees] produced for *Saturday Night Fever* and that success and its relationship to the success of that film just speaks for itself. They created history when they wrote those songs and performed them for the film.

"We sold 750,000 copies of the album in four days between Christmas and New Years. We knew we had the makings of a major hit album if we promoted it as an album."

Barry laughed, "We thought we'd been big *before*. We didn't realise that you could reach this stage!"

David English says he will certainly never forget his involvement in the album's promotion. "We were in Paris and we were at the very top of the Hotel Intercontinental, well up into the sky, and we all got out of the window onto the balcony and walked round the ledge. We went past the room next to us and there was a couple in there actually making love! His young lady was sitting on top of him and the bloke looked up and saw the three Bee Gees walk past the window . . . and then they walked back again. The next day we were on the plane to London and this couple were actually on the plane, and as we walked by Barry said, "Hello darling, very nice to see you with your clothes on!"

Blue Weaver revealed that, in the studio at any rate, production was less of a priority than on their previous two albums. "We didn't take as much trouble with that even as we did with *Main Course*, and nowhere near as long as *Children Of The World*, and it just sort of happened so quickly; nobody knew it was going to evolve into such a monster. I mean, it was huge!"

"As far as I know, it's still the best selling soundtrack," Maurice said recently, "and that was an incredible thing for me because I used to love *Sound Of Music* and that was number one for years. I never thought we'd knock Rogers and Hammerstein off.

"We got inducted into the Songwriters Hall Of Fame, and above our picture was Rogers and Hammerstein. I can't believe that we're with these people or even classed in the same class. That was an amazing thing for me," he marvelled.

Whilst no one was prepared for the smash hit that *Fever* became, Barry said that it hadn't come as a complete shock. "We always had an idea that if we kept doing what we were doing long enough, someone might listen and something special might happen to us," he explained.

★　★　★

The phenomenon that was *Saturday Night Fever* brought about an astonishing change to the personal lives of The Bee Gees and their families. "It's starting to feel very much like 1967 and '68," Barry said. "It gets so everybody's running your life, or trying to, and you can't breathe. Ask our wives. If anybody knows, they do. You have to protect yourself or else you end up like distant friends, passing in the corridor between appointments."

He admitted, "Success hits you in a way that you never expect. No one can prepare you for it. You think everybody around you has changed; they think *you* have. They think they ought to listen to you, and you sit there scratching your head, thinking, 'Well, what if I don't say anything?' Eventually you feel you are a commodity instead of the person."

Robin celebrated the group's new found success in his own way. According to Barry, Robin has an "idiosyncrasy" – whenever anything good happens, he likes to lie back in his bath and savour the moment. The Bee Gee with a constant eye on the charts, Robin would find plenty to celebrate that year.

All three of The Bee Gees' singles had become chart toppers in the United States. 'How Deep Is Your Love' was the initial release in October, which remained in the charts for an unprecedented 26 weeks, reaching the top by Christmas Eve. It was joined in the States in December by 'Stayin' Alive' although British fans would have to wait until after the New Year for its release on seven-inch format. By the time 'Night Fever' completed the trio in February, 'Stayin' Alive' had taken over the peak position, where it remained for four weeks until it was displaced by youngest brother Andy's '(Love Is) Thicker Than Water'. 'Night Fever' regained the pinnacle for the elder Gibbs two weeks later with 'Stayin' Alive' at number two, and the Barry and Robin Gibb composition, 'Emotion' by Samantha Sang at number three. On March 4, those five songs comprised half of the American Top 10. Referring back to Robin's idiosyncrasy, Barry quipped, "That week, Robin was clean as a whistle." 'Night Fever' held the top spot for the next eight weeks, before being replaced by Yvonne Elliman's rendition of The Bee Gees' 'If I Can't Have You' in mid-May.

Criteria Studios would also claim a share of the Gibbs' achievements too. Although technically entitled to do so, they were stretching the point a little as not all five songs had been recorded there. Only the remixing and overdubs on the *Fever* songs were done at Criteria.

In Britain, 'Night Fever' also achieved the top spot, while 'Stayin' Alive' and 'How Deep Is Your Love' reached the fourth and third position respectively.

When 'How Deep Is Your Love' entered the British charts, it was a sweet victory for The Bee Gees. "You have no idea what a thrill it is to have a Top Five single in England," Barry exclaimed. "With all the new wave and punk rock out, I would have thought something like 'How Deep Is Your Love' wouldn't have a chance. We always kept going forward and we're getting stronger every day."

In Chile, Portugal, Italy and Australia, The Bee Gees' version of 'More Than A Woman' would also be released as a single, giving them another Australian Top 40 hit.

For Maurice, their success could be measured by the impact it would have on the brothers' children. "It ended up providing security for our kids. When they were first born, that was always our main goal, to make sure they'd have nothing to want for in life if anything ever happened to us. We're not that materialistic. Sure, I have a house [in Miami Beach] and in England, where most people who have supposedly earned as much as us have four or five houses. We're very sensible, we don't flaunt it, but we do make sure it works for us and that it's there for the kids."

After the completion of the *Saturday Night Fever* tracks and mixing the live album, Barry and Lynda Gibb had rented out their house in the Isle of Man to the estate agent who had sold it to them in the first place and had moved to Miami Beach. It was a way of trying to bring some stability and permanence into their lives, making their home base near the recording studio. Within months, Barry was urging the whole family to move there. Lynda's parents, George and May Gray, were soon Miami-bound and installed in Barry and Lynda's new home.

By this time, Andy and his wife Kim were already in Miami, and Barbara, Hugh and Beri were persuaded to leave Australia and settle nearby. In early August, Maurice and Yvonne arrived in Miami to live, with Yvonne's parents and brother Herbie joining them.

The only hold-outs were Robin and Molly, still staunchly determined that Britain was the best place to raise their two children, in spite of the punitive tax rate in Britain at the time.

"Taxes for people under a high earning bracket pay 83 per cent tax," Barry explained in qualifying his decision to become a tax exile. "If you have shares in a company or dividends coming in, that is taxed at 98 per cent."

"Lots of rock stars complain about the tax situation, but you can still get things done. It's my home and where my family is. I have a good accountant, and I don't pay that much tax in England," Robin countered. "The average fool does. I'm waiting to see what happens in the next elections. If the Conservatives get in, I'm sure they will reduce the maximum tax to 50 per cent."

In early 1977, Robin and Molly had moved to a larger house, complete with swimming pool and tennis court, near their former home in Virginia Water, Surrey. "Molly wants to stay at home and won't travel around, so there's some tension," he admitted. "But she's a human being too. I don't own her. She wants the kids to grow up in one place. As kids, we never lived in one place for more than two years. As a result, we didn't really have a childhood. We don't want our families to grow up like that."

"I don't think America is the best country to raise children in. I don't like the whole commercial aspect of life out there," Molly added. "Besides, I prefer to live in England and so does Robin. He's happy working in the States, but I think he keeps his sanity by coming back [to England] where he can relax."

"I fish in the river, play tennis. I spend lots of time with my wife and kids. A quite sane life," Robin explained. "You see, we never had this as kids. We were always too busy working, singing on the road. We had to make our own lives stable. In the early days, we practically had to work to live. Our family didn't have much money so I think they had to make it on us . . . My father was 41 when we moved from Manchester to Australia. We left nothing behind, except Manchester, and I wouldn't want to die there. I suppose I've got to look back fondly on my childhood. I've got no other life."

It was reported that back in Australia, even sister Lesley was considering a return to the music industry, but although she recorded a song, family commitments severely curtailed her promotion of it, and it disappeared without a trace.

The Bee Gees were said to be taping a television special in August but it never aired. They had also begun plans for their first tour of Russia, scheduled for November, 1978, but this too would fall by the wayside.

On September 8, Barry and Lynda's second son was born at the Mount Sinai Hospital in Miami. The baby, christened Ashley Robert Crompton Gibb, was born with a heart disorder and spent the first month of his life in a special care unit. He weighed only four pounds and 11 ounces and measured 18 inches long.

Four days after Ashley's birth, Robin and Maurice flew to Los Angeles to begin recording at Cherokee Studio, and Barry joined them two days later.

★   ★   ★

On December 11, with 'Stayin' Alive' topping the American charts, The Bee Gees acted as co-hosts for the *Billboard Rock Awards Show* recorded live for television in the USA. They also received the Don Kirshner Rock Award for Public Service.

In February they picked up the Grammy Award in the category of "Best

Vocal Pop Performance by a Duo, Group or Chorus" for 'How Deep Is Your Love', the only single from the *Saturday Night Fever* soundtrack released in time for the 20th Annual Grammy Award.

The awards and recognition were all very welcome, but Barry insisted, "We don't want to sit on our laurels. We knew we always had a lot more to offer people than they thought we had.

"We feel the pressure to make the perfect album. Before, nobody much cared what we were working on. Now we feel like we've got to please the world and his uncle. People used to say that The Bee Gees would never be a lasting influence on music and we hated that. We always knew that we could make music that would last and influence other people, but we had to find the right time."

As the only one not a tax exile at the time, Robin was the sole Gibb brother present for the London premiere of the film on March 22, well over three months later than its American equivalent. For the party afterwards, Stigwood had arranged for the Sundown Club in London to be revamped at a cost of over £30,000 to resemble 2001 Odyssey, the disco of the film. Special lighting effects, smoke machines and film equipment added to the atmosphere, as nearly everyone took to the dance floor. The film's star, John Travolta, whom Robert Stigwood described with his usual hyperbole as "the new Robert Redford, the new Rudolph Valentino", was a notable exception – he remained sitting, chatting with Bianca Jagger. Robin and Molly Gibb were also sitting out the dancing, with Robin complaining to a journalist that he was losing his voice. "It's dreadful trying to talk over this noise," he said, as a Bee Gees song blared from the club's speakers.

28

I *JUST* WANT TO BE YOUR EVERYTHING

" 'I JUST WANT TO BE YOUR EVERYTHING' was one of the most meaningful songs of all for me, you know," Andy revealed. "It all came about that I had just got married in Australia at the time, and Robert Stigwood and my brother Barry asked me to fly out to Bermuda as kind of a honeymoon come-working set-up to meet with Barry and to sign up with Robert for RSO Records."

It appeared to be a logical progression for Andy to sign up with the manager who had masterminded The Bee Gees' career. "Obviously, I wasn't going to refuse an offer from RSO Records," he said. "They don't come along every day, you know." Robert Stigwood had watched Andy grow up from the youngster who wanted more than anything to be just like his eldest brother. It now seemed likely that Stigwood could work the same magic on Andy's career as he had on his elder brothers' 10 years earlier.

Andy's follow-up to his Australian début single, 'Words And Music' was intended to be his version of the Ray Stevens' song, 'Can't Stop Dancing'. He had performed the song on the Australian *Bandstand* television show, and the single, backed by Andy's own composition, 'In The End', was actually pressed and scheduled for release in September. Andy had even recorded an album at Col Joye's ATA studio consisting of all original compositions with the exception of Don McLean's 'Winter Has Me In Its Grip'. "I'm very much influenced by Don McLean," Andy revealed, "which is funny because critics have said they haven't heard a song of mine they could possibly relate to Don McLean. But if I'm ever musically dry, all I have to do is put on an album of his songs and suddenly I can write."

Both the single and the album Andy recorded in Australia were scrapped, although at least one copy of the unreleased single is known to exist. With his eyes firmly on the future, Andy wanted a fresh start with new songs.

"So, once we discussed it all and got the deal together . . . me and Barry locked ourselves in a bedroom, and Barry just started writing," Andy recalled. "When Barry writes, it is very hard to collaborate with him, because he is so quick. And before I knew it he was starting to do the chorus [of 'I Just Want To Be Your Everything], and I thought, 'Wow, what a hook!' It was right in there.

"He's an expert at his craft. Within about 20 minutes, he'd written a number one record; and then we went right into another one; and then we co-wrote the next one . . . in about 40, 50 minutes, it's just unbelievable when you are working with him."

After cutting the demos of the tracks, Andy and Kim returned briefly to Australia before getting the call to return to Florida. One of the first things Andy did on his return was to phone Trevor Norton, his former Zenta band mate. "I still kept in contact with him after he went to America . . . As soon as he arrived at the airport and got back to the hotel, he'd ring me straight away and say, 'Come over, man, come over!'" Trevor recalled. "Andy actually wanted to take me to the States with him, because he'd gone over a couple of times just after we'd finished playing with him and that was his idea, to take me with him over there . . . but his brothers said, 'We can get you the best drummers in the bloody world over here, you know?'"

Andy and Kim travelled to the sunny beaches of Miami, where they stayed at the oceanfront Key Biscayne Hotel. Although she said she liked America, native Australian Kim remained unimpressed with her new surroundings. "The beaches are not a patch on ours," she said. "I used to be really sarcastic and say, 'Come on, surf's up!' when there was a little ripple on the water."

Andy went into the studio to begin work with Barry, Albhy Galuten and Karl Richardson to lay down the tracks for his first album. With his experience in the Miami music scene, Albhy Galuten put a band together for the sessions. Harold Cowart on bass and Ron "Tubby" Ziegler on drums were from Louisiana. "They had been session musicians for Atlantic Records earlier, back before I got down there," Albhy recalled. "They were the session musicians in a band called Cold Grits that played on some of the Atlantic records like 'Rainy Night in Georgia' . . . so I knew those two and others from playing on other records doing session work. George Terry [guitar] was in a band called Game and had done some session work. Joey Murcia [guitar] was a session musician over at Tone, which is a studio where they did all that KC & The Sunshine Band stuff and all those records. They were a good band, good musicians. So Barry was very impressed."

Karl explained what they described as "The Andy Gibb Sound". "We don't put the vocals too loud. We want it to sound like a band. And I put a lot of rhythm into the songs. After we find the right mix, we feature people whose parts seem more integral to the record."

Andy's career was off to a promising start, but things were beginning to change for the newlyweds. Andy told his new bride that now she must consider the Gibb brothers and their wives her family, but her own family ties remained strong. Kim said Maurice, Yvonne and Robin were kind to her, but she was beginning to feel that the "Gibb commune" was closing in on her, just as she noticed a change in Andy. "He tried hard not to let what happened to him happen," she said. "But Andy adapts to the environment he's in. When he's in the [Gibb] family's company, he's a different person.

They're not entirely to blame. Andy didn't have to do the things they said."

Still, despite some homesickness, Kim remained supportive of Andy's goals. "We were very happy – he wanted to be famous and I helped him," she said simply.

The song selected to be Andy's first single outside Australia was the first song written in one of the bedrooms of Stigwood's Bermuda home. "The word 'just' was vital," Barry explained. "It came about because I was looking for a way to sing it and place the emphasis on that particular word. When it first went into the charts and was listed only as 'I Want To Be Your Everything', I could have screamed. The whole idea of that title was the word 'just' . . . 'I *Just* Want To Be Your Everything'; 'just' meaning 'That's *all* I want!' That was the sentiment. So I had to figure out a way to put that line into a chorus where it would lay on a nice melody line and emphasise 'just'."

Andy burst onto the scene with a good collection of songs written mostly by himself. His youthful good looks made him a popular teen idol. Innate musical talent may have been no more than an added bonus to some people, but talent there was.

Both singles from this album were written by Barry. While it is hard to argue with number one singles, the fact that Andy's own songs were consistently not used calls into question what his goals were and whether they were being achieved. 'I Just Want to Be Your Everything' is a great example of Barry's ability to knock out a catchy pop tune inspired by his idea of what a specific artist would sing. The light-disco style suits the fluffy lyrics – the song is not really about anything – and foreshadows The Bee Gees' somewhat darker stuff to come for *Saturday Night Fever*.

The second single '(Love is) Thicker Than Water' has an unusual guitar break and long rhythmic ending. Andy says he didn't contribute much to it, but if so then Barry had been listening to Andy because it sounds more like an Andy song.

In a strange twist to the credits, apart from the two singles, all the songs on the album were listed as written by Andy only; however, 'Dance To The Light Of The Morning' and 'Too Many Looks In Your Eyes' were filed as copyright Andy Gibb-Albhy Galuten. The songs show a real gift that was sadly not developed much further. He sounds more like the older Bee Gees than the dance tracks on The Bee Gees' last album, but this was not the direction he was to follow. 'Words And Music', a remake of his Australian single, has quiet verses and rolls into a melodic chorus that forces his voice as high as it can go.

The Eagles just happened to be recording at one of Criteria's other studios at the same time as Andy was working on his album and lent a little of their style – not to mention their lead guitarist – to the youngest Gibb. "Originally, I had no intention of doing a country-rock album," said Andy, "but I was influenced by The Eagles' sessions just from having them nearby and hearing their songs all the time. That got me wrapped up in country-rock. Joe Walsh came over and did lead guitar tracks on two of the songs. The whole structure of my session started to lean towards country-rock." Many of the songs on the album did take on a distinct Eagles' flavour, with ballads and pop songs adding variety.

Both 'Words And Music' and 'Flowing Rivers', which dated back to his days with John Stringer and John Alderson, were given the Gibb & Karlbhy treatment to give them a totally new sound. 'Flowing Rivers' would lose an entire verse as part of this process.

"Most of the songs on *Flowing Rivers* were written over a period of two years in Australia," Andy revealed. "But Albhy Galuten has a very off-the-wall approach to producing and he took those songs and turned them around and came up with some incredible grooves." 'Flowing Rivers' sounds as if it was inspired by The Eagles, but it is another old song that sounded just as country-rock as when Andy did it in Australia.

With the recording finished, Andy and Kim moved to Los Angeles, renting a small apartment in West Hollywood in late 1976. Kim hoped that away from his family, Andy would revert to the devoted, protective young man she knew in Australia. Unfortunately, he would change even more. Although it would take more than 10 years, Barry believes that in many ways, moving to Los Angeles was the beginning of Andy's undoing.

"I've often said, although I know it's not entirely true," he asserted, "Hollywood is the reason that Andy died. It's a very dangerous environment for someone who's susceptible to drugs or who has an addictive kind of personality because you can get anything you want in Hollywood. It's readily available. While he was in Miami, the whole time we were making records, it was good and he was good . . . He was healthy, and he was living a healthy lifestyle. At some point, he got in with the wrong people and decided he had to live in Hollywood and went to Hollywood and, from then on, everything started to go the wrong way."

On a trip to New York, Andy played some club dates, mixing his original songs with the occasional cover of songs by The Beatles and The Hollies. Kim was fascinated by the variety of New York's shops and bought clothes and cosmetics – "marvellous things we'd never seen before" – and sent gifts to both the Gibb and the Reeder families. But soon Andy began to discourage her from wearing the new clothes that she bought. She bought two wigs; one for herself and one for her twin sister, Kerrie, but while she was allowed to send Kerrie's to her, Andy attempted to flush Kim's down the toilet. "He was very jealous," she said.

Eventually, he became reclusive. "We couldn't do much in New York because Andy wouldn't go to many places," Kim explained. "He had this thing about how he's a superstar and everybody would recognise him."

Back in Los Angeles, the "hangers-on", as Kim called them, surrounding Andy began to invade the couple's lives. "They had keys to our apartment and car – there was never any privacy," she said. "They had access to my cheque account, which they would close off when it suited them. We couldn't move without these people being there, and Andy, a really mixed-up fellow, has been easily led by them."

Andy began to disappear for days at a time. "All of a sudden, Andy wanted to go to the mountains by himself," Kim recalled. "He became depressed and paranoid." A naïve girl from a working class family, Kim didn't immediately suspect drugs, but soon she could no longer deceive herself. "He became ensconced in the drug scene. Cocaine became his first love," she said. "When he was living in Australia, he never seemed to want or need drugs."

Trevor Norton and Glen Greenhalgh, his friends and former band mates from Zenta, agreed. "All the stories I hear about Andy is all the drugs and all that," Glen said. "Well, gee whiz, you know, that sort of thing never happened down here . . . that just didn't happen . . . The Andy Gibb that I read about in the papers years later, I just couldn't believe that it was him . . ."

Trevor recalled his parents pointing out articles in the papers about Andy, telling him that his former band mate had fallen in with a bad crowd, but Trevor staunchly defended his friend. "I told them it was just publicity and bullshit. It was Andy's rule," he insisted, "you smoke or drink before a show and you're out! He was *very* anti-drugs and alcohol. All the little rumours I would read . . . I could not believe them because that was not the Andy Gibb I knew. Something happened to him in America . . . something bad . . ."

"The hangers-on in the rock industry are like piranhas," Kim said. "They hang around stars and offer drugs as a way of making friendships. I suppose they think the stars will become dependent on them for drugs."

In Andy's case, they were right. In Los Angeles in the Seventies, just as today, cocaine seemed to be omnipresent, and for a young man who was trying to convince the world – and himself – that he was confident and self-assured, it proved a powerful anodyne.

When he was using the drug, Andy *felt* confident, witty, astute, energetic – but only for as long as the drug's effects lasted. Soon, as his body became accustomed to it, he would need more and more to get that high.

'I Just Want To Be Your Everything' was released in May, 1977, backed with 'In The End' – Andy's own composition from his Australian days – and began its ascent up the American charts. With the record's release, the RSO publicity machine went into overdrive, creating a perfect squeaky clean boy next door, an image that Andy was never comfortable with. "I never put myself in a teen idol bracket," Andy protested. "I've always been scared of falling into that category because, you know, it's not a very long-lived career."

Like it or not, the American teen magazines were only too ready to embrace the young pop star. Only 19 years old, Andy's toothy grin graced them all, with such headlines as "Could *You* Be Andy's Everything?", "How To Be Andy's Best Girl", "The ABC's Of Loving Andy" and "The Bee

Gees' Baby Brother Wants To Be Your Everything" calling out to young girls across the land. The combination of Andy's good looks, talent and soft-spoken charm could only help sell the teen idol image.

Andy made no secret of his marriage at the start, but as his début single climbed the charts, that marriage already seemed doomed. Success had come too easily, bringing with it more temptations and feelings of guilt that it *was* all too effortless.

"I kept finding buckets of bleach around the flat," Kim said. "I finally understood that's how cocaine was tested for purity. If a substance floated to the top, then talcum powder had been added. If the drug sank, it was pure. So we argued. But he was trapped so quickly. Some people have addictive personalities, and he was one of them. He wasn't a bad person; he was a wonderful person. I just don't think he could handle the fame, the pace – everything – so quickly. It all happened so fast. He seemed to have it all, but really, he had nothing."

When Kim discovered she was pregnant, she hoped the news would help him to get his life back on track, and in the beginning, she said, "He was thrilled and excited about the baby. He had only one misgiving, that it had come at a bad point in his career – but he got over that and told everyone the news . . . We planned to have four kids, and everything was going to coast along just normally like everybody else.

"But as usual, dope and cocaine took priority over everything else. He blew most of our money – we had an income of $200 a week – on drugs."

Kim had threatened many times before to leave him if he didn't give up drugs, but her pregnancy made the decision final, and a record industry appearance helped her carry out her plans. "I just couldn't carry on with the responsibility of having a child and looking after him as well. So one day when he was out of town, I left him."

Distressed and ill, she fled to Pasadena, to the home of friends of her family, Judi and Bill Daniels. The Daniels and Reeder family had corresponded for years about their common interest in dogs, but Andy had discouraged Kim from seeing them when they first arrived in Los Angeles. Bill and Judi took her in and put her on a plane back to Australia, back to her parents in Rydalmere.

Kim was two months pregnant and suffering from a congenital disease of the kidneys. The Air New Zealand flight crew "were beautiful to me," she said. "They didn't know who I was, but they laid me down in the plane and couldn't do enough for me. When I came back, I was pretty sick. I'd been worrying to death. I was eating like a horse, but the weight just kept dropping off me. I was really ill and deeply depressed."

Andy phoned her the week after she left and promised to return to Australia for the birth. It was a promise that he would not keep.

The Australian press had a field day with the story that Andy refused to send any money for support – possibly in an effort to press Kim to return to him. Kim's medical bills were heavy but had to be paid, so she went on the dole, collecting a $45 a week welfare cheque. "He refuses to maintain me, and I am just existing on the paltry Australian Social Security hand-out. He thinks that now he has had a hit and become a star, he can walk all over anyone. Every time I call, one of his protectors picks up the phone and tells me he is not available. I won't be calling again – he knows where to get in touch with me."

On July 29, with 'I Just Want To Be Your Everything' at number one in the American charts, Andy played the first of two concert appearances in Canada, as the support act for April Wine. With him were Tony Messina, still in tow as his personal assistant, The Bee Gees' American tour manager, Alan LaMagna, and Andy's new personal manager, Jim Dayley. Replacing the session musicians who recorded with him were a young band of musicians he'd met in California: Phoenix, Arizona natives, Richard Page and Steve George on keyboards and backing vocals, Peter Lyon [Leinheisen] on lead guitar, Jerry Manfredi on bass and Russ Battelene on drums.

Andy admitted that he suffered from stage fright. "For live appearances . . . there's always those few minutes of nerves. Especially before a big show, I get really scared."

Still, he preferred the immediate feedback that he got from being before a live audience. "I like touring," he said. "Recording is nice when you see the end result . . . But the stage is nice – spontaneous."

On August 3, he began a 23-date tour of the Unites States at the Saratoga Performing Arts Center in upstate New York, supporting Gibb family friend, Neil Sedaka. "Some of [the venues] were big open-air arenas, and the audience reaction was incredible," Andy said later. "It's been a great thing to go by. I mean, going out to Neil Sedaka's audience . . . and seeing twenty-one thousand people and seeing the banners across the audience with my name on. It was amazing."

Drugs were all too present before and after the concerts, although he insisted, "Personally, I'm not a very typical rock'n'roll star you might come across elsewhere. We're a very close-knit family, and we don't even go out that often. We don't really socialise; we just basically all sit at home with cups of tea and watch television. I suppose we must be like a slightly cool Osmond family. As we don't mix too much with other people, I don't have any fears about the pressures getting to me.

"You build up before the show so much, and you're such a bag of nerves, you go on and you're releasing this energy, getting the response from the audience, and it builds you up even higher, even though you become much more relaxed with the audience. It's funny because it seems as quick as you start, you're running up the stairs to your dressing room. Then you just sit there and think, 'Well, that's it.' It's all over again. It's a strange feeling coming off, I find, and it takes me about three hours to totally unwind."

There were also a growing number of teenage groupies. "I didn't really expect anything like that – I just thought I was a songwriter, and I knew I loved performing before audiences," Andy said. "But I didn't think for a moment that I could be a strong attraction for girls. Going on tour and seeing it all, I still couldn't believe it. It was just funny in some places – these young girls, 12 or 13, who were following me around!"

At times, the adulation of his young fans took a more serious tone. "They worry me sometimes," he revealed. "They get so much emotion inside them. Crying. It's emotional to see them from the stage. It's hard to sing and watch them at the same time. To see kids at that age crying – that much broken up over a concert – it makes me feel pretty strange. They lose their mind and get hysterical – it's really frightening sometimes."

His single continued to dominate the airwaves. "It's the hit song of the year," Andy raved. "It just won't stop selling."

Questioned by a journalist whether Kim had accompanied him on the tour, he replied, "No, not this time. It gets to be a bit much, and she's enjoying the sun in Miami. She's near the rest of my family, so she doesn't get too lonesome."

The final show of the Sedaka tour was an appearance at the Nebraska State Fair in Lincoln, Nebraska on September 4. Before the show, Andy was on edge, asking if it would be safe for him to go out and see the attractions at the fair before his set. With the ever-present Tony Messina and members of his band along, Andy wandered unnoticed through the crowds, climbing aboard a helicopter on display at a Navy recruitment post with childlike glee.

After the show, Andy and his band members were full of plans for future recordings and personal appearances. Both Richard Page and Steve George were also budding songwriters, and there was talk of Andy recording one of their songs.

"I was so lucky to have a chance to go on tour with Neil Sedaka," Andy enthused. "Neil had three generations of audiences: he had his original following and a new following, plus my following in the audience. I found that when I was going out there, all my following was out front for my show, and I was still getting response from the older people, who were . . . waiting for Neil to come on. It was very encouraging to have people, especially older people, respect my music and like it. That meant a lot to me."

He was still very aware that his pedigree had made things much easier for him. "I feel very lucky," he admitted. "I know that people try for years to break into even the lowest level of show business, and I just stepped into the top level. I never even had to audition. So it doesn't bother me when people connect my break with my brothers, because I realise that, without them, I would not be where I am."

He commented to The Bee Gees' fan club, which had been reporting regularly on his progress since 1973, "I was amazed to find that so many people have been following my career for so long. I am really pleased and surprised that everyone seems to know so much about me. What can I say? It's really fantastic and I really appreciate it."

Andy and his band headlined at some club dates after the tour, where he continued to be amazed at the reaction of girls in the audience. Still, he was realistic about the advantages he'd had. "I don't think I would ever have had my first hit if my brothers hadn't been The Bee Gees, and if I hadn't been with my manager, Robert Stigwood. I know they did it all," he said modestly. "They gave me the push to go ahead. I think they're responsible for everything that's happened to me so far. Things just started jumping and wouldn't stop, like a dream come true. I never thought it would happen to me.

"It was incredible to me that the single itself – my *first* single – didn't show any signs of slowing down. I couldn't believe it because I know how hard it is to have a hit record, especially when you stop to think that there are hundreds of records released every week. How could I expect my single to compete with all of them?"

But compete it did. For the first time in the history of *Billboard*'s record charts, a single reached the top of the chart and remained there for five weeks, then dropped to number four, before retaking the number one position and holding for a further five weeks. 'I Just Want To Be Your Everything' went on to become the most-played song of 1977.

"I think Barry, my brother, really pinpointed the reason [for its success]," Andy said. "He said it all works with the time of year. If you release a song in the summer that's right for the summer, it's a happy song, and 'I Just Want To Be Your Everything' was the perfect happy song. I mean, everybody sang along to it. It was a big hit with the industry before it was even released."

Shortly before the release of his début album, Andy returned to Australia with his parents to open a three-day music festival at Vision Valley in Sydney. One of the first things he did was to contact drummer Trevor Norton. "He called me up to see what I was doing," Trevor recalled. "He said he wanted me to get a band together 'pronto' to open a three day music festival with him at Vision Valley in Sydney."

By this time, Trevor had moved on from Zenta and was playing with a much heavier outfit called Alcatraze, whose style was radically different from Andy's pop approach. "I told him that I didn't think they would be able to cut it," he said, "so he told me to get some other players together to do this set for the concert."

Trevor brought together Paddy Lelliott, the former Zenta bass man; Carlton Spencer on keyboards from the Stevie Wright Band and Garry Rowley from Nightshift on lead guitar. "Two days later, we were rehearsing with Andy," he recalled. "We only had three days to learn the songs, which were 'I Just Want To Be Your Everything', '(Love Is) Thicker Than Water', 'Flowing Rivers', 'Words And Music' and a couple of Bee Gees' songs.

"It was great to play with him again, and I could see a great change in him – more professional than ever. He was obviously learning a lot over in America and his voice was sounding great. It all went over quite well and Andy was happy enough. The ABC television cameras were there to capture the whole set, and it was on the news that night.

"That was the last time I saw Andy," Trevor added sadly. "We kept in touch by phone after that day. He was very excited about his first album and sent me a copy personally, but after about 12 months, he stopped communicating."

The *Flowing Rivers* album, spurred on by the success of the its first single, 'I Just Want To Be Your Everything', entered the *Billboard* Top 40 on August 27 and remained there for the next 18 weeks, reaching number 19 at its highest position. It would remain on the *Billboard* Top 100 album chart for the next year – an impressive feat for a new artist. "I don't think you can pin any one thing on the way my voice and songwriting have developed. A lot of people say my album, *Flowing Rivers*, sounds like The Bee Gees, but if I sang or wrote any differently than I do now, it wouldn't be me at all," he explained. "This is my voice and these are mostly my songs. I know the single has helped sell the album, but I want people to listen to the album for what I put into it."

He later admitted that he wasn't really as confident about the album as his words seemed to indicate. "I was worried about my own material really, really badly. I didn't think I was a good songwriter at all. I was a bit doubtful about my own performance. Even today, I don't like what I did on it. I did one song with Barry, 'Thicker Than Water', which I thought was good. And 'Everything' I thought would be a hit."

Andy's second single, written less than an hour after the first one, was '(Love Is) Thicker Than Water'. It was issued first in Britain in September, where 'Flowing Rivers' was the B-side, but in America where its release was delayed until November, its companion title was 'Words And Music'. Although 'Thicker' was credited as a collaboration between the eldest and youngest Gibb brothers, Andy explained, "Even though it says on the credits 'B. & A. Gibb', it is really Barry's song . . . It is very hard to write with Barry, but he said, 'Help me think of a great title.' That was a period where Barry was thinking of titles first and seeing how they would inspire him to write a song . . .We were thinking of good titles, and I said, 'How about Thicker Than Water?' I did not say 'Love Is', just 'Thicker Than Water'. He said, 'That's great!' and then he came up with 'Love is higher than a mountain . . .' and he just went on from there, but the title was totally my idea."

It would seem a strange division of credits, but Albhy's insight into Barry's modus operandi might shed some light. "At some point, he would feel it was appropriate for you to be a writer, and then he would always split it in half. He didn't do the 70 per cent 30 per cent thing. If people wrote the song, it was always split in half . . . It's much easier if you just divide everything by the numbers. You don't have to deal with the psychological implications of telling somebody this is how much their participation was worth. It's a difficult thing even for people who are good at that, and that was not Barry's strong suit. The issue for him was not ever about money; it was about success in music."

During a four-day stint at the Roxy in Los Angeles, Robert Stigwood

433

presented Andy with his first gold record for 'I Just Want To Be Your Everything'. The presentation brought the show to a close, with thunderous applause and screams continuing long after he had left the stage.

As the year came to its end, so did Andy's association with the band who had toured with him. The band, now called Pages, continued to work together without Andy, playing mostly jazz fusion. A demo tape came to the attention of A&R man, Bobby Colomby, the former Blood, Sweat & Tears drummer, who signed them to Epic Records. Their eponymous début album contained original songs written by Richard Page, Steve George, Jerry Manfredi and Page's cousin, John Lang. Guitarist Peter Leinheisen and drummer Russell Battelene left the group soon after the recording of the album.

Richard Page and Steve George had attracted the attention of several record companies for their background vocals on the tour, and were kept busy with session work for Toto, Kenny Loggins, REO Speedwagon, Donna Summer, Quincy Jones, The Village People, Barry Manilow, James Ingram and Twisted Sister. They would again work with Andy on his 1982 live dates, providing backing vocals.

Eventually, they formed a band with guitarist Steve Farris and drummer Pat Mastelotto, releasing their first album in 1983 under the name Mr. Mister, but it was their second album, 1985's *Welcome To The Real World*, which would bring them fame. The album was RCA's first number one in more than a decade, and all three singles released from the LP made the American Top 10, with 'Broken Wings' and 'Kyrie' both reaching the top spot.

★   ★   ★

After his concert dates, Andy returned to the Gibb family fold in Florida, moving onto a houseboat reportedly once owned by a Miami's drug lord, who had been shot to death in the master bedroom. In the December issue of *Superteen* magazine, he said, "I live in Miami now . . . my wife and I live on a houseboat.

"I have two king-sized beds pushed together in my bedroom. The walls and floor are black carpet. The whole ceiling is mirrors and the headboard of the bed is mirrored also and meets the ceiling. The bathroom is designed for two people. There are two sinks and mirrors and you face each other as you're washing. It's really incredible."

Back in Australia for six months by the time the article was published, Kim said, "I think the houseboat sounds unpleasant and kinky. I categorically deny ever living on a houseboat of any kind with Andy. I can't understand why he would say that I did . . .

"We discussed it and decided that our marriage and Andy's career were two different identities. We agreed we would not speak publicly about each other. But that's only one of a number of agreements Andy broke . . . I am very disappointed in [him] and his tactics of using me as a stepping-stone to gain publicity."

Kim was rumoured to be expecting twins, living on welfare while he was living in the lap of luxury, and it did not take long before the news began to break in the United States.

Forced to admit to the breakdown in his marriage, he said, "My wife has said I'm a slave to fame but it's just not true. She left me even before my first record was a hit. Her mother came and took her away from me. It's all very sad – she's a lovely girl. But she came from a working class family in Sydney, and she couldn't cope with show business. If I had to go out in the afternoon and do an interview, she'd blow her top. We were together 98 per cent of the time and I worshipped her. I would never look at anyone else. I used to think, 'Oh God, it's such a shame – we have so much more to come but she's not going to be able to handle it.'

"Getting together again is something I am still hoping for, but with my career as hectic as it now is, it's hard. There's so much going on today with my career, with what I'm doing at the moment, plus the split – wow! We are still hoping and talking about getting back together. But Kim is back with her folks in Sydney, and I am here in New York."

Rumours had begun to circulate about Andy's alleged drug use, but he took pains to contradict them by admitting to smoking grass and, on one occasion, trying cocaine. "It was at a Hollywood party right after my first big record hit," he said. "I was getting crazed being 'Andy Gibb' all the time. Luckily, it didn't do any harm. I've cut myself off from that stuff. Everyone likes some kind of high, but I have enough trouble handling myself without it. I've become a health nut."

The Bee Gees' road manager, Tom Kennedy, remembers Andy fondly. "Most people wouldn't buy a lion at an auction – well, they might buy it to donate to a zoo, but he took it home to live on his houseboat!" he said. Andy kept the lion cub, named Samantha, on his houseboat until she began to grow too large, and only then was she donated to a Miami zoo.

His sister Lesley remembered what happened next. She got an urgent phone call from her youngest brother, asking her if she could get him a kangaroo. Later, he made another call, Lesley said. "He [wanted] me to see if I can get a kangaroo for Olivia Newton-John too. I think I'll quietly shelve the whole thing. I mean, where would he keep a kangaroo – on his boat? Anyway, Mum would probably end up having to look after it."

★   ★   ★

"After Kim left me, I was really depressed," Andy said. "Like for months and months, I didn't want to do anything. Susie just lifted me right out of everything. She was incredible. I met Susie at a celebrity sports thing in Los Angeles. We had two days of filming together, and in those two days, she virtually heard my whole life story. We came close to being in love. But we never got so involved that we talked about marriage or even living together. We just had a beautiful relationship . . . At one time it was a bit more – but now we have a kind of brother and sister relationship."

435

"Susie" was British film star Susan George, eight years Andy's senior. Following their appearance on the *US Against The World* television sports special, the two were seen together at various show business functions. "Andy and I were the best of friends but there was no affair," she said later.

Publicly, Andy was still denying a drug problem, going so far as to criticise his brothers for once using drugs. "It totally puts me off," he said. "But I can understand the pressures, and they didn't do themselves any permanent damage."

The ruse didn't deceive Susan George. She recognised his dependence on drugs and tried to help him through it. "Those nights were terrible," she recalled. "I would try my best and, to be fair, so would he. But it became too much . . . in the end, you feel helpless. It is really hard to judge what causes that unhappiness that led him into drugs. He was such a natural boy – never a bit fazed by all the success. He had tremendous charisma and vitality, he was always very special to me and always will be."

Back in Australia, his estranged wife was waiting for him. "There I was," Kim recalled, "sitting at home with Mum and Dad, pregnant, believing Andy would be with me for the baby's birth because he'd promised, no matter what, he would be there."

Instead, she received a cruel shock. "Suddenly, the Sydney press were calling me, telling me a press release had gone out saying that Andy and I were getting a divorce," she recalled. "The divorce papers arrived two weeks before Peta was due. I don't think I stopped crying until her birth."

Not only was Andy breaking his promise to be there for the birth; in a callous twist, the divorce papers served to the 19-year old stated that there were no children from the marriage; in effect, making the unborn child illegitimate. It was that which distressed Kim the most.

"Everyone thought, back then, that I was after money," she explained. "They always think that. But it was the principle I was fighting for, not money. The divorce lawyers in America were trying to pretend Andy and I didn't have a child. They were trying to pretend she didn't exist. I couldn't accept that so I fought long and hard [that] it nearly killed me. My weight dropped to 45 kg, and I believe I had a breakdown."

A few days after the papers were served, Andy's personal manager Jim Dayley phoned to find out if the child was born, telling Kim that Andy was off fishing.

After a difficult 40 hour labour, Kim gave birth on January 25 to a daughter, whom she christened Peta Jaye after her obstetrician. "Kim was very lucky to have Peta," said Yvonne Reeder. "The doctor thought she was going to lose her. She is heaven-sent, our baby."

Andy didn't contact Kim at all after the birth. "He didn't even send me a card," she added.

As soon she and baby Peta were released from hospital, Kim and her parents began looking through the Yellow Pages to find a lawyer to represent her in the divorce case. It wasn't going to be an easy fight. With earnings of over $2 million in his first year, Andy could afford the best lawyers money could buy. Kim's parents mortgaged the family home to finance the legal battle, to try to ensure that Peta would have the acknowledgement that she deserved.

Back in the United States, Andy told reporters that he did not wish to see the new arrival.

His parents were a little more forthcoming. Barbara explained that at 18, Andy had become "obsessed" with Kim. "Barry and Andy both married at 18, and in eight months, they were finished."

"You get kids of 18 getting married just because they think they can do what they want," Hugh added.

"They moved to Los Angeles," Barbara continued, "and Andy had to go off to do a promotional appearance. It was only overnight, but when he returned, Kim had gone back to Australia. He couldn't follow her because he had work commitments. So the Australian press wrote that he'd abandoned her without a penny.

"Then she had a daughter Peta, and the press got on to Andy and asked if he wanted to see Peta, the baby. He said, 'No.' Well, the truth is, of course, he'd love to see her. If Andy and Kim had come to live near us, none of this would have happened," she insisted.

"My family is keeping me alive, not Andy's," Kim said bitterly. "He is giving money to his parents and to his niece, but he doesn't seem to care for his own little girl. I haven't got a cent. Andy refused to give me money and he said he would refuse to support me and my daughter."

But paradoxically, Kim clung to the memories of the old Andy. "He was just so loving," she said.

"That's why we believe all these things he's been saying to the press are out of character," her mother added. "We can't believe that he didn't want to see his baby, that he absolutely refuses to give Kim even the minimum support money. That he was cruel to her."

Kim flew to New York in early April, and the divorce settlement was fought out in the American courts. When it was all over, Kim was awarded $225,000, of which $60,000 went into trust for Peta. Out of the balance, Kim had to pay all her own expenses; her doctor's bills, plane fare to and from the States and accommodation there, as well as her legal fees to three international lawyers and the Australian QC representing her. "I tell that story so that people will know what really happens to money when you have to get involved with lawyers," she said. "There was very little left after all the expenses. And you know, I really didn't mind. I'd made my point – Peta was officially recognised. That's all that mattered to me."

Kim and her lawyer, Mr L. Gruzman, returned to Australia on April 23 and were met by her family at the Sydney Airport. After a joyful reunion with her daughter, Kim told the waiting reporters that she was looking forward to "some peace and quiet." She gave no details of the settlement and said she had had no contact with Andy during her three weeks in America.

"All the discussions were handled by lawyers, we had about 15 between us." she said. "All I want to do now is settle down with Peta.

"I just want to look after my baby. I'll try to give her the best education she can have. If she wants to learn the piano, or if she has a talent for anything, I'll help her and foster it. But I'll never force her into anything she doesn't want to do. I want her to grow up to be a lady, a daughter Andy and I could both be proud of. But most of all, I want her to be happy."

★ ★ ★

Just before Christmas, Andy went back into the studio to begin recording his second album, again produced by Barry with Albhy Galuten and Karl Richardson.

"Andy's got a lot of energy," Karl said, "and each time, like the first album we did, it has been so amazing to watch him grow to do the second album . . . I am sure when we do the third one, it will be even another quantum leap. Each time he grows, the songs come through with more stuff, and he's feeling it more. He spends a lot more time getting involved in the studio, so I'm looking forward to the next one. There is always a quantum leap when you are dealing with someone that young."

"The strongest characteristic to come to mind about Andy is the fact that he's 20 now, and he's just growing out of being a teenager," Albhy explained. "He's very inspirational. His brothers are more scientific. He's doing something that they have been doing for years. With Andy, the quality of performance depends on the mood he's in. He's sort of a raw talent, very much unharnessed at this point."

Andy agreed that his mood was vital to all aspects of his career. "I believe you're only good when you're in the mood. If I feel like playing, I'll play. When I feel like writing a song, I will. On the other hand, my brother Barry has the urge to write every day. He's constantly writing. It's his main hobby. I know I can write, but I just get lazy sometimes.

"I can't write when I'm depressed," he explained. "But if I'm feeling okay, I can write about what it feels like when you are depressed. And if all else fails, I can always listen to Randy Newman or Don McLean and feel lifted again. They both construct marvellous songs."

Albhy tried to encourage Andy to work with other composers, in an effort to help him develop as a writer and broaden his horizons. "The first one that I got him together with was John Oates of Hall & Oates," Albhy said, "because he's a great facilitator . . . When Robert [Stigwood] heard about it, he called me up and he said, 'Don't let him do this, I don't want him writing with anyone but his brothers.'

"To me, that was a turning point in his life," he added sadly. "What could have been . . . but instead he became The Bee Gees' little brother, the fourth Bee Gee . . . When you love somebody, it's very, very hard to push them out on their own and tell them succeed or fail on your own."

In 1979, Andy discussed the possibility of writing with other artists. "There

438

have been times when it's been arranged, but I always back out," he said. "I was set to write with Hall & Oates, but I backed out. The only people I can write with are my brothers. I'd be terrified to write with anyone else. Yet the thing is, I know I should be more terrified writing with them because they are – in my mind, which I admit is biased – the very best!"

Like his earlier singles, 'Shadow Dancing' was in sharp contrast to what Andy was writing himself. His most well known songs were a little at odds with what was coming from his own creative soul, but he was to "throw it all away" after this album.

Barry's songs for Andy were more ephemeral than those he wrote for The Bee Gees. 'Shadow Dancing' was a catchy chorus and a good dance groove, great for radio, not great for close listening. 'An Everlasting Love' might rely a little too much on the Barry falsetto backing, and the cycling repeating line of the chorus can become tiresome. But at the other extreme '(Our Love) Don't Throw It All Away' by Barry and Blue Weaver is a classic song, as suitable for an older singer as for Andy, and even the unnecessary bridge section Barry added for this version can only slightly detract from its beauty (but compare the older Bee Gees take, released later, with Barry and Blue).

Andy's own songs continue in the mould of the 'Flowing Rivers' songs, like 'Melody'. Notably, at the UNICEF show in 1979 Andy chose to do one, 'I Go For You', instead of one of his hits. None really stand out, but they have a consistent flow. At times, he relied on Albhy's musical expertise to help translate his ideas into reality. "He'll sit down at the keyboards and find chords that we're hearing," Andy marvelled. "He's magic. He hears exactly what you're hearing. 'One More Look [At The Night]' – that came across in 10 or 15 minutes."

For the song, 'Why', Andy revealed, "I wrote all the melody . . . and I took it to Barry, pretty desperate with it, saying, 'I just can't put lyrics to this song. I've tried.' I had tried; I tried for over a month on this song, and I was just on the verge of throwing it over my shoulder and going for another one. Barry put lyrics to it, and it's now turned out as his favourite song on the album."

When *Shadow Dancing* was complete, Andy said, "I am so much more confident now after doing this second album, dealing with the pressures of proving to myself that the first one wasn't a 'fluke' and that I could write a second album. So now I am a lot more confident." With the benefit of hindsight, his words sound like whistling in the dark.

RSO arranged a mini-tour of Europe to promote the new album, with planned appearances in England, Scotland, Belgium, Holland, Switzerland, France, Germany, Italy and Sweden. It was less than a resounding success. On March 6, Andy arrived in London for the start of the tour, but soon there were warning signs that all was not well. During a live radio interview, he fell asleep while he was on the air. Some ten days later he arrived in Amsterdam, where he recorded 'Shadow Dancing' and '(Love Is) Thicker Than Water' for the Dutch television programme *Top Pop*, but the following day, he collapsed during a photo shoot. The tour was cut short, and he flew home to Miami that same day.

"I broke down, it certainly wasn't mental," Andy told Robert W. Morgan in a radio interview. "It was a sort of physical collapse and we had to cut the tour a few weeks short and bring me home to Miami; and that was like a month ago, so that's it, I just get very tired, very quickly. Having to constantly talk about being successful, until you get used to that, I suppose, is a different thing for a person.

"I haven't had a lot of years struggling in the business of non-stop touring and everything else," he further explained, "so I went out to do a promotional tour of Europe. Well, I'm not really big there, nothing like America. To go out there, naturally, they are really ready there for me to work and we had five weeks promotion and for three weeks we would be going from like six in the morning until two in the morning. I wasn't eating all my meals, I was getting called away to all these meetings, not being able to finish my meals."

After the success of 'I Just Want To Be Your Everything', sales of '(Love Is) Thicker Than Water' had proved initially worrying. "It slowed down," Andy explained. "We were all scared. There's lots of points where all the record people at RSO said they were a little worried that it was stopping. It didn't lose its 'bullet', but it really heavily lost its jump in sales activity. And then, it picked up and nothing stopped it. So it was not predictable . . . but it's still a commercial song. We believed in it. I think the momentum of the first record obviously helped the second a little, but it was, again, a different record."

'(Love Is) Thicker Than Water' eventually entered the Top 10 of the American singles chart several weeks after its release, finally achieving the top spot on March 4 by muscling aside The Bee Gees' 'Stayin' Alive'. It remained there for two weeks, before his brothers once again took control with 'Night Fever'.

'Flowing Rivers' had been intended for release as a single in the UK at the same time as 'Thicker Than Water' reached number one in the USA but was withdrawn in favour of 'Shadow Dancing', which was released worldwide in April. It would only achieve number 42 in the British chart, but it became his third consecutive American number one, remaining at the peak position for the next seven weeks and making him the first solo artist in the history of the American Top 40 to have their first three singles top the charts. The song would also be named the number one song of the year on Casey Kasem's year-end countdown, giving him the top spot two years in a row.

It was an amazing run of success, but Hugh Gibb observed, "It's like the old story, too much too soon. I think he was about . . . 19, when he had his first number one. I think he's the only person at that time to have three number ones in a row from starting. His brothers didn't. The Beatles didn't, but bang bang bang, three number ones in a row . . . He couldn't handle it."

"[It was] very exciting, of course," Barbara added, "because this was something he'd worked for and he wanted to be a big star. Of course, it did go to his head. I mean, it really did go to his head. He was young, you know."

"I got carried away at first on material things," Andy admitted later, "and I bought . . . a 308 Ferrari, which was very expensive and very flashy. I don't suppose it was money – the cost of upkeep and insurance – as much as the boredom that caused me to get rid of it. The novelty wore off. It just wasn't the right kind of car for Miami."

Andy's appearances on American television were helping to boost his already thriving career. After his first appearance on the *Donny & Marie Show*, there were rumours that it had been love at first sight for the youngest Gibb brother and the only Osmond sister.

Initially, Andy confirmed the stories. "She's a beautiful girl. I never thought it would happen to me but we met and wham! That was it," he said. "And vice versa. It's gone a lot further since then. We speak a lot on the phone. And I've sent her flowers. Two dozen yellow roses with one red one in the middle."

"There's nothing to it on Marie's side," said Marie's mother, Olive Osmond. "It's ridiculous. As far as she's concerned, he's just a friend. We laugh about it. I don't think my daughter would marry outside her faith. She's basically religious. She wants a temple marriage and thinks the ideal age is around 23. Then she'll settle down and have a family. She and Andy are working together on some records, and there's no room for anything else. She told me Andy had been calling her. Sometimes he gets kind of lonely and sometimes it's business."

"Andy had a crush on Marie," Albhy Galuten verified, "and they had seen each other, but . . . he was doing tons of drugs, and she was not even drinking Coca-Cola. Talk about unrequited love!"

Beri Gibb was Andy's confidante in those days, and she claimed, "Andy was in love with Marie and marriage was discussed. But during all the time Andy and Marie went out together, they were never on a date alone. Sometimes it was Marie's unmarried brothers, sometimes her mother and father but always a chaperone or guardian. Religion was always a factor in the relationship. Marie said she would only marry someone who was a Mormon."

Lesley Evans also said that she believed that her youngest brother would like to marry Marie, but she too felt that there was little chance of that ever happening. "The point is that Marie has been raised a Mormon and her greatest desire is to marry in the Mormon Temple," she said. "So Andy would have to become a Mormon, and that would mean him having to do two years in the field, as they say. Well, you know, I can't ever see Andy doing that."

Andy began a week of rehearsals in Baltimore for his upcoming American tour on May 19, and the 44-city tour opened in Richmond on May 28. On his first tour, he looked like the boy next door. He played guitar, clinging to it almost like a security blanket, and remained with feet planted firmly in front of his microphone.

But it was a very different Andy Gibb who took to the stage this time around. "Before, I was terrified on stage," he confessed. "I never moved, just stood there with my guitar. Now I'm running and jumping and I only play guitar during the acoustic songs. After a while, you can elicit certain responses from the crowd, like Elvis. The more I do body-wise, the more they react. I hope as I go along, the fans will realise I've got a good, hot band that can really play. Now I hear the screams ringing in my ears hours after the show is over."

Dressed in skin-tight satin trousers which he admitted were "verging on obscene," he pranced, gyrated and strutted his way through the concert to the screams of his adoring fans. "I definitely have a sexual ego thing," he confessed. "But if I'm suggestive, it's in a nice way. Luckily, no one's ever been hurt – a few girls have passed out, that's all. I'll worry when they stop."

Three very special guests joined Andy on stage for his concert at the Jai Alai Fronton in Miami. A crowd of 6,000 thrilled to the sight and sound of Barry, Robin and Maurice Gibb joining their little brother for 'Shadow Dancing'.

Barbara Gibb was as excited as any teenager in the audience. "I haven't seen Andy perform since last year when he opened for Neil Sedaka," she said. "I told him then to move around a little more. Tonight my boy moved around, wouldn't you say? Andy is basically very shy off stage, but he's learned how to make the audience respond and in such a short time."

"I don't know where Andy got those moves," Barry added. "Certainly not from me!"

But Hugh Gibb took it all in his stride. "I'm not all that surprised," he asserted. "I taught Andy and The Bee Gees their stage technique: how to walk on, smile, bow, dress. And I arrange Andy's stage programme and lighting. Once he walks out there, he almost never stops moving. The sweat pours out – he shakes his head and sprays the first four rows."

In early June, Andy participated in the March of Dimes Superwalk in Detroit and took time out to attend the West Coast premiere of *Grease* in Los Angeles.

Between the first and second legs of the tour, he flew to Honolulu for a short holiday, before resuming his tour with a concert at the Honolulu NBC Arena. As it happened, Donny and Marie Osmond were also in Honolulu filming their movie, *Goin' Coconuts*, which only fuelled the rumours about a relationship between Andy and Marie. There were news reports that the Osmond family asked that Andy leave Hawaii, and when pressed for comment, The Bee Gees' personal manager, Dick Ashby, replied, "Yes, there was a phone call of this nature, but it's such a personal matter I don't feel at liberty to discuss it."

Marie herself denied any rumours of a romance, saying, "That's really funny. You just have to laugh at that. Andy came up to our studio complex in Utah to do the *Donny And Marie Show,* and our families are friends. That's all."

Andy's fourth single, 'An Everlasting Love' was released in July, just as *Shadow Dancing* achieved platinum status. It reached number five on the American charts and number 10 in the UK. The following month, *Flowing Rivers* also went platinum.

The *Shadow Dancing* Tour came to its conclusion at the Omni in Atlanta, Georgia, on September 1, coinciding with the release of the LP and his fifth single, the Barry Gibb and Blue Weaver ballad, 'Our Love (Don't Throw It All Away)' in the United States. In Britain, the single's release was delayed until January, and was released with 'Shadow Dancing' as the B-side. It was also released in a special edition blue vinyl 12-inch format, with the A-side incorrectly credited to B., R. & M. Gibb. The song reached number nine on the American charts but failed to break into the British charts.

The year had been a hectic one for Andy, and with the benefit of hindsight, a radio interview from 1978 seems eerily prophetic. Andy jokes, "They're going to bury me tomorrow," and then in a more serious vein, he continued, "I still feel pretty much . . . the same about it as I did before. Because though everything has happened in a short time and so as much as, you know, I get tired sometimes and have done quite a few things, I can handle it. And yet, it is weird as I suppose I must really remember 'cause 20 years old and three number one's is a lot, and I'm just worried about 10 years or all those years until I'm 30.

"Sometimes it is a strange thought, thinking if all this can happen . . . Some days you get depressed and think that it's been a long year. What is it going to be like having to fight through 10 years? I know that success and everything that is happening now is great, and it seems like it's gonna last forever, as it's happening to you now, but it's amazing how short that space in time was when you look back on it and how quick things can all turn around."

29

IF AT FIRST YOU DON'T SUCCEED . . .

THE BEE GEES have never let failure overly discourage them, always maintaining that if they just kept doing what they did long enough, success
would eventually come their way. During the remainder of the Seventies,
perseverance became a watchword for many others too, as several attempts
were made to achieve a hit with songs that had failed to chart previously,
sometimes on more than one occasion.

'One Bad Thing' was a case in point. Following on from Ronnie Burns'
Australian release, in March 1970, New Horizon were next to pin their
hopes on it. The main men behind the group were Tony Burrows and Bob
Saker.

Burrows is best known by many for his involvement in The Flowerpot
Men, the group who made number four in the UK charts in 1967 with
'Let's Go To San Francisco', a hit that earned them a support act billing on
The Bee Gees' Saville Theatre shows in November of that year.

The other main protagonist behind the group was a character called Bob
Saker who would have much to do with Maurice Gibb and Billy Lawrie
over the coming months. Like Burrows, Saker was a session musician, albeit
with a less varied history behind him. " 'One Bad Thing Leads To Another'
[sic] was one of their songs, and I recorded that," said Bob. "I used to do fake
groups; I was in a lot of these Seventies groups. I was in New Horizon. That
one, we made up a group of sessions guys; the singers on it are Tony
Burrows and I."

Bob is very much one for plain speaking, even if it involves an element of
self deprecation. "I probably wrote the B-side, so it was shit. I think it might
have been 'Cider Rosey'. You always put duff B-sides on in case they flip
the bugger. You put a good record on the B-side and they'll split your
plays." Bob would probably happily debate his theory with you until the
cows came home; whether it's better to have the radio play one song only,
against the other belief that by having two good songs, you double your
chances of gaining a hit.

In this instance, it was something of an academic argument. New Horizon's
version of 'One Bad Thing' fared as badly in the charts as Ronnie Burns'
version had.

Not in the slightest put off by this failure were The Freshmen. Although

444

low on profile, they were high in output, 'One Bad Thing' this being their seventh and penultimate single release. None of their releases had provided any indication of a bright future for the band, and this CBS single was certainly no exception.

The final attempt of the four was probably the most obscure. Wildwood were a little known band from New Zealand, and in 1972 they too issued 'One Bad Thing' as an A-side, this time on Festival's Interfusion subsidiary. Somewhat predictably, it suffered the same fate as all the others.

★   ★   ★

The Bell label released a second Gibb composition on April 16, 1971. Originally from Adelaide, Bev Harrell is best known in Australia for her 1967 hit with her début release, 'What Am I Doing Here With You', on the EMI's HMV label. She was voted Australia's top female vocalist in 1968 but, despite the Australian connection, she had never met Maurice Gibb before travelling to England, following visits to South Africa and Germany. Her recording of 'Back To The People', came mainly through the urgings of the music publishing company who were pushing it.

Maurice, who wrote the song with Billy Lawrie, played piano and bass, and Lulu provided back-up vocals. Bev still recalls Richard Harris recording in the studio next door. She also has memories of Maurice having a red open top Rolls-Royce and of enjoying riding around London in such luxury.

This was the second occasion that Bev had sung a Gibb composition. In the mid to late Sixties, she had also recorded Robin's 'I Am The World' back in Australia under the careful eye of producer David Mackay who would himself work directly with The Bee Gees in the future. Bev remains in show business, and lives in Melbourne.

In May 1971, introduced by Tony Blackburn, Lulu performed her new single 'Everybody Clap' on *Top Of The Pops*. The song had come from Maurice's blossoming songwriting partnership with Billy Lawrie and is the only known occasion where Maurice and Lulu appeared together on one of her records, although there were probably several other such instances, which remain unreleased. Amongst others, Lulu's band for the night included Maurice, Billy Lawrie and Zoot Money.

Maurice and Billy had offered Lulu several titles from which to choose, but this was the number she liked best. A fairly impressive line-up of studio musicians was assembled for the January 11 session, as she herself explained proudly. "It was recorded with John Bonham of Led Zeppelin on drums, Jack Bruce of Cream on bass, and Leslie Harvey of Stone The Crows on guitar, not forgetting Maurice on piano. The result was a lovely, very pleasant record, but it did nothing very much and never hit the charts." Maggie Bell, another Stone The Crows member, was also said to have had an involvement, probably on backing vocals.

In spite of the lack of commercial success for Atlantic, it was still a good experience for Maurice. After all, there can be few who can rightfully claim

445

to have produced a record with members of Led Zeppelin and Cream on it!

Buoyed up by the occasion, Maurice and Billy had stayed on at the studios after the others had gone to continue work on some other projects. One was 'Take It Easy Greasy', first demoed by them on December 9. Another was their jingle for Ultrabrite, but for which they required the services of another vocalist, little realising that they would be launching the career of an anonymous legend. If that seems a contradiction in terms, Bob Saker can be relied on for clarification.

"We used to be both signed to Robert Stigwood at the same time, we used the same pubs as it were and all that. I was signed as a writer, and so was [Maurice] of course, and I was signed as an artist too." In fact, Bob released five singles between 1968 and 1971 either under his own name, or as plain Saker.

"What was strange was that I started picking up doing sessions and things, and Maurice was given a job writing jingles. He wrote a jingle but couldn't sing it himself for contractual reasons, so I sang the jingle, it was for Ultrabrite, the first one he did, and it was really peculiar, because since then I really took off. He was the first guy to record me doing a jingle and I became the biggest jingle guy in the country within about six months. There were articles in the papers and stuff about me.

"I was doing four or five sessions a day," he continued. "I remember turning the TV on once, and I had a whole commercial break to myself! It was ridiculous, but it was all different voices, that's how you can get away with it.

"Remember the Hofmeister [Beer] Bear? 'Hey, hey,' that was me. The [Sugar Puffs] Honey Monster, that's me! Isn't it great to be famous . . . gets me tables in restaurants! I say, 'Do you know who I am?' 'No not really!' 'I'm the talking lavatory' [Domestos – Big Bad Dom]. I get a good table then!" Another product to benefit from Bob's exuberant persona was Wagon Wheels biscuits. The list is virtually endless.

Barry's unreleased solo album still continued to be a source of potential new material, and Genaro Louis Vitaliano, a native of New York City's Bronx borough, became the latest to plunder from it. Better known by his stage name of Jerry Vale, the American crooner chose to record what is arguably the best of the bunch. 'Moonlight' is right up there with 'Words' as one of Barry's finest compositions and, even 30 years after its creation, it remains a hit in waiting. Perhaps "The Ambassador of Song for contemporary romantic music", as Jerry was once described, can persuade someone else to take a chance on 'Moonlight', even though his own version failed to take off in the manner it deserved to.

Katja Ebstein was next to record one of Barry's solo efforts. Originally titled 'Peace In My Mind', her German language version appeared on her *Freunde* album for United Artists as 'Frieden In Mir', its literal translation being 'Peace In Me'.

Barry's publishers were obviously hard at work because his songs continued to turn up on obscure albums. Although an impromptu acoustic version of 'Summer Ends' was included on his 1970 Fan Cub single, its first official airing was discovered on the 1972 album by Company, of the same name. Released solely in the USA on the Playboy Music label – a brand name not immediately connected with record production – this was Company's début album and the trio, who comprised David Stuart, Jack Moran and Joe Croyle, could best be described as belonging to the easy listening category. Barry's song may have looked out of place beside some standards like 'I'd Like To Teach The World To Sing' and 'Without You', but the group knew the rarity value of the song and plugged it on the reverse cover by promoting it as "surprise! – a previously unreleased Bee Gees gem", which they had performed on their own original audition tape.

Another LP released Stateside that year was *Paid My Dues* by Atlantic solo artist Jimmy Stevens. Born in Liverpool's dockland area during the Second World War, the bookmaker's son was no angel as a child, and soon had a natty collection of leather jackets, none of them his! Thinking of his long-term gain, his mother decided on short-term pain and reported him to the police which led to him spending a while in Borstal at Her Majesty's pleasure.★

After "paying his dues", he found work in a variety of trades such as digging roads and mining coal. But he needed a means of escape, and as he wasn't built for football, he followed the other route open to him and worked hard on his songwriting. Offered the chance of appearing in some of the city's less salubrious nightspots, he earned the nickname of Jimmy Some-time. "Sometimes I turned up, and sometimes I didn't," he put it succinctly.

The Daily Mirror once unkindly referred to him as "a fat John Lennon [who] writes like a broken-down poet and sings like he chews gravel for breakfast". Years before, Brian Epstein had seen something in him, and offered him the chance to make a record. Jimmy didn't believe him, and the opportunity was gone. Maurice's intervention offered him the option of making up for lost time

In his native Britain, the album went by the name of *Don't Freak Me Out*, but it didn't contain any Gibb compositions. It was the first of two LPs to be released that year in which Maurice was heavily involved, and in Stevens' case, Maurice contributed bass, organ and backing vocals; being joined in the singing by Billy Lawrie and Peter Frampton. Alan Kendall was on guitar, as indeed was Frampton, while Bill Shepherd and Gerry Shury shared the arrangements. It was also another credit for Moby productions with Maurice taking the producer's chair, and Billy Lawrie getting an additional name-check in the associate capacity. Maurice, naturally, appeared by arrangement with The Robert Stigwood Organisation, a standard footnote whenever he was involved outside The Bee Gees.

Atlantic had given Billy and Maurice a budget of £4,000 to complete the

---

★ A young offenders correction system used in Britain at that time.

album and, by the time they had done all they originally intended to do, the bill stood at £2,200. It never occurred to them to keep the money for themselves, but neither had they any intention of giving the money back either. If certain parts of the album sound as if they have a preponderance of strings on them, it doesn't require too much imagination to work out why.

Jimmy was a very down-to-earth character who enjoyed his music for its own sake, rather than for the rich rewards that a successful career could bring. In that sense, he was regarded by some as an under-achiever, who could have made a greater name for himself in the industry than he ultimately did. His motivation came from wanting to provide for his family. His wife and four children lived in a Liverpool council house while he recorded in London, and he would go back each week with money to pay the rent. As he said, "You've got to keep the kids in shoes." Jimmy was scheduled to support The Bee Gees on their 1973 UK tour but, like the headlining act themselves, only ended up playing the one concert on June 24 at the London Palladium. Still, he had enjoyed opening for The Bee Gees on their 16-date tour of the States in March, so at least he had those memories to look back on.

The other male performer to enjoy Maurice's participation on vinyl that year was the man of a thousand jingles, Bob Saker. Encouraged by his success on the advertising front, Bob was persuaded to record a solo album entitled *They've Taken Back My Number*, but it didn't exactly set the heather on fire. However, that was more down to administrative and distribution problems than any lack of quality on the LP itself, an aspect that Bob was quick to highlight.

"It was a complete flop. York Records was a mess up. They pressed the wrong records, and they didn't send the right ones to the DJs, they sent the wrong records, all the wrong pressings; it was a complete mess. York Records closed after about six months in complete chaos. It was attached to Yorkshire Television."

The disarray notwithstanding, the actual songs were pleasant on the ear, and quite representative of the music of the period. Maurice was on his by then favoured bass, and Jack Winsley produced the album. Winsley and Saker worked together on quite a number of records during this period, "a Winsak production" being their particular trademark.

The recordings took place just as problems were surfacing between Maurice and Lulu, and after each session was completed, the pair would socialise together, each receiving a sympathetic ear from the other, as Bob explained. "I used to knock about with Maurice when he was getting divorced, and I was getting divorced, so we used to get wrecked together and whine about the women."

It was during this period that Bob noted one of Maurice's little character traits, not normally to the fore while sober, but which in those days became painfully obvious to his drinking companions. Many have hinted at this aspect of his persona, but Bob was never one for subtle inferences, simply being one of those people who are used to plain speaking.

"Maurice is famous for embroidering stories," he divulged. "He exaggerates completely! It used to annoy me, because he used to tell stories about me in front of people and he'd made them up, but he'd convinced himself that they were true like an apocryphal story. 'Remember that time you set fire to yourself, and there were these three girls going down on you', and all this, and of course you'd say, 'No, Maurice, that never happened.' 'Oh yes it did, I was there.' He's a fantasy merchant," Bob continued. "You wouldn't think that he was the most famous guy in the world, you'd think he was a guy who actually worked in Woolworths and pretends he knows The Bee Gees; makes up stories about famous people."

Talking to Bob though, it's clear he retains nothing but affection for his old buddy. "He's a nice guy, they're all nice fellers. Maurice is a very good musician and so's Barry, but Robin for some reason, he just busks along, they fit around him."

Another album released that year, this time in Australia, was *Restless*, by Ian B. McLeod. This one did feature a Gibb song, 'Give Your Best, but what really raised the eyebrows of those who recognised its significance, was the identity of his co-singer, Lesley Gibb. She also sang on two other tracks, and those who missed out on her performance three years earlier on *Talk Of The Town* would be able to ascertain that she is indeed quite a talented singer in her own right. Curiously, the album was released on three different independent labels, Festival, Troubadour and Bunnyip; the latter two being subsidiaries of Festival Records. The re-issues on the subsidiaries were released during the following year. The other songs that Lesley participated on were 'Rings Of Gold' and 'Keep On Smiling', and the back cover showed three photos of her which had been taken at the recording sessions.

One of Robert Stigwood's former office boys came good for him in the end. After years performing other duties, Norman Hitchcock had made his way into the recording studios on November 12, 1971 and January 17, 1972. The fruits of his labours appeared during 1972, the first single, 'Just Another Minute' backed with 'One Wheel On My Wagon' appearing in the spring while 'Baby Come On Home'/'Angelina' was delayed until autumn. All were original Hitchcock compositions; the last named being written in conjunction with Billy Lawrie. All four songs were Moby productions.

Steve Hodson's single, 'Crystal Bay', also a Winsak production issued on the terminal York label, closed off the year. Written by the Gibb/Lawrie partnership, promotional copies were issued with a biography sheet and a photo which showed Steve sitting on a fence outside Follyfoot Farm, a less than subtle reminder of the singer's acting role in the *Follyfoot* TV series.

Former Marble Graham Bonnet was back on the scene in 1973, and he chose 'Castles In The Air' from the unreleased Bee Gees' *A Kick In The Head Is Worth Eight In The Pants* album as the B-side to his 'Trying To Say Goodbye' single on RCA.

Continuing with The Marbles theme, Philips released Rosetta Hightower's powerful version of 'The Walls Fell Down' as the A-side of a single.

449

It had taken until 1973 for Billy Lawrie to finally release a solo album, even though the talented singer-songwriter had been recording his own material for a number of years beforehand. His first single, 'Roll Over Beethoven', was released in 1970, but another title, 'Visitor From America', which he had written with Maurice, had also been considered at one point, but this remains unreleased.

Like Bob Saker, Billy had also supplemented his income in the advertising market. One surviving demo tape from October 13, 1971 was referred to as "TV single" and included 'Cabory's' (presumably chocolate manufacturers Cadburys?), and 'Spangles', a brand of boiled sweets remembered fondly by British children of the Seventies, as much for their sharp edges when bitten, as for their fruity flavours.

It was no surprise that one of the tracks on Billy's *Ship Imagination* LP involved Maurice, although 'Freedom' introduced a third writer into the partnership. Leslie Harvey was a member of Glasgow rock band, Stone The Crows, a discovery of Led Zeppelin's manager Peter Grant. Harvey is credited as acoustic guitarist on the song, whilst Jimmy McAnonymous provided guitar, and Mags McGlint joined Lulu on backing vocals. It seems more than just a coincidence that Stone The Crows had a guitarist by the name of Jimmy McCulloch and a singer by the name of Maggie Bell, and contractual problems may have reared their ugly head once again. Stone The Crows broke up later that year. McCulloch joined Wings whilst Bell began a solo career which failed to capitalise on her wide acceptance as one of Britain's top female singers of the time. She would return to prominence in the Eighties as the voice behind 'No Mean City', the theme song of the *Taggart* television series. Tragically, by the time the album came out, Les Harvey – brother of "Sensational" Alex Harvey – was dead, having been electrocuted while on stage during a concert at Swansea University.

It might have been expected that Maurice would have played a bigger part on his brother-in-law's only album, repaying the favour extended to him on his own unreleased solo album, but it is likely that the cracks appearing in his marriage with Lulu were starting to make it difficult for him to continue his working relationship with Billy.

Two more of Barry's solo compositions surfaced that year, again demonstrating the international appeal of his music. Peter Maffay's German LP *Du Bist Wie Ein Lied* contained 'Mando Bay' and 'Ich Bin Dein Freund'. The album's title was the same as the first song on the disc; the German language version of Barry and Robin's 'When Do I' from the *Trafalgar* LP. Fortunately, for those fans who only spoke English, Maffay also went down a treat in South Africa, and the singer displayed his command of the language by reprising all three songs on his *It's You I Want To Live With* album there, released that same year. 'Mando Bay' lost nothing in its translation, whilst those who had a limited knowledge of German, and would swear that Freund meant friend, were confused by title of the remaining song being revealed as 'If I Were The Sky'.

In 1974, The Bee Gees had sunk to uncharted depths, and there was little to encourage them on the cover versions front either. However, the first green shoots of a recovery poked their heads into the American charts in March 1975 when Elton John's drummer, Nigel Olsson, took 'Only One Woman' to number 91 in the US Hot 100. In doing so, he became the first artist in almost five years to achieve a chart placing with a Gibb composition. The record was also issued in Britain and Australia on Elton's Rocket label.

It would also be the last significant release of a song not released by the Gibbs themselves, for the next couple of years. A move to Miami for the brothers was imminent and their strategy was simple. Sort out their own lack of commercial success, before even attempting to remedy the suffering of others.

★   ★   ★

If there was a definitive golden period for the Brothers Gibb, it was most definitely the Eighties when they recorded five albums for internationally renowned artists; each of which spawned at least one hit record. The seeds of this success were sown in the mid-to-late Seventies when The Bee Gees achieved unprecedented levels of popularity. However, for one of the brothers, this new era of fulfilment had a false dawn.

Over the years, Maurice's name had been linked with many uncredited appearances on other artists' records so it was quite amusing to find him denying his suggested involvement on one. Henry Cooper, the British boxer famous for flooring Cassius Clay and promoting Brut aftershave, had released a single in 1976 called 'Knock Me Down With A Feather'. In his official biography he claimed that Maurice had written the song for him, attributing, "Give It A Try Surprise Yourself" to the surprised Gibb. Perhaps Henry had taken one punch too many during his career, as it seems unlikely that he would easily confuse Maurice with the real writer, Richard Cassman. Blue Weaver wrote the B-side 'Knocked Out By Your Love'. In any event, it wasn't a hit. Indeed, Henry played the record to one of his friends, and proudly invited him to, "Guess who that is?"

"That's easy," came the response. "Max Bygraves!"

However, 1976 did at least provide some chart action on the cover version front. In March, Olivia Newton-John coasted to number 23 in the USA with 'Come On Over' which had been lifted off The Bee Gees' *Main Course* album from the previous year. Yvonne Elliman then took 'Love Me' from *Children Of The World* and made number 14, whilst it fared even better in Britain by reaching number 6.

That British chart feat was also achieved by Candi Staton in July of the following year with 'Nights On Broadway'. There then followed the hit that never was, according to one of its participants that is. Its co-producer and co-writer, Albhy Galuten, felt strongly that Network's 'Save Me, Save Me' was the right song at the right time.

"I was really bummed that wasn't a hit. That's where I met George Bitzer.

That group was managed by Tommy Mottola, and Karl Richardson and I were producing the record. I knew Tommy . . . and he wanted us to do Network.

"George is still a great keyboard player, and he shows up on Andy's records," Albhy continued. "So we produced that record and Barry and I wrote a song that was a great song and I thought, 'God you know it's too bad that wasn't a hit, it was an excellent song'. But it was not a hit, for who knows what reason. To break a band, you know, it was a brand new band.

"Actually the record wasn't as good as we wanted it to be, 'cause . . . it was a case of managers fucking with things. The singer sang a lot in falsetto and they particularly wanted a song that could feature his voice. The song was written with that range in mind, and then I think Tommy decided they didn't like the sound of the band, not that song, but the band with so much falsetto. So they really wanted to make the song work in natural voice. So we had to change it."

Two of the Gibb's strongest ever ballads resurfaced on albums that year too. 'Only One Woman' was recorded by Swedish group Christers for their strangely titled *5:e* LP on the Tor label while Patricia Paay included 'The Love Of A Woman' on *The Lady Is A Champ* for EMI in Holland.

However, the best was still to come.

Eight years after a Gibb composition had brought her an initial but all too brief fame, Samantha Sang was back, and taking the American charts by storm. However, the story behind the song that launched her comeback begins on the other side of the Atlantic.

"I had a clever manager," Samantha began, inferring that the forthcoming meeting arranged by Bill May was no coincidence, "who found out that The Bee Gees were in France recording, and I was travelling and playing around the world at that time. We contacted Barry and told him we were in France and he told us to come over. So we met and spoke, and he said he would write a song for me. I love the big emotional ballads, but Barry said, 'I'm gonna write one to show off your soft voice'. After about a month he called me and asked me to come to Florida to record with him."

Written at Chateau d'Herouville in Paris immediately during the initial *Saturday Night Fever* sessions, the song that Barry had written for her with Blue Weaver was '(Our Love) Don't Throw It All Away', which she soon got a tape of. When she arrived in Miami, Barry announced, "I think I've topped myself," and played her 'Emotion' which he and Robin had just written.

After a few bars, Samantha said, "I'm gonna take that, thank you." She didn't want to sound like she was copying The Bee Gees' "but that was the basic sound, that's what the song demanded."

Barry sang backing vocals on the record, saying, "We decided it's better to have her sound like that, with everyone knowing that Barry Gibb is on the record as an excuse for sounding like that." The instrumental intro is inspired by the opening of the old ballad 'September In The Rain', something which Albhy Galuten thinks nobody has ever noticed.

'Emotion' was recorded at Criteria studios by the Gibb, Richardson, Galuten combination, and it took a whole month to complete. The B-side was 'When Love Is Gone', a non–Gibb composition written by Francis Lai and was the theme song of the popular film of the time, *Bilitis*.

The single entered the US charts in November and sold phenomenally well, eventually climbing to number three. In Britain, release of 'Emotion' was delayed until February, 1978 where it attained a highly respectable number 11. The album of the same name followed shortly thereafter, and it contained two additional Gibb songs. There was a re-recording of Samantha's original 1969 hit, which still has very special meaning for her.

"I think 'The Love Of A Woman' is one of the best songs ever written and never got the attention it was due. It's still in my live repertoire. Also, because Barry specifically wrote it for me, that's why I recorded it again'. Barry suggested the other song, 'Charade' – taken from The Bee Gees' *Mr. Natural* album – because it seemed well suited to her voice."

Initially Samantha's success was dwarfed by the attention being focused on The Bee Gees themselves at that point, and she had to fight to achieve the recognition her singing deserved. "I had to get out and prove myself on the road, on the circuit," she said. "Most people thought I was an overnight success, but I had been performing for over 10 years."

Nowadays, she continues to perform in her native Australia, but is ready to resume her partnership with Barry at any time. "Working and being associated with Barry Gibb has been the highlight of my career. If Barry wants to write another song, I'll be there tomorrow, and I'd do it all again!"

Considering the incredible success enjoyed by the RSO label at that time, it seems incredible that 'Emotion' wasn't part of it as, in a rare error of judgement, Stigwood had refused first option on it. Instead it was picked up by Franki Valli's Private Stock label. However, a strange twist of fate would soon restore the smile to Robert's face. Barry Gibb tells the story.

"Robert [Stigwood] rang up and said, 'Can there be a song called "Grease"? I have another song called "Grease" by another artist who I won't mention, but it doesn't work.' I said, 'What do you want?' He said, 'I want a hit record that's called "Grease".' I says, 'How can anybody write a big hit record called "Grease"? I mean, d'you write about combing your hair, d'you write about Brylcreem or what, how can you make that romantic?' It clicked later on. If you write a song about the word 'Grease', it would work, and that's all I did."

All Barry did was to write one of the biggest hits of the year: a number one in America, a number two in Germany, and a number three in Britain. Not bad for an off the cuff little number. Franki Valli certainly wasn't complaining either.

"How bad can it be, working with people who are responsible for the biggest record success of the decade and possibly of all time? All that, and nice people, too. It was fabulous in every way."

Paul Nicholas, also then fresh from the filming of *Sgt. Pepper's*, was equally effervescent about the song. "Barry wrote that great tune, one of my favour-ite, favourite tunes of all time. It's fantastic. It really, again, caught the mood, and again it was an enormous success. I think he wrote it very quickly, Robert told me. I think Robert said, 'Can you write me a song blah, blah, for *Grease*,' and he came up with that. I mean, it's fantastic."

For anyone else, to miss out on a hit the size of 'Emotion' would be a severe blow. Stigwood hardly blinked. Not only did he have one of the songs of the year in 'Grease', he had one of the films of the year too, as crowds all over the world flocked to the cinemas to view the on-screen romance develop between John Travolta and co-star Olivia Newton-John.

Barry's co-producer on the recording, did rather nicely out of it too. " 'Grease' was the most money I ever made per hour," Albhy Galuten divulged. "I think it took two days, start to finish, soup to nuts including mix, and my first check was like $200,000. Any time I can make $100,000 a day . . .

"I remember that pretty well," Albhy continued. "We were in Barry's living room in Miami when Robert called. I was there when he took the call. I think it was Barry's idea [to ask Franki Valli]. He was a big fan of those records back then, so this would be a great person to do it with. We cut it in LA, not Miami. The horns were done by George Bohannon, the contractor. The guitar players were Peter Frampton, along with probably George Terry, two guitar players. I think the rest were the regular band, like on an Andy record, Harold and Tubby. The girl singers were The Sweet Inspirations. The arrangement was my stuff. The intro was Barry's idea, and I remember going how weird, just da daaaaa, dadadadada, but then the groove stuff is mine."

One musician Albhy didn't mention was Gary Brown. 'Grease' was released with an instrumental version on the B-side, but the American single differed from the rest of the world as its instrumental version featured Gary providing an overdubbed sax solo. Exactly the same formula would be repeated a couple of years later on the American release of Robin and Marcy Levy's 'Help Me'.

The year 1978 also witnessed a strange series of connecting releases. Franki Valli's attempt at a follow-up was 'Save Me, Save Me' on Warner Brothers, and Rare Earth also recorded the same song for their *Grand Slam* LP for Prodigal. Shortly prior to that, they had issued 'Warm Ride' as single; Graham Bonnet's version of the song also appearing as a single, this time on the Ringo Starr's short-lived Ring O' Records label. Both Rare Earth and Bonnet issued an extended remix of the song too. The best either performer could achieve in Europe or America was the number 39 that Rare Earth's version reached in America. However, Graham Bonnett's version was very successful in Australia and New Zealand where it reached number two and number six respectively.

'Save Me, Save Me' was proving to be a very popular cover indeed. Teri De Sario was next to try her hand at it, but gave it little chance by relegating it to the relative obscurity of a slot on her *Pleasure Train* album. The song-stress fared well with the Barry Gibb composed title that did make it onto a single though, and again Albhy Galuten was involved.

"This was someone who I had just heard in a club somewhere, and said to Barry, 'She's got a great voice, let's do something and see what happens.' It turned out not to be a big hit. I think it was a marketing and momentum thing. She did have a hit after that with somebody. If I'd been smarter then, I'd have signed for ongoing royalties on her future records! She was very sweet. Her husband was Bill Purse, the trumpet player."

The song that Barry came up with was called 'Ain't Nothing Gonna Keep Me From You', but the Casablanca single fared better than Albhy gives it credit for, climbing to number 43 in the USA Hot 100.

'Emotion' is a song that will forever be associated with Samantha Sang, but this didn't prevent Johnny Mathis & Deniece Williams from recording their own version, which they placed on the B-side of their big hit, 'Too Much, Too Little, Too Late'.

The year 1978 was also the year that Rita Coolidge provided A&M with a Top 30 hit in Britain, taking 'Words' to the number 25 spot. It was the year of the "cash-in" too, as Carol Douglas and Richard Ace took 'Night Fever' and 'Stayin' Alive' respectively to the same position of number 66 in Britain.

The activity continued unabated when the brothers even found time to provide backing vocals for 'Little Miss Loving' on Chicago's *Hot Streets* album. The fourth brother Andy got in on the act too, singing with Stephen Stills on two songs on Stephen's *Thoroughfare Gap* LP.

A New Year, an old song. Dusty Springfield became the latest to record the much vaunted 'Save Me, Save Me' when it made a discreet appearance on her *Living Without Your Love* album.

Visitors to Criteria studios in 1979 were The Osmonds, and Maurice shared the producer's chair with Steve Klein for their *Steppin' Out* album for Mercury, which also included 'Rest Your Love On Me', the recent B-side to The Bee Gees' 'Too Much Heaven'.

The decade came to a close with some chart success from an unlikely source. The Bee Gees had left 'You Stepped Into My Life' as an album track on 1976's *Children Of The World*, but Melba Moore turned it into a reasonable hit in January 1979 when she took it to number 47 in the American charts. The same title reached number 90 in the USA when none other than Wayne Newton, almost fifteen years after recording 'They'll Never Know', also released as a single.

As a group, The Bee Gees had reached saturation point, and they would need to find new ways to get their songs heard.

Barry explained the group's thinking behind writing for others. "It's great input for us, because it gives us another dimension to our songwriting. It tells us what else we can do. If we just use our own voices all the time, you can get locked into that syndrome of just our own voices as the instruments. Writing for other people tells you what else you can do, like stretching if you're acting."

The words almost had a hollow ring to them, as their own acting careers had not stretched them by any manner of means.

30

BEING FOR THE BENEFIT OF
MR STIGWOOD

Iₙ ₙₒᵥₑₘᵦₑᵣ, 1976, plans had been announced for a new RSO film. In theory, it sounded like the perfect idea – take the music from The Beatles' masterpiece, *Sgt. Pepper's Lonely Hearts Club Band*, add The Bee Gees and "Flavour Of The Month" rock star, Peter Frampton, whose *Frampton Comes Alive* had topped the charts, and with The Bee Gees' and Frampton's respective managers, Robert Stigwood and Dee Anthony, at the helm, what could possibly go wrong?

The project began with mutually patronising statements to the press from Messrs. Stigwood and Anthony. "I am happy and proud to be associated with Dee Anthony," Stigwood announced. "His expertise and sensitivity will add greatly to the filmisation of this wonderful Lennon-McCartney musical. Peter Frampton's presence brings the ultimate in true stardom to *Sgt. Pepper*. His portrayal of Billy Shears as his first music role will prove to be the first definite marriage of contemporary music and film. I couldn't be more delighted."

Dee Anthony responded, "We are deeply privileged and honoured to be associated with Robert Stigwood and are looking forward to a rewarding experience. Both Peter and I have every confidence in Mr Stigwood's artistic integrity, talent and ability to make this an important milestone in Peter Frampton's career."

Barry Gibb told reporters that, "*Sgt. Pepper's Lonely Hearts Club Band* is a great opportunity for us. It's going to be a fantastic film. Chris Bearde, the creator of *Laugh-In* and *The Gong Show,* is going to direct and his fluid style should work well with The Bee Gees' natural humour.

"The *Sgt. Pepper* album was always very special to me . . . I first heard The Beatles' album ten years ago in Robert Stigwood's office the first day it came out. The next day there was a copy of the album on every music industry desk. No one could believe the album. It was a milestone in recording. It pushed everyone forward."

The original casting plans called for such diverse artists as Elton John, Olivia Newton-John, Donna Summer, Barry Manilow, Doris Day, Rock Hudson and Bob Hope to join The Bee Gees and Peter Frampton. Most wisely bowed out.

Paul Nicholas said, "I suppose by then Robert Stigwood had made so much money with *Saturday Night Fever* and *Grease* that he decided to do what was described as The Robert Stigwood Home Movie, which was *Sgt. Pepper's Lonely Hearts Club Band*."

Robert Stigwood had been contemplating making a film based on the *Sgt. Pepper* album for several years. "For a long time, I looked at those long lines of people at rock concerts and wondered why you couldn't have the same kind of crowd for a film," he explained. His theory was that if you made a film which appealed to the people who go to rock concerts, you would get the same people turning out in droves to go to the cinema. He had had some success with *Jesus Christ, Superstar* and *Tommy*, so why not *Sgt. Pepper*?

He might have guessed there was trouble ahead – he reportedly turned down ten scripts before he enlisted the aid of the *New York Times* critic, Henry Edwards, to write the "ultimate fantasy", an allegorical tale of good triumphing over evil in the music world. He had similar trouble choosing a director, finally settling on Michael Schultz, whose previous works included *Car Wash*, *Which Way Is Up?* And *Cooley High*.

"It's fun simply because it's so berserk . . . The idea is to take people on a trip," Schultz said, "even those die-hard people who say, 'Oh, Peter Frampton and The Bee Gees, they're not going to be The Beatles.' Well, they're *not* The Beatles. They're goody-goody singers who have been entrusted with the magic music of *Sgt. Pepper* to bring joy to the world. And if you accept that premise, you don't have any trouble with the picture."

Robert Stigwood had always envisaged The Bee Gees as Sgt. Pepper's band, but when the movie was being cast, "Peter Frampton was the hottest property," Maurice explained. "He became the grandson of Sgt. Pepper." The Bee Gees became The Henderson Brothers, taking their name from a line in 'Being For The Benefit Of Mr. Kite'.

"It was a battle all the way for us," Barry would say later. "Robert had verbally promised us the starring roles, and then this red-hot young man called Peter Frampton came along, and Robert wanted him to play Billy Shears. The film didn't work for The Bee Gees. It worked for Peter – and I think you'd be blind not to see it – The Bee Gees had no place in the story. We just weren't consequential to the story line, and we tried to point that out along the way. I just wish they'd given people a chance to act."

While The Bee Gees had met Peter Frampton in 1968 when he was a member of The Herd, and Maurice had been friendly with Peter in the early Seventies, they had lost touch after Frampton's phenomenal rise to success. Maurice found himself thinking, "I only hope he's the same cat I knew in England in 1972 . . ." He needn't have worried; Peter hadn't changed. "It was great because the four of us got on like a house on fire. We had bad moments during the film, but not between the four of us," he said. "By the time we finished the film, we had become the band."

The chemistry between Frampton and The Bee Gees as a band took some time though. "We were wary of each other," Barry admitted. "[Peter] was a little worried about singing with us because we'd sung together all our lives, and he didn't know how he fitted in. So a lot of our sessions were done separately."

The soundtrack album was recorded at Cherokee Studios in Los Angeles under the auspices of George Martin, The Beatles' legendary producer who had produced the original LP. When Stigwood first approached Martin with the idea for the project, Martin's first inclination was to refuse. "I didn't want to do the project at first," he said, "but I was persuaded because Peter Frampton was riding so high back then, and I admired The Bee Gees very much. The premise was that it was a film score and not a record album.

"I knew in my heart of hearts that The Beatles would not have approved," Martin continued, "and, although I don't need their permission to run my life, I still wondered if it was right to go over old ground. On the other hand, Robert assured me that if I took the job on I would have complete artistic control over the music, and would be able to dictate exactly what it should sound like."

Stigwood offered a powerful incentive to take on the task. The generous commission he proposed would be enough to make anyone stop and consider, and George Martin was no different. After much soul searching, it was his wife who made the decision for him in the end. "She said, 'I understand the problems you're going through,'" Martin recalled. "'You want to be sure that you're doing the right thing artistically. But have you ever considered that if you don't do it, someone else will, and you will hate what they've done? If you do it, you'll be in a position to ensure that the music isn't maltreated.' That, and Robert's promise of total freedom, which in the event was fully honoured, finally decided me."

Before the filming could begin, Martin had to prepare all the music tracks. "Since it was a musical film, all the musical sequences had to be mimed to existing recorded performances. It didn't mean making finished tracks, but providing them with the nucleus, the rhythm and voices. With nearly two hours of music in the film, there was obviously a mountain of material to record before they could even start shooting," he explained.

When Martin began work on September 1, he had assembled a first class band of session musicians. On keyboards was Max Middleton, formerly of The Jeff Beck Group, as was the bass player, Wilbur Bascombe. Bernard Purdie, a fine drummer from New York and Robert Awhai, a guitarist who had done a great body of work with Middleton, completed the ensemble.

For The Bee Gees, working with The Beatles' producer seemed like a dream come true. "The greatest thing about making *Sgt. Pepper* was working with George Martin," Maurice raved, "to recreate the songs he did with The Beatles . . . wow!"

Martin seemed equally pleased to be working with The Bee Gees. "I first heard about The Bee Gees soon after I started recording The Beatles because they were kind of connected with Brian Epstein. They were kind of junior rivals. They were so professional, all three of them," he said. "When they came into the studio, they would fool around and joke a lot, but once that red light was on, they were in there, and they were dead serious. Their harmony singing . . . they were very careful about precision of ensemble, and in fact, they wanted to do things over and over much more than I did. I would be inclined to say, 'That's human, that's lovely.' 'Oh no. We've got to get it right.' When they double tracked, they double tracked so accurately that you could hardly tell it was double tracked. They were very, very good."

Barry's uncanny precision for staying perfectly in tune turned out to be a bit of a drawback for Martin. "I actually found myself telling him that by being so exactly in tune he was tending to spoil the nice parts of the double-tracking. He was so accurate, it almost sounded like a single track."

But Barry explained his approach to recording. "I don't agree with the process where the artist goes into the studio, sings one vocal, and it feels right so everyone says, 'Wow! That's all right, that's it.' I say let's have a vocal that feels right and is an impeccable vocal at the same time. Why not? You just do it till it's right. You can accomplish that without doing it so often that it becomes bland."

Paul Nicholas was cast as Frampton's brother, Dougie Shears. Not dissimilar in appearance to Peter, he had the benefit of previous theatrical experience – a dubious advantage in this case, as he noted, "Looking at the script, there's no real focus. I think it must be very different for Frampton and The Bee Gees coming to this – I've done a lot of stage musicals and *Tommy*, and I still think it's hard to react in this situation.

"It should have been a hit . . . It had all the right elements in the sense that it had Peter Frampton and The Bee Gees and a very good English cast and a good director. Unfortunately, the problem with it was that it had a terrible script, and there was a very poor presentation of what really was a very heavy album."

Barry claimed that working on the film was great fun, and that he felt very comfortable in front of the camera. Robin echoed those sentiments, adding, "There's no tension at all while you're doing it. That's because everything on a movie set happens so slowly there's plenty of time to think about what you're doing and relax."

As the Lonely Hearts Club Band, Peter Frampton was the lead guitarist, but The Bee Gees all took on different instrumental roles. On Barry's recommendation Maurice, ordinarily a bass player, became the drummer because of his time-keeping ability. "Robin knew that he wouldn't be good as a drummer 'cause he'd be very stiff, where I'm very loose," Maurice added. "And I could follow a beat, 'cause being a bass player, you always follow the drums a lot."

Even so, Maurice said that he practised for nearly two months with a practise kit with session musician Bernie Purdy, who played the drums on the soundtrack album. "He's a bloody good drummer, and it was very difficult," he admitted. "When I first met him, I said, 'You're the hardest guy to mime to that I've ever come across.' And he said, 'I'm glad they picked you 'cause in that last filming, you didn't miss one beat, and you hit every drum I hit when I recorded it.' I was very knocked out from his compliments. He's one of the best."

Barry took on Maurice's usual instrument, and Robin became the rhythm guitarist almost by default.

George Burns took the role of Heartland's mayor, Mr Kite, the narrator and only speaking role in the film. Other stars involved in the film included Frankie Howerd as Mr Mustard, Aerosmith as The Future Villain Band, Alice Cooper as Father Sun, Steve Martin as Dr Maxwell Edison, Billy Preston in one of the strangest pieces of casting as the reincarnation of Sgt. Pepper and Earth, Wind & Fire, as themselves. The female leads were played by relative unknowns; Sandy Farina as Billy Shears's innocent girlfriend, Strawberry Fields, and Dianne Steinberg as the vampish Lucy.

Aerosmith were actually the second choice for The Future Villain Band. Kiss turned down the roles out of concern that it might hurt their image. Lead guitarist Joe Perry of Aerosmith recalled that their agents phoned them to say, " 'They want you as the Future Villain Band. You get to kill Frampton and The Bee Gees.' Sounded cool, so that spring we went to California and moved into the Beverly Hills Hotel . . ."

Aerosmith's first day was spent filming close-ups, and the second performing 'Come Together'. On the third day, they filmed the famous fight scene with The Bee Gees and Peter Frampton, which took place on a platform illuminated by glowing dollar signs. The script called for Peter Frampton to kill Aerosmith's lead singer, Steven Tyler, but the group threatened to walk off the film.

"We're saying, 'There's no fucking way that Steven is gonna get directly offed by Frampton. No way. It's gotta be an accident, the way it was in the original script we fucking agreed to,' " Joe Perry recalled. Oddly enough, Tyler had no objection to being pushed to his death by the petite Sandy Farina, who in turn was killed by the surviving Future Villains.

"We noticed it took The Bee Gees hours in makeup to get their hair right," Perry added. "Then we heard these three guys were getting a million dollars to be in this movie, which we didn't like, because we were getting considerably less. Joey Kramer [Aerosmith's drummer] goes, 'Let's not beat them up in the fight scene. Just mess up their hair. That'll really fuck 'em up!' "

During the filming of Strawberry's funeral, Peter Frampton had little need of crocodile tears as fate stepped in to give him a genuine cause for mourning. "I thought about the Lynyrd Skynyrd plane crash, which happened about the time we were filming that scene. All my road crew died on that crash," he reflected.★

★ Frampton is exaggerating. Six people died in the Lynyrd Skynyrd plane crash in Mississippi on October 20, 1977: singer Ronnie Van Zant, guitarist Steve Gaines, his sister Cassie Gaines, personal roadie Dean Kilpatrick, and two pilots.

Part of the film included the Lonely Hearts Club Band jumping and tumbling on a trampoline, but the film's insurers refused to allow its highly paid stars to participate so stunt doubles were employed. Peter Frampton was annoyed as he had been the first in his school to do a double somersault on the trampoline. Robin Gibb was simply bewildered by the uncanny likeness of his counterpart. "He looks like me. Nobody told me about the doubles. I was in the bog and came out and saw *me* on the bandstand. I thought, 'They don't need me – I'm already *there*,' " he said.

An early scene, in which the Lonely Hearts Club band is leaving Heartland in a hot air balloon, nearly turned serious, when Barry was almost burnt. He was rescued by the prompt action of Paul Nicholas, who managed to extinguish the fire before Barry suffered any injury.

The filming of *Sgt. Pepper* paused for Christmas and the New Year, resuming on January 2, 1978, for the final two weeks. The film's finale was to be an all star reprise of the title track, in an effort to recreate the original *Sgt. Pepper's Lonely Hearts Club Band* sleeve. Robert Stigwood invited 400 major and minor celebrities to participate, providing each with a first class plane ticket. He hired rock impresario Bill Graham to organise the accommodation for the stars, who weren't paid a penny for their services, but had all their expenses paid and limousines at their disposal round the clock. Graham booked every available suite in Los Angeles and organised for more limousines to be shipped in from other cities, as there were fewer than a hundred in LA. The total cost for the single day of filming was over half a million dollars, and that didn't even take into account the bill for the hugely extravagant party held later that evening.

Sgt. Pepper's Lonely Hearts Club Band was launched with a gala premiere at the Palladium on Sunset Boulevard in Los Angeles on July 18, 1978. All the movie's stars were present, with the exception of Peter Frampton, who was hospitalised in New York after he was seriously injured in a car accident. More than a thousand guests celebrated at the Beverly Hills Hilton afterwards.

The film's East Coast premiere took place just three days later at the Radio City Music Hall in New York. With excitement running high, it was declared *Sgt. Pepper* Day in New York, and the city's Police Athletic League benefited once again, as all proceeds from the premiere were donated to the charity.

Robin Gibb's solo single of 'Oh! Darling' and the much anticipated soundtrack album were released in conjunction with the film. Never had an album received that sort of promotion – the film even shows the production and packing of the two disc-set. The album was a guaranteed smash hit. It *did* seem likely – from Christmas of 1977 through May 20, 1978, RSO Records had retained the top spot of the *Billboard* Hot 100 singles chart. No other record label had ever before managed to score six consecutive number ones, and by the end of summer, RSO had attained an additional 11 weeks at number one. A Hollywood insider predicted, "Even if the movie sinks like *The Titanic*, Stigwood will still make a fortune from the soundtrack album." The prediction couldn't have been less accurate.

Barry Gibb laughed, "There's a good story about the *Sgt. Pepper* album . . . They shipped about two million and then found about a million of them by the side of the road. In those days, you could actually go platinum based on your shipping. You can't do that these days. The mechanic doesn't work anymore. They had shipped all these albums to stores, but there was no demand. So somebody had dumped a million albums by the side of the road."

Rumour has it that the *Sgt. Pepper's Lonely Hearts Club Band* soundtrack was the only album in history to ship double platinum and return triple platinum, meaning that even the counterfeit copies of the two LP set were being returned by retailers.

One quirk of the album's distribution was that, in Britain, it was released on A&M, the label to which Peter Frampton was contracted. A&M's marketing department scored a minor victory over their RSO counterparts, who had distribution rights elsewhere in the world, by issuing an extremely limited edition pressing of the double album set on pink vinyl. While black vinyl copies soon became "10 a penny", the pink vinyl ones were quickly snapped up by collectors and are virtually impossible to find nowadays.

Of the nearly 30 songs on the soundtrack, only two charted on the American Top 20. Earth, Wind & Fire's 'Got To Get You Into My Life' reached number nine, and Robin's soulful take on 'Oh! Darling' achieved the number 15 spot.

Everyone involved in the project went into it with high hopes, but little more than a year later, all were singing a different tune. In an industry dominated by sales, no one dares to admit they actually might have enjoyed something which turned out to be a monumental turkey of the scale of *Sgt. Pepper's Lonely Hearts Club Band*, but The Bee Gees' road manager, Tom Kennedy, insisted, "They *did* enjoy it at the time. The camaraderie of all the people who worked on it and the whole carnival atmosphere was excellent. Whether it was sound financially, whether it was the wrong time or just the wrong film, it was a fairy tale in the making. I took reels and reels of photographs, and there were all these smiling faces. They might not have enjoyed it in retrospect, but at the time they did enjoy it apart from the long hours – it was hard work, having to get up at 6.00 a.m.

"George Burns [was] a lovely man; Peter Frampton, a great, fun character; Paul Nicholas – all these people, it was like a circus atmosphere all the time."

Alice Cooper is one of the few involved in the film who readily admits that he had no idea that the film would be a disaster, but he also reveals that he was only on the set for three days, including the time it took to record his track, 'Because', for his role of Father Sun. "The crazy thing about it was that I was in the hospital at the time undergoing treatment for alcoholism. They arranged for a three-day pass for me to leave the hospital to do the filming," he said.

He especially enjoyed his work with George Martin. "When I did the first take of the song, I did it in my best John Lennon impersonation. George said it was fine, but then told me to do it like Alice Cooper would do it. He seemed really happy with it."

The director, Michael Schultz, said, "When I read the script and saw it was one great fantasy, then I knew how much trouble I was in for."

Robin Gibb said, "It wasn't a terribly pleasant experience because we were between albums at the time, and we had finished recording *Saturday Night Fever*, and it was a contractual commitment for everyone at that time, including our manager, Robert Stigwood, which we had to complete. It was a very undecided venture, nobody really knew where we were going with it."

Barry calls it, "The movie that should never have been made. If somebody said to you, 'I want to make the film *Sergeant Pepper*, and I want you to play a member of the band, you wouldn't say, 'No'. You'd say, 'Wow, fantastic.' You wouldn't imagine for a second it would turn out quite as bad as it did. I think the movie *Sergeant Pepper* should have been *The Making Of The Sergeant Pepper* because I thought that was where the real story was going on. The craziness of Hollywood, all those pop artists thrown together making a movie where they weren't allowed to speak, it was just madness."

"It should have had more excitement poured into it," Robin added. "As we were making it, I was thinking, 'I hope they are going to put some visual effects in here.' When I saw it, it was exactly as we shot it; nothing was improved. On the set, the camera is pointed at you and you're thinking to yourself, 'It's *gotta* be more than just me sitting here in this room 'cause nothing's happening.' But then you see the film and that's all there is."

Tom Kennedy probably summed it up best when he said, "It was a great film to make. When you see it up on the screen, it was a different thing – sometimes when you live something, you can't record it. It's like not being able to take a picture of the Grand Canyon. It was more fun to make than it was to watch."

★   ★   ★

When the Academy Award nominations were announced early in 1978, there was a curious omission – the biggest selling soundtrack album of all time hadn't even received a mention. *Saturday Night Fever* received only one nomination for John Travolta in the Best Actor category.

The Bee Gees and their manager were stunned. Robert Stigwood lodged a formal complaint with the Academy of Motion Picture Arts and Sciences' music branch, stating, "Music critics and audiences have responded to the fresh sounds of The Bee Gees' compositions in unprecedented numbers . . . Furthermore, the music is hand and glove with the script's development and is completely integral to the action of the film . . . We emphatically insist that a serious omission has been made which would seem to reflect an unwillingness on the part of the music branch to recognise the more innovative and popular currents in the music world today."

Months later, Robert Stigwood was still unwilling to put it behind him and live with it, as Oakes had suggested. "I was shocked and still am shocked," he declared. "I think the governors of the music branch of the Academy were out of their minds because I don't think there has ever been a more perfect marriage of music and movie together. I know in the heart of everyone in the world who is a movie goer, they agree with me, and I think by popular consensus that The Bee Gees won the Academy Award for their music."

Back in Britain, the 23rd Annual Ivor Novello Awards were presented at Grosvenor House Hotel in London on May 12, and The Bee Gees' contribution to film was given the acknowledgement Stigwood sought. 'How Deep Is Your Love' scooped the awards in the categories for Best Pop Song and Best Film Music or Song.

The group also collected their third AMPEX Golden Reel Award for *Saturday Night Fever*. This time The Bee Gees donated their $1,000 award to The Bertha Abbess Children's Center, a mental health facility for severely mentally disturbed children.

In August, Molly Gibb travelled to Germany to receive awards for *Saturday Night Fever* on behalf of The Bee Gees.

Molly, six-year-old Spencer and four-year-old Melissa had also joined Robin in the States for a visit to *Sesame Street*. As both children were fans of the Public Broadcasting System's award winning television programme, Robin had agreed to participate in the recording of the *Sesame Street Fever* album, with the stipulation that his son and daughter be allowed to meet the *Sesame Street* characters they loved. Robin found himself sharing vocals on the title track with The Count, Grover, Ernie and Cookie Monster, and providing a spoken intro to 'C Is For Cookie'. His song, 'Trash', was released as a single in October and remains a novelty favourite for many Bee Gees' fans today. As Robin put it, "How often does one get the chance to work with Cookie Monster?"

The LP went gold less than four months after its release, and Robin and his family travelled to New York to be presented with the award by none other than Big Bird.

★　★　★

In May, 1978, The Bee Gees held a press conference with Robert Stigwood and David Frost at the United Nations General Assembly Building. While all three Gibbs admitted that they were "not very political", all felt the importance of UNICEF's work in helping needy children, whom they referred to as "the most defenceless people on earth".

"The idea came up when Robert Stigwood and David Frost were on holiday in Miami spending some time with us in one of our homes," Barry explained. "What really went down was a long conversation and a lot of laughs about what the year had given us, and how hard everyone had worked and of course, Robert's enormous success apart from ours. It was

Maurice. (*Harry Goodwin*)

Reunited – the three brothers phone the press with the news that Robin is back in the band, evidently a tiring day's work. (*Barry Plummer*)

Barry welcomes Aussie pop star Ronnie Burns to London. (*Courtesy Ronnie Burns*)

Drummer Geoff Bridgeford with Maurice and Robin. (*LFI*)

Barry's wedding to Lynda Gray, September 1, 1970. Left to right: George Gray, Barbara Gibb, Lynda, Barry, May Gray and Hugh Gibb. (*LFI*)

Barry, Robin and Maurice with moustache, in 1972. (*Harry Goodwin*)

Barry Gibb at the Golden Garter, Wythenshawe, Manchester, 1974. (*Harry Goodwin*)

Andy Gibb and his first band Melody Fayre. Left to right: John Alderson, Andy, John Stringer and Jerry Callaghan. (*Courtesy John Stringer*)

Maurice marries Yvonne Spenceley at Haywards Heath, October, 1975. (*LFI*)

Andy Gibb marries Kim Reeder in Sydney, July 11, 1976. (*Courtesy Gibb Family*)

Clockwise from top left - The Bee Gees Band in Los Angeles : drummer Dennis Bryon, Maurice, keyboard player 'Blue' Weaver, guitarist Alan Kendall, Barry and Robin. (*Ed Caraeff*)

Robin and Molly Gibb at the Empire, Leicester Square, London, for the premier of *Saturday Night Fever*, March 1978. (*David Wainwright/Relay*)

The Bee Gees with Robert Stigwood and Dee Anthony at the time of the disastrous *Sergeant Pepper* movie. (*Chris Walter/Relay*)

The Bee Gees outside their 'Tour Headquarters', their shop on New York's 57th Street. (*LFI*)

Ron and Joanne Selle leaving the Federal Court during their copyright suit against The Bee Gees, February 1983. (*Rex*)

The UNICEF *A Gift Of Song Concert*, New York, 1979. Left to right: Hugh Gibb, Danny Kaye (background), Henry Fonda, Barbara Gibb, Andy, Robert Stigwood's mother, Barry and Linda Gibb. (*LFI*)

The Bee Gees with manager Robert Stigwood immediately after they settled their 1981 law suit. (*Rex*)

Andy Gibb with Susan George (left) and Olivia Newton-John. (*LFI/Rex*)

Andy. (*Harry Goodwin*)

Maurice, Robin and Barry reunited with former Rattlesnakes Kenny Horrocks and Paul Frost, 1981. (*Courtesy Gibb Family*)

Andy Gibb as Frederick in *The Pirates Of Penzance* and in the starring role in *Joseph And The Amazing Technicolour Dreamcoat*. (*Rex*)

Andy with *Dallas* star Victoria Principal. (*LFI*)

Robin with Dwina Murphy and their son Robin John.
(*D. White/Camera Press*)

Barry in a scene cut from his *Now Voyager* video. (*LFI*)

A mini-Bunbury's convention at a polo match in Windsor Great Park in 1986. Left to right: Barry and Linda, Ian and Cathy Botham, David English and Eric Clapton. (*Camera Press*)

Robin, Beri and Hugh Gibb at Heathrow Airport immediately after Andy's death. (*Rex*)

Peta and Kim Gibb, daughter and widow of Andy. (*Rex*)

Maurice and family in 1983. Daughter Samantha is held by her parents, son Adam stands below. (*Camera Press*)

Left to right: Dwina Gibb, Robin's second wife, Spencer and Melissa, Robin's son and daughter from his first marriage, and Robin. In the foreground is Robin John, his son with Dwina. (*Rex*)

The Barry Gibb family Christmas card, 1999. Left to right: Travis, Ashley, Michael, Steven and (seated) Ali.
(*Therese Hallman/background photo: Claude Zick*)

Reunited with Vince Melouney and Colin Petersen in Sydney, 1989. (*Glenn A. Baker Archives*)

Maurice, Barry and Robin with Hugh and Barbara in 1989. (*Camera Press*)

Prince Albert of Monaco presents a World Music Lifetime Achievement Award to The Bee Gees, 1997. (*PA News*)

The Bee Gees receive a presentation board of stamps issued in their honour by the Isle of Man Post Office. Left to right: Robin, Janet Bridge, Dot Tilbury, Maurice and Barry. (*Courtesy Isle of Man Post Office*)

Dick Ashby, the fourth Bee Gee. (*Mark Crohan*)

The Bee Gees in 1998. (*Rex*)

"This is where we came in"… with Barbara in 1997, the three brothers outside their old home in Keppel Road, Manchester. (*Harry Goodwin*)

just a very happy time for us; we were sort of celebrating. The idea came up from us that we should give something back, we should form some sort of charity or form something that gave something to kids, and we suggested donating the proceeds of a song or donating a song, which we found out later you could not do. You can't donate a physical song, but you can donate the all the proceeds, and this was how the idea came about."

As The Bee Gees left the United Nations General Assembly Building following the press conference, their limousine was immediately surrounded by fans, who slowed the car's progress down the street. Barry related, "One called, 'Put your window down! I want to shake hands with you.' It was pouring, but she kept saying, 'Please, please,' so we rolled down the window. The rain came in, we shook hands, then put the window up again. A few yards farther, the girl rushed back and shouted, 'Where's my watch? You guys ripped off my watch!' So she had us lower the window, then she found it on her. That's New York. First, 'I want to shake your hand'; next, it's 'Get the police!' " he laughed.

The Bee Gees had begun recording their follow-up to the *Saturday Night Fever* soundtrack at Criteria Studio in March. Following their summer holidays and the *Sgt. Pepper* premieres, they returned to Criteria to complete the album in late July.

The success of *Fever* had not made The Bee Gees complacent about the future. "We're scared of the next album," Barry admitted. "We're scared of whatever we do. We're the same desperate, worried, insecure songwriters we've ever been."

The Bee Gees' return to the studio kept things interesting for the Criteria staff, who likened the group's popularity to that of The Beatles. "We get about 20–25 Bee Gee fan letters a day. They call up all day. I don't know what it is that they've got in their heads, but they're really crazy," said the studio's receptionist, Patti Romano. "I remember one day when we had 25 girls out here screaming."

The group's new high profile meant round two of the pressures of super-stardom which had spelled disaster for the group in the late Sixties, but this time around, the brothers were older and wiser. The competition between them had gone, even as Andy's single looked set to replace his older brothers'.

"So now our baby brother's sneaking up to knock us off. I'll kill him, I will!" Maurice joked. "It's funny; years ago, we'd have been furious if Andy bumped us from number one. Jesus, the three of us were fighting amongst *ourselves* to be the biggest star. Now, like Barry says, it's all in the family. Barry wrote and produced the bloody song, anyhow."

Even as the press tried to instigate another family feud by focusing on Barry as the group leader and sex symbol, they refused to be drawn into it, although Barry confessed, "I think this sex symbol talk affects Robin and Maurice more than it does me. They see that I get more attention and there's nothing they can do. They know it gives me more . . . opportunities.

"There was an adjustment period five years ago, but all the little hassles and hang-ups have disappeared. We began to relate to each other as brothers. For a while, when we came back together, and I'm talking about five or six years ago, we weren't working at full capacity. The personal crisis we went through provided extra incentive and the records we put out now, especially the last few, are full of drive and ambition. We can feel it."

Robin agreed, "I know what people think of me. I used to be very insecure. There was a lot of pressure around me, and I had trouble coping with initial stardom and touring. That's changed, as I've come from this boy-to-man period over the last five years. A new era has started. I feel great about the people around me."

While the brothers had put the quarrels of the past behind them, there was nothing they could do about the growing intrusion of their adoring fans into their private lives. "You can't go to a cinema or restaurant without being chased for autographs," Maurice complained. "We can't even take a commercial plane."

As the group went back into the studio, Lynda Gibb observed, "Soon Barry will disappear again. The studio is his drug. During the last album, Stevie asked if he was getting a new daddy."

"Stevie tells me he's going to get three daddies – he says he needs more than one," Barry admitted, adding, "We need some time with our families. I see Lynda and the children about two hours a day. I think it's wrong. I'm always working; even when I'm home, my mind is somewhere else. As far as she's concerned, it's no good. We don't get a chance to talk, to be husband and wife."

The group's workday usually started about three o'clock in the afternoon and carried on until midnight, which did preclude spending much time with the family. "You're not a slave to the music," Albhy Galuten said, "but you're very dependent on their inspiration at the moment, or maybe even your own. In other words, if you're excited about something and something is working, you can't leave."

"Success creates energy," Barry explained, "and we were very fortunate that . . . we were pretty much number one in the charts the whole time we were making *The Spirits Having Flown* album from previous material, including material from Andy, Samantha Sang, Yvonne [Elliman] . . . There were a lot of records that we made around that period, not just the *Fever* album, that were very successful.

"We went to pop heaven for about two years. There's a good side and a bad side to that. The good side is that you get a hit no matter what, which can be unhealthy. The bad side is you can't answer your own phone, you can't go to the cinema or a restaurant, and you have people climbing over your walls. That's not the life I wanted to lead.

"We were just reflecting what was going on around us. We were suddenly living in a goldfish bowl and we couldn't perceive real life. We couldn't go and hang out like we used to and go sit in a club where we used to get our ideas . . . Writing became different.

"This might sound corny," he confessed, "we make our records like we paint a picture, but it's true. It's like a mental picture; you paint it, you know where the instrumental should be, you know the instrumental areas have got to be just as strong as the vocal areas. You can't have a low for an instrumental area and go back to the . . . vocals for a rise. It doesn't work – the whole thing has got to go up and go down and the instrumental must be just as important."

Blue Weaver believes that the secret of The Bee Gees' success during this period was not down to any virtuosity but rather the willingness to work together until everyone was pleased with the final result. "None of us were incredible musicians, as such," he admitted. "Barry is probably the most outstanding one, inasmuch as, even if he can't *play* the instrument, he can sing a brass part or a string part . . . Vocally, they're brilliant, all three of them. Whereas maybe myself, Dennis and Alan were not great individually, but worked incredibly well together. I think if you'd had so-called great players, it wouldn't have worked as well as it did. Everything all fits together as a *whole* – the voices, the backing, everything."

"I always wanted Barry to sing in real voice again," Blue said, "because I just love his real voice, but I was getting off on the songs, you know, it was great, so I wasn't really thinking, 'Oh, this is falsetto.'

"I don't analyse things, I just *do* it. I mean, it's *there*, it happens, I don't think *why* has it happened, or why did we do that, I just go ahead and do it. If you think it's right at the time, and I obviously thought . . . it was all right, but I wished there had been some real voice."

"The control in Barry's voice is actually better in falsetto," Karl Richardson explained. "On a powerful, complex song like 'Tragedy', the lead vocal has to stand out, and a lower ranger would have little impact and be harder to mix. The first time I heard 'Tragedy' was at Barry's house, with all three of The Bee Gees singing to an acoustic guitar. They even sang the explosion near the end, which ended up in the studio as five tracks of Barry cupping his hands over the microphone combined with Blue Weaver hitting random notes on the bottom end of the piano run through a product generator."

New technology was beginning to play its part in the recording process, as Albhy pointed out. "It was the first time we had the technology to give Barry the control he'd always wanted [with two 24-track machines, 44 usable tracks]."

'Too Much Heaven', a song that took full advantage of the upgraded technology, became a particular favourite of their friend David English. "I met a girl out there called Cindy Lee Johnson," he explained. Cindy and her business partner, Jeri, had a company called "Home At Last" and rented out the house at 461 Ocean Boulevard to Eric Clapton, which gave him the title of his album.

"When [The Bee Gees] went to Miami to record at Criteria Studios with Arif Mardin, Cindy and Jeri were the people that found them a house to live in, but they stayed in 461 Ocean Boulevard first . . . and I met Cindy and

Jeri through Barry and the boys. Barry kept saying, 'You've got to meet this girl, you're going to really like her, her name's Cindy Lee Johnson.' Sure enough, I walked into the studio when they were having a playback of 'Spirits (Having Flown)', and in walks Cindy and I said, 'Christ, they're right, you're great,' and she laughed, and it took me two weeks of phoning her and pursuing her . . . They all knew that I had kind of fallen for her, and I did in a big way. She was probably the love of my life . . . I went there for three weeks and ended up staying there for two years. We had a little house together in North Miami. Very happy memories and, at that time, 'Too Much Heaven' came out and that was marvellous because every time it went on, it kinda helped me in my love affair. It's lovely if you're with someone and that lovely song comes on."

'Too Much Heaven' was recorded with The Chicago Horns. Chicago were recording their *Hot Streets* album at Criteria at the same that The Bee Gees were working on their new album. The Chicago Horns also played on 'Stop (Think Again)', and in return, The Bee Gees provided backing vocals for Chicago's 'Little Miss Lovin' '.

Blue Weaver revealed that most of the recording process for *Spirits Having Flown* was a painstaking series of takes. "My piano parts – don't think that on things like 'How Deep Is Your Love' or 'Too Much Heaven' I just went out . . . and played . . . I'd be out there for hours – days – there could be hundreds of tracks of me playing the piano, and in the end, we'd just go in and sort out, and make one good one out of it," he said.

Maurice was credited as bass player on the album, along with "guest musician" Harold Cowart. At the time, he explained that he was unable to play bass because of a back injury. "I had to sit there and tell the bass player what to play. It was a bitch," he added.

In recent years, Maurice has admitted that he was going through a critical period in his life. His drinking would begin in the morning and continue throughout the day, and he would hide bottles from his family and friends. "I could get up in the morning and have a Scotch and coke for breakfast," he confessed. "I'd be doing bass work . . . and behind my back, [Barry and Robin] would bring someone in to play a part that I was supposed to be playing and stuff like that. I played fine, but it was just that they couldn't rely on me."

"It was very important to Barry to have stuff in tune and time," Albhy explained, "and the meter was critical and the feel was critical, and so he would have liked to use Harold from the day he met him. But it was delicate with Maurice. Harold was a great bass player and had incredible meter . . . He'd listen to a track that would slow down or speed up a little in some place . . . Harold had incredible meter, which was so important to Barry . . . Switching was just a matter of finding a way where Maurice could feel comfortable and save face. So he was a songwriter and singer and major in the band, so he didn't need to do trivial stuff like playing bass on the record. A lot of life is about saving face."

Both Barry and Robin have admitted that by covering for Maurice, they were enabling him to continue drinking, to pretend to himself and the world that he didn't have a problem.

Being outside the family circle, Albhy Galuten could observe the mechanics of co-dependency. "There was a lot of stuff around Maurice constructed so he could keep the facade going, and then even in the social environment, when the family's sitting around, they'd all pretend . . . which for me never helps anyone solve their problem. You need to say, 'Fine, we spoke to the press, but you're fuckin' up, dude.' And I'm sure they told him a lot he was screwing up, when not drinking . . . There was a lot of . . . unclarity . . . a lot of going overboard to not hurt someone's feelings, to the point where you really are not telling the truth."

The album went through working titles of *Spirits* and *Reachin' Out* before the final title of *Spirits Having Flown* was chosen. It was a change in title for both the album and the song, which had originally been called 'Passing Thought'. "[It] started in the studio," Barry recalled. "It wasn't written at home . . . We sat down with a guitar and just strummed, and we found different chords on the guitar that we don't normally look for . . . That's really how it was written and without words and without a title, we put the backtrack down the way you heard it. Then we worked on the lyrics, and we worked on the additional, the overdub structures and things like that.

"It was really an experimentation of us trying to move away from *Saturday Night Fever*," he added. "We were trying to follow up such a mammoth album, but not really knowing how to do that, and we were trying to get back to the mind-set we had before *Saturday Night Fever*. It was sort of a scatter-brained scenario. We were looking for a focus, and *Spirits Having Flown* as a title reflects that."

The first single from the album, 'Too Much Heaven', was released in November, with all proceeds to be donated to UNICEF. It is a slow ballad with an enormous number of Barry vocal tracks in falsetto and whispery voice, repeating a limited amount of melodic and lyrical material over and over to a slow but steady rhythm and an ample horn accompaniment. In no way could it be described as a disco song. The B-side was the totally different country number 'Rest Your Love On Me', a clear indication that someone wanted to show off The Bee Gees' versatility.

The single soared to the top of the American charts and reached the number three spot in Britain. It was also a number one in Norway, number 10 in Germany and a Top Five single all over Europe, Australia and New Zealand. Much to the group's delight, it also rapidly gained recognition on the American soul radio stations. "At the moment, it's really taken off big on the black stations," Robin said. "We've got a lot of black people buying our records, but we've never had [acceptance from] black stations." And while the A-side was getting airplay on American black radio stations, the country stations were playing the B-side, resulting in The Bee Gees' 'Rest Your Love On Me' climbing into the Top 50 of the US Country charts.

'Heaven' was one of three songs written in one very productive day during a break in the filming of *Sgt. Pepper's Lonely Hearts Club Band.* "We had an afternoon off and we wrote 'Tragedy' and 'Too Much Heaven' in about an hour and a half," Maurice revealed. The title track of Andy Gibb's second album, 'Shadow Dancing', completed the trio that evening.

"Three number ones in about two hours!" Robin exclaimed. "Robert Stigwood was there [when] we wrote ['Tragedy'], actually. He was downstairs, and we were talking. He went upstairs for half an hour, and we had written it. That's how we write – we get an idea, and we got straight through it . . . He heard it, and he said, 'Amazing, a number one record.'"

"The Bee Gees have the tendency to disobey the laws of music because they are not formally schooled in it," Richardson said. "They don't even know the names to all the chords they write with. But if they studied formally, they'd never have sung the melodies they do."

While The Bee Gees have always taken their songwriting very seriously, the atmosphere in the studio was hardly sombre. "If a group gets too serious and stops bantering when they record, you stagnate and lose your creativity," Karl continued.

While Maurice has always been the comedian of the group in public, it was his seemingly more reserved twin who livened up the studio. "Robin may be shy alone but not when he gets with his brothers," Dick Ashby revealed, adding that even on his first meeting with the group in Polydor's studios in 1967, "Robin turned out to be hilarious – totally crazy – constantly cracking one-liners."

"Robin's into blue humour," Karl added, "and I don't know if you'd be able to print a lot of his jokes. He also draws caricatures of everybody and hangs them up in the studio."

"We have a serialisation called *The Adventures of Sunny Jim,*" Barry divulged. "It only happens at recording sessions, and no one else ever hears them. We do them to relax ourselves when we're singing. So we do them first, have a bit of a laugh, and then we're ready."

With Robin revelling in the role of the hapless Sunny Jim with his high pitched, vacuous whine and Barry as the suave voice-over announcer, the adventures began with the recording of the *Main Course* album and are best described by Maurice as "wonderfully dirty and sick!"

"We start the stories off the tops of our heads and call them *The Continuing Adventures of Sunny Jim,*" Barry said, "and there's always an echo chamber effect there. Then we go off into *Sunny Jim In Brazil, Sunny Jim Joins The Army* and strange stuff like *Sunny Jim Steals Surgical Instruments.* He's just an imaginary character. A lunatic, I suppose."

A cleaner tale of Gibb inspired lunacy, *The Rescue Of Bonnie Prince Wally* was recorded as a members-only single for The Bee Gees Fan Club. "What they used to do, in between takes, they used to just lark around in the writing room upstairs at [the studio]," David English said. "They were very influenced by The Goons so that was just something that they came up with.

It happened, just like when they write, they get very prolific."

One can only wonder what Senator Ted Kennedy made of all this when he dropped by the recording studio to meet them during a visit to Miami that September.

Later in the month, Barry organised a soccer match for family and friends on Yvonne's birthday. Although Andy had always been athletic and Barry had become an accomplished tennis player, by no stretch of the imagination could any of the brothers be considered keen footballers. Working as they had since childhood, The Bee Gees never really took time out for sport when growing up, so the game was strictly for fun.

The Bee Gees' work was finished for the year, and it was time for quiet family Christmases all around. While Maurice, Yvonne and little Adam flew back to Leeds for a white Christmas in Yorkshire, Robin, Molly, Spencer and Melissa spent Christmas in New York. Barry and Lynda and their family had a low key Christmas in Miami Beach as little Ashley was recovering from an illness.

Robert Stigwood opined, "[The Bee Gees] are all family people, which is very strange in this business. They don't create scandals just to see their names in print."

Barbara Gibb explained it further. "It's a very big thing, this family thing. People are either family or they're not. And if they are; well, that's that. Robert Stigwood is family. When Brian Epstein asked Stiggy to manage The Beatles and Cilla Black, Stiggy said no, he had The Bee Gees. Families take care of each other."

Contrasting the difference between his first and second marriages, Maurice said, "[Yvonne is] a lovely Yorkshire girl who's not in show business. Of course, she knows a thing or two about the business but doesn't want to get involved in it."

But in Molly Gibb's eyes, the Gibb family togetherness was something from which she was happy to remain distant. "I couldn't stand it – I mean, could you?" she asked. "Barry, Maurice and their mother all within half a kilometre of each other in America – much too close. I wouldn't even like to live that close to my own mother, and I love her dearly."

Even Lynda Gibb admitted that she had her own doubts about the living arrangements in the first place, but she explained, "To Barry, family is *everything*. His parents live five minutes from us. His brother Maurice lives six blocks away with *his* in-laws and their kids. And Barry moved my family here from Scotland. Quite honestly, I couldn't see it. I love them and all, but I'm a 28-year-old married woman; living with my parents seemed a bit odd. But Barry really wanted it and he's been right. For him, having family around is vital."

471

31

TOO MUCH HEAVEN?

"POWER IS FLEETING; so is ego," Barry noted. "When you start putting religion or whatever into it and tell the world how it can be saved, it just rubs against people. Politicians have no idea how to save the world, so why should pop stars? Instead you can do things like the UNICEF thing, which is just a positive move to help children."

The Bee Gees arrived in New York at the start of the new year with a flurry of publicity. On January 8, 1979, they were the guests of honour at the Police Athletic League's dinner at the Americana Hotel, the first musical group ever to receive the PAL's Superstars Of The Year Award.

The following evening, all eyes were on the group as they topped the bill as the founder-organisers of the *Music For UNICEF* concert, held at the General Assembly Hall of the United Nations. Andy Gibb, Olivia Newton-John, John Denver, Donna Summer, ABBA, Rita Coolidge, Kris Kristofferson, Rod Stewart and Earth, Wind & Fire all performed live and donated songs to the project, while The Bee Gees lip-synched their way through 'Too Much Heaven'. The event, which raised $100 million, was televised in 70 countries worldwide as a television special and recorded for release as an album. *A Gift Of Song – The MUSIC FOR UNICEF Concert* was the official recording of the concert and continued to raise funds to provide food, health care, shelter and education for the children in greatest need in 100 developing countries.

Robin reported that they were "very happy with the results", but he added, "The television show was secondary. More important is that all the copyrights from all those songs were donated to UNICEF, and hopefully other songwriters will follow. And we are willing to take every measure to make sure the money reaches the kids it's intended for."

"We started by talking about wanting to give something back," said Barry. "We'd all been in sympathy with disadvantaged children and with starvation in the world. And starving children all over the world really haven't been thought about on this scale before. I know that so far 'Too Much Heaven' has probably made close to one million dollars, just in publishing royalties. If we can get 20 artists to contribute one song, and five of them become top three records, that's five million dollars."

While The Bee Gees were in New York for the UNICEF concert, they stayed at the posh Waldorf Astoria Hotel. Blue Weaver recalled that Robin, always the Gibb brother most careful with his money, got quite a shock when he saw the prices for the rooms. "I think Robin said he had the Cole Porter suite and saw the price was $1,500 a night or something," Blue said. It was a revelation that horrified his thrifty soul, but Dick Ashby put it all into perspective for him, saying, "Look, you make more than that every hour, so go and put your head on that pillow tonight and think that by the time you've thought of that, you've made what you're paying for that room!"

"It's hard – it's not living in the real world because you haven't got to give up anything," Blue admitted. "I think [The Bee Gees] *do* try as hard as they possibly can to be approachable and to be normal . . . The trouble is when you're pop stars, you . . . don't want to be normal, you always think of yourself as being different than other people because you're fortunate enough to make money and do something that you enjoy, where most other people have to go out and work. This is how managers can exploit you as well, because they know they can keep you happy giving you five or 10 pounds a week in your pocket and paying for your cleaning and your rent and everything because they know you love what you're doing."

Just three days after their UNICEF triumph, The Bee Gees received a star on Hollywood's Walk Of Fame, which was officially unveiled in March. The group flew to Los Angeles for the unveiling and caused a near riot. "There were about five thousand people there, the largest crowd they've ever had for one of those ceremonies," Robin recalled.

What began as a moment of glory rapidly turned to something of a mob scene. "Before I knew it, I barely had room to breathe," he continued. "Strangers were sweating all over me, and I was scared to death because I had my kids, four-year-old Melissa and six-year-old Spencer, with me. When we finally got back in the limousines, fans were climbing all over them, and they followed our cars for miles. We almost didn't get away."

At the beginning of the year, The Bee Gees rented a warehouse in Miami initially for the storage of their equipment, but they would later purchase the building, which became Middle Ear Studio. "It was owned by an accountancy company," Tom Kennedy recalled. "They were accountants for KC & The Sunshine Band and their record company, which is now defunct, and this warehouse was brimming with their returns . . . We emptied it out – it took us about two weeks to burn all the records, because you couldn't *give* them away. Then we had the studio built and the offices, and I was there for the next ten years."

Nominations for the twenty-first Annual Grammy Awards were announced by the National Academy of Recording Arts and Sciences, with The Bee Gees receiving nominations in six major categories. *Saturday Night Fever* was nominated for album of the year and best pop vocal performance by a group. 'Stayin' Alive' was nominated in the record of the year, song of the year and best arrangement for voices categories.

On January 26, the *Spirits Having Flown* album was rush-released by RSO, after a few disc jockeys began playing illicitly obtained tapes of the album before the promotional copies were distributed to radio stations. The record company served cease-and-desist orders against those radio stations that participated in the advance previews, as Robin professed, "Playing a record too early can spoil sales." Later, a limited edition picture disc was also released, but only in the United States. The album's front cover shows tight shots of the three brothers on the front and gatefold, with a silhouette of them on the beach on the rear. The inner sleeve, not reproduced in the CD version, has pictures of the brothers and the other band members.

Being in the public eye more at this time than at any in their career, the brothers had been determined to create an album worthy of the attention it was guaranteed to get. They remained true to their ideal of making each song different by ranging widely in style, but Barry's falsetto vocal on almost all the songs tends to minimise the differences.

Spirits Having Flown is not a disco album as only a few tracks are dance numbers although the second single certainly was. 'Tragedy' followed its predecessor's meteoric rise to top the charts in the USA, the UK, Australia and New Zealand. It was also a Top Five single in Germany, Norway and Holland.

"They use the word and the word becomes the chorus almost and just that one word almost sums it up," George Martin said of the song. "They keep coming back to that word time and time again. They spit it out, and as it comes out, it kind of takes you back a bit. Then they go into the other words that pad it out and rhythmically, beautifully but always leads back, always leads back to those words. 'Tragedy' keeps pointing at you and it's so effective."

On February 15, The Bee Gees came out the winners in four of the six categories in which they were nominated at the Grammy Awards in Los Angeles, scooping up the awards for Best Single for 'Stayin' Alive' and also Best Production, Best Pop Vocal Performance By A Duo, Group or Chorus and Best Album for the *Saturday Night Fever* soundtrack, losing out in the Record and Songwriter Of The Year to Billy Joel for 'Just The Way You Are'.

After the ceremony, Barry enthused, "This is unbelievable! We have worked long and hard for this and we have had our disappointments along the way."

"We are pleased not only for ourselves but also for Britain, where we were born," Maurice added.

For Robin, the awards ceremony was most memorable for host John Denver's performance of the Best Song candidates. "When he started singing the nominations, I thought, 'Oh, no, he's *not* gonna sing 'Stayin' Alive'! He was all right singing the ballads, but Denver didn't exactly have the same moves as John Revolting, did he? But he did go for two hours without saying, 'Far-out'," he added.

474

Although their spare time was becoming more and more curtailed, The Bee Gees continued to make their own bizarre films. "We used to do a lot of home movies," David English said. "Maurice was good at that, always the one on the camera, Barry was kind of the director type and Robin was always very kind of off the wall, very zany . . . extremely funny lads. They were like The Goons, Monty Python, the three of them together were just as funny and, of course, a lot of people never saw that side of them.

"David Frost was doing a special for NBC on The Bee Gees and we were always doing home movies together, and I always did the daft parts in there, and we did a thing called *The Amateurville Horror* and NBC sent down a film unit to actually film this. It's quite extraordinary, just like The Beatles with *A Hard Days Night*, and that was the only time really they were ever seen clowning about and being barmy, apart from being The Bee Gees."

There was also a serious side to Barry's and David English's creativity, as David English recounted. "Whenever I get together with BG, we always come up with some ideas, and I went to Miami in 1979 for a few weeks and stayed there six months! This was before *Miami Vice* had come out and we started writing this thing every day called *Whirlpool* about the dope dealing and whatever, you know the boats coming out of Miami and it was terrific. We sent it to Robert who said, 'We're going to make a feature film on this,' which didn't come off, but very mysteriously only a matter of a few months later, *Miami Vice* came on which was exactly our story. It was an extraordinary coincidence. It's a shame that because we'd got all the Cubans, all the characters, but of course the drug business in Miami was prevalent then anyway and so it was just a time when somebody must have got the same idea."

This was not their only good idea that failed to come to fruition. "Barry is fascinated by ghost stories and haunted stories," said David, "and we actually wrote an idea and we gave it to a man called Barney Broom to see if he could place it and it never came off. But he was definitely commissioned to actually push that story around about the haunted houses of Europe, all famous true stories."

The Bee Gees third single from the *Spirits* LP, 'Love You Inside Out', was released in April, giving the group their sixth consecutive American number one, a feat matched only by The Beatles at their peak. According to *Billboard* magazine, 'Love You Inside Out' was the ninth number one single for The Bee Gees, tying them for fourth place on the list of artists with the most American number ones. The top three were The Beatles with 20, Elvis Presley with 17, and Michael Jackson and The Supremes tied for third place with 12 each. In Britain, the single stalled at number 13.

With so much success, it was perhaps inevitable that stories were printed about internal problems within the group that might lead to another split. *People* magazine quoted an unnamed source as saying, "Everyone is jealous of Barry. He writes the stuff, he produces the albums, he's the big lead vocalist, all the girls think he's the sexiest one. It's really too much for Robin and Maurice." The rumours were hotly denied by The Bee Gees' camp.

"Rapport within the Bee Gees has never been better," Stigwood proclaimed. "They're working together better than they've ever done. The current 'story' has no foundation whatsoever."

"I know there are rumours that Barry does more on our records than Robin and I," Maurice said. "I don't know how that rot got started, but I hate it and resent it. It's a load of shit. People get that impression because Barry's out front a lot and gets quite a bit of attention for his work with Karl and Albhy on other people's songs and for his work with Andy. But as far as our records are concerned, we all contribute equally and all produce equally."

Barry, meanwhile, emphasised the group's outside projects, as well as the immediate future for The Bee Gees. "I am currently finishing Andy's album and will start work on Barbra Streisand's next record in January," he announced. "Robin and Blue Weaver are producing a record for Jimmy Ruffin, and Maurice is writing the music for Robert Stigwood's film called *The Fan*." As it turned out, Maurice's music for *The Fan* was abandoned in favour of original music by Pino Donaggio and Marvin Hamlisch, with lyrics by Tim Rice.

★ ★ ★

Although both denied that it affected their marriage, the hectic lifestyle was beginning to take its toll on Robin and Molly's relationship. Molly revealed, "I think you have to be very level-headed to survive in this business. If a woman is to survive, there is no time for being helpless or jealous – that's what causes so many break-ups." She also admitted that when, "Robin came home for a month in April, the first time for a year, I'd spent so long without him that I was quite nervous just wondering what it was going to be like to have him home. Suddenly I had to change my habits and routine and fit back into being a married person again.

"We always have such a lovely time together when he's home – we go out to our favourite restaurants and to see movies at the local cinema – we generally relax. Then, for a couple of days before his departure date, I find myself getting very tense – I've become so used to having him back that it's as if he's never been away."

She explained that being on her own with the children so much meant that, "If something goes wrong, there's invariably no one here to put an arm around me and tell me it'll be all right. I suppose it does tend to make you a bit . . . not so much hard as independent. For example, once when I was away, friends rang to say there'd been a burglary at our house. I had to go back and face it alone – that was one time I really wished Robin could have been with me."

It was difficult for Spencer and Melissa, as well. One family friend observed that whenever Robin was at home, little Melissa used to follow him around like a puppy, afraid to let him out of her sight. It was up to

Molly to be the disciplinarian, as Robin was so rarely there that when he was, he wanted to spoil the children.

"Of course, the children miss their father," Molly conceded, "but they have grown up with the situation. It's not a sudden thing, and they have a very secure and happy home life here. And there's always Concorde – I pop over to the States fairly frequently. Sometimes I leave the children with my mother, but I usually try to make my visits coincide with their school holidays."

Molly said that she planned to "pop over" to the States soon, to look for a house. "Then at least we'll have a home to go to when we stay for the holidays," she explained. "It'll be better for the kids . . . it'll be better for *me*.

"I never go to the airport to see him off – we both get so emotional. It's better if he just walks out the front door."

In May, Robin walked out the front door to return to the States, and the group began preparations for their most ambitious American tour to date. They didn't even take time out from rehearsals to attend the *Billboard* Awards Banquet in Los Angeles. Instead, they sent their mother, Barbara, and 13-year-old Beri Gibb to collect 11 awards on the group's behalf.

The Bee Gees' absence added fuel to the rumours of another break-up, but Blue explained that the complex staging and special effects of the *Spirits* tour simply required more rehearsal time than any of the previous tours. "I actually found some tapes the other day of rehearsals of the tours and was listening to them," he said. "I think on all these tapes, I was the stubborn one . . . It was only years afterwards that Dennis told me I was very bossy, and I think musically I was probably very bossy as well."

"I've never seen them as nervous as they were before the tour started," Dick Ashby recalled. "They're at the pinnacle of their careers, and people will try to tear them down. If they hadn't been up and down before, they'd be going haywire now. They can handle anything thrown at them."

As usual, Lynda and Yvonne Gibb accompanied their husbands on tour, and as usual, Molly Gibb stayed behind in England. "The greatest thing . . . is that my wife and I can go anywhere together," Maurice said. "We can always go touring. Eventually, as our son grows up, he'll be able to come too if he wants to. The same goes for Barry's wife. Robin's wife doesn't particularly like travelling that much. She has two older children, so it's more of a responsibility for her, and she's not really hot on touring. But in our case – mine and Barry's – our wives love it and they get on together like a house on fire."

"I went on tour once and that was enough for me," Molly said. "It was so regimented – everyone had to meet in the foyer at the same time. I'm far too independent to be pushed and shoved around. I vowed I'd never go again and I haven't."

With the popularity of the group at its highest, extraordinarily stringent security precautions were taken for the 41-date North American tour. The Bee Gees based themselves out of hotels in only five cities in the USA.

Instead of the usual flying into the city on the day of the concert, checking into a hotel, playing the show, and going back to the hotel, then travelling to the next concert the following day, the group would fly out of the home city to the venue on the day, returning to their home base immediately after the concert. This eliminated the need to set up security each day in hotels in all of the individual cities.

The tour began on June 28 in Fort Worth, Texas, at the Tarrant County Convention Center. The group arrived in their 55-seat Boeing 707 jet, leased at a cost of over a million dollars and custom-painted with a specially designed *Spirits Having Flown* tour logo. Inside, the plane was like a plush living room, with four video TV screens, 12-channel stereo system customised to the group's musical tastes. Credit for this refurbishment belonged to Bill Hardy, who was also responsible for organising the flight crew. Four stewardesses in designer jeans and Hawaiian blouses served gourmet meals to the band and assorted family members, including their parents and grandmother Nora Pass, who had flown in from Australia to see her famous grandsons perform.

While the Gibbs and their fellow musicians were living it up in one of the five plush hotels and flying in comfort to and from gigs, The Bee Gees' road crew had to make do with two customised buses with 32 bunk beds, catching up on their sleep as they rode their way to the next gig.

The Bee Gees were accompanied on the tour by a film crew capturing highlights of the concerts, for use in a 90-minute NBC-TV special hosted by David Frost.

The three Gibb brothers took their places front and centre stage, identically dressed in tight white satin trousers and dazzling white spangled jackets, opened to reveal hairy chests and medallions. Robin's long wavy hair had changed from its natural brown to a bright red, allegedly dyed to match his Irish Setter, Penny. "He's very doggy-minded," explained their sister Lesley. The deafening shrieks from the audience threatened to drown out the opening strains of 'Tragedy'. Al Coury, RSO Records President, who flew in for the first show, claimed, "I couldn't take it. I had to break off two cigarette filters and stick them in my ears."

Two nights later, at their concert at the Summit in Houston, a bearded John Travolta, in Texas filming *Urban Cowboy* on location, joined the group on stage to reprise some of his fancy footwork from *Saturday Night Fever*.

By the time that The Bee Gees had made their way to Los Angeles, some enterprising souls were getting as much as $700 for a pair of $15 concert tickets; and before the concert began, it was estimated that concessionaires were taking in nearly $3,000 each minute on Bee Gees' programmes, t-shirts, jewellery and posters. "We have our own merchandising company," Barry said, "and it's done with taste, I hope. We're doing things like nice t-shirts. We deal in jewellery but only real gold plate. If you're an innovator, you've gotta be real careful not to get involved with all the spin-offs because they're highly dangerous."

478

Among the 60,000 fans at their concert at LA's Dodger Stadium were some famous faces: Barbra Streisand, Olivia Newton-John, Karen Carpenter, KC and The Jacksons. Barbra Streisand was recognised as she and Jon Peters attempted to slip unnoticed into their seats. "The audience spotted me and started to applaud," she recalled. "And it was like I was in shock. I couldn't believe they would respond to me in that way. It was really thrilling."

Streisand, in search of a new producer to bring flair and continuity to her next LP, was impressed. "I really love their music," she said.

"We used to play to half-filled halls," said Barry. "We always felt people were never really listening to us. Now we're having the time of our lives."

But Robin pointed out that, "For all intents and purposes, this tour is like being in prison." The group were whisked into limousines after each concert and deposited 10 yards from their tour plane after each night's concert.

Any thought of leading any sort of a normal life on the road was hastily dismissed as too much trouble. "To go out and buy a shirt would require two hours' planning for logistics and security," Robin claimed.

But Barry protested that it was much the same at home. "If I want to acquire something," he said, "I call someone in the organisation who then goes out and gets it. You can go crazy like that, living in a controlled, concealed world. It's like Presley."

When the Gibbs and assorted band members wanted to see the film *Alien* on a rare evening off, Robert Stigwood had to make the theatre manager an offer he couldn't refuse to cordon off the entire balcony for them.

Robin and Molly continued their long distance marriage with nightly telephone calls. "[Groupies] don't worry me," Molly said. "But it's really sad that these people think by sleeping around with pop stars they are going to somehow become involved and maybe even find a husband. I know they haven't got a hope in hell. I usually keep my distance from them, but there's no way I'm going to grab Robin off if he happens to be talking to them. I'd know immediately [if Robin were to have an affair] – I'd be able to tell by his voice on the telephone. I can't say how I'd react. I don't know whether I'd forgive him or not."

She insisted, "I trust Robin completely – so far no one has ever threatened our relationship. We're always totally honest with each other. If he wants to go to a party or take a girl to the cinema, that's fine by me, and I'm free to do what I want too. It's something we've always agreed on – okay, you can be married and love each other, but you don't own your partner."

With so many concerts and being in a different city every night, there were sure to be a few mistakes. With his dry humour and willingness to laugh at himself, Blue Weaver described some of the little glitches that kept the tour interesting.

'Tragedy' was accompanied by dramatic explosions, which had to be carefully synchronised with the music, and Blue was the man with his finger on the button. "I used to set off the explosions," he revealed, "and the first one would be in the lights above the top . . . of the stage, and all this sort of fairy dust would come down – it was quite spectacular. To create that – the actual explosions themselves wouldn't make that much noise . . . So there was this one explosion, which was above the stage."

After the first explosion, one of the group's roadies would have to crawl underneath the stage and flick a relay switch, to reset for the following explosion at the side of the stage. "If you can imagine, there's a relay switch under the stage . . . and I had this big button on the side of the keyboard that I used to hit to set off the explosions . . . because to make the explosions more effective, I used to hit the keyboard, and I had this sort of explosive sound . . . The first explosion went off, and the button must have stuck down so . . . when he's crawling underneath the stage and flicked the switch, of course, the explosion went off right away, right at the wrong point. You can imagine, it threw everybody, but as true performers, we sort of carried on."

Barry's biggest crowd-pleaser would have to be 'Words', which was always accompanied by whoops and screams from the audience. "You know how Barry used to sort of milk the audience on ['Words']," Blue said. "The song would start off . . . I'd be doing a piano intro like that, and it could go on for several minutes. Barry would talk and every time he'd go to sing the first word, which is 'Smile', everybody – women would scream – the whole place would erupt so he would sort of stop, and then he would carry on and it would happen again . . . Well, I started off – the whole song is in G – so I had a mental block, and I was playing in F, and then I suddenly realised – and he did 'Smile' a couple of times and he didn't quite get into the song – and I looked down and suddenly realised that I'm in F, and just as he was going to start the song, I changed so Barry actually went 'S-m-i-i-i-l-e'," Blue sang, his voice rising sharply mid-word. "I had to do it – it was either then or no time at all."

"One other time, on 'How Deep Is Your Love' – the record was actually in E Flat, but some nights on stage, we would do it in E, depending on how Barry's voice was . . . which sounds odd because it's a higher key than E flat," he said. "I think I had the habit of saying, 'How are we doing 'How Deep Is Your Love' tonight, and he'd say . . . 'E flat', or whatever . . . This one night, I just started to do it and I started it off in E . . . thinking that was the usual key, and there was this cacophony, and Barry had to say, 'Okay, let's start this again' . . . but that only happened one time."

In August, the group took a well-earned three-week break from touring, resuming the second leg of the tour on August 26. The Bee Gees were presented with the Golden Ticket, an award presented to artists who draw audiences of more than 100,000, following sell-out concerts at Madison Square Garden.

At a party after the final New York concert, Barry was in a pensive mood. "Having families keeps us sane," he said. "With all the ups and downs we've experienced, we have to have someone to sit at home with who'll tell us, 'Hey, you're just a person. Knock it off.' "

On September 24, they were invited to the White House to be congratulated by President Carter for their work with UNICEF, along with the St. Louis Cardinals baseball player, Lou Brock, who was invited in recognition of his 3000th major league baseball hit.

Talking to reporters outside the West Wing of the White House, Barry said The Bee Gees had personally raised about $2.5 million for UNICEF so far. As for the President, "He didn't tell us he was a Bee Gees fan. He said his family was," he added.

It was a great honour for Barry, Robin and Maurice, but at least one member of their party remained unfazed by meeting the former peanut farmer from Georgia. "Hughie thought he was a twerp! I said, 'He's the President of the United States, Hughie!' 'He's still a bloody twerp!' He was never impressed by politicians," Tom Kennedy chuckled.

Still riding high, *Bee Gees' Greatest,* a two LP set in an embossed gatefold sleeve was released in October in the US and Britain, with their *20 Greatest Hits* album released in mainland Europe. In the UK, RSO also released *Short Cuts*, a promotional only album for *Bee Gees' Greatest*, which consisted of two separate six track medleys, one slow, the other fast.

The tour came to its conclusion on October 6 in their adopted hometown with a concert at the Miami Baseball Stadium. It would be The Bee Gees' last concert in Miami for almost 13 years, until they took part in the Hurricane Andrew Relief Concert in 1992.

The strain of the tour had begun to tell on the group. "It looks like we can't go on being The Bee Gees," Barry confessed. "With this tour, all the hyperactivity began to take its toll. I found myself either on top of the world or totally depressed. A couple of times, I was at the point of bursting into tears. Being Bee Gees is like three people being one person. It's impossible. We are each of us having an identity crisis. It could drive all of us crazy."

"I can't see us together singing 'You Should Be Dancing' at 40," Maurice added, with all the arrogance of youth. "We'd probably have seizures from the strain."

While Maurice still played the clown during the group's medley of their earlier hits – checking his watch, wandering off and mimicking Robin's cupped hand to his ear – as with many comedians, the jokes hid a darker side.

Recently, all three brothers have admitted that Maurice's drinking was putting pressure on everyone during the tour. "There were instances where Maurice would actually have to feel his way along the wall to get to the stage," Barry revealed, "and these were times when Robin and me would start to get apprehensive about what was going on. Because at that point, it was [Robin] and me that had to make sure that everything works right because Maurice doesn't look like he's going to make it happen, like he's going to be able to play his part. So then it becomes tense, and you end up filling in for where Maurice isn't doing it."

"You're not worrying so much about what the act's going to be like when you're going on," Robin added, "you're worried more about if Maurice is going to be able to come up with his part of the act. So you're worried about him, more than you're worried about whether it's going to go down well."

Until Maurice himself was ready to confront his alcoholism, worrying and trying to cover for him were all that they could do. "I would always escape, so something wasn't right," he said later. "My biggest defect of character, if you like, is unworthiness. I just didn't feel worthy of what I was doing, or my contribution. It came from the boozing. This is what happens to your mind when you do this, you know with the disease of alcoholism. It's totally, it's very cunning, it sneaks up on you. You can't love anybody else unless you love yourself, it's impossible." For the time being, he wasn't ready to love himself.

But there were no signs of any discord when NBC aired *The Bee Gees Special* on November 15. The 90-minute programme covered the full spectrum of the group's career, as they were shown working in the studio, performing live across the United States, and relaxing at home with their wives and children. It represented an idyllic family life that was becoming severely curtailed by the demands of their profession.

Robin had joined his brothers as a tax exile from Britain, so he and Molly and their children would meet up in Paris for short breaks as an alternative to the home in Long Island, New York, which they had bought earlier in the year. The couple were still insistent that Spencer and Melissa grow up in England, so Molly was back to being a pop widow for most of the year.

Maurice had teamed up with another celebrity friend, Neil Sedaka, to buy a Falcon 20 private jet. "Neither of us can quite afford it on our own," Sedaka explained, "so it seemed a good idea to buy it between us. We're going to use it ourselves and also rent it out a bit."

It was rumoured that Barry had been offered the role of Ché Guevara in a film version of *Evita*; a rumour which he vigorously denied. With his production work with Andy and the forthcoming Barbra Streisand project, he was beginning to sound jaded. "I spend all of my time in the studio," he confessed. "It will probably ruin my marriage. My house is never empty. There are always people passing through. Dick Ashby, our personal manager, lives in my house. All the business flows through there. I used to like being close to it. Now I want a retreat."

32

ALL I HAVE TO DO IS DREAM

B Y THE MIDDLE of 1979, as his elder brothers reached a pinnacle of success, Andy Gibb's personal and professional lives were in turmoil. The recording sessions had begun for his third album while The Bee Gees were still on tour but were soon shelved. "He tried recording without Barry, but he felt uncomfortable and had to wait," a friend said. As insecurity and drugs – reportedly cocaine and Quaaludes★ – took their toll, Andy became more and more unreliable.

The Bee Gees' *Spirits Having Flown* tour ended in October, and Barry went back into the studio to try to help his youngest brother. The process was slow and painful to all involved. At this point, Andy was no longer able to contribute much, so *After Dark* was Barry creating an album of songs he thought would suit Andy's voice, which due to his failing health was not so strong here, with its thin raspy qualities more emphasised.

"By the time we got to that last Andy album," said Albhy Galuten, "he [was] in such bad shape that we were just doing something to put on it. It wasn't an Andy album any more, it was a big contractual obligation."

Time after time, Andy wouldn't appear for recording sessions, leaving Barry to sing lead on the demos for the album. "He broke studio dates," Maurice recalled. "He loved making records, but he didn't show up for the vocal tracks."

In 1985, Andy himself admitted, "I am sure you heard of my drug problem that I had. I checked myself into a place for it, it started around then very lightly. The kind of drug that I was doing was very big in Florida about that time and of course the rest of the world . . . cocaine. What happened is I started not turning up for recording sessions, leaving Barry to cover for me. On a couple of my albums you will hear Barry singing a line and you think it's me, but it was really him. Me and Barry have an uncanny similarity vocally. We are the closest mentally too, and writing style,

---

★ Methaqualone, a central nervous system depressant. In small doses, it causes a feeling of euphoria; in larger doses, it causes a reduction in heart and breathing rates and a drop in blood pressure. Speech becomes slurred and reflexes are affected. Users rapidly become dependent and withdrawal is said to be more intense than withdrawal from heroin. The mixture of alcohol and Quaaludes is a deadly combination.

everything. He is the first boy born, and I am the last boy born and it's funny. The other two, there is no resemblance . . ."

Copyright filings tell a story: there were a few Andy-written songs that were not used, leaving only two co-written with Barry on the finished album. Two songs were left over Bee Gees' tracks written by Barry, Robin and Maurice. Barry collaborated with Albhy on 'Falling In Love With You', and wrote all the other songs himself. The album began to take on the feel of a Barry Gibb solo album, "except that it wasn't Barry doing his vision," Albhy observed, "it was Barry trying to rescue his brother, which is always somewhat disingenuous."

To be fair, Barry wrote some very good songs for this album: the up-tempo 'After Dark' and 'Wherever You Are' surround 'Desire' to lead off the first side, and Andy does a good job with the quiet beat of 'Dreamin' On' at the end of the album. The two songs by Barry and Andy are both quiet ballads, 'One Love' and 'Someone I Ain't', needlessly buried in the middle of side two.

" 'After Dark' is a single that was never released and I wish it was," Andy said in 1981. "To this day, it still should have been a single. I believe it was the strongest cut on that album."

"I . . . remember the song 'After Dark'," Albhy said. "That *was* a great track . . . We used Michael and Randy Brecker and David Sanborne on, and it was incredible, the horn parts on it. If you listen to that, all the background chorus parts were all sung by Barry. The stuff that sounds great is all actually Barry. Andy was pretty absent."

The production team of Barry, Karl and Albhy had their work cut out for them, trying to pull together an album with an unreliable star. "By that point, Andy was hard to work with," Albhy recalled. "So you would have songs that would not quite make the grade, start to work on it and put it away, and say maybe it'll resurface later . . . It was not as easy to get stimulated about writing good Andy songs because he was a basket case. He wouldn't show up, he wasn't there."

The lead single 'Desire' is the only released recording featuring all four Gibb brothers. The copyright office copy is labelled "Bee Gees". There was some talk of Andy appearing on the 'Spirits Having Flown' album although in the end he did not. This song might have been a little close to 'Too Much Heaven' in sound. The Bee Gees' harmonies at any rate help cover for Andy's lead voice.

Blue Weaver, Alan Kendall and Dennis Bryon were listed among the musicians playing on the album, but Blue explained, " 'Desire' actually started out as a Bee Gees track, so that's why we're credited on that. It was only really for the one song. We'd already done that with Barry singing lead – we'd worked on it for weeks, actually . . . Then we thought, 'Well, it's all right, but it's not really happening,' so it was set aside. The same thing happened with the track that I got onto the Ruffin album, 'Where Do I Go'. That started off as a Bee Gees song and 'Nobody' as well." Barry's lead vocals were simply removed from the mix and replaced by Andy's. The song would reach number four on the American charts but failed to place in the UK.

Albhy observed that one of the difficulties that Barry had when writing for Andy was that he would rely on his falsetto. "Andy's falsetto was nowhere near Barry's," he added. "Andy's natural voice was much more his strength, so that . . . sometimes he had to do more work because his facility with falsetto made it naturally easier for him to write for female singers."

Olivia Newton-John appeared on the album to reprise her duet of 'Rest Your Love On Me' from the UNICEF concert – yet another recording of the song after its recent appearances on a Bee Gees B-side, The Osmonds' *Steppin' Out* album (which Maurice produced) and the country hit by Conway Twitty. She also lent her voice to a new Barry Gibb composition, 'I Can't Help It'.

"It was so sad, the duet with Olivia," Albhy said. "When we had done the first demo vocals with Olivia and Barry, it was magical. But it was supposed to be an Andy record, it was kind of like you feel guilty, like, 'Oh gee, we did this thing, and now we had to try to get Andy to do the same things Barry had done.' Originally, we were in the studio in Miami, and it was Barry and Olivia singing together. I think Andy was not showing up. Barry had sung the demo, and Olivia sang to that. I think Andy showed up late. It was a problematic period for Andy. He sang some with her, [but] he was not making the notes . . . Andy's voice was horrible in those days; he was in really bad shape. It was wispy, there was no character to it . . . It's one thing to fix somebody's pitch or meter, but you can't fix the timbre of their voice or the emotion of their singing. So it was a lost opportunity."

Although publicly Olivia raved that the Gibb brothers "never cease to amaze me", privately, she was said to have complained that the album took so long to be completed that the two duets were stale by the time they were finally released. Her appearance on the LP led to more rumours of romance, but once again, these were denied. "Olivia was total publicity, and there was nothing into that at all. Any guy would love to have her," Andy sighed. "I'd like the rumours to be true, but it takes two to tango."

While he admitted that he had taken full advantage of all that life as a pop star had to offer, he said, "I went through a period where it was always right in front of me . . . just so much sex, girls, and dates who were around me because I was 'Andy Gibb', and I just started to back away from it. I didn't like to date so much; I started looking for that special girl. I think, I'm like my brothers, I'm a romantic, and I don't like 'one night stands'. I'm really not into that. I'm a guy like anybody else and I've had my fun, but I think I was looking for that nice lady to live with or settle down with . . ."

He admitted that he still had feelings for Marie Osmond, but added, "There's no love affair going on with Marie. She's a great person, always smiling. Very bubbly, she lives life every minute. Marie spends most of her time with her family. They're all very close. I just can't wheedle her away. I fancy her like mad. She knows I do. I've liked her for a long time, but there's no love affair. We haven't progressed any further than that. We have talked about it and we've got to the point where we both understand each other.

"She's a smashing girl, and although we've had roughly the same upbringing – the show business family, the fame the money – she's very different from me. I've been spoiled – she hasn't. She doesn't take anything for granted. She's very level-headed. So she's very special to me. She's the only one who is."

The following year, he admitted, "There was only one, and I have never said it in any interviews – as a matter of fact, I denied it in most interviews – there was only one girl I was really crazy about and that was Marie. And I think, even though nothing really happened, once I met her I just totally relaxed, calmed down and I stopped dating so much. I think it was a 'saving myself' thing, and it was stupid because now we are just good friends. There is nothing there now. We both felt something at the time and she is just a really unique lady. That was the one that was not just publicity, for my part it was pretty true."

For a brief time, Andy was linked with Olympic ice skater, Tai Babilonia, whom he met when both appeared on *Bob Hope's 77th Birthday Special* on NBC. "We hit it off right away and started dating," Tai recalled. "But we were never alone. He was always with a bodyguard. You might say I was in love with him from afar."

In January, family business gave Kim Gibb the opportunity to fly to Los Angeles. She had had no contact at all with Andy since before the birth of their daughter, claiming that "The record moguls and the family had moved in to put a brick wall between us." Despite all this, she decided that it was time that Andy met his two-year-old daughter.

When she arrived in Los Angeles, she called the RSO offices to find out if he was in town. "I put on an American accent so they wouldn't know it was me," she said, "and they assured me he was there. Then I told them who I was, and that I'd brought Peta to see her father, as it was her second birthday tomorrow.

"I was referred to his lawyers, who told me in no uncertain terms, 'Andy doesn't want to see you.' They then asked me how much money I wanted. God, I didn't want money – all I wanted was his recognition and his love. Finally, after some persuading, they agreed that they would get him to call me."

Kim waited nervously for the phone in her hotel room to ring. When Andy finally did call her, she said his first words to her were, "Hello, Kim, how much money do you want?"

She continued, "When I explained that I only wanted him to see his child, he replied typically, 'I don't know if I can cope with that.' I was devastated, but at least I was hearing it from his lips."

Clearly, the temptation to see his only child must have been too much for him, and he relented. He asked Kim if she could drive to the Beverley Hills Hilton Hotel, where he had a suite. She arrived to find a man she could hardly recognise. "He was clearly not well," she recalled, "but he was gentle with Peta and bought her a bracelet engraved with the words 'All my love, A.G.' "

Peta's sole memory of her only meeting with her father was of him handing her a glass of Coca-Cola. Kim and Peta returned to their own hotel. "I didn't know it then," said Kim, "but that was the last time I would ever see Andy alive. The next day I called the hotel, but he had gone."

When the *After Dark* LP arrived in the shops in the following month, it was seen as something of a comeback for Andy. Andy himself said, "I was kind of on ice for a year, but now I feel I've got a new start. It took me over a year to record [the] album. I finished it just before Christmas. I thought I was never going to see the outside of the studio. It was too long to be away," he admitted.

Andy flew to Britain to promote the release of the *After Dark* album. An interviewer described the young Gibb as "not what you would expect from someone who will be just 22 next month". Andy seemed to have aged more than the two years which had passed since his last album. His hair was dull, his skin pallid, there were wrinkles under his eyes; all the tell-tale signs of the dangerous lifestyle he had adopted.

Still, Andy tried to downplay his dependency by confessing just a little. "My first success went to my head," he admitted. "I did some very silly things. Life was just a big party. I don't say I got into heavy drugs, but it was definitely silly. Just not worth it. Not conducive to creativity and certainly not good for my health. But I've grown out of it now and I'm glad I have.

"I guess I got a little cocky, a little big-headed. I became a bit of a bad boy and tried to get out of doing things. I became a bit of a recluse. What got to me was that anything and everything was connected with *what* I was, not *who* I was. It got to the stage where I didn't know who I was anymore. So last year was spent getting back to me again. Now I am 100 per cent better than I was. I'm much more confident. I have a purpose and have big plans."

Andy claimed, "I just want to settle down. I want to be very mellow, very secure, like my brother Barry. That's the way it used to be. And that's the way I'm determined it's going to be in the future.

"I'm really just getting over my divorce," he added. "I saw my ex-wife Kim and my daughter Peta, who is two . . . for the first time just a couple of weeks ago in Los Angeles. They live in Australia. It's the only fair way for them to live."

While he said that the meeting "went real well", he admitted that, "In a way I wish I had not seen Peta. I can't not see her again. She's absolutely gorgeous, a little doll. I've just lost my heart to her. And in looks, she's a real Gibb. I couldn't stop taking pictures of her."

Andy and Olivia's duet, 'I Can't Help It', was the second single released from the album. It too made no impact on the British charts but reached number 12 in the United States. Andy was also said to have sung lead on the first verse of an unreleased take of 'Play The Game', a Freddie Mercury composition included on Queen's 1980 LP, *The Game*.

Once again mirroring his eldest brother's career, rumours abounded that Andy would soon make the transition to film. He was touted for the role of Olivia Newton-John's younger brother in *Grease II* and even went so far as a screen test. There was also talk of a role in a science fiction movie, *Nebula's Run*. "There are plans again for a movie this year, so things are happening," he declared. "I'm very into acting, and I want to make a film badly . . . I often worry if my Australian character would not work in the movies, but that is something I feel I can do. It would have to be the right type of script, it has to be the right concept, everything."

Ostensibly to make himself more available to the film world, he moved away from the family compound in Florida and back to Los Angeles. Barry believes it was for another reason. "Once he realised that everyone in Miami was trying to stop him doing [drugs], then he moved to LA."

Hugh, Barbara and Beri also made the move to Los Angeles in June, but the closeness of his family did little to deter Andy from falling back into his old ways.

Just as his brother Maurice had done, Andy bought a private jet in partnership with a famous friend; in this instance, Robert Redford. While it may seem an unlikely friendship, Andy explained, "Robert Redford and I both love the country. He's heavily into ecology, and he's also working in politics in Utah where he owns this big ski resort and I snow-ski heavily. I go up there every Christmas time and ski on his resort."

In September, *Andy Gibb's Greatest* was released, a compilation of his hits with three new tracks, which marked Andy's career wrap-up.

The house band really let loose on 'Time Is Time' by Andy and Barry and turn it into a great record, with the chugging rhythm section, a super synthesizer break, organ backing as it raves up, and wonderful offhand complete finish that was inexplicably faded off the song on the post-humous *Andy Gibb* CD. "I wrote ['Time Is Time'] out here in Los Angeles on my own," Andy said. "'Without You' I wrote out [in Miami]. It took me about two weeks to write that song. It is not a personal experience or anything like that, it is just a song I sat down and I had a deadline to write and I sat down and I wrote it. A lot of people that have heard it think it is one of the prettiest I have ever written; but then again I am very critical, I don't know."

'Time Is Time', was released as the first single from the *Greatest* LP. It reached number 15 in the US but was a no show in the British charts. Andy was becoming slightly defensive about the amount of input that Barry had on his albums by this time. "'Time Is Time' is very interesting," he said. "It was written about the same period out here in LA. When we went out to record them in Florida, Barry heard 'Time Is Time', and he altered one little thing in the song and for that reason you will see A. & B. Gibb, but it is mostly my record."

The third new track was a duet with Pat Arnold of the Carole King classic, 'Will You Still Love Me Tomorrow', a US chart topper for The Shirelles in 1960. By coincidence Arnold, an American-born soul singer who had some success in the UK in the late Sixties, had previously recorded with The Bee Gees as a back-up singer on the *Cucumber Castle* album and recorded several Bee Gees' songs under the name P.P. Arnold.

Andy's second American single from the LP was his own composition, 'Me (Without You)', released in February. It peaked at number 40.

While he tried to convince himself that it wasn't his problem, his old feelings of unworthiness and the insecurity that came from feeling that he hadn't really made it on his own merit still haunted him. "I read reviews and everything about, they always relate to The Bee Gees sound, how Gibb is . . . helped, and 'sounds like The Bee Gees' and everything," he said. "I always thought that people were buying my records as an extension to The Bee Gees. I was automatically getting The Bee Gee fans who liked that sound, and I never thought there was any individual thing in there that they liked . . . I just felt that anything I would say would not be as valuable as the ideas that they were working on, and that it would not matter that much. You know, that it really wasn't good enough, and so I used to hold back and they would say, 'Well, it's Andy's baby, we want Andy to give us an idea about how he feels about it.' And I never really did until the last two albums. I felt that I really wasn't good enough, they had just brought me up from Australia. I didn't have any confidence."

Admittedly, having a greatest hits album at such an early age was uncommon, but Andy was resolute that it didn't mark the end of his career. "There's a lot to do yet, and I can't imagine retiring at 23," he said. "I'd hate to think that everything that's happened so far is the high point of my life."

★   ★   ★

Rarely can a television chat show be credited – or blamed – with changing a guest's life, but in the case of Andy's appearance on the *John Davidson Show* on January 6, 1981, it did just that.

Researchers for the show found an interview which he had done for *People* magazine in which he claimed to have two dream girls. The first was Bo Derek, "the most beautiful thing on two legs". The other was "that girl on *Dallas*. Every time I see her I kind of tingle all over," he said. "She's so beautiful, there's a kind of haunted look about her that really turns me on."

As it happened, January 6 was also the night that Victoria Principal was scheduled to appear on *The Tonight Show*, which was taped in the studio next door. The *John Davidson Show* staff plotted to sneak Victoria onto the show during Andy's segment as a surprise. In the course of the interview, John Davidson casually mentioned Victoria Principal, and Andy eagerly admitted his infatuation.

"*People* magazine asked me my favourite show," Andy would explain later. "I said, '*Dallas* but only because of Victoria Principal.' Victoria wrote a thank you note because of that . . . John started bringing up Victoria. I thought, 'What's this to me?' and Victoria suddenly appeared behind me and came and sat next to me."

Andy's response was to blush like a schoolboy and stammer a few words. "He was acting like a 16-year-old," recalled a Davidson spokesman.

"I thought his reaction was so natural that I just sat and talked to him," Victoria said. She explained that she had read the story and had written Andy a note of thanks, put it in her purse and forgotten to post it. Newly separated from her husband of 20 months, 24-year-old actor Christopher Skinner, Victoria had spent the past few years trying to live down her "party girl" image after highly publicised relationships with Frank Sinatra, Desi Arnaz Jr., football player Lance Rentzel and financier Bernie Cornfeld, among others.

Andy managed to regain his composure enough to ask for her phone number. "Our rapport was immediate," he recalled. "Two days later, I called her. She was sick in bed with a heavy case of flu. I made some chicken soup and brought her some beautiful red roses with just one white rose in the centre, but when I got to the house, I was too scared to ring the bell. I just left the soup and the roses on the doorstep, got about halfway home to Malibu, and stopped in Westwood to call her and tell her to look on the doorstep."

"I said, 'Why didn't you ring the bell?' But I loved his shyness and his thoughtfulness," Victoria added. "Even now, when he sends me flowers, he always includes that one white rose."

The couple spent the next three days on the telephone, learning each other's life history, and soon became inseparable. "I moved in with her a couple of days later," Andy recalled. "I was head over heels in love. I wanted to spend my life with this woman. Nobody else existed."

Although he would insist that for him, it was love at first sight, he added, "By the time we broke up 13 months later, I still loved her, but in the same breath, I also hated her."

Despite evidence to the contrary, his parents would later cite the relationship as the beginning of Andy's drug abuse, but Maurice Gibb said years later, "I think his relationship with Victoria Principal was absolutely beautiful, it was everything he dreamed of. And that's the only important thing here, it's not what I think or what anybody else thinks. Andy thought the world of her."

It was rumoured that Andy's brothers tried to discourage him from the relationship, but Maurice denied that this was ever the case. "We hardly ever met Victoria, but they seemed happy living together. Andy always found it hard to shrug off the baby brother image – it was widely assumed that we three always took it upon ourselves to approve his girlfriends, but that was never the case. He was into his twenties when he was with Victoria

490

and a big enough boy to handle himself. Who really knows what goes on behind closed doors in a relationship? None of us is blameless in that department."

For a time, it did seem to be a fairy tale relationship. Despite the age difference of anywhere from eight to 14 years, depending upon whom you choose to believe about the actress's date of birth, they seemed to be well-suited. "People think I have been cradle-snatching since puberty. That's not true," Victoria protested. "I have dated men my own age and men older than me, but these relationships never made headlines . . . Some people seem to find it immoral that Andy and I should be together, with our age gap. So what?"

"I'm tired of being a teen love object," Andy insisted. "I'm 23 going on 45. I've had a lot of adventures and I've already travelled to most countries of the world. Sometimes I feel old because I've never mixed with kids my own age. I've always been around older people and been accepted as an adult equal. My feelings and my outlook on life are adult experiences."

"It's not that I'm attracted to younger men but to a certain kind of spirit," Victoria protested. "I love spontaneity, enthusiasm, courage and a positive, unjaded attitude."

Andy enthused, "Since I have met Victoria, she's been a great source of inspiration and happiness to me. She's a very special lady."

Andy and Victoria managed to keep their relationship a secret from the press for three months. "They were three of the most delicious, wonderfully happy months of my life," Andy would later tell Neil Blinkow. "Victoria was just as much in love with me as I was with her. We could not bear to be apart for a single second. We were like two lovers shipwrecked on a desert island. There was no world outside our love.

"She would come to my home by the Pacific Ocean. We would cook meals, and as the sun sank in those great glowing West Coast sunsets that reddened the entire sky, we would walk barefoot through the sand, heads down, locked in our own thoughts, talking about our careers, our future together."

Victoria agreed, "It's been wonderful for both of us. I finally finished decorating the house. And professionally, it's been great because we're so supportive of each other work-wise. I'm wild to know all that he's doing. And he's been so successful in his own right, there's no jealousy. He's never said to me, 'Oh, I haven't seen enough of you. Don't take that job or don't do that talk show.' It's the first time ever that someone I've cared for hasn't tried to suppress my work, and my work's important to me."

"Victoria didn't tell a soul about our love affair, nor did I," Andy added. "We spent time at each other's homes, sneaking in and out like criminals, although we were so profoundly happy it was ridiculous. Then I felt outraged; I wanted the world to know that I was in love with Victoria, that she felt the same way about me. Why should we hide our feelings for one another?"

Victoria was still legally married to Skinner at the time, and she explained, "I had been separated from my husband for three months when I met Andy. At first it frightened me to love him, so I hid it from myself. After all, we both had broken marriages. I don't want to do anything that reflects discredit on my relationship with Christopher. That wasn't something undertaken lightly. I'm not exactly going out on the town. I anticipate that Andrew and I will enjoy each other's company for a time."

While at the time, both painted an idyllic picture of true romance, Andy would later allege, "When I met Victoria she was in a depression over her broken marriage; she was depressed around the clock. I could never really deal with Victoria's moods, but love is blind, so I stuck it out.

"While she was worldly and sophisticated, she was actually an insecure, very mixed-up little girl. She would sit in bed at night reading the *National Enquirer* and getting so upset about publicity that other actresses were getting. There were nights when she just used to cry on me like a little baby because she was so scared – she didn't know where she was going or what she was going to do . . ."

"I'd not been seen for so long, I could have been in a convent," Victoria added. "Then we decided to go public with it, to make the American Music Awards our first outside date. When we emerged from the limo, photographers were so startled, they forgot to take pictures and we ran right through them. Not one photograph of us going in. But they were waiting for us when we came out." The resulting photographs appeared in the newspapers all over America, Australia and Britain.

The following week, Andy and Victoria flew to New York, where persistent reporters and photographers soon tracked them to the Waldorf-Astoria. When the time came for Victoria to return to Los Angeles to resume filming for *Dallas*, Andy was supposed to remain in New York to discuss the possibility of taking on the role of Frederic in *The Pirates Of Penzance*, replacing singer/actor Rex Smith, and to stay on for an appearance at the Grammy Awards. On his own, he missed her so much that he flew back to Los Angeles, leaving his responsibilities behind in New York. A pattern would soon begin to emerge.

On June 2, 1981, he opened with the Los Angeles production of *The Pirates Of Penzance,* starring opposite Pam Dawber, at that time best known for her role as Robin William's sidekick in television's *Mork & Mindy*. Andy loved the excitement and the brilliance of opening night, but the reality of appearing on stage night after night, and juggling the demands of the challenging Gilbert and Sullivan role with his relationship with Victoria soon proved too much for him.

On July 7, as he was getting ready to leave for the theatre, he was suddenly doubled over in pain. Concerned and frightened, Victoria rushed him to the emergency room of the Cedars-Sinai Medical Center. From there, he was wheeled up to the VIP eighth floor of the hospital, where he remained for four days. It wasn't the first time he had been rushed to hospital with mysterious pains, but once again, the doctors' tests would prove inconclusive.

August saw the release of Andy's latest single, a saccharine duet with Victoria of 'All I Have To Do Is Dream, which he co-produced with Michael Barbeiro. The record sustains little in musical merit and reached only number 52 on *Billboard*'s Hot 100, in spite of the couple's appearances on various American television shows promoting it. Andy revealed that there might be more records to come. "We have another one in the can," he said. "We did two songs when we did this one. We did 'Will You [Still] Love Me Tomorrow', the Carole King song."

In addition to his recording with Victoria, he lent his vocals to one track on the Dutch recording artist Flower's eponymous LP.

Returning to the opening scene of their romance, the couple made another appearance on the *John Davidson Show*.

On the *Donahue* show, Andy and Victoria spoke frankly about their relationship and their previous marriages, admitting to host Phil Donahue that they were living together and had discussed marriage, but Victoria was still waiting for her divorce from Christopher Skinner.

"I was curious what my fans would think of me having a serious relationship, which I have not had before," Andy confessed. "Well, I was married for 10 months once. I still consider myself an infant when I got married. I was married at 18 . . . and I don't consider that a true marriage. I believe in the old expression, 'You know when it's real,' and I know.

"I believe that if you have dated for a long time there is a fear of parting. I think that is how it was for me. I dated Kim for two years in Australia, and I had to leave to come to America to do my first record here. And I felt deep down that if I came and was successful I may not come back. I stumbled into marriage that way. I was scared of splitting up at the time."

That same month, he made the transition from recording artist and star of the stage to star of the small screen, when he signed a 46-show contract as co-host with Marilyn McCoo for the hit syndicated television series, *Solid Gold*. It all began with such promise, as Andy's charm and talent made him an ideal candidate for the show. The format for the show gave Andy the opportunity to sing the hits of the day, as well as his own material, and to establish himself as a personality rather than just a pop star. It was seen as yet another fresh start for the 23-year-old.

In the late Seventies, when Andy first came to fame, teenagers just wanted to dance and have a good time, and Andy's brand of sweet pop music and his clean-cut good looks were ideal. By the Eighties, although traditional love songs still made the charts, the US music industry was moving towards the big-haired, heavy metal headbangers. Music by bands like Poison, Cinderella, Quiet Riot, Mötley Crüe and Bon Jovi couldn't have been further from the sweet innocence of 'I Just Want To Be Your Everything'.

The discos of the Seventies remained in business but resorted to theme nights to draw in the crowds. Wet t-shirt contests and male strippers came into vogue, and the *Solid Gold* dancers capitalised on this sexy image as they rolled and writhed to the hits every week.

Andy remained a big star although he hadn't released an album since 1980. Millions of teenagers tuned in each week to watch him present *Solid Gold*. But soon a pattern of dysfunction would become apparent once again.

Despite their public protestations of an idyllic romance, behind the scenes, trouble was brewing. Victoria confided to an interviewer, "I was frightened he was only in love with my Pam Ewing character. That's one of the dangers of being attracted to a character. There are elements of you that aren't that character. The first time I did or said something that wasn't Pam Ewing, it was a shock to him."

Andy later admitted, "Sometimes being with Victoria was like tiptoeing through a mine field. Put one foot wrong and everything is going to be blown sky-high. It was exciting, but often frightening. She had a terrible temper at times."

He alleged that the pressure to constantly prove himself to her was tearing away his self-esteem. Andy had always secretly worried that his success was firmly linked to having famous brothers, and she intensified these feelings of doubt. "I could feel this strong sense of competition between us," he said. "I didn't thrust my career success to the front all the time. She did, and she was quick to point out that she got it all for herself, that she didn't come from a family that already included famous performers."

Andy would later claim that their relationship was stormy almost from the start, saying, "Within the first week I thought to myself, 'I can't live with her, she's so crazy.' I had heard a lot of stories about Victoria's background and the men she had dated. She was a Hollywood socialite who had played around. Many people tried to warn me, but I wouldn't listen to it." Each new argument brought him close to despair. He would frequently disappear, travelling to Northern California and registering under a false name so neither his family nor his management could find him.

Hugh Gibb observed, "Andy always seems to come out of these arguments the worst. He is always upset after them. He is an emotional boy and apparently gets more upset than she does."

Andy would subsequently admit that a contributory cause of their final break-up may have been the exclusive nature of their relationship. "We were so into each other that we gave up all our friends. We didn't have any friends and I think that's very important in a relationship. When she left, I had nobody, only my parents and my brothers. They pulled me right through it, all the worst of it."

A fiercely driven and ambitious woman, Victoria soon realised that a former teen idol with a drug problem didn't fit into her plans for the future. Andy believed that if they were married, everything that was wrong in their relationship would magically disappear.

"One night at the Waldorf-Astoria Hotel in New York, we had both had a couple of drinks and were in bed watching TV," he revealed. "I leaned across to Victoria and said, 'Let's get married.' And she said, 'All right.' I said, 'Right now.' And she said, 'Okay . . . right now.' It was three in the morning. I called my manager, Mark Hulett, and told him he was going to be a witness. But then we decided, 'No, we'll do it in a church somewhere, like St. Patrick's Cathedral.' We were genuinely in love.

"I just know that if we'd have married, I could have saved our relationship. I think that if I'd have got on with my career, proved to Victoria that I was a man she could really rely on, a man who would have allowed her to pursue her own career to the upper limits, she would have been happy. But by then I was freaking her out by using cocaine. I was freaking myself out because I couldn't get off the stuff."

His family were already concerned over his behaviour. "I talked to him in the *Solid Gold* dressing room and said, 'What are you taking this rubbish for?' Hugh Gibb recalled. He said, 'It's the only way I can handle her.'"

Victoria would later say, "It became very apparent to me that his behaviour was becoming erratic and that he was very, very thin. And Andy was a very kind person and a very gentle person and some of his behaviour seemed so the antithesis of who I knew him to be. And over a period of deduction, I finally realised that it had to be drugs.

"I asked him either to choose me or to choose drugs and, though I know with all his heart he wanted to choose me, he chose drugs. It put me in an incredible position of a terrible dilemma because to speak out on my own behalf and to reveal that the problem had been ongoing, and that was the reason for the break-up, would have been to add to the already tremendous burden that Andy was carrying, and so I chose to remain silent.

"Watching someone you care about destroyed because of drugs is a horrifying experience. I did everything I humanly could to stop him," she insisted. "It broke my heart, the torment that he went through."

Andy was included in the American Music Awards salute to Australian music, with his elder brothers appearing live via a video link from London.

But it was yet another awards ceremony which would mark the end of Andy and Victoria's relationship. In March, 1982, the couple made their final public appearance together, attending the People's Choice Awards. "We turned up arm in arm," he said. "But we started arguing at the table . . . and muttering under our breath at each other.

"Victoria got up to receive an award with the *Dallas* cast, and when she came back, it was like she didn't know me. She was talking to her friends and I called out, 'Victoria, I *am* here, you know.' She looked at me and walked away. I felt like killing her.

"Victoria and I went to pick up some Indian curry and went back to her house. We were fighting in the car and when we got back to the house we just started ranting and screaming and pushing and shoving. In the end, it got a little physical. I stormed out and drove back to my house at Malibu Beach. That was the last time I saw Victoria."

The next day, he telephoned her, desperately pleading with her for forgiveness and offering to call again in a week when they had both had time to let things cool down. She told him that their relationship was finished.

"I still loved her desperately," he said. "It was as though my world was going to pieces. I didn't believe her. I didn't wait until the following week, I called her at home, I called her on the set . . . She was cold and angry. She just didn't want to hear from me."

"They have been splitting up every other week since the middle of last year," Barbara Gibb said. "Whenever they have a falling-out, it's always a big fight and Andy moves back to his Malibu beach house. I've never known anyone who fights like these two. But this time, he was really rundown and at a very low ebb."

Andy suffered a complete collapse after the break-up. "I wasn't eating," he said. "I wasn't sleeping. I was so devastated by the split-up I fell apart and just didn't care about anything. I think subconsciously I wanted to commit suicide. I started to do cocaine around the clock – about a thousand dollars a day. I stayed awake for about two weeks, locked in my bedroom. I went down from 142 pounds to 110 pounds. It sounds awfully weak for a man to let a woman get to him in that way. But Victoria's not just any woman."

"For about four months, he was devastated. We had a bad time with him, and he was crying for hours and hours," Barbara recalled.

His recording contract with RSO ended in March, and Robert Stigwood regretfully declined to renew it. It made little difference to Andy at the time, nor did his commitment to *Solid Gold*.

"Nothing existed for me except Victoria. I just stopped turning up for work," he confessed. "I didn't care. I forgot the show existed. The producers kept calling up, coming to the house, sending cars for me, but I refused to go. I locked myself in my room and nobody could get me out. I couldn't have worked in front of a camera any way, I looked so bad – like a human skeleton."

In May, Brad Lachman had had enough. He fired the no-show co-host and ironically hired Rex Smith, Andy's predecessor in *The Pirates Of Penzance*, to replace him.

Andy ignored his other commitments as well. "The most embarrassing thing for me was the day Bob Hope called me up," he recalled, "and I was spaced out on cocaine. I was supposed to do his TV special, and I didn't turn up. He said, 'Andy, I know what's going on, but we need you down here. Everything's been written around you.' I said, 'I'm sorry, Bob, but I really can't make it.' I hung up on him. Consequently, I was blacklisted by NBC for a long time. I damaged my career and almost ruined my whole life."

Rumours circulated that Andy had attempted to commit suicide with a massive drug overdose. The Bee Gees' manager, Dick Ashby, told reporters, "We heard rumours about Andy's suicide attempt, and the family called to make sure he was okay. Barry Gibb's wife spoke to him last night, and he sounded very calm."

Andy would later say that the turning point came when he was at his lowest ebb. "I was sitting in my house with my mother and father about midnight, not wanting to feel this way anymore," he said.

"It was the worst feeling of my life, and I was crying my eyes out, and I said, 'I know a psychiatrist who lives two doors down from me.' I had heard about him in Malibu and that was the turning point. He has been fantastic to me. We see each other every day and he literally saved my life."

A family friend said later, "[Andy] lost all control. The doctor and the family decided there was no alternative. Andy needed round-the-clock hospital care. They chose St. Francis Hospital in Santa Barbara because it was secluded and quiet."

Andy registered at the hospital under the pseudonym of Roy Lipton, his middle name teamed with the name of one of America's most popular brands of teabags. As the hospital catered principally to aged patients, it seemed unlikely that the teen idol would be recognised. "Doctors at the hospital said Andy was suffering from nervous exhaustion," said the friend. "His father called it a nervous breakdown."

During his three-day hospital stay, doctors ordered complete bed rest and tranquillisers, but he remained obsessed with the thought of a reconciliation with Victoria. Time after time, he made desperate telephone calls begging her to come and see him, pleading with her to give their relationship one last chance. She tried to comfort him with platitudes about remaining friends, but to no avail.

Andy left the hospital with his parents and spent some time recuperating on a friend's ranch before returning to his Malibu home. Seventeen-year-old Beri briefly abandoned drama school and moved in with him to keep a watchful eye on him. "I missed five weeks of school being with Andy, but I felt better being there. It helped him a lot that I was there and that he didn't have to look for me. He could just walk from his bedroom to mine when he needed to talk."

Barbara Gibb was a frequent visitor, too, providing "some fabulous meals" for her two youngest children. "I can only cook spaghetti and Andy only cooks for himself," Beri explained.

For awhile, Andy seemed to have made a recovery. "He's writing music again, and he may go back to *Solid Gold*. Now he's taking it easy," Beri said.

Soon, a healthy-looking Andy Gibb appeared on *Good Morning, America*, telling Joan Lunden, "I have been to hell and back. I had a very, very bad nervous breakdown. There was a lot of pressure on me and Victoria. There was a sweet dream of a relationship, and also a nightmare at some point. She's a very ambitious girl, and I think it was mutual. I think we both pressured each other too much. We couldn't spend five minutes apart from each other. We split up several times before the final split. It was inevitable, it had to happen. I thought so much of the girl and I still do . . ."

Although he told Joan, "I think it is very important to my fans to know *exactly* what has happened to me, to know that they should not do this to themselves. I think it's very vital," he was still not ready to admit the extent of his drug problem. "I just fell apart. I turned to drugs for a month," he said. "I did an awful lot of cocaine, which I no longer do . . . I gave up everything . . . I started missing tapings of *Solid Gold*. I would not turn up for tapings, very bad boy. I didn't care. I didn't care about people. I didn't care about life."

Andy was still mindful of his image, trying desperately not to disappoint the fans who had been "through ups and downs" with him. "They've never really quite known the truth of what I've been through or the things that I've done. I'm no longer a teenybopper idol," he said.

The story of the innocent young pop star whose life was nearly destroyed by the older woman was the stuff of tabloid headlines. "I felt like a black-widow spider," Victoria was quoted as saying. "I know how it looks from the outside, especially as I didn't come forward. Everybody just assumed I split with Andy. But I didn't want to go into it at the time, and that is something I will have to live with. There is no point in defending or explaining what actually happened, but it would be unfair to say it was my choice to end the relationship. What I know is that I tried everything that I was capable of, that I think any human being would be capable of in an effort to rescue someone that you love very much. And, there came a point in time, when I had to face the fact that I could go on trying to rescue Andy and sacrifice my own life, or I had to stand apart and hope that he would, that he would be able to help himself."

Understandably bitter after the break-up, Andy claimed that Victoria's obsession with her age and appearance indirectly led her to her second husband. "We went to this plastic surgeon, Dr Harry Glassman," he said. "I waited in his office while the surgery was being done. I used to joke with her about her refusal to come out of her darkened bedroom for two weeks after the operation and she'd get hysterical. She wouldn't let anybody in the room except me. She's dead scared of getting old. That was her big problem."

In 1985, he further told interviewer Bob Durant, "I want to state that I am very happy for her marriage now, and we have made amends as I have congratulated her and wish her all the happiness in the future, but Victoria is a woman that has done everything that it would take to get where she is today. She has done it all, believe me. She had a drug problem when I met her, she was an alcoholic, and a coke problem and I was off it. Just because of sexual things and other things, we got back onto it together and that got me heavily back into it . . . and then we stopped. When we really fell in love, we agreed to stop everything, because we didn't like each other on drugs. At the very end of it all, after about 15 months or something, we just started arguing, I don't think we were meant to be. She is a very seductive woman . . . very few men can resist her . . . But I will say that she took me basically back to it . . . but I wish her all the best."

33

MEANINGFUL SONGS
(IN VERY HIGH VOICES)

AFTER THE GRUELLING schedule of The Bee Gees' *Spirits Having Flown* tour, 1980 marked the beginning of an emphasis on projects outside the confines of the group. "Up until then," explained Barry, "we'd always used our own voices as the instruments for our songs and it's like switching instruments. Suddenly you can stretch the songs, you can make them do other things because it's someone else."

There were also the awards to collect, a tribute to the group's resurgence in popularity. At the seventh annual American Music Awards, The Bee Gees took away the trophies for Favourite Band, Duo or Group in the Pop/Rock category and Favourite Album in the Pop/Rock categories for both. The group also made recordings and filmed commercials for TDK Japan.

As he had been at the end of the previous decade, Robin was the first to break away from The Bee Gees' activities in late 1979 by working with Blue Weaver to produce the *Sunrise* album for soul singer, Jimmy Ruffin. "I've known Jimmy for years, and one day he simply phoned me up and asked if I would like to produce some tracks for him," Robin explained. "I said yes, and it all evolved from there."

"I met Robin Gibb years ago – a really nice person, he was even more reclusive than I, so we got on well," Jimmy recalled. "We talked a lot about working together then suddenly with *Saturday Night Fever* and all the other stuff, they became so hot [that] we couldn't work together until 1979. So we made an album and almost immediately the record company went out of business."

They began with the two songs from The Bee Gees' recording sessions, 'Where Do I Go' and 'Nobody'. Of the latter, Blue said, "It was written during the *Spirits* time but rejected. That was a Bee Gees' backing track and I used it." Robin reworked the lyrics, and 'Nobody' became 'Forever'. Jimmy also recorded a soulful version of the first Gibb/Weaver collaboration, 'Songbird'.

A very different and almost country number was 'Where Do I Go?', written by all four Gibb brothers for *Spirits Having Flown*. For the *Sunrise* album, it became a duet with Jimmy and Marcy Levy★, then best known as Eric Clapton's backing vocalist and the co-writer of his hit, 'Lay Down Sally'.

Blue and Robin collaborated on the remainder of the songs, including the first single. "The original lyric that Robin came up with for 'Hold On (To My Love)' was, 'I can't laugh, I can't cry'," Blue recalled. The single was released in February on both sides of the Atlantic and reached number seven in the UK and number 10 in the US. The single, however, failed to showcase Jimmy's voice. A disco number, the track was not representative of the album. On the other hand, almost nothing would have been representative, as the producers handed Jimmy quite a variety of fare.

Robin's R&B ballad style all the way back to 'I Can't See Nobody' was modelled after singers like Jimmy, and his rougher voice adds a warmth to these songs.

The most successful song was 'Searchin'', a fine piano melody by Blue in the tradition of his songs with Barry, married in this case to Robin's bluesy "if I could live my life over again" lyrics. 'Two People' and 'Changin' Me' owe a lot to Jimmy's vocals to be convincing but they work.

The album followed in May. The cover photo appears to be from Miami, where part of the album was recorded. The earlier songs were recorded at a studio in Syosset, not far from Robin's house on Long Island, where both he and Blue lived at the time. Another single, 'Night Of Love', was released but failed to reach the charts.

Following their work with Jimmy Ruffin, Robin and Blue collaborated on a song for the soundtrack of the RSO movie *Times Square*, and Blue was credited with composing the film score. If Stigwood was hoping for a repeat of the success of *Saturday Night Fever* with this film, he was disappointed. Robin recorded their composition, 'Help Me!' as a duet with Marcy Levy, which featured in the end credits of the film. The pair recorded a video for the song, which was released as a single, but it reached only number 50 on *Billboard*'s Hot 100 and failed to chart at all in Britain.

They also composed another song, 'Touch Me', originally written for fellow RSO recording artist Linda Clifford, which Robin convinced Marcy to demo, against her better judgement, according to Blue. "I don't think she sang those lyrics willingly," he said. Robin's suggestive words like "Touch Me . . . hold me there . . . feel me there . . ." proved to be a little too hot to handle, and the track never went beyond that initial working demo stage.

Maurice and his family had returned to their home for a quiet Christmas, but in late December, he was admitted to a private London clinic.

On his release two weeks later, he was met by Yvonne and the couple's

★ Born Marcella Levy in Detroit, Michigan, she went on to study and eventually teach drama at the Lee Strasberg Institute in Los Angeles, while continuing as a songwriter for such artists as Chaka Khan and Al Jarreau. She moved to London in 1989, and, adopting her birthplace as her new surname, came to fame with Siobhan Fahey in the duo, Shakespear's Sister, as Marcella Detroit, the name she uses to this date as a solo artist.

four-year-old son Adam. While in light of subsequent revelations, it might be assumed that he was receiving treatment for alcoholism, Maurice insisted at the time, "There was nothing seriously wrong with me. I was just shattered from a heavy concert and recording schedule. My doctor thought it would be a good idea for me to get away from it all. Now I feel on top of the world."

Back in good spirits, Maurice began composing incidental music, which he described as "a sort of *Star Wars* come *Love Story*, for the soundtrack for *The Geller Effect*, a proposed RSO film based on psychic spoon-bender, Uri Geller, which would ultimately be shelved. When this project fell through, he turned his hand to an instrumental album, tentatively titled *Strings And Things*.

★ ★ ★

Barry had by far the highest profile of the group – producing Barbra Streisand's album. Maurice recalled that The Bee Gees were asked which artist they would most like to produce. "We said, 'Barbra Streisand.' . . . Then, about a week later, Charles [Koppelman] called and said 'I heard in the papers that you'd love to do Barbra.' So this is how the Barbra situation came about. She said she was very interested."

Barry claimed she had been his favourite singer ever since he first heard her perform 'People' and raved, "She's a thoroughbred. I mean, she's been around as long as any artist has been around. She's the lady, in fact, who sang the demo for 'Our Day Will Come' which Ruby & The Romantics sang eventually. She's always regretted the fact that she never got to make the record at all on the album for her. She's been through so many patches where she's never sold records at all, not unlike ourselves, and seems to just come out and surface again at the time that's right for her, and everyone falls in love with her again."

Although it has come to be seen as Barry's project, the idea actually had begun as a group concept. Koppelman suggested a few songs to The Bee Gees. They listened to them and felt they could do better.

"We then submitted five of our own songs," Barry recalled. "Barbra liked them and asked us to write five more . . . We set out to make the great Streisand LP that she never made." While Maurice was hospitalised, Barry and Robin wrote 'Woman In Love', 'Run Wild', 'Promises' and 'Life Story'.

'Guilty' was written with Robin and Maurice, the only three-way collaboration of the LP. "When we wrote that stuff for Streisand," Maurice explained, "we knew what her voice was, so we heard it in our head, so could you imagine her singing something like . . . this? And we'd go into the writing. And we'd use her voice as the instrument to interpret the song . . ."

Once the decision was made, the songs seemed to appear out of nowhere. "I'm pretty sure when we did the Streisand album, [Barry] wrote and demo'd the whole album in a week," Albhy Galuten marvelled. "Well, maybe not the demos, but a week's worth of writing, for 10 or 12 songs, a few of them which became smashes. I think the normal process would be

501

about half a day to write a song, which is not that far away from most people. The 80 per cent on the creative stuff happens almost instantly, like it would form in his head, and the rest would be details."

In the process of writing the songs, Barry said, "[Barbra] became the adventure. I knew what she was capable of doing. I mean, if you write the script for an actor, you know what the spectrum of the actor is, what the actor can do, so you can write scenes that you would not write for another actor. So in this case, this is what happened with Barbra Streisand. I was able to almost write a screenplay for her, to make her do something."

There were still some early concerns. "I'd heard about the time 'Evergreen' was written and how Paul Williams was sent backwards and forwards to write lyrics — and I was afraid that was going to happen to me," Barry confessed. "But the wonderful thing is, it never did. Apart from the fact that Barbra's a total professional, she's a very nice lady. You can't go wrong with an artist like that."

Although there were no altercations, Barbra was not afraid to speak her mind when she had concerns. "She questioned the line, 'It's a right I defend/Over and over again'," Barry recalled. "At first she felt that it was a little bit liberationist; that it might be a little too strong for a pop song." She allowed herself to be convinced, and the line stayed.

According to one industry insider, "Streisand's group spoke to Stigwood, and all was very jolly until they asked him for a cut of the publishing. But Stigwood wouldn't give up one lousy E-flat to them. Not this tycoon. In making deals and pulling in money he was a pro; he could outwit the best of them."

Not only did Robert Stigwood keep the publishing rights, he was said to have asked for three-quarters of the CBS advance and royalties, a deal which he saw as only fair since Streisand was only one voice and there were three Bee Gees. Rumour has it that Streisand replied, "But they all sound alike. How much for just one?"

It was finally agreed that Barry would perform and co-produce the LP with Karl Richardson and Albhy Galuten. He would receive half the royalties on the duets with the full producer's fee and royalty for each record and tape sold. It was said that Stigwood later billed Barbra Streisand for the use of Barry's face and body on the album cover, but she refused to pay.

Robin recalled that the album was intended as a change of styles for the singer. "She wanted to make an album that was a popular music album as opposed to Broadway orientated songs that she had been used to doing," he explained. "She wanted to do a contemporary album of songs that would be heard generally on Top 40 radio."

"She wasn't into doing live performances at that point," Barry added. "She wanted to make an album and she wanted to make it very contemporary, and I suppose we were the most contemporary people around at that point. So she aimed right at us and we did the project."

Initially, Barry admitted to some reservations about working with the

502

diva. "Only because I'd heard all those stories about Barbra – that's she's a tough lady to work with. People feel that she comes on very strong, that you'll get all kinds of arguments from her. That's the rumour around the business, and Barbra's heard it herself.

"I wasn't going to do the album at one point. I was an absolute nervous wreck before we started . . . And she is this enormous star. That's got to intimidate anyone. I didn't want to work with her at first, but my wife told me she'd divorce me if I didn't!"

As Albhy recalled it, "Barry just wanted to work with Streisand. It was an incredible opportunity . . . I've come to know her and we've had a good relationship. I worked on a record for her after that on my own."

Charles Koppelman, the president of the New York based Entertainment Company, which produced the four previous Barbra Streisand albums, admitted, "This project could have been a disaster. You're dealing with a lot of egos, mine included. And this wasn't one song, it was an entire album. But it went much smoother than any of us anticipated."

Although Barry admitted, "We treaded on eggs until we actually got to know one another," in the end, he said, "I have to say she was extremely pleasant to work with, and this is not just show business talk. She seemed to come across as an absolute lady."

Charles Koppelman credits Barry's ease in the role of producer as one of the reasons that everything went so smoothly. "If he'd walked in as 'singer-star' as opposed to producer, we could have had difficulties," he explained.

But the credit must be shared by his co-producers, Albhy and Karl. "The record was pretty incredible," Albhy enthused. "We did the demos, the way we do, with the drum machine and whatever, and then we hired a band and made a real record. We had never done that before. The Streisand demos are the first ones."

Albhy recalled an early encounter with the singer. "I went to her house in Malibu – it was full of Tiffany stuff. I think this was the first time we met . . . She asked Barry what he'd like to drink, and he said, 'I'd love a cup of tea.' She said, 'Oh, that sounds good, I'll have one too.' And in her style . . . a New York cup of tea . . . she's like, 'Oh, just bring one teabag and we can share it.' "

It was obviously a conciliatory gesture on Barbra's part, but for Albhy, knowing Barry's obsession with the perfect cup of tea, the moment was hysterical. "Barry, of course, would be too shy to say anything," he laughed. "I don't know how much you know about Barry's tea ritual, but, I mean, they had a road case called scientific instruments that was full of tea-making gear . . . Electric kettles so you don't burn the water, you pour boiling water over a tea bag . . . the tea doesn't taste right if you don't do that. So here's Barry, tea being his ritual, and sharing it, doing it like you're at Nedick's★, they'd bring you two glasses of hot water and a tea bag to share.

★ A chain of New York lunch counters.

503

"It was very funny. Being a New York Jew, I can totally understand, and knowing Barry very well, I can totally see these are two universes, and absolutely no way to translate!"

Shared teabags aside, the working relationship soon blossomed.

The demos were made with Barry singing the pilot vocals. Although the task was made easier by his facility with falsetto, differences between Barry's style of singing and Barbra's had to be overcome. "Barbra's vocal ability is really a different style," Albhy explained. "She didn't listen to R&B music, she didn't listen to rhythmic music, so she has . . . long time instead of short time; her sense of time is long phrasing. In Broadway theatre, great singers can do that . . . The other thing is pitch. Barry liked, if you were singing in E flat, he doesn't *slide* into notes, except very rarely on purpose, he hits it. To him, people who slide into notes are like correcting, like you start low and you get up to there. For Barbra, it's a style, and her pitch ends up being quite good, but she *floats* into notes, again, as a stylistic thing . . ." As Barry had said, it was definitely writing for a different instrument.

The results were incredible, according to Charles Koppelman. "I was always a Barry Gibb fan from way back," he said. "When we talked about the collaboration, the idea was to go back to the old Barry Gibb songwriter of years back and all those wonderful old songs: 'To Love Somebody' and 'Massachusetts' and some great melodies.

"When I first heard Barry's demos, I was blown away. I said to myself, 'Holy mackerel, I sure hope Barbra will make me forget I ever heard Barry singing these songs.' Well, that concern lasted about two minutes, until the first time Barbra opened her mouth to sing."

"Barbra sings something once and it's *magic*," Barry raved. "You can't cut into it or mess with it because each time she sings it's good. We could tell about halfway through that we had something very different than she'd been doing and that it could be an extremely big album."

Koppelman agreed. "As the album progressed, it became more and more a collective effort between Barbra and Barry. The whole thing kind of evolved into a real team involvement."

The involvement carried on after working hours as well. Tom Kennedy recalled a pleasant evening at Barbra's ranch home with some unexpected guests. "She was really very nice and she invited us to dinner," he said. "I went along with Barry and Lynda, and afterwards we were just sitting around making small talk and rats started running around. Barry was about to say something, and I just nudged him. So when we were in the car on the way home, Barry said to Lynda, 'Did you see the rats?' She said, 'What rats?' and he said, 'There were rats running along the wall – *he* saw them!' and I said 'Yeah, there were rats walking along the wall.' She said, 'Why didn't you say something?' I said, '*I'm* not going to tell Barbra Streisand she's got rats – she's one of the biggest stars in the world! You can't tell her she's got rats – it would have ruined the evening!' We just laughed about it . . . She was a lot of fun, and Jon Peters was very nice, too."

According to composer Mickey Leonard, Jon Peters and Charles Koppelman kept the world at bay during the recording sessions. "They had a guard posted outside the door to the studio," he recalled. "I ran into Barbra and Koppelman in the parking lot one day. She was wonderful, very friendly. She mentioned a new song of mine that she had heard, but then Koppelman got nervous. She wanted to talk, but he said, 'Oh, Barry's waiting and he'll be angry.' So he led her away. It was as if he was afraid I'd give her some material without his sanction. To me that kind of behaviour is counterproductive, counter-creative, counter-*everything*."

The cover design for *Guilty* had been planned almost from the start. Tony Lane from Columbia Records had decided that Barbra should be photographed in the studio, with a saint on one shoulder and a devil on the other.

Mario Casilli, a Hollywood photographer who had photographed Streisand for her *Playboy* cover and for her *Wet* LP, arrived at one of the recording sessions to take a few shots of the work in progress. "I wasn't hired to shoot the cover . . . So when I got to the session I took some test shots, with no concept at all in mind," he explained. "They were just production shots of her with Barry, wearing a white blouse and white slacks. She looked at the shots and said, 'Let's do more of these.'"

Tony Lane, realising that this was a perfect opportunity, said, "I figured we better do something . . . With Barbra in those days, you had to take advantage of whatever time you were given. Mario sent one of his assistants out for some white background paper. We decided to set up part of the recording studio as a photo studio. A messenger was sent over to Barry's hotel to get his white shirt and slacks. It was rather quick and was the most offhand way of trying to do a cover."

"There was no pressure from Barbra, from anyone," Casilli said. "When you're shooting for a cover, which we weren't; well, that's a tougher situation. We shot for about an hour. It was fun. Sometimes you're lucky enough to ride on a wave. Something happens and you've got your camera going."

Casilli went out to Barbra's ranch with the processed slides from the photo session and his projector. Barbra was delighted with the results.

He recalled that she told him, "These photographs are so flattering to me. How the hell did you do that?"

He quickly responded, "Barbra, I've got to do something well. I can't sing!"

Any thought of saints or devils was immediately set aside, and the "production shots" became the sleeve, with a generous set of the photos for the gatefold cover inside and out. The photos led to some speculation as to how close the pair had actually become, but Barry took pains to set the record straight. "My whole life revolves around my family. My wife Lynda and I have been married for 10 years and it gets better every year. She is just as beautiful as when I first met her. Barbra and I are both extremely happily married, she in her way to Jon. Our whole relationship was on a business level, although I'm happy to be as close to Barbra as I am."

In total, Barbra recorded 11 Gibb compositions. Nine of the tracks appeared on the album. 'Secrets', perhaps too similar to 'Woman In Love' to use, and 'Carried Away' were later rejected but were released by Elaine Paige and Olivia Newton-John respectively. Barry, Albhy and Karl also produced Barbra singing Chuck Berry's 'Kansas City' and The Beatles' 'Lady Madonna', but these were also dropped from the final LP.

In the 1985 biography, *Barbra Streisand, The Woman, The Myth, The Music*, one engineer on the project gave his views about the evolution of Barry and Barbra's duet of 'What Kind Of Fool'. "They kept overdubbing on that song and they still had a problem," he alleged. "Barbra's performance was so pure, so good – too good, in fact. She made Barry sound like an intrusion. She didn't need his voice or any other voice on the song. Her advisors kept telling her, 'Do it alone, drop Barry.' But she wouldn't. It was written as a duet, and the guy only had one other song to sing on the album, so she insisted that he stay with her. They must have overdubbed the thing 20 times in Los Angeles, and it was eventually finished at Media Sound in New York."

But Albhy Galuten's memory of events differs. "The other very interesting, amazing thing that I remember about that . . . I think this is correct, the duets were done after the fact. This record was put together by Charlie Koppelman – he was the executive producer . . . It was Barry's idea to do the record, but it was Charlie's idea that they should do some duets. Charlie's probably all along thinking, 'Barry's a hot property, we should do some duets, it'll make the record sell.' None of the songs were originally planned as duets, so we ended up trying to figure out how to turn two songs into duets. Well, we converted the songs to duets *after* Barbra was gone. She had already come and sung."

On 'What Kind Of Fool', a song written at the piano in Albhy's house when Barry and Lynda had come to see his newborn son Jason, Albhy recalled that the complicated changes to make it a duet caused problems with the sound of the drums. Steve Gadd played drums on the bridge, but for the main part of the song, the drummer credited was a certain Bernard Lupe.

"The track never really felt right, so we ended up using our famous drum loop," Albhy explained, referring to the tape loop from *Saturday Night Fever*. "It's very quiet. It was not an important part; it was meant to be just keeping time."

Barry and Albhy chose the pieces, but it fell to Karl to put them together without any tell-tale noise on the tape. "The pitch changes and the meter changes were so complicated that while we were doing it in the studio, it took Karl at least a hundred hours separately just to perform the punches so they wouldn't click and pop."

Barry would later say, "The album represented six months work for me, and two weeks for Barbra," but he modestly added, "I'd have to say at least 80 per cent of the success of the record belongs to her."

All the hard work paid off – the result was an album which would produce three American Top 10 singles over the following nine months.

The initial set of songs by Barry and Robin included the lead-off single

'Woman In Love', a verse-chorus ballad "in the Russian modalities" as the New York *Times* reviewer put it. Barbra's voice rides up and down on the melody, sustaining the long notes in the chorus, and it was a quick hit. The quiet reuse of the 'Stayin' Alive' drum loop may have given it a subconscious familiarity. Many people think Barry sings the high backing but he does not; it is girl singers on this song. Released in August, 'Woman In Love' topped the charts in Britain, Australia and the United States and was a Top Five hit in Norway.

The two duets by Barry and Barbra became the second and third singles, partly to capitalise on the collaboration, but mainly on the merits. 'Guilty', the only song on the album written by all three Gibb brothers, is set to an island beat, with Barbra and Barry soloing the first and second verses, and together in the choruses. Barry sings the back-up, therefore backing his own lead vocal in places. The single was released in October, reaching number three in the US, but only achieving number 34 in the UK.

The third single, 'What Kind Of Fool', is a more sophisticated song by Barry and Albhy with some nice interplay between the two voices singing solo and together. Barry uses both natural voice and falsetto, and Barbra goes from quiet control at the start to her loudest stage voice, which could have overwhelmed Barry's voice but never does. 'What Kind Of Fool' was released in January, reaching the number 10 spot in the US but failing to place in Britain.

A fourth single was tried, 'Promises' by Barry and Robin, the most up-tempo song of the nine on the album. Side one ends with the traditional song that is hard to follow, 'The Love Inside', a slow piano song by Barry that Barbra sings beautifully and with great feeling. The only song not written specifically for the project, it dates from the *Spirits Having Flown* period when it was given a copyright by all four Gibb brothers, but must have been almost entirely Barry's song from the start as indicated in the revised credit.

"The album itself was the biggest album she'd ever had, as a studio album," Maurice said. "It sold in countries where she couldn't sell before . . . so it really broke a lot of ground for her." *Guilty* reached number one in 15 different countries, including Russia. With sales of over eight million, the profits from the album carried Columbia Records over its recession slump.

With that sort of success, Barry speculated on future collaborations. "I'm pretty sure we could follow it with an even better album because we know each other better," he said.

Although Charles Koppelman and Jon Peters were equally willing, "Barbra does not like to repeat herself" was the official final word at that time. Through the years since then, the possibility has been bandied about, but to date, there has been no firm commitment.

★   ★   ★

Early in 1980, Maurice entered a private clinic in California seeking treatment for his alcoholism, but the recurrence of an old back problem caused a

507

necessary hiatus. "He was actually in a clinic for addiction in Santa Barbara, and Yvonne refused to go with him, so I went as his family member," Tom Kennedy explained. "His back went out, and he wasn't even allowed pain-killers. They actually thought it might be . . . a ploy to get some sort of medicine . . . It got so bad, he was like an old man . . ."

The doctors' examination proved that this was no mere chicanery and that Maurice would need to have a disc removed. Obviously, the surgery could not be carried out without the use of painkillers so he left the programme at Pinecrest Hospital, and Maurice and Tom flew back to Miami. Maurice had initial concerns about the risks of the surgery, fearing that he would never walk again, but the doctors reassured him.

"He had the operation in Santa Barbara, and true to their word, they had him up the same day," Tom recalled. "He did go back into the programme, and Yvonne went there with him."

Barry's back injury would come later, occurring during a friendly tennis match with the group's personal manager, Dick Ashby. Like Maurice, Barry had long suffered with back pain, the legacy of various accidents in his youth, but he managed to get along with only pain-killing injections.

Maurice had barely recovered from the surgery when The Bee Gees received a staggering professional blow. Ronald H. Selle, an amateur song-writer from Illinois, filed a lawsuit against the group accusing them of steal-ing his tune, 'Let It End' for 'How Deep Is Your Love'.

Selle claimed that in May 1978, he was out raking his lawn when a neigh-bour's son put on the *Saturday Night Fever* soundtrack. "I heard what was *my* music," he alleged. Hiring lawyer Allen Engerman, he filed suit against The Bee Gees, Paramount Pictures and PolyGram.

For the brothers, who have always considered themselves songwriters before anything else, it was probably the most painful accusation anyone could make about them. They would have to live with the allegations for the next four years.

⋆   ⋆   ⋆

Robin's 12-year marriage was rapidly becoming a casualty of the group's resurgence between 1975 and 1979. The marriage was the longest running of the three brothers, but judging by various statements made on behalf of both parties, it was apparent the relationship was finally on the rocks. The first hint that something might be amiss had come in 1978 when Robin said, "Molly wants to stay at home and won't travel around, so there's some tension. But she's a human being too. I don't own her."

On May 22, 1980, Molly told reporters, "I have hardly seen Robin for the past three years, and I have sadly come to the conclusion that our mar-riage is over. There is no one else involved, but there comes a point when a woman has to say she has had enough. I have filed for divorce and the papers are due to be served tomorrow.

"The more successful the group became, the less I saw of Robin," she added. "It's really due to the pressures of the pop business and the length of time Robin is now away. When we married, Robin was not such a big star and life was easier to manage."

Robin was not immediately available for contact, but The Bee Gees' lawyer, Michael Eaton, said on his behalf, "I know Robin does not want the marriage dissolved. He is in Britain, but I have not been able to contact him."

Tom Kennedy said sympathetically, "Molly's a nice person. Down to earth would be the best way to describe her. She's done a very good job of bringing up Robin's children. A forthright lady, who would call a spade a spade . . . She was a strong-willed person, obviously, and I think she was what Robin needed at the time . . ."

Acknowledging the problems of the long distance marriage they had maintained for so many years, he added, "Of course, he *was* away a lot of the time, and when they had the children, she brought them up on her own . . . The discipline came from Molly . . . because Robin would spoil them because he didn't see them all that often. There were times when she was living in [England] and he was a tax exile. It was a difficult existence."

While Molly maintained, "I do not want to air private grievances in public and I hope everyone will respect our wish for privacy through this difficult time," Robin countered, "I think her announcement is a little premature. We are still talking, and it is too soon to say if we are heading for a divorce."

A close family friend revealed, "This hit Robin like a hammer blow. He would do anything to get back with Molly. He misses the kids very much. If Molly names her terms, Robin is so anxious to get back with her that he'd accept them."

But Molly remained resolute. There would be no reconciliation.

★   ★   ★

As if Robin's personal problems weren't enough, The Bee Gees suddenly found themselves at loggerheads with Robert Stigwood. The ugly and – as it turned out – largely unnecessary confrontation was fought out in public in an unseemly manner and resulted in claims and counter claims running into hundreds of millions of dollars. The spark that lit this particular inferno was RSO's claim that Barry could not undertake the Barbra Streisand project without the company's direct consent. The dictatorial tone did not sit well with the brothers. On October 2, after more than 13 years under contract to Stigwood, The Bee Gees sued for release from all their ties with Stigwood, charging that he had controlled virtually every aspect of their professional lives leading to a conflict of interests as their personal manager as well as head of their record company and music publishing company, he had deliberately mismanaged the group to his own advantage and had withheld millions of dollars in royalties.

The Bee Gees announced they were suing Stigwood individually, the Robert Stigwood Organisation, the Robert Stigwood Group of Companies and RSO Records and seeking termination of their recording contract with RSO Records. The Bee Gees were seeking $75 million from Stigwood, $75 million from the PolyGram Group (which owned half of the Stigwood Group Companies), $50 million in punitive damages, millions more in interest and back royalties, the return of all The Bee Gees' master recordings and copyrights, and the cancellation of all their "many and tangled contracts" with Stigwood.

Robert responded by issuing the following statement: "I am angry, dismayed, revolted. I will fight this attack on my integrity. I have instructed counsel to see that the truth is told and that those responsible for this travesty are made to account for their misconduct." He remained sequestered in his Bermuda home.

The allegations rocked the music world. The brothers were depicted as ingrates, biting the hand which had fed them for so many years. Gershon labelled the lawsuit "revolting" and countered, "What you're dealing with is a bunch of guys who are trying to renegotiate their contracts through the press. The Bee Gees have reached a certain point in their careers, and they're trying to capitalise on it, and they're frustrated because, for the last year and a half, Robert has refused to renegotiate. I don't believe that The Bee Gees believe in this lawsuit. Barry Gibb looked me in the eye and said, 'We have to start with a high number, Freddie, so we can renegotiate down to a new deal.' I know that Robin and Maurice told Robert Stigwood that they'd never read or seen these papers."

Gershon further declared that Stigwood had never discouraged the Gibbs from working on outside projects, and indeed, had been instrumental in negotiating the deal for Barry's collaboration with Barbra Streisand.

Robert Stigwood remained in Bermuda, but Freddie Gershon insisted that he would not go down without a fight. "Robert has a Victorian sense of morality," he explained. "He will see to it that this goes on and on until it's proven publicly and clearly that he has done no wrong."

RSO Records president Al Coury also leapt to Robert's defence, outraged at what he saw as "a betrayal of Stigwood, in light of the relationship he has had with the group for the past 20 years."

It wasn't just blind devotion to his leader. Coury had felt in the past that Stigwood's generosity to the group had compromised his position as head of the company. Coury had even threatened to resign over what he felt were unreasonable demands made by The Bee Gees relating to songs on the *Saturday Night Fever* soundtrack. Due to Stigwood's friendship with the boys, he had insisted that the record company spend far beyond what might be considered the normal budget for marketing, such as deluxe advertising campaigns, lavish album packaging and extraordinary special promotions for The Bee Gees' product, to the detriment of the company.

"The group has made more than $56 million over the last five years while the record company has made less than half that amount," Coury added. "If you took the cumulative profits of our company from its inception, I could show you that The Bee Gees have earned more than twice as much money as the entire record company. I can't *possibly* pay them any more money. If I gave them any more money, I'd put my company out of business."

On October 27, Robert Stigwood struck back, filing a $310 million suit against The Bee Gees in the New York Supreme Court. In it, he claimed that the Gibb brothers had libelled him. He also accused them of extortion and breach of contract, stating that he had "transformed the Gibbs from penniless youths into multi-millionaires." An RSO spokesman stated, "Relations between us and The Bee Gees are best described as frozen."

★   ★   ★

In Miami, Yvonne gave birth to a daughter on July 2, 1980, with Maurice again by her side. The new arrival was named Samantha Amanda, and the entire family was delighted. Maurice revealed that four-year-old Adam had taken a proprietary interest in his little sister, saying, "He thinks it's *his* baby!"

Meanwhile, Barry applied to the Miami Beach zoning officials for permission to put up a nine foot high fence around his property following a spate of intrusions into his family's privacy.

In September, Maurice became the first – and to date only – traveller to be put off a Concorde flight. After the rigorous "drying-out" programme at Pinecrest Hospital, and commenting, "The strongest drink I touch now is a Pepsi, but I guess I'll probably have that image of being a lush for quite some time," he had fallen back off the wagon. Arriving at Heathrow Airport over an hour and a half before the flight was due to depart, he waited in the Concorde departure lounge, where free food and drink are served. Yvonne, upset and afraid that he was in no fit condition for the journey, tried to curtail his drinking but eventually gave up the battle. Taking the children with her, she returned to the couple's Surrey home. Maurice boarded the plane, bound from Heathrow to Washington DC, without her. The supersonic aircraft was ready for take-off, when the captain, judging Maurice "unsuitable for travel", radioed for steps to be brought to the jet. He was carried off the plane and escorted back to the departure lounge.

After a 90-minute wait in the lounge, he was taken away in a white estate car to a hotel, where the party continued. Maurice was eventually tracked down by a member of The Bee Gees' crew and duly escorted home.

Later that month, all four Gibb brothers were in Miami for the wedding of Candi Marshall and Karl Richardson.

The transformation of the warehouse had been completed at the start of year, and Middle Ear Recording Studio was ready for business. Tom Kennedy, The Bee Gees' road manager, now took over the management of the studio. The new studio gave the group the freedom to record on their own terms, without having to work around Criteria's busy schedule. Although the cost of converting the studio was high, Tom put it into perspective when he pointed out, "I think our last album at Criteria cost $700,000 . . ."

The group began work on their next album, tentatively titled *Sanctuary*, with the usual band of Alan Kendall, Blue Weaver and Dennis Bryon. The sessions soon broke down for reasons the Gibbs have never made public, and Dick Ashby informed the three musicians that their services were no longer required. The recording of the album would be completed with session musicians.

"We were there one day and gone the next," Blue recalled.

"Well, it happened just like that, but we all knew it was coming because we weren't producing anything," he acknowledged. "It was stale, nothing was happening, we were in the studio for six months or something . . . We got complacent – we *all* just got complacent . . . We weren't hungry, the incentive wasn't there anymore."

Although Blue admitted, "I think you're a bit hurt at first that the split is there." He said that he realised, "It had to happen at some point . . . I don't blame them, I blame myself. It was my fault, it wasn't their fault – I wasn't putting in as much as I did in the beginning; *none* of us were, really, if they were completely honest with themselves.

"The pressure was on us because we were trying to create things using computers and things . . . We were trying to create songs in other ways as well, to be a bit different . . . We turned more to technology and that was wrong."

Searching for new ideas for what turned out to be the *Living Eyes* album, the group turned to the Fairlight synthesizer and the synclavier as a new focus. "Albhy sort of took over the synclavier part and I got into the Fairlight," Blue explained. "I think we were trying to make computer music rather than make real music . . . We were spending so much time on technology . . ."

Albhy Galuten verified the problems that arose from over reliance on computer technology. One of the drummers credited on the LP was Solly Noid. "Seth Synder, an engineer who built studios down there, developed a solenoid drum machine that we had out in the maintenance area. The drums themselves were real, but the trigger to play it, rather than a human, was an electronic impulse.

"What technology has enabled people to do is to infinitely save and try again. There's no need for this emotional commitment that was required to get things done. We could fix anything, so you could make stuff perfect, and making things perfect doesn't make it soulful and emotional," Albhy added.

Blue is philosophical about the end of The Bee Gees' band. "I think it had run its course, I don't think *I* was particularly good for The Bee Gees during that period – I wasn't coming up with anything new . . . I don't think Albhy was a particularly good influence at that time . . . I'm not putting the blame on Albhy . . ."

Albhy agreed with Blue's perspective on the times. The *Living Eyes* album is not one he looks back on with great affection. "There was a tremendous fear . . . that we had fallen into a rut, and I felt strongly on *Living Eyes* that it was time to change. When we started working on [it] and it was not being fun . . .

I remember sitting around with my friends at the time . . . and saying, 'It's just not working and I think that I'm going to leave.'

"The problem was we had a formula that worked, but the formula was not the reason for success, the formula was the means."

Blue's own thoughts echoed Albhy's. "I most probably should have gone off and done something else, but just being lazy, just going along day to day with what we were doing . . . I came back to England," he recalled, "and most probably that gave them the breathing space to sit down and say, 'We're going nowhere – what are we gonna do? Okay, well, we've gotta do something as radical as what we did in 1975 . . .'

"That whole process of the *Living Eyes* album . . . if you consider what had just been done, myself and Robin had done Jimmy Ruffin, and we were really hyped up on that, they'd done Barbra Streisand . . . The process of making a new album after *Spirits Having Flown* was very difficult.

"If you think of all the things that they'd done, how can you top that, how can you actually make things better? We'd done everything that you could possibly do at that stage," Blue said, "and everything reached such highs that it was hard to go from there."

★   ★   ★

On January 10, 1981, Barry and Lynda's third son, Travis Ryan, was born nearly two months prematurely, weighing four pounds and five ounces. His anxious parents waited as he spent the first seven weeks of his life in an incubator.

Finally, the day came when they were allowed to take their youngest son home, but the struggle wasn't over. Within days, little Travis had contracted pneumonia and returned to Variety Children's Hospital in South Miami.

"Our ordeal started all over again," Barry said. "Pneumonia is bad enough for anybody, but for a premature baby, it's usually fatal. It was an experience Lynda and I just don't want to go through again – but it hasn't put us off having more children."

After Travis had recovered, Barry, Robin and Maurice paid a surprise visit to the hospital, with photographer Bob Sherman in tow, to spend an hour and a half talking to the 20 young people in the adolescent psychiatric unit and signing autographs.

Nearly a week after the visit, the Miami *Herald* reported that the visit had produced a "miracle cure" in an 11-year-old girl who had been virtually crippled by a brain inflammation. "The prognosis for her was very bad," declared the hospital publicist, "but now the doctors say the possibilities for her recovery are limitless."

Barry was once again touted for a starring role in a film, this time, *A Face In The Crowd*, the story of a pop star who finds success but loses everyone important to him as it all goes to his head.

On February 25, the twenty-third annual Grammy Awards were held in New York City's Radio City Music Hall, hosted by Paul Simon. Barry and

Robin were the only composers not to perform their nominated song, 'Woman In Love', in the Best Song category. The track didn't win, but Barbra Streisand and Barry did collect the award for Best Pop Performance by a duo or group for 'Guilty'.

In May, 'Woman In Love' was the winner in the Best Song Musically or Lyrically category at the twenty-sixth annual Ivor Novello Awards in Britain.

Whether or not there was any connection to the litigation involving The Bee Gees and Robert Stigwood, it was announced that RSO Records had fired about 80 per cent of its employees, reducing its American staff from about 60 to 12.

Al Coury admitted, "The chances of us having another *Saturday Night Fever* or Bee Gees aren't good these days so we have to approach things differently than we did five years ago, or even 20 minutes ago. It didn't make sense to have a big field staff pushing just a few records."

After similar cutbacks the previous year, Casablanca, Phonogram/Mercury and Polydor Records had all been absorbed by PolyGram Records, which also distributed RSO Records, leading to speculation that Robert Stigwood was also planning to sell out to the parent company.

Coury explained, "Because we're owned by one person, we've always had the ability to expand or contract to meet conditions." He added that he was encouraged by Robert Stigwood's plans to settle his differences with The Bee Gees, re-sign Eric Clapton to the company and to bring out more soundtracks.

"If he decides he wants to get out of the record industry, he could very easily sell the company to PolyGram," he added. "But there's been every indication that he plans on staying in this business."

That month saw the settlement out of court of the lawsuits between Robert Stigwood and The Bee Gees. Apart from the escalating costs of the legal battle, the brothers were anxious to pursue a settlement with Stigwood rather than continue the fight. Sidelining their American attorneys, they re-engaged Michael Eaton, who had represented them as their solicitor in the early Seventies, and who had only recently returned to private practice after a period of work "in house" for Dick James Music. An RSO press release declared, "The Bee Gees deeply regret the distress caused by allegations made ostensibly in their name. The Bee Gees and Robert Stigwood . . . are delighted to continue their immensely successful long-term association."

A Bee Gees' spokesman told reporters, "Things will open up down the line, but for now, the press release is all we have to say."

"The status quo remained," Freddie Gershon gloated. "If you've been in the business long enough, you know that all artists go through periods of temporary insanity.

"The Bee Gees started investigating the facts, and I think they realised [that] it wasn't worth it to go through several years of litigation, only to have a judge or jury tell them the same thing they found out for themselves: that Robert Stigwood has always treated them fairly and correctly. I believe they were embarrassed to find that out, and they dropped the suit and went away with their tails between their legs."

His remarks did little to soothe matters, and in response The Bee Gees took out full page advertisements in both *Rolling Stone* and *Variety*, with the following declaration:

A STATEMENT FROM THE BEE GEES

TO WHOM IT MAY CONCERN

Up to this point in time we had intended there to be no further press statement regarding the recent settlement between the Robert Stigwood Organisation and The Bee Gees, apart from the single statement from both parties that was agreed and issued on 8th May 1981. However, it has now become necessary, in response to a recent interview given by Mr Freddie Gershon, the President of RSO, Inc., to Rolling Stone *published in the June 25th edition to set the record straight once and for all.*

First and foremost, The Bee Gees have never 'apologised' to Robert Stigwood or RSO; this has never been the case, nor will it ever be the case, no matter what any other press article may claim.

Secondly, it should be said that, as well as those connected with RSO, The Bee Gees themselves also have personal opinions about the situation which arose and its outcome.

The Bee Gees have never revealed these personal opinions and this will hopefully continue to be the case.

We believe the venting of personal feelings in music trade magazines is a highly negative vocation and it displays an extreme disrespect for the very thing and the very reason we are all doing what we do, namely – the music.

We will now set before you – for the entertainment industry and the general public to digest – the actual terms of the recent settlement.

Recording
The Bee Gees will deliver to RSO the album currently being recorded by them and one more album. (These will constitute the seventh and eighth albums which were already required under the existing Agreements the terms of which were originally agreed in 1975.) The Bee Gees' remuneration in respect of these last two albums has been improved; the advances have been greatly increased to what are now extremely substantial sums, the US royalty rate marginally improved (it was already considerable) and the rest of the world royalty substantially improved. In addition, the royalty rates on all product recorded prior to the commencement of the current Agreements have been very substantially improved.

515

There is no other recording obligation on the part of The Bee Gees to RSO.

The revised terms were agreed by the respective advisers of RSO and The Bee Gees, having regard to prevailing market conditions. An increase in the royalty rate had never (notwithstanding speculation to the contrary) been for The Bee Gees a material consideration in the litigation.

Management
The Management Agreements with RSO have been terminated. Accordingly, Robert Stigwood is no longer The Bee Gees' Manager. The Bee Gees are free to undertake whatever projects they choose (including outside production work and 'guest' recording appearances) without any right of RSO to be consulted in connection with or approve any such projects.

Songwriting
The existing arrangements, whereby all works written by The Bee Gees are published by RSO in perpetuity, have been terminated. All works written by The Bee Gees or any of them will be vested in a new entity being formed by The Bee Gees. Similarly, RSO have agreed that all previous compositions written by The Bee Gees (right back to 1967) will likewise be vested in the new venture with RSO merely retaining a modest financial interest in those compositions as well as the compositions recorded and released on or before 31st December 1985 and cease altogether after 31st December 1989.

Audit Claims
Claims were made against RSO by The Bee Gees for substantial arrears of royalties. Many of the claims (totalling millions of dollars) have been paid in full, other claims have been compromised and other claims have been conceded by The Bee Gees. In addition, various other outstanding claims for substantial royalties remain to be resolved primarily because further investigation is needed by both parties. Furthermore, other audits are in progress which may well give rise to further claims. It is not unusual where high selling records are involved for audits to give rise to substantial claims, but any suggestion made by RSO that The Bee Gees' claims for arrears of royalties were without foundation is totally untenable.

General
The more general claims made in the name of The Bee Gees in the litigation seeking a repudiation of the Agreements from the outset and substantial damages were dropped by The Bee Gees. Similarly, we would like to point out that the counterclaims made by RSO against The Bee Gees amounting to some $310,000,000 were likewise dropped.

The statement you have just read is the true one; it has been witnessed, confirmed and co-signed by our personal attorney, Mr Michael Eaton.

Mr Gershon and any other member of the entertainment industry is free to challenge this statement at any time he or she wishes.

B.A.C. Gibb   M.E. Gibb   R.H. Gibb
Co-signed
M.C.A. Eaton

It came as little surprise that RSO took up The Bee Gees' invitation to challenge their remarks with a terse statement. "The press release issued by The Bee Gees is inconsistent with the terms of the settlement. Indeed, as was clearly understood, any settlement with The Bee Gees was conditional on a worldwide apology . . . and without it no settlement would have been concluded." The increase in The Bee Gees' royalties was referred to as "modest" and "The claim to an underpayment of recording and publishing royalties was settled by a payment, which, in the context of what they had earned, was not material."

For The Bee Gees, the financial aspects had never been of importance in the litigation; rather, it was the freedom to make decisions for themselves. Although the young Gibbs had initially required the support and the guiding hand of Robert Stigwood to develop their fledgling career; by 1980, they were ready to leave the nest. Their multifaceted management contract to RSO had failed to acknowledge the fact that the young lads, whom Stigwood had signed in 1967, had indeed grown up.

"It was a total misunderstanding and we patched it up," Robin would later explain. "We made friends with each other. At that time, RSO was folding up anyway as a record company, and everybody was parting ways. It was just that time where everybody was moving on, and I think it was the right thing to do. Robert didn't really feel like he wanted to keep managing artists all the time . . .

"With Polydor and RSO splitting, and Robert wanting to do personal things with his life, and we coming off the back of all this huge chaos, we needed to clean our heads out, we needed a break. We just wanted to concentrate on writing and producing other people, which we did."

★   ★   ★

In July, 1981, Robin and Molly's acrimonious separation took a bizarre turn. Robin alleged in the press that his estranged wife had conspired with black show business lawyer, Ashley Adams, to try to get him to accuse her of adultery so that they could hit him with a £5 million slander action.

He alleged that, with the knowledge of the local police, he and a private detective had broken into the couple's Weybridge home the previous summer to get evidence of the purported conspiracy. Police confirmed that an incident was reported in August, 1980, in which he broke into his home after telling police that he needed to do this because he had no keys. "I got into the house by smashing a window. Then I broke into the safe and uncovered all the evidence. I discovered signed documents and letters which made it clear they had been planning to set me up for about a year – and were ready to put that plan into action.

"By breaking into my own home, I was able to get hold of papers and documents, including letters from Molly," Robin told the *Daily Mirror*. "At the time she was in New York. After what has happened, I can never forgive her. I haven't said anything about this until now. My London lawyer has prepared the case, which will come up in London in a few months. The whole thing has been a terrible shock, but I am determined to go ahead. The papers containing the proof have been shown to Scotland Yard and the FBI."

Molly retorted, "The allegations are absolutely untrue. The only part of what he said that has any truth in it is that he *did* break in here while I was away. But he certainly didn't find anything incriminating."

While the accusations might once have come as a shock, Molly claimed, "I have got past being surprised by anything Robin says now." She added that Robin was making life miserable for her and the children.

"The whole matter is now in the hands of my solicitor, who has advised me to say nothing more at the moment except that all the allegations against me are completely untrue," she said.

Ashley Adams, who had offices on Manhattan's Fifth Avenue and on Broadway, was unavailable for comment, but an associate stated, "It's an astonishing allegation that Robin is making."

★　★　★

In September, the first single from the forthcoming *Living Eyes* LP was released. 'He's A Liar' reached number 30 on the American charts but failed to make a showing in Britain.

"A few people thought it had something to do with Stigwood," Barry said later. "It was wrongly timed. At another time, it could have been the right single. It doesn't reflect the rest of the album.

"We originally felt the single should have been 'Living Eyes' but I don't want to put the blame on anyone's shoulders. 'He's a Liar' was the choice of everyone involved . . . We still believe it is the one to go with first because of its radical differences and because we simply have to break new ground. We can't go on being the falsetto singers . . . 'Oh no, not that again,' and as with the whole of this album, there's only one falsetto song on this album. We went out of our way to show that . . . the original Bee Gees are still there, those voices are still there and we know how to use them."

"The Bee Gees were suing Robert at the time, and radio thought it was a personal vendetta," Albhy confirmed. "It had never been meant that way. It was meant to be about a love triangle. They thought it was all subtle. The radio stations, programme directors, always give people too much credit for subtlety. When you think people are working on subtle levels, you're usually fooling yourself.

"I thought that, at that time . . . it was a great song with great vocals and great hooks . . . We had political backlash, but at the time, I believed it was a great track."

Unlike the rest of the album, 'He's a Liar' is a rock song, with former Eagle Don Felder contributing a solid lead guitar line and Barry singing full voice for the first time since *Mr. Natural* back in 1974. Barry and Maurice play rhythm, Albhy and George Bitzer play keyboards and synthesizer, Harold Cowart plays bass as usual, and top drummer Steve Gadd rounds out what was the basic personnel list for all the songs on the album, although Jeff Porcaro drummed on some others. The near total lack of success for 'He's A Liar' calls for some explanation. The Bee Gees had reached saturation point by 1980, so much so that people probably wanted to move on, yet paradoxically it's possible that this release sounds so unlike The Bee Gees of the Seventies that they were unrecognisable. The group's management dispute with RSO and the collapse of the label cannot have helped garner enthusiasm among the promotion staff either. Maybe it was just doomed to failure.

'He's A Liar' was the group's first single to be released commercially on 12-inch with an extended version of the song, whilst both vinyl formats contained an instrumental version on the B-side, another trend they would flirt with briefly for the next few years.

The album followed in October. In Japan, there was a special promotional record from the album for DJs and dealers, which played the six songs – three on each side – from the centre outwards. *Living Eyes* was also chosen by Philips to be the very first album manufactured in compact disc format, as could be seen in close-up when the new technology was first demonstrated on the BBC's futuristic television programme, *Tomorrow's World*.

The album's cover photos were taken in New York. The front photo shows a well-dressed trio on a Manhattan rooftop at sunset, somewhere in east Midtown, within a few blocks of 46th Street and Second Avenue judging by the perspective, looking west by southwest towards the Chrysler Building and Pan Am Building. The inner gatefold shows them in the lobby of Radio City Music Hall in Rockefeller Center, while on the back, still wearing the same clothes, they are at Robin's house on the North Shore of Long Island, about 25 miles east of Manhattan.

Living Eyes was certainly an album of change. There were no dance tunes, and Barry avoided singing everything in falsetto. Robin, who'd conspired to showcase Barry for a few years by adopting a role as co-writer, production adviser, and harmony singer, once again took lead vocal on several songs, which probably also influenced the sound of those songs since they tend to write for the singer. However, it was Maurice, newly sober, who positively bewildered Albhy Galuten, who had never seen him take such an active role in every aspect of the production. While the idea had been to break with the past, the project lost its sense of direction with so many hands at work.

Although sessions had started with Blue Weaver, Dennis Bryon, and Alan Kendall, they were stopped and picked up again later using top session players instead; some the same as on the Andy Gibb and Barbra Streisand projects. The Bee Gees were no longer going to play live, and consequently were no longer a band. This had been coming ever since Barry's eyes were opened at the Andy Gibb sessions. Hiring session men could fulfil Barry's desire for perfect timing and pitch.

With this album, Barry completed a transition from the Beatles-like concept of a self-contained band to the R&B concept of a hot house band backing the featured singers. It is a remarkable change of philosophy because most artists prefer one of the two concepts and cannot stand the other. It was a case of the authenticity of friends and brothers playing the best they can with great, but limited, ability, against the professionalism of the best musicians that money can buy who can play with great skill and beauty.

One song written at this time, Barry and Maurice's 'Hold Her In Your Hand', would come out as a solo single for Maurice three years later, but three others from these sessions, 'Heat Of The Night', 'Loving You Is Killing Me' and 'City Of Angels', remain unreleased.

At the time *Living Eyes* was released, Barry declared, "It's our finest album in terms of depth, performance, and quality of the production. It's been about 11 months working on this album, and we do tend to work an awful long time on our albums because we want to be sure."

Three years later, his views had changed considerably. "Obviously we had a scare with *Living Eyes*," he admitted. "It wasn't the kind of album we should have brought out at that point. It was a little too downbeat, as opposed to having energy. But we were trying to go for a change, to draw ourselves away from the falsetto vocals and do something that might be a little different. We knew the risks when we did that."

Reflecting on the album's failure to make any significant impact on the charts, Robin insisted that that had been their plan all along. "*Living Eyes* was a turkey, I think, for a good reason," he explained. "I don't think that last album does any harm but I'm really glad it was a turkey."

"*Living Eyes* . . . was just what was needed for us," Barry claimed in 1990. "We needed to stop being what we were. It was driving us all round the twist. We needed at that point to step back and look at our lives as individuals."

"We were suffering burn out and the public had OD'd," Robin added. "I believe when people do too much or have that kind of phenomena to go through, they become parodies of themselves to the public. You don't become art for arts' sake, your credibility is ignored. We were pressured to bring out [*Living Eyes*] by our record company and by certain individuals because of the cashing-in process."

The brothers admitted that having their own studio had given them the freedom to take as long as they wanted.

"We knew how much we had to do this time, we knew it was going to take a year," Barry explained. "We talked about the fact that, no, we're not going to spend a year on the next album, it's ridiculous, but we've ended up doing it again. We've become more fortunate than the average artist and in that way we get to be able to do virtually anything we want sound wise. All we have to do is be creative. All we have to do is think what sound we want and we can probably get it. And that's where the money helps us. What we do with our money is, is we put it back into what we do.

"It's a fallacy that money doesn't mean happiness. Money can be very good to you," he laughed.

The second single from the album was the title track, released in November. Despite promoting it with appearances on the *Donahue* show in the US and on *Parkinson* in Britain, 'Living Eyes' was not destined to be a hit, reaching only number 45 in the States and 41 in Holland, while failing to chart in the UK. Barry described 'Living Eyes' as "an up tempo, philosophical . . . ballad . . . Basically the message in the song, if there is to be a message, is that, 'God, if only everyone felt like this!' There was a slight paranoia on our part on being afraid to change with the falsettos, you know. You get into that thing where, 'God, every falsetto record we're putting out is a monster, we shouldn't change yet.' That's what stopped us from saying, 'Well, it's time Robin had a lead.' . . . But now it's no longer a sales point, it's important that Robin's voice gets heard. It's equally important that Maurice's voice gets heard. And it's becoming less important that I get heard. And that's the way we work. There's no ego within the three of us, whoever's singing most or whoever has the most hits is irrelevant."

In Britain, the backlash against The Bee Gees was exemplified by the appearance of a new musical/comedy trio called The Hee Bee Gee Bees. Dressed in the flying jackets and scarves (but in their case, the scarves were held fully extended) of the *Children Of The World* album cover, Philip Pope as Dobbin, Angus Deayton as Garry, both Oxford University students, and Mike Stevens as Norris, a graduate of Oxford Polytechnic, performed a merciless Bee Gees parody that was brutally funny.

Angus Deayton explained, "The Hee Bee Gee Bees act was part of a show that we did at The Edinburgh Festival, which was the Oxford Revue, where the final part of the revue, 'Meaningless Songs', was a parody of The Bee Gees. There were a couple of record producers from a company called Original Music who came to see it, and they basically offered us a recording contract for a single there and then."

Phil Pope wrote all the music, with Pope and Deayton collaborating on the lyrics for 'Ah!'. 'Meaningless Songs' and 'Posing In The Moonlight' featured lyrics by Richard Curtis, MBE, who wrote *Four Weddings And A Funeral* and *Notting Hill* and has been involved in several other high profile activities such as *Comic Relief*.

" 'Ah!' was *inspired* by 'Children Of The World' " Deayton said. "We were always slightly touchy about that [word] because The Barron Knights did use the same tunes and put different words on them, so we slightly prided ourselves on the fact that the music was an original composition, as were the lyrics."

521

The Bee Gees' reaction was swift and furious. While the group would later profess to find Kenny Everett's parody of them hilarious, they were outraged at the implication that their lyrics were meaningless.

"I don't think that we were aware that The Bee Gees would react so unkindly towards us," Angus said. "Obviously you never quite know. We did do parodies of a large number of artists on our two albums in the ensuing years, and there were very few, with the possible exception of Abba, who were really *against* their parody. In fact, a lot of them, like Francis Rossi of Status Quo, were actually quite a fan of it.

"If you look at Kenny Everett's parody, effectively what that was, was Kenny miming to 'Children Of The World' and taking three pills, one of which gives you a hairy chest, and another a medallion, so it wasn't particularly offensive. Also, The Bee Gees maintain that Kenny Everett's one came first, trying to make out that we pinched his idea, but actually ours a), came first and b), was quite a lot more hard hitting and satirical, so that's probably why they objected to it. I think also in retrospect, with the hindsight that one has and, for example on the *Clive Anderson show*, I think it's quite clear that they don't really have that much of a sense of humour about themselves.

"We did get the feeling that we did upset them more than others. We only got feedback through third parties, but we got the impression that Maurice was about the only one who had any time for it. I don't think it did much damage. I mean in a way, I think it does more damage if you object to satirical comments than if you simply go along with every one else and laugh at it. I think if they'd laughed at it, and seen the funny side of it, they probably would have scored more brownie points than objecting to it and slamming the phone down on music journalists, as they did whenever they were after something. I think it just sort of gave people the impression that they don't have a sense of humour about themselves," he repeated.

One such journalist was Chas de Whalley of *Record Mirror*, whose ears were smarting after an attempt to get a quote from the brothers.

As Angus pointed out, Kenny Everett's sketch would appear in October of the following year.

"Oh, Kenny's brilliant, Kenny's was the best without a doubt," Maurice declared. "The best impression I've ever seen. He had me on the floor. I could not believe how good that was. We'll miss him, he was a real good guy."

"It never offended me," Barry commented in 1997. "I thought it was one of the best giggles I've ever seen. When you look at The Bee Gees, you don't look at yourself. I guess you're not objective about how you're perceived, but he nailed us. Big hair, big teeth, medallions . . . The hair's not so big now!"

In November, 1993, The Bee Gees would take the opportunity for revenge on The Hee Bee Gee Bees, pretending to blow up the group after their performance of 'Meaningless Songs' on the *Children In Need* programme.

"The producer . . . was, strangely enough, a Hee Bee Gee Bees fan," Angus explained, "and it was his idea that we should bury the hatchet although, because of the unavailability of us and them, we had to record it on two different days so we were never actually in the studio at the same time.

"I was invited to *An Audience With [The Bee Gees]* . . . but I thought that would probably be too near falling into a trap."

It was a mark of how well their single, 'Meaningless Songs', was done that Blue Weaver admitted to being taken in by the parody the first time he heard it. "I'd come home from America for a couple of days, and I was driving my wife in Chiswick, driving up to our house with the radio on, and I'm just humming along and she says, 'This is great, I haven't heard that one before, when did you do that?' and at that point I suddenly listened and the chorus came in, and I'd been sub-consciously thinking it was us!

"I hadn't even thought anything about it," Blue continued, "because I was driving, it was background music, and then when 'Meaningless songs in very high voices' came in, I stopped in the middle of the road and just couldn't believe it. I said, 'This isn't us, this is a joke.' It was absolutely brilliant, it fooled me. Honestly, I was going along, you know – just driving, not tuning in to anything specific, and just thinking of it as a Bee Gees track! It was great."

Angus was amused by Blue's story, adding, "Well, that's fantastic news because that means that one day we might actually end up on a compilation album of The Bee Gees. If the producer makes the same mistake, we could earn more money than we ever did from The Hee Bee Gee Bees. I think it's an enormous compliment, although it's more down to Phil Pope because he was the one who was responsible for the music, but I think he did a good job of making something sound as if it was by a particular artist. There was a sort of music copyright law where no more than three or four bars can be identical, so he was ruled by that and at the same time he made it sound like an original artist's song."

Despite the incisive parody of The Hee Bee Gee Bees, Angus Deayton admitted, "I was a fan in the Seventies, as indeed, I'm sure everyone was when they sort of caught the mood of disco fever. I had *Children Of The World* and *Spirits Having Flown*, but I did run a discotheque in the Seventies so I was sort of professionally obliged to have those sort of albums. *Saturday Night Fever* was a classic . . . In some respects, I probably should represent the opinions of Richard Curtis, who wrote the original lyrics, as well, because I know that he is much more conciliatory and much keener to make peace with them. I know that he picked one of their songs when he was on *Desert Island Discs* and hoped they knew there were no hard feelings."

34

TO BE OR NOT TO BEE GEE

AFTER *LIVING EYES*, The Bee Gees as a group took the year off and concentrated on outside projects. Barry accepted the role of Lord Byron in a film of the same name to be shot in Italy, although by August, he would pull out of the picture when the producers requested a postponement which conflicted with his schedule. Robin turned his thoughts to a solo album, while Maurice appeared on American television as an interviewer for *Good Morning America* and playing himself on the long running soap opera, *Guiding Light*.

An auction of Bing Crosby memorabilia caught Barry's attention, and he made several purchases. "He never went to the auction – it was an over-the-phone bid by someone for him, and he bought a desk, some golf clubs, walking canes, bits and pieces. It was quite a nice desk, I'll have to say – whether it was Bing Crosby's, we may never know . . . Might have been his son's or some distant relative's who thought they'd get money for this," Tom Kennedy chuckled.

The Barry-Albhy-Karl team followed up the amazing success of the Streisand project with an album of songs by Dionne Warwick, best known for her many hits by Hal David and Burt Bacharach some years earlier. They took the same approach as they had done with Streisand: songwriting was again partly by the three Gibb brothers and partly by Barry and Albhy together, and again Barry played rhythm guitar and sings backing vocals along with the house band.

According to Albhy, the original idea was not to be a Dionne Warwick solo album. "We were talking about people that we loved, singers," he explained, "and I had this idea to do an album with three woman singers: Gladys Knight, Dionne Warwick, and . . . the girl who worked with Earth, Wind & Fire all the time. She had a high voice. It would be three people in three different ranges, low medium and high. Barry was totally jazzed about writing it. You could have duets, three-way things; it would be a great writing stimulus. That's what the original record was going to be. But once Barry got on the phone with Clive Davis, Clive was very persuasive, and he talked Barry, who can't say no, into doing a Dionne Warwick record instead . . . which we did fine with. The Dionne Warwick record was great. It was the first record where we used some synclavier stuff."

The lead single, and title track of the LP was 'Heartbreaker', written by Barry, Robin and Maurice.

For Maurice, the song's title was particularly apt. "I cried my eyes out after we wrote it," he recalled. "I drove home and thought, 'We should be doing this one,' and when she did it, it was brilliant. We sang on it, and it still became like a duet between The Bee Gees and Dionne Warwick.

"That became her biggest single since 'Do You Know The Way To San Jose', which, when we were kids, we adored. Burt Bacharach & Hal David and John Lennon & Paul McCartney are probably the best songwriters I have ever heard in my life. Burt's chords and Hal David's lyrics and things, and it was just [that] the melodies that Burt was coming up with were dynamite. We were working with Dionne Warwick, she was like their instrument and doing a song that Burt Bacharach and Hal David usually only did, we felt really honoured. It was a great experience."

The other singles were 'Yours', a slower ballad with a plenty of emotion but less commercial, and 'All The Love In The World', a lighter pop tune neither of which were up to high standard of 'Guilty'.

During the recording of *Heartbreaker*, an old friend dropped in. "I was working down [in Miami] at the time and caught up with them," Geoff Bridgeford said. "Barry asked me to come over as Steve Gadd was drumming and to come and check him out. So I did and we hung out together and it was cool. At the time, he had just received a new vehicle that had been built specially for him and was saying, 'Geoff, this could have all been yours, man!' But, you know, I have no regrets. I'm happy, and they are happy, so it all worked out."

Barry, Robin and Maurice wrote seven songs for the project. Two of those, 'Broken Bottles' and 'Oceans And Rivers', were turned down, and more songs were written by Barry with Albhy to make up the album. Once again, Barry's falsetto proved a valuable instrument in writing and performing the demos of the songs, so much so that Clive Davis was still playing the Dionne Warwick demos five years later.

Heartbreaker was released in October and gave Dionne a best selling LP. The title track topped the Australian singles charts for four consecutive weeks and was a Top 10 hit on both sides of the Atlantic, reaching number two in Britain and number 10 in the States and Germany. The follow-up, 'All The Love In The World', reached number 10 in Britain but reached only number 50 in Germany.

"What we're most proud of is that just about every record we made with all those people set some sort of record for that artist," Barry marvelled. "It's amazing. I think Dionne Warwick had the biggest album of her career in Europe with that album."

Dionne was not the only artist who would have a hit that year with a Gibb composition. Leo Sayer reached number 22 in the British charts with the Arif Mardin produced 'Heart (Stop Beating In Time)'.

Earlier in the year, it was reported that Maurice was being considered as a possible composer for a British television special of *A Christmas Carol*. In December, he took time out to fly to Los Angeles to discuss the film score he was composing with Jimmie Haskell for the movie *Misunderstood*, starring Gene Hackman. Jimmie was as much impressed by Maurice's skill for mimicry as for his musical talent. "I was working with Maurice in his hotel room in Beverly Hills when he said, 'Let's order lunch to be brought up.' He picked up the phone and ordered hamburgers in the most typical American accent I have ever heard. I had never before heard an Englishman/Australian 'put on' a USA accent, and Maurice did it so well that it bowled me over!"

As it turned out, both projects were destined to go to other composers. "I think they get three or four people doing these things and just pick whichever one suits the films best," Tom Kennedy explained.

The Gibb family all came together for a triple christening for Maurice and Yvonne's daughter, Samantha, and Barry and Lynda's sons, Ashley and Travis. Barry and Lynda were Samantha's godparents, while Maurice and Yvonne did the honours for Ashley, and Travis's godparents were Lynda's brother and sister-in-law, Tommy and Shirley Gray.

★　★　★

Since Molly filed for divorce, Robin's life had been tumultuous, causing concern for his well-being within the family. "We hope in time things will work out all right for Robin, although he's very, very unhappy about his personal life just now," Barbara Gibb said. "You can't blame him, can you?"

It was around this time that Robin recruited his personal assistant, former policeman, Ken Graydon. "It was kind of funny actually," he said. "I needed somebody to look after me when I came to London from America. This was where Ken stepped in, because I had been told to remove myself from the premises, as one does in a divorce, so I said, 'Right, I'm off!' Anyway, I was in a hotel in London, wondering what to do, because I'd never *stayed* in a hotel in England before, and suddenly there was a knock on the door and there's Ken . . . and that was how we met and he looked after me at that time."

It was also around this time that one of Ken's relations, an Irish artist called Dwina, came into the picture. "Ken is my cousin, and I hadn't seen him for about 12 years so I called him up," Dwina recalled.

Ken told her his new employer's name, but she said, "I didn't know who Robin Gibb was. If he had said The Bee Gees, I'd have thought, 'Wow!'"

Ken mentioned that Robin was interested in meeting the actress Sarah Miles, who happened to be one of Dwina's friends. She gave him Sarah's phone number, and a meeting was arranged.

"One night I had dinner with Sarah Miles, who was a friend of Dwina's . . . I was sitting there in her apartment, and there was a picture on the television that Dwina had drawn, a great pen and ink drawing. I said, 'Wonderful drawing, I like it,' and she said, 'It's a friend of mine, that's Dwina.'"

While there was to be no relationship with the actress, Robin's interest in his minder's cousin was piqued. "Luckily, the date with Sarah didn't work out romantically," Dwina said. "Then I met him, and yes, it was all magic and stars. I was terribly excited because someone as creative as Robin appreciated *my* creativity . . . So he commissioned me to do some drawings, which I never finished – he paid me for them, but I never finished them and I shan't finish them now.

"I kept making them more and more detailed so I could keep seeing him," she admitted. "I didn't want to finish because I thought I'd never see him again. They're still unfinished for the same reason."

Robin and Dwina soon discovered that in addition to sharing an interest in art and the unconventional, they also shared a birthday. Edwina Elizabeth Murphy was born on December 22, 1952, in County Tyrone, Northern Ireland. When Robin first told her that his birthday was the same, "I thought he was just playing around, giving me a chat-up line," she recalled. "But it was true and, what's more, it's the date of the winter solstice. With my interest in Druidism, I thought that was a good omen."

"I wasn't actually looking for anybody to have a relationship with," Robin said. "It was a pretty heavy period for me, but in the end, we were both won over."

For her part, Dwina claimed, "I was too busy working to give any thought to romance, living in brick dust in a house in south-east London while trying to do it up. I didn't have a roof over my kitchen, and I was using the electric fire to cook three-course meals."

Robin asked her advice about properties he was thinking of buying, and she advised him to buy a small cottage they had seen, never anticipating that she would soon be sharing it with him. "I'd been a loner for about 10 years when I met Robin," Dwina explained. "I'd had a little girl who was born prematurely and, sadly, she died . . . Not long after Robin and I met, we both knew we wanted a child together before actually *being* with each other. We felt ours would be good genes to put together. But the baby never came along until we started living together."

Just coming out of a failed marriage, Robin wanted to keep the relationship secret, and the couple succeeded in keeping all but their closest friends and family in the dark.

★   ★   ★

Following all the accusations and denials of the previous two years, Robin and Molly's marriage ended in an acrimonious divorce near the end of 1982. In May of the following year, Robin shared some of his heartbreak with readers of the *Scottish Daily Express* in an exclusive interview with Garth Pearce, the paper's show business writer.

Refuting Molly's claims that the break-up in the relationship was caused by long periods away from home, he stated, "It was nothing to do with me being away on tour all the time. She was having an affair with a New York lawyer and it took me a long time to find out.

"She began staying in our New York home when I wasn't there," Robin continued. "I thought she was falling in love with America, when all the time she was falling in love with a lawyer down the road! I was distraught to learn the truth, I really was. I honestly believe she was in love with this man. Once a wife falls in love with someone else, you can do nothing about it. Marriage is out of the window."

Robin went on to reveal that a considerable financial burden had been placed on him over and above any emotional ones. Clearly hurt by the whole business, he explained that the money aspect was only part of his unhappiness, claiming to have seen his children Spencer and Melissa only once during a three-year period. "I have had to pay out at least £1 million, but there were other things, too, that destroyed me emotionally."

He clearly couldn't understand why it had to be such a messy divorce. After all, he said, "She was still the mother of my children, despite everything."

The article pictured Robin with his new love, Dwina Waterfield, described by the *Express* as an 'erotic artist'. Also known as Dwina Brown in connection with her acting and modelling career, she used her real name, Dwina Murphy, for her writing activities.

Concluding on a happier note, and with one eye firmly on the future, Robin confirmed that despite the traumatic experience of his parting of the ways with Molly, "I have not been put off marriage."

Sadly, that was not the end of the matter. None too pleased at Robin's assertions, Molly instructed her (other) lawyers to sue Robin for breaching certain confidential aspects of their settlement. A writ was served as Robin was appearing on a breakfast television programme, "Rather unnecessarily, I might add," he observed.

On the eve of The Bee Gees' scheduled Verona concert, Robin hired a plane to appear in court on September 9, 1983. Despite his contention that it was just "an emotional outburst", he was found guilty of breaking a court order not to discuss his former marriage with the press, but when he was sentenced to two weeks in jail by Judge Phelan, Molly Gibb broke down, saying, "I didn't want that."

A stunned Robin left the courtroom, although he was relieved to note, "I didn't go into the cells at all . . . I went outside and I was waiting in the hallway, and one of the police officers said, 'We have to go out and arrest people to get sentences like this.' But that's just everyday life, these things happen," he added philosophically.

Lord Justice Ackner, sitting with Lord Justice O'Connor, overturned the sentence a few hours later but added that Judge Phelan had been right to regard the singer's breach of a court order made the previous July as serious.

Robin returned to *Good Morning Britain* after the case was concluded. While the experience had served to make him slightly more cautious with his words, he remained outraged at the treatment he had received.

"It's been a strange year, on reflection," he mused. "Obviously, I can't talk about it, otherwise they'll probably end up serving me with another writ . . . They found me in contempt of court for talking about my previous marriage, which in America they find against the freedom of speech act . . .

"It's very difficult, really, because I don't even *have* to talk about my marriage to be in contempt of court. The law took a very wrong view of it, and they should not have done what they did to me, because there are so many different factors involved in this situation.

"I'm in a very vulnerable position for a start. There are other people, such as journalists . . . For instance, I could go to a party, and I could be speaking to someone who I don't know is a journalist, and if they say something, 'Blah blah blah have you seen such and such?' and I say, 'No, blah blah blah,' that's a quote. 'No' becomes a quote," he explained

"Getting down to that, the one thing I am against in this situation is that they should not have found for 14 days in prison. *Anybody* who does what I did, an article talking about my previous marriage in the paper, it should not have gone that far, and I think that the people involved in finding that kind of sentence [were] irresponsible in doing that.

"People like us are in a vulnerable position. You don't know whether or not the judge on the day is being biased because you are in the business that you're in, or because you may have a bit more money than he's got, which is a very wrong view to take. There are so many factors . . . I do hear that high court judges don't get paid very much," Robin added recklessly.

Although Robin and Dwina had now gone public with their relationship, they still managed to keep a few secrets from the public. On January 21, Dwina had given birth to their son, Robin John, in Miami, but the baby's existence was only known to a few of the couple's closest friends.

On October 28, the *Daily Mail* printed a story about Robin's "secret family" with Dwina, this time identified as Dwina Waterford.

"We wanted little Robin and he's wonderful," Robin said, "but neither Molly, my former wife, nor my other two children know about him yet. I will be introducing the children to their little brother, but it's still too early and the situation is too fragile."

He claimed that his divorce had affected him badly, adding, "I developed a terrible mistrust of women. It's taken a while for me to get over it. But having the baby with Dwina has sealed our happiness."

★　★　★

When The Bee Gees were first approached by Ronald Selle's lawyers in 1980, Dick Ashby said that they were advised by their own lawyers to "offer something like $25,000 just to sort of [make him] go away."

"Everyone was fair game . . . Rather than spend the millions of dollars [defending it]," explained Tom, "most people would just give them a few thousand to go away."

But Selle wasn't going to be bought off so easily. "He said he wanted six figures," Dick Ashby recalled. "That was when we said, 'See you in court.' But, of course, we were pretty new to this whole thing."

For Selle, an antiques dealer in Illinois with a master's degree in music education who played keyboards locally with a trio, the story began in 1975. Whilst shaving one morning, he came up with a melody, which he later worked out and recorded a demo tape in a small home studio. After paying six dollars to obtain a copyright, he sent out 14 copies of the tape with lead sheets to record companies, but notably not to The Bee Gees or any company directly connected to the group. Eleven companies returned the tapes to him, whilst three never responded.

On February 20, 1983, the case came to trial in federal court in Chicago, heard before the Honourable George N. Leighton, United States District Judge for the Northern District of Illinois.

The brothers were confident as they approached the opportunity to clear their names. With nearly 20 years as published songwriters, there seemed no reason for anyone to believe that they would suddenly resort to stealing songs from an unknown composer – and indeed, there had been no opportunity for them to have heard the song in the first place. Knowing they were in the right, losing the case didn't even seem a possibility, especially with Dick Ashby, Blue Weaver and Albhy Galuten along to give testimony about the composing process, and expert witnesses on hand.

"I have no malice towards this man," Barry said. "I believe that he acted in good intentions on his behalf that certain notes in these songs resemble each other enough for him to believe that we took his song. I only hope that at the end of the day, no matter how this goes down, he just takes into consideration that he could be wrong."

Plagiarism is a difficult crime to prove, rarely witnessed, so by necessity, any evidence must be circumstantial. Ordinarily, the plaintiff would be expected to prove that the defendant had access to the work in question. Selle's attorneys never attempted to indicate how The Bee Gees might have gained access to the unpublished song. Instead, Selle obtained an analytical and comparative study of the two songs from an expert witness, Arrand Parsons, a professor of music at Selle's alma mater, Northwestern University, and a doctor of philosophy in music theory. A music theorist whose work had previously concentrated on classical music, he had never made a comparative analysis of popular songs prior to his involvement in the trial.

Graphs and charts prepared by Parsons compared the two songs bar by bar. He testified that the first eight bars, known as Theme A, of each song had 24 notes – out of 34 notes in 'Let It End' and 40 notes in 'How Deep Is Your Love' – which were identical in pitch and symmetrical positions. Out of 35 rhythmic impulses in Selle's tune and 40 in the Gibbs', 30 were identical. In the last four bars of both songs, Theme B, 14 notes were identical in pitch. Of the 14 rhythmic impulses in Theme B of each song, 11 were identical. Finally, both Theme A and Theme B occur in the same position in each song.

Based on his structural analysis of the two songs, Parsons stated his conclusion, "The two songs have such striking similarities that they could not have been written independently of one another."

According to Selle's attorney, "Once you establish such striking similarity, you have also established what the law recognises as inferred access."

When cross-examined by The Bee Gees' attorney, Robert Osterberg, Parsons sounded much less certain. Osterberg asked, "Is it your opinion, Mr Parsons, that the only way the B Theme of 'How Deep Is Your Love' could come about was as a result of copying?"

Parsons responded, "I don't believe . . . put it positively. I believe that The Bee Gees' song, with these elements which we have described in common with the Selle song, I believe that The Bee Gees' song could not have come into being with the . . . I must correct that because that is again dealing with a conjecture. I believe that elements, if I may just wipe that away and start again, because it's gotten twisted up. I believe that elements which are in common between the songs in question are of such striking similarity that the second song could not have come into being without the first."

Osterberg countered that similarities alone could not prove copying, and coincidental similarities, attributed to the limited number of notes, provided no legal redress. In cross-examining Selle, Osterberg confronted him with similarities between 'Let It End' and The Beatles' 'From Me To You'.

One of the most damning testimonies came from Maurice, who was called by the plaintiff as an adverse party witness. In Maurice's taped deposition before the trial, he was asked to identify a piece of music. He identified it as 'How Deep Is Your Love'. The same tape was played, and Maurice was asked if he could "identify that example as being from any piece of music that you are familiar with?"

Maurice agreed that he could, and when asked to identify it, he responded, "I believe that's 'How Deep Is Your Love'. Yes, I'm sure it's 'How Deep Is Your Love'."

Selle's lawyer, Allen Engerman, then read a stipulation of the parties that the music which Maurice had identified was, in fact, "the melody of Theme B, the first two phrases of Ronald Selle's 'Let It End'." With that, the plaintiff rested his case. As a final point, it left a powerful impression.

For the defence, Blue Weaver's working tape of the sessions which resulted in 'How Deep Is Your Love' was played, and Barry explained the inception of the song. "The idea was to get [Blue] to play the chords that I could hear in my head and turn that into a song," he said. Robin and Maurice joined in later that night and the following day, helping with the lyrics, harmonies and "shorter melodies within the song."

Much was made of the fact that there was a 12-minute blank gap on the tape with implications that the tape had been falsified.

"If you listen to that tape, there's no way that you could *contrive* anything like that," Blue insists. "Really – if you *were* contriving it, it would sound differently – you would do it so people could understand what was going on . . . you wouldn't have the repetition, the trying to hone in . . ."

The trial took an unusual course when, during a routine scheduling meeting with Judge Leighton, he expressed his impatience with the trial and requested that the attorneys finish up the following day. When Engerman said that he intended to spend four hours cross-examining one witness, Leighton retorted, "Let me say something to you in all candour. There is a lot of time we have taken in this matter which I think could be cut down a great deal . . . If I were hearing this case without a jury, I could make all the findings of fact and reach conclusions of the law on the evidence already heard. Just remember that."

The Bee Gees' attorneys, Robert Osterberg and Robert Bergstrom, had originally planned to call two experts of their own to counter Parsons' testimony, but interpreting Judge Leighton's remarks to mean that the case might be dismissed without reaching the jury, Osterberg announced he was resting the case without calling any experts.

"The judge gave us indications at least two times during the trial that we should rest our case," Barry mused. "It told us that these people do not have a strong enough case. Maybe we were just being overconfident because we were innocent, but why belabour the point? If it was obvious to us that the court didn't think we were guilty, why not rest our case?

"The judge also did give signals that he was getting very tired of the hours and hours of interrogation."

On the fourth day of the trial, after five hours deliberation, the jury foreman, Earl Wilke, announced their decision, ruling in favour of Ronald Selle. "There was nothing to contradict the plaintiff's witness," Wilke said. "There was no expert for the defence . . . Dr Parsons talked of the improbability of independent composition, and nobody disputed that."

"It was a big monopoly of lawyers from New York that had done all this and the judge knew it was scam from the word go," Maurice said.

Judge Leighton declared, "The longer I stay in this job as a judge, the more appalled I get at what people will seize for litigation."

Shocked and stunned, The Bee Gees returned to their hotel.

"On the day of the judgement, I stayed at the hotel to pack up," Tom Kennedy recalled, "and they came back, very downcast. I said, 'What's going on?' and they said, 'They found for Ronald Selle.' I said, 'You're joking' – I thought it was a group joke, that they were going to say, 'Ha ha, we had you!'

"When they questioned the jury, the jury literally said, 'Well, if we made a mistake, they can afford it,' and that's why they found for Selle."

While Selle called it "a victory for the little guy", his lawyer, Allen Engerman gloated, "The Gibbs' lawyer told me, 'Allen, if you win, there'll be a pot of gold at the end of the rainbow.'"

Robin tersely declared it, "A lie!"

Barry still seemed dazed by the verdict, saying, "I feel like I've somehow stepped into *The Twilight Zone*. It's been a nightmare." While he conceded that there were "similarities in those portions of the two melodies as written, what hasn't been established is that that means we stole the song.

"I can understand a conviction based on one well-known song on another well-known song, but this is a song that we have never heard in our lives," he insisted. "Look, between the ages of 12 and 18 . . . when I lived in Australia, I had 65 songs that I wrote that were sung by other artists – this was before I ever left Australia to come to England or America. Now, am I going to steal someone else's songs? That's just pure madness," he added.

There can be no doubt when looking at the *transcribed* musical lead sheets that there are similarities in the first eight and last four bars of the songs, but when the songs are played back to back, significant variations in rhythm, phrasing and overall style become apparent. On paper, one can find melodic similarities between any number of pop songs. With only 12 notes in the scale and a limited number of ways those notes can be harmonised, this resemblance seems inevitable.

Since the Fifties, rhythmic style, harmonisation, phrasing, bass lines and other aspects of what used to be regarded as strictly part of a song's arrangement have come to be regarded as integral to the song as distinguishing characteristics. In seeking only the opinion of an expert schooled in classical music, these characteristics were never recognised in the trial.

The Bee Gees immediately filed a motion to overturn the decision. "If that fails," Barry added, "of course we'll appeal. We intend to fight this to the end."

"I guess you have to be accused of something you didn't do to really feel how we feel. We're outraged; it's very difficult to describe," he added.

Robin described his feelings as "rotten", adding, "It's only going to hurt the poor, unknown songwriters who are going to have their tapes turned away by publishing companies. It's a tragedy for songwriters who genuinely want their music heard but will have it returned to them unopened. That's what this case has done, and we tried to fight it on those grounds."

Selle told reporters he was unconcerned about the possibility of the counter action. "I don't look at it as a problem; it's a common post-trial motion." He added that after the verdict, his nephew had sent him a telegraph which read, "Forget the money. Did you get their autographs?"

Steve Massarsky, a former manager of The Allman Brothers who was then the principal lawyer for the Entertainment Center of Jacoby and Meyers, predicted that the jury's decision could have serious long term consequences. "This case will create a whole batch of litigants who will say, 'This guy beat The Bee Gees; so-and-so has my song.' Ninety-nine out of 100 times [the band or record company] will win. But the problem is not so much winning as having to defend it. The cost of lawyers is not inexpensive."

It was a fact that The Bee Gees well knew. "The legal fees they paid were in the millions," Tom Kennedy said, but the money was never the issue. What was important to them was their reputation, and whatever the cost, they wanted to clear their names.

On July 8, Judge Leighton nullified the jury's verdict, granting the defence motion for a judgement notwithstanding the verdict, ruling that the evidence could not support the verdict.

"The jury's original verdict was that we had done it," Barry explained on

CNN's *Freeman Report*. "The judge had to overrule the decision simply based on the fact that, without any proof of any kind of access or copying, you do not have a case at all really. You cannot prove what didn't happen, and the truth of the matter is the song was never heard by any of us so there really isn't a case. There has to be at least some sort of proof of access or some reasonable evidence that we would have heard his song and that is simply not the case. So the judge had to, what we like to call, give us our honour back, which was taken away and should not have been.

"In my mind and in my heart, the question is why we would do this. Why would three people who have been writing all their lives and who have had considerable success with many, many songs, why would they stoop to stealing an unknown writer's song who lives in Chicago? Why? It's quite possible that Ronald Selle really believes when he took action against us that he really believes that we took his song. But he was wrong. He was wrong now, and he will always be wrong about that and this forum gives me the chance to say that, wherever he is, he's most definitely wrong and we'd like to get on with our lives and we'd like him to get on with his."

As had been predicted, the case seemed to bring other litigants out of the woodwork. "We're being sued again now for 'Woman In Love', just for the title," Robin said gloomily. "The girl who's bringing the suit had about 30 lawyers turn her down. Then they finally found one. The record sounds about as much like our 'Woman In Love' as 'Chattanooga Choo-Choo'."

Even though the decision had been reversed in their favour, Barry admitted that the experience had left its mark. "I guess now we'll have to live with the feeling that somewhere, somehow, somebody's going to take action against us again based on another song that we didn't take," he said ruefully. "We've written a lot of songs and had a lot of successes, so we're a good target. But hopefully this case and the way it's gone down is going to stop people from really wanting to hit established songwriters quite so easily."

He would later explain, "It was just a piece of melody that resembled ours a little bit . . . But the fact that there were two different people who came up with this idea halfway around the world from each other, a new step was created in the law, and you now have to prove that the other person had to have access to your idea . . . What was heartbreaking was the six months waiting to be vindicated by the judge . . . and when we were found innocent, nobody publicised it so that was even more devastating. People have said nice things to us since because we fought. Billy Joel said, 'I wish I'd fought a case that I was sued for – I was innocent but I settled and I wish I'd fought. And you guys, because you fought, now every time someone gets sued, they don't settle, they fight.' And Michael Jackson also said the same thing, because he'd been sued. You fight, you don't pay off people that do that."

But the nightmare was far from over. Ronald Selle appealed the decision. There would be yet another trial, yet more attempts to discredit them.

★   ★   ★

534

In 1983, The Bee Gees finished out their recording contract to RSO with five songs contributed to the soundtrack for the sequel to *Saturday Night Fever, Staying Alive*. Once again starring John Travolta as Tony Manero, the film was not destined to be a blockbuster like its predecessor.

"My first impression when I first heard about it happening was, naturally, we were very knocked out that John was going to do it again with our music," Maurice said, "and also the fact that Sylvester Stallone was directing was an added bonus. The people involved in this picture now . . . this is obviously going to be in a completely different direction, and the script, when we eventually read it, it read like a Rocky script, it was bang bang bang. I mean, a lot of people refer to it as 'Rocky In Legwarmers', because John . . . built himself up and Sylvester really worked hard with him for about three months before the film . . . and he looks great in it."

Robin Gibb, in Europe on a promotional tour, said, "The new music, of course, is different now. It's 1983 now and probably our new music would not have worked in 1978. The new film *Staying Alive* is nothing like *Saturday Night Fever*. It has John Travolta in it and Bee Gees music, but it's not a disco film."

In retrospect, it is easy to find fault with the project. Perhaps the problem lay in the fact that five years was too long a gap between the two films. Possibly *Saturday Night Fever* just captured the mood of its time, and that time had passed. Maybe it was a problem with the choice of director for the film, Sylvester Stallone. Whatever the reasons, *Staying Alive* as a film just didn't seem to work, and as a vehicle for the music of The Bee Gees, it was even less effective.

While the music of Sylvester's brother, Frank Stallone, a heretofore unknown in the music world, featured prominently in the film, The Bee Gees' tracks were lost, not so much edited as merely chopped.

"Even still today," Maurice mused, "the directors and producers still regard music as second class and regard it as something that's not important . . . 'Let's work that out last, we'll get all this done first,' and then they think, 'Huh, what about the music?' "

"There is a sort of a barrier [between the composer and the filmmaker]," Barry added, "and it would be nice one day if that could be actually overcome. If the people who write the music for films and the people who make the films could actually sit down at the same table long before the film gets made, and discuss how the music will be treated or how the film will be made compared to the music."

The brothers rapidly disassociated themselves not only with the latest project, but also from the film which started the whole disco phenomenon.

Robin insisted, "We didn't think there should be a follow-up at all. The moment had passed. Kids know when you're overdoing it; they know when they're being patronised. Still, the original script wasn't as bad as the movie turned out, so we agreed to some songs. But then it became clear it was Sylvester and Frank Stallone's movies, so we gave 'em what we had and got out. It was a dreadful movie. Sylvester Stallone should never direct a musical. *Gone With The Wind* had a better musical pace than *Staying Alive*."

These five new Bee Gees songs were essentially the next Barry-Albhy-Karl project, as again all three brothers wrote the songs to be handed over to the production team. Robin and Maurice are barely noticeable on the recordings, which feature Barry on lead and backing vocals, together with the house band. This set of songs is better than those on *Living Eyes* but the film did not do well, and even if it had done, the songs are not well used within it.

The lead single, 'The Woman In You', is a return to the funk sound Barry had avoided with Streisand and Warwick, and the song itself is more like the songs Barry wrote with Albhy. Only the harmonies in the chorus sound much like The Bee Gees that people remembered from *Saturday Night Fever*. The second single was the quiet ballad, 'Someone Belonging To Someone', another long and winding melody sung by Barry. The slow and fast dance grooves respectively of 'I Love You Too Much' and 'Breakout' deserved a better fate than they got. The second to last track on side one, 'Life Goes On', is a bouncy little pop song that's pleasant enough on the ear but lacks that certain something to justify its worldwide release as a single, although it found its way onto seven-inch format in Japan.

A drastically edited version of 'Stayin' Alive' finished The Bee Gees' involvement on the album. Its inclusion appeared to be something of an afterthought, perhaps in recognition of its importance as the title track of the film.

Despite the negativity, the first single, 'The Woman In You' was released in May, 1983, and started out strong. Always the Gibb with an eye on the charts, Robin told interviewer Louis Bakens in Holland, "The new Bee Gees' single is out in America now, which is a very big hit, and that in just a few days. Today's it's [gone] from 49 to 33, and it's going very fast. Everyone is very excited over there, and they're counting that it is gonna be a number one there in only a few weeks' time. 'The Woman In You' is the fastest breaking single. The President of Polygram in New York said the other night that it is the fastest breaking single in the last five years. It is excellent news, considering that 'Stayin' Alive' went on the charts as 75, 'Night Fever' as 71 and 'How Deep Is Your Love' as 89."

Although it didn't reach the expected number one spot, it was a Top 40 hit in the US, Germany and Holland, reaching number 24, 23 and 26 respectively in those countries. It was also released as a 12-inch single with a special 'Saturday Night Mix', a medley of *Fever* songs on the B-side.

The soundtrack LP followed in June, and the film had its premiere in Los Angeles on July 11 and in New York two days later.

The second single, the romantic ballad 'Someone Belonging To Someone', followed in July, inexplicably reaching only number 49 in both the UK and the USA, although it did feature in the Dutch charts in the number 30 spot.

★   ★   ★

536

In late 1982, Robin began work on his first "solo" album in more than 12 years. He had been disappointed that prior commitments prevented Arif Mardin from producing the LP, but rather than work with anyone else, he opted to co-produce the disc with Maurice.

Although billed as a Robin Gibb album, this is primarily a duo record by Robin and Maurice, who wrote all the songs together. Maurice's extensive work as songwriter, musician, arranger, producer, and back-up singer should rate him a co-credit but he chose – characteristically – to put himself in the background. Of the former Bee Gees band, Dennis Bryon, Alan Kendall, and the Boneroo Horns reappeared, along with "house band" player George Bitzer. Notably, however, Barry, Albhy, and Karl had nothing at all to do with this record.

The lead single 'Juliet', released in June, packs everything into it to make a hit: the pseudo 'Also Sprach Zarathustra' opening, the dance beat, the high but not falsetto vocal, a stutter on "J-J-Juliet", and after the second chorus, a bridge section ("close your eyes . . .") rocketing through a new melody in different vocal styles before bringing it home for one last chorus. And it worked, at least in Europe, where "Euro-pop" was being born from the ashes of disco. "The story is about a man, really having his fantasies. It's a love fantasy and she doesn't really exist in the song," he said. With a romantic video for the song filmed in Sussex, the single topped the German charts, although it reached only number 94 in the UK.

The lively title song 'How Old Are You' was also issued as a single in October in some parts of the world, and the enjoyable video, set in a girls' boarding school, mocks the singer's melodramatic situation of finding himself with an underage girl. Robin starred not only as the schoolteacher, but he took on the George Cole type role of a "spiv" as well. Apparently, Dwina makes a cameo appearance as a hockey girl too, although she disguises herself well if indeed she is there. "It's cheeky . . . it's not a fantasy," Robin said. "I think it's a lot of fun. I just liked the *St. Trinian*'s idea of the English school." The song reached number 37 in Germany, but only 93 in Britain.

A better follow-up single was 'Another Lonely Night In New York', released January of the following year. Although the melody owes a glaring debt to Foreigner's 1981 hit 'Waiting For A Girl Like You', the single, with a video incongruously filmed in Holland, reached number 16 in Germany, and number 71 in the UK. Its failure to progress higher in Britain must have disappointed Robin who aggressively promoted it with live performances on various TV shows including *Cannon & Ball*, *The Leo Sayer Show* and *Rod Hull & Emu*. The performance on the last named show is of particular interest, audibly at least, as the backing tape includes instrumentation which would not be heard on either the single or album version.

"The Bee Gees are not breaking up; however, it's the Gibb brothers together that will always [have] something going on because the Gibb brothers are songwriters," Robin clarified.

"Even though I know I'm producing with my brother, or whatever, I see it as a team," he said. "I don't think you can get things done if you see your-self as a leader. You've got to be able to take feedback and input. Maurice is very good at that. If either one of us had an idea the other didn't like, we'd talk about it. We could discuss it. When you're in the studio awhile, it becomes very relaxed."

While *How Old Are You* might have some links to The Bee Gees' more recent work, it bore no resemblance at all to its predecessor, *Robin's Reign*. "I was still in my teens and I was doing stuff that was just off the wall," he said of his first solo effort. "I wasn't following any set musical direction at all. But I've matured musically and I'm developing in a certain direction. I could never have done this kind of stuff then.

"During the years, the styles of music change. My style of music also changes because I get older. I still like a lot of black groups . . . I still like Smokey Robinson . . . and from the English new wave groups, I like Culture Club and Human League and things like that.

"Now in our careers, we're writing more for other artists as the Gibb brothers. There's only a certain amount one can do writing-wise just for the entity of The Bee Gees – that doesn't mean The Bee Gees are breaking up, it's just that the format of The Bee Gees will be limited to less albums possibly than there were six or seven years ago."

How Old Are You was released in July, but Robin had doubts about issuing the LP in the States. "I was in the middle of changing labels . . . and I didn't want Polygram to release it because I was not able to support it," he explained. "I didn't want it to come out and die without my support. I didn't feel they had its best interests at heart. I felt it would be better if I started with a new label, and one which was more into the kind of music I was doing." In spite of this, 40,000 copies leaked through to the US in October and most were sold.

Although Robin made the rounds of television shows promoting the album, he insisted, "I don't really look for a steady solo career as an artist. It's really a project with Maurice outside The Bee Gees, but I'm not looking to be separate from The Bee Gees. My priority is still The Bee Gees."

★　★　★

Barry was also looking towards outside projects. In late 1982, he participated in both *Dynasty* star Linda Evans' International Tennis Tournament to benefit a Spina Bifida charity, and Illie Nastase's Tournament to benefit the American Cancer Society. Barry and his wife Linda – note the subtle change late in life to the spelling of her Christian name – also flew with Kenny Rogers in Kenny's own plane to his home to discuss the possibility of writing and producing an album for him. "Kenny Roger's private jet was a BAC 111 with about 20 seats in white kid leather," Tom Kennedy recalled. "He *did* live a rather opulent lifestyle."

Kenny had approached Barry, asking for a song, and as Barry explained, it snowballed from there. "Someone may say, 'Would you do a couple of tracks?', and if I really love that artist, I'd say, 'Well, I'd actually love to do a whole project, do an album rather than just do two songs.' Because I think an album has an identity, and I think you work for the whole identity and you do it as a project . . . Then your heart's in it, and it's better than doing just two songs. I don't think it works otherwise."

Although the visit was successful in that Barry and Kenny were able to agree to the project, for Linda the visit had a painful outcome. An afternoon of go-karting resulted in a broken arm. "It was one of those things . . . Odysseys, they're called, with a roll cage. She turned it over and put her hand out to save herself, which was apparently quite a bad move," Tom explained.

For the casual listener of the late Seventies and early Eighties, familiar only with the falsetto-driven R&B hit singles, the pairing of the country music star and The Bee Gees may have raised many an eyebrow, although long-term Bee Gees' fans would already have known about Barry's predilection for country music. In fact, earlier that year, Barry had even received a BMI Country Citation of Achievement for composing 'Rest Your Love On Me'. Kenny Rogers, seeking to broaden his image, maintained, "You have to stick your neck out and hope that your audience will stretch out their musical tastes with you. Just the thought of me working with The Bee Gees has to make people a little curious about these two different musical styles."

Once the suggestion was made, there was never any doubt that the project would come to fruition, with the team of Gibb, Galuten and Richardson producing. "Barry wanted to work with Kenny," Albhy explained. "The basic rule of thumb was, if there was anybody who was inspirational for Barry to work with, then it would be great to work with them. Everything was tied to Barry writing great songs. If Barry was inspired that was all that was needed. If he wasn't, you were wasting your time."

"We've been very fortunate because being songwriters first, we've been able to adapt ourselves to different people like Kenny Rogers," Maurice explained.

The project was done around the same time as *Staying Alive*. The same methodology was used as for Streisand and Warwick, although here Maurice plays rhythm guitar on some songs, and he and Robin even sing back-up on one, 'Living With You'. Viewed as a whole, the project was much less successful than its comparable predecessors.

"We sent all the songs and when he came to start singing, he didn't know the words," Maurice complained.

Barry agreed that it was a drawback to Kenny's performance. "The fact that they have to have a piece of paper in front of them, and they've been working on this album with you for three months, and they haven't actually learnt the songs. You think . . . if I was the artist and you were the producer, I'd be at home memorising these words and making sure that I didn't have to read when I sang 'cause it's a different thing when you read and sing."

According to Albhy, Kenny had some difficulty interpreting the songs in his own distinctive style. The set of demos Barry and Albhy made for this album has surfaced on bootleg CD, and for all its rough edges, it is much more enjoyable to listen to than the finished album. The exception is 'Islands In The Stream', sung in duet by Kenny and Dolly Parton, which is not only the artistic highlight but was a huge chart success as well in both country and pop.

The only song by Barry and Albhy, 'This Woman', was a follow-up single and reached number 23 in the USA charts although it failed to make any impact in Europe. 'Evening Star' by Barry and Maurice might be the best of the album cuts, possibly because it uses country musicians instead of the house band and has The Gatlin Brothers singing back-up. Barry's demos of 'You And I', 'Hold Me', and 'Eyes That See In The Dark' show how good the songs themselves are.

Albhy's memories of the album are coloured by the fact that it was not a particularly pleasant experience for him. In past productions, the demos would be made to be used as guides for the finished song, to be replaced by tracks recorded by session musicians. He felt that in his performances, Kenny was trying to duplicate Barry's voice on the demos, rather than allowing his own style to come through. Always forthright, Albhy voiced his concerns to Kenny.

"It just was not Kenny Rogers at all, I thought . . . so I was candid," he recalled, "and I said to Kenny, perhaps not as tactful then as I would learn to be later, but nonetheless I said, 'You need to sing it like *you*.' And all I know is his manager came in and spoke to Dick and said, 'You know, we think it would be better off if Albhy wasn't there when Kenny sings his vocals.'" Albhy claims he spent much of the remainder of the *Eyes That See In The Dark* sessions wind-surfing.

Eyes That See In The Dark was released in August in the States and two months later in Britain. The first single was the title track, which failed to break into the Top 40 in either Britain or the United States, reaching only number 61 and number 79 on the respective charts of each.

While the album's sales overall were disappointing, the next single, 'Islands In The Stream', became the biggest selling single in RCA's (Elvis Presley's label) long and successful history, and the biggest country hit ever, eventually reaching platinum status. It was the number one single for two weeks in a row in the US charts, as well as achieving that ranking in the US Country charts for two weeks and the American adult contemporary charts for four weeks. It was also a massive number one in both Australia and New Zealand, and reached number seven in Britain. Although seen as a country styled song, it initially had a very different slant. "We wrote it as a black-feeling song. It could easily have been done by Marvin Gaye," said Robin.

"We were writing a song for Diana Ross," Barry revealed, "but she never got round to hearing it and Kenny wanted a song and we came up with this one. It was written as an R&B song so it just shows you the relationship between the two types of songs that it could, in fact, turn into a country song very easily. It has become the most successful country song in history, which is overwhelming in itself."

The single teamed Kenny with the effervescent Dolly Parton. "Dolly Parton, now there's a lady that is *the* pleasure to work with," Barry enthused. "I mean, [what a] fantastic voice!"

"When we did 'Islands In The Stream', we imagined Dolly singing the other part," Maurice recalled, "because she was the queen of country, he was the king, [but] they never sang together [before]. So it's a perfect sort of marriage.

"That was an R&B song, and yet as soon as Kenny and Dolly sang it, we got country crossover. We have the [original] demo of it. It's very R&B; in fact, it's Smokey Robinson type of R&B."

The song earned The Bee Gees the National Music Publishers' Association award for the Country Song Of The Year in Los Angeles the following March.

Despite his disappointment with some aspects of the album, Albhy had to concede that he was thrilled that the next single, 'This Woman', which he co-wrote with Barry, garnered them an Academy of Country Music award and a *Billboard* award for a country record, "so personally I am glad the record was made in some ways. ['This Woman'] was more in Kenny's regular range, more of a regular Kenny song," he said. The single was released in January of 1984, and reached number 23 in the US.

★   ★   ★

In August, 1983, plans were announced for a new *Best Of Bee Gees* album to be released in January. The proposed album was to feature their hits from *Children Of The World* and *Spirits Having Flown*, as well as three new tracks: 'It's My Neighbourhood', 'Dimensions' and 'Toys', the latter described as a Christmas song.

That same month, the brothers attended a book signing at Liberty's in London for David English's updated *Legend*, donating their proceeds from the sale of the book to the World Wildlife Fund.

In September, The Bee Gees were Noel Edmonds' guests on his *Late Late Breakfast Show* and to their embarrassment were shown a film of their first television appearance, singing 'Time Is Passing By', as children in Australia.

Barry also joined Stevie Wonder on stage on November 6 in Sunrise, Florida, to sing 'Happy Birthday' for Martin Luther King.

Maurice made a 15-minute film with soundtrack, at a cost of $60,000, which he donated to the Metro-Dade Tourism Department.

In November, The Bee Gees participated in the *Salute To Neil Sedaka* television special, paying tribute to the singer/songwriter with a rendition of his 'Happy Birthday, Sweet Sixteen'.

Christmas Eve was a time for happy families, and Cilla Black's Christmas special featured a live satellite link to Miami bringing Barry and Linda with their sons, Stevie, Ashley and Travis; Maurice and Yvonne with Adam and Samantha; and in their first real public appearance, Robin and Dwina with baby Robin John. It had been an eventful year, but all was calm as the family joined Cilla in singing 'Silent Night'.

35

PRICE OF FAME

W ITH HIS LOVE affair with Victoria Principal behind him, Andy returned to the role of Frederic, this time in the critically acclaimed Canadian version of *The Pirates Of Penzance* in Toronto in August. Once again, he began with high hopes and good intentions, but once again he left the company a short time later.

In the autumn, a new role beckoned; this time the starring role in the national company of the Andrew Lloyd Webber and Tim Rice musical, *Joseph And The Amazing Technicolour Dreamcoat*.

After his *Pirates* experience, Andy was reluctant to commit himself to another stage show. The challenging Gilbert and Sullivan operetta required a trained tenor voice, and accustomed to singing pop music, his voice couldn't hold up. Besides, Andy said ingenuously, "It sounded kind of biblical. I didn't know if I wanted to be in something like that. It was a big transition from being a rock singer to a biblical thing."

Andy was unfamiliar with both the musical and the story of Joseph from the book of Genesis, but he saw the show on a trip to New York and found that the music was more in keeping with his pop background. He was instantly sold on the idea. "I wanted to be in it," he said. "I just knew I wanted to do it, no doubt about that. It was so colourful, I wanted to be up on that stage."

Andy read the story of Joseph in the Bible and found himself enjoying it. He made his début in the national company of *Joseph And The Amazing Technicolour Dreamcoat* in Philadelphia in November, the final month of the national tour of the show, and later that month appeared in costume on a float in Macy's Thanksgiving Day Parade performing songs from the show including 'Any Dream Will Do'. Andy couldn't make the immediate transition from the national company to Broadway until he first fulfilled a previous commitment.

The director and choreographer for *Joseph*, Tony Tanner, was also the director for Andy's next project, a made for cable television musical comedy entitled *Something's Afoot,* filmed for Showtime Cable TV. Andy's co-stars were the veteran actress, Jean Stapleton, best known for her role of Archie Bunker's wife Edith in the long-running American television series, *All In The Family*, and Lenore Zann. The play was a musical murder mystery inspired by

542

Agatha Christie and Sir Arthur Conan Doyle, who even rate a mention in the lyrics. Ten guests at an English country manor house are being murdered one by one; a real *Ten Little Indians* affair. The set was elaborate. Andy explained, "They had a huge mansion built on stage, a six-ton set."

The tedium of filming a play for television was something that Andy hadn't encountered in his *Solid Gold* days, and just as the characters in the play were diminishing so were the audience numbers. "We'd start every evening with a live audience," he recalled. "We kept stopping to get things right, and they'd get bored and leave until in the end, there was nobody in the audience at all."

Soon, he found himself escaping into music during quiet moments in the filming of the show. While his co-stars studied their lines, "I'd find myself slipping in the tape of the *Joseph* soundtrack. I loved the music," he confessed.

When *Something's Afoot* first aired on December 9, 1982, Andy's performance was given full marks. Showtime repeated the show three more times during the month.

On December 1, 1982, Andy made his Broadway début in *Joseph And The Amazing Technicolour Dreamcoat* at New York's Royale Theater, opening to rave reviews. His parents, Barry and Maurice were there to cheer him on for his opening night, and Andy's name proved to have a powerful drawing power, ensuring sold-out houses. Nearly every night brought another round of standing ovations, and Andy seemed to be on top of the world.

The show's producer, Zev Bufman, said, "When he started rehearsals, his brothers were jumping up and down with excitement. His mum and dad came over from England."

In Manhattan's Celebrity Café, Andy met the country music star, Tanya Tucker, with whom he was romantically linked for a very short time. Tanya had recently ended a well publicised relationship with an older star; in her case, singer Glen Campbell. Her publicist rather tactlessly revealed, "Tanya had a two-night with [boxer Gerry] Cooney and a three-night stand with Gibb." Tanya's mother confirmed, "Tanya called me from New York at four a.m., and this man said, 'Hello, Mama Tucker. This is Gerry Cooney.' I talked with Andy Gibb one morning too. It was really exciting." Tanya has since said that her feelings for Andy were almost maternal, explaining, "You just wanted to baby him."

While Andy enjoyed the music and the spectacle of *Joseph*, he admitted wistfully, "I miss performing in front of my fans, singing my own hits and stuff."

But the following month, Andy missed a full week of performances and was threatened with firing if he didn't return. "He used to say it was because of his throat," his mother explained, "but of course, it wasn't. They bought that for a while, and then they realised what was happening. We couldn't get him out of bed, you know, his door was locked. It happened and it'd break his heart, you know, he was sorry. But then it would happen again."

"He was always talking about it as a new start," Bufman recalled. "But we'd lose him over long weekends. He'd come back on Tuesday, and he'd look beat. He was like a little puppy – so ashamed when he did something wrong."

Bufman added, "He was all heart, but he didn't have enough muscle to carry through." His words were more prophetic than he could ever have imagined.

On January 12, Andy didn't appear for either the matinée or the evening performance at the Royale Theater. His scheduled TV appearances were cancelled, and his understudy Doug Voet took his place on stage. Bufman said, "Doug has been great. He gets standing ovations so he'll be the logical one to replace Andy."

Unfortunately, no matter how talented he might be, Doug Voet was not a familiar name, and in the long term, the show needed a star. Other former teen idols stepped into the role of Joseph. First David Cassidy and later Donny Osmond would wear the multicoloured "dreamcoat", with the latter recording both the soundtrack and a video of the show.

Three years later, Andy admitted, "My past history has shown what the drug has done to me. I lost a lot of work through it. I lost *Solid Gold*. I lost *Joseph* on Broadway," but in the months after his dismissal from the show, he simply blamed immaturity and insisted that he would love to return to the theatre sometime in the future. "I'd really want to be ready for it, though," he said. "I didn't work out and get in shape for those other things. I just wasn't ready for them. I guess I'll have to wait until I'm older. Right now, my attention span over three months is very bad, doing the same thing night after night. But maybe when I get older, more mature, maybe then I can cut it."

He felt that his time with both *Pirates* and *Joseph* had given him valuable experience. "I'm just sorry I wasn't able to stick it out [in *Joseph* for] the full six months," he said. "But it was very demanding on me at the time, doing eight shows a week."

Like his eldest brother before him, Andy was tempted by a career in Hollywood. "I have had some offers, but nothing I'd want to do the first time out," he explained. "They always want me to play a rock singer, but I don't want to take a film role and then play myself. When the right thing comes along, though, I'll know it."

In the meantime, he was still in demand as a famous face, making the rounds of talk shows and awards presentations. At the 1983 American Music Awards, Andy teamed up with a member of another famous singing family, LaToya Jackson, to present the Favourite Pop Group award to Hall & Oates.

In June, he began his first South American tour, with scheduled appearances in Brazil, Columbia, Argentina, Venezuela and Puerto Rico. It was an unfortunate coincidence, given its reputation, that Columbia was the one country where problems were encountered. But it had nothing whatsoever to do with drugs, more to do with the expectations of the promoter outweighing those of the performer. As the disagreement between the two gained momentum, Andy felt threatened and eventually sought refuge in the country's American Embassy when the promoter refused to return his passport. Being a famous face undoubtedly helped his cause, and although Andy was a resident alien rather than an American citizen, members of the elite United States Special Forces Unit escorted him back to the US without incident.

Recovering from his ordeal, which was kept out of the press, Andy insisted that reports of his condition after his well-publicised split from Victoria Principal were exaggerated, and that he now was off drugs and completely over his emotional crisis, with no desire to discuss what had passed. "I'm not saying it wasn't bad. It certainly wasn't good," he admitted. "It's something everybody wants to talk about. It just seems to me, why does it have to be brought up? The point is, it's not something I'm ashamed of. It's something I learned a lesson from.

"To me, it's just an old memory," he said. "I'm so much healthier now and really together."

Andy and his band and managers went on a camping trip on a lake near Santa Barbara, California, between gigs. "The idea was to just relax and catch some bass and have a good time," he said.

In August, he launched his nightclub act with a one-week engagement at The Resorts International Hotel Casino in Atlantic City, New Jersey, with former Bee Gees' band member, Dennis Bryon, on drums. It was yet another fresh start for the 25-year-old.

"This is a whole new thing to me," Andy said. "I've never done anything quite like this before, and we have been working hard putting the show together, rehearsing every day. In fact, right now my voice is really sore. The difference between this and the big concerts is that the setting is more intimate. I'll be talking more than I have before, chatting with the audience. And besides that, we'll have a few surprises up our sleeves – some dance routines, things that I've never done before."

Two days after his Resorts International Casino appearance was over, Andy opened a one-week stand at the MGM Grand in Las Vegas, Nevada.

Press reports described him as a young Tom Jones with wholesome appeal, adding, "Versatility seems to be Andy's calling card." Andy's set included 'Old Time Rock'n'Roll', 'Show Me' 'How Deep Is Your Love', 'Massachusetts', 'Words' and a Mills Brothers medley with his own songs, 'Time Is Time', 'Me (Without You)' and 'Shadow Dancing'.

Next he planned to return to the recording studio to begin work on an album, scheduled for release in the spring of 1984.

"I'm looking forward to it," said Andy. "It's time that I get back to recording. It's just that there were so many hits in a rather short time, and I needed to get away from it for a while, to try other things. But now I'm looking forward to getting back at it. I have six of my own songs. They aren't quite finished yet, but I think they're pretty good songs." But the album was not to be.

In November, Andy co-hosted the *Penthouse* Magazine One Million Dollar Pet Of The Year awards at the Sands Hotel and Casino in Atlantic City.

Despite the time that had passed since his last record, he continued to be in demand for television appearances throughout 1983, featuring on the situation-comedy, *Gimme A Break* (with Dennis Bryon), *Battlestars* and *Fantasy*, which he co-hosted on several episodes. He also continued to perform live in Denver and at the MGM Grand Hotel in Las Vegas, and opened on December 26 at the Diplomat Hotel in Hollywood, Florida. He began the New Year at the Riviera Hotel in Las Vegas with his *Solid Gold* co-star, Marilyn McCoo, playing from January 13–19, 1984, and returning for a repeat engagement from May 3–30.

In February he gave a concert at Vina Del Mar in Chile, playing before 35,000 fans, and was honoured with The Silver Torch award for his performance. From there he went on to a week's engagement at the Sun City Resort Hotel in South Africa, ending the day before his twenty-sixth birthday.

Returning to North America, Andy made appearances in Minneapolis, Montreal and Lake Tahoe in the spring, before kicking off his summer season with a week at Caesar's in Atlantic City.

Once again teaming up with his former co-star Marilyn McCoo, Andy kicked off a 10-date tour in Dallas, performing with the Dallas Symphony Orchestra. On his final concert of the tour at the James. L. Knight Center in Miami Beach on September 1, Andy was joined on stage by his brother Maurice and his eight-year-old nephew, Adam. The proceeds of the concert, which was filmed, were donated to benefit the American Diabetes Foundation.

Later that month, Andy appeared on a television show about heart disease called *For The Sake Of Heart Life*. No one could possibly have guessed at that time that the athletic, fit young man could have any health concerns in that direction.

Returning to his Malibu ranch, Andy took on the task of singing the national anthem before a Los Angeles Raiders football game. 'The Star Spangled Banner' is a difficult piece of music for anyone to sing in those circumstances, since football stadiums are not built for acoustics and your own voice echoes back at you. For someone who grew up in Australia and Britain, it must be even more daunting, but Andy performed it faultlessly.

On December 18, Andy made another sitcom appearances, this time on *Punky Brewster*, playing the piano teacher of the young title character. He reappeared on the programme a month later, this time acting as the master of ceremonies – even taking part in a magic trick – for the "Miss Adorable Pageant".

In January, 1985, it was reported that Andy was due to start filming a movie called *Satan And Eve* in Rome. Andy was cast as Adam, with Orson Welles as God and Malcom McDowell as Satan, but the project fell through.

Andy was very briefly romantically linked with another actress, 17-year-old daytime soap star Melissa Brennan Reeves, who played Jade on *Santa Barbara* and currently appears on another soap opera, *Days Of Our Lives*, in the part of Jennifer Horton.

He appeared live at the Olympic Velodrome in Montreal in February and was asked to head the Royal Command Performance of *Australia Salutes The UK* for Princess Anne. He insisted that there was "no drug problem, no way. I only had one drug problem in my life and I'm never gonna go through that again," he stated emphatically, but by early spring, it was clear that he was once again losing the battle with substance abuse.

Barbara watched helplessly as the son she adored turned into a stranger. "When he was under the influence, that wasn't him at all," she insisted. "That was [when] somebody else took over. The next day, he would be back apologising to everybody. He wouldn't know what he'd done, but he would be sorry."

He became demanding and abusive to the people he worked with, ordering them to supply him with cocaine. "He would threaten them that he wouldn't go on stage if they didn't get him some . . . I don't know where they got it from, but somebody always managed to get him some," Barbara said sadly. Her naïve remarks about the comparative dangers of drugs in the Seventies must have haunted her as she watched Andy's decline.

Andy's problems ran much deeper than the drugs and alcohol which he used as a crutch to cope with his extreme lack of self-esteem. His agent at the time, Jeff Witjas, said, "Sometimes I'd say, 'Andy, look in the mirror. You've got everything – good looks, talent. Women love you.' Men liked him too. But when he looked in the mirror, you always had the feeling he didn't see anything."

In April, Andy again sought help for his addiction, checking into the Betty Ford Treatment Clinic at Rancho Mirage in Southern California for six weeks.

Maurice, himself a recovering alcoholic, was well aware of Andy's problems but felt that there was little anyone could do to help. "Andy was always the golden boy, but he got into cocaine as well as booze," he said. "We all knew he was dabbling, but we didn't know how deep he was into drugs. It began to show. He got nasty . . . We all did what we could to help Andy, but I had to accept that all I could do was plant the seed for his recovery. When he finally went into the Betty Ford Clinic, we thought, 'Thank God.'"

At first, the Betty Ford Clinic appeared to have worked, and Andy returned to the road in May, performing in Jackson, New Jersey. Soon, he had slipped back into addiction. Marc Gurvitz, who managed Andy from 1983 to 1985, observed, "It was hard on him not having the royal treatment any more. Whenever he was depressed on tour, he wanted to cancel the engagement."

Often, Andy would complain of unbearable pain, insisting that his mother take him to the hospital, "because if you're in pain, they give you a shot . . . and you go to sleep. I'd got to the point where I'd take him to the hospital . . .

not believing him, of thinking he was crying wolf again," Barbara admitted.

His cardiologist, Dr William Shell, said that in some cases, Andy's pains were not only very real, but also very serious. "These weren't heart attacks in the lay sense," he explained. "They were heart attacks in the sense that he destroyed small amounts of heart muscle."

In the autumn, Andy played two shows in Minneapolis, before beginning a week's engagement in Toronto at the Royal York Hotel. On his first night at the Royal York, Andy's performance was well received, although one heckler in the audience insisted upon chanting "Victoria" ad infinitum throughout his performance of 'Me (Without You)'. As a result, Andy dropped that particular number from his repertoire during the remainder of his engagement there, substituting more Bee Gees' and Mills Brothers' tunes.

After each show, a large number of people would congregate in the lounge area located immediately outside of the dinner room, hoping to meet the young star. Dawn Martin, a young woman who worked in hospitality, making sure the entertainers were fed and kept relatively happy, also happened to be a fan, and she recalled that Andy entered the room followed by an entourage of people including his mother. Leaning casually on one of the partitions, Andy waited receptively for people to approach him and shortly thereafter, he began to mingle.

"Gosh, Andy spoke to each of us like we'd been long lost friends," Dawn recalled. "His mother would also jump in every now and then as well. I am not sure if the family likes to joke around a lot, or if they were just trying to put all of us ladies at ease as we met Andy, but it was such a warm, receptive experience. When it came to pictures, he was so inviting and he'd sort of give you a little squeeze as if to let me know that I was special. Although the night was getting on, he graciously remained until everyone had spoken to him, signed autographs and had completed their photos."

Dawn's work put her in contact with many celebrities whose personal and professional personas were not the same, but in Andy's case, "he still came across as a sincere, gracious, and 'down to earth' guy even in a room full of female admirers flocking to see him after a performance."

The gremlins were at work for the performance on Andy's third evening. In the middle of a song, his microphone died, which he took in his stride. Unfortunately, the replacement microphone was also dead, which seemed to particularly annoy him.

After the show, Dawn went backstage and spoke to Andy's tour manager, Michael Sterling, with a view towards beginning an "official" Andy Gibb fan club as well as to present some of the photos that she had taken of Andy during the previous evenings' performances.

"When I arrived, Mr Sterling ushered me into the dressing room. The dressing room itself was not overly decorated but it was filled with flowers, cards, and teddy bears from other admirers," Dawn said.

The strain of the nightly performances seemed to show on Andy when he appeared. "Unlike the previous evenings . . . this night he was dressed

casually in a sweat suit. He looked very thin and appeared to be very tired
. . . Andy and I began to talk briefly about my intentions. He listened and
responded enthusiastically, and in the end we agreed that I'd get Mr
Sterling's mailing address and we'd take it from there. Prior to leaving I presented Andy with a couple of 8x10's which I'd taken the previous night, for
him to autograph. Andy was quite critical of his appearance and commented
about his 'poor make-up job'."

Andy was often disparaging about his own appearance, often referring to
Barry as his "older and better looking brother". Despite the adulation of
thousands, his low self-esteem and insecurity about his talent, looks – even
his own worth as a person – continued to plague him, and he sought
comfort in whatever substance it took to make him feel self-confident.

In December, Andy performed one of two scheduled shows at Caesar's in
Lake Tahoe but cancelled the second, due to the poor sound quality of the
initial concert.

Andy had a new manager, Dana Miller, who also handled soap opera star
turned singer, Rick Springfield. There was a new lady in his life as well,
Kansas native Nicole Romaine, who had also choreographed his nightclub
act.

"I think the biggest thing that really helped me is that I'm in love at the
moment, intensely in love," he said. "I have found the girl of my dreams,
and we're talking marriage. She's a *Solid Gold* dancer and I am just crazed,
crazed about her. She only adds to my sobriety."

Andy recognised the problems of his meteoric rise and fall, saying,
"Looking back, almost a little too much too soon, too young, because I
peaked and then I died for a while and I am just now starting to try and get
my feet back on the ground."

He also admitted that he had fallen victim to the materialism and
one-upmanship of the "Me Decade", where materialism was the name of
the game and image was everything.

"I didn't think it was going to be [a disadvantage] at the time, 'cause it was
wonderful! Great big beautiful roller coaster ride. I was making a couple of
million a week, literally, it was just pouring in. I was buying cars, yachts . . .
Looking back, I suppose I could blame a few people 'cause I was too young
to know any better, but nobody advised me. Maybe I wouldn't have listened
if they had thinking back, 'cause I was pretty head strong, but nobody
advised me how to invest it, what to do with it."

Andy finished off the year with a well-received Asian tour. In Bangkok,
he starred in a Royal Command Performance at the Royal Orchard Hotel
before the King and Queen of Thailand, even performing a duet with the
Crown Princess on 'All I Have To Do Is Dream'.

In Kuala Lumpur, he played to a crowd of 6,000, and in Tai Pei, Hong
Kong, the attendance more than doubled, with 12,500 excited fans. His
over-enthusiastic admirers pulled him from the stage, bumping his head and
dislocating his thumb in the process. After all that, it was little wonder that

Andy cancelled the second scheduled Hong Kong concert, although he pleaded only "throat problems".

Andy played a New Year's Eve concert in Singapore followed by two shows on New Year's Day and had an unexpected reunion with his former sister-in-law, Lulu, who was also touring the Far East.

There was yet another fresh start planned for the coming year, as Andy vowed, "I've got a feeling that deep down in the pit of my stomach that '86 is going to be good for me. Because I am clean now, and I know what I'm doing and to work with my brothers, joining my brothers at the end of the year as a Bee Gee at the end of '86 is what we're doing. We're going to be one group, and we will start my new album in May with Barry again, now we have confidence in me."

Like many other acts who enjoyed brief stardom during the Seventies, Andy was finding that he could earn a living by playing many smaller club dates instead of a few big stadiums, but the clubs weren't nearly as lucrative as the major venues had been. He wistfully recalled the days when he performed before thousands of screaming fans and looked forward to that next new beginning when a new album would put him back on top.

He had a busy schedule of concert dates lined up, playing various Fairmont Hotels during March and April He opened at the San Francisco Fairmont on March 9, just four days after his twenty-eighth birthday.

One fan who saw Andy performing on several occasions during his engagement there, Marty Hogan, recalled that he was surprised that the 500-seat capacity room was only about one fifth full. "The show, however, was excellent and Andy was doing as much talking as he was singing, being very intimate with the audience. The crowd was older and too polite, probably as there was a 21-year-old minimum age requirement," Marty explained.

Marty had become friendly with one of Andy's backing vocalists, Leonard, who asked him if he would mind sitting with Barbara Gibb at one of the shows. On that occasion, Andy left abruptly, without finishing with 'Shadow Dancing', usually his closing number.

Marty accompanied Leonard to return Andy's show jacket to his hotel room, with the offer that he could briefly meet the star. Barbara Gibb let the two young men into the suite, where a wet-haired Andy clad in a bathrobe was kicking the television set with his bare feet because the reception was poor.

Marty recalled that Andy was "talking a mile a minute, telling gruesome stories about the old prison Alcatraz in the San Francisco Bay. Some of the remarks were startling and I kept watching Barbara for reactions to some of Andy's comments. She just smiled," he said.

That evening, Marty was treated to a full private concert of 26 Bee Gees' songs performed by Andy, accompanying himself on a gold plated guitar, said to be worth $100,000, that Barry had given him for his birthday.

Andy mentioned that he had a new single due for release later that year,

'It's My Neighbourhood'. "I think it's a number one hit, don't you, mum?" he added to Barbara.

Marty continued, "Somehow, Victoria Principal's name came up and Andy simply replied, 'But we don't talk about actresses, do we, mum?' He quickly changed the subject. Before anyone realised, it was 5.00 a.m. We finally prepared to depart and Andy completely caught me off guard. He said, 'Thanks for coming up tonight' and gave us all hugs. He was so well mannered," he added.

From San Francisco, Andy went on to play at the Fairmont Hotels in Orlando, Reno, New Orleans and Dallas.

In May, he was in the studio for the first time in four years recording demos for a new album, tentatively titled, *It's My Neighbourhood*, to be co-produced by Jimmy Studer. Eventually, the working title for the album was changed to *Man On Fire*. "I think it'll be my best album by far," Andy enthused. One of the tracks for the album was a Phil Collins composition that his new manager, Dana Miller, had secured for him.

That summer, he played concerts in the Catskill Mountains, Cleveland and Atlantic City. Andy claimed that Miller "just turned everything around" for him. "It's been really amazing. He's changed my image completely. We're working on it day by day. We haven't been together that long, but he's just making me see what I need to do to get away from the old Andy Gibb and attract a new audience.

"I've had to overcome this stigma that I've been through in the past two years. Obviously, the problems have been hard to overcome, but I think with time and positive thinking, I'm ready again. I was in a rut and staying in it. I was being the old Andy Gibb. I never changed my looks or my appearance or the way I dressed. I think it's about time I caught up with the times."

On one occasion, some Girl Scout campers had a rare treat. There was a call to the camp director that Andy Gibb was eating at a local restaurant in the nearby resort town. Several of the girls were interested in meeting him, but some of the camp counsellors had had bad experiences with other celebrities and were none too keen to risk a repeat performance. One counsellor, Daisy, was a little more daring. "I figured, okay, what's the worst that can happen . . . He could scream and be obnoxious like many of the others . . . After all, the girls really wanted to see him," she explained.

She needn't have worried. "Andy was a perfect gentleman," she recalled. "He was very patient and took time with each girl. He was a breath of fresh air."

Late in 1986, Andy returned to Miami to once again live near his brothers. He briefly dated model Donna Rice, whose 15 minutes of fame had come when she was linked with Presidential candidate Gary Hart, effectively ending his dreams for the White House.

He ended 1986 with a New Year's Eve concert in Indianapolis and dreams of his long-awaited recording comeback for the coming year.

36

YOU DON'T SAY "US" ANYMORE

"WE JUST TOOK a year out just to do these separate things," Maurice explained. "We've all been helping each other out with our separate things too. We did actually, the three of us, collectively decide that this year we would do everything that we've always wanted to do a little bit of."

For Robin, it was house-hunting and a new LP; for Barry, a solo video album; for Maurice, it was scoring films.

In 1984, when their son Robin John was a year old, Robin and Dwina began searching for a place to put down roots. They discovered just the place on the edge of Thame, in Oxfordshire. As Dwina put it, "We came to the arches of the gate house and stepped into paradise. It was just what we were looking for."

It might not have been the conventional idea of paradise, but Robin and Dwina have never made any pretence of being a conventional couple. A medieval mansion, The Prebendal was built in the twelfth century by the English theologian Robert Grosseteste and for 500 years played a strictly ecclesiastical role as a place where priests trained to become bishops. The property still has its own chapel and refectory. A heated swimming pool and tennis courts were later additions to the 20 acre estate.

A Bee Gee was not the first celebrity to inhabit The Prebendal. "Elizabeth I was here," Robin revealed. "So was Henry VIII. George III had some exiles from the French Revolution stay here, about 50 of them . . . This house is a fantastic base. Amazing to think it's older than Hampton Court and the same age as the Tower of London." It later became the home of the last member of the Rolls-Royce family.

After buying the house, the couple decided to restore the property to its medieval glory. They searched the country for authentic doors, wood panelling and furnishings – even a suit of armour. Inspired by Ryecote Chapel, Dwina hand-painted the ceilings in a soft, pale blue with gold stars. The chapel on the estate was carefully restored and remains a consecrated Christian chapel.

"It all adds up to a very expensive undertaking, but it's been worth it," Robin said. "You don't really own a property like this. You're merely custodians for the next generation. But we love what we're doing, love the ambience of the place – we even love the ghosts!"

The renovation wasn't easy in the beginning. "When we first moved in here, the house wouldn't accept anything new," Dwina claimed. "Washing machines would break down, televisions, video machines. Telephone systems – they wouldn't function properly. An engineer from BT came out and said, 'It's not us, it's the house.'"

Despite the mechanical problems, Dwina credited the "500 years of prayer" during its religious history for giving The Prebendal an air of tranquillity. Robin agreed, "It is just so peaceful . . . I have never felt anything other than utterly relaxed here."

Robin's second album of the Eighties, with its emphasis on the techno-pop sound, could hardly be farther removed from the medieval splendour of The Prebendal. Despite his love for history, Robin's musical taste is modern. "I don't like songs of the past," he explained. "I like to get ahead; these songs are very 1984, maybe even more futuristic. You'd never associate them with The Bee Gees."

Perhaps not, but once again, *Secret Agent* was a Robin and Maurice collaboration all the way, and this time two songs were even co-written with Barry. Except for some electric guitar, the instrumental tracks are all synthesizers and drum sequencers, so the album has a cold and crisp sound to it.

The lead single, 'Boys Do Fall In Love', was released in May, 1984, and just cracked the Top 40 in the United States, coming in at number 37. It did slightly better in Germany, where it peaked at 21. There was a 12-inch single with a "long version" – what would become known soon as a "dance remix" – not strictly mixing but very free editing, including even the insertion of newly recorded material. "'Boys Do Fall In Love' is quite tongue-in-cheek," he explained. "I'm very cynical about love ballads right now because I went through a dreadful divorce back in 1980. I don't feel like doing love ballads, quite honestly."

The B-side 'Diamonds', with a little bit of Maurice vocal, was one of the more successful songs on the album, and its storyline as well as its title harks back to 1969's 'Black Diamond'.

The LP followed in June. The second single was the title track, 'Secret Agent', but this did not fare as well as its predecessor.

This album was distributed in the US by Mirage, an Atlantic custom label owned by Jerry Greenberg, a long-time friend of The Bee Gees from their Atlantic days.

"It's a different sound," Robin maintained. "Very black and urban, with strong story lines. It reflects street music. I'm not singing at all the same as I did on our early records."

While Robin conceded that people would always regard him as a Bee Gee, he still held out hope that eventually people would see him simply as Robin Gibb. "I'll always be a Bee Gee, but I'd like to think that as kids discover this record, they'll see me as a new artist. It's not difficult to establish a solo identity, but it *does* take time. Look at Phil Collins. He will always be associated with Genesis, but now he has a completely separate profile. I want to build a personal repertoire and not simply go on stage singing songs The Bee Gees made famous – that's too easy."

In the immediate future, he had no plans to take his new songs on the road. "There's no point in touring solo until I've built a solo base," he said. "Otherwise, people just expect Bee Gees songs."

Robin revealed that he and Barry both had plans for another solo album in January, 1985, with the next Bee Gees album planned for the following autumn. "It will be different," he claimed. "Adventuresome. Something that will bury the disco business. We have deliberately done other things because we felt our image needed a rest. We needed to rebuild our credibility."

★   ★   ★

In August, 1983, Barry had signed a recording and film deal with Irving Azoff of MCA in New York, with plans for a "visual album".

"It's something I always wanted to do," Barry revealed, "but I never quite felt comfortable enough to do it. The man who really made me think seriously about it was Irving Azoff, who convinced me that there was possibly a market out there for me."

Reflecting back over his career, Barry said, "You tend to know a lot more people over the years. The ones that thought you were very green in the first place now treat you with a little more respect, and I think length of time really helps your career. The fact that people know you've been around a long time, give you just a little more attention than they would if you'd just come on the scene, you know. It's interesting, we've been very lucky in that respect because we're a group that went up, down and then up again, and it's very like an education when that happens to you because you really find out about who your friends are . . . We were lucky. We hit the bottom and all the people that hung around when we were successful at first disappeared, and people like our personal manager, Richard Ashby, and our original road manager, Tom Kennedy, who've been with us now for 14 years are still with us. So they went through the bad times too, and all the people that were no use have now disappeared. So we had success again, and we're all together, and the people who really care – and the people we really care about – are still with us."

Barry recorded his first solo album with Karl Richardson but not Albhy Galuten. He co-wrote most of the songs with George Bitzer and some with Maurice, with Robin contributing to one. He again used the house band, "the same musicians that I have used for many years now," to make the recordings, as well as Jimmie Haskell's arrangement skills. "George Bitzer, who is a co-writer on this album, is a very fine pianist and he helped me to broaden some of my scope with my chord progressions," Barry explained. "Albhy went to live in California so he is not involved in this project." It was the first sign that all was not well with the production team who had worked together so successfully.

"I would have loved to have worked on it," Albhy asserted, "if he would have done it in the way that I thought . . . But what I had said to Barry when he was looking to do the new album, there were incredible musicians that he loved working with. I said, 'Your ability to write songs is great, let's book a Broadway theatre, some nice sounding theatre in New York for a week or two week's worth of shows, and rehearse a band . . . You love working with The Sweet Inspirations, and Steve Gadd, Richard Tee, Randy Brecker, David Sanborne, Harold the bass player, George Terry the guitar player, Cornell Dupree . . .'

"We could have put together the ideal band, even string section, the whole nine yards," he continued, "written about 15 songs, more than enough for an album, and record it, like seven shows, and put together a live album of solo Barry Gibb. I said, 'This would be great, it would so much more stimulating and inspiring than sitting in a room by ourselves for nine months with a click track.' And he just said, 'I can't do it, man.' And I said, 'Well, I just can't stay and do another one of these records.'"

Although they would do one more project together, the relationship was never the same. "We haven't *really* spoken since," Albhy said. "I know he was very hurt by my leaving."

Albhy still muses over the album that he had dreamed of. "At that point, it would have been so unbelievable," he said. "His ability to sing is great, and we would have had background singers. And with seven or eight versions of each song, we could have had *unbelievable* takes. At that point, the technology was such that you could repair anything in a live take you wanted to. We could have had guest appearances by people coming in and singing verses. It would have been an amazing record."

So Albhy left for California and Karl Richardson stayed behind. "Karl never wanted to leave Florida," he explained. "Florida was a one band town. I wasn't Latin so I wasn't in the Gloria Estefan circle . . . Nobody came and stayed in Florida and had a great career: The Bee Gees and that was it. So, Karl didn't want to leave."

To this point, Barry's traditional strength had been short, catchy pop tunes, but here he was striving for something more substantial than that, and he built up the songs into a longer form with extended lyrics and additional sections of melody. It's a denser album than one might have expected, and the experiment does not always work, but some of the songs are rewarding. Unfortunately, the direction he was taking worked against mass popularity.

Now Voyager was named after one of Barry's favourite films, starring Bette Davis, although the album has nothing to do with the 1942 classic. There was no song of that title on the album, although an instrumental written by Barry called 'Theme From *Now Voyager*' was heard on the feature length video released in conjunction with the album.

The "video album" version of *Now Voyager* has a storyline loosely connecting videos for most of the songs. The protagonist, played by Barry, is plunged into a limbo, and made to reflect on his life, which is shown

555

through the songs. Playing the role of part conscience/part guardian angel was the distinguished British actor, Sir Michael Hordern.

The videos for the album were filmed on location in Tallahassee and St. Petersburg, Florida; Chester, Norfolk, London, Manchester and Sidmouth.

The filming was not an altogether pleasant experience for him. He shaved off his beard for the first time in years – something he described as "absolute hell". He explained, "I did it because I thought it was important. I hate myself without my beard."

For the segments filmed at Manchester's Victoria Baths, not too far from the Gibbs' old home in Chorlton, Barry claimed, "We worked virtually on a sea of cockroaches. They were all in my shoes, you know, and they were everywhere we were working, especially in bare feet. I can't be objective about it . . . It was a nightmare to do.

"I definitely think that acting is hard work. I like the idea of being hungry. When I'm not hungry, I don't work as well, I don't work or create the kind of stuff that really works for me. You have to keep working, keep rolling. You can't sit on your laurels," he added.

While shaving, cockroaches and acting proved to be something less than pleasant for Barry, a stunt during the filming nearly proved fatal for the stuntman, Ken Shepherd. The car he was driving was meant to plunge off the bridge and into the river, landing flat on the water and sinking slowly, giving him enough time to release his seatbelt, put on a breathing apparatus and escape from the car. Instead, weights inside the car shifted, causing the vehicle to go into a nose-dive into nine feet of water at Wretton, Norfolk, sinking immediately. The stuntman was rescued and taken to hospital.

"Ken is an amazing guy," Barry marvelled. "When I spoke to him in the ambulance, he wanted to know if the director was happy and would he need to shoot it again."

The first single from the album, 'Shine Shine', was released in August, 1984. The first impression of the track, written by Barry, Maurice, and George Bitzer, is its very fast beat and Caribbean feel, and the chorus was catchy enough to crack the American Top 40, coming in at number 37. It was less successful in the UK, where it only reached 95, and in Germany, where it achieved number 45.

The album was released in September, one month after the first single and Barry described the making of *Now Voyager* as a lonely time for him. "I don't mean it in the unhappy sense of the word," he explained, "but I do miss working with Maurice and Robin. It's mutual, all three of us need some time to work as individuals, but it doesn't mean we don't miss working together. I believe that, with the album, I have gone out of my way to create something for everybody."

In fact, that is one of the main problems of the album – the sense that Barry was trying to appeal to every market, to be all things to all people. The change from calypso to rap, from easy listening to funk, give the album a slightly disjointed feel. Four years earlier, Barry Gibb was the hottest songwriter on the planet and had this album been released then, it would have been hugely successful with just his name on the cover. The album certainly deserved better chart success than it received, but by mid-1984 with the *Fever* backlash still in overdrive, particularly in the US, the album was bound to struggle. Whilst credit should be given to Barry for not taking the easy road and releasing an album of very commercial Bee Gees-style songs, this was not the great Barry Gibb solo album anticipated by fans.

★   ★   ★

Maurice's first solo single in 14 years was 'Hold Her In Your Hand' from the soundtrack of *A Breed Apart*. For him, the project was something of a dream come true.

"I always wanted to write film scores," he explained. "I always have since *Saturday Night Fever*. I've been so over the moon about making a certain picture with the music, help it and make a great marriage of music and movie. I'm doing another score called *Ghost Soldiers*."

Since Maurice, like all his brothers, cannot read or write music, he enlisted the expert assistance of Jimmie Haskell, with whom he had worked on the unreleased *Misunderstood* soundtrack and The Bee Gees' similarly ill-fated *A Kick In The Head Is Worth Eight In The Pants*.

Haskell rated the experience as a great pleasure. "I went to Miami to work with Maurice during the preliminary stages of scoring the film," he recalled. "Maurice is an accomplished composer and plays synthesizer very well. He created the entire music score on synthesizer and even played the arrangements which were needed to enhance the music.

"My job was essentially to orchestrate his music and then conduct for the recordings. We recorded with a real orchestra of symphonic size in Hollywood. I wrote Maurice's synthesizer recordings as readable music and assigned each portion of the various notes he played to the instruments which I knew would play those notes with the best sound and meaningful character so as to best enhance the scene being scored."

The visit to Miami was not confined strictly to the business of the *A Breed Apart* soundtrack. He also worked with Barry on his solo LP as well as finding time for some socialising with the brothers and their families. "The Bee Gees' wives are all lovely, and they and their children are all matter of fact, down to earth, charming, fun-loving (without being overly boisterous) people," he said. "If you didn't already know they are stars, you would not suspect it from their manner."

Maurice's brooding and atmospheric instrumental music created the dark mood that the film required. "The film is about a rare breed of eagle that nests on this man's island in the Carolinas," he explained, "and it's basically about a rich man's desire to get this bird's eggs. He's a mad avid egg collector. I did the eagle sounds. You can make up any kind of sounds if you have the working knowledge of your synthesizer." *A Breed Apart* was described as a "picturesque but illogical, uninvolving tale" upon its premiere in December.

In January, Maurice had began scoring the film *Ghost Soldiers*, which later became *The Supernaturals*. The film featured Nichelle Nicholls, best known as *Star Trek*'s Uhura, and also a cameo appearance by Maurice himself as a Civil War Yankee soldier. In the end, Maurice's music wasn't used in the film, but video copies of *The Supernaturals* have turned up with his original film score.

It wasn't to be his last flirtation with the film world. In March, 1985, plans were made for him to appear in a film with Omar Sharif, and later he was rumoured to be writing the music for *Two By Forsyth*.

★　★　★

On December 1, 1984, Barry's family had cause for a double celebration. Not only was it their eldest son Stevie's eleventh birthday, but at 6.03 that morning, Linda gave birth to the couple's fourth son at Mount Sinai Hospital in Miami. The baby weighed seven pounds eight ounces and was named Michael David.

Just five days later, Barry played host to what would be the first of a series of Love & Hope Tennis Festivals, to benefit Miami's Diabetes Research Institute. Celebrities and socialites mingled with Bee Gees' fans at the celebrity tennis tournament at the Doral Country Club in Miami. Andy joined Barry to play tennis and helped to entertain the guests at a gala dinner and ball in the evening.

It wasn't the only charity function to involve the Gibbs. On April 25, 1985, Maurice was the guest of honour at the National Police Athletic League dinner, where he received a plaque "in recognition of his outstanding service and contribution to the youth of our nation".

★　★　★

After being together for nearly five years, Robin and Dwina were married in Wheatley in Hampshire on July 31, 1985, with Robin's unique wedding gift for his bride a 1910 gypsy caravan. Their wedding date was carefully chosen by Dwina – it's the eve of Lughnasad, a Druid festival marking the turning of the year.

While Druidism was nothing new to Dwina – she traces her interest in it back to her childhood – marriage was something she had never previously considered. "If Robin hadn't come along, I would never have married. Definitely not," she said firmly.

"We weren't really that interested in the idea of being married," Robin agreed. "We didn't even contemplate it, let alone expect it."

The idea of marriage grew slowly, as their commitment to each other became stronger. Their new home also played a part, according to Robin. "Since we've been here our relationship has got better and better. I never want to leave the place when I'm here. It's where my roots are. This place and the family, they're my world.

"I never expected all this. I never expected to end up with three wonderful kids and a woman like Dwina. But I thank God every single day that I did, and I thank God we found The Prebendal," he added fervently.

Former 'Marmalade' band member, Pat Fairley, had remained with RSO for many years and was on the invitation list to Robin and Dwina's ceremony. However, as he explained, the joyful occasion was a source of some embarrassment for him. "When I went to Robin's wedding, I hadn't got round to getting a present and when we got to his house, there were pressies everywhere. All the cards had been knocked off. Anyway, a week later I got a card thanking me for my lovely gift. Still owe you, Robin," he apologised.

★　　★　　★

The last of the Barry-Albhy-Karl projects was the album for Diana Ross that they had begun talking about a few years earlier. The magic was almost gone by this time and the result had few high points. The songs are as usual mostly by all three Gibb brothers, with Andy collaborating on two, and Albhy, George Bitzer, and Michael Jackson on one each. Of the brothers, only Barry worked on the recording sessions. For the first time, the team also worked with a different engineer. After Albhy's return to California, he had begun working with Jack Puig. "We used him on the Diana Ross stuff along with Karl . . . Karl is an excellent engineer, but there are some engineers who are brilliant, like Bob Clearmountain certainly, Bill Schnee, who are another order of magnitude. Karl did the engineering, but we went to do the mixing with Jack," Albhy explained.

Diana Ross has long been rumoured to play the diva, but Albhy claimed that although they had heard the tales, the project was completed without incident. "Now *she* was a piece of work," he added, "not particularly troublesome for us, because we got along fine, but the stories about her are legion. I know a lot of people who've worked for her, and she is an unbelievable piece of work. Makes everybody call her Miss Ross. But we did fine."

Barry revealed some problems during the recording, saying, "It's only difficult because she's very much in control of her own destiny and it's very difficult to work with an artist who is very single-minded like that," although he admitted that he, too, could be accused of single-mindedness. "That's why there's a clash," he acknowledged.

Comparing Diana Ross to his first major production, he explained, "Barbra was totally focused and studying the songs and learning the songs. Being a record producer, when you put the other hat on, it's very frustrating to see that the artist doesn't always learn the songs when they're supposed to be recording them."

The lead single was 'Eaten Alive', a song by Barry and Maurice reworked with them by Michael Jackson and produced with him. It's not a bad song, but neither is it the something special one might hope for with all the famous names involved.

Albhy recalled how the Michael Jackson connection first came about. "It's so funny, when he first called me, the first time, I was at home . . . I got the phone call, and I thought it was someone pulling my leg, because he has that characteristic voice. He'd been able to get my number but not Barry's number," he explained, "and he'd never met Barry before then, but he'd always wanted to."

Michael Jackson became a co-producer on the song, but Albhy said, "Even though I spent a week sitting between Michael and Barry . . . Michael never let his barrier down. He was very much – I guess control freak is the right [term] – but certainly emotionally challenged."

Albhy calls 'Eaten Alive' "the most amazing track we cut", adding, "Now there is another record where if you were to ask Barry a song that you thought should have been a hit but wasn't, it might have been 'Eaten Alive'."

Barry agreed. "'Eaten Alive' . . . should have been the big hit off that album, but incidentally just wasn't. Michael was lovely, he's a very shy person. He came along one day to the house we were renting in LA, and he heard the songs from the Diana Ross album . . . He heard part of 'Eaten Alive', which was unfinished, and it was just the verses, you know. And he just said that there should be something else in this song, there should be another place to go to. And I was cheeky enough to say, 'Well . . . Michael, if you feel like there's somewhere, something else to put in there . . . If you have any thoughts, you let me know because we'd be delighted to share the song with you if you want to do that.' So he said, 'Well, give me a cassette of . . . the piece of the song,' and he went away and in a few days later he came back with the chorus area."

"It's good," Maurice added. "It was quite funny hearing him with a drum machine and a keyboard in his lounge room somewhere, singing the song with his bit in the middle that he put in. But it's a lovely tape, and we value [it] very much."

While Albhy raves about the song itself, he calls it "one of those cases where I would say we lost it in the mix."

Both the album and the single were released in September, 1985, with the single reaching number 38 in Germany, but only a disappointing 71 in the UK and 77 in the US.

The surprise big hit of the album was the second single, 'Chain Reaction' – "the one song that wasn't going to be on the album," Barry said. "It was, in fact, the last song we cut. We'd done the whole album and she said, 'Well, we still need one more song from somewhere.' We'd had 'Chain Reaction' all along but hadn't the nerve to play it to her because it was so Tamla Motown-ish that we were scared she wouldn't want to go back there."

Robin recalled, "We said, 'We think it's time you did something which you would have done with The Supremes, not as Diana Ross. It's time to do that again.' She didn't really think it was going to be appropriate at the time. It wasn't 'til after she'd recorded it and sat down and heard it, that she thought it was right, and it was a credible tribute to her past."

Released in December, The Supremes-like number with Barry singing the back-up was a massive hit in some countries, topping the charts in

Britain★ and Australia and reaching number 11 in Germany. It did nothing at all in the United States, where a new Diana Ross release was as welcome as a Bee Gees release at that time.

The single was well supported by a brilliant video of Ross looking much as she did in her Supremes days, singing the song against a black and white set in a Sixties-type television studio with a live audience, à la *Hullabaloo*; then as the song goes into its chorus, the video changes to colour and an Eighties-style Diana Ross. The song captured the Motown/Supremes era so perfectly that the black singers miming Barry's backing vocals looked perfectly natural. The single was even reissued in the UK eight years later in October, 1993, and placed number 20 in its second outing.

A third single, 'Experience', was written by all four Gibb brothers. It reached number 47 in the British charts in April, 1986, but failed to make a showing elsewhere.

The overlooked gem of the album would be 'More And More', a cocktail lounge piano number by Barry, Andy and Albhy that Miss Ross coos in a nice Marilyn Monroe voice.

Barry summed up the experience by saying, "Diana Ross is a woman of many parts, and I think, it's not really a criticism, but I think she concentrates on about a dozen things at once. She might be hosting the Academy Awards on the same week as she's doing her vocal and you won't see her 'cause she's at rehearsals when she should be singing . . . I wouldn't call it unprofessional, I wouldn't have the *right* to call it unprofessional – this woman was having hits when I was having my diapers changed. I'm not going to have the *audacity* to say that Diana Ross is unprofessional. All I'm saying was, it wasn't *comfortable*."

★　　★　　★

The first sign of trouble within The Bee Gees' camp was the discord between Barry and Albhy, but there were rumblings of discontent elsewhere. While Barry was enjoying the independence that Middle Ear afforded him, Robin and Maurice were not enjoying quite the same use of the facility. Maurice had been heard to grumble about having to use Criteria's studio when all three brothers had one of their own. Barry enthused, "One of the nicest things about having your own studio is the ability to leave complicated set-ups on the console or in the studio and know that no other act is going to be booked in the morning, so you will have to change it all back again in the afternoon. We can make our own hours and fine tune set-ups for days, if necessary, which enables us to complete projects in a way that gives us much more creative freedom."

"All three of them shared the ownership [of Middle Ear], so all three of them shared the expenses," Tom Kennedy explained. "Any project that went through there was billed.

★ Despite many subsequent releases, to date, it remains Diana's last number one single in the UK.

"It was really that Barry got first tabs on it, and it cost them a third each to run it . . . If it costs $175 an hour to break even, that's what they would pay . . . I always thought if Robin and Maurice weren't going to get the use out of it, it shouldn't cost them money, and I actually voiced that opinion on many occasions and got away with it . . . Why should it cost 25 grand to Robin and Maurice, you know, why have a studio at all?"

Barry teamed up with country star Larry Gatlin to write 'Indian Summer', which was included on The Gatlin Brothers' *Smile* LP in October, 1985 and was also issued as a single in Australia. The song featured lead vocals by Larry, with Barry and Roy Orbison providing backing vocals. Barry also played synthesizer and Maurice keyboards on the track. It has since appeared on several Roy Orbison anthologies and, as far as David English is concerned, the song is deserving of a wider audience than it has thus far received. "I continually talk to BG about 'Indian Summer'," he lamented. "If ever there was a song which would go to number one, it's 'Indian Summer'. That and 'My Eternal Love'," he reflected.

Barry was also rumoured to be considering album projects for Neil Diamond and fellow Miami resident, Julio Iglesias.

Walls Have Eyes, Robin's third album of the Eighties, was recorded at Criteria and Middle Ear. It was again a joint project with Maurice, who provided keyboards, bass, and backing vocals, and produced it together with Atlantic veteran Tom Dowd. Barry co-wrote eight of the 10 songs, and sang on one. The brothers were inching towards a Bee Gees reunion.

Dowd recalled the album as something of "an exercise", elaborating, "It wasn't really a worthy recording endeavour. We tried and did the best we could with the material and the concept and the budget which we had available. But in all sincerity, I don't think it was the best Robin could do. It wasn't my cup of tea, finally."

The instigator for the project was the head of A&R for Polygram in the UK. "I think he was a loyal Bee Gees fan," Dowd explained. "He wasn't heavy-handed about what he wanted, but he didn't give us the artistic freedom we'd like to have [had] . . . It was never a dispute, but just not the way you'd like it to be."

An animated and gifted storyteller who changes voices and character to fit the tale, he continued, "It was 'I want this, and something that'll do that, and it's got to fit this.' He's not giving the artist the freedom of expressing what the artist is best at. That's normal, because when they sign somebody they're thinking, 'If we can get them into this market, we can do this and that.' They're living in a different world. All of a sudden you realise that, 'Wait a minute, I'm not in here to make the best record that this artist is capable of making, I'm here to make a record that will fill this guy's concept of what he can sell,' which is a little bit different, you know! Sometimes you can pull it off, and sometimes it isn't a very good marriage."

"We were sitting on a tight monetary consideration, and here we were recording in the United States for a record company that's in England, and once in a while somebody shows up, and the rest of the time it's like, 'What did you do, you should have told me,' and all of a sudden, the reins are getting tighter."

Both the album and first single were released in November, 1985. The lead single was 'Like A Fool', similar in feel to 'Another Lonely Night in New York'. Unlike the songs on *Now Voyager*, all the tracks on *Walls Have Eyes* are all pretty straight verse-chorus songs, so Robin seems to have directed the songwriting using contributions from Barry, not the way a Bee Gees album would be written by the same three. 'Like A Fool' is nicely done, but nothing they hadn't done before just as well.

The second single 'Toys' was released in February, 1986, and features all three brothers. "I think at this point, because things weren't going the way they 'were planned to go'," Tom Dowd intoned slowly, shifting into his Dr Evil voice for the final four words, "it was, 'Hey, maybe if we get the brothers on it, we'll be able to come out smelling better.' I am guessing that – I can't determine what goes on in record companies' minds. That was an unusual record company. It wasn't like Atlantic, where we were always exchanging information and in touch with each other. Here we were working with record companies that were not as well organised and not as sensitive to artists and artists' facilities."

Barry's second Love & Hope Tennis Festival was held on December 13 and 14, 1985. Once again, Andy was on hand to lend support to the charity and in addition to his own 'Shadow Dancing', also joined his eldest brother for a seasonal favourite, 'White Christmas'.

★   ★   ★

In September, 1985, a young songstress called Carola visited Barry and Maurice in Miami to record some demos, hopefully for an album. She stayed only one week on that first visit, returning to Sweden with her demos and the promise of a whole album in the future.

Carola Maria Häggkvist was born on September 8, 1966, in Hägersten, Sweden. Like the Gibb brothers, singing was always her first love and Carola rapidly became Sweden's hottest singer and developed a strong following in the Far East as well, although European stardom outside Scandinavia eluded her. In April, 1985, she signed with Polydor International with her next album to be produced by Maurice. She met with Maurice in London just before Christmas to further discuss the project, returning to Miami early in the new year to begin recording.

"It was a wonderful experience to work with The Bee Gees," Carola said. "A fabulous thing, in fact. Maurice and Robin were in the studio everyday. Maurice is very modest, and we do have the same kind of humour. Robin is very concentrated when he is working. He helped me with the pronunciation, and he does have much musical specialities.

"Most of the studio work was done in the afternoons and evenings. In the daytime I went out to the beach and relaxed. It was great," she enthused.

Maurice was equally impressed with her. He raved, "Her voice is remarkably perfect, and she is easy to work with. She is really fantastic!"

The resulting album, *Runaway* was issued only in Sweden. Maurice co-wrote all the songs with Robin, some also with Barry, and one with keyboard player Rhett Lawrence, the only musician on the album besides Maurice, and one with Lawrence and Carola herself. Robin adds some backing vocals but Barry was not involved with the recording itself.

Carola has a good clear voice somewhat reminiscent of the Scottish singer, Sheena Easton, that combines well with Maurice's usual clean production. The lead single, 'The Runaway', written by Robin and Maurice, was a good representative of an album that, as far as most non-European fans are concerned, was so hard to obtain that its release went virtually unnoticed. A video for the single was shot in Miami, and the song topped the charts in Sweden and reached the Top 10 in other Scandinavian countries.

"I think *Runaway* still today ranks as a very modern, and up-to-date album, having been made in the Eighties. It was in forefront of the technology in those days. I still like it a lot," Carola said.

She explained that she had little input on the album. "I was too young and inexperienced to get fully involved in the making of the songs, although I did a bit on one track. I had very little to say all in all in the project. I was just the voice. The songs were also a bit too high for me, I think. Maurice made me sing so high! Especially on the track 'We Are Atomic'. These days I like to sing a bit lower on the scale, so I have something to balance with if I go up."

Shortly after the release of the album in July, 1986, Carola joined the Livets Ord fundamentalist sect, and it was rumoured that she refused to promote the album, a charge she denied years later. "I wanted to do a lot of promotion. In fact, I was up to it. But the communication between me and The Bee Gees was not up and running. They heard things from other sources, and they probably believed those stories. Anyway, the album died, and I went on to other projects."

The album was withdrawn after a short time. "There was this person responsible for the project in Polydor," Carola explained, "and when he quit, the whole project sort of disappeared." Despite its short release time, it was a platinum seller in her native country, selling 200,000 copies in Scandinavia. "In retrospect, I was perhaps not ready for eventual international stardom," she added.

★   ★   ★

During 1986, Barry commenced recording his second solo album that was never released, probably because of his American label MCA. Many of the songs appeared on his *Hawks* soundtrack two years later. They are similar in style to *Now Voyager* for the most part, although with greater variety since there was a country ballad and a few sung in falsetto. For whatever reasons, this project was pushed back until it collided with The Bee Gees' reunion album *E.S.P.* Three songs that appeared on *Hawks* also appeared on non-American copies of the 1990 box set, *Tales From The Brothers Gibb*, of which Barry said he was especially proud of 'Letting Go', one of the falsetto ballads.

Another Barry project begun at this same time was The Bunburys, with the single of 'We're The Bunburys' issued on Island in June with no reference to Barry or The Bee Gees as performers, although the writer credit to Barry and David English was visible on the disk. The 45 rpm came in the back cover of a thin children's book about a team of cricket-playing rabbits, written by David English, who narrates the story for the B-side, and illustrated by Jan Brychta. Barry Gibb contributes a short and uncredited speaking part on the track, doing his best Australian imitation.

"It's for under-privileged children, the charity that we've chosen for The Bunburys," Barry explained. "In other words, charities that will be involved with us having to find a large piece of land in Scotland, which hopefully with local government permission, we can get to name Bunbury for about two weeks a year . . . to take under-privileged children or children without parents for the holiday of their lives. Pony rides, hiking, camping. Ian Botham, in fact, will drive the children up there, and other star players will come up there and play cricket with the kids."

At the beginning of the year, The Bee Gees sang 'The Star Spangled Banner' at the annual football game between Florida's Metro Dade's Deputy Dawgs and The Force.

Robin also participated in the all-star assembly at Abbey Road to record 'Live In World' as part of an anti-heroin project for the Phoenix House Charity Drug Rehabilitation Centre.

It was reported that Barry was working with Burt Bacharach and Carole Bayer Sager to write the title song for the next Jane Fonda film, but nothing ever came of the project.

In September, Barry joined Barbra Streisand in her first live concert appearance in eight years, a Democratic senatorial fundraiser. Dressed in white, the pair reprised their duets of 'Guilty' and 'What Kind Of Fool' at Barbra's California ranch before a celebrity audience, and the concert was recorded and filmed as an album, HBO television special and video, *One Voice*. For the eagle-eyed viewer, 'What Kind Of Fool' provides some inadvertent entertainment, watching Barry's belt mysteriously turn from white to black to white again. Look even closer, and you notice that it's not even the same white shirt that he's wearing all the way through the song. Apparently, someone was not pleased with all the close-up shots in the video footage, and parts needed to be re-filmed. No one bothered to check all the fine details in continuity, although the editing is so smoothly done that apart from the changing belt, it appears to be all one seamless performance.

That same year, Alcatrazz, with former Marble Graham Bonnet as lead singer, reprised 'Only One Woman' on their LP.

Barry held his third Love & Hope Tennis Festival on November 15 and

16, with Andy once again supporting the cause. Barry was also joined on stage for the finale by Andy, Larry Gatlin and long time Australian friend, Noeleen Batley Stewart, who joined for a lively version of 'What'd I Say'.

With the non-release of Barry's album, the limited release of Carola's album in Sweden, and the limited release of The Bunburys single in England, it looked to most people as if the group had taken a year off. This would have to be the fewest records sold for the most Gibb work since their aborted solo projects of 1970.

"We'd lost our management and our record company," Barry explained, "and all of those legal problems associated with both led us into a vacuum for three years. And so, for those years we weren't a pop group and we enjoyed it. It was good for us. Then I think we basically just got tired of listening to everything that was on the radio and knowing we could do just as well, if not better."

★   ★   ★

On October 30, 1986, The Bee Gees had signed a long-term contract with Warner Brothers Records in New York. In honour of the change of record companies, Warner Brothers issued an official promotional cassette entitled *Words & Music*, celebrating the past, present and future careers of The Bee Gees, while in Brazil, Polydor issued one last Bee Gees promo LP, *Bee Gees Mix*.

Early in the year, Beri — at that time called Bobbi — Gibb and her band, Social Fact, produced a demo and video of a 1985 composition by all four Gibb brothers called 'Girl Gang'.

In April, 'Chain Reaction' picked up the Most Performed Work trophy at the 32nd Annual Ivor Novello Awards in London.

In the latter part of 1986, the Gibb brothers began working on the first Bee Gees album in five years. They had not really been apart, with all the work they'd contributed to each others' solo albums and productions, but this was to be the first project they all worked on fully as a team in a long time. The idea of doing another Bee Gees record had been percolating for some time.

Doing solo albums and productions no longer looked as good as it once had. Although Barry said that he and Robin had wanted to do solo albums, neither was satisfied with the way they had turned out in the end. "Principally because we are not solo artists, that's what it is," Robin explained. "We're not used to working alone. We work better as a team, we don't work well on our own very well."

"We definitely fire up off each other," Barry agreed. "We want to be The Bee Gees, we *enjoy* being The Bee Gees."

They had a valid point. The Diana Ross and Robin Gibb albums of 1985 had both been artistically compromised and commercially weak, and the next year was even worse, as the Barry and Carola projects were going nowhere. It was time to cast that aside and start fresh under the group banner. It was a reunion with Arif Mardin as well, because Warner Brothers was under the same corporate umbrella as Atlantic. It was in some ways an attempt to return to happier days, when they had last worked themselves out of a slump and into records they'd been proud of. Robin summed it up for the group when he said, "What we're trying to do is reinstate the kind of level that The Bee Gees were at before *Fever*."

The session band were new to the group except Rhett Lawrence (five songs) who had been on Carola's album, and Greg Phillinganes (four) who had been on Diana Ross's album. Robbie Kondor appeared the most with eight tracks. Barry and Maurice are credited with programming drums and bass lines, in addition to their usual credits to both for rhythm guitar and to Maurice for keyboards.

Arif shared the production duties with Barry, Robin and Maurice and Brian Tench. The working title for the LP was *Tokyo Nights*, but by the time it was released in September, the title had changed to *E.S.P.* Promotional copies of the album were sent out to radio stations accompanied by a small black drawstring bag marked with *E.S.P.* and containing a crystal for good vibes.

The title track itself went through a name change – originally, the brother's had planned to call it 'XTC' or 'Ecstasy' until they were made aware of the drug connection.

But it was the lead single with its distinctive stomping beat that brought The Bee Gees back to the public's eye. "The success [of 'You Win Again'] sustained us," Barry said. "It proved our belief in what we were doing and that was encouraging. So we carried on."

Barry recalled the origin of the song. "I woke up at about three in the morning with this melody and I thought 'What is that? . . . If I wake up tomorrow morning, I won't remember it.' So I had to go and find a tape recorder and put that little bit of melody on tape. Sometimes I do that and the next day, it's rubbish and I throw it away, but the next day it still meant something . . . So I played it to Maurice and Robin, and they said 'Yeah, let's finish it and see what happens.

"Maurice concocted 20 different drum sounds to create one, and he'd keep adding something and Robin and me would go, 'Yeah?' and he'd add something else and we'd go, 'Yeah? Yeah!' and then it suddenly hit, this is it! That drum sound is it, don't touch a thing."

Not everyone shared their view of the distinctive sound.

"A lot of the songs, people say, 'Well, that's not what's happening out there.' We've been very fortunate to have the success like 'You Win Again'," Maurice added. "That record, everybody said, 'Take the stomps off, take those banging stomps off! You're going to kill the song, you know. Can we lower them in the mix, can we take them off the intro, can we take them off the record?'

"That was the whole *signature* of 'You Win Again'. With the stomps, you hear those stomps on the radio and you know it's us! And everyone was really against it, but we stuck to our guns and said, 'No, we're not changing the mix, that's it.' Now people are asking me for a sample of it!"

"It really draws the listener in," Robin explained. "It starts with nothing, and again, it was something we wanted to do that was a little different to what other people were doing. Just something off the wall that started the song and went through the song."

'You Win Again' was released in August and turned into a great comeback single, topping the charts in the UK, Germany and Norway and reaching number six in Holland and eight in Australia, even though the American market again proved resistant. The intro starts off with a great stomping drum track by Maurice and Rhett Lawrence, and then Robbie Kondor's bright keyboards and synthesizer bass, with Barry's subliminal rhythm guitars the only other ingredient aside from "additional keyboard" by Maurice. Barry sings lead in his best natural voice, avoiding falsetto throughout, with exclamations by Robin and harmonies that really sound like all three brothers. They seem to have agreed also on more carefully worked out lyrics that make the whole song count, here and on the rest of the album.

But with the new found success in Europe, it was a unified front the group presented to the public. "I don't think that any other group could make it three times in row unless they were brothers," Barry asserted. "It isn't possible because you drift and your lives change. With us, our families support the same things we do, so it all comes to one point. There's nobody in our families, wives or in-laws that says 'You shouldn't go with them – you're better on your own, lad.' That stuff doesn't go on anymore."

'E.S.P' leads off the album and was the second single in October in the States, November in the UK. It opens unexpectedly with a rich a capella harmony, then two lines of Barry's falsetto, before jumping into the instrumental opening and the beat that propels the rest of the song.

The title track was less successful than its predecessor, achieving number 13 in Germany and 26 in Holland, while only reaching number 51 in the UK.

In Germany and Australia, 'Angela' – a song which Arif had originally wanted to omit from the album – was the single, but the song reached only number 52 on the German charts and didn't chart at all in Australia.

The project was a good return to form for the band, and it received good reviews and healthy sales around the world with the exception of the US where they still struggled with the *Fever* backlash. The brothers worked hard at promoting the album too, offering themselves to the media for countless interviews, particularly in the US, to try to counter the preconceptions people may have of their music and image.

The cover photos were taken at Brimham Rocks near Hull at sunset. The album is dedicated to their old Australian friend and supporter of many years past, Ozzie [sic] Byrne, who had died recently.

In November, Barry held his fourth Love & Hope Tennis Festival, with Maurice bidding successfully for an Akita puppy at the festival's charity auction. The puppy, named Alf by Adam and Samantha, was a beloved family pet for many years.

In December, The Bee Gees sang a brief a capella segment of 'Holiday' and provided a "Don't drink and drive" message for a Warner Brothers promotional album called *Yulesville*. Pressed in red vinyl, it was released only in the US.

It was around this time that Tom Kennedy, their stalwart road manager and studio manager for so many years, decided to leave his work with the group behind and return to England. The man who came for six weeks and stayed for "20-odd years" had resolved to call it a day.

"I should have left years before, really . . . There were certain things I didn't agree with. The whole thing *did* get out of control," Tom admitted. "There were a lot of bad feelings within the group – within the camp, to be honest with you. I felt it myself, because I always had the group's interests at heart. I was just unhappy with the whole thing . . . There was friction over little things that didn't matter."

In his comfortable English home where he lives with his wife Stephanie and their children, Kathryn and Ben, there is little evidence that for nearly 20 years, Tom played a major part in The Bee Gees' career. There is one black and white glossy reminder, but few people would realise its significance or its link to his earlier career. It's not an 8×10 promotional shot; it's the family's sleek black and white cat, Ada.

Back in Miami, Tom had begun feeding a stray cat at Middle Ear, and she duly gave birth to a litter of kittens in the studio. The Gibb children were *Star Wars* fans, so all the kittens were given names from their favourite film. Homes were found for the kittens, with Andy taking one, although when it came to the question of ownership, Tom says, "*He* belonged to *her*," rather than the other way about. With the problems in his personal life, pet ownership was a difficult task for Andy, and the kitten was given to Tom and Stephanie's care.

"She was originally Darth Vader, then when Andy took her, he called her Cessna because he loved flying, then it came back to Darth Vader again," Tom said. "Then it was gradually changed to Daft Ada, because she *is* a bit daft, and now it's just Ada."

When the Kennedys landed at Heathrow Airport on March 1, Ada was with them. She came through her six months' quarantine with no problems, although she tactfully declined to comment on what she thought of the change in climate from sunny Miami to an English winter. If she remembers that as a youngster, she once owned a famous singer, she keeps that to herself as well.

Tom looks back with great affection on his years with The Bee Gees, adding, "I like to think that everything I did for the boys, I did with their best interests at heart. Whether they believed it at the time or not, I think time will tell that I did."

37

A SPIRIT HAVING FLOWN

ANDY BEGAN 1987 performing the National Anthem at the annual Pig Bowl football game at Tamiami Park in Florida, before beginning a 12-night engagement at the Sahara Hotel and Casino in Las Vegas on January 27. Andy had come to love Las Vegas, particularly the bright lights and dazzle of the nightclubs.

"He just loved to perform for live audiences," Barbara Gibb recalled. "He liked the response, especially in Vegas, where he used to get standing ovations after every show. He loved that."

Barbara was there with her youngest son, cheering him at every performance. She was also gradually coming to realise that he was still using cocaine.

In the spring of 1987, Andy checked into another drug rehabilitation centre and became a member of Alcoholics Anonymous. He faced his problem honestly, and his friends and family all believed that he really had made a clean and sober restart.

Andy returned to Miami, with hopes of making a comeback with the original formula of his first success. "The fact that we'd done it together in the first place was what brought him back," Barry explained. "You know, 'Let's do it again, let's go into the studio again and this time, I'll keep my grip, I'll hold on and I won't slip again.' "

The brothers began working on demos to re-launch Andy's career. They even found time for writing and recording demos for Beri, the latest Gibb to seek a career in music.

To all outward appearances, Andy still seemed to be living the life of a superstar. His new home was a luxurious penthouse apartment in the exclusive Venetia apartment complex overlooking Biscayne Bay. But the apartment came to him rent-free in exchange for promoting the development in which it was located. His brothers were providing him with a $200 a week allowance for his living expenses.

Despite Andy's career and personal setbacks, he remained a tireless worker for charities, always willing to give of his time and effort to help the causes that were important to him. In April, he played in the Jockey Club's Pro-Celebrity Tennis Classic, benefiting Pet Rescue.

He also hosted his own tennis tournament at the Sea Oaks Beach Club in Vero Beach, Florida, to benefit the American Cancer Society. The tournament began with a cocktail party launch, at which Andy performed 'Unchained Melody', 'Blue Bayou', 'Yesterday' and 'Twist And Shout'.

On September 9, 1987, Andy filed a personal bankruptcy petition which stated that he had less than $50,000 but more than $1.5 million in outstanding debts.

Filing for Chapter 7 relief under the US Bankruptcy Code, Andy would be allowed to keep only $1,000 in personal property in addition to one primary residence. A plan of repayment to his creditors would have to be established.

As far back as 1982, Andy had been selling off jewellery and other personal items for cash on Sunset Boulevard in Los Angeles. It was a painful admission for the young man who had been at the peak of his career just 10 years earlier, dropping from an annual income of over two million dollars to less than $8,000 for 1986. He was humiliated by the sense of failure.

"I think that was a crippling blow to him," Barry reflected sadly. "I don't think he survived that. I think he was embarrassed by it."

Barry insisted, "For two years, he was straight before he died . . . He was very energetic and healthy and playing tennis. I'm the only other brother who plays, so we'd play all the time, and we wrote songs together and recorded them. We were going to be together, to go out as a force. He wanted to do another solo album to prove he was good at what he did and then he was going to join us."

During those brotherly tennis matches, they would play five or six sets. Barry noticed that Andy would become very flushed, but he never knew the cause. "What he wasn't telling me was that he really shouldn't be doing it," he said.

Andy didn't admit to his family or friends that he had been treated by physicians in California for heart inflammation on several occasions. Although he was now clean, the years of substance abuse had taken their toll.

He had fulfilled a long-time dream of taking flying lessons, and in January, he gained his pilot's license and flew solo around Florida several times. With childlike enthusiasm, he claimed, "This is what has taken the place of drugs for me. The only time I get high these days is when I'm flying an aeroplane."

With the benefit of hindsight, Robin thinks that flying should have been his career. "I feel that he really didn't want to make another album," he explained. "He didn't want to be successful in the music business. What he really wanted to do was to join the Navy and be a pilot. But he had this feeling that he had to prove himself to us, which was a mistake. If he had pursued another course, I genuinely feel that he would be alive today."

His former wife Kim agreed. "I just wish, sometimes, that he'd never had anything to do with the music industry," she said. "He wanted to be a pilot, and he was bright. He could have done anything that he wanted to. But his career was decided for him. I believe it killed him."

Flying was to remain a brief but pleasurable pastime for Andy. He signed a lucrative contract with Caribbean Connection to promote a new line of beach clothes, suntan oils and surfing products. After Christmas, Barry took

Andy to meet with executives at Island Records in London. On the strength of the four demos he had recorded with his brothers in Miami, Island offered him a contract in February 1988. Yet another new beginning seemed imminent.

"This is an opportunity for me to make a fresh start," Andy enthused. "Sometimes you have to hit rock bottom before you can lift your head up again and get back on the right track.

"Unfortunately, I've had some rocky times in the past few years, but I am over them and fully back to health, fully recovered, free from any drug or alcohol problems. I was very young when I was on top . . . I feel confident that I can make a significant contribution once again."

Saying that he couldn't wait to get to get back to Britain, he added, "I'll do nothing but work on my music. I can promise you one thing – no matter what happened to me in recent years, I've had the most wonderful 18 clean months in Florida. The future has never been brighter. I know inside me that things will be fantastic in England."

It was an outwardly confident Andy who claimed, "I'm going to devote myself 100 per cent to my singing career. I know I'm going to make it big again with my contract with Island Records."

Maurice recalled, "He was enthusiastic, bounding with energy and told everyone he was determined to make a go of it now that he had been given a second chance."

For Kim and Peta, it also felt like a new beginning. "He rang me in January to say he was coming over to see me," Kim said. "I was so excited. He told me, 'Kim, I'm clean. I've finally stopped doing any drugs. I've really got myself together, and I'm coming over to Australia to see you and Peta.' "

It was news she had been longing for. In spite of the nearly 10 years that had passed since their divorce, Kim had always clung to the hope that one day, they would be reunited. Even through his highly publicised romance with Victoria Principal, that hope remained strong. "He never remarried, did he?" Kim said. "Neither did I. We were never out of touch – not through all the years we were apart. He would ring me from whatever part of the world he was in and sometimes talk for hours. I'm sure he loved me as much as I loved him.

"If we hadn't kept in touch over the years, I suppose it would have been easier to accept that the relationship was over. But he would call so often, and when Peta was old enough to talk, he'd ask to speak to her."

"He was just like my friend," Peta said. "He asked me what groups I liked, who were my favourite celebrities, and he promised to introduce me to them when I visited him in Los Angeles. He was really nice."

The long telephone calls always came at Andy's instigation by necessity. "I wasn't ever able to contact him – his managers put a block on that – and I wasn't in any way assisted by his family," Kim explained. "So if I wanted to speak to Andy, I had absolutely no choice but to wait until he picked up the phone. But during this conversation, he sounded so positive. He wasn't raving on about dashing off to the Seychelles, or some exotic place, as he had in the past. Because he sounded so rational and sensible, I honestly believe that he really meant it.

"But most of all, he was desperate to see Peta. I think he had at last realised he had a daughter, and he could cope with that," she added. It was the acceptance she had longed for. "Quite simply, Peta and I were outcasts from the Gibbs. I longed to write to Andy sometimes, but I wasn't allowed to. I once sent him some pictures of Peta, but I had to do it through the fan club."

Kim was especially pleased that Andy had returned to England. "America was the ruin of him. I think that's why he finally returned to Britain. He thought he'd be safe there," she explained.

Andy settled into the Chancery, a cottage at Robin's Oxfordshire home, to write more songs for his comeback album. "It was a relief that he chose to live with Robin and his family," said Maurice. "We all knew he'd be well looked after, and that there would always be members of the family around just in case there were any problems."

At first, it seemed to be working out well. "He was great fun and we shared our sense of humour," Robin said. "We were forever watching Tony Hancock tapes and listening to The Goons."

Soon it became clear to Robin that all was not well. Andy had begun taking elaborate measures to avoid contact with anyone. He tried to encourage Andy, but to little avail. "I had to keep reassuring him, you know, of his talent and to build up his confidence. It actually affected his mind, that he had to really start again . . . And he wouldn't come out of his cottage for days. He'd miss appointments, he wouldn't take phone calls. There was something going on, and I couldn't figure out was going on in his head.

"Andy had developed a fear of life, and what he did to himself – almost driving himself to oblivion – was born out of that fear. It was an extremely destructive emotion.

"There were obviously bad times . . . and because he was living with me up until the end, I experienced them with him. He was going to make a new album and get his feet back on the ground. Unfortunately, his confidence was shot, and he was afraid of the world and not succeeding. He had the talent to succeed, but he was frightened that people wouldn't like him. He was terribly insecure."

Barry explained, "He always seemed to have a zest for life. But beneath all that fun was an incredible sadness that only a few of us could see. He was the most insecure man in the world, and even when he had hit records, he felt it was still not good enough. Whatever I'd say to reassure him, he would still go away and hide in the depths of depression.

"I was either on the phone or seeing him, giving him encouragement. I would say to him, 'Just get up and sing. Do what you do best. No one does it better.' I would tell him this everyday."

Robin believed that Andy's problems began anew when he arrived in Britain. "He had just signed a recording contract and was about to start with two new songwriters," he said. "But it terrified him because he was scared stiff that he would not be able to prove a success again. He became scared of everything, including me and his own family. He locked himself in the Chancery . . . and refused to see anyone.

"He kept a watch at the window for hours because he was petrified of anyone coming up to see him. He did not want to have contact with anyone. It was very strange. He went to elaborate lengths to avoid everyone.

"He would watch all the cars coming down the road, and when he spotted mine turning into the drive, he would disappear and start dashing around turning all the lights off. He pretended the whole time that he was not there."

Robin and his family were forced into the uncomfortable position of being shut out while watching someone they loved spiral out of control. "We saw him sliding downhill again and tried to help, but he would not take help from anyone. It was dreadful being so close to him and yet being unable to do anything. He did not want to see any of us," he explained.

For Barry, Andy's problems seemed at least partially due to homesickness. "He was missing Miami, and he felt he just could not go out. Perhaps I did not realise the extent to which he was folding up inside," he added. "He didn't really need to be away from his family and we didn't want him away from us. I think he went into a decline because of that."

Barbara Gibb was concerned about her youngest son and made plans to join him in England. "I got on to Robin and Robin said, 'Don't come, Mum, you're babying him too much, he's fine.' But I was on the plane that next day because I knew something was wrong."

She arrived to find that Andy had turned back to alcohol in his depression. "He was drinking again, he was drinking, definitely," she admitted. "He was getting those little tiny bottles. He was ringing the little liquor store in Thame at two o'clock in the morning. They close at 10 o'clock, everybody goes to sleep. Andy thought this was terrible, he was going back to America, he couldn't stand it."

Barry said that David English, with whom he was working on the *Hawks* project, had suggested that they go over to visit Andy. "We had heard stories he was not behaving himself." But neither of them realised just how serious Andy's depression had become.

Barry revealed, "I'd always be telling him, 'Andy, you look great. You look incredible. Let's go out'. He'd say 'Okay'. Then five minutes later, he'd ask, 'Are you sure that I look all right?' He never knew how much talent he had, and the more I told him, the less he seemed to believe it."

"He was to the point where he couldn't even stand up, he kept falling down. He smashed his face against the wall and lost all his teeth. Oh, it was just a mess, I could go on and on," Robin said grimly. "And my mother had to be there to see it, which was a nightmare for her. He wasn't even aware of his existence anymore."

Andrew Roy Gibb, the person, seemed to have disappeared in the struggle to recapture Andy Gibb, the star. He lost his sense of self. He was afraid of failing to make a comeback in the music business, yet terrified that he couldn't do anything else. "The biggest thing on his mind was, 'Can I make it back to the top?' That's what he really wanted to do, and under all the pressure, his mind and heart gave way," Barry said.

Maurice recalled a missed opportunity to connect with Andy. "I called him up and Robin said he couldn't come to the phone 'cause he was drunk, and I said, 'Oh, sod him then,' and I put the phone down . . . I never spoke to him so I never forgave myself for that for a long time, I thought I should have spoken to him."

Barbara remembered, "He kept walking in and out and saying, 'I might as well be dead, there's nothing going on.' Because there was nobody there, you see."

Even at the height of his success, Andy had always admitted that his moods played a major role in his songwriting, explaining he could only write, "when I'm most relaxed." He added, "I don't seem to be too good at writing songs when I'm troubled for some reason. I don't know what it is." Now he was depressed and afraid of failure, with the fear compounding the depression in a vicious cycle. He needed six more songs for his album, but it might as well have been 600. He couldn't write.

"You can't just *make* yourself write, you know," Barbara explained. "It's not something you can just sit down and do. He got a block and he couldn't write and that upset him, it upset him very much."

"Andy went downhill in the last three weeks of his life," Barry explained. "Maybe it was the idea that he was going back in the studio. To me, Andy's problems were not drugs and booze – to me, they were a massive insecurity, psychological problems compounded by the drink and cocaine. Maybe they also caused it, but at the end of the day, you were dealing with a person who was tremendously insecure and had no confidence in himself at all, yet had a lot of talent . . . He seemed to have lost the will or desire to use it.

"Andy had so many problems . . . You see it everywhere. Lots of success to young people, I believe, is very dangerous. They have to grow into it, and they either do or they don't. I'm afraid Andy didn't. We would tell him over and over again that he could compete with anybody, and that he should get up and get going and be counted again rather than worry about what people think. But those feelings, that lack of confidence in him, perhaps what drugs had done in the past to him . . . I don't know. I've never seen anybody cope well with phenomenal success. I've spoken with Michael Jackson, Dolly Parton and Kenny Rogers about this, and a lot of people, and with respect to them, they're very insecure. With most major artists you'll find a cupboard of insecurity. Everybody wants reassurance from somebody else, even if they're gigantic superstars."

Towards the end of February, Andy had been rushed to hospital, but he checked himself out again before the doctors could ascertain the cause. Unbeknownst to his English physicians, this was not the first time that Andy had suffered such symptoms. He mentioned to no one the previous seizures for which he had been treated in Los Angeles.

"Andy didn't die of drugs, although drugs had done a lot of damage to his heart in previous years," Robin said. "He'd had four seizures and things like that, so he was not in good nick. A week and a half before he died, in fact, he had gone into hospital suffering from severe chest pains but checked himself out before doctors could do tests. If he hadn't left, his condition might have been diagnosed, the right treatment prescribed for him and who knows . . . he might have stood a fighting chance."

★   ★   ★

"Superstars usually have a tough hide from having doors slammed in their face and hustling," said Freddie Gershon, the former president of RSO Records. "Andy never built up those layers, because he never had to. Andy grew older, but he didn't grow up. He froze in time at about age 17."

It's a sentiment that's echoed by Barbara Gibb, who said of her youngest child, "He was just like Peter Pan. He was just like a little boy all his life."

Success had come so easily to Andy; but his career, which had shown such bright promise at the start, declined just as rapidly as he fell victim to the temptations of the condition his brothers describe as "first fame". Although his income at the height of his career had averaged nearly $2 million a year, selling more than 20 million albums, the money had disappeared; most of it on cocaine. Through stints in Californian drugs rehabilitation centres, he did manage to beat his cocaine addiction, but giving up drink had proven more difficult, despite confiding in his long time friend, Marie Osmond, how proud he was to be a recovering member of Alcoholics Anonymous.

Just days after celebrating his thirtieth birthday on March 5, 1988, with his mother Barbara at brother Robin's Oxfordshire estate, he checked into John Radcliffe Hospital in Oxford, complaining of stomach and chest pains.

Robin recalled, "When he was on his way to hospital the day before he died, I said to him, 'You've got to start getting yourself together. You are the master of your own destiny.' He said, 'Yes, I know I am. I keep telling myself this.' Those were the last words we spoke to each other."

Although tests revealed no signs of drugs or alcohol in his system, the years of abuse had taken their toll. His American cardiologist, Dr William Shell, said, "I thought that the physicians in London would have been well served by talking to some of us, because some of these events were pretty frightening. They probably could have aborted one of these events if they had known what the treatment was."

Barbara had been reluctant to leave her son. "I said I'd stay with him, I thought, give me the paper, I'll stay here all night, but they don't let you in England, you can't stay in the ward all night so I had to go, so I said, 'I'll be back in the morning.' . . . [The nurse] said, 'Well, you better go because he'll sleep all night now, we've given him something to sleep.' And he was . . . fast asleep."

The following morning, March 10, his doctor told him he needed more tests. Andy agreed, then slumped into unconsciousness. Moments later, at

8.45 a.m., he was pronounced dead. Poignantly, his last words to his mother, uttered the night before, were, "You can't die from this, can you?"

Robin broke the news to his brothers back in Miami. "That has to be the saddest, most desperate moment of my life, when I heard he had gone," Barry said. "Since then, I've asked myself a thousand times, could I have done more or said more to help him?"

Maurice's reaction was stunned disbelief and prompted his own break in his recovery from alcoholism, as he admitted later. "Andy was in Miami doing great, getting his pilot's licence . . . He's in England for about a month – and he's *dead*," he said incredulously. "It took me three years to cry over that – *three years*. When it happened, I just drank and drank to numb my mind.

"The death of Andy was just one of those things that I refused to recognise for a while . . . You'd think I would have learned directly from Andy's tragedy, but when you're not ready, you're just not ready. Of course, somewhere in my subconscious, it helped me learn that the time had come for me to do something about my problem."

The media were quick to leap to conclusions when the news leaked. Andy's death was called a massive cocaine overdose, or a drink and drug binge. One article in an Australian women's magazine even claimed, "After his death, his mother Dorothy [*sic*], found a huge hoard of more than 20 vodka bottles under his bed." It seemed to typify how little importance they placed on printing the truth about Andy's death.

Barbara Gibb angrily denied the rumours. "I was with him in England when he died and they assured me at the hospital that there was not anything in his bloodstream at all. He was clean."

It was even suggested that he had died from a broken heart over the end of his relationship with Victoria Principal. Barbara insisted that he had completely recovered years earlier. "All this stuff in the papers about him breaking his heart for Victoria Principal, four years after it was all over, was just a myth. I don't know who dreamed that one up."

Hugh put it more succinctly. "Garbage," he termed it.

The official cause of death was viral myocarditis, an inflammation of the tissue surrounding the heart. The condition is more common in those with weakened immune systems, which in turn can be caused by long-term drug or alcohol abuse. As with any virus, antibiotics are useless in treating viral myocarditis; doctors can only prescribe massive doses of steroids and painkillers, and hope that it clears up.

For Maurice, the pain was only intensified by the fact that the press seemed disappointed by the lack of a hot story. Setting themselves up in a pub called Thatcher's down the road from Robin's estate, the journalists seemed to wait like vultures. "What upsets us more is what certain sections of the media did," Maurice explained. "One national newspaper declared Andy had taken a massive cocaine overdose before we'd even got him to hospital, because he'd done it before. We were also accused of taking drugs at the funeral ourselves. When our mum used to give money to Andy when he was going through bad patches, we'd see headlines like, 'Mum gives drug money to Andy'. It's okay for us because we are used to pressures of that kind, but we ask why the press takes it out on the families of the people involved because they are devastated enough as it is. The bit that got me was a reporter from one paper who phoned his editor and said, 'I've got bad news for you, chief, it was natural causes.' . . . That, to me, put the whole thing in a nutshell."

Robin Gibb's personal assistant, Ken Graydon, described the family as "devastated by grief".

The Gibb family closed ranks, issuing a statement to the press. "His passing was completely unexpected and occurred just as he was looking forward to resuming his career and working on a new recording contract."

Dick Ashby commented, "It looks as if Andy went off the straight and narrow after he arrived back in England. It's a terrible shame."

Hugh Gibb flew to London from his home in Los Angeles and was met by Robin at Heathrow Airport. Hugh was responsible for getting the news of Andy's death to his former wife and daughter, who also immediately headed for London. "He said he didn't think it would have been right for me to read about it in the paper," Kim said. "I'll always be grateful to him for that."

She claimed that she wasn't surprised when the news came. "I always knew that one day I would get a call like this," she said. "It was only a matter of time."

But even the knowledge that the lifestyle Andy had led could lead to an untimely death didn't prepare her for her own reaction to the news. "It's really only now that he has gone that I have stopped hoping he'd come back," she admitted. "I always thought we would eventually get back together. But now, he's dead. And the story will never be resolved. I will never know what might have happened."

She added, "It's so bloody sad, Andy died when he was clear of drugs, he was free and it seemed to me that he had finally grown up. Since I heard the news about his death, I have been crying solidly. I keep thinking how our daughter will never see him, never know him. Peta is the one good thing that came out of our marriage, and she is all there is left of Andy."

On March 13, Kim and Peta went to The Prebendal for Sunday lunch with the whole Gibb family, with the hopes of putting the past behind them. "I want once and for all to end the rift between us for Peta's sake," Kim said. "She should know who her grandparents are – she will never know her dad. This meeting should have happened years ago. Andy would be happy to know we are here. All there is left to do is pray that Andy is all right now, that the pain and the suffering are over for him."

A memorial service for Andy was held in the private chapel on Robin's estate, but Andy's funeral was held on March 21 in his adopted home city of Los Angeles. He was laid to rest at Forest Lawn Cemetery, with the simple epitaph provided by one of his hit singles, 'An Everlasting Love'. The entire Gibb clan were present, but Kim and Peta still didn't feel as if they were part of the family. Of all Andy's famous friends, Olivia Newton-John was the only celebrity to attend his funeral. During the service, Barry read a poem written by Andy in Las Vegas three years earlier.

'Andy's Song'

Am I all that I appear
when the spotlight dims and dies
or only a reflection
of the glitter etched in lies

Been far from home for much too long
not sure what I should feel
and even if I felt it
could I be sure it's real

So dim the lights and set the stage
they want to see the show
all the time and effort
Lord, I hope they know

'Cause with every song a part of me
is what I give to you
and when the show is over
may the memory shine through

It's hard to form relationships
when you're on the road a lot
I've yet to find a lady
who'll forgive the things I'm not

There's a side of me that's worked so hard
for all I've come to know
a dream achieved throughout the years
I just can't let it go

So dim the lights and set the stage
they want to see the show
all the time and effort
Lord, I hope they know

'Cause with every song a part of me
is what I give to you
and when the show is over
may the memory shine through.

© *Andy Gibb, 1985*

Another memorial service was held in Miami, and a plaque dedicated to Andy's memory was placed at St. Mary's Chapel in Thame.

★   ★   ★

579

In the aftermath, Andy's family and friends struggled to come to terms with their loss. "It was a devastating experience for us, obviously," Barry explained, "but you know, I think it was *more* devastating for our mum and dad than it was for us. He was our youngest brother, but when it's the youngest in the family, I think Mum and Dad really feel it the hardest.

"But you know, the fascinating thing about all of that situation is, three months before he died, this boy learnt to fly a plane. Now, you have to think about that. You know, it takes an awful lot for a person to learn to fly a plane. *We* haven't done it; Maurice would probably like to. But you know it takes an awful lot of mental, you know, concentration to learn to fly. And he did this three months before he died. So you have to at least assume that his head was in the right place."

It is indicative of the way that that everyone who knew Andy thought of him; that at 30 years old, Barry still referred to him as a boy.

"It's like the old Shakespeare saying – Andy *did* have success thrust upon him," Robin said. "He wasn't born into it, he wasn't prepared for it. He went from being a young kid to being a young star who could get anything he wanted, and he'd spend it until there was nothing left."

Barry agreed, "He is a perfect example of what happens if the business gets you and you don't get the business. He was not strong enough to deal with it."

"Andy's problem wasn't drugs or alcohol," Barry reiterated. "It was the *lack* of things. He lacked confidence. He had forgotten how to grab life. That was the sad thing. He'd lost faith."

"We wanted to revitalise him, get his confidence back, refocus him," Robin added. "He was really young when he died. There was a hell of a lot he could have done. Maybe he never should have pursued a solo career. Maybe he should have got confidence without having success first; maybe it would have been better for his first four or five records to have died."

A year on, Maurice maintained, "In many ways, I think we've all refused to accept he's gone for good. I suppose because he was taken from us so suddenly, we still find it impossible to accept. His death has definitely brought the rest of the family closer together. We are united in our devastation."

For Barry, the memories of his last telephone conversation with his youngest brother are painful. "I regret that we didn't spend more time. We were always too busy and of course, you always have that after somebody's gone. You always feel remorse because you could have given them more time, there were things you could have said you didn't say and vice versa. The last thing that happened between me and Andy was an argument, which is devastating for me because I have to live with that all my life. In that phone call between him and me, I was sort of saying, 'You know, you've really got to get your act together, and this is no good.' Instead of being gentle about it, I was angry because someone had said to me at some point, you know, tough love is the answer. For me it wasn't, because that was the last conversation we had. So that's my regret, that's what I live with.

"In hindsight, you could always see things clearer," Barry added, "how it could have been or what we should have done, or the words that we didn't say and we should have done and the arguments that we should never have had. All these things go through your mind when you lose someone like Andy. And the guilt, I'm afraid, is part of that. People say we shouldn't feel responsible or that we shouldn't feel guilty, but we do. We do."

Robin, with whom Andy had spent his last few weeks, was philosophical about his brother's life. "He was a great artist out of control, and his personality and his emotions just couldn't deal with what was going on around him and the success that he had. I don't think he liked the world that was going on out there so he kind of constructed his own; which, in the end when he did have to deal with the real world, was kind of hard for him."

Maurice shared similar emotions saying, "I hope people particularly remember his kindness, because he helped a lot of people. He just couldn't help himself."

"Andy is out there, somewhere," Barry said. "When you lose someone close to you, your concept of death is changed. You can't believe it is just dust."

He insisted, "Both my wife Linda and my mother have seen Andy's ghost. They both saw him at the same time – in different parts of the world. It was just a few weeks after he'd died. He appeared in front of Linda, unshaven, and kissed her on the cheek. He woke her up! The very next day, my mother phoned from Nevada and told me exactly the same story."

"I was sleeping alone and felt something very strange," Linda explained. "The light was on at the end of the bedroom, as one of the children had been in. It was about four a.m. I felt a kiss and a little bit of bristle on my face. I opened my eyes and looked up and Andy was there. He was smiling."

Maurice, too, claimed to have ghostly visitations. "Andy always came by boat; he never used the front door. He'd park and say, 'Hey, buddy!' He always used to say 'buddy', which I think he picked up from The Osmonds. I was having this barbecue with the family, and then we went inside. I heard, 'Hey, buddy!' as loud as anything. It was his voice. It had this slight nasalness to it." He has also mentioned Andy's favourite chair moving in the studio, or seeing Andy's face in the audience when The Bee Gees have performed live.

While Kim made no claims of apparitions, she said, "I think Andy will haunt me for the rest of my life. I know that I will never find anyone who will love me as much as Andy did." She and Peta returned to Australia with much unresolved.

"There were times when he thought I might have turned [Peta] against him," Kim explained, "but I never dreamed of doing that. I wanted her to love him. And I wanted her to know that Andy loved her."

In that, at least, she was successful. Peta, whose only meeting with her father took place when she was just two years old, knew him through his phone calls. "Well, my main memories of him are on the phone, and he was always, you know, my father, sweet and gentle, and he seemed to love me," she said, "so I grew up with that."

"In quite a few phone calls that he made, he did tell me that not a day went by when he didn't think of us," Kim revealed. "I think we were the only touch with reality he ever had."

A year after Andy's death, she mused, "It was all so long ago and yet the interest in Andy has never faded. Why? I know Andy worshipped his older brother, Barry, but I always thought that Andy had the greatest potential of the lot. Maybe that's why he still generates so much interest."

In 1989, Kim appealed to the executors of Andy's estate on her daughter's behalf. "I have never been interested in money," she insisted, "especially Andy's money." She continued to live with her parents, staying home with Peta and existing on the Australian welfare, until Peta began school at age five. "At the time, Andy was making millions, but I never asked him for a penny," she added.

"But Peta is older now, and her needs have grown. And she is the only heir to Andy's estate. I want justice for her. I want to establish what Andy left – if anything – and I want her to receive what is rightfully hers."

Kim's main goal for her daughter was to see that she received the education that both her parents lacked. With understandable pride, she stated, "Peta is special. She's bright, always at the top of her class. She's a great little poet, and she loves to write songs and sing and dance."

While Kim admitted that she had reservations about "the song and dance part" after seeing the destructive side of show business, she said, "I'd never stop her from doing whatever she wants. The only thing that I'm adamant about is that she gets an education. I don't want her to be forced into a career she doesn't want because she doesn't have the right qualifications."

She reflected back to her last court battles, saying, "The one thing I remember out of the divorce proceedings is a line my QC said to me. He said Andy and I didn't matter, that a child takes precedence over everything. Peta is the most important person in my life, and I intend to take care of her to the best of my ability. And if it means going through the horrors of another legal battle, I'll do it. I just hope it doesn't come to that. This may sound odd, but I believe Andy would have wanted me to do battle for Peta. I feel this is the last thing I can do for him, the last wish I can fulfil."

Barry, Robin and Maurice agreed with Kim's assessment that Peta's education should be everyone's first concern, and they arranged for funds to be made available for her school and college fees in later years. Additionally, mindful of the family's responsibility to Peta as Andy's sole beneficiary, they were also instrumental in negotiating appreciable increases in the royalty rate payable on Andy's record sales which, although far from the level that they were in his heyday, remain meaningful if not substantial. In any event, Peta seems to be enjoying life away from the public eye and, at the time of writing, is pursuing a career in the fashion industry.

★   ★   ★

Everyone who knew Andy displays genuine affection for him and deep regret for what might have been.

For Robert Stigwood, who had launched Andy's career, the fight to persuade Andy to seek help for his alcohol and substance abuse left its own scars. "I tried and tried and tried and broke my heart," he said, yet he remained sympathetic about the pressures of teenage adulation which drove Andy in that direction. "It is terribly hard to cope with. He got devoured because he was the current celebrity."

Family friend David English fondly remembers the high-spirited "little boy [of] about 14 or 15, whom he first met with Barry. "I saw a lot of signs of great enthusiasm, he was just like a Barry junior. He was very keen and very funny, a chip off the old block. He was somebody who was so versatile; he flew planes, he was wonderful on boats, he was a good singer . . . but the problem with Andy was that he never really realised how good he was, he always had to be continually reminded how good he was. He was always living in the shadow of his brothers, but he didn't have to because he was certainly exceptional in his own right . . . He used to run around, always very keen . . . He used to get bored very easily, always needed to be on the go all the time."

John Stringer and John Alderson, members of Andy's first band Melody Fayre on the Isle of Man, both remember hearing the news of Andy's death on the radio as they were driving to work. "It was a complete shock," said John Stringer, now a police sergeant on the island. "My own personal feelings are that I would have liked to have met him again as a bit more grown up. We had far more good times with him than we ever had bad times. I've always been a little bit upset that Andy never contacted me or John [Alderson], for old time's sake more than anything, because we did get on well with him, and we didn't have any arguments with him."

Down Under, the radio also brought the sad news to Trevor Norton from Zenta. "The people I was with that morning could see I was quite upset," he recalled. "I could not believe it. Even though I had not seen him for quite a few years, it really hit me. He was one of the nicest guys I've ever met."

His *Pirates Of Penzance* co-star, Pam Dawber, said, "I felt like he died of a broken heart. I felt like he just checked out; he just couldn't do it anymore."

"Andy had everything," Marie Osmond said. "He had fame and popularity and the money and anything you could want, but he was still empty."

For actress Victoria Principal, Andy's death left much unspoken but like his brothers, she too was able to find her own way to resolve things. "Several years after Andy died, I had a dream and in that dream, Andy came to me, knowing that I was haunted by our unfinished business. So we sat down, and we had the talk that I certainly wanted to have and that we probably needed to have. I thought it was so like Andy, even after his death to find a way to bring me solace because he was simply the nicest person I've ever known." However, she reflected, "I had to live for many years with the awareness it wasn't *if* Andy would die, it would be *when* Andy would die."

Brad Lachman, who signed him to co-host the American television show *Solid Gold*, remembered Andy as "a very charming, vulnerable and charismatic performer. He wanted everyone to love him. He had so much going for him, but he just couldn't believe it."

★ ★ ★

Just two months after Andy's death, The Andy Gibb Memorial Foundation was formed by Renée Schreiber, Beverly Burke and Karen Witkowski to continue to raise funds through the charities he had supported throughout his lifetime. It still thrives to this day.

On March 10, 1989, the Gibbs' adopted hometown of Miami, Florida named a street in Andy's honour, Andy Gibb Drive. The Mayor of Miami Beach, Alex Daoud, and Miami Beach commissioners named the street in South Point Park in Miami Beach in honour of Andy's accomplishments and charitable work for the community. The mayor brought Barry, Robin and Maurice on stage to present them with the proclamation, which Barry accepted, saying that he felt that Andy was there in the park with everyone, enjoying the sunshine. A cheque for $5,000 from the Andy Gibb Memorial Foundation was presented by Renée Schreiber to the American Heart Association.

"We promised ourselves when Andy died that something would be done in his memory," Barry explained. "We want to thank the Mayor, the City Commission and the people of Miami Beach for helping us to fulfil that dream." The sign later disappeared but was restored with the change of name to Andy Gibb Way.

In 1991, Polydor released a CD, entitled simply *Andy Gibb*, consisting of Andy's greatest hits with one track from his final recording sessions, 'Man On Fire'. Another, 'Arrow Through The Heart', remains officially unreleased, but the Gibb family agreed to its use in VH1's *Behind The Music: Andy Gibb*, whilst 'Price Of Fame' and 'Hell Or High Water' were never released. Andy's first three albums would finally be released in CD format in 1997.

The world around him changed, but Andy Gibb never did. Whether he could have regained the early promise of his career, we will never know, but he remains forever young in the memories of those closest to him; the bright star that burned out far too quickly.

The haunting final words come from Andy himself. In one of his last songs, 'Arrow Through The Heart', the eerily prophetic lyrics describe the protagonist's anguish in his quest for an everlasting love.

> *But an arrow through the heart,*
> *Arrow through the heartbreak over you,*
> *Steady hand, your aim is true,*
> *Bring me to my knees again,*
> *I'm too young to die.*

> *Andrew Roy Gibb, March 5, 1958–March 10, 1988.*

38

WISH YOU WERE HERE

"THEY SAY IT causes soul growth when you lose somebody," Barry mused. "Before, you don't look at the metaphysical side of life much at all. After, you start looking at everything like that . . ."

Barry believes that the loss of their brother was the catalyst for The Bee Gees' decision to go back to live performances. "Andy's death kicked us in the pants and got us going again. It got us motivated to go back on the road. Andy's death stopped us in our tracks and woke us up.

"The trauma of losing Andy, the idea that we were wasting what we were doing, everything compounded to make us start performing again," he explained. "We were a live group before we ever made a record. We're out to show that that's the kind of energy we're prepared to put in our work. We don't want to hide behind our records, which we've done for the last 10 years."

Although they were still unwilling to commit to a full tour, the three surviving Gibb brothers made their first live appearance at the Atlantic Records 40th Anniversary Concert at Madison Square Garden in New York on May 15, 1988. Backed by Paul Schaffer & The World's Most Dangerous Band★, The Bee Gees performed 'To Love Somebody', 'Lonely Days' and 'Jive Talkin' ' to an appreciative audience.

This was followed on June 6 by their first live appearance in Great Britain in 14 years. The group took part in The Prince's Trust Rock Gala Concert at the Royal Albert Hall, where they performed 'Jive Talkin'' and 'You Win Again' and were presented afterwards to the Prince and Princess of Wales. Five days later, they joined in the Nelson Mandela 70th Birthday Tribute Concert at Wembley Stadium, performing 'You Win Again' and 'I've Gotta Get A Message To You'. As with the Prince's Trust concert, Phil Collins was their guest drummer for the performances.

The following week, Barry took part in the Harrod's Pro-Celebrity Tennis Tournament at the Royal Albert Hall in London.

★   ★   ★

★ Best known for their residency on the *David Letterman Show*.

As far back as 1981, Barry Gibb and David English had begun to formulate the idea for a film. "We often chew over silly ideas," Barry explained, "but nothing had ever come to fruition. Then one day there was a hurricane forecast."

David English continued the story. "We were on the way to the studios in an old Ford Mustang, which was kind of shaky, but BG loved it and I used to drive him along. One day we went along the coastal road and we saw a big storm out at sea, and I thought it could be our last day on earth and I said, 'Barry, what would happen if we only had a limited time to live, what would you do?' "

Barry mused, "What would your idea of fulfilment be if there was not time left on earth and you knew it? For some people, I think it would be to sit with their families and wait to die. For others, it would be to go out and do everything that they ever had wanted to do."

David said, "We started writing it, about two lads in a hospital, and it took seven years to make, from actually writing the idea, getting Roy Clarke to do the screenplay, Steve Lanning to produce it, to actually raise the money . . .

"What Barry and I normally do with ideas, it comes quickly, and if we both like it, it's like the eclipse of the sun. Two stars go together, you know – occasionally, it happens like that . . . It's very much better to do it with a friend. You know if you've got a game of tennis, if the ball doesn't come back over the net, you haven't got a game," he explained. "But you know if it's going well, the idea came in about twenty minutes."

"If it takes one of us a little while to get to like the idea, then we probably won't use it," Barry added.

Barry was determined that the film be made in the UK. "The British make the best films in the world, as far as I'm concerned," he enthused. "And as long as I can – in my own small way – I'm going to try and support the industry.

"The key to making a good film is if everybody functions the right way at the right time," he continued. "It's a whole team of people. And if the sound people don't function, then the film doesn't work. If the film people don't function, the sound doesn't work, none of it works. Everybody has to do something special like wardrobe, makeup; all of these things if they're not all done right, everything falls down, you know. Take the main card out and the whole pack falls down so that's what it's like . . . That's why you have to rely on so much expertise to make a film . . . It's quite crazy and I don't know how a lot of films get made, especially in Hollywood."

The concept of two terminally ill young men seems unusual for a comedy, but Roy Clarke took Barry and David's idea and wrote a script that manages to combine humour, emotion, strength and resilience, concentrating on living even when dying. The film's star, Timothy Dalton, explained, "*Hawks* is about living and the value of life. It teaches that you can approach the problems of life and death with courage and humour."

The film also starred Anthony Edwards, then best known as Tom Cruise's co-star in *Top Gun*, but who would go on to greater fame in the American television series, *ER*. Edwards plays Deckermensky – abbreviated to Decker – an American football player, who falls ill during a tour of Britain and finds himself sharing a ward with the acerbic lawyer, Bancroft. The two men decide to make their last days on earth pleasurable by stealing an ambulance and heading for the brothels of Amsterdam. Along the way, they meet Hazel and Maureen, played by Janet McTeer and Camille Coduri respectively, and their plans go awry. While Dalton and Edwards already had impressive filmographies to display to their latest employers, *Hawks* came relatively early in the careers of six foot one inch tall McTeer and the more diminutive Coduri. For each it was their third film, and both would move onto bigger and better things; in particular, *Nuns On The Run* for Coduri, while in 1999, McTeer appeared in *Tumbleweeds* and received an Academy Award nomination for her role as Mary Jo Walker.

Timothy Dalton was eager to take on the role of Bancroft, in spite of – or perhaps because of – the contrast to his suave screen persona as Agent 007. "I jumped at the chance of playing in *Hawks* because scripts of the calibre Roy Clarke has written come along once in a blue moon," he explained. "I enjoy playing Bond and those movies are great of their type, but I'm an actor who craves variety."

He reflected that playing James Bond hadn't changed his life, although the money and fame which it brought allowed him to be more selective in his choice of roles. "I know that having me in the movie helped to get it financed because I'm considered bankable as Bond," he added. "I don't say that in any egotistical way, but if that leverage means small budget films [that] I want to do can get made, then that's useful."

"He's a man faced with a huge problem and he faces it with great pugnacity, verve and humour. *Hawks* is really more about life than death. The lives of Decker and Bancroft have been brought into very sharp focus through their illness. The film is about the course of action that they take and how they deal with it. It's a film of resilience and courage, good humour and toughness. It's a terrific story, a worthwhile story.

"It's a story so international in its theme, it should touch everybody. There's learning, wisdom, dependence, independence, need . . . all about life in the little time," Dalton summarised, "and it's all enchanted by Barry Gibb's haunting score."

That haunting score had been through several transformations before its eventual release. It began its life as Barry's 1986 follow-up to his *Now Voyager* album, with the working title *When Tomorrow Comes*, which later became *My Eternal Love*, before changing to *Moonlight Madness*.

David English described the film as "another way of getting Barry's music over to the public" during the *Fever* backlash, when American radio in particular turned against The Bee Gees. "It's another medium; it's a good way of actually getting through while this silly period is going on," he added.

Barry explained, "*Hawks* was actually turned down by my record company twice. A lot of those songs were done for the second solo album, which never came out, so I was more or less caught with a lot of songs that MCA didn't particularly want to release [which] I thought should still go out. It's a matter of creative opposition. I opposed MCA's opinion not to put it out. And that's why I forced a lot of that music through this film and through the album, because I think the music *ought* to get heard, whether or not they're what you'd call hit singles . . . I hate dealing with the idea that you can only write music if it's bracketed as a hit single by a record company's opinion. I think it's wrong."

The *Hawks* soundtrack combines two new songs, the Diana Ross recording of 'Chain Reaction', and seven songs from Barry's unreleased 1986 solo album. Credited as a Barry Gibb album, it was not released by MCA for North America, but Polygram did release it to the rest of the world in September.

"MCA turned it down when it was in its original form as an album, and they turned it down when I presented it to them as a soundtrack so, there's really nothing I can do about that," Barry disclosed.

Three of the 1986 songs were not in the movie and are listed as "bonus cuts" in the CD notes.

August 4 marked the world premiere of the film *Hawks* at the Odeon West End in London, with general release on the following day. "What Barry and I did beforehand," David English revealed, "we had a look at the underground, at the posters on the wall, just to see our names. "We couldn't believe we'd actually pulled it off!"

For Barry, the occasion was tinged slightly by the sorrow that his youngest brother could not be there to share in the achievement. Andy had seen two early previews of the film shortly after his arrival in England. "Those pre-views were virtually the only times he went out," said Barry.

In the United States, the film would have a limited release some three months after its British premiere.

The single 'Childhood Days', backed by 'Moonlight Madness', was also released in August, supported by a film clip showing co-writer Maurice playing bass. It remains the only time any of the Gibbs had appeared in one of their brother's solo promotional film clips.

August also saw the release of *One Moment In Time*, a compilation of songs by various artists for the 1988 Olympics. The Bee Gees contributed 'The Shape Of Things To Come', one of the finest singles that never was. Arista Records opted for Whitney Houston's title track for the lead-off single.

"It was a great song," Barry asserted. "We gave it to them, but you know, it's a strange business. Whitney came first. We're not on Arista Records. So we gave a song to Arista Records to put on an album that also included people like Whitney Houston, who *is* on Arista Records. So they're going to promote the people on their own label because that's where their money's going to get made. And people like us, little did we realise, are going to get pushed into the background . . . It should have been out as a single, but they screwed around with it. You know, that's what happens."

The Bee Gees with Eric Clapton also appeared incognito on the LP as The Bunburys with 'Fight (No Matter How Long)'. Earlier that year, Clapton explained, "The first single was 'We're The Bunburys' by The Bunburys, who at the time were The Bee Gees. David English invented The Bunburys as a cartoon. Those two started writing, and Barry wrote a song for me to do which hasn't been released yet, called 'Fight', and will be out on The Bunburys album. Elton's on it and George Harrison is on it. It has been held up for one reason or another because I don't know what label it's coming out on yet. But it's good stuff and I think it's going to be an ongoing thing for David."

While The Bunburys project was on hold, the *One Moment In Time* album seemed a good opportunity to get at least one of the songs heard.

The project had expanded from its inception as a children's story. "I'd written six books on *Bunbury Tails*," David English explained, "then I got a deal with Channel 4 to have a series out and we thought we'd write a song for each one of the episodes. So 'Fight', we wrote it together, Barry and I."

Once the song was completed with Robin and Maurice, Barry and David approached Clapton to involve him in the project. "We trapped him at the polo at Windsor. [It was] a very sociable day," David recalled, "and we said, 'We've written this demo for you, we'd love you to hear it,' and he said, 'Where is it?' We got it out of our pockets so, as he was eating, he was listening to it on the Walkman. So he said, 'Okay, I'll do that,' so we went down to Dave Mackay's studios and recorded it . . . Ian Botham was on the 'Fight' track doing back-up vocals – it was really getting all your mates together, but singing is a gift and, with The Bee Gees' writing, it does help when you've got some songs of that kind of quality."

The song was recorded over the summer holidays, so all the Gibb and Mackay children, as well as Ian Botham's young son, had a fine time together while their fathers toiled away in the studio. Dave Mackay recalled that during the recording, the air conditioning in his studio had broken down, and as it was a hot summer's day, all the windows and doors were open. Eric Clapton, immersed in his guitar solo with his eyes tightly closed in concentration, was brought abruptly back to earth by Mackay's dog's impudent snuffling.

Mackay was accustomed to getting up starting his work day at about seven each morning, and finishing up for the day at around five, in sharp contrast to The Bee Gees' usual routine of beginning work late in the afternoon and working until the early morning hours. Dave recalled Linda Gibb wistfully wondering if Barry could ever be convinced to "work to live" as he did, striking a better balance between work and family, rather than living for his work.

The Bunburys 'Fight' was released in January, 1989, as a single in some parts of the world, notably not in the USA although it was heavily promoted there on a promotional only 12-inch single. Despite the superstar collaboration, the song failed to make an impact on the charts.

Barry hosted his fifth Love & Hope Tennis Festival for the Diabetes Research Institute at the Turnbury Isle Yacht And Country Club in

Aventura, Florida, on November 18, 1988. Despite the usual complement of celebrity guests, Andy's absence was almost tangible at the event, after the years of lending his support to the cause. One of the features of the evening's entertainment was the performance of Barry and old Australian family friend Noeleen Batley Stewart – now a resident of Miami – of 'Islands In The Stream'.

★   ★   ★

Months after Andy's death, The Bee Gees gathered in Middle Ear Studio to commence the recording of material written over the previous 18 months for the *One* album. In an ironic twist of fate, the title reflected their intention to tour with Andy in 1989 under the "all for one, one for all" principles of *The Three Musketeers*. Memories of their youngest brother were still strong, and the group subconsciously exorcised their individual demons in the lyrics of two songs in particular, 'Tears' and 'Wish You Were Here'. While to outsiders, the connection seems patently obvious, the three brothers were so wrapped up in their emotions, that it was not until recordings were complete that they would realise the extent of Andy's influence upon them.

The album is simply "dedicated to our brother, Andy." The only cover art is overlapping black and white photos of their three faces, none shown in its entirety, but which merge from the neck down.

The Bee Gees were once again producing themselves along with engineer Brian Tench, who has been listed as "co-producer" on *E.S.P.* They used a small group of four musicians: Tim Cansfield on guitar, Peter John Vettese on keyboards, Nathan East on bass, and Steve Ferrone on drums, along with Alan Kendall on three songs. Of the four, Vettese had probably the most varied history having previously worked with Annie Lennox, Frankie Goes To Hollywood, Jethro Tull, Chicago's Peter Cetera and Tommy Shaw of Styx.

In most places, the lead single and first song on the album, was 'Ordinary Lives', released in April, 1989, followed by 'One'; the order was reversed in the United States. The demo of 'Ordinary Lives' was made around the time of Andy's death under the title 'Cruel World', a phrase that is still in the opening line of the second verse. Ordinary Lives' reached number 27 in Holland and number 54 in the UK.

'One' was released in June and reached a disappointing number 71 in Britain and 46 in Holland. When it was released in the USA in July, coinciding with the start of their American tour, it was their first Top 10 smash since 1979, peaking at number seven.

The album *One* was released in April, 1989, in most of the world, with its American release delayed until July. Less than a month after the album's European release, The Bee Gees opened their first concert tour in nearly a decade. "We're enthusiastic about our new music," Maurice said, "and we'd like to play it live now. Besides, we'd like to present many of our former hits in a new polished up version to all our new and of course to all our old fans."

"In 1988, after our performances at the 40th Anniversary of Atlantic

Records, the Prince's Trust [Concert] and at the Nelson Mandella concert, we decided to use the chance that came up after the release of our new album to go on tour again," Robin explained. "We hadn't been playing live for nearly ten years. And when it suddenly started to be fun again, we decided to go on tour. It is extremely exciting. And we haven't been playing live in many countries, like France for example.

"I've looked forward to this tour for a long time, even though I know it's going to be a lot of hard work. You've got to make every night your first night. That's important to the audience because, for them, it is your first night and they want everything you've got."

"We've got a lot of thanking to do," Barry added. "There's a lot of people that've been really good to us over so many years, and I think it would be nice to see them sitting in front of us and be able to please them the same way. The band is in our blood. I just can't wait for the energy you get when it's 10 seconds before you go on stage."

The touring band was quite impressive for, as well as Barry, Robin, Maurice and Alan Kendall, it also featured Tim Cansfield on guitar, Vic Martin and Gary Moberley each on keyboards and synthesizer, George Perry on bass and Chester Thompson on drums. Tampa Lann, Linda Harmon and Phyllis St James on vocals and percussion completed the band. It was quite a change from their first tour of Germany back in 1968.

The *One For All* tour began on May 3 at Westfalenhalle in Dortmund, Germany, taking the group to 19 cities throughout Europe. The final concert, on July 1, brought them back to Germany with a show at the Niedersachsenstadion, a huge football stadium in Hannover, where 50,000 were in attendance. Hugh was literally dragged on stage and introduced to the audience, while during his brothers' performance of 'Holiday', Maurice disappeared to fetch his video camera and proceeded to film the audience. During the medley version of 'Islands In The Stream', Maurice grabbed hold of his jumper at strategic points in a clear tribute to one of the two performers who turned the song into a hit.

Germany has always held special memories for The Bee Gees, going right back to their first international success. "For us it is the most fanatical place," Robin asserted. "The shows there sell out very fast, and the fans have got every album we've made. At a hotel in Munster once, the manager turned a fire hose on a whole crowd of our fans in the lobby and washed them out into the street, so they promptly got hold of the hose and turned it back on him. All the while, we were watching and laughing from a window above." Tennis star Steffi Graf attended the Hamburg concert, and was clearly thrilled when 'You Win Again' was dedicated to her.

Although the tour included a show in Copenhagen, where Linda celebrated her birthday, other Scandinavian fans were disappointed since there were no concerts in Oslo and Stockholm, shows in these cities having been dropped shortly before the tour had begun. Three shows in Italy would also be cancelled, apparently due to Barry's continuing back problems.

591

"The *E.S.P.* album was so successful over in Europe, we thought it would be a great place to start the tour because they've already accepted us back over there," Maurice explained.

Acceptance was the key for the brothers. After the disco backlash of the early Eighties, they wanted to prove to their detractors that there was more to The Bee Gees than *Saturday Night Fever.* Referring to John Travolta's trademark pose on the album cover, Barry joked, "Let's be clear, here. We never did point at the ceiling!

"I don't think we really wanted a *Fever*," he added seriously. "As a career move, we would have liked a couple of Top 10 records and maybe to have had a successful soundtrack. But it was such a really huge social phenomenon which nobody could have predicted. It was a stroke of luck in one sense, and a lot of people who loved the film discovered The Bee Gees for the first time. But it also created an image for us which was out of control. When that sort of thing occurs, your life turns upside down.

"First of all, you don't think you are that famous . . . you have got five singles in the Top 10 in America, two albums in the Top 20 . . . you can't be any bigger than you are. At that point, you start doubting everything that you are. You feel insecure. Then you realise it's not being there which is great but getting there – the trip there and the camaraderie of everyone making it together."

"We are actually quite simple in our needs," Robin explained. "All we want is to be around for a long time, make nice hit albums with a few hit singles every now and again and have people come and see our shows. We are keeping our image at a low profile and making the music speak for itself. *Fever* was really all about John Travolta, not us. He can dance – we can't!"

"I want to see The Bee Gees where they are not made fun of," Barry declared. "That's my cause. And I'll go on until that happens. It may never happen, but I don't care. I'm prepared for the fight.

"We have taken a lot of flak over the years. We've spent too many years on the defensive, and now that we're on the attack, it feels a damn sight better. This band has been around for 30 years, so it's a little unfair to tag us with a disco label. Paul McCartney made disco records. Rod Stewart did. Even Ethel Merman★, which shows you how outrageous the times were."

The brothers were distinctly perplexed by the public response. "It's amazing how praise turns to scorn when it suits people," Barry said. "It's very confusing. If everybody said no, I would understand and maybe go off and buy a farm and raise pigs. On the other hand, I hear people say, 'Your music is the most beautiful I ever heard.'"

Despite their longevity in the pop music business, they were still young men. "We see ourselves as coming into our prime," said Barry. "We don't see ourselves as having been around a long time. I'm 42 and Maurice and

★ A Broadway and film star most famous for her inimitable rendition of 'There's No Business Like Show Business'.

Robin are 39. If you're that age as a banker or accountant, you're coming into your prime."

The group returned to the United States and on July 13, they appeared on David Letterman's show, performing 'One'. On July 29, they began their American tour – Michael Murphy replaced Chester Thompson on drums – with an outdoor concert before an enthusiastic crowd at Riverfest on Harriet Island, St. Paul, Minnesota. Teens too young to have seen *Saturday Night Fever* when it was first released were on their feet and dancing to the driving beat.

"Journalists would actually say to our faces, 'How can you carry on after *Saturday Night Fever* – it's a bit of a joke, isn't it?' Well, to me, it wasn't a joke," Barry declared. "I mean, we had material success, but creatively nobody would take us seriously. It took a while but finally we decided to go out there and do Bee Gees music the best way we could.

"The press would say, 'The guys who brought you *Saturday Night Fever* are here to take you back to the lights and glamour of disco.' But once they came, they went away with quite a different attitude. Hopefully, the image of being disco wimps is now gone. What we are finding is that there are a lot of girls in the audience around the age of 20. When they were 10 or 11, that's when the *Fever* syndrome was very, very hot so they were our fans when they were just reaching that age. Consequently, a lot of our fans are still under 20 and it's marvellous to see, especially the girls."

The concert began with the strong opening track from the *One* album, 'Ordinary Lives' and moved straight into another new song, 'Giving Up The Ghost'. The *Main Course* to *Saturday Night Fever* period was well represented with 'Jive Talkin' ', 'Nights On Broadway', 'You Should Be Dancing', 'How Deep Is Your Love' and 'Stayin' Alive'.

"I don't mind singing the old songs as long as there is a new song out there, a new single, an album that's happening now," Robin explained. "Then the old stuff has its place and the show isn't just a retrospective. Audiences really want to hear the hits."

'One', 'It's My Neighbourhood' and 'House Of Shame' received as enthusiastic response as the old standards, 'To Love Somebody', 'I've Gotta Get A Message To You', 'Words' and 'Lonely Days', No Bee Gees' concert would be complete without 'New York Mining Disaster 1941', 'Holiday', 'Too Much Heaven', 'Run To Me' and 'World', and all were included in the acoustic medley, which also highlighted the first time that The Bee Gees themselves had ever been heard to sing their compositions, 'Heartbreaker' and 'Islands In The Stream'. 'How Can You Mend A Broken Heart', 'I Started A Joke' and 'Massachusetts' completed the "essentials", and Robin's solo hits even featured, with a snippet of 'Saved By The Bell' in the medley and all three brothers turning in an energetic performance of 'Juliet'. The "disco wimp" image was well and truly laid to rest.

The tour crossed the country, ending on September 2 with a show at the Shoreline Amphitheatre in San Francisco.

The group made an appearance on the *Arsenio Hall Show* in November, performing 'One' and 'You Win Again', before setting off on the Australian leg of the tour.

The promoters of the 1989 Australian Tour, The Bee Gees' first tour there in 15 years, were David Trew and Garry Van Egmond. It was the fourth time Trew had been the promoter of a Bee Gees Australian Tour; the previous tours being 1971, 1972 and 1974. The Gibb Brothers' friendship with Trew went back to their Australian days as teenagers performing in a regional Victorian city named Geelong, about 60 miles from Melbourne. Trew, about the same age as the twins, was something of a teenage entrepreneur and he took the time to give the exhausted teenagers a cold drink and meat pie after one of their shows. The Gibb brothers were impressed – never having witnessed such benevolence from a promoter before – and never forgot the favour. Trew also had the foresight to bring them to Australia during their relatively quite periods elsewhere in the world and was rewarded with sell-out tours every time. When The Bee Gees were touring the US during the Fever tour in 1979, the Gibbs invited Trew to join them for a few shows.

The sell-out tour opened on November 7 in Canberra, with a concert in Adelaide two nights later. A pair of concerts in Perth followed, with three dates in Sydney, two in Melbourne and two in Brisbane. As with previous Australian tours, the November 18 Melbourne concert was captured on film, to be shown as a television special just after the band's departure from the country.

In 1990 the special was issued as a Video Cassette for commercial release under the title *One For All*. Although the video market was relatively new, for a band that had been internationally successful since 1967 with hundreds of live performances under their belt, it was still somewhat of a belated launch into the live video market. Their earliest foray into this genre had come in 1985 when MGM/United Artists released *The Story Of The Bee Gees* whilst Virgin Music Video issued *Bee Gees Biography*; both being similar in content, but sufficiently different to merit the purchase of both as far as their visually starved fans were concerned.

Prior to the show in Sydney there was also a reunion of the 1967 Bee Gees band. Vince Melouney and Colin Petersen, both now Sydney residents, had been invited to catch up with the boys and be their guests at the show later that evening. Colin was later to describe the meeting as "quite tentative at first", but once they relaxed – while not quite like old times – it was very friendly.

From Australia, the *One For All* tour took them to Japan for six concerts, opening at Yokohama Arena, Kanagawa-ken on November 28 and ending on December 7 at Ehime Kenmin Bunka Kaikan, Matsuyama, Ehime-ken.

On March 3, 1990, The Bee Gees lent their support to the VH1 cable television channel's fund-raiser in aid of cystic fibrosis research at Crested Butte Mountain Resort in Colorado, playing an acoustic set.

Later that month, Maurice began writing music for the proposed film, *Sonja*. It was a project close to his heart. Andy had read a book entitled *Doctor And The Damned*, based on the life of Albert Haas, a wartime resistance leader who spied on the Nazis for the Allies. He and his wife Sonja were betrayed by a member of the Hitler Youth and spent the next six years in the concentration camps at Auschwitz and Dachau respectively. Reunited after the war, Haas went on to be a leading consultant at New York's University Hospital.

Andy was gripped by the story and convinced his brothers of its potential as a film, and Maurice planned to co-produce it for Robin's Redbreast Films. "It's a chilling tale, but it has a great message of love conquering all . . . and survival against the odds.

"I don't think we ever thought for a moment that we should drop the project after Andy died," Maurice declared. "Instead it will be a tribute to him, Andy's name will be the main credit on the film, and we will dedicate it to him."

Although Kevin Costner was touted for the role of Albert Haas, the project was eventually shelved.

In April, the brothers came together again for Barry's sixth Love & Hope Tennis Festival at Turnbury Isle Yacht and Country Club in Aventura, Florida. This time they performed a full set comprising 'To Love Somebody', 'New York Mining Disaster 1941', 'Holiday', 'Too Much Heaven', 'Heartbreaker', 'Islands In The Stream', 'Run To Me', 'World', 'Words', 'Lonely Days', 'Jive Talkin'' and 'You Should Be Dancing'.

★   ★   ★

In August 1990, a live version of 'How Can You Mend A Broken Heart', taken from the Melbourne concert, appeared on *Nobody's Child*, a Warner Brothers Record's album to benefit the Romanian Angel Appeal launched by Olivia Harrison, Barbara Bach, Linda McCartney and Yoko Ono the previous April.

By the end of the year, The Bee Gees' status in the music world was recognised with a career retrospective entitled *Tales From The Brothers Gibb – A History In Song, 1967–1990*, a boxed set of four CDs or cassettes, released in November.

"Looking back, as we've been doing for this compilation, the songs have a certain naïveté to them but we were finding our own sound," Barry explained. "There were the harmonies, that particular vocal style, and a sort of Sixties folksy feel that runs through those songs."

In addition to The Bee Gees' hit singles, the set included some rare B-sides and 10 live tracks from the 1989 tour. Outside the United States, the set included three tracks from Barry's *Hawks* soundtrack. It would have seemed a perfect opportunity for more rarities – perhaps previously unreleased tracks from *A Kick In The Head Is Worth Eight In The Pants*. Indeed, Polygram's box set co-ordinator Bill Levenson disclosed that this was one of the ideas discussed for the set, but they all finally decided not to do so for this particular project, with the sole exception of the demo version of 'E.S.P.' possibly included to reduce the number of songs licensed from Warner Brothers' records. Some of the B-sides, however, had originally had such limited release that, even in England and the United States, a claim could be made that the box included "previously unreleased" songs.

Perhaps with the lucrative Christmas market in mind, outside the USA, a 21-track CD called *The Very Best Of The Bee Gees* was also issued, specifically aimed at those who preferred a briefer trip down Bee Gees' memory lane. In November, a four-track CD single of 'How Deep Is Your Love' was released in the UK. The CD also featured 'Too Much Heaven', 'To Love Somebody' and a Bruce Forrest remix of 'You Should Be Dancing'. A special 7.15 dub version also appeared on a promo–only 12–inch single.

To further promote the album in mainland Europe, 'Words' and 'Run To Me' were the selected tracks on a CD single manufactured in Holland early in the New Year. The marketing strategy paid off as *The Very Best Of The Bee Gees* scaled the charts in the UK, Europe and Australia.

By the time *Tales From The Brothers Gibb* was in the shops, The Bee Gees had already completed their next album, and Barry re-enforced the brothers' claim that financial gain wasn't the reason for their continued presence in the studios.

"We don't make records to make money – we don't need to anymore. But we are creative people and we want to have hits, to make records that people like. I don't see anything wrong with that. The new album will surprise a lot of people, and it's perfectly timed after this greatest hits package, the old and the new."

In February, 1991, The Bee Gees were under the impression that they were about to be filmed for a Channel Four documentary called *A Day In The Life Of Steve Wright*, appearing on the disc jockey's popular radio programme when television presenter Michael Aspel entered the studio with his requisite big red book and announced, "The Bee Gees, This Is Your Life."

"We always used to watch *This Is Your Life* as kids and wondered if we would ever be on it one day," Maurice said.

The brothers were whisked away to the television studio, where their families and friends were waiting to surprise them. As Hugh Gibb quipped, "It took a television show in England to get your mother away from the slot machines in Las Vegas." The programme didn't run to plan at first; the taping was delayed for 40 minutes when the projector malfunctioned. Frankie Howerd, Kenny Everett and Susan George were among the celebrities on hand to share their anecdotes about the group, with taped messages from Robert Stigwood, their sister Lesley and her family, as well as such luminaries as Barbra Streisand, Michael Jackson, Dionne Warwick, Kenny Rogers and Neil Sedaka, who was returning the favour from their appearance on his *This Is Your Life*.

Video clips of the very young Bee Gees from Australian television reduced the brothers to fits of embarrassed laughter, but the mood turned sombre as the focus shifted to Andy. Although disc jockey Bill Gates was there to represent the early days in Australia, it seemed odd that there was no sign of their Manchester friends, nor indeed any of the various band members who had worked with the group through the years. Considering The Bee Gees' long and prestigious history, to those not used to the show's low key format, it came over as a rather bland special on the band, although it was well received according to TV audience figures. The occasion also marked the last official appearance of Hugh Gibb.

On March 2, Beri Gibb married Harry "Chino" Rhoades at a chapel in Las Vegas. Although Barry, Robin and Maurice weren't there to see Hugh give the bride away, their gifts enabled the couple to take a honeymoon in Mexico. At the reception in the ballroom at the Holiday Casino, the newlyweds danced to a recording of a love song written and sung by Beri for her new husband.

The Bee Gees, meanwhile, were kept busy promoting their latest album, *High Civilization* and its first single, 'Secret Love', released in March in most parts of the world, although American fans would have to wait two more months. The album was again recorded with just a small group of musicians: returning favourites Alan Kendall on guitar and Chocolate Perry on bass, and Tim Moore on keyboards and programming and Lenny Castro on percussion. As usual, Barry and Maurice played guitars and Maurice also played keyboards.

The overall sound of the album, as well as its follow-up, has been described by some as cold and mechanical and by others as sharp and clear, and the man most associated with this difference is Prince's engineer Femi Jiya, who worked on only these two albums. The most obvious change is that the percussion tracks, a mix of real and synthesized sound, are loud in the mix, but that's not the whole answer.

This was the first Bee Gees album issued essentially on CD. The natural dividing point of two sides was gone, and the album length also increased, this one clocking in at just over 60 minutes.

The second single was released in May. 'When He's Gone' is a genuinely exciting track which again has Robin singing a strong lead most of the way, and a thumping syncopated beat propels the song along. A strong single, it nonetheless failed to make any impact on the charts, despite the sleeve featuring a great picture of Maurice with his hands crossed over his face.

'The Only Love' sounds like a classic Bee Gees ballad, and it was released as a single in some parts of the world in August but reached only number 88 in Britain. Barry himself must have favoured the song as he featured it as his solo spot, relegating his long time favourite ballad 'Words' to a less prominent position during the 1991 European concert tour. The single's cover artwork featured a photo of Maurice's daughter Samantha.

On May 2, The Bee Gees appeared on Arsenio Hall's late night talk show, performing 'When He's Gone' and 'To Love Somebody' but pointedly not being interviewed, amidst rumours of dissatisfaction with the way Hall conducted their chat on a previous appearance. The following night they appeared on fellow former RSO artist Rick Dees' *Into The Night*, performing 'When He's Gone' and 'One', as well as an interview, the only promotion in the United States for the album and single. Later in the year, a *Going Home* one-hour special for cable TV's Disney Channel would highlight the group's career.

American radio proved resistant to The Bee Gees once again, with a general feeling of astonishment that the group was still recording. The attitude rankled with the brothers. "You wouldn't be surprised if Fleetwood Mac, Eric Clapton, David Bowie or Elton John had a new album out. We're younger than any of them," Robin protested. "Why do you think we should retire? We've a long way to go yet."

On May 25, The Bee Gees kicked off their 23-city *High Civilization* European tour in Kiel in Germany. During that first evening's concert, they included their tribute to Andy, 'Wish You Were Here', but perhaps the memories were still too fresh, as the song was dropped from the set list for the remainder of the tour.

For those who attended, there were other memories and highlights. In Dortmund, Robin's thumb was noticeably bandaged, the result of an accident with a razor. There was a full five-minute standing ovation for 'Words' in Frankfurt. At Saarbrücken, the first in a run of five open-air concerts, a point was made of sound-checking 'Secret Love' as the band had lost their timing of the song due to audience clapping becoming faster and faster at each show. During the concert itself, there was a total power outage midway through Robin's 'Juliet'. No problem for the crowd though, they finished the song off for him while Barry led the clapping to sustain the correct tempo and Maurice performed one of his little dances.

In Berlin, Barry wore a different combination of fingerless cycling gloves at each of the three shows, ostensibly in an attempt to keep his arthritic hands warm. Each of these shows at the Waldbuhne Stadium were filmed, a one-hour TV special and limited edition video release being the end result. An over-zealous security guard wrestled a camera from one fan's grasp. Barry was having none of it and interrupted his song to demand, "Give that man his camera back!" The guard dutifully complied. The Berlin concerts were also recorded by a mobile studio as there were plans to issue a live album too. Over 50,000 turned up for the gig at Bremen's Weserstadion. Those who turned up early enough heard Barry's rendition of 'Blowing In The Wind' at the sound check!

After completing the German leg of the tour, they moved on to Holland where, in Rotterdam, a large inflatable globe was thrown on-stage during 'World'.

Although concerts in Madrid, La Coruna, Milan, Lyon and Montpelier were cancelled, the one in Brussels was reprieved late in the day. On hearing that it was going to be cancelled due to poor ticket sales, fan club representative Ann Grootjans intervened. "The promoter helped eventually in fact," she said. "It was the record company's fault, combined with a promoter who started promoting too late. 'When He's Gone' was supposed to be in the shops, but it wasn't, and it got no airplay either." Ann argued that the lack of response was more down to insufficient awareness than the public's apparent apathy. To prove her point, she organised a group of like-minded supporters to go around Belgium's capital and the whole of Flanders putting up posters. They even covered the city of Liège in Wallonia. Within days, the show was a sell-out. Fan-power 1 – Warner Bros 0. Showing the extent of some fans' devotion, the front row comprised followers from not just Belgium, but also Holland, Norway, Hong Kong, Germany, France and Great Britain, a fact acknowledged by Barry in his introduction to 'Words'. "First of all, I'd like to say that there are numerous fans, although we call them friends, because they mean so much more to us than that, they travel to see so many shows, and we don't quite understand it," Barry laughed, "but we love them very much for it." Gesturing specifically to the front row, he added, "To all of you – thank you!"

Although the July 4 Independence Day concert in Dublin – there were Stars & Stripes hanging either side of the stage – was not technically one of the Gibbs' best-ever shows, both the band and the audience were having a blast so the uncharacteristic errors went largely unnoticed. The tour ended in England on a triumphant note. They were at Birmingham's NEC Arena on July 6 where the sound check unusually included 'Marley Purt Drive', and even more amazingly, Barry's unreleased 'Words Of A Fool'. Next up was the concert at Wembley Arena, which was broadcast live on BBC Radio One. Although originally scheduled as the final show of the tour, to satisfy the unprecedented demand, they returned to Birmingham for an additional date. Barry, Robin and Maurice got some unexpected vocal help that evening when assorted Gibb children suddenly joined them on stage for the final two numbers, 'Party With No Name' and 'You Should Be Dancing'.

When the tour came to its end, Maurice and his family left Britain for Miami for what he described as a well-deserved break. "I've been living like a gypsy and just want to put my feet up at home."

Barry and Linda and their sons also returned to their home in Miami. Barry, too, was ready for some respite from life on the road. "The tour went very well, but I don't know when we'll be back again," he said. As for future projects, he added, "There is nothing to speak of just yet. It is all quiet right now."

39

SIZE IS EVERYTHING

Although Linda Gibb claimed that she never wanted children at all, she and Barry have raised the largest family of the three brothers. "Stephen was an accident; when he was such a good baby, I thought this is a piece of cake," she laughed. "Then along came Ashley. We'd both always wanted a girl – Stephen was going to be Stephanie, Ashley was going to be Ashley whether it was a boy or a girl – and I guess we wanted one of both so we kept trying . . . then a couple of years ago, Barry said we should try one more time. I said, 'Oh Barry, I'm too old for this!' and he said, 'Come on, one more time.'"

"After four boys, both of us really wanted a little girl and neither of us expected to have one," Barry explained. "The last resort, for want of a better term, was to adopt one and that would have been our next move."

But first Barry and Linda consulted a fertility specialist in helping couples conceive a child of a certain sex in order to guarantee the longed for daughter. "We thought about artificial insemination, but then I found out I was pregnant," Linda related. "I was utterly shocked."

As it happened, her pregnancy was first detected by an unlikely consultant. "A friend's little girl said to me, 'You've got five babies!' I said no, I had four," Linda recalled. "Then she pointed at me and said, 'There's one in your tummy!'

"I thought well, that's funny, my period was a bit strange last month. I thought it was because I was away on tour. I had an old pregnancy kit in the cupboard, left over from Michael. When it showed positive, I thought it must be out of date."

Unable to believe the results, Linda went out and bought three more test kits and got three more positive results. Finally convinced, she made an appointment for tests and waited anxiously to hear the result of the amniocentesis. "I thought, it'll be another boy. I was convinced it was because that's all we've had, boys, why should it be a girl," she said.

When she phoned the doctor to find out the results, her relief was so great to hear that there were no health problems that she nearly forgot to ask the sex of the baby. The doctor then confirmed the news she had been hoping for; it was a girl. "When he said everything was fine and that it was a girl, I must have screamed so hard down that phone! I couldn't believe it was a girl.

"The tears were flying down my face," Linda said. "I ran upstairs to tell Barry and he started crying too."

According to Linda, they weren't the only ones pleased with the result. "I think that my sons would have thrown me out if it had been another boy," she laughed. The boys even decided on a name for this unborn sister. "I had wanted to call her Leanna, but they all wanted Alexandra so I was out-voted." Linda's choice would become the baby's middle name.

Christmas in the Gibb house was exceptionally merry in 1991. Barry made a cameo appearance as himself on the Christmas special episode of the popular British television series, *Only Fools And Horses*. Everything seemed to be perfect.

Although Linda said, "I did everything I could to be healthy while I was pregnant," there were complications just after Christmas. Their youngest son Michael came down with a virus, and Linda also fell ill.

"I think while I was ill, I must have slipped on the floor. I didn't feel anything, but my waters must have broken," she explained. "The next night I didn't feel right, and the next morning my shape had changed – there wasn't the same kind of bump. By the time I got to hospital, my temperature was still 104°."

The doctors decided that both the mother and child were in grave danger if they didn't operate immediately to get the baby out before the virus passed through the placenta. So although the baby wasn't due for another 16 weeks, on December 29, Linda underwent an epidural caesarean section. Conscious throughout the surgery, Linda couldn't stop crying with despair. "How was a baby going to survive at 25 weeks?" she asked. "I knew she was a girl, I knew how much Barry wanted her. I was numb with distress and sadness . . . I was just so frightened I was going to lose this little girl."

"The moment of her birth was extremely spiritual," Barry said. "Everyone else in the operating theatre seem to disappear, and I felt alone with her as I cut the cord.

"I was shocked that something so beautiful could come from a situation so chaotic. It all happened in a scenario of chaos."

Linda recalled, "It was amazing – she came out crying. Her lungs were as developed as those of a seven and a half month baby, and I think that's what pulled her through – she was breathing on her own straightaway.

"The doctors said that because my waters had been leaking gradually for a couple of weeks, the baby had gone into stress. When that happens, it sends messages around the body saying, 'Forget the hair, forget the fingernails; finish those lungs, work on the major parts.' "

Only one pound and nine ounces, the new-born was rushed to the neo-natal intensive care unit. "As small as she was – and she was 12½ inches, or ruler length – she was just so perfect," Linda said.

With any premature baby, the first 24 to 48 hours are crucial. Even past those critical early days, it would be months before the baby would be out of danger. As Linda was still recovering from the virus, she wasn't allowed to see her daughter for the first five days, although Barry saw her everyday. Linda could only watch helplessly through a window at the fragile little life in the incubator, distressed by the tubes in her nose and throat.

"Right away, the doctors told us it was touch and go," Barry recalled. "It was terrifying. For the first week, we weren't convinced she'd make it, so we were holding back. I tried not to love her too much, seeing her only a few minutes each day."

"It's really difficult because you are almost too frightened to get too close to them because you don't know if they are going to survive or not," Linda agreed.

"Then the doctor called us in and said, 'You've got to love this child. It's that commitment that may save her life.' So we made the commitment," Barry said, "all or nothing. For three months, I lived and breathed the thought of that child. I hung a little cross around the mirror of my car. To have my little girl at this time of my life is the thing that's most special of all to me."

Linda said that those first months were terrifying. "You just never knew if something might go wrong. She could have had a bleed in the head, which a lot of premature babies do. But she never had anything. We were very lucky . . .

"After the first few weeks, I could hold her everyday and feed her, even if it was through the tubes. The doctors like you to have as much contact as possible with the babies, so that they can feel the love from you." Linda even taped photos of Alexandra's brothers and the family's dogs to the incubator so little Ali would know her family.

When Linda had first discovered she was pregnant, Barry had decided to go ahead with surgery for his troublesome back, so that he would be able to bend down and pick up the new baby. "I'd been in pain for about 12 years and it interrupted everything – touring, promotion work, even recording. It was the bane of my life. I got to the point where the idea of being fixed was far more attractive than the idea of going on with the pain."

As little Alexandra wasn't due until April, Barry's surgery had been scheduled for January and went on as planned; a nightmare scenario for Linda. "It was unbelievable," she recalled. "Ali was in one hospital, and while she was there, Barry was in another having back surgery. He had an allergic reaction to morphine and stopped breathing. I had to keep him talking while the nurse ran to turn off the morphine drip.

"In the middle of the night, he had a cardiac arrest; the next night I heard my mother had a serious eye injury.

"Everything seemed to be going wrong. I had three of them in hospital. Fortunately, my mother was in the same hospital as the baby, so I was up and down floors there, across to the hospital where Barry was, and he didn't like the food so I had to take him a food hamper!"

It was all too much for Linda's disturbed hormones. "I came home, sat in the bath and cried," she said.

In the midst of this stressful period, Hugh Gibb, the brothers' father who had encouraged their music since they were old enough to walk, died from internal bleeding. He was 76 and he died on Andy's birthday, March 5, 1992, and was laid to rest near his youngest son at Forest Lawn Cemetery in Los Angeles.

"We think Dad lost any kind of will to live after Andy," Barry explained. "The spark went out of his life. When you lose your youngest child something else happens. He willed it on himself in the end.

"He knew all about the baby, but he didn't get the chance to see her. That's the way it goes . . . It's a great shame Dad never saw Alexandra because he would have absolutely idolised her. She's so beautiful."

"Ali was the saviour of it all," Linda said. "If it hadn't been for her doing so well, I wouldn't have been able to go on. She was a little life, getting better each day."

Although naturally saddened by the loss of his father, Barry was philosophical. "I believe all this was meant to happen. I miss my father, of course, but he stopped living when Andy died and I'm sure he's happier now."

He mused, "It was just a matter of time. He knew where Andy was and he wanted to be with him. He didn't say that to us directly, but we knew he was saying those things. He used to hide behind his masculine persona. Mum was the backbone; she still is very strong . . . She's suddenly got a new life. She's going to travel and do things she's never done before."

By then, Barry and Linda were looking forward to the day when they could take their baby daughter home. It had been a stressful three months during which time Linda went to the hospital everyday to feed and bathe her. Now in preparation for her homecoming, Barry explained, "Linda is going back into the hospital to get used to sleeping next to her . . . She's going to have to spend the night next to her, to be there when she awakens suddenly. We're both learning to operate the monitor that's attached to her. When premature babies suddenly waken, they get a terrible shock and it can damage their hearts."

The couple had to take a resuscitation course for babies, learning what to do if their tiny daughter should stop breathing. The entire experience was an education for them, seeing what other parents went through at the same time and noting that there was no preferential treatment for superstars – all the babies in the neonatal intensive care unit were equally important.

When they finally brought little Ali home, it was with the monitor, which was to be strapped to her chest, but after nerve-shattering false alarms when the monitor wasn't put on properly, they took the monitor back. "We've been told to treat her like any normal baby but to be careful for the first few weeks," Linda said. "Ali will need regular check-ups for the foreseeable future. But I still feel so blessed. When I was in hospital there were a couple of babies much bigger and full-term who died. I was scared right down the line. We were so lucky."

"When we first took her home, the boys were a wee bit fragile with her,"

Linda admitted. "They were nervous of touching her. But now they pat her on the head as they go by or give her a kiss. They are great with her . . . There's no jealousy at all – at least, not yet."

Although their "little miracle", as Barry called her, was making exceptional progress, it would take nearly six months before they felt confident that all would be well.

The back surgery hadn't cured Barry's back problems in the way he had hoped. "I have to deal with twinges and stiffness, but I'm dealing with it, and I'm not having the same pain I had before," he said. "At the time, there were so many other little crises going on it was a bit difficult to focus on your own problems, but maybe that was a good thing."

★   ★   ★

A drama of a very different sort had been unfolding just down the street at Maurice and Yvonne's Miami home. After Andy's death, Maurice's resolve to fight his alcoholism had weakened. "I hadn't had a drink for years," he said. "My wife Yvonne went away for a weekend, and I was like a kid in a toy shop." After a weekend binge during which he claimed to have drunk eight gallons of Guinness, four bottles of whisky and two bottles of brandy, he said, "I was still sober. That's when the wife sussed out that I was sick again."

Maurice credited Yvonne with helping him beat his drinking problem. Without her, he said, "If I were lucky, I'd be in some gutter, drunk – but I probably would be dead."

Despite previous attempts at conquering his problem "going into one luxury rehab after the other", he had never really managed to kick the habit. "As an alcoholic, you have no appreciation for your wife or children's feelings. But I'm making up for that now. I'm winning my kids' trust back and it really is great.

"Before there was no way they would believe me because I lied to them so many times. For 14 years I've been an alcoholic – often a really nasty person, wrecking new Rolls-Royces and Aston Martins – blacking out, even taking transatlantic trips without knowing it! My whole life – everything – was just a haze, a blur."

Maurice began drinking during The Bee Gees' "first fame" period in 1967. A teenager suddenly thrust into the limelight and exalted company, he claimed, "John Lennon was the first one that gave me a drink. A Scotch and Coke, that was the drink of the day. I mean everybody drank Scotch and Coke. The Beatles drank Scotch and Coke, that's what you drank. If he'd have given me cyanide I would've drank the cyanide, I mean it's just that I was in awe of the man. In those days, I was 17 so I could drink just like the next guy. I could drink anybody under the table, the next day feel fabulous, no hangover, nothing.

"At 17 you're very gullible," he added. "When you meet your heroes for the first time and all of a sudden you're having a drink with them – jeez!"

At first, he considered himself a social drinker. "When I was married to

Lulu, for six years we both drank. We didn't have any responsibilities, we partied, we never ate at home and I could handle it okay, but I would always go off somewhere and be sick, I would never let her see me," he admitted.

"I crossed into alcoholism when I was about 25. Because I was drinking every day, I started to drink in the morning. I was starting to be sick in the morning, I was hugging the toilet every morning, you know and things like that. So I knew there was something wrong but I never once thought it was the drink. I always used to think it was something else, I've got a bug or I've got a virus, or something like that."

Although he was never physically abusive to the family, he admitted, "I was verbally abusive, very arrogant, obnoxious, belligerent, you know. Inconsiderate, it was all me, me, me, whatever *I* had to do. I was a loving dad and still am, but I was very selfish about everything. I would always put myself before my wife and my children, which is what the disease does to you."

After the excitement and challenge of the *High Civilization* tour of Europe, when the family had returned home to Miami, the tedium of everyday life quickly set in for Maurice. "I was bored. Absolutely bored stiff. And then I just drove to Walgreen's, a supermarket place, and bought a bottle of brandy. And I had a month, just a complete binge," he confessed.

Although Yvonne immediately recognised the signs, Maurice was unwilling to acknowledge the extent of his problem. "I was in denial of my *denial*. I mean, it was that ridiculous," he said. When she finally confronted him, he was indignant, as he would later confess to actress Lyn Redgrave on her *Fighting Back* television series in May, 1992.

"I said, 'You silly cow. How dare you?', totally off guard, you know, defending myself . . . I went straight down to my studio, poured out a large brandy and I said, 'How dare she,' and drank it."

It was the start of a four-week binge unlike any he had ever experienced before. "I didn't get drunk," he confessed. "I didn't get merry. I just got sicker and sicker. I just drank, trying to get normal again, because it would start off with those two drinks. Three drinks the next night. Four drinks the next night. All of a sudden, I'm running out. I have to go and get another bottle. I have to have back-up. And then it would be just straight brandy with just ice, and I'd have like four or five of those . . . I got very verbally violent."

Normally easy-going and sociable, alcohol had begun to make him aggressive towards his wife and children. "I would use anything for an argument," he said. "I hit rock bottom so hard I couldn't even function. I'd become arrogant . . . and called my family names I would never have dreamed of calling them if I hadn't drunk. I hurt them so much. I was Jekyll and Hyde; the children didn't know when Daddy was going to be all right. Yvonne would go shopping not knowing whether I'd be drunk or sober when she got back."

So blind was he to the effect his drinking had on the family, he claimed that nothing mattered to him at the time but the drink. He no longer cared that he was disturbing Yvonne, Adam and Samantha. "They were very upset," he admitted. "See, as far as they were concerned, Daddy had lied to them all this time."

The binge culminated when he brandished a gun at the family he had begun to feel were just getting in his way.

"I was like, 'Oh my God' . . . I couldn't believe it," recalled his son Adam, then 15 years old, "and then my mom said, 'Go upstairs, get some clothes,' and so, when we came downstairs that's when he had the gun and I thought, 'Oh my God, he's gonna shoot us.' "

Maurice's actions were completely out of character, although they had kept a gun in the house for years and he maintained that the gun was unloaded. He added, "Normally I didn't even like guns."

It was too much for the family to cope with. "He's been angry before . . . [but] he's never really been a violent person. It's always been verbally. But the kids were scared to death. That's when I saw what it was doing to the kids. I said, 'This is it.' So I packed a bag, and we went up to Barry's house, and I weren't coming back," Yvonne said with quiet conviction. "I were determined. This time I weren't gonna come back, until he did something. And we stayed there all night." It was apparent that her years in America had done little to diminish her broad Yorkshire dialect, which, to the uninitiated, appears grammatically incorrect.

"The family all came to my home . . . and we isolated him . . . That's another tactic I think you have to do, and he really needed to bottom out," Barry said. "He needed to realise that everyone around him was no longer going to support what he was doing and smile about it. We just turned into a brick wall, and it really hurts to do that . . . to have to stand and say to somebody, 'We're isolating you; you no longer have our support. You no longer have a job.' "

As well as frightening the family, the episode terrified Maurice. "You see, I didn't have a blackout over that," he said. "I remembered all of it, and that scared the hell out of me . . . I said 'That's not me. That's just not me.' . . . I just said 'That's it. I've gotta do something about this.' . . . It was very emotional for me. I'd reached a bottom and I just couldn't take it any more . . . I surrendered. I just gave up, I just didn't like being that person. That was a completely alien person to me . . . Think of the worst word you could think of, but I became that monster."

When Yvonne came back after three days to pick up a few things from the house, Maurice broke down. "He was so sorry and it was the worst bottom that he'd ever had," she recalled. He said, 'I have to do something about this problem.' And something inside of me knew, you know, he just cried and cried."

Maurice realised that it was something he could not do on his own and he went into detox for two days. On the couple's sixteenth wedding anniversary, Yvonne sent him a card saying, "We've gone this far together. It can only get better."

For Maurice, it was a turning point; the realisation that he had come so close to losing his wife and family. Still, he said, "I had to come to the decision to do it for *me*. I couldn't do it for Yvonne or the kids. I couldn't do it for anybody else but me."

He believed that for him, like Andy, the main problem behind the addiction was a feeling of inadequacy. "My biggest defect of character, if you like, is unworthiness," he explained. "I just didn't feel worthy of what I was doing, or my contribution. It came from the boozing. This is what happens to your mind . . . with the disease of alcoholism . . . It's very cunning, it sneaks up on you."

He entered the New Life rehabilitation programme, conducted by Dr Jules Trop, himself a recovering alcoholic. "I started first with a 28-day non-stop programme."

The follow-up programme, called 'Transition', aimed to put the patients into as nearly normal a lifestyle as possible, without drugs or alcohol. Maurice shared an apartment with three other men. "We learned to support ourselves; shopping, cooking and cleaning. In the afternoons, I was allowed to visit my wife and my kids."

The transitional period worked on the buddy system. "Whenever you need support, there is someone there for you," Maurice said.

When he came back home, there was still a period of adjustment for the family. "We were frightened he'd left all his support system there, you know," Yvonne admitted, "coming home to us and sleeping at home. Each time he went to the studio, the kids were thinking, 'He's down there a long time,' and 'What's he doing?' But you see, we had to get used to that too, you know. We have to give him a little trust, although it was hard in the beginning."

"It's a family disease," Maurice explained. "It's not just the person or the spouse who has it, it affects everybody. Tentacles reach out and touch everybody except for the person who has the problem, and in my case, it was my wife, my children, my brothers, all the people around me it affected . . . Adam remembers from when he was three, hearing me shouting and yelling when I was drunk."

Undoing those effects didn't happen overnight, but the family relationship was strengthened. "I couldn't get back any trust from my wife and kids until I proved to them that I was an example, and that took a while.

"The family have been through a lot with me. I didn't know what love was really like until I married Yvonne. I never lost their love, but I had to win back their respect."

Part of the New Life Transitions programme involves treating the whole family. Both Adam and Samantha received guidance in dealing with an alcoholic parent, and Yvonne was not left out either. Maurice said, "There's a lovely lady at Transitions who has a one-to-one with Yvonne each week just to chat things through. It means that, like me, she has someone to talk to who can guide her in different ways.

"I still go regularly to meetings at the Centre and keep in touch with the people I've met there," he added, "especially the family therapist, who helped my family enormously and who has become my big buddy. I owe a lot to him and my other friends in Alcoholics Anonymous. Without them, I probably wouldn't be here today.

"My children can at last see Daddy in a good light. He's sensible, not stupid or incoherent. He's not falling over, he's not angry. Anger was the worst thing that used to happen to me."

"He likes to do more things with us now and he's really easy going," Adam said. "He's not really agitated easily. The drink was always talking, it was never really him. He was really under there. The real person that was inside all these years is finally out."

Although he had been able to stop drinking, he recognised that it was by no means a cure; that a recovering addict is never fully recovered. "There's no graduation in this," he said. "You don't graduate at all. There's no big medal at the end of the day . . . It's an ongoing process."

When he went back to the studio, he found that Barry and Robin had been waiting for him. "They didn't write a single note while I was in treatment and it's been beautiful," Maurice enthused. "The album's turning out great. It's nice to go in the next day and know that you don't have to replace the part that you did the day before, and I can see it with my brothers as well, they see the change in me. They're just glad to see that I did something about it, and they were totally supportive."

On February 23, 1992, their son Adam's sixteenth birthday, the family had cause for celebration. With Samantha as maid of honour and Adam as best man, Maurice and Yvonne renewed their wedding vows before a Justice of the Peace in the garden of their Miami home. It was a joyous re-affirmation of the love which had triumphed over the problems of the past.

His family and his new friends from the New Life Treatment Center were there to join in the happy occasion. "We had a huge party with no alcohol at all and everyone still managed to have a great time. It was to signify the start of a new lease on life."

In May, The Bee Gees would also make a new start. Their contract with Warner Brothers had concluded, and the group once again signed with Polydor Records.

★   ★   ★

On June 21, 1992, more than 300 white-robed Druids gathered on Hampstead Heath to celebrate the summer solstice and elected Dwina Murphy Gibb their patroness.

"I am a member of The Order Of Ovates And Druids," Dwina explained, "and their chief is a wonderful man called Philip Carr-Gamm. He decided that women should take up a higher profile within the order and that I was suitable to act as their patroness – the first woman to do so for 300 years. It is a wonderful honour.

"I was overwhelmed by the ceremony. It was the first time that Druids from Ireland, France, Scotland and Wales all came together. It was a very moving moment."

Dwina's interest in Druidry began when she was a nine-year-old girl living in the tiny village of Kilkeery in County Tyrone, Northern Ireland. "When I was about nine," she recalled, "I started to have very vivid dreams about nature and natural life forces. Since then I have studied just about every religion – from Tibetan Buddhism through to Hinduism and Christianity – and I ended up with Druidism, which to me feels like coming home. I read several books and knew instinctively it was right. I never had any difficulty following it, and I officially joined the Druids at 16."

To mark her new position, Dwina decided to have the tennis courts at The Prebendal bulldozed to make way for her own stone circle. "Stonehenge is the main solar temple, but there are others," she explained. "I plan to build a special stone calendar aligned with the winter solstice at our Oxfordshire home.

"When it is completed, I will be able to tell what time of year it is just by looking at which stone the sun is shining on. That's what Stonehenge was partly used for. Then we will have a ceremony to inaugurate it."

Dwina added seriously, "It will be a natural extension to the religious history of the house – and it will be of far more use than a tennis court."

★   ★   ★

On August 24, 1992, Florida witnessed the onslaught of Hurricane Andrew, the costliest hurricane in the history of the US. A category four hurricane★, it would go on to cause an estimated $26 billion worth of damage, destroying thousands of homes and damaging many more. It also claimed more than 60 lives either directly or indirectly. Dade County (of which Miami is a part) was hardest hit.

The Bee Gees' Middle Ear Studio and the Gibbs' homes all escaped the hurricane's devastation with minor damage, but they realised that many were not so fortunate. For some time, Robin and Dwina had been making regular visits to the Miccosukee Indian Reservation in the Everglades, calling on 90-year-old Lillie Tigertail and her tribe. "They are wonderful people but very wary of outsiders," Dwina said.

After the hurricane ended, Robin and Dwina learned that the reservation where their new friends lived had been ravaged by the storm. With the couple's nine-year-old son Robin John, Dwina made a television appeal for donations for the tribe to be made to a special bank account. The Bee Gees were the first contributors to the account, and Linda and Yvonne gave their support to Dwina.

★ Hurricanes are classified by degrees of intensity using the Saffir-Simpson Hurricane Damage Potential Scale, ranging from a category one hurricane, which offers the weakest wind speeds and highest pressures, up to a category five, which produces the fiercest wind speeds and lowest pressures. By the time Hurricane Andrew made landfall in southern Florida, it registered a central pressure of 922 mb, the third lowest pressure of the century for a landfall hurricane in the United States, with wind speeds of 145 miles per hour.

Next, the couple organised a relief operation. Along with Robin John and Robin's two children from his first marriage, Spencer and Melissa, they began to help in the clean-up, and enlisted the aid of friends to help with the reconstruction. "The Miccosukee live in trailers which have been totally destroyed," Dwina explained, "so we've gathered together some friends to help – they need manpower to rebuild their homes. We were very lucky with just the odd tree blown down. But the Indians were not, and we are going to make it up to them."

On September 26, The Bee Gees were among the artists who performed at the Hurricane Andrew Relief Concert at Joe Robbie Stadium in Miami. It was their first concert in their adopted home town in 13 years. They played a 40-minute set with Barry's eldest son, Stephen, playing guitar with the group. Although they were eager to help out, the concert was not altogether a pleasant experience for them.

Maurice described the atmosphere before the show. "I mean nobody said hello to anybody backstage, it was very unfriendly," he said. "We were supposed to go to the press tent after the show and we said no, we'll go home. We did this for Miami. We didn't do this for publicity."

"We were hyped and we were angry because we were never given the chance to check our sound," Barry explained.

"Anyway it was a good show," Robin added.

"Look you've got to at least say one thing. Everybody's heart was in the right place," Barry conceded, "and if you were in Miami when that hurricane struck. The following days was like the whole city had lost somebody in the family. It was a very grievous situation. You were actually on the verge of tears for about three days following it."

The Bee Gees also opened Middle Ear Studios to the public for a week, as a way of thanking all the fans who supported the Hurricane Andrew Relief Concert.

★   ★   ★

Barry and David English still hadn't given up on those cricket-playing rabbits, The Bunburys. In 1992, *The Bunbury Tails* CD was finally released, a compilation of tracks by various artists, including the previously issued singles of 'We're The Bunburys' and 'Fight' and new songs by The Bee Gees, Elton John, No Hat Moon, and newcomer Kelli Wolfe. David English co-wrote lyrics on most of them.

The new Bee Gees song, 'Bunbury Afternoon', has a happily loping beat, and lyrics celebrating all things English, sunny afternoons and cricket on the village green. Unlike 'We're The Bunburys', also credited to The Bee Gees on the CD, 'Bunbury Afternoon' clearly has all three brothers singing and Robin takes a line or two. It probably dates from 1986, before the 'E.S.P' reunion.

No Hat Moon were a group who just happened to be in the right place at the right time when Barry and David came to David Mackay's studio, The

Factory, in the garden of his Woldingham, Surrey home. Consisting of Paul Carman on bass, Peter King on guitars and Sheryl and Sheila Parker on vocals, the group didn't actually do any concerts, concentrating instead on studio work only. They had worked previously with David Mackay.

"I think we were doing backing vocals for an album [by] Cilla Black," Peter King explained. "We were recording this stuff and it was coming to the end of it, and Dave said, 'Why don't you hang on until tomorrow and they'll be here?' . . . So we waited and they turned up too, I think they were sounding out the place . . . but I'm not sure. We played them a bit of [our] stuff . . .

"They'd written this tune, called 'Seasons' and Barry just suggested that we have a go at it. Barry was strumming along and singing it so we just got together, did a few guitars and built it up. We went away and did the vocal arrangements up at the house, and they got on with the track and then we just came back and did it then. When we left, I think Barry stayed until it was mixed."

According to the album notes, this was "the following day" from Eric Clapton's recording of 'Fight', which does not quite match with King's recollection, but any rate it was probably close to the same date in the summer of 1986. Despite the season, it is a Christmas song, and a beautiful one. Barry has proudly used its lyrics for his Christmas cards in the Nineties. The two women singers take alternating leads with their clear pure voices, and truly "sing like birds" as the notes put it. Even the Gibb brothers' famous harmony could not top this performance. Although the song seemed a strong possibility for a hit single, lack of promotion caused it to die an untimely death.

"Barry was very upset that [Polygram] didn't promote it well enough," Peter King said. "It was having a lot of radio play, Radio One were playing it and everything, many times a day. I was hearing it all the time, in petrol stations, in the car, it was going out all the time. Steve Wright was the one – he tipped it for a number one! But again, they just weren't in the shops, Polygram failed, but that's the way it is. When you're getting mega Radio One plays, you think, 'Great, people will want to buy this' – and they can't! Barry was upset about that. I know it was his song but he was genuinely concerned; he thought it was a good record and they let everybody down.

"We were looking forward to maybe doing more, but the record company put the kibosh on it as usual – they just didn't support it."

A news item from 1986 reports that the Bunburys project also included the song 'Up The Revolution' sung by Errol Brown and Hot Chocolate, and an unnamed song by Shaking Stevens. Neither of those recordings made it out, but 'Up The Revolution' appeared in a recording by Elton John made in 1988.

"Elton John was . . . a friend of mine too," English explained. "We wrote to him, sent him a cassette of the demo, and he came and did 'Revolution' in Mayfair studios in Camden Town." Elton's rendition of 'Up The Revolution' is one of the many highlights of what is a surprisingly – considering its subject matter and the number of years the project took – good collection of songs. Like 'We're The Bunburys', it has a real Caribbean feel and bounces along to an almost honky tonk sounding piano. It would be one of the rare occasion where Elton would record other artist's material.

In the same year, George Harrison contributed an original song he wrote with David English. George sings lead vocal, his young son Dhani sings backing vocals, and David English speaks the character voice of the Katman of Katmandu in an excruciating Indian accent. Instrumentally, the song was a reunion after many years between George and sitar master Ravi Shankar. David English recalls, "George we saw through Eric. We saw him at Friar Park [Harrison's home] and I wrote that with George. So they were really my four contacts, The Bee Gees, Eric and the other two."

In 1990 Kelli Hartman was a teenager fresh out of high school and attending the New World School Of The Arts in Miami. At school during the day, in the evenings she was working as a hostess at Dick Clark's American Bandstand Grill.

Barry and Maurice were there one evening for dinner with Dick Clark, when the manager of the restaurant told Clark that he had to "hear this kid sing". Kelli sang 'Wind Beneath My Wings', and when she had finished, Clark came down, telling her, "I have to take you to meet somebody." That somebody was Barry Gibb.

Although Kelli said that she considered The Bee Gees "an older group", she added ingenuously, "I knew who they were and I loved their music, and more so, my mom loved their music. He said, 'You're fantastic, give me your number.' . . . Sure enough he called me the very next day, and then he called my parents, and said, 'I want to talk business. I think Kelli really has what it takes to break into the music business, and I want to work with her.' . . . He said, 'I have a few things that I've written.' " One of the songs he had in mind for her was 'The Only Love'. Another was a track called 'Born To Be Loved By You' which he had written specifically for her, with participation from Maurice in its final stages.

Kelli continued, "My parents had called the studio to get directions how to get to Bay Road in Miami Beach, but we ended up in some dangerous looking part of Miami. We were scared, but I got out of the car and called Barry from a phone booth and asked, 'So how do we get there?' He said, 'I don't really know my way around town either,' and had me talk to Dick Ashby. Meanwhile, my mom was urging me to get back in the car! But Barry said he'd stand outside, because you'd never know it's a studio and might go right by it. So we pulled off the causeway into Bay Road, and then we see this little figure standing outside a white building waving his arms, and my mom goes, 'That ain't him!' but it was. He's only five nine, and pretty thin. They're all tiny. You would never guess from the photographs where they look like these big guys, but they're not."

Over the next few days, Kelli's parents dropped her off at the studio and picked her up again later. "We recorded 'Born [To Be Loved By You]' in a few days, in September 1990. I was there when they did some of the instrumental tracks too, with Stevie [Gibb] playing guitar. Then for a while Barry would call on the phone and speak to me or to my parents about how I was doing, and he'd call at odd hours, in the middle of the night sometimes. But then he stopped calling. There was a 15-month gap in there because he wasn't speaking with us. Meanwhile I had pulled out of school because I had joined the union and it looked like I was going to work professionally. Finally I called [the studio] and said, 'What's going on, are we going to do this or not?' and then he came out with 'Eyes', which we recorded in December 1991. He apologised to me and my mom for the delay. But then after that, again nothing happened for a long time."

She chose the professional name Kelli Wolfe, borrowing the surname of the surgeon who had done extensive surgery on her larynx. She explained, "I had developed polyps on my vocal cords. I was told that I may never sing again. He helped me so that I could. I had laser surgery in 1989 and couldn't speak one word for a month. I had to relearn to talk and sing so that I was not creating calluses on my cords."

Kelli was told that the two tracks she had recorded would be released as a single first in Britain, because Barry explained to her that American artists usually do better in Europe. "I don't know if that's true or it was just for some reason what Polydor wanted," she added. "I spoke to John Merchant on the phone the night before, and he was congratulating me on the record coming out. But the next day I get a phone call from Barry and he said, 'I'm really sorry things didn't work out,' I never got to deal with Barry again. I didn't want to pester, but I did send a letter asking for an explanation, but I never got one. Barry's solicitor sent me a letter explaining that Barry was a very busy man.

"I finally called Dick in 1995 and said, 'You know it's been two years, and I just want to hear from you guys what happened.' Barry called me back and said, something about not wanting anyone else to work with me if he couldn't. Polydor sent me a legal document about breach of contract. Later I was sent the master tapes of the two songs, and I still have them."

Although she was completely unaware of it at the time, some CD singles did leak out in Britain, but even more puzzling was the appearance of her version of 'Eyes' on The Bunburys' CD. "I was never told I was on The Bunburys' album until I saw it on your web site!" she told Joseph Brennan. "That blew me away. I never got a copy of it, or even of my two songs."

Whilst Kelli was understandably upset, viewing events from her own perspective, there was more to things than met the eye. When the brothers had re-signed as recording artists with Polydor in 1992, part of the overall negotiations centred around the possibility of their being able to release other artists' recordings on their own "Brothers Gibb" label. However, very shortly after the agreements were signed, the people who had been most instrumental in signing The Bee Gees, David Munns and Andrew Jenkins, were no longer in charge of Polydor UK. The new Managing Director was Jimmy Devlin, and it would appear that he had other priorities in his new role. As a result, the subject of creating a new label found its way to the bottom of the agenda.

Additionally, promotional copies of the CD single received a poor response from the radio stations so Devlin "pulled" the release, leaving George McManus in the unfortunate role of messenger, delivering the bad news to Barry. Obviously feeling bad about the situation, Barry instructed his own lawyers to obtain a release for Kelli from Polydor and tried very hard to obtain a new deal for her on both sides of the Atlantic. Unfortunately, although there was initially some favourable response, no one ever followed through with a firm offer, leaving the talented Kelli Wolfe to contemplate what might have been.

★   ★   ★

On December 27, 1992, Barry and Linda's two youngest children were christened at St. Mary's Church in Hendon, North London, along with Amy Rose, the infant daughter of David and Robyn English, followed by a reception for 40 at a nearby hotel. Charlie Burkett was Alexandra's godfather, and David English stood in for Michael Jackson, Michael's godfather, who was in Japan. Dwina was chosen as Michael's godmother.

"It is a very pretty church and it was a lovely service," Linda said afterwards. "I couldn't believe how good Ali was. We had got her up earlier than normal from her nap so she was awake much longer and she hadn't really been fed properly because we were all rushing around. She was an angel.

"She gave the vicar a funny look, though, when he poured the water over her. But she didn't cry – she was wonderful. The only time she cried was when the photos were being taken."

Little Ali had made amazing progress during her first year. "She's catching up more quickly than most premature babies," said her proud mother. "She can stand and walk around her playpen, so she's about right for her age."

The welfare of children everywhere was a cause close to The Bee Gees' hearts. On June 5, 1993, they joined Duran Duran, Barry White, The Temptations and The Four Tops, performing in KISS Radio's concert at Great Woods, Massachusetts. The 11-hour benefit concert raised more than $50,000 for the Genesis Fund for The National Birth Defects Center in Boston.

The following month, they returned to Britain and raised money on a smaller scale. Taking part in a televised busking contest against a Covent Garden regular called Wally, The Bee Gees sang 'Massachusetts', 'New York Mining Disaster 1941' and 'To Love Somebody' and collected £100 from passers-by who dropped coins into Barry's open guitar case. The Great Ormond Street Children's Hospital was the chosen recipient.

The year also saw the first of several 'tribute' albums to The Bee Gees or more specifically, the Gibb brothers' songwriting, that would be released over the next few years. *The Bee Gees Songbook – The Gibb Brothers By Others* was released on the UK-based Connoisseur Collection label. A compilation of previously released cover versions recorded from 1967 to 1992, it must have sold reasonably well as it has been reissued twice since.

In August, The Bee Gees announced their intention to play a benefit concert for the children of war-torn Bosnia. "I really am angry that our governments can't unite in some way and do something to stop this kind of violence when it occurs," Barry declared. "To stop the conflict that is going on in the former Yugoslavia as well as just be able to stop conflicts that go on all over the world. My greatest fear, personally, is that all of these things are going to start occurring at the same time, and the United Nations is going to become impotent. And, if it isn't already happening, it's definitely foreseeable."

Although the concert didn't come off, they dedicated a song from their forthcoming album to the children whose young lives were blighted.

"At the end of the First World War, there was an enormous amount of spiritualism. This is probably because so many millions of people died in the . . . war that there was an upheaval of families wanting to contact their lost ones. Now from that came a combined opinion from spiritualists that the other side . . . what we call heaven . . . in fact is blue and it's an island. And from there, for the want of a better word, we're *processed* before we move on to our next reality. Good or bad, this is where we all end up. So we [wrote] a song called 'Blue Island' and dedicated it for the children of Yugoslavia, because even though they may not survive, the hope is that they, as well as us, are all going to this beautiful place."

★   ★   ★

In August, 'Paying The Price Of Love' was the first single released after The Bee Gees' return to Polydor. The song combines the heavy percussion sound characteristic of this album, and modern hip hop rhythm, with some of the old Barry falsetto that had not appeared on a Bee Gees single for a decade.

The strong B-side was not on the album. 'My Destiny' is a great rocker with an Alan Kendall electric guitar lead reminiscent of Barry's 'System Of Love', and some fine harmony vocal.

'Paying The Price Of Love' reached number 23 on the British charts. The brothers were gratified by the reception of the single.

"Other artists, the media and deejays are treating us with the type of respect we wish we could have had five or six years ago," Robin said. "We've been getting more respect these past 12 months than we did in the past 10 years."

Barry agreed. "A few years ago, my kids would come home and say, 'Why don't people like your group, Dad?' 'All things pass,' I'd say, but I'd be disturbed. Now they come home and say, 'People think your group's really hip now, what's going on? How come you're doing the same thing and sometimes it's credible and sometimes it's not?' "

He admitted that he found it as perplexing as his sons. "I'm confused by a culture that invents things, destroys them, only to reinvent them. We're enjoying a sudden resurgence; in five years time, we won't be."

615

September saw the release of their latest album in most parts of the world, although its release was delayed until November in the US. The album's title, *Size Isn't Everything*, received nearly as much attention as the music. Maurice explained that it "was more of a fun title. It also means basically, 'Don't judge a book by its cover.' No matter how you perceived us or what we are or what we've been or what we're doing, just listen to the music."

Size was the second of the pair of albums featuring the crisp sound of engineer Femi Jiya. The vocal recording is superb: all three brothers can be clearly heard weaving in and out of the harmonies and alternating lead parts. Rarely have the vocal assignments been so well balanced on a Bee Gees album, or the variety of musical styles been so broad. No one dominates the sound on this one. It sounds like three people all bursting with ideas, and many old fans got the same feeling from it as they did from Bee Gees albums of long ago, and yet the sound itself was very contemporary. It's hard to pull off a union of opposites, crisp but warm, harmonies with each voice heard, memories of the with sounds from the present, but they manage to walk the fine line.

Many of the same small group of players carry over from *High Civilization*: Alan Kendall on guitar, Chocolate Perry on bass and Tim Moore on keyboards, are joined here by a musician from some earlier projects, Tim Cansfield on guitar. The drums and percussion are a mix of real playing by Trevor Murrell and Luis Jardim, and programming by Moore and probably Maurice. Ed Calle adds sax and Gustavo Lezcano plays harmonica on one song.

Released in November, the second single was 'For Whom The Bell Tolls', a remarkable combination of old and new Bee Gees style. Somewhat like 'The Only Love', it sounds like it is a combination of the twisting verse melodies Barry favours with the big melodic chorus Maurice and Robin tend to come up with, but here Barry and Robin sing lead on their sections, much as they did on older numbers like 'Run To Me'. But the harmony singing here is more complex than in the old days, and it builds in intensity in a much more subtle way than the old songs where they just piled on more instruments.

Barry described the song as "a piece of melody that popped up at home." He explained, "I collared Robin in the studio one day. Maurice hadn't come in yet, and we were towards the end of the album . . . I said, 'I've got a little bit of melody I want to sing to you.' And we went upstairs and sat in the room upstairs in the writing room, and it was just . . . [the chorus] and that was it. Then I repeated that line, I thought it seems like it wants to keep repeating itself. And Robin sort of went 'Yeah, yeah, it seems OK. Have we got enough tracks already, shall we develop it?' . . . I said, 'Well, I feel we ought to be developing it.' So that's where we were." Aimed at the Christmas market, it unfortunately had to compete with novelty records like 'Mr. Blobby'★ for the number one slot. Although it did well in reaching number

---

★ A Noel Edmonds creation consisting of an actor in a multi-coloured "Blobby" costume which briefly attained cult status amongst his younger viewers of his *House Party* television programme.

four in the UK, perhaps with the benefit of hindsight, a release earlier in the year could have seen it top the charts.

The album included two other singles, depending on the market – but again not in the USA – 'Kiss Of Life' and 'How To Fall In Love, Part One', two very different songs.

'Kiss Of Life', an April 1994 single in continental Europe, rocks energetically along behind a Robin lead switching to Barry for the bridges. Above all, the harmony singing on much of the song is incredible, pure Bee Gees magic as they shift effortlessly from one vocal combination to another.

In contrast the quieter rhythmic ballad 'How To Fall In Love, Part One', the simultaneous single release in the UK, sounds like mainly Barry's idea, and he sings all the lead. The long repeating ending is one of the purest examples of Bee Gees songs being music with words – there's no reason to concentrate on the lyric, which is just the rhythm section for the instrumental work. As with 'Town Of Tuxley Toymaker' back in the mid-Sixties, to date there has been no Part Two for this song either.

European copies of the album included an extra cut at the end, 'Decadance', which was a "remix" in the new sense of 'You Should Be Dancing' – that is, a combination of the original with a great deal of newly recorded and synthesized material.

The other non-album B-side which came with 'Kiss Of Life' or 'How To Fall In Love', was called '855-7019', with alternating Barry and Robin verses, a catchy chorus of "eight double five, seven oh one nine", and a long instrumental ending continuing the bassline and beat into a fade, after which the hapless singer hears an answering machine inform him that the object of his affections is "tied up at the moment".

About the same time, Barry, Maurice and Femi Jiya also produced a track for Lulu's forthcoming *Independence* LP. 'Let Me Wake Up In Your Arms' was written by all three brothers three years earlier, and Barry provided guitar and backing vocals on the song.

Using some rare spare time, The Bee Gees also collaborated with a Brazilian duo who recorded 'Words' in Spanish, 'Palabras', as Jose & Durval, and in Portuguese, 'Palavras' as Chitaozhino & Xororo.

In preparation for the upcoming tour to promote *Size Isn't Everything*, The Bee Gees played a 16-song concert at the Sunrise Musical Theater as part of the Y-100 Radio Birthday Month.

Kelli Wolfe attended the concert with her mother, an occasion she found memorable for several reasons. "I had called Dick," she explained, "because Barry had said to me, if they ever did a concert in Miami that we could come. I don't think he spoke to Barry, but he got me tickets, my mom and I. So we went up there and stayed in the hotel and went to the show, and we got backstage passes . . .

"None of them were speaking to each other. They got off stage, and Maurice went one way, Barry went the other, and Robin went to the far side of the room, and I don't think they said a word to each other the rest of the night. My mom asked John Merchant what was going on, and he said, 'They're fighting as usual.'

"Right after the show, we went to the party room backstage. At any concert I've ever been backstage, they have champagne and wine and food, but you know what they had there? *Popcorn*," she announced in disgust. "My mom and I looked at each other. All they had was popcorn, and there were all these people that were all dressed up, and I thought this was really weird! Maurice saw me and waved me over and told me how excited they were that my record was coming out and so on. Barry spoke to me too for a few minutes before Linda pulled him away, and that was the last time I ever saw him in person."

The Bee Gees reprised the 16-song set at Rupert's Nightclub in Atlanta, Georgia on November 5 and again two days later at Orlando for VH1's *Center Stage*.

On November 25, they performed four songs on the Royal Variety Performance before the Queen at London's Dominion Theatre. Maurice expressed what a privilege they considered the appearance. "I can vividly remember as kids watching The Beatles make their famous appearance on the show," he said, "when John Lennon came out with his immortal comment about the rattling of jewellery. The Beatles were our heroes, our gods. We had just made our first records in Australia and I remember thinking, 'I wonder if one day it'll be us up there.' Now it's actually happened, and it's a treat. We've done things for Charles and Diana, but this is the first time we've appeared in front of the Queen. We feel greatly honoured."

Earlier that month, they had also made an appearance on American "shock jock" Howard Stern's syndicated radio show. Ostensibly there to talk about their career and the new album, Barry's discomfort with Stern's style was audible as he attempted to steer the conversation back to business. He lost any hope of salvaging the interview when Stern asked if they were faithful to their wives, and Robin announced, "My wife cheats on me now, but not with men. Yeah, she's gay. She's proud of it."

Maurice observed, "I think it's turned out to be the Robin show," adding, "I don't suppose there's much that we can say now after Robin's . . ."

Howard, interrupted, "No, no one's interested in you two. You guys just sit back now and relax, all right?"

Barry responded tersely, "We'll just sit here and keep our big mouths shut."

Urged on by Howard and his female sidekick, Robin Quivers, Robin went on to elaborate, "Everything is confined within the relationship. She only likes women . . . She's got a steady girlfriend at the moment, her lover . . . and I get to join in. It works. It works for us . . . but there's a lot of people out there that get threatened by that kind of situation. I see it as completely normal."

Howard observed, "Barry, you seem upset by this."

Barry's voice was icy as he replied, "I'm not upset at all. Actually I'm very,

very calm. I just don't talk about my personal life. Whatever I've got up to in the past 25 years is not for everybody's ears."

The brothers performed a ribald version of their own 'To Love Somebody' with new lyrics provided by Stern. It was certainly a new image for The Bee Gees. They continued the theme the following month on Tribute Entertainment TV with a mock commercial for "The National Addadicktome Foundation Appeal" in which they lampooned the unfortunate Mr Bobbit with yet another set of alternative lyrics to the music of 'To Love Somebody'. This time, the song was called 'To Lose Your Penis'!

Back on the show, Howard continued, "You want my advice, I mean, you guys never need me to tell you how to make an album, but I would dump two of the tracks and just put the lesbian stories on. I would be immediately in the store, I mean I wouldn't know what to do."

The following day, the story was in newspapers around the globe. Robin had flown back to England, while Dwina stayed in Miami. At four o'clock in the morning, she got a phone call. "He called me up from London and said, 'There's been an article in *The Sun*,'" she recalled.

"I said, 'Well, read it to me,' but he wouldn't. A friend read it. Robin was very apologetic, but I was stunned, shocked and hurt. I couldn't go back to sleep."

The immediate reaction by both Robin and Dwina was to treat the entire episode as a joke which got out of hand. "Robin is normally a good practical joker but he went too far this time. I'm going to kill him," Dwina said. "I have my son Robin John here with me in Miami. He's only 10 so he doesn't understand attraction. I am afraid of other children ribbing him at school.

"And my family in England think it is serious. I have dozens of relatives in Britain and I'm sure I have ancestors turning in their graves. But I am keeping a brave face on it. I haven't spoken to my mother yet, but she'll be on his warpath for this."

Barbara Gibb wasn't so easily shocked. "I get on extremely well with my mother-in-law," Dwina continued. "She's very broad-minded and never even mentioned you know what."

Robin attempted some damage control on *Pebble Mill*, telling Judi Spiers, "That was basically a radio show in New York called *Howard Stern* . . . They don't have anything like it in England, it just went completely awry because, he just likes to shock. He talks about everybody including his own family."

Judi responded, "So, the allusions you were making about sexual activities were a joke?"

"Absolutely," Robin agreed, "but it just totally backfired and again it wasn't a sort of serious statement about my life. It was more of a conversation that sort of rolled on early in the morning, and it happened to have gone to 17 cities, and it was the number one show in the country so, when people hear things like that, even in jest, it just gets picked up."

Dwina told *The Sun*'s Piers Morgan, "It might have been a little dig at me because I am writing a novel in which there are things pertaining to lesbian activities. I suppose he was having a little dig which turned into a very big dig, and almost dug his own grave. If he doesn't dig it, I am sure my mother will!

"It will cost him dearly. He'll pay in his own way. I am going to extract from him one of the biggest diamonds I have ever extracted in my life. The diamond is getting bigger by the minute, the more I reflect on it!"

After all the uproar, most people would agree with Robin Quivers when she said, "I thought he'd keep his mouth shut after he saw what happened." Indeed, one might have expected Robin to be a little more discreet in the future – but few who know him were surprised that discretion was the last thing on his mind. In an on-air phone call from London to *The Howard Stern Show* just over a week later, he denied that Dwina had been angry. "She actually loved the whole thing," he insisted.

Robin Quivers said, "Well yeah, you could tell it was sort of tongue in cheek because she said she was going to extract a big diamond from you."

"That's right you see, so there's a little method to her madness here," he replied.

Far from denying any of the previous revelations, Robin gave even more details. With Howard urging him on, he went on to describe their three in the bed lifestyle.

"Not only could I [not] believe that we got Robin Gibb to tell us this story, I can't believe we're getting him to tell us it again! It's great. I love it," Howard gloated.

For the next year or so, there was the "Is she or isn't she?" game being played, with Robin alternately telling interviewers that it was a joke or that it was all true.

Dwina proudly showed off her new Jaguar XJRS with a number plate reading DRU 1 D, saying, "Robin bought it for me after his . . . indiscretion. I told him he owed me the biggest diamond ever, so he bought me this car in diamond blue."

But in 1995, the couple spoke frankly with *OK!* magazine. "I was being interviewed by the biggest shock jockey in the US on live radio," Robin explained. "You have to shock with him, or you become the butt of his treatment so I got in first. It wasn't until I got on the plane later to go to London that I realised what a can of worms I'd opened . . . but yes, it's true, Dwina is bisexual with me."

"He was trying to shock – and he certainly shocked my mother! His comments did upset me," Dwina admitted, "but only because I was worried about how my family, my mother and our son Robin John would take it. I didn't have any feelings of shame about what Robin said, and I still don't. No one can hurt me in anything they do or say. I just carry on living my life."

Although Barry had sounded distinctly uncomfortable with the revelations at the time, Dwina insisted that neither he nor Maurice had been surprised. "They're used to Robin," she explained. "On one radio show, they were asked what past lives they might have lived, and Robin piped up,

'Barry was probably a rent-boy for Oscar Wilde.' He tends to throw in these bombshells. Maybe that's why we're attracted to each other."

Although the couple's close friends had known about Dwina's sexuality from the beginning of their relationship, there were still shockwaves when they revealed all.

According to Robin, they disproved the old axiom that opposites attract. "I couldn't live with someone who was opposite to me, or who held grudges," he said. "We never go to bed on an argument."

Saying that they had made their "commitments in the eyes of God", Robin divulged, "I knew Dwina was gay when we married, but that didn't matter because I was in love with her. I still am very much in love with her. She is the best wife any husband could want."

Dwina continued, "We have a spiritual/physical bond whereby we know we're always going to be together."

She insisted that bond wasn't weakened by the fans who tried to get close to Robin. "I find it flattering that so many women find my husband sexy. Women write to me and tell me they think he's sexy and how lucky they think I am.

"Although Robin still has lots of fans from the Seventies, as I get older, the fans seem to get younger," she laughed. "Often they're very beautiful, and they can be very nice to me. It's only the odd one . . . who oversteps the mark. But that's probably because things aren't working in their lives."

Robin added, "No disrespect to anyone who likes us, but there are people out there who write in and say the strangest things. We keep a list of them, just in case they show up somewhere."

In April, one of Robin's fans crossed that boundary between fan devotion and obsession when she showed up in a most unexpected place – a wardrobe in the couple's English home. Robin and Dwina received a phone call at their Miami home from Robin's personal assistant, Ken Graydon back in England. "Someone's broken into your house," Ken said. "We found her in the wardrobe. She seems to be a fan."

A 43-year-old housewife and mother of four travelled more than 150 miles from her home to The Prebendal. It was no spur of the moment whim; she had prepared for her mission well, arming herself with a camera, camcorder, tape recorder, rubber gloves, screwdriver and Stanley knife. After strolling through the grounds taking photos, she used her tools to prise open one of the latticed windows and climbed inside, seeking the ultimate fan souvenir, her own video of the medieval mansion's interior.

She hadn't reckoned on the sophisticated security system which alerted the police and tracked her movements through the house. As the deafening alarm sounded, she stowed her bag of burglary gear under a bed. Within minutes, the police and Ken Graydon were on the scene, and found the woman cowering in the wardrobe of the nanny's bedroom. She was led away in shame.

"Her only concern seemed to be that she'd be banned from [The Bee Gees] fan club," Dwina said.

Robin instructed the fan club not to end her membership and asked the police to drop the charges of criminal damage against the woman. "I'm not so materialistic that I'd feel this was important to me," he said. "Anyway, it wasn't a vicious revengeful break-in." The police declined to drop the charges.

"I'm not angry about the break-in, and I feel no resentment towards [her]," he explained. "I don't feel like my house has been violated either."

Dwina didn't fully agree. "It's a very strange sensation knowing someone's been in your house rummaging around," she said. "She wasn't a thief, however, just a very ardent fan and quite harmless. If she'd just come and asked me if she could take pictures inside the house, I might have been able to sort something out."

A psychiatrist testified that she had been suffering from menopausal depression at the time of the break-in, and that she had also been distressed after the death of her dog.

The defendant claimed she had not intended to steal anything from the house but wanted only to take photos. She stressed that she was shocked by what she had done and offered to pay compensation for the damages. She pleaded guilty to going equipped to burgle and guilty to damaging the window. She was ordered pay £402 compensation − £314 for damage to the window plus £88 to reset the alarm − and £25 costs.

Robin donated the money to a children's leukaemia charity. "I still think it would have been better if the police hadn't charged her," he said. "There are, I believe, a lot of worse people out there."

★   ★   ★

In early 1994, the tabloids in Britain reported that Maurice was "back in booze clinic", a rumour which he denied.

"They got it wrong. A lot of people said I'd relapsed and gone back into treatment. But in fact, I'd gone back to do treatment, to facilitate the group, and that's a different thing," he explained. "I don't have to keep going to the meetings, but if it makes me feel good when I do go to them, then there's no reason why I should stop. Now I also have a wonderful AA support group in England around the Surrey area. It's a boon."

Polydor announced plans, subject to planning permission, to decorate the towers at Battersea Power Station with the Gibbs' images from the *Size Isn't Everything* album. It was also announced that the promotional tour for the album would take The Bee Gees to 18 cities throughout Europe, beginning in April in Toulon.

But in February, the proposed tour was cancelled due to concerns about Barry's health. The arthritis in his back, right hand and right knee had become worse, and during tests at Mount Sinai Hospital, the doctors discovered a problem with his heart. Their solicitor, Michael Eaton, stated, "We don't think it's going to stop him doing most things, but it's one of those things you don't take liberties with."

He added that the group were very disappointed. "They get their greatest thrill playing to live audiences. I can't remember them ever having to pull out before. They'll try to reschedule the tour as soon as possible."

The group's agent, Pete Bassett announced, "Barry's suffering from arthritis, which is why the group called off the tour. But he is soldiering on and is in Britain with the other two brothers for the release of their single."

Explaining that the warm climate of Miami was more beneficial, he added, "It could be a long time before the tour is back on. At the moment, Barry has had exploratory surgery to see how bad the trouble is. He even wears a glove on stage when he is playing guitar to keep his hand warm, which helps stop the pain."

Robin and Maurice did some promotional appearances, making excuses for their absent brother. "It was pretty hairy for Barry as he's normally so healthy," Maurice commented. "He'd been run down for a while, and after a check-up at the doctor's, he was told he had a viral infection which had affected his heart. We were very concerned for him, but he's had treatment and is okay now."

He later said, "Barry has had back problems but didn't keep up the physiotherapy. His current heart problem is being taken good care of, and he is looking forward to getting back to England soon, even if he can't appear live."

With the memory of Andy's death from myocarditis still fresh, rumours spread quickly about the state of Barry's health. Although initially grateful for the concern shown by the group's fans, the attention soon grated on Barry. "There's an abnormality with my heart," he said. "I didn't have a heart attack, but everybody goes and talks to the press. It was my feeling that people should mind their own business – and I refer to my brothers in the nicest possible way."

In April, both of the CD single releases included a non-album B-side, '855–7019'. In Britain, 'How To Fall In Love, Part One' reached number 30, whilst on the European mainland, the best that its counterpart 'Kiss Of Life' could achieve in Germany was a disappointing 51.

On June 1, The Bee Gees were inducted into the Songwriters Hall Of Fame at a ceremony at the Sheraton Hotel in New York.

Later that month, they were asked to write the title song for the remake of the Christmas classic, *Miracle On 34th Street*. The resulting song, 'Miracles Happen', would be left out of the film after the last minute decision to restrict the music to traditional Christmas songs only.

In September, Polydor announced that the next Bee Gees' album, a compilation entitled *Love Songs*, was appropriately scheduled for a Valentine's Day 1995 release. The album would be partly previously released recordings, plus the new song 'Rings Around The Moon' and The Bee Gees' own versions of two older songs they had written for other artists, 'Emotion' and 'Heartbreaker'. With the decision not to use 'Miracles Happen' in the film, it was also earmarked for the album.

1994 also saw the release of another tribute album containing some interesting cover versions. *Melody Fair*, a 21-track CD released on the Eggbert label in the USA, featured new cover versions of Bee Gees' songs by American new wave and 'grunge' artists and bands. Taking a refreshingly different look at the songs, the album draws heavily from hitherto obscure album tracks from the 1966 to 1972 period, with 'How Deep Is Your Love' the only hit represented. Among many highlights were Sneetches' cover of 'Mrs. Gillespie's Refrigerator', a 1967 track never released by The Bee Gees, and Phil Seymour's cover of Barry's 'The First Mistake I Made', as well as a Dick Dale-influenced surf instrumental version of 'How Deep Is Your Love'. There is also one other notable inclusion, 'I'm Not Wearing Make-Up', a 1987 composition by Barry, Maurice and Andy and recorded by their niece, Beri Rhodes, with Barry singing back-up.

The 1969 song 'Melody Fair' itself was resurrected for a Japanese TV advert to promote Suzuki cars and was scheduled to air 12,000 times. Always a big favourite with their Japanese fans, Polydor took the opportunity to re-release it as a single, taking the same approach with *The Very Best* album with 'Melody Fair' being added to the original track listing.

Soul singer Percy Sledge recorded a 1975 *Main Course* out-take, 'Your Love Will Save The World', and Bad Boys Inc. released 'Ain't Nothing Gonna Keep Me From You', the 1978 single by Teri De Sario.

There was also a 12-inch promotional single of *Saturday Night Fever* megamixes released in France.

In March, 1995, it was announced that the *Love Songs* album concept had been dropped in favour of a new studio album.

In June, Barry was named as the executive producer for the UK Channel 4 TV film, *Making Waves*, about a pirate radio station in the Sixties. He was also said to be writing the musical score, but the project never came to fruition.

That month, Ronal & Peter, two celebrity supporters of the Dutch football club Ajax, the recent winners of the European Champions League, recorded a revised version 'I.O.I.O', which had become a terracing chant at matches. It became a hit in Holland.

The Bee Gees were back in Britain on September 1 to switch on the Blackpool illuminations in conjunction with a Radio One Special.★ The Gibbs' first appearance on the Radio One show came at 1.00 p.m. when they waved to the crowds on the beach and did a short interview to promote the official opening later that evening. As darkness fell, they reappeared to perform 'For Whom The Bell Tolls' and 'You Win Again' before turning on the illuminations at 9.00 p.m. "We are slightly overwhelmed," Barry said. "We came to Blackpool hoping to enjoy the honour of turning the lights on, and we are proud to have done it. It has been a stunning day."

"It is a big honour," Maurice said. "It's a *huge* honour to do that. So it wasn't something belittling or anything like that."

★ Blackpool is a seaside resort in the north of England and each year a celebrity switches on festive street lighting to signal the start of the autumn season.

They were back in Florida later that month, where they were inducted into Florida's Artists Hall Of Fame in Tallahassee.

"Seriously, isn't it amazing that it could be happening," Barry marvelled. "The dream was to be famous and, if you imagine that 10 years after you are dead, people will still be playing your records; well, that's the dream. There's no ego with us. We can't believe we are still around – that people are still listening to us. That is the truth. I do think, though, that most of our career, most of our success, has come from luck. We always feel, 'My God, we've fooled them again!' "

"We've been written off so many times," Maurice added, "but because of being persistent and doing something we love so much, it has made us stronger as people, as brothers, as songwriters."

Robin continued, "I don't think we have anything to prove. We genuinely do have a lot to contribute to the music business because we still feel we're doing things that a lot of artists are not doing, like writing our own music. When we first began, artists who wrote their own music got a tremendous amount of respect. Nowadays, it's not true.

"The three of us are tremendously ambitious. We have the same feeling about life, that we are here for a very short time, so it is important when you do what you do to cram as much of it and achieve as much as you can into that space you have. I don't think we'll stop until we drop.

"When one of your songs is on the radio, it is a wonderful thing, an extension of yourself. People, strangers that you have never met, speak different languages. It is marvellous, greater than governments and politics in breaking down barriers."

Maurice further elaborated, "It's wonderful to have some people that we see, groups and people that we bump into, say that we were their inspiration, if it wasn't for us they wouldn't be in the business . . . It's wonderful to hear things like that. I used to say that about The Beatles. There's people today that were brought up in the Seventies that were fond of our music, like The Pet Shop Boys, people like that. They're wonderful guys, and a funny connection, because we thought, there's something that we like about that, something that's very like our early stuff. 'You've got the looks, I've got the brains, let's make lots of money'. 'Lonely days, lonely nights, where would I be without my woman.' It's exactly the same, so they told us, 'oh yeah, we're influenced by it.' Oh, nice one!"

In 1996, the group joined forces with other artists to pay homage to another singer/songwriter they had long admired, when their October 1995 recording of 'Will You Love Me Tomorrow' was included on the *Tapestry Revisited* tribute to Carole King's best selling album. The song must have been a family favourite as Andy Gibb had also released his own version of the same song as a duet with Pat Arnold on his 1980 *Greatest Hits* LP. The Bee Gees' track was released as a promotional only CD single in Australia; although some doubt still remains as to the legitimacy of its release.

Barry provided backing vocals and arrangements on 'Too Much Heaven' on American female vocalist, Jordan Hill's eponymous LP. The chanteuse was exuberant in her praise of the Gibbs, when thanking them on the CD's liner notes thus: "Bee Gees. Wow!!!! Not only do I get to sing one of your incredible songs, but I also get you on backgrounds . . . is it real or am I dreaming?"

Soul Of The Bee Gees, another tribute album, was also released in 1996. Again, a compilation of previously released cover versions that could only loosely be described as "soul", it sold quite well. Curiously, it also included Robin Gibb's own version of 'Toys', a Barry, Robin and Maurice composition from Robin's 1985 solo album, *Walls Have Eyes*.

On October 24, The Bee Gees opened VH1's Fashion Awards in New York. The following day, they performed at a special charity event, where they were introduced by John Travolta. Frank Sinatra, Sylvester Stallone and Antonio Banderas were among the famous names in attendance.

On November 25, The Bee Gees were featured in VH1's *Storytellers* series, performing some of their best known songs in Coral Springs, Florida, accompanied only by Ben Stivers on synthesizer and telling the background of the songs. As usual Barry was on rhythm guitar, whilst Maurice alternated between guitar and keyboards. There were no pre-recorded parts and they still sounded great. 'Stayin' Alive' was a highlight of the show because of its very different arrangement, which made it all the more disappointing that it wasn't one of the tracks featured on a bonus CD that accompanied their new album in some American stores the following year.

"We're always perceived as making comebacks, but we've never been away," Barry said. "We're just carrying on like we always have. We're moving into our prime now because we've got so much experience behind us.

"The best time is now because we've lived through it all and come out the other end. Our music is being played again on the radio and the media doesn't perceive us as being strange or silly any more and our families are healthy and growing up. Now we can look back on it all. I feel more content . . . than I've ever felt in my life."

40

SEVERAL NIGHTS ONLY

A<small>T THE START</small> of 1997, Barry declared, "It's one more time on the merry-go-round . . . If they like us this time round, maybe we'll go on a little bit longer. We're aware of being criticised; we're aware that we get ridiculed. It's like water off a duck's back to us. But the key to it is that we're doing the kind of music we like, and we believe that if we like it, others will too."

The group's music was reaching a whole new generation of fans with boy bands Take That and Boyzone both topping the British charts with their covers of Bee Gees' songs, 'How Deep Is Your Love' and 'Words' respectively.

For The Bee Gees, this particular ride on the merry-go-round of fame was marked not only by the recognition of their music but also by accolades from the public and their peers. The honours began in Los Angeles on January 27, 1997, at the *American Music Awards Show* produced by the former *American Bandstand* host Dick Clark.

In a taped message, John Travolta thanked the group for the role they had played in his success. "I just wanted to say congratulations to you guys," he said. "Nobody deserves this award more than The Bee Gees and that's the truth. I've always felt that when Barry, Robin and Maurice get behind the mic, it's pure magic."

After an introduction which included rare live footage of the group throughout their careers and brief clips from home movies, Quincy Jones presented them with the International Artist Award, in recognition of more than 30 years of making music on a global playing field.

Handing his award to Robin before making his acceptance speech, Barry was every bit the eldest brother, admonishing him, "Don't drop it!" as Robin replied indignantly, "I won't!"

Assured that his award was in safe hands, Barry announced, "I've got a little list here because we've got a lot of people to thank so we've gotta be real quick. Our mum and dad, our wives and our children . . . the fourth Bee Gee, Dick Ashby; all our fans everywhere – we love you, thank you so much. Our managers, Allen Kovac and Carol Peters and everybody at Left Bank; our record company, Polydor; our original mentor, Mr Robert Stigwood; Ahmet Ertegun; Nesuhi [Ertegun]; Arif Mardin; John Travolta – there's more folks! Bill Gates, Col Joye, Kevin Jacobsen, John Merchant, our brother Andy, who we know is watching, and of course, Mr Dick Clark for making this the proudest day of our lives – thank you so much!"

In February, the first single from their forthcoming album, 'Alone', was released and entered the charts at number five in Britain, while achieving the eighth position in Australia.

'Alone' has a driving rhythm, acoustic rhythm guitars and a bagpipe-like organ. Maurice maintained that he originally saw the song as a Byrds-type rambling song with a bit of Fifties influence thrown in, but it took a very different path when he came up with a bagpipes sound on the synthesizer. "We weren't too sure about the bagpipes," he admitted, "but Robin actually persisted. He said, 'They're great; you gotta keep the bagpipes.' "

Robin explained, "They were just an idea to make it rock. I don't know . . . there's just something haunting about bagpipes in rock music. It's very driving. It's been used on Phil Collins' records. I think it just worked on that song."

The song has some problems as a single. The arrangement reminded many of Bruce Springsteen records like 'Glory Days' that have similar organ backing, and reminded others of the rhythm guitar sound of The Traveling Wilburys and Roy Orbison's last hit 'Anything You Want'. Neither is fatal, since other records borrow those sounds too, but what really hurt the song was the light lead vocal, when something harsher would have made greater impact.

The single was delayed until June in the USA, where it failed to make an impression on the charts. The CD single had two B-sides, 'Closer Than Close' from the album and the remarkable 'Rings Around The Moon' left over from the unissued *Love Songs* album of 1995. Robin's great crying lead vocal on most of the song only points up by contrast how little his voice is used on 'Still Waters'.

The Bee Gees went through several working titles as the album progressed, considering *Crusader*, *Obsessions* and *Irresistible Force* before deciding upon *Still Waters*.

For this project, The Bee Gees worked with several top producers. Their stated goal was to get some new ideas into their music, and Barry commented, "I learnt something technically from each producer, and I learnt something spiritually from each producer. Spiritually, in terms of the faith that somebody has in the creative process, we have learnt an awful lot working with each of the producers, but in no way has any of them brought us into the Nineties."

Despite Barry's praise, several of the producers were quoted saying happily that they didn't need to do much since The Bee Gees knew what they wanted. This was borne out by the release of the demo of the song 'Still Waters' as a B-side, which proves to be nearly identical to the finished recording.

Initial plans for the album called for the group to work with former Eurythmic, Dave Stewart; Jimmy Jam and Terry Lewis, the prolific R&B

producers best known for their work with Janet Jackson; Attrel and Jarrett Cordes, of the hip-hop/rap/pop group PM Dawn; Raphael Saadiq, of the R&B/hip-hop crossover act Tony! Toni! Toné!, but the final selection consisted of their old favourite, Arif Mardin; Hugh Padgham, best known for his work with The Police, Sting and Phil Collins; Russ Titelman, whose previous work included discs for Eric Clapton, Paul McCartney and Steve Winwood; and David Foster, whose production credits read like a veritable Who's Who of pop music.

Foster considered himself a Bee Gees fan as well as a producer. "They sing as magnificently now as I remember them 30 years ago," he enthused. "They haven't lost any range. You know, the voice is a muscle and like everything, we all get a little older, lose your range, whatever. I see no difference in the way they sing now than when I was a fan like everyone else. Next to The Beatles, they were probably the most creative group ever."

The crisp sound of Femi Jiya was lost, and so was the sense of a band working together. Barry dominates this album, both vocally and in the type of songwriting, for reasons never clarified. Robin seems limited to chipping in ideas to Barry's songs, and Maurice's role is as subtle as ever. This may be just the impression given by the vocal assignments, but the difference from *Size Isn't Everything* to this is striking.

The album was unusually long in the making, with the proposed release date slipping from August 1996 to October 1996 to January 1997, before its eventual release in March 1997 in the UK, Europe and Asia. Ten of the 12 songs are from 1994 and 1995. The first recordings were probably 'Obsessions' and 'I Will' with Arif Mardin in October 1995. 'I Could Not Love You More' and 'I Surrender' were done with David Foster in February 1996, and 'Irresistible Force' with Hugh Padgham in March 1996. Russ Titelman worked on 'Alone', 'Smoke And Mirrors', and 'My Lover's Prayer'. One set of sessions did not work out – 'Fire With Fire' and 'Still Waters' with the group P M Dawn (Attrel Cordes and Jarett Cordes) were never used, and 'Still Waters' was remade with Hugh Padgham. The last songs done may have been the two 1996 songs, 'With My Eyes Closed' with Raphael Saadiq, and finally 'Closer Than Close' produced by the group towards the autumn of 1996.

Robin explained, "I think that the longer you've been around, you have to really focus on what you're gonna put out . . . I mean, artists like Elton John and Phil Collins and people like that spend more time making an album than . . . new groups. Because it's more important what you put out."

No consistent group of musicians was used across all the sessions, with the different producers selecting top session players as appropriate, a state of affairs from which The Bee Gees could only benefit.

The second single featured another *Love Songs* original on the B-side, the island beat, 'Love Never Dies', with another excellent Robin lead vocal on verses and soaring to a chorus, and Maurice's somewhat Lennon-like lead on an alternating section. Both these B-side songs were appended to the album itself in Japan, but they are rare and sought after elsewhere.

Barry declared, "If you listen to the album before this or the one before that, you will get a better perspective. But a lot of those albums weren't being listened to simply because we weren't in vogue, so we were dealing with that, too. Radio, a couple of years ago, wouldn't have touched a Bee Gees record. Being in fashion simply means that you'll eventually go out of fashion.

"We've seen a lot of adversity, and that's why the songs on *Still Waters* are so personal. You can learn from the bad things. Musically, there's more R&B in what we're doing now, but our subject matter still runs deep. This album reflects 35 years of the things that have influenced us.

"Music is a life trip for me. I love it – whether it's being in a group, producing other people or writing songs. There's still a lot I want to do – I don't feel like an old man just yet!"

He summarised the album by saying, "All of these songs are not just songs as such. I think this is a really important statement. The world of illusion, the idea that none of us are really what we seem to be. There's a lot of examination of yourself in these songs. The album itself is about a romanticism, mysticism, looking inward, self-examination, relationships, so it's a lot more than a bunch of songs. Somebody who is looking for a hit single won't notice that, but a true listener will."

★　★　★

The Bee Gees made the rounds of British television, beginning with an appearance on *Noel's House Party* on February 8, when they performed the newly released single 'Alone' and were the hapless victims of one of Noel Edmond's "gotcha" pranks. Just four days later, they appeared on *Des O'Connor Tonight*.

On February 24, they were the proud recipients of the British Phonographic Industry's Lifetime Achievement Award at the Brit Awards, televised live from Earl's Court in London.

Although Barry said that the award "really means a lot to us", he turned a thumbs down on their choice of Jarvis Cocker, who famously disrupted Michael Jackson's performance at the previous Brit Awards. "I don't want to seem ungrateful, but they wanted to get this Jarvis guy to give us the award," he complained. "What's Jarvis Cock-Up got to do with The Bee Gees? I don't want to be associated with anyone who might have pushed small children over." He was successful on that point; Sir Tim Rice was the one to present the award on the night.

In accepting the award, Barry said, "We'd like to thank our mum and dad, of course; our wives, Linda, Yvonne and Dwina; and the fourth Bee Gee, Dick Ashby." He then read aloud a statement by Robert Stigwood and exclaimed, "Robert, as the greatest showman of all time, if you don't accept this alongside us tonight, we won't accept it either. We love you."

All the problems of the Eighties seemed to be forgotten as a frail-looking Robert Stigwood joined them on stage and embraced each brother. He then read a prepared speech, concluding, "I would like you to take a Bee Gees' song, 'I've Gotta Get A Message To You', and I send that out to all young performers and composers – be like The Bee Gees and never give up!"

Behind the scenes, Barry confessed that he was less than pleased that the Brit Awards producers wanted them to perform 'Stayin' Alive'. "I don't like singing it," he claimed. "We were delighted they decided to give us this award but that was another thing altogether." Despite his declared reservations about performing the song, it was included in the show. The Bee Gees performed a spirited medley of their hits, to the obvious delight of the star-studded audience. 'To Love Somebody', 'Massachusetts', 'Words' and 'How Deep Is Your Love' all received a warm reception, but when they went into 'Jive Talkin'', the crowd were on their feet and dancing as a snowstorm of confetti dropped on the group. The audience danced and clapped their way through 'Stayin' Alive' and 'You Should Be Dancing' as the confetti continued to fall.

In March, Melvyn Bragg's *The South Bank Show* dedicated an hour to the lives and careers of the group, taking them back to their childhood haunts of Keppel Road and Oswald Road School in Manchester, right up to the future, with 'Just In Case', a work in progress in the studio.

According to producer Andrew Bell, the programme was 14 months in the making, after he had originally been contacted by Sam Wright, the head of television promotion for Polydor in the UK. Although he said he thought it surprising that The Bee Gees' contribution to songwriting had never received the recognition he thought it deserved, he had never actually developed the thought into a project until the Polydor executive expressed interest in a collaboration. "The first six months entailed developing and researching the idea," Bell explained, "including trips to Miami where we spent several hours with each brother, financing the project with advances from distributors and sales to broadcasters."

What followed was two months of pre-production, followed by about two months of shooting in Manchester, at the brothers' homes in Miami and England and a multi-cam performance shot at Middle Ear Studio. Then came the months of post-production editing.

Bell said that he went into the project with few preconceptions about The Bee Gees but added, "Having met the brothers, I was stunned by their intelligence, their articulacy [*sic*] and an aura. As a child, I had listened to John Lennon, particularly in the mid-Seventies. I was stunned then by Lennon's presence and perception. When I discussed this idea with *The South Bank Show* in the UK, I could only compare the impact, and in many ways, that was a big turn on for Melvyn Bragg. I think Melvyn was intrigued by the songwriting achievements of the brothers but also cerebrally."

In addition to its screening in the UK, the programme was syndicated for television broadcast worldwide. A 90-minute version of the programme was released the following June on home video as *Keppel Road: The Life And Music Of The Bee Gees*.

The World Music Awards, hosted by Prince Albert and Princess Stephanie of Monaco, were the next to honour the group with the Lifetime Contribution To Music Award on April 17. Prince Albert presented the award to the group, and Barry once again acted as spokesman, thanking the usual cast of characters and wishing Robert Stigwood a happy birthday. The Bee Gees performed a live medley of 'I've Gotta Get A Message To You', 'How Deep Is Your Love', 'Jive Talkin'', 'Alone', Stayin' Alive' and 'You Should Be Dancing'. David Adelson, the managing director of *Hits* magazine noted, "They were the only band in Monaco that brought a very staid and jaded audience to its feet."

He added, "The Bee Gees are once again a combination of cool and kitsch. They evoke favourable memories and seem to have won renewed respect, proving that longevity enables certain artists to become hip again. If you survive long enough, you can thrive again."

On May 6, The Bee Gees were inducted into the Rock'n'Roll Hall Of Fame in Cleveland, Ohio. "It's like the pinnacle of everything you've worked for," Maurice enthused. "It vindicates everything you've believed in."

The same day saw the American release of the *Still Waters* album. In the second week of sales, a limited edition package of *Still Waters* plus a special bonus CD, *VH1 Storytellers*, containing live versions of 'Words', 'I've Gotta Get A Message To You', 'I Started A Joke', 'To Love Somebody' and 'Jive Talkin'', was sold only in Target stores across the country. The bonus package rapidly sold out as album sales in the US exceeded Polydor's expectations, but a lack of the product in the stores may have hurt its chart position. The album entered the American charts at number 11, with first week sales of 65,558. By comparison, the group's previous album, *Size Isn't Everything*, peaked at 153 on the *Billboard* Top 200.

Jim Caparro, the CEO of Polygram Group Distribution, confessed, "The band delivered a terrific record, and everyone got juiced from that, but to say we were expecting 65,000 records sold in the first week – no. It shows that great music doesn't die."

The American success pleasantly surprised The Bee Gees themselves, in spite of the album's Top 10 status in Britain and Europe. "We were stunned, absolutely," Barry admitted. "We would have been happy to enter the charts at 100. The idea of actually reaching the public in the US is a new one for us."

"You've got moms in the forties and their teenage kids liking this record – and these kids weren't even born when *Saturday Night Fever* was out," said Left Bank Management's Vice President of Sales, Jordan Berliant. "It's clear you don't sell these kinds of numbers for such an act without it being multi-generational. This represents the leading edge of a phenomenon in the music industry, a rare example where an act still appeals to its original audience, with a surprisingly high popularity among younger demographics."

"We feel we're into our third period of fame now," Barry explained, "but after *Saturday Night Fever*, there was a huge backlash against us. Radio wouldn't touch us – we were censored. Now it appears we're fashionable again. It's quite confusing how suddenly you can be 'in' again when no one wanted to know before.

"Fact is, your popularity will fail and people will start to disappear. We were wonderboys for a while, but I think having low spells is healthy. We had to work our way back, but we've always just written what we wanted. We never pandered to what we thought was popular at any time."

On September 22, The Bee Gees were inducted into the Hall Of Fame of the Australian Music Industry Association (ARIAs) for their Lifetime Contribution to Music. The audience was shown a pre-recorded video of the brothers thanking the Association before the award was formally accepted on their behalf by Bill Gates. The following month, it was Germany's turn to honour the group, when they were awarded the BAMBI Award in Cologne and a lifetime achievement award at the Goldene Europa Awards.

Despite all the attention to their past body of work, The Bee Gees bridled at any suggestion that they were perceived as a nostalgia act, as one unfortunate journalist found at a press conference in Australia.

"We take issue with that, pal," Barry retorted. "Actors and great comedians, like Ernie Wise for instance, are applauded for longevity and I would think that pop artists and rock stars are not applauded for longevity, and there's something wrong with that."

"There's no room for being just a part of yesterday," Robin explained. "We want to be part of the now . . . contemporary. We want to have some relation to music as it is today."

★　★　★

Barry and Linda were going through some trying times behind the scenes of The Bee Gees' Nineties career revival. The previous year, they had been horrified to discover that their eldest son, Stephen, was using heroin. A family friend revealed, "The truth is he has had a drink problem for some years, but a while ago a female friend offered him heroin. He was hooked in no time."

With memories of Andy's dangerous downward spiral fresh in their minds, the thought of losing another family member to addiction was unbearable. Stephen was quickly admitted to a drugs rehabilitation centre, and his parents were pleased with his progress.

In March, Barry told *OK!* magazine, "He's been clean and sober for some time now. His mother and I are very proud of him."

But in the autumn, it was Barry's own condition which was cause for concern. A 21-date American tour was cancelled because of his arthritis.

Although it had been troublesome in the past, his condition had seemed to deteriorate after the surgery for degenerating discs in his spine.

Anxious to dispel the belief that the malady was connected with growing old, Barry declared, "Arthritis is something you can have at any age, and I think mine was really triggered off by my back surgery five years ago."

"A joint can swell up to the point where it's like a blister and you think his skin is going to burst," Linda said.

"When he walks out on a stage, you'd think there was nothing wrong with him, but he suffers badly . . . He can still sing and write music, but sometimes the arthritis is so bad, it's hard for him to grip the guitar and play it."

While the tour cancellation made his condition public, all aspects of Barry's life had been affected.

"I can actually hear him crying from the pain as he turns over in the middle of the night," Linda revealed. "It wakes me up. He doesn't hear the cries because he sleeps with ear-plugs, but I do. It is heartbreaking."

The family were only able to spend about two months of the year in their English home because of his condition. "I can't handle the cold weather," Barry explained. "I become very stiff and the arthritis can be quite chronic here, as the cold and damp affects me. Having lived in Australia when I was growing up, I'm used to a tropical climate and Miami is a compromise."

Even his favourite pastimes were no longer possible for him. Always a keen tennis player, he had been forced to give up the game. The couple's 19-year-old son, Ashley, showed great promise as a young tennis player, even attending tennis academy with the hope of turning professional, but father-son tennis matches were now a thing of the past.

"Physically, I'm not going to play at Wimbledon," Barry admitted, "but mentally, I'm as strong as I ever was. It can be agony but I don't take pills for it. I refuse to take anything – I'm completely drug-free."

"He's seen so many doctors," Linda said, "and I think he's now a little tired of trying to find ways of relieving the pain."

But she refused to give up hope. "We're not going to stop trying and hopefully one day we'll find something or someone who can do something to help him. I believe there are injections you can have in Canada which you only need every six months, but they're not available in America yet."

★   ★   ★

When The Bee Gees had completed the *Still Waters* album, Barry revealed, "We overwrote a little bit for this album. We had about four more songs, which we didn't use, but they're great for other people. We've had some good offers, so we're considering some of those."

Earlier that year, Robert Stigwood had approached the brothers with his idea to turn *Saturday Night Fever* into a stage musical. In addition to the original music, he requested something new. "Robert called us up and asked for one more song," Barry recounted, "a big ballad if possible and that is what we came up with but, really, 'Immortality' is about anyone's dreams."

Often during the songwriting process, the brothers will pick an artist to influence the direction that the song will take. "Then you get two different styles," Robin explained. "You get your own style coming in with theirs, you then come up with something unique."

So it happened that they wrote 'Immortality'. Although the song was intended for the new stage production of *Fever*, they wrote it in the style of French-Canadian pop diva, Celine Dion, and were delighted to offer it to her when she approached them with her request. "We always seize the chance to work with someone else that we really like," said Barry. "If we're always writing for ourselves, then I think you can become bored with that. Your voice is constantly the instrument by which your song becomes heard. If you've got someone else's voice . . . someone who puts their personality into your song, it's the cream on the cake. That's what makes it happen. It stretches your songwriting. It makes you write songs that you would not write otherwise."

"We asked them if they could maybe write a song for the new album. You know, if you don't ask," Celine said with a Gallic shrug, "things will never happen, so we asked and they have sent me this amazing song."

"We just happened to have this one song that would suit Celine right down to the ground. In fact, it was written with Celine in mind," Barry said. "The demo itself is almost identical to her record. That's a perfect example of saying, 'Well, here's the song, here's the demo and this makes the song shine. This brings out the personality of the person singing the song – that's it, it's a record.' So they changed almost nothing, apart from Celine herself singing the song. That's when it works right."

After Celine had finished recording her vocals against the backing vocals done by the brothers, The Bee Gees went to New York to give their approval to the recording. "I just wanted them to be happy," she said.

If she had been worried about their reaction beforehand, her doubts were quickly laid to rest. "That was a great moment when we went and heard the vocal for the first time," Maurice enthused. "It was magic."

Celine marvelled, "They listened to the song, and they were *crying*. They didn't have to tell me anything because when you see somebody with emotion and crying, it says it all. I was very touched by it."

Barry has even gone on record as saying that of all the recordings of their songs, "I think our favourite at this point in time, of *all* time, is Celine doing 'Immortality'. That, to us, is extremely special. That's the finest cover version of any of our songs."

For Celine's part, she declared, "I'm so glad I have this song – I just love it so much."

On October 4, The Bee Gees got another chance to relive their favourite cover version. The audience also got a special treat when they joined Celine on stage at her concert at Miami's Sunrise Musical Theater to perform 'Immortality'.

There was yet another special cover version in 1997. 'Nobody's Some-one' on *Million Dollar Movie*, a CD by an artist simply credited as Andrew, would have to take the prize for the longest gap between the writing and release of a Gibb composition. 'Nobody's Someone' had been written in 1968 at the start of the *Odessa* sessions, according to copyright information. Andrew Sandoval explained how he came to record the track some 28 years later.

"I first heard the song around 1990 when I was working for Bill Inglot and Bill Levenson on a non-Bee Gees project for PolyGram," said Andrew. "At the time, it was strongly being considered for the [*Tales From The Brothers Gibb*] box set they were working on.

"Later, when I was gathering ideas for some of my own recordings, I decided to do some productions with orchestration in the early Bee Gees/Bill Shepherd style. I almost did 'Never Say Never Again' from *Odessa*, but I remembered this song, 'Nobody's Someone', and thought I could join the long list of artists who recorded exclusive material by the brothers. The main difference being that they did not write the song for me, nor have they ever heard of me! The other factor being that I wanted to highlight the style of songs that they created during the Sixties, which were very unique, and not the modern songwriting/production style of today."

Taking his inspiration from the first four internationally released Bee Gees' albums, Andrew elaborated on The Bee Gees' original demo for the song to create a sound that he describes as "more a tribute than a pastiche".

On October 21, Barry, Robin and Maurice joined Robert Stigwood at a press conference at the London Palladium for the official launch of the new *Saturday Night Fever*. "The timing is perfect because the Seventies are so popular again," Barry declared. "It is about the peak period that *Saturday Night Fever* captures – the music and the fashion styles. I think the Seventies are still part of everyone's hearts and minds. Young people are wanting to live through what they didn't the first time."

The transition from film to stage musical was complicated by the fact that Stigwood was anxious to maintain as much of the film's storyline as possible, while cleaning up the language and the more controversial aspects to attract a broader audience. To this end, he hired Nan Knighten to write a new script, and Arlene Phillips as choreographer and director. Long-time RSO stalwart Paul Nicholas came on board as co-producer.

The Bee Gees agreed to provide two new songs for the project, 'Immortality' and 'First And Last' (the latter actually a short new Gibb com-position used as an opening and closing to the 1979 hit, 'Tragedy'), as well as sanctioning the inclusion of more of their earlier hits than were originally featured in the film. "You're gonna have 'Nights On Broadway', you're gonna have 'Words', 'Tragedy', 'To Love Somebody'. We're on a consul-tancy fee, £5 an hour," Barry jested. "And they will call us up if they want any input on how the music is presented. But that's basically it. These people are veterans. They're experts at what they do. Every one of the people involved in the show, in the making of the show, is in fact a star in their own right."

The year wasn't to be all kudos. While in Britain, the group caused a stir with their brief appearance on Clive Anderson's *All Talk* television programme. Apparently unfamiliar with Anderson's interview style of rapid-fire comedic insults, the brothers laughed good-naturedly at the beginning of the interview, but as the jibes continued, Barry in particular grew visibly agitated. Ultimately, his patience exhausted by Anderson's merry quips, Barry walked off in disgust before being joined by his brothers.

The response to the show from Bee Gees' fans was mixed between outrage at the maltreatment of their idols at the hands of the baneful barrister and bewilderment at the reaction of a group who pride themselves on their senses of humour.

Defending himself later in a letter to an irate Bee Gees fan, Clive Anderson explained, "Most people, including virtually all the studio audience, were completely puzzled by The Bee Gees' sudden departure. In the few minutes they were with me, I had praised their songwriting skills, stressed that they had been highly successful over three or four decades and mentioned their immense commercial success. However, it is a comedy show and along the way, I cracked a couple of gags about their high-pitched singing style, the clothes they wore in the Seventies and the like. Barry Gibb chose to mention they had previously been known as Les Tossers which invited, I thought, a humorous response. Or was that a serious name? At the time of their leaving, I was doing my best to praise Robin Gibb's solo success, 'Saved By The Bell'. Barry interrupted his brother to mention his own, 'Don't Forget To Remember' and I said I had forgotten that one. A fairly obvious joke, I suppose, but not cruel enough to provoke a walk-out. But off Barry went calling me a tosser, still brooding, it would appear on my riposte of a few minutes before. Robin went straight away with him. I am not sure that Maurice immediately appreciated that his brother was being serious, but he left apparently in solidarity with his brothers rather than in any state of annoyance of his own . . . I am sorry to have upset you and The Bee Gees so much, but I was subjecting them to no more than light-hearted banter which . . . is more or less standard on my show. I was not trying to annoy them . . . I was very pleased to have them there. I have done much tougher interviews in the past [and] nobody else has taken umbrage and taken off like that . . ."

Barry's immediate response was guarded. "With the greatest respect in the world, we've never commented on that story," he said. "We don't want to. It was a very upsetting experience and the guy was really out to sort of ridicule us if he could and every remark he made was, in a sense, created to try to ridicule us. I had just about had enough of it and walked off. And Maurice and Robin followed me. It was not a nice experience. That was it. We never commented when it happened. Apart from what I've just said, I don't want to say any more. The details were not pleasant."

Nearly a year later, he was eager to make amends. "We'd had a bad day and didn't expect to be insulted with every line," he explained. "I'd be happy to go for a drink with him now. I like Clive Anderson, I'm a fan."

★　　★　　★

The question of Barry's fitness for the rigors of a full-scale concert tour had left The Bee Gees with a bit of a dilemma.

"I did about two or three trips to Europe earlier this year, and that made me exceptionally tired," Barry explained. "I couldn't imagine committing to a year of touring the world. I would not be able to fulfil those commitments."

They were, of course, in the enviable position of not actually *needing* to tour to earn a living, but at the same time, they craved the immediate response of a live audience. They weren't ready to bow out yet, especially with their newly regained credibility in the music world.

Barry observed, "It seems that the past couple of years we've stopped being this camp joke and become a genuine part of pop culture again."

"We're durable, persistent little buggers," Robin joked, "and no matter how many people have written us off, we've always overcome adversity. We're well aware of the fact that The Bee Gees are the band that should never have made it, but we've got no plans to disappear. There's life in these old boys yet!"

Still, he admitted, "Performances can be gruelling. If you do them back to back, you are not always on form."

"We don't feel that we should be constantly touring now," added Barry. "We have all got families and children and they take priority."

They needed a new way to bring their music to their audience, and the solution was summarised in three words: *One Night Only*. Rather than taking their concert tour to 20 or 30 cities across the country, they decided to play one major concert, to be initially televised in the United States as a cable Pay Per View special.

On November 10, Barry, Robin and Maurice were given a warm welcome to their mother's adopted hometown of Las Vegas. They were presented with the keys to the city by the Mayor. The Governor of the state of Nevada declared it Bee Gees' Week, and Las Vegas Boulevard was renamed Bee Gees Boulevard for the week.

Years earlier, with the arrogance of youth, Barry had declared, "My greatest fear is that we'll always be The Bee Gees. You can't go on past 40. I don't want to end up in Vegas." In his wildest dreams, he could never have imagined that Las Vegas would be the scene of triumph some 30 years after The Bee Gees' first international hit, with the group's first major American concert since 1989. The *One Night Only* concert at the MGM Grand Hotel's Grand Garden Arena was a far cry from the nightclub appearances that Barry had wanted to avoid all those years ago.

At age 51, Barry, the man who had once thought that 40 was the optimum retirement age, now enthused, "Right now, we are at the best part of our lives in regard to what we do best!"

When the familiar driving beat of 'You Should Be Dancing' filled the air at the MGM Grand, the audience of more than 15,000 seemed to agree. They surged to their feet as the brothers, dressed in black, took the stage amidst riotous applause. A smooth segue into their latest hit single, 'Alone', received an equally warm response.

Accompanying Barry on vocals and rhythm guitar, Robin on vocals, and Maurice, alternating between keyboards and guitar and vocals, were a backing band of Matt Bonelli on bass, Steve Rucker on drums, Ben Stivers on keyboards, Stephen Gibb on guitar and, as Maurice introduced him, "the man who's been with us longer than we have", Alan Kendall on lead guitar.

Barry greeted the audience, saying, "Thank you very, very much. Good evening to all of you. Thank you for coming so far – many of you have come a long way and we really appreciate you caring and it means the world to us."

He added, "Now we're gonna shoot back 30 years – if we can remember that far back – and try and bring you up to date slowly but surely. It starts here."

'Massachusetts' and 'To Love Somebody' represented 1967, followed by 1968's 'I've Gotta Get A Message To You' and 'Words'. They then "shot back" to the present with Maurice's featured spot, 'Closer Than Close', from the *Still Waters* album. Their own version of 'Islands In The Stream' followed.

Barry introduced the next number with a simple, "This is our song for Andy." As video footage of Andy through the years was projected on the screens behind them, The Bee Gees began 'Our Love (Don't Throw It All Away)', with Barry taking the lead. The footage on screen changed to Andy in concert as his voice took over for the second verse of the song, with his brothers providing backing vocals to his taped lead vocal.

It was an emotional moment that the brothers all admitted wouldn't have been possible in the first few years after Andy's death. Although Maurice vehemently declared, "All I can say is thank God we're lucky enough to have records and videos and films of Andy that will always remind us of him – there are not many people who lose someone that young and have those sorts of memories," it had taken time before the hurt had healed enough that they could watch the videos. The idea of a posthumous duet would have seemed unthinkable in those early days.

As the brothers and their audience surreptitiously wiped away the tears, it seemed to be time for another change in mood, and a medley of 'Night Fever' and 'More Than A Woman' brought the necessary light-hearted relief.

Bee Gees classics like 'New York Mining Disaster 1941', 'I Can't See Nobody', 'Lonely Days', 'Nights On Broadway' and 'How Can You Mend A Broken Heart' mingled with songs written for other artists, such as 'Heartbreaker' and 'Guilty'.

Celine Dion returned the favour that The Bee Gees had paid her at her Florida concert by joining them for a heartfelt 'Immortality'. 'Tragedy' got the crowd back on their feet, before another abrupt change of mood with 'I Started A Joke'.

It was then time for another duet. 'Grease' alternated Frankie Valli's taped vocal with The Bee Gees. In the audience, the film's star, Olivia Newton-John, laughingly covered her daughter Chloe's eyes as footage of her from the now 20-year-old film flashed on the screen behind the group.

'Jive Talkin' ', 'How Deep Is Your Love' and 'Stayin' Alive' followed, with the evening coming full circle to end as it began with 'You Should Be Dancing'. There could be no doubt that The Bee Gees were back.

The initial Pay-Per-View broadcast on New Year's Eve, 1997, achieved top ratings, as did the edited version which made its début on HBO on February 14, 1998, and in Britain on BBC One on May 31, 1998.

The success of that single concert became the impetus for a series of *One Night Only* concerts that would take The Bee Gees around the world. "We wanted to do something a little special," Maurice explained, "and . . . rather than do a back to back city tour, this was the sort of idea we came up with."

"This way they will be more of an event," Robin added.

"I'd like for us to continue the road we're on and hope that that happens," Barry mused. "I really love doing the gigs. The isolated stage show here and there is where the fun is for me . . . We're actually in our prime, believe it or not. I think vocally and mentally, we've managed to stay intact, somehow. We're very strong. Two of us don't smoke at all. Maurice still smokes, but Robin and I stopped years back. I think that's made an enormous difference to the strength of our throats and our muscles. So we've maintained our voices. I'm the eldest at 51, and I think if the Stones can drag themselves around the country one more time . . . As long as you're having fun, that's the key. It's got to be fun. The moment it becomes a grind, it's over."

★   ★   ★

On Christmas Day, listeners to Manx Radio in The Bee Gees' birthplace, the Isle of Man, were treated to a radio special, *The Bee Gees Come Home To Ellan Vannin*. Disc jockey Bernie Quayle spoke with Barry, Robin, Maurice and Barbara Gibb about their memories of life on the island, as well as The Bee Gees' career. Knowing that they had once recorded a demo of 'Ellan Vannin', the "unofficial national anthem" of the Isle of Man based on Eliza Craven Green's original poem printed in the newspaper *The Manx Sun* on July 22, 1854 and later set to music, Quayle asked the brothers if they would record a new version of the song in aid of Manx Children In Need.

The Bee Gees immediately replied in the affirmative. "When it comes to children, there's no argument," Maurice explained. "Being parents our-selves, we've been very blessed with our kids. We just don't take it for granted, and there's a lot of children out there that need a lot of help, and as I say, when it comes to children, there's nothing too great."

The result was a CD single in a limited edition of only 1,000 copies, featuring Robin's distinctive voice against a Celtic background of Maurice's synthesized bagpipes and James Kelly's fiddle. The brothers slightly altered the lyrics to the original song. They signed 10 copies of the CD, which were auctioned on the Internet for The Lion's Club annual Dial-A-Lion Appeal, raising £15,000 for the children's charity.

Maurice phoned in to Manx radio to tell listeners about the recording of the track. "Oh, I tell you something, it was wonderful doing it," he exclaimed. "It was such a proud moment for us. I'm playing the pipes on it as well. We wanted to do something that was very patriotic; we wanted to do something that was warm, well, *heart-warming*; something that would be really pleasant to listen to, and the melody of 'Ellan Vannin' is so gorgeous, so we had to do it in the original way that we visualised it. That's what we wanted to do, we just wanted to give it a beautiful, wonderful, Isle of Man touch, whatever.

"Doing this particular track brought us very close to home again, and it brought back a lot of memories. It was just a wonderful thing to do, especially for the kids. Believe you me, it was wonderful to do something for home."

Plans were also announced to create a Bee Gees museum on the island; a project which is still in development.

On January 31, 1998, The Bee Gees joined Yvonne Elliman, KC & The Sunshine Band, Tavares, Kool & The Gang and The Tramps for a special *Saturday Night Fever* Reunion Concert at Madison Square Garden in New York. An earlier outdoor Reunion Concert had been planned by radio station WKTU for the previous November 1 but had been cancelled due to rain. Not limiting themselves strictly to their *Fever* hits, The Bee Gees performed 'Night Fever', 'More Than A Woman', 'I've Gotta Get A Message To You', 'To Love Somebody', 'Jive Talkin'', 'How Deep Is Your Love', 'Stayin' Alive' and 'You Should Be Dancing'. They received the same enthusiastic response as they had in Las Vegas. It was still a bit mystifying to the group.

"For about 15 years, we had some kind of leprosy," Barry mused. "There was many a single, many a record which we put out in the last 15 years that the radio stations wouldn't even *listen to*, never mind *play*. I don't know, but where I'm sitting it exists and has existed, and now I think the veil is falling slowly because of this new obsession with the Seventies. So suddenly The Bee Gees are not so bad after all and I'm bewildered again. Now it's okay to like us. 'Stayin' Alive' has been in fifteen movies since *Saturday Night Fever* so, for a song that was so shunned or from an album title that was so shunned, why is it that everybody wants it?"

That same shunned title drew standing room only crowds when *Saturday Night Fever*, the stage show, opened at the London Palladium on March 5. A standing ovation greeted the Gibbs as they arrived with their wives for the premiere. Robert Stigwood arrived with the Duchess of York, Sarah Ferguson, who told reporters, "I have seen the film and really enjoyed it. Now I am really looking forward to the stage show."

Benny Anderson and Bjorn Ulvaeus, the former Abba music men, were also on hand. "This is not just a swing in fashion," Ulvaeus insisted. "These are classic pop songs. Lennon and McCartney and The Bee Gees are the best and most consistent songrwriters. I am green with envy."

Five hundred tickets and other donations raised £50,000 for Childline that evening. With £4 million advance bookings, producer Paul Nicholas could easily afford to gloat, "The Seventies are alive and kicking. We brought *Grease* successfully to the stage, and we have done it again with *Saturday Night Fever*."

After the performance, Maurice raved, "Adam [Garcia] was fantastic! What energy! He is a great dancer."

Barry agreed, "He looks like Travolta and moves like Travolta. He is one of the best dancers I have ever seen. You cannot take your eyes off him."

The original cast recording, featuring Adam Garcia in the role of Tony Manero, with Anita Louise Combe, Simon Greiff, Sebastian Torkia, Michael Rouse, Tara Wilkinson and Adrian Sarple, was released later in the year, with Adam Garcia's version of 'Immortality' and Simon Greiff's 'First And Last/Tragedy' of special interest.

A new tribute album entitled *We Love The Bee Gees*, a collection of new cover versions done mainly in hip-hop, rap and techno styles was released in Germany in December 1997 and in Australia in February 1998 with a slightly different track listing. Take That, Boyzone, N-Trance, 'N Sync, Nana, C-Block, Masterboy and Vivid were among the artists included on the album.

In another tribute, 13 of the biggest names in pop music all recorded Bee Gees' songs in aid of Live Challenge 99 to raise money for homeless young people. The songs were included in a Bee Gees Tribute Album entitled *Gotta Get A Message To You*. Boy band 911 had a smash hit with their version of the *Fever* classic 'More Than A Woman'. 911's lead singer Jimmy raved, "Maybe because the bands on the tribute album are from a younger generation, we don't have the preconceptions other people seem to have . . . Everyone I know thinks they are legends in music. The Bee Gees are brilliant songwriters, the best in the business. They've written so many different songs for so many different artists. 'Chain Reaction' for Diana Ross doesn't sound anything like 'Immortality', their duet with Celine Dion. Actually, I shouldn't be saying this, but we're in talks with them about co-writing a song if we can ever get our schedules to match."

UK teen idols Steps topped the charts in Britain and Australia with their version of the 1979 hit, 'Tragedy'. Boyzone, who had had their first number one with their version of 'Words' in 1996, said they "were more than happy" to record an updated 'Words '98' for the tribute. Ultra Naté,

Cleopatra, Adam Garcia, Space, Louise, Robbie Williams & The Orb, Monaco, Spikey T & Gwen Dickey, Dana International and The Lightning Seeds all recorded tracks.

In July, Celine Dion's version of 'Immortality' featuring The Bee Gees on backing vocals was eventually released as a single in most of the world, although notably not in the US. It was a number five hit in Britain and reached number eight in Australia.

Barry also lent backing vocals to 'Do I Love You' on Paul Anka's *A Body Of Work*, the English language version of his 1996 South American album.

★　★　★

On August 28, The Bee Gees played the first of four sold-out stadium concerts in 1998. Brian Kennedy opened the show at RDS Stadium in Dublin, before The Bee Gees took to the stage before a crowd of 39,000. Tim Cansfield had replaced Stephen Gibb in the line-up this time around, and on this occasion, Boyzone heart-throb Ronan Keating joined the group for 'Words'.

The concert was also memorable from a fan perspective as the first live performance of 'Ellan Vannin' — and as the first sighting of Robin's new hair. Instead of adopting his twin's solution of covering his balding pate with an ever-present hat, the brother whose hair style had gone through the most transitions through the years had augmented his thinning locks with a toupee.

On September 5, Australian Tina Arena was the support act, when The Bee Gees appeared before an audience of 55,000 at Wembley Stadium in London.

Two days later, the *One Night Only* live album and video recorded at their Las Vegas concert were released.

On September 13, *An Audience With The Bee Gees* television special was taped in London for broadcast on November 7. Boyzone joined the group for a special performance of 'Words'.

"It's a real honour actually to have anyone, especially . . . the younger artists that are doing the songs because it was written [30] years ago," Maurice enthused. "So when Boyzone did it, we were blown away because it was just a lovely version. It's the first time we'd actually heard it fresh again and also be successful. I think for any songwriters, it's a wonderful, wonderful feeling."

Former Rolling Stone Bill Wyman, *Saturday Night Fever*'s Adam Garcia and soap star Patsy Palmer were among those in the celebrity audience, asking questions of the group. Clive Anderson and Angus Deayton notably declined invitations to appear.

In October, Stephen Gibb's absence from the shows was explained, when a "family friend" chose to speak to the press. A relapse into heroin use had placed him first in a Missouri rehabilitation centre, and then in a halfway house drugs centre in Miami.

"He'll be in the halfway house for the next month or so and we're all hoping that will be the end of it," said the friend. "Barry is nervously optimistic. But after what happened to his kid brother Andy, it's fair to say he is going through a personal nightmare. Don't forget Andy went to clinics – and he told Barry a million times he'd kicked drugs. But he never did. We hope this terrible business has been nipped in the bud. Stephen has faced up to things like a man."

In covering the story, the *Mirror* showed little compassion and even less concern for the truth when they added, "In 1988, [Andy] was found dead in a rundown Miami motel room after suffering a heart attack during a marathon cocaine and drink session" – a statement in which only the year of Andy's death was correct.

October 1998 saw the release of two long-awaited collections from The Bee Gees' Australian days from Festival Records. The first was a 63-track two CD set called *Brilliant From Birth*, which was a confusingly similar title to their previous collection in 1978 of early Bee Gees' recordings called *Birth Of Brilliance*. This 1998 version is the definitive collection of The Bee Gees' Australian years which, as well as containing the fairly easy to obtain 35 recordings, also included another 20 less common demos and four previously unreleased songs. The four unreleased tracks are recordings made by The Bee Gees at Festival Records' studios in 1964 to provide backing tapes for the Australian television show *Sing, Sing,* and were never intended for release on record. 'Can't You See That She's Mine' was a big hit for the Dave Clark 5 and it's clear that the very young Bee Gees had a lot of fun with this one. Perhaps the highlight of the compilation is the sound of the Gibbs' harmonies on their cover of The Beatles' 'From Me To You' – Barry's voice is just that little bit deeper than that of his younger brothers at this point. 'Yesterday's Gone' had been a big hit for English duo Chad & Jeremy in the mid-Sixties, and The Bee Gees' own version doesn't stray far from the arrangement of the original. The fourth song was their near identical rendition of The Hollies' 'Just One Look'. It's no surprise that the harmonies of both groups are so similar because both were brought up in Manchester.

The sound quality on the collection was excellent as Festival Records had gone to considerable expense, having the sound of each recording restored at Australia's National Film and Sound Archives in Canberra. Great care had obviously been taken to authenticate the information in the CD's booklet, but a couple of mistakes slipped through the net in the songwriting credits section. 'You're The Reason' by Edwards, Henley and Fell is a different song from Bobby Darrin's 'You're The Reason I'm Living', which is the one sung here. Also, it was Payne & Carroll who wrote 'Just One Look' and not Hicks & Clarke, while a revision is needed for 'The End' where Jacobsen & Krondes are the correct writers. Otherwise, Warren Fahey's team can be well pleased with their efforts.

The other Festival records release that month was titled *Assault The Vaults – Rare Australian Cover Versions Of The Brothers Gibb*. The set contained 31 recording of songs written by the Gibb brothers for other Australian artists from 1963 to 1966 and never released by The Bee Gees themselves. It was the first time that most of these recordings, now very rare and very expensive in their original vinyl, had appeared on album format let alone CD. Members of The Bee Gees appear on many of the tracks as back-up singers or musicians. What was particularly unique about this release was that it resulted from two Australian fans approaching a somewhat sceptical record company of the commercial viability of such a collection. At times acting almost as surrogate Bee Gees themselves, the two fans, Mark Crohan and Mark Byfield, argued successfully with the record company to protect the authenticity of the collection. Rather than use a new photo of the Gibbs they recommended a 1965 photo of the brothers to reflect the period the songs were written. They also successfully pushed for the use of the term "Brothers Gibb" in lieu of the more familiar and more commercial "Bee Gees" to reflect that this was no mere collection of covers of well-known Bee Gees songs. Festival Record's support of the project was rewarded when it sold well on its release – well enough that plans are well on the way for a second volume of these rare recordings.

On October 17, The Bee Gees played the first South American concert of their career at Boca Junior Stadium in Buenos Aires before a crowd of 42,000. The support act for the evening was a blues band, Memphis La Blusera.

On November 28, it was *One Night Only* at Loftus Versveld Stadium at Pretoria, South Africa. The Bee Gees added 'First Of May' and 'Melody Fair' to the set list for the show, which was broadcast live into 2,200 Walmart stores across the United States.

On January 23, 1999, Barry performed a concert of Frank Sinatra classics with The Peter Graves Orchestra, as a charity fund-raiser for the Diabetes Research Institute's Love & Hope Silver Anniversary Ball at the Fontainbleu Hilton Hotel in Miami. The Andy Gibb Memorial Foundation sponsored the orchestra for the event, the realisation of a long time dream for Barry.

On March 20, The Bee Gees took their *One Night Only* show to New Zealand. The concert at Western Springs Stadium in Auckland was their first in New Zealand since 1974. At a press conference the day before the show, Maurice declared, "It's too long since we've been to New Zealand. We've wanted to come back." The brothers were presented with Auckland Blues rugby shirts with their names on, which they wore during their encore at the concert before 61,000. They were also presented with multi-platinum discs for the New Zealand sales of the *One Night Only* CD, the biggest selling album in the country for 1998, which made another journey to the top of the charts during the week of the show.

A week later, The Bee Gees made a triumphant return to Australia for the first concert at the new Stadium Australia, the new Olympic stadium, where they played to a crowd of 70,000. The support act for the show was Wendy Matthews. The promoter for the Australian leg of the tour was their long term friend, Kevin Jacobsen, but there was a more familiar face joining The Bee Gees on stage. Vince Melouney, still playing the pub circuit around Australia as a solo performer, joined his old band-mates to play guitar on 'Massachusetts', 'To Love Somebody' and 'I've Gotta Get A Message To You'.

"Things are going great for me," Vince maintained. "I'm enjoying what I'm doing, and it's getting better all the time. It hasn't always been easy. Sometimes I felt I could have been as big as Paul McCartney and nobody wanted to book me. The only thing I regret is the time I spent running around partying and having a great time overseas when I could have been doing something musically. We hold no bad feelings towards each other, and I still keep in touch with the band and with Colin. It [was] tremendous to catch up with them again."

Another old friend, David Trew, joined them in Sydney for the *One Night Only* concert; this time not as a promoter but as their guest. He was in ill health by this time, suffering the ravages of cancer, but was treated as a member of the family by the Gibbs, staying with them at their hotel for the duration of the tour. Tragically, Trew would die a few months after the concert, not yet 50 years of age.

In April, 2000, VH1 released *Storytellers*, a CD compilation of tracks from their popular television series, to benefit City of Hope, a research and treatment centre for cancer and other deadly diseases. The Bee Gees dedicated 'How Deep Is Your Love' to their late friend, David Trew.

As was almost traditional for Bee Gees' tours in Australia, the concert was filmed and on this occasion shown live across the country. The evening before the concert, the *Audience with The Bee Gees* special was also broadcast in Australia, and the *Keppel Road* special was also repeated on television, all to good ratings.

Such was The Bee Gees "fever" in Sydney in March 1999 that the New South Wales Premier Bob Carr, in the midst of an election, made a surprise visit to The Bee Gees' press conference, formally welcoming them back to Australia and reminding them that one of the old homes in Maroubra was in his electorate.

Buoyed by the success of the Australian tour, the *One Night Only* CD was re-released in that country as a 'Special Limited Tour Edition', with a bonus CD of the six additional live tracks from their 1997 MGM concert not included on the original live album. It immediately shot to the number one position in the album charts, where it stayed for six consecutive weeks. It was The Bee Gees' first number one album in Australia since 1979.

In October, the Isle of Man Post Office issued a series of stamps to commemorate The Bee Gees' contribution to music. Since no living person outside the royal family can be depicted on stamps, each stamp featured a different Bee Gees song. The Gibb brothers' birthplace had long been considering honouring its famous sons in this way — indeed, the idea had first been proposed as far back as April 1985 — and the issue of the stamps had to be approved by the Queen. A special, limited edition set of the 'Ellan Vannin' CD with the stamps included in the CD insert booklet was also issued.

"Barry, Robin and Maurice are most enthusiastic to be honoured in this manner by the nation of their birth," said Dick Ashby. "They consider this to be a milestone achievement."

Representatives for the Isle of Man Post Office, Dot Tilbury and Janet Bridge, presented Barry, Robin and Maurice Gibb with the stamps in New York on October 21. Maurice enthused, "We are just tickled by this entire tribute. These stamps really span our careers through the decades and cover a lot of ground. I know our fans will be very pleased with them."

Robin commented, "The best thing about these stamps is that they have a deep connection to us because they have been issued by the country where we were born. Our mum once worked there as a postal official many years ago, so I guess these stamps bring everything full circle. The stamps are really colourful and turned out even better than we could have expected."

"We are proud of this unique accomplishment," Barry added. "We have a special fondness for the Isle of Man, and we look forward to perhaps a visit there next year. Maybe I'll even send a few postcards with our stamps on them to some of our friends just to prove that they are real."

After the stamps presentation, it was off to the Minskoff Theater for the opening night of the *Saturday Night Fever* stage show's Broadway run. There was a strong sense of déjà vu. Just as they had at the London premiere, The Bee Gees received a standing ovation when they entered the theatre. John Travolta was also on hand, as was Robert Stigwood, again with the Duchess of York, who apparently enjoyed the London premiere.

Once again produced by Robert Stigwood and Paul Nicholas and choreographed by Arlene Phillips, the Broadway production starred James Carpinello and Paige Price as Tony and Stephanie.

Stigwood had taken a hands-on approach to setting up the move to Broadway, checking out three theatres before settling on the Minskoff, and sitting in on the final auditions for the five major roles.

In November, the latest Bee Gees composition, 'I Will Be There', was released on Tina Turner's album, *Twenty-Four Seven*. 'End Of Time', a track originally written for Bette Midler, was earmarked for recording by Tina Arena, and The Backstreet Boys, Deana Carter and Lara Fabian were all rumoured to be recording new Gibb compositions.

Recording sessions for The Bee Gees themselves were moving along at a snail's pace. Although the brothers had begun writing new songs for their next album as far back as February, 1998, nearly two years on, the proposed release date for the album was being pushed further into the future. Even the album's working title, *Technicolour Dream*, had run into problems when their management was informed that Technicolour was a registered trademark.

Whilst the new album had not seen light of day by the close of the Nineties, it had nonetheless been an impressive decade of releases for The

Bee Gees. Since 1990, fans had been witness to a whole array of recordings including a four CD box set, three studio albums, one *Best Of* album, a two CD collection of their Australian recordings, a live album, a soundtrack album, no less than five tribute CDs, three videos, one DVD and numerous singles.

At a press conference before their Sydney concert, Barry had mentioned The Bee Gees' hope to return to Australia for a New Year's Eve concert. "It's New Year here before it's New Year anywhere else, so it would be great to come home and do that," he said.

"So we'll be at Balmain Leagues Club," quipped Maurice, "and we might get to play South Sydney Juniors."

But New Year's Eve, 1999, found them celebrating in their other adopted home with a concert at the National Car Rental Center auditorium in Sunrise, Florida. Devoted fans from around the world paid up to $600 a seat for the event, and indeed, the $600 tickets even entitled them to keep their folding chair, emblazoned with BG2K, the date and the venue. Coupons for free champagne after the show were taped to each seat.

Although debates continue as to whether it was this New Year or the next which marked the new Millennium, the faithful who assembled to see The Bee Gees weren't concerned. As a nod to the importance of the occasion, the group added their 1967 song, 'Turn Of The Century' to their acoustic medley.

Just after Barry, Robin and Maurice left the stage, it turned midnight. The giant screens on stage showed Times Square in New York, and the audience counted down as the large ball dropped on screen. The band played 'Auld Lang Syne' as the arena was showered with balloons, confetti and silver and white streamers which fell from the ceiling as people kissed in celebration.

The Brothers Gibb rejoined the rest of their band on stage for an encore of 'You Should Be Dancing'. Years earlier, Barry had said, "We believe that on New Year's Eve 2000, people will still be dancing to *Saturday Night Fever*." Twelve thousand fans in Sunrise, Florida, proved him right.

41

THE NEXT GENERATION

"OUR FAMILIES AND our kids [are] the fundamental basis of everything else we do," Barry declared. "That's our anchor, that's what keeps our feet on the ground, that's what keeps our egos in check, 'cause our kids don't see us as pop artists or a pop group. They see us as dad, and it's just totally different. It's not like you would expect it to be. Home is just home."

When asked in 1997 if any of the Gibb children showed any signs of following their famous fathers into the pop business, he replied, "They're all musical. But it took more than being musical for us – you had to be passionate and hungry. To be honest, I don't see that in any of our kids yet. We started this because we *had* to, we knew nothing else. They've got other choices. I just hope we're around to stop them making the same mistakes we made."

As the eldest of the Gibb offspring, it naturally follows that Robin's son Spencer (born 1972) was the first to get involved with music, as a guitarist and songwriter, when he was growing up in Surrey. "I've been a musician since I was about 15," he explained. "I played in a bunch of different bands when I lived in England and was a solo artist for a long time."

He got his first real taste of the music business when Robin took him along for The Bee Gees' 1989 *One For All* tour.

Although it may seem strange to some, Spencer claims that it was his mother, Molly, who most influenced his musical tendencies by playing her favourite music around the house. "That's what rubs off, totally," he said. "My mum, even more than my dad, was such a music fan, and I was turned on to so much music that hardly anyone in my generation has heard. She is just heavily into all kinds of stuff, especially a lot of Stax and Motown stuff. There was some Beatles and some other English music, but really mostly Stax and Motown. I grew up listening to Otis Redding and all that stuff . . . A lot of people our age aren't that familiar with it. I think that's sad."

By 1994, Spencer had relocated to Miami where he formed a band called Spencer, which played around local clubs. That year he registered a US copyright on a tape of 10 songs, possibly a demo for an album which was never released. 'Days Like These', 'Amber', 'Competition', 'Falling', 'Crazy Old World', 'Talk To My Angel', 'What Have You Done?', 'Sad And Blue', 'Miami Blues' and 'Water Into Wine' were all written by Spencer Gibb. The following year, he would add 'Seeing Blue', 'Hoping It Won't

Be Long' and 'Let Me Down Easy' to the list.

Disillusioned after a few years of the Florida club scene, he decided it was time for another move, this time to Austin, Texas. "It sounds really cheesy . . . but I moved to Austin because I had a dream that I moved here," Spencer revealed. Shortly after he arrived, he met up with J.J. Johnson, one of the city's most respected drummers, whose work as a session musician features on a host of recordings.

"J.J. and I played together for awhile [as Jez Spencer] and decided starting a band was the only way to go," said Spencer. After auditioning a number of musicians, the pair decided that they really wanted band members who could contribute as equals rather than backing players. Keyboard wizard Stewart Cochran was next on board, and Glenn McGregor on bass followed shortly after. Like Johnson, Cochran and McGregor were veterans of the Austin music scene. All four members write the band's music, although Cochran added, "Spencer handles most of the lyrics 'cause he's the only one who can spell."

All they needed was a name, and that came courtesy of a remark made by the band's first manager. "He thought the hooks came too late in our songs," Spencer explained. " 'In the perfect pop song, the chorus comes in at 54 seconds,' he told us. We didn't agree, but after we fired him, we had ourselves a name." 54 Seconds it was.

In 1997, 54 Seconds made their début at the South By Southwest (SXSW) Music Conference in Austin. The band became favourites of the local club scene, attracting the interest of several record labels, although at the time of writing, they remained unsigned. "I don't want to appear bitter or cynical, but I'm definitely a realist," Spencer declared. "It's like, these days, you're at someone else's mercy. It wasn't engineered to be that way. It wasn't always that way."

In the meantime, they have independently recorded a nine-song CD entitled *ep*, produced by the band with Dave McNair, and a live album is in the works. The group play a weekly Monday night gig at Austin's Speakeasy, in which Stewart Cochran jokes that clubbers can expect, "Spencer will say 'How're y'all doing?' but his 'y'all' never sounds authentic!"

Bee Gees' fans expecting a carbon copy of Robin Gibb may be surprised. Despite Spencer's strong physical resemblance to his father and the vibrato in his vocals, his style is very much his own. 54 Seconds' music has been described as "psychedelic yet melancholic, ambient, enigmatic, lyrical, moody ethereal, pneumatic pop with elements of trance, funk and world music".

Spencer tries to downplay the importance of having such a celebrated father. "If my father were a famous welder, nobody would care," he said.

Robin's daughter, Melissa (born 1974), has remained in England, and perhaps because they don't see each other on a daily basis, Robin said, "We've had friendship rather than father/child conflict . . . We have little rows, not huge arguments. It's usually about what Melissa's going to do with her life."

Robin admitted that when she was a teenager, he worried because she wanted "to leave home without a proper job" or that she might become involved with drugs. "I do have rules," he said. "I don't allow Melissa to drink or smoke in my presence. I say that if I don't need to, she doesn't."

Melissa is quick to allay her father's fears. "I don't smoke or take drugs," she said. "I like to be healthy and clean, the way I was brought up. I respect both my parents very much. I think there is a mutual trust."

She admitted that she went through a rebellious stage in her early teens, when she hated the girls' public school she attended. She left that school and began college at 16.

Although Melissa has shown no interest in a musical career, she is creative in other ways, concentrating on her artwork and writing. She enjoys foreign travel, as well as languages – she speaks Arabic, French and Italian. She has also helped her stepmother, Dwina, with research for one of her books.

Until recently, Robin and Dwina's son, Robin John (born 1983), seemed to be more interested in sport than music, even though he began violin, trumpet and piano lessons at a very early age, winning an award from the National Guild of Piano Playing. As goalie for his ice hockey team, he played at the President's Day Hockey Tournament at a junior rematch of the Stanley Cup Playoff. Lately, he has hung up his ice skates – at least part time – to consider a career as a rapper with the group Hi Rollaz. RJ writes the group's songs, which they have been recording at Middle Ear, and one of his rap lyrics, 'Golden Age', shows remarkable promise.

★　★　★

In 1997, Maurice commented, "My daughter loves singing, she loves writing. She's phenomenal. And my son, he's got the same interests, he just wants to play. She's got a great voice, they both write well together, and I am doing some demos with them right now actually. So they're coming along real good."

Samantha (born 1980) had begun to show an interest in music early on, as a talented pianist and singer. In June, 1994, she and her actress friend Majandra Delfino began performing as The China Dolls. On January 20, 1995, the duo performed at the Love & Hope Ball benefit for the Diabetes Research Institute in Miami.

The following December, Maurice and John Merchant produced demos for the two girls at Middle Ear Studio. Samantha and Majandra recorded a Barry, Robin and Maurice Gibb composition, 'Angel Of Mercy', and the Lennon and McCartney classic, 'Here, There And Everywhere'. Samantha also sang lead on 'Without You', a song written and recorded by her brother Adam (born 1976) and his college friend Fred. Majandra has since gone on to earn a starring role in the hit US TV show *Roswell*.

Adam studied the business side of the music industry at the University of Miami, but in early 1998, he opted for the performing side.

"My son loves publishing," Maurice explained, "and he loves the management, the industry side . . . and yet he can programme, he can work board and produce and stuff like that if he wants to. If he puts his mind to it, he probably could, 'cause he's got a great ear. But whatever he wants to do, I'll help him . . . I'm not going to push him into something he doesn't want to do, or my daughter, because [I want them to] have a happy and healthy life doing what they love to do.

"There's that lovely expression: 'We are but bows and they're arrows and they fly into the air and wherever they land, good luck!' They're going to fly away soon, so you can imagine what it's like for me right now," he added.

Adam and Samantha, along with her boyfriend Lazaro Rodriguez, formed Luna Park. The trio composed 'Until You' and 'How Was I To Know', and Adam and Samantha also wrote 'Hummingbird Love' with Sarah Henderson. With Samantha on lead vocals, Adam handling keyboards and backing vocals, and Laz on guitar, Luna Park recorded a demo album produced by Maurice and John Merchant, and are looking for a record label as of writing.

★   ★   ★

Barry's eldest son, Stephen (born 1973), also turned to music at around age 15. His first instrument had been piano, but he changed when he decided that playing guitar "looked cooler". In 1989, Stephen and some school friends formed a band which they called NNY – for No Name Yet – and in February, they appeared at Woody's, a Miami club owned by Rolling Stone Ron Wood. The band would later change their name to ZEX. Later that year, Stephen picked up extra pocket money when he worked as a guitar technician on The Bee Gees' *One For All* tour.

By 1991, he was a student at a Miami music school, where he studied for about a year. He had also begun writing. 'Whiskey Jam' was the name of his first solo effort, and he soon added 'Shadows Of Your Dreams' with Emerson Forth and Deniz Kose, and 'Hole In My Soul', written with Deniz, to his list. The following year, he collaborated with Middle Ear engineer Scott Glasel and Scott's girlfriend Amanda Green on 'Ren And Stevie', a title that refers to the Gibb family's dog, Ren, and to the *Ren & Stimpy* cartoon series.

In 1992, a long-haired and heavily tattooed Stephen Gibb had joined a heavy metal band called Skillet Head, which performed on the Miami club circuit. He continued to play gigs in the Miami area and made occasional appearances as a guitarist backing The Bee Gees.

In February, 1997, he joined The Underbellys, a five man hard rock band based in Miami, and recorded demos with them for Columbia Records. After his appearance with The Bee Gees at their *One Night Only* concert in Las Vegas, he reportedly toured with The Smithereens in early 1998, before drug problems intervened.

Stephen had originally been scheduled to tour with Stevie Nicks, but the proposed tour was cancelled. Instead, towards the end of 1999, he joined Mötley Crüe bassist Nikki Sixx's side project 58, along with David Darling of Boxing Ghandis and drummer Bucket Baker, who previously toured with Boz Scaggs and Kenny Loggins. Sixx teamed up with Beyond Music CEO Allen Kovac to create what he described as a "pro-artist" label, Americoma Records. 58's début album, *Diet For A New America*, has been described as "rock oriented, but with a twist . . . a sort of cross between David Bowie's *Diamond Dogs* era and a little bit of Nine Inch Nails vibe."

At the time of writing, Stephen was set to tour Japan with Zakk Wylde, Ozzy Osbourne's former guitarist. Wylde's band (including Stephen) were also the scheduled support for Mötley Crüe's American tour on their return.

Barry's second son, Ashley (born 1977), proposed to his girlfriend, Therese, just before midnight at The Bee Gees' Millennium New Year's Eve concert, and the couple plan to be married in England on July 21, 2001.

Ashley showed great promise as a tennis player and considered making it his career, when a problem with his ankle convinced him to give it up, although he still does the odd bit of coaching. After a brief stint in California with hopes of going into acting, Ashley returned to Miami and entered the family business behind the scenes, as an intern engineer at Middle Ear Studios. One of his first projects was as assistant engineer for Ronan Keating's 1999 collaboration with The Bee Gees', 'Lovers And Friends'.

Although he seems to be blossoming a little later than other Gibb offspring in music, Ashley recently had a taste of the spotlight when he went on stage in Miami to sing with the resident band, performing 'How Deep Is Your Love'. Those who heard him were favourably impressed by the effort.

Barry's third son, Travis (born 1981) is an avid reader and sports enthusiast who graduated from high school in June, 1999. He plays keyboards and has formed a group with some of his friends, but at the moment, music is more a pastime than a career choice. A student at the Johnson and Wales University in Miami, Travis is studying catering and hotel management with the intention of one day running his own restaurant or nightclub.

Michael (born 1984) is also keen on sports and, along with Ashley, attended the Bollettieri Academy in Bradenton, Florida, the tennis camp run by famed tennis coach Nick Bollettieri, who counts Andre Aggassi among his successful students. Michael attends high school in Miami.

The baby of the family, little Alexandra (born 1991), has already appeared in several school plays. She seems to have inherited the musical genes as well. Ali plays piano and loves to sing, and her doting family say she has a very good voice, so she may also be destined for the family business.

Although many of The Bee Gees' offspring are now involved in the music business, the brothers reiterate that none of them need to follow in their fathers' footsteps. "They all have great ambitions," Maurice concluded proudly, "and if we can be there to support them, and always be there for them if anything happens, that's all that we can give them. I know that whatever they do, they'll be good at it."

42

TURN OF THE CENTURY

A T THE DAWN of the new Millennium, The Bee Gees endure. "I think the most amazing thing, what still overwhelms us," Barry marvelled, "is that our music still gets played today. I mean, when you go back that far, and you realise that these songs are still being played, that's a stunning factor to us, you know."

The unwieldy illuminated Bee Gees' logo designed for their 1979 *Spirits Having Flown* tour had been brought out for the New Year's Eve concert after more than 20 years in storage cases. However, following the show, it was packed away once more, probably for the final time.

Although Barry, at age 54, and twins Robin and Maurice, at age 50, no longer choose to pursue the frenetic pace that defined their career in the late Sixties and Seventies, the suggestion of leaving the music business behind is still an anathema to them. So what does drive them to continue to write new songs – not only for themselves but also for other artists – to make albums, and to stage the occasional major concert event?

"It's something we've been doing since we were kids, and we just keep on wanting to do it," Maurice explained. "It's also our hobby and our love. There is no other life for us. We're really just three brothers . . . who love to write, to sing in front of an audience. It's never been the money. We just wanted to be famous."

"We've just got to keep on doing what we do because we love it," Robin agreed. "We enjoy doing what we do. There's no cut-off moment. We just feel that as long as we feel that we've got something good to contribute, and we enjoy what we're doing, then we'll keep on doing it. It's like painting, you just have to do what you do.

"I see no reason to retire when I'm 65," he continued. "Picasso didn't stop painting then, did he? Maybe someone will have to carry the colostomy bag onto the stage, but asking me about retirement is like asking me about death!"

Whilst Robin can still be relied upon to provide the trademark poignant quips that must make his public relations people cringe, Barry can usually be trusted to give the carefully considered response of the responsible eldest brother. "First of all," he maintained, "you gotta care about each other and we really do. We are brothers and we love making music. That's infectious

654

and extremely addictive for us. It's the best drug in the world, and we can't stay away from it. So whether something really works for us or not, we have to keep making music that's instinctive and we love it."

The fraternal link may be the all important key. None of the brothers would deny that they have had – and will continue to have – their disagreements. No family is completely without conflict and discord; most grow apart as they grow older. Few brothers spend more than four decades working together, as The Bee Gees have done; fewer still all live minutes apart, as the Gibbs do in Miami Beach.

"Barry lives next door but one," Robin said, "and Maurice lives [nearby]. In England our houses are 50 miles apart. We have our own independent lives and our own circle of friends. We get on very well but we work so much together that you need your own space for your own lives . . . spending so much time together you need that space."

"It's been fun and friction," Barry admitted. "We've developed tough skins . . . Now we don't get hurt anymore and we don't hurt each other. If we hadn't been brothers, we would have split up. But if you're brothers, it's a dream you've shared right from the beginning of your childhood.

"All along the way, we've always been reminded by experts that our music is now 'out' and it can no longer apply to what's going on today, so we're sort of used to it. We're used to the idea of having failures as well as successes, but the up and down process is much more helter-skelter than others might see it, and it's much more emotional and traumatic to us. We've gotten pretty hungry from it and pretty persistent because of it, pretty determined, and very close. As much as we get laughed at here and there, or we get told we're 'out' here or there, we just continue on and keep our fingers crossed. As a family, we fight pretty hard now, and we're not about to give up what we do. We're not about to be rejected by anybody."

Despite the success they have achieved, all three brothers are reluctant to point to any particular composition as their masterpiece. "You don't know that the next piece of work that you do may be the best you ever did in your life," Barry explained. "It may be the most successful . . . We believe that there's work for us to do yet . . . and we're working towards that. We're working to become the best, not just becoming good."

A new generation of artists discovered The Bee Gees in the Nineties, and it seems likely that their musical influence will continue through the years. Boyzone heart-throb Ronan Keating is the most recent artist to work with the group. When he began work on his first solo album, he enlisted the assistance of the Gibb brothers. In August 1999, he travelled with his wife and their young son to Miami, where he visited Barry and Maurice while Robin was working in England with keyboard player, Peter John Vettesse.

"Working with Barry and Maurice was a hugely memorable experience," he said. "Meeting those guys inspires me to try to make music for the rest of my life. I hope in 25 years if I am still doing this I can just be like them."

Ronan collaborated with Barry and Maurice to write and produce a track

655

called 'Lovers And Friends', for possible inclusion on the album, on which all three brothers contributed backing vocals. "It's sounding great," he revealed. "They've helped out a lot and it's come together really well."

The Bee Gees' manager, Dick Ashby, was enthusiastic about the commercial appeal of 'Lovers And Friends'. "[It's] one of those songs that you hear and want to hear again," he declared. "It gets you, so you want to hear more, rather than it over gets you."

As a long time Bee Gees fan, Ronan was clearly delighted not only with the assistance he had received from his fellow Polydor stars, but also for the friendship which developed. "It was amazing, you know," he explained. "Barry and his family . . . took me and Yvonne and Jack in [and] made us feel one of the family. We had such a wonderful time in Miami, and Robin and Maurice, their family are fantastic. I feel like one of their sons, you know, it's really cool, just getting invited to parties and weddings. They are just special people."

So what does the future hold for The Bee Gees? At time of writing, their latest album is scheduled for a February 2001 release. While they hope it will be successful, topping the charts is not the most important thing to them.

"I've reached that point in my life when I feel liberated," Barry confessed. "At long last I'm not a teenager trying to make it. I'm not that person who was desperately changing everything about himself in order to have a hit record."

Maurice's laid-back attitude, which has long endeared him to audiences, has also come to the fore. "I used to look in the mirror and just see darkness," he said. "Now I look and see little cherubs with flowers flying around my head. Well, it's not quite like that, but I do know I'm one hell of a contented guy."

Maurice's new found repose has manifested itself in a song called 'The Bridge'. The song had some input from an emerging source. Adam and Samantha each contributed a verse in which they tell the story of how they've crossed "the bridge of tears" created by their father's drinking, but how they've now come out the other side.

Whether that track finds its way onto the new album remains to be seen. Originally due to be called *Technicolour Dreams*, after another of the new songs, copyright problems intervened. A new title, *This Is Where I Came In*, was adopted, and the song by that name is a strong possibility for the lead single.

Other working titles of songs which are currently being considered for inclusion on the album are 'She Keeps On Coming', 'Sacred Trust', 'Wedding Day', 'Promise The Earth', 'Sensuality', 'Angel Of Mercy', 'The Extra Mile' and 'Just In Case'. Those which do not make it onto the albums original release may well appear on the subsequent Japanese CD for which two bonus tracks are planned. The Bee Gees have also recorded 'I Will Be There', the song included on Tina Turner's *Twenty-Four Seven* album, which is likely to be a bonus track on the first CD single, while 'Angel Of Mercy' is tipped for inclusion on the follow-up.

The new album will showcase each brother's individual styles as never before. Working titles of Barry's contributions include 'Voice In The Wilderness' and 'Loose Talk Costs Lives', while Robin's numbers include 'Embrace' and 'Déjà Vu'. Maurice has added 'Walking On Air' and the aptly titled, 'Man In The Middle', a phrase he has often used to describe his role in the group.

The album's release was originally timed to coincide with plans for the group to perform a nine-minute medley featuring at least a one-minute segment of the lead single at the closing ceremony of the Olympics in Sydney, a performance which was expected to be seen by an audience of more than two billion people. However, at the time of writing their involvement seems unlikely after all.

In October, the Rock'n'Roll Hall Of Fame plan to open a special exhibit dedicated to teen idols throughout the years, and Andy Gibb will be featured along with such diverse artists as Frank Sinatra and Michael Jackson.

Left Bank Management continues to discuss television programming, with the possibility of a special for an American network, as well as a tribute programme for VH1, featuring guest artists performing Bee Gees' songs, with the brothers finishing off the show.

An offer was made for The Bee Gees to play a New Year's Eve concert in Hong Kong, but the brothers decided to decline the engagement.

June, 2001, may see them playing a few of the One Night Only-style concerts which marked the end of the Nineties. Germany, where The Bee Gees have always maintained its most ardent fan base, and Twickenham, England's national rugby stadium, are the probable locations for the events, after which they plan to return to the States.

An American concert, which is intended to include a full orchestral backing for the first time since 1974, is also in the planning stages. A television special which will take them back to their birthplace in the Isle of Man is still in the offing, with the possibility of the first ever Bee Gees' concert on the island. The site of the proposed concert is the Gaiety Theatre in Douglas. While negotiations continue, the timing for both events will probably be linked with a new *Greatest Hits* CD at the end of 2002.

Following its successful runs in London's West End and New York's Broadway, the *Saturday Night Fever* stage show is scheduled to open in late 2001 at the Lyric Theatre in Sydney. A British cast will also begin a national tour of the show in November.

Although through the years, they have suggested that The Bee Gees as a group couldn't go on past a certain point, the optimum quitting point seems to move further away with each passing year. Barry had once insisted that a pop group couldn't possibly go on when its members were past the age of 40, but by 1997, he predicted another five years for The Bee Gees, adding, "I'll be 55 – too old to be playing in a band. But now I can do another five years." In the long term, even as The Bee Gees' albums come fewer and farther between, it seems indisputable that the Brothers Gibb will continue as songwriters, producers and occasional performers. There will always be new goals to achieve, new records to make, new artists to work with, new dreams.

"The three of us are tremendously ambitious," Robin explained. "We have this same feeling about life, that we're here for a very short time, so it's important when you do what you do to cram as much of it and achieve as much as you can into that space . . . I don't understand people who say, 'I've done enough; I'm gonna sit back and relax.' It's beyond my comprehension. The three of us are driven, a feeling that will never let us stop. It's in our blood – I don't think we'll stop until we drop."

Barry revealed one ambition that has yet to be realised. "I think we'd like to have a really good song in a really good movie," he said. "I think that has never happened to The Bee Gees, apart from *Fever* and *Grease*, of course, but they were sort of novelty things in our minds. We've never had that serious shot at being nominated for an Academy Award for a song in a film, and I think that's one of our dreams . . . That would be wonderful."

Sharing in the dream is the often mentioned fourth Bee Gee, Dick Ashby, who continues to act as their personal manager. "We've grown up together and learned the music business together," Dick said. "I've seen them become adults, get married and have kids. I feel about this family, about their kids, as if they were my own.

"There's incredible work and external pressure . . . but I've been fortunate to have an open and honest relationship with Barry, Robin and Maurice. Because of our long, close relationship, there's a great deal of mutual respect."

★   ★   ★

As the eldest brother, Barry has long carried the additional burden of automatically being perceived as the leader and main spokesperson for the group. With that responsibility has come an extra drive, more than just from his obvious love of what he does.

The basic need for love and approval is the force which has driven many a performer. Barry Gibb has always had a burning desire that The Bee Gees should be accepted for what they are and should gain the recognition he feels that they deserve. When he first led his brothers onto that Gaumont stage on December 28, 1957, he dreamed of the day that they would become famous.

"We're on the same path today," he admitted. "We'd still like to be a famous pop group. Hopefully, we're going to make it. The dream is still there.

"What the end thing is, no one knows," he reflected, "[but my final goal is] to walk through the Golden Gates and have someone standing there saying, 'Liked ya!' "

APPENDIX I – A NICE LITTLE EARNER

WHILE ATTENTION IS often focused on those artists who have recorded songs especially written for them by the Brothers Gibb, these pale into insignificance compared with the number of performers who have covered material previously released by The Bee Gees themselves. Clearly, the vast majority of cover versions are of songs that have been previously recorded by The Bee Gees either as a group or in solo efforts.

The Bee Gees are one of the most prolific composing teams in the history of recorded music. Cover artists in almost every country in the world have recorded their compositions. The vast majority, however, have been released in the United States, Western Europe, Australia and New Zealand, Eastern Asia and Japan, Canada, and Southern Africa.

Artists have been recording Gibb songs for more than 35 years. They continue to do so today and, undoubtedly, will continue to do so in the future. Performers who have recorded Gibb songs range from the most famous singers in the world to obscure musicians who have never experienced any commercial success. Indeed, it would be fair to say that most of these cover artists are not well known. Many covers are released by budget labels who either create a generic artist name or don't even bother to identify the performer at all. For the most part, though, cover artists make serious attempts to do justice to Gibb songs.

Cover versions run the gamut in musical categories from pop to rock to rhythm & blues to disco to easy listening to country to reggae to rap to folk to jazz to semi-classical to soul to psychedelic to comedy to children's music to heavy metal to gospel to karaoke music. In most cases, cover artists closely follow the arrangement and style of the original Gibb versions, but there are countless examples of cover versions with very unique arrangements.

One good example was The Searchers' version of 'Spicks And Specks'. "We try and change songs to suit how we felt at the time," their lead guitarist, John McNally, explained. "We were playing heavier stuff on stage at that point, so we thought, let's give it a bit more beef, and we did so on that one. In fact, we played around with it quite a lot, because we didn't particularly like the song, so we ad-libbed a bit with it and tried to make it something it wasn't. A lot of people liked it; RCA liked it; they liked it that much they were thinking of putting it out as an A-side."

Many cover artists, if not so already, quickly become fans too as they come to appreciate the quality of the material they are recording. The Searchers were no exception. "I went to see The Bee Gees in '89 when they were doing Wembley Arena," McNally continued. "I was impressed with The Bee Gees that night – unbelievable. They did that acoustic thing in the middle – I thought it was brilliant! They were great that night, I really enjoyed them. I thought they were superb."

Praise indeed for their performance, but what about their compositions?

"Brilliant!" John enthused. "I think they've got to be the best songwriters after Lennon & McCartney. They've probably had more hits than Lennon & McCartney when you put them all down."

Songs are sung in many different languages although, as might be expected, English predominates. Approximately 85 per cent of cover versions are vocals, the remainder instrumentals.

Best known are the albums that the Gibbs have written and produced for Jimmy Ruffin, Barbra Streisand, Kenny Rogers, Dionne Warwick, Diana Ross and Carola. In addition, there have been dozens and dozens of "tribute" albums and maxi-singles. These involve various well-known, as well as obscure, cover artists who perform an entire record of Gibb songs without any Bee Gees production involvement. To date, 151 different albums and maxi-singles, either Gibb produced or "tributes", have been identified worldwide. New "tributes" are being released around the world continuously but the vast majority of cover versions appear

659

on albums on which only one or two Gibb compositions are included.

One indicator of the greatness of The Bee Gees as composers has been the commercial success of cover artists performing their songs. This alternative barometer of their status has contributed to seemingly arbitrary guesses being made by the media as to the extent of their wealth. *The Sunday Times* 2000 "Rich List" valued the brothers' collective worth at some £100 million (Paul McCartney's was £550 million) while issue 199 of *OK!* magazine estimated their annual income as now being in the region of £10 million. The figures themselves are meaningless. Far more relevant was the astute editorial comment which accompanied the *OK!* feature about the Top 100 showbiz earners which said, "Hit covers of their songs by the likes of Boyzone and Celine Dion bring the money rolling in for this ever popular band. The stage production of *Saturday Night Fever* and a clever tour – in which they played a very limited number of huge venues – have kept them firmly in the public eye. TV specials have helped boost their album sales." Much of the credit for this clever marketing of the group belongs to their professional advisers, Left Bank Management.

The most common method by which observers determine the relative commercial success of a song is to monitor how well it does on record charts. Most major countries have had "official" or "semi-official" record charts during the last 40 years. *Billboard* magazine in the USA has, for many years now, published record charts for about 15 to 20 countries in every issue. The problem faced by researchers is not the absence of record charts for most of the world's major countries but, rather, finding published compilations covering the period in question. Published data is extremely difficult to locate and, in most cases, only covers parts of the time period desired. There are 14 countries for which significant historical chart data could be located, namely United States, United Kingdom, Germany, France, Italy, Australia, Canada, South Africa, Zimbabwe, Sweden, Norway, The Netherlands, Belgium, and New Zealand. The most complete data is available for the United States, United Kingdom, and Germany which represent three of the four biggest record markets in the free world. To a lesser extent, some chart data is also available for Japan, the second largest. The data for the other listed countries is not as complete because some time periods are missing. Among the countries where historical chart data could not be found are: China, Thailand, Hong Kong, Singapore, Spain, Ireland, Greece, Switzerland, Austria, Denmark, Portugal, Finland, Mexico, the countries of the former Eastern Bloc, nearly all of the African countries, and all of the countries of South America.

Over the past 35 years many cover versions of Gibb compositions have reached number one on the record charts in major countries around the world. Several other cover versions have hit number two while countless others have reached the Top 10 and Top 20. In the absence of published chart histories for many countries, there is no way to determine an exact number of worldwide cover version chart successes. However, to obtain a representative "sampling", the chart data of the 15 countries for which statistics are available, can be examined. 50 different cover versions have reached the Top 10 in one or more of these countries accounting for a total of 144 Top 10 chart entries. Included are 25 different cover versions which reached the top two and which account for 40 number one's and 19 number two's. These very impressive totals would be significantly higher if data for additional countries were available. It should also be noted that similar records of chart success for The Bee Gees and Andy Gibb, impressive as they already are, would be likewise affected.

In some countries, record charts are based solely on sales. In other countries, they are based on a combination of sales and radio play. Sometimes, competing charts exist within one country. In the United States, *Billboard* magazine is generally considered as the "official" chart source. However, in the Seventies, three independent charts existed in the United States – *Billboard*, *Cash Box*, and *Record World*. This led to a very unusual occurrence on March 11, 1978. On this date each chart had a different Gibb-related number one song – Andy Gibb's '(Love Is) Thicker Than Water' in *Billboard*, Samantha Sang's 'Emotion' in *Cash Box*, and The Bee Gees' 'Night Fever' in *Record World*.

Success for the cover artist obviously means success for the writer, and there is no doubt that the Gibbs have benefited enormously from this branch of their activities. One man who has viewed them from both sides of the fence is guitarist, Pat Fairley.

Pat left Marmalade towards the end of 1971 to concentrate on a career in publishing. Gradually he began to make a name for himself in that area of the business, and it wasn't long before others began to take notice of his abilities. "During the 'hungry' days, I got a personal call from Robert Stigwood to join him as head of publishing and I admired his catalogue," he said. The deal was quickly concluded and Pat headed back to hand in his resignation but news travels fast in London. "When I got back to my office there was a big red cross painted on the door with 'traitor' on it. But that move helped Thin Lizzy on its way as I signed them to Stigwood."

Taking into account that the Gibbs, as writers, were indirectly responsible for Marmalade's sole failure before he left, Pat is generous in his appraisal of their songwriting talents. "They had tremendous sales as Bee Gees material was getting recorded by every other major star in the world, you name them. They are on a par with The Beatles and have made more money from their songs (publishing) than sales of records."

Pat Fairley is not the only person well placed to be judgmental of the Gibbs' impact on music sales. As Vice President of BMG, the International music-publishing concern, Andrew Jenkins is uniquely positioned to offer insight, not only on the brothers themselves, but also on the workings of that particular sector of the industry.

"The job of the music publisher is to represent the songwriter in all areas of the entertainment business," he began. "Sheet music is probably the first thing that springs to most people's minds, but in fact this accounts for a relatively small amount of a songwriter's income. Far more money is generated from the sales of albums and singles, from the use of music in films, TV and commercials, and from the performance of songs on the radio, film & TV and in bars, clubs and restaurants and live performance in concert.

"In many cases the songwriter is different from the artist who performs the song, and therefore his interests are different. The Gibb brothers are fantastically successful artists and songwriters, and as their music publisher, it is in their role as songwriters that I am principally concerned. We are all aware of their versions of their own songs," Andrew continued, "which are for the most part definitive versions, but of course as songwriters they have had an incredible impact on the music industry. Obvious examples of artists who have covered their songs include Kenny Rogers and Dolly Parton, Barbra Streisand, Diana Ross, Take That and Dionne Warwick, but there are literally thousands of other covers, some better known than others."

It would be all too easy to accuse Andrew of having a vested interest in saying nice things about his charges, but to do so would be churlish, and there should be no doubting the sincerity of his words. "Their songs remain as popular and in demand today as they ever were. Indeed, Barry, Robin and Maurice, could probably write songs full-time for other artists and do nothing else, such is the demand.

"They are without doubt one of the greatest songwriting teams of all time," he opined. "In my view, they have no peers. They have written number one singles in the UK in each of the four decades that they have been writing music. Quite simply they are the finest writers I have ever had the privilege of working with. Barry, Robin and Maurice are very serious about their music, but are also great fun to be around."

Adding a personal touch, he concluded, "I feel like part of the family and it is this combination of warmth and professionalism that characterises our business relationship. They have added so much to my career in the music business through knowing them, and working with them, and have enriched my life as they have so many people that work with them on a regular basis. Quite simply, they are the best!"

★　　★　　★

A complete list of all of the cover versions that have charted in the United States, United Kingdom, and Germany is provided in Appendix VI. Since 1967, a total of 73 different cover versions involving 51 different Gibb songs performed by 62 different artists have charted in one or more of these three countries. The two songs which have appeared the most times are 'Grease' and 'Stayin' Alive' at six times each.

A short summary of the complete cover version chart history in the United States, United Kingdom and Germany is as follows:

No. of Cover Versions which reached:	USA	UK	Germany
Number 1	4	5	2
" 2–5	2	10	4
" 6–10	3	10	4
" 11–20	3	6	3
" 21–40	4	7	4
" 41–100	17	20	6
	33	58	23

The chart success of Gibb cover versions in the United Kingdom during the Nineties was truly amazing. There were a total of 26 cover version chart hits of which 11 reached the Top 10, eight reached the Top 5, and three reached number one. The number one's were 'How Deep Is Your Love' by Take That, Boyzone's 'Words', and 'Tragedy' by Steps.

All three bands freely admitted to being Bee Gees fans themselves but the most fulsome in their praise of the Gibbs were 911 whose version of 'More Than A Woman' made runners-up position in the UK charts, a month before Steps went one better.

Referring to The Bee Gees as "the kings of disco" is not widely considered to be the most flattering method of endearing yourself to the brothers, but lead singer Jimmy Constable quickly recovered from his early mistake. "We can't understand," he said, acting as the band's spokesperson, "why anyone could think they are tacky. [The] younger generation don't have the preconceptions other people seem to have. Everyone I know thinks they're legends. The Bee Gees are brilliant songwriters, the best in the business. They've written so many different songs for so many different artists."

★   ★   ★

Songs written by The Bee Gees are highly sought after by today's leading performers, and The Bee Gees are now recognised by their peers within the industry as writers of quality.

Changed days from 1977 when their then biographer, Saul Davis, justifiably complained, "They are the most overlooked tunesmiths in the rock era," before citing a random *Billboard* survey which revealed that, in a three month period alone, four Gibb songs had been covered by five different artists or groups. These were Rhoda Curtis, and also separately, Michelle Phillips – 'Baby As You Turn Away', Jackie De Shannon – 'To Love Somebody', Coyote – 'Marley Purt Drive' and Network – 'Save Me Save Me'. Also released during that same period, however, were Samona Cooke – 'Subway' and Flower – 'Run To Me'. Just for good measure though, Saul also reminded journalist Tamara Handy that Narvel Felts had recently taken 'To Love Somebody' into the country charts and that Gibb songs were regularly interpreted by Tom Jones and Paul Anka in their Las Vegas acts.

In contrast to the flurry of cover version successes in the United Kingdom and much of the rest of the world during the last decade, chart entries in the United States have been few in number. During the late-Seventies and early-Eighties, chart successes there were very numerous. However, since 'Islands in The Stream' by Kenny Rogers & Dolly Parton reached number one in the USA in 1983, there have only been two other cover versions to crack the Top 20. These were 'To Love Somebody' by Michael Bolton, a number 11 in 1992, and 'Ghetto Supastar (That Is What You Are)' by Pras Michel, Ol' Dirty Bastard & Mya which got as far as number 15 in 1998.

This decline in popularity for Gibb cover versions, and indeed for The Bee Gees themselves, is due to the so called "disco backlash", a stigma which has proven to be very hard to overcome. The relative lack of singles chart success in the USA is likely to continue. In late-1998 *Billboard* changed the way they compile the Top 100 singles list so that radio play dominates and sales count for very little. One week prior to the change, L. F. O.'s version of 'If I Can't Have You' was number 70 because of good sales results. However, they dropped out of the Top 100 immediately after the change because of the lack of radio play. This disparity is even more apparent in the case of the Steps' version of 'Tragedy'. This former UK number one was released in the USA at the beginning of 2000 and, in spite of being one of the Top 30 best selling singles for several weeks, it failed to penetrate the Top 100 because of the continuing radio boycott of Gibb songs. Had *Billboard* been using the current methodology when 'Alone' by The Bee Gees was released in 1997, it would not have reached anywhere near the number 28 that it ultimately achieved, because most of its strength came from sales with only minimal help from radio play.

So just how many cover versions of Gibb songs actually exist? Music publishing companies such as BMG might have some idea because they collect royalties for the brothers. Unfortunately, due to its confidential nature, this information is not available to Gibb fans and collectors.

Robert F. Sommerville, the recognised authority in the field of cover versions, has conducted extensive research in this area. He has identified more than 5,000 cover versions by over 2,500 artists of 340 different Gibb songs. Even though this total is very impressive, the actual figure is much higher because there are undoubtedly hundreds, if not thousands, of additional cover versions that remain undiscovered, plus new cover versions are being released around the world every week. The current total includes 426 vocal versions sung in languages other than English. A look at the Top 10 reveals that the Scandinavian countries are particularly well represented. Swedish (93) is the most popular, followed by Italian (64), Spanish (61), German (53), Hungarian (31), French (28), Norwegian (22), Finnish (18), Danish (16) and Chinese (11).

It perhaps comes as no surprise to learn that 'How Deep Is Your Love' is the Gibb composition most requested of publishers and, at the time of writing, Bob had identified 382 different versions.

Most of the older cover versions are only available on vinyl records and these are becoming more and more difficult to find with each passing year. Even if these can be located, their sound quality may leave a lot to be desired. In some cases, especially if major artists are involved, the older cover versions have been reissued on CDs. However, the vast majority of them will never be reissued on CD, leaving the original vinyl recordings as the only source of this invaluable material. This is unfortunate, as many of these "gems" may soon become lost forever.

APPENDIX II – 5339.338

THE PREMATURE DEATH of Andy Gibb was a devastating blow to his friends and family, but it also came as a massive shock to those fans who had stuck with him through his bad times, and who were looking forward to hearing the new music he was in the midst of recording.

New Yorker Renée Schreiber had experience of running various fan clubs in the early to mid-Seventies, so when she had expressed a desire to run the first International Andy Gibb Fan Club in 1977, she seemed an ideal candidate. In time, she would also come to be involved in the running of the Official Bee Gees Fan Club too, continuing to play an active role to this day.

Renée had moved to Miami soon after her appointment, and quickly formed close friendships with two other young women who shared her willingness to take an active role in organising various fan club events; Beverly Burke and Karen Witkowski. For these three in particular, after the initial grieving period had passed, there was a determination that Andy's name should live on through the causes that he himself held so dearly. Renée summed up this largely unseen part of Andy's life when she said, "Andy was a strong supporter of many charities and always made himself available to lend a helping hand, whether it be playing in a tennis tournament, performing at a benefit concert, or just making a public appearance."

Bev has similarly fond memories of the man who was more of a friend to her than the idol he was to millions. "I was fortunate enough to meet Andy on several occasions," she said, "and found him to be one of the most caring, giving persons that I've ever met. Any time a cause needed help and Andy could be of any assistance, he went above and beyond to help out any way he could, always there with a smile on his face.

"Shortly after Andy's death," she continued, "a group of us were together talking about all of the good times we had had at many of these charity functions, and how sad it was that Andy's charity work would have to come to an end. But we started thinking, it didn't have to end. We could continue raising money and donate it to various charities in Andy's name."

Thus, with the co-operation and blessings of the entire Gibb family, The Andy Gibb Memorial Foundation was formed in 1988.

It is clear that, apart from being an important part of the healing process for all three, their creation has provided a common cause for fans and family alike. Bev is particularly enthusiastic about this aspect of her involvement.

"My work with the Foundation has allowed me to see first-hand the kind of generous fans that The Bee Gees and Andy Gibb have. Whatever sale or event that we may have to generate money for the Foundation, the fans are the ones we can always count on, and we truly appreciate them. The Gibb family has been there for the Foundation since the beginning and has been a constant source of inspiration to us. Their generosity and enthusiasm for the cause has been incredible. The entire family gets involved, from the brothers and their wives, as well as their mom Barbara, attending our many functions, to Steven and Spencer of the next generation of Gibbs performing at one of the events.

"I think Andy would be proud to know that the Foundation continues to raise money for his favourite charities, as well as uniting Gibb fans from around the world in a common cause."

Karen Witkowksi is equally passionate about her involvement in the Foundation.

"It's a way of keeping Andy's name and memory alive," she confirmed. "That was our original goal, and it has always been for Andy, first and foremost, on top of having the opportunity to help worthy charities.

"I know I would have never have had the opportunity to help charities on a large scale without the AGMF, and that has been a humbling and rewarding experience. I've also met a lot of caring, dedicated people, and that has also had a positive impact on my life. I'm proud of Andy for all the charity work he did, and I'm proud we were able to help continue his charitable legacy, with the help of family, friends, and fans."

Karen is being modest when she claims that the three co-founders have "made a difference in a small way". March 1998 marked the 10th anniversary of AGMF and, since its inception, donations totalling in excess of $250,000 have been made by the Foundation to the five nominated charities with whom Andy had been previously linked. These are the Diabetes Research Institute, the American Heart Association, the American Cancer Society, the National Music Foundation and the National Drug Abuse Council. In 1998, the University of Miami School of Music was added to the list of recipients, replacing the National Drug Abuse Council.

The Foundation raises money from donations, no matter how large or small, from fans of The Bee Gees and Andy Gibb. In addition, the AGMF also raises money through fund-raisers, and special offers and sales through the various Bee Gees Fan Clubs. The first AGMF fund-raiser was held at the Fontainebleau Hilton on Miami Beach in November, 1988, where a screening of the movie *Hawks* was held, in addition to a memorabilia sale and auction. Barry Gibb and David English attended this event and, encouraged by their presence, fans raised over $6,000 at this event alone.

In April of 1990, the screening of *The Bee Gees' One For All Concert Live in Australia* took place at the Diplomat Hotel in Hollywood, Florida, in addition to the memorabilia sale and auction. This time, all three Bee Gees were there to lend their personal support, boosting proceeds to $14,000.

The fund-raiser expanded to an entire weekend in November of 1994. The Saturday was spent enjoying a cruise on the charter boat *Lady Lucille* for an afternoon cruise on Biscayne Bay and Maurice Gibb graciously joined the revellers for that. On Sunday, the festivities moved to the Fontainebleau Hilton for an afternoon of auctions, sales, a screening of the VH-1 *Center Stage* concert and another appearance by The Bee Gees. All in attendance were lucky enough to receive autographs from the group and over $25,000 was raised from the activities of the two days.

Another event was held in Miami Beach at the end of May during the Memorial Day weekend of 1999, this time at the Shelborne Resort.

In addition to these occasional fund-raising events, throughout the year the various Bee Gees fan clubs have their own special sales, auctions, contests, lotteries etc. to raise money, and these funds are added to by the many private donations made directly to the AGMF.

In addition to the three co-founders, there is an Advisory Committee which consists of eldest brother Barry Gibb, Renée Schreiber and Joe Teichman. The Founders, along with the Advisory Committee, decide when the money is to be distributed to its recipients and the size of the donation. The entire Gibb family are constant supporters of the Foundation and are kept informed of its progress at all times, while the Dade Community Foundation in Miami oversees its running and handles all of the paperwork.

★   ★   ★

Fan power can manifest itself in many forms. Apart from raising huge amounts of money, fans can also create the demand, which results in the availability of otherwise unreleased recordings; most of which manifest themselves in the form of bootleg CDs.

In Britain, the growing problem of music piracy is the responsibility of the British Phonographic Industry, originally formed in 1972 by the record companies to address such concerns.

David Martin, Director of Anti-Piracy at the BPI since 1993, confirmed that the BPI have had problems with Bee Gees pirated repertoire in places like the United States. "It's been possible for me to speak to my opposite numbers in the States and succeed in stopping some of that piracy.

"Generically we talk about music piracy," David continued, "and then we split that up into categories. 'Counterfeits' are copies of genuine sound recordings, dressed up to look like the genuine article, but of course, they're not. These are very easy to identify because the disc itself will be bluey-green on the under-surface." Bee Gees fans may well have come across examples of these over Internet auctions too, as the scarcity of CDs like *Now Voyager* and *Walls Have Eyes* make these plum targets for counterfeiters who can "burn" copies of these discs at home for a couple of dollars each.

"The second category would be what we call 'pirate recordings'. These are compilations of albums made up from different sources . . . genuine albums, radio, etc., which might appear as things like *Simply Red's Greatest Hits* which has never been officially produced.

"The third category is what we call 'bootlegs'. There is a lot of confusion here because a lot of people in the industry talk about 'bootlegs' in the sense that they think that they're counter-feits. But bootlegs are unauthorised live recordings or studio out-takes or perhaps recordings from TV or radio."

The top artists who are being counterfeited at the moment are certainly the likes of The Spice Girls, Robbie Williams and Boyzone but, due to the longevity of The Bee Gees' career, David concedes that the Gibbs could conceivably have lost more potential income in the long run, when compared to the popular new artists of today. However, a different picture emerges on the bootleg front where acts from the Sixties and Seventies appear most affected. "For the older sort of artists like The Bee Gees, The Rolling Stones and The Beatles," confirms David, "there is a constant demand – mainly for unreleased material. With The Bee Gees, I think there have been more bootlegs around over the last few years rather than copies of genuine released recordings, but it's very interesting to note that we've recently discovered a very, very sophisti-cated attempt by South East Asian pirates to duplicate official releases of The Bee Gees, and dressed up very, very well with full artwork and full on-body printing. There is still a market for this type of recording, and the pirates will respond to that market."

By being able to listen to these compact discs, or some of the poor quality cassette tapes that have been circulating amongst a lucky few for years, fans have been pleasantly surprised to dis-cover that some of the Gibbs' best work is included amongst these recordings. Indeed, it would be a relatively easy task to put together an album of quality unreleased tracks over and above those that appeared on *A Kick In The Head* . . . or the solo albums.

Twelve songs that are certainly worthy of acclaim from a wider audience are 'In The Heat Of The Night' and 'City Of Angels' from the *Living Eyes* sessions, Andy's 'Arrow Through The Heart', 'Every Morning, Every Night', 'Irresponsible, Unreliable, Indispensable Blues', 'Alexandria Good Time', 'Christmas Eve Or Halloween' from the split era, 'Human Being' & 'Saying Goodbye' which were written for Jimmy Ruffin and Kenny Rogers respectively, 'Merrily Merry Eyes' from the *Trafalgar* collection of out-takes, 1968's 'I Can Lift A Mountain' and finally, the classy instrumental 'The Love Was That Lost'. It can only be hoped that some of these may one day become commercially available on a bonus disc to some future greatest hits package.

★　　★　　★

The entity known as The Bee Gees has been around for almost 40 years now. Much is made of this fact, but less so of the parallel statistic that some of their admirers have been following their career for that length of time too.

The earliest fan club started in Australia and was run firstly by their sister Lesley, and then by Barry's then future wife, Maureen Bates. Probably their biggest supporter at that time was Dorothy Gliksman from Maroubra who constantly badgered music papers and radio stations in an effort to ensure that her favourites received the publicity and airplay that she felt they deserved. One surviving example is a letter she wrote to Sydney radio station 2SM in October, 1964. To the station's credit, they didn't just bin it, as might happen nowadays. Instead, she received the following prompt and courteous response on October 16:

Dear Dorothy,

Thanks very much for writing in. I like Barry Gibb and The Bee Gees' new record myself and I hope it does become a hit.

I'll see what I can do about playing it more.

Yours sincerely,

Mike Walsh

When The Bee Gees moved to Britain in 1967, the level of their success meant that it was no longer possible to run their fan club on a part-time basis from their home. Full-time professional help was required and the group were indeed fortunate to be able to call on the dedication and expertise that Julie Barrett was able to provide. For one thing, she was just delighted that she could get rid of the identity crisis with which she had been burdened during the previous 24 months.

"I started with NEMS Enterprises in 1965 when I was 17, working in The Beatles' fan club in Monmouth Street along with a couple of other girls with fictitious names. One was known as Anne Collins, she was secretary. Mary was her proper name, and when she left I took on her name so that, in effect, The Beatles' fan club secretary hadn't left. I also did the fan clubs of Gerry & The Pacemakers under the name of Roseanna Scott, Billy J. Kramer under the name of Pat Strong and The Moody Blues under the name of Jill Brady, so all these fan clubs were run out of that one office in Monmouth Street. It was all under the name of NEMS, but they made out that there were all these people. Sometimes you'd forget whom you were signing as, who you were at the time. I'd receive letters addressed to three or four different people in the morning's post and you'd think, 'Oh dear! Who am I today?' Originally, they did have three people who were doing the Beatles' one, then one by one they all left, so they decided that it didn't look good to have all the fan club secretaries leaving so they just kept the names as they were all fictitious names you see.

"This was my full time job for NEMS but I didn't meet Brian Epstein until the Christmas party at Argyle Street, which is where their offices were.

"That was around the time when he amalgamated with Robert Stigwood and I went into the Press Office for a while as a clerk/typist. When NEMS took on The Bee Gees, I said, 'Could I run their fan club?' because all the other fan clubs had really run down by then, and The Beatles one had been taken over by someone in Liverpool. Brian and Robert said, 'Yes,' and I was actually allowed to keep my real name of Julie Barrett. So I started their fan club which officially opened in July, and this was the first time I'd done one under my own name!

"The first office was in Gerard Street and then I was sent to Old Compton Street where above us we actually had a couple of 'hostesses', for want of a better word. We ran the club from there, alongside a girl who was doing Georgie Fame's fan club, and we were all a little worried because it got very, very seedy – Soho wasn't the best of places to go to. Then I got transferred to Brook Street in Mayfair and was given a nice office in the basement."

Strange requests that are made of today's pop idols are not just the domain of the current batch of teenagers. Julie had more than her fair share of unusual inquiries in those days too.

"There's lots I remember from that time, because it was quite exciting and I was only young myself. I remember some of the things that fans asked . . . one wanted Robin's bath water so I said that Barbara had managed to get some and sent it; it was really only dirty water so I'm sorry if that disappoints someone! Another wanted leftover crumbs from their breakfast. It was ludicrous what the girls were asking for."

Fan club secretaries, then and now, occupy a very privileged role as intermediaries between fans and their favourites. As chief BeeGeeBopper, Julie was therefore well placed to gauge the attitude of the stars to those who worshipped their every move, and agreed that The Bee Gees of the Sixties, and one in particular, were more considerate towards their fans than many other performers she had encountered.

"Vince Melouney was always very good at coming in and signing photos, I liked him very much. You used to ask them if they would come in, and the others were a bit naughty, although not as bad as some. Compared to the other groups like The Beatles, where you sometimes had to forge their signatures, The Bee Gees actually signed quite a lot, but Vince spent ages doing them and he was always so good, and one time he spent six hours signing Christmas cards for members. Vince was the one who would always put himself out and sign as much as he could, because I think he knew how important it was to the fans. He'd always stop and talk to any fans when he was coming out of the offices too. I found him very, very good with them."

Over the years, various Bee Gees fan clubs have come and gone. The UK fan club continued after Julie went to Greece in May, 1969; their first new newsletter being issued by Theresa Daligan just two months later. This continued in various formats under the stewardship of the likes of Barbara Gibb and Maureen Du-Four until January, 1977. The editors of these newsletters were kept very well informed and each issue was packed with interesting little snippets of information. How else, for example, could you be expected to know what Robert Stigwood had given the boys for Christmas in 1971? Well, Robin obtained Henry, Maurice received Alfred, while Barry took possession of Jock; Myna birds we are told.

There was also a Robin Gibb Fan Club which operated briefly between March and June of 1970. Its main souvenir was a colour reproduction of a picture which Robin had painted while on honeymoon in Geneva in December 1968. There soon followed the Barry Gibb Fan Cub, which ran from December 1970 to July 1972. Theresa Daligan wrote the newsletters from information provided to her by Lynda Gibb. The highlight of the club's existence was the limited edition 1970 pressing of 200 copies of its own single on the Lyntone label, which had also been responsible for issuing the famous Beatles' fan club EPs of the early Sixties. The disc contained the exclusive 'King Kathy', as well as the first hearings of 'Summer Ends' and 'I Can Bring Love'. The club also issued a booklet containing 28 of Barry's "poems", although these were actually all from songs he had written during the split period.

Fans were active in Europe too. In 1971, a Dutch-German fan club was formed under the banner of *Bee Gees Information*. Reflecting international trends, it was re-baptised *Brothers Gibb Information* in the early Eighties. Followers of Maurice's music were well served in 1976 by the issue of an EP on Germany's New Blood label. Thanks to the combined efforts of Norbert Lippe for BGI and the Dutch fan club, Maurice had agreed to donate four tracks from his unreleased solo album from 1970. Thus, accompanied by its own picture sleeve, this became the only official release of 'Laughing Child', 'Soldier Johnny', 'Something's Blowing' and 'Journey To The Misty Mountains'.

Lamplight was very much a torch bearer for the Gibbs when it was formed by Louis Bakens in April 1974, and it continued until December 1985. Its successor, *The Spirit*, kept the faith right up to December 1998, closing down after its 52nd issue; the 100th to emanate from fans in Holland when the 48 magazines produced by *Lamplight* are taken into account.

The main officially recognised club is *Bee Gees Quarterly*, which has been in existence since December, 1990 when it arose from the ashes of *Gibbstyle*. An international club with members in 58 countries worldwide, it benefited greatly from the closure of BGI whose key staff transferred to *BGQ* as did much of *The Spirit*'s readership. *BGQ* is professionally designed by Belgium's top comic strip artist Wim Swerts, whose creations include "Samson & Gert" and "Ambionix"; both of which have their own web-sites. Until recently, *BGQ*'s main competitor was *The Bee Gees UK Fan Club*, but its demise at the start of the new Millennium – when it merged with *BGQ* – has left Britain with just the unofficial *The Rural HG Times*, a Robin-oriented fanzine, to represent British viewpoints.

Bee Gees fans can be found in every corner of the globe and represent all walks of life. Some write poetry about their heroes, others have even written books. The more musically inclined have even written songs. Not all of it is simple idolatry by nature either, and there are some examples of genuine talent. One who illustrates this point is the American writer David Leaf.

David Leaf has made a career out of writing and, as a long-time fan of the group himself, was thrilled to be asked to write *The Authorised Biography* which was first published in 1979. As he recently said, "I just wrote a book that I, as a fan, would want to read." One advantage of writing an official book is that you get to spend time with its subjects. David flew to Miami to interview the brothers and, while there, was able to appreciate the energy being generated by them. "At the time," he began, "they were recording *Spirits* so it was an incredible time to be in the studio."

David was a fan of the group to begin with, and in record stores could always be found at the 'B' section where The Beach Boys' and The Beatles' records preceded those of The Bee Gees. "We called these groups 'The Killer Bees'," he enthused. If anything, the passing of the last 20 years or so has only served to increase David's admiration for the brothers. "I probably am a bigger fan today than I ever was," he admitted. "I don't know of any group that has lived up to their reputation better than The Bee Gees – they are so consistent."

Many other Bee Gees fans have remained loyal to the group throughout the peaks and valleys of their career, and they are now raising second and even third generations of fans. A typical concert will include both grans and grandchildren, and that's just in the seats reserved for the Gibb family, with Barbara and Ali happily clapping along with all the rest.

Children in particular are a constant source of inspiration and invention. Who else could tell you to punch the numbers 8819 or 5339.338 into a pocket calculator, and then turn it 180 degrees before you read the digital display?

APPENDIX III

ALBUM DISCOGRAPHY

(# = was subsequently released on CD) (★ = compilation) (+ = compilation with new material)

YEAR	ARTIST	FORMAT	TITLE	UK	USA	ELSEWHERE
1965	Barry Gibb &		Barry Gibb & The Bee Gees Sing			
	The Bee Gees	LP	And Play 14 Barry Gibb Songs	x	x	Australia
1966	Bee Gees	LP	Monday's Rain (withdrawn)	x	x	Australia
	Bee Gees	LP	Spicks And Specks	x	x	Australia
1967	Bee Gees	LP #	Bee Gees First (also mono)	✓	✓	✓
	Bee Gees	LP	Turn Around Look At Us	x	x	Australia
1968	Bee Gees	LP #	Horizontal (also mono)	✓	✓	✓
	Bee Gees	LP	Rare, Precious and Beautiful ★	✓	✓	✓
	Bee Gees	LP #	Idea (also mono)	✓	✓	✓
	Bee Gees	LP	Rare, Precious and Beautiful Volume 2 ★	✓	✓	✓
1969	Bee Gees	LP	Rare, Precious and Beautiful Volume 3 ★	✓	x	✓
	Bee Gees	2 LPs #	Odessa (also mono)	✓	✓	✓
	Bee Gees	LP #	Best Of Bee Gees ★	✓	✓	✓
1970	Robin Gibb	LP #	Robin's Reign	✓	✓	✓
	Bee Gees	LP #	Cucumber Castle	✓	✓	✓
	Bee Gees	2 LPs	Inception/Nostalgia +			Germany
				x	x	France, Japan
	Bee Gees	2 LPs	Bee Gees Best ★	x	x	Germany
	Various	LP	Sing A Rude Song	✓	x	x
	Bee Gees	LP #	2 Years On	✓	✓	✓
1971	Bee Gees	LP #	Melody (also called S.W.A.L.K. in the UK)	✓	✓	✓
	Bee Gees	LP #	Trafalgar	✓	✓	✓
1972	Bee Gees	LP #	To Whom It May Concern	✓	✓	✓
1973	Bee Gees	LP #	Life In A Tin Can	✓	✓	✓
	Bee Gees	LP	Massachusetts ★	✓	x	x
	Bee Gees	LP #	Best Of Bee Gees Volume 2 ★	✓	✓	✓
1974	Bee Gees	LP #	Mr Natural	✓	✓	✓
	Bee Gees	LP	Gotta Get A Message To You +	✓	x	x
1975	Bee Gees	LP #	Main Course	✓	✓	✓
1976	Bee Gees	LP #	Children Of The World	✓	✓	✓
	Various	LP	All This And World War II			
			(limited edition box set in the USA)	✓	✓	x
1977	Bee Gees	2 LPs #	Here At Last ... Bee Gees ... Live	✓	✓	✓
	Andy Gibb	LP #	Flowing Rivers	✓	✓	✓
	Various	2 LPs #	Saturday Night Fever			
			(limited edition platinum vinyl in Australia)	✓	✓	✓
1978	Andy Gibb	LP #	Shadow Dancing	✓	✓	✓
	Various	2 LPs #	Sgt. Pepper's Lonely Hearts Club Band			
			(limited edition pink vinyl in the UK)	✓	✓	✓
	Various	LP #	Sesame Street Fever (CD in Japan only)	✓	✓	x
	Bee Gees	LP	The Words And Music Of ... (promo) +	x	✓	x

Year	Artist	Format	Title				Country
	Bee Gees	2 LPs #	Birth Of Brilliance +	x	x		Australia
1979	Bee Gees	LP #	Spirits Having Flown				
			(limited edition picture disc in the USA)	✓	✓	✓	
	Various	LP	The Music For UNICEF Concert	✓	✓	✓	
	Bee Gees	2 LPs #	Bee Gees Greatest +	✓	✓	x	
	Bee Gees	LP	Short Cuts (promo) ★	✓	x	x	
1980	Andy Gibb	LP #	After Dark	✓	✓	✓	
	Andy Gibb	LP	Greatest Hits +	✓	✓	✓	
1981	Bee Gees	LP #	Living Eyes	✓	✓	✓	
1983	Robin Gibb	LP/CD	How Old Are You?	✓	✓	✓	
	Various	LP/CD	Staying Alive	✓	✓	✓	
	Bee Gees	LP	Rarities				
			(in 20th Anniversary Box Set) +	x	x		Germany
1984	Robin Gibb	LP/CD	Secret Agent	✓	✓	✓	
	Barry Gibb	LP/CD	Now Voyager	✓	✓	✓	
1985	Robin Gibb	LP/CD	Walls Have Eyes	✓	x	✓	
1987	Bee Gees	LP/CD	E.S.P.	✓	✓	✓	
1988	Various	LP/CD	One Moment In Time	✓	✓	✓	
	Barry Gibb	LP/CD	Hawks	✓	x	✓	
1989	Bee Gees	CD	Rare Collection ★	x	x		Japan
	Bee Gees	CD	16 Greatest Hits (edit remixes) ★	x	x		Mexico
	Bee Gees	LP/CD	One (CD only in USA)	✓	✓	✓	
1990	Bee Gees	LP/CD	The Very Best Of The Bee Gees ★	✓	x	✓	
	Bee Gees	4 CDs	Tales From The Brothers Gibb +	✓	✓		Holland
(6LPs)							
1991	Bee Gees	LP/CD	High Civilization (CD only in USA)	✓	✓	✓	
	Andy Gibb	CD	Andy Gibb +	✓	✓	✓	
1992	Various	CD	Bunbury Tails	✓	x	x	
1993	Bee Gees	LP/CD	SIZE Isn't Everything				
			(CD only ex-Germany)	✓	✓	✓	
1997	Bee Gees	CD	Still Waters	✓	✓	✓	
	Bee Gees	2 CDs	Still Waters (limited edition issued in				
			Target Stores with "VH1 Storytellers")	x	✓	x	
	Bee Gees	2 CDs	Come Home To Ellan Vannin				
			(charity interview disc)	x	x		Isle of Man
1998	Bee Gees	CD	One Night Only	✓	✓	✓	
	Bee Gees	2 CDs	Brilliant From Birth	x	x		Australia

APPENDIX IV

BEE GEES/ANDY GIBB ALBUMS WHICH CHARTED IN USA, UK & GERMANY

(Compiled by Norbert Lippe as of March, 2000)

ENTRY DATE	ARTIST	TITLE	USA	UK	GER.
Aug-67	Bee Gees	Bee Gees 1st	7	8	4
Feb-68	Bee Gees	Horizontal	12	16	1
Aug-68	Bee Gees	Rare, Precious & Beautiful	99	–	15
Aug-68	Bee Gees	Idea	17	4	3
Feb-69	Bee Gees	Odessa	20	10	4
Jul-69	Bee Gees	Best Of	9	7	26
Mar-70	Robin Gibb	Robin's Reign	–	–	19
Mar-70	Bee Gees	Rare, Precious & Beautiful Vol. 2	100	–	–
May-70	Bee Gees	Cucumber Castle	94	57	36
Jan-71	Bee Gees	2 Years On	32	–	–
Sep-71	Bee Gees	Trafalgar	34	–	–
Nov-72	Bee Gees	To Whom It May Concern	35	–	–
Feb-73	Bee Gees	Life In A Tin Can	69	–	–
Aug-73	Bee Gees	Best Of Vol. 2	98	–	n/a
Jun-74	Bee Gees	Mr. Natural	178	–	–
Jun-75	Bee Gees	Main Course	14	–	29
Oct-76	Bee Gees	Children Of The World	8	–	–
Nov-76	Bee Gees	Bee Gees Gold Vol. 1	50	n/a	n/a
Jun-77	Bee Gees	Here At Last - Live	8	–	44
Jul-77	Andy Gibb	Flowing Rivers	19	–	–
Nov-77	Soundtrack	Saturday Night Fever	1	1	1
Apr-78	Bee Gees	20 Greatest Hits	n/a	n/a	4
Jun-78	Andy Gibb	Shadow Dancing	7	15	–
Aug-78	Soundtrack	Sgt. Pepper's Lonely Hearts' Club Band	5	38	29
Feb-79	Bee Gees	Spirits Having Flown	1	1	1
Nov-79	Bee Gees	Greatest	1	6	43
Mar-80	Andy Gibb	After Dark	21	–	–
Dec-80	Andy Gibb	Andy Gibb's Greatest Hits	46	–	–
Nov-81	Bee Gees	Living Eyes	41	73	37
Mar-83	Bee Gees	Gold & Diamonds	n/a	n/a	4
May-83	Robin Gibb	How Old Are You	–	–	6
Jul-83	Soundtrack	Staying Alive	6	14	8
Jun-84	Robin Gibb	Secret Agent	–	–	31
Oct-84	Barry Gibb	Now Voyager	72	85	38
Oct-87	Bee Gees	E.S.P.	96	5	1
Apr-89	Bee Gees	One	68	29	4
Nov-90	Bee Gees	The Very Best Of	n/a	6	9
Apr-91	Bee Gees	High Civilization	–	24	2
Sep-93	Bee Gees	SIZE Isn't Everything	153	23	12
Mar-97	Bee Gees	Still Waters	11	2	2
Sep-98	Bee Gees	One Night Only	72	4	5

672

APPENDIX V

BEE GEES/ANDY GIBB SINGLES WHICH CHARTED IN USA, UK & GERMANY
(Compiled by Norbert Lippe as of March, 2000)

ENTRY DATE	ARTIST	TITLE	HIGHEST CHART POSITION USA	UK	GER.
Apr-67	Bee Gees	New York Mining Disaster 1941	14	12	10
Jun-67	Bee Gees	To Love Somebody	17	41	19
Aug-67	Bee Gees	Spicks And Specks	n/a	–	28
Sep-67	Bee Gees	Holiday	16	n/a	–
Sep-67	Bee Gees	Massachusetts (The Lights Went Out In)	11	1	1
Nov-67	Bee Gees	World	–	9	1
Jan-68	Bee Gees	Words	15	8	1
Mar-68	Bee Gees	Jumbo/The Singer Sang His Song	57	25	5
Aug-68	Bee Gees	I've Gotta Get A Message To You	8	1	3
Dec-68	Bee Gees	I Started A Joke	6	n/a	–
Feb-69	Bee Gees	First Of May	37	6	3
May-69	Bee Gees	Tomorrow, Tomorrow	54	23	6
Jul-69	Robin Gibb	Saved By The Bell	–	2	5
Aug-69	Bee Gees	Don't Forget To Remember	73	2	9
Jan-70	Robin Gibb	One Million Years	n/a	–	14
Feb-70	Robin Gibb	August October	n/a	45	12
Mar-70	Bee Gees	If Only I Had My Mind On Something Else	91	n/a	n/a
Mar-70	Bee Gees	I.O.I.O.	94	49	6
Dec-70	Bee Gees	Lonely Days	3	33	25
Jun-71	Bee Gees	How Can You Mend A Broken Heart	1	–	–
Oct-71	Bee Gees	Don't Wanna Live Inside Myself	53	n/a	n/a
Jan-72	Bee Gees	My World	16	16	41
Jul-72	Bee Gees	Run To Me	16	9	–
Nov-72	Bee Gees	Alive	34	–	–
Mar-73	Bee Gees	Saw A New Morning	94	–	–
Mar-74	Bee Gees	Mr. Natural	93	–	–
May-75	Bee Gees	Jive Talkin'	1	5	23
Oct-75	Bee Gees	Nights On Broadway	7	–	17
Dec-75	Bee Gees	Fanny Be Tender With My Love	12	–	42
Jul-76	Bee Gees	You Should Be Dancing	1	5	16
Sep-76	Bee Gees	Love So Right	3	41	38
Jan-77	Bee Gees	Boogie Child	12	n/a	n/a
Apr-77	Andy Gibb	I Just Want To Be Your Everything	1	26	–
Jul-77	Bee Gees	Edge Of The Universe (live)	26	–	–
Sep-77	Bee Gees	How Deep Is Your Love	1	3	21
Nov-77	Andy Gibb	(Love Is) Thicker Than Water	1	–	–
Dec-77	Bee Gees	Stayin' Alive	1	4	2
Feb-78	Bee Gees	Night Fever	1	1	2
Apr-78	Andy Gibb	Shadow Dancing	1	42	44
Jul-78	Andy Gibb	An Everlasting Love	5	10	–
Aug-78	Robin Gibb	Oh! Darling	15	–	–

673

Date	Artist	Title			
Oct-78	Andy Gibb	(Our Love) Don't Throw It All Away	9	32	–
Nov-78	Bee Gees	Too Much Heaven	1	3	10
Feb-79	Bee Gees	Tragedy	1	1	2
Apr-79	Bee Gees	Love You Inside Out	1	13	21
Jan-80	Bee Gees	Spirits (Having Flown)	n/a	16	–
Jan-80	Andy Gibb	Desire	4	–	36
Mar-80	Andy Gibb	I Can't Help It (with Olivia Newton-John)	12	–	–
Nov-80	Robin Gibb	Help Me (with Marcy Levy)	50	–	–
Nov-80	Andy Gibb	Time Is Time	15	–	44
Mar-81	Andy Gibb	Me (Without You)	40	–	–
Aug-81	Andy Gibb	All I Have To Do Is Dream	52	–	–
Sep-81	Bee Gees	He's A Liar	30	–	68
Nov-81	Bee Gees	Living Eyes	45	–	58
May-83	Robin Gibb	Juliet	–	94	1
May-83	Bee Gees	The Woman In You	24	81	23
Aug-83	Robin Gibb	Another Lonely Night In New York	n/a	71	16
Aug-83	Bee Gees	Someone Belonging To Someone	49	49	55
Nov-83	Robin Gibb	How Old Are You	n/a	93	37
Jun-84	Robin Gibb	Boys Do Fall In Love	37	–	21
Sep-64	Barry Gibb	Shine Shine	37	95	45
Sep-87	Bee Gees	You Win Again	75	1	1
Dec-87	Bee Gees	E.S.P.	–	51	13
Feb-88	Bee Gees	Crazy For Your Love	n/a	79	n/a
Mar-88	Bee Gees	Angela	n/a	n/a	52
Oct-88	Barry Gibb	Childhood Days	n/a	–	60
Apr-89	Bee Gees	Ordinary Lives	n/a	54	8
Jun-89	Bee Gees	One	7	71	37
Mar-91	Bee Gees	Secret Love	n/a	5	2
Feb-91	Bee Gees	The Only Love	n/a	–	31
Aug-93	Bee Gees	Paying The Price Of Love	74	23	36
Nov-93	Bee Gees	For Whom The Bell Tolls	–	4	52
Apr-94	Bee Gees	How To Fall In Love Part One	n/a	30	n/a
Apr-94	Bee Gees	Kiss Of Life	n/a	n/a	51
Mar-97	Bee Gees	Alone	28	5	6
Jun-97	Bee Gees	I Could Not Love You More	–	14	88
Nov-97	Bee Gees	Still Waters Run Deep	57	18	79

APPENDIX VI

GIBB COVER VERSION SINGLES & ALBUMS WHICH CHARTED IN USA, UK & GERMANY
(Compiled by Norbert Lippe as of March, 2000)

ENTRY DATE	COVER ARTIST	SINGLE TITLE	USA	UK	GER.
Sep-67	Esther & Abi Ofarim	Morning Of My Life	n/a	–	2
Jul-68	Sweet Inspirations	To Love Somebody	74	n/a	n/a
Sep-68	Marbles	Only One Woman	–	5	6
Jan-69	Nina Simone	To Love Somebody	–	5	–
Mar-69	Marbles	The Walls Fell Down	–	28	–
May-69	Jose Feliciano	Marley Purt Drive	70	–	–
Oct-69	Jose Feliciano	And The Sun Will Shine	–	25	–
Sep-70	Engelbert Humperdinck	Sweetheart	47	22	n/a
Mar-75	Nigel Olsson	Only One Woman	91	–	–
Mar-76	Olivia Newton-John	Come On Over	23	–	–
Oct-76	Yvonne Elliman	Love Me	14	6	–
Jul-77	Candi Staton	Nights On Broadway	–	6	–
Nov-77	Samantha Sang	Emotion	3	11	–
Nov-77	Tavares	More Than A Woman	32	7	–
Jan-78	Yvonne Elliman	If I Can't Have You	1	4	–
Feb-78	Rita Coolidge	Words	–	25	–
Apr-78	Rare Earth	Warm Ride	39	–	–
May-78	Frankie Valli	Grease	1	3	24
Jul-78	Teri De Sario	Ain't Nothing Gonna Keep Me From You	43	–	–
Jul-78	Carol Douglas	Night Fever	n/a	66	–
Dec-78	Richard Ace	Stayin' Alive	n/a	66	–
Jan-79	Melba Moore	You Stepped Into My Life	47	–	n/a
Sep-79	Wayne Newton	You Stepped Into My Life	90	–	n/a
Mar-80	Jimmy Ruffin	Hold On (To My Love)	10	7	–
Sep-80	Barbra Streisand	Woman In Love	1	1	1
Nov-80	Barbra Streisand	Guilty (with Barry Gibb)	3	34	15
Jan-81	Barbra Streisand	What Kind Of Fool (with Barry Gibb)	10	–	–
May-81	Barbra Streisand	Promises	48	–	–
Aug-81	Startrax	Startrax Club Disco (medley)	n/a	18	–
Jun-82	Leo Sayer	Heart (Stop Beating In Time)	n/a	22	–
Oct-82	Dionne Warwick	Heartbreaker	10	2	10
Dec-82	Dionne Warwick	All The Love In The World	n/a	10	50
Feb-83	Dionne Warwick	Yours	n/a	66	n/a
Feb-83	Dionne Warwick	Take The Short Way Home	41	85	–
Aug-83	Kenny Rogers & Dolly Parton	Islands In The Stream	1	7	25
Oct-83	Kenny Rogers	Eyes That See In The Dark	79	61	–
Jan-84	Kenny Rogers	This Woman	23	–	–
Mar-85	Dionne Warwick & Barry Manilow	Run To Me	–	86	–
Sep-85	Diana Ross	Eaten Alive	77	71	38
Nov-85	Diana Ross	Chain Reaction	66	1	11
May-86	Diana Ross	Experience	n/a	47	–

675

Jul-87	Boogie Box High	Jive Talkin'	n/a	7	—
Oct-87	This Way Up	If I Can't Have You	n/a	76	—
Feb-89	The Bunburys (BRM + Eric Clapton)	Fight (No Matter How Long)	—	88	—
Nov-90	Jimmy Somerville	To Love Somebody	n/a	8	20
Feb-91	Mixmasters	The Night Fever Megamix	n/a	23	—
Mar-91	Frankie Valli	Grease– The Dream Mix	n/a	47	—
Feb-92	Ochsenknecht	Only One Woman	n/a	n/a	21
Oct-92	Michael Bolton	To Love Somebody	11	16	61
Jul-93	Kim Wilde	If I Can't Have You	—	12	51
Sep-93	Lulu	Let Me Wake Up In Your Arms	n/a	51	n/a
Dec-93	Craig McLachlan	Grease	n/a	44	n/a
Jul-95	Portrait	How Deep Is Your Love	93	41	79
Jul-95	Fever Featuring Tippa Irie	Stayin' Alive	n/a	48	—
Sep-95	N-Trance Featuring Ricardo Da Force	Stayin' Alive	62	2	3
Mar-96	Take That	How Deep Is Your Love	n/a	1	7
Oct-96	Boyzone	Words	n/a	1	7
Nov-96	Total	When Boy Meets Girl (★1)	50	n/a	n/a
May-97	Rebekah Ryan	Woman In Love	n/a	64	—
Jun-97	Wyclef Jean	We Trying To Stay Alive	45	13	72
Dec-97	Nana	Too Much Heaven	n/a	n/a	2
May-98	Adam Garcia	Night Fever	n/a	15	n/a
Jun-98	Celine Dion	Immortality (with The Bee Gees)	n/a	5	2
Jun-98	Pras Michel Feat. ODB & Mya	Ghetto Supastar (That Is What You Are) (★2)	15	2	1
Oct-98	Black Eyed Peas	Joints & Jams (★3)	n/a	53	n/a
Oct-98	911	More Than A Woman	n/a	2	—
Nov-98	Pras Michel	Blue Angels (★4)	n/a	6	75
Nov-98	Faith No More	I Started A Joke	—	49	—
Nov-98	Lyte Funkie Ones (L.F.O.)	If I Can't Have You	70	54	—
Nov-98	Steps	Tragedy –	1	—	—
Dec-98	Dope Smugglaz	The Word (★5)	n/a	62	—
Jan-99	Blockster	You Should Be . . . (Dancing)	n/a	3	—
Dec-99	Martine McCutcheon	Love Me	n/a	6	n/a

(★1) Lyrics and melody from 'Love You Inside Out' used in parts of song.

(★2) Includes lyrics and melody from 'Islands In The Stream' along with non-Gibb rap music.

(★3) Includes snippets of 'Grease' in rap song otherwise unrelated to The Bee Gees.

(★4) Includes lyrics and melody from 'Grease' along with non-Gibb rap music.

(★5) Repeats the lyrics "Is The Word" from 'Grease' throughout otherwise technopop instrumental.

ENTRY			HIGHEST CHART POSITION		
DATE	COVER ARTIST	ALBUM TITLE	USA	UK	GER.
May-80	Jimmy Ruffin	Sunrise	152	—	—
Oct-80	Barbra Streisand	Guilty	1	1	4
Oct-82	Dionne Warwick	Heartbreaker	25	3	18
Sep-83	Kenny Rogers	Eyes That See In The Dark	6	53	—
Sep-85	Diana Ross	Eaten Alive	45	11	20
Jan-98	Various Artists	We Love The Bee Gees	n/a	n/a	48
Aug-98	Original London Cast	Saturday Night Fever	n/a	17	n/a

BIBLIOGRAPHY

1. BOOKS

Grant, Ian and Madden, Nicholas, *The Countryside At War,* Jupitor Books (London) Ltd., UK, 1975

Stevens, Kim, *The Bee Gees,* Quick Fox, USA, 1978

Riley, Joe, *Today's Cathedral The Cathedral Church Of Christ, Liverpool,* SPCK, UK, 1978

Leaf, David, *The Authorised Biography,* Dell Publishing Inc., USA, 1979

Tatham, Dick, *The Incredible Bee Gees,* Futura Publications, UK, 1979

Berman, Connie, and Daly, Marsha, *Andy Gibb,* Xerox Corporation, USA, 1979

Pryce, Larry, *The Bee Gees,* Granada Publishing, UK, 1979

Martin, George, with Hornsby, Jeremy, *All You Need Is Ears,* St. Martins Press, USA, 1979

Pye, Michael, *Moguls,* Holt, Rinehart & Winston, USA, 1980

Hayton, John and Isackson, Leon, *Behind The Rock,* Select Books, Australia, 1980

English, David and Brychta, Alex, *The Legend (updated),* Quartet Books Ltd., UK, 1983

Patey, Dean Edward H., *My Liverpool Life,* Mowbray's Popular Christian Paperbacks, UK, 1983

Brown, Peter, *The Love You Make,* McGraw Hill, USA, 1983

Mac Cana, Proinsias, *Celtic Mythology,* Newnes Books, UK, 1984

Beck, Christopher, *On Air : 25 Years Of TV In Queensland,* One Tree Hill Publishing, Australia, 1984

Lulu, *Lulu-Her Autobiography,* Granada Publishing, UK, 1985

Considine, Shaun, *Barbra Streisand, The Woman, The Myth, The Music,* Delacorte Press, USA, 1985

Sheridan, Dorothy, *Wartime Women,* William Heineman Ltd., UK, 1990

Coleman, Ray, *Brian Epstein – The Man Who Made The Beatles,* Penguin Books, UK, 1990

Windsor, Barbara, with the assistance of Flory, Joan, *Barbara, The Laughter And Tears Of A Cockney Sparrow,* Arrow Books, UK, 1991

Froggatt, Raymond, *Raymond Who?,* Scala Music Ltd., UK, 1992

Tobler, John, *This Day In Rock,* Simon & Schuster, UK, 1993

Wexler, Jerry and Ritz, David, *Rhythm And The Blues,* Alfred A. Knopf, USA, 1993

Strong, Martin C., *The Great Rock Discography,* Canongate Press, UK, 1994

Rosen, Craig, *Billboard Book Of Number One Albums,* Billboard Books, an imprint of Watson-Guphill Publications, USA, 1996

Spencer, Chris, *Who's Who Of Australian Rock,* Five Mile Press, Australia, 1997

Weller, Helen (Editor), *British Hit Singles – 11th Edition,* Guinness Publishing Ltd, UK, 1997

Barnes, Jim and Scanes, Stephen, *The Book – Top 40 Research 1956–1997,* Barscan Music Research, Australia, 1998

Haden-Guest, Anthony, *The Last Party: Studio 54, Disco, And The Culture Of The Night,* William Morrow & Co., USA, 1998

Larkin, Colin, *The Encyclopaedia Of Popular Music,* MacMillan/Muze, UK, 1998

Aerosmith and Davis, Stephen, *Walk This Way : The Autobiography Of Aerosmith,* Avon, USA, 1999

McFarlane, Ian, *The Encyclopaedia Of Australian Rock & Pop,* Allen and Irwin, Australia, 1999

2. PRIMARY MAGAZINE ARTICLES

(various), *20th Anniversary Salute,* Record World, USA, 14th June 1975

(various), *Salutes The Bee Gees,* Billboard, USA, 2nd Sept. 1978

Dasch, David, *The Bee Gees Story,* Rockin' Aware Research Mag. USA, 1979

Doggett, Peter, *The Bee Gees 1962–67,* Record Collector, UK, Sept. 1986

Grant, Mike, *The Bee Gees 1967–75*, Record Collector, UK, Dec. 1987

Howlett, Scott, *Barry Gibb*, Australian Playboy, Australia, Nov. 1990

Badman, Keith, *Happening For Lulu*, Record Collector, UK, Apr. 1999

Dwyer, Kate, *I'm The Girl Barry Gibb Left Behind,* Take 5, Australia, July 7, 1999 – various fan club magazines were also used; details of which can be found in Appendix II.

3. MAJOR NEWSPAPER/MAGAZINE SOURCES

Billboard; *Daily Express / Scottish Daily Express*; *Daily Record*; *Disc & Music Echo*; *Goldmine*; *Melody Maker*; *New Musical Express*; *Record Mirror*; *Rolling Stone*

4. SLEEVE NOTES

Gibb, Robin, *Bee Gees Hits* LP (Robert Stigwood Orchestra), Polydor, UK, 1968

Shepherd, Bill, *Aurora* LP (Bill Shepherd Singers), ATCO, USA, 1968

Baker, Glenn A., *Birth Of Brilliance* LP (The Bee Gees), Festival, Australia, 1978

Currie, Brent, *Marble-ized* CD (The Marbles), Polydor, Australia, 1994

Baker, Glenn A. and Byfield, Mark, *Brilliant From Birth* CD (The Bee Gees), Festival, Australia, 1998

Byfield, Mark and Crohan, Mark, *Assault The Vaults* CD (Various Artists), Festival, Australia, 1998

Mcloughlin, Rob and Hartley, Joanna, *Gotta Get A Message To You* CD (Various Artists), Polydor, UK, 1998

5. INTERNET WEB SITES

Bonnet, Graham, *Bonnet Rocks*, http://www.bonnet-rocks.com

Brennan, Joe, *The Brothers Gibb*, http://www.columbia.edu/~brennan/beegees/

Hogan, Marty, *Bee Gees Index*, http://www.slip.net/~martyho/indexbg.html

Shadrick, Kristi, *One More Look At The Night*, http://www.geocities.com/Hollywood/Interview/5986/index.html

Stigwood, Robert, *Robert Stigwood Organisation*, http://www.rsogroup.com/Robert.html

INDEX

Index

Index